THE FACTS ON FILE
ENGLISH/CHINESE
Visual Dictionary

THE FACTS ON FILE
ENGLISH/CHINESE
Visual Dictionary

LOOK UP THE WORD FROM THE PICTURE
FIND THE PICTURE FROM THE WORD

Jean-Claude Corbeil/Mein-ven Lee

Facts On File® Publications
New York, *New York* • Oxford, *England*

英漢對照萬物圖解大詞典

主　編：李勉民

出版者：讀者文摘遠東有限公司

地　址：香港筲箕灣阿公岩村道三號

排　版：合衆排版有限公司

地　址：香港中環擺花街廿九號中環大廈303室

印　刷：讀者文摘遠東有限公司

地　址：香港筲箕灣阿公岩村道三號

ⓒ 一九八八年。讀者文摘遠東有限公司。

ⓒ 一九八八年。讀者文摘亞洲有限公司。

English/Chinese Visual Dictionary

Reader's Digest Association Far East Limited

3, A Kung Ngam Village Road

Shaukiwan, Hong Kong

Published in the United States by Facts On File, Inc., 460 Park Avenue South, New York, NY 10016.

Published in the United Kingdom by Facts On File, Ltd., Collins Street, Oxford.

Published in Hong Kong under license from Les Éditions Québec/Amérique Inc., Montreal.

Printed in Hong Kong.

ISBN 0-8160-2043-4

Library of Congress Card Number 88-16609

INTRODUCTION

PURPOSE OF THE DICTIONARY

Initially, we set ourselves two goals:

a) List all the terms and notions which designate or portray the many elements of everyday life in an industrial, post-industrial or developing society, and which one needs to know to buy an object, discuss a repair, read a book or a newspaper, etc.

b) Visualize them through graphic representation; i.e., assign to an illustration the role played by the written definition in a conventional dictionary.

The latter implies a constraint: The selected notions must lend themselves to graphic representation. Hence, the list must omit abstract words, adjectives, verbs and adverbs, even though they are part of the specialized vocabulary. Terminologists have not yet adequately solved this problem.

Following a series of tests and consultations, technical graphics were deemed the best form of visual presentation because they stress the essential features of a notion and leave out the accessories, like the fashion details of clothing. The resulting illustration gains in conceptual clarity what it loses in detail and provides a better definition.

To achieve our goals, we assembled two production teams, one of terminologists and another of graphic artists, who worked together under one scientific supervisor.

THE INTENDED USER

The VISUAL DICTIONARY is meant for the active member of the modern industrial society who needs to be acquainted with a wide range of technical terms from many assorted areas, but not to be specialist in any.

The profile of the typical user guided our selection of items in every category. We included what may be of use to everybody and deliberately left out what is in the exclusive realm of the specialist.

Varying levels of specialization will be noted from one category to another, however, depending on one's degree of familiarity with a subject or the very constraints of specialization. Thus, the vocabulary of clothing or electricity is more familiar to us than that of nuclear energy. Or again, to describe the human anatomy, one is confined to medical terminology but to describe the structure of a fruit, one may use both the scientific and popular terms. Familiarity with a subject also varies from one user to another or with the degree of penetration of a specialty. The best example no doubt is the propagation of the vocabulary of data processing brought on by the widespread use of the personal computer.

Be that as it may, the aim was to reflect as best as possible the specialized vocabulary currently used in every field.

CHARACTERISTICS OF THE DICTIONARY

What distinguishes THE FACTS ON FILE VISUAL DICTIONARY from other lexicons?

Conventional works

Dictionaries come in four basic types:

a) Language dictionaries

Language dictionaries are divided into two parts.

The first is the nomenclature, i.e., the list of words that are the object of a lexicographical commentary. It forms the macrostructure of the dictionary. For practical purposes, words are

listed in alphabetical order. The nomenclature generally includes words of the common modern language, archaic words — often incorporated in a text — whose knowledge is useful to understand the language's history, and some technical terms that are fairly widespread.

The second is a lexicographical commentary whose microstructure varies according to lexicographical tradition. It generally deals with the word's grammatical category, its gender (if the case may be), its pronunciation in the international phonetic alphabet, its etymology, its various meanings, often in chronological order, and, finally, its uses according to a rather impressionistic typology that includes the *colloquial*, the *popular* and the *vulgar*.

b) Encyclopedic dictionaries

These add on to, the former type of dictionary commentaries on the nature, the function or the history of things, allowing the layman or the specialist to better understand the import of a word. They devote much more space to technical terms and closely follow the development of science and technology. Illustrations are assigned an important role. These works are more or less bulky, depending on the extent of the nomenclature, the importance of the commentaries and the space allotted to proper nouns.

c) Encyclopedias

Contrary to the preceding, encyclopedias do not include a full word list. They are essentially concerned with the scientific, technical, geographical, historical and economic aspects of their subjects. The structure of the nomenclature is arbitrary since every classification, be it alphabetical, notional, chronological or otherwise, is legitimate. The number of such works is potentially unlimited as are the activities of civilization, although a distinction must be drawn between universal and specialized encyclopedias.

d) Specialized lexicons or vocabularies

These works are generally meant to enhance communications or to answer particular needs arising from the evolution of science or technology. They vary from one another in every respect: the method of compilation, the relationship of the authors to the subject, the size of the nomenclature, the number of languages dealt with at once and the manner of establishing equivalents, either through translation or comparison between unilingual terminologies. There is intense activity in this field nowadays. Works abound in every area and in every language combination deemed useful.

THE FACTS ON FILE VISUAL DICTIONARY is not an encyclopedia. For one, it does not describe but names items. Secondly, it avoids the enumeration of items within a category. Rather than list the different types of trees, for instance, it selects a typical representative of the tree family and lists each of its parts.

It is even less a language dictionary. It contains only substantives — without written definitions — few adjectives, and very often complex terms, which is common to all terminologies.

Neither is it a compendium of specialized vocabularies —, as it favors words useful to the average person over terms known only to specialists, who may find it too elementary.

The VISUAL DICTIONARY is the first basic dictionary of terminological orientation, comprising within a single volume, with high regard for accuracy and easy access, thousands of more or less technical terms for which knowledge becomes a necessity in this modern world where science, technology and their by-products permeate and influence daily life.

METHODOLOGY

The preparation of this dictionary followed the methodology of systematic and comparative terminological research developed in Quebec in the early Seventies, now widespread in the whole of Canada, Europe, South America, North Africa and Sub-Saharan Africa.

We worked in the two languages, English and French, that are the most widely used throughout the world. The research available in both languages ensures a comprehensive stock of notions and terms, thanks to the interrelationship of approaches and specialties proper to

each language and their different perception and expression of the same realities. Eventually, we propose to apply the same methods to other languages, particularly Arab and Spanish.

The methodology of systematic terminological research involves many stages that follow one another in logical order. This progression applies to each language under study, their comparison intervening only at the end of the process with the compilation of terminological files. Thus, the pitfalls of literal translation are avoided.

A brief description of each stage follows:

Field delimitation

First, the content and size of the project must be carefully determined according to its goals and its prospective users.

In the case of the VISUAL DICTIONARY, we selected the major themes we felt should be dealt with, then divided each one into categories and sub-categories, keeping sight of our initial goal to steer clear of encyclopedism and ultraspecialization. The result was a detailed interim table of contents, providing the structure of the dictionary, to be used as a guide and refined in subsequent stages. The actual table of contents emerged from this process.

A dummy was then submitted to the contributing editors, lexicographers and terminologists, for their opinion on the content and the graphic style of the illustrations. Enriched from their comments, the project moved onto the production stage.

The collection of documentary sources

The production plan first called for researching and collecting the material likely to yield the required information on each subject. The research covered both French and English texts.

Here, without prejudice, is the list of documentary sources in order of the confidence placed in them for reflecting correct usage:
— English-French language dictionaries.
— Specialized dictionaries or vocabularies, whether unilingual, bilingual (French-English) or multilingual, whose quality and reliability should be carefully appraised.
— Encyclopedias or encyclopedic dictionaries, language dictionaries.
— Catalogues, commercial texts, advertisements in specialized magazines and large dailies.
— Technical documents from the International Standard Organization (ISO), the American Standard Association (ASA) and the Association française de normalisation (AFNOR); directions for use of commercial products; comparative product analyses; technical information supplied by manufacturers; official government publications, etc.
— French or English articles or works by specialists with an adequate level of competence in their field. In translation, these prove highly instructive as to word usage, although caution should be exercized.

On the whole, some four to five thousand references. The selective bibliography contained in the dictionary lists only the general reference works, not the specialized sources.

Sifting through the documentation

For every subject, the terminologist must sift through the documentation, searching for specific notions and the words used by various authors to express them. From this process emerges the notional structure of the subject, its standard or differing designations. In the latter case, the terminologist pursues his research, recording each term with supporting references, until he has formed a well-documented opinion on each of the competing terms.

Since the dictionary is visual, terminologists at this stage searched for appropriate ways of graphically depicting each coherent group of notions in one or several illustrations

depending on the subject. The graphic artists drew from these elements to design each page of the dictionary.

The make-up of documentary files

The elements of each terminological file were assembled from the mass of documentation.

Once identified and defined through illustration, each notion was assigned the term most frequently used by the best authors and the most reliable sources to express it. If the terminological file suggested competing terms, one was selected upon discussion and agreement between the terminologist and the scientific director.

Specialists were called upon to discuss highly technical files subject to a greater risk of error.

Graphic visualization

The terminological file, along with a proposal for graphic representation, was then turned over to the graphics team for the design and production of the final illustrated page.

Each terminologist revised the plates pertaining to his files to ensure the accuracy of illustrations, terms and spelling.

General revision of plates

The terminological research was carried out subject by subject following a plan, but not necessarily in order.

The final version of the dictionary underwent two complete verifications. Three revisers in each language were first asked to proofread the entire work, with emphasis on the spelling, without disregarding the terminology. With the help of their commentaries, the written form was standardized throughout the dictionary. Each instance of every word or notion was checked to insure the greatest possible degree of coherence.

All the documentation and terminological files on which the dictionary is based remain in archives.

PARTICULAR PROBLEMS

Users of THE FACTS ON FILE VISUAL DICTIONARY may want to know how regional disparities in English usage were resolved.

American, Canadian or British English?

English usage, particularly spelling, but also vocabulary, varies with every region.

We elected to follow American standards, using the various editions of Webster's and the Random House Dictionary of the English Language, Unabridged Edition (1983), as our basic references.

In a later edition of the dictionary, it might be worthwhile to list the terms in usage in each English-language community.

Terminological variation

Our research revealed a number of cases of terminological variation, i.e., designation of a notion by different terms.

Here is a partial list of such cases:

— A particular term may have been used by only one author or occurred only once throughout the documentation; we then chose the most frequent competing term;

— Technical terms are often in compound form, hyphenated or not, incorporating a preposition or preceded by a noun. This characteristic gives rise to at least two types of terminological variants:

a) The compound technical term may be shortened by the deletion of one or many of its elements, especially when the context is significant. Within limits, the shorter term becomes the usual designation of the notion. For instance, *objective lens* becomes *objective*, *fine adjustment knob* becomes *fine adjustment*, *revolving nose piece*, *nose piece*. We retained the compound form, leaving it to the user to shorten it according to the context.

b) One of the elements of the compound may itself have equivalent forms, generally synonyms in the common language. For instance, *magnetic needle* is equivalent to *magnetized needle*, *eye lens* to *ocular lens*. We then retained the most frequent form.

— Finally, the variation may stem from a difference of opinion, with no bearing on terminology, making it unnecessary to give up the best known term. For instance, the *first condenser lens* and *second condenser lens* of the electronic microscope are called *upper condenser lens* and *lower condenser lens* by some authors. The difference is not sufficient to cause a problem. In these cases, the most frequent or best known form was preferred.

Terminological sense

This calls for a brief commentary on the terminological sense as compared to the lexicographical sense.

The long history of language dictionaries, the fact that they are familiar reference works, known and used by everyone from schooldays, means that a certain tradition has been set that is known and accepted by all. We know how variants designating the same notion are classified and treated ; therefore, we know how to interpret the dictionary and how to use the information it gives or does not give us.

Terminological dictionaries are either recent or intended for a specialized few. There is no real tradition guiding the preparation of such dictionaries. If the specialist knows how to interpret a dictionary pertaining to his own area of expertise because he is familiar with its terminology, the same cannot be said of the layman who may be confused by variants. Finally, language dictionaries have to some extent disciplined their users to a standard vocabulary. But since they relate to recent specialties, the terms listed in specialized vocabularies are far from set.

This aspect of the vocabulary sciences must be taken into account in the evaluation of the VISUAL DICTIONARY.

Spelling variations

The spelling of English words varies considerably. It sometimes differs according to the variety of English : for instance, *center* is American while *centre* is British. Often, the problem lies in determining whether a word should be written as a single word or in two words, with or without a hyphen : for example, *wave length* and *wavelength*, *grand-mother* and *grandmother*, *cross bar* and *crossbar*. Finally, there is some question as to the doubling of consonants in words like *levelling* and *traveller*. In every case, we used the spelling favored by Merriam Webster's and the Random House Dictionary.

Jean-Claude CORBEIL

P.S. In this edition, the British English terms are shown in *italics*.

前　言

　　有些事物用文字解說，遠不及採用圖畫表示那樣生動鮮明和容易記牢，刺繡針法、糕點麵食、機械零件等就是例子。《萬物圖解大詞典》收錄與現代日常生活息息相關的名詞術語，約一萬五千條，採用圖解代替文字釋義，讀者可一目了然，準確理解詞義。

　　本詞典取材廣汎，包括衣、食、住、行、天文、地理、工藝、園藝、運動、遊戲、人體構造、能源、機械、儀器、武器等，可以說是應有盡有。各類常見的名詞術語，凡可以用圖畫表示的，大都在收錄之列。

　　本詞典既有別於百科全書，也不是專科詞彙簡編。書中沒有詳列各門學科的所有詞條，以免龐雜；也沒有收錄專家才用得着的術語，以求實用。這是特別為一般讀者編纂的名詞術語詞典，不求卷帙浩繁，不以艱深為尚，力求精確簡明，便於翻檢，以滿足讀者日常應用的需要。

　　全書圖畫都盡量突出事物的特徵，罥去枝葉，極其清楚明確。舉例來說，在服裝篇裏，各種裙子的名稱一一臚列，配合圖解，一望而知，至於有多少褶子，有沒有緄邊，就不加以贅述了。

　　原書在北美出版，已有英文版本和英法文對照版本兩種。英文版本只收錄美式英語詞，英法文對照版本則在美式英語詞後用斜體字標出常用的英式英語詞，供讀者參考。英漢對照版本根據英法文版本編成。讀者既可看圖識詞，也可以藉索引和圖解找出英語詞的中譯，或反過來找到所需的英語詞。由於文化背景和生活習慣不同，有些東西在英語裏劃分得很精細，在漢語裏則只有概括的名稱。就馬蹄和鞋子來說，各部分都有特定的英語名稱；長短不同的項鏈在英語裏也各有專名，在漢語裏卻沒有對應名稱。遇到類似的情況，在漢英詞典中根本無法找到所需的英語詞，本詞典正好有助於解決這種難題。因此，《萬物圖解大詞典》不僅是掌握林林總總名詞術語必備的詞典，更是學習英語不可缺少的案頭工具書。

THE FACTS ON FILE VISUAL DICTIONARY
FOR A *NEW* DICTIONARY A *NEW* USAGE GUIDE

THE FACTS ON FILE VISUAL DICTIONARY is divided into three parts:

— TABLE OF CONTENTS

— ILLUSTRATIONS depicting the ENTRIES

— ALPHABETICAL GENERAL INDEXES

There are two ways of finding what you are looking for. You may refer either to the illustration or the word.

Starting from the **illustration**	Starting from the **word**
You want to know what an object is called	You want to know what a word stands for
• Look in the **table of contents** for the **theme** which best corresponds to your query	• Look for the word in the alphabetical **general index**
• You will find **references** to **illustrations**	• You will find **references** to the **illustrations** in which the word appears
• Alongside the illustration, you will find the corresponding **word**.	• You will see from the **illustration** what the word stands for.

用法指南

《萬物圖解大詞典》主要分為三部分：

（一）分類目錄
（二）詞條圖解
（三）詞條索引

翻檢時可以按圖索詞，也可以據詞找圖。

按圖索詞	據詞找圖
想要知道某種東西的名稱：	想要了解某個名詞的意義：
● 從分類目錄找出所屬細目的頁碼	● 依筆畫或字母順序在索引中找出該詞
● 按頁碼查閱圖解	● 按頁碼查閱圖解
● 在圖中找出該詞	● 找出該詞所指示的圖形

THEMES   檢目表

ASTRONOMY	17	天文	25
GEOGRAPHY	17	地理	25
VEGETABLE KINGDOM	17	植物	25
ANIMAL KINGDOM	18	動物	26
HUMAN BEING	18	人	26
FOOD	18	食物	26
FARM	18	農場	26
ARCHITECTURE	18	建築	26
HOUSE	19	房屋	27
HOUSE FURNITURE	19	家具	27
GARDENING	19	園藝	27
DO-IT-YOURSELF	19	自行修理用具	27
CLOTHING	19	服裝	27
PERSONAL ADORNMENT	20	儀容修飾	27
PERSONAL ARTICLES	20	個人用品	27
COMMUNICATIONS	20	通訊	27
TRANSPORTATION	20	交通運輸	28
OFFICE SUPPLIES AND EQUIPMENT	21	辦公室用品與設備	29
MUSIC	21	音樂	29
CREATIVE LEISURE ACTIVITIES	21	消閒工藝	29
SPORTS	21	運動與遊戲	29
MEASURING DEVICES	22	量度儀器	30
OPTICAL INSTRUMENTS	23	光學儀器	30
HEALTH	23	醫護復健	30
ENERGY	23	能源	30
HEAVY MACHINERY	23	重型機械	30
WEAPONS	23	武器	31
SYMBOLS	23	標識	31
GENERAL INDEX	725	索引	761

TABLE OF CONTENTS

INTRODUCTION 6
USAGE GUIDE 12
THEMES 15

ASTRONOMY 33
Earth co-ordinate system........................ 35
Celestial co-ordinate system.................... 35
Seasons of the year 35
Planets of the solar system..................... 36
Symbols of the planets 36
Sun 37
    Structure of the Sun, solar eclipse
Moon 38
    Lunar features, lunar eclipse, phases of the Moon
Galaxy, Hubble's classification................ 39
Comet ....,.......... 39
Constellations of the northern hemisphere 40
Constellations of the southern hemisphere 41
Astronomical observatory....................... 42
Planetarium....................................... 43
Planetarium projector........................... 43

GEOGRAPHY..................................... 45
Structure of the Earth........................... 47
Profile of the Earth's atmosphere 47
Space achievements 47
Section of the Earth's crust 48
Configuration of the continents.............. 49
Ocean floor....................................... 50
Wave... 51
Common coastal features 51
Clouds and meteorological symbols 52
Volcano 53
Earthquake 53
Mountain.. 54
Cave... 54
Desert 55
Glacier 56
Water forms 57
    Classification of snow crystals, kinds of precipitation

Hydrologic cycle................................. 58
Climates of the world 59
International weather symbols 60
    Meteors, fronts, sky coverage, wind
Meteorology...................................... 62
    Weather map, station model, meteorological ground
Meteorological measuring instruments 64
    Direct-reading rain gauge, sunshine recorder
Meteorological satellite........................ 65

VEGETABLE KINGDOM....................... 67
Structure of a plant............................. 69
    Root, stem, leaf, leaf margin, types of leaves, simple leaves, compound leaves
Structure of a tree 71
    Tree, cross section of a trunk, stump
Structure of a flower 72
    Types of inflorescences
Mushrooms....................................... 73
    Structure of a mushroom, edible mushrooms, poisonous mushroom, deadly mushroom
Fleshy fruits : berry fruits 74
    Section of a berry : grape, major types of berries
Compound fleshy fruits........................ 74
    Section of a strawberry, section of a wild blackberry or raspberry
Stone fleshy fruits 75
    Section of a stone fruit : peach, major types of stone fruits
Pome fleshy fruits 76
    Section of a pome fruit : apple, principal types of pome fruits
Fleshy fruits : citrus fruits 77
    Section of a citrus fruit : orange, major types of citrus fruits
Dry fruits : nuts 78
    Section of a hazelnut, section of a walnut, major types of nuts
Various dry fruits 79
    Section of a follicle : star anise, section of a legume : pea, section of a silique : mustard, section a capsule : poppy, section of a grain of wheat
Tropical fruits 80
    Major types of tropical fruits

Vegetables.. 81
  *Fruit vegetables. inflorescent vegetables. leaf
  vegetables. section of a bulb. bulb vegetables.
  tuber vegetables. root vegetables. stalk vegetables. seed vegetables*
Cell 86
  Plant cell, animal cell

ANIMAL KINGDOM 87
Deer family 89
  Deer antlers, kinds of deer
Types of jaws.................................... 90
  *Carnivore's jaw: leopard, rodent's jaw: beaver,
  herbivore's jaw: horse*
Horse 91
  *Morphology, skeleton, hoof, plantar surface of
  the hoof, horseshoe*
Cat 94
  Head, foreleg, retracted claw, extended claw
Bird 95
  *Morphology, wing, contour feather, principal
  types of bills, principal types of feet, egg*
Fish 98
  Morphology, gills, anatomy
Butterfly 100
  Caterpillar, pupa, butterfly
Univalve shell 101
Bivalve shell 101
  Left valve. dorsal view
Mollusk.. 102
  Oyster, principal edible mollusks
Crustacean 103
  Lobster, principal edible crustaceans
Gastropod 104
  Snail, principal edible gastropods
Batrachian 105
  *Frog, life cycle of the frog, skeleton of the
  hindlimb*
Honeybee.. 106
  *Worker, queen, drone, hind legs of the worker,
  hive, honeycomb section*
Bat 108
Reptile... 109
  Venomous snake's head, turtle

HUMAN BEING 111
Fertilized egg development 113
  Egg, embryo, fetus
Human body..................................... 114
  Anterior view, posterior view
Genital organs, male 116
  Sagittal section, spermatozoon
Genital organs, female.......................... 117
  Sagittal section, anterior view
Breast, sagittal section......................... 117
Muscles 118
  Anterior view, posterior view
Skeleton... 120
  Anterior view, posterior view
Osteology of skull 122
  *Lateral view, anterior view, superior view, inferior
  view*

Teeth 123
  Cross section of a molar, human denture
Blood circulation 124
  *Schema of circulation. heart, principal veins and
  arteries*
Respiratory system, lungs...................... 126
Digestive system................................ 127
Urinary system.................................. 128
Nervous system................................. 129
  *Peripheral nervous system, central nervous sys-
  tem, medullar axis of lumbar vertebra*
Sense organs: sight 131
  Eye. eyeball
Sense organs: hearing 132
  External ear, internal and middle ear
Sense organs: smell 133
  *External nose, nasal fossae, sense of smell and
  taste*
Sense organs: taste 134
  Mouth, dorsum of tongue
Sense organs: touch 135
  Skin. sensory impulse
Neuron.. 135
Skin... 136
Nail.. 137
Hair.. 137
Family relationships............................. 138

FOOD 141
Herbs 143
Pasta.. 144
Bread 146
Veal 147
  North American cut, Parisian cut
Beef... 148
  North American cut, Parisian cut
Pork... 150
  North American cut, Parisian cut
Lamb 151
  North American cut, Parisian cut
Beef... 152
  British cut
Veal, pork, lamb................................ 153
  British cut
North American cheeses 154
French cheeses 154
Desserts.. 156

FARMING 159
Buildings.. 161
Agricultural machinery 162

ARCHITECTURE................................ 167
Traditional houses.............................. 169
Architecture styles 170
  *Doric order, ionic order, corinthian order, column
  base*
Greek temple.................................... 171
  Basic plan of the Greek temple
Arches... 172
  Semicircular arch, types of arches
Roman house 173

Gothic cathedral........................... 174
  Cathedral, plan, façade, vault
Vauban fortification 176
Castle.. 177
Downtown 178
Theater 179
  Hall, wings, cross section of a stage
Elevator 181
Escalator 182
City houses 183

HOUSE 185
Exterior of a house 187
Plan reading.................................. 188
  Lot plan, ground floor, upper floor
Rooms of the house........................... 189
  Ground floor, upper floor, basement
Structure of the house 190
  Roof structure, types of roofs, frame, foundations
Building materials 193
Wood flooring................................. 196
  Wood flooring on wooden structure, wood floor-ing on cement screed, wood flooring arrange-ments
Stairs 197
Door 198
  Exterior door, types of doors, plan symbols
Window 199
  Structure, types of windows
Heating....................................... 200
  Fireplace, wood stove, firetending tools, log car-rier, andiron, forced warm-air system, chimney, forced hot-water system, heating unit, convector, column radiator, baseboard radiator, boiler, split system heating pump, electric furnace, oil burner
Air conditioning.............................. 206
  Room air conditioner, ceiling fan, dehumidifier

HOUSE FURNITURE 207
Table 209
  Gate-leg table, major types of tables
Armchair 210
  Parts, principal types of armchairs
Seats... 212
Side chair 213
  Parts, stretchers, types of chairs
Bed 214
  Parts, linen
Storage furniture 215
Window accessories 217
  Curtain, pole, rod, track, roller shade, roll-up blind, shutters, Venetian blind
Lights.. 220
Glassware.................................... 222
Dinnerware 223
Silverware.................................... 224
  Knife, major types of knives, fork, major types of forks, spoon, major types of spoons
Kitchen utensils.............................. 227
  Kitchen knife, types of kitchen knives, utensils for straining and draining, utensils for grinding and grating, set of utensils, utensils for opening,

  utensils for measuring, baking utensils, miscel-laneous utensils
Cooking utensils.............................. 232
Coffee makers................................ 234
Domestic appliances.......................... 235
  Blender, table mixer, hand mixer, hand blender, beaters, food processor, ice-cream freezer, juicer, citrus juicer, microwave oven, grill and waffle baker, toaster, griddle, electric range, frost-free refrigerator, washer, dryer, dishwasher, steam iron, can opener, kettle, canister vacuum cleaner, cleaning tools

GARDENING 245
Pleasure garden 247
Tools and equipment 248
Chainsaw 253

DO-IT-YOURSELF 255
Carpentry : tools.............................. 257
  Claw hammer, mallet, plane, screwdriver, wrenches, pliers, vise, C-clamp, brace, hand drill, router, drill press, electric drill, bench saw, hacksaw, handsaw, circular saw
Carpentry : fasteners 264
  Nail, screw, bolt, nut, washer
Carpentry..................................... 265
  Board, peeled veneer, panel, plywood
Lock 266
  Mortise lock, cylinder, tubular lock
Plumbing..................................... 267
  Plumbing system, toilet, bathroom, sink, faucet, branching, electric water-heater tank, connectors, union, fittings, plumbing tools, septic tank, sump pump
Painting upkeep 278
  Ladders and stepladders, spray paint gun, brush, scraper, paint roller
Soldering and welding......................... 281
  Soldering iron, soldering gun, soldering torch, oxyacetylene welding, arc welding, welding torch, cutting torch, butt welding, pressure regulator, protective clothing
Electricity.................................... 284
  Incandescent lamp, mercury-vapor lamp, fluo-rescent lamp, electrical supplies, electrician's tools, distribution board

CLOTHING 289
Men's clothing 291
  Trench coat, raincoat, sheepskin jacket, duffle coat, parka, inverness cape, three-quarter coat, vest, double-breasted jacket, single-breasted coat, pants, suspenders, belt, shirt, collar, necktie, ascot tie, bow tie, V-neck cardigan, pullovers, sock, underwear, headgear
Glove 299
Women's clothing 300
  Coats, dresses, skirts, pockets, blouses, sleeves, vests and pullovers, types of collars, necklines and necks, pants, nightwear, hoses, underwear, headwear

Children's clothing 315
  *Christening set, wraparound diaper shirt bathing
  wrap, grow sleepers, blanket sleepers, nylon
  rumba thights, plastic pants, diaper, vest, bib,
  crisscross back straps overall, high-back overall,
  jumpsuit, bunting bag, sleeper, body stocking,
  polojama, gym rompers, jumper, Eton suit, snowsuit*
Shoes.. 318
  *Parts of a shoe, principal types of shoes, acces-
  sories for shoes*
Costumes 321
  Bullfighter, ballerina, diving suit, clown

PERSONAL ADORNMENT 323
Jewelry.. 325
  *Diversity of jewelry, bracelets, charms, rings,
  necklaces, cuts for gemstones, brilliant cut facets*
Eyeglasses.. 328
  *Front, temple, nose pad, principal types of
  eyeglasses*
Hair styles 330
  *Kinds of hair, components of hair styles, wigs
  and hairpieces*
Makeup.. 332
  *Makeup kit, makeup products, makeup acces-
  sories*

PERSONAL ARTICLES 335
Razors... 337
Scissors... 338
Combs... 338
Hairbrushes 338
Toothbrush 339
Oral hygiene center 339
Hair dryer 340
Lighted mirror.................................... 340
Salon-style hair dryer 340
Curling iron....................................... 341
Curling brush 341
Hairsetter 341
Manicure set...................................... 342
Manicuring instruments 343
Hairstyling implements 343
Smoking accessories 344
Umbrella 346
Luggage... 347
Handbags.. 348
Leather goods.................................... 350

COMMUNICATIONS 353
Writing systems of the world................... 355
Braille alphabet 356
Deaf-mute alphabet 357
Punctuation marks 357
Diacritic symbols 357
International phonetic alphabet 358
Typical letter, *American model* 359
Typical letter, *Canadian model*............... 360
Typical letter, *British model*................... 361
Proofreading 362
Writing instruments 367

Photography 368
  *Single-lens reflex camera, still cameras, objective
  and accessories, Polaroid Land camera, films,
  flash unit, exposure meter, spotmeter, studio
  lighting, photographic accessories, studio acces-
  sories, darkroom, enlarger, slide projector, pro-
  jection screen*
Sound reproducing system 378
  *System elements amplifier-tuner, turntable, record,
  tape deck*
Video tape recorder 382
Cinematography.................................. 383
  *Sound camera, sound projector, video camera,
  dynamic microphone*
Telegraph 385
  *Diagram of a circuit, receiver, transmitter, Morse
  code*
Telex : teleprinter................................ 386
Telephone set 387
  *Receiver, transmitter, types of telephones, tele-
  phone answering machine*
Television.. 389
  *Studio and control rooms, studio floor, produc-
  tion control room, television set, picture tube*
Telecommunication satellites................... 393
  *Hermes satellite, examples of satellites, trajectory
  of a satellite, telecommunications network*

TRANSPORTATION.............................. 395
Transportation by Road 397
Automobile 397
  *Body, types of bodies, headlight, back of a
  station wagon, windshield wiper, dashboard, in-
  strument board, door, steering, seats*
Service station 401
  Gasoline pump
Semitrailer 402
  Platform, truck trailer
Engines 404
  *Diesel engine, turbo-compressor engine, gasoline
  engine*
Battery 406
Radiator 406
Spark plug 406
Exhaust system 406
Tires 407
Brakes 407
Snowmobile 408
Motorcycle.. 409
Bicycle 411
Cross section of a street........................ 413
Cross section of a road 413
Fixed bridges..................................... 414
Movable bridges 417

Rail transport 418
Diesel-electric locomotive...................... 418
Box car 419
Types of cars..................................... 420
Types of passenger cars........................ 421
  Coach car, sleeping car, dining car
Railroad track 422

Highway crossing 423
Railroad station 424
Train yard................................... 425
Container 425
Station hall 426
Station platform.............................. 427
Transportation by Subway..................... 428
Subway station.............................. 428
Underground railway 429
Subway train, passenger car interior, truck and track
Transportation by Sea.......................... 430
Four-masted bark............................ 430
Masting and rigging, sails
Types of sails................................ 432
Types of rigs 432
Passenger liner 433
Ferry....................................... 434
Container ship 434
Hovercraft 435
Hydrofoil boat............................... 436
Bathyscaphe 437
Submarine................................... 438
Frigate...................................... 439
Canal lock 440
Harbor...................................... 441
Navigation devices 442
Echo sounder, sextant, liquid compass
Maritime signals 444
Buoys, lighthouse, lantern of lighthouse, cardinal
system of marking, lateral system of marking
Anchor 447
Ship's anchor, types of anchors
Transportation by Air.......................... 448
Long-range jet 448
Wing structure 449
Wing shape................................. 449
Tail shape................................... 449
Turbo-jet engine............................. 450
Flight deck.................................. 451
Airport..................................... 452
Ground airport equipment
Passenger terminal.......................... 454
Helicopter................................... 455
Space Transportation 456
Rocket...................................... 456
Space shuttle................................ 457
Space shuttle at takeoff, space shuttle in orbit
Space suit................................... 458
OFFICE SUPPLIES AND EQUIPMENT........ 459
Stationery................................... 461
Office furniture.............................. 465
Typewriter 466
Microcomputer 468
Functions in a system, configuration of a system,
keyboard, peripheral equipment, dot matrix
printer, acoustic coupler, joystick
Computer room 472
MUSIC..................................... 473

Musical notation............................. 475
Stringed instruments......................... 477
Violin family, violin, bow, harp
Keyboard instruments 479
Upright piano, upright piano action
Organ...................................... 481
Production of sound, console, mechanism of the
organ, organ pipes
Wind instruments............................ 483
Woodwind family, saxophone, reeds, brass family,
trumpet
Percussion instruments....................... 485
Traditional musical instruments............... 487
Instrumental groups.......................... 490
Musical accessories 492
Symphony orchestra......................... 493
Electric and electronic instruments........... 494
Electric guitar, synthesizer
CREATIVE LEISURE ACTIVITIES.............. 497
Sewing 499
Sewing machine: tension block, presser foot,
needle, sewing accessories, fasteners, zipper,
fabric structure, underlying fabrics, pattern
Knitting.................................... 504
Knitting machine: tension block, needle bed,
carriage, latch needle
Bobbin lace................................. 506
Embroidery.................................. 507
Frame, groups of stitches
Weaving.................................... 508
Low warp loom, high warp loom, accessories,
diagram of weaving principle, basic weaves
Fine bookbinding............................. 512
Bound book
Intaglio printing process 515
Relief printing process........................ 516
Equipment, etching press
Lithography 517
Equipment, lithographic press
Printing.................................... 518
Diagram of letterpress printing, diagram of in-
taglio printing, diagram of planographic printing
Pottery 519
Turning wheel, tools, baking
Stained glass 521
SPORTS.................................... 523
Team Games................................ 525
Baseball.................................... 525
Field, catcher, player, bat, glove
Football 527
Playing field for Canadian football, playing field
for American football, scrimmage in American
football, scrimmage in Canadian football, protec-
tive equipment, uniform, football
Rugby 531
Field, team, ball
Soccer...................................... 532
Field, ball
Ice hockey 533
Rink, goalkeeper, ice hockey player, player's
stick, goalkeeper's stick, puck

Basketball. 535
  Court, basket
Volleyball 536
  Court, volleyball
Tennis 537
  Court, tennis players, tennis racket
Handball 539
  Court, handball
Squash 540
  International singles court, squash racket
Racquetball. 541
  Four-wall court, racquetball racket
Badminton. 542
  Court, shuttlecock
Table tennis 543
  Table
Curling 544
  Curling rink

Water Sports 545
  Water polo. 545
    Playing area
  Swimming 546
    Swimming competition, starting position, types
    of strokes
  Diving 548
    Diving installations, starting positions, groups of
    dives
  Skin diving. 550
  Sailboard. 551
  One-design sailboat. 552
    Points of sailing, upperworks
  Water skiing 554

Aerial Sports 555
  Parachuting 555
    Parachute, free fall
  Gliding 556
    Glider, cockpit
  Hang gliding. 557
    Hang glider

Winter Sports 558
  Skiing. 558
    Ski resort, alpine skier, ski boot, safety binding
  Cross-country skiing. 561
    Cross-country skier, cross-country ski
  Skating 562
    Figure skate, hockey skate, speed skate, roller
    skate
  Snowshoes 563
    Michigan snowshoe, snowshoe types
  Bobsleigh 564
  Toboggan. 564

Equestrian Sports 565
  Riding 565
    Dress and equipment, obstacles, course of obsta-
    cles, bridle, saddle
  Harness racing. 568
    Standardbred pacer, racing program, stand and
    track

Athletics 570

Track and field athletics 570
  Arena, throwings
Gymnastics. 573
  Men's apparatus, women's apparatus, trampoline
Weightlifting. 575

Combat Sports 576
  Fencing 576
    Piste, fencer, parts of the weapon, fencing weap-
    ons, positions
  Judo 578
    Mat, judo suit, holds
  Boxing. 579
    Ring

Leisure Sports 580
  Fishing 580
    Fly rod, spinning rod, fly reel, open-face spinning
    reel, fishhook, float, lures, accessories
  Billiards 583
    Billiards equipment, pool and carom billiards,
    English billiards and snooker
  Golf 585
    Course, hole, types of golf clubs, golf accessories
  Mountaineering 588
    Equipment, mountaineer
  Bowling 590

Indoor Games 591
  Chess. 591
    Men, chessboards, chess notation
  Backgammon 592
  Card games. 592
  Dice. 593
  Dominoes. 593
  Mah-jongg 593
  Roulette table 594
    Roulette wheel, betting layout
  Slot machine 595

Camping 596
  Tents 596
    Family tents, pup tent, major types of tents
  Sleeping bags 598
  Bed-mattress and accessories. 598
  Propane or butane accessories. 599
  Cooking set. 599
  Combination knife. 599
  Tools 600
  Knots 601

MEASURING DEVICES 603
  Measure of time. 605
    Mechanical watch, tuning fork watch, hourglass,
    sundial, weight-driven clock mechanism, grand-
    father clock
  Measure of weight. 608
    Steelyard, beam balance, spring balance, Rober-
    val's balance, analytical balance, self-indicating
    scales, bathroom scales, electronic scales
  Measure of temperature 611
    Bimetallic thermometer, clinical thermometer,
    room thermostat
  Measure of pressure 612
    Aneroid barometer, sphygmomanometer

Tape measure 613
Pedometer 613
Micrometer caliper 613
Theodolite 614
Watt-hour meter 615
Horizontal seismograph 616
Vertical seismograph.......................... 616
OPTICAL INSTRUMENTS........................ 617
Binocular microscope 619
Electron microscope........................... 620
Prism binoculars............................... 621
Telescopic sight 621
Reflecting telescope 622
Refracting telescope 623
Radar 624
Lens 625
Conveging lens, diverging lens
Magnetic compass 625
HEALTH...................................... 627
First aid kit................................... 629
Syringes.. 629
Walking aids................................... 630
Crutches, canes
Wheelchair..................................... 631

ENERGY...................................... 633
Coal mine...................................... 635
Open-pit mine, strip mine, mining, underground mine, pithead, pneumatic hammer, jackleg drill
Oil... 640
Drilling rig, beam pump, gas lift, Christmas tree, offshore drilling, production platform, pipeline, tanker, tank car, tank trailer, tank truck, floating-roof tank, fixed-roof tank, refinery, refinery products, oil sands mining plant
Electricity..................................... 651
Hydroelectric complex, cross section of an embankment dam, cross section of a concrete dam, major types of dams, steps in production of electricity, cross section of an hydroelectric power station, generator, cross section of an hydraulic turbine, tower, overhead connection, tidal power plant
Nuclear energy................................. 661
Candu nuclear generating station, Candu reactor, nuclear reactor, fuel bundle, generating station flow diagram, fuel handling sequence, control room, production of electricity by nuclear energy, nuclear fuel cycle
Solar energy................................... 668
Solar furnace, tower-type solar power station, solar house, solar cell, solar collector
Windmill....................................... 671
Tower mill, post mill
Wind turbine................................... 672
Horizontal-axis wind turbine, vertical-axis wind turbine, wind turbine electricity production
HEAVY MACHINERY............................. 673
Dragline....................................... 675
Fire engine.................................... 676
Aerial ladder truck, pumper

Bulldozer...................................... 678
Wheel loader 679
Grader... 680
Hydraulic shovel............................... 681
Scraper.. 682
Dump truck.................................... 682
Material handling 683
Crane, forklift truck, forklift reach truck, handling engines
WEAPONS 687
Stone Age arms................................. 689
African warrior................................ 689
Roman legionary 689
Armor.. 690
Bows and crossbow............................ 691
Swords 692
Bayonets....................................... 693
Major types of bayonets, parts of a hilted bayonet
Seventeenth century cannon 694
Muzzle loading, tube, projectiles, accessories for firing
Arquebus 696
Flintlock, loading
Hand grenade.................................. 696
Mortar 697
Modern, seventeenth century
Submachine gun................................ 697
Modern howitzer............................... 698
Automatic rifle 699
Bazooka.. 700
Recoilless rifle 700
Heavy machine gun 701
Light machine gun 701
Hunting weapons............................... 702
Rifle, shotgun, cartridge
Pistol 703
Revolver....................................... 703
Tank 704
Combat aircraft 705
Missiles....................................... 706
Structure of a missile, command system, major types of missiles
SYMBOLS.................................... 707
Heraldry....................................... 709
Parts of a flag, shield, examples of symbols, flag shapes
Signs of the zodiac 712
Information symbols 713
Graphic elements for symbols, international road signs, common symbols, fabric care
Common scientific symbols 723
GENERAL INDEX — ENGLISH 725
SELECTIVE BIBLIOGRAPHY 823

目 錄

前言 11
用法指南 13
檢目表 15

天文 33
  座標系 35
  太陽系行星 36
  行星符號 36
  太陽 37
  月球 38
  星系 39
  彗星 39
  北天球星座圖 40
  南天球星座圖 41
  天文台 42
  天文館 43

地理 45
  地球構造 47
  地球大氣層縱剖面 47
  太空成就 47
  地殼剖面 48
  各大洲輪廓 49
  洋底 50
  波浪 51
  常見的海岸地形 51
  雲及其氣象符號 52

火山 53
地震 53
山 54
溶洞 54
荒漠 55
冰川 56
水的形態 57
水分循環 58
世界氣候 59
國際天氣符號 60
氣象學 62
氣象測量儀器 64
「雨雲」三號氣象衞星 65

植物 67
  植物構造 69
  樹的構造 71
  花的構造 72
  蕈類 73
  肉質果:漿果 74
  複漿果 74
  核果 75
  梨果 76
  肉質果:柑果 77
  乾果:堅果 78
  乾果種類 79
  熱帶水果 80
  蔬菜 81
  植物細胞 86

動物細胞 86

動物 87

鹿科 89
頜的類型 90
馬 91
貓 94
鳥 95
魚 98
蝴蝶 100
單殼貝 101
雙殼貝 101
軟體動物 102
甲殼類動物 103
腹足類動物 104
無尾兩棲動物 105
蜜蜂 106
蝙蝠 108
爬蟲類動物 109

人 111

受精卵發育 113
人體 114
男性生殖器官 116
女性生殖器官 117
肌肉 118
骨骼 120
顱骨構造 122
牙齒 123
血液循環 124
呼吸系統 126
消化系統 127
泌尿系統 128
神經系統 129
感覺器官：視覺 131
感覺器官：聽覺 132
感覺器官：嗅覺 133
感覺器官：味覺 134
感覺器官：觸覺 135

神經元 135
皮膚 136
指甲 137
毛髮 137
親屬關係 138

食物 141

香草 143
麵食 144
麵包 146
小牛肉 147
牛肉 148
豬肉 150
羊肉 151
牛肉 152
小牛肉 153
北美乾酪 154
法國乾酪 154
甜點 156

農場 159

建築物 161
農業機械 162
機械構造 165

建築 167

不同民族的房屋 169
建築風格 170
希臘神廟 171
拱券 172
羅馬房屋 173
哥德式教堂 174
符邦堡壘 176
城堡 177
商業區 178
劇院 179
升降機 181
自動扶梯 182
城市房屋 183

房屋 185

　　房屋外觀 187
　　平面圖 188
　　屋內房間 189
　　結構 190
　　屋頂類型 190
　　結構 192
　　建築材料 193
　　木地板 196
　　樓梯 197
　　門 198
　　窗 199
　　供暖 200
　　空氣調節設備 206

家具 207

　　桌子 209
　　扶手椅 210
　　凳、椅 212
　　無扶手椅子 213
　　床 214
　　儲物家具 215
　　窗簾 217
　　窗簾安裝用具 218
　　軟、硬窗簾 219
　　照明設備 220
　　玻璃器皿 222
　　餐具 223
　　銀餐具 224
　　廚房用具 227
　　炊具 232
　　煮咖啡壺 234
　　家用電器 235

園藝 245

　　花園 247
　　園藝工具和機械 248
　　鏈鋸 253

自行修理用具 255

　　木工工具 257
　　木工緊固用具 264
　　木工 265
　　鎖 266
　　管道工程 267
　　髹漆和粉刷 278
　　軟銲和熔銲 281
　　電氣 284

服裝 289

　　男裝 291
　　手套 299
　　女裝 300
　　童裝 315
　　鞋 318
　　特殊服裝 321

儀容修飾 323

　　珠寶飾物 325
　　眼鏡 328
　　髮型 330
　　化妝品 332

個人用品 335

　　刮鬍刀 337
　　理髮工具 338
　　護齒用品 339
　　電吹風機 340
　　燙髮工具 341
　　修指甲工具 342
　　整髮工具 343
　　烟具 344
　　傘 346
　　行李 347
　　手提包 348
　　皮革製品 350

通訊 353

　　世界各地文字 355

凸點文字	....	356
聲啞人手語	....	357
標點符號	....	357
變音符號	....	357
國際音標	....	358
書信格式	....	359
校對符號	....	362
書寫工具	....	367
攝影	....	368
音響器材	....	378
錄影機	....	382
電影攝影	....	383
電視攝影機	....	384
電報	....	385
電話機	....	387
電話機數種	....	388
電視	....	389
電信衛星	....	393

交通運輸 395

道路交通	....	397
汽車	....	397
服務站	....	401
半掛貨車	....	402
載台掛車	....	402
貨運掛車	....	403
引擎	....	404
輔助系統	....	406
輪胎	....	407
制動器	....	407
雪地機車	....	408
摩托車	....	409
腳踏車	....	411
街道橫斷面	....	413
行車道橫斷面	....	413
固定橋	....	414
活動橋	....	417
鐵路運輸	....	418
內燃電力傳動機車	....	418

貨車車廂	....	419
載貨車廂種類	....	420
載客車廂種類	....	421
火車軌	....	422
信號裝置	....	423
火車站	....	424
貨櫃	....	425
調車場	....	425
車站大廳	....	426
車站月台	....	427
地下鐵路運輸	....	428
地下鐵路車站	....	428
地下鐵路	....	429
水路運輸	....	430
四桅帆船	....	430
帆的種類	....	432
帆式	....	432
定期客船	....	433
渡船	....	434
貨櫃船	....	434
氣墊船	....	435
水翼船	....	436
深海潛水器	....	437
潛艇	....	438
驅逐艦	....	439
水道船閘	....	440
港口	....	441
航海儀器	....	442
航海標識	....	444
錨	....	447
航空運輸	....	448
遠程噴射機	....	448
機翼結構	....	449
渦輪噴射引擎	....	450
駕駛艙	....	451
機場	....	452
機場大樓	....	454
直升飛機	....	455
太空航行	....	456

火箭	456
太空穿梭機	457
太空衣	458

辦公室用品與設備 459

辦公室用品 461
文具 461
辦公室設備 465
打字機 466
微型電腦 468
系統功能示意 468
系統組合 469
鍵盤 470
附加設備 471
電腦室 472

音樂 473

記譜法 475
弦樂器 477
鍵盤樂器 479
風琴 481
管樂器 483
敲擊樂器 485
民族樂器 487
樂器合奏 490
輔助用具 492
交響樂團 493
電樂器與電子樂器 494

消閒工藝 497

縫紉 499
編織 504
編織機 505
枕結花邊 506
刺繡 507
織造 508
精裝書籍裝訂 512
凹版印刷 515
凸版印刷 516

平版印刷 517
印刷 518
陶瓷工藝 519
彩色玻璃 521

運動與遊戲 523

球類運動 525
棒球 525
美式橄欖球 527
英式橄欖球 531
足球 532
冰球 533
籃球 535
排球 536
網球 537
手球 539
壁球 540
短拍壁球 541
羽毛球 542
乒乓球 543
冰上溜石 544
水上運動 545
水球 545
游泳 546
泳式 547
跳水 548
跳水動作 549
潛水 550
帆板 551
帆船 552
航向 553
滑水 554
空中運動 555
跳傘 555
滑翔 556
翼滑翔 557
冬季運動 558
滑雪 558
高山滑雪 559

越野滑雪 561
溜冰 562
雪鞋 563
有舵雪橇 564
平底雪橇 564
馬術運動 565
騎術 565
賽馬車 568
體育運動 570
田徑運動 570
體操 573
舉重 575
格鬥運動 576
劍術 576
柔道 578
拳擊 579
消閒運動 580
垂釣 580
撞球遊戲用具 582
落袋撞球和四球撞球 583
英式撞球和彩球撞球 584
高爾夫球 585
登山 588
保齡球 590
室內遊戲 591
國際象棋 591
西洋雙陸棋 592
紙牌遊戲 592
骰子 593
骨牌 593
麻將 593
輪盤賭枱 594
吃角子老虎 595
露營 596
帳篷 596
露營裝備 598
航海技術 601
繩結 601
纜索 601

量度儀器 603
計時 605
秤重量 608
測溫 611
量壓 612
量度長度和厚度 613
經緯儀 614
電表 615
地震儀 616

光學儀器 617
雙筒顯微鏡 619
電子顯微鏡 620
雙筒稜鏡望遠鏡 621
望遠瞄準器 621
反射望遠鏡 622
折射望遠鏡 623
透鏡 625
探測儀器 624
雷達 624
磁羅盤 625

醫護復健 627
急救藥箱 629
助行工具 630
輪椅 631

能源 633
煤礦 635
石油 640
電力 651
核能 661
太陽能 668
風車 671
風力渦輪機 672

重型機械 673
拉鏟挖土機 675

消防車 676
推土機 678
輪式裝載機 679
平路機 680
液壓挖土機 681
刮土機 682
自卸載重車 682
器材搬運 683
起重機 683
起重車 684
手推車 685
貨盤 685

武器 687

古代武器 689
甲冑 690
弓與弩 691
刀劍 692
匕首 692
刺刀 693
十七世紀火砲 694
火繩槍 696
手榴彈 696
迫擊砲 697
衝鋒槍 697
現代榴彈砲 698
自動步槍 699
火箭筒 700

無座力砲 700
重機關槍 701
輕機關槍 701
獵槍 702
手槍 703
左輪手槍 703
坦克 704
戰鬥機 705
導彈 706

標識 707

旗幟紋章 709
旗幟與盾牌 709
紋章圖案 710
旗形 711
黃道十二宮 712
星座 712
告示標識 713
表意符號 713
國際路標 714
常用標識 718
織物洗熨 722
常用科學符號 723

英文索引 725
中文索引 761

ASTRONOMY

天文

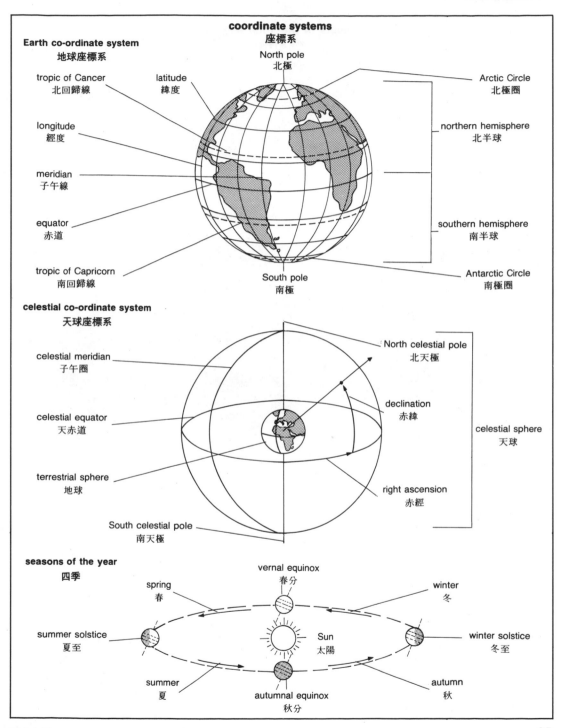

coordinate systems
座標系

Earth co-ordinate system
地球座標系

tropic of Cancer
北回歸線

latitude
緯度

North pole
北極

Arctic Circle
北極圈

northern hemisphere
北半球

longitude
經度

meridian
子午線

equator
赤道

southern hemisphere
南半球

tropic of Capricorn
南回歸線

South pole
南極

Antarctic Circle
南極圈

celestial co-ordinate system
天球座標系

celestial meridian
子午圈

North celestial pole
北天極

declination
赤緯

celestial equator
天赤道

celestial sphere
天球

terrestrial sphere
地球

right ascension
赤經

South celestial pole
南天極

seasons of the year
四季

vernal equinox
春分

spring
春

winter
冬

summer solstice
夏至

Sun
太陽

winter solstice
冬至

summer
夏

autumnal equinox
秋分

autumn
秋

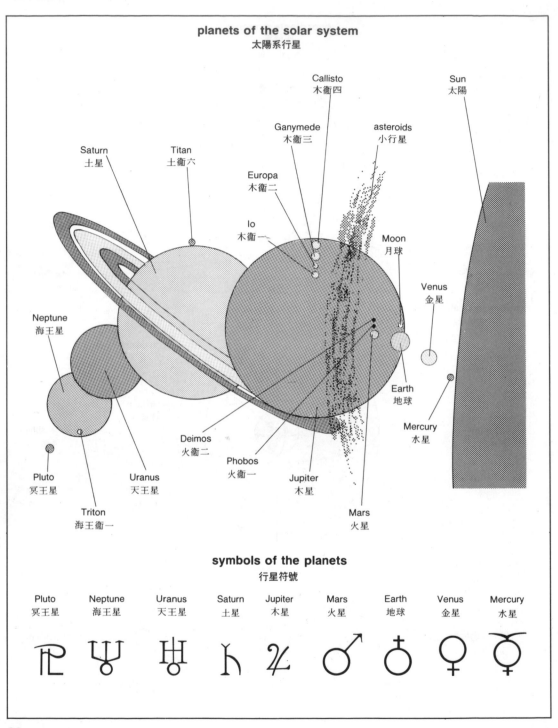

planets of the solar system
太陽系行星

Callisto 木衞四

Ganymede 木衞三

Europa 木衞二

Io 木衞一

asteroids 小行星

Sun 太陽

Saturn 土星

Titan 土衞六

Moon 月球

Venus 金星

Neptune 海王星

Earth 地球

Deimos 火衞二

Phobos 火衞一

Jupiter 木星

Mercury 水星

Pluto 冥王星

Uranus 天王星

Triton 海王衞一

Mars 火星

symbols of the planets
行星符號

Pluto 冥王星	Neptune 海王星	Uranus 天王星	Saturn 土星	Jupiter 木星	Mars 火星	Earth 地球	Venus 金星	Mercury 水星

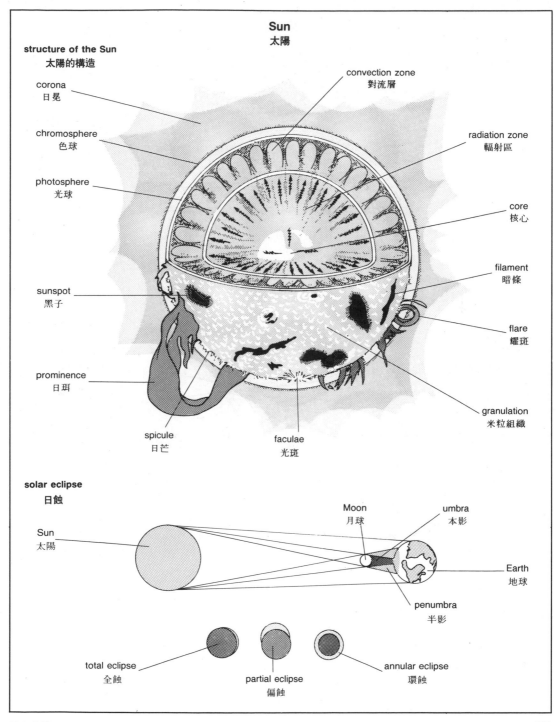

Sun
太陽

structure of the Sun
太陽的構造

corona
日冕

convection zone
對流層

chromosphere
色球

radiation zone
輻射區

photosphere
光球

core
核心

filament
暗條

sunspot
黑子

flare
耀斑

prominence
日珥

granulation
米粒組織

spicule
日芒

faculae
光斑

solar eclipse
日蝕

Moon
月球

umbra
本影

Sun
太陽

Earth
地球

penumbra
半影

total eclipse
全蝕

partial eclipse
偏蝕

annular eclipse
環蝕

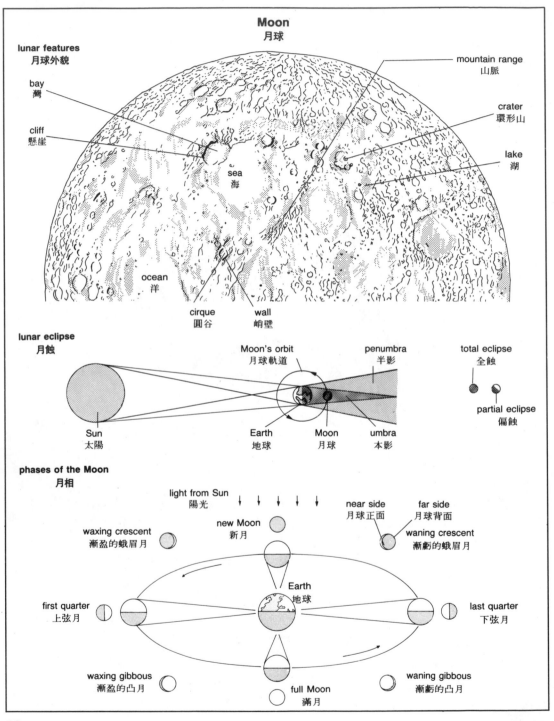

Moon
月球

lunar features
月球外貌

bay
灣

cliff
懸崖

sea
海

ocean
洋

mountain range
山脈

crater
環形山

lake
湖

cirque
圓谷

wall
峭壁

lunar eclipse
月蝕

Moon's orbit
月球軌道

penumbra
半影

total eclipse
全蝕

partial eclipse
偏蝕

Sun
太陽

Earth
地球

Moon
月球

umbra
本影

phases of the Moon
月相

light from Sun
陽光

new Moon
新月

near side
月球正面

far side
月球背面

waxing crescent
漸盈的蛾眉月

waning crescent
漸虧的蛾眉月

first quarter
上弦月

Earth
地球

last quarter
下弦月

waxing gibbous
漸盈的凸月

full Moon
滿月

waning gibbous
漸虧的凸月

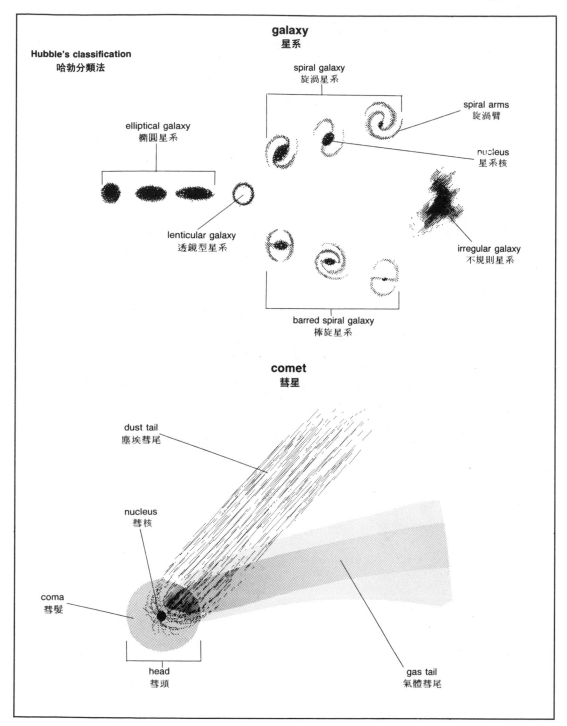

galaxy
星系

Hubble's classification
哈勃分類法

elliptical galaxy
橢圓星系

spiral galaxy
旋渦星系

spiral arms
旋渦臂

nucleus
星系核

lenticular galaxy
透鏡型星系

irregular galaxy
不規則星系

barred spiral galaxy
棒旋星系

comet
彗星

dust tail
塵埃彗尾

nucleus
彗核

coma
彗髮

gas tail
氣體彗尾

head
彗頭

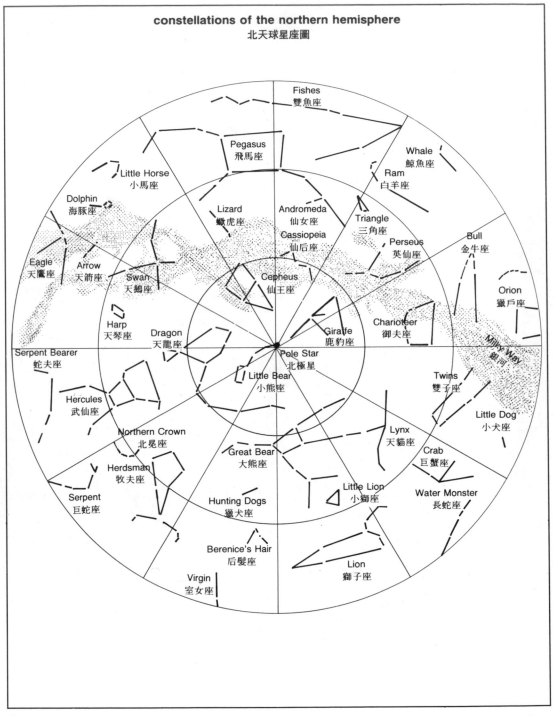

constellations of the northern hemisphere
北天球星座圖

constellations of the southern hemisphere
南天球星座圖

Water Bearer
寶瓶座

Whale
鯨魚座

Southern Fish
南魚座

Sculptor
玉夫座

Crane
天鶴座

Sea Goat
摩羯座

Eagle
天鷹座

Furnace
天爐座

Phoenix
鳳凰座

Indian
印第安座

Eridanus
波江座

Toucan
杜鵑座

Southern
Crown
南冕座

Archer
人馬座

Shield
盾牌座

Hare
天兔座

Swordfish
劍魚座

Sea Serpent
水蛇座

Telescope
望遠鏡座

Serpent
巨蛇座

Dove
天鴿座

Net
網罟座

Octant
南極座

Peacock
孔雀座

Orion
獵戶座

Flying Fish
飛魚座

Chameleon
蝘蜓座

Bird of Paradise
天燕座

Serpent Bearer
蛇夫座

Big Dog
大犬座

Altar
天壇座

Ship's Keel
船底座

Fly
蒼蠅座

Southern Triangle
南三角座

Scorpion
天蠍座

Unicorn
麒麟座

Southern Cross
南十字座

Ship's Stern
船尾座

Wolf
豺狼座

Compass
羅盤座

Ship's Sails
船帆座

Centaur
半人馬座

Balance
天秤座

Water Monster
長蛇座

Cup
巨爵座

Crow
烏鴉座

Virgin
室女座

astronomical observatory
天文台

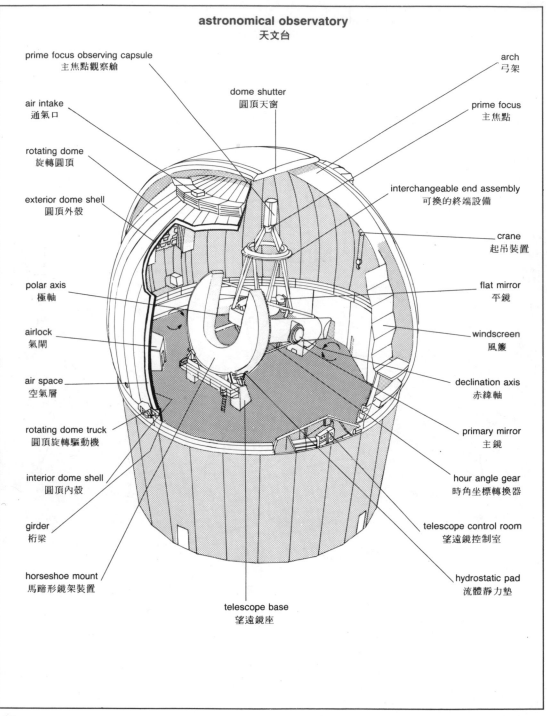

prime focus observing capsule
主焦點觀察艙

arch
弓架

dome shutter
圓頂天窗

prime focus
主焦點

air intake
通氣口

rotating dome
旋轉圓頂

interchangeable end assembly
可換的終端設備

exterior dome shell
圓頂外殼

crane
起吊裝置

polar axis
極軸

flat mirror
平鏡

airlock
氣閘

windscreen
風簾

air space
空氣層

declination axis
赤緯軸

rotating dome truck
圓頂旋轉驅動機

primary mirror
主鏡

interior dome shell
圓頂內殼

hour angle gear
時角坐標轉換器

girder
桁梁

telescope control room
望遠鏡控制室

horseshoe mount
馬蹄形鏡架裝置

hydrostatic pad
流體靜力墊

telescope base
望遠鏡座

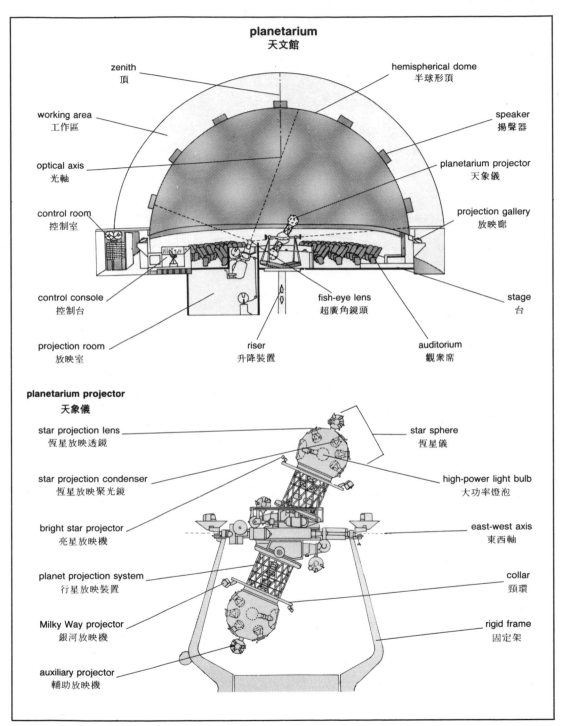

planetarium
天文館

zenith
頂

hemispherical dome
半球形頂

working area
工作區

speaker
揚聲器

optical axis
光軸

planetarium projector
天象儀

control room
控制室

projection gallery
放映廊

control console
控制台

fish-eye lens
超廣角鏡頭

stage
台

projection room
放映室

riser
升降裝置

auditorium
觀衆席

planetarium projector
天象儀

star projection lens
恆星放映透鏡

star sphere
恆星儀

star projection condenser
恆星放映聚光鏡

high-power light bulb
大功率燈泡

bright star projector
亮星放映機

east-west axis
東西軸

planet projection system
行星放映裝置

collar
頸環

Milky Way projector
銀河放映機

rigid frame
固定架

auxiliary projector
輔助放映機

GEOGRAPHY

地理

structure of the Earth
地球構造

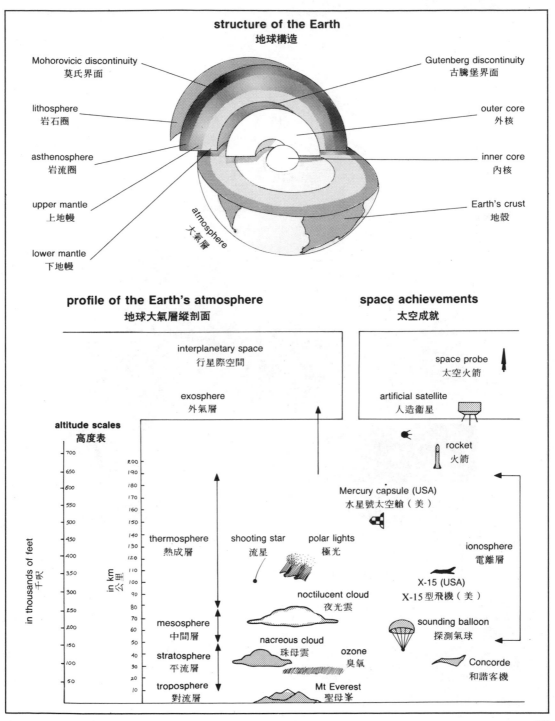

Mohorovicic discontinuity
莫氏界面

Gutenberg discontinuity
古騰堡界面

lithosphere
岩石圈

outer core
外核

asthenosphere
岩流圈

inner core
內核

upper mantle
上地幔

Earth's crust
地殼

lower mantle
下地幔

atmosphere
大氣層

profile of the Earth's atmosphere
地球大氣層縱剖面

space achievements
太空成就

interplanetary space
行星際空間

space probe
太空火箭

exosphere
外氣層

artificial satellite
人造衛星

altitude scales
高度表

rocket
火箭

in thousands of feet
千呎

700
650
600
550
500
450
400
350
300
250
200
150
100
50

in km
公里

200
190
180
170
160
150
140
130
120
110
100
90
80
70
60
50
40
30
20
10

Mercury capsule (USA)
水星號太空艙（美）

thermosphere
熱成層

shooting star
流星

polar lights
極光

ionosphere
電離層

X-15 (USA)
X-15型飛機（美）

noctilucent cloud
夜光雲

mesosphere
中間層

nacreous cloud
珠母雲

sounding balloon
探測氣球

stratosphere
平流層

ozone
臭氧

Concorde
和諧客機

troposphere
對流層

Mt Everest
聖母峯

section of the Earth's crust
地殼剖面

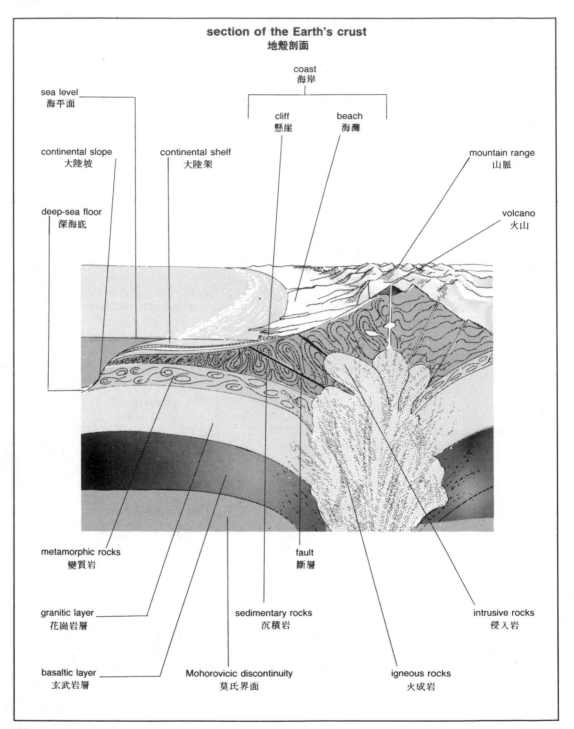

coast
海岸

sea level
海平面

cliff
懸崖

beach
海灘

mountain range
山脈

continental slope
大陸坡

continental shelf
大陸架

volcano
火山

deep-sea floor
深海底

metamorphic rocks
變質岩

fault
斷層

granitic layer
花崗岩層

sedimentary rocks
沉積岩

intrusive rocks
侵入岩

basaltic layer
玄武岩層

Mohorovicic discontinuity
莫氏界面

igneous rocks
火成岩

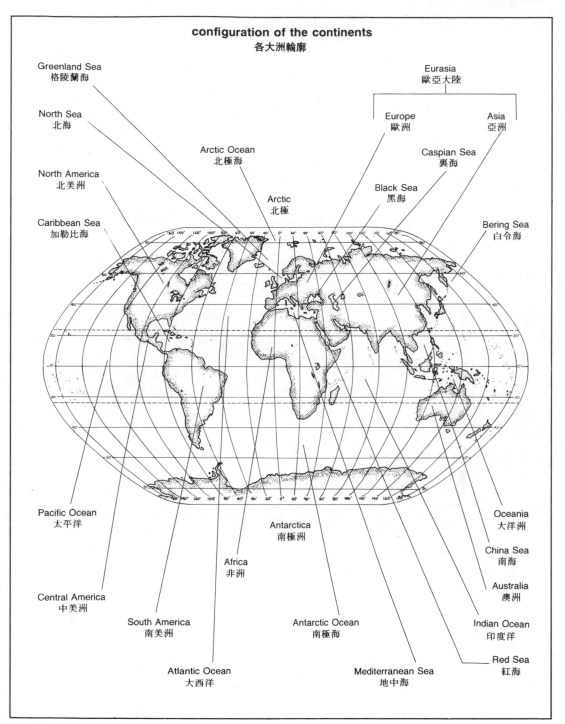

configuration of the continents
各大洲輪廓

Greenland Sea
格陵蘭海

North Sea
北海

Arctic Ocean
北極海

Eurasia
歐亞大陸

Europe
歐洲

Asia
亞洲

Caspian Sea
裏海

North America
北美洲

Black Sea
黑海

Arctic
北極

Caribbean Sea
加勒比海

Bering Sea
白令海

Pacific Ocean
太平洋

Oceania
大洋洲

Antarctica
南極洲

China Sea
南海

Africa
非洲

Australia
澳洲

Central America
中美洲

South America
南美洲

Antarctic Ocean
南極海

Indian Ocean
印度洋

Atlantic Ocean
大西洋

Mediterranean Sea
地中海

Red Sea
紅海

ocean floor
洋底

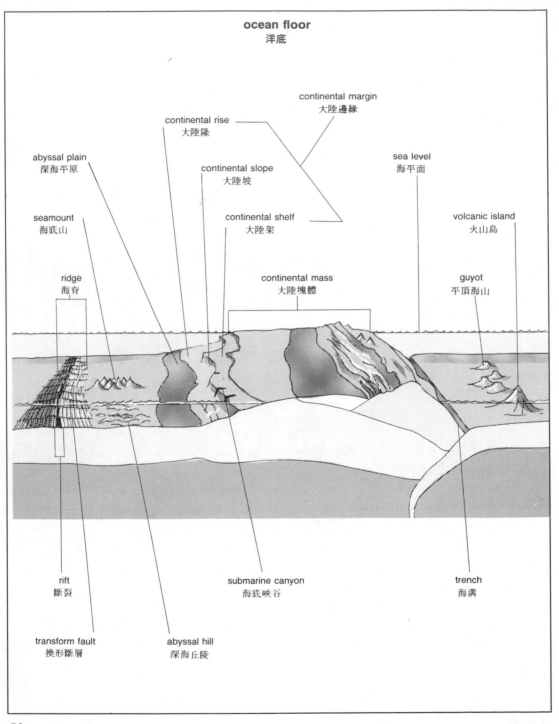

continental margin
大陸邊緣

continental rise
大陸隆

abyssal plain
深海平原

continental slope
大陸坡

sea level
海平面

seamount
海底山

continental shelf
大陸架

volcanic island
火山島

ridge
海脊

continental mass
大陸塊體

guyot
平頂海山

rift
斷裂

submarine canyon
海底峽谷

trench
海溝

transform fault
換形斷層

abyssal hill
深海丘陵

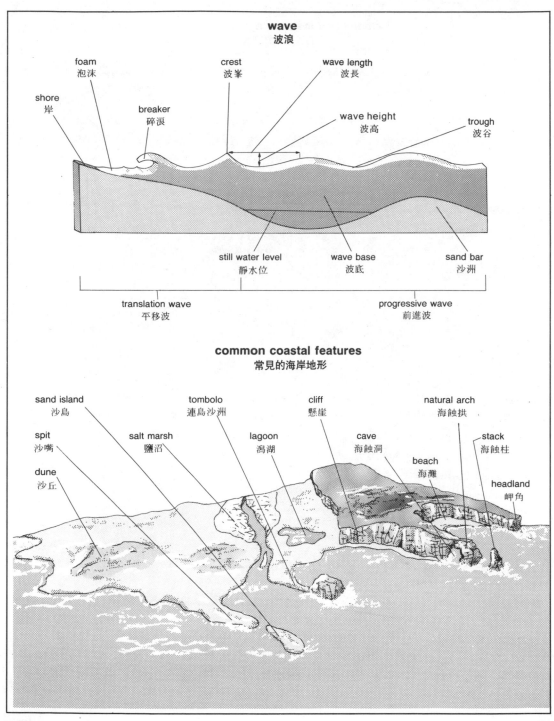

wave
波浪

shore
岸

foam
泡沫

breaker
碎浪

crest
波峯

wave length
波長

wave height
波高

trough
波谷

still water level
靜水位

wave base
波底

sand bar
沙洲

translation wave
平移波

progressive wave
前進波

common coastal features
常見的海岸地形

spit
沙嘴

dune
沙丘

sand island
沙島

salt marsh
鹽沼

tombolo
連島沙洲

lagoon
潟湖

cliff
懸崖

cave
海蝕洞

beach
海灘

natural arch
海蝕拱

stack
海蝕柱

headland
岬角

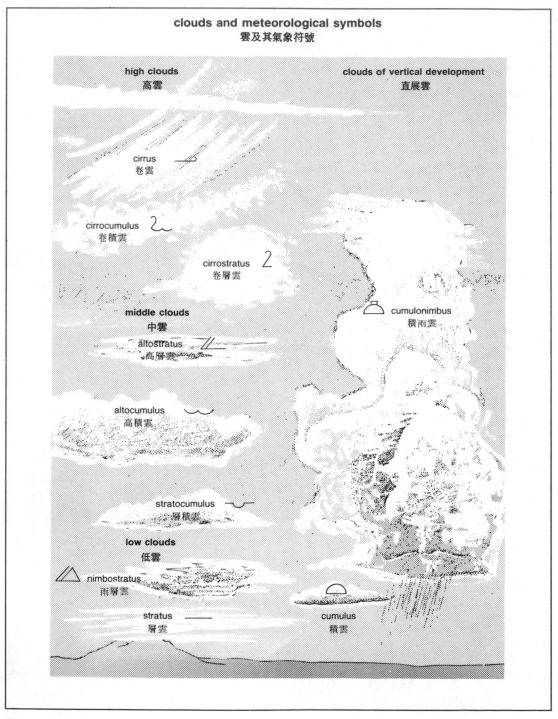

clouds and meteorological symbols
雲及其氣象符號

high clouds
高雲

clouds of vertical development
直展雲

cirrus
卷雲

cirrocumulus
卷積雲

cirrostratus
卷層雲

cumulonimbus
積雨雲

middle clouds
中雲

altostratus
高層雲

altocumulus
高積雲

stratocumulus
層積雲

low clouds
低雲

nimbostratus
雨層雲

stratus
層雲

cumulus
積雲

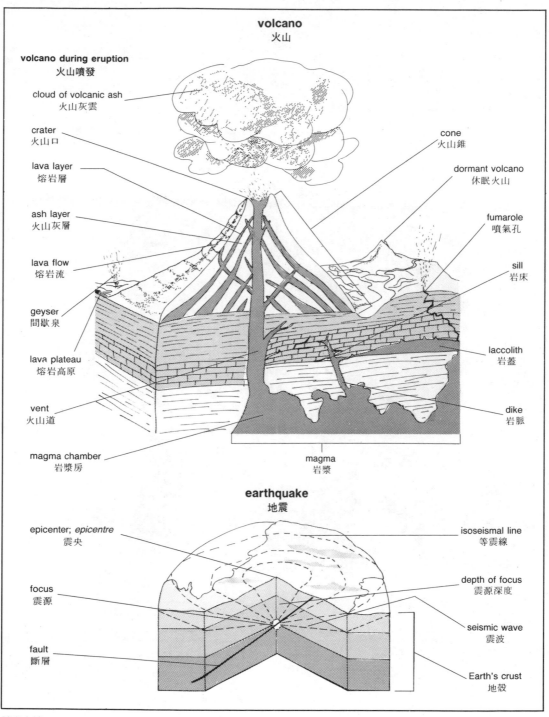

volcano
火山

volcano during eruption
火山噴發

cloud of volcanic ash
火山灰雲

crater
火山口

lava layer
熔岩層

ash layer
火山灰層

lava flow
熔岩流

geyser
間歇泉

lava plateau
熔岩高原

vent
火山道

magma chamber
岩漿房

cone
火山錐

dormant volcano
休眠火山

fumarole
噴氣孔

sill
岩床

laccolith
岩蓋

dike
岩脈

magma
岩漿

earthquake
地震

epicenter; *epicentre*
震央

focus
震源

fault
斷層

isoseismal line
等震線

depth of focus
震源深度

seismic wave
震波

Earth's crust
地殼

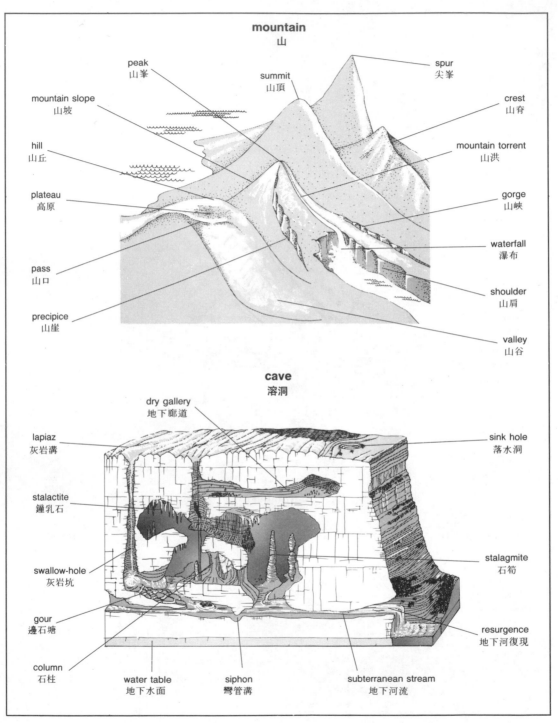

mountain
山

peak
山峯

spur
尖峯

summit
山頂

crest
山脊

mountain slope
山坡

mountain torrent
山洪

hill
山丘

plateau
高原

gorge
山峽

waterfall
瀑布

pass
山口

shoulder
山肩

precipice
山崖

valley
山谷

cave
溶洞

dry gallery
地下廊道

lapiaz
灰岩溝

sink hole
落水洞

stalactite
鐘乳石

swallow-hole
灰岩坑

stalagmite
石筍

gour
邊石塘

resurgence
地下河復現

column
石柱

water table
地下水面

siphon
彎管溝

subterranean stream
地下河流

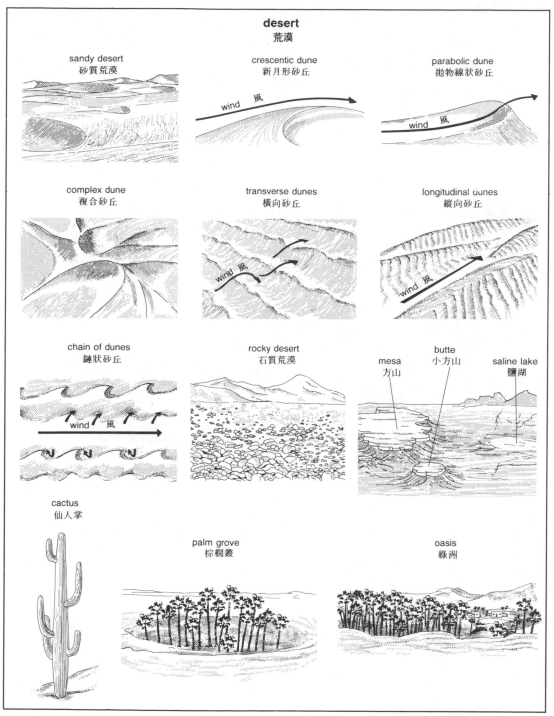

desert
荒漠

sandy desert
砂質荒漠

crescentic dune
新月形砂丘

wind 風

parabolic dune
拋物線狀砂丘

wind 風

complex dune
複合砂丘

transverse dunes
橫向砂丘

wind 風

longitudinal dunes
縱向砂丘

wind 風

chain of dunes
鏈狀砂丘

wind 風

rocky desert
石質荒漠

mesa
方山

butte
小方山

saline lake
鹽湖

cactus
仙人掌

palm grove
棕櫚叢

oasis
綠洲

glacier
冰川

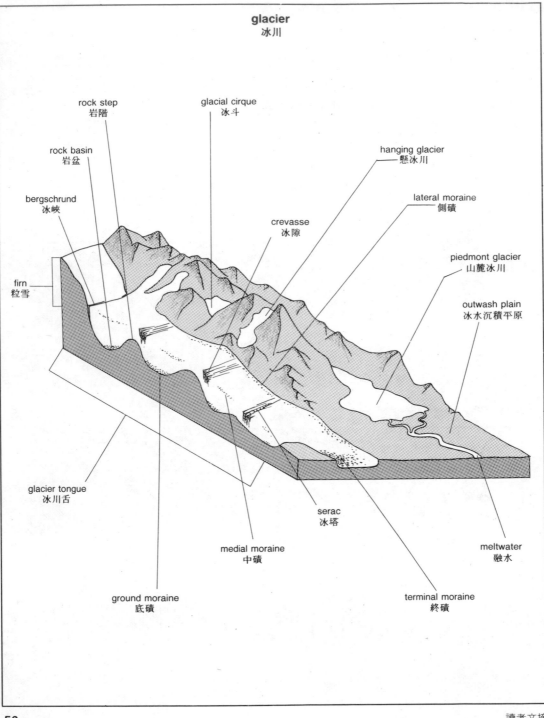

rock step
岩階

glacial cirque
冰斗

hanging glacier
懸冰川

rock basin
岩盆

lateral moraine
側磧

bergschrund
冰峽

crevasse
冰隙

piedmont glacier
山麓冰川

outwash plain
冰水沉積平原

firn
粒雪

glacier tongue
冰川舌

serac
冰塔

meltwater
融水

medial moraine
中磧

ground moraine
底磧

terminal moraine
終磧

water forms
水的形態

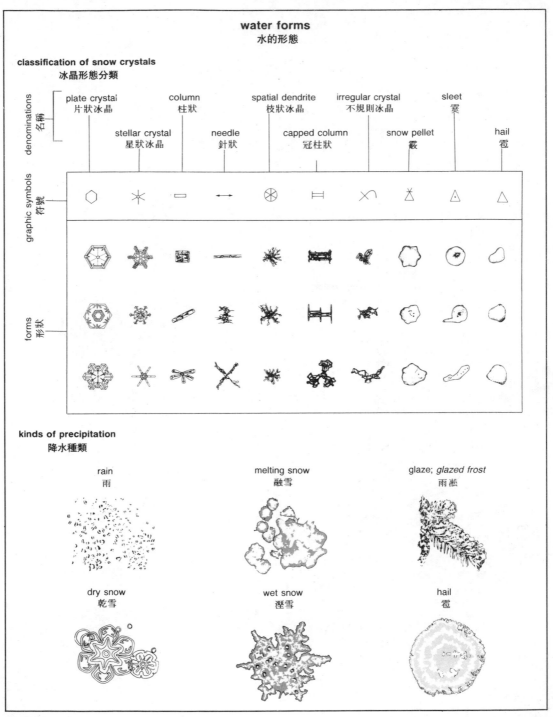

classification of snow crystals
冰晶形態分類

denominations 名稱

plate crystal 片狀冰晶

stellar crystal 星狀冰晶

column 柱狀

needle 針狀

spatial dendrite 枝狀冰晶

capped column 冠柱狀

irregular crystal 不規則冰晶

snow pellet 霰

sleet 霙

hail 雹

graphic symbols 符號

forms 形狀

kinds of precipitation
降水種類

rain 雨

melting snow 融雪

glaze; *glazed frost* 雨凇

dry snow 乾雪

wet snow 溼雪

hail 雹

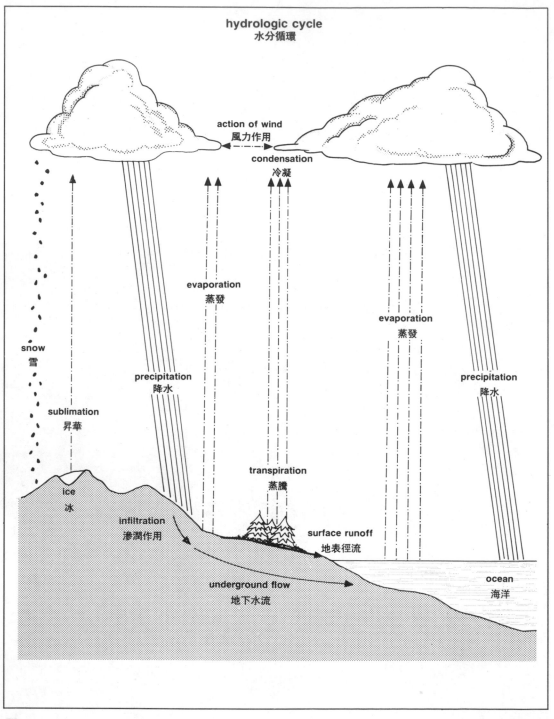

hydrologic cycle
水分循環

action of wind
風力作用

condensation
冷凝

evaporation
蒸發

evaporation
蒸發

snow
雪

sublimation
昇華

precipitation
降水

precipitation
降水

transpiration
蒸騰

ice
冰

infiltration
滲潤作用

surface runoff
地表徑流

underground flow
地下水流

ocean
海洋

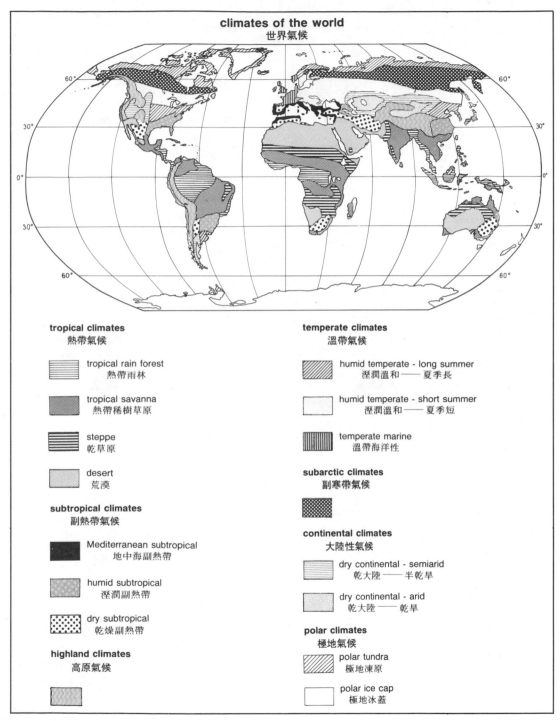

climates of the world
世界氣候

tropical climates
熱帶氣候

- tropical rain forest
  熱帶雨林
- tropical savanna
  熱帶稀樹草原
- steppe
  乾草原
- desert
  荒漠

subtropical climates
副熱帶氣候

- Mediterranean subtropical
  地中海副熱帶
- humid subtropical
  溼潤副熱帶
- dry subtropical
  乾燥副熱帶

highland climates
高原氣候

temperate climates
溫帶氣候

- humid temperate - long summer
  溼潤溫和——夏季長
- humid temperate - short summer
  溼潤溫和——夏季短
- temperate marine
  溫帶海洋性

subarctic climates
副寒帶氣候

continental climates
大陸性氣候

- dry continental - semiarid
  乾大陸——半乾旱
- dry continental - arid
  乾大陸——乾旱

polar climates
極地氣候

- polar tundra
  極地凍原
- polar ice cap
  極地冰蓋

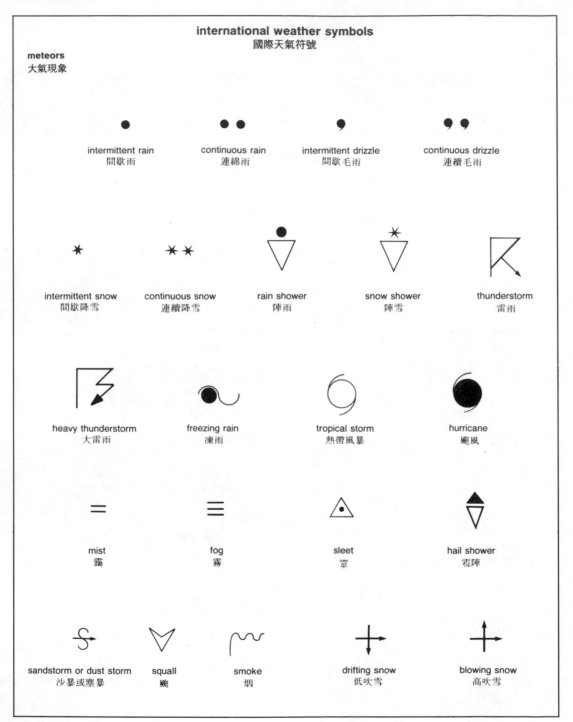

international weather symbols
國際天氣符號

meteors
大氣現象

intermittent rain
間歇雨

continuous rain
連綿雨

intermittent drizzle
間歇毛雨

continuous drizzle
連續毛雨

intermittent snow
間歇降雪

continuous snow
連續降雪

rain shower
陣雨

snow shower
陣雪

thunderstorm
雷雨

heavy thunderstorm
大雷雨

freezing rain
凍雨

tropical storm
熱帶風暴

hurricane
颶風

mist
靄

fog
霧

sleet
霙

hail shower
雹陣

sandstorm or dust storm
沙暴或塵暴

squall
颮

smoke
烟

drifting snow
低吹雪

blowing snow
高吹雪

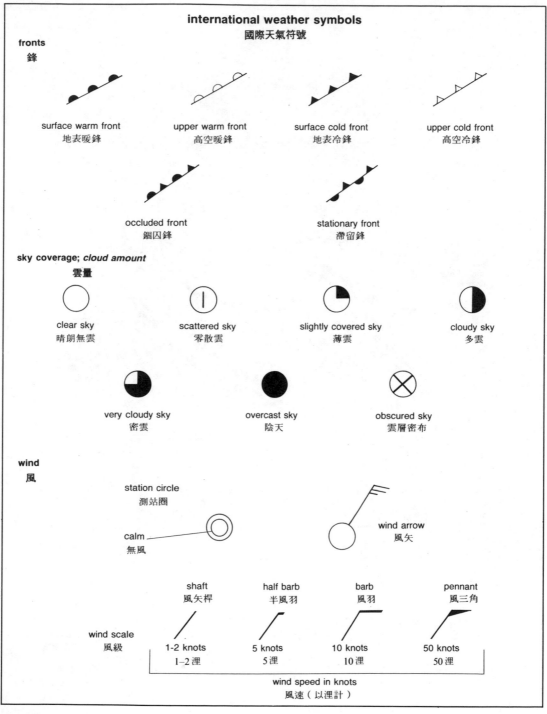

international weather symbols
國際天氣符號

fronts
鋒

surface warm front
地表暖鋒

upper warm front
高空暖鋒

surface cold front
地表冷鋒

upper cold front
高空冷鋒

occluded front
錮囚鋒

stationary front
滯留鋒

sky coverage; *cloud amount*
雲量

clear sky
晴朗無雲

scattered sky
零散雲

slightly covered sky
薄雲

cloudy sky
多雲

very cloudy sky
密雲

overcast sky
陰天

obscured sky
雲層密布

wind
風

station circle
測站圈

calm
無風

wind arrow
風矢

shaft
風矢桿

half barb
半風羽

barb
風羽

pennant
風三角

wind scale
風級

1-2 knots
1-2浬

5 knots
5浬

10 knots
10浬

50 knots
50浬

wind speed in knots
風速（以浬計）

meteorology
氣象學

weather map
天氣圖

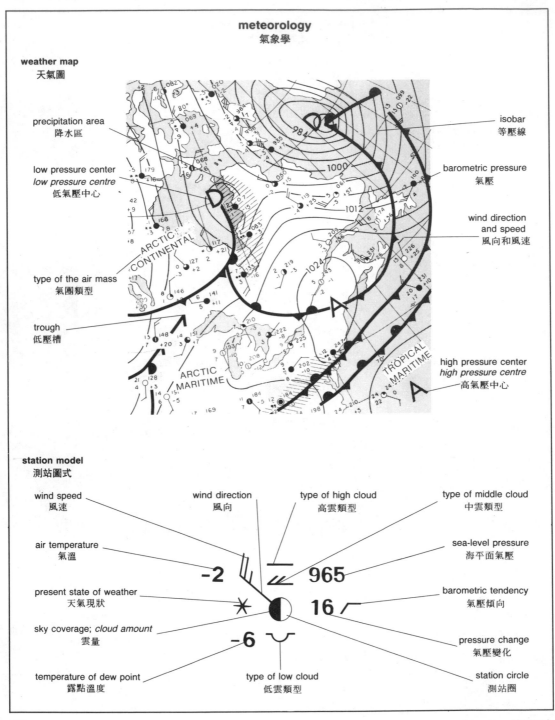

precipitation area
降水區

low pressure center
low pressure centre
低氣壓中心

type of the air mass
氣團類型

trough
低壓槽

isobar
等壓線

barometric pressure
氣壓

wind direction
and speed
風向和風速

high pressure center
high pressure centre
高氣壓中心

ARCTIC CONTINENTAL

ARCTIC MARITIME

TROPICAL MARITIME

station model
測站圖式

wind speed
風速

air temperature
氣溫

present state of weather
天氣現狀

sky coverage; *cloud amount*
雲量

temperature of dew point
露點溫度

wind direction
風向

type of high cloud
高雲類型

type of low cloud
低雲類型

type of middle cloud
中雲類型

sea-level pressure
海平面氣壓

barometric tendency
氣壓傾向

pressure change
氣壓變化

station circle
測站圈

-2   965

16

-6

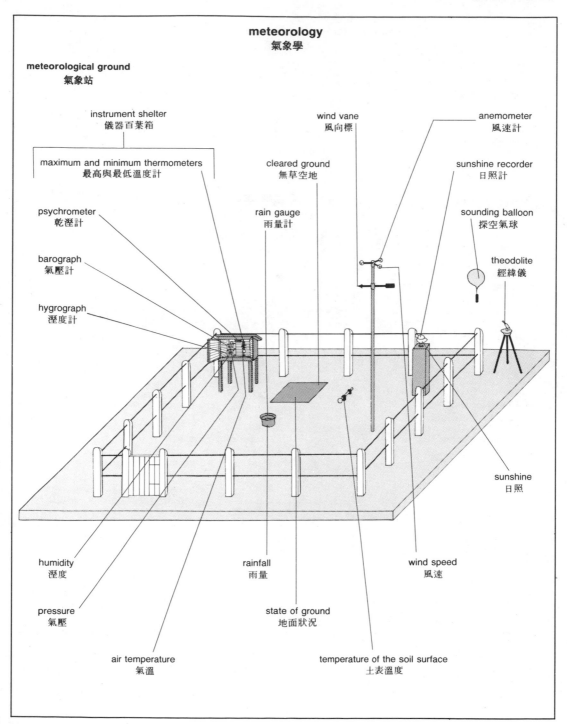

meteorology
氣象學

meteorological ground
氣象站

instrument shelter
儀器百葉箱

maximum and minimum thermometers
最高與最低溫度計

psychrometer
乾溼計

barograph
氣壓計

hygrograph
溼度計

wind vane
風向標

cleared ground
無草空地

rain gauge
雨量計

anemometer
風速計

sunshine recorder
日照計

sounding balloon
探空氣球

theodolite
經緯儀

sunshine
日照

humidity
溼度

pressure
氣壓

air temperature
氣溫

rainfall
雨量

state of ground
地面狀況

temperature of the soil surface
土表溫度

wind speed
風速

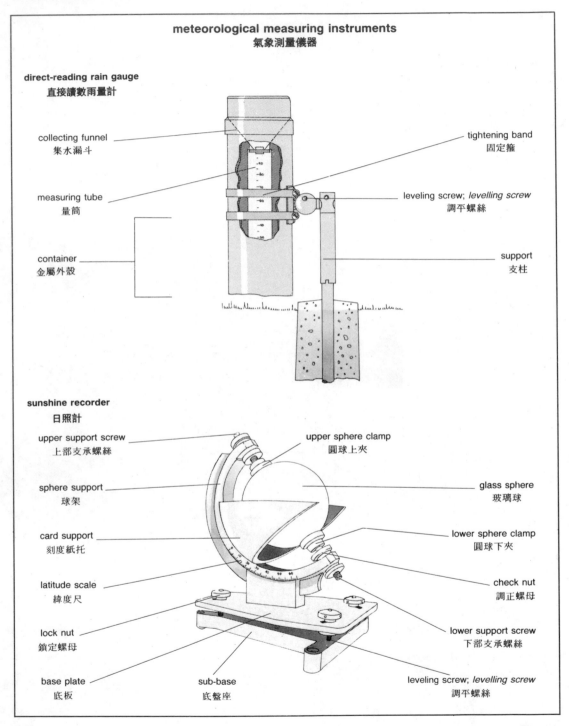

meteorological measuring instruments
氣象測量儀器

direct-reading rain gauge
直接讀數雨量計

collecting funnel
集水漏斗

tightening band
固定箍

measuring tube
量筒

leveling screw; *levelling screw*
調平螺絲

container
金屬外殼

support
支柱

sunshine recorder
日照計

upper support screw
上部支承螺絲

upper sphere clamp
圓球上夾

sphere support
球架

glass sphere
玻璃球

card support
刻度紙托

lower sphere clamp
圓球下夾

latitude scale
緯度尺

check nut
調正螺母

lock nut
鎖定螺母

lower support screw
下部支承螺絲

base plate
底板

sub-base
底盤座

leveling screw; *levelling screw*
調平螺絲

NIMBUS III meteorological satellite
「雨雲」三號氣象衛星

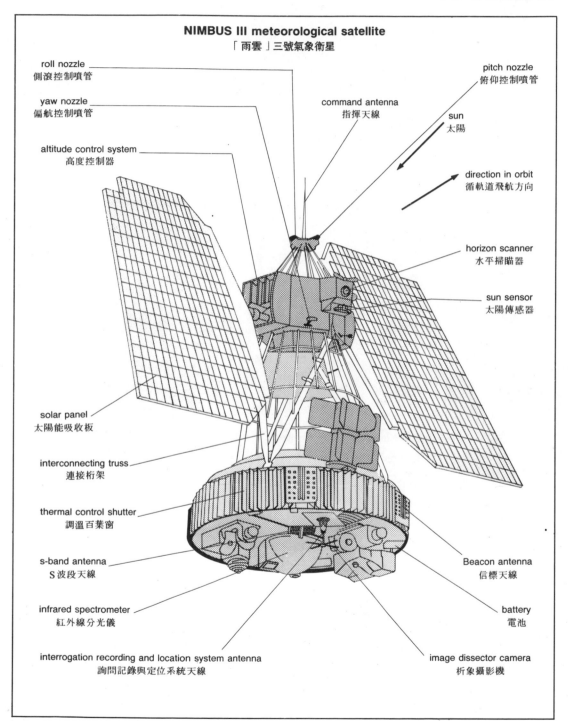

roll nozzle
側滾控制噴管

yaw nozzle
偏航控制噴管

altitude control system
高度控制器

command antenna
指揮天線

pitch nozzle
俯仰控制噴管

sun
太陽

direction in orbit
循軌道飛航方向

horizon scanner
水平掃瞄器

sun sensor
太陽傳感器

solar panel
太陽能吸收板

interconnecting truss
連接桁架

thermal control shutter
調溫百葉窗

s-band antenna
S 波段天線

infrared spectrometer
紅外線分光儀

interrogation recording and location system antenna
詢問記錄與定位系統天線

Beacon antenna
信標天線

battery
電池

image dissector camera
析象攝影機

VEGETABLE KINGDOM

植物

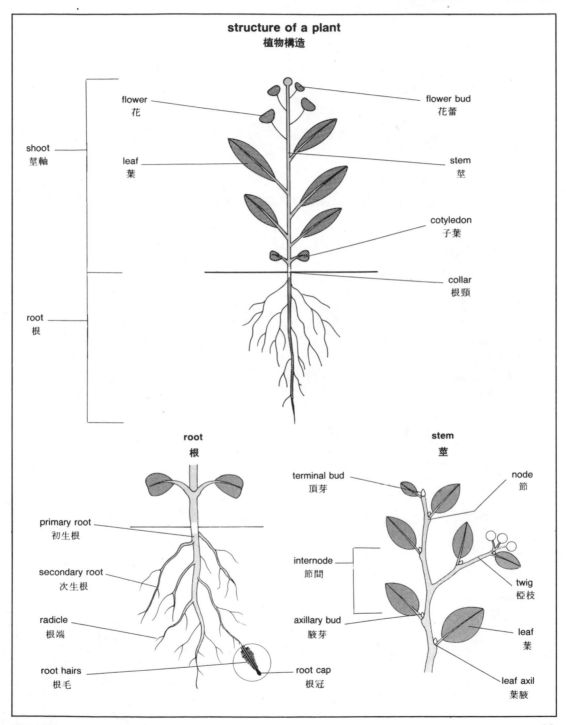

structure of a plant
植物構造

shoot
莖軸

flower
花

leaf
葉

flower bud
花蕾

stem
莖

cotyledon
子葉

collar
根頸

root
根

root
根

stem
莖

primary root
初生根

secondary root
次生根

radicle
根端

root hairs
根毛

root cap
根冠

terminal bud
頂芽

internode
節間

axillary bud
腋芽

node
節

twig
椏枝

leaf
葉

leaf axil
葉腋

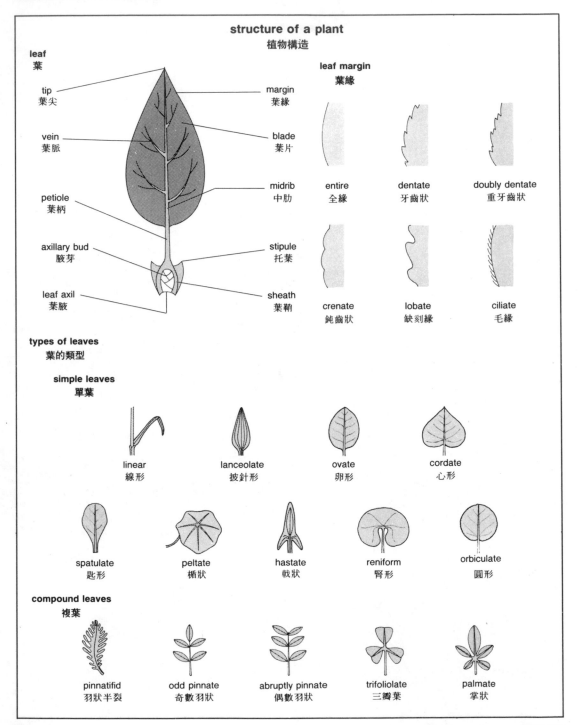

structure of a plant
植物構造

leaf
葉

tip
葉尖

vein
葉脈

petiole
葉柄

axillary bud
腋芽

leaf axil
葉腋

margin
葉緣

blade
葉片

midrib
中肋

stipule
托葉

sheath
葉鞘

leaf margin
葉緣

entire
全緣

dentate
牙齒狀

doubly dentate
重牙齒狀

crenate
鈍齒狀

lobate
缺刻緣

ciliate
毛緣

types of leaves
葉的類型

simple leaves
單葉

linear
線形

lanceolate
披針形

ovate
卵形

cordate
心形

spatulate
匙形

peltate
楯狀

hastate
戟狀

reniform
腎形

orbiculate
圓形

compound leaves
複葉

pinnatifid
羽狀半裂

odd pinnate
奇數羽狀

abruptly pinnate
偶數羽狀

trifoliolate
三鰴葉

palmate
掌狀

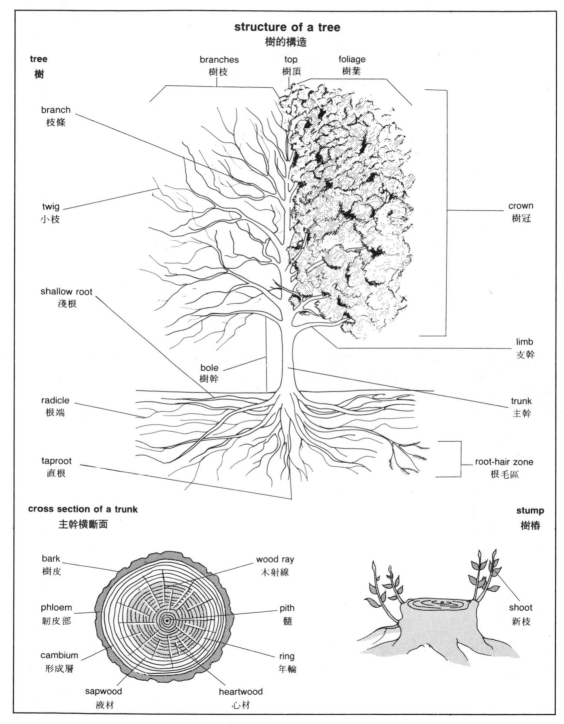

structure of a tree
樹的構造

tree
樹

branches
樹枝

top
樹頂

foliage
樹葉

branch
枝條

twig
小枝

shallow root
淺根

bole
樹幹

radicle
根端

taproot
直根

crown
樹冠

limb
支幹

trunk
主幹

root-hair zone
根毛區

cross section of a trunk
主幹橫斷面

stump
樹樁

bark
樹皮

wood ray
木射線

phloem
韌皮部

pith
髓

cambium
形成層

ring
年輪

sapwood
液材

heartwood
心材

shoot
新枝

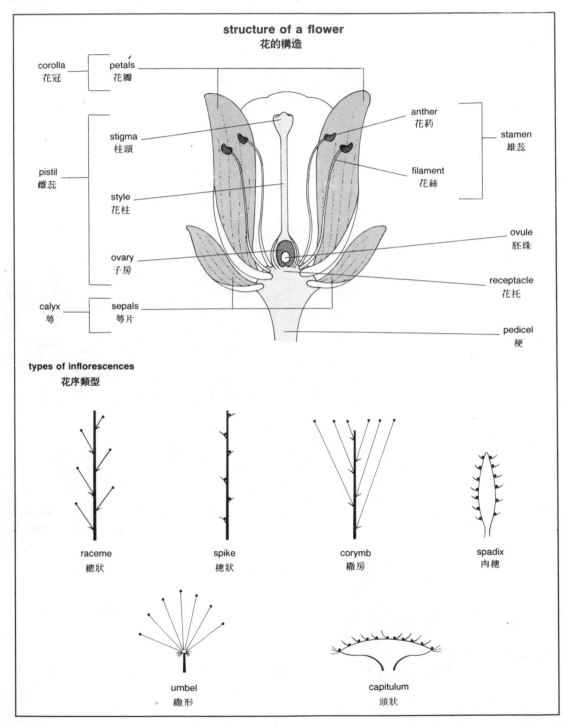

structure of a flower
花的構造

corolla
花冠

petals
花瓣

stigma
柱頭

anther
花葯

stamen
雄蕊

pistil
雌蕊

filament
花絲

style
花柱

ovary
子房

ovule
胚珠

receptacle
花托

calyx
萼

sepals
萼片

pedicel
梗

types of inflorescences

花序類型

raceme
總狀

spike
穗狀

corymb
繖房

spadix
肉穗

umbel
繖形

capitulum
頭狀

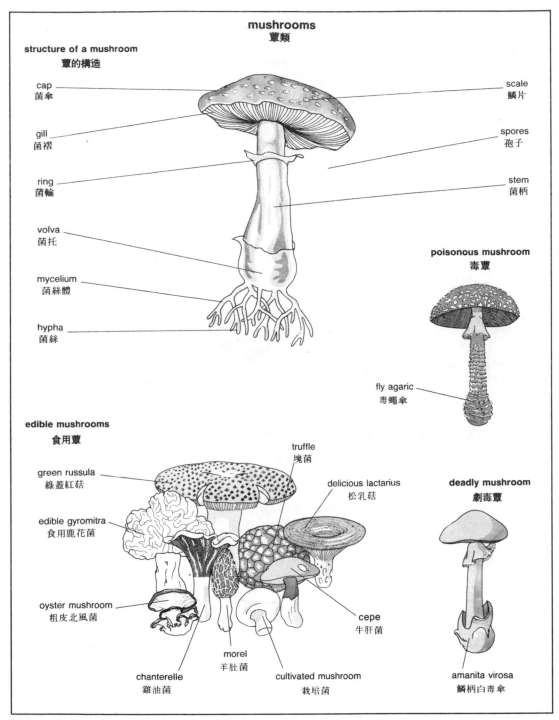

mushrooms
蕈類

structure of a mushroom
蕈的構造

cap
菌傘

scale
鱗片

gill
菌褶

spores
孢子

ring
菌輪

stem
菌柄

volva
菌托

mycelium
菌絲體

hypha
菌絲

poisonous mushroom
毒蕈

fly agaric
毒蠅傘

edible mushrooms
食用蕈

green russula
綠蓋紅菇

truffle
塊菌

delicious lactarius
松乳菇

deadly mushroom
劇毒蕈

edible gyromitra
食用鹿花菌

oyster mushroom
粗皮北風菌

cepe
牛肝菌

morel
羊肚菌

chanterelle
雞油菌

cultivated mushroom
栽培菌

amanita virosa
鱗柄白毒傘

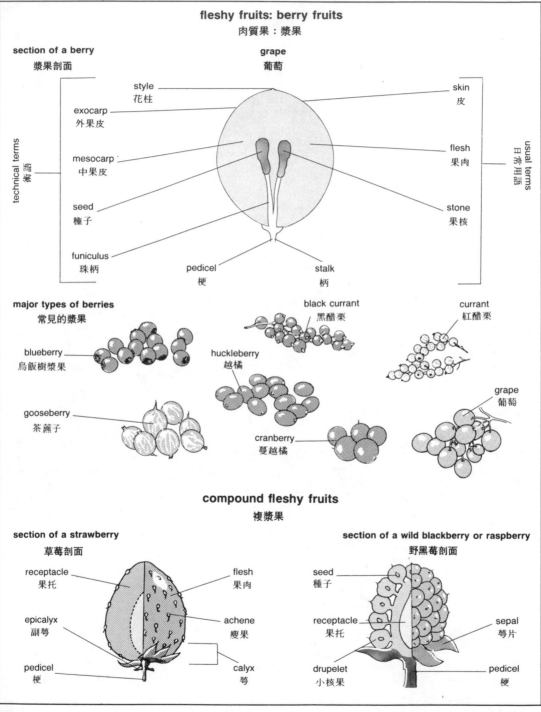

fleshy fruits: berry fruits
肉質果：漿果

section of a berry
漿果剖面

grape
葡萄

technical terms
術語

usual terms
日常用語

style
花柱

skin
皮

exocarp
外果皮

mesocarp
中果皮

flesh
果肉

seed
種子

stone
果核

funiculus
珠柄

pedicel
梗

stalk
柄

major types of berries
常見的漿果

black currant
黑醋栗

currant
紅醋栗

blueberry
烏飯樹漿果

huckleberry
越橘

gooseberry
茶藨子

cranberry
蔓越橘

grape
葡萄

compound fleshy fruits
複漿果

section of a strawberry
草莓剖面

section of a wild blackberry or raspberry
野黑莓剖面

receptacle
果托

flesh
果肉

seed
種子

epicalyx
副萼

achene
瘦果

receptacle
果托

sepal
萼片

pedicel
梗

calyx
萼

drupelet
小核果

pedicel
梗

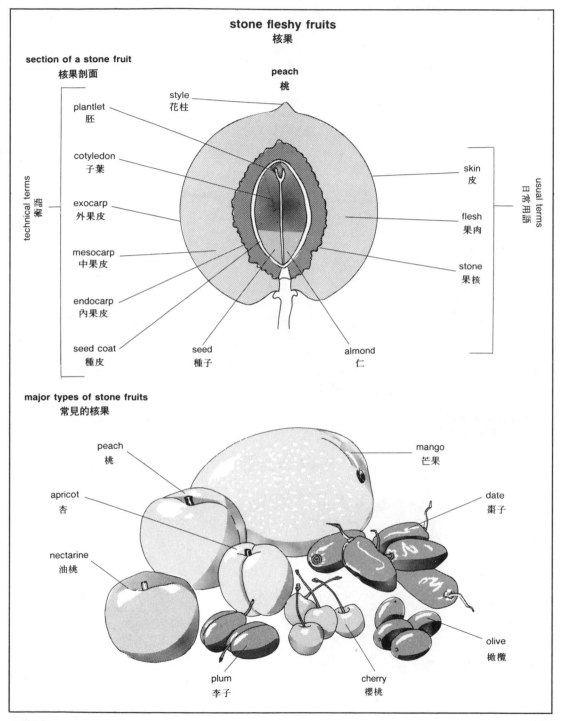

stone fleshy fruits
核果

section of a stone fruit
核果剖面

peach
桃

style
花柱

plantlet
胚

cotyledon
子葉

exocarp
外果皮

mesocarp
中果皮

endocarp
內果皮

seed coat
種皮

seed
種子

almond
仁

technical terms
術語

usual terms
日常用語

skin
皮

flesh
果肉

stone
果核

major types of stone fruits
常見的核果

peach
桃

mango
芒果

apricot
杏

date
棗子

nectarine
油桃

plum
李子

cherry
櫻桃

olive
橄欖

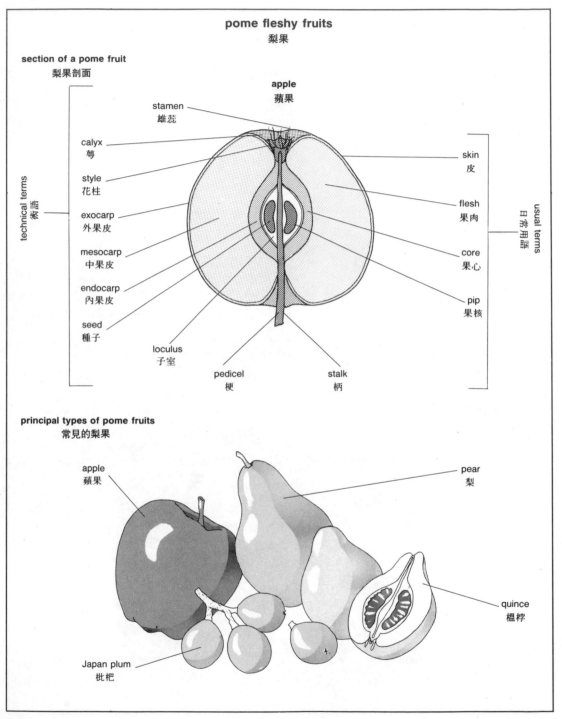

pome fleshy fruits
梨果

section of a pome fruit
梨果剖面

apple
蘋果

technical terms
術語

stamen
雄蕊

calyx
萼

style
花柱

exocarp
外果皮

mesocarp
中果皮

endocarp
內果皮

seed
種子

loculus
子室

pedicel
梗

stalk
柄

skin
皮

flesh
果肉

core
果心

pip
果核

usual terms
日常用語

principal types of pome fruits
常見的梨果

apple
蘋果

pear
梨

quince
榅桲

Japan plum
枇杷

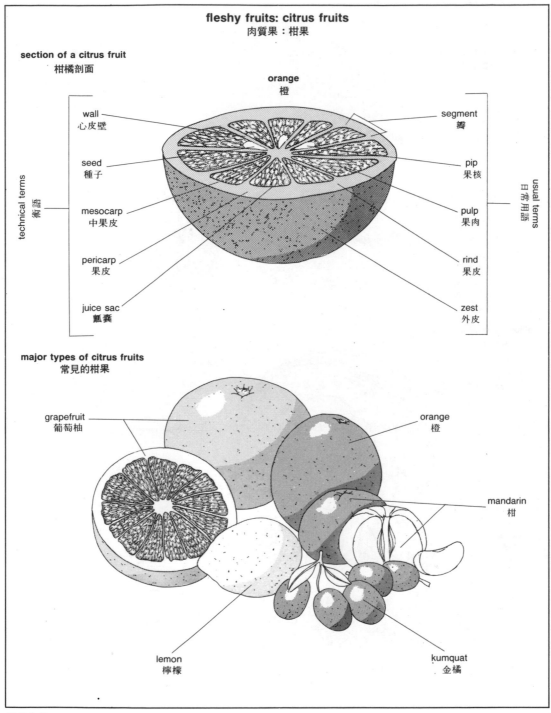

fleshy fruits: citrus fruits
肉質果：柑果

section of a citrus fruit
柑橘剖面

orange
橙

technical terms
術語

usual terms
日常用語

wall
心皮壁

segment
瓣

seed
種子

pip
果核

mesocarp
中果皮

pulp
果肉

pericarp
果皮

rind
果皮

juice sac
瓤囊

zest
外皮

major types of citrus fruits
常見的柑果

grapefruit
葡萄柚

orange
橙

mandarin
柑

lemon
檸檬

kumquat
金橘

dry fruits: nuts
乾果：堅果

section of a hazelnut
榛子剖面

section of a walnut
核桃剖面

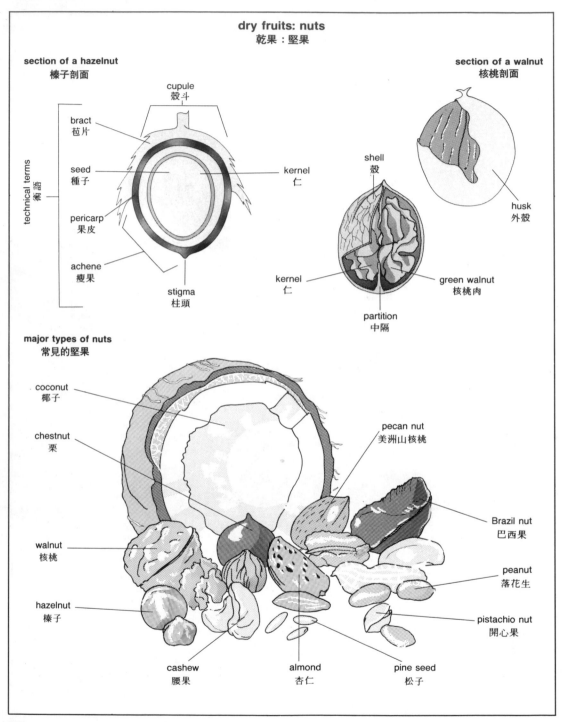

technical terms
術語

cupule
殼斗

bract
苞片

seed
種子

pericarp
果皮

achene
瘦果

stigma
柱頭

kernel
仁

shell
殼

husk
外殼

kernel
仁

green walnut
核桃肉

partition
中隔

major types of nuts
常見的堅果

coconut
椰子

chestnut
栗

pecan nut
美洲山核桃

Brazil nut
巴西果

walnut
核桃

peanut
落花生

hazelnut
榛子

pistachio nut
開心果

cashew
腰果

almond
杏仁

pine seed
松子

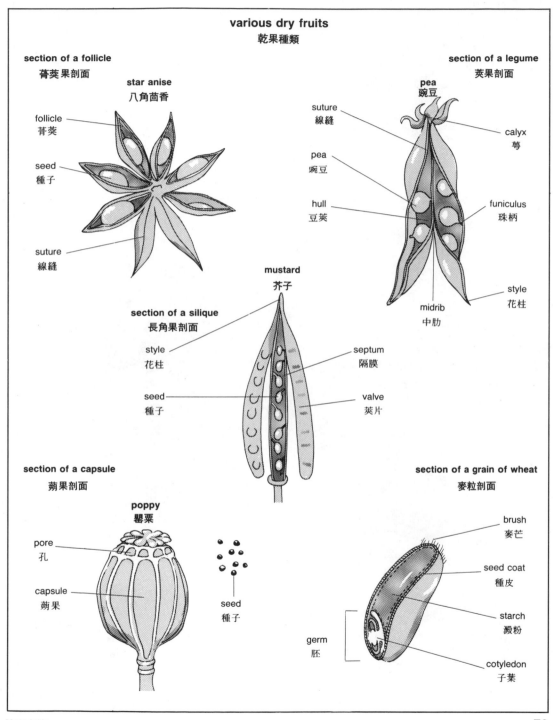

various dry fruits
乾果種類

section of a follicle
菁葜果剖面

star anise
八角茴香

follicle
菁葜

seed
種子

suture
線縫

section of a legume
莢果剖面

pea
豌豆

suture
線縫

calyx
萼

pea
豌豆

hull
豆莢

funiculus
珠柄

style
花柱

midrib
中肋

mustard
芥子

section of a silique
長角果剖面

style
花柱

septum
隔膜

seed
種子

valve
莢片

section of a capsule
蒴果剖面

poppy
罌粟

pore
孔

capsule
蒴果

seed
種子

section of a grain of wheat
麥粒剖面

brush
麥芒

seed coat
種皮

starch
澱粉

germ
胚

cotyledon
子葉

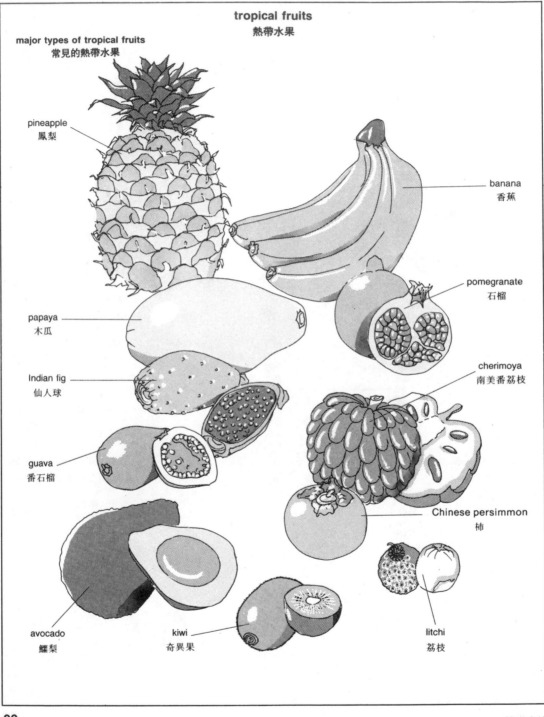

tropical fruits
熱帶水果

major types of tropical fruits
常見的熱帶水果

pineapple
鳳梨

banana
香蕉

pomegranate
石榴

papaya
木瓜

cherimoya
南美番荔枝

Indian fig
仙人球

guava
番石榴

Chinese persimmon
柿

avocado
鱷梨

kiwi
奇異果

litchi
荔枝

vegetables
蔬菜

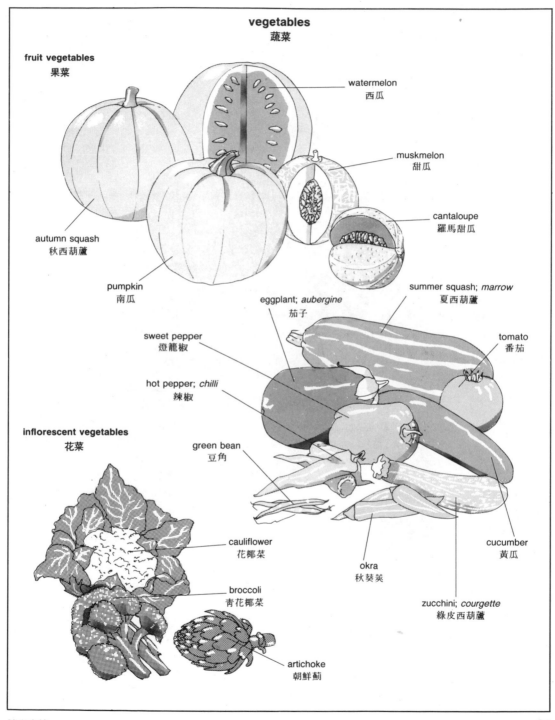

fruit vegetables
果菜

watermelon
西瓜

muskmelon
甜瓜

cantaloupe
羅馬甜瓜

autumn squash
秋西葫蘆

pumpkin
南瓜

summer squash; *marrow*
夏西葫蘆

eggplant; *aubergine*
茄子

tomato
番茄

sweet pepper
燈籠椒

hot pepper; *chilli*
辣椒

inflorescent vegetables
花菜

green bean
豆角

cucumber
黃瓜

cauliflower
花椰菜

broccoli
青花椰菜

okra
秋葵莢

zucchini; *courgette*
綠皮西葫蘆

artichoke
朝鮮薊

vegetables
蔬菜

leaf vegetables
葉菜

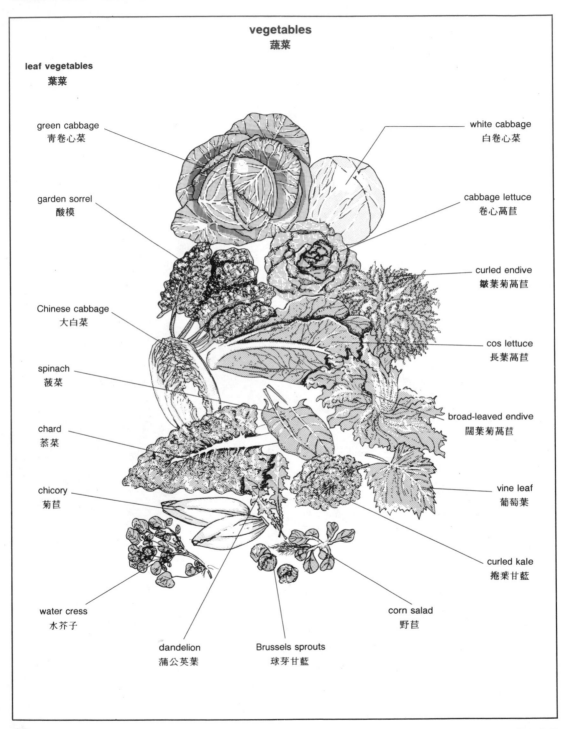

green cabbage
青卷心菜

white cabbage
白卷心菜

garden sorrel
酸模

cabbage lettuce
卷心萵苣

curled endive
皺葉菊萵苣

Chinese cabbage
大白菜

cos lettuce
長葉萵苣

spinach
菠菜

broad-leaved endive
闊葉菊萵苣

chard
莙荙菜

vine leaf
葡萄葉

chicory
菊苣

curled kale
捲葉甘藍

water cress
水芥子

corn salad
野苣

dandelion
蒲公英葉

Brussels sprouts
球芽甘藍

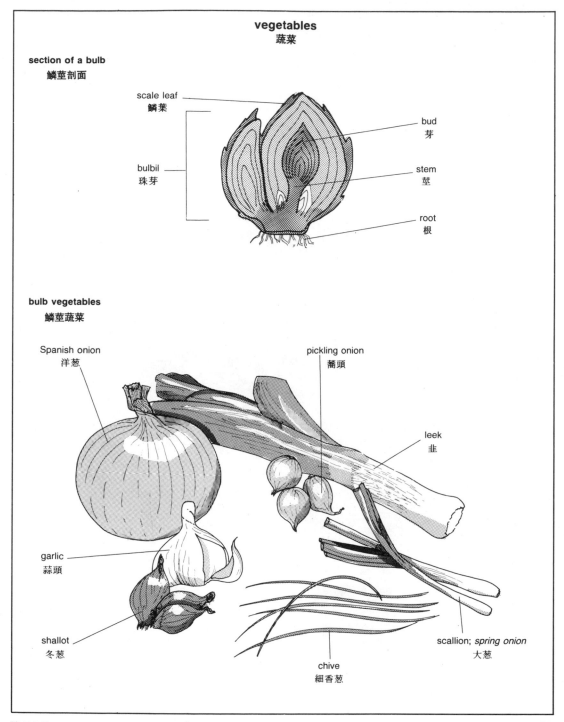

vegetables
蔬菜

section of a bulb
鱗莖剖面

scale leaf
鱗葉

bud
芽

bulbil
珠芽

stem
莖

root
根

bulb vegetables
鱗莖蔬菜

Spanish onion
洋葱

pickling onion
蕎頭

leek
韭

garlic
蒜頭

shallot
冬葱

chive
細香葱

scallion; *spring onion*
大葱

vegetables
蔬菜

tuber vegetables
塊莖菜

sweet potato
甘薯

potato
馬鈴薯

Jerusalem artichoke
菊芋

root vegetables
根菜

kohlrabi
球莖甘藍

turnip
蕪菁

celeriac
塊根芹

beet; *beetroot*
甜菜根

parsnip
防風根

rutabaga
蕪菁甘藍

salsify
婆羅門參根

carrot
胡蘿蔔

black salsify
細卷鴉蔥

horseradish
辣根

radish
萊菔

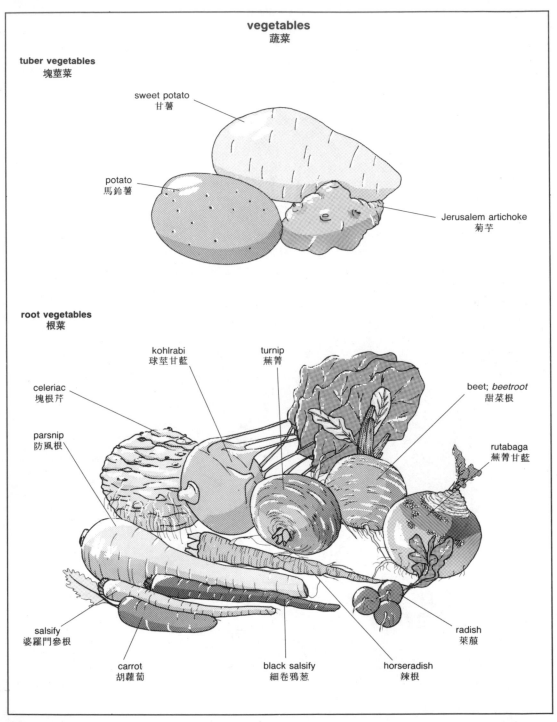

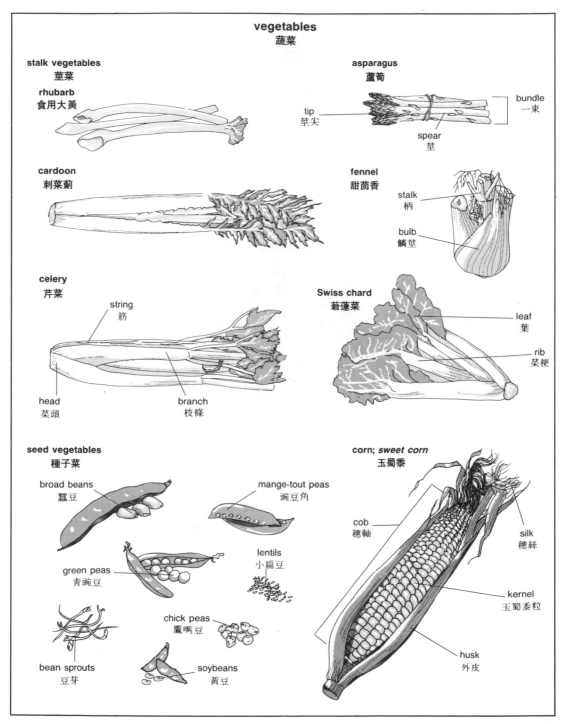

vegetables
蔬菜

stalk vegetables
莖菜

rhubarb
食用大黃

asparagus
蘆筍

bundle
一束

tip
莖尖

spear
莖

cardoon
刺菜薊

fennel
甜茴香

stalk
柄

bulb
鱗莖

celery
芹菜

string
筋

Swiss chard
莙蓬菜

leaf
葉

rib
菜梗

head
菜頭

branch
枝條

seed vegetables
種子菜

corn; *sweet corn*
玉蜀黍

broad beans
蠶豆

mange-tout peas
豌豆角

cob
穗軸

silk
穗絲

green peas
青豌豆

lentils
小扁豆

kernel
玉蜀黍粒

chick peas
鷹嘴豆

bean sprouts
豆芽

soybeans
黃豆

husk
外皮

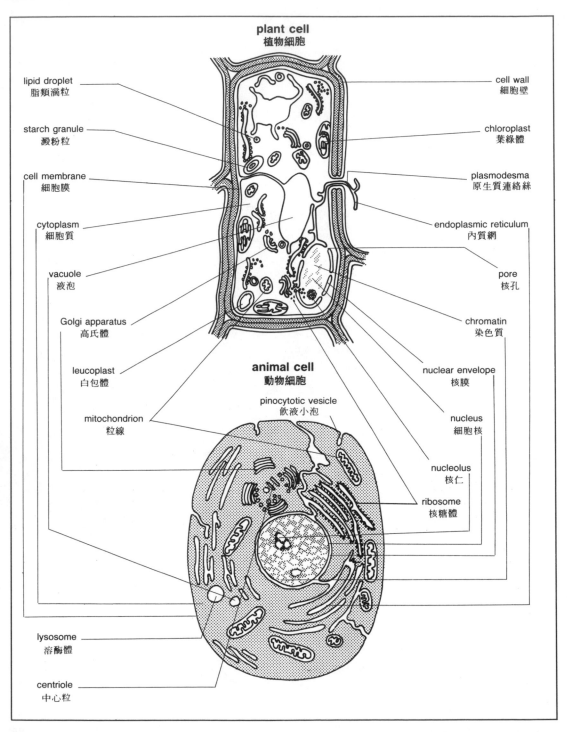

plant cell
植物細胞

lipid droplet
脂類滴粒

starch granule
澱粉粒

cell membrane
細胞膜

cytoplasm
細胞質

vacuole
液泡

Golgi apparatus
高氏體

leucoplast
白包體

mitochondrion
粒線

cell wall
細胞壁

chloroplast
葉綠體

plasmodesma
原生質連絡絲

endoplasmic reticulum
內質網

pore
核孔

chromatin
染色質

nuclear envelope
核膜

nucleus
細胞核

nucleolus
核仁

ribosome
核糖體

animal cell
動物細胞

pinocytotic vesicle
飲液小泡

lysosome
溶酶體

centriole
中心粒

ANIMAL KINGDOM

動物

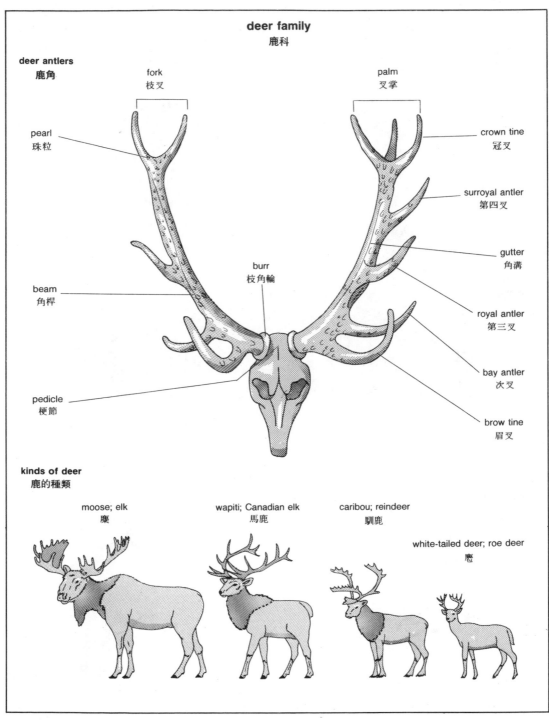

deer family
鹿科

deer antlers
鹿角

fork
枝叉

palm
叉掌

pearl
珠粒

crown tine
冠叉

surroyal antler
第四叉

gutter
角溝

burr
枝角輪

beam
角桿

royal antler
第三叉

bay antler
次叉

pedicle
硬節

brow tine
眉叉

kinds of deer
鹿的種類

moose; elk
麋

wapiti; Canadian elk
馬鹿

caribou; reindeer
馴鹿

white-tailed deer; roe deer
麀

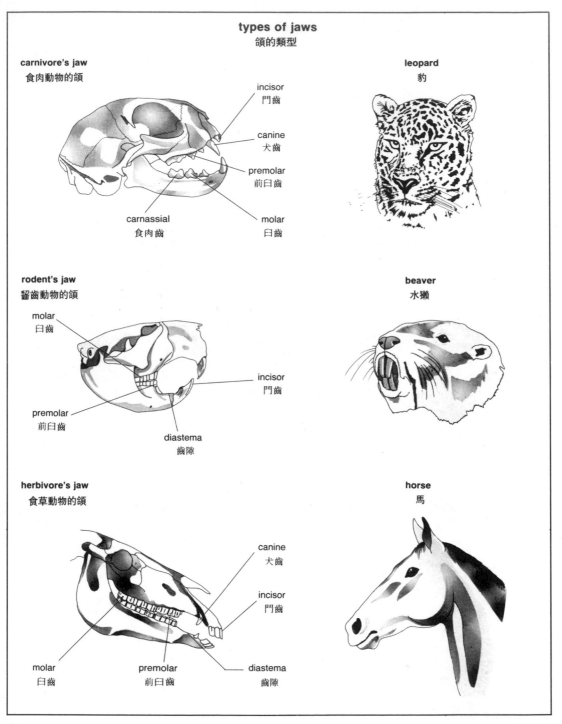

types of jaws
頜的類型

carnivore's jaw
食肉動物的頜

incisor
門齒

canine
犬齒

premolar
前臼齒

carnassial
食肉齒

molar
臼齒

leopard
豹

rodent's jaw
齧齒動物的頜

molar
臼齒

premolar
前臼齒

incisor
門齒

diastema
齒隙

beaver
水獺

herbivore's jaw
食草動物的頜

canine
犬齒

incisor
門齒

diastema
齒隙

molar
臼齒

premolar
前臼齒

horse
馬

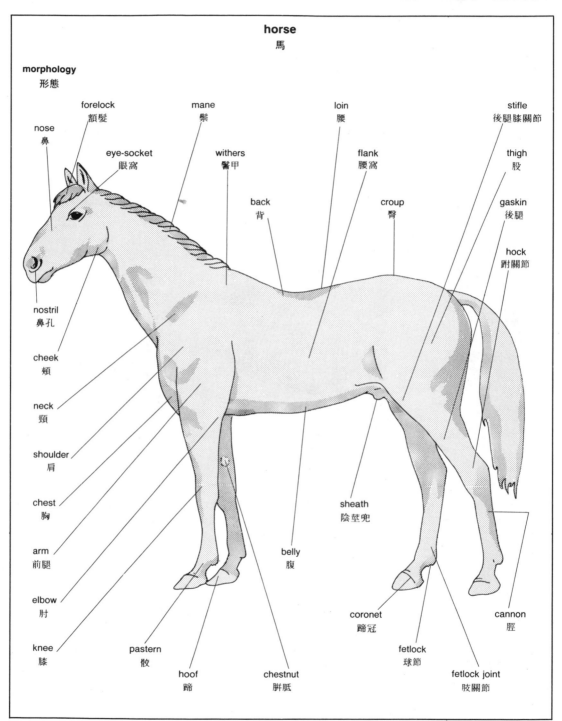

horse
馬

morphology
形態

nose
鼻

forelock
額髮

eye-socket
眼窩

mane
鬃

withers
鬐甲

loin
腰

stifle
後腿膝關節

flank
腰窩

thigh
股

back
背

croup
臀

gaskin
後腿

hock
跗關節

nostril
鼻孔

cheek
頰

neck
頸

shoulder
肩

chest
胸

arm
前腿

elbow
肘

knee
膝

pastern
骹

hoof
蹄

chestnut
胼胝

belly
腹

sheath
陰莖兜

coronet
蹄冠

fetlock
球節

fetlock joint
肢關節

cannon
脛

horse
馬

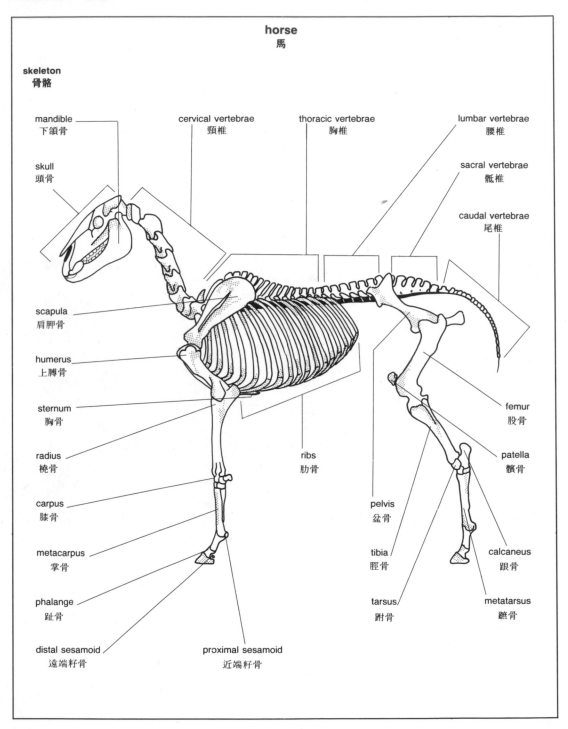

skeleton
骨骼

mandible
下頜骨

skull
頭骨

cervical vertebrae
頸椎

thoracic vertebrae
胸椎

lumbar vertebrae
腰椎

sacral vertebrae
骶椎

caudal vertebrae
尾椎

scapula
肩胛骨

humerus
上膊骨

sternum
胸骨

radius
橈骨

carpus
膝骨

metacarpus
掌骨

phalange
趾骨

distal sesamoid
遠端籽骨

proximal sesamoid
近端籽骨

ribs
肋骨

pelvis
盆骨

tibia
脛骨

tarsus
跗骨

femur
股骨

patella
髕骨

calcaneus
跟骨

metatarsus
蹠骨

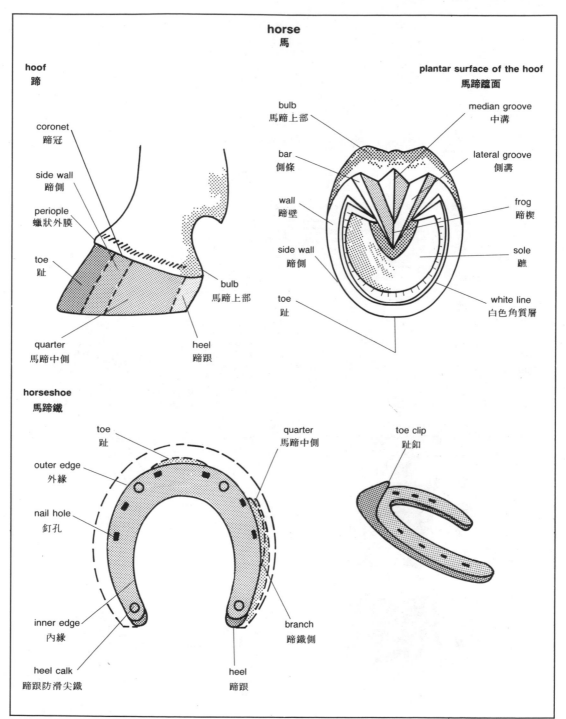

horse
馬

hoof
蹄

coronet
蹄冠

side wall
蹄側

periople
蠟狀外膜

toe
趾

quarter
馬蹄中側

bulb
馬蹄上部

heel
蹄跟

plantar surface of the hoof
馬蹄蹠面

bulb
馬蹄上部

bar
側條

wall
蹄壁

side wall
蹄側

toe
趾

median groove
中溝

lateral groove
側溝

frog
蹄楔

sole
蹠

white line
白色角質層

horseshoe
馬蹄鐵

toe
趾

outer edge
外緣

nail hole
釘孔

inner edge
內緣

heel calk
蹄跟防滑尖鐵

quarter
馬蹄中側

branch
蹄鐵側

heel
蹄跟

toe clip
趾釦

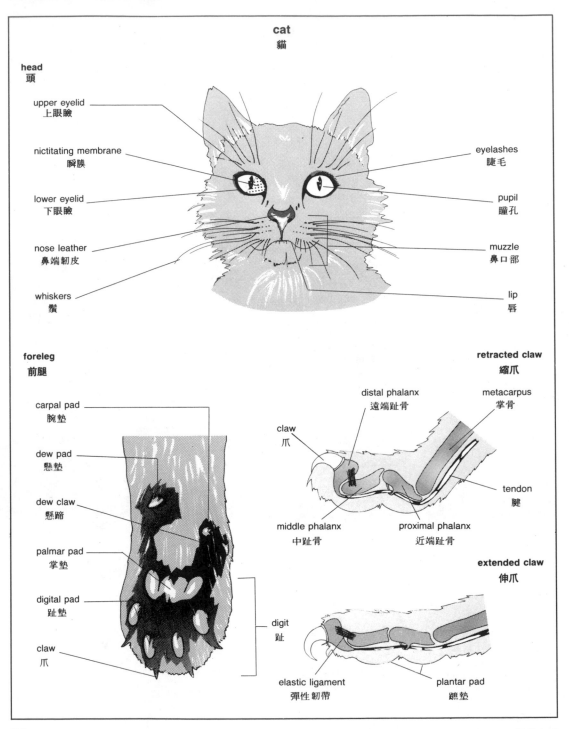

cat
貓

head
頭

upper eyelid
上眼瞼

nictitating membrane
瞬膜

lower eyelid
下眼瞼

nose leather
鼻端韌皮

whiskers
鬚

eyelashes
睫毛

pupil
瞳孔

muzzle
鼻口部

lip
唇

foreleg
前腿

carpal pad
腕墊

dew pad
懸墊

dew claw
懸蹄

palmar pad
掌墊

digital pad
趾墊

claw
爪

digit
趾

retracted claw
縮爪

distal phalanx
遠端趾骨

metacarpus
掌骨

claw
爪

tendon
腱

middle phalanx
中趾骨

proximal phalanx
近端趾骨

extended claw
伸爪

elastic ligament
彈性韌帶

plantar pad
蹠墊

bird
鳥

morphology
形態

nostril
鼻孔

lore
眼先

forehead
額

crown
頭頂

upper mandible
上喙

lower mandible
下喙

chin
頦

malar region
頰

throat
喉

breast
胸

flank
脅

belly
腹

thigh
腿

inner toe
內趾

middle toe
中趾

outer toe
外趾

claw
爪

tarsus
跗骨

hind toe
後趾

foot
足

eye ring
眼圈

eyebrow stripe
眉斑

auricular
耳羽

nape
後頸

back
背

wing covert
覆羽

rump
腰

tail feather
尾羽

upper tail covert
尾上覆羽

under tail covert
尾下覆羽

wing
翼

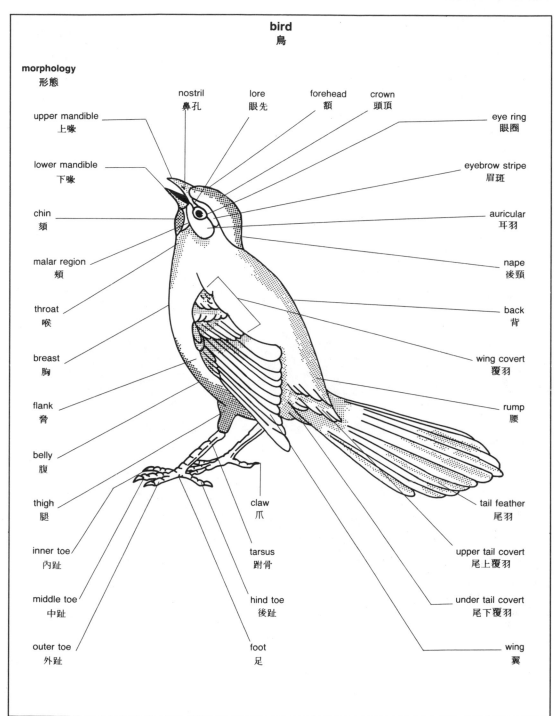

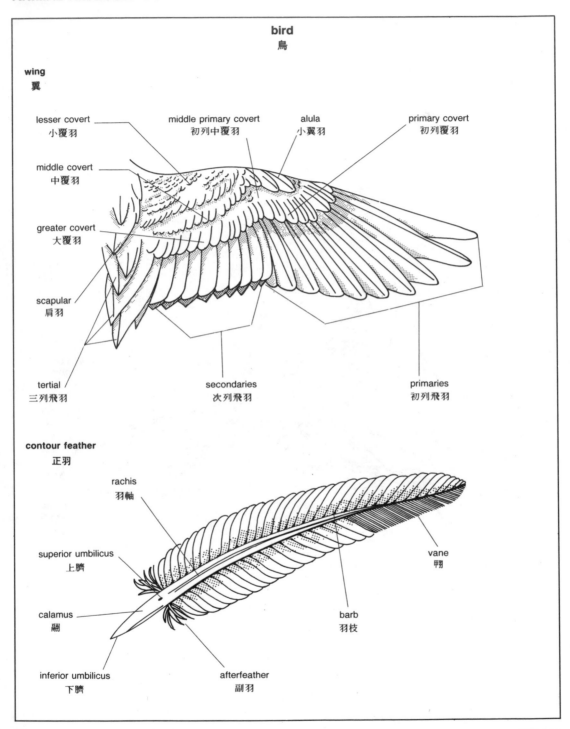

bird
鳥

wing
翼

lesser covert
小覆羽

middle primary covert
初列中覆羽

alula
小翼羽

primary covert
初列覆羽

middle covert
中覆羽

greater covert
大覆羽

scapular
肩羽

tertial
三列飛羽

secondaries
次列飛羽

primaries
初列飛羽

contour feather
正羽

rachis
羽軸

superior umbilicus
上臍

vane
羽

calamus
翮

barb
羽枝

inferior umbilicus
下臍

afterfeather
副羽

bird
鳥

principal types of bills
鳥喙主要類型

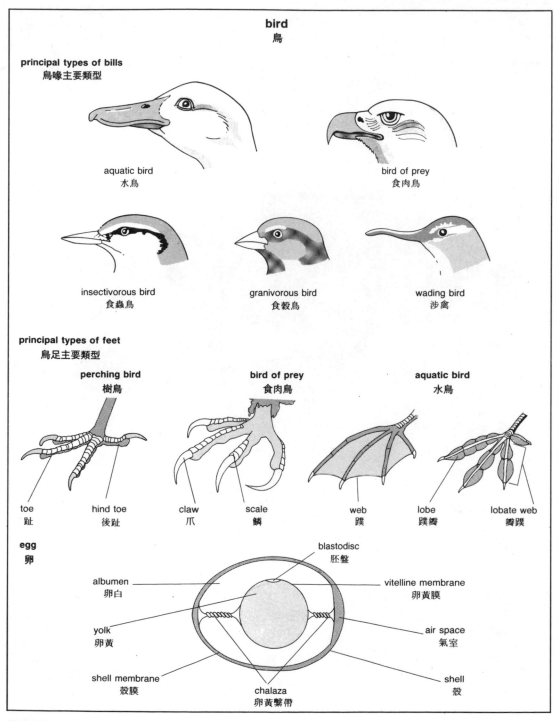

aquatic bird
水鳥

bird of prey
食肉鳥

insectivorous bird
食蟲鳥

granivorous bird
食穀鳥

wading bird
涉禽

principal types of feet
鳥足主要類型

perching bird
樹鳥

bird of prey
食肉鳥

aquatic bird
水鳥

toe
趾

hind toe
後趾

claw
爪

scale
鱗

web
蹼

lobe
蹼瓣

lobate web
瓣蹼

egg
卵

blastodisc
胚盤

albumen
卵白

vitelline membrane
卵黃膜

yolk
卵黃

air space
氣室

shell membrane
殼膜

chalaza
卵黃繫帶

shell
殼

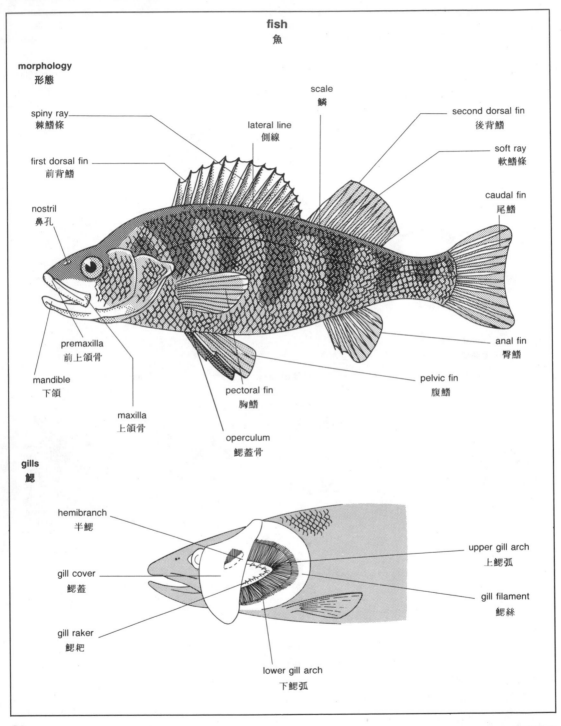

fish
魚

morphology
形態

scale
鱗

spiny ray
棘鰭條

lateral line
側線

second dorsal fin
後背鰭

first dorsal fin
前背鰭

soft ray
軟鰭條

nostril
鼻孔

caudal fin
尾鰭

premaxilla
前上頜骨

mandible
下頜

anal fin
臀鰭

maxilla
上頜骨

pelvic fin
腹鰭

pectoral fin
胸鰭

operculum
鰓蓋骨

gills
鰓

hemibranch
半鰓

upper gill arch
上鰓弧

gill cover
鰓蓋

gill filament
鰓絲

gill raker
鰓耙

lower gill arch
下鰓弧

fish
魚

anatomy
解剖

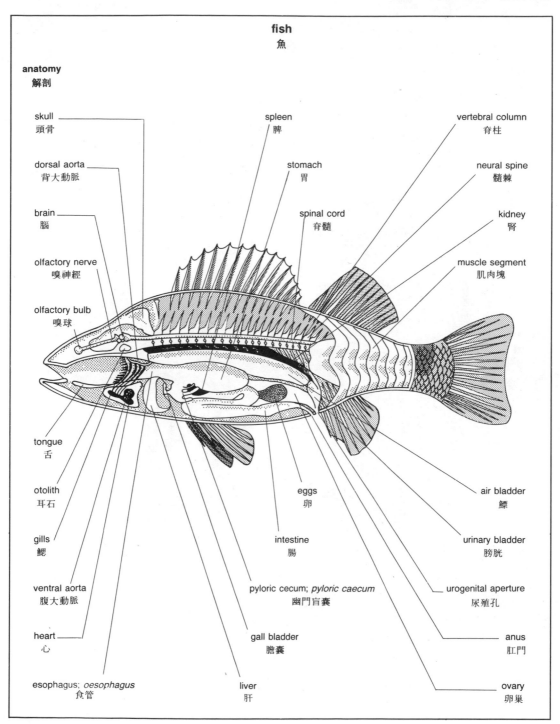

skull
頭骨

spleen
脾

vertebral column
脊柱

dorsal aorta
背大動脈

stomach
胃

neural spine
髓棘

brain
腦

spinal cord
脊髓

kidney
腎

olfactory nerve
嗅神經

muscle segment
肌肉塊

olfactory bulb
嗅球

tongue
舌

otolith
耳石

eggs
卵

air bladder
鰾

gills
鰓

urinary bladder
膀胱

intestine
腸

ventral aorta
腹大動脈

pyloric cecum; *pyloric caecum*
幽門盲囊

urogenital aperture
尿殖孔

heart
心

gall bladder
膽囊

anus
肛門

esophagus; *oesophagus*
食管

liver
肝

ovary
卵巢

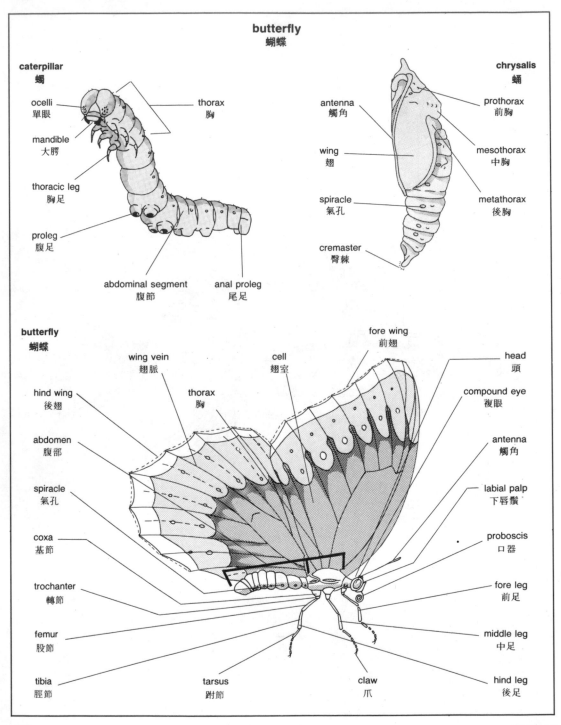

butterfly
蝴蝶

caterpillar
蝎

ocelli
單眼

thorax
胸

mandible
大腭

thoracic leg
胸足

proleg
腹足

abdominal segment
腹節

anal proleg
尾足

chrysalis
蛹

antenna
觸角

prothorax
前胸

wing
翅

mesothorax
中胸

spiracle
氣孔

metathorax
後胸

cremaster
臀棘

butterfly
蝴蝶

wing vein
翅脈

fore wing
前翅

cell
翅室

head
頭

hind wing
後翅

thorax
胸

compound eye
複眼

abdomen
腹部

antenna
觸角

spiracle
氣孔

labial palp
下唇鬚

coxa
基節

proboscis
口器

trochanter
轉節

fore leg
前足

femur
股節

middle leg
中足

tibia
脛節

tarsus
跗節

claw
爪

hind leg
後足

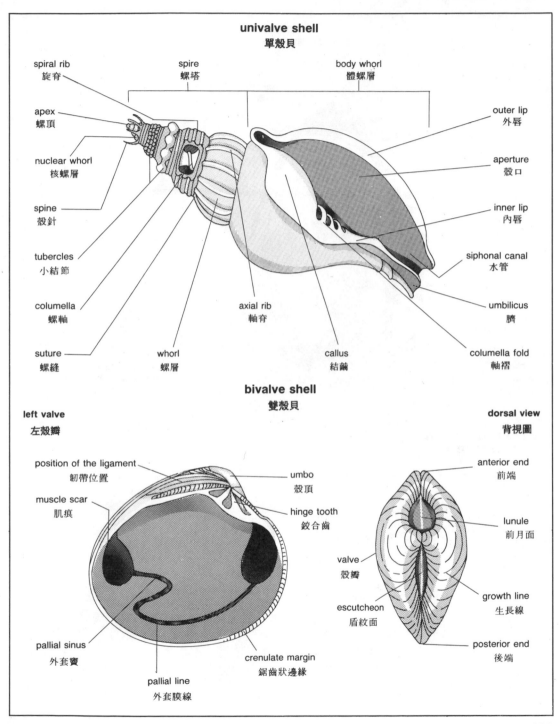

univalve shell
單殼貝

spiral rib
旋脊

spire
螺塔

body whorl
體螺層

apex
螺頂

outer lip
外唇

nuclear whorl
核螺層

aperture
殼口

spine
殼針

inner lip
內唇

tubercles
小結節

siphonal canal
水管

columella
螺軸

axial rib
軸脊

umbilicus
臍

suture
螺縫

whorl
螺層

callus
結繭

columella fold
軸褶

bivalve shell
雙殼貝

left valve
左殼瓣

dorsal view
背視圖

position of the ligament
韌帶位置

umbo
殼頂

muscle scar
肌痕

hinge tooth
鉸合齒

anterior end
前端

lunule
前月面

valve
殼瓣

pallial sinus
外套竇

escutcheon
盾紋面

growth line
生長線

pallial line
外套膜線

crenulate margin
鋸齒狀邊緣

posterior end
後端

mollusk
軟體動物

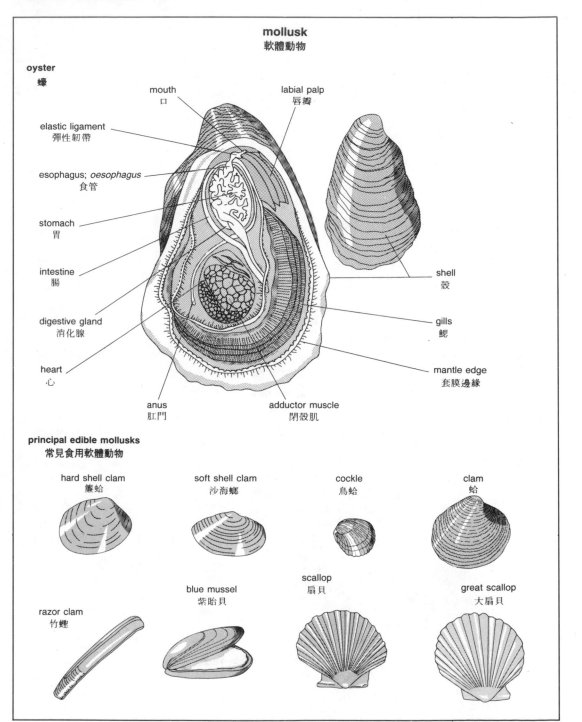

oyster
蠔

mouth
口

labial palp
唇瓣

elastic ligament
彈性韌帶

esophagus; *oesophagus*
食管

stomach
胃

intestine
腸

digestive gland
消化腺

heart
心

anus
肛門

adductor muscle
閉殼肌

shell
殼

gills
鰓

mantle edge
套膜邊緣

principal edible mollusks
常見食用軟體動物

hard shell clam
簾蛤

soft shell clam
沙海螂

cockle
鳥蛤

clam
蛤

razor clam
竹蟶

blue mussel
紫貽貝

scallop
扇貝

great scallop
大扇貝

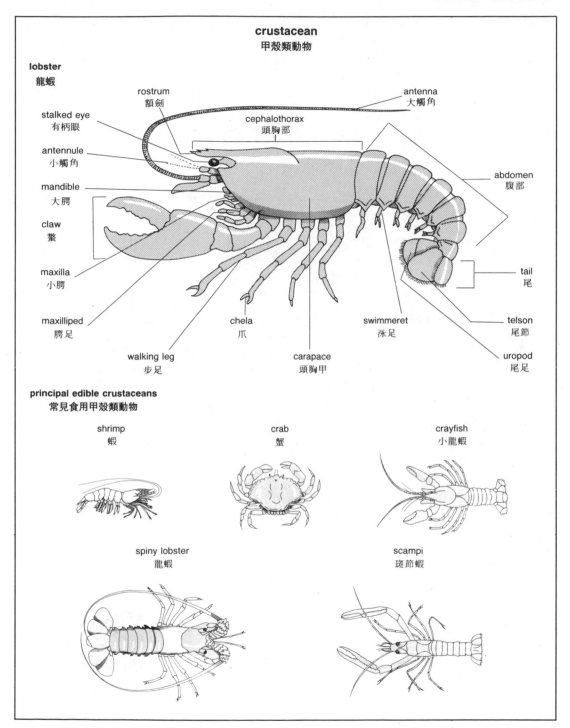

crustacean
甲殼類動物

lobster
龍蝦

rostrum
額劍

antenna
大觸角

stalked eye
有柄眼

cephalothorax
頭胸部

antennule
小觸角

mandible
大腭

abdomen
腹部

claw
螯

maxilla
小腭

tail
尾

maxilliped
腭足

chela
爪

swimmeret
泳足

telson
尾節

walking leg
步足

carapace
頭胸甲

uropod
尾足

principal edible crustaceans
常見食用甲殼類動物

shrimp
蝦

crab
蟹

crayfish
小龍蝦

spiny lobster
龍蝦

scampi
斑節蝦

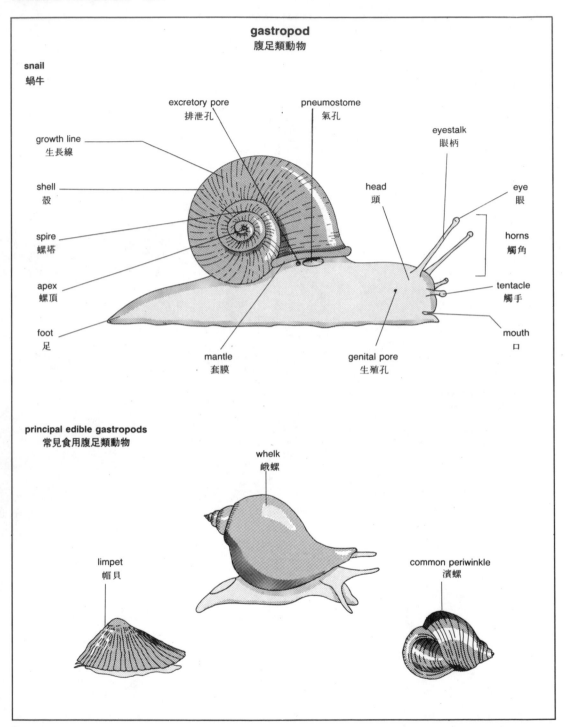

gastropod
腹足類動物

snail
蝸牛

excretory pore
排泄孔

pneumostome
氣孔

eyestalk
眼柄

growth line
生長線

shell
殼

head
頭

eye
眼

horns
觸角

spire
螺塔

apex
螺頂

tentacle
觸手

foot
足

mantle
套膜

genital pore
生殖孔

mouth
口

principal edible gastropods
常見食用腹足類動物

whelk
峨螺

limpet
帽貝

common periwinkle
濱螺

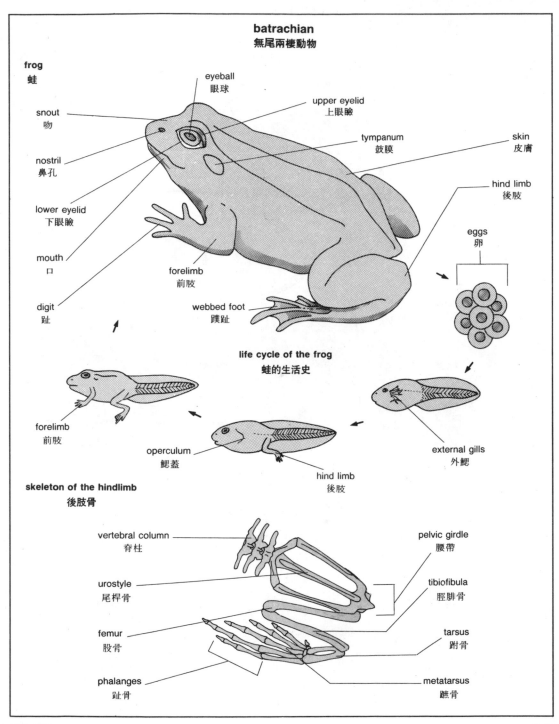

batrachian
無尾兩棲動物

frog
蛙

eyeball
眼球

upper eyelid
上眼瞼

tympanum
鼓膜

skin
皮膚

snout
吻

nostril
鼻孔

lower eyelid
下眼瞼

mouth
口

digit
趾

forelimb
前肢

webbed foot
蹼趾

hind limb
後肢

eggs
卵

life cycle of the frog
蛙的生活史

forelimb
前肢

operculum
鰓蓋

hind limb
後肢

external gills
外鰓

skeleton of the hindlimb
後肢骨

vertebral column
脊柱

urostyle
尾桿骨

femur
股骨

phalanges
趾骨

pelvic girdle
腰帶

tibiofibula
脛腓骨

tarsus
跗骨

metatarsus
蹠骨

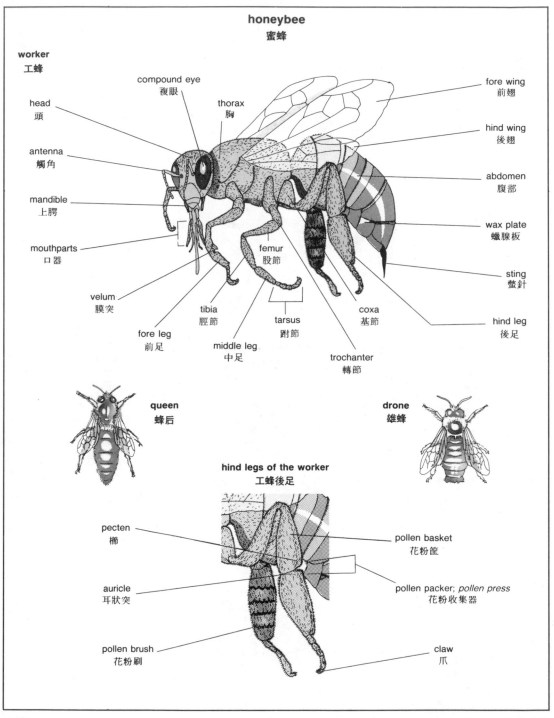

honeybee
蜜蜂

worker
工蜂

compound eye
複眼

thorax
胸

fore wing
前翅

head
頭

hind wing
後翅

antenna
觸角

abdomen
腹部

mandible
上腭

wax plate
蠟腺板

mouthparts
口器

femur
股節

sting
螫針

velum
膜突

coxa
基節

hind leg
後足

tibia
脛節

tarsus
跗節

fore leg
前足

middle leg
中足

trochanter
轉節

queen
蜂后

drone
雄蜂

hind legs of the worker
工蜂後足

pecten
櫛

pollen basket
花粉筐

auricle
耳狀突

pollen packer; *pollen press*
花粉收集器

pollen brush
花粉刷

claw
爪

honeybee
蜜蜂

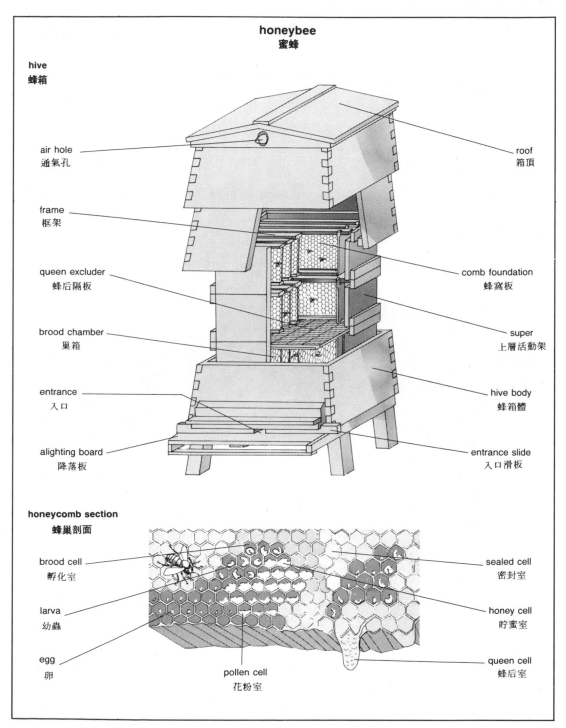

hive
蜂箱

air hole
通氣孔

roof
箱頂

frame
框架

queen excluder
蜂后隔板

comb foundation
蜂窩板

brood chamber
巢箱

super
上層活動架

entrance
入口

hive body
蜂箱體

alighting board
降落板

entrance slide
入口滑板

honeycomb section
蜂巢剖面

brood cell
孵化室

sealed cell
密封室

larva
幼蟲

honey cell
貯蜜室

egg
卵

queen cell
蜂后室

pollen cell
花粉室

bat
蝙蝠

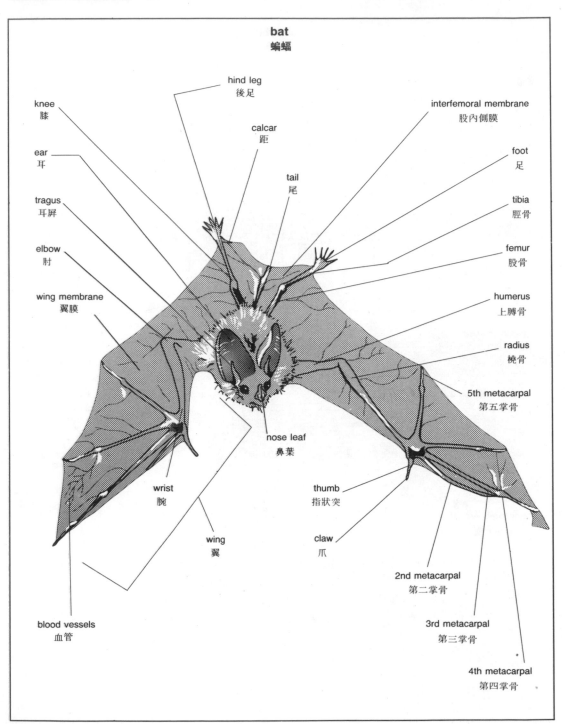

knee
膝

ear
耳

tragus
耳屏

elbow
肘

wing membrane
翼膜

hind leg
後足

calcar
距

tail
尾

interfemoral membrane
股內側膜

foot
足

tibia
脛骨

femur
股骨

humerus
上膊骨

radius
橈骨

5th metacarpal
第五掌骨

nose leaf
鼻葉

wrist
腕

thumb
指狀突

wing
翼

claw
爪

blood vessels
血管

2nd metacarpal
第二掌骨

3rd metacarpal
第三掌骨

4th metacarpal
第四掌骨

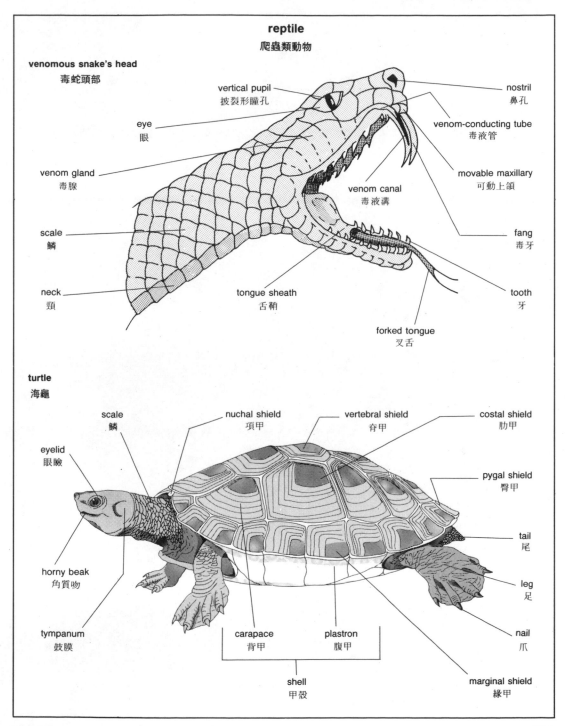

reptile
爬蟲類動物

venomous snake's head
毒蛇頭部

vertical pupil
披裂形瞳孔

nostril
鼻孔

eye
眼

venom-conducting tube
毒液管

venom gland
毒腺

movable maxillary
可動上頜

venom canal
毒液溝

scale
鱗

fang
毒牙

neck
頸

tongue sheath
舌鞘

tooth
牙

forked tongue
叉舌

turtle
海龜

scale
鱗

nuchal shield
項甲

vertebral shield
脊甲

costal shield
肋甲

eyelid
眼瞼

pygal shield
臀甲

horny beak
角質吻

tail
尾

leg
足

tympanum
鼓膜

nail
爪

carapace
背甲

plastron
腹甲

shell
甲殼

marginal shield
緣甲

HUMAN BEING

人

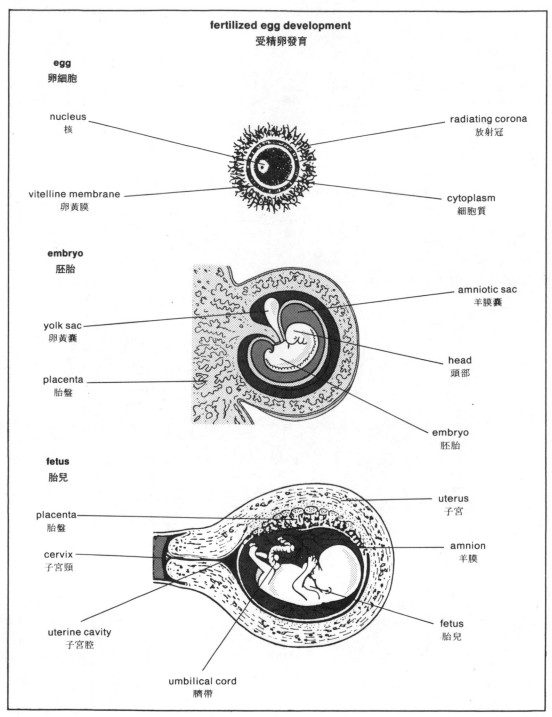

fertilized egg development
受精卵發育

egg
卵細胞

nucleus
核

radiating corona
放射冠

vitelline membrane
卵黃膜

cytoplasm
細胞質

embryo
胚胎

yolk sac
卵黃囊

amniotic sac
羊膜囊

placenta
胎盤

head
頭部

embryo
胚胎

fetus
胎兒

placenta
胎盤

uterus
子宮

cervix
子宮頸

amnion
羊膜

uterine cavity
子宮腔

fetus
胎兒

umbilical cord
臍帶

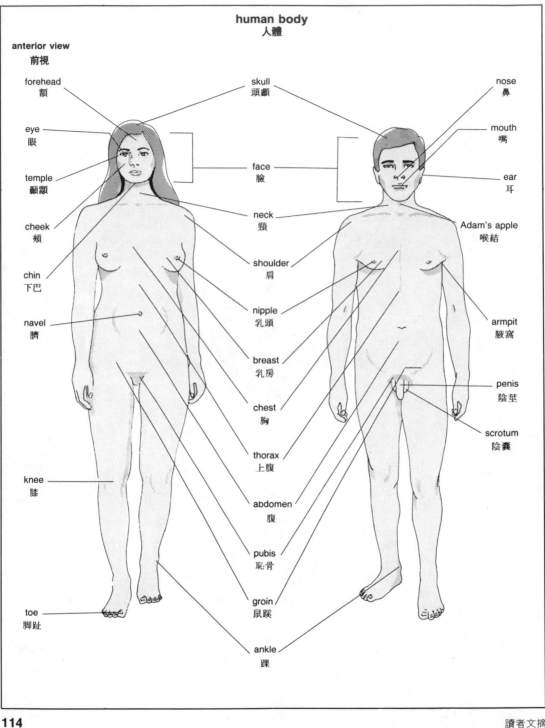

human body
人體

anterior view
前視

forehead
額

eye
眼

temple
顳顬

cheek
頰

chin
下巴

navel
臍

knee
膝

toe
脚趾

skull
頭顱

face
臉

neck
頸

shoulder
肩

nipple
乳頭

breast
乳房

chest
胸

thorax
上腹

abdomen
腹

pubis
恥骨

groin
鼠蹊

ankle
踝

nose
鼻

mouth
嘴

ear
耳

Adam's apple
喉結

armpit
腋窩

penis
陰莖

scrotum
陰囊

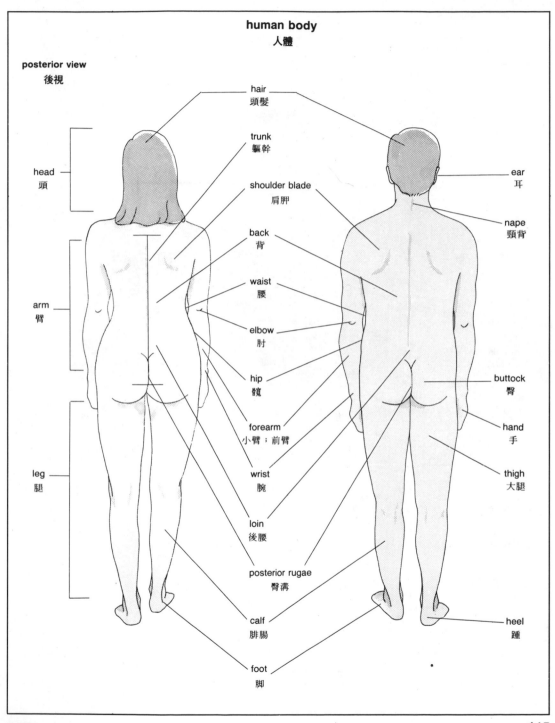

human body
人體

posterior view
後視

hair
頭髮

trunk
軀幹

shoulder blade
肩胛

back
背

waist
腰

elbow
肘

hip
髖

forearm
小臂；前臂

wrist
腕

loin
後腰

posterior rugae
臀溝

calf
腓腸

foot
脚

head
頭

arm
臂

leg
腿

ear
耳

nape
頸背

buttock
臀

hand
手

thigh
大腿

heel
踵

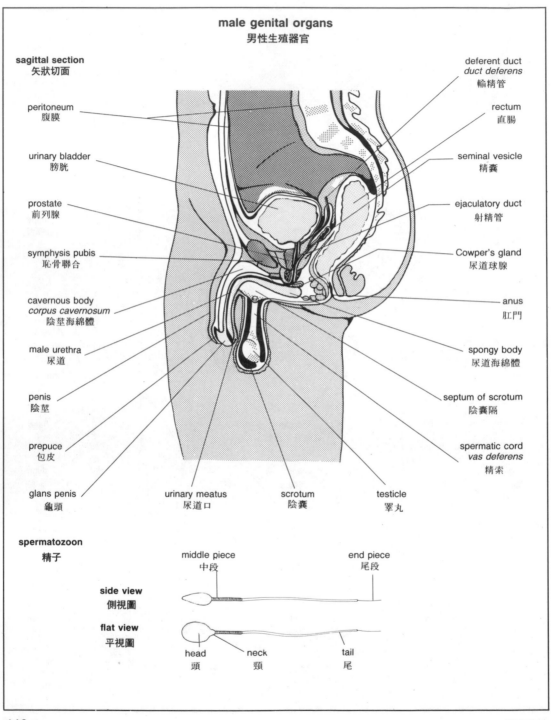

male genital organs
男性生殖器官

sagittal section
矢狀切面

peritoneum
腹膜

urinary bladder
膀胱

prostate
前列腺

symphysis pubis
恥骨聯合

cavernous body
corpus cavernosum
陰莖海綿體

male urethra
尿道

penis
陰莖

prepuce
包皮

glans penis
龜頭

urinary meatus
尿道口

scrotum
陰囊

testicle
睪丸

deferent duct
duct deferens
輸精管

rectum
直腸

seminal vesicle
精囊

ejaculatory duct
射精管

Cowper's gland
尿道球腺

anus
肛門

spongy body
尿道海綿體

septum of scrotum
陰囊隔

spermatic cord
vas deferens
精索

spermatozoon
精子

middle piece
中段

end piece
尾段

side view
側視圖

flat view
平視圖

head
頭

neck
頸

tail
尾

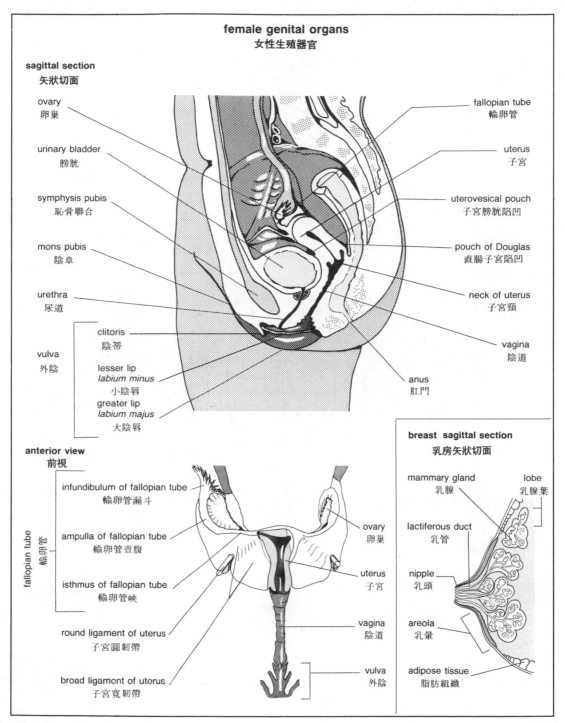

female genital organs
女性生殖器官

sagittal section
矢狀切面

ovary
卵巢

urinary bladder
膀胱

symphysis pubis
恥骨聯合

mons pubis
陰阜

urethra
尿道

vulva
外陰

clitoris
陰蒂

lesser lip
labium minus
小陰唇

greater lip
labium majus
大陰唇

fallopian tube
輸卵管

uterus
子宮

uterovesical pouch
子宮膀胱陷凹

pouch of Douglas
直腸子宮陷凹

neck of uterus
子宮頸

vagina
陰道

anus
肛門

anterior view
前視

fallopian tube
輸卵管

infundibulum of fallopian tube
輸卵管漏斗

ampulla of fallopian tube
輸卵管壺腹

isthmus of fallopian tube
輸卵管峽

round ligament of uterus
子宮圓韌帶

broad ligament of uterus
子宮寬韌帶

ovary
卵巢

uterus
子宮

vagina
陰道

vulva
外陰

breast sagittal section
乳房矢狀切面

mammary gland
乳腺

lobe
乳腺葉

lactiferous duct
乳管

nipple
乳頭

areola
乳暈

adipose tissue
脂肪組織

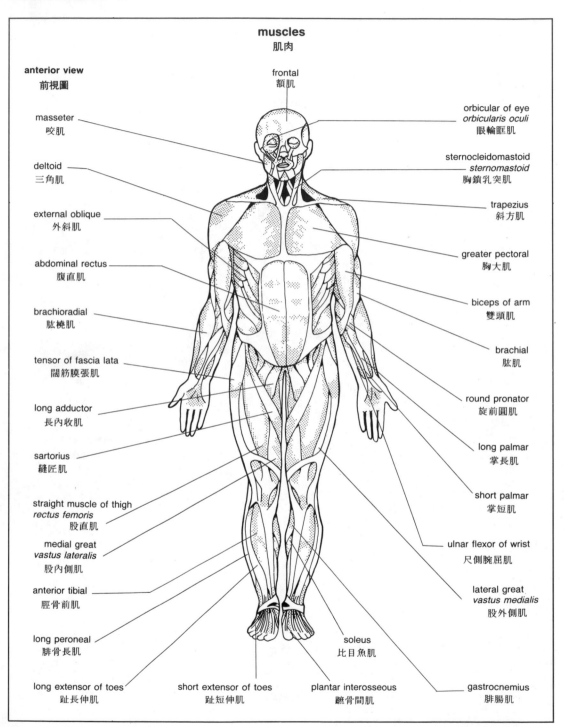

muscles
肌肉

anterior view
前視圖

frontal
額肌

orbicular of eye
orbicularis oculi
眼輪眶肌

masseter
咬肌

sternocleidomastoid
sternomastoid
胸鎖乳突肌

deltoid
三角肌

trapezius
斜方肌

external oblique
外斜肌

greater pectoral
胸大肌

abdominal rectus
腹直肌

biceps of arm
雙頭肌

brachioradial
肱橈肌

brachial
肱肌

tensor of fascia lata
闊筋膜張肌

round pronator
旋前圓肌

long adductor
長內收肌

long palmar
掌長肌

sartorius
縫匠肌

short palmar
掌短肌

straight muscle of thigh
rectus femoris
股直肌

medial great
vastus lateralis
股內側肌

ulnar flexor of wrist
尺側腕屈肌

anterior tibial
脛骨前肌

lateral great
vastus medialis
股外側肌

long peroneal
腓骨長肌

soleus
比目魚肌

long extensor of toes
趾長伸肌

short extensor of toes
趾短伸肌

plantar interosseous
蹠骨間肌

gastrocnemius
腓腸肌

muscles
肌肉

posterior view
後視圖

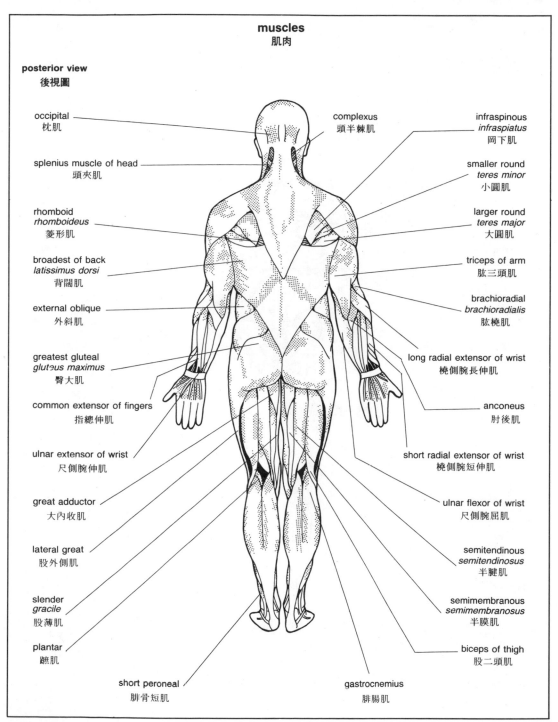

occipital
枕肌

complexus
頭半棘肌

infraspinous
infraspiatus
岡下肌

splenius muscle of head
頭夾肌

smaller round
teres minor
小圓肌

rhomboid
rhomboideus
菱形肌

larger round
teres major
大圓肌

broadest of back
latissimus dorsi
背闊肌

triceps of arm
肱三頭肌

external oblique
外斜肌

brachioradial
brachioradialis
肱橈肌

greatest gluteal
gluteus maximus
臀大肌

long radial extensor of wrist
橈側腕長伸肌

common extensor of fingers
指總伸肌

anconeus
肘後肌

ulnar extensor of wrist
尺側腕伸肌

short radial extensor of wrist
橈側腕短伸肌

great adductor
大內收肌

ulnar flexor of wrist
尺側腕屈肌

lateral great
股外側肌

semitendinous
semitendinosus
半腱肌

slender
gracile
股薄肌

semimembranous
semimembranosus
半膜肌

plantar
蹠肌

biceps of thigh
股二頭肌

short peroneal
腓骨短肌

gastrocnemius
腓腸肌

skeleton
骨骼

anterior view
前視圖

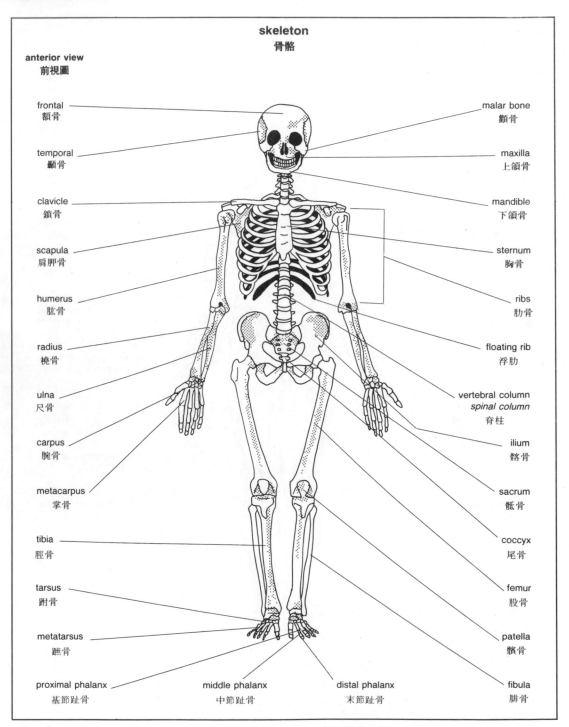

frontal
額骨

temporal
顳骨

clavicle
鎖骨

scapula
肩胛骨

humerus
肱骨

radius
橈骨

ulna
尺骨

carpus
腕骨

metacarpus
掌骨

tibia
脛骨

tarsus
跗骨

metatarsus
蹠骨

proximal phalanx
基節趾骨

middle phalanx
中節趾骨

distal phalanx
末節趾骨

malar bone
顴骨

maxilla
上頜骨

mandible
下頜骨

sternum
胸骨

ribs
肋骨

floating rib
浮肋

vertebral column
spinal column
脊柱

ilium
髂骨

sacrum
骶骨

coccyx
尾骨

femur
股骨

patella
髕骨

fibula
腓骨

skeleton
骨骼

posterior view
後視圖

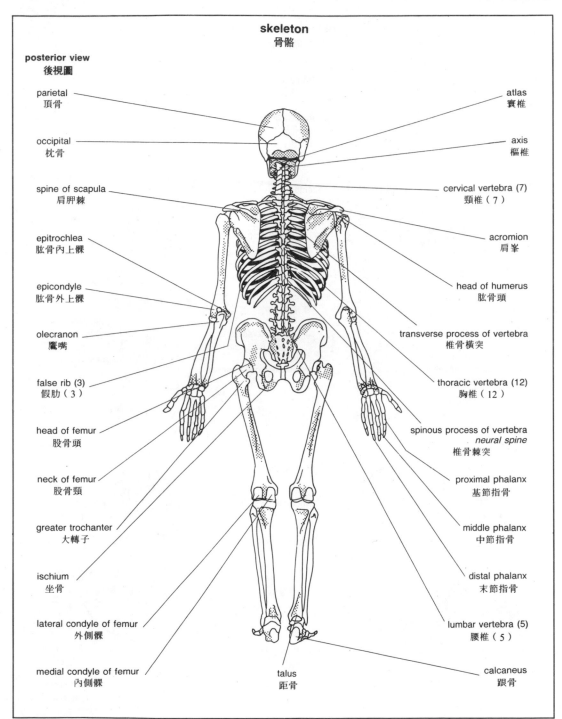

parietal
頂骨

occipital
枕骨

spine of scapula
肩胛棘

epitrochlea
肱骨內上髁

epicondyle
肱骨外上髁

olecranon
鷹嘴

false rib (3)
假肋（3）

head of femur
股骨頭

neck of femur
股骨頸

greater trochanter
大轉子

ischium
坐骨

lateral condyle of femur
外側髁

medial condyle of femur
內側髁

atlas
寰椎

axis
樞椎

cervical vertebra (7)
頸椎（7）

acromion
肩峯

head of humerus
肱骨頭

transverse process of vertebra
椎骨橫突

thoracic vertebra (12)
胸椎（12）

spinous process of vertebra
neural spine
椎骨棘突

proximal phalanx
基節指骨

middle phalanx
中節指骨

distal phalanx
末節指骨

lumbar vertebra (5)
腰椎（5）

calcaneus
跟骨

talus
距骨

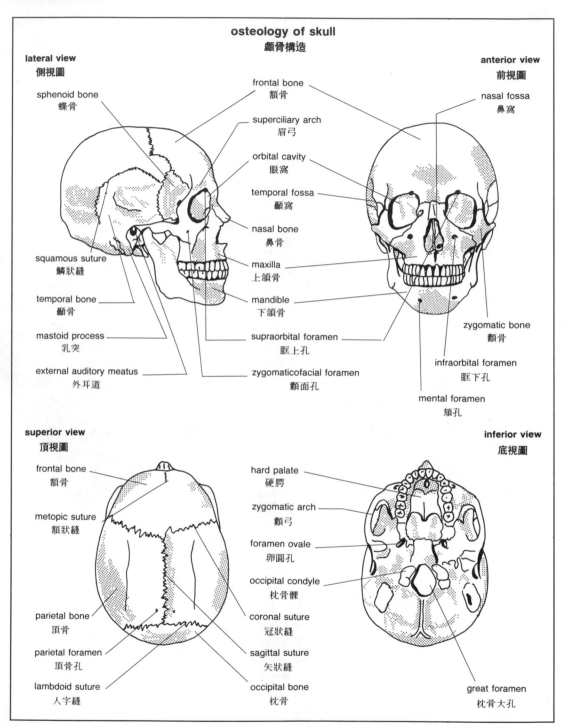

osteology of skull
顱骨構造

lateral view
側視圖

sphenoid bone
蝶骨

squamous suture
鱗狀縫

temporal bone
顳骨

mastoid process
乳突

external auditory meatus
外耳道

frontal bone
額骨

superciliary arch
眉弓

orbital cavity
眼窩

temporal fossa
顳窩

nasal bone
鼻骨

maxilla
上頜骨

mandible
下頜骨

supraorbital foramen
眶上孔

zygomaticofacial foramen
顴面孔

anterior view
前視圖

nasal fossa
鼻窩

zygomatic bone
顴骨

infraorbital foramen
眶下孔

mental foramen
頦孔

superior view
頂視圖

frontal bone
額骨

metopic suture
額狀縫

parietal bone
頂骨

parietal foramen
頂骨孔

lambdoid suture
人字縫

hard palate
硬腭

zygomatic arch
顴弓

foramen ovale
卵圓孔

occipital condyle
枕骨髁

coronal suture
冠狀縫

sagittal suture
矢狀縫

occipital bone
枕骨

inferior view
底視圖

great foramen
枕骨大孔

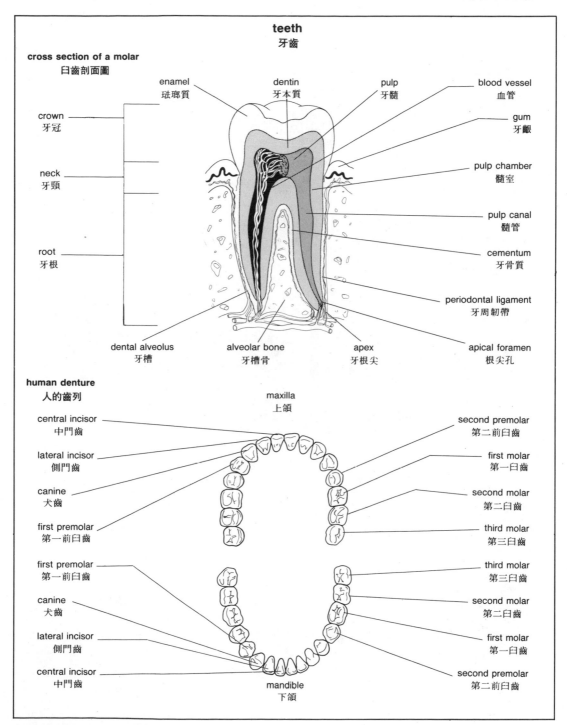

teeth
牙齒

cross section of a molar
臼齒剖面圖

enamel
琺瑯質

dentin
牙本質

pulp
牙髓

blood vessel
血管

crown
牙冠

gum
牙齦

neck
牙頸

pulp chamber
髓室

pulp canal
髓管

cementum
牙骨質

root
牙根

periodontal ligament
牙周韌帶

dental alveolus
牙槽

alveolar bone
牙槽骨

apex
牙根尖

apical foramen
根尖孔

human denture
人的齒列

maxilla
上頜

central incisor
中門齒

second premolar
第二前臼齒

lateral incisor
側門齒

first molar
第一臼齒

canine
犬齒

second molar
第二臼齒

first premolar
第一前臼齒

third molar
第三臼齒

first premolar
第一前臼齒

third molar
第三臼齒

canine
犬齒

second molar
第二臼齒

lateral incisor
側門齒

first molar
第一臼齒

central incisor
中門齒

second premolar
第二前臼齒

mandible
下頜

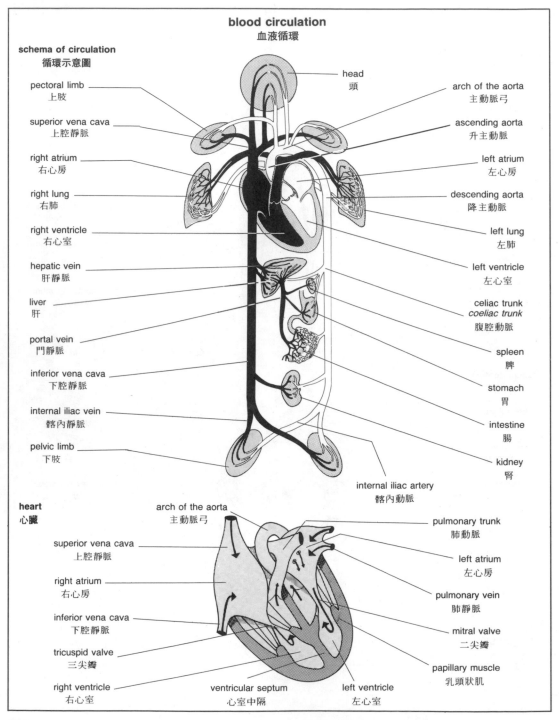

blood circulation
血液循環

schema of circulation
循環示意圖

pectoral limb
上肢

superior vena cava
上腔靜脈

right atrium
右心房

right lung
右肺

right ventricle
右心室

hepatic vein
肝靜脈

liver
肝

portal vein
門靜脈

inferior vena cava
下腔靜脈

internal iliac vein
髂內靜脈

pelvic limb
下肢

head
頭

arch of the aorta
主動脈弓

ascending aorta
升主動脈

left atrium
左心房

descending aorta
降主動脈

left lung
左肺

left ventricle
左心室

celiac trunk
coeliac trunk
腹腔動脈

spleen
脾

stomach
胃

intestine
腸

kidney
腎

internal iliac artery
髂內動脈

heart
心臟

arch of the aorta
主動脈弓

superior vena cava
上腔靜脈

right atrium
右心房

inferior vena cava
下腔靜脈

tricuspid valve
三尖瓣

right ventricle
右心室

ventricular septum
心室中隔

left ventricle
左心室

pulmonary trunk
肺動脈

left atrium
左心房

pulmonary vein
肺靜脈

mitral valve
二尖瓣

papillary muscle
乳頭狀肌

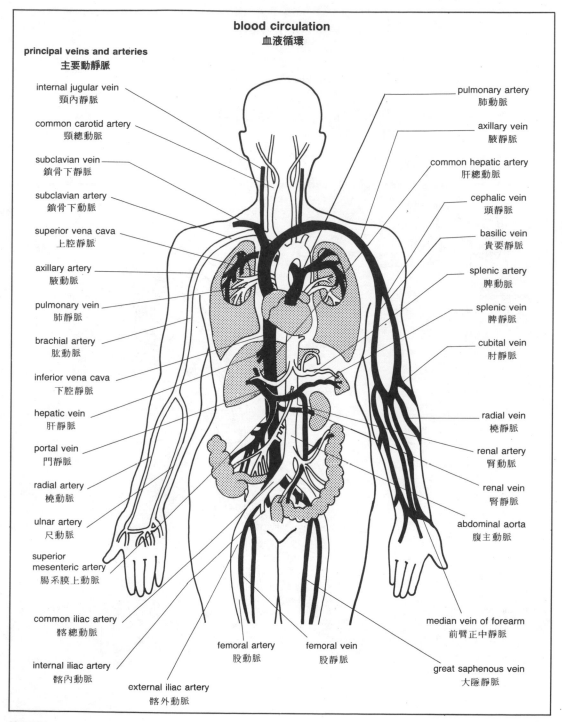

blood circulation
血液循環

principal veins and arteries
主要動靜脈

internal jugular vein
頸內靜脈

common carotid artery
頸總動脈

subclavian vein
鎖骨下靜脈

subclavian artery
鎖骨下動脈

superior vena cava
上腔靜脈

axillary artery
腋動脈

pulmonary vein
肺靜脈

brachial artery
肱動脈

inferior vena cava
下腔靜脈

hepatic vein
肝靜脈

portal vein
門靜脈

radial artery
橈動脈

ulnar artery
尺動脈

superior
mesenteric artery
腸系膜上動脈

common iliac artery
髂總動脈

internal iliac artery
髂內動脈

external iliac artery
髂外動脈

femoral artery
股動脈

femoral vein
股靜脈

pulmonary artery
肺動脈

axillary vein
腋靜脈

common hepatic artery
肝總動脈

cephalic vein
頭靜脈

basilic vein
貴要靜脈

splenic artery
脾動脈

splenic vein
脾靜脈

cubital vein
肘靜脈

radial vein
橈靜脈

renal artery
腎動脈

renal vein
腎靜脈

abdominal aorta
腹主動脈

median vein of forearm
前臂正中靜脈

great saphenous vein
大隱靜脈

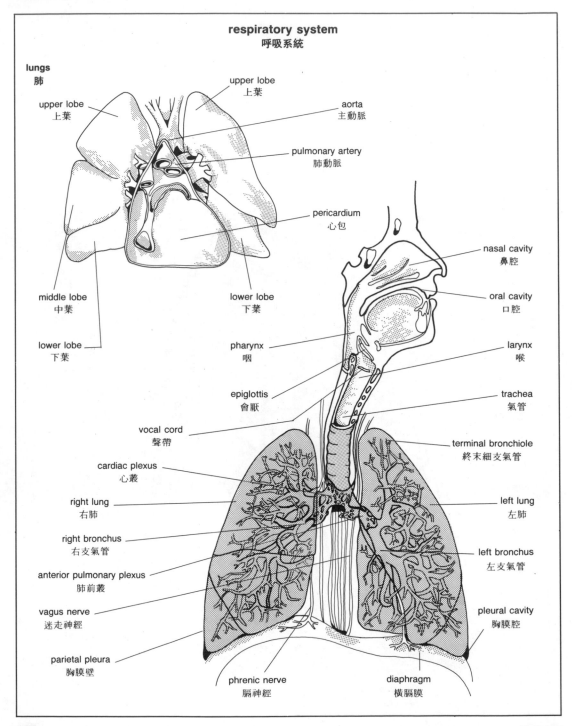

respiratory system
呼吸系統

lungs
肺

upper lobe
上葉

upper lobe
上葉

aorta
主動脈

pulmonary artery
肺動脈

pericardium
心包

nasal cavity
鼻腔

oral cavity
口腔

middle lobe
中葉

lower lobe
下葉

lower lobe
下葉

pharynx
咽

larynx
喉

epiglottis
會厭

trachea
氣管

vocal cord
聲帶

terminal bronchiole
終末細支氣管

cardiac plexus
心叢

right lung
右肺

left lung
左肺

right bronchus
右支氣管

left bronchus
左支氣管

anterior pulmonary plexus
肺前叢

vagus nerve
迷走神經

pleural cavity
胸膜腔

parietal pleura
胸膜壁

phrenic nerve
膈神經

diaphragm
橫膈膜

digestive system
消化系統

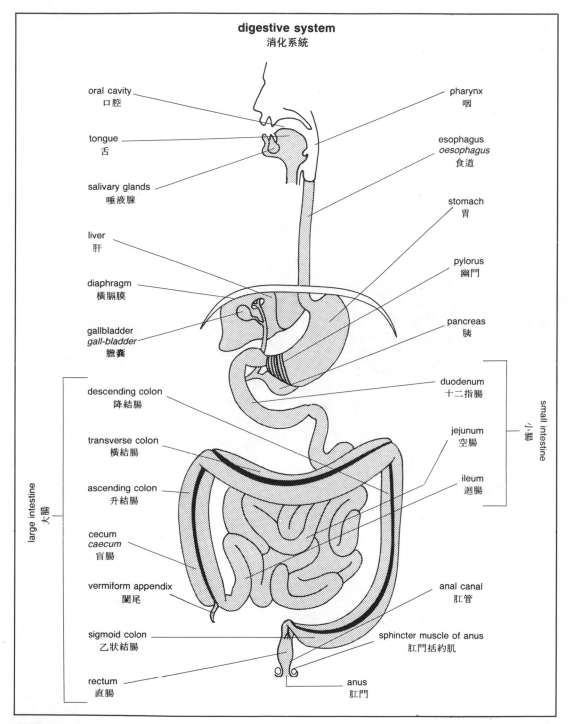

oral cavity
口腔

pharynx
咽

tongue
舌

esophagus
oesophagus
食道

salivary glands
唾液腺

stomach
胃

liver
肝

pylorus
幽門

diaphragm
橫膈膜

pancreas
胰

gallbladder
gall-bladder
膽囊

duodenum
十二指腸

descending colon
降結腸

jejunum
空腸

transverse colon
橫結腸

small intestine
小腸

ascending colon
升結腸

ileum
迴腸

cecum
caecum
盲腸

large intestine
大腸

vermiform appendix
闌尾

anal canal
肛管

sigmoid colon
乙狀結腸

sphincter muscle of anus
肛門括約肌

rectum
直腸

anus
肛門

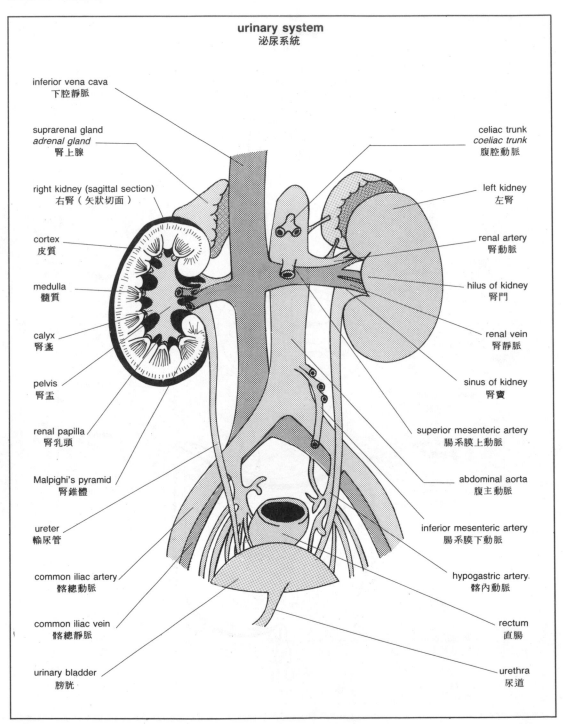

urinary system
泌尿系統

inferior vena cava
下腔靜脈

suprarenal gland
adrenal gland
腎上腺

right kidney (sagittal section)
右腎（矢狀切面）

cortex
皮質

medulla
髓質

calyx
腎盞

pelvis
腎盂

renal papilla
腎乳頭

Malpighi's pyramid
腎錐體

ureter
輸尿管

common iliac artery
髂總動脈

common iliac vein
髂總靜脈

urinary bladder
膀胱

celiac trunk
coeliac trunk
腹腔動脈

left kidney
左腎

renal artery
腎動脈

hilus of kidney
腎門

renal vein
腎靜脈

sinus of kidney
腎竇

superior mesenteric artery
腸系膜上動脈

abdominal aorta
腹主動脈

inferior mesenteric artery
腸系膜下動脈

hypogastric artery
髂內動脈

rectum
直腸

urethra
尿道

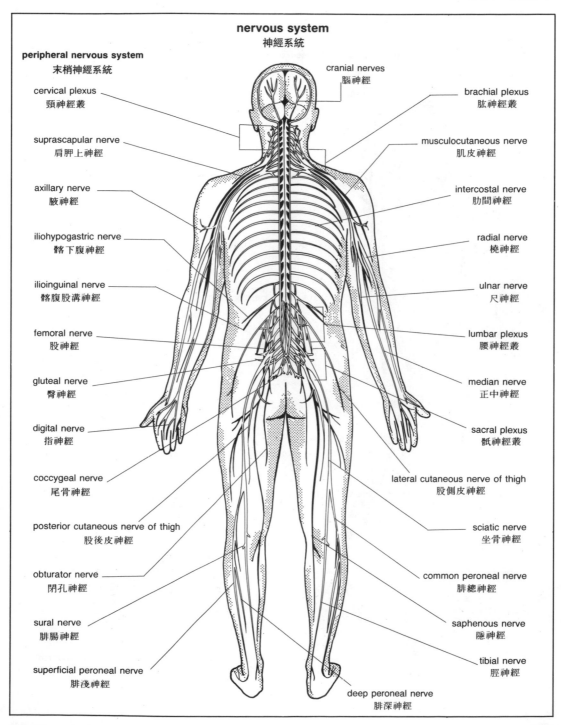

nervous system
神經系統

peripheral nervous system
末梢神經系統

cranial nerves
腦神經

cervical plexus
頸神經叢

brachial plexus
肱神經叢

suprascapular nerve
肩胛上神經

musculocutaneous nerve
肌皮神經

axillary nerve
腋神經

intercostal nerve
肋間神經

iliohypogastric nerve
髂下腹神經

radial nerve
橈神經

ilioinguinal nerve
髂腹股溝神經

ulnar nerve
尺神經

femoral nerve
股神經

lumbar plexus
腰神經叢

gluteal nerve
臀神經

median nerve
正中神經

digital nerve
指神經

sacral plexus
骶神經叢

coccygeal nerve
尾骨神經

lateral cutaneous nerve of thigh
股側皮神經

posterior cutaneous nerve of thigh
股後皮神經

sciatic nerve
坐骨神經

obturator nerve
閉孔神經

common peroneal nerve
腓總神經

sural nerve
腓腸神經

saphenous nerve
隱神經

superficial peroneal nerve
腓淺神經

tibial nerve
脛神經

deep peroneal nerve
腓深神經

nervous system
神經系統

central nervous system cerebrospinal axis (sagittal section)
中樞神經系統（矢狀切面）

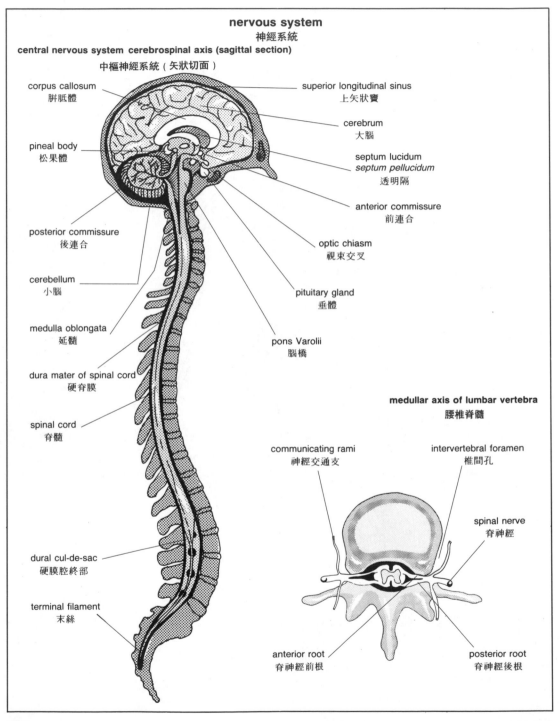

corpus callosum
胼胝體

superior longitudinal sinus
上矢狀竇

cerebrum
大腦

pineal body
松果體

septum lucidum
septum pellucidum
透明隔

anterior commissure
前連合

posterior commissure
後連合

optic chiasm
視束交叉

cerebellum
小腦

pituitary gland
垂體

medulla oblongata
延髓

pons Varolii
腦橋

dura mater of spinal cord
硬脊膜

medullar axis of lumbar vertebra
腰椎脊髓

spinal cord
脊髓

communicating rami
神經交通支

intervertebral foramen
椎間孔

spinal nerve
脊神經

dural cul-de-sac
硬膜腔終部

terminal filament
末絲

anterior root
脊神經前根

posterior root
脊神經後根

sense organs: sight
感覺器官：視覺

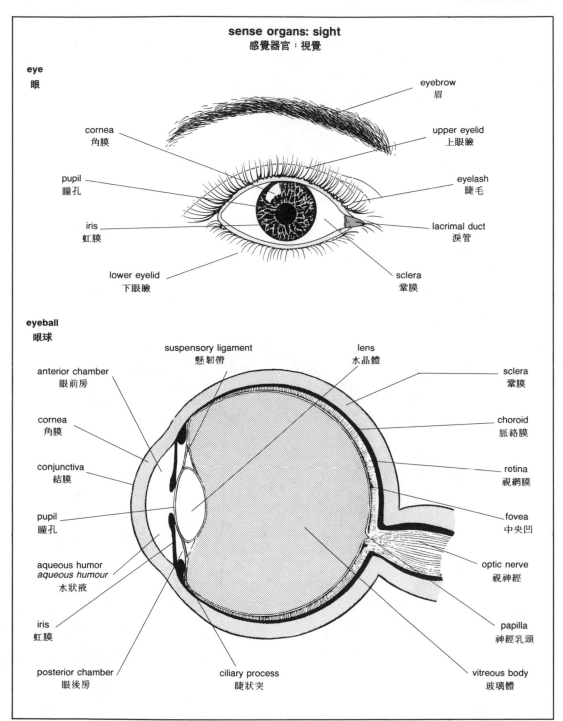

eye
眼

eyebrow
眉

cornea
角膜

upper eyelid
上眼瞼

pupil
瞳孔

eyelash
睫毛

iris
虹膜

lacrimal duct
淚管

lower eyelid
下眼瞼

sclera
鞏膜

eyeball
眼球

suspensory ligament
懸韌帶

lens
水晶體

sclera
鞏膜

anterior chamber
眼前房

choroid
脈絡膜

cornea
角膜

retina
視網膜

conjunctiva
結膜

fovea
中央凹

pupil
瞳孔

optic nerve
視神經

aqueous humor
aqueous humour
水狀液

iris
虹膜

papilla
神經乳頭

posterior chamber
眼後房

ciliary process
睫狀突

vitreous body
玻璃體

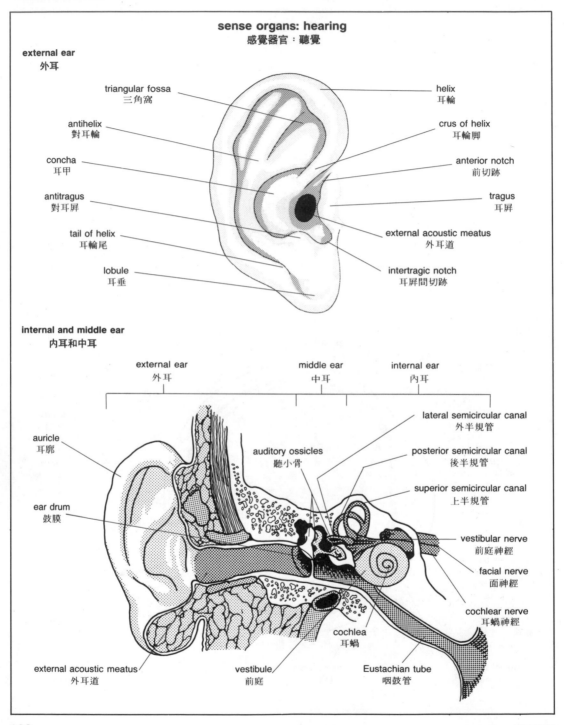

sense organs: hearing
感覺器官：聽覺

external ear
外耳

triangular fossa
三角窩

helix
耳輪

antihelix
對耳輪

crus of helix
耳輪腳

concha
耳甲

anterior notch
前切跡

antitragus
對耳屏

tragus
耳屏

tail of helix
耳輪尾

external acoustic meatus
外耳道

lobule
耳垂

intertragic notch
耳屏間切跡

internal and middle ear
內耳和中耳

external ear
外耳

middle ear
中耳

internal ear
內耳

auricle
耳廓

lateral semicircular canal
外半規管

auditory ossicles
聽小骨

posterior semicircular canal
後半規管

superior semicircular canal
上半規管

ear drum
鼓膜

vestibular nerve
前庭神經

facial nerve
面神經

cochlear nerve
耳蝸神經

cochlea
耳蝸

external acoustic meatus
外耳道

vestibule
前庭

Eustachian tube
咽鼓管

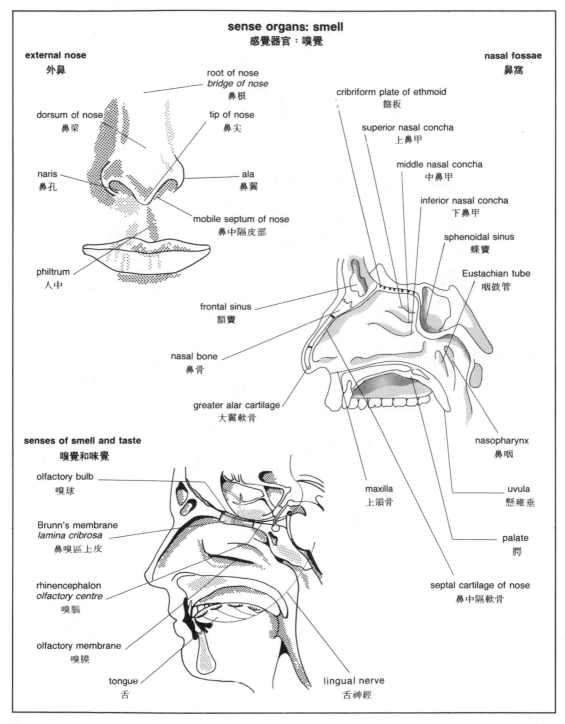

sense organs: smell
感覺器官：嗅覺

external nose
外鼻

root of nose
bridge of nose
鼻根

dorsum of nose
鼻梁

tip of nose
鼻尖

naris
鼻孔

ala
鼻翼

mobile septum of nose
鼻中隔皮部

philtrum
人中

frontal sinus
額竇

nasal bone
鼻骨

greater alar cartilage
大翼軟骨

nasal fossae
鼻窩

cribriform plate of ethmoid
篩板

superior nasal concha
上鼻甲

middle nasal concha
中鼻甲

inferior nasal concha
下鼻甲

sphenoidal sinus
蝶竇

Eustachian tube
咽鼓管

nasopharynx
鼻咽

maxilla
上頜骨

uvula
懸雍垂

palate
腭

septal cartilage of nose
鼻中隔軟骨

senses of smell and taste
嗅覺和味覺

olfactory bulb
嗅球

Brunn's membrane
lamina cribrosa
鼻嗅區上皮

rhinencephalon
olfactory centre
嗅腦

olfactory membrane
嗅膜

tongue
舌

lingual nerve
舌神經

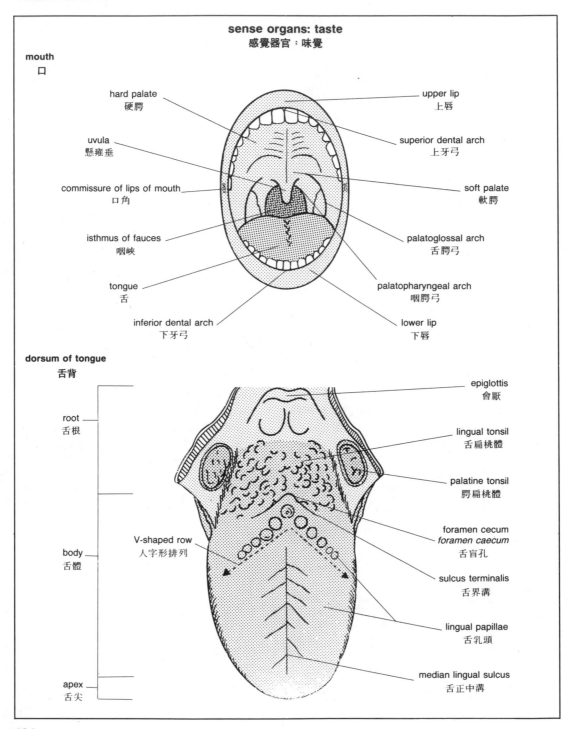

sense organs: taste
感覺器官：味覺

mouth
口

hard palate
硬腭

upper lip
上唇

uvula
懸雍垂

superior dental arch
上牙弓

commissure of lips of mouth
口角

soft palate
軟腭

isthmus of fauces
咽峽

palatoglossal arch
舌腭弓

tongue
舌

palatopharyngeal arch
咽腭弓

inferior dental arch
下牙弓

lower lip
下唇

dorsum of tongue
舌背

epiglottis
會厭

root
舌根

lingual tonsil
舌扁桃體

palatine tonsil
腭扁桃體

foramen cecum
foramen caecum
舌盲孔

V-shaped row
人字形排列

sulcus terminalis
舌界溝

body
舌體

lingual papillae
舌乳頭

median lingual sulcus
舌正中溝

apex
舌尖

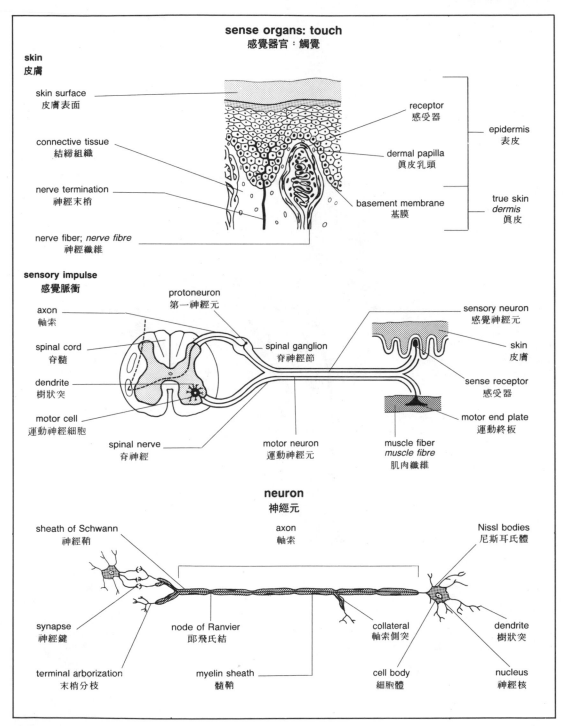

sense organs: touch
感覺器官：觸覺

skin
皮膚

skin surface
皮膚表面

connective tissue
結締組織

nerve termination
神經末梢

nerve fiber; *nerve fibre*
神經纖維

receptor
感受器

dermal papilla
真皮乳頭

basement membrane
基膜

epidermis
表皮

true skin
dermis
真皮

sensory impulse
感覺脈衝

axon
軸索

spinal cord
脊髓

dendrite
樹狀突

motor cell
運動神經細胞

spinal nerve
脊神經

protoneuron
第一神經元

spinal ganglion
脊神經節

motor neuron
運動神經元

sensory neuron
感覺神經元

skin
皮膚

sense receptor
感受器

motor end plate
運動終板

muscle fiber
muscle fibre
肌肉纖維

neuron
神經元

sheath of Schwann
神經鞘

axon
軸索

Nissl bodies
尼斯耳氏體

synapse
神經鍵

node of Ranvier
郎飛氏結

collateral
軸索側突

dendrite
樹狀突

terminal arborization
末梢分枝

myelin sheath
髓鞘

cell body
細胞體

nucleus
神經核

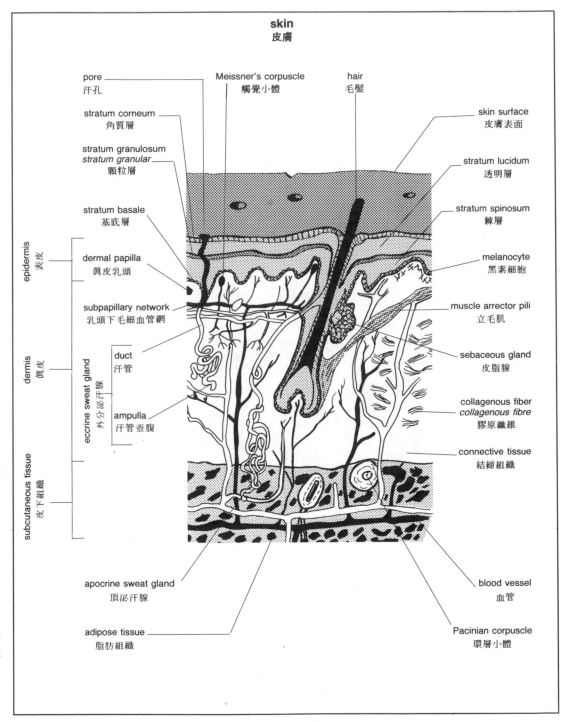

skin
皮膚

pore
汗孔

Meissner's corpuscle
觸覺小體

hair
毛髮

skin surface
皮膚表面

stratum corneum
角質層

stratum lucidum
透明層

stratum granulosum
stratum granular
顆粒層

stratum basale
基底層

stratum spinosum
棘層

epidermis
表皮

dermal papilla
真皮乳頭

melanocyte
黑素細胞

subpapillary network
乳頭下毛細血管網

muscle arrector pili
立毛肌

dermis
真皮

eccrine sweat gland
外分泌汗腺

duct
汗管

sebaceous gland
皮脂腺

ampulla
汗管壺腹

collagenous fiber
collagenous fibre
膠原纖維

connective tissue
結締組織

subcutaneous tissue
皮下組織

apocrine sweat gland
頂泌汗腺

blood vessel
血管

adipose tissue
脂肪組織

Pacinian corpuscle
環層小體

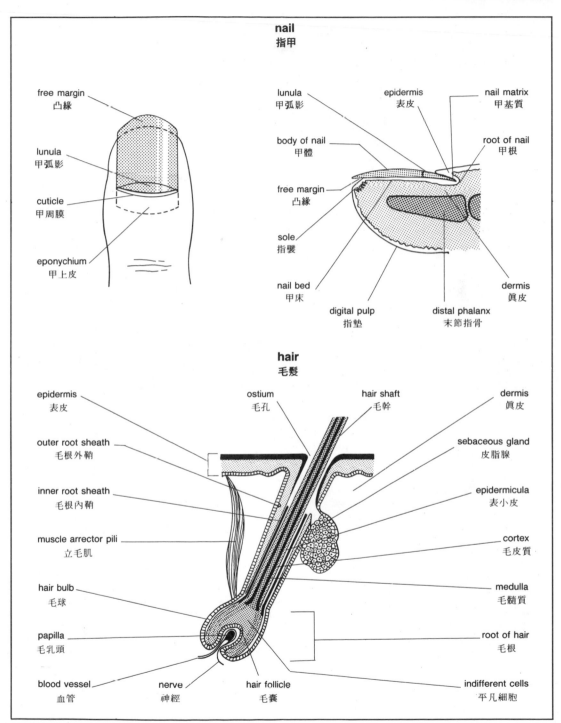

nail
指甲

free margin
凸緣

lunula
甲弧影

cuticle
甲周膜

eponychium
甲上皮

lunula
甲弧影

epidermis
表皮

nail matrix
甲基質

body of nail
甲體

root of nail
甲根

free margin
凸緣

sole
指甖

nail bed
甲床

digital pulp
指墊

distal phalanx
末節指骨

dermis
眞皮

hair
毛髮

epidermis
表皮

ostium
毛孔

hair shaft
毛幹

dermis
眞皮

outer root sheath
毛根外鞘

sebaceous gland
皮脂腺

inner root sheath
毛根內鞘

epidermicula
表小皮

muscle arrector pili
立毛肌

cortex
毛皮質

hair bulb
毛球

medulla
毛髓質

papilla
毛乳頭

root of hair
毛根

blood vessel
血管

nerve
神經

hair follicle
毛囊

indifferent cells
平凡細胞

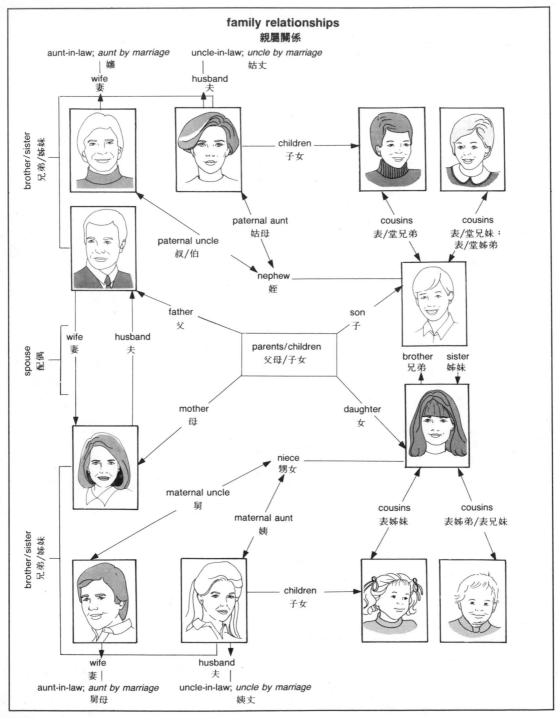

family relationships
親屬關係

aunt-in-law; *aunt by marriage* 嬸

uncle-in-law; *uncle by marriage* 姑丈

wife 妻

husband 夫

brother/sister 兄弟/姊妹

children 子女

paternal aunt 姑母

cousins 表/堂兄弟

cousins 表/堂兄妹; 表/堂姊弟

paternal uncle 叔/伯

nephew 姪

father 父

son 子

spouse 配偶

wife 妻

husband 夫

parents/children 父母/子女

brother 兄弟

sister 姊妹

mother 母

daughter 女

niece 甥女

brother/sister 兄弟/姊妹

maternal uncle 舅

cousins 表姊妹

cousins 表姊弟/表兄妹

maternal aunt 姨

children 子女

wife 妻

aunt-in-law; *aunt by marriage* 舅母

husband 夫

uncle-in-law; *uncle by marriage* 姨丈

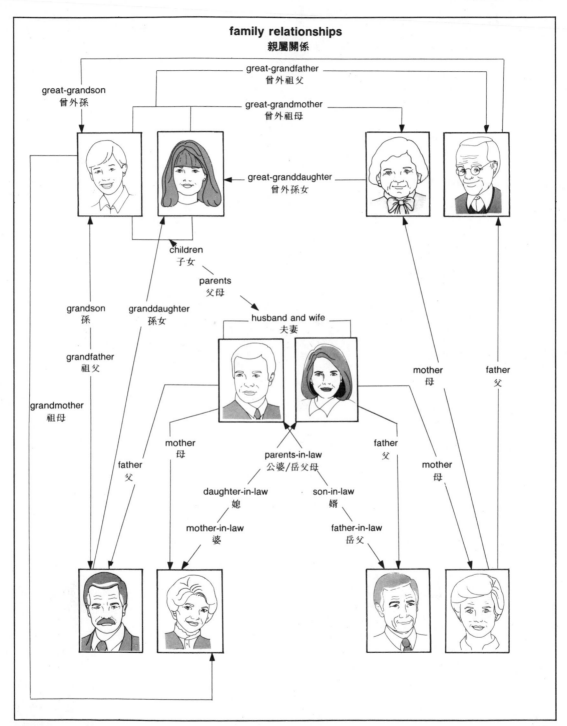

family relationships
親屬關係

great-grandfather 曾外祖父

great-grandson 曾外孫

great-grandmother 曾外祖母

great-granddaughter 曾外孫女

children 子女

parents 父母

grandson 孫

granddaughter 孫女

grandfather 祖父

husband and wife 夫妻

mother 母

father 父

grandmother 祖母

father 父

mother 母

father 父

mother 母

parents-in-law 公婆/岳父母

mother 母

daughter-in-law 媳

son-in-law 婿

mother-in-law 婆

father-in-law 岳父

FOOD
食物

herbs
香草

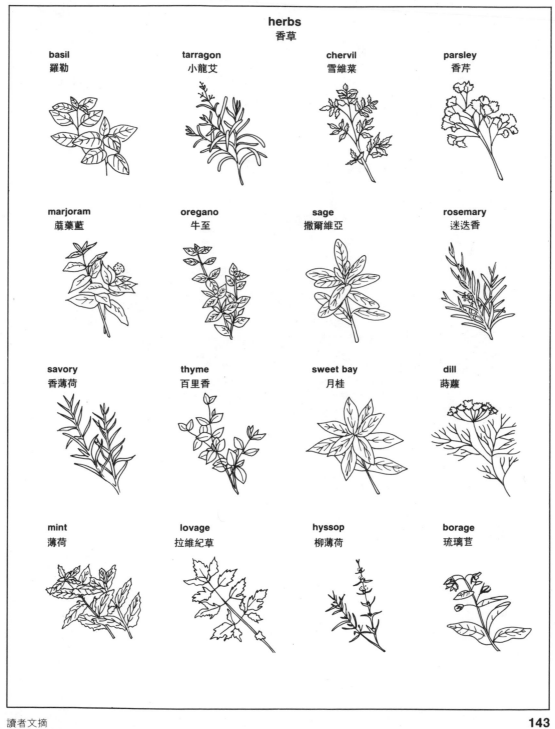

basil
羅勒

tarragon
小龍艾

chervil
雪維菜

parsley
香芹

marjoram
蘪葽藍

oregano
牛至

sage
撒爾維亞

rosemary
迷迭香

savory
香薄荷

thyme
百里香

sweet bay
月桂

dill
蒔蘿

mint
薄荷

lovage
拉維紀草

hyssop
柳薄荷

borage
琉璃苣

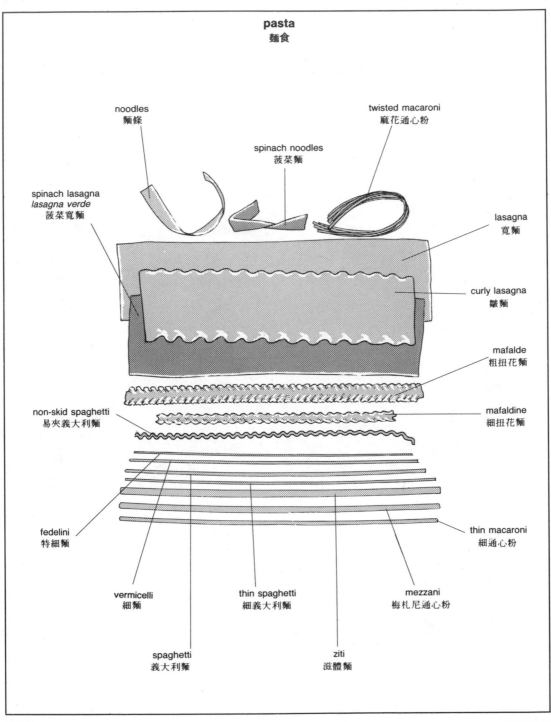

pasta
麵食

noodles
麵條

twisted macaroni
麻花通心粉

spinach noodles
菠菜麵

spinach lasagna
lasagna verde
菠菜寬麵

lasagna
寬麵

curly lasagna
皺麵

mafalde
粗扭花麵

non-skid spaghetti
易夾義大利麵

mafaldine
細扭花麵

fedelini
特細麵

thin macaroni
細通心粉

vermicelli
細麵

thin spaghetti
細義大利麵

mezzani
梅札尼通心粉

spaghetti
義大利麵

ziti
滋體麵

pasta
麵食

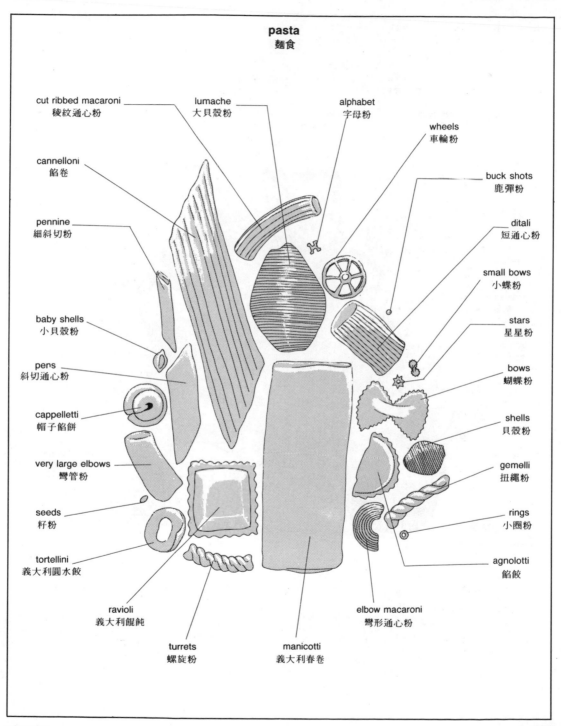

cut ribbed macaroni
稜紋通心粉

lumache
大貝殼粉

alphabet
字母粉

wheels
車輪粉

buck shots
鹿彈粉

cannelloni
餡卷

ditali
短通心粉

pennine
細斜切粉

small bows
小蝶粉

stars
星星粉

baby shells
小貝殼粉

pens
斜切通心粉

bows
蝴蝶粉

cappelletti
帽子餡餅

shells
貝殼粉

very large elbows
彎管粉

gemelli
扭繩粉

seeds
籽粉

rings
小圈粉

tortellini
義大利圓水餃

agnolotti
餡餃

ravioli
義大利餛飩

elbow macaroni
彎形通心粉

turrets
螺旋粉

manicotti
義大利春卷

bread
麵包

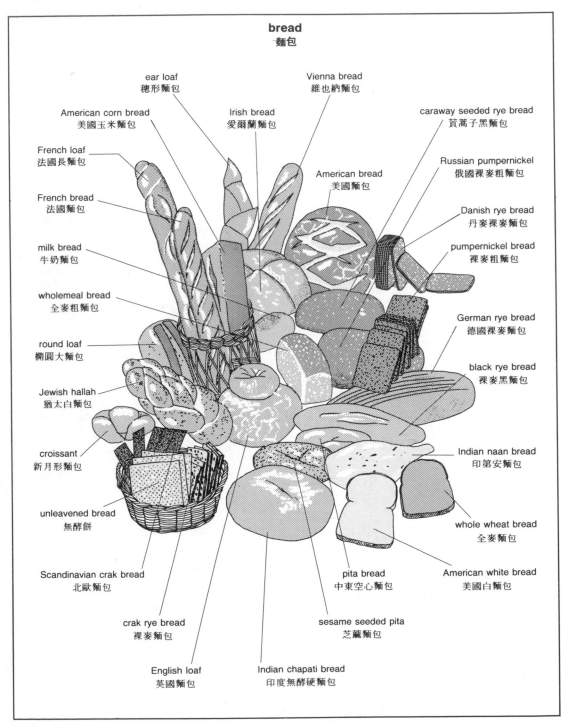

ear loaf
穗形麵包

Vienna bread
維也納麵包

American corn bread
美國玉米麵包

Irish bread
愛爾蘭麵包

caraway seeded rye bread
葛蔞子黑麵包

French loaf
法國長麵包

American bread
美國麵包

Russian pumpernickel
俄國裸麥粗麵包

French bread
法國麵包

Danish rye bread
丹麥裸麥麵包

milk bread
牛奶麵包

pumpernickel bread
裸麥粗麵包

wholemeal bread
全麥粗麵包

German rye bread
德國裸麥麵包

round loaf
橢圓大麵包

black rye bread
裸麥黑麵包

Jewish hallah
猶太白麵包

croissant
新月形麵包

Indian naan bread
印第安麵包

unleavened bread
無酵餅

whole wheat bread
全麥麵包

Scandinavian crak bread
北歐麵包

American white bread
美國白麵包

pita bread
中東空心麵包

crak rye bread
裸麥麵包

sesame seeded pita
芝蔴麵包

English loaf
英國麵包

Indian chapati bread
印度無酵硬麵包

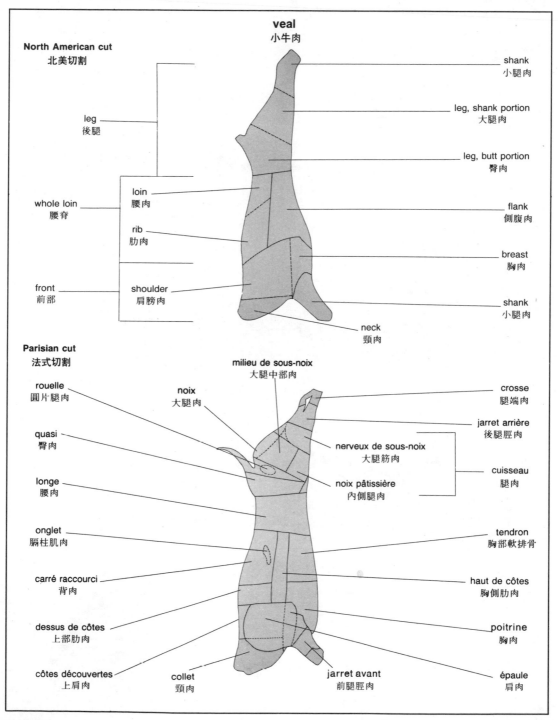

veal
小牛肉

North American cut
北美切割

leg
後腿

whole loin
腰脊

front
前部

loin
腰肉

rib
肋肉

shoulder
肩膀肉

shank
小腿肉

leg, shank portion
大腿肉

leg, butt portion
臀肉

flank
側腹肉

breast
胸肉

shank
小腿肉

neck
頸肉

Parisian cut
法式切割

rouelle
圓片腿肉

quasi
臀肉

longe
腰肉

onglet
膈柱肌肉

carré raccourci
背肉

dessus de côtes
上部肋肉

côtes découvertes
上肩肉

milieu de sous-noix
大腿中部肉

noix
大腿肉

nerveux de sous-noix
大腿筋肉

noix pâtissière
內側腿肉

collet
頸肉

jarret avant
前腿脛肉

crosse
腿端肉

jarret arrière
後腿脛肉

cuisseau
腿肉

tendron
胸部軟排骨

haut de côtes
胸側肋肉

poitrine
胸肉

épaule
肩肉

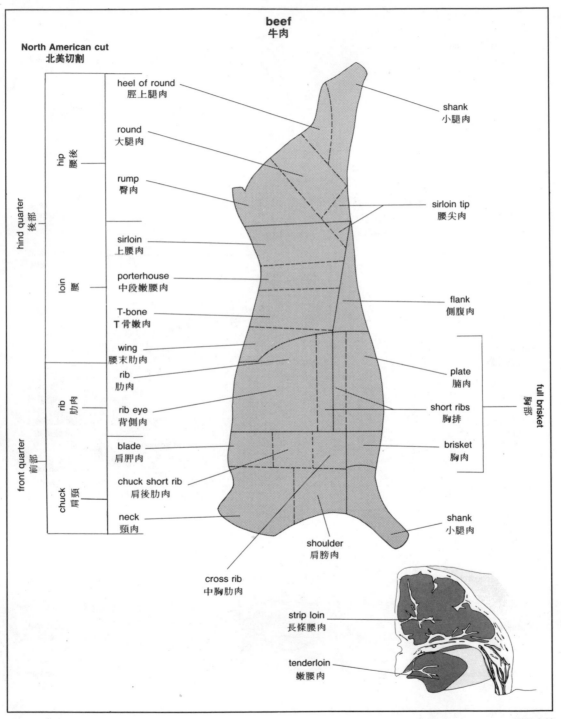

beef
牛肉

North American cut
北美切割

heel of round
脛上腿肉

round
大腿肉

rump
臀肉

sirloin
上腰肉

porterhouse
中段嫩腰肉

T-bone
T骨嫩肉

wing
腰末肋肉

rib
肋肉

rib eye
背側肉

blade
肩胛肉

chuck short rib
肩後肋肉

neck
頸肉

cross rib
中胸肋肉

shank
小腿肉

sirloin tip
腰尖肉

flank
側腹肉

plate
腩肉

short ribs
胸排

brisket
胸肉

shank
小腿肉

shoulder
肩膀肉

hip
腰後

loin
腰

rib
肋肉

chuck
肩頸

hind quarter
後部

front quarter
前部

full brisket
胸部

strip loin
長條腰肉

tenderloin
嫩腰肉

beef
牛肉

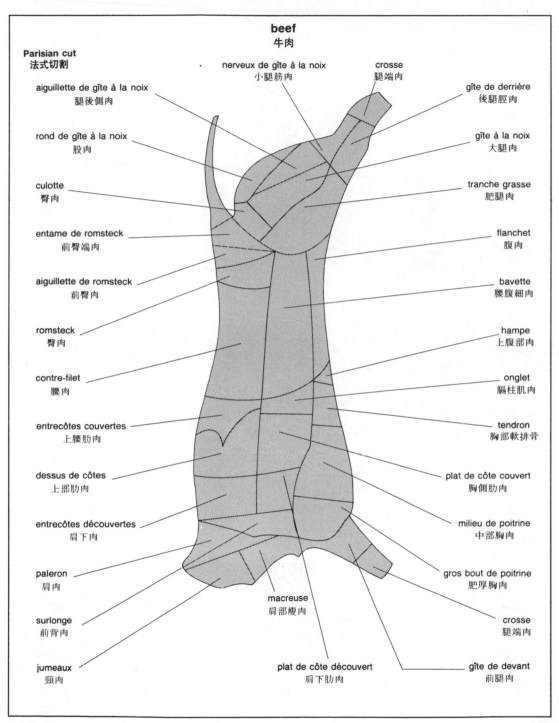

Parisian cut
法式切割

nerveux de gîte à la noix
小腿筋肉

crosse
腿端肉

aiguillette de gîte à la noix
腿後側肉

gîte de derrière
後腿脛肉

rond de gîte à la noix
股肉

gîte à la noix
大腿肉

culotte
臀肉

tranche grasse
肥腿肉

entame de romsteck
前臀端肉

flanchet
腹肉

aiguillette de romsteck
前臀肉

bavette
腰腹細肉

romsteck
臀肉

hampe
上腹部肉

contre-filet
腰肉

onglet
膈柱肌肉

entrecôtes couvertes
上腰肋肉

tendron
胸部軟排骨

dessus de côtes
上部肋肉

plat de côte couvert
胸側肋肉

entrecôtes découvertes
肩下肉

milieu de poitrine
中部胸肉

paleron
肩肉

gros bout de poitrine
肥厚胸肉

surlonge
前背肉

crosse
腿端肉

jumeaux
頸肉

macreuse
肩部瘦肉

plat de côte découvert
肩下肋肉

gîte de devant
前腿肉

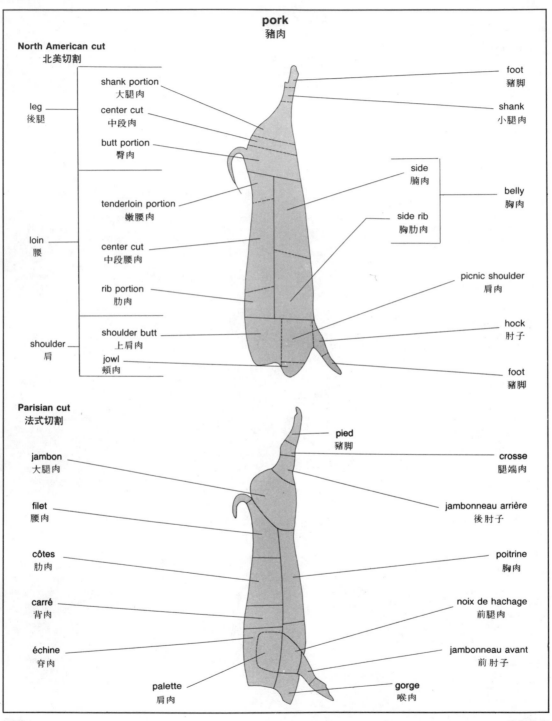

pork
豬肉

North American cut
北美切割

foot
豬脚

shank portion
大腿肉

shank
小腿肉

center cut
中段肉

leg
後腿

butt portion
臀肉

side
腩肉

belly
胸肉

tenderloin portion
嫩腰肉

side rib
胸肋肉

loin
腰

center cut
中段腰肉

picnic shoulder
肩肉

rib portion
肋肉

hock
肘子

shoulder
肩

shoulder butt
上肩肉

jowl
頰肉

foot
豬脚

Parisian cut
法式切割

pied
豬脚

jambon
大腿肉

crosse
腿端肉

filet
腰肉

jambonneau arrière
後肘子

côtes
肋肉

poitrine
胸肉

carré
背肉

noix de hachage
前腿肉

échine
脊肉

jambonneau avant
前肘子

palette
肩肉

gorge
喉肉

lamb
羊肉

North American cut
北美切割

leg
後腿

whole loin
腰脊

loin
腰肉

rib
肋肉

shoulder
肩肉

neck
頸肉

front
前部

shank
小腿肉

shank portion
大腿肉

butt portion
臀肉

flank
側腹肉

breast
胸肉

shank
小腿肉

Parisian cut
法式切割

côtelettes premières et secondes
一、二級肋肉

haut de côtelettes
胸側肋肉

côtelettes découvertes
上肩肋肉

collet
頸肉

gigot
後腿

selle
脊肉

filet
腰肉

poitrine
胸肉

épaule
肩肉

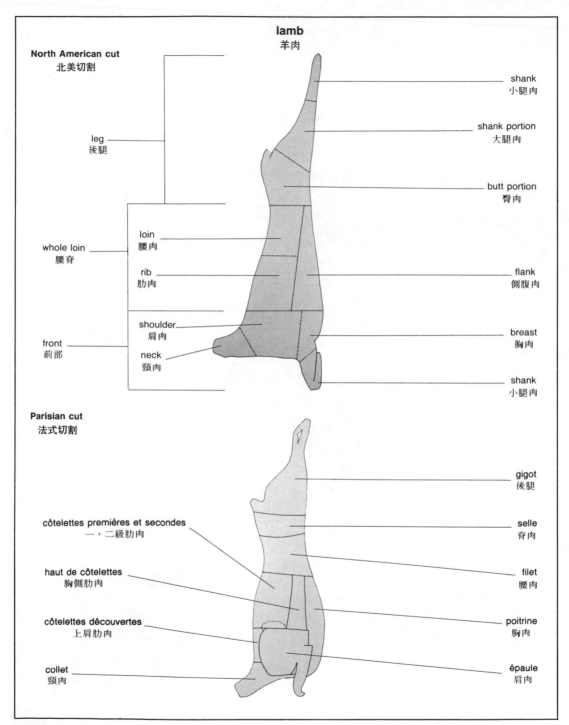

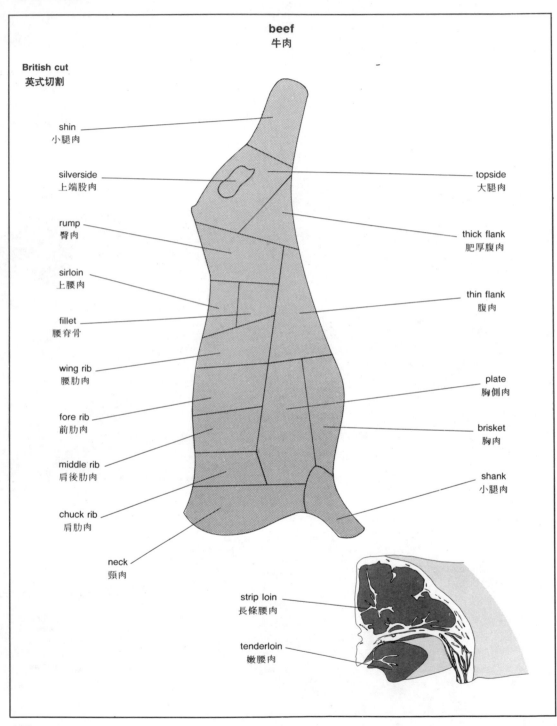

beef
牛肉

British cut
英式切割

shin
小腿肉

silverside
上端股肉

rump
臀肉

sirloin
上腰肉

fillet
腰脊骨

wing rib
腰肋肉

fore rib
前肋肉

middle rib
肩後肋肉

chuck rib
肩肋肉

neck
頸肉

topside
大腿肉

thick flank
肥厚腹肉

thin flank
腹肉

plate
胸側肉

brisket
胸肉

shank
小腿肉

strip loin
長條腰肉

tenderloin
嫩腰肉

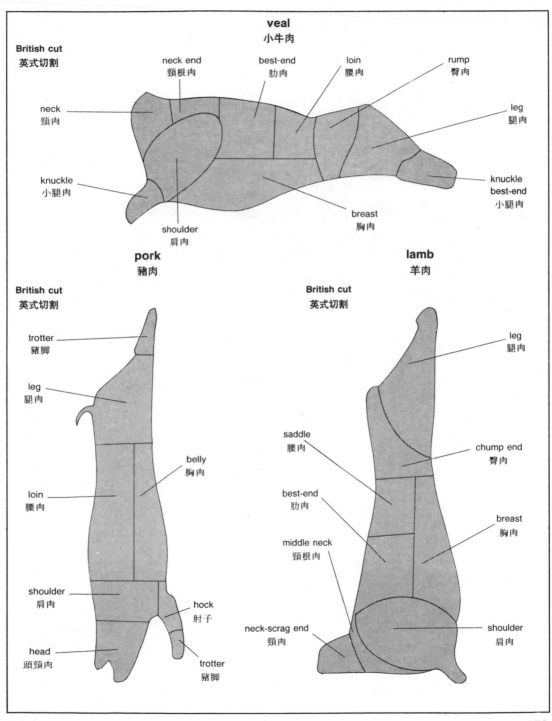

veal
小牛肉

British cut
英式切割

neck end
頸根肉

best-end
肋肉

loin
腰肉

rump
臀肉

neck
頸肉

leg
腿肉

knuckle
小腿肉

knuckle
best-end
小腿肉

shoulder
肩肉

breast
胸肉

pork
豬肉

lamb
羊肉

British cut
英式切割

British cut
英式切割

trotter
豬脚

leg
腿肉

leg
腿肉

belly
胸肉

saddle
腰肉

chump end
臀肉

loin
腰肉

best-end
肋肉

breast
胸肉

middle neck
頸根肉

shoulder
肩肉

hock
肘子

neck-scrag end
頸肉

shoulder
肩肉

head
頭頸肉

trotter
豬脚

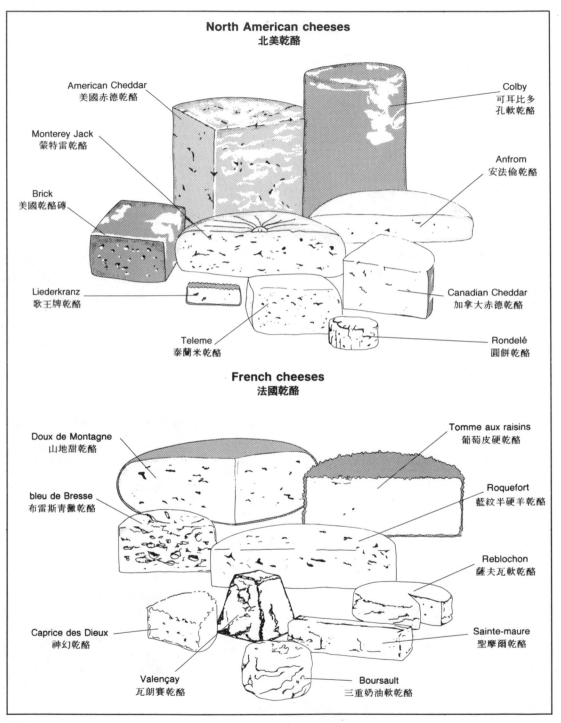

North American cheeses
北美乾酪

American Cheddar
美國赤德乾酪

Colby
可耳比多
孔軟乾酪

Monterey Jack
蒙特雷乾酪

Anfrom
安法倫乾酪

Brick
美國乾酪磚

Liederkranz
歌王牌乾酪

Canadian Cheddar
加拿大赤德乾酪

Teleme
泰蘭米乾酪

Rondelé
圓餅乾酪

French cheeses
法國乾酪

Doux de Montagne
山地甜乾酪

Tomme aux raisins
葡萄皮硬乾酪

bleu de Bresse
布雷斯青黴乾酪

Roquefort
藍紋半硬羊乾酪

Reblochon
薩夫瓦軟乾酪

Caprice des Dieux
神幻乾酪

Sainte-maure
聖摩爾乾酪

Valençay
瓦朗賽乾酪

Boursault
三重奶油軟乾酪

French cheeses
法國乾酪

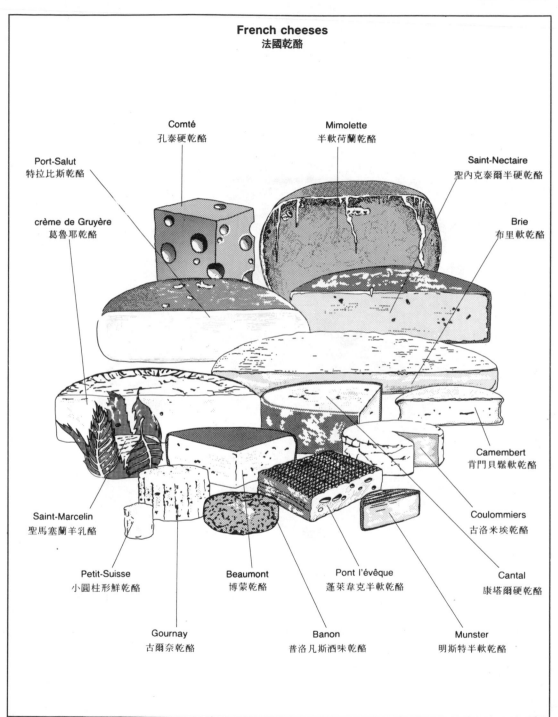

Comté
孔泰硬乾酪

Mimolette
半軟荷蘭乾酪

Saint-Nectaire
聖內克泰爾半硬乾酪

Port-Salut
特拉比斯乾酪

Brie
布里軟乾酪

crème de Gruyère
葛魯耶乾酪

Camembert
肯門貝鬆軟乾酪

Saint-Marcelin
聖馬塞蘭羊乳酪

Coulommiers
古洛米埃乾酪

Petit-Suisse
小圓柱形鮮乾酪

Beaumont
博蒙乾酪

Pont l'évêque
蓬萊韋克半軟乾酪

Cantal
康塔爾硬乾酪

Gournay
古爾奈乾酪

Banon
普洛凡斯酒味乾酪

Munster
明斯特半軟乾酪

desserts
甜點

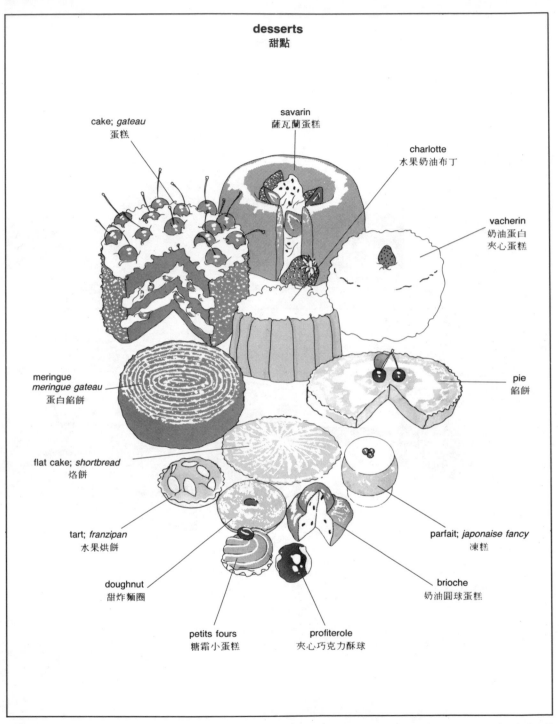

cake; *gateau*
蛋糕

savarin
薩瓦蘭蛋糕

charlotte
水果奶油布丁

vacherin
奶油蛋白
夾心蛋糕

meringue
meringue gateau
蛋白餡餅

pie
餡餅

flat cake; *shortbread*
烙餅

tart; *franzipan*
水果烘餅

parfait; *japonaise fancy*
凍糕

doughnut
甜炸麵圈

brioche
奶油圓球蛋糕

petits fours
糖霜小蛋糕

profiterole
夾心巧克力酥球

desserts
甜點

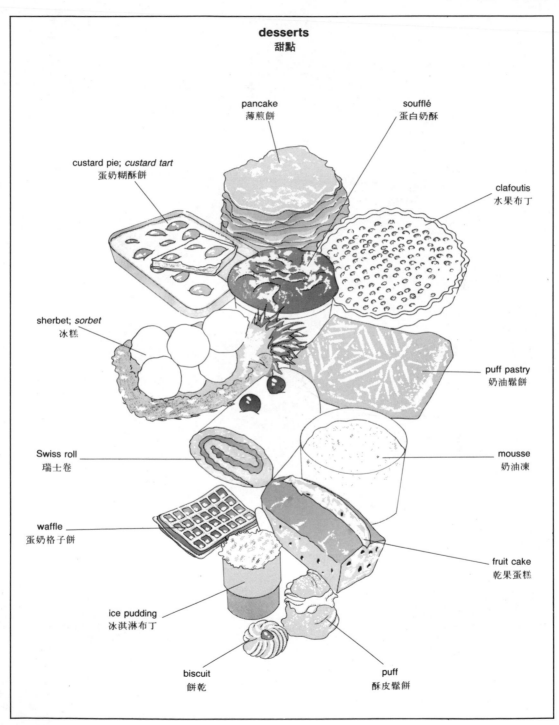

pancake
薄煎餅

soufflé
蛋白奶酥

custard pie; *custard tart*
蛋奶糊酥餅

clafoutis
水果布丁

sherbet; *sorbet*
冰糕

puff pastry
奶油鬆餅

Swiss roll
瑞士卷

mousse
奶油凍

waffle
蛋奶格子餅

fruit cake
乾果蛋糕

ice pudding
冰淇淋布丁

biscuit
餅乾

puff
酥皮鬆餅

FARM

農場

buildings
建築物

open housing
敞開式農場

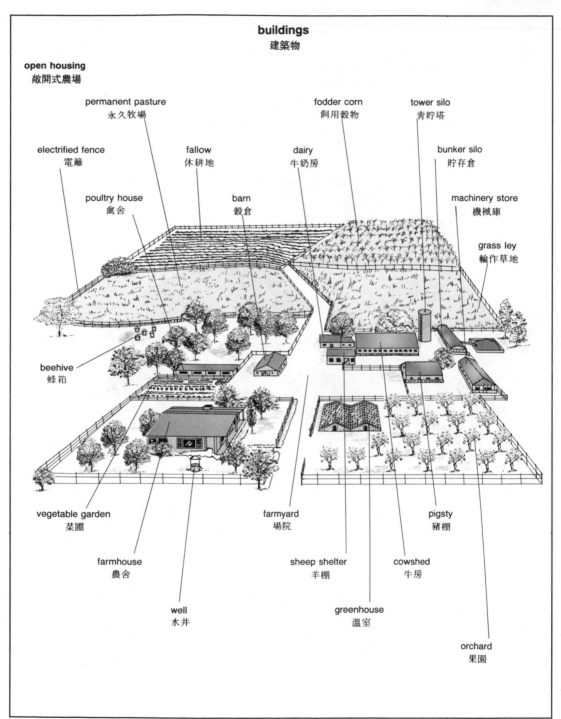

permanent pasture
永久牧場

fodder corn
飼用穀物

tower silo
青貯塔

electrified fence
電籬

fallow
休耕地

dairy
牛奶房

bunker silo
貯存倉

poultry house
禽舍

barn
穀倉

machinery store
機械庫

grass ley
輪作草地

beehive
蜂箱

vegetable garden
菜圃

farmyard
場院

pigsty
豬棚

farmhouse
農舍

sheep shelter
羊棚

cowshed
牛房

well
水井

greenhouse
溫室

orchard
果園

agricultural machinery
農業機械

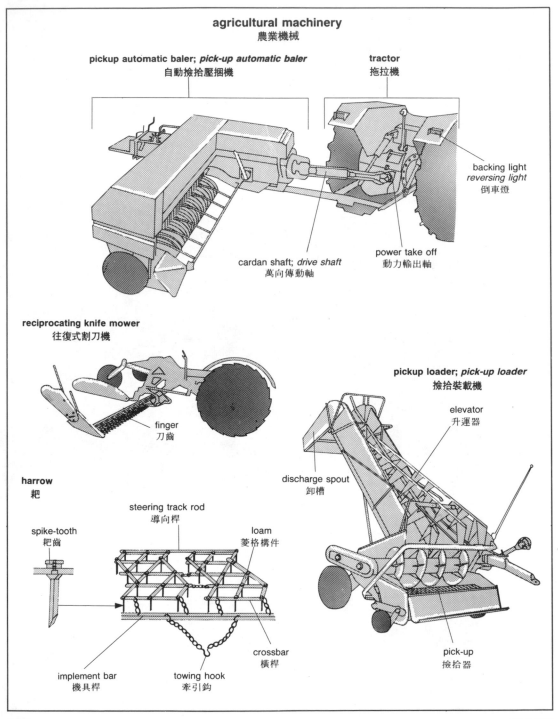

pickup automatic baler; *pick-up automatic baler*
自動撿拾壓捆機

tractor
拖拉機

backing light
reversing light
倒車燈

power take off
動力輸出軸

cardan shaft; *drive shaft*
萬向傳動軸

reciprocating knife mower
往復式割刀機

finger
刀齒

pickup loader; *pick-up loader*
撿拾裝載機

elevator
升運器

discharge spout
卸槽

harrow
耙

steering track rod
導向桿

spike-tooth
耙齒

loam
菱格構件

crossbar
橫桿

pick-up
撿拾器

implement bar
機具桿

towing hook
牽引鈎

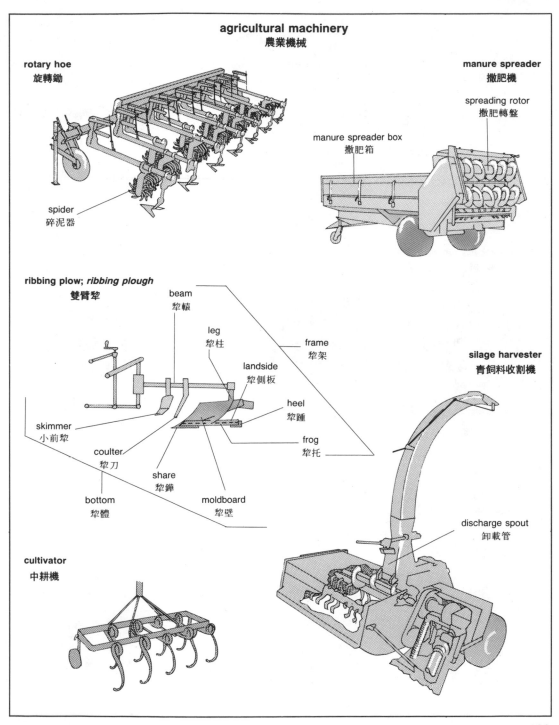

agricultural machinery
農業機械

rotary hoe
旋轉鋤

spider
碎泥器

manure spreader
撒肥機

spreading rotor
撒肥轉盤

manure spreader box
撒肥箱

ribbing plow; *ribbing plough*
雙臂犁

beam
犁轅

leg
犁柱

landside
犁側板

frame
犁架

heel
犁踵

frog
犁托

skimmer
小前犁

coulter
犁刀

share
犁鏵

moldboard
犁壁

bottom
犁體

silage harvester
青飼料收割機

discharge spout
卸載管

cultivator
中耕機

agricultural machinery
農業機械

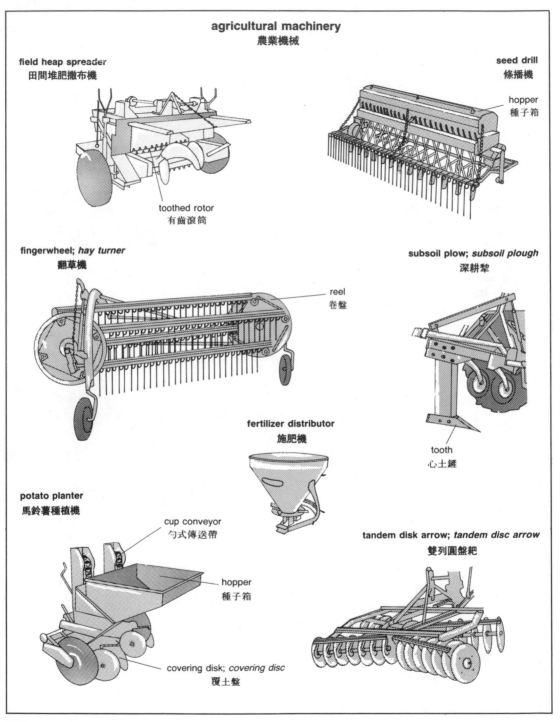

field heap spreader
田間堆肥撒布機

toothed rotor
有齒滾筒

seed drill
條播機

hopper
種子箱

fingerwheel; *hay turner*
翻草機

reel
卷盤

subsoil plow; *subsoil plough*
深耕犁

tooth
心土鏟

fertilizer distributor
施肥機

potato planter
馬鈴薯種植機

cup conveyor
勺式傳送帶

hopper
種子箱

covering disk; *covering disc*
覆土盤

tandem disk arrow; *tandem disc arrow*
雙列圓盤耙

machinery
機械構造

combine harvester
聯合收割機

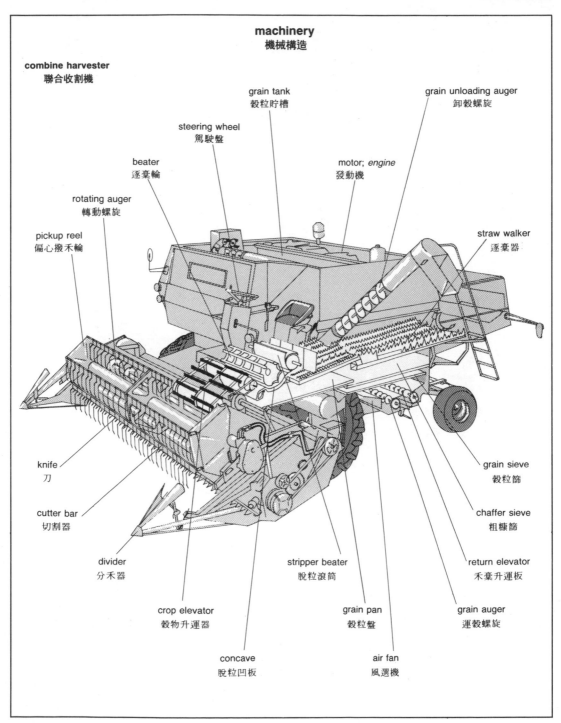

grain tank
穀粒貯槽

grain unloading auger
卸穀螺旋

steering wheel
駕駛盤

motor; *engine*
發動機

beater
逐藁輪

rotating auger
轉動螺旋

straw walker
逐藁器

pickup reel
偏心撥禾輪

knife
刀

cutter bar
切割器

divider
分禾器

stripper beater
脫粒滾筒

return elevator
禾藁升運板

crop elevator
穀物升運器

grain pan
穀粒盤

grain auger
運穀螺旋

concave
脫粒凹板

air fan
風選機

grain sieve
穀粒篩

chaffer sieve
粗糠篩

ARCHITECTURE
建築

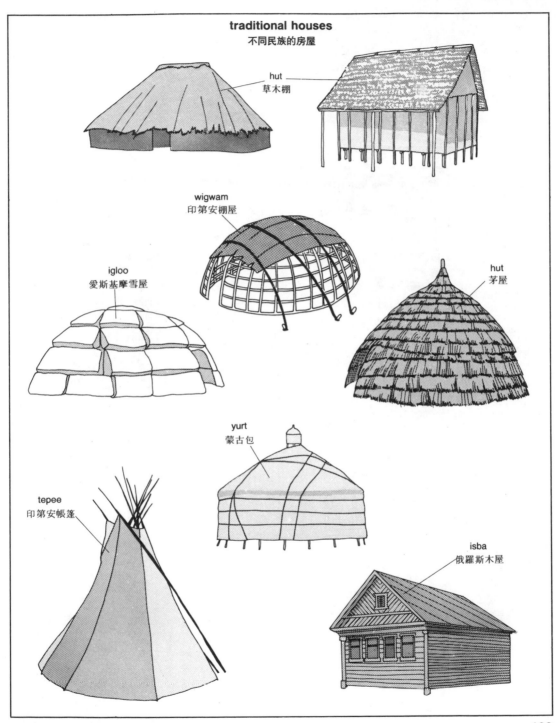

traditional houses
不同民族的房屋

hut
草木棚

wigwam
印第安棚屋

igloo
愛斯基摩雪屋

hut
茅屋

yurt
蒙古包

tepee
印第安帳篷

isba
俄羅斯木屋

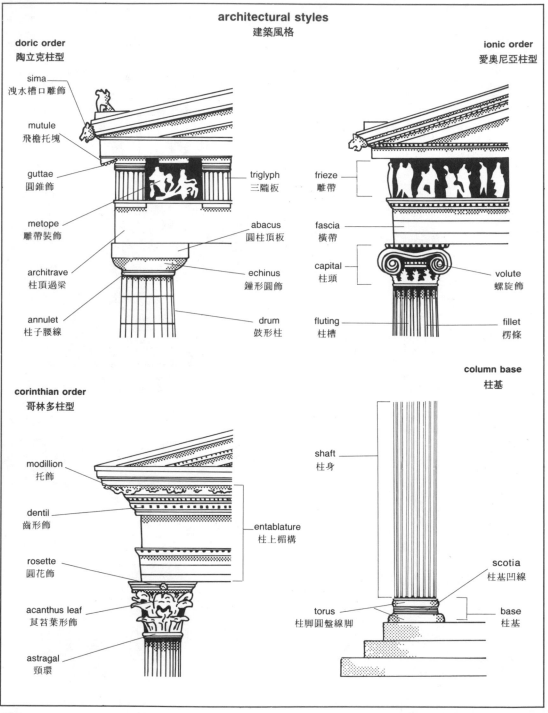

architectural styles
建築風格

doric order
陶立克柱型

sima
洩水槽口雕飾

mutule
飛檐托塊

guttae
圓錐飾

metope
雕帶裝飾

architrave
柱頂過梁

annulet
柱子腰線

triglyph
三隴板

abacus
圓柱頂板

echinus
鐘形圓飾

drum
鼓形柱

ionic order
愛奧尼亞柱型

frieze
雕帶

fascia
橫帶

capital
柱頭

fluting
柱槽

volute
螺旋飾

fillet
楞條

corinthian order
哥林多柱型

modillion
托飾

dentil
齒形飾

rosette
圓花飾

acanthus leaf
莨苔葉形飾

astragal
頸環

entablature
柱上楣構

column base
柱基

shaft
柱身

scotia
柱基凹線

torus
柱脚圓盤線脚

base
柱基

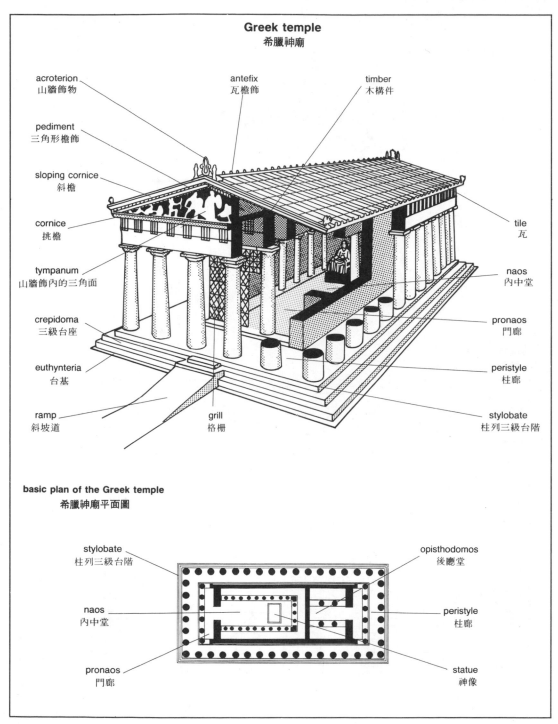

Greek temple
希臘神廟

acroterion
山牆飾物

antefix
瓦檐飾

timber
木構件

pediment
三角形檐飾

sloping cornice
斜檐

cornice
挑檐

tympanum
山牆飾內的三角面

crepidoma
三級台座

euthynteria
台基

ramp
斜坡道

grill
格柵

tile
瓦

naos
內中堂

pronaos
門廊

peristyle
柱廊

stylobate
柱列三級台階

basic plan of the Greek temple
希臘神廟平面圖

stylobate
柱列三級台階

opisthodomos
後廳堂

naos
內中堂

peristyle
柱廊

pronaos
門廊

statue
神像

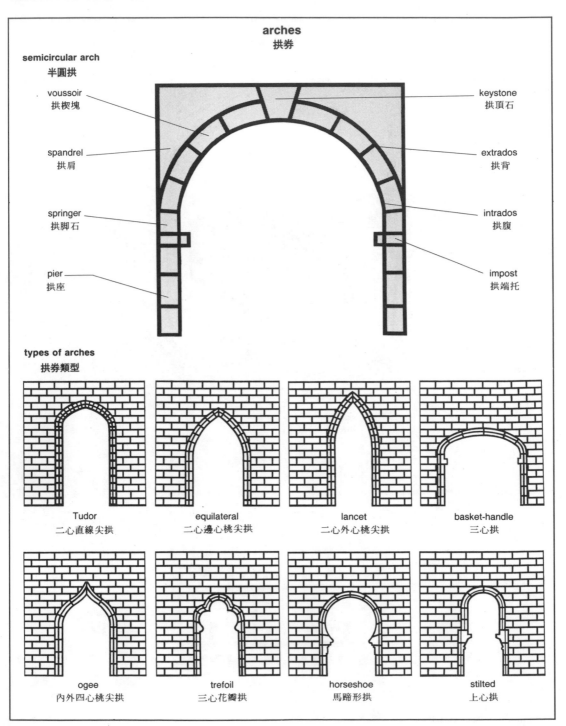

arches
拱券

semicircular arch
半圓拱

voussoir
拱楔塊

keystone
拱頂石

spandrel
拱肩

extrados
拱背

springer
拱脚石

intrados
拱腹

pier
拱座

impost
拱端托

types of arches
拱券類型

Tudor
二心直線尖拱

equilateral
二心邊心桃尖拱

lancet
二心外心桃尖拱

basket-handle
三心拱

ogee
內外四心桃尖拱

trefoil
三心花瓣拱

horseshoe
馬蹄形拱

stilted
上心拱

Roman house
羅馬房屋

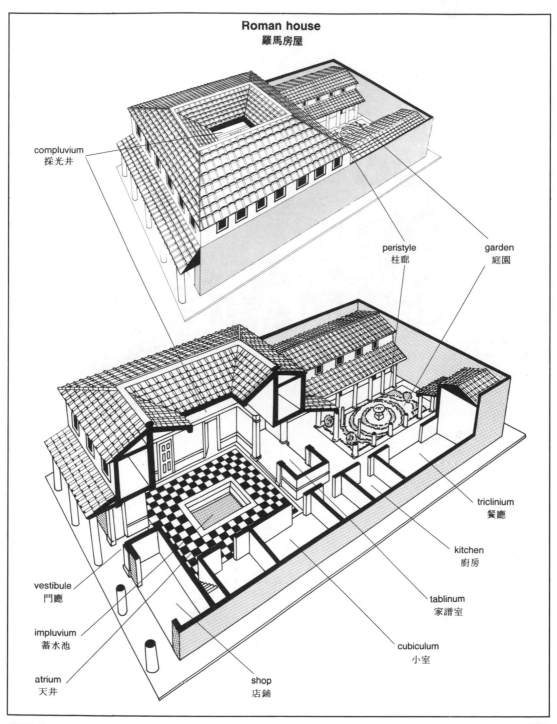

compluvium
採光井

peristyle
柱廊

garden
庭園

triclinium
餐廳

kitchen
廚房

vestibule
門廳

tablinum
家譜室

impluvium
蓄水池

cubiculum
小室

atrium
天井

shop
店鋪

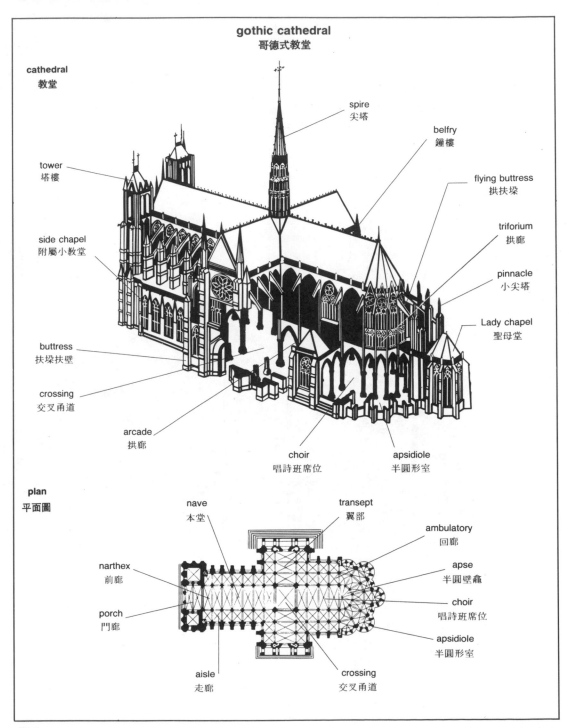

gothic cathedral
哥德式教堂

cathedral
教堂

spire
尖塔

belfry
鐘樓

tower
塔樓

flying buttress
拱扶垜

side chapel
附屬小教堂

triforium
拱廊

pinnacle
小尖塔

Lady chapel
聖母堂

buttress
扶垜扶壁

crossing
交叉甬道

arcade
拱廊

choir
唱詩班席位

apsidiole
半圓形室

plan
平面圖

nave
本堂

transept
翼部

ambulatory
回廊

narthex
前廊

apse
半圓壁龕

choir
唱詩班席位

porch
門廊

apsidiole
半圓形室

aisle
走廊

crossing
交叉甬道

gothic cathedral
哥德式教堂

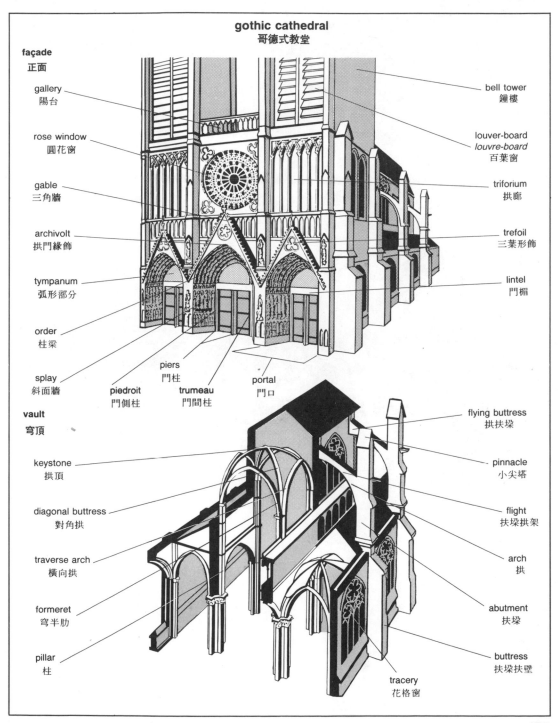

façade
正面

gallery
陽台

rose window
圓花窗

gable
三角牆

archivolt
拱門緣飾

tympanum
弧形部分

order
柱梁

splay
斜面牆

piedroit
門側柱

piers
門柱

trumeau
門間柱

portal
門口

bell tower
鐘樓

louver-board
louvre-board
百葉窗

triforium
拱廊

trefoil
三葉形飾

lintel
門楣

vault
穹頂

keystone
拱頂

diagonal buttress
對角拱

traverse arch
橫向拱

formeret
穹半肋

pillar
柱

tracery
花格窗

flying buttress
拱扶垛

pinnacle
小尖塔

flight
扶垛拱架

arch
拱

abutment
扶垛

buttress
扶垛扶壁

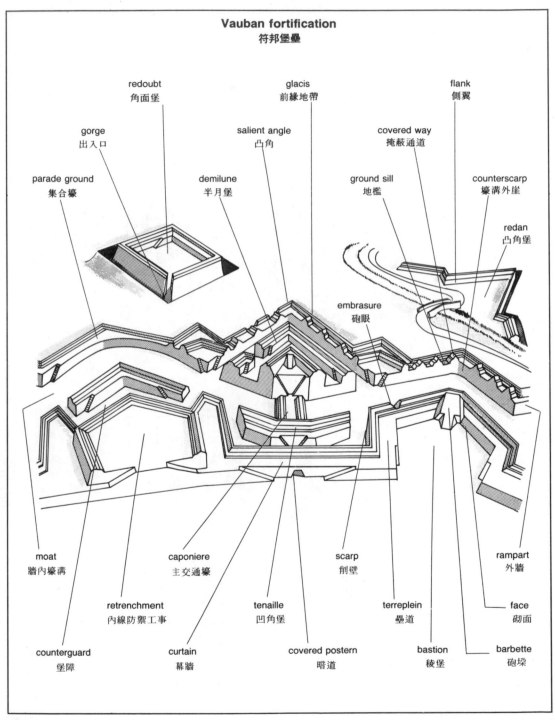

Vauban fortification
符邦堡壘

redoubt
角面堡

glacis
前緣地帶

flank
側翼

gorge
出入口

salient angle
凸角

covered way
掩蔽通道

parade ground
集合壕

demilune
半月堡

ground sill
地檻

counterscarp
壕溝外崖

redan
凸角堡

embrasure
砲眼

moat
牆內壕溝

caponiere
主交通壕

scarp
削壁

rampart
外牆

retrenchment
內線防禦工事

tenaille
凹角堡

terreplein
壘道

face
砲面

counterguard
堡障

curtain
幕牆

covered postern
暗道

bastion
稜堡

barbette
砲垛

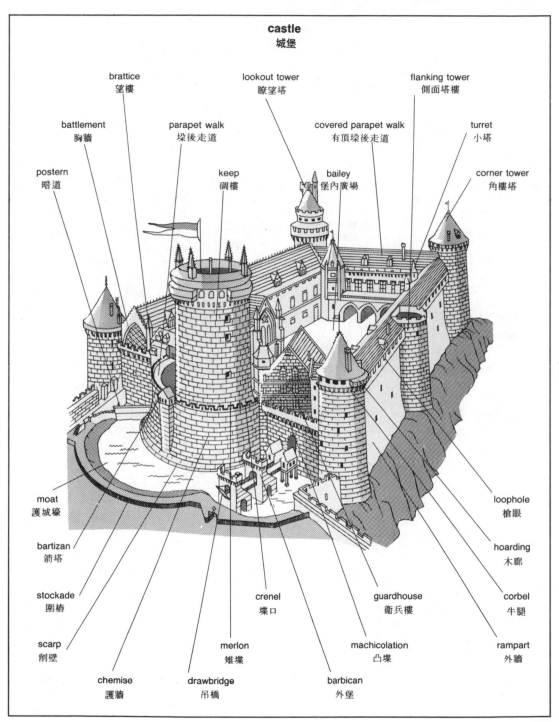

castle
城堡

brattice
望樓

lookout tower
瞭望塔

flanking tower
側面塔樓

battlement
胸牆

parapet walk
垛後走道

covered parapet walk
有頂垛後走道

turret
小塔

postern
暗道

keep
碉樓

bailey
堡內廣場

corner tower
角樓塔

moat
護城壕

loophole
槍眼

bartizan
箭塔

hoarding
木廊

stockade
圍樁

crenel
垛口

guardhouse
衛兵樓

corbel
牛腿

scarp
削壁

merlon
雉堞

machicolation
凸垛

rampart
外牆

chemise
護牆

drawbridge
吊橋

barbican
外堡

downtown
商業區

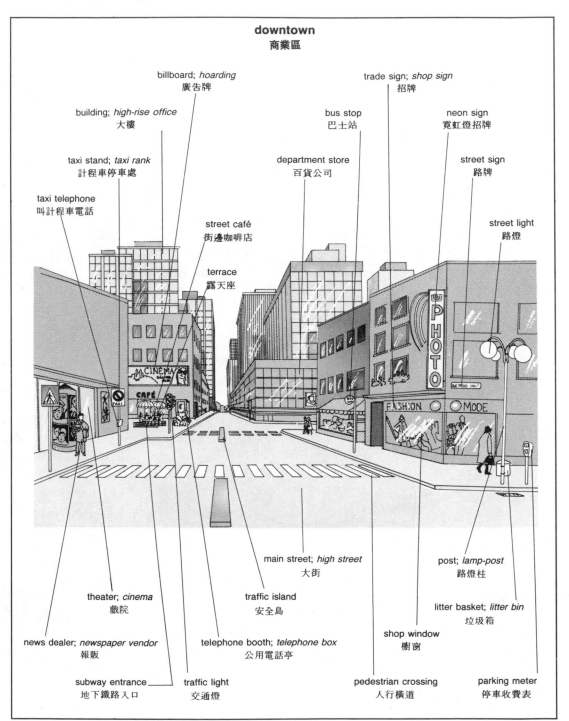

billboard; *hoarding*
廣告牌

trade sign; *shop sign*
招牌

building; *high-rise office*
大樓

bus stop
巴士站

neon sign
霓虹燈招牌

taxi stand; *taxi rank*
計程車停車處

department store
百貨公司

street sign
路牌

taxi telephone
叫計程車電話

street café
街邊咖啡店

street light
路燈

terrace
露天座

main street; *high street*
大街

post; *lamp-post*
路燈柱

theater; *cinema*
戲院

traffic island
安全島

litter basket; *litter bin*
垃圾箱

news dealer; *newspaper vendor*
報販

telephone booth; *telephone box*
公用電話亭

shop window
櫥窗

subway entrance
地下鐵路入口

traffic light
交通燈

pedestrian crossing
人行橫道

parking meter
停車收費表

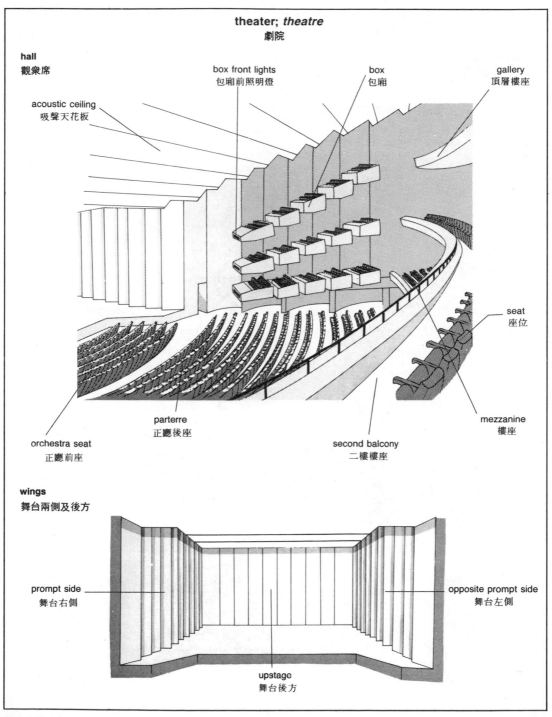

theater; *theatre*
劇院

hall
觀眾席

box front lights
包廂前照明燈

box
包廂

gallery
頂層樓座

acoustic ceiling
吸聲天花板

seat
座位

mezzanine
樓座

orchestra seat
正廳前座

parterre
正廳後座

second balcony
二樓樓座

wings
舞台兩側及後方

prompt side
舞台右側

opposite prompt side
舞台左側

upstage
舞台後方

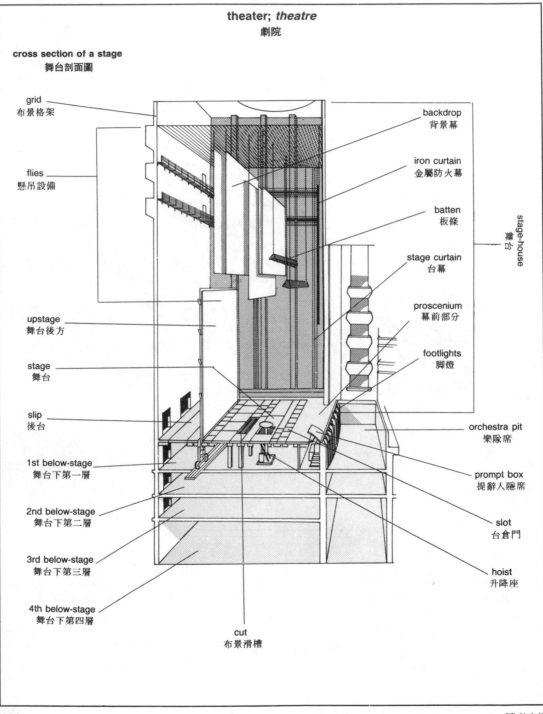

theater; _theatre_
劇院

cross section of a stage
舞台剖面圖

grid
布景格架

flies
懸吊設備

upstage
舞台後方

stage
舞台

slip
後台

1st below-stage
舞台下第一層

2nd below-stage
舞台下第二層

3rd below-stage
舞台下第三層

4th below-stage
舞台下第四層

cut
布景滑槽

backdrop
背景幕

iron curtain
金屬防火幕

batten
板條

stage curtain
台幕

proscenium
幕前部分

footlights
脚燈

stage-house
舞台

orchestra pit
樂隊席

prompt box
提辭人隱席

slot
台倉門

hoist
升降座

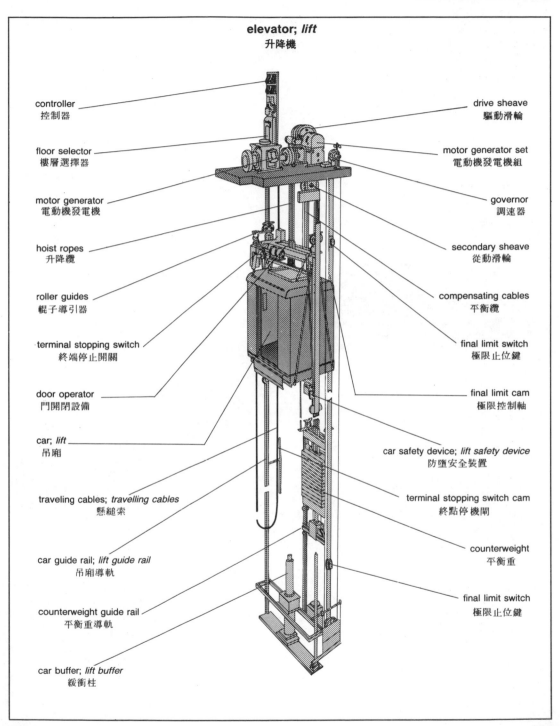

elevator; *lift*
升降機

controller
控制器

floor selector
樓層選擇器

motor generator
電動機發電機

hoist ropes
升降纜

roller guides
輥子導引器

terminal stopping switch
終端停止開關

door operator
門開閉設備

car; *lift*
吊廂

traveling cables; *travelling cables*
懸繩索

car guide rail; *lift guide rail*
吊廂導軌

counterweight guide rail
平衡重導軌

car buffer; *lift buffer*
緩衝柱

drive sheave
驅動滑輪

motor generator set
電動機發電機組

governor
調速器

secondary sheave
從動滑輪

compensating cables
平衡纜

final limit switch
極限止位鍵

final limit cam
極限控制軸

car safety device; *lift safety device*
防墮安全裝置

terminal stopping switch cam
終點停機閘

counterweight
平衡重

final limit switch
極限止位鍵

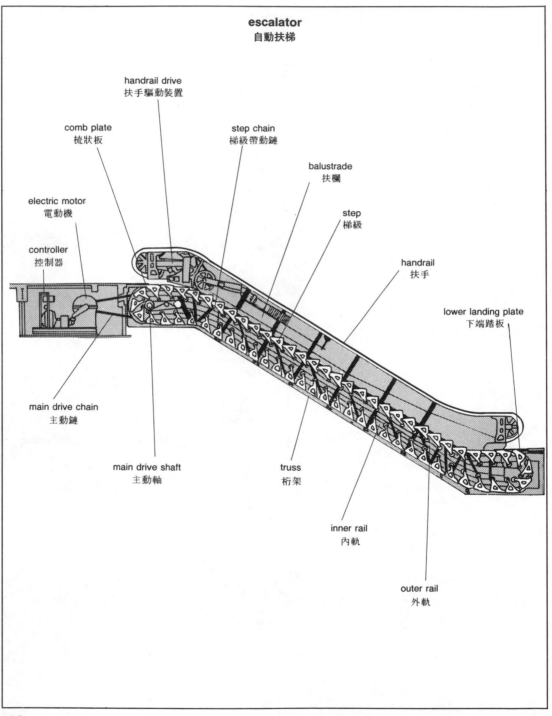

escalator
自動扶梯

handrail drive
扶手驅動裝置

comb plate
梳狀板

step chain
梯級帶動鏈

balustrade
扶欄

electric motor
電動機

step
梯級

controller
控制器

handrail
扶手

lower landing plate
下端踏板

main drive chain
主動鏈

main drive shaft
主動軸

truss
桁架

inner rail
內軌

outer rail
外軌

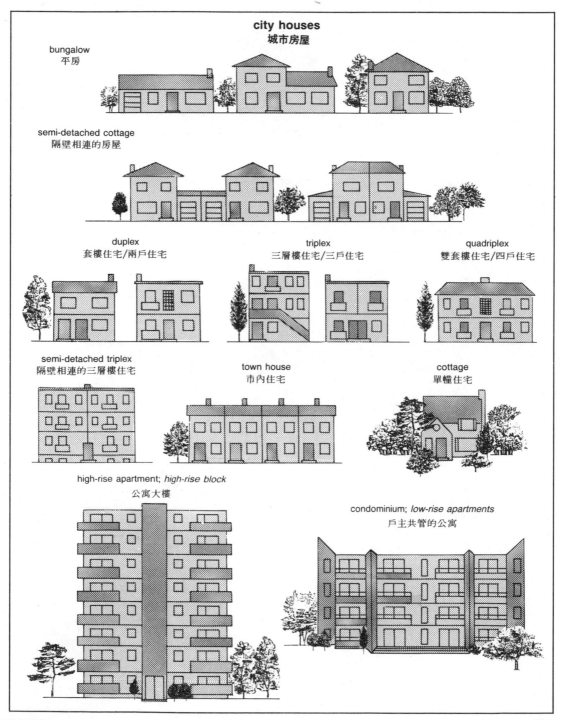

city houses
城市房屋

bungalow
平房

semi-detached cottage
隔壁相連的房屋

duplex
套樓住宅/兩戶住宅

triplex
三層樓住宅/三戶住宅

quadriplex
雙套樓住宅/四戶住宅

semi-detached triplex
隔壁相連的三層樓住宅

town house
市內住宅

cottage
單幢住宅

high-rise apartment; *high-rise block*
公寓大樓

condominium; *low-rise apartments*
戶主共管的公寓

HOUSE
房屋

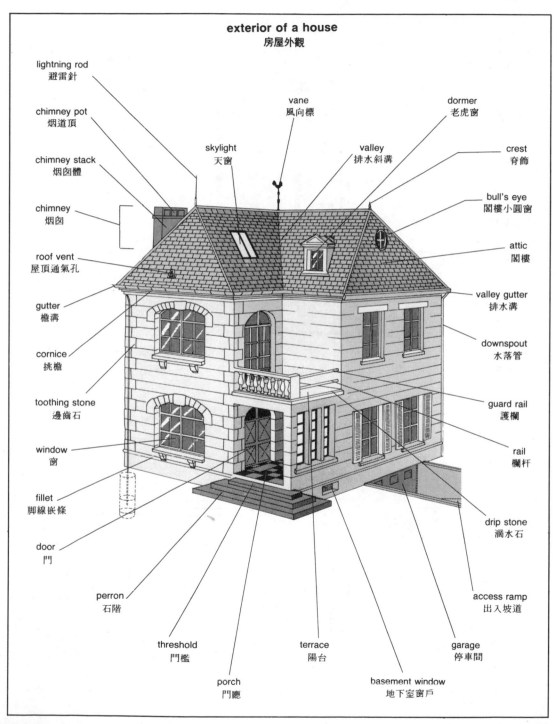

exterior of a house
房屋外觀

lightning rod
避雷針

chimney pot
烟道頂

chimney stack
烟囪體

chimney
烟囪

roof vent
屋頂通氣孔

gutter
檐溝

cornice
挑檐

toothing stone
邊齒石

window
窗

fillet
脚線嵌條

door
門

skylight
天窗

vane
風向標

valley
排水斜溝

dormer
老虎窗

crest
脊飾

bull's eye
閣樓小圓窗

attic
閣樓

valley gutter
排水溝

downspout
水落管

guard rail
護欄

rail
欄杆

drip stone
滴水石

access ramp
出入坡道

garage
停車間

basement window
地下室窗戶

terrace
陽台

porch
門廳

threshold
門檻

perron
石階

plan reading
平面圖

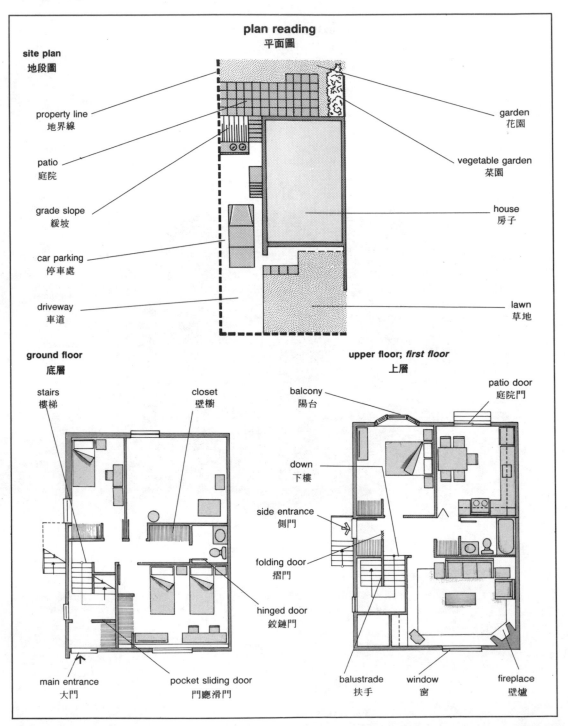

site plan
地段圖

property line
地界線

patio
庭院

grade slope
緩坡

car parking
停車處

driveway
車道

garden
花園

vegetable garden
菜園

house
房子

lawn
草地

ground floor
底層

stairs
樓梯

closet
壁櫥

main entrance
大門

pocket sliding door
門廳滑門

hinged door
鉸鏈門

upper floor; *first floor*
上層

balcony
陽台

patio door
庭院門

down
下樓

side entrance
側門

folding door
摺門

balustrade
扶手

window
窗

fireplace
壁爐

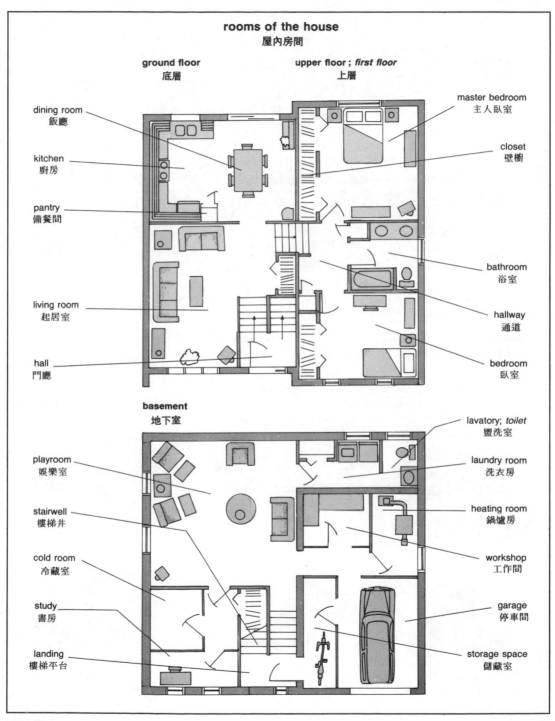

rooms of the house
屋內房間

ground floor
底層

upper floor ; *first floor*
上層

dining room
飯廳

master bedroom
主人臥室

kitchen
廚房

closet
壁櫥

pantry
備餐間

bathroom
浴室

living room
起居室

hallway
通道

hall
門廳

bedroom
臥室

basement
地下室

lavatory; *toilet*
盥洗室

playroom
娛樂室

laundry room
洗衣房

stairwell
樓梯井

heating room
鍋爐房

cold room
冷藏室

workshop
工作間

study
書房

garage
停車間

landing
樓梯平台

storage space
儲藏室

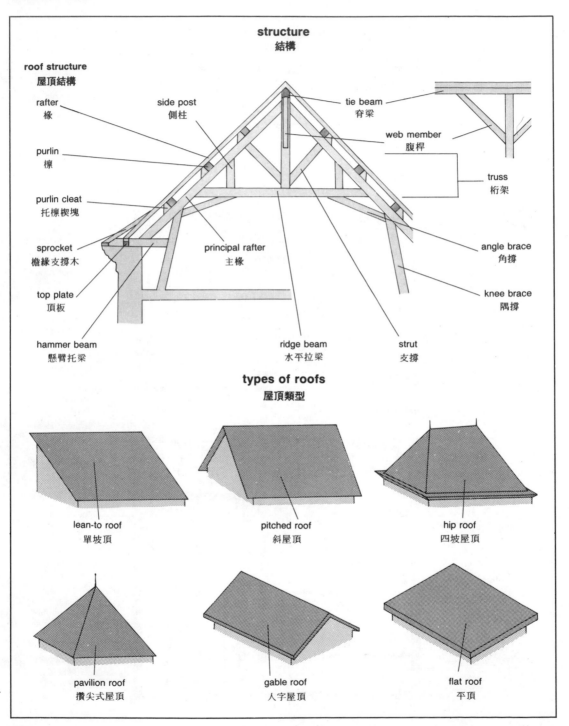

structure
結構

roof structure
屋頂結構

rafter
椽

side post
側柱

tie beam
脊梁

web member
腹桿

truss
桁架

purlin
檁

purlin cleat
托檁楔塊

sprocket
檐緣支撐木

principal rafter
主椽

angle brace
角撐

top plate
頂板

knee brace
隅撐

hammer beam
懸臂托梁

ridge beam
水平拉梁

strut
支撐

types of roofs
屋頂類型

lean-to roof
單坡頂

pitched roof
斜屋頂

hip roof
四坡屋頂

pavilion roof
攢尖式屋頂

gable roof
人字屋頂

flat roof
平頂

types of roofs
屋頂類型

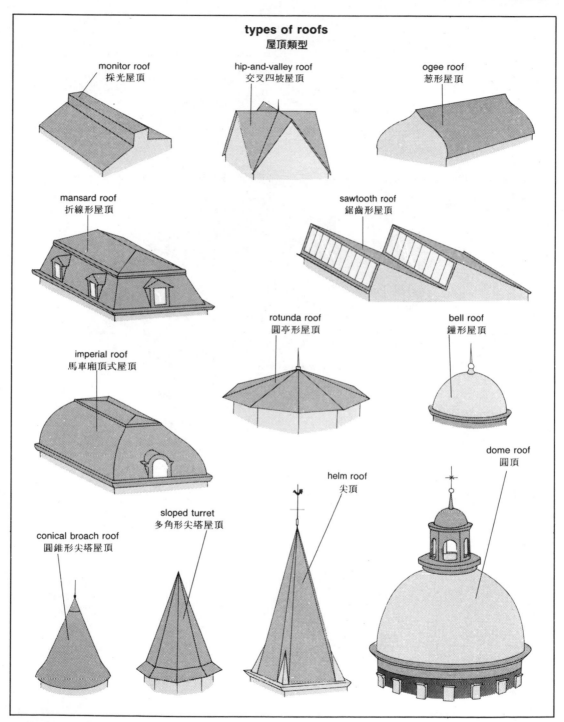

monitor roof
採光屋頂

hip-and-valley roof
交叉四坡屋頂

ogee roof
葱形屋頂

mansard roof
折線形屋頂

sawtooth roof
鋸齒形屋頂

imperial roof
馬車廂頂式屋頂

rotunda roof
圓亭形屋頂

bell roof
鐘形屋頂

dome roof
圓頂

helm roof
尖頂

sloped turret
多角形尖塔屋頂

conical broach roof
圓錐形尖塔屋頂

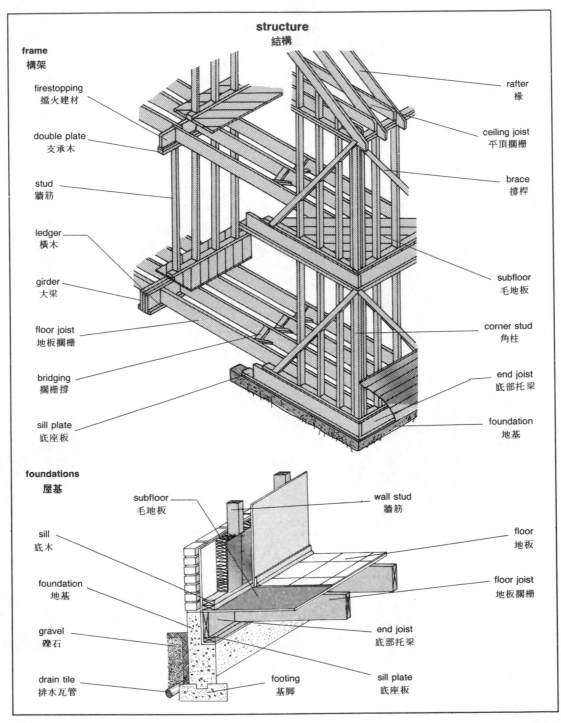

structure
結構

frame
構架

firestopping
擋火建材

double plate
支承木

stud
牆筋

ledger
橫木

girder
大梁

floor joist
地板擱柵

bridging
擱柵撐

sill plate
底座板

rafter
椽

ceiling joist
平頂擱柵

brace
撐桿

subfloor
毛地板

corner stud
角柱

end joist
底部托梁

foundation
地基

foundations
屋基

subfloor
毛地板

wall stud
牆筋

sill
底木

floor
地板

foundation
地基

floor joist
地板擱柵

gravel
礫石

drain tile
排水瓦管

footing
基腳

end joist
底部托梁

sill plate
底座板

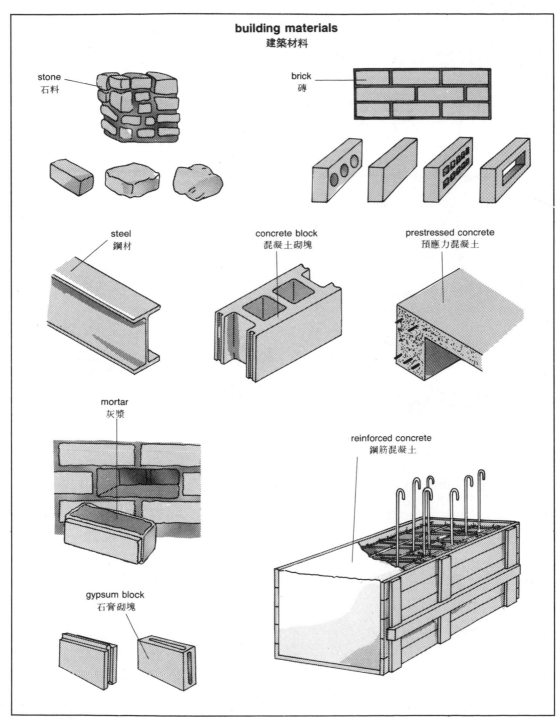

building materials
建築材料

stone
石料

brick
磚

steel
鋼材

concrete block
混凝土砌塊

prestressed concrete
預應力混凝土

mortar
灰漿

reinforced concrete
鋼筋混凝土

gypsum block
石膏砌塊

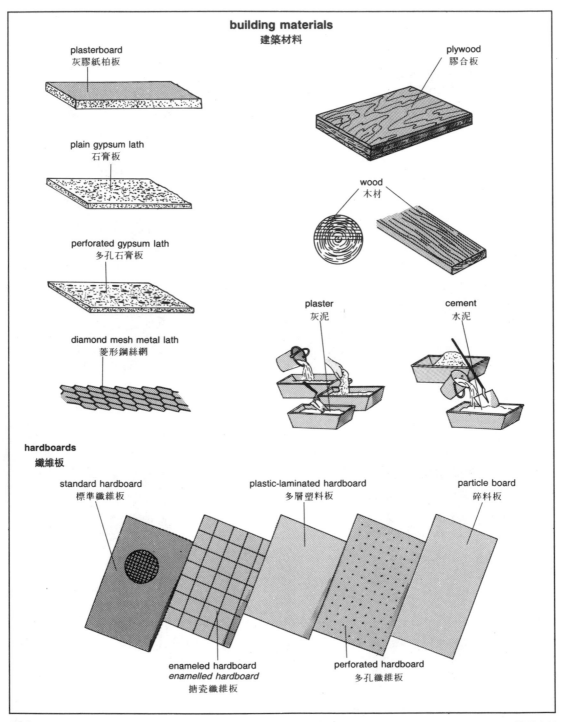

building materials
建築材料

plasterboard
灰膠紙柏板

plywood
膠合板

plain gypsum lath
石膏板

wood
木材

perforated gypsum lath
多孔石膏板

plaster
灰泥

cement
水泥

diamond mesh metal lath
菱形鋼絲網

hardboards
纖維板

standard hardboard
標準纖維板

plastic-laminated hardboard
多層塑料板

particle board
碎料板

enameled hardboard
enamelled hardboard
搪瓷纖維板

perforated hardboard
多孔纖維板

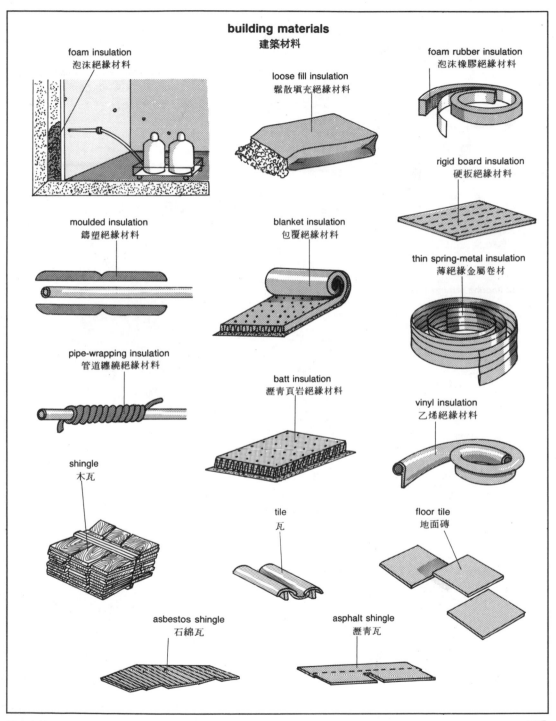

building materials
建築材料

foam insulation
泡沫絕緣材料

loose fill insulation
鬆散填充絕緣材料

foam rubber insulation
泡沫橡膠絕緣材料

rigid board insulation
硬板絕緣材料

moulded insulation
鑄塑絕緣材料

blanket insulation
包覆絕緣材料

thin spring-metal insulation
薄絕緣金屬卷材

pipe-wrapping insulation
管道纏繞絕緣材料

batt insulation
瀝青頁岩絕緣材料

vinyl insulation
乙烯絕緣材料

shingle
木瓦

tile
瓦

floor tile
地面磚

asbestos shingle
石綿瓦

asphalt shingle
瀝青瓦

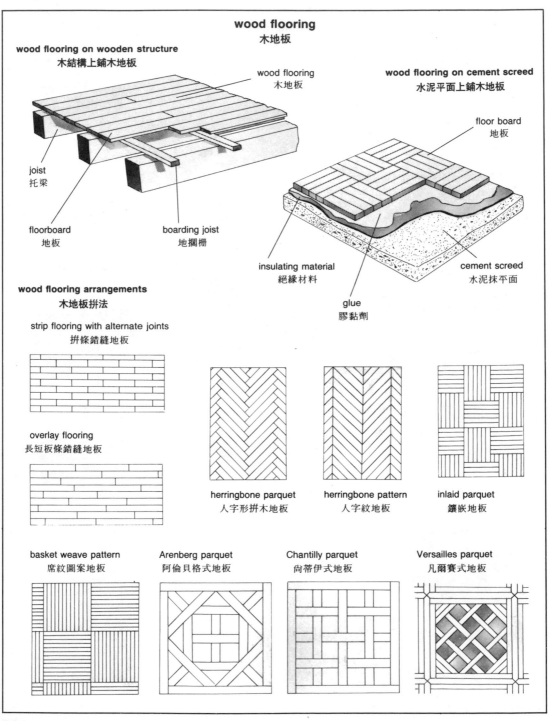

wood flooring
木地板

wood flooring on wooden structure
木結構上鋪木地板

wood flooring
木地板

wood flooring on cement screed
水泥平面上鋪木地板

floor board
地板

joist
托梁

floorboard
地板

boarding joist
地擱柵

insulating material
絕緣材料

cement screed
水泥抹平面

glue
膠黏劑

wood flooring arrangements
木地板拼法

strip flooring with alternate joints
拼條錯縫地板

overlay flooring
長短板條錯縫地板

herringbone parquet
人字形拼木地板

herringbone pattern
人字紋地板

inlaid parquet
鑲嵌地板

basket weave pattern
席紋圖案地板

Arenberg parquet
阿倫貝格式地板

Chantilly parquet
尚蒂伊式地板

Versailles parquet
凡爾賽式地板

stairs
樓梯

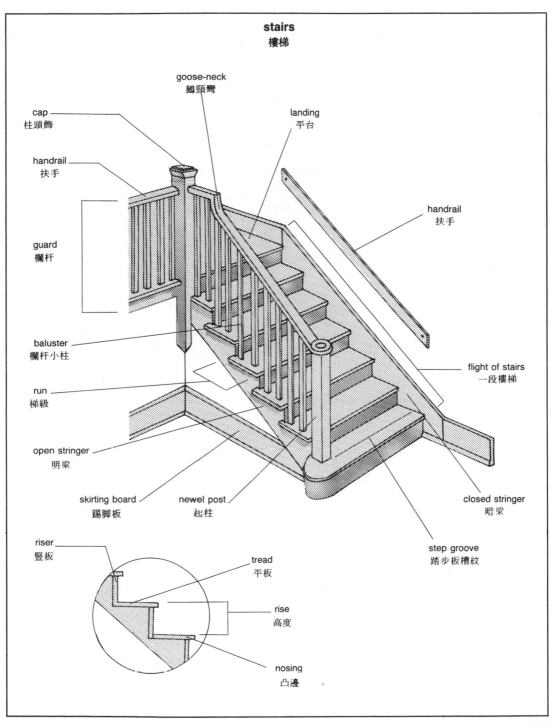

goose-neck
鵝頸彎

cap
柱頭飾

landing
平台

handrail
扶手

handrail
扶手

guard
欄杆

baluster
欄杆小柱

run
梯級

flight of stairs
一段樓梯

open stringer
明梁

skirting board
踢腳板

newel post
起柱

closed stringer
暗梁

step groove
踏步板槽紋

riser
豎板

tread
平板

rise
高度

nosing
凸邊

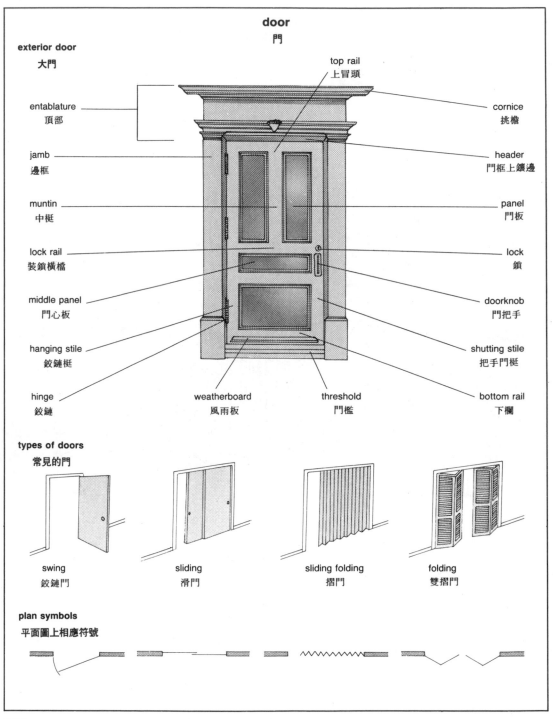

door
門

exterior door
大門

top rail
上冒頭

entablature
頂部

cornice
挑檐

jamb
邊框

header
門框上鑲邊

muntin
中梃

panel
門板

lock rail
裝鎖橫檔

lock
鎖

middle panel
門心板

doorknob
門把手

hanging stile
鉸鏈梃

shutting stile
把手門梃

hinge
鉸鏈

weatherboard
風雨板

threshold
門檻

bottom rail
下欄

types of doors
常見的門

swing
鉸鏈門

sliding
滑門

sliding folding
摺門

folding
雙摺門

plan symbols
平面圖上相應符號

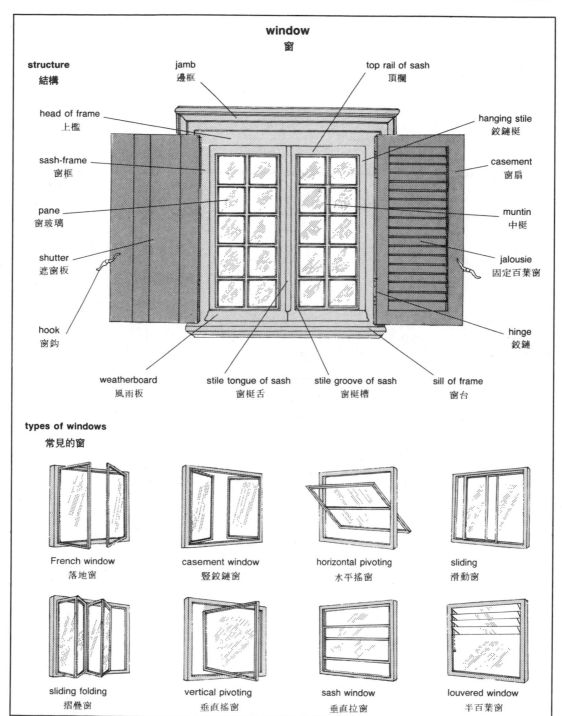

window
窗

structure
結構

jamb
邊框

top rail of sash
頂欄

head of frame
上檻

hanging stile
鉸鏈梃

sash-frame
窗框

casement
窗扇

pane
窗玻璃

muntin
中梃

shutter
遮窗板

jalousie
固定百葉窗

hook
窗鉤

hinge
鉸鏈

weatherboard
風雨板

stile tongue of sash
窗梃舌

stile groove of sash
窗梃槽

sill of frame
窗台

types of windows
常見的窗

French window
落地窗

casement window
豎鉸鏈窗

horizontal pivoting
水平搖窗

sliding
滑動窗

sliding folding
摺疊窗

vertical pivoting
垂直搖窗

sash window
垂直拉窗

louvered window
半百葉窗

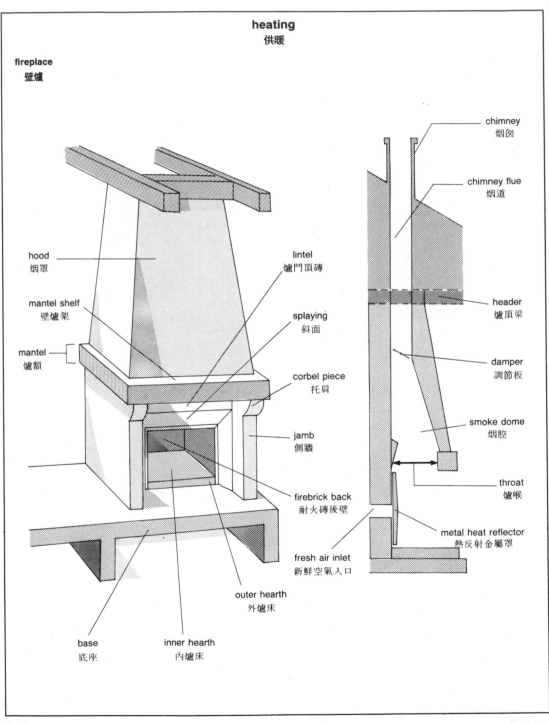

heating
供暖

fireplace
壁爐

hood
烟罩

mantel shelf
壁爐架

mantel
爐額

lintel
爐門頂磚

splaying
斜面

corbel piece
托肩

jamb
側牆

firebrick back
耐火磚後壁

fresh air inlet
新鮮空氣入口

outer hearth
外爐床

base
底座

inner hearth
內爐床

chimney
烟囪

chimney flue
烟道

header
爐頂梁

damper
調節板

smoke dome
烟腔

throat
爐喉

metal heat reflector
熱反射金屬罩

heating
供暖

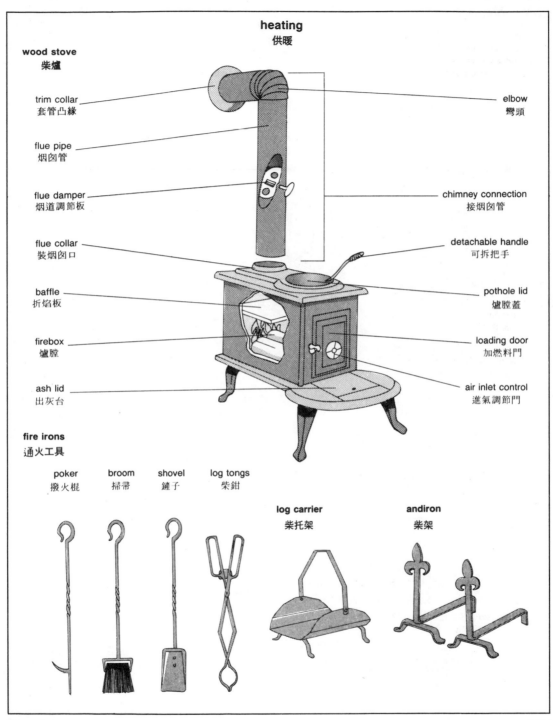

wood stove
柴爐

trim collar
套管凸緣

flue pipe
烟囱管

flue damper
烟道調節板

flue collar
裝烟囱口

baffle
折焰板

firebox
爐膛

ash lid
出灰台

elbow
彎頭

chimney connection
接烟囱管

detachable handle
可拆把手

pothole lid
爐膛蓋

loading door
加燃料門

air inlet control
進氣調節門

fire irons
通火工具

poker
撥火棍

broom
掃帚

shovel
鏟子

log tongs
柴鉗

log carrier
柴托架

andiron
柴架

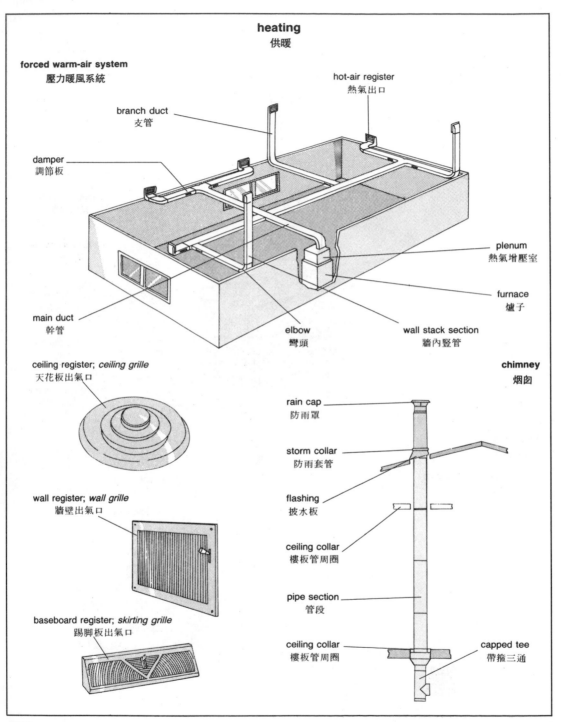

heating
供暖

forced warm-air system
壓力暖風系統

hot-air register
熱氣出口

branch duct
支管

damper
調節板

plenum
熱氣增壓室

furnace
爐子

main duct
幹管

elbow
彎頭

wall stack section
牆內豎管

ceiling register; *ceiling grille*
天花板出氣口

chimney
烟囱

rain cap
防雨罩

storm collar
防雨套管

flashing
披水板

ceiling collar
樓板管周圈

pipe section
管段

ceiling collar
樓板管周圈

capped tee
帶擓三通

wall register; *wall grille*
牆壁出氣口

baseboard register; *skirting grille*
踢脚板出氣口

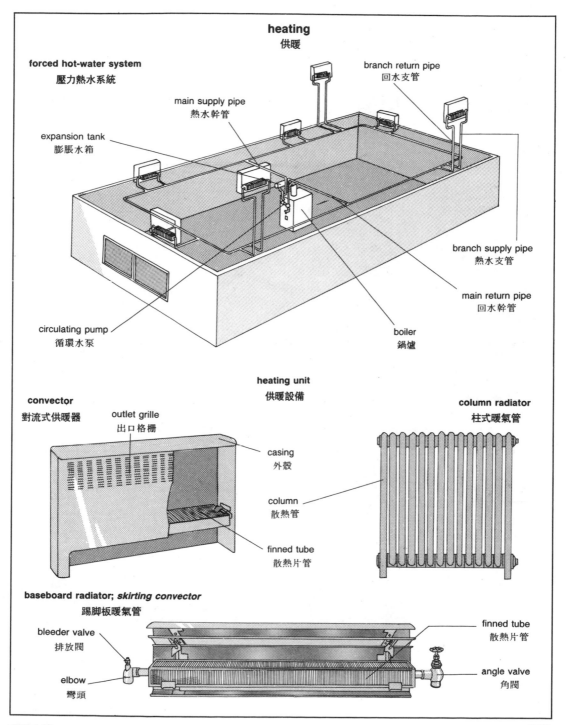

heating
供暖

forced hot-water system
壓力熱水系統

main supply pipe
熱水幹管

branch return pipe
回水支管

expansion tank
膨脹水箱

branch supply pipe
熱水支管

main return pipe
回水幹管

circulating pump
循環水泵

boiler
鍋爐

heating unit
供暖設備

convector
對流式供暖器

outlet grille
出口格柵

casing
外殼

column
散熱管

finned tube
散熱片管

column radiator
柱式暖氣管

baseboard radiator; *skirting convector*
踢腳板暖氣管

bleeder valve
排放閥

finned tube
散熱片管

elbow
彎頭

angle valve
角閥

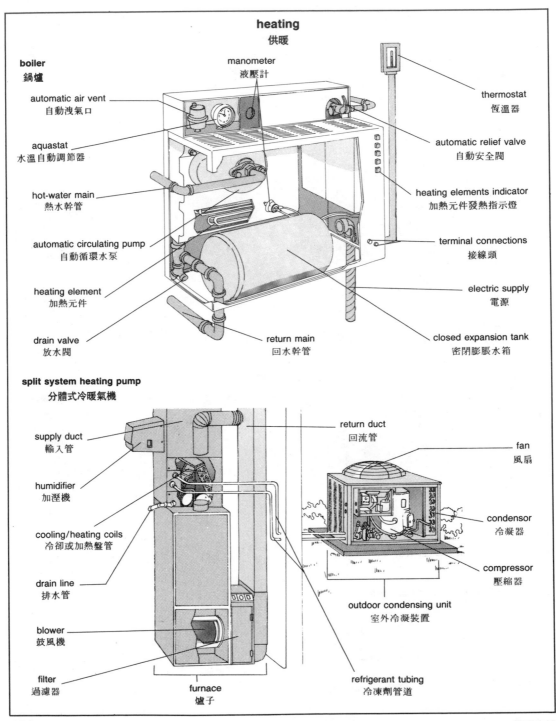

heating
供暖

boiler
鍋爐

manometer
液壓計

thermostat
恆溫器

automatic air vent
自動洩氣口

aquastat
水溫自動調節器

automatic relief valve
自動安全閥

hot-water main
熱水幹管

heating elements indicator
加熱元件發熱指示燈

automatic circulating pump
自動循環水泵

terminal connections
接線頭

heating element
加熱元件

electric supply
電源

drain valve
放水閥

return main
回水幹管

closed expansion tank
密閉膨脹水箱

split system heating pump
分體式冷暖氣機

return duct
回流管

supply duct
輸入管

fan
風扇

humidifier
加溼機

condensor
冷凝器

cooling/heating coils
冷卻或加熱盤管

compressor
壓縮器

drain line
排水管

outdoor condensing unit
室外冷凝裝置

blower
鼓風機

filter
過濾器

furnace
爐子

refrigerant tubing
冷凍劑管道

heating
供暖

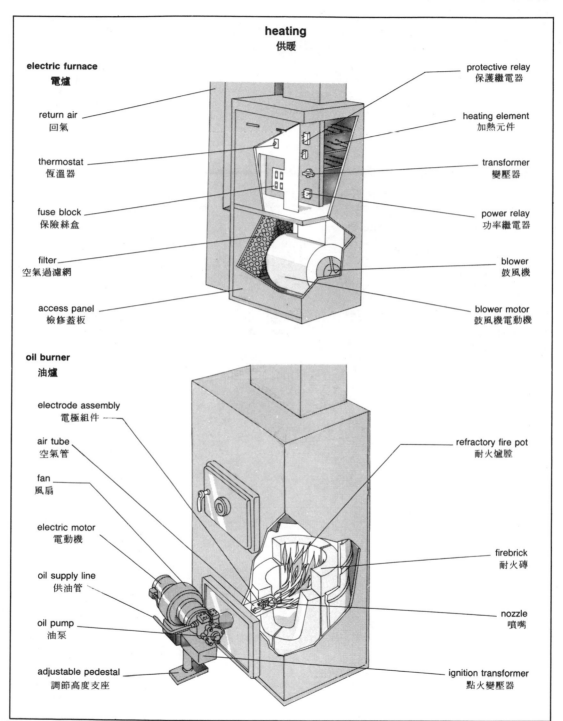

electric furnace
電爐

return air
回氣

thermostat
恆溫器

fuse block
保險絲盒

filter
空氣過濾網

access panel
檢修蓋板

protective relay
保護繼電器

heating element
加熱元件

transformer
變壓器

power relay
功率繼電器

blower
鼓風機

blower motor
鼓風機電動機

oil burner
油爐

electrode assembly
電極組件

air tube
空氣管

fan
風扇

electric motor
電動機

oil supply line
供油管

oil pump
油泵

adjustable pedestal
調節高度支座

refractory fire pot
耐火爐膛

firebrick
耐火磚

nozzle
噴嘴

ignition transformer
點火變壓器

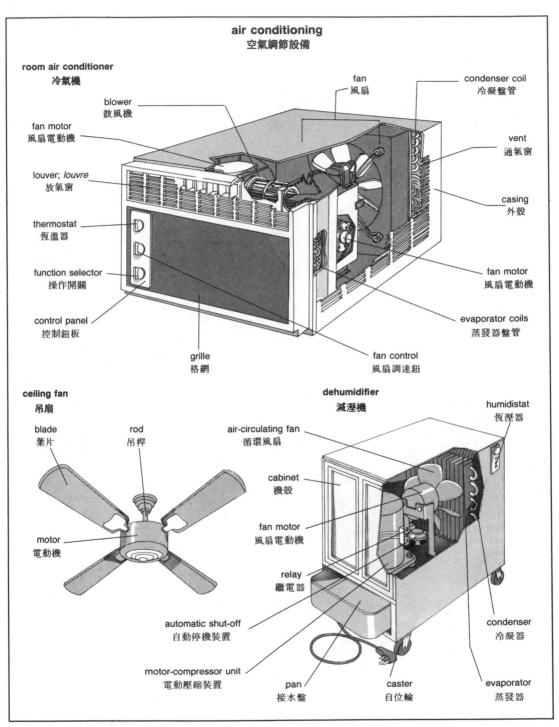

air conditioning
空氣調節設備

room air conditioner
冷氣機

fan
風扇

condenser coil
冷凝盤管

blower
鼓風機

fan motor
風扇電動機

vent
通氣窗

louver; *louvre*
放氣窗

casing
外殼

thermostat
恆溫器

function selector
操作開關

fan motor
風扇電動機

control panel
控制鈕板

evaporator coils
蒸發器盤管

grille
格網

fan control
風扇調速鈕

ceiling fan
吊扇

dehumidifier
減溼機

humidistat
恆溼器

blade
葉片

rod
吊桿

air-circulating fan
循環風扇

cabinet
機殼

fan motor
風扇電動機

motor
電動機

relay
繼電器

condenser
冷凝器

automatic shut-off
自動停機裝置

motor-compressor unit
電動壓縮裝置

pan
接水盤

caster
自位輪

evaporator
蒸發器

HOUSE FURNITURE

家具

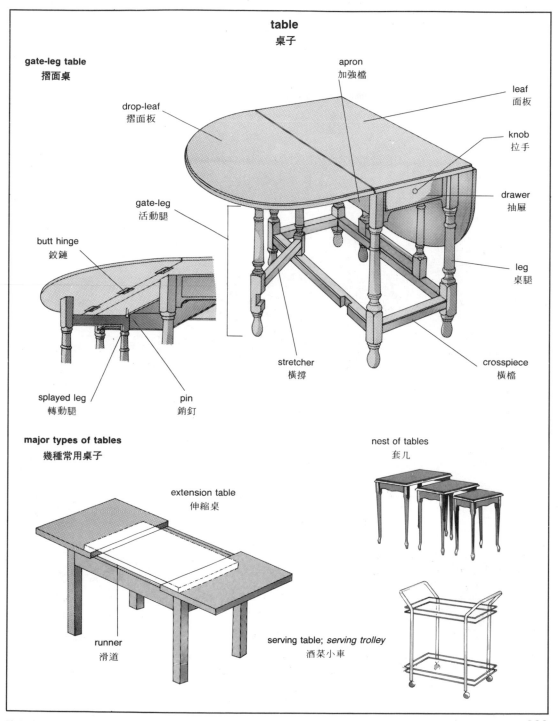

table
桌子

gate-leg table
摺面桌

apron
加強檔

leaf
面板

drop-leaf
摺面板

knob
拉手

drawer
抽屜

gate-leg
活動腿

butt hinge
鉸鏈

leg
桌腿

splayed leg
轉動腿

pin
銷釘

stretcher
橫撐

crosspiece
橫檔

major types of tables
幾種常用桌子

nest of tables
套几

extension table
伸縮桌

runner
滑道

serving table; *serving trolley*
酒菜小車

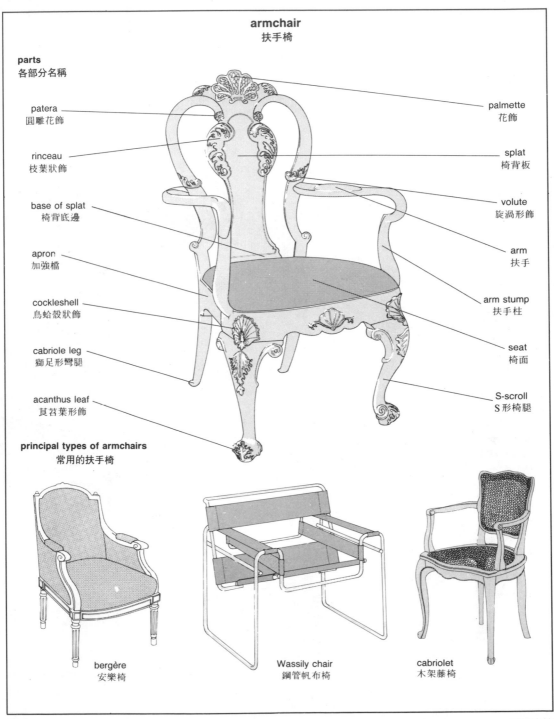

armchair
扶手椅

parts
各部分名稱

patera
圓雕花飾

rinceau
枝葉狀飾

base of splat
椅背底邊

apron
加強檔

cockleshell
鳥蛤殼狀飾

cabriole leg
獅足形彎腿

acanthus leaf
莨苕葉形飾

palmette
花飾

splat
椅背板

volute
旋渦形飾

arm
扶手

arm stump
扶手柱

seat
椅面

S-scroll
S 形椅腿

principal types of armchairs
常用的扶手椅

bergère
安樂椅

Wassily chair
鋼管帆布椅

cabriolet
木架藤椅

armchairs
扶手椅

principal types of armchairs
常用的扶手椅

récamier
法式躺椅

sofa
長沙發

love seat; *two-seater settee*
雙人沙發

director's chair
帆布摺椅

club chair
單人沙發

chesterfield
靠背連扶手長沙發

rocking chair
搖椅

méridienne
法式午睡沙發

seats
凳、椅

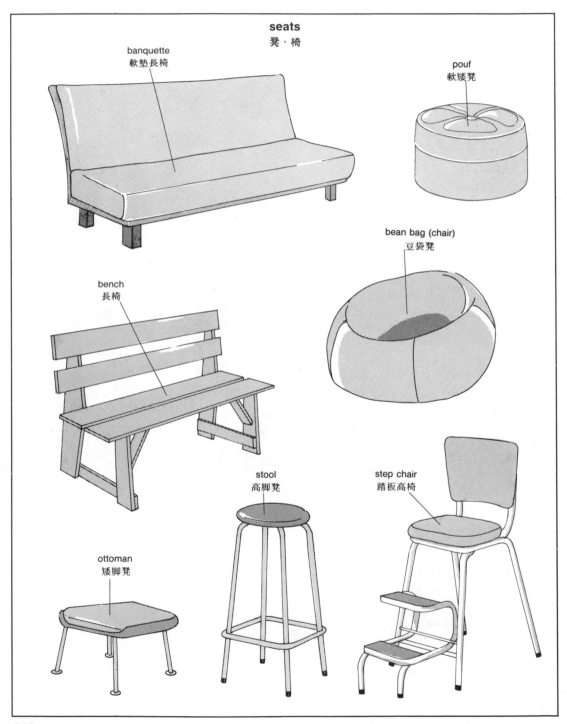

banquette
軟墊長椅

pouf
軟矮凳

bean bag (chair)
豆袋凳

bench
長椅

ottoman
矮腳凳

stool
高腳凳

step chair
踏板高椅

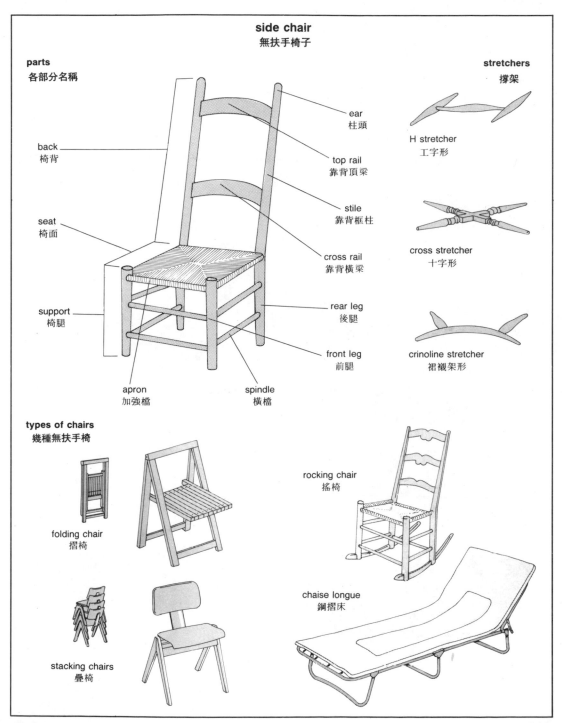

side chair
無扶手椅子

parts
各部分名稱

ear
柱頭

back
椅背

top rail
靠背頂梁

stile
靠背框柱

seat
椅面

cross rail
靠背橫梁

support
椅腿

rear leg
後腿

front leg
前腿

apron
加強檔

spindle
橫檔

stretchers
撐架

H stretcher
工字形

cross stretcher
十字形

crinoline stretcher
裙襯架形

types of chairs
幾種無扶手椅

folding chair
摺椅

stacking chairs
疊椅

rocking chair
搖椅

chaise longue
鋼摺床

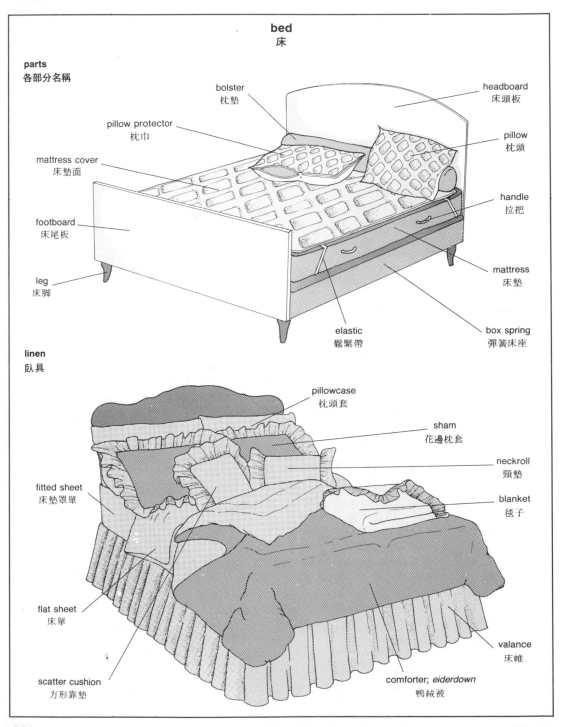

bed
床

parts
各部分名稱

bolster
枕墊

headboard
床頭板

pillow protector
枕巾

pillow
枕頭

mattress cover
床墊面

handle
拉把

footboard
床尾板

mattress
床墊

leg
床脚

elastic
鬆緊帶

box spring
彈簧床座

linen
臥具

pillowcase
枕頭套

sham
花邊枕套

neckroll
頸墊

fitted sheet
床墊罩單

blanket
毯子

flat sheet
床單

valance
床帷

scatter cushion
方形靠墊

comforter; *eiderdown*
鴨絨被

storage furniture
儲物家具

armoire
雕飾衣櫃

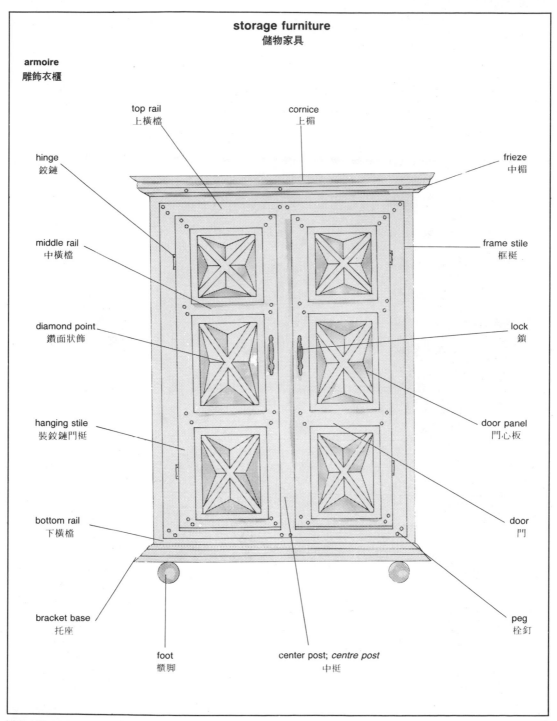

top rail
上橫檔

cornice
上楣

frieze
中楣

hinge
鉸鏈

middle rail
中橫檔

frame stile
框梃

diamond point
鑽面狀飾

lock
鎖

hanging stile
裝鉸鏈門梃

door panel
門心板

bottom rail
下橫檔

door
門

bracket base
托座

peg
栓釘

foot
櫃腳

center post; *centre post*
中梃

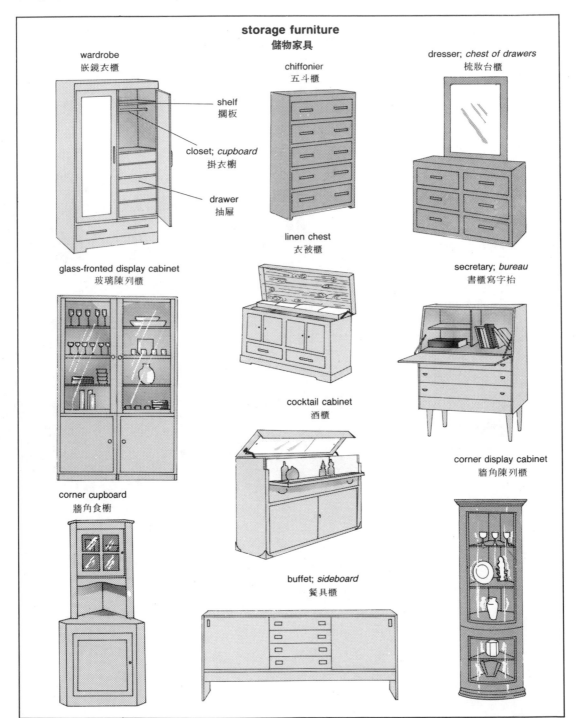

storage furniture
儲物家具

wardrobe
嵌鏡衣櫃

shelf
擱板

closet; *cupboard*
掛衣櫥

drawer
抽屜

chiffonier
五斗櫃

dresser; *chest of drawers*
梳妝台櫃

glass-fronted display cabinet
玻璃陳列櫃

linen chest
衣被櫃

secretary; *bureau*
書櫃寫字枱

cocktail cabinet
酒櫃

corner display cabinet
牆角陳列櫃

corner cupboard
牆角食櫥

buffet; *sideboard*
餐具櫃

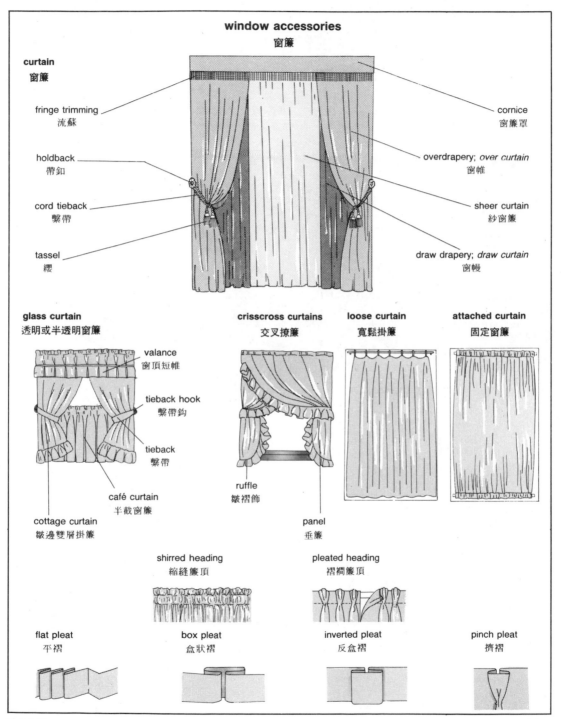

window accessories
窗簾

curtain
窗簾

fringe trimming
流蘇

cornice
窗簾罩

holdback
帶鈕

overdrapery; *over curtain*
窗帷

cord tieback
繫帶

sheer curtain
紗窗簾

tassel
纓

draw drapery; *draw curtain*
窗幔

glass curtain
透明或半透明窗簾

valance
窗頂短帷

tieback hook
繫帶鈎

tieback
繫帶

café curtain
半截窗簾

cottage curtain
皺邊雙層掛簾

crisscross curtains
交叉撩簾

ruffle
皺褶飾

panel
垂簾

loose curtain
寬鬆掛簾

attached curtain
固定窗簾

shirred heading
縮縫簾頂

pleated heading
褶襇簾頂

flat pleat
平褶

box pleat
盒狀褶

inverted pleat
反盒褶

pinch pleat
擠褶

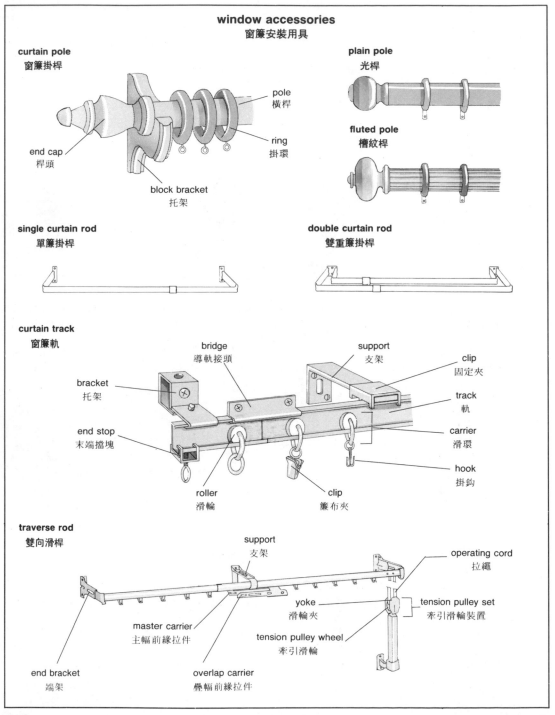

window accessories
窗簾安裝用具

curtain pole
窗簾掛桿

pole
橫桿

ring
掛環

end cap
桿頭

block bracket
托架

plain pole
光桿

fluted pole
槽紋桿

single curtain rod
單簾掛桿

double curtain rod
雙重簾掛桿

curtain track
窗簾軌

bridge
導軌接頭

support
支架

clip
固定夾

bracket
托架

track
軌

end stop
末端擋塊

carrier
滑環

hook
掛鈎

roller
滑輪

clip
簾布夾

traverse rod
雙向滑桿

support
支架

operating cord
拉繩

yoke
滑輪夾

tension pulley set
牽引滑輪裝置

master carrier
主幅前緣拉件

tension pulley wheel
牽引滑輪

end bracket
端架

overlap carrier
疊幅前緣拉件

window accessories
軟、硬窗簾

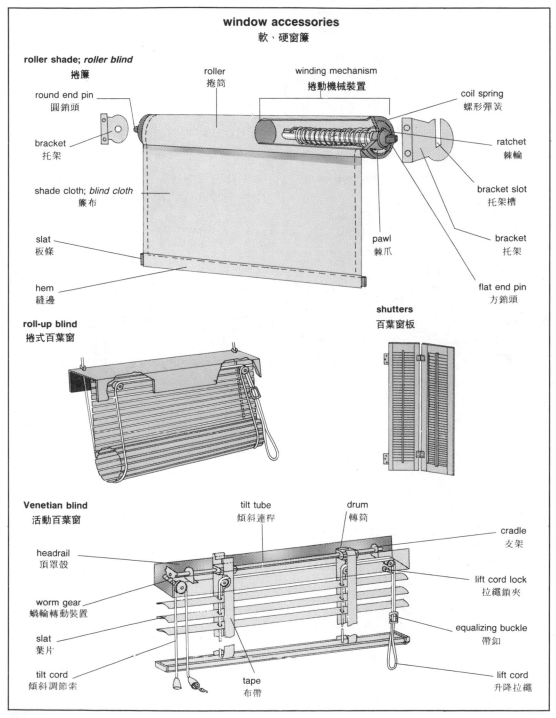

roller shade; *roller blind*
捲簾

round end pin
圓銷頭

bracket
托架

shade cloth; *blind cloth*
簾布

slat
板條

hem
縫邊

roller
捲筒

winding mechanism
捲動機械裝置

coil spring
螺形彈簧

ratchet
棘輪

bracket slot
托架槽

bracket
托架

pawl
棘爪

flat end pin
方銷頭

roll-up blind
捲式百葉窗

shutters
百葉窗板

Venetian blind
活動百葉窗

tilt tube
傾斜連桿

drum
轉筒

cradle
支架

headrail
頂罩殼

lift cord lock
拉繩鎖夾

worm gear
蝸輪轉動裝置

equalizing buckle
帶釦

slat
葉片

tilt cord
傾斜調節索

tape
布帶

lift cord
升降拉繩

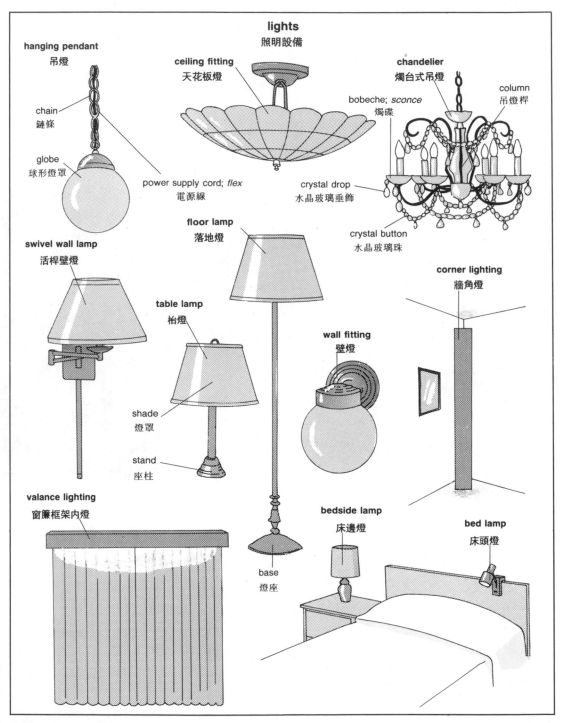

lights
照明設備

hanging pendant
吊燈

chain
鏈條

globe
球形燈罩

ceiling fitting
天花板燈

power supply cord; *flex*
電源線

chandelier
燭台式吊燈

bobeche; *sconce*
燭碟

column
吊燈桿

crystal drop
水晶玻璃垂飾

crystal button
水晶玻璃珠

swivel wall lamp
活桿壁燈

floor lamp
落地燈

table lamp
枱燈

wall fitting
壁燈

corner lighting
牆角燈

shade
燈罩

stand
座柱

valance lighting
窗簾框架內燈

base
燈座

bedside lamp
床邊燈

bed lamp
床頭燈

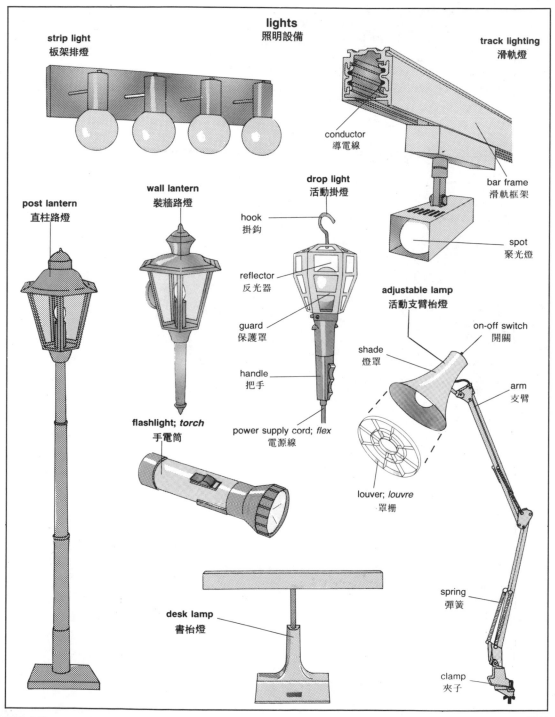

lights
照明設備

strip light
板架排燈

track lighting
滑軌燈

conductor
導電線

bar frame
滑軌框架

post lantern
直柱路燈

wall lantern
裝牆路燈

drop light
活動掛燈

hook
掛鉤

reflector
反光器

guard
保護罩

handle
把手

power supply cord; *flex*
電源線

spot
聚光燈

adjustable lamp
活動支臂枱燈

shade
燈罩

on-off switch
開關

arm
支臂

louver; *louvre*
罩柵

flashlight; *torch*
手電筒

desk lamp
書枱燈

spring
彈簧

clamp
夾子

glassware
玻璃器皿

champagne flute
鬱金香形香檳杯

champagne glass
香檳杯

bordeaux
波爾多酒杯

burgundy
勃艮第酒杯

white wine
白葡萄酒杯

Alsace glass
萊茵白酒杯

water goblet
高脚水杯

cocktail
雞尾酒杯

port
砵酒杯

brandy
白蘭地酒杯

liqueur
甜酒杯

old-fashioned; *tumbler*
攙酒矮杯

highball; *tall tumbler*
攙酒高杯

beer mug
啤酒杯

decanter
葡萄酒瓶

dinnerware
餐具

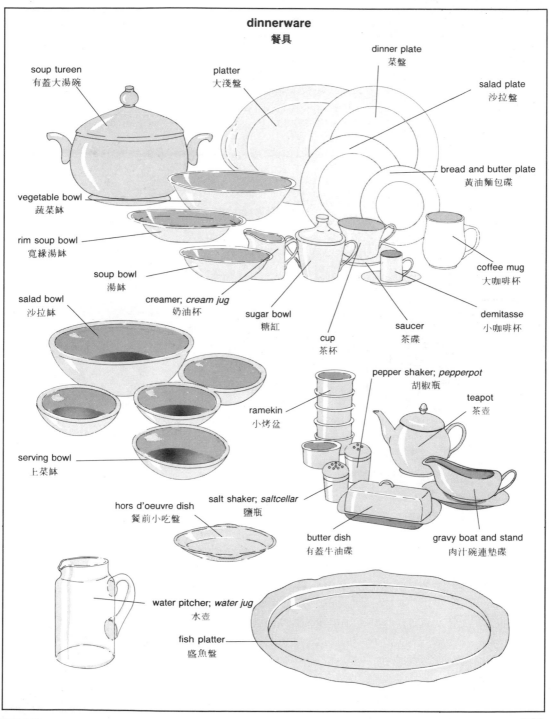

soup tureen
有蓋大湯碗

platter
大淺盤

dinner plate
菜盤

salad plate
沙拉盤

bread and butter plate
黃油麵包碟

vegetable bowl
蔬菜缽

rim soup bowl
寬緣湯缽

soup bowl
湯缽

creamer; *cream jug*
奶油杯

sugar bowl
糖缸

cup
茶杯

saucer
茶碟

coffee mug
大咖啡杯

demitasse
小咖啡杯

salad bowl
沙拉缽

ramekin
小烤盆

pepper shaker; *pepperpot*
胡椒瓶

teapot
茶壺

serving bowl
上菜缽

hors d'oeuvre dish
餐前小吃盤

salt shaker; *saltcellar*
鹽瓶

butter dish
有蓋牛油碟

gravy boat and stand
肉汁碗連墊碟

water pitcher; *water jug*
水壺

fish platter
盛魚盤

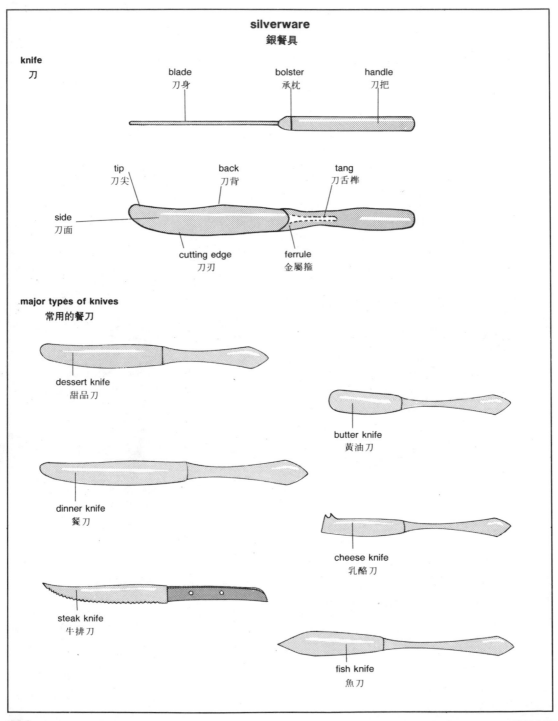

silverware
銀餐具

knife
刀

blade
刀身

bolster
承枕

handle
刀把

tip
刀尖

back
刀背

tang
刀舌榫

side
刀面

cutting edge
刀刃

ferrule
金屬箍

major types of knives
常用的餐刀

dessert knife
甜品刀

butter knife
黃油刀

dinner knife
餐刀

cheese knife
乳酪刀

steak knife
牛排刀

fish knife
魚刀

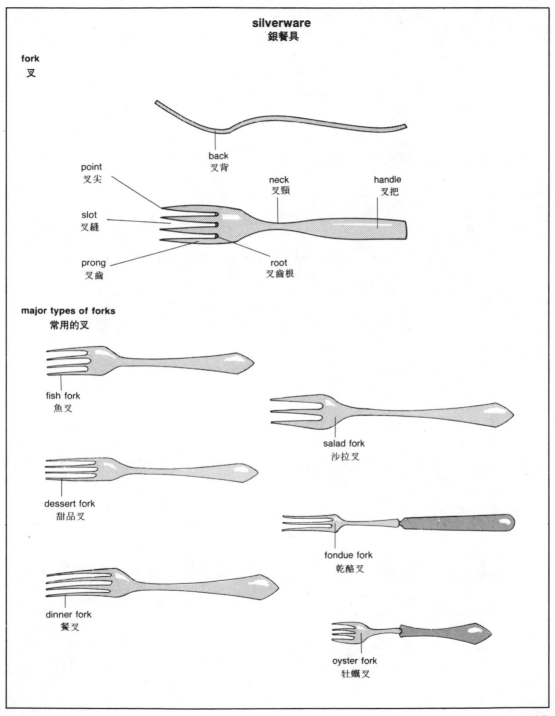

silverware
銀餐具

fork
叉

back
叉背

point
叉尖

neck
叉頸

handle
叉把

slot
叉縫

prong
叉齒

root
叉齒根

major types of forks
常用的叉

fish fork
魚叉

salad fork
沙拉叉

dessert fork
甜品叉

fondue fork
乾酪叉

dinner fork
餐叉

oyster fork
牡蠣叉

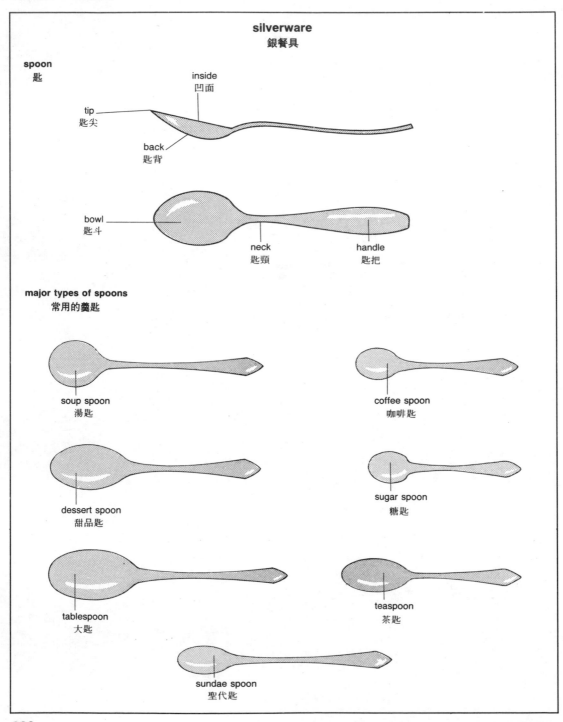

silverware
銀餐具

spoon
匙

inside
凹面

tip
匙尖

back
匙背

bowl
匙斗

neck
匙頸

handle
匙把

major types of spoons
常用的羹匙

soup spoon
湯匙

coffee spoon
咖啡匙

dessert spoon
甜品匙

sugar spoon
糖匙

tablespoon
大匙

teaspoon
茶匙

sundae spoon
聖代匙

kitchen utensils
廚房用具

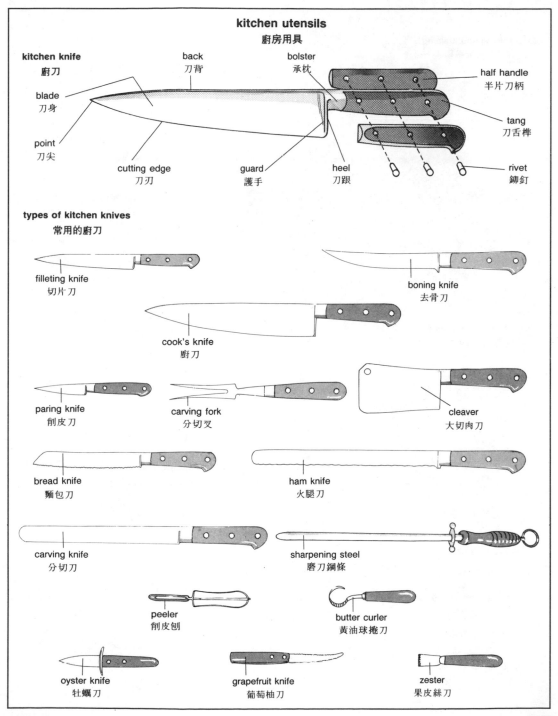

kitchen knife
廚刀

back
刀背

bolster
承枕

half handle
半片刀柄

blade
刀身

tang
刀舌榫

point
刀尖

cutting edge
刀刃

guard
護手

heel
刀跟

rivet
鉚釘

types of kitchen knives
常用的廚刀

filleting knife
切片刀

boning knife
去骨刀

cook's knife
廚刀

paring knife
削皮刀

carving fork
分切叉

cleaver
大切肉刀

bread knife
麵包刀

ham knife
火腿刀

carving knife
分切刀

sharpening steel
磨刀鋼條

peeler
削皮刨

butter curler
黃油球捲刀

oyster knife
牡蠣刀

grapefruit knife
葡萄柚刀

zester
果皮絲刀

kitchen utensils
廚房用具

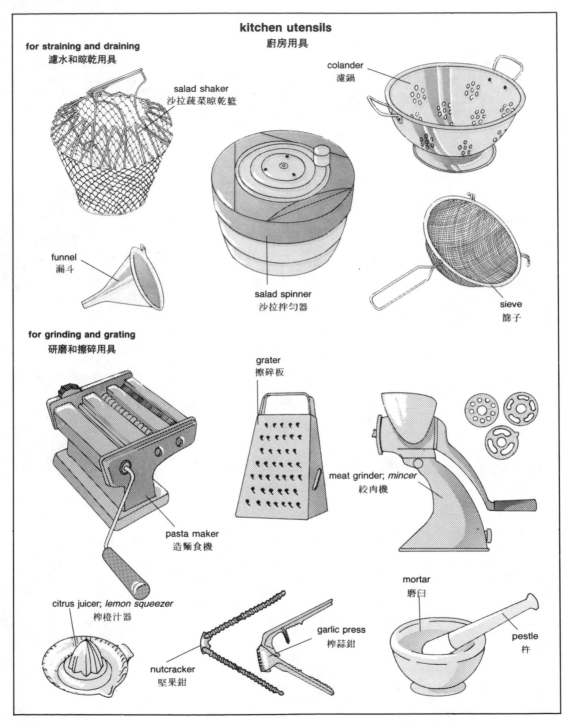

for straining and draining
濾水和晾乾用具

salad shaker
沙拉蔬菜晾乾籃

colander
濾鍋

funnel
漏斗

salad spinner
沙拉拌勻器

sieve
篩子

for grinding and grating
研磨和擦碎用具

grater
擦碎板

meat grinder; *mincer*
絞肉機

pasta maker
造麵食機

mortar
磨臼

citrus juicer; *lemon squeezer*
榨橙汁器

nutcracker
堅果鉗

garlic press
榨蒜鉗

pestle
杵

kitchen utensils
廚房用具

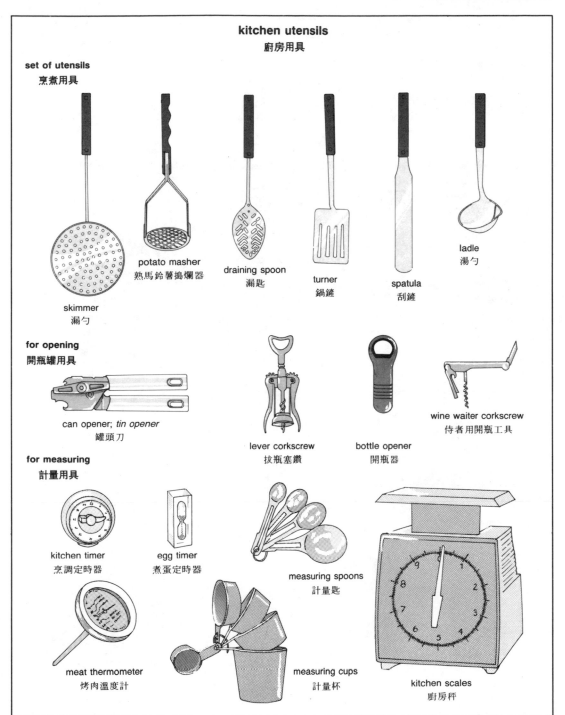

set of utensils
烹煮用具

potato masher
熟馬鈴薯搗爛器

draining spoon
漏匙

turner
鍋鏟

spatula
刮鏟

ladle
湯勺

skimmer
漏勺

for opening
開瓶罐用具

can opener; *tin opener*
罐頭刀

lever corkscrew
拔瓶塞鑽

bottle opener
開瓶器

wine waiter corkscrew
侍者用開瓶工具

for measuring
計量用具

kitchen timer
烹調定時器

egg timer
煮蛋定時器

measuring spoons
計量匙

meat thermometer
烤肉溫度計

measuring cups
計量杯

kitchen scales
廚房秤

kitchen utensils
廚房用具

baking utensils
製麵包糕餅用具

rolling pin
擀麵杖

pastry brush
塗刷

whisk
攪拌器

pastry cutting wheel
切餅輪

egg beater
打蛋器

sifter
篩

pastry bag and nozzles
捏奶油花紋的袋和嘴

mixing bowls
混和盆

pie pan; *pie tin*
餡餅烤盤

flan pan; *flan tin*
水果蛋糕盤

cookie cutters; *biscuit cutters*
小甜餅模

cookie press; *biscuit press*
小甜餅成形擠管

quiche plate; *quiche tin*
芝士蛋糕盤

cake pan; *cake tin*
蛋糕烤盤

muffin pan; *bun tin*
鬆餅烤盤

cookie sheet; *biscuit sheet*
烘小甜餅板

icing syringe
糖衣擠管

kitchen utensils
廚房用具

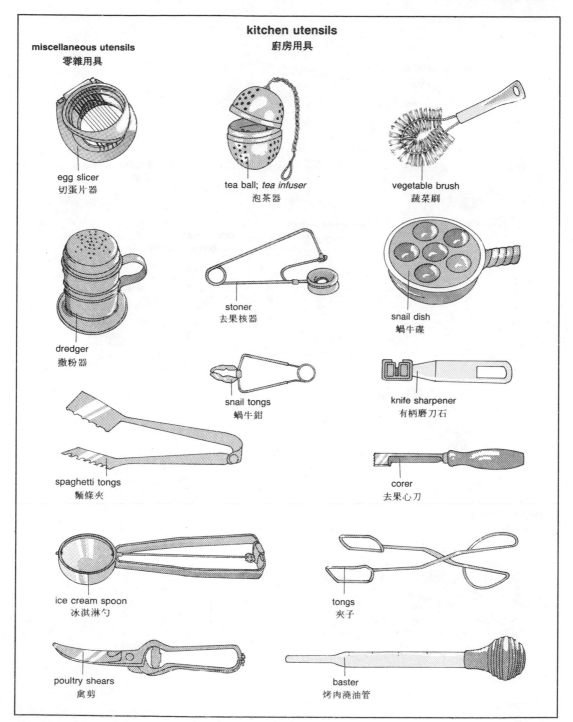

miscellaneous utensils
零雜用具

egg slicer
切蛋片器

tea ball; *tea infuser*
泡茶器

vegetable brush
蔬菜刷

dredger
撒粉器

stoner
去果核器

snail dish
蝸牛碟

snail tongs
蝸牛鉗

knife sharpener
有柄磨刀石

spaghetti tongs
麵條夾

corer
去果心刀

ice cream spoon
冰淇淋勺

tongs
夾子

poultry shears
禽剪

baster
烤肉澆油管

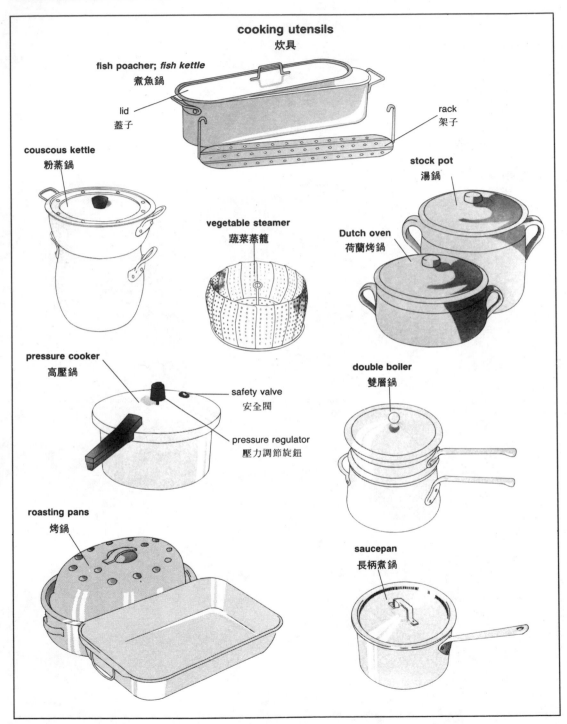

cooking utensils
炊具

fish poacher; _fish kettle_
煮魚鍋

lid
蓋子

rack
架子

couscous kettle
粉蒸鍋

vegetable steamer
蔬菜蒸籠

stock pot
湯鍋

Dutch oven
荷蘭烤鍋

pressure cooker
高壓鍋

safety valve
安全閥

pressure regulator
壓力調節旋鈕

double boiler
雙層鍋

roasting pans
烤鍋

saucepan
長柄煮鍋

cooking utensils
炊具

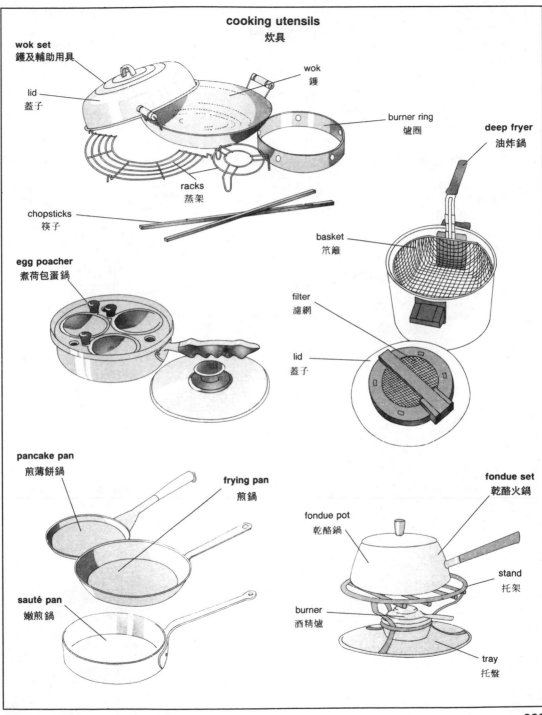

wok set
鑊及輔助用具

lid
蓋子

wok
鑊

burner ring
爐圈

deep fryer
油炸鍋

racks
蒸架

chopsticks
筷子

basket
笊籬

egg poacher
煮荷包蛋鍋

filter
濾網

lid
蓋子

pancake pan
煎薄餅鍋

frying pan
煎鍋

fondue set
乾酪火鍋

fondue pot
乾酪鍋

stand
托架

sauté pan
嫩煎鍋

burner
酒精爐

tray
托盤

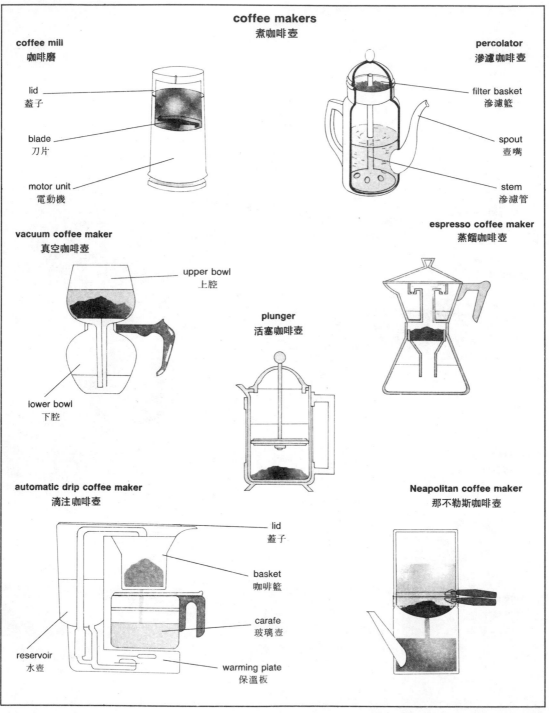

coffee makers
煮咖啡壺

coffee mill
咖啡磨

lid
蓋子

blade
刀片

motor unit
電動機

percolator
滲濾咖啡壺

filter basket
滲濾籃

spout
壺嘴

stem
滲濾管

vacuum coffee maker
真空咖啡壺

upper bowl
上腔

lower bowl
下腔

espresso coffee maker
蒸餾咖啡壺

plunger
活塞咖啡壺

automatic drip coffee maker
滴注咖啡壺

lid
蓋子

basket
咖啡籃

carafe
玻璃壺

reservoir
水壺

warming plate
保溫板

Neapolitan coffee maker
那不勒斯咖啡壺

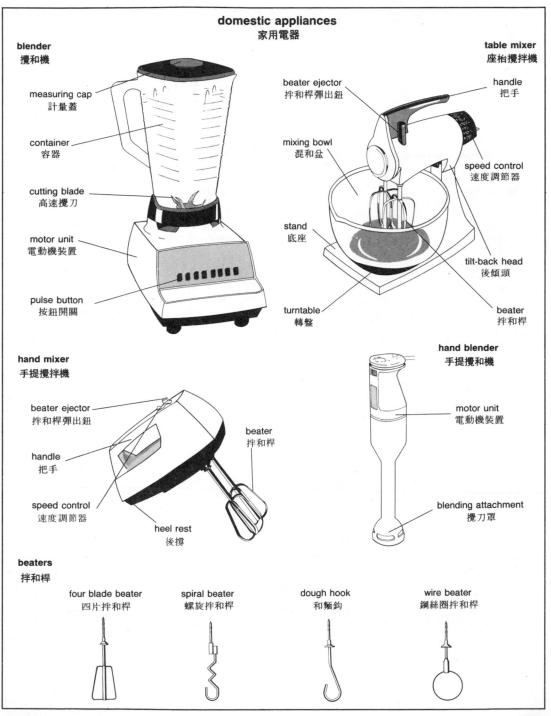

domestic appliances
家用電器

blender
攪和機

measuring cap
計量蓋

container
容器

cutting blade
高速攪刀

motor unit
電動機裝置

pulse button
按鈕開關

table mixer
座枱攪拌機

beater ejector
拌和桿彈出鈕

handle
把手

mixing bowl
混和盆

speed control
速度調節器

stand
底座

tilt-back head
後傾頭

turntable
轉盤

beater
拌和桿

hand mixer
手提攪拌機

beater ejector
拌和桿彈出鈕

beater
拌和桿

handle
把手

speed control
速度調節器

heel rest
後撐

hand blender
手提攪和機

motor unit
電動機裝置

blending attachment
攪刀罩

beaters
拌和桿

four blade beater
四片拌和桿

spiral beater
螺旋拌和桿

dough hook
和麵鈎

wire beater
鋼絲圈拌和桿

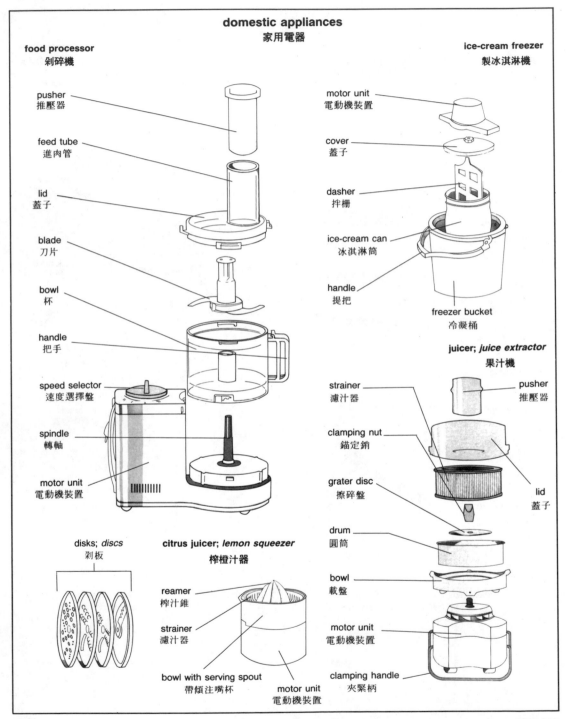

domestic appliances
家用電器

food processor
剁碎機

pusher
推壓器

feed tube
進肉管

lid
蓋子

blade
刀片

bowl
杯

handle
把手

speed selector
速度選擇盤

spindle
轉軸

motor unit
電動機裝置

disks; *discs*
剁板

citrus juicer; *lemon squeezer*
榨橙汁器

reamer
榨汁錐

strainer
濾汁器

bowl with serving spout
帶傾注嘴杯

motor unit
電動機裝置

ice-cream freezer
製冰淇淋機

motor unit
電動機裝置

cover
蓋子

dasher
拌柵

ice-cream can
冰淇淋筒

handle
提把

freezer bucket
冷凝桶

juicer; *juice extractor*
果汁機

strainer
濾汁器

clamping nut
錨定銷

grater disc
擦碎盤

drum
圓筒

bowl
載盤

motor unit
電動機裝置

clamping handle
夾緊柄

pusher
推壓器

lid
蓋子

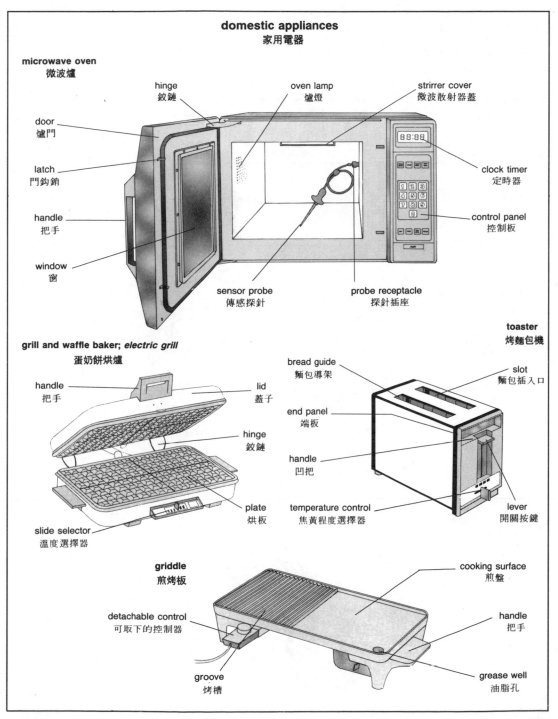

domestic appliances
家用電器

microwave oven
微波爐

hinge
鉸鏈

oven lamp
爐燈

stirrer cover
微波散射器蓋

door
爐門

latch
門鈎銷

clock timer
定時器

handle
把手

control panel
控制板

window
窗

sensor probe
傳感探針

probe receptacle
探針插座

toaster
烤麵包機

grill and waffle baker; *electric grill*
蛋奶餅烘爐

bread guide
麵包導架

slot
麵包插入口

handle
把手

lid
蓋子

end panel
端板

hinge
鉸鏈

handle
凹把

plate
烘板

temperature control
焦黃程度選擇器

lever
開關按鍵

slide selector
溫度選擇器

griddle
煎烤板

cooking surface
煎盤

detachable control
可取下的控制器

handle
把手

groove
烤槽

grease well
油脂孔

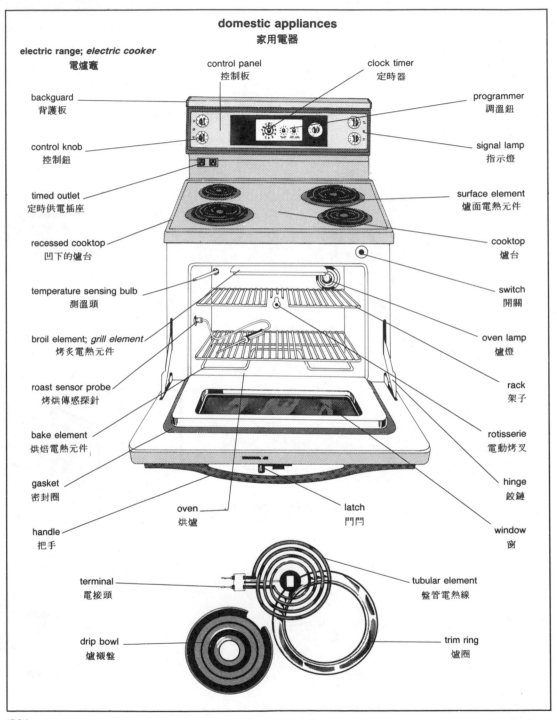

domestic appliances
家用電器

electric range; *electric cooker*
電爐竈

control panel
控制板

clock timer
定時器

backguard
背護板

programmer
調溫鈕

control knob
控制鈕

signal lamp
指示燈

timed outlet
定時供電插座

surface element
爐面電熱元件

recessed cooktop
凹下的爐台

cooktop
爐台

temperature sensing bulb
測溫頭

switch
開關

broil element; *grill element*
烤炙電熱元件

oven lamp
爐燈

roast sensor probe
烤烘傳感探針

rack
架子

bake element
烘焙電熱元件

rotisserie
電動烤叉

gasket
密封圈

hinge
鉸鏈

oven
烘爐

latch
門閂

window
窗

handle
把手

terminal
電接頭

tubular element
盤管電熱線

drip bowl
爐襯盤

trim ring
爐圈

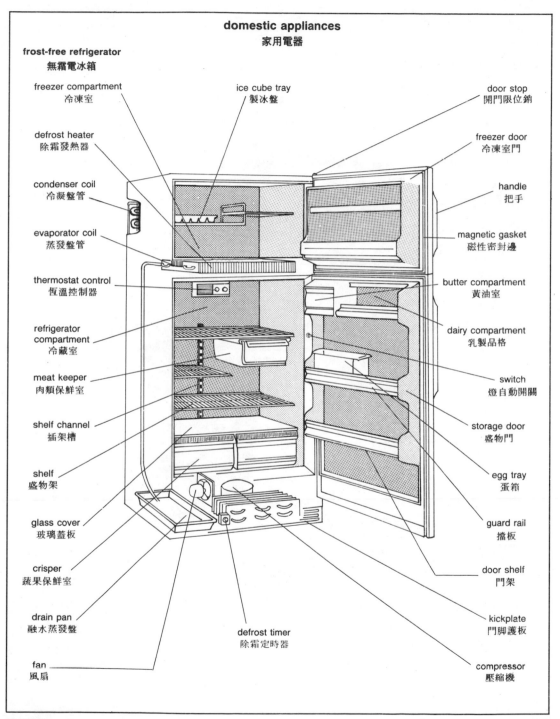

domestic appliances
家用電器

frost-free refrigerator
無霜電冰箱

freezer compartment
冷凍室

ice cube tray
製冰盤

door stop
開門限位銷

defrost heater
除霜發熱器

freezer door
冷凍室門

condenser coil
冷凝盤管

handle
把手

evaporator coil
蒸發盤管

magnetic gasket
磁性密封邊

thermostat control
恆溫控制器

butter compartment
黃油室

refrigerator
compartment
冷藏室

dairy compartment
乳製品格

meat keeper
肉類保鮮室

switch
燈自動開關

shelf channel
插架槽

storage door
盛物門

shelf
盛物架

egg tray
蛋箱

glass cover
玻璃蓋板

guard rail
擋板

crisper
蔬果保鮮室

door shelf
門架

drain pan
融水蒸發盤

defrost timer
除霜定時器

kickplate
門腳護板

fan
風扇

compressor
壓縮機

domestic appliances
家用電器

washer; *washing machine*
洗衣機

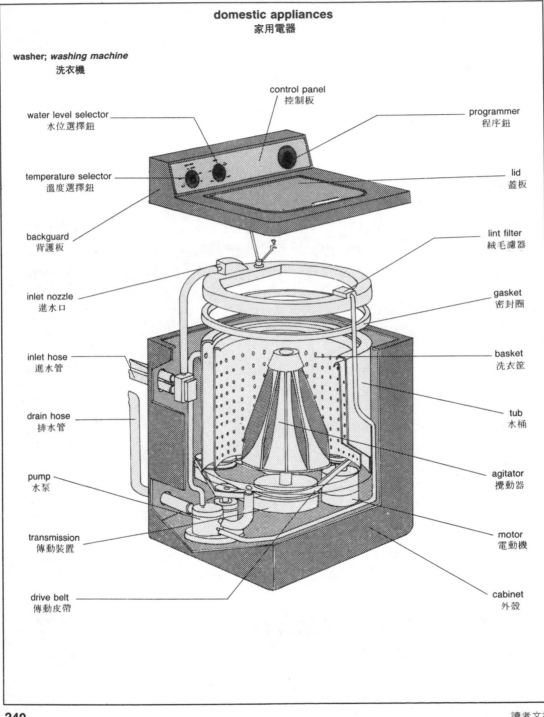

control panel
控制板

water level selector
水位選擇鈕

programmer
程序鈕

temperature selector
溫度選擇鈕

lid
蓋板

backguard
背護板

lint filter
絨毛濾器

inlet nozzle
進水口

gasket
密封圈

inlet hose
進水管

basket
洗衣筐

drain hose
排水管

tub
水桶

pump
水泵

agitator
攪動器

transmission
傳動裝置

motor
電動機

drive belt
傳動皮帶

cabinet
外殼

domestic appliances
家用電器

dryer; *tumble dryer*
乾衣機

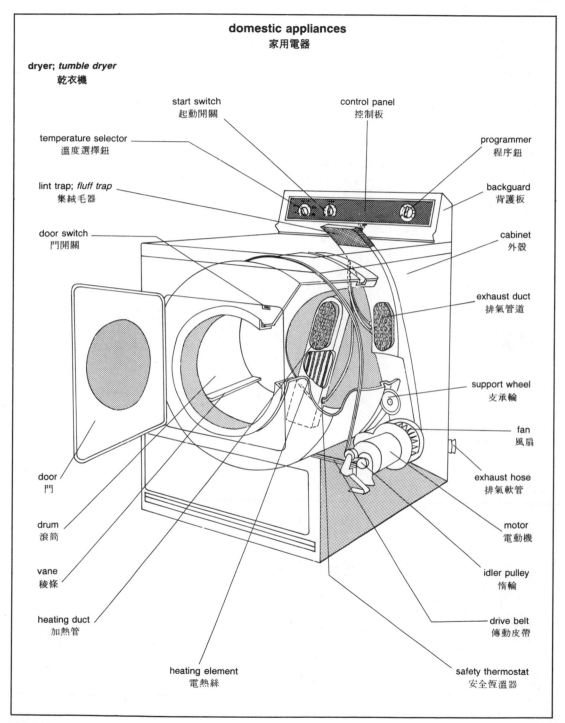

temperature selector
溫度選擇鈕

start switch
起動開關

control panel
控制板

programmer
程序鈕

lint trap; *fluff trap*
集絨毛器

backguard
背護板

door switch
門開關

cabinet
外殼

exhaust duct
排氣管道

support wheel
支承輪

fan
風扇

door
門

exhaust hose
排氣軟管

drum
滾筒

motor
電動機

vane
稜條

idler pulley
惰輪

heating duct
加熱管

drive belt
傳動皮帶

heating element
電熱絲

safety thermostat
安全恆溫器

domestic appliances
家用電器

dishwasher
洗碗碟機

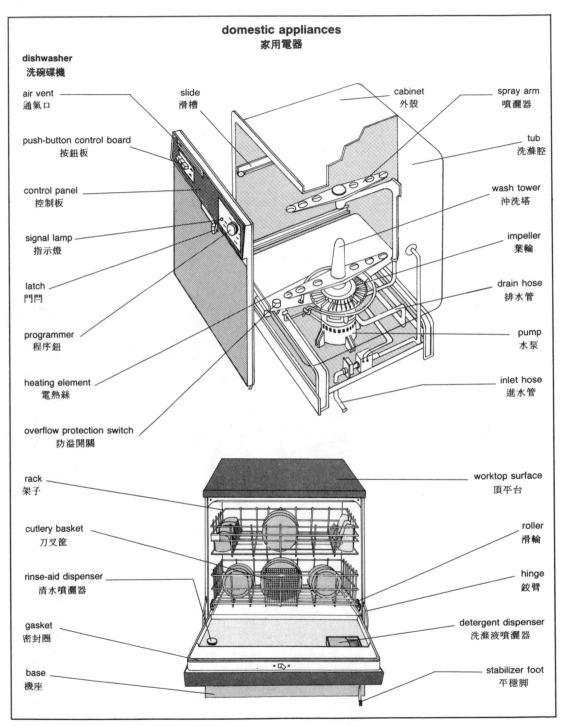

air vent
通氣口

slide
滑槽

cabinet
外殼

spray arm
噴灑器

push-button control board
按鈕板

tub
洗滌腔

control panel
控制板

wash tower
沖洗塔

signal lamp
指示燈

impeller
葉輪

latch
門閂

drain hose
排水管

programmer
程序鈕

pump
水泵

heating element
電熱絲

inlet hose
進水管

overflow protection switch
防溢開關

rack
架子

worktop surface
頂平台

cutlery basket
刀叉筐

roller
滑輪

rinse-aid dispenser
清水噴灑器

hinge
鉸臂

gasket
密封圈

detergent dispenser
洗滌液噴灑器

base
機座

stabilizer foot
平穩腳

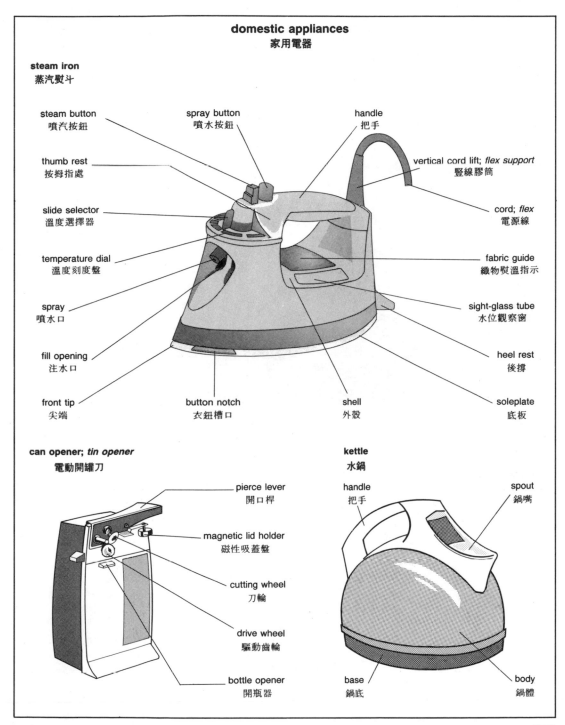

domestic appliances
家用電器

steam iron
蒸汽熨斗

- steam button 噴汽按鈕
- spray button 噴水按鈕
- handle 把手
- vertical cord lift; *flex support* 豎線膠筒
- thumb rest 按拇指處
- slide selector 溫度選擇器
- cord; *flex* 電源線
- temperature dial 溫度刻度盤
- fabric guide 織物熨溫指示
- spray 噴水口
- sight-glass tube 水位觀察窗
- fill opening 注水口
- heel rest 後撐
- front tip 尖端
- button notch 衣鈕槽口
- shell 外殼
- soleplate 底板

can opener; *tin opener*
電動開罐刀

- pierce lever 開口桿
- magnetic lid holder 磁性吸蓋盤
- cutting wheel 刀輪
- drive wheel 驅動齒輪
- bottle opener 開瓶器

kettle
水鍋

- handle 把手
- spout 鍋嘴
- base 鍋底
- body 鍋體

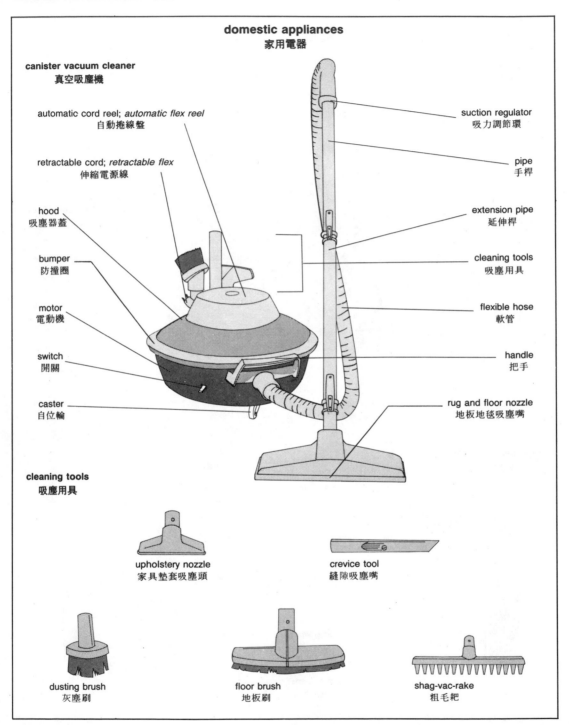

domestic appliances
家用電器

canister vacuum cleaner
真空吸塵機

automatic cord reel; *automatic flex reel*
自動捲線盤

retractable cord; *retractable flex*
伸縮電源線

hood
吸塵器蓋

bumper
防撞圈

motor
電動機

switch
開關

caster
自位輪

suction regulator
吸力調節環

pipe
手桿

extension pipe
延伸桿

cleaning tools
吸塵用具

flexible hose
軟管

handle
把手

rug and floor nozzle
地板地毯吸塵嘴

cleaning tools
吸塵用具

upholstery nozzle
家具墊套吸塵頭

crevice tool
縫隙吸塵嘴

dusting brush
灰塵刷

floor brush
地板刷

shag-vac-rake
粗毛耙

GARDENING

園藝

pleasure garden
花園

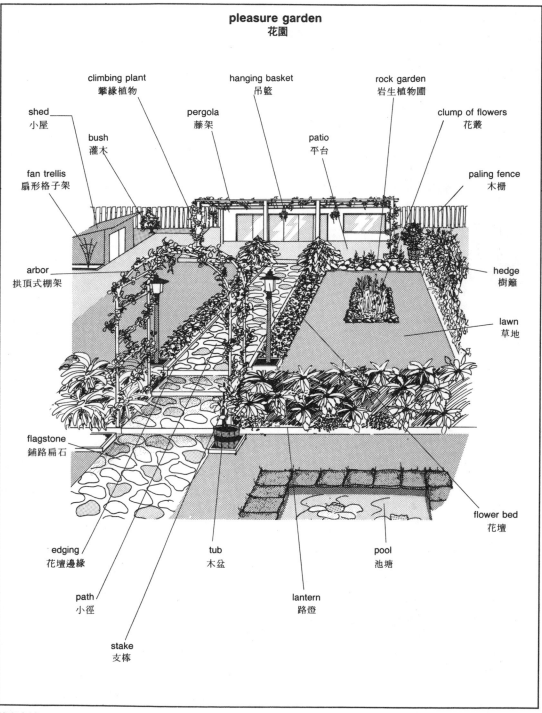

climbing plant
攀緣植物

hanging basket
吊籃

rock garden
岩生植物圃

shed
小屋

pergola
藤架

clump of flowers
花叢

bush
灌木

patio
平台

fan trellis
扇形格子架

paling fence
木柵

arbor
拱頂式棚架

hedge
樹籬

lawn
草地

flagstone
鋪路扁石

flower bed
花壇

edging
花壇邊緣

tub
木盆

pool
池塘

path
小徑

lantern
路燈

stake
支棒

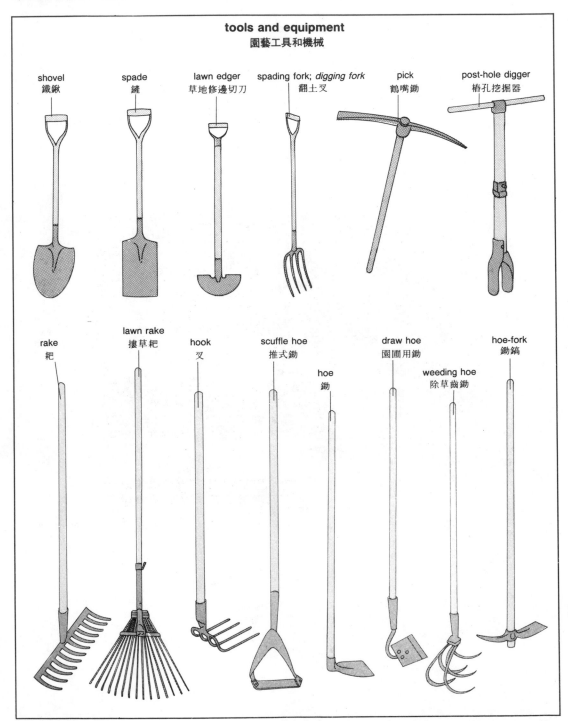

tools and equipment
園藝工具和機械

shovel
鐵鍬

spade
鏟

lawn edger
草地修邊切刀

spading fork; *digging fork*
翻土叉

pick
鶴嘴鋤

post-hole digger
樁孔挖掘器

rake
耙

lawn rake
摟草耙

hook
叉

scuffle hoe
推式鋤

hoe
鋤

draw hoe
園圃用鋤

weeding hoe
除草齒鋤

hoe-fork
鋤鎬

tools and equipment
園藝工具和機械

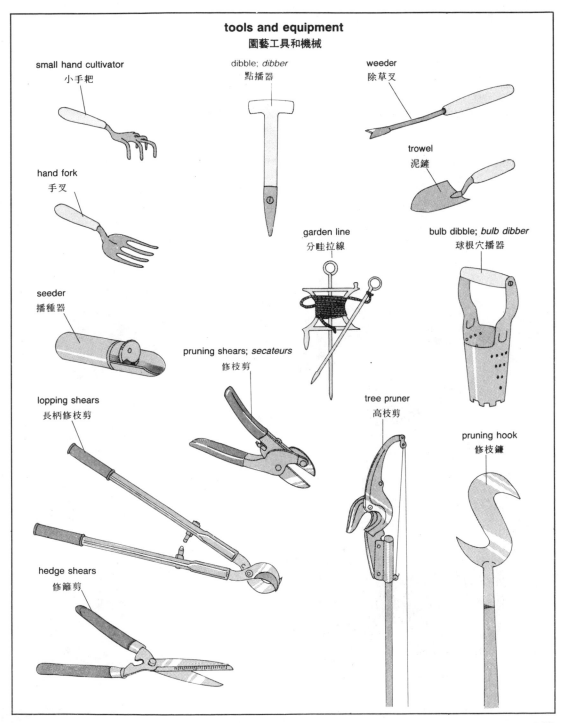

small hand cultivator
小手耙

hand fork
手叉

seeder
播種器

lopping shears
長柄修枝剪

hedge shears
修籬剪

dibble; *dibber*
點播器

garden line
分畦拉線

pruning shears; *secateurs*
修枝剪

weeder
除草叉

trowel
泥鏟

bulb dibble; *bulb dibber*
球根穴播器

tree pruner
高枝剪

pruning hook
修枝鐮

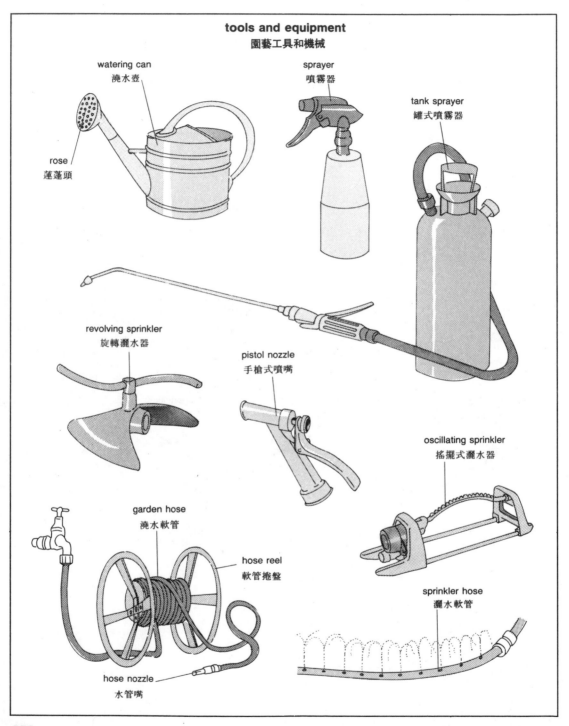

tools and equipment
園藝工具和機械

watering can
澆水壺

sprayer
噴霧器

tank sprayer
罐式噴霧器

rose
蓮蓬頭

revolving sprinkler
旋轉灑水器

pistol nozzle
手槍式噴嘴

oscillating sprinkler
搖擺式灑水器

garden hose
澆水軟管

hose reel
軟管捲盤

sprinkler hose
灑水軟管

hose nozzle
水管嘴

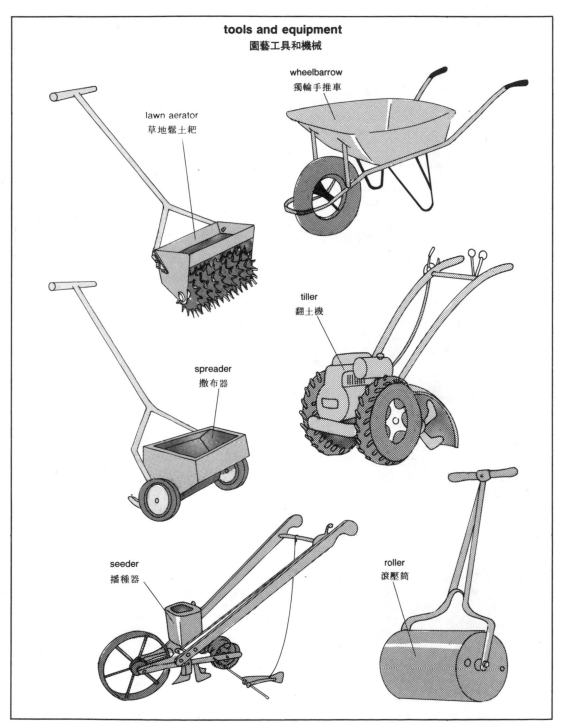

tools and equipment
園藝工具和機械

wheelbarrow
獨輪手推車

lawn aerator
草地鬆土耙

tiller
翻土機

spreader
撒布器

seeder
播種器

roller
滾壓筒

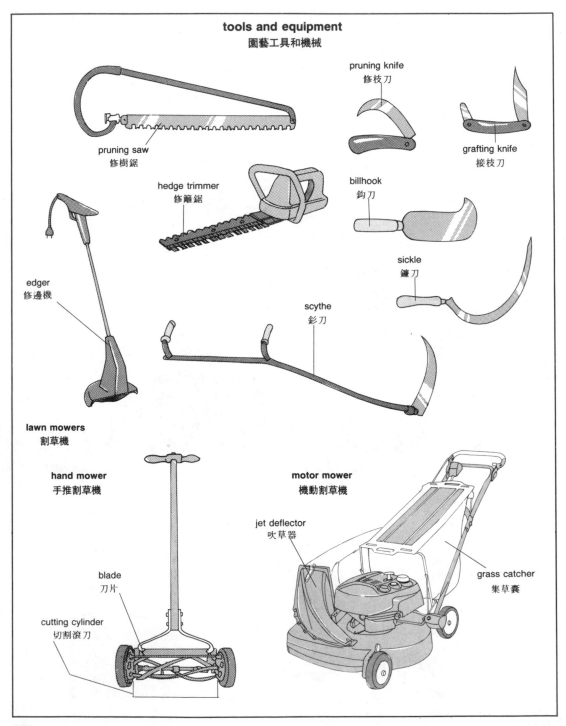

tools and equipment
園藝工具和機械

pruning knife
修枝刀

pruning saw
修樹鋸

grafting knife
接枝刀

hedge trimmer
修籬鋸

billhook
鈎刀

edger
修邊機

sickle
鐮刀

scythe
釤刀

lawn mowers
割草機

hand mower
手推割草機

motor mower
機動割草機

jet deflector
吹草器

blade
刀片

grass catcher
集草囊

cutting cylinder
切割滾刀

chainsaw
鏈鋸

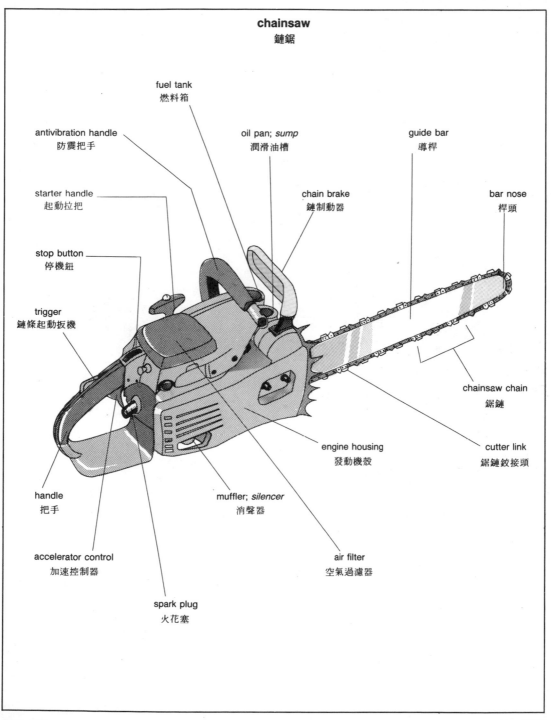

fuel tank
燃料箱

antivibration handle
防震把手

oil pan; *sump*
潤滑油槽

guide bar
導桿

starter handle
起動拉把

chain brake
鏈制動器

bar nose
桿頭

stop button
停機鈕

trigger
鏈條起動扳機

chainsaw chain
鋸鏈

engine housing
發動機殼

cutter link
鋸鏈鉸接頭

handle
把手

muffler; *silencer*
消聲器

accelerator control
加速控制器

air filter
空氣過濾器

spark plug
火花塞

DO-IT-YOURSELF

自行修理用具

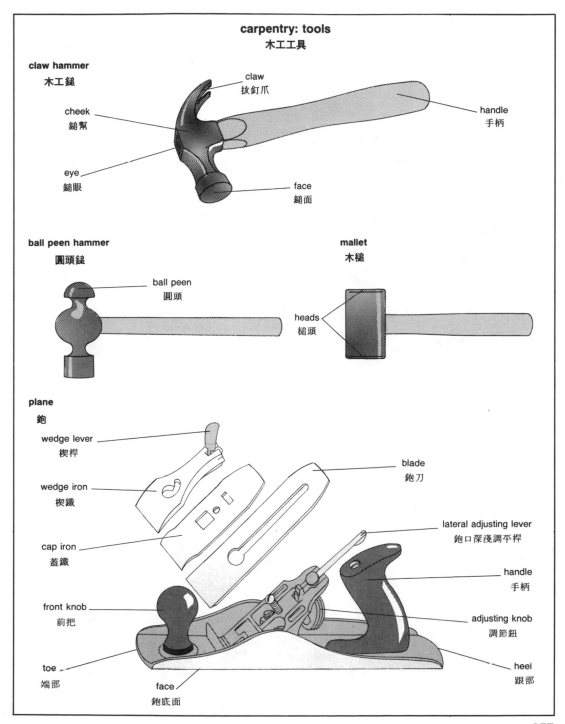

carpentry: tools
木工工具

claw hammer
木工鎚

claw
拔釘爪

cheek
鎚幫

handle
手柄

eye
鎚眼

face
鎚面

ball peen hammer
圓頭鎚

ball peen
圓頭

mallet
木槌

heads
槌頭

plane
鉋

wedge lever
楔桿

wedge iron
楔鐵

cap iron
蓋鐵

front knob
前把

toe
端部

face
鉋底面

blade
鉋刀

lateral adjusting lever
鉋口深淺調平桿

handle
手柄

adjusting knob
調節鈕

heel
跟部

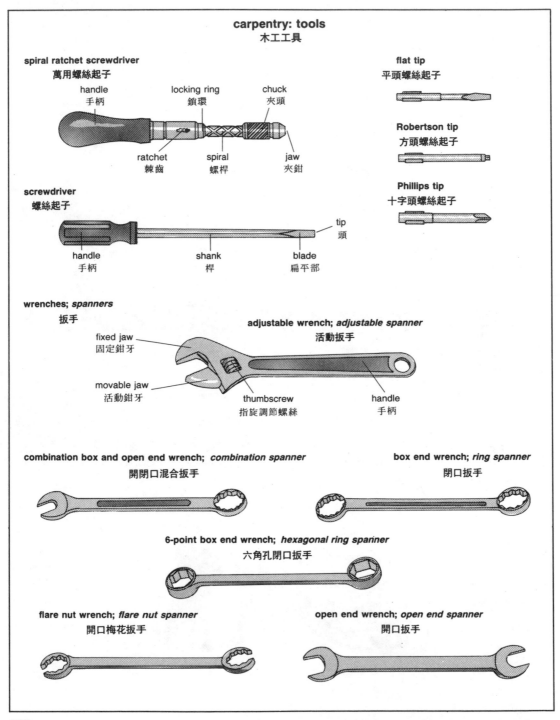

carpentry: tools
木工工具

spiral ratchet screwdriver
萬用螺絲起子

handle
手柄

locking ring
鎖環

chuck
夾頭

ratchet
棘齒

spiral
螺桿

jaw
夾鉗

flat tip
平頭螺絲起子

Robertson tip
方頭螺絲起子

Phillips tip
十字頭螺絲起子

screwdriver
螺絲起子

tip
頭

handle
手柄

shank
桿

blade
扁平部

wrenches; *spanners*
扳手

adjustable wrench; *adjustable spanner*
活動扳手

fixed jaw
固定鉗牙

movable jaw
活動鉗牙

thumbscrew
指旋調節螺絲

handle
手柄

combination box and open end wrench; *combination spanner*
開閉口混合扳手

box end wrench; *ring spanner*
閉口扳手

6-point box end wrench; *hexagonal ring spanner*
六角孔閉口扳手

flare nut wrench; *flare nut spanner*
開口梅花扳手

open end wrench; *open end spanner*
開口扳手

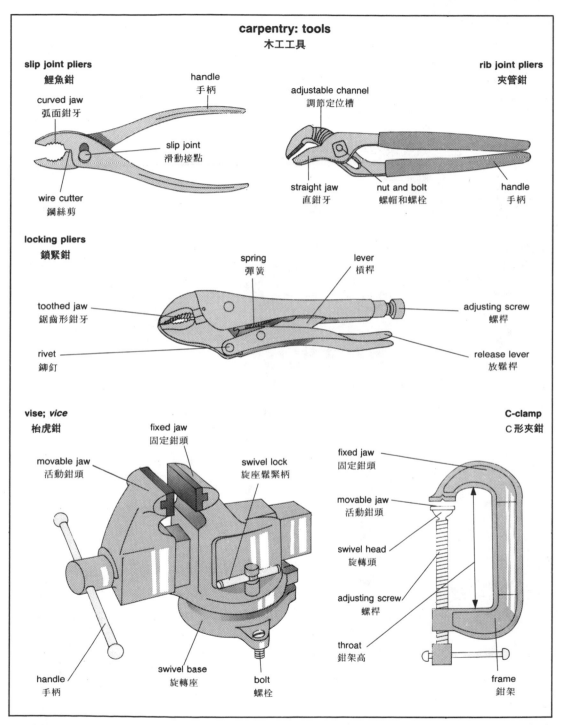

carpentry: tools
木工工具

slip joint pliers
鯉魚鉗

curved jaw
弧面鉗牙

handle
手柄

slip joint
滑動接點

wire cutter
鋼絲剪

rib joint pliers
夾管鉗

adjustable channel
調節定位槽

straight jaw
直鉗牙

nut and bolt
螺帽和螺栓

handle
手柄

locking pliers
鎖緊鉗

spring
彈簧

lever
槓桿

toothed jaw
鋸齒形鉗牙

adjusting screw
螺桿

rivet
鉚釘

release lever
放鬆桿

vise; *vice*
枱虎鉗

fixed jaw
固定鉗頭

movable jaw
活動鉗頭

swivel lock
旋座鬆緊柄

handle
手柄

swivel base
旋轉座

bolt
螺栓

C-clamp
C形夾鉗

fixed jaw
固定鉗頭

movable jaw
活動鉗頭

swivel head
旋轉頭

adjusting screw
螺桿

throat
鉗架高

frame
鉗架

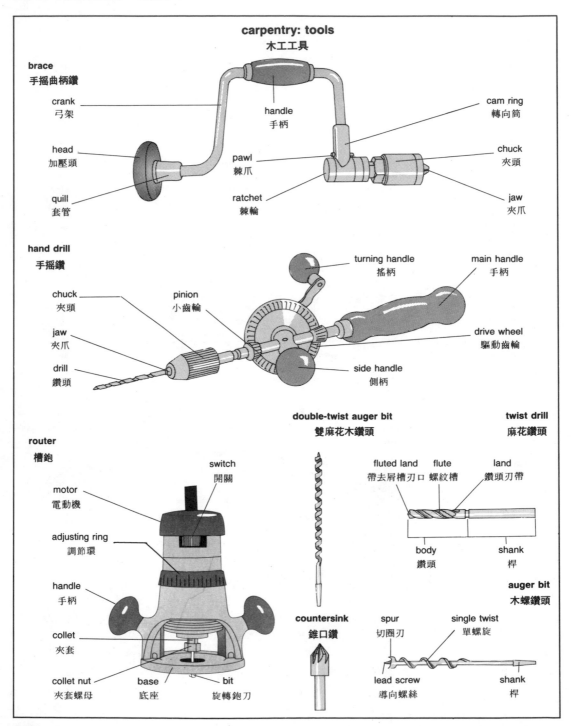

carpentry: tools
木工工具

brace
手搖曲柄鑽

crank
弓架

handle
手柄

cam ring
轉向筒

head
加壓頭

pawl
棘爪

chuck
夾頭

quill
套管

ratchet
棘輪

jaw
夾爪

hand drill
手搖鑽

turning handle
搖柄

main handle
手柄

chuck
夾頭

pinion
小齒輪

jaw
夾爪

drive wheel
驅動齒輪

drill
鑽頭

side handle
側柄

double-twist auger bit
雙麻花木鑽頭

twist drill
麻花鑽頭

router
槽鉋

switch
開關

fluted land
帶去屑槽刃口

flute
螺紋槽

land
鑽頭刃帶

motor
電動機

adjusting ring
調節環

body
鑽頭

shank
桿

handle
手柄

auger bit
木螺鑽頭

collet
夾套

countersink
錐口鑽

spur
切圈刃

single twist
單螺旋

collet nut
夾套螺母

base
底座

bit
旋轉鉋刀

lead screw
導向螺絲

shank
桿

carpentry: tools
木工工具

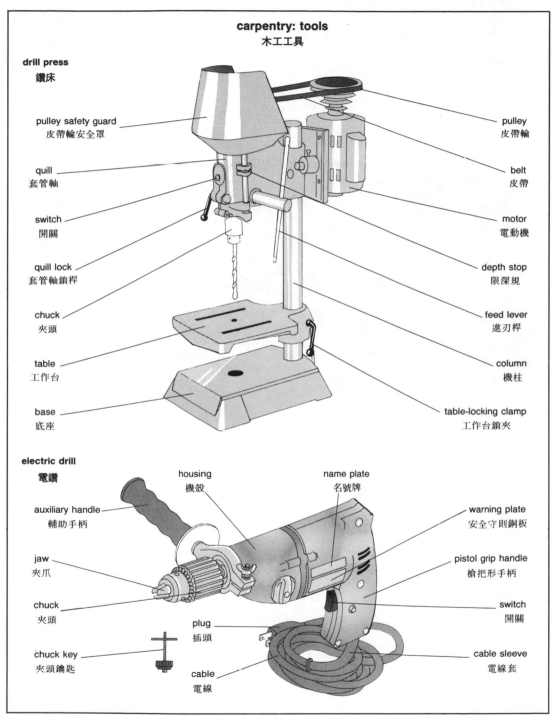

drill press
鑽床

pulley safety guard
皮帶輪安全罩

quill
套管軸

switch
開關

quill lock
套管軸鎖桿

chuck
夾頭

table
工作台

base
底座

pulley
皮帶輪

belt
皮帶

motor
電動機

depth stop
限深規

feed lever
進刃桿

column
機柱

table-locking clamp
工作台鎖夾

electric drill
電鑽

housing
機殼

name plate
名號牌

auxiliary handle
輔助手柄

warning plate
安全守則銅板

jaw
夾爪

pistol grip handle
槍把形手柄

chuck
夾頭

switch
開關

chuck key
夾頭鑰匙

plug
插頭

cable
電線

cable sleeve
電線套

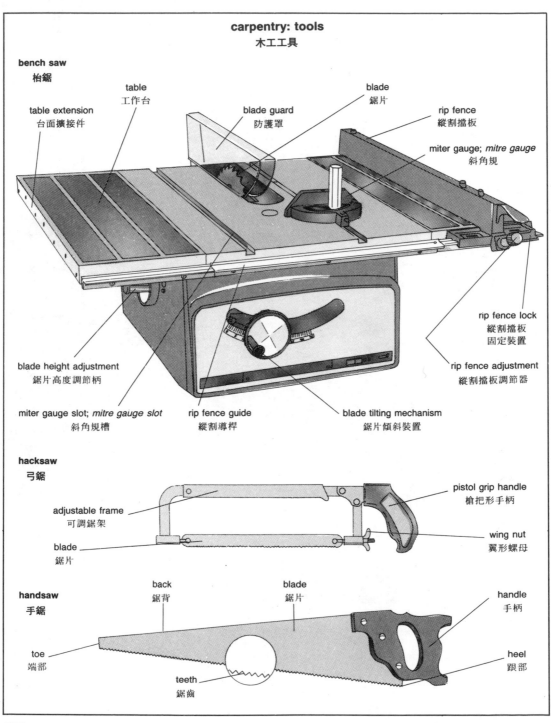

carpentry: tools
木工工具

bench saw
枱鋸

table extension
台面擴接件

table
工作台

blade guard
防護罩

blade
鋸片

rip fence
縱割擋板

miter gauge; *mitre gauge*
斜角規

rip fence lock
縱割擋板
固定裝置

rip fence adjustment
縱割擋板調節器

blade height adjustment
鋸片高度調節柄

miter gauge slot; *mitre gauge slot*
斜角規槽

rip fence guide
縱割導桿

blade tilting mechanism
鋸片傾斜裝置

hacksaw
弓鋸

adjustable frame
可調鋸架

blade
鋸片

pistol grip handle
槍把形手柄

wing nut
翼形螺母

handsaw
手鋸

back
鋸背

blade
鋸片

handle
手柄

toe
端部

teeth
鋸齒

heel
跟部

carpentry: tools
木工工具

circular saw
圓鋸

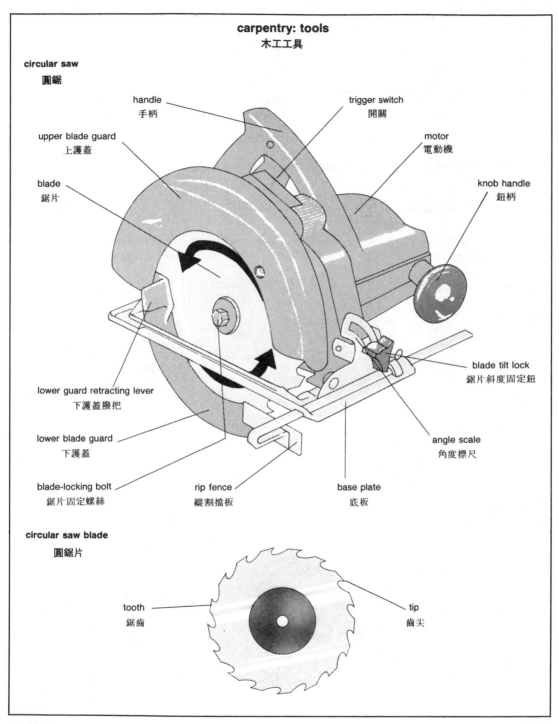

handle
手柄

trigger switch
開關

upper blade guard
上護蓋

motor
電動機

blade
鋸片

knob handle
鈕柄

lower guard retracting lever
下護蓋撥把

blade tilt lock
鋸片斜度固定鈕

lower blade guard
下護蓋

angle scale
角度標尺

blade-locking bolt
鋸片固定螺絲

rip fence
縱割擋板

base plate
底板

circular saw blade
圓鋸片

tooth
鋸齒

tip
齒尖

carpentry: fasteners
木工緊固用具

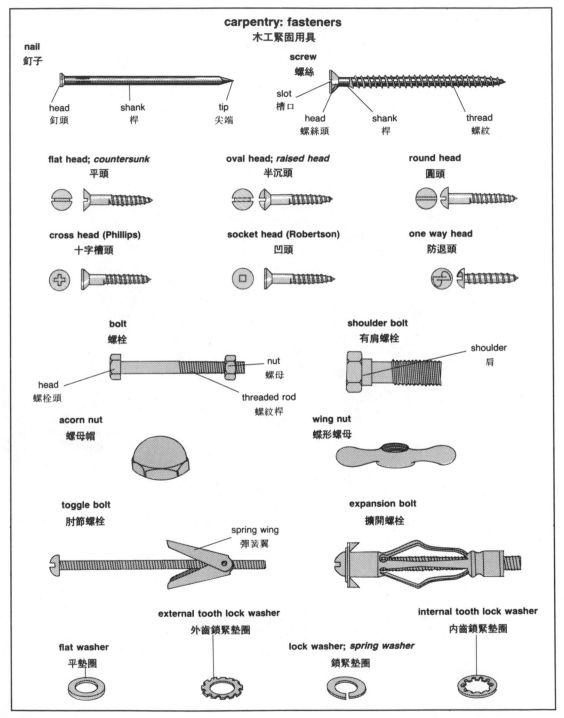

nail
釘子

head
釘頭

shank
桿

tip
尖端

screw
螺絲

slot
槽口

head
螺絲頭

shank
桿

thread
螺紋

flat head; *countersunk*
平頭

oval head; *raised head*
半沉頭

round head
圓頭

cross head (Phillips)
十字槽頭

socket head (Robertson)
凹頭

one way head
防退頭

bolt
螺栓

nut
螺母

head
螺栓頭

threaded rod
螺紋桿

shoulder bolt
有肩螺栓

shoulder
肩

acorn nut
螺母帽

wing nut
蝶形螺母

toggle bolt
肘節螺栓

spring wing
彈簧翼

expansion bolt
擴開螺栓

external tooth lock washer
外齒鎖緊墊圈

internal tooth lock washer
內齒鎖緊墊圈

flat washer
平墊圈

lock washer; *spring washer*
鎖緊墊圈

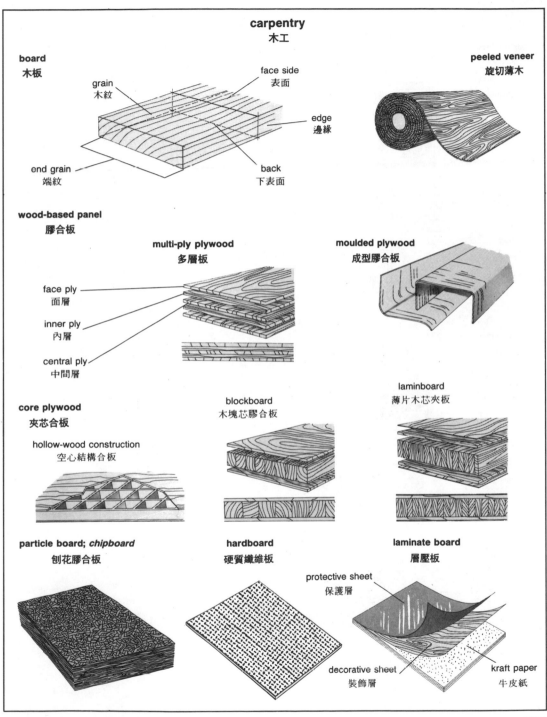

carpentry
木工

board
木板

grain
木紋

face side
表面

edge
邊緣

end grain
端紋

back
下表面

peeled veneer
旋切薄木

wood-based panel
膠合板

multi-ply plywood
多層板

moulded plywood
成型膠合板

face ply
面層

inner ply
內層

central ply
中間層

core plywood
夾芯合板

blockboard
木塊芯膠合板

laminboard
薄片木芯夾板

hollow-wood construction
空心結構合板

particle board; *chipboard*
刨花膠合板

hardboard
硬質纖維板

laminate board
層壓板

protective sheet
保護層

decorative sheet
裝飾層

kraft paper
牛皮紙

lock
鎖

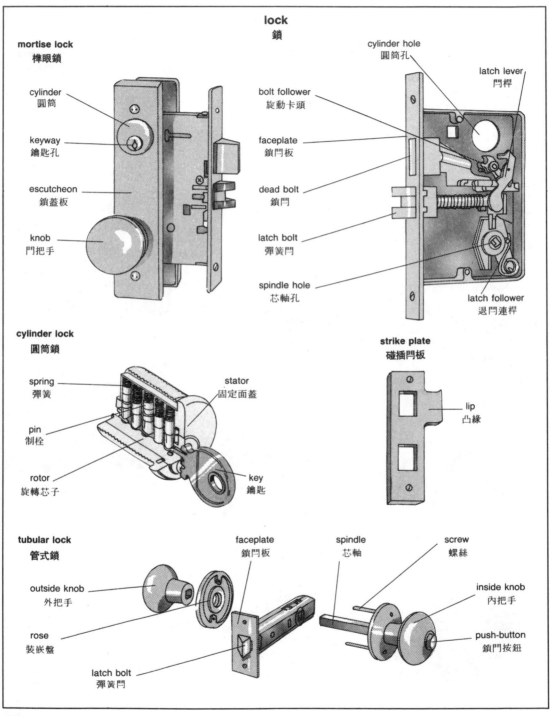

mortise lock
榫眼鎖

cylinder
圓筒

keyway
鑰匙孔

escutcheon
鎖蓋板

knob
門把手

cylinder hole
圓筒孔

bolt follower
旋動卡頭

faceplate
鎖門板

dead bolt
鎖門

latch bolt
彈簧門

spindle hole
芯軸孔

latch lever
門桿

latch follower
退門連桿

cylinder lock
圓筒鎖

spring
彈簧

pin
制栓

rotor
旋轉芯子

stator
固定面蓋

key
鑰匙

strike plate
碰插門板

lip
凸緣

tubular lock
管式鎖

outside knob
外把手

rose
裝嵌盤

faceplate
鎖門板

latch bolt
彈簧門

spindle
芯軸

screw
螺絲

inside knob
內把手

push-button
鎖門按鈕

plumbing
管道工程

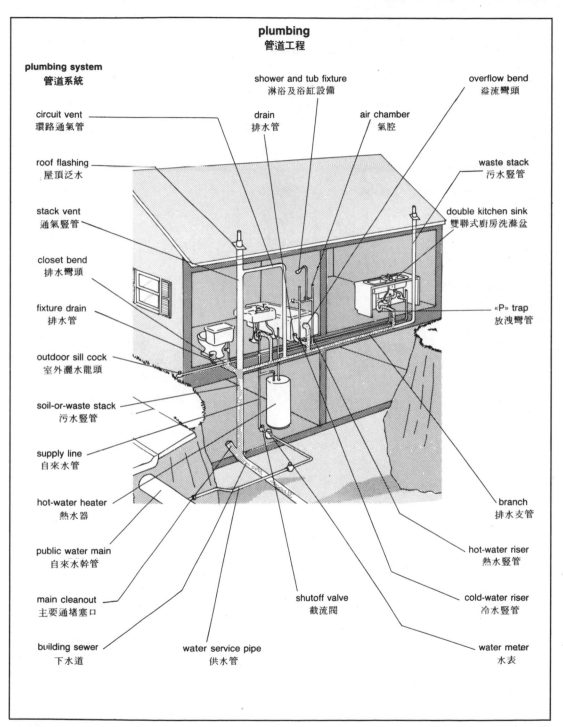

plumbing system
管道系統

shower and tub fixture
淋浴及浴缸設備

overflow bend
溢流彎頭

circuit vent
環路通氣管

drain
排水管

air chamber
氣腔

roof flashing
屋頂泛水

waste stack
污水豎管

double kitchen sink
雙聯式廚房洗滌盆

stack vent
通氣豎管

closet bend
排水彎頭

«P» trap
放洩彎管

fixture drain
排水管

outdoor sill cock
室外灑水龍頭

soil-or-waste stack
污水豎管

branch
排水支管

supply line
自來水管

hot-water heater
熱水器

hot-water riser
熱水豎管

public water main
自來水幹管

cold-water riser
冷水豎管

main cleanout
主要通堵塞口

shutoff valve
截流閥

water meter
水表

building sewer
下水道

water service pipe
供水管

plumbing
管道工程

toilet
抽水馬桶

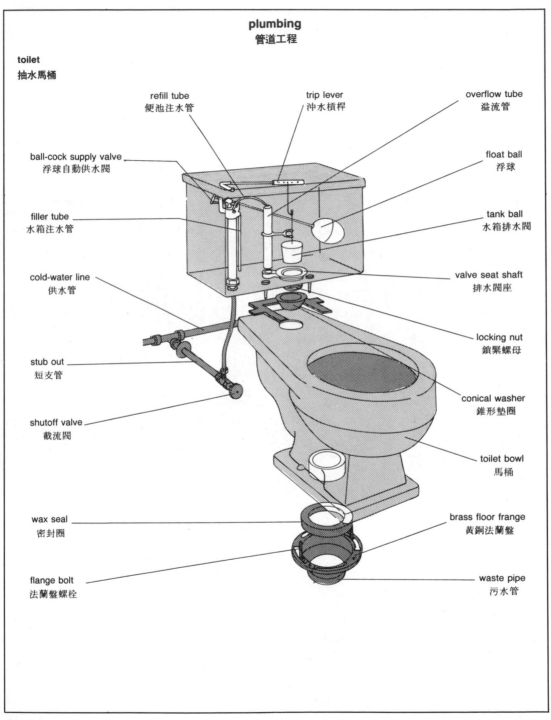

refill tube
便池注水管

trip lever
沖水槓桿

overflow tube
溢流管

ball-cock supply valve
浮球自動供水閥

float ball
浮球

filler tube
水箱注水管

tank ball
水箱排水閥

cold-water line
供水管

valve seat shaft
排水閥座

stub out
短支管

locking nut
鎖緊螺母

shutoff valve
截流閥

conical washer
錐形墊圈

toilet bowl
馬桶

wax seal
密封圈

brass floor frange
黃銅法蘭盤

flange bolt
法蘭盤螺栓

waste pipe
污水管

讀者文摘

plumbing
管道工程

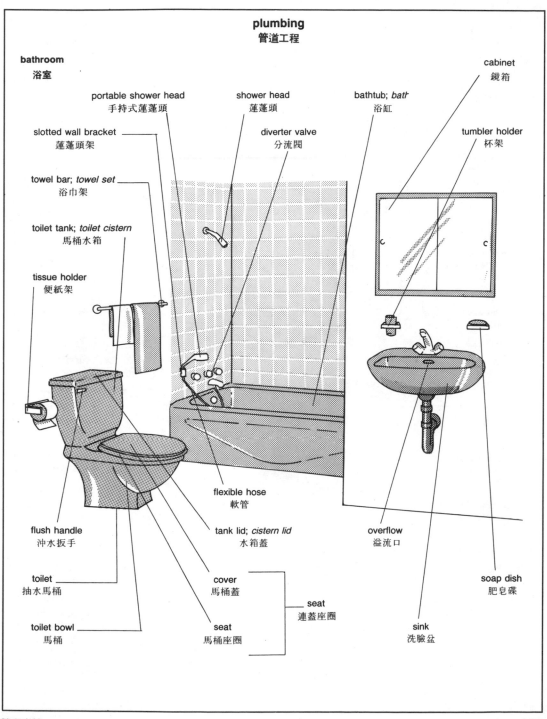

bathroom
浴室

portable shower head
手持式蓮蓬頭

shower head
蓮蓬頭

bathtub; *bath*
浴缸

cabinet
鏡箱

slotted wall bracket
蓮蓬頭架

diverter valve
分流閥

tumbler holder
杯架

towel bar; *towel set*
浴巾架

toilet tank; *toilet cistern*
馬桶水箱

tissue holder
便紙架

flexible hose
軟管

flush handle
沖水扳手

tank lid; *cistern lid*
水箱蓋

overflow
溢流口

soap dish
肥皂碟

toilet
抽水馬桶

cover
馬桶蓋

seat
連蓋座圈

toilet bowl
馬桶

seat
馬桶座圈

sink
洗臉盆

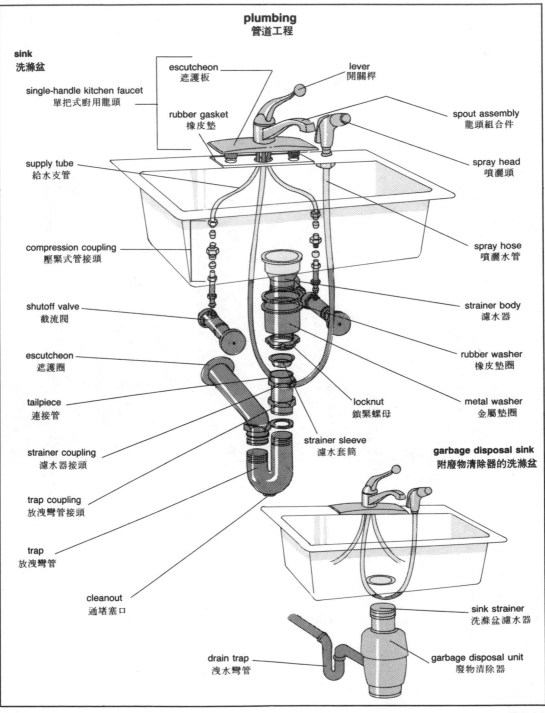

plumbing
管道工程

sink
洗滌盆

single-handle kitchen faucet
單把式廚用龍頭

escutcheon
遮護板

lever
開關桿

spout assembly
龍頭組合件

rubber gasket
橡皮墊

spray head
噴灑頭

supply tube
給水支管

compression coupling
壓緊式管接頭

spray hose
噴灑水管

shutoff valve
截流閥

strainer body
濾水器

escutcheon
遮護圈

rubber washer
橡皮墊圈

tailpiece
連接管

locknut
鎖緊螺母

metal washer
金屬墊圈

strainer coupling
濾水器接頭

strainer sleeve
濾水套筒

garbage disposal sink
附廢物清除器的洗滌盆

trap coupling
放洩彎管接頭

trap
放洩彎管

cleanout
通堵塞口

sink strainer
洗滌盆濾水器

drain trap
洩水彎管

garbage disposal unit
廢物清除器

plumbing
管道工程

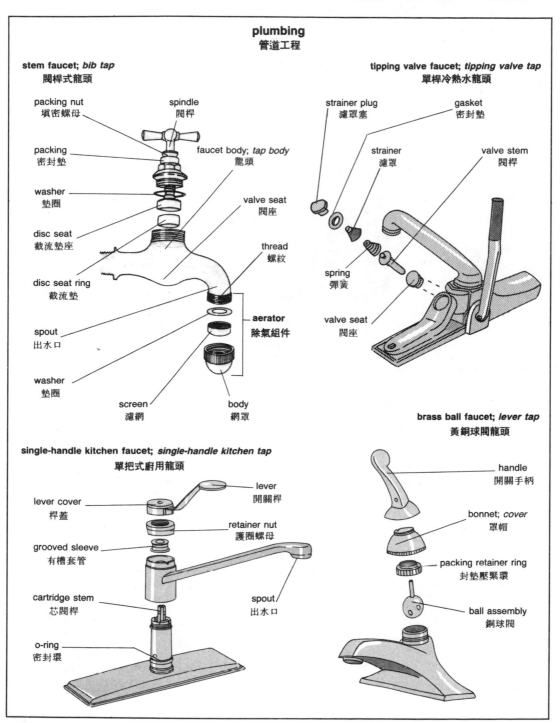

stem faucet; *bib tap*
閥桿式龍頭

packing nut
填密螺母

spindle
閥桿

packing
密封墊

faucet body; *tap body*
龍頭

washer
墊圈

valve seat
閥座

disc seat
截流墊座

thread
螺紋

disc seat ring
截流墊

aerator
除氣組件

spout
出水口

washer
墊圈

screen
濾網

body
網罩

tipping valve faucet; *tipping valve tap*
單桿冷熱水龍頭

strainer plug
濾罩塞

gasket
密封墊

strainer
濾罩

valve stem
閥桿

spring
彈簧

valve seat
閥座

single-handle kitchen faucet; *single-handle kitchen tap*
單把式廚用龍頭

lever
開關桿

lever cover
桿蓋

retainer nut
護圈螺母

grooved sleeve
有槽套管

cartridge stem
芯閥桿

spout
出水口

o-ring
密封環

brass ball faucet; *lever tap*
黃銅球閥龍頭

handle
開關手柄

bonnet; *cover*
罩帽

packing retainer ring
封墊壓緊環

ball assembly
銅球閥

plumbing
管道工程

examples of branching
接管方式數種

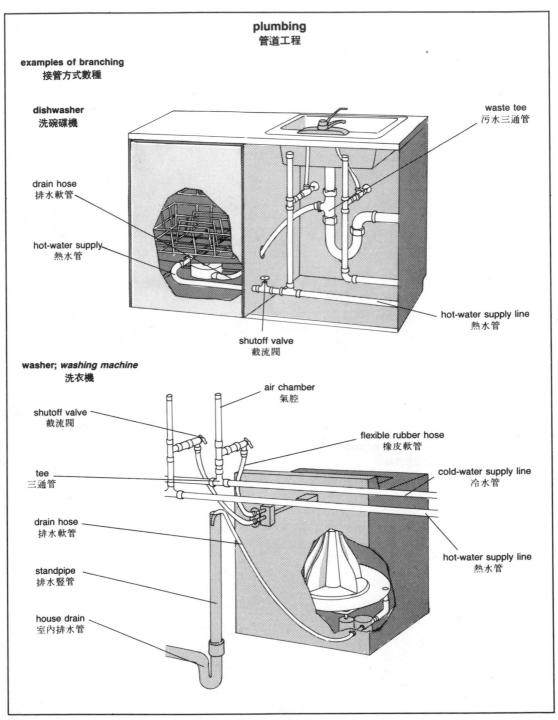

dishwasher
洗碗碟機

waste tee
污水三通管

drain hose
排水軟管

hot-water supply
熱水管

hot-water supply line
熱水管

shutoff valve
截流閥

washer; *washing machine*
洗衣機

air chamber
氣腔

shutoff valve
截流閥

flexible rubber hose
橡皮軟管

tee
三通管

cold-water supply line
冷水管

drain hose
排水軟管

hot-water supply line
熱水管

standpipe
排水豎管

house drain
室內排水管

plumbing
管道工程

electric water-heater tank
電熱水器水箱

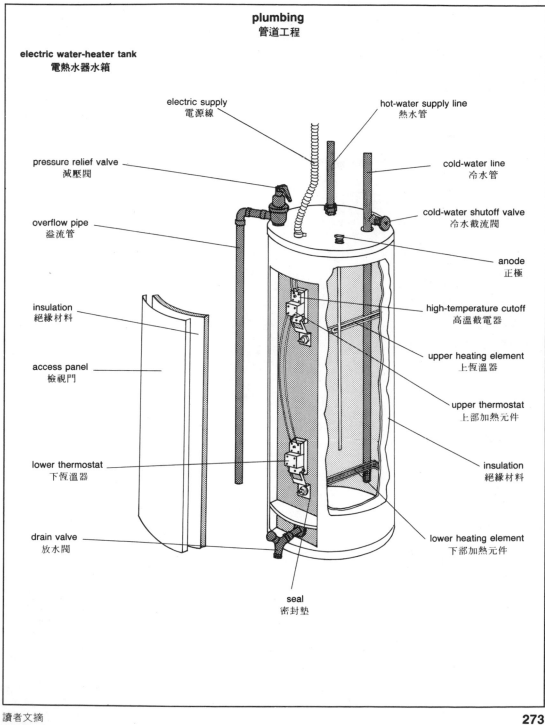

electric supply
電源線

hot-water supply line
熱水管

pressure relief valve
減壓閥

cold-water line
冷水管

cold-water shutoff valve
冷水截流閥

overflow pipe
溢流管

anode
正極

high-temperature cutoff
高溫截電器

insulation
絕緣材料

upper heating element
上恆溫器

access panel
檢視門

upper thermostat
上部加熱元件

insulation
絕緣材料

lower thermostat
下恆溫器

lower heating element
下部加熱元件

drain valve
放水閥

seal
密封墊

plumbing
管道工程

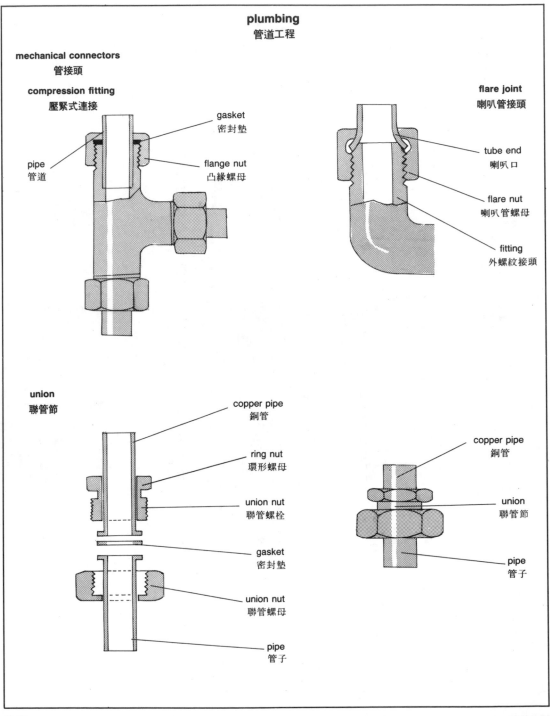

mechanical connectors
管接頭

compression fitting
壓緊式連接

gasket
密封墊

pipe
管道

flange nut
凸緣螺母

flare joint
喇叭管接頭

tube end
喇叭口

flare nut
喇叭管螺母

fitting
外螺紋接頭

union
聯管節

copper pipe
銅管

ring nut
環形螺母

union nut
聯管螺栓

gasket
密封墊

union nut
聯管螺母

pipe
管子

copper pipe
銅管

union
聯管節

pipe
管子

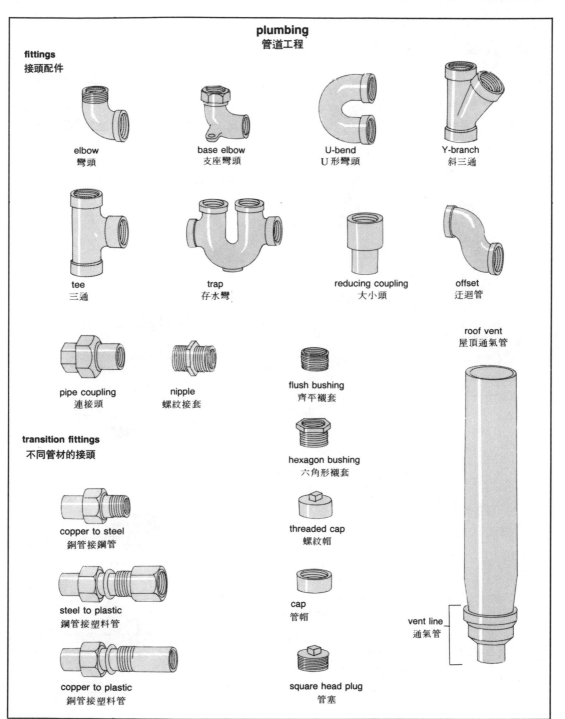

plumbing
管道工程

fittings
接頭配件

elbow
彎頭

base elbow
支座彎頭

U-bend
U形彎頭

Y-branch
斜三通

tee
三通

trap
存水彎

reducing coupling
大小頭

offset
迂迴管

pipe coupling
連接頭

nipple
螺紋接套

flush bushing
齊平襯套

hexagon bushing
六角形襯套

threaded cap
螺紋帽

cap
管帽

square head plug
管塞

roof vent
屋頂通氣管

vent line
通氣管

transition fittings
不同管材的接頭

copper to steel
銅管接鋼管

steel to plastic
鋼管接塑料管

copper to plastic
銅管接塑料管

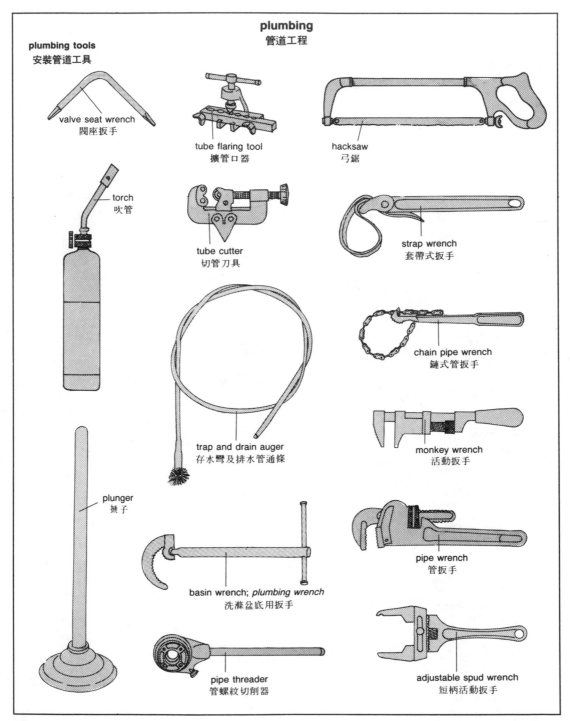

plumbing
管道工程

plumbing tools
安裝管道工具

valve seat wrench
閥座扳手

tube flaring tool
擴管口器

hacksaw
弓鋸

torch
吹管

tube cutter
切管刀具

strap wrench
套帶式扳手

chain pipe wrench
鏈式管扳手

trap and drain auger
存水彎及排水管通條

monkey wrench
活動扳手

plunger
搋子

basin wrench; *plumbing wrench*
洗滌盆底用扳手

pipe wrench
管扳手

pipe threader
管螺紋切削器

adjustable spud wrench
短柄活動扳手

plumbing
管道工程

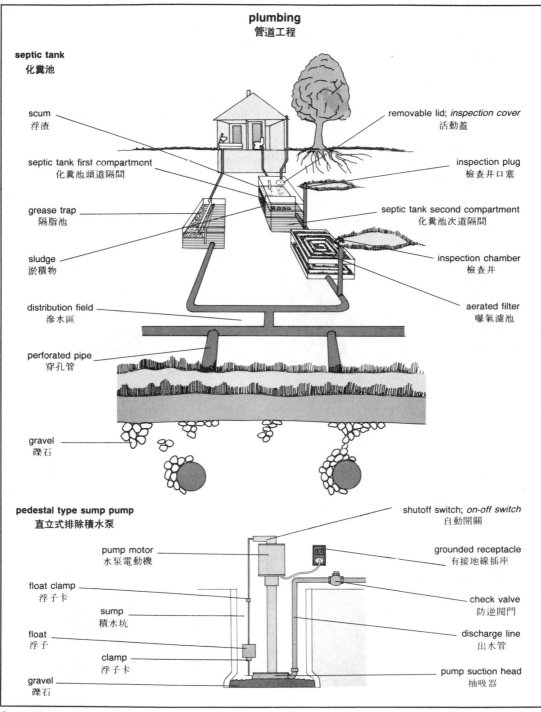

septic tank
化糞池

scum
浮渣

removable lid; *inspection cover*
活動蓋

septic tank first compartment
化糞池頭道隔間

inspection plug
檢查井口塞

grease trap
隔脂池

septic tank second compartment
化糞池次道隔間

sludge
淤積物

inspection chamber
檢查井

distribution field
滲水區

aerated filter
曝氣濾池

perforated pipe
穿孔管

gravel
礫石

pedestal type sump pump
直立式排除積水泵

shutoff switch; *on-off switch*
自動開關

pump motor
水泵電動機

grounded receptacle
有接地線插座

float clamp
浮子卡

check valve
防逆閥門

sump
積水坑

discharge line
出水管

float
浮子

clamp
浮子卡

pump suction head
抽吸器

gravel
礫石

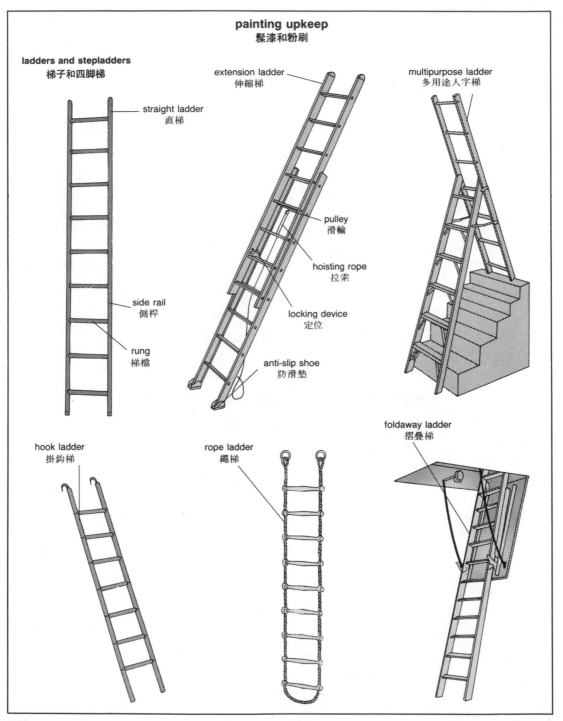

painting upkeep
髹漆和粉刷

ladders and stepladders
梯子和四脚梯

straight ladder
直梯

extension ladder
伸縮梯

multipurpose ladder
多用途人字梯

pulley
滑輪

hoisting rope
拉索

side rail
側桿

locking device
定位

rung
梯檔

anti-slip shoe
防滑墊

foldaway ladder
摺疊梯

hook ladder
掛鈎梯

rope ladder
繩梯

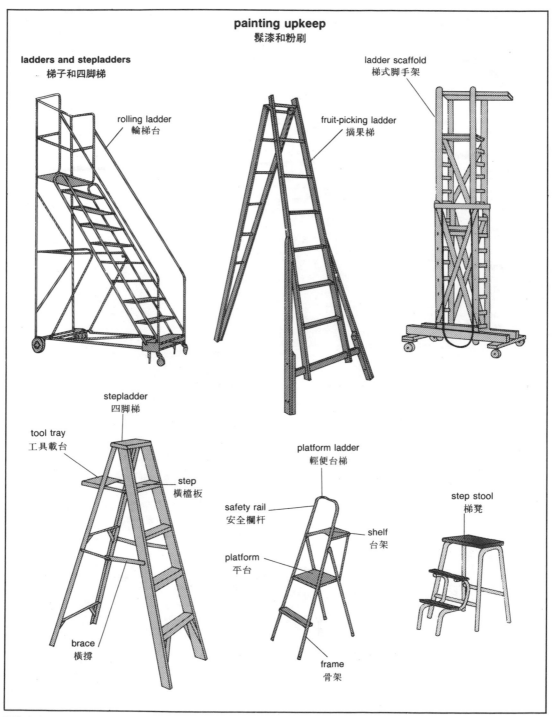

painting upkeep
髹漆和粉刷

ladders and stepladders
梯子和四脚梯

ladder scaffold
梯式脚手架

rolling ladder
輪梯台

fruit-picking ladder
摘果梯

stepladder
四脚梯

tool tray
工具載台

step
橫檔板

platform ladder
輕便台梯

safety rail
安全欄杆

shelf
台架

platform
平台

step stool
梯凳

brace
橫撐

frame
骨架

painting upkeep
髹漆和粉刷

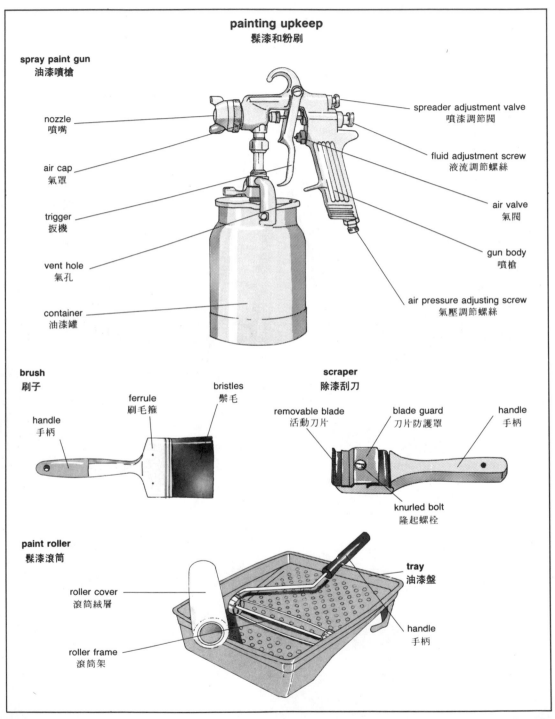

spray paint gun
油漆噴槍

nozzle
噴嘴

air cap
氣罩

trigger
扳機

vent hole
氣孔

container
油漆罐

spreader adjustment valve
噴漆調節閥

fluid adjustment screw
液流調節螺絲

air valve
氣閥

gun body
噴槍

air pressure adjusting screw
氣壓調節螺絲

brush
刷子

ferrule
刷毛箍

bristles
鬃毛

handle
手柄

scraper
除漆刮刀

removable blade
活動刀片

blade guard
刀片防護罩

handle
手柄

knurled bolt
隆起螺栓

paint roller
髹漆滾筒

roller cover
滾筒絨層

roller frame
滾筒架

tray
油漆盤

handle
手柄

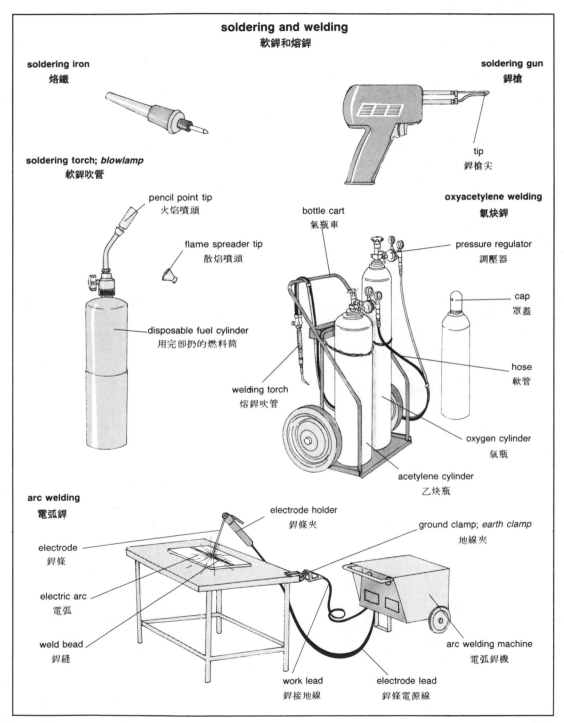

soldering and welding
軟銲和熔銲

soldering iron
烙鐵

soldering gun
銲槍

tip
銲槍尖

soldering torch; *blowlamp*
軟銲吹管

pencil point tip
火焰噴頭

oxyacetylene welding
氧炔銲

bottle cart
氣瓶車

pressure regulator
調壓器

flame spreader tip
散焰噴頭

cap
罩蓋

disposable fuel cylinder
用完卽扔的燃料筒

hose
軟管

welding torch
熔銲吹管

oxygen cylinder
氧瓶

acetylene cylinder
乙炔瓶

arc welding
電弧銲

electrode holder
銲條夾

ground clamp; *earth clamp*
地線夾

electrode
銲條

electric arc
電弧

weld bead
銲縫

arc welding machine
電弧銲機

work lead
銲接地線

electrode lead
銲條電源線

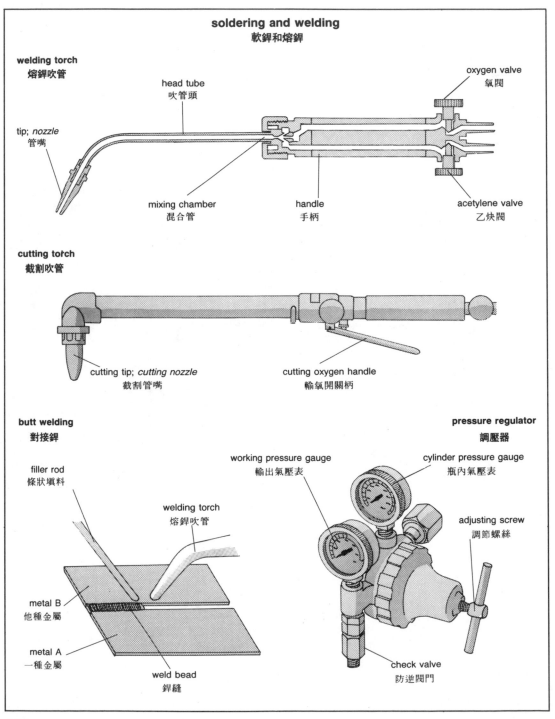

soldering and welding
軟銲和熔銲

welding torch
熔銲吹管

head tube
吹管頭

oxygen valve
氧閥

tip; *nozzle*
管嘴

mixing chamber
混合管

handle
手柄

acetylene valve
乙炔閥

cutting torch
截割吹管

cutting tip; *cutting nozzle*
截割管嘴

cutting oxygen handle
輸氧開關柄

butt welding
對接銲

pressure regulator
調壓器

filler rod
條狀填料

working pressure gauge
輸出氣壓表

cylinder pressure gauge
瓶內氣壓表

welding torch
熔銲吹管

adjusting screw
調節螺絲

metal B
他種金屬

metal A
一種金屬

weld bead
銲縫

check valve
防逆閥門

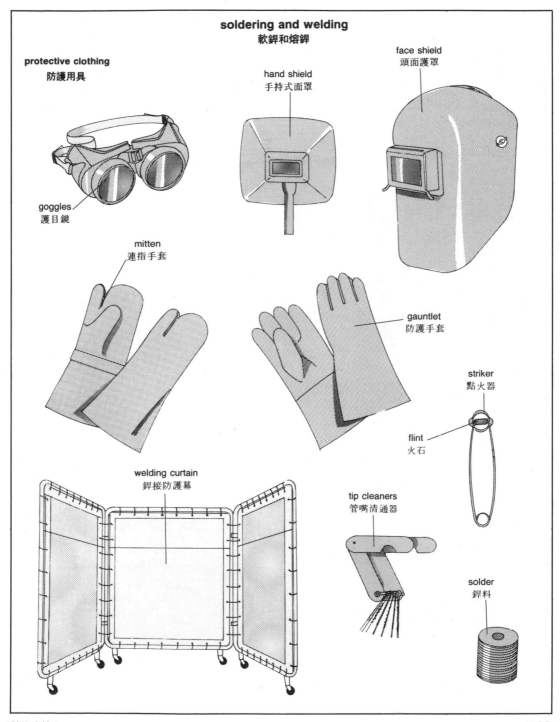

soldering and welding
軟銲和熔銲

protective clothing
防護用具

hand shield
手持式面罩

face shield
頭面護罩

goggles
護目鏡

mitten
連指手套

gauntlet
防護手套

striker
點火器

flint
火石

welding curtain
銲接防護幕

tip cleaners
管嘴清通器

solder
銲料

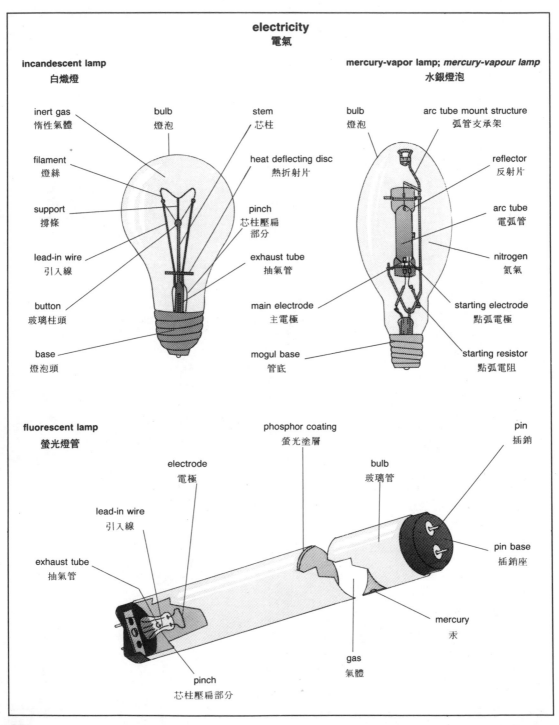

electricity
電氣

incandescent lamp
白熾燈

inert gas
惰性氣體

filament
燈絲

support
撐條

lead-in wire
引入線

button
玻璃柱頭

base
燈泡頭

bulb
燈泡

stem
芯柱

heat deflecting disc
熱折射片

pinch
芯柱壓扁
部分

exhaust tube
抽氣管

main electrode
主電極

mogul base
管底

mercury-vapor lamp; *mercury-vapour lamp*
水銀燈泡

bulb
燈泡

arc tube mount structure
弧管支承架

reflector
反射片

arc tube
電弧管

nitrogen
氮氣

starting electrode
點弧電極

starting resistor
點弧電阻

fluorescent lamp
螢光燈管

phosphor coating
螢光塗層

pin
插銷

electrode
電極

bulb
玻璃管

lead-in wire
引入線

exhaust tube
抽氣管

pin base
插銷座

mercury
汞

gas
氣體

pinch
芯柱壓扁部分

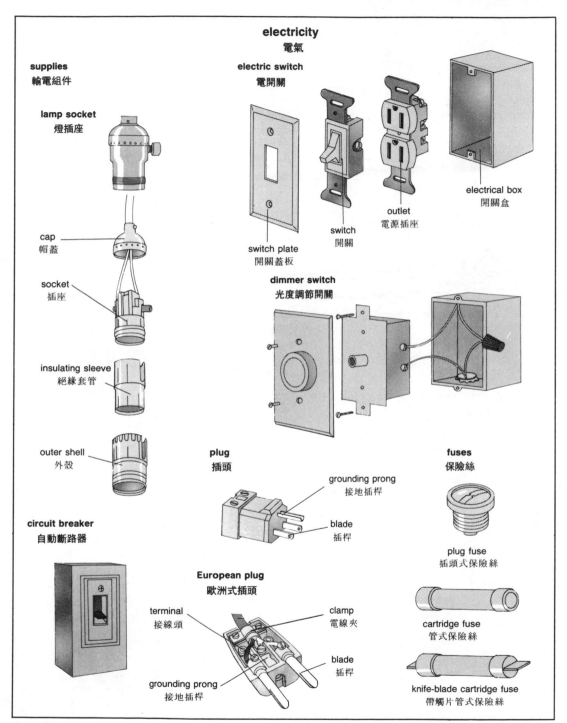

electricity
電氣

supplies
輸電組件

lamp socket
燈插座

cap
帽蓋

socket
插座

insulating sleeve
絕緣套管

outer shell
外殼

circuit breaker
自動斷路器

electric switch
電開關

switch plate
開關蓋板

switch
開關

outlet
電源插座

electrical box
開關盒

dimmer switch
光度調節開關

plug
插頭

grounding prong
接地插桿

blade
插桿

European plug
歐洲式插頭

terminal
接線頭

clamp
電線夾

blade
插桿

grounding prong
接地插桿

fuses
保險絲

plug fuse
插頭式保險絲

cartridge fuse
管式保險絲

knife-blade cartridge fuse
帶觸片管式保險絲

electricity
電氣

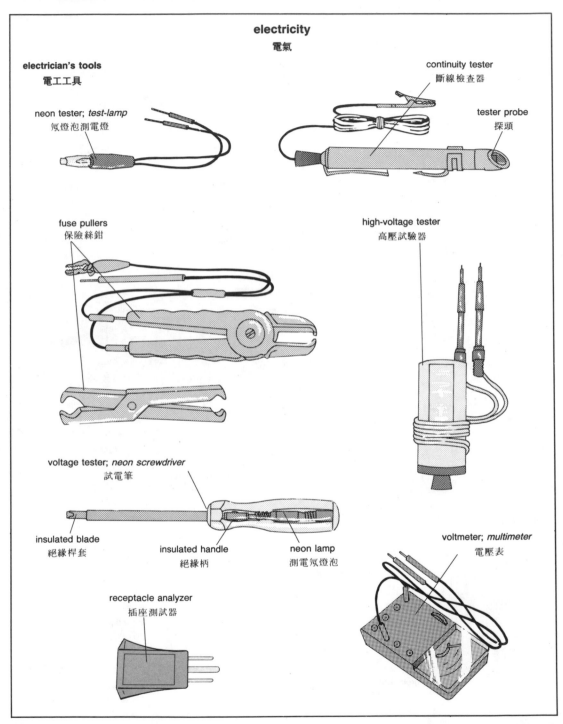

electrician's tools
電工工具

neon tester; *test-lamp*
氖燈泡測電燈

continuity tester
斷線檢查器

tester probe
探頭

fuse pullers
保險絲鉗

high-voltage tester
高壓試驗器

voltage tester; *neon screwdriver*
試電筆

insulated blade
絕緣桿套

insulated handle
絕緣柄

neon lamp
測電氖燈泡

voltmeter; *multimeter*
電壓表

receptacle analyzer
插座測試器

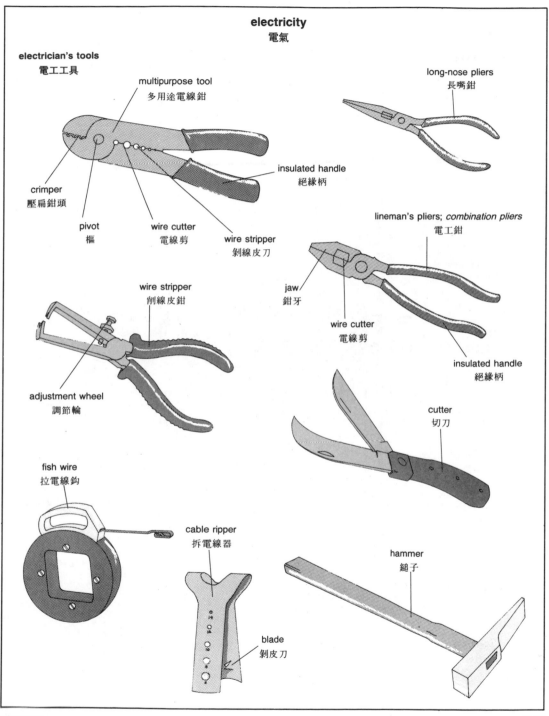

electricity
電氣

electrician's tools
電工工具

multipurpose tool
多用途電線鉗

long-nose pliers
長嘴鉗

crimper
壓扁鉗頭

pivot
樞

wire cutter
電線剪

wire stripper
剝線皮刀

insulated handle
絕緣柄

lineman's pliers; *combination pliers*
電工鉗

wire stripper
削線皮鉗

jaw
鉗牙

wire cutter
電線剪

insulated handle
絕緣柄

adjustment wheel
調節輪

cutter
切刀

fish wire
拉電線鉤

cable ripper
拆電線器

hammer
鎚子

blade
剝皮刀

electricity
電氣

distribution board
配電盤

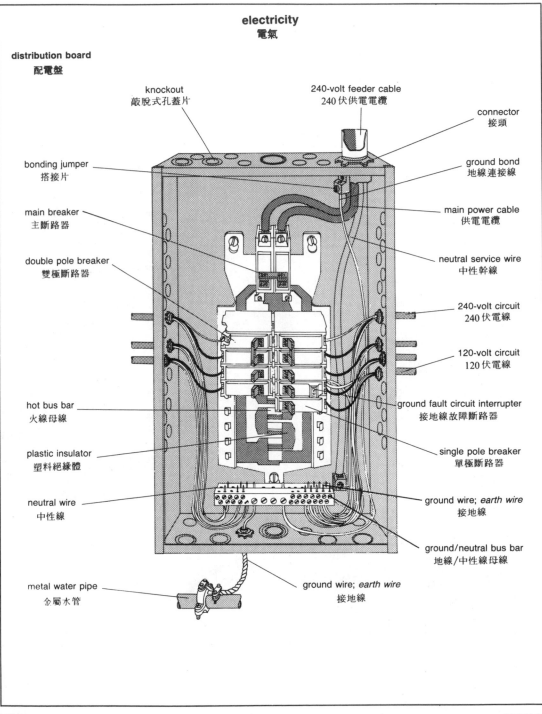

knockout
敲脫式孔蓋片

240-volt feeder cable
240 伏供電電纜

connector
接頭

bonding jumper
搭接片

ground bond
地線連接線

main power cable
供電電纜

main breaker
主斷路器

neutral service wire
中性幹線

double pole breaker
雙極斷路器

240-volt circuit
240 伏電線

120-volt circuit
120 伏電線

hot bus bar
火線母線

ground fault circuit interrupter
接地線故障斷路器

plastic insulator
塑料絕緣體

single pole breaker
單極斷路器

neutral wire
中性線

ground wire; *earth wire*
接地線

ground/neutral bus bar
地線/中性線母線

metal water pipe
金屬水管

ground wire; *earth wire*
接地線

CLOTHING

服装

men's clothing
男裝

trench coat
軍裝雨衣

raincoat
雨衣

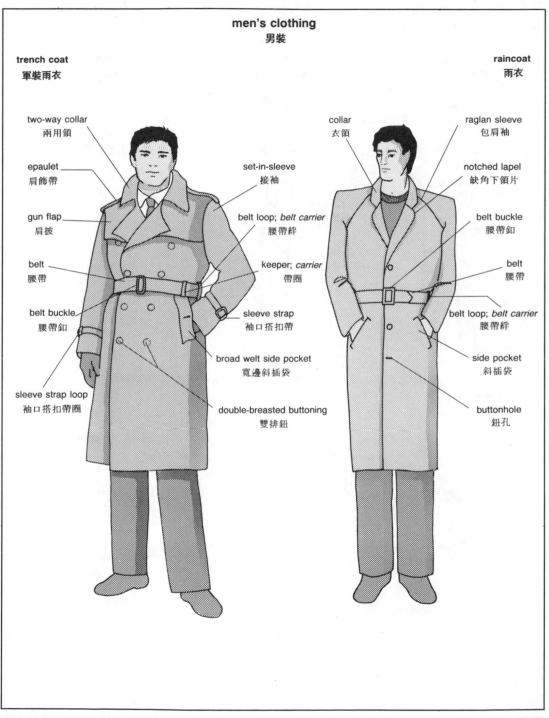

two-way collar
兩用領

epaulet
肩飾帶

gun flap
肩披

belt
腰帶

belt buckle
腰帶釦

sleeve strap loop
袖口搭扣帶圈

set-in-sleeve
接袖

belt loop; *belt carrier*
腰帶絆

keeper; *carrier*
帶圈

sleeve strap
袖口搭扣帶

broad welt side pocket
寬邊斜插袋

double-breasted buttoning
雙排鈕

collar
衣領

raglan sleeve
包肩袖

notched lapel
缺角下領片

belt buckle
腰帶釦

belt
腰帶

belt loop; *belt carrier*
腰帶絆

side pocket
斜插袋

buttonhole
鈕孔

men's clothing
男裝

sheepskin jacket
羊皮外套

duffle coat
連帽粗呢上衣

parka
風雪大衣

hood
兜帽

frog
盤花鈕釦

toggle fastening
鈕襻

flap pocket
有蓋口袋

drawstring
繫帽帶

inverness cape
披風大衣

overcoat
大衣

three-quarter coat
中長大衣

peaked lapel
尖角下領片

breast dart
腰褶

breast pocket
胸前口袋

flap pocket
有蓋口袋

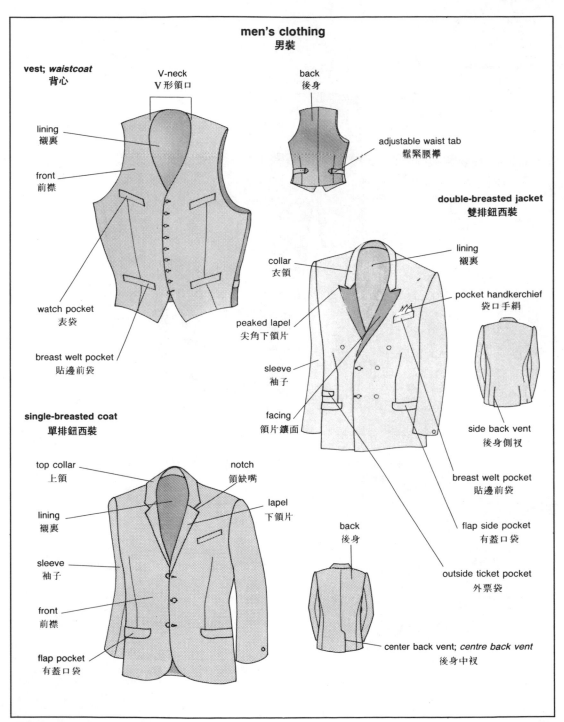

men's clothing
男裝

vest; *waistcoat*
背心

V-neck
V形領口

back
後身

lining
襯裏

adjustable waist tab
鬆緊腰襻

front
前襟

double-breasted jacket
雙排鈕西裝

collar
衣領

lining
襯裏

pocket handkerchief
袋口手絹

peaked lapel
尖角下領片

watch pocket
表袋

sleeve
袖子

breast welt pocket
貼邊前袋

facing
領片鑲面

side back vent
後身側裉

single-breasted coat
單排鈕西裝

top collar
上領

notch
領缺嘴

lapel
下領片

lining
襯裏

breast welt pocket
貼邊前袋

sleeve
袖子

back
後身

flap side pocket
有蓋口袋

front
前襟

outside ticket pocket
外票袋

flap pocket
有蓋口袋

center back vent; *centre back vent*
後身中裉

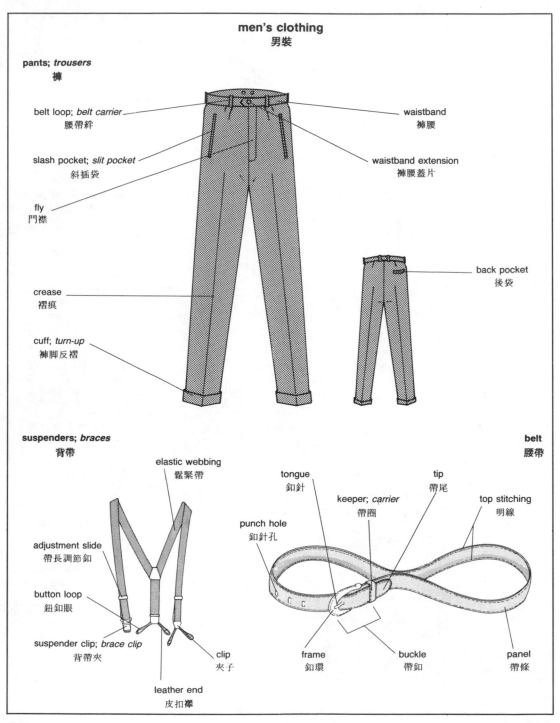

men's clothing
男裝

pants; *trousers*
褲

belt loop; *belt carrier*
腰帶絆

slash pocket; *slit pocket*
斜插袋

fly
門襟

crease
褶痕

cuff; *turn-up*
褲脚反褶

waistband
褲腰

waistband extension
褲腰蓋片

back pocket
後袋

suspenders; *braces*
背帶

elastic webbing
鬆緊帶

adjustment slide
帶長調節釦

button loop
鈕釦眼

suspender clip; *brace clip*
背帶夾

clip
夾子

leather end
皮扣襻

belt
腰帶

tongue
釦針

keeper; *carrier*
帶圈

punch hole
釦針孔

tip
帶尾

top stitching
明線

frame
釦環

buckle
帶釦

panel
帶條

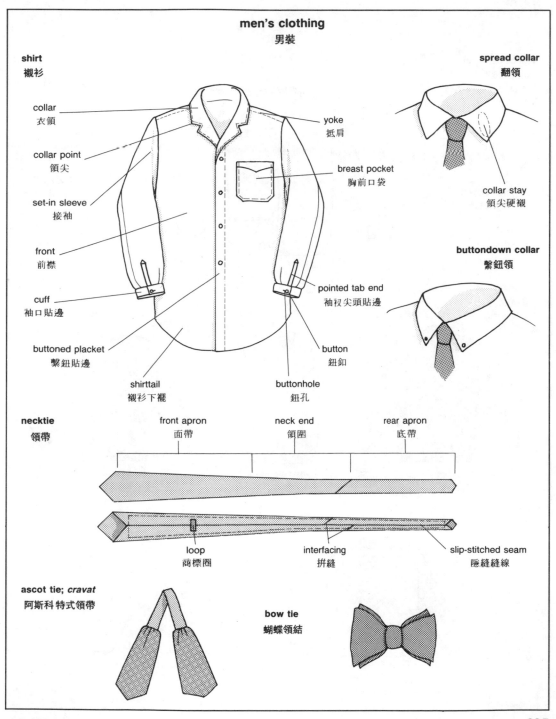

men's clothing
男裝

shirt
襯衫

collar
衣領

collar point
領尖

set-in sleeve
接袖

front
前襟

cuff
袖口貼邊

buttoned placket
繫鈕貼邊

shirttail
襯衫下襬

yoke
抵肩

breast pocket
胸前口袋

pointed tab end
袖衩尖頭貼邊

button
鈕釦

buttonhole
鈕孔

spread collar
翻領

collar stay
領尖硬襯

buttondown collar
繫鈕領

necktie
領帶

front apron
面帶

neck end
領圍

rear apron
底帶

loop
商標圈

interfacing
拼縫

slip-stitched seam
隱縫縫線

ascot tie; *cravat*
阿斯科特式領帶

bow tie
蝴蝶領結

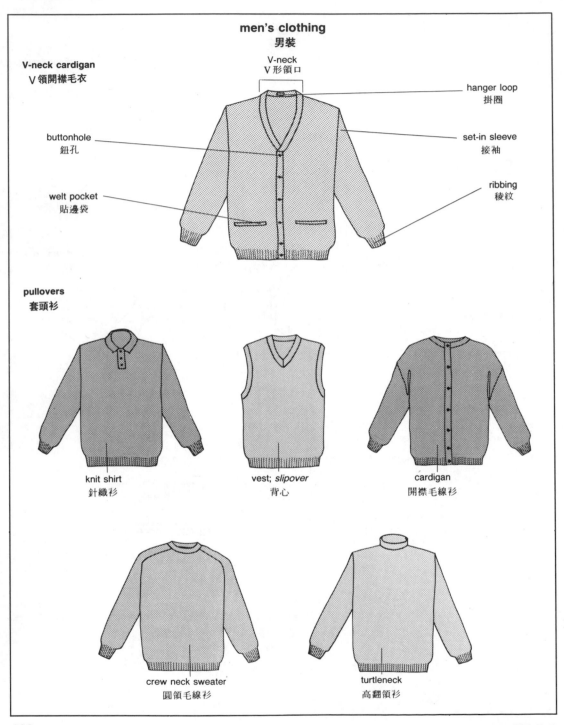

men's clothing
男裝

V-neck cardigan
Ｖ領開襟毛衣

V-neck
Ｖ形領口

hanger loop
掛圈

buttonhole
鈕孔

set-in sleeve
接袖

ribbing
稜紋

welt pocket
貼邊袋

pullovers
套頭衫

knit shirt
針織衫

vest; *slipover*
背心

cardigan
開襟毛線衫

crew neck sweater
圓領毛線衫

turtleneck
高翻領衫

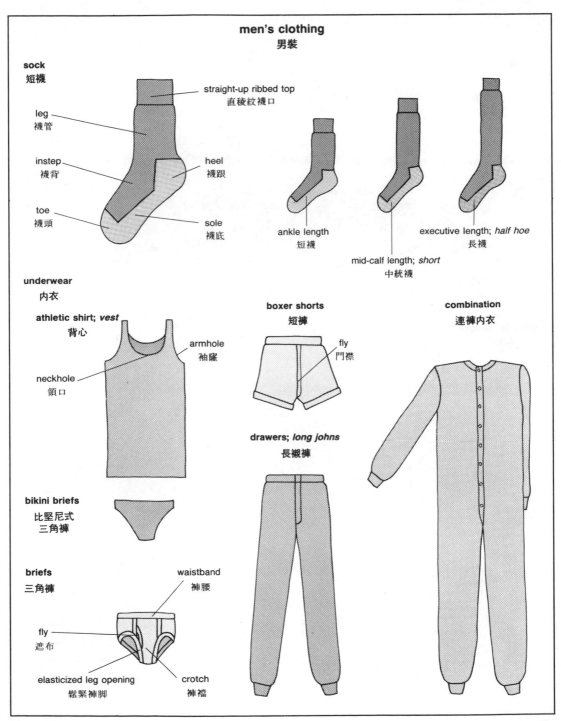

men's clothing
男裝

sock
短襪

leg
襪管

straight-up ribbed top
直稜紋襪口

instep
襪背

heel
襪跟

toe
襪頭

sole
襪底

ankle length
短襪

mid-calf length; *short*
中統襪

executive length; *half hoe*
長襪

underwear
內衣

athletic shirt; *vest*
背心

armhole
袖窿

neckhole
領口

boxer shorts
短褲

fly
門襟

combination
連褲內衣

bikini briefs
比堅尼式
三角褲

drawers; *long johns*
長襯褲

briefs
三角褲

waistband
褲腰

fly
遮布

elasticized leg opening
鬆緊褲腳

crotch
褲襠

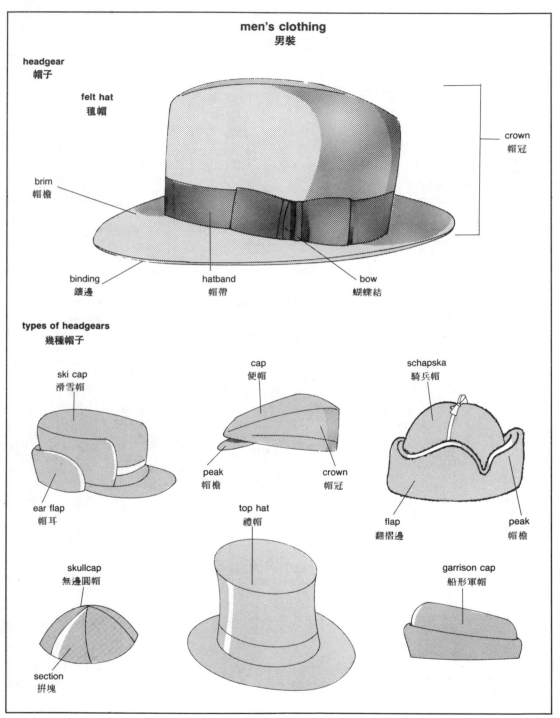

men's clothing
男裝

headgear
帽子

felt hat
氈帽

crown
帽冠

brim
帽檐

binding
鑲邊

hatband
帽帶

bow
蝴蝶結

types of headgears
幾種帽子

ski cap
滑雪帽

cap
便帽

schapska
騎兵帽

peak
帽檐

crown
帽冠

ear flap
帽耳

flap
翻摺邊

peak
帽檐

skullcap
無邊圓帽

top hat
禮帽

garrison cap
船形軍帽

section
拼塊

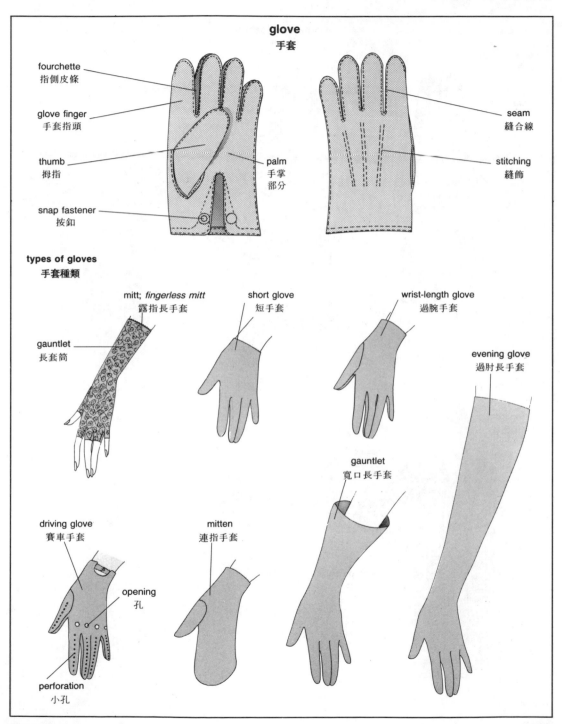

glove
手套

fourchette
指側皮條

glove finger
手套指頭

thumb
拇指

snap fastener
按鈕

palm
手掌
部分

seam
縫合線

stitching
縫飾

types of gloves
手套種類

mitt; *fingerless mitt*
露指長手套

gauntlet
長套筒

short glove
短手套

wrist-length glove
過腕手套

evening glove
過肘長手套

gauntlet
寬口長手套

driving glove
賽車手套

opening
孔

mitten
連指手套

perforation
小孔

women's clothing
女裝

coats
外衣

car coat
短大衣

raglan
包肩大衣

raglan sleeve
包肩袖

pelerine
披肩大衣

pelerine
披肩

broad welt
寬貼邊

patch pocket with turn-down flap
翻邊貼袋

fly front closing
暗門襟

seam pocket
縫線暗袋

top coat
薄大衣

seaming
裝飾縫

patch pocket
貼袋

back belt
後腰帶

women's clothing
女裝

coats
外衣

cape
斗篷

buttoned placket
繫鈕門襟

arm slit
伸手縫

tailored collar
西裝領

pea jacket
粗呢上衣

notched lapel
缺角下領片

hand warmer pocket
暖手插袋

mock pocket
假袋

double breasted buttoning
雙排鈕

poncho
套頭披肩

windbreaker; *windcheater*
防風上衣

windbreaker; *windcheater*
防風上衣

ribbing
稜紋

waistband
下襬貼邊

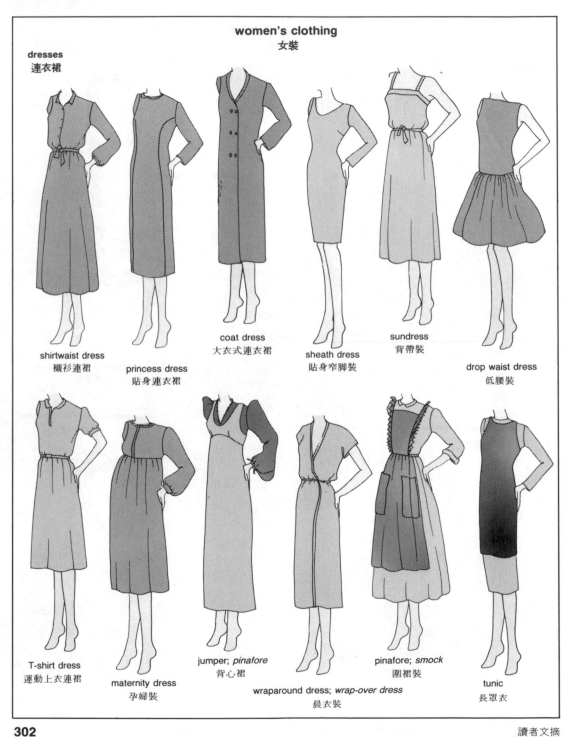

women's clothing
女裝

dresses
連衣裙

shirtwaist dress
襯衫連裙

princess dress
貼身連衣裙

coat dress
大衣式連衣裙

sheath dress
貼身窄脚裝

sundress
背帶裝

drop waist dress
低腰裝

T-shirt dress
運動上衣連裙

maternity dress
孕婦裝

jumper; *pinafore*
背心裙

wraparound dress; *wrap-over dress*
晨衣裝

pinafore; *smock*
圍裙裝

tunic
長罩衣

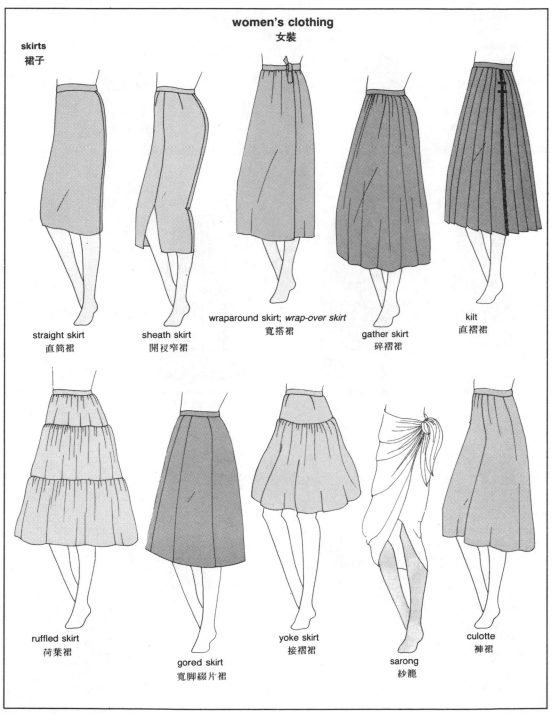

women's clothing
女裝

skirts
裙子

straight skirt
直筒裙

sheath skirt
開衩窄裙

wraparound skirt; *wrap-over skirt*
寬搭裙

gather skirt
碎褶裙

kilt
直褶裙

ruffled skirt
荷葉裙

gored skirt
寬腳綴片裙

yoke skirt
接褶裙

sarong
紗籠

culotte
褲裙

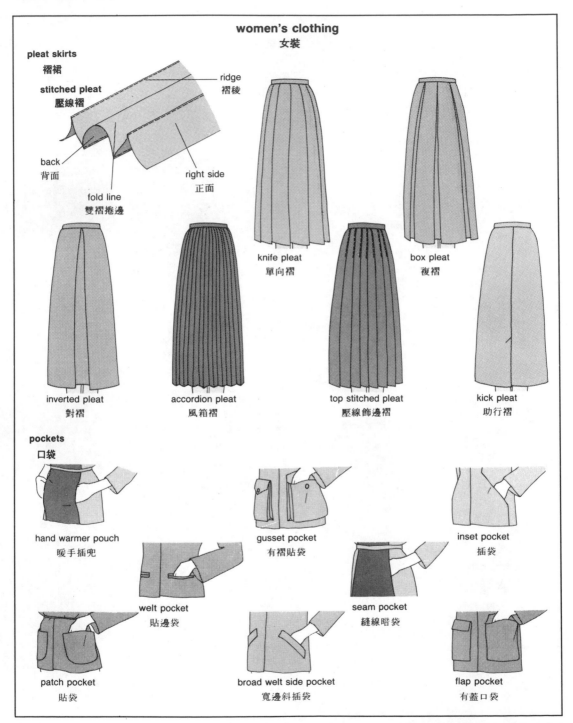

women's clothing
女裝

pleat skirts
褶裙

stitched pleat
壓線褶

ridge
褶稜

back
背面

right side
正面

fold line
雙褶捲邊

knife pleat
單向褶

box pleat
複褶

inverted pleat
對褶

accordion pleat
風箱褶

top stitched pleat
壓線飾邊褶

kick pleat
助行褶

pockets
口袋

hand warmer pouch
暖手插兜

gusset pocket
有褶貼袋

inset pocket
插袋

welt pocket
貼邊袋

seam pocket
縫線暗袋

patch pocket
貼袋

broad welt side pocket
寬邊斜插袋

flap pocket
有蓋口袋

women's clothing
女裝

blouses
上衣

classic
傳統式

tunic; *smock*
寬鬆長上衣

middy; *sailor tunic*
水手裝

yoke
抵肩

gather
褶裥

smock; *button-through smock*
罩衫

buttoned placket
繫鈕襟

breast pocket
胸前口袋

polo shirt; *T-shirt*
運動衫

wrap over top; *wrap-over top*
無領疊襟衫

bottom of collar
領底

shirt collar
襯衫領

shirttail
襯衫下襬

shirt sleeve
襯衫袖

crotch piece
褲襠片

over-blouse; *tunic*
長罩衫

mini shirtdress; *overshirt*
連短裙上衣

body shirt
緊身衣褲

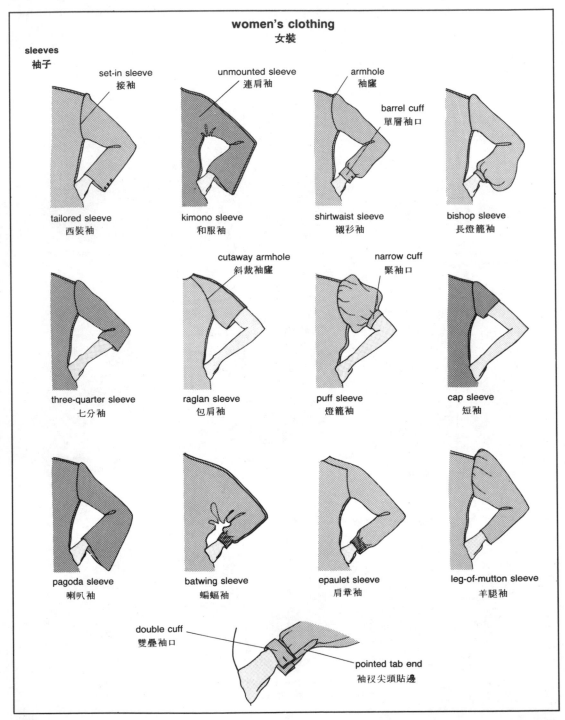

women's clothing
女裝

sleeves
袖子

set-in sleeve
接袖

tailored sleeve
西裝袖

unmounted sleeve
連肩袖

kimono sleeve
和服袖

armhole
袖窿

barrel cuff
單層袖口

shirtwaist sleeve
襯衫袖

bishop sleeve
長燈籠袖

three-quarter sleeve
七分袖

cutaway armhole
斜裁袖窿

raglan sleeve
包肩袖

narrow cuff
緊袖口

puff sleeve
燈籠袖

cap sleeve
短袖

pagoda sleeve
喇叭袖

batwing sleeve
蝙蝠袖

epaulet sleeve
肩章袖

leg-of-mutton sleeve
羊腿袖

double cuff
雙疊袖口

pointed tab end
袖衩尖頭貼邊

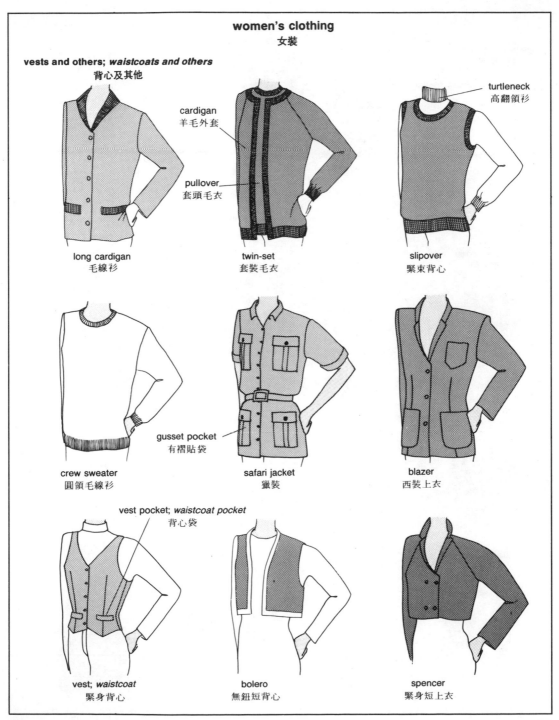

women's clothing
女裝

vests and others; *waistcoats and others*
背心及其他

cardigan
羊毛外套

pullover
套頭毛衣

turtleneck
高翻領衫

long cardigan
毛線衫

twin-set
套裝毛衣

slipover
緊束背心

crew sweater
圓領毛線衫

gusset pocket
有褶貼袋

safari jacket
獵裝

blazer
西裝上衣

vest pocket; *waistcoat pocket*
背心袋

vest; *waistcoat*
緊身背心

bolero
無鈕短背心

spencer
緊身短上衣

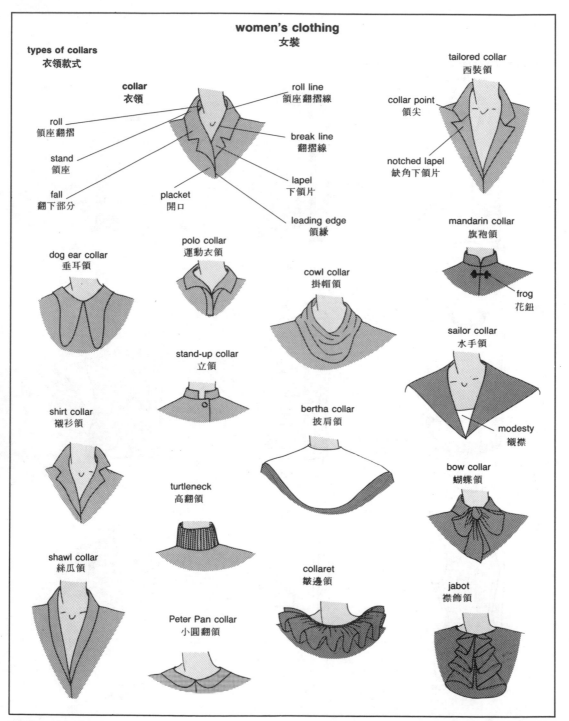

women's clothing
女裝

types of collars
衣領款式

collar
衣領

roll
領座翻摺

stand
領座

fall
翻下部分

roll line
領座翻摺線

break line
翻摺線

lapel
下領片

placket
開口

leading edge
領緣

tailored collar
西裝領

collar point
領尖

notched lapel
缺角下領片

dog ear collar
垂耳領

polo collar
運動衣領

cowl collar
掛帽領

mandarin collar
旗袍領

frog
花鈕

stand-up collar
立領

sailor collar
水手領

shirt collar
襯衫領

bertha collar
披肩領

modesty
襯襟

turtleneck
高翻領

bow collar
蝴蝶領

shawl collar
絲瓜領

collaret
皺邊領

Peter Pan collar
小圓翻領

jabot
襟飾領

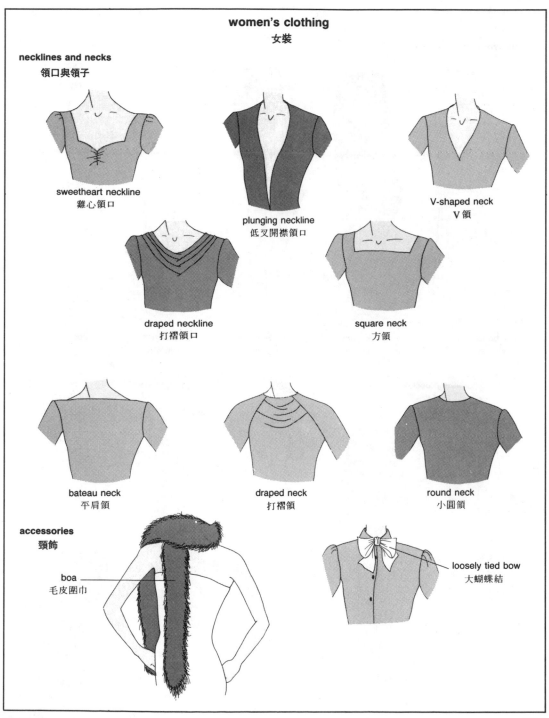

women's clothing
女裝

necklines and necks
領口與領子

sweetheart neckline
雞心領口

plunging neckline
低叉開襟領口

V-shaped neck
V領

draped neckline
打褶領口

square neck
方領

bateau neck
平肩領

draped neck
打褶領

round neck
小圓領

accessories
頸飾

boa
毛皮圍巾

loosely tied bow
大蝴蝶結

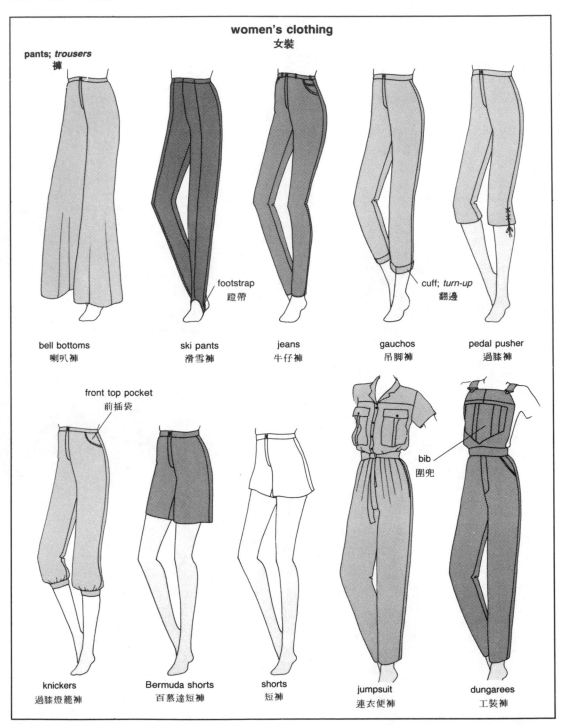

women's clothing
女裝

pants; *trousers*
褲

footstrap
蹬帶

cuff; *turn-up*
翻邊

bell bottoms
喇叭褲

ski pants
滑雪褲

jeans
牛仔褲

gauchos
吊脚褲

pedal pusher
過膝褲

front top pocket
前插袋

bib
圍兜

knickers
過膝燈籠褲

Bermuda shorts
百慕達短褲

shorts
短褲

jumpsuit
連衣便褲

dungarees
工裝褲

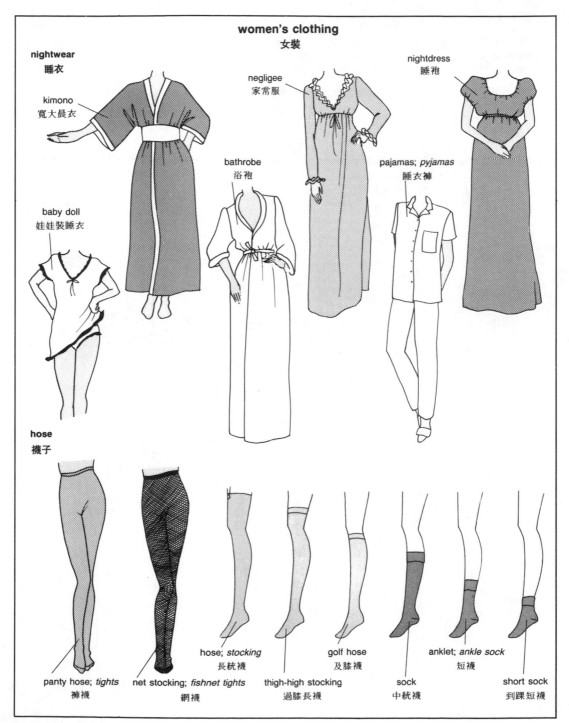

women's clothing
女裝

nightwear
睡衣

kimono
寬大晨衣

baby doll
娃娃裝睡衣

negligee
家常服

bathrobe
浴袍

nightdress
睡袍

pajamas; *pyjamas*
睡衣褲

hose
襪子

panty hose; *tights*
褲襪

net stocking; *fishnet tights*
網襪

hose; *stocking*
長統襪

thigh-high stocking
過膝長襪

golf hose
及膝襪

sock
中統襪

anklet; *ankle sock*
短襪

short sock
到踝短襪

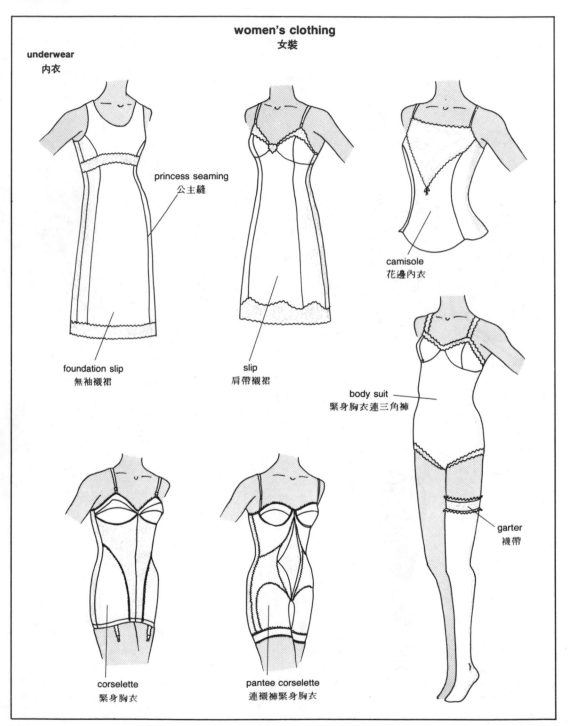

women's clothing
女裝

underwear
內衣

princess seaming
公主縫

foundation slip
無袖襯裙

slip
肩帶襯裙

camisole
花邊內衣

body suit
緊身胸衣連三角褲

garter
襪帶

corselette
緊身胸衣

pantee corselette
連襯褲緊身胸衣

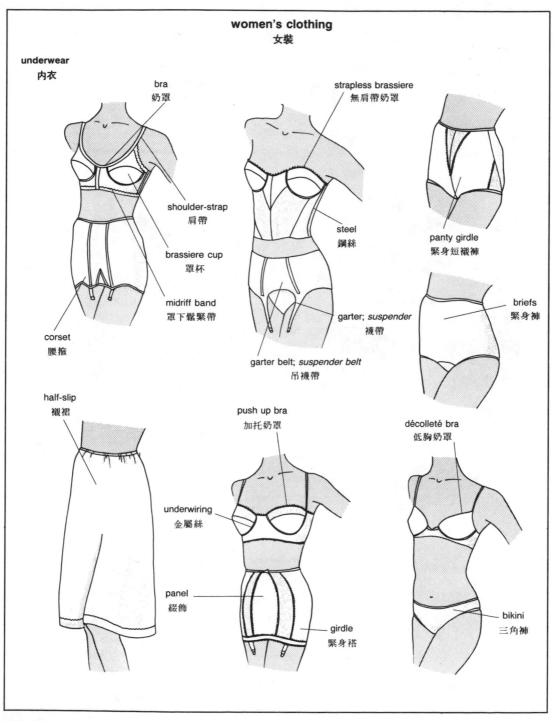

women's clothing
女裝

underwear
内衣

bra
奶罩

shoulder-strap
肩帶

brassiere cup
罩杯

midriff band
罩下鬆緊帶

corset
腰箍

strapless brassiere
無肩帶奶罩

steel
鋼絲

garter; *suspender*
襪帶

garter belt; *suspender belt*
吊襪帶

panty girdle
緊身短襯褲

briefs
緊身褲

half-slip
襯裙

push up bra
加托奶罩

underwiring
金屬絲

panel
綴飾

girdle
緊身褡

décolleté bra
低胸奶罩

bikini
三角褲

women's clothing
女裝

headgear
帽子和頭巾

fur hood
風雪帽

balaclava
兜帽

stocking cap
毛線帽

kerchief
頭巾

pompom
絨球

head band
束頭帶

tam-o'-shanter
蘇格蘭便帽

string
繫帽帶

southwester
雨帽

crown
帽冠

brim
帽檐

gob hat
軟邊帽

toque
無檐軟帽

hat veil
帽子
面紗

pillbox hat
圓盒形小帽

mob-cap
室內便帽

turban
頭巾帽

boater
平頂硬草帽

cartwheel hat
闊邊帽

felt hat; *trilby*
氈帽

cap
便帽

beret
貝雷帽

cloche
鐘形帽

children's clothing
童裝

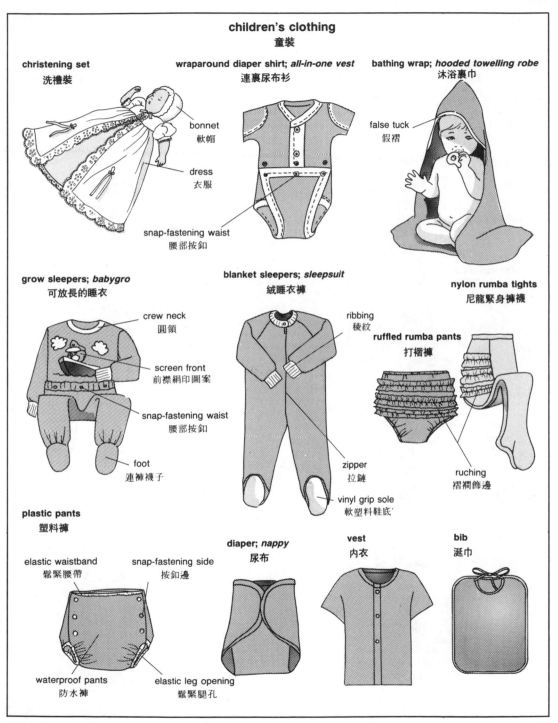

christening set
洗禮裝

bonnet
軟帽

dress
衣服

snap-fastening waist
腰部按鈕

wraparound diaper shirt; *all-in-one vest*
連裹尿布衫

bathing wrap; *hooded towelling robe*
沐浴裹巾

false tuck
假褶

grow sleepers; *babygro*
可放長的睡衣

crew neck
圓領

screen front
前襟絹印圖案

snap-fastening waist
腰部按鈕

foot
連褲襪子

blanket sleepers; *sleepsuit*
絨睡衣褲

ribbing
稜紋

zipper
拉鏈

vinyl grip sole
軟塑料鞋底

nylon rumba tights
尼龍緊身褲襪

ruffled rumba pants
打褶褲

ruching
褶襉飾邊

plastic pants
塑料褲

elastic waistband
鬆緊腰帶

snap-fastening side
按鈕邊

waterproof pants
防水褲

elastic leg opening
鬆緊腿孔

diaper; *nappy*
尿布

vest
内衣

bib
涎巾

children's clothing
童裝

crossover back straps dungarees
交叉背帶褲

high-back dungarees
高背背帶褲

button strap
繫釦帶

snap-fastening adjustable strap
可調長短的按釦帶

bib
圍兜

zipper
拉鏈

top stitching
明線

rope belt
繩帶

patch pocket
貼袋

belt loop; *belt carrier*
腰帶絆

inside-leg snap-fastening
按釦內縫

ribbing
稜紋

jumpsuit
連衣便褲

snap-fastening shoulder strap
肩部按釦

sleeper; *sleeping-suit*
睡衣

bunting bag
嬰兒暖套

raglan sleeve
包肩袖

screen print
絹印圖案

ribbing
稜紋

vest
貼身衣

snap-fastening front
前面按釦

foot
連褲襪子

inside-leg snap-fastening
按釦內縫

vinyl grip sole
軟塑料鞋底

children's clothing
童裝

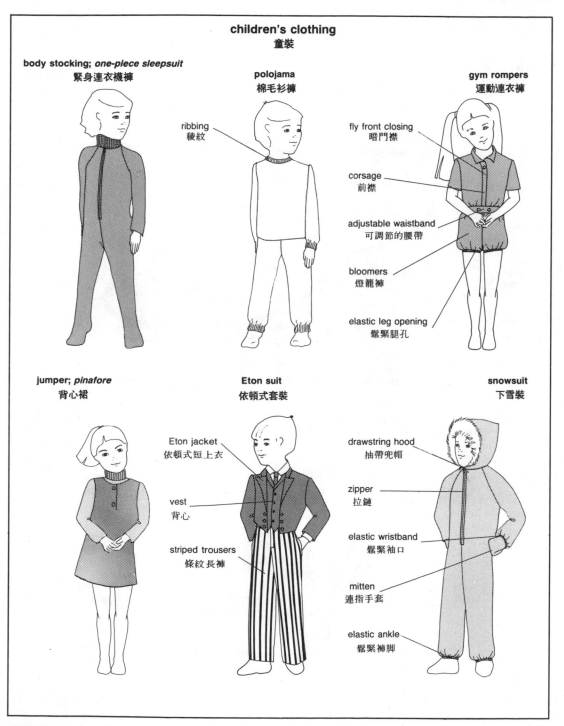

body stocking; *one-piece sleepsuit*
緊身連衣襪褲

polojama
棉毛衫褲

ribbing
稜紋

gym rompers
運動連衣褲

fly front closing
暗門襟

corsage
前襟

adjustable waistband
可調節的腰帶

bloomers
燈籠褲

elastic leg opening
鬆緊腿孔

jumper; *pinafore*
背心裙

Eton suit
依頓式套裝

Eton jacket
依頓式短上衣

vest
背心

striped trousers
條紋長褲

snowsuit
下雪裝

drawstring hood
抽帶兜帽

zipper
拉鏈

elastic wristband
鬆緊袖口

mitten
連指手套

elastic ankle
鬆緊褲脚

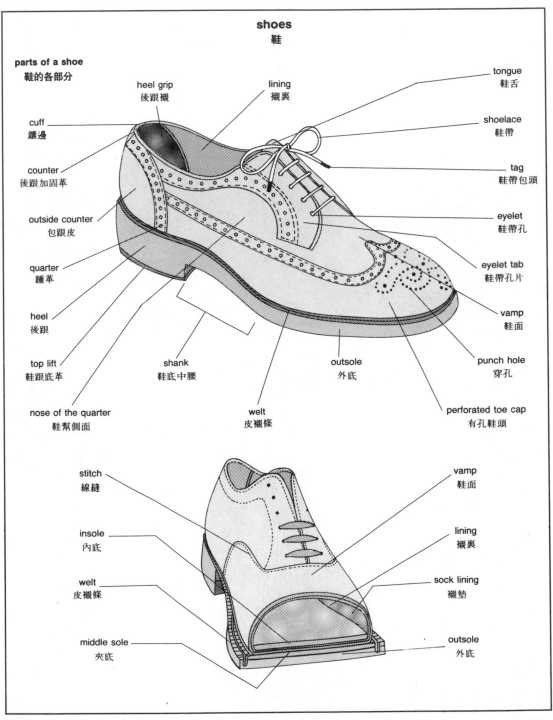

shoes
鞋

parts of a shoe
鞋的各部分

heel grip
後跟襯

lining
襯裏

tongue
鞋舌

cuff
鑲邊

shoelace
鞋帶

counter
後跟加固革

tag
鞋帶包頭

outside counter
包跟皮

eyelet
鞋帶孔

quarter
踵革

eyelet tab
鞋帶孔片

heel
後跟

vamp
鞋面

top lift
鞋跟底革

shank
鞋底中腰

outsole
外底

punch hole
穿孔

nose of the quarter
鞋幫側面

welt
皮襯條

perforated toe cap
有孔鞋頭

stitch
線縫

vamp
鞋面

insole
內底

lining
襯裏

welt
皮襯條

sock lining
襯墊

middle sole
夾底

outsole
外底

shoes
鞋

principal types of shoes
各種常見的鞋

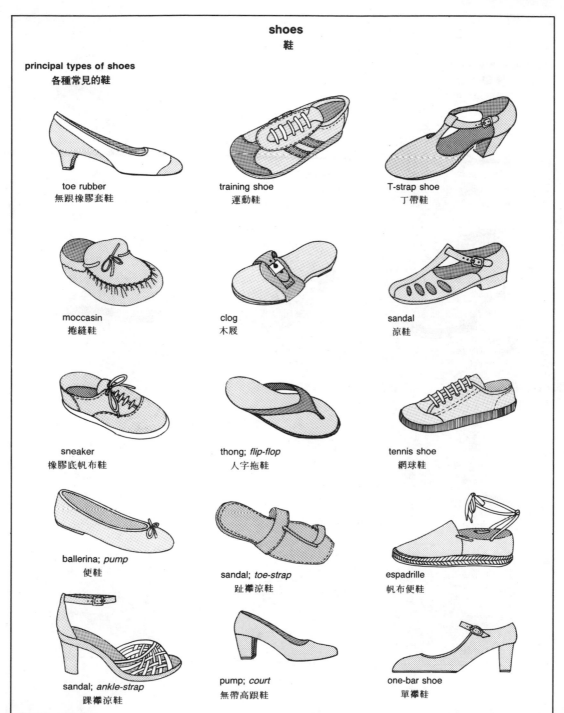

toe rubber
無跟橡膠套鞋

training shoe
運動鞋

T-strap shoe
丁帶鞋

moccasin
捲縫鞋

clog
木屐

sandal
涼鞋

sneaker
橡膠底帆布鞋

thong; *flip-flop*
人字拖鞋

tennis shoe
網球鞋

ballerina; *pump*
便鞋

sandal; *toe-strap*
趾襻涼鞋

espadrille
帆布便鞋

sandal; *ankle-strap*
踝襻涼鞋

pump; *court*
無帶高跟鞋

one-bar shoe
單襻鞋

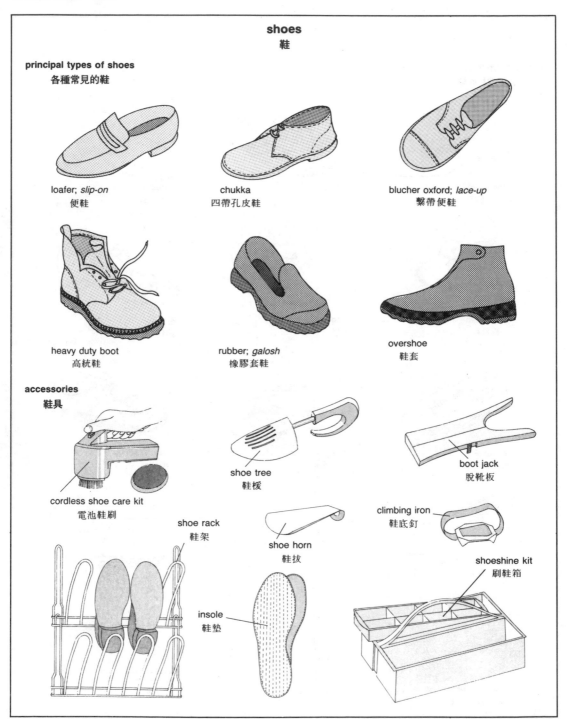

shoes
鞋

principal types of shoes
各種常見的鞋

loafer; *slip-on*
便鞋

chukka
四帶孔皮鞋

blucher oxford; *lace-up*
繫帶便鞋

heavy duty boot
高統鞋

rubber; *galosh*
橡膠套鞋

overshoe
鞋套

accessories
鞋具

cordless shoe care kit
電池鞋刷

shoe tree
鞋楦

boot jack
脫靴板

shoe rack
鞋架

shoe horn
鞋拔

climbing iron
鞋底釘

shoeshine kit
刷鞋箱

insole
鞋墊

costumes
特殊服裝

bullfighter
門牛裝

shirt
襯衫

tie
領帶

vest
背心

sash
腰帶

frog
綴飾

pants
褲

tassel
繐

pink stocking
粉紅色襪

slippers
淺口便鞋

ballet slippers
芭蕾舞鞋

drawstring
抽緊帶

sole
鞋底

hat
帽子

pigtail
辮子

epaulet
肩飾

jacket
外套

cape
斗篷

ballerina
芭蕾舞裝

tights
褲襪

ribbon
繫帶

tutu
芭蕾舞裙

toe
鞋頭

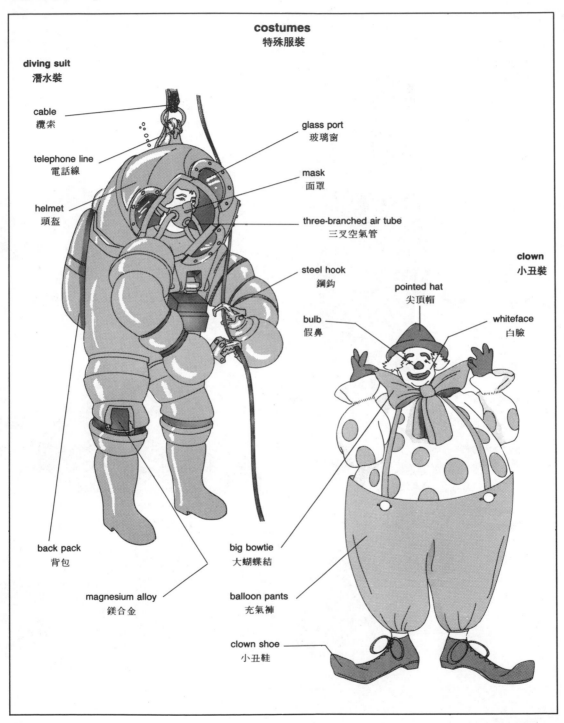

costumes
特殊服裝

diving suit
潛水裝

cable
纜索

telephone line
電話線

helmet
頭盔

glass port
玻璃窗

mask
面罩

three-branched air tube
三叉空氣管

steel hook
鋼鈎

clown
小丑裝

pointed hat
尖頂帽

whiteface
白臉

bulb
假鼻

back pack
背包

magnesium alloy
鎂合金

big bowtie
大蝴蝶結

balloon pants
充氣褲

clown shoe
小丑鞋

PERSONAL ADORNMENT
儀容修飾

jewelry; *jewellery*
珠寶飾物

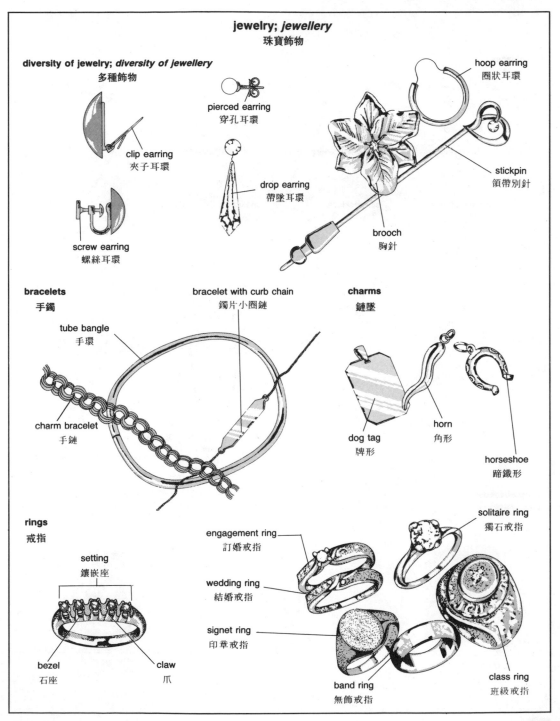

diversity of jewelry; *diversity of jewellery*
多種飾物

pierced earring
穿孔耳環

hoop earring
圈狀耳環

clip earring
夾子耳環

drop earring
帶墜耳環

stickpin
領帶別針

screw earring
螺絲耳環

brooch
胸針

bracelets
手鐲

bracelet with curb chain
鐲片小圈鏈

charms
鏈墜

tube bangle
手環

charm bracelet
手鏈

dog tag
牌形

horn
角形

horseshoe
蹄鐵形

rings
戒指

solitaire ring
獨石戒指

engagement ring
訂婚戒指

setting
鑲嵌座

wedding ring
結婚戒指

signet ring
印章戒指

bezel
石座

claw
爪

band ring
無飾戒指

class ring
班級戒指

jewelry; *jewellery*
珠寶飾物

necklaces
項鏈

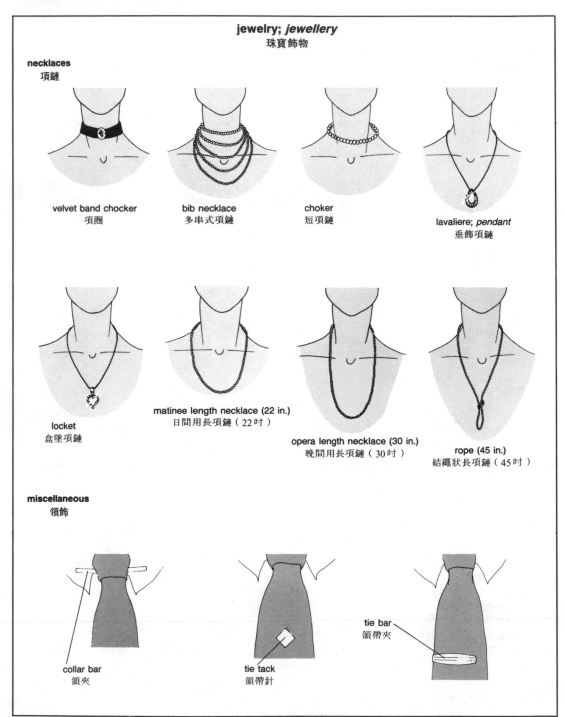

velvet band chocker
項圈

bib necklace
多串式項鏈

choker
短項鏈

lavaliere; *pendant*
垂飾項鏈

locket
盒墜項鏈

matinee length necklace (22 in.)
日間用長項鏈（22吋）

opera length necklace (30 in.)
晚間用長項鏈（30吋）

rope (45 in.)
結繩狀長項鏈（45吋）

miscellaneous
領飾

collar bar
領夾

tie tack
領帶針

tie bar
領帶夾

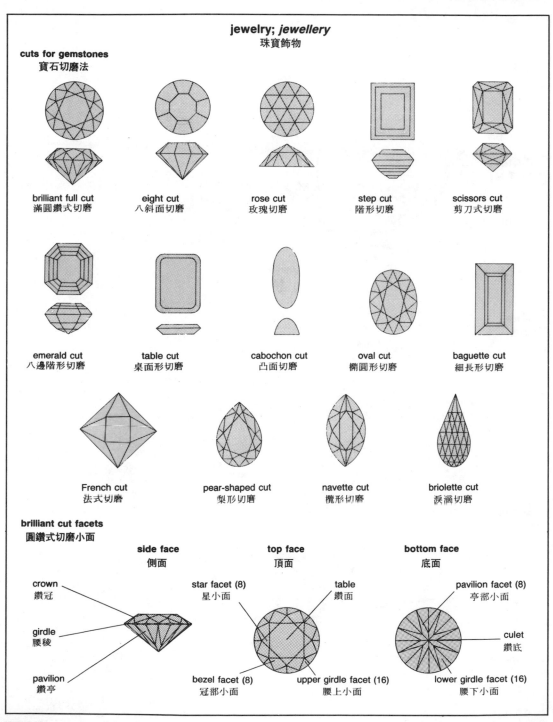

jewelry; *jewellery*
珠寶飾物

cuts for gemstones
寶石切磨法

brilliant full cut
滿圓鑽式切磨

eight cut
八斜面切磨

rose cut
玫瑰切磨

step cut
階形切磨

scissors cut
剪刀式切磨

emerald cut
八邊階形切磨

table cut
桌面形切磨

cabochon cut
凸面切磨

oval cut
橢圓形切磨

baguette cut
細長形切磨

French cut
法式切磨

pear-shaped cut
梨形切磨

navette cut
欖形切磨

briolette cut
淚滴切磨

brilliant cut facets
圓鑽式切磨小面

side face
側面

top face
頂面

bottom face
底面

crown
鑽冠

girdle
腰稜

pavilion
鑽亭

star facet (8)
星小面

table
鑽面

bezel facet (8)
冠部小面

upper girdle facet (16)
腰上小面

pavilion facet (8)
亭部小面

culet
鑽底

lower girdle facet (16)
腰下小面

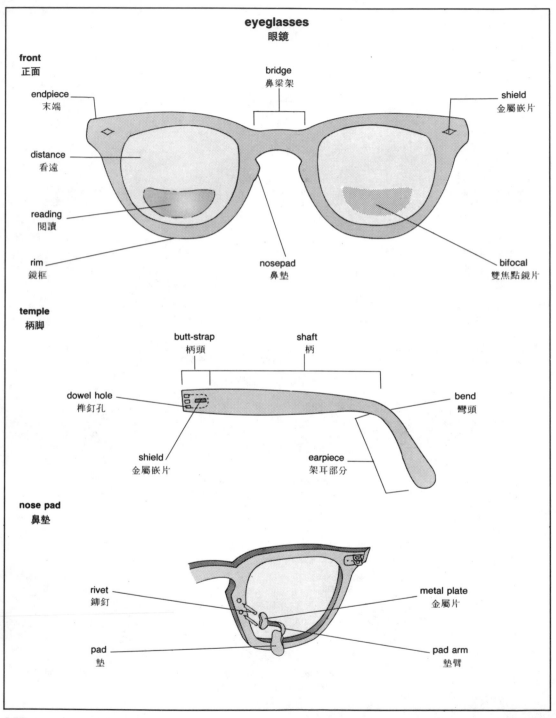

eyeglasses
眼鏡

front
正面

endpiece
末端

bridge
鼻梁架

shield
金屬嵌片

distance
看遠

reading
閱讀

rim
鏡框

nosepad
鼻墊

bifocal
雙焦點鏡片

temple
柄脚

butt-strap
柄頭

shaft
柄

dowel hole
榫釘孔

bend
彎頭

shield
金屬嵌片

earpiece
架耳部分

nose pad
鼻墊

rivet
鉚釘

metal plate
金屬片

pad
墊

pad arm
墊臂

eyeglasses
眼鏡

principal types of eyeglasses
各種常見的眼鏡

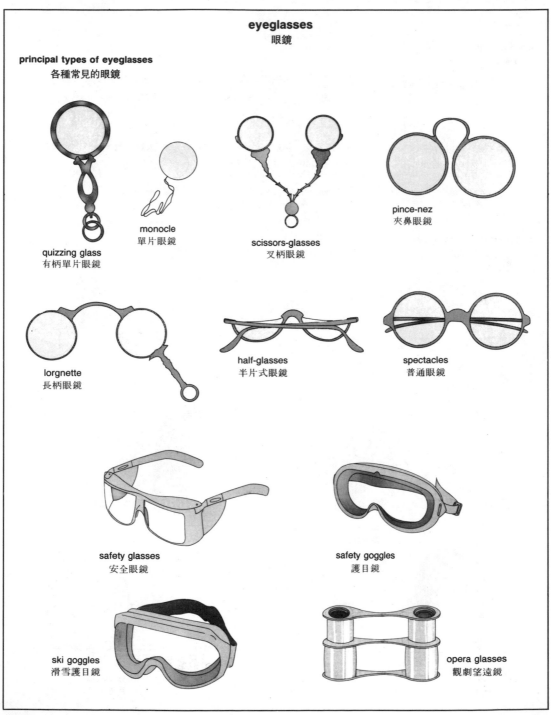

quizzing glass
有柄單片眼鏡

monocle
單片眼鏡

scissors-glasses
叉柄眼鏡

pince-nez
夾鼻眼鏡

lorgnette
長柄眼鏡

half-glasses
半片式眼鏡

spectacles
普通眼鏡

safety glasses
安全眼鏡

safety goggles
護目鏡

ski goggles
滑雪護目鏡

opera glasses
觀劇望遠鏡

hair styles
髮型

kinds of hair
頭髮類型

straight hair
直髮

wavy hair
曲髮

curly hair
鬈髮

components of hair styles
常見髮型

bun
髻

bouffant
蓬蓬頭

page boy
清湯掛麵

corkscrew curls
螺旋鬈

braids
辮子頭

pigtails
雙辮子

pony tail
馬尾

fingerwaves
指捲波紋

hair styles
髮型

components of hair styles
常見髮型

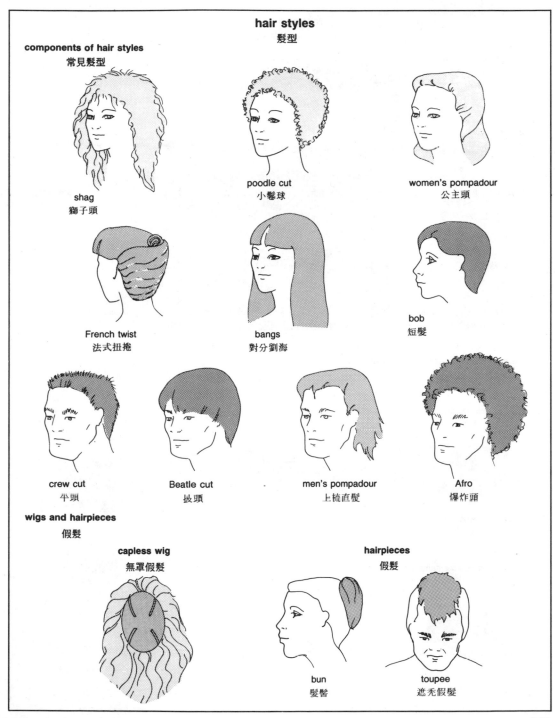

shag
獅子頭

poodle cut
小鬈球

women's pompadour
公主頭

French twist
法式扭捲

bangs
對分劉海

bob
短髮

crew cut
平頭

Beatle cut
披頭

men's pompadour
上梳直髮

Afro
爆炸頭

wigs and hairpieces
假髮

capless wig
無罩假髮

hairpieces
假髮

bun
髮髻

toupee
遮禿假髮

makeup; *make-up*
化妝品

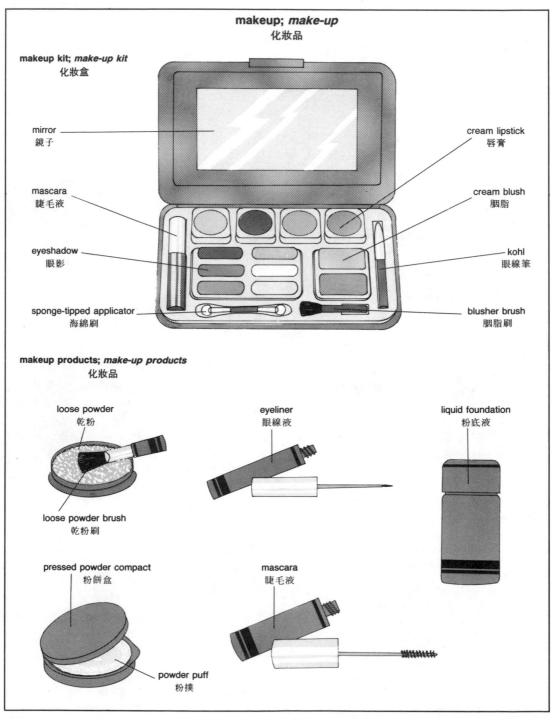

makeup kit; *make-up kit*
化妝盒

mirror
鏡子

cream lipstick
唇膏

mascara
睫毛液

cream blush
胭脂

eyeshadow
眼影

kohl
眼線筆

sponge-tipped applicator
海綿刷

blusher brush
胭脂刷

makeup products; *make-up products*
化妝品

loose powder
乾粉

eyeliner
眼線液

liquid foundation
粉底液

loose powder brush
乾粉刷

pressed powder compact
粉餅盒

mascara
睫毛液

powder puff
粉撲

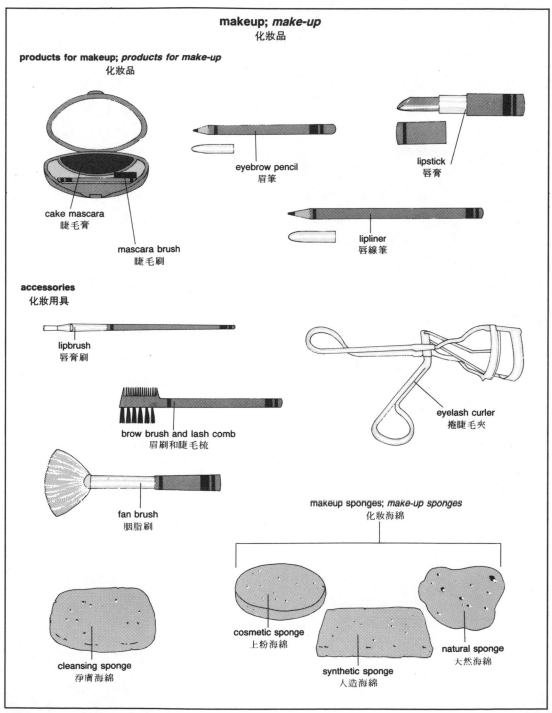

makeup; *make-up*
化妝品

products for makeup; *products for make-up*
化妝品

eyebrow pencil
眉筆

lipstick
唇膏

cake mascara
睫毛膏

mascara brush
睫毛刷

lipliner
唇線筆

accessories
化妝用具

lipbrush
唇膏刷

brow brush and lash comb
眉刷和睫毛梳

eyelash curler
捲睫毛夾

fan brush
胭脂刷

makeup sponges; *make-up sponges*
化妝海綿

cosmetic sponge
上粉海綿

natural sponge
大然海綿

synthetic sponge
人造海綿

cleansing sponge
淨膚海綿

PERSONAL ARTICLES

個人用品

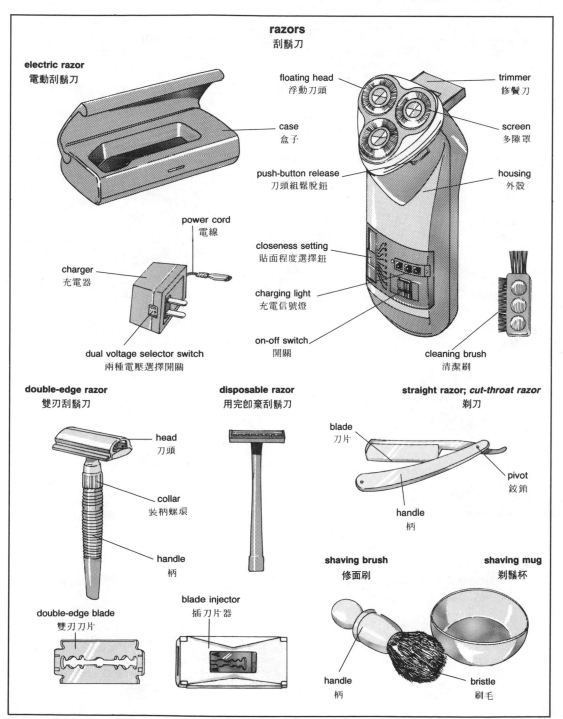

razors
刮鬍刀

electric razor
電動刮鬍刀

floating head
浮動刀頭

trimmer
修鬢刀

case
盒子

screen
多隙罩

push-button release
刀頭組鬆脫鈕

housing
外殼

power cord
電線

closeness setting
貼面程度選擇鈕

charger
充電器

charging light
充電信號燈

cleaning brush
清潔刷

dual voltage selector switch
兩種電壓選擇開關

on-off switch
開關

double-edge razor
雙刃刮鬍刀

head
刀頭

collar
裝柄蝶墊

handle
柄

disposable razor
用完卽棄刮鬍刀

straight razor; _cut-throat razor_
剃刀

blade
刀片

pivot
鉸銷

handle
柄

double-edge blade
雙刃刀片

blade injector
插刀片器

shaving brush
修面刷

shaving mug
剃鬍杯

handle
柄

bristle
刷毛

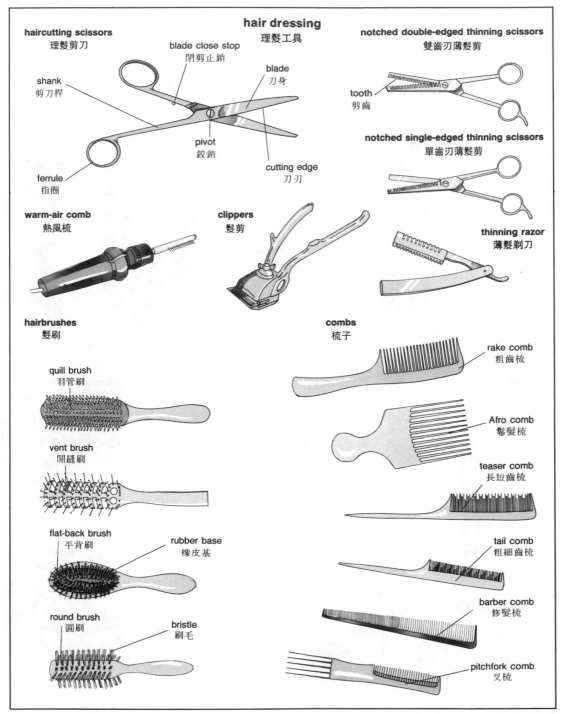

hair dressing
理髮工具

haircutting scissors
理髮剪刀

blade close stop
閉剪止銷

blade
刀身

shank
剪刀桿

pivot
鉸銷

ferrule
指圈

cutting edge
刀刃

notched double-edged thinning scissors
雙齒刃薄髮剪

tooth
剪齒

notched single-edged thinning scissors
單齒刃薄髮剪

warm-air comb
熱風梳

clippers
髮剪

thinning razor
薄髮剃刀

hairbrushes
髮刷

combs
梳子

quill brush
羽管刷

vent brush
開縫刷

flat-back brush
平背刷

rubber base
橡皮基

round brush
圓刷

bristle
刷毛

rake comb
粗齒梳

Afro comb
鬆髮梳

teaser comb
長短齒梳

tail comb
粗細齒梳

barber comb
修髮梳

pitchfork comb
叉梳

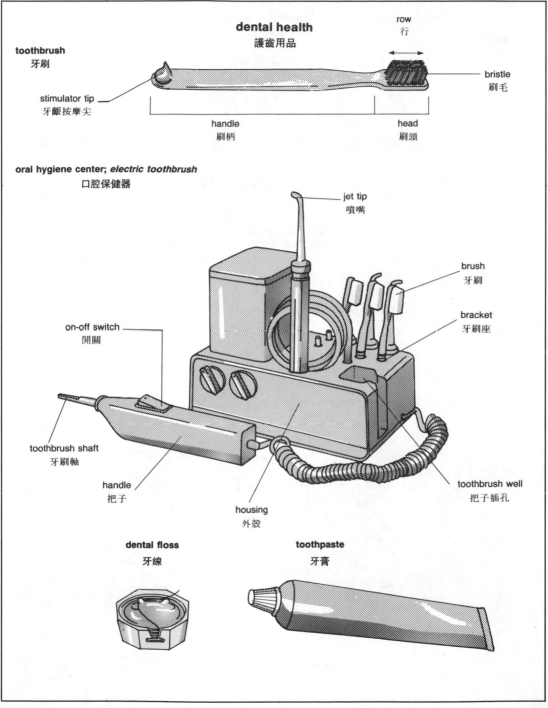

dental health
護齒用品

toothbrush
牙刷

row
行

bristle
刷毛

stimulator tip
牙齦按摩尖

handle
刷柄

head
刷頭

oral hygiene center; *electric toothbrush*
口腔保健器

jet tip
噴嘴

brush
牙刷

bracket
牙刷座

on-off switch
開關

toothbrush shaft
牙刷軸

handle
把子

housing
外殼

toothbrush well
把子插孔

dental floss
牙線

toothpaste
牙膏

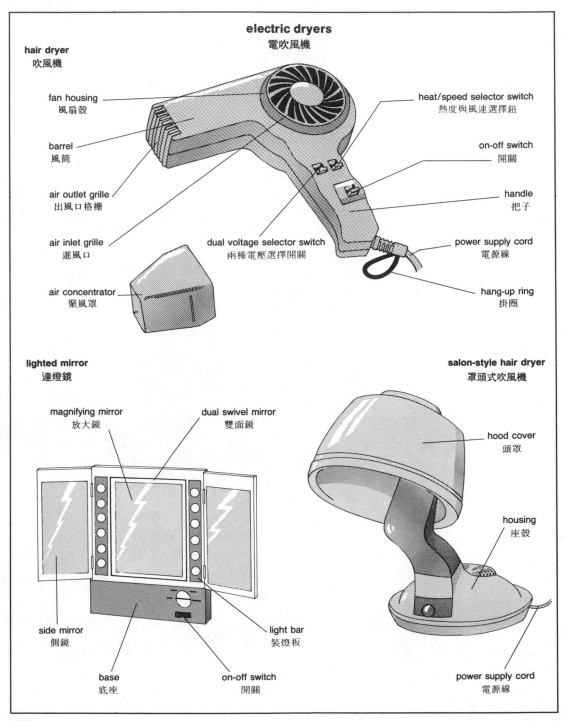

electric dryers
電吹風機

hair dryer
吹風機

fan housing
風扇殼

barrel
風筒

air outlet grille
出風口格柵

air inlet grille
進風口

air concentrator
聚風罩

dual voltage selector switch
兩種電壓選擇開關

heat/speed selector switch
熱度與風速選擇鈕

on-off switch
開關

handle
把子

power supply cord
電源線

hang-up ring
掛圈

lighted mirror
連燈鏡

magnifying mirror
放大鏡

dual swivel mirror
雙面鏡

side mirror
側鏡

base
底座

on-off switch
開關

light bar
裝燈板

salon-style hair dryer
罩頭式吹風機

hood cover
頭罩

housing
座殼

power supply cord
電源線

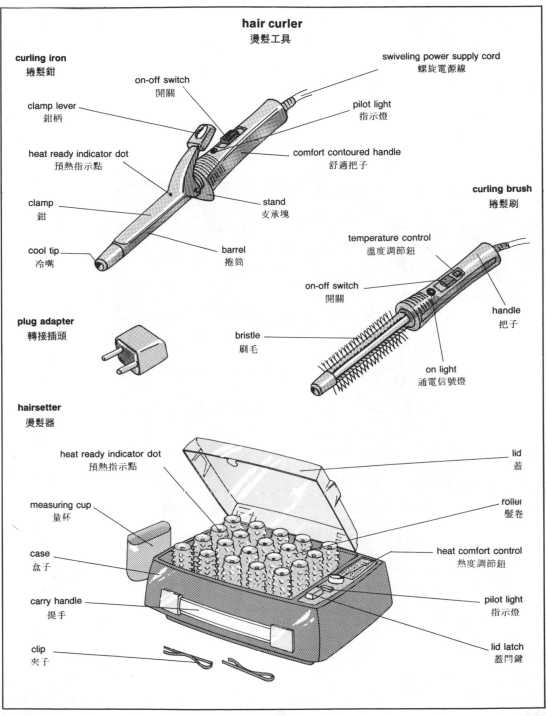

hair curler
燙髮工具

curling iron
捲髮鉗

on-off switch
開關

swiveling power supply cord
螺旋電源線

clamp lever
鉗柄

pilot light
指示燈

heat ready indicator dot
預熱指示點

comfort contoured handle
舒適把子

curling brush
捲髮刷

clamp
鉗

stand
支承塊

temperature control
溫度調節鈕

cool tip
冷嘴

barrel
捲筒

on-off switch
開關

handle
把子

plug adapter
轉接插頭

bristle
刷毛

on light
通電信號燈

hairsetter
燙髮器

heat ready indicator dot
預熱指示點

lid
蓋

measuring cup
量杯

roller
髮卷

case
盒子

heat comfort control
熱度調節鈕

carry handle
提手

pilot light
指示燈

clip
夾子

lid latch
蓋門鍵

manicure set
修指甲工具

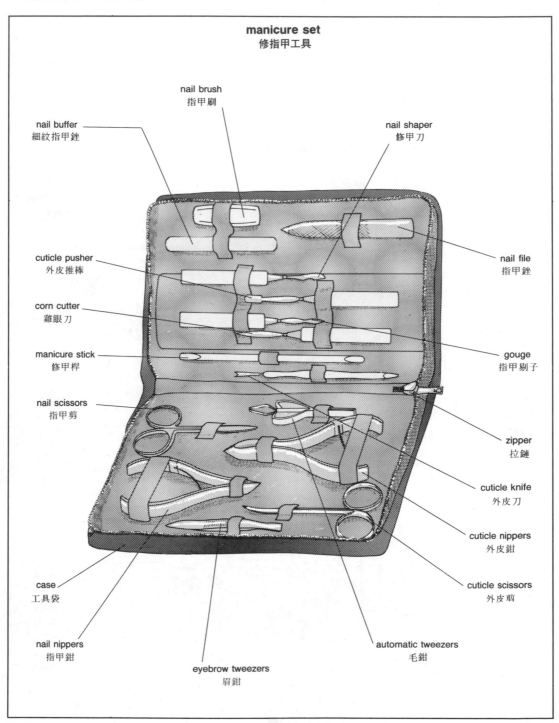

nail brush
指甲刷

nail buffer
細紋指甲銼

nail shaper
修甲刀

nail file
指甲銼

cuticle pusher
外皮推棒

corn cutter
雞眼刀

manicure stick
修甲桿

gouge
指甲剔子

nail scissors
指甲剪

zipper
拉鏈

cuticle knife
外皮刀

cuticle nippers
外皮鉗

cuticle scissors
外皮剪

case
工具袋

nail nippers
指甲鉗

automatic tweezers
毛鉗

eyebrow tweezers
眉鉗

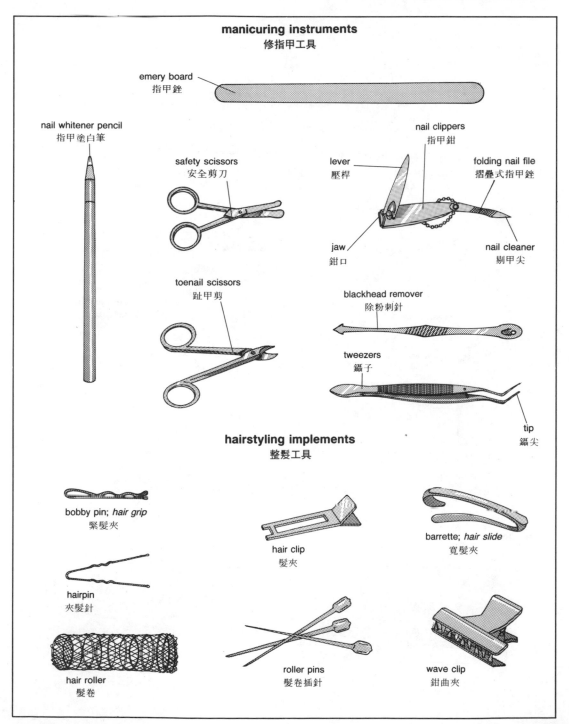

manicuring instruments
修指甲工具

emery board
指甲銼

nail whitener pencil
指甲塗白筆

safety scissors
安全剪刀

nail clippers
指甲鉗

lever
壓桿

folding nail file
摺疊式指甲銼

jaw
鉗口

nail cleaner
剔甲尖

toenail scissors
趾甲剪

blackhead remover
除粉刺針

tweezers
鑷子

tip
鑷尖

hairstyling implements
整髮工具

bobby pin; *hair grip*
緊髮夾

hair clip
髮夾

barrette; *hair slide*
寬髮夾

hairpin
夾髮針

hair roller
髮卷

roller pins
髮卷插針

wave clip
鉗曲夾

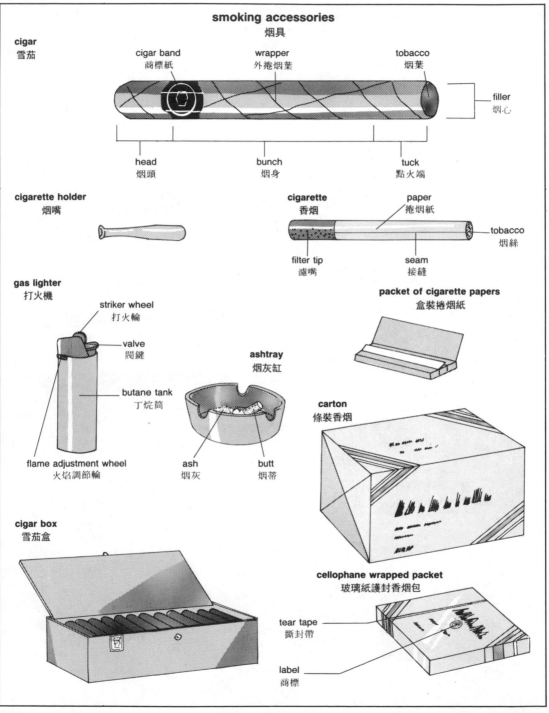

smoking accessories
烟具

cigar
雪茄

cigar band
商標紙

wrapper
外捲烟葉

tobacco
烟葉

filler
烟心

head
烟頭

bunch
烟身

tuck
點火端

cigarette holder
烟嘴

cigarette
香烟

paper
捲烟紙

tobacco
烟絲

filter tip
濾嘴

seam
接縫

gas lighter
打火機

striker wheel
打火輪

valve
閥鍵

butane tank
丁烷筒

flame adjustment wheel
火焰調節輪

packet of cigarette papers
盒裝捲烟紙

ashtray
烟灰缸

ash
烟灰

butt
烟蒂

carton
條裝香烟

cigar box
雪茄盒

cellophane wrapped packet
玻璃紙護封香烟包

tear tape
斷封帶

label
商標

smoking accessories
烟具

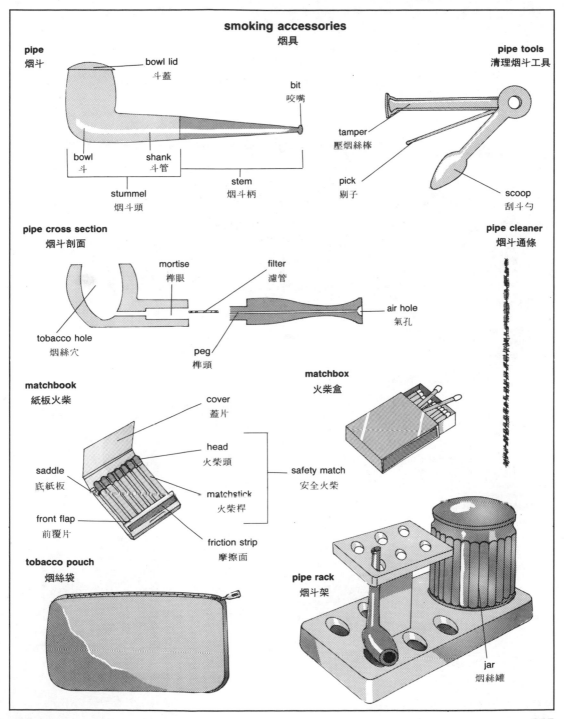

pipe
烟斗

bowl lid
斗蓋

bit
咬嘴

bowl
斗

shank
斗管

stummel
烟斗頭

stem
烟斗柄

pipe tools
清理烟斗工具

tamper
壓烟絲棒

pick
剔子

scoop
刮斗勺

pipe cross section
烟斗剖面

mortise
榫眼

filter
濾管

tobacco hole
烟絲穴

peg
榫頭

air hole
氣孔

pipe cleaner
烟斗通條

matchbook
紙板火柴

cover
蓋片

head
火柴頭

matchstick
火柴桿

saddle
底紙板

front flap
前覆片

friction strip
摩擦面

matchbox
火柴盒

safety match
安全火柴

tobacco pouch
烟絲袋

pipe rack
烟斗架

jar
烟絲罐

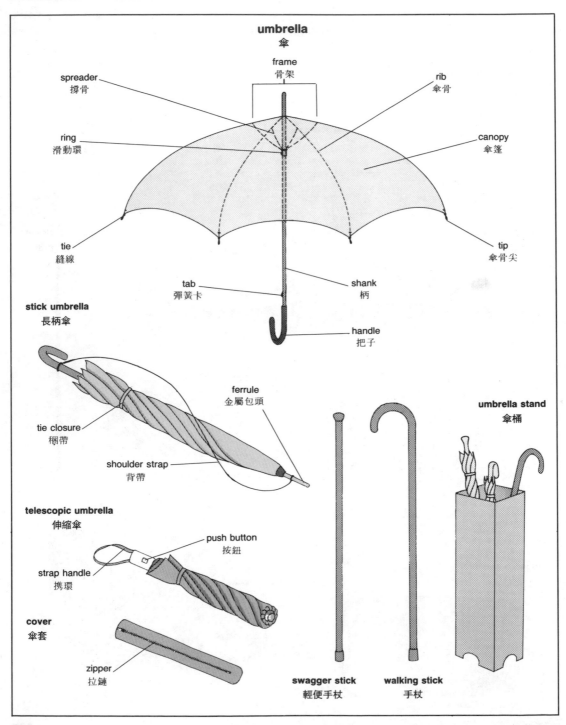

umbrella
傘

frame
骨架

spreader
撐骨

rib
傘骨

ring
滑動環

canopy
傘篷

tie
縫線

tip
傘骨尖

tab
彈簧卡

shank
柄

stick umbrella
長柄傘

handle
把子

ferrule
金屬包頭

umbrella stand
傘桶

tie closure
綑帶

shoulder strap
背帶

telescopic umbrella
伸縮傘

push button
按鈕

strap handle
携環

cover
傘套

zipper
拉鏈

swagger stick
輕便手杖

walking stick
手杖

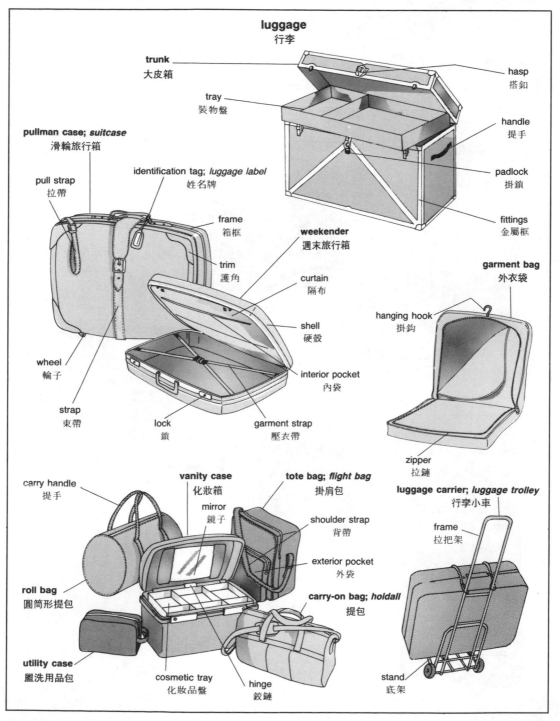

luggage
行李

trunk
大皮箱

tray
裝物盤

hasp
搭釦

handle
提手

padlock
掛鎖

fittings
金屬框

pullman case; *suitcase*
滑輪旅行箱

pull strap
拉帶

identification tag; *luggage label*
姓名牌

frame
箱框

weekender
週末旅行箱

trim
護角

curtain
隔布

shell
硬殼

interior pocket
內袋

wheel
輪子

strap
束帶

lock
鎖

garment strap
壓衣帶

garment bag
外衣袋

hanging hook
掛鈎

zipper
拉鏈

carry handle
提手

vanity case
化妝箱

mirror
鏡子

tote bag; *flight bag*
掛肩包

shoulder strap
背帶

exterior pocket
外袋

luggage carrier; *luggage trolley*
行李小車

frame
拉把架

roll bag
圓筒形提包

carry-on bag; *holdall*
提包

utility case
盥洗用品包

cosmetic tray
化妝品盤

hinge
鉸鏈

stand
底架

handbags
手提包

barrel bag
筒狀手提包

zipper
拉鏈

clutch bag
腋挾包

accordion bag
摺疊包

press-stud
按鈕

box bag
箱狀手提包

tote bag
大手提袋

gusset
凹褶

beach bag
沙灘袋

lining
襯裏

carrier bag
購物長袋

shopping bag
購物袋

handbags
手提包

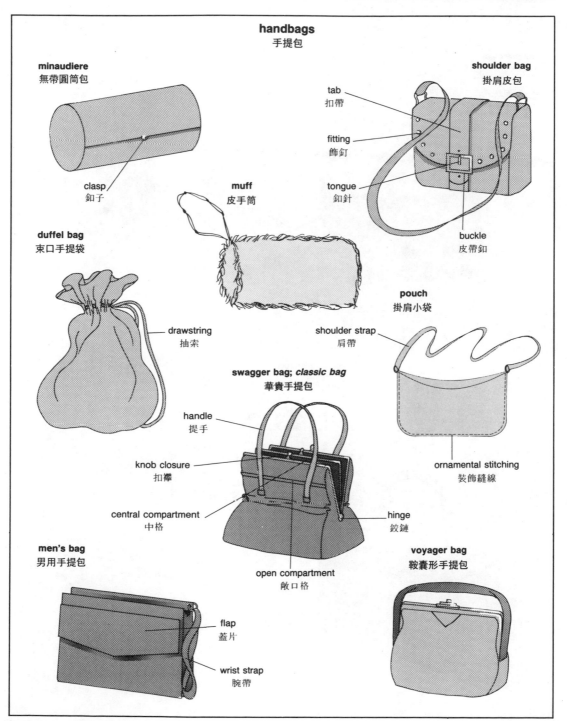

minaudiere
無帶圓筒包

clasp
釦子

shoulder bag
掛肩皮包

tab
扣帶

fitting
飾釘

tongue
釦針

buckle
皮帶釦

muff
皮手筒

duffel bag
束口手提袋

drawstring
抽索

pouch
掛肩小袋

shoulder strap
肩帶

swagger bag; *classic bag*
華貴手提包

handle
提手

knob closure
扣攀

central compartment
中格

hinge
鉸鏈

ornamental stitching
裝飾縫線

men's bag
男用手提包

open compartment
敞口格

voyager bag
鞍囊形手提包

flap
蓋片

wrist strap
腕帶

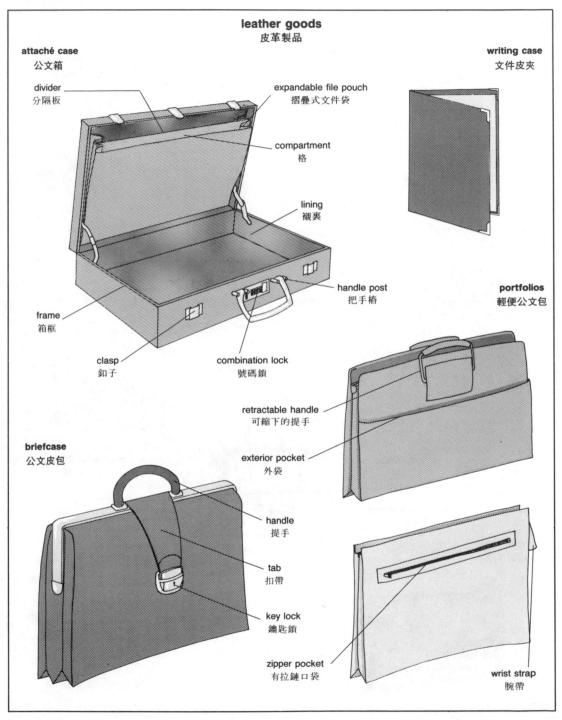

leather goods
皮革製品

attaché case
公文箱

divider
分隔板

expandable file pouch
摺疊式文件袋

compartment
格

lining
襯裏

frame
箱框

clasp
釦子

handle post
把手樁

combination lock
號碼鎖

writing case
文件皮夾

portfolios
輕便公文包

retractable handle
可縮下的提手

exterior pocket
外袋

briefcase
公文皮包

handle
提手

tab
扣帶

key lock
鑰匙鎖

zipper pocket
有拉鏈口袋

wrist strap
腕帶

leather goods
皮革製品

billfold; *wallet*
鈔票夾

pocket
鈔票兜

checkmate; *cheque book cover*
支票夾

strap
帶

stamp pocket
郵票兜

ticket pocket
票兜

passport case
護照夾

bill compartment; *wallet section*
紙幣夾層

card case; *credit card wallet*
卡片夾

window
透明夾

accordion windows
覆疊式透明卡片袋

slot
插縫

face
面

checkbook/secretary clutch
calculator/cheque book holder
支票簿夾/秘書夾

wallet
皮夾

money clip
錢夾

tab
閂片

press-stud
按鈕

notepad
記事簿

trimming
邊飾

card and photo case
證件和相片套

interior pocket
內夾層

coin purse
零錢口袋

hidden pocket
暗夾層

calculator
計算機

bill compartment; *wallet section*
紙幣夾層

gusseted pocket
摺疊口袋

pen holder
插筆套

purse
零錢包

knob closure
扣襻

key case
鑰匙包

flap
蓋片

hook
鑰匙圈

checkbook holder; *cheque book holder*
支票簿夾層

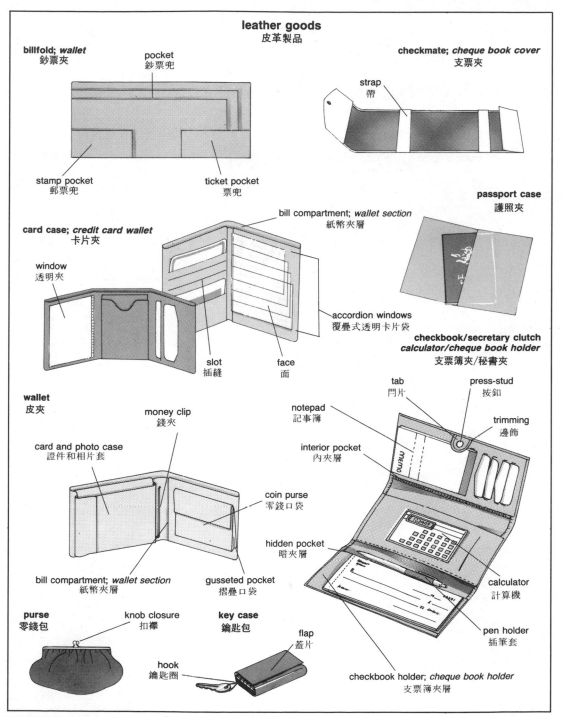

COMMUNICATIONS

通訊

writing systems of the world
世界各地文字

Merry Christmas
Happy New Year

English
英文

Joyeux Noël
Bonne année

French
法文

クリスマス
おめでとう

初光リ

Japanese
日文

God
Jul
Godt
Nytt Ar

Norwegian
挪威文

Vrolijk Kerstfeest
en een
Gelukkig Nieuwjaar

Dutch
荷蘭文

Feliz
Navidad
Próspero
Año Nuevo

Spanish
西班牙文

C Рождеством
С новым годом

Russian
俄文

חג שמח
שנה טובה

Hebrew
希伯來文

عيد شما مبارك
كريسمس مبارك

Iranian
伊朗文

BUON
NATALE
FELICE
ANNO NUOVO

Italian
義大利文

Glædelig Jul
og
Godt Nytaar

Danish
丹麥文

Hyvaa Joulua Ja
Onnellista
Uutta Vuotta

Finnish
芬蘭文

ΚΑΛΑ ΧΡΙΣΤΟΥΓΕΝΝΑ
ΚΑΙ ΕΥΤΥΧΙΣΜΕΝΟΣ Ο
ΚΑΙΝΟΥΡΓΙΟΣ ΧΡΟΝΟΣ

Greek
希臘文

CHÚC MỪNG GIÁNG SINH
CUNG CHÚC TÂN XUÂN

Vietnamese
越南文

God Jul
och
Gott Nytt
Ar

Swedish
瑞典文

عام سعيد
وكل عام وانتم بخير

Arabic
阿拉伯文

नव वर्ष की शुभकामनाएँ

Hindi
印地文

Armenian
亞美尼亞文

SĂRBĂTORI FERICITE
ȘI
LA MULTI ANI

Rumanian
羅馬尼亞文

XPUCTOC
РОДИВСЯ
ШАСЛИВОГО
HOBOTO POKY

Ukrainian
烏克蘭文

FELIZ NATAL
PRÓSPERO ANO NOVO

Portuguese
葡萄牙文

Fröhliche Weihnachten
und alles Gute
zum Neuen Jahr

German
德文

Sinhalese
僧伽羅文

Wesołych Świąt
i
Szczęśliwego
Nowego Roku

Polish
波蘭文

聖誕快樂
新年愉快

Chinese
中文

Nadolig Llawen
Blwyddyn Newydd
Dda

Welsh
威爾斯文

KELLEMES KARÁCSONYI
ÜNNEPEKE
BOLDOG ÚJÉVET

Hungarian
匈牙利文

Inuktitut
愛斯基摩文

Braille
凸點文字

letters
字母

a b c d e f g h i j k l m

n o p q r s t u v w x y z

numerals
數字

numeral sign
數字符號

1 2 3 4 5 6 7 8 9 0

mathematical symbols
數學符號

: :: + − × / = > < √

punctuation marks
標點符號

, ; : . ! ( ) " " * ?
« »

apostrophe
所有格或縮畧符號

—

majuscule
大寫字母

capital sign
大寫符號

" ?

French language signs
法語音標

ì ò ou § æ ç é à è ù

â ê î ô û ë ï ü œ

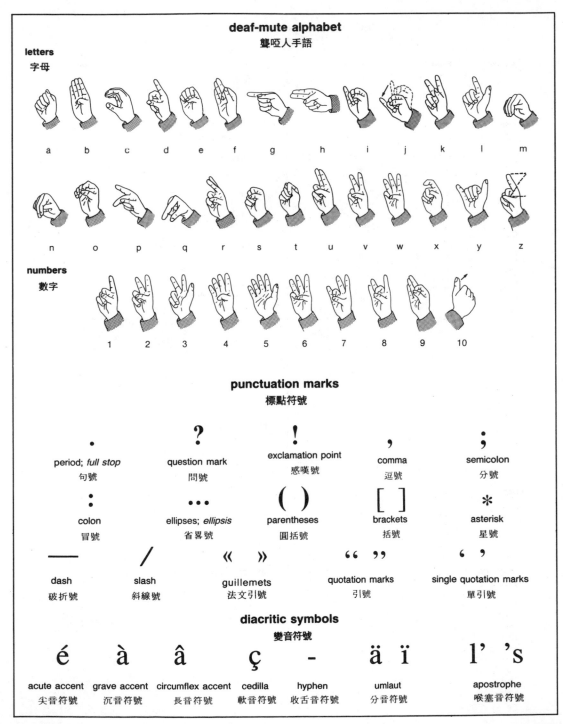

deaf-mute alphabet
聾啞人手語

letters
字母

a b c d e f g h i j k l m

n o p q r s t u v w x y z

numbers
數字

1 2 3 4 5 6 7 8 9 10

punctuation marks
標點符號

.
period; *full stop*
句號

?
question mark
問號

!
exclamation point
感嘆號

,
comma
逗號

;
semicolon
分號

:
colon
冒號

...
ellipses; *ellipsis*
省畧號

( )
parentheses
圓括號

[ ]
brackets
括號

*
asterisk
星號

—
dash
破折號

/
slash
斜線號

《 》
guillemets
法文引號

" "
quotation marks
引號

' '
single quotation marks
單引號

diacritic symbols
變音符號

é
acute accent
尖音符號

à
grave accent
沉音符號

â
circumflex accent
長音符號

ç
cedilla
軟音符號

-
hyphen
收舌音符號

ä ï
umlaut
分音符號

l' 's
apostrophe
喉塞音符號

international phonetic alphabet
國際音標

signs 符號	French 法語	English 英語		signs 符號	French 法語	English 英語
vowels 母音				**fricative consonants** 摩擦子音		
[a]	lac	—		[f]	fou	life
[ɑ]	mât	arm		[v]	vite	live
[æ]	—	back		[θ]	—	thin
[e]	thé	elite		[ð]	—	then
[ɛ]	poète	yet		[h]	—	hot
[ə]	—	ago		[s]	hélas	pass
[ɜ]	—	earth		[z]	gaz	zoo
[i]	île	beet		[ʒ]	page	rouge
[ɪ]	—	bit		[ʃ]	cheval	she
[ɔ]	note	ball				
[o]	dos	note				
[œ]	peur	—		**liquid consonants** 流音		
[u]	loup	rule		[l]	mal	real
[ʊ]	—	bull		[r]	rude	rue
[ʌ]	—	but		[m]	blême	him
[y]	mur	cure		[n]	fanal	in
[ø]	feu	—		[ɲ]	agneau	rang
[ɒ]	—	hot				
[:]	longueur / length					
nasal vowels 鼻母音				**stop consonants** 閉塞音		
[ã]	blanc	—		[p]	pas	mop
[ɛ̃]	pain	—		[b]	beau	bat
[ɔ̃]	bon	—		[d]	dur	do
[œ̃]	brun	—		[t]	tu	two
				[k]	que	lake
glides 滑音				[g]	gare	bag
[j]	yeux	you				
[ɥ]	nuit	—				
[w]	oui	we		**affricate consonants** 塞擦音		
diphthongs 雙母音				[tʃ]	—	chin
[aɪ]	—	my		[dʒ]	—	joke
[aʊ]	—	how				
[ɔɪ]	—	toy				
[ju]	—	amuse				
[eɪ]	—	may				
[ɛə]	—	dare				
[ɪə]	—	here				
[əʊ]	—	no				
[ʊə]	—	here				

typical letter
書信格式

American model
美國式

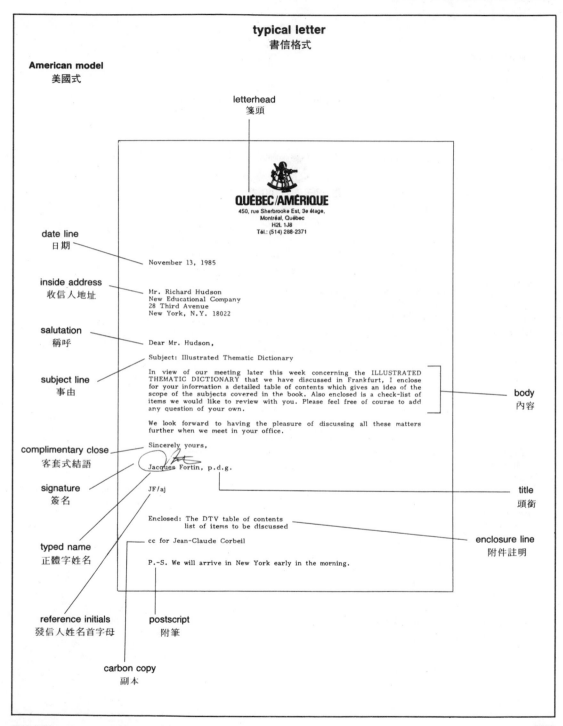

letterhead
箋頭

QUÉBEC/AMÉRIQUE
450, rue Sherbrooke Est, 3e étage,
Montréal, Québec
H2L 1J8
Tél.: (514) 288-2371

date line
日期

November 13, 1985

inside address
收信人地址

Mr. Richard Hudson
New Educational Company
28 Third Avenue
New York, N.Y. 18022

salutation
稱呼

Dear Mr. Hudson,

Subject: Illustrated Thematic Dictionary

subject line
事由

In view of our meeting later this week concerning the ILLUSTRATED THEMATIC DICTIONARY that we have discussed in Frankfurt, I enclose for your information a detailed table of contents which gives an idea of the scope of the subjects covered in the book. Also enclosed is a check-list of items we would like to review with you. Please feel free of course to add any question of your own.

body
內容

We look forward to having the pleasure of discussing all these matters further when we meet in your office.

complimentary close
客套式結語

Sincerely yours,

Jacques Fortin, p.d.g.

title
頭銜

signature
簽名

JF/aj

typed name
正體字姓名

Enclosed: The DTV table of contents
list of items to be discussed

enclosure line
附件註明

cc for Jean-Claude Corbeil

P.-S. We will arrive in New York early in the morning.

reference initials
發信人姓名首字母

postscript
附筆

carbon copy
副本

COMMUNICATIONS 通訊

typical letter
書信格式

Canadian model
加拿大式

en-tête
箋頭

lieu et date
地點和日期

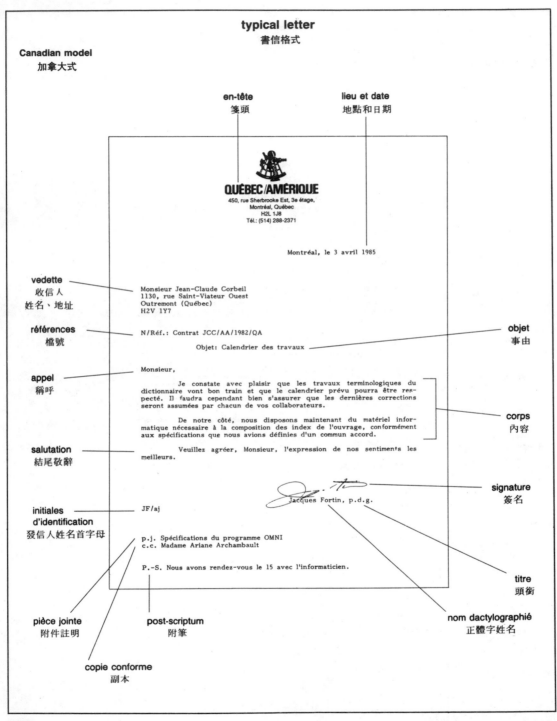

QUÉBEC/AMÉRIQUE
450, rue Sherbrooke Est, 3e étage,
Montréal, Québec
H2L 1J8
Tél.: (514) 288-2371

Montréal, le 3 avril 1985

vedette
收信人
姓名、地址

Monsieur Jean-Claude Corbeil
1130, rue Saint-Viateur Ouest
Outremont (Québec)
H2V 1Y7

références
檔號

N/Réf.: Contrat JCC/AA/1982/QA

Objet: Calendrier des travaux

objet
事由

appel
稱呼

Monsieur,

Je constate avec plaisir que les travaux terminologiques du dictionnaire vont bon train et que le calendrier prévu pourra être respecté. Il faudra cependant bien s'assurer que les dernières corrections seront assumées par chacun de vos collaborateurs.

De notre côté, nous disposons maintenant du matériel informatique nécessaire à la composition des index de l'ouvrage, conformément aux spécifications que nous avions définies d'un commun accord.

corps
內容

salutation
結尾敬辭

Veuillez agréer, Monsieur, l'expression de nos sentiments les meilleurs.

signature
簽名

Jacques Fortin, p.d.g.

**initiales
d'identification**
發信人姓名首字母

JF/aj

p.j. Spécifications du programme OMNI
c.c. Madame Ariane Archambault

P.-S. Nous avons rendez-vous le 15 avec l'informaticien.

titre
頭銜

pièce jointe
附件註明

post-scriptum
附筆

nom dactylographié
正體字姓名

copie conforme
副本

typical letter
書信格式

British model
英國式

letterhead
箋頭

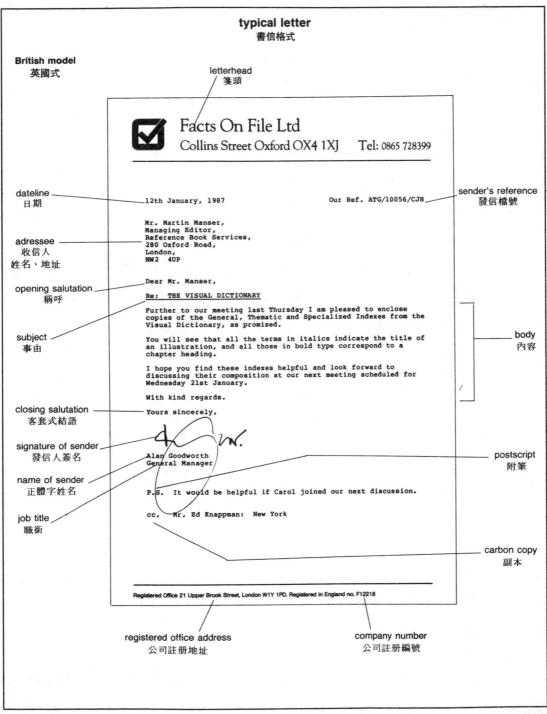

Facts On File Ltd
Collins Street Oxford OX4 1XJ   Tel: 0865 728399

dateline
日期

12th January, 1987

Our Ref. ATG/10056/CJH

sender's reference
發信檔號

adressee
收信人
姓名、地址

Mr. Martin Manser,
Managing Editor,
Reference Book Services,
280 Oxford Road,
London,
NW2 4UP

opening salutation
稱呼

Dear Mr. Manser,

subject
事由

Re: THE VISUAL DICTIONARY

Further to our meeting last Thursday I am pleased to enclose
copies of the General, Thematic and Specialized Indexes from the
Visual Dictionary, as promised.

You will see that all the terms in italics indicate the title of
an illustration, and all those in bold type correspond to a
chapter heading.

I hope you find these indexes helpful and look forward to
discussing their composition at our next meeting scheduled for
Wednesday 21st January.

With kind regards.

body
內容

closing salutation
客套式結語

Yours sincerely,

signature of sender
發信人簽名

name of sender
正體字姓名

Alan Goodworth
General Manager

job title
職銜

postscript
附筆

P.S. It would be helpful if Carol joined our next discussion.

cc. Mr. Ed Knappman: New York

carbon copy
副本

Registered Office 21 Upper Brook Street, London W1Y 1PD. Registered in England no. F12218

registered office address
公司註册地址

company number
公司註册編號

proofreading
校對符號

corrections of errors 改正錯誤	French 法式	American 美式	British 英式
align vertically 排成直行	‖	‖	‖
align horizontally 排成橫行	=	=	=
begin a new paragraph 分段	⌈	⌙	⌐
augmenter le blanc 增加空位	—#—		
center; *centre* 分中	][	][	[ ]
correct a letter 改字母	*a*/	*a*/	*a*/
correct a word 改詞	/ demi /	heel /	heel /
insert space 插入空位	#/	#	Y
run in; *run on* 接上文	à jouer. On pourrait	heel. The doctor	heel. The doctor
insert here 在此插入	⋏	⋏	h
insert a letter 插入字母	*u*⋏	*a*⋏	
insert a word 插入一個詞	*la* ⋏	*low* ⋏	
close up 移密	⌒	⌒	⌒
justifier à gauche 左移	⌐		
justifier à droite 右移	⌐		
take over to next line 移到下行	⌐à	_⌐break	⌐break

proofreading
校對符號

corrections of errors
改正錯誤

	French 法式	American 美式	British 英式
take back to previous line 移到上行	*la]*	*move up*	*move up]*
let it stand 保留原樣	*bon H*	...*stet*	*stet*
move to left 左移	⎣	⎣	⊢←⎣
move to right 右移	⎤	⎤	⎤→⊣
rapprocher sans joindre 移開	↕⎮		
reduce space 減少空位	→	*reduce #*	↑
delete 刪去	♂	*e*	*e⟋*
transpose two words 兩詞調換	la ⎣solution⎦bonne	order⎦the *tr*	order⎦the
transpose lines 兩行調換	⊃	⊃ *tr*	⊃
transpose two letters 兩字母調換	*eg*	*uo tr*	*uo*
something omitted 有所遺漏	*v. copie*	*see copy*	*see copy*

corrections of punctuation marks
改正標點

	French 法式	American 美式	British 英式
period; *full stop* 句號	⊙	⊙	⊙
comma 逗號	⌄	⌄	⌄
apostrophe 所有格或縮畧符號	⌄	⌄	⌄

proofreading
校對符號

corrections of punctuation marks 改正標點	French 法式	American 美式	British 英式
colon 冒號	: /	: /	(⦂)
semicolon 分號	; /	; /	; /
hyphen 連字號	– /	= /	⊢⊣
quotation marks 引號	˯˯ / ˰˰	˯˯ / ˯˯	˯˯ / ˯˯
parentheses 圓括號	(/)	(/)	(/)

corrections of diacritic symbols
改正上下標符號

	French	American	British
superscript 上標	a^2	a^2	a^2
subscript 下標	H_2O	H_2O	H_2O

corrections of type
改正字體

	French	American	British
set in lower case 改爲小寫	bdc	lc	≠ lc
set in capitals 改爲大寫	cap	cap	≡
set in small capitals 改爲小體大寫	p.c.	sc	=
set in italic 改爲斜體	ital.	ital	___
set in roman 改爲羅馬體	rom.	rom	⊣/
set in boldface 改爲黑體	gr.	bf	∿∿∿
set in lightface 改爲線體	léger	lf	

proofreading
校對符號

indication of types
字體指示

italic 斜體	<u>bible</u>	*bible*·
boldface; *bold* 黑體	<u>bible</u>	**bible**
small capitals 小體大寫	<u>bible</u>	BIBLE
capitals 大寫	<u>bible</u>	BIBLE
italic capitals 斜體大寫	bible	*BIBLE*
boldface capitals; *bold capitals* 黑體大寫	bible	**BIBLE**
italic boldface capitals 斜黑體大寫	bible	***BIBLE***
capitals for initials, small capitals for the rest 起首字母大寫，其餘的小體大寫	HENRY MILLER	HENRY MILLER

American proofreading model
美式校對舉例

1.1 - The phoneme. It is important to keep in mind that the sounds of human language are more that just sounds. The p of pin is exploded with a puff of air following it, where as the p of capture is not those sound are quite different as mere sounds. But english we say they are the same, and they are, because they functions as the same unit in the sound system of English.

The functioning units like English /p/ are called phonemes by structural linguists and with usually be enclosed in plant bars in the text.

Robert Lado

from Linguistics across cultures

proofreading
校對符號

French proofreading model
法式校對舉例

]Alchimie du verbe[

J'inventais la couleur des voyelles. A noir, !/ —人

/blanc/ E /beige/, I rouge, O bleu, U vert.- Je réglais la

forme et le mouvement de chaque consonne et, avec des

h人me人 rythmes instinctifs, je flottais d'inventer un verbe a/ e/

poétique accessible, un jour ou l'autre, à tuós les sens.

Je réservais la traduction. [D'abord ce fut] une étude. bdc

J'écrivais des silences, des nuits, je notais l'inexpri-

mable.

Je fixais des vertiges.

Arthur Rimbaud

extraits de Un saison en enfer e人

British proofreading model
英式校對舉例

ш/1.1 - The phoneme. It is important to keep in mind

that the sounds of human language are more that just n/

ʒ/ш/p/ш/ sounds. The p of pin is exploded with a puff of air d/

ひ/ᄃ/ fllowing it, where as the p of capture is not/ those ш/ш/0/²/

rwo人 s人 sound are quite different as mere sounds. But english ʒ/in人 ²/

we say they are the same, and they are, because they ʸ ʸ

ʔ/ functions as the same unit in the sound system of

English.

ᄃ ᵃh ʔ/ The functioning units like English p are called ʔ/ш/ʔ/

ш/ɣ/ phonemes by structural linguists and (with) usually be ʔ/will 人

s/ enclosed in plant bars in the text.

Robert Lado

from Linguistics across cultures

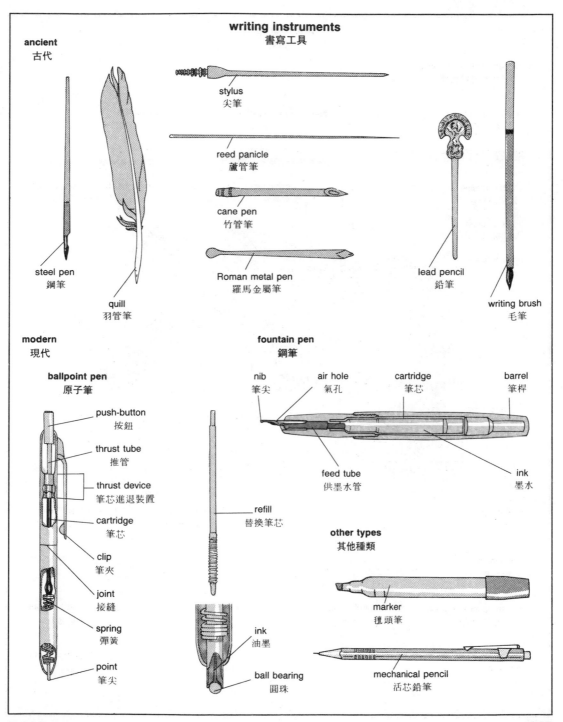

writing instruments
書寫工具

ancient
古代

stylus
尖筆

reed panicle
蘆管筆

cane pen
竹管筆

Roman metal pen
羅馬金屬筆

steel pen
鋼筆

quill
羽管筆

lead pencil
鉛筆

writing brush
毛筆

modern
現代

fountain pen
鋼筆

ballpoint pen
原子筆

push-button
按鈕

thrust tube
推管

thrust device
筆芯進退裝置

cartridge
筆芯

clip
筆夾

joint
接縫

spring
彈簧

point
筆尖

nib
筆尖

air hole
氣孔

cartridge
筆芯

barrel
筆桿

feed tube
供墨水管

ink
墨水

refill
替換筆芯

other types
其他種類

marker
氈頭筆

ink
油墨

mechanical pencil
活芯鉛筆

ball bearing
圓珠

photography
攝影

single-lens reflex camera
單鏡頭反光照相機

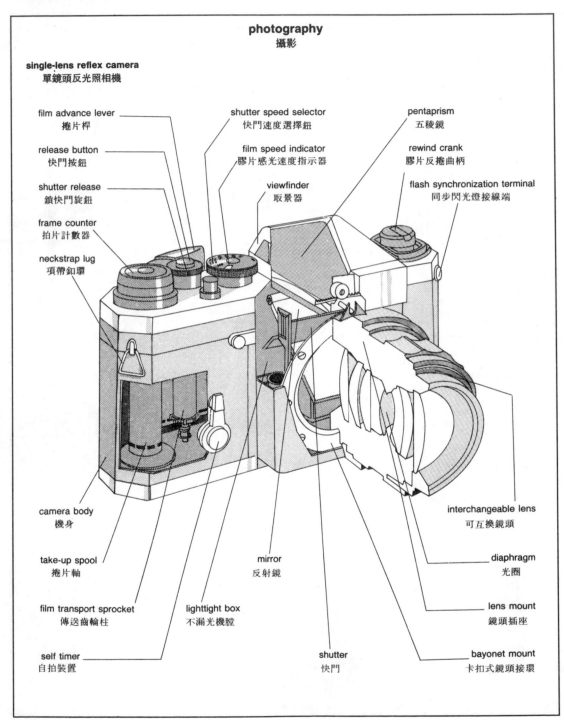

film advance lever
捲片桿

release button
快門按鈕

shutter release
鎖快門旋鈕

frame counter
拍片計數器

neckstrap lug
項帶釦環

shutter speed selector
快門速度選擇鈕

film speed indicator
膠片感光速度指示器

viewfinder
取景器

pentaprism
五稜鏡

rewind crank
膠片反捲曲柄

flash synchronization terminal
同步閃光燈接線端

camera body
機身

take-up spool
捲片軸

film transport sprocket
傳送齒輪柱

self timer
自拍裝置

mirror
反射鏡

lighttight box
不漏光機腔

shutter
快門

interchangeable lens
可互換鏡頭

diaphragm
光圈

lens mount
鏡頭插座

bayonet mount
卡扣式鏡頭接環

photography
攝影

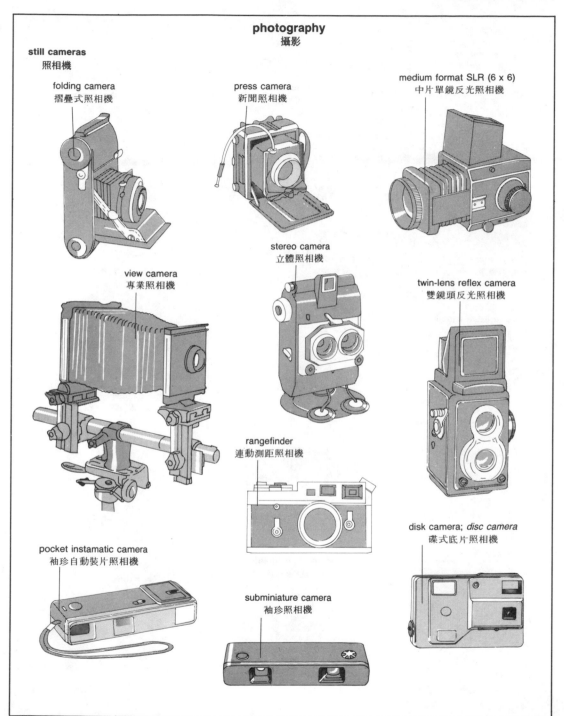

still cameras
照相機

folding camera
摺疊式照相機

press camera
新聞照相機

medium format SLR (6 x 6)
中片單鏡反光照相機

view camera
專業照相機

stereo camera
立體照相機

twin-lens reflex camera
雙鏡頭反光照相機

rangefinder
連動測距照相機

pocket instamatic camera
袖珍自動裝片照相機

subminiature camera
袖珍照相機

disk camera; *disc camera*
碟式底片照相機

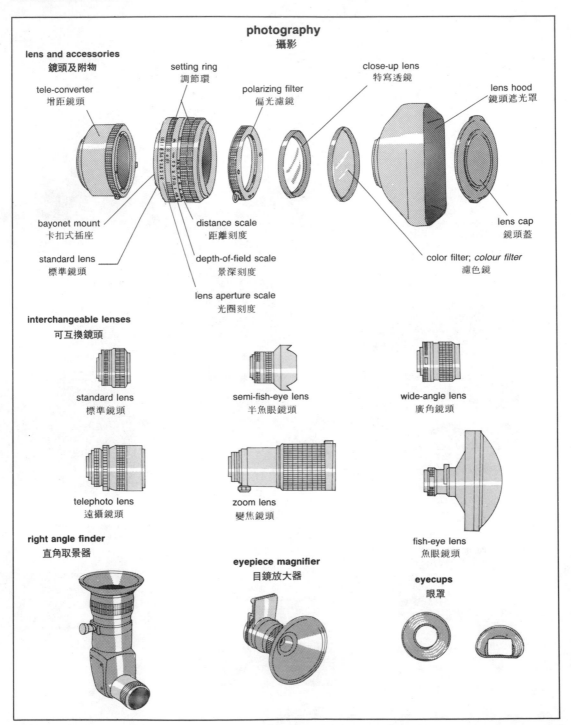

photography
攝影

lens and accessories
鏡頭及附物

tele-converter
增距鏡頭

setting ring
調節環

polarizing filter
偏光濾鏡

close-up lens
特寫透鏡

lens hood
鏡頭遮光罩

bayonet mount
卡扣式插座

standard lens
標準鏡頭

distance scale
距離刻度

depth-of-field scale
景深刻度

lens aperture scale
光圈刻度

lens cap
鏡頭蓋

color filter; *colour filter*
濾色鏡

interchangeable lenses
可互換鏡頭

standard lens
標準鏡頭

semi-fish-eye lens
半魚眼鏡頭

wide-angle lens
廣角鏡頭

telephoto lens
遠攝鏡頭

zoom lens
變焦鏡頭

fish-eye lens
魚眼鏡頭

right angle finder
直角取景器

eyepiece magnifier
目鏡放大器

eyecups
眼罩

photography
攝影

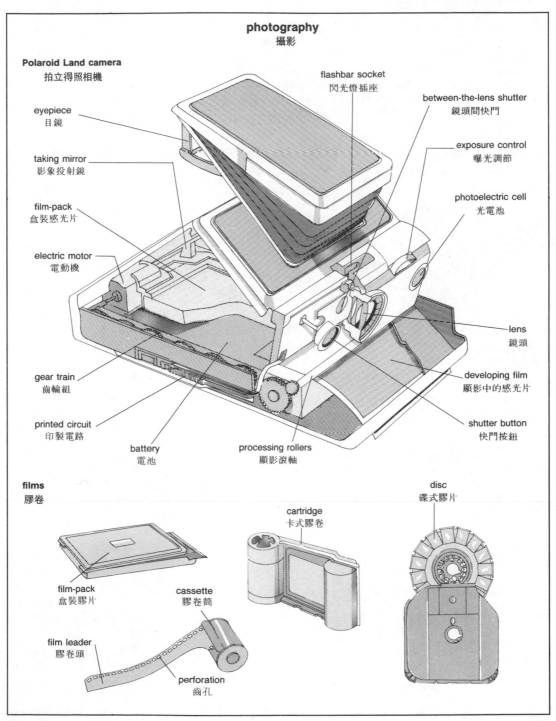

Polaroid Land camera
拍立得照相機

eyepiece
目鏡

taking mirror
影象投射鏡

film-pack
盒裝感光片

electric motor
電動機

gear train
齒輪組

printed circuit
印製電路

battery
電池

processing rollers
顯影滾軸

flashbar socket
閃光燈插座

between-the-lens shutter
鏡頭間快門

exposure control
曝光調節

photoelectric cell
光電池

lens
鏡頭

developing film
顯影中的感光片

shutter button
快門按鈕

films
膠卷

film-pack
盒裝膠片

cassette
膠卷筒

film leader
膠卷頭

perforation
齒孔

cartridge
卡式膠卷

disc
碟式膠片

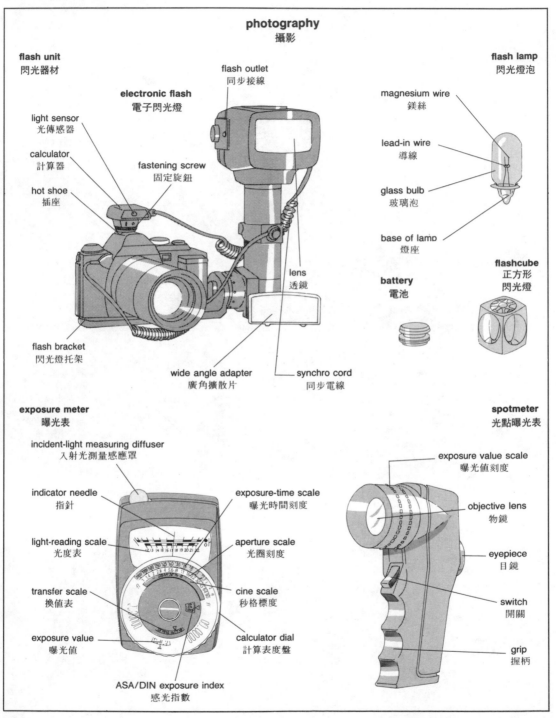

photography
攝影

flash unit
閃光器材

flash outlet
同步接線

electronic flash
電子閃光燈

light sensor
光傳感器

calculator
計算器

fastening screw
固定旋鈕

hot shoe
插座

lens
透鏡

flash bracket
閃光燈托架

wide angle adapter
廣角擴散片

synchro cord
同步電線

flash lamp
閃光燈泡

magnesium wire
鎂絲

lead-in wire
導線

glass bulb
玻璃泡

base of lamp
燈座

battery
電池

flashcube
正方形
閃光燈

exposure meter
曝光表

incident-light measuring diffuser
入射光測量感應罩

indicator needle
指針

exposure-time scale
曝光時間刻度

light-reading scale
光度表

aperture scale
光圈刻度

transfer scale
換值表

cine scale
秒格標度

exposure value
曝光值

calculator dial
計算表度盤

ASA/DIN exposure index
感光指數

spotmeter
光點曝光表

exposure value scale
曝光值刻度

objective lens
物鏡

eyepiece
目鏡

switch
開關

grip
握柄

photography
攝影

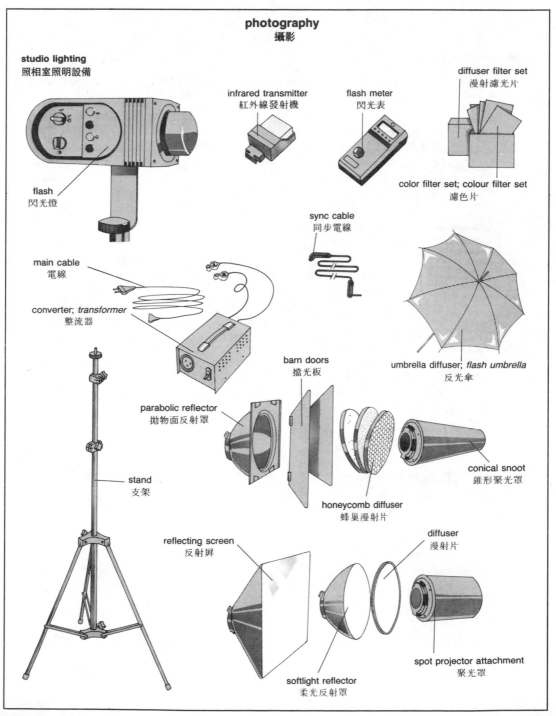

studio lighting
照相室照明設備

infrared transmitter
紅外線發射機

flash meter
閃光表

diffuser filter set
漫射濾光片

color filter set; colour filter set
濾色片

flash
閃光燈

sync cable
同步電線

main cable
電線

converter; *transformer*
整流器

umbrella diffuser; *flash umbrella*
反光傘

barn doors
擋光板

parabolic reflector
拋物面反射罩

conical snoot
錐形聚光罩

stand
支架

honeycomb diffuser
蜂巢漫射片

reflecting screen
反射屏

diffuser
漫射片

spot projector attachment
聚光罩

softlight reflector
柔光反射罩

photography
攝影

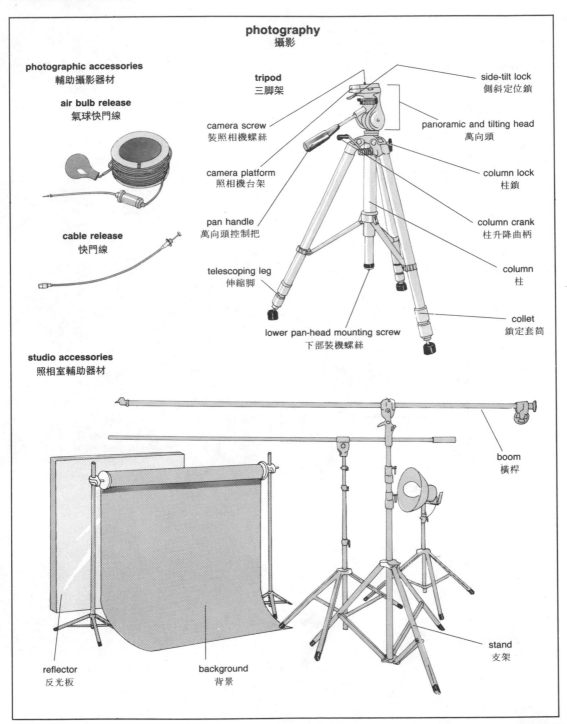

photographic accessories
輔助攝影器材

air bulb release
氣球快門線

cable release
快門線

tripod
三脚架

camera screw
裝照相機螺絲

camera platform
照相機台架

pan handle
萬向頭控制把

telescoping leg
伸縮脚

lower pan-head mounting screw
下部裝機螺絲

side-tilt lock
側斜定位鎖

panoramic and tilting head
萬向頭

column lock
柱鎖

column crank
柱升降曲柄

column
柱

collet
鎖定套筒

studio accessories
照相室輔助器材

boom
橫桿

stand
支架

reflector
反光板

background
背景

photography
攝影

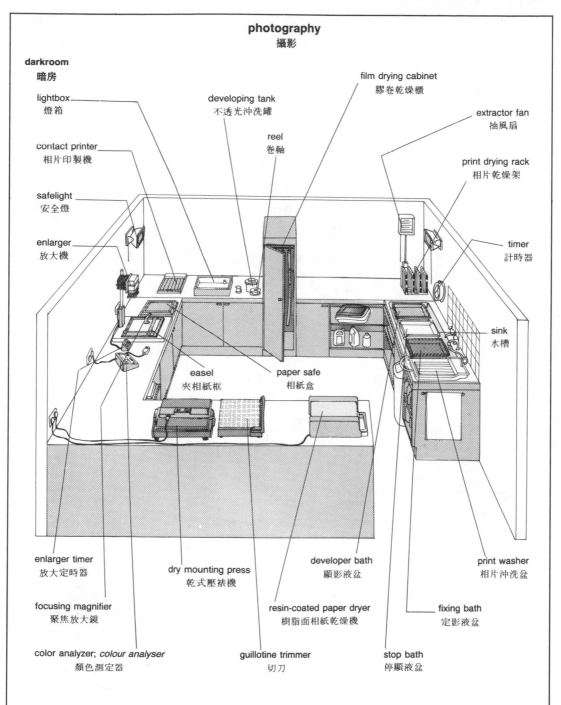

darkroom
暗房

lightbox
燈箱

contact printer
相片印製機

safelight
安全燈

enlarger
放大機

developing tank
不透光沖洗罐

reel
卷軸

film drying cabinet
膠卷乾燥櫃

extractor fan
抽風扇

print drying rack
相片乾燥架

timer
計時器

sink
水槽

easel
夾相紙框

paper safe
相紙盒

enlarger timer
放大定時器

focusing magnifier
聚焦放大鏡

color analyzer; *colour analyser*
顏色測定器

dry mounting press
乾式壓裱機

guillotine trimmer
切刀

resin-coated paper dryer
樹脂面相紙乾燥機

developer bath
顯影液盆

stop bath
停顯液盆

fixing bath
定影液盆

print washer
相片沖洗盆

讀者文摘

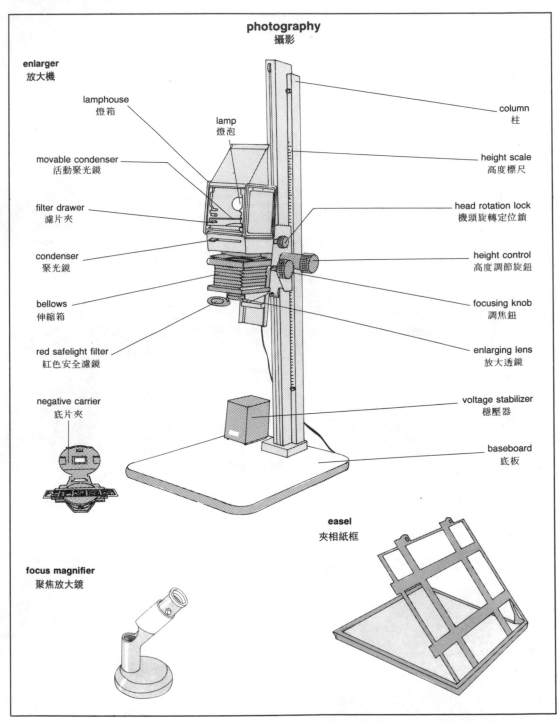

photography
攝影

enlarger
放大機

lamphouse
燈箱

lamp
燈泡

movable condenser
活動聚光鏡

filter drawer
濾片夾

condenser
聚光鏡

bellows
伸縮箱

red safelight filter
紅色安全濾鏡

negative carrier
底片夾

column
柱

height scale
高度標尺

head rotation lock
機頭旋轉定位鎖

height control
高度調節旋鈕

focusing knob
調焦鈕

enlarging lens
放大透鏡

voltage stabilizer
穩壓器

baseboard
底板

easel
夾相紙框

focus magnifier
聚焦放大鏡

photography
攝影

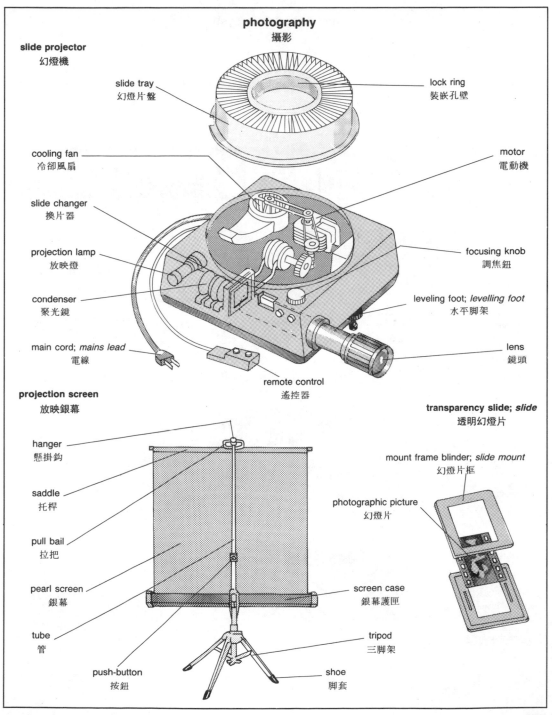

slide projector
幻燈機

slide tray
幻燈片盤

lock ring
裝嵌孔壁

cooling fan
冷卻風扇

motor
電動機

slide changer
換片器

focusing knob
調焦鈕

projection lamp
放映燈

condenser
聚光鏡

leveling foot; *levelling foot*
水平腳架

main cord; *mains lead*
電線

lens
鏡頭

remote control
遙控器

projection screen
放映銀幕

transparency slide; *slide*
透明幻燈片

hanger
懸掛鈎

mount frame blinder; *slide mount*
幻燈片框

saddle
托桿

photographic picture
幻燈片

pull bail
拉把

pearl screen
銀幕

screen case
銀幕護匣

tube
管

tripod
三腳架

push-button
按鈕

shoe
腳套

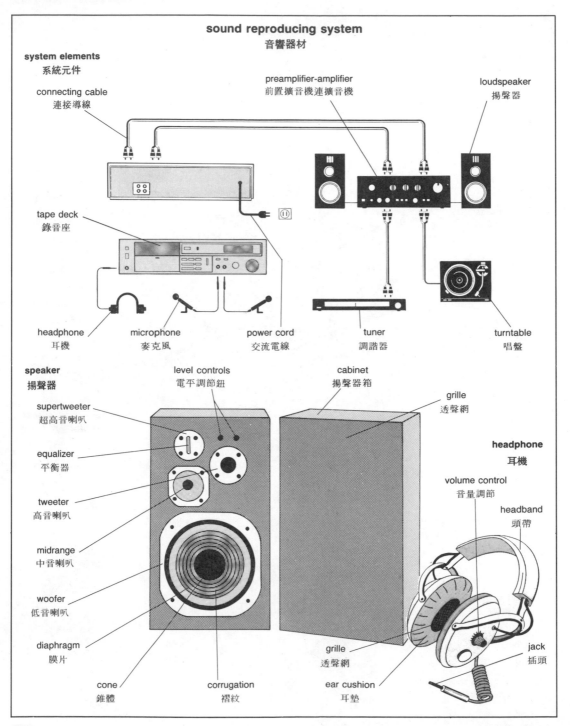

sound reproducing system
音響器材

system elements
系統元件

preamplifier-amplifier
前置擴音機連擴音機

loudspeaker
揚聲器

connecting cable
連接導線

tape deck
錄音座

headphone
耳機

microphone
麥克風

power cord
交流電線

tuner
調諧器

turntable
唱盤

speaker
揚聲器

level controls
電平調節鈕

cabinet
揚聲器箱

grille
透聲網

supertweeter
超高音喇叭

equalizer
平衡器

headphone
耳機

volume control
音量調節

headband
頭帶

tweeter
高音喇叭

midrange
中音喇叭

woofer
低音喇叭

diaphragm
膜片

grille
透聲網

jack
插頭

cone
錐體

corrugation
褶紋

ear cushion
耳墊

sound reproducing system
音響器材

amplifier-tuner
擴音調諧器

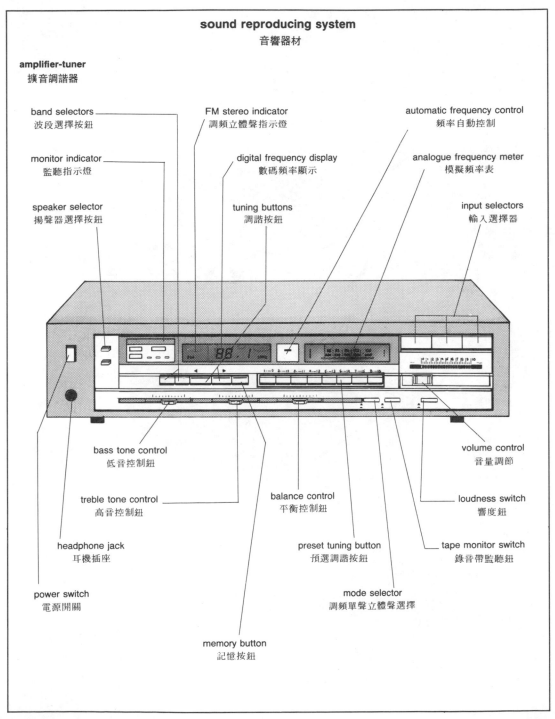

band selectors
波段選擇按鈕

monitor indicator
監聽指示燈

speaker selector
揚聲器選擇按鈕

FM stereo indicator
調頻立體聲指示燈

digital frequency display
數碼頻率顯示

tuning buttons
調諧按鈕

automatic frequency control
頻率自動控制

analogue frequency meter
模擬頻率表

input selectors
輸入選擇器

bass tone control
低音控制鈕

treble tone control
高音控制鈕

balance control
平衡控制鈕

volume control
音量調節

loudness switch
響度鈕

headphone jack
耳機插座

preset tuning button
預選調諧按鈕

tape monitor switch
錄音帶監聽鈕

power switch
電源開關

mode selector
調頻單聲立體聲選擇

memory button
記憶按鈕

sound reproducing system
音響器材

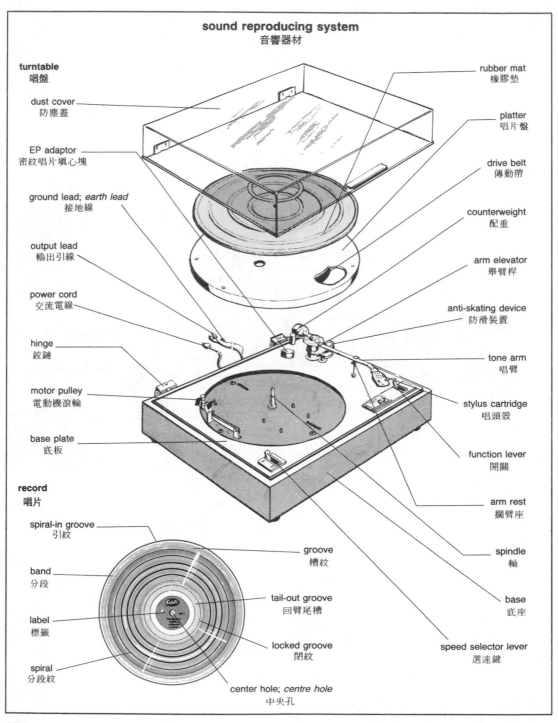

turntable
唱盤

dust cover
防塵蓋

EP adaptor
密紋唱片填心塊

ground lead; *earth lead*
接地線

output lead
輸出引線

power cord
交流電線

hinge
鉸鏈

motor pulley
電動機滾輪

base plate
底板

record
唱片

spiral-in groove
引紋

band
分段

label
標籤

spiral
分段紋

groove
槽紋

tail-out groove
回臂尾槽

locked groove
閉紋

center hole; *centre hole*
中央孔

rubber mat
橡膠墊

platter
唱片盤

drive belt
傳動帶

counterweight
配重

arm elevator
舉臂桿

anti-skating device
防滑裝置

tone arm
唱臂

stylus cartridge
唱頭殼

function lever
開關

arm rest
擱臂座

spindle
軸

base
底座

speed selector lever
選速鍵

sound reproducing system
音響器材

tape deck
錄音座

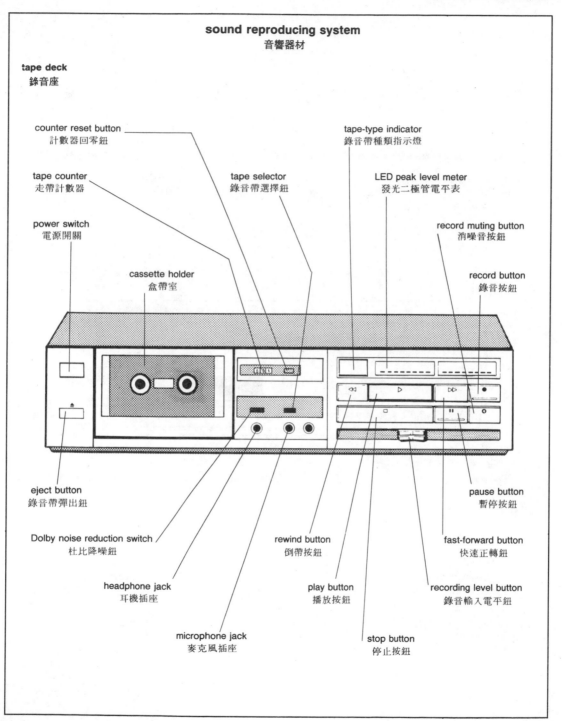

counter reset button
計數器回零鈕

tape-type indicator
錄音帶種類指示燈

tape counter
走帶計數器

tape selector
錄音帶選擇鈕

LED peak level meter
發光二極管電平表

power switch
電源開關

record muting button
消噪音按鈕

record button
錄音按鈕

cassette holder
盒帶室

eject button
錄音帶彈出鈕

pause button
暫停按鈕

Dolby noise reduction switch
杜比降噪鈕

rewind button
倒帶按鈕

fast-forward button
快速正轉鈕

headphone jack
耳機插座

play button
播放按鈕

recording level button
錄音輸入電平鈕

microphone jack
麥克風插座

stop button
停止按鈕

video tape recorder
錄影機

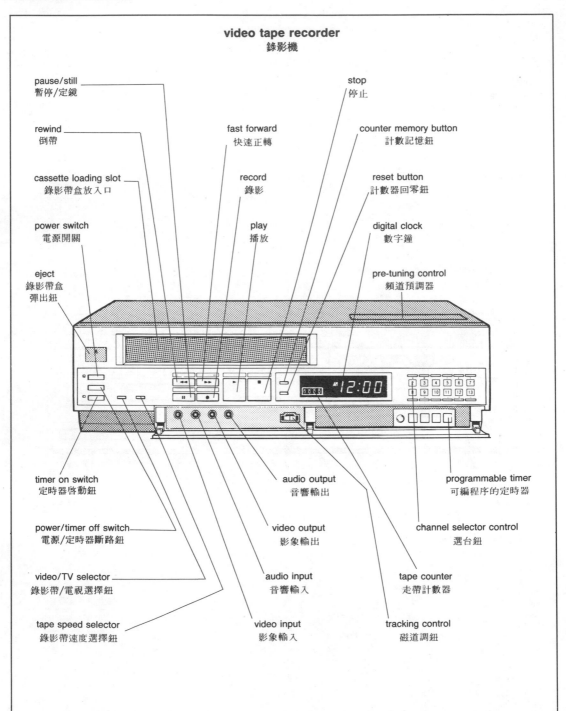

pause/still
暫停/定鏡

stop
停止

rewind
倒帶

fast forward
快速正轉

counter memory button
計數記憶鈕

cassette loading slot
錄影帶盒放入口

record
錄影

reset button
計數器回零鈕

power switch
電源開關

play
播放

digital clock
數字鐘

eject
錄影帶盒
彈出鈕

pre-tuning control
頻道預調器

timer on switch
定時器啓動鈕

audio output
音響輸出

programmable timer
可編程序的定時器

power/timer off switch
電源/定時器斷路鈕

video output
影象輸出

channel selector control
選台鈕

video/TV selector
錄影帶/電視選擇鈕

audio input
音響輸入

tape counter
走帶計數器

tape speed selector
錄影帶速度選擇鈕

video input
影象輸入

tracking control
磁道調鈕

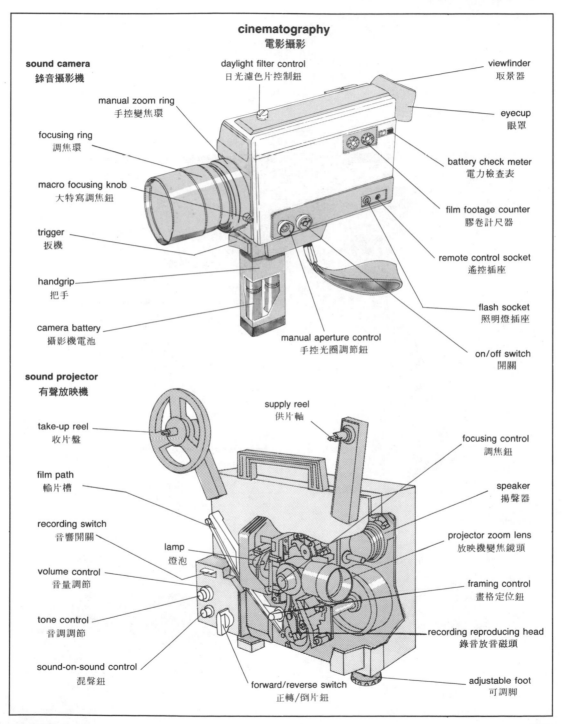

cinematography
電影攝影

sound camera
錄音攝影機

daylight filter control
日光濾色片控制鈕

viewfinder
取景器

manual zoom ring
手控變焦環

eyecup
眼罩

focusing ring
調焦環

battery check meter
電力檢查表

macro focusing knob
大特寫調焦鈕

film footage counter
膠卷計尺器

trigger
扳機

remote control socket
遙控插座

handgrip
把手

flash socket
照明燈插座

camera battery
攝影機電池

manual aperture control
手控光圈調節鈕

on/off switch
開關

sound projector
有聲放映機

take-up reel
收片盤

supply reel
供片軸

focusing control
調焦鈕

film path
輪片槽

speaker
揚聲器

recording switch
音響開關

lamp
燈泡

projector zoom lens
放映機變焦鏡頭

volume control
音量調節

framing control
畫格定位鈕

tone control
音調調節

recording reproducing head
錄音放音磁頭

sound-on-sound control
混聲鈕

forward/reverse switch
正轉/倒片鈕

adjustable foot
可調脚

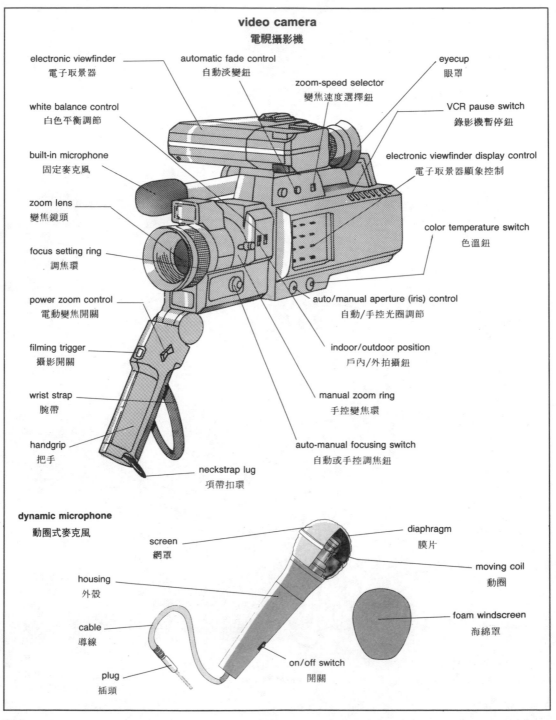

video camera
電視攝影機

electronic viewfinder
電子取景器

automatic fade control
自動淡變鈕

zoom-speed selector
變焦速度選擇鈕

eyecup
眼罩

white balance control
白色平衡調節

VCR pause switch
錄影機暫停鈕

built-in microphone
固定麥克風

electronic viewfinder display control
電子取景器顯象控制

zoom lens
變焦鏡頭

color temperature switch
色溫鈕

focus setting ring
調焦環

power zoom control
電動變焦開關

auto/manual aperture (iris) control
自動/手控光圈調節

filming trigger
攝影開關

indoor/outdoor position
戶內/外拍攝鈕

wrist strap
腕帶

manual zoom ring
手控變焦環

handgrip
把手

auto-manual focusing switch
自動或手控調焦鈕

neckstrap lug
項帶扣環

dynamic microphone
動圈式麥克風

screen
網罩

diaphragm
膜片

moving coil
動圈

housing
外殼

cable
導線

foam windscreen
海綿罩

on/off switch
開關

plug
插頭

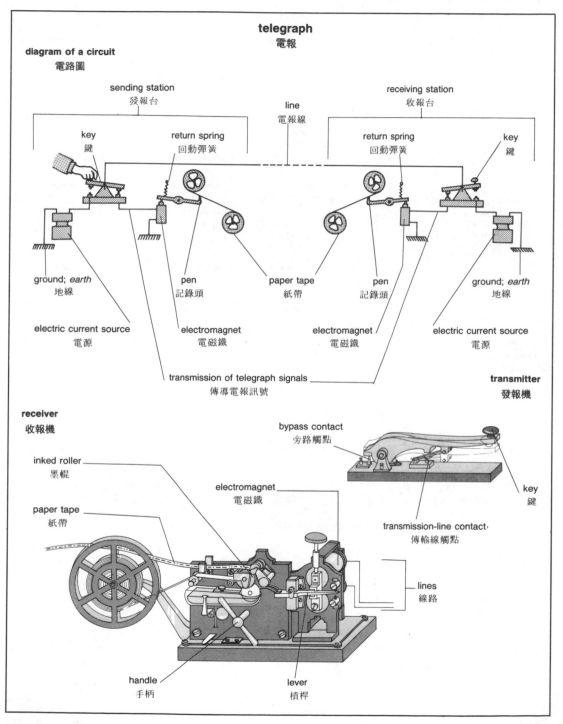

telegraph
電報

diagram of a circuit
電路圖

sending station
發報台

line
電報線

receiving station
收報台

key
鍵

return spring
回動彈簧

return spring
回動彈簧

key
鍵

ground; *earth*
地線

pen
記錄頭

paper tape
紙帶

pen
記錄頭

ground; *earth*
地線

electric current source
電源

electromagnet
電磁鐵

electromagnet
電磁鐵

electric current source
電源

transmission of telegraph signals
傳導電報訊號

transmitter
發報機

receiver
收報機

bypass contact
旁路觸點

key
鍵

inked roller
墨輥

electromagnet
電磁鐵

transmission-line contact
傳輸線觸點

paper tape
紙帶

lines
線路

handle
手柄

lever
槓桿

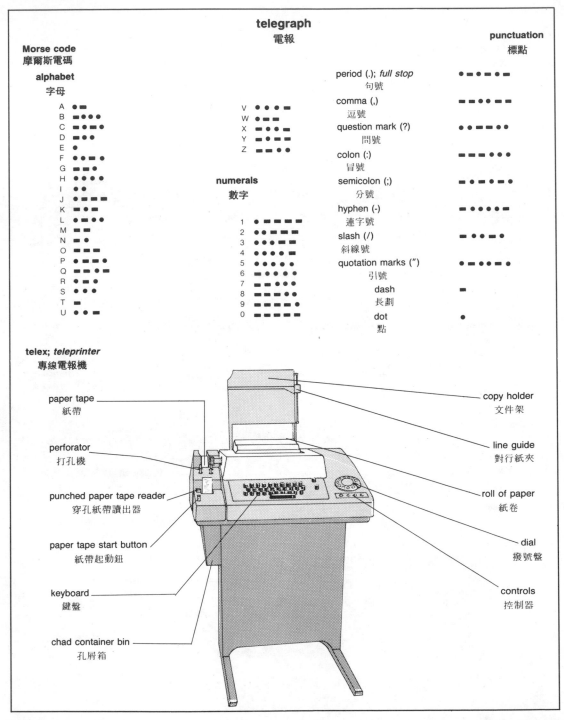

telegraph
電報

Morse code
摩爾斯電碼

alphabet
字母

A ●▬
B ▬●●●
C ▬●▬●
D ▬●●
E ●
F ●●▬●
G ▬▬●
H ●●●●
I ●●
J ●▬▬▬
K ▬●▬
L ●▬●●
M ▬▬
N ▬●
O ▬▬▬
P ●▬▬●
Q ▬▬●▬
R ●▬●
S ●●●
T ▬
U ●●▬

V ●●●▬
W ●▬▬
X ▬●●▬
Y ▬●▬▬
Z ▬▬●●

numerals
數字

1 ●▬▬▬▬
2 ●●▬▬▬
3 ●●●▬▬
4 ●●●●▬
5 ●●●●●
6 ▬●●●●
7 ▬▬●●●
8 ▬▬▬●●
9 ▬▬▬▬●
0 ▬▬▬▬▬

punctuation
標點

period (.); *full stop* ●▬●▬●▬
句號

comma (,) ▬▬●●▬▬
逗號

question mark (?) ●●▬▬●●
問號

colon (:) ▬▬▬●●●
冒號

semicolon (;) ▬●▬●▬●
分號

hyphen (-) ▬●●●●▬
連字號

slash (/) ▬●●▬●
斜線號

quotation marks (") ●▬●●▬●
引號

dash ▬

dot ●
點

telex; *teleprinter*
專線電報機

paper tape
紙帶

perforator
打孔機

punched paper tape reader
穿孔紙帶讀出器

paper tape start button
紙帶起動鈕

keyboard
鍵盤

chad container bin
孔屑箱

copy holder
文件架

line guide
對行紙夾

roll of paper
紙卷

dial
撥號盤

controls
控制器

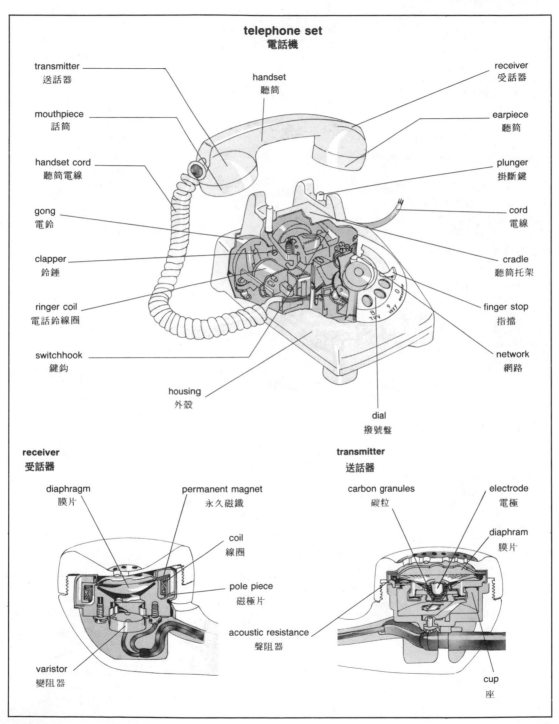

telephone set
電話機

transmitter
送話器

handset
聽筒

receiver
受話器

mouthpiece
話筒

earpiece
聽筒

handset cord
聽筒電線

plunger
掛斷鍵

gong
電鈴

cord
電線

clapper
鈴錘

cradle
聽筒托架

ringer coil
電話鈴線圈

finger stop
指擋

switchhook
鍵鈎

network
網路

housing
外殼

dial
撥號盤

receiver
受話器

diaphragm
膜片

permanent magnet
永久磁鐵

coil
線圈

pole piece
磁極片

acoustic resistance
聲阻器

varistor
變阻器

transmitter
送話器

carbon granules
碳粒

electrode
電極

diaphram
膜片

cup
座

types of telephones
電話機數種

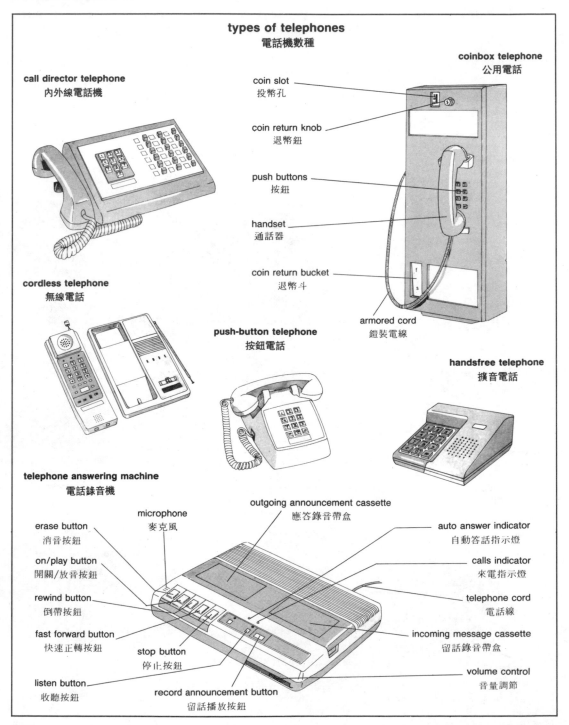

call director telephone
內外線電話機

coinbox telephone
公用電話

coin slot
投幣孔

coin return knob
退幣鈕

push buttons
按鈕

handset
通話器

coin return bucket
退幣斗

cordless telephone
無線電話

armored cord
鎧裝電線

push-button telephone
按鈕電話

handsfree telephone
擴音電話

telephone answering machine
電話錄音機

outgoing announcement cassette
應答錄音帶盒

microphone
麥克風

auto answer indicator
自動答話指示燈

erase button
消音按鈕

calls indicator
來電指示燈

on/play button
開關/放音按鈕

rewind button
倒帶按鈕

telephone cord
電話線

fast forward button
快速正轉按鈕

incoming message cassette
留話錄音帶盒

stop button
停止按鈕

listen button
收聽按鈕

volume control
音量調節

record announcement button
留話播放按鈕

television
電視

studio and control rooms
演播室和控制室

lighting and vision control room
燈光與影象控制室

video technician; *video operator*
影象技術員

lighting director
燈光指導

dimmer control; *lighting control panel*
光度調節

control panel
控制台

videotape recorder
磁帶錄影機

amplifier
擴音機

studio
演播室

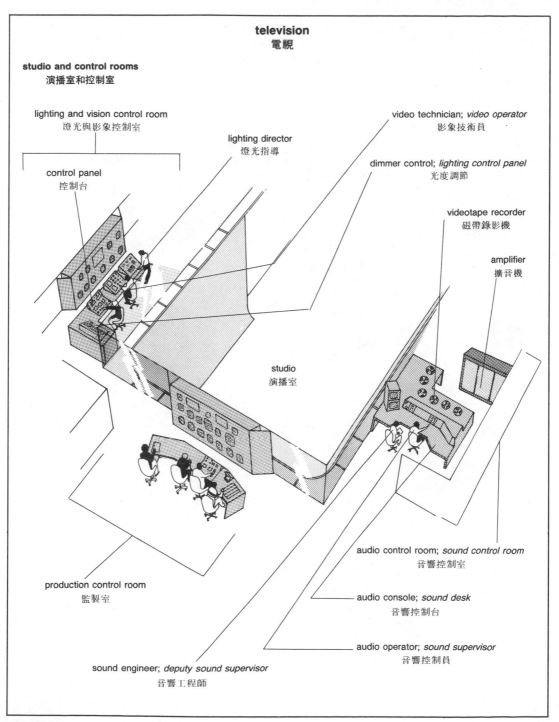

audio control room; *sound control room*
音響控制室

production control room
監製室

audio console; *sound desk*
音響控制台

audio operator; *sound supervisor*
音響控制員

sound engineer; *deputy sound supervisor*
音響工程師

television
電視

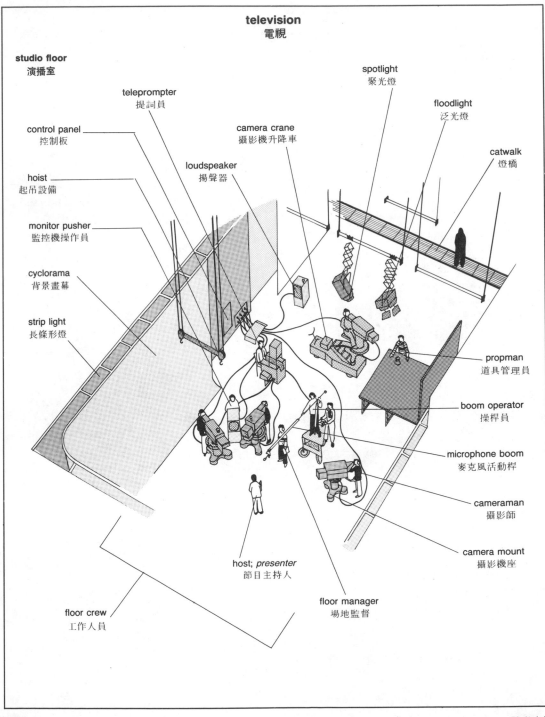

studio floor
演播室

teleprompter
提詞員

spotlight
聚光燈

floodlight
泛光燈

control panel
控制板

camera crane
攝影機升降車

catwalk
燈橋

loudspeaker
揚聲器

hoist
起吊設備

monitor pusher
監控機操作員

cyclorama
背景畫幕

strip light
長條形燈

propman
道具管理員

boom operator
操桿員

microphone boom
麥克風活動桿

cameraman
攝影師

camera mount
攝影機座

host; *presenter*
節目主持人

floor manager
場地監督

floor crew
工作人員

television
電視

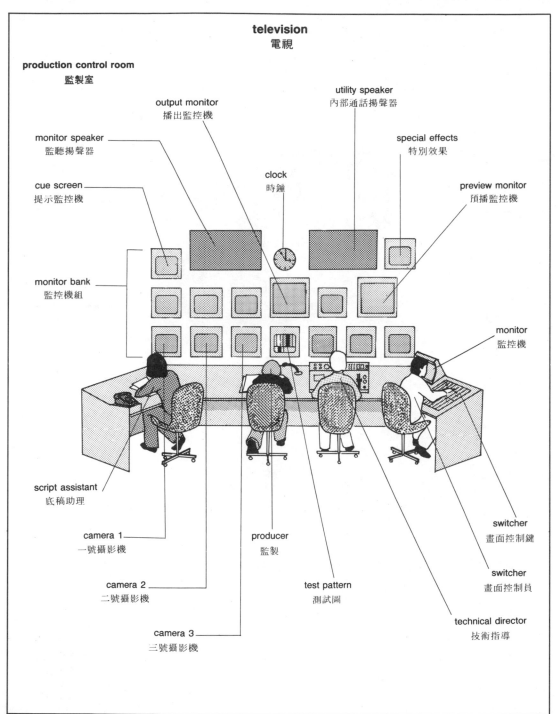

production control room
監製室

output monitor
播出監控機

utility speaker
內部通話揚聲器

monitor speaker
監聽揚聲器

special effects
特別效果

cue screen
提示監控機

clock
時鐘

preview monitor
預播監控機

monitor bank
監控機組

monitor
監控機

script assistant
底稿助理

camera 1
一號攝影機

producer
監製

switcher
畫面控制鍵

switcher
畫面控制員

camera 2
二號攝影機

test pattern
測試圖

technical director
技術指導

camera 3
三號攝影機

television
電視

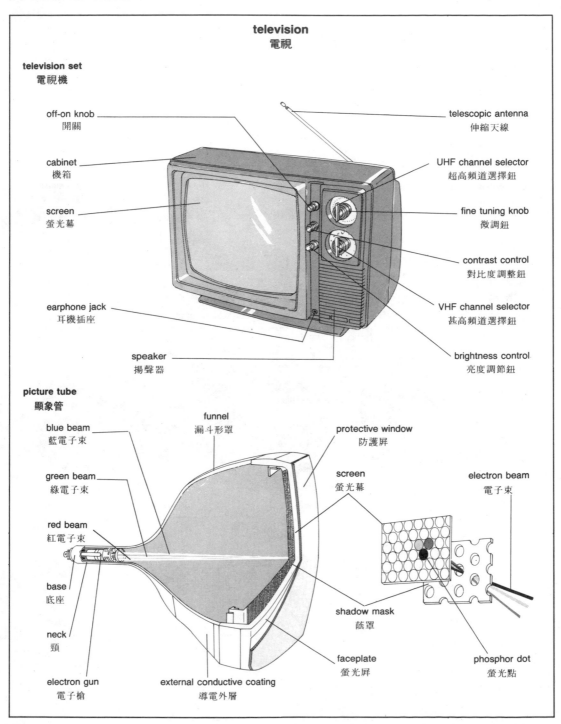

television set
電視機

off-on knob
開關

telescopic antenna
伸縮天線

cabinet
機箱

UHF channel selector
超高頻道選擇鈕

screen
螢光幕

fine tuning knob
微調鈕

contrast control
對比度調整鈕

earphone jack
耳機插座

VHF channel selector
甚高頻道選擇鈕

speaker
揚聲器

brightness control
亮度調節鈕

picture tube
顯象管

blue beam
藍電子束

funnel
漏斗形罩

protective window
防護屏

green beam
綠電子束

screen
螢光幕

electron beam
電子束

red beam
紅電子束

base
底座

shadow mask
蔭罩

neck
頸

faceplate
螢光屏

phosphor dot
螢光點

electron gun
電子槍

external conductive coating
導電外層

telecommunication satellites
電信衛星

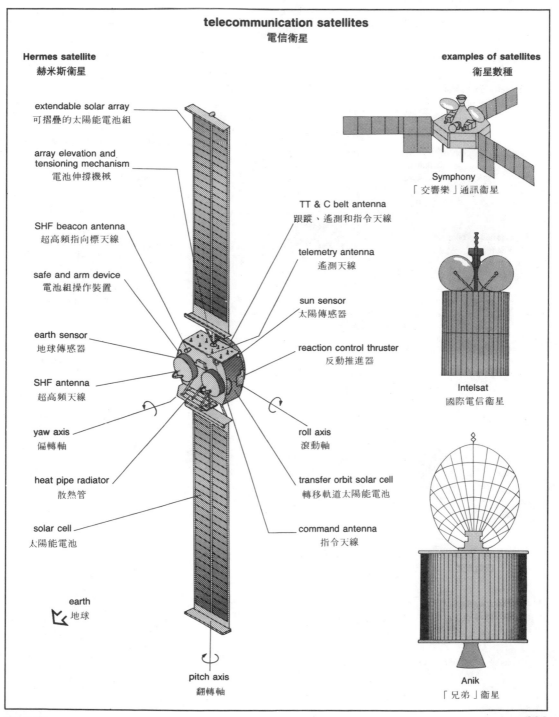

Hermes satellite
赫米斯衛星

extendable solar array
可摺疊的太陽能電池組

array elevation and tensioning mechanism
電池伸撐機械

SHF beacon antenna
超高頻指向標天線

safe and arm device
電池組操作裝置

earth sensor
地球傳感器

SHF antenna
超高頻天線

yaw axis
偏轉軸

heat pipe radiator
散熱管

solar cell
太陽能電池

earth
地球

pitch axis
翻轉軸

TT & C belt antenna
跟蹤、遙測和指令天線

telemetry antenna
遙測天線

sun sensor
太陽傳感器

reaction control thruster
反動推進器

roll axis
滾動軸

transfer orbit solar cell
轉移軌道太陽能電池

command antenna
指令天線

examples of satellites
衛星數種

Symphony
「交響樂」通訊衛星

Intelsat
國際電信衛星

Anik
「兄弟」衛星

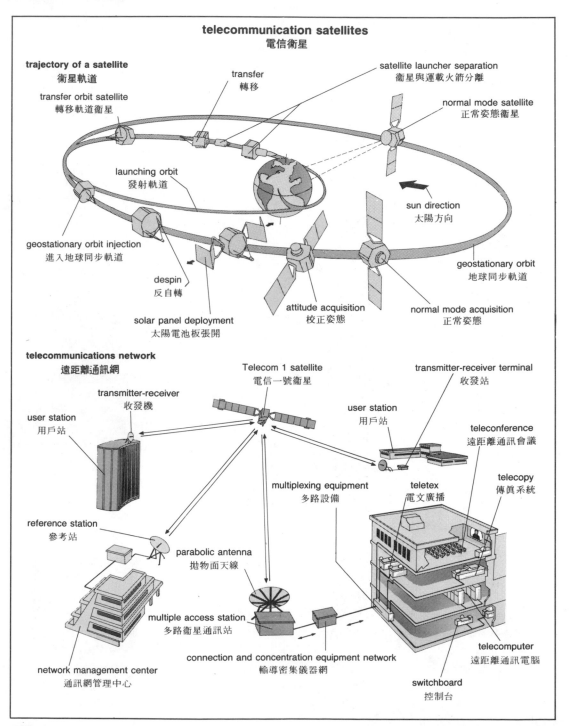

telecommunication satellites
電信衛星

trajectory of a satellite
衛星軌道

transfer
轉移

satellite launcher separation
衛星與運載火箭分離

transfer orbit satellite
轉移軌道衛星

normal mode satellite
正常姿態衛星

launching orbit
發射軌道

sun direction
太陽方向

geostationary orbit injection
進入地球同步軌道

geostationary orbit
地球同步軌道

despin
反自轉

solar panel deployment
太陽電池板張開

attitude acquisition
校正姿態

normal mode acquisition
正常姿態

telecommunications network
遠距離通訊網

Telecom 1 satellite
電信一號衛星

transmitter-receiver terminal
收發站

transmitter-receiver
收發機

user station
用戶站

teleconference
遠距離通訊會議

user station
用戶站

telecopy
傳真系統

multiplexing equipment
多路設備

teletex
電文廣播

reference station
參考站

parabolic antenna
拋物面天線

multiple access station
多路衛星通訊站

telecomputer
遠距離通訊電腦

connection and concentration equipment network
輸導密集儀器網

network management center
通訊網管理中心

switchboard
控制台

TRANSPORTATION
交通運輸

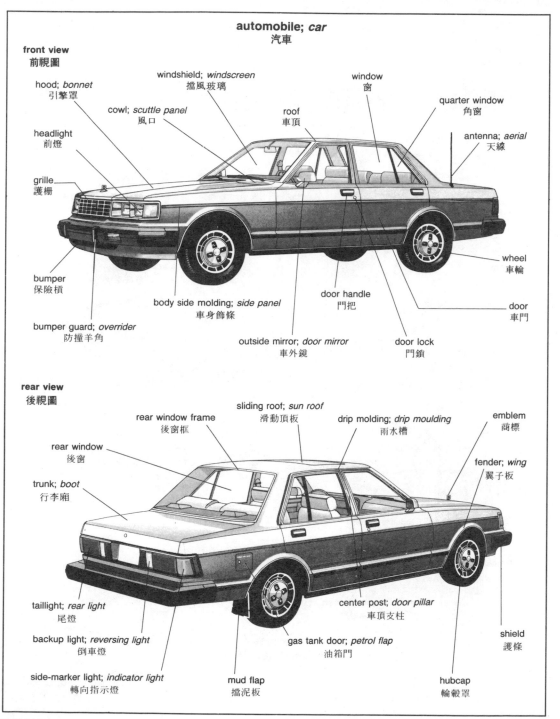

automobile; *car*
汽車

front view
前視圖

hood; *bonnet*
引擎罩

windshield; *windscreen*
擋風玻璃

window
窗

quarter window
角窗

cowl; *scuttle panel*
風口

roof
車頂

antenna; *aerial*
天線

headlight
前燈

grille
護柵

wheel
車輪

bumper
保險槓

body side molding; *side panel*
車身飾條

door handle
門把

door
車門

bumper guard; *overrider*
防撞羊角

outside mirror; *door mirror*
車外鏡

door lock
門鎖

rear view
後視圖

sliding roof; *sun roof*
滑動頂板

rear window frame
後窗框

drip molding; *drip moulding*
雨水槽

emblem
商標

rear window
後窗

fender; *wing*
翼子板

trunk; *boot*
行李廂

taillight; *rear light*
尾燈

center post; *door pillar*
車頂支柱

shield
護條

backup light; *reversing light*
倒車燈

gas tank door; *petrol flap*
油箱門

side-marker light; *indicator light*
轉向指示燈

mud flap
擋泥板

hubcap
輪轂罩

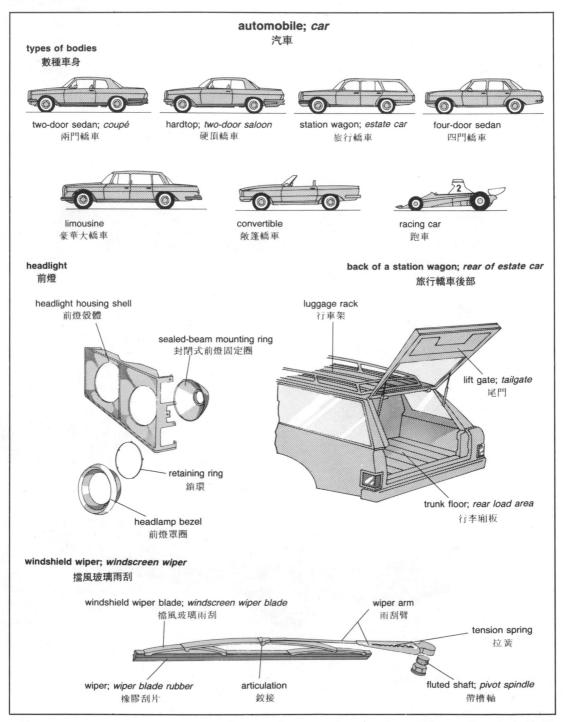

automobile; *car*
汽車

types of bodies
數種車身

two-door sedan; *coupé*
兩門轎車

hardtop; *two-door saloon*
硬頂轎車

station wagon; *estate car*
旅行轎車

four-door sedan
四門轎車

limousine
豪華大轎車

convertible
敞篷轎車

racing car
跑車

headlight
前燈

headlight housing shell
前燈殼體

sealed-beam mounting ring
封閉式前燈固定圈

retaining ring
鎖環

headlamp bezel
前燈罩圈

back of a station wagon; *rear of estate car*
旅行轎車後部

luggage rack
行車架

lift gate; *tailgate*
尾門

trunk floor; *rear load area*
行李廂板

windshield wiper; *windscreen wiper*
擋風玻璃雨刮

windshield wiper blade; *windscreen wiper blade*
擋風玻璃雨刮

wiper arm
雨刮臂

tension spring
拉簧

wiper; *wiper blade rubber*
橡膠刮片

articulation
鉸接

fluted shaft; *pivot spindle*
帶槽軸

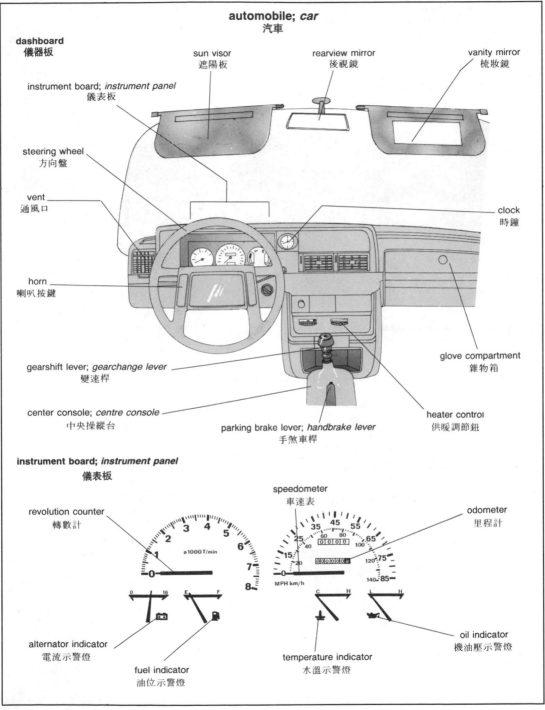

automobile; *car*
汽車

dashboard
儀器板

sun visor
遮陽板

rearview mirror
後視鏡

vanity mirror
梳妝鏡

instrument board; *instrument panel*
儀表板

steering wheel
方向盤

clock
時鐘

vent
通風口

horn
喇叭按鍵

glove compartment
雜物箱

gearshift lever; *gearchange lever*
變速桿

center console; *centre console*
中央操縱台

heater control
供暖調節鈕

parking brake lever; *handbrake lever*
手煞車桿

instrument board; *instrument panel*
儀表板

speedometer
車速表

revolution counter
轉數計

odometer
里程計

a 1000 T/min

MPH km/h

alternator indicator
電流示警燈

oil indicator
機油壓示警燈

fuel indicator
油位示警燈

temperature indicator
水溫示警燈

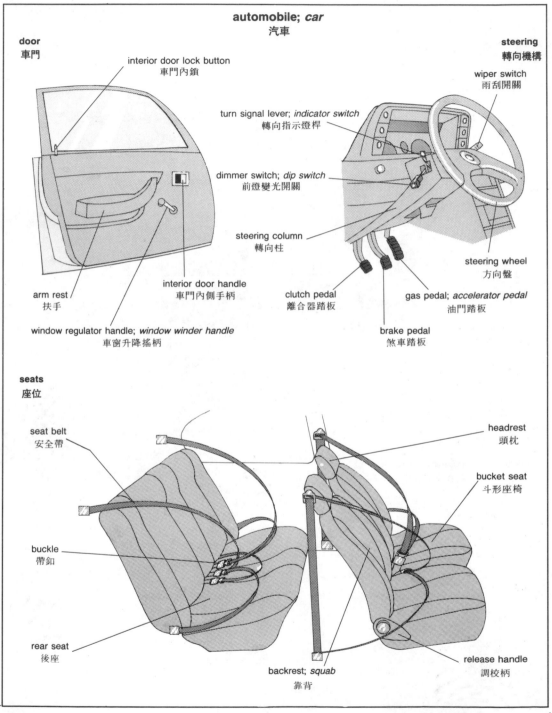

automobile; *car*
汽車

door
車門

interior door lock button
車門內鎖

turn signal lever; *indicator switch*
轉向指示燈桿

dimmer switch; *dip switch*
前燈變光開關

steering column
轉向柱

arm rest
扶手

interior door handle
車門內側手柄

window regulator handle; *window winder handle*
車窗升降搖柄

clutch pedal
離合器踏板

brake pedal
煞車踏板

gas pedal; *accelerator pedal*
油門踏板

steering
轉向機構

wiper switch
雨刮開關

steering wheel
方向盤

seats
座位

seat belt
安全帶

buckle
帶釦

rear seat
後座

backrest; *squab*
靠背

headrest
頭枕

bucket seat
斗形座椅

release handle
調校柄

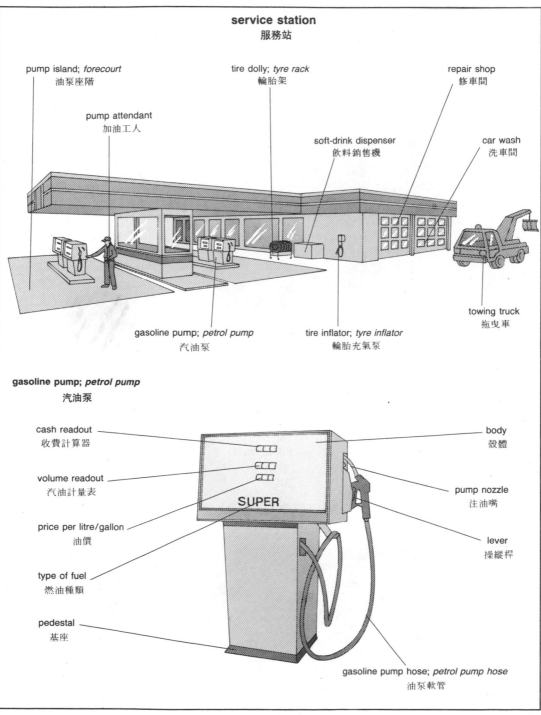

service station
服務站

pump island; *forecourt*
油泵座階

pump attendant
加油工人

tire dolly; *tyre rack*
輪胎架

soft-drink dispenser
飲料銷售機

repair shop
修車間

car wash
洗車間

gasoline pump; *petrol pump*
汽油泵

tire inflator; *tyre inflator*
輪胎充氣泵

towing truck
拖曳車

gasoline pump; *petrol pump*
汽油泵

cash readout
收費計算器

volume readout
汽油計量表

price per litre/gallon
油價

type of fuel
燃油種類

pedestal
基座

body
殼體

pump nozzle
注油嘴

lever
操縱桿

gasoline pump hose; *petrol pump hose*
油泵軟管

SUPER

semitrailer
半掛貨車

refrigeration unit
製冷裝置

clearance light
示廓燈

electrical connection
電路接頭

sidewall
側壁

roof
箱頂

reflector
反光器

vent door
通氣門

upper side-rail
上側梁

frontwall
前壁

battery box
電池箱

partlow chart
記溫圖表

kingpin
主銷

support leg
停放支架

auxiliary tank
備用油箱

lower side-rail
下側梁

sand shoe
寬底脚座

support leg crank
停放支架曲柄

mud flap
擋泥板

red marker light
紅色尾燈

platform
載台掛車

bulkhead
橫隔板

deck
載台
面板

turn signal; *indicator*
轉向指示燈

taillight; *rear light*
尾燈

support leg crank
停放支架曲柄

rub rail
防擦擋條

stake pocket
豎柱凹槽

bumper
檔板

mud flap
擋泥板

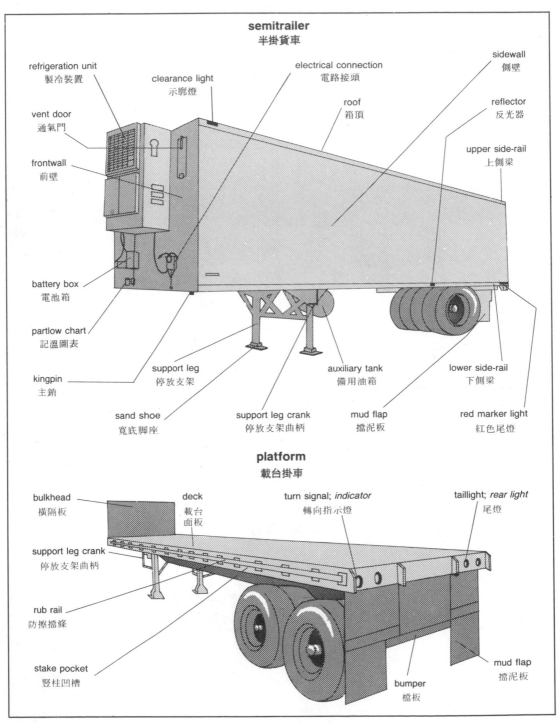

truck trailer; *tractor unit*
貨運掛車

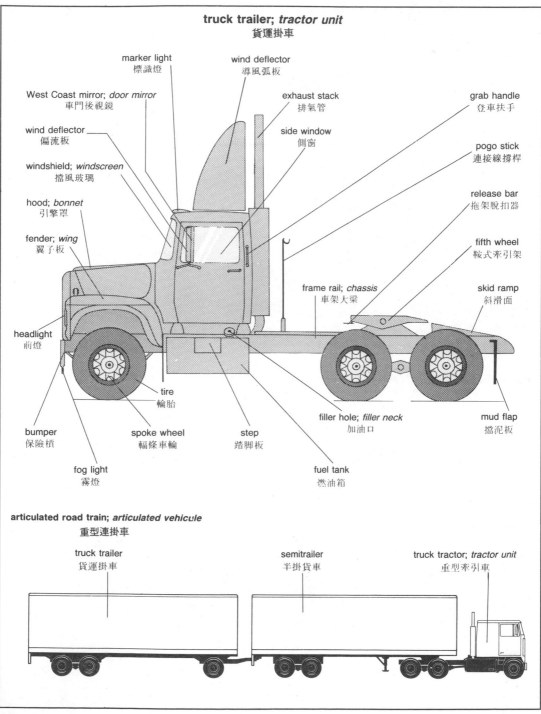

marker light
標識燈

wind deflector
導風弧板

exhaust stack
排氣管

West Coast mirror; *door mirror*
車門後視鏡

side window
側窗

grab handle
登車扶手

wind deflector
偏流板

pogo stick
連接線撐桿

windshield; *windscreen*
擋風玻璃

release bar
拖架脫扣器

hood; *bonnet*
引擎罩

fender; *wing*
翼子板

fifth wheel
鞍式牽引架

frame rail; *chassis*
車架大梁

skid ramp
斜滑面

headlight
前燈

tire
輪胎

filler hole; *filler neck*
加油口

mud flap
擋泥板

bumper
保險槓

spoke wheel
輻條車輪

step
踏腳板

fog light
霧燈

fuel tank
燃油箱

articulated road train; *articulated vehicle*
重型連掛車

truck trailer
貨運掛車

semitrailer
半掛貨車

truck tractor; *tractor unit*
重型牽引車

engines
引擎

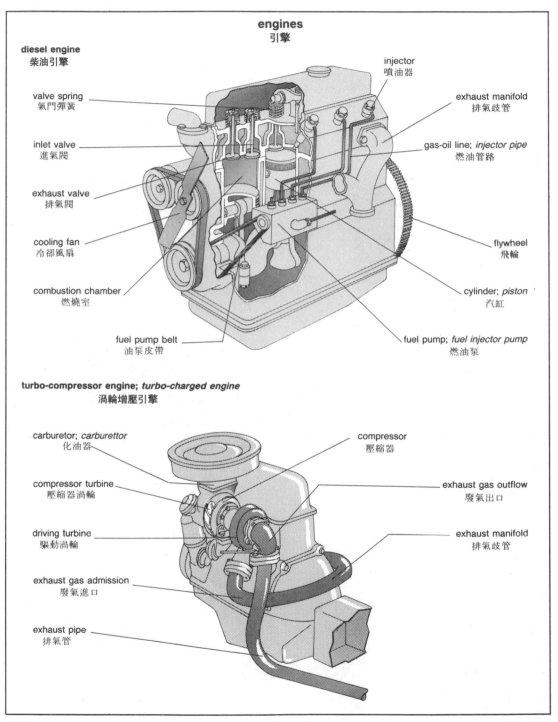

diesel engine
柴油引擎

injector
噴油器

valve spring
氣門彈簧

exhaust manifold
排氣歧管

inlet valve
進氣閥

gas-oil line; *injector pipe*
燃油管路

exhaust valve
排氣閥

flywheel
飛輪

cooling fan
冷卻風扇

cylinder; *piston*
汽缸

combustion chamber
燃燒室

fuel pump belt
油泵皮帶

fuel pump; *fuel injector pump*
燃油泵

turbo-compressor engine; *turbo-charged engine*
渦輪增壓引擎

carburetor; *carburettor*
化油器

compressor
壓縮器

compressor turbine
壓縮器渦輪

exhaust gas outflow
廢氣出口

driving turbine
驅動渦輪

exhaust manifold
排氣歧管

exhaust gas admission
廢氣進口

exhaust pipe
排氣管

engine
引擎

gasoline engine; *petrol engine*
汽油引擎

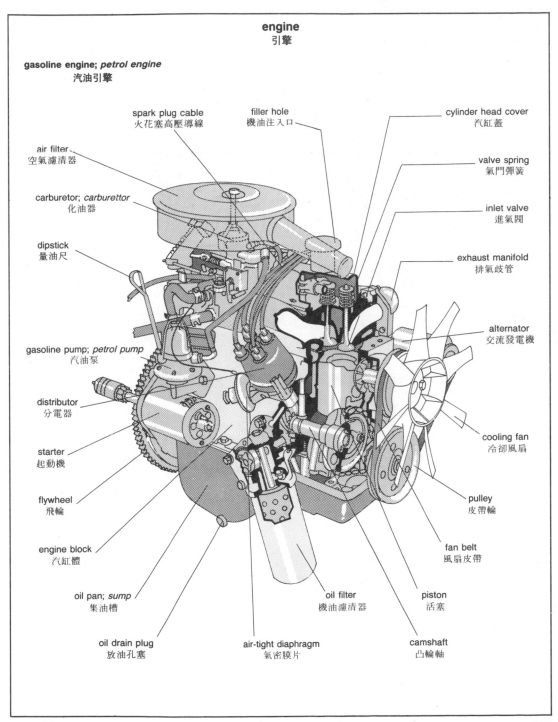

spark plug cable
火花塞高壓導線

filler hole
機油注入口

cylinder head cover
汽缸蓋

air filter
空氣濾清器

valve spring
氣門彈簧

carburetor; *carburettor*
化油器

inlet valve
進氣閥

dipstick
量油尺

exhaust manifold
排氣歧管

alternator
交流發電機

gasoline pump; *petrol pump*
汽油泵

distributor
分電器

cooling fan
冷卻風扇

starter
起動機

pulley
皮帶輪

flywheel
飛輪

fan belt
風扇皮帶

engine block
汽缸體

oil pan; *sump*
集油槽

oil filter
機油濾清器

piston
活塞

oil drain plug
放油孔塞

air-tight diaphragm
氣密膜片

camshaft
凸輪軸

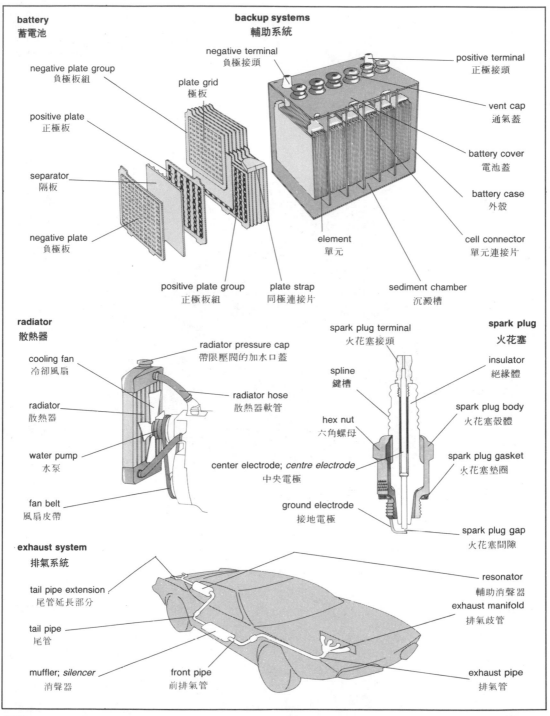

battery
蓄電池

backup systems
輔助系統

negative plate group
負極板組

plate grid
極板

positive plate
正極板

negative terminal
負極接頭

positive terminal
正極接頭

vent cap
通氣蓋

battery cover
電池蓋

separator
隔板

battery case
外殼

negative plate
負極板

element
單元

cell connector
單元連接片

positive plate group
正極板組

plate strap
同極連接片

sediment chamber
沉澱槽

radiator
散熱器

radiator pressure cap
帶限壓閥的加水口蓋

cooling fan
冷卻風扇

radiator hose
散熱器軟管

radiator
散熱器

water pump
水泵

fan belt
風扇皮帶

spark plug
火花塞

spark plug terminal
火花塞接頭

insulator
絕緣體

spline
鍵槽

spark plug body
火花塞殼體

hex nut
六角螺母

spark plug gasket
火花塞墊圈

center electrode; *centre electrode*
中央電極

ground electrode
接地電極

spark plug gap
火花塞間隙

exhaust system
排氣系統

tail pipe extension
尾管延長部分

resonator
輔助消聲器

exhaust manifold
排氣歧管

tail pipe
尾管

muffler; *silencer*
消聲器

front pipe
前排氣管

exhaust pipe
排氣管

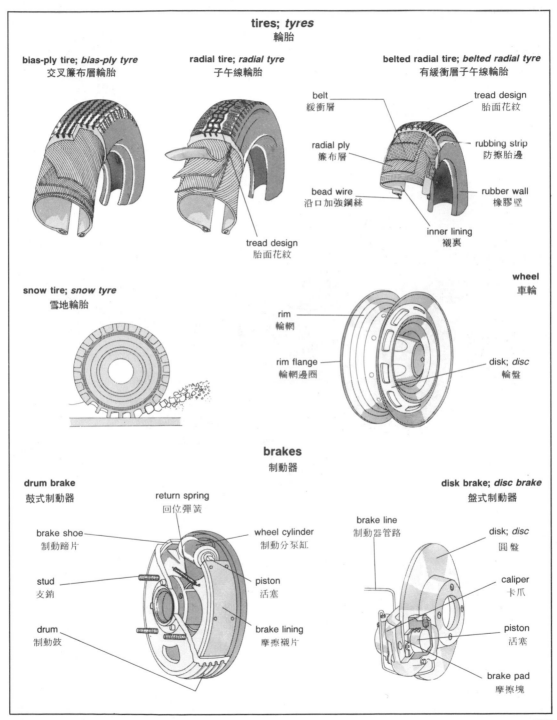

tires; *tyres*
輪胎

bias-ply tire; *bias-ply tyre*
交叉簾布層輪胎

radial tire; *radial tyre*
子午線輪胎

belted radial tire; *belted radial tyre*
有緩衝層子午線輪胎

belt
緩衝層

tread design
胎面花紋

radial ply
簾布層

rubbing strip
防擦胎邊

bead wire
沿口加強鋼絲

rubber wall
橡膠壁

inner lining
襯裏

tread design
胎面花紋

snow tire; *snow tyre*
雪地輪胎

wheel
車輪

rim
輪輞

rim flange
輪輞邊圈

disk; *disc*
輪盤

brakes
制動器

drum brake
鼓式制動器

return spring
回位彈簧

disk brake; *disc brake*
盤式制動器

brake shoe
制動蹄片

wheel cylinder
制動分泵缸

brake line
制動器管路

disk; *disc*
圓盤

stud
支銷

piston
活塞

caliper
卡爪

drum
制動鼓

brake lining
摩擦襯片

piston
活塞

brake pad
摩擦塊

snowmobile
雪地機車

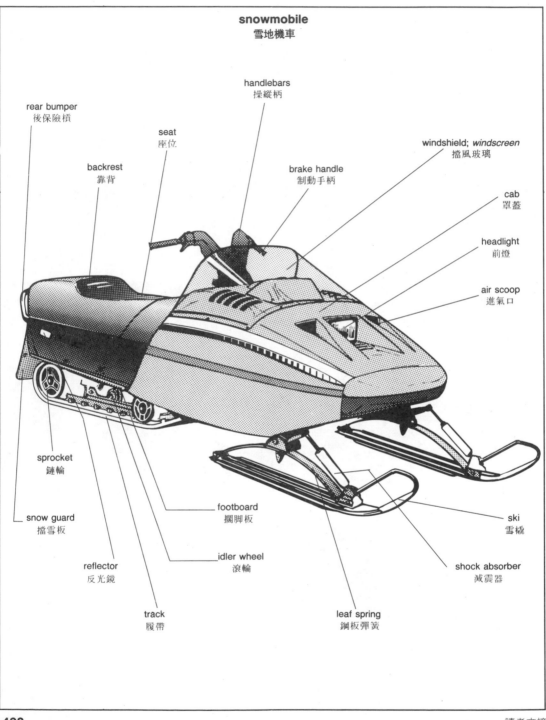

handlebars
操縱柄

rear bumper
後保險槓

seat
座位

windshield; *windscreen*
擋風玻璃

backrest
靠背

brake handle
制動手柄

cab
罩蓋

headlight
前燈

air scoop
進氣口

sprocket
鏈輪

snow guard
擋雪板

footboard
攔腳板

ski
雪橇

reflector
反光鏡

idler wheel
滾輪

shock absorber
減震器

track
履帶

leaf spring
鋼板彈簧

motorcycle
摩托車

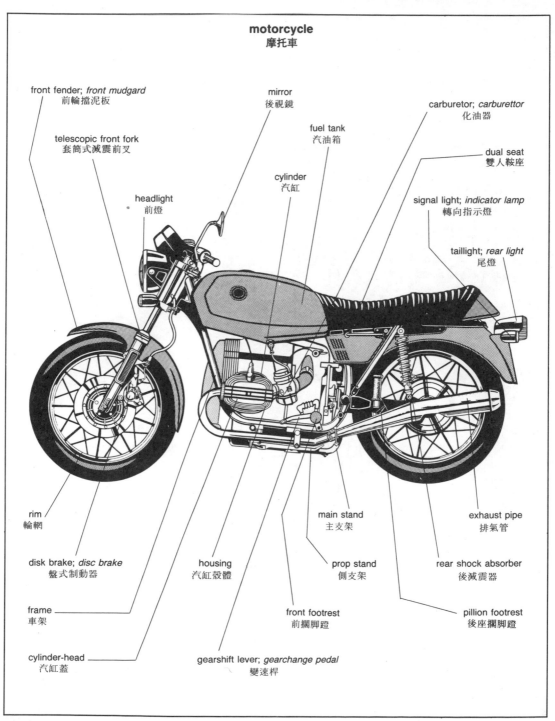

front fender; *front mudgard*
前輪擋泥板

mirror
後視鏡

carburetor; *carburettor*
化油器

telescopic front fork
套筒式減震前叉

fuel tank
汽油箱

dual seat
雙人鞍座

cylinder
汽缸

signal light; *indicator lamp*
轉向指示燈

headlight
前燈

taillight; *rear light*
尾燈

rim
輪輞

main stand
主支架

exhaust pipe
排氣管

disk brake; *disc brake*
盤式制動器

housing
汽缸殼體

prop stand
側支架

rear shock absorber
後減震器

frame
車架

front footrest
前擱腳蹬

pillion footrest
後座擱腳蹬

cylinder-head
汽缸蓋

gearshift lever; *gearchange pedal*
變速桿

motorcycle
摩托車

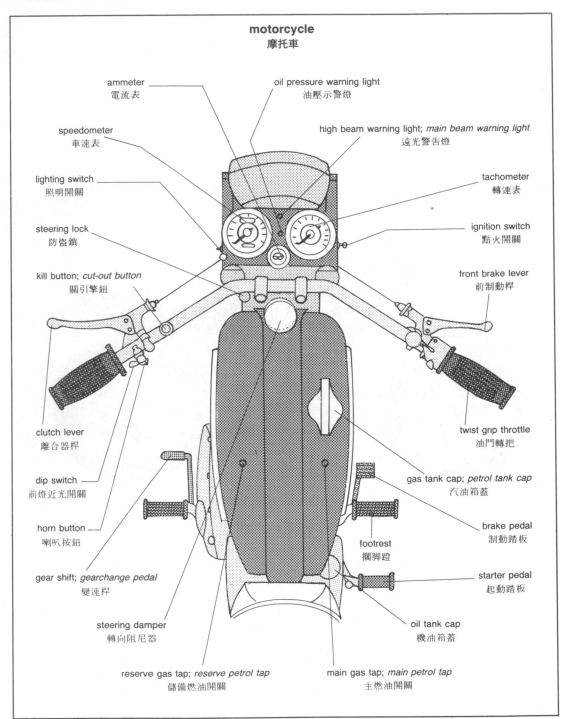

ammeter
電流表

oil pressure warning light
油壓示警燈

high beam warning light; *main beam warning light*
遠光警告燈

speedometer
車速表

lighting switch
照明開關

tachometer
轉速表

steering lock
防盜鎖

ignition switch
點火開關

kill button; *cut-out button*
關引擎鈕

front brake lever
前制動桿

clutch lever
離合器桿

twist grip throttle
油門轉把

dip switch
前燈近光開關

gas tank cap; *petrol tank cap*
汽油箱蓋

horn button
喇叭按鈕

brake pedal
制動踏板

footrest
擱脚蹬

gear shift; *gearchange pedal*
變速桿

starter pedal
起動踏板

steering damper
轉向阻尼器

oil tank cap
機油箱蓋

reserve gas tap; *reserve petrol tap*
儲備燃油開關

main gas tap; *main petrol tap*
主燃油開關

bicycle
脚踏車

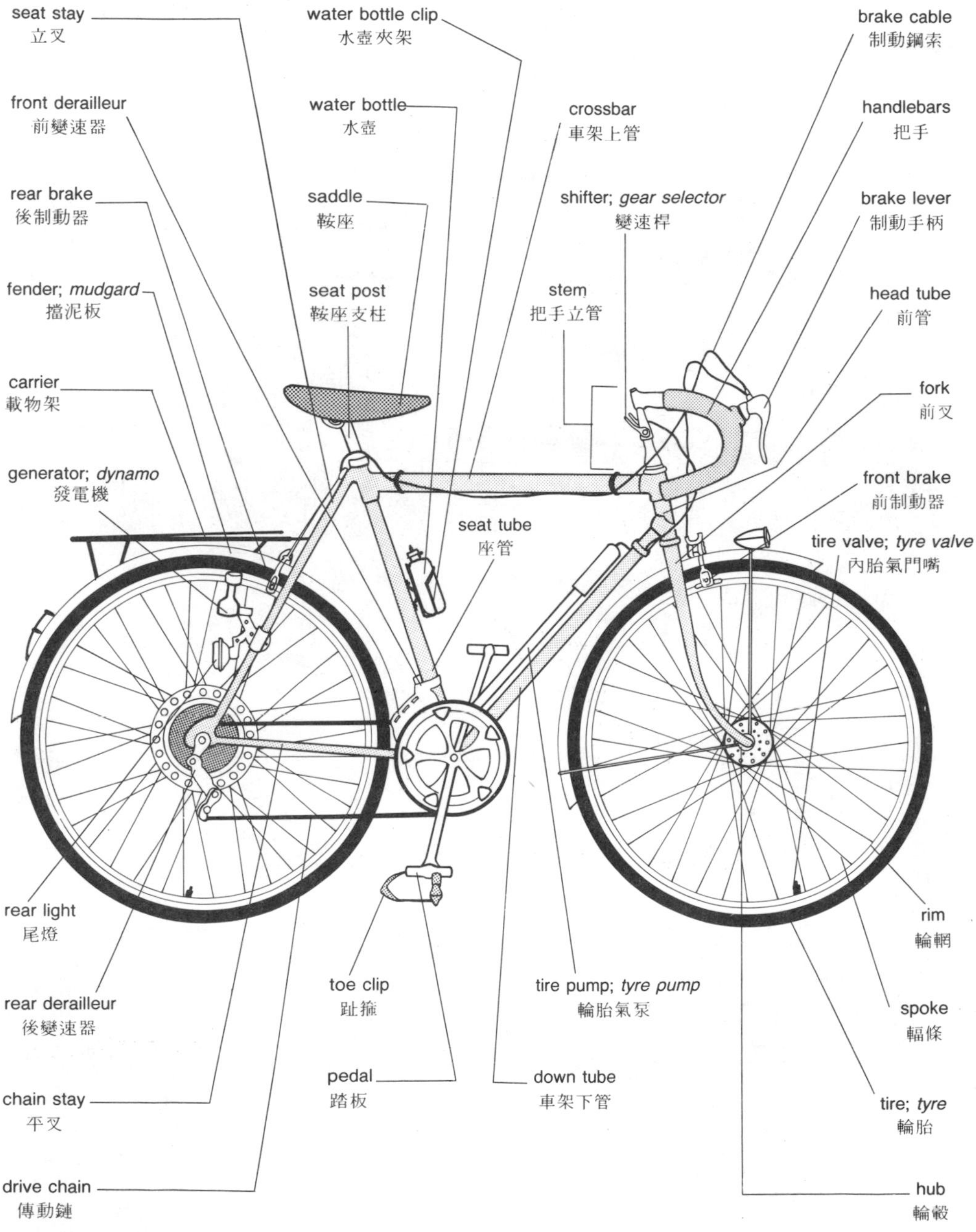
seat stay
立叉
front derailleur
前變速器
rear brake
後制動器
fender; *mudgard*
擋泥板
carrier
載物架
generator; *dynamo*
發電機
rear light
尾燈
rear derailleur
後變速器
chain stay
平叉
drive chain
傳動鏈
water bottle clip
水壺夾架
water bottle
水壺
saddle
鞍座
seat post
鞍座支柱
seat tube
座管
toe clip
趾箍
pedal
踏板
crossbar
車架上管
shifter; *gear selector*
變速桿
stem
把手立管
tire pump; *tyre pump*
輪胎氣泵
down tube
車架下管
brake cable
制動鋼索
handlebars
把手
brake lever
制動手柄
head tube
前管
fork
前叉
front brake
前制動器
tire valve; *tyre valve*
內胎氣門嘴
rim
輪輞
spoke
輻條
tire; *tyre*
輪胎
hub
輪轂

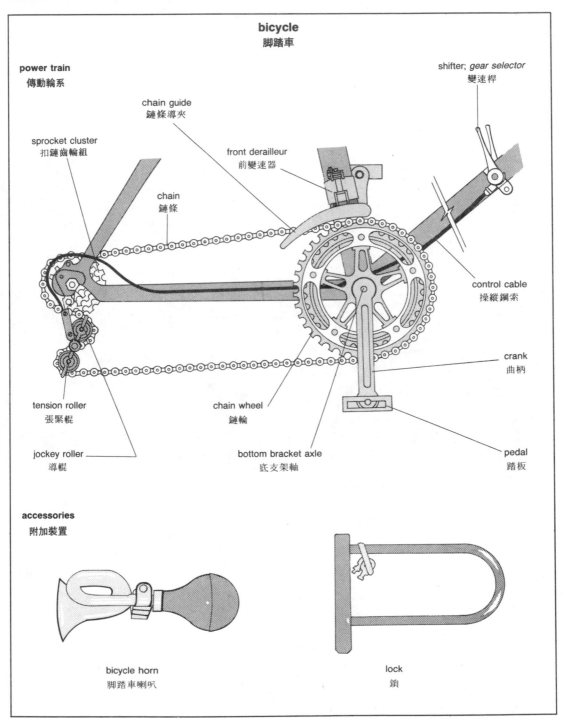

bicycle
腳踏車

power train
傳動輪系

shifter; *gear selector*
變速桿

chain guide
鏈條導夾

sprocket cluster
扣鏈齒輪組

front derailleur
前變速器

chain
鏈條

control cable
操縱鋼索

crank
曲柄

tension roller
張緊輥

chain wheel
鏈輪

jockey roller
導輥

bottom bracket axle
底支架軸

pedal
踏板

accessories
附加裝置

bicycle horn
腳踏車喇叭

lock
鎖

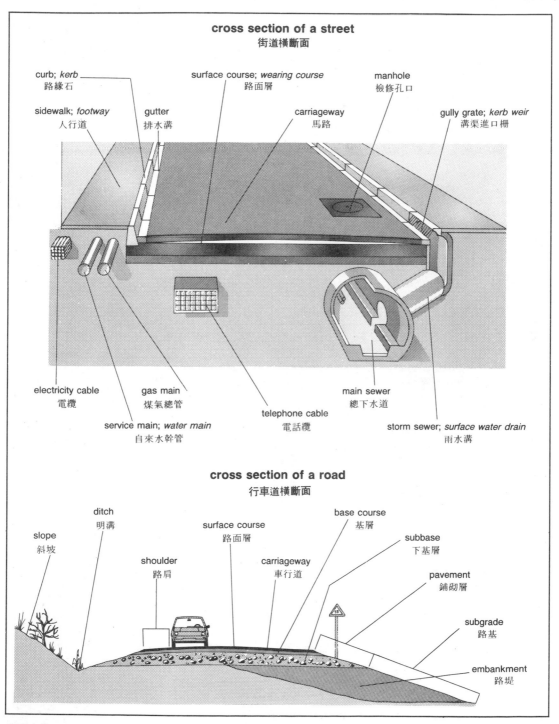

cross section of a street
街道橫斷面

curb; *kerb*
路緣石

sidewalk; *footway*
人行道

gutter
排水溝

surface course; *wearing course*
路面層

carriageway
馬路

manhole
檢修孔口

gully grate; *kerb weir*
溝渠進口柵

electricity cable
電纜

gas main
煤氣總管

service main; *water main*
自來水幹管

telephone cable
電話纜

main sewer
總下水道

storm sewer; *surface water drain*
雨水溝

cross section of a road
行車道橫斷面

slope
斜坡

ditch
明溝

shoulder
路肩

surface course
路面層

carriageway
車行道

base course
基層

subbase
下基層

pavement
鋪砌層

subgrade
路基

embankment
路堤

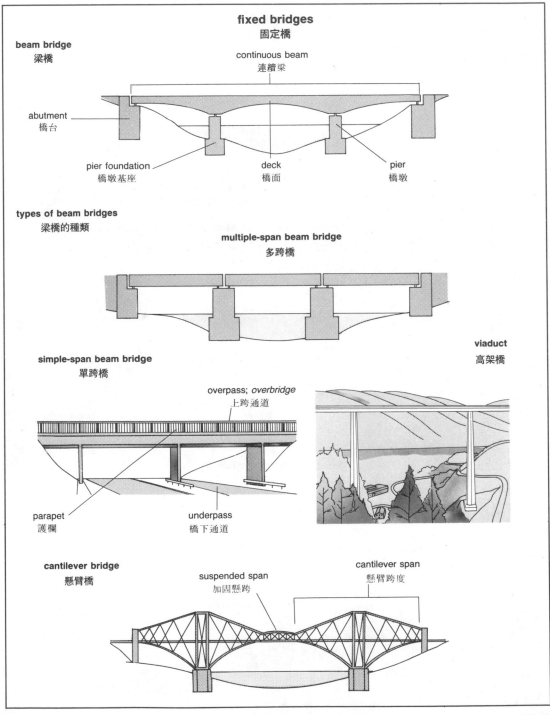

fixed bridges
固定橋

beam bridge
梁橋

continuous beam
連續梁

abutment
橋台

pier foundation
橋墩基座

deck
橋面

pier
橋墩

types of beam bridges
梁橋的種類

multiple-span beam bridge
多跨橋

viaduct
高架橋

simple-span beam bridge
單跨橋

overpass; *overbridge*
上跨通道

parapet
護欄

underpass
橋下通道

cantilever bridge
懸臂橋

suspended span
加固懸跨

cantilever span
懸臂跨度

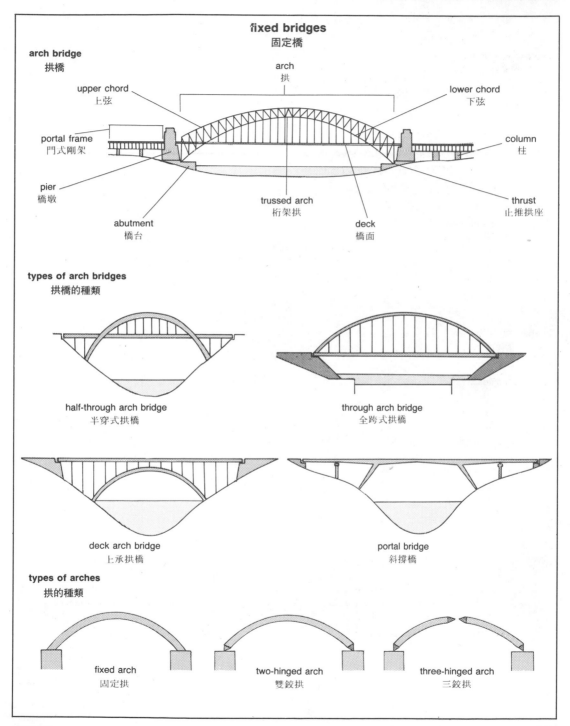

fixed bridges
固定橋

arch bridge
拱橋

arch
拱

upper chord
上弦

lower chord
下弦

portal frame
門式剛架

column
柱

pier
橋墩

trussed arch
桁架拱

thrust
止推拱座

abutment
橋台

deck
橋面

types of arch bridges
拱橋的種類

half-through arch bridge
半穿式拱橋

through arch bridge
全跨式拱橋

deck arch bridge
上承拱橋

portal bridge
斜撐橋

types of arches
拱的種類

fixed arch
固定拱

two-hinged arch
雙鉸拱

three-hinged arch
三鉸拱

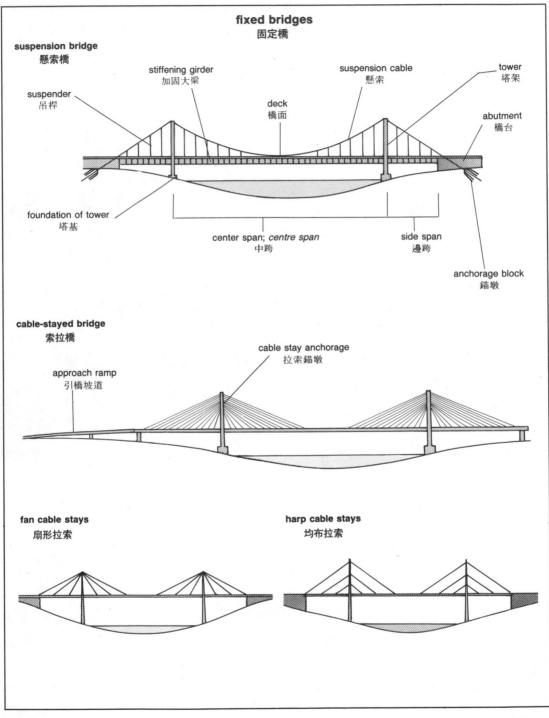

fixed bridges
固定橋

suspension bridge
懸索橋

suspender
吊桿

stiffening girder
加固大梁

deck
橋面

suspension cable
懸索

tower
塔架

abutment
橋台

foundation of tower
塔基

center span; *centre span*
中跨

side span
邊跨

anchorage block
錨墩

cable-stayed bridge
索拉橋

approach ramp
引橋坡道

cable stay anchorage
拉索錨墩

fan cable stays
扇形拉索

harp cable stays
均布拉索

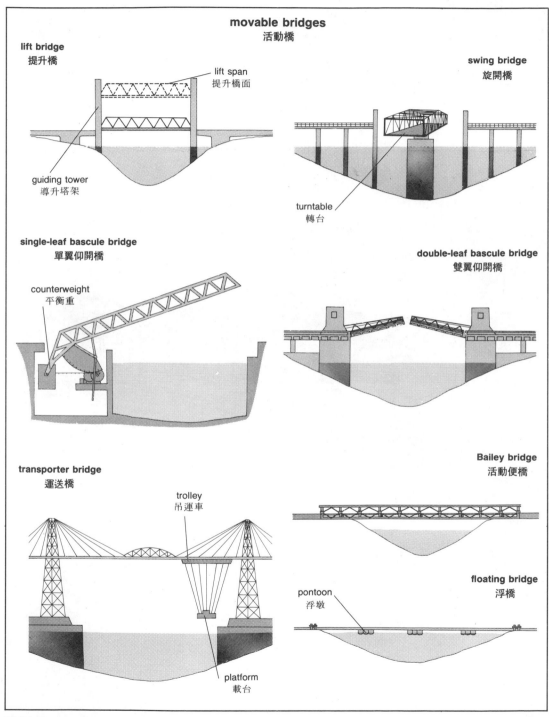

movable bridges
活動橋

lift bridge
提升橋

lift span
提升橋面

guiding tower
導升塔架

swing bridge
旋開橋

turntable
轉台

single-leaf bascule bridge
單翼仰開橋

counterweight
平衡重

double-leaf bascule bridge
雙翼仰開橋

transporter bridge
運送橋

trolley
吊運車

Bailey bridge
活動便橋

floating bridge
浮橋

pontoon
浮墩

platform
載台

diesel-electric locomotive
內燃電力傳動機車

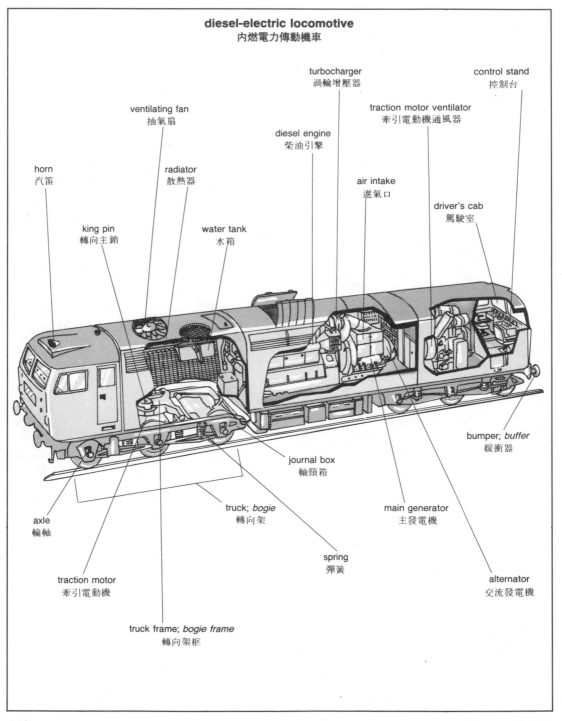

turbocharger
渦輪增壓器

control stand
控制台

ventilating fan
抽氣扇

traction motor ventilator
牽引電動機通風器

diesel engine
柴油引擎

horn
汽笛

radiator
散熱器

air intake
進氣口

driver's cab
駕駛室

king pin
轉向主銷

water tank
水箱

bumper; *buffer*
緩衝器

journal box
軸頸箱

axle
輪軸

truck; *bogie*
轉向架

main generator
主發電機

spring
彈簧

alternator
交流發電機

traction motor
牽引電動機

truck frame; *bogie frame*
轉向架框

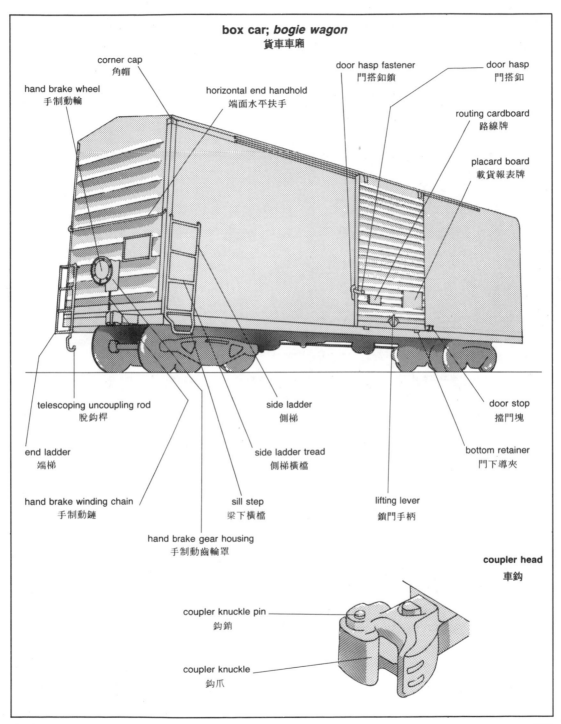

box car; *bogie wagon*
貨車車廂

corner cap
角帽

hand brake wheel
手制動輪

horizontal end handhold
端面水平扶手

door hasp fastener
門搭釦鎖

door hasp
門搭釦

routing cardboard
路線牌

placard board
載貨報表牌

telescoping uncoupling rod
脫鈎桿

side ladder
側梯

door stop
擋門塊

end ladder
端梯

side ladder tread
側梯橫檔

bottom retainer
門下導夾

hand brake winding chain
手制動鏈

sill step
梁下橫檔

lifting lever
鎖門手柄

hand brake gear housing
手制動齒輪罩

coupler head
車鈎

coupler knuckle pin
鈎銷

coupler knuckle
鈎爪

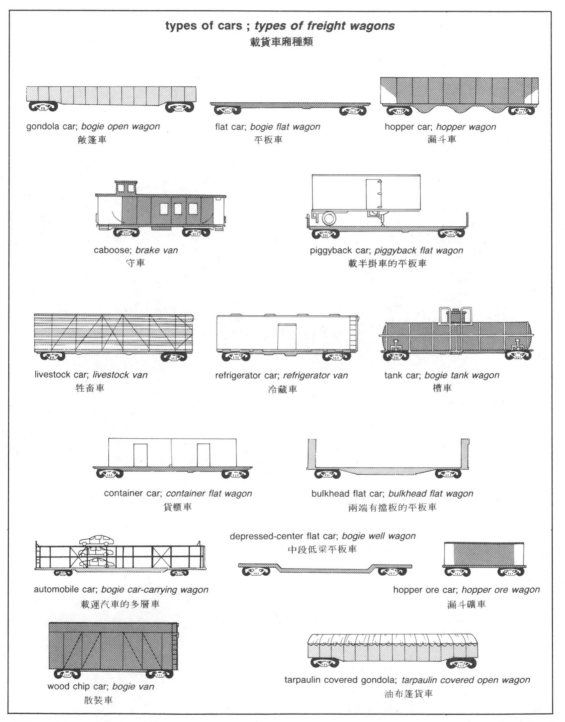

types of cars ; *types of freight wagons*
載貨車廂種類

gondola car; *bogie open wagon*
敞篷車

flat car; *bogie flat wagon*
平板車

hopper car; *hopper wagon*
漏斗車

caboose; *brake van*
守車

piggyback car; *piggyback flat wagon*
載半掛車的平板車

livestock car; *livestock van*
牲畜車

refrigerator car; *refrigerator van*
冷藏車

tank car; *bogie tank wagon*
槽車

container car; *container flat wagon*
貨櫃車

bulkhead flat car; *bulkhead flat wagon*
兩端有擋板的平板車

automobile car; *bogie car-carrying wagon*
載運汽車的多層車

depressed-center flat car; *bogie well wagon*
中段低梁平板車

hopper ore car; *hopper ore wagon*
漏斗礦車

wood chip car; *bogie van*
散裝車

tarpaulin covered gondola; *tarpaulin covered open wagon*
油布篷貨車

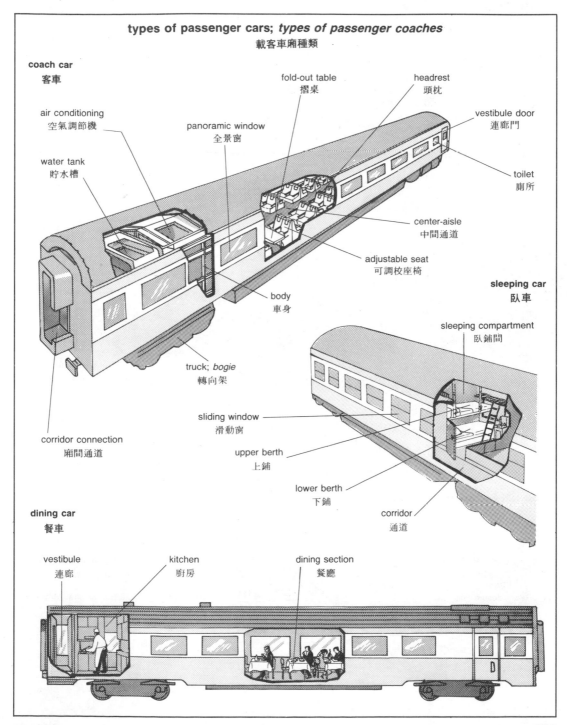

types of passenger cars; *types of passenger coaches*
載客車廂種類

coach car
客車

air conditioning
空氣調節機

water tank
貯水槽

fold-out table
摺桌

panoramic window
全景窗

headrest
頭枕

vestibule door
連廊門

toilet
廁所

center-aisle
中間通道

adjustable seat
可調校座椅

body
車身

truck; *bogie*
轉向架

corridor connection
廂間通道

sleeping car
臥車

sleeping compartment
臥鋪間

sliding window
滑動窗

upper berth
上鋪

lower berth
下鋪

corridor
通道

dining car
餐車

vestibule
連廊

kitchen
廚房

dining section
餐廳

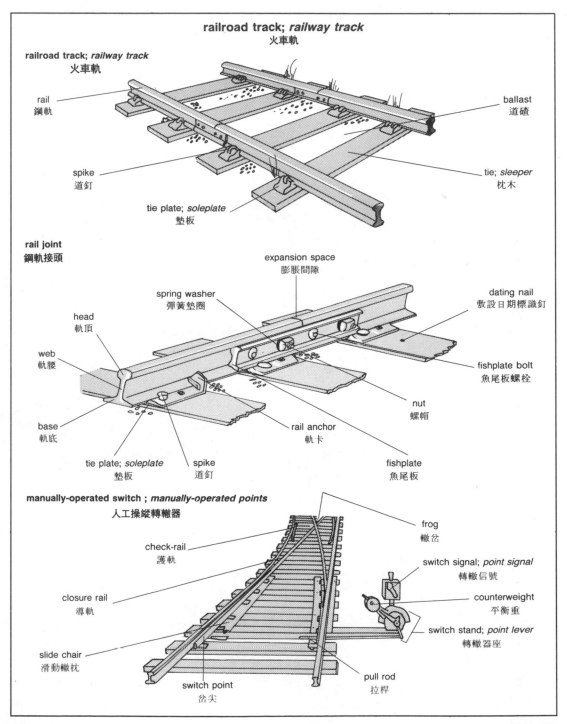

railroad track; *railway track*
火車軌

railroad track; *railway track*
火車軌

rail
鋼軌

ballast
道碴

spike
道釘

tie; *sleeper*
枕木

tie plate; *soleplate*
墊板

rail joint
鋼軌接頭

expansion space
膨脹間隙

spring washer
彈簧墊圈

dating nail
敷設日期標識釘

head
軌頂

web
軌腰

fishplate bolt
魚尾板螺栓

base
軌底

nut
螺帽

rail anchor
軌卡

tie plate; *soleplate*
墊板

spike
道釘

fishplate
魚尾板

manually-operated switch ; *manually-operated points*
人工操縱轉轍器

frog
轍岔

check-rail
護軌

switch signal; *point signal*
轉轍信號

closure rail
導軌

counterweight
平衡重

switch stand; *point lever*
轉轍器座

slide chair
滑動轍枕

switch point
岔尖

pull rod
拉桿

railroad track; *railway track*
火車軌

remote-controlled switch; *remote-controlled points*
遙控轉轍器

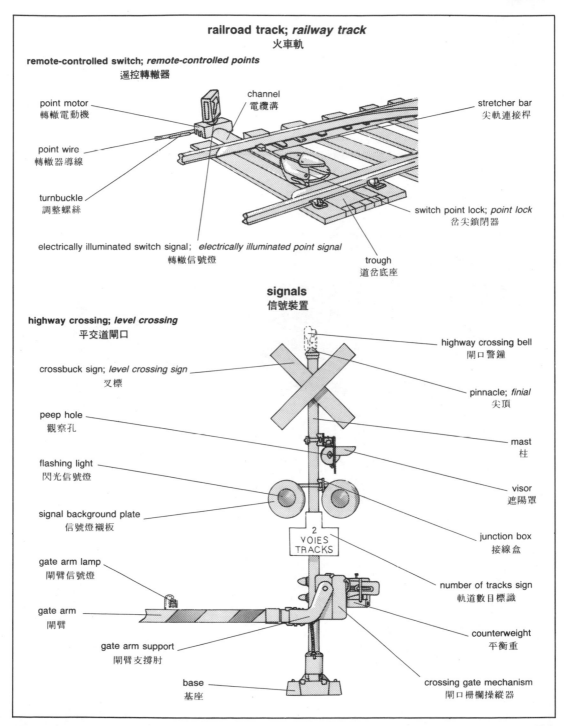

point motor
轉轍電動機

channel
電纜溝

stretcher bar
尖軌連接桿

point wire
轉轍器導線

turnbuckle
調整螺絲

switch point lock; *point lock*
岔尖鎖閉器

electrically illuminated switch signal; *electrically illuminated point signal*
轉轍信號燈

trough
道岔底座

signals
信號裝置

highway crossing; *level crossing*
平交道閘口

highway crossing bell
閘口警鐘

crossbuck sign; *level crossing sign*
叉標

pinnacle; *finial*
尖頂

peep hole
觀察孔

mast
柱

flashing light
閃光信號燈

visor
遮陽罩

signal background plate
信號燈襯板

2
VOIES
TRACKS

junction box
接線盒

gate arm lamp
閘臂信號燈

number of tracks sign
軌道數目標識

gate arm
閘臂

counterweight
平衡重

gate arm support
閘臂支撐肘

base
基座

crossing gate mechanism
閘口柵欄操縱器

railroad station; *railway station*
火車站

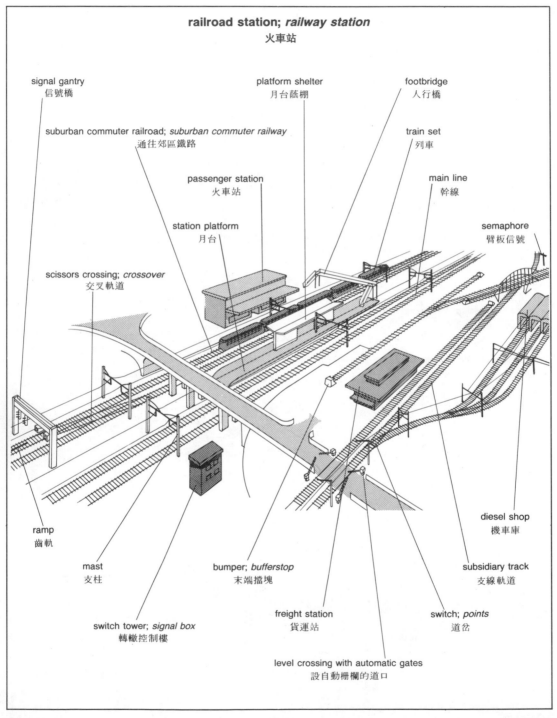

signal gantry
信號橋

platform shelter
月台蔭棚

footbridge
人行橋

suburban commuter railroad; *suburban commuter railway*
通往郊區鐵路

train set
列車

passenger station
火車站

main line
幹線

station platform
月台

semaphore
臂板信號

scissors crossing; *crossover*
交叉軌道

diesel shop
機車庫

ramp
齒軌

mast
支柱

bumper; *bufferstop*
末端擋塊

subsidiary track
支線軌道

switch tower; *signal box*
轉轍控制樓

freight station
貨運站

switch; *points*
道岔

level crossing with automatic gates
設自動柵欄的道口

container
貨櫃

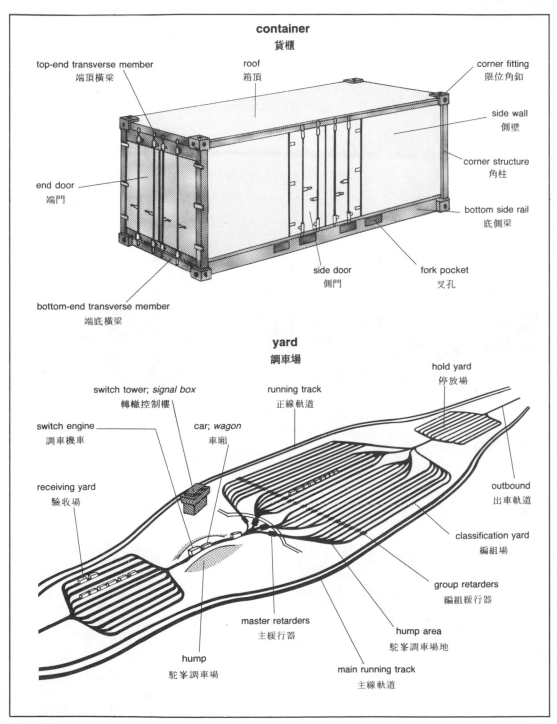

top-end transverse member
端頂橫梁

roof
箱頂

corner fitting
限位角釦

side wall
側壁

corner structure
角柱

end door
端門

bottom side rail
底側梁

side door
側門

fork pocket
叉孔

bottom-end transverse member
端底橫梁

yard
調車場

switch tower; *signal box*
轉轍控制樓

running track
正線軌道

hold yard
停放場

switch engine
調車機車

car; *wagon*
車廂

receiving yard
驗收場

outbound
出車軌道

classification yard
編組場

group retarders
編組緩行器

master retarders
主緩行器

hump area
駝峯調車場地

hump
駝峯調車場

main running track
主線軌道

station hall; *station concourse*
車站大廳

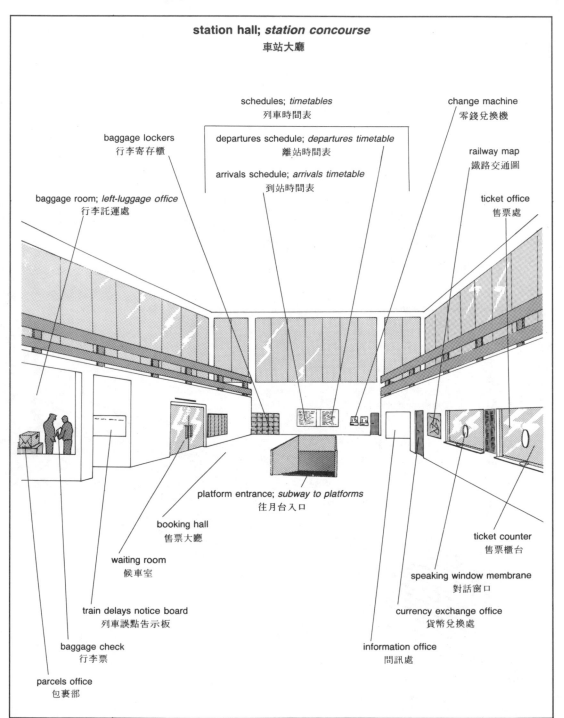

schedules; *timetables*
列車時間表

change machine
零錢兌換機

baggage lockers
行李寄存櫃

departures schedule; *departures timetable*
離站時間表

railway map
鐵路交通圖

arrivals schedule; *arrivals timetable*
到站時間表

baggage room; *left-luggage office*
行李託運處

ticket office
售票處

platform entrance; *subway to platforms*
往月台入口

booking hall
售票大廳

ticket counter
售票櫃台

waiting room
候車室

speaking window membrane
對話窗口

train delays notice board
列車誤點告示板

currency exchange office
貨幣兌換處

baggage check
行李票

information office
問訊處

parcels office
包裹部

station platform
車站月台

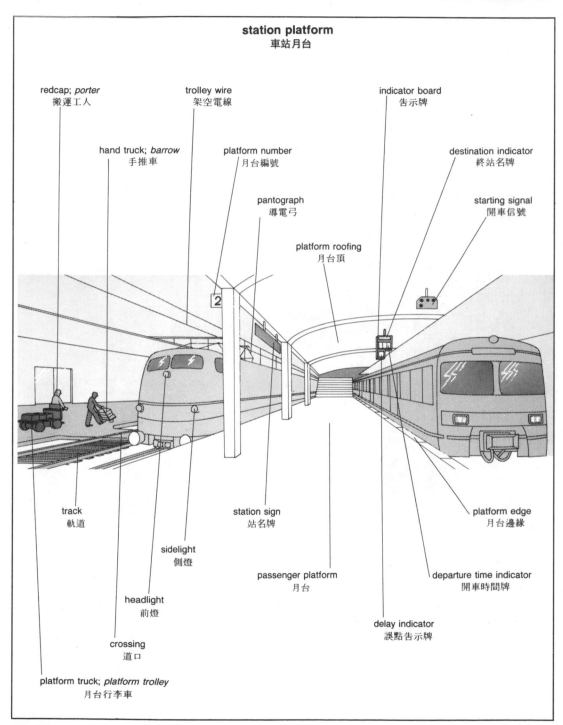

redcap; *porter*
搬運工人

hand truck; *barrow*
手推車

trolley wire
架空電線

platform number
月台編號

pantograph
導電弓

platform roofing
月台頂

indicator board
告示牌

destination indicator
終站名牌

starting signal
開車信號

track
軌道

sidelight
側燈

headlight
前燈

crossing
道口

platform truck; *platform trolley*
月台行李車

station sign
站名牌

passenger platform
月台

delay indicator
誤點告示牌

platform edge
月台邊緣

departure time indicator
開車時間牌

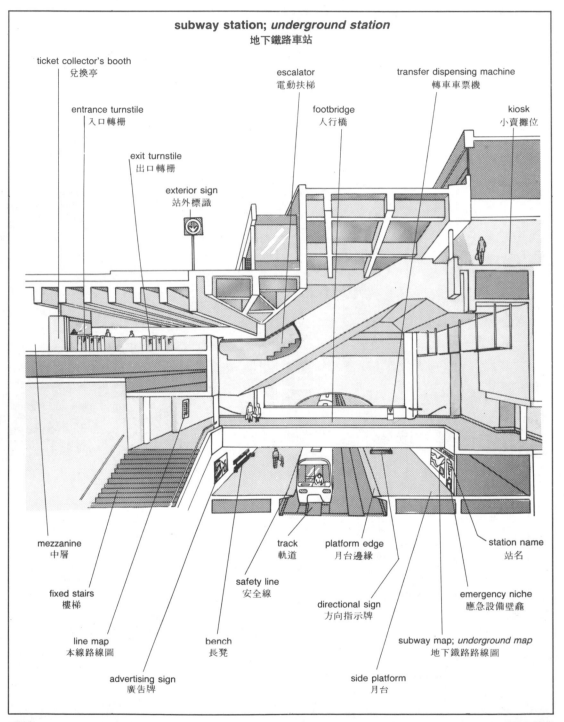

subway station; *underground station*
地下鐵路車站

ticket collector's booth
兌換亭

entrance turnstile
入口轉柵

exit turnstile
出口轉柵

exterior sign
站外標識

escalator
電動扶梯

footbridge
人行橋

transfer dispensing machine
轉車車票機

kiosk
小賣攤位

mezzanine
中層

track
軌道

platform edge
月台邊緣

station name
站名

fixed stairs
樓梯

safety line
安全線

emergency niche
應急設備壁龕

directional sign
方向指示牌

line map
本線路線圖

bench
長凳

subway map; *underground map*
地下鐵路路線圖

advertising sign
廣告牌

side platform
月台

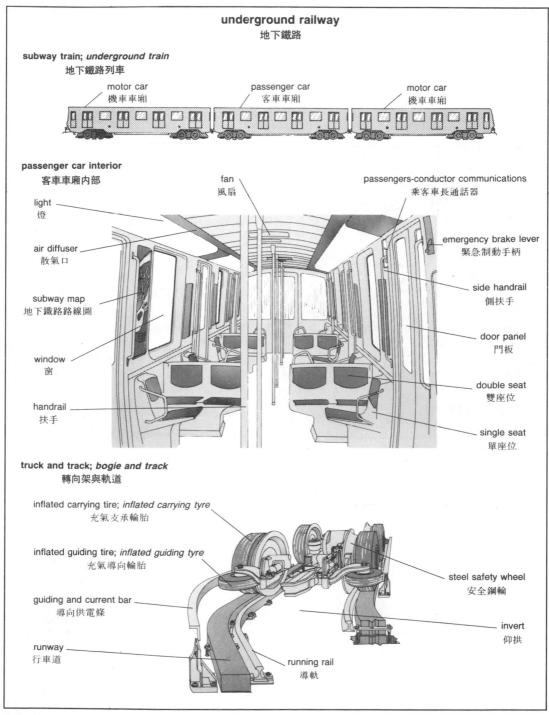

underground railway
地下鐵路

subway train; *underground train*
地下鐵路列車

motor car
機車車廂

passenger car
客車車廂

motor car
機車車廂

passenger car interior
客車車廂內部

light
燈

air diffuser
散氣口

subway map
地下鐵路路線圖

window
窗

handrail
扶手

fan
風扇

passengers-conductor communications
乘客車長通話器

emergency brake lever
緊急制動手柄

side handrail
側扶手

door panel
門板

double seat
雙座位

single seat
單座位

truck and track; *bogie and track*
轉向架與軌道

inflated carrying tire; *inflated carrying tyre*
充氣支承輪胎

inflated guiding tire; *inflated guiding tyre*
充氣導向輪胎

guiding and current bar
導向供電條

runway
行車道

running rail
導軌

steel safety wheel
安全鋼輪

invert
仰拱

four-masted bark
四桅帆船

masting and rigging
桅杆與索具

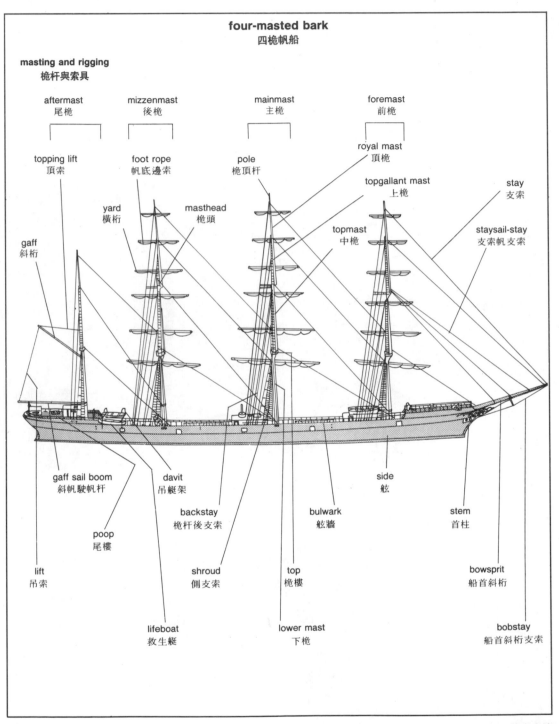

aftermast
尾桅

mizzenmast
後桅

mainmast
主桅

foremast
前桅

topping lift
頂索

foot rope
帆底邊索

pole
桅頂杆

royal mast
頂桅

topgallant mast
上桅

stay
支索

yard
橫桁

masthead
桅頭

topmast
中桅

staysail-stay
支索帆支索

gaff
斜桁

gaff sail boom
斜帆駛帆杆

davit
吊艇架

side
舷

stem
首柱

poop
尾樓

backstay
桅杆後支索

bulwark
舷牆

bowsprit
船首斜桁

lift
吊索

shroud
側支索

top
桅樓

lower mast
下桅

bobstay
船首斜桁支索

lifeboat
救生艇

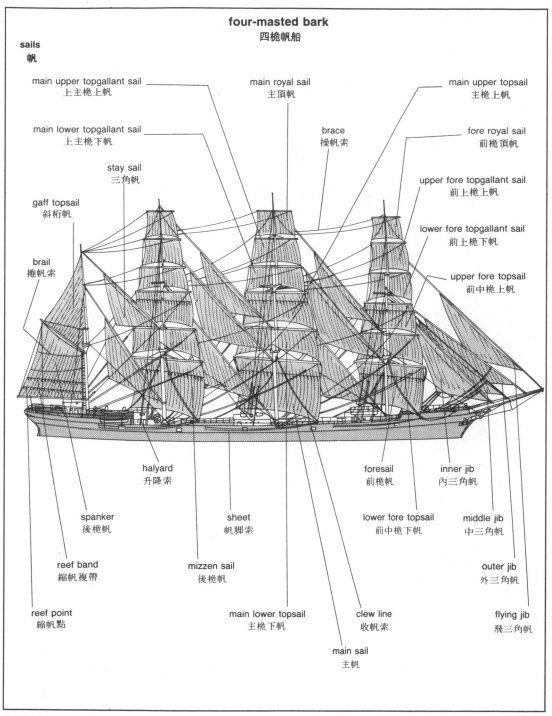

four-masted bark
四桅帆船

sails
帆

main upper topgallant sail
上主桅上帆

main royal sail
主頂帆

main upper topsail
主桅上帆

main lower topgallant sail
上主桅下帆

brace
操帆索

fore royal sail
前桅頂帆

stay sail
三角帆

upper fore topgallant sail
前上桅上帆

gaff topsail
斜桁帆

lower fore topgallant sail
前上桅下帆

brail
捲帆索

upper fore topsail
前中桅上帆

halyard
升降索

foresail
前桅帆

inner jib
內三角帆

spanker
後桅帆

sheet
帆脚索

lower fore topsail
前中桅下帆

middle jib
中三角帆

reef band
縮帆複帶

mizzen sail
後桅帆

outer jib
外三角帆

reef point
縮帆點

main lower topsail
主桅下帆

clew line
收帆索

flying jib
飛三角帆

main sail
主帆

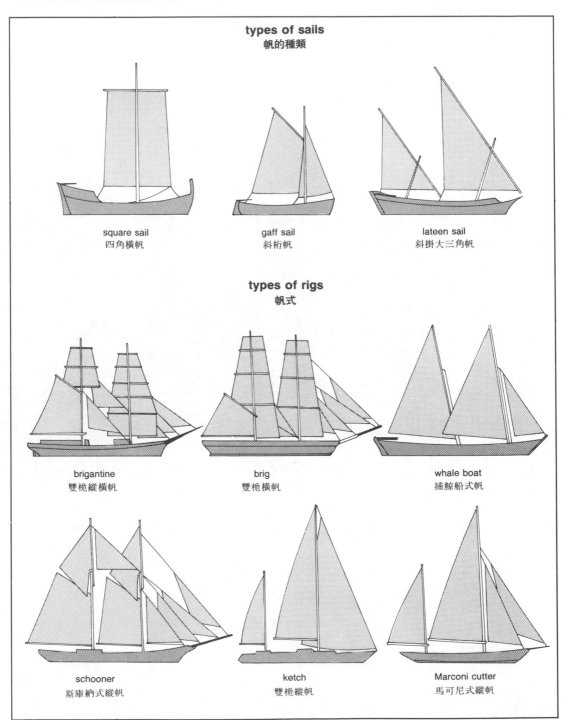

types of sails
帆的種類

square sail
四角橫帆

gaff sail
斜桁帆

lateen sail
斜掛大三角帆

types of rigs
帆式

brigantine
雙桅縱橫帆

brig
雙桅橫帆

whale boat
捕鯨船式帆

schooner
斯庫納式縱帆

ketch
雙桅縱帆

Marconi cutter
馬可尼式縱帆

passenger liner
定期客船

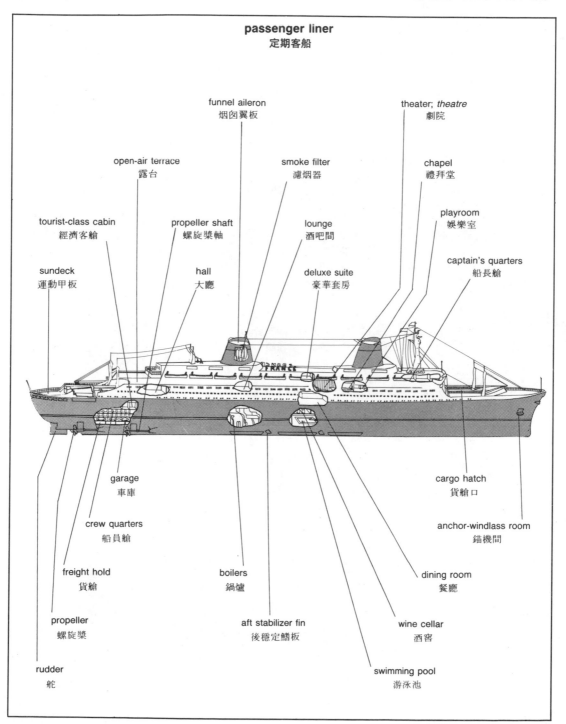

funnel aileron
烟囱翼板

theater; *theatre*
劇院

open-air terrace
露台

smoke filter
濾烟器

chapel
禮拜堂

tourist-class cabin
經濟客艙

propeller shaft
螺旋槳軸

lounge
酒吧間

playroom
娛樂室

captain's quarters
船長艙

sundeck
運動甲板

hall
大廳

deluxe suite
豪華套房

garage
車庫

cargo hatch
貨艙口

crew quarters
船員艙

anchor-windlass room
錨機間

freight hold
貨艙

boilers
鍋爐

dining room
餐廳

propeller
螺旋槳

aft stabilizer fin
後穩定鰭板

wine cellar
酒窖

rudder
舵

swimming pool
游泳池

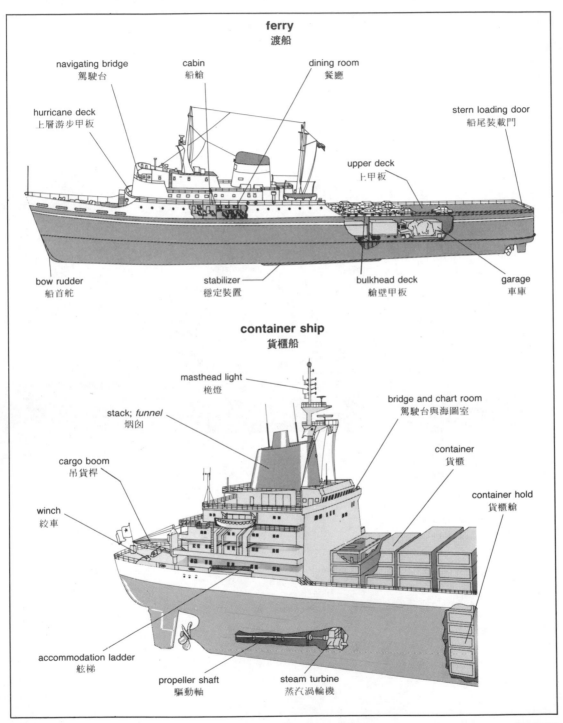

ferry
渡船

navigating bridge
駕駛台

cabin
船艙

dining room
餐廳

stern loading door
船尾裝載門

hurricane deck
上層游步甲板

upper deck
上甲板

bow rudder
船首舵

stabilizer
穩定裝置

bulkhead deck
艙壁甲板

garage
車庫

container ship
貨櫃船

masthead light
桅燈

bridge and chart room
駕駛台與海圖室

stack; *funnel*
烟囱

container
貨櫃

cargo boom
吊貨桿

container hold
貨櫃艙

winch
絞車

accommodation ladder
舷梯

propeller shaft
驅動軸

steam turbine
蒸汽渦輪機

hovercraft
氣墊船

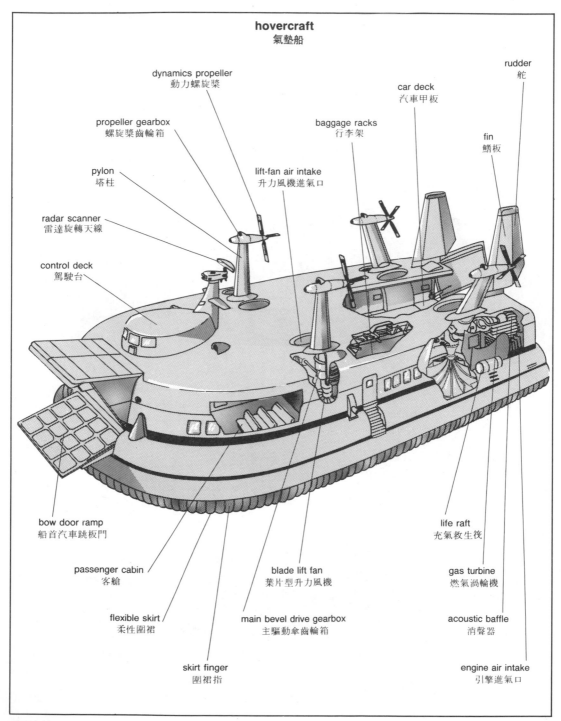

dynamics propeller
動力螺旋槳

propeller gearbox
螺旋槳齒輪箱

pylon
塔柱

radar scanner
雷達旋轉天線

control deck
駕駛台

lift-fan air intake
升力風機進氣口

car deck
汽車甲板

baggage racks
行李架

rudder
舵

fin
鰭板

bow door ramp
船首汽車跳板門

passenger cabin
客艙

flexible skirt
柔性圍裙

skirt finger
圍裙指

blade lift fan
葉片型升力風機

main bevel drive gearbox
主驅動傘齒輪箱

life raft
充氣救生筏

gas turbine
燃氣渦輪機

acoustic baffle
消聲器

engine air intake
引擎進氣口

hydrofoil boat
水翼船

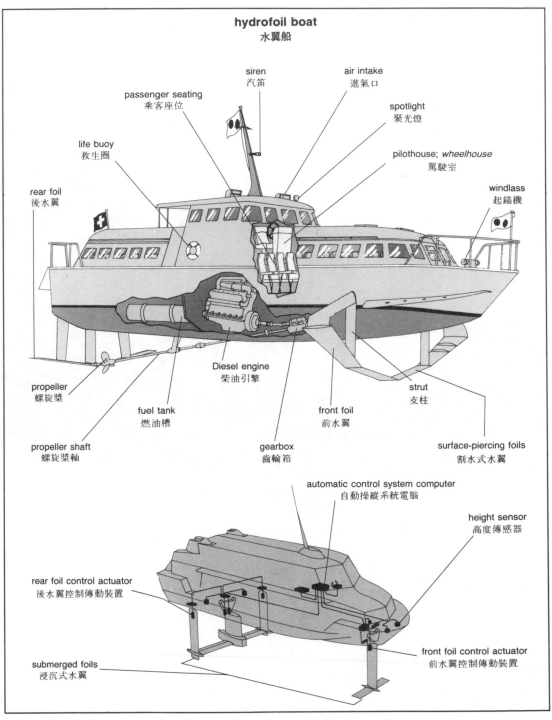

siren
汽笛

air intake
進氣口

passenger seating
乘客座位

spotlight
聚光燈

life buoy
救生圈

pilothouse; *wheelhouse*
駕駛室

rear foil
後水翼

windlass
起錨機

propeller
螺旋槳

Diesel engine
柴油引擎

strut
支柱

fuel tank
燃油槽

front foil
前水翼

propeller shaft
螺旋槳軸

gearbox
齒輪箱

surface-piercing foils
割水式水翼

automatic control system computer
自動操縱系統電腦

height sensor
高度傳感器

rear foil control actuator
後水翼控制傳動裝置

front foil control actuator
前水翼控制傳動裝置

submerged foils
浸沉式水翼

bathyscaphe
深海潛水器

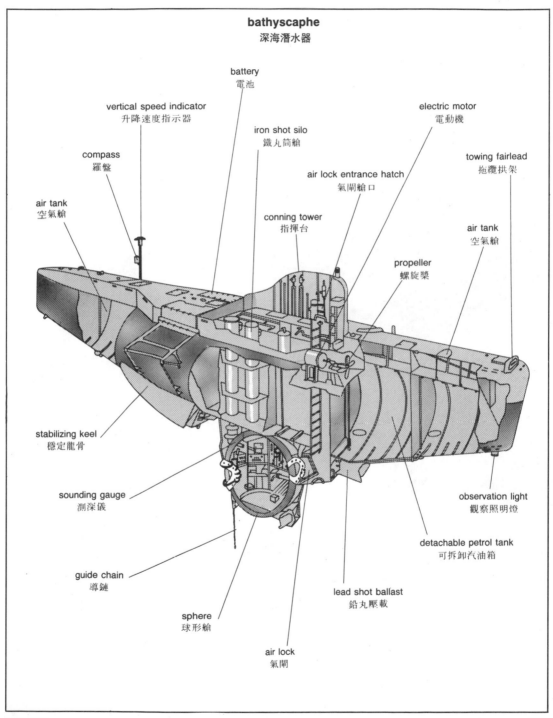

vertical speed indicator
升降速度指示器

battery
電池

iron shot silo
鐵丸筒艙

electric motor
電動機

compass
羅盤

air lock entrance hatch
氣閘艙口

towing fairlead
拖纜拱架

air tank
空氣艙

conning tower
指揮台

air tank
空氣艙

propeller
螺旋槳

stabilizing keel
穩定龍骨

sounding gauge
測深儀

observation light
觀察照明燈

detachable petrol tank
可拆卸汽油箱

guide chain
導鏈

sphere
球形艙

lead shot ballast
鉛丸壓載

air lock
氣閘

submarine
潛艇

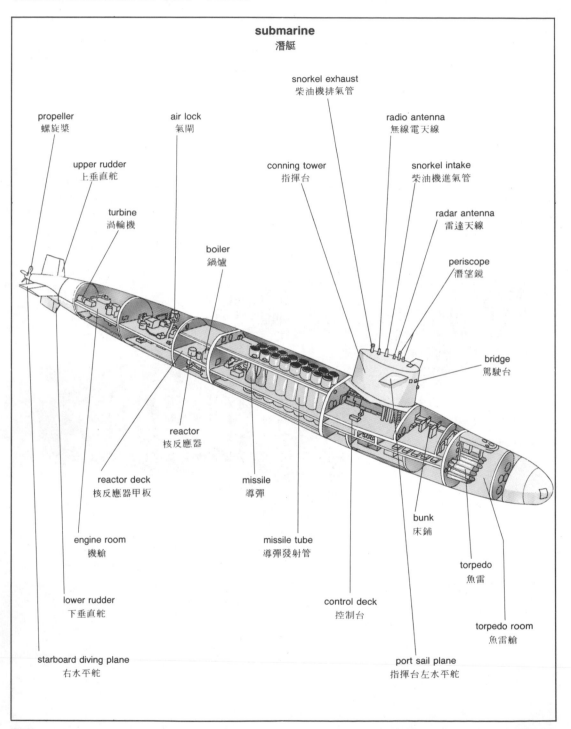

propeller
螺旋槳

air lock
氣閘

snorkel exhaust
柴油機排氣管

radio antenna
無線電天線

upper rudder
上垂直舵

conning tower
指揮台

snorkel intake
柴油機進氣管

turbine
渦輪機

radar antenna
雷達天線

boiler
鍋爐

periscope
潛望鏡

bridge
駕駛台

reactor
核反應器

reactor deck
核反應器甲板

missile
導彈

engine room
機艙

missile tube
導彈發射管

bunk
床鋪

torpedo
魚雷

lower rudder
下垂直舵

control deck
控制台

torpedo room
魚雷艙

starboard diving plane
右水平舵

port sail plane
指揮台左水平舵

frigate
驅逐艦

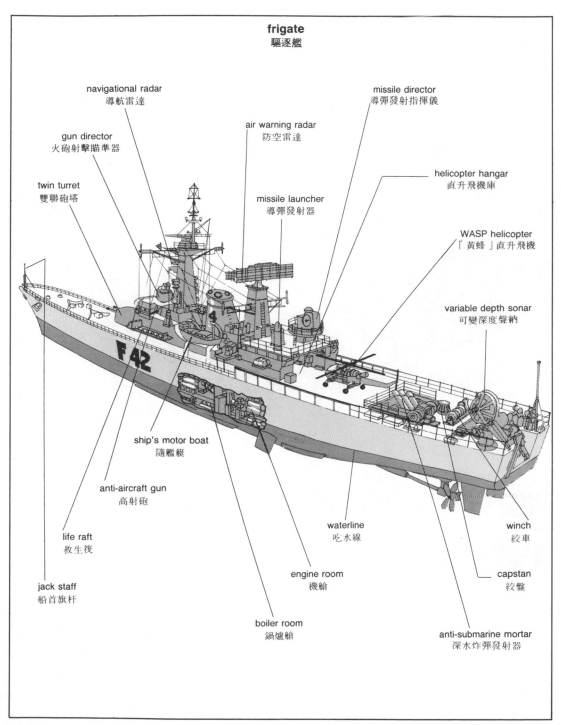

navigational radar
導航雷達

missile director
導彈發射指揮儀

air warning radar
防空雷達

gun director
火砲射擊瞄準器

helicopter hangar
直升飛機庫

twin turret
雙聯砲塔

missile launcher
導彈發射器

WASP helicopter
「黃蜂」直升飛機

variable depth sonar
可變深度聲納

ship's motor boat
隨艦艇

anti-aircraft gun
高射砲

waterline
吃水線

winch
絞車

life raft
救生筏

capstan
絞盤

jack staff
船首旗杆

engine room
機艙

boiler room
鍋爐艙

anti-submarine mortar
深水炸彈發射器

canal lock
水道船閘

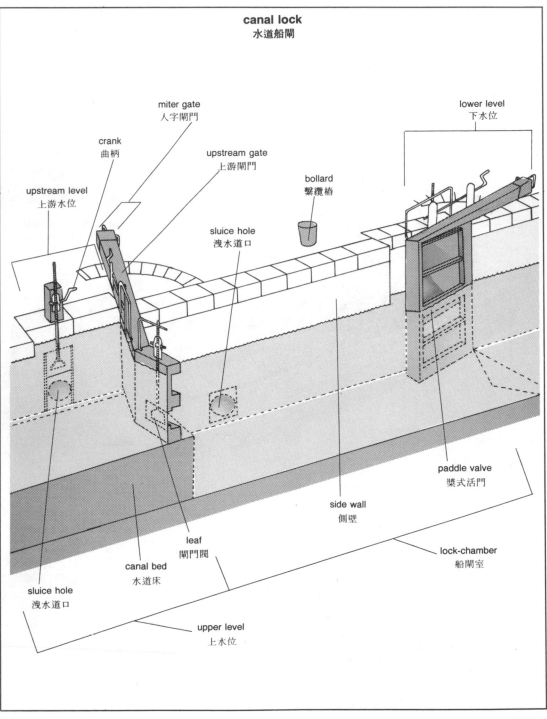

miter gate
人字閘門

crank
曲柄

upstream gate
上游閘門

lower level
下水位

upstream level
上游水位

bollard
繫纜樁

sluice hole
洩水道口

paddle valve
槳式活門

side wall
側壁

leaf
閘門閥

lock-chamber
船閘室

canal bed
水道床

sluice hole
洩水道口

upper level
上水位

harbor; *harbour*
港口

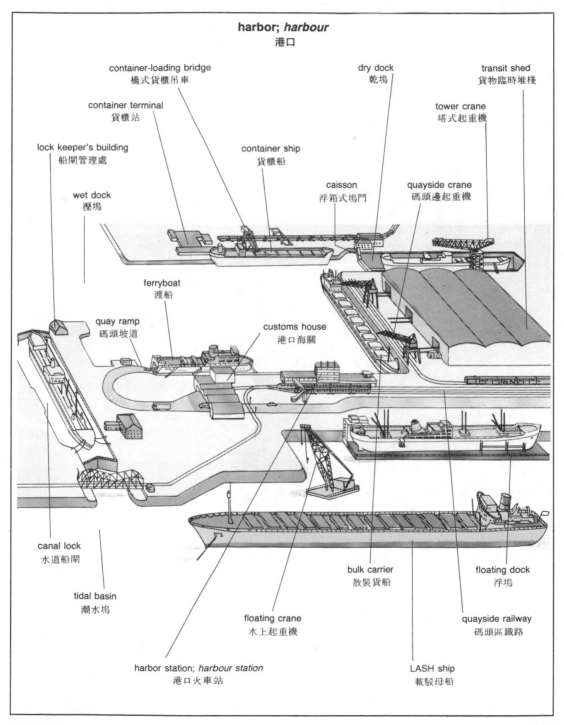

container-loading bridge
橋式貨櫃吊車

dry dock
乾塢

transit shed
貨物臨時堆棧

container terminal
貨櫃站

tower crane
塔式起重機

lock keeper's building
船閘管理處

container ship
貨櫃船

wet dock
湮塢

caisson
浮箱式塢門

quayside crane
碼頭邊起重機

ferryboat
渡船

quay ramp
碼頭坡道

customs house
港口海關

canal lock
水道船閘

bulk carrier
散裝貨船

floating dock
浮塢

tidal basin
潮水塢

quayside railway
碼頭區鐵路

floating crane
水上起重機

harbor station; *harbour station*
港口火車站

LASH ship
載駁母船

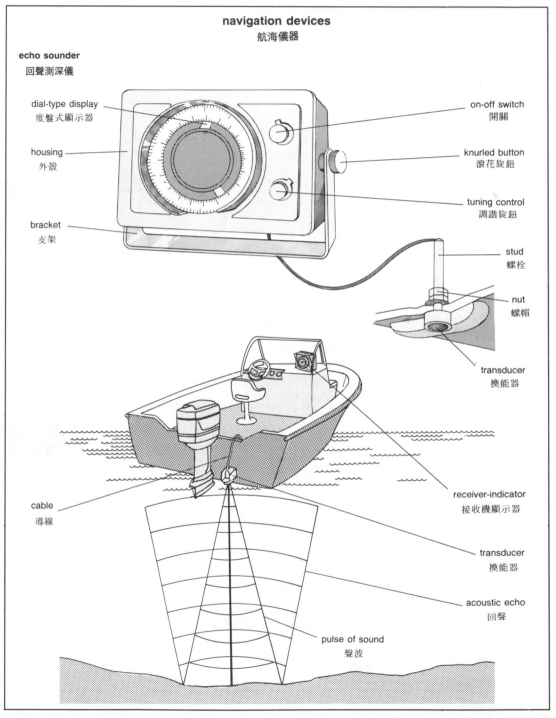

navigation devices
航海儀器

echo sounder
回聲測深儀

dial-type display
度盤式顯示器

housing
外殼

bracket
支架

on-off switch
開關

knurled button
滾花旋鈕

tuning control
調諧旋鈕

stud
螺栓

nut
螺帽

transducer
換能器

cable
導線

receiver-indicator
接收機顯示器

transducer
換能器

acoustic echo
回聲

pulse of sound
聲波

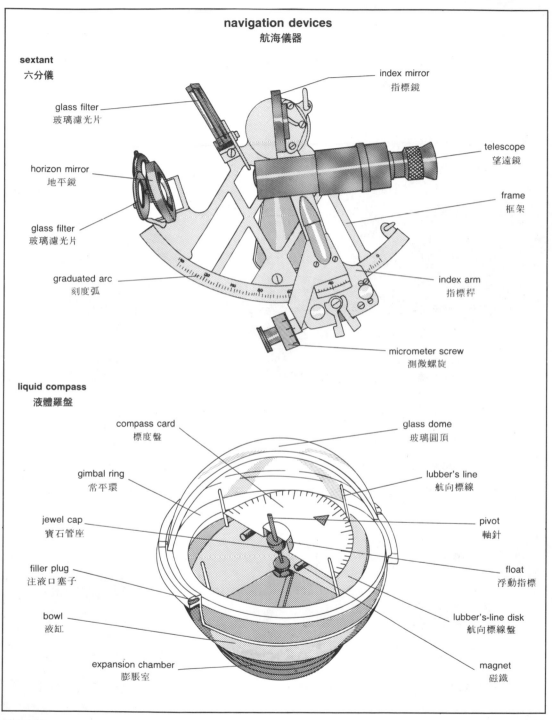

navigation devices
航海儀器

sextant
六分儀

index mirror
指標鏡

glass filter
玻璃濾光片

telescope
望遠鏡

horizon mirror
地平鏡

frame
框架

glass filter
玻璃濾光片

graduated arc
刻度弧

index arm
指標桿

micrometer screw
測微螺旋

liquid compass
液體羅盤

compass card
標度盤

glass dome
玻璃圓頂

gimbal ring
常平環

lubber's line
航向標線

jewel cap
寶石管座

pivot
軸針

filler plug
注液口塞子

float
浮動指標

bowl
液缸

lubber's-line disk
航向標線盤

expansion chamber
膨脹室

magnet
磁鐵

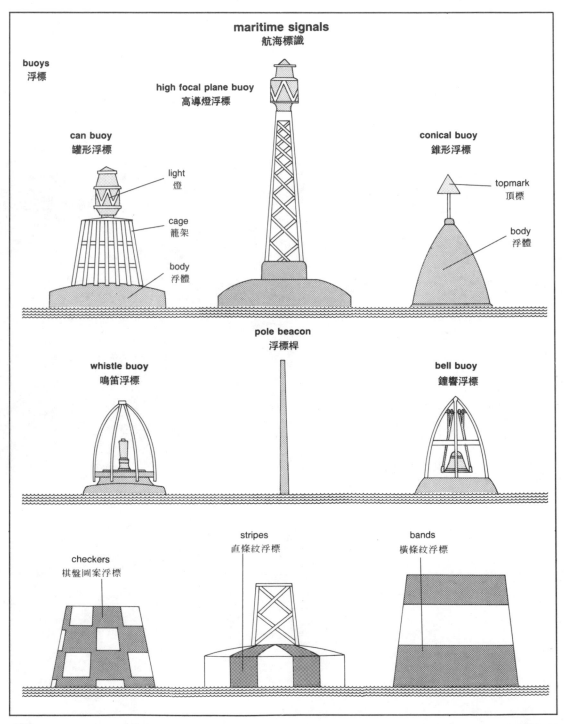

maritime signals
航海標識

buoys
浮標

high focal plane buoy
高導燈浮標

can buoy
罐形浮標

conical buoy
錐形浮標

light
燈

cage
籠架

body
浮體

topmark
頂標

body
浮體

whistle buoy
鳴笛浮標

pole beacon
浮標桿

bell buoy
鐘響浮標

checkers
棋盤圖案浮標

stripes
直條紋浮標

bands
橫條紋浮標

maritime signals
航海標識

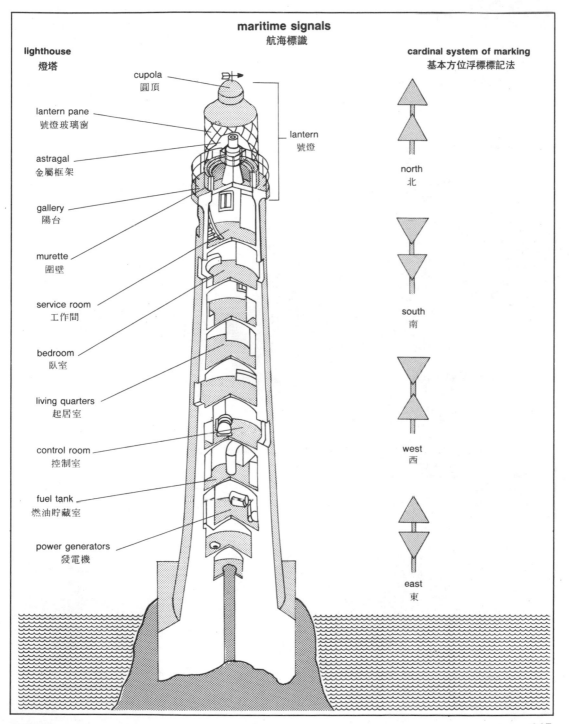

lighthouse
燈塔

cupola
圓頂

lantern pane
號燈玻璃窗

astragal
金屬框架

gallery
陽台

murette
圍壁

service room
工作間

bedroom
臥室

living quarters
起居室

control room
控制室

fuel tank
燃油貯藏室

power generators
發電機

lantern
號燈

cardinal system of marking
基本方位浮標標記法

north
北

south
南

west
西

east
東

maritime signals
航海標識

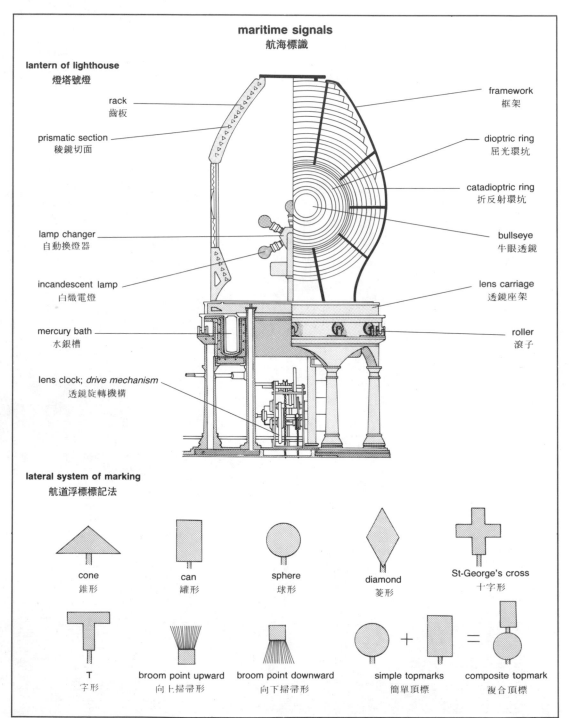

lantern of lighthouse
燈塔號燈

rack
齒板

prismatic section
稜鏡切面

lamp changer
自動換燈器

incandescent lamp
白熾電燈

mercury bath
水銀槽

lens clock; *drive mechanism*
透鏡旋轉機橫

framework
框架

dioptric ring
屈光環坑

catadioptric ring
折反射環坑

bullseye
牛眼透鏡

lens carriage
透鏡座架

roller
滾子

lateral system of marking
航道浮標標記法

cone
錐形

can
罐形

sphere
球形

diamond
菱形

St-George's cross
十字形

T
字形

broom point upward
向上掃帚形

broom point downward
向下掃帚形

simple topmarks
簡單頂標

composite topmark
複合頂標

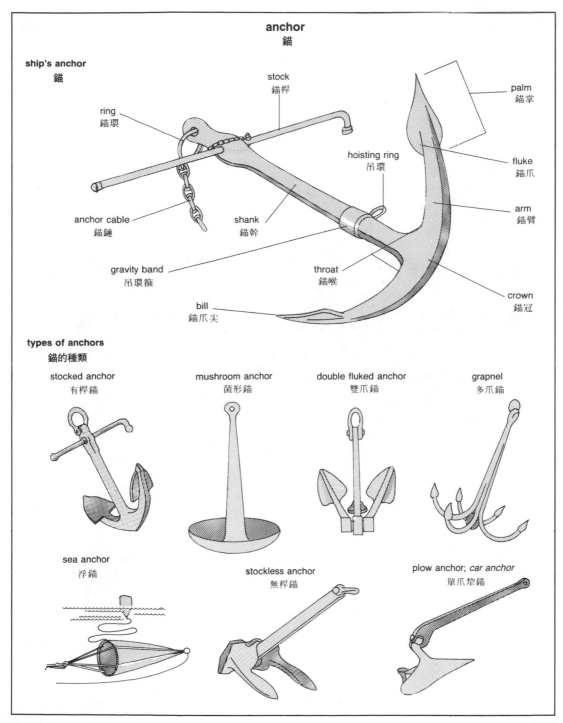

anchor
錨

ship's anchor
錨

stock
錨桿

ring
錨環

palm
錨掌

hoisting ring
吊環

fluke
錨爪

anchor cable
錨鏈

shank
錨幹

arm
錨臂

gravity band
吊環箍

throat
錨喉

crown
錨冠

bill
錨爪尖

types of anchors
錨的種類

stocked anchor
有桿錨

mushroom anchor
菌形錨

double fluked anchor
雙爪錨

grapnel
多爪錨

sea anchor
浮錨

stockless anchor
無桿錨

plow anchor; *car anchor*
單爪犁錨

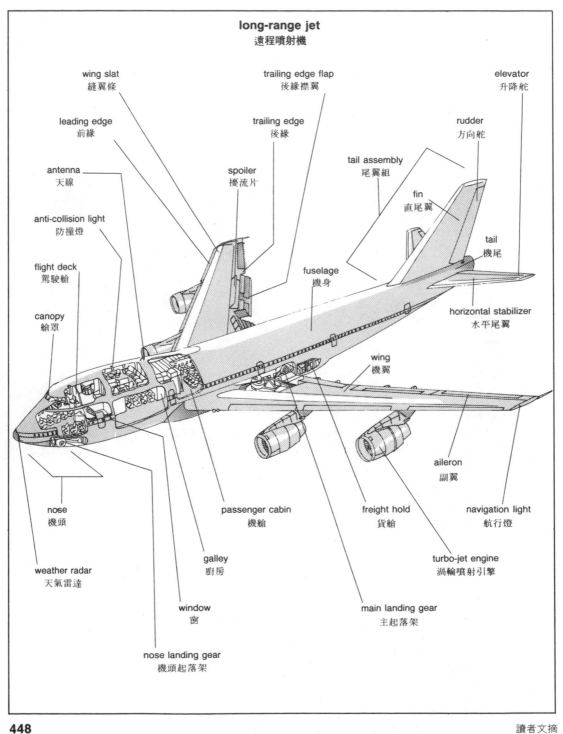

long-range jet
遠程噴射機

wing slat
縫翼條

trailing edge flap
後緣襟翼

elevator
升降舵

leading edge
前緣

trailing edge
後緣

rudder
方向舵

antenna
天線

spoiler
擾流片

tail assembly
尾翼組

anti-collision light
防撞燈

fin
直尾翼

tail
機尾

flight deck
駕駛艙

fuselage
機身

canopy
艙罩

horizontal stabilizer
水平尾翼

wing
機翼

aileron
副翼

nose
機頭

passenger cabin
機艙

freight hold
貨艙

navigation light
航行燈

weather radar
天氣雷達

galley
廚房

turbo-jet engine
渦輪噴射引擎

window
窗

main landing gear
主起落架

nose landing gear
機頭起落架

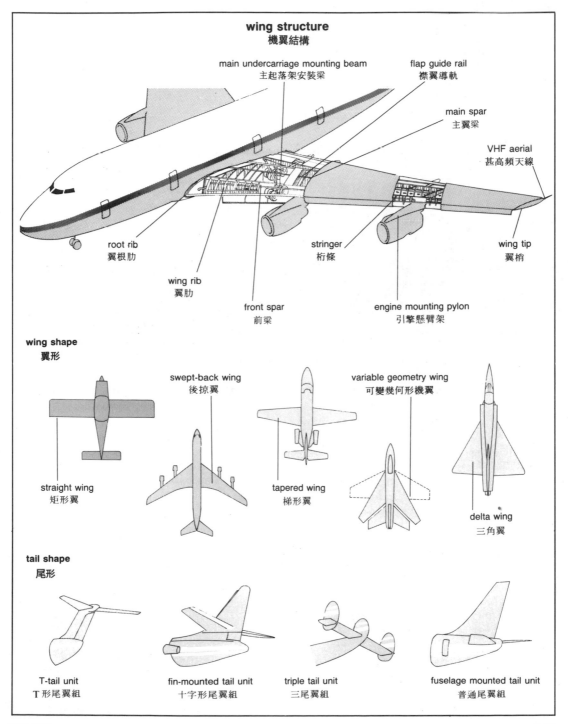

wing structure
機翼結構

main undercarriage mounting beam
主起落架安裝梁

flap guide rail
襟翼導軌

main spar
主翼梁

VHF aerial
甚高頻天線

root rib
翼根肋

wing rib
翼肋

front spar
前梁

stringer
桁條

engine mounting pylon
引擎懸臂架

wing tip
翼梢

wing shape
翼形

straight wing
矩形翼

swept-back wing
後掠翼

tapered wing
梯形翼

variable geometry wing
可變幾何形機翼

delta wing
三角翼

tail shape
尾形

T-tail unit
T形尾翼組

fin-mounted tail unit
十字形尾翼組

triple tail unit
三尾翼組

fuselage mounted tail unit
普通尾翼組

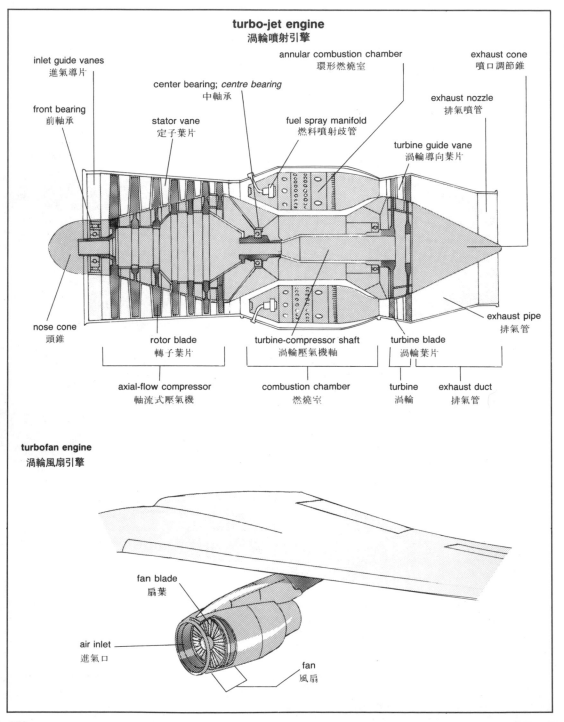

turbo-jet engine
渦輪噴射引擎

inlet guide vanes
進氣導片

annular combustion chamber
環形燃燒室

exhaust cone
噴口調節錐

center bearing; *centre bearing*
中軸承

exhaust nozzle
排氣噴管

front bearing
前軸承

stator vane
定子葉片

fuel spray manifold
燃料噴射歧管

turbine guide vane
渦輪導向葉片

nose cone
頭錐

rotor blade
轉子葉片

turbine-compressor shaft
渦輪壓氣機軸

turbine blade
渦輪葉片

exhaust pipe
排氣管

axial-flow compressor
軸流式壓氣機

combustion chamber
燃燒室

turbine
渦輪

exhaust duct
排氣管

turbofan engine
渦輪風扇引擎

fan blade
扇葉

air inlet
進氣口

fan
風扇

flight deck
駕駛艙

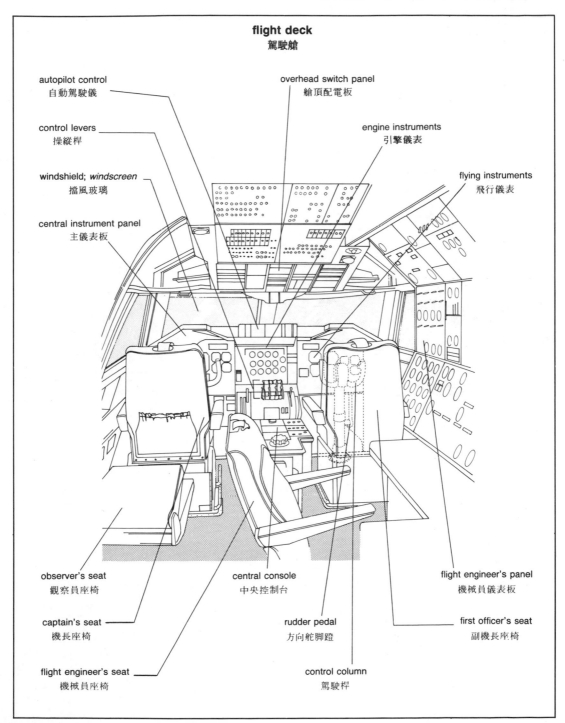

autopilot control
自動駕駛儀

overhead switch panel
艙頂配電板

control levers
操縱桿

engine instruments
引擎儀表

windshield; *windscreen*
擋風玻璃

flying instruments
飛行儀表

central instrument panel
主儀表板

observer's seat
觀察員座椅

central console
中央控制台

flight engineer's panel
機械員儀表板

captain's seat
機長座椅

rudder pedal
方向舵腳蹬

first officer's seat
副機長座椅

flight engineer's seat
機械員座椅

control column
駕駛桿

airport
機場

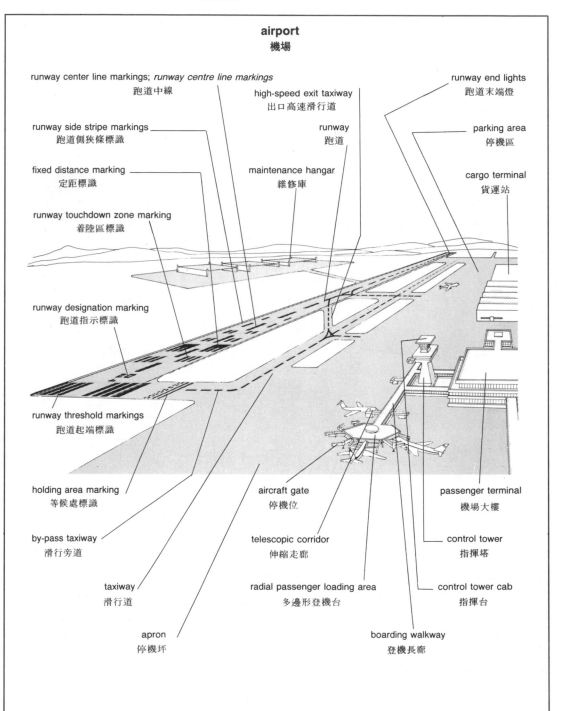

runway center line markings; *runway centre line markings*
跑道中線

high-speed exit taxiway
出口高速滑行道

runway end lights
跑道末端燈

runway side stripe markings
跑道側狹條標識

runway
跑道

parking area
停機區

fixed distance marking
定距標識

maintenance hangar
維修庫

cargo terminal
貨運站

runway touchdown zone marking
着陸區標識

runway designation marking
跑道指示標識

runway threshold markings
跑道起端標識

holding area marking
等候處標識

aircraft gate
停機位

passenger terminal
機場大樓

by-pass taxiway
滑行旁道

telescopic corridor
伸縮走廊

control tower
指揮塔

taxiway
滑行道

radial passenger loading area
多邊形登機台

control tower cab
指揮台

apron
停機坪

boarding walkway
登機長廊

airport
機場

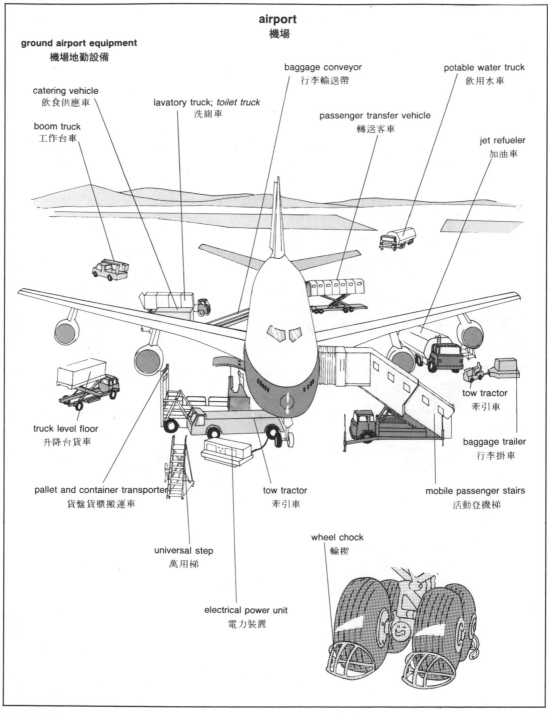

ground airport equipment
機場地勤設備

catering vehicle
飲食供應車

boom truck
工作台車

lavatory truck; *toilet truck*
洗廁車

baggage conveyor
行李輸送帶

passenger transfer vehicle
轉送客車

potable water truck
飲用水車

jet refueler
加油車

truck level floor
升降台貨車

pallet and container transporter
貨盤貨櫃搬運車

universal step
萬用梯

electrical power unit
電力裝置

tow tractor
牽引車

wheel chock
輪楔

tow tractor
牽引車

baggage trailer
行李掛車

mobile passenger stairs
活動登機梯

TRANSPORTATION BY AIR 航空運輸

passenger terminal
機場大樓

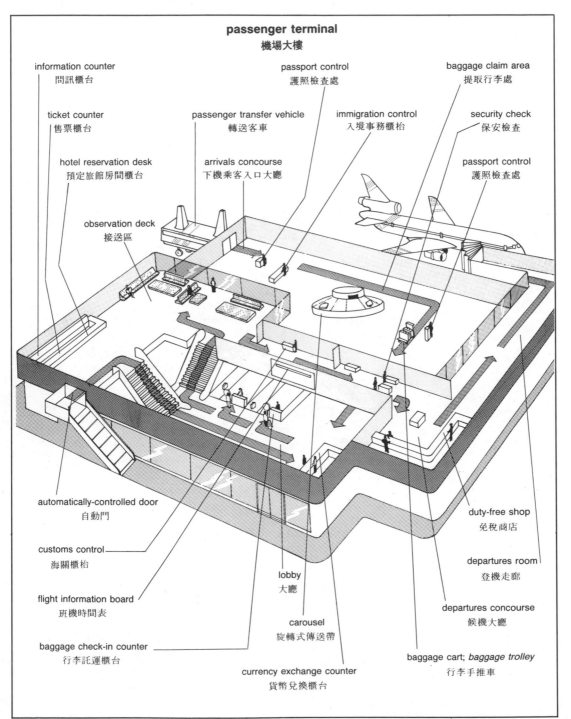

information counter
問訊櫃台

passport control
護照檢查處

baggage claim area
提取行李處

ticket counter
售票櫃台

passenger transfer vehicle
轉送客車

immigration control
入境事務櫃枱

security check
保安檢查

hotel reservation desk
預定旅館房間櫃台

arrivals concourse
下機乘客入口大廳

passport control
護照檢查處

observation deck
接送區

automatically-controlled door
自動門

duty-free shop
免稅商店

customs control
海關櫃枱

lobby
大廳

departures room
登機走廊

flight information board
班機時間表

carousel
旋轉式傳送帶

departures concourse
候機大廳

baggage check-in counter
行李託運櫃台

currency exchange counter
貨幣兌換櫃台

baggage cart; *baggage trolley*
行李手推車

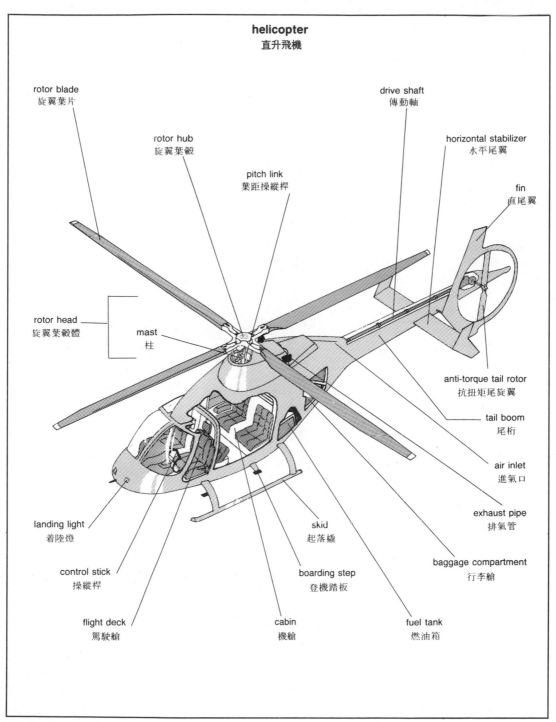

helicopter
直升飛機

rotor blade
旋翼葉片

rotor hub
旋翼葉轂

pitch link
葉距操縱桿

drive shaft
傳動軸

horizontal stabilizer
水平尾翼

fin
直尾翼

rotor head
旋翼葉轂體

mast
柱

anti-torque tail rotor
抗扭矩尾旋翼

tail boom
尾桁

air inlet
進氣口

exhaust pipe
排氣管

baggage compartment
行李艙

landing light
着陸燈

skid
起落橇

control stick
操縱桿

boarding step
登機踏板

flight deck
駕駛艙

cabin
機艙

fuel tank
燃油箱

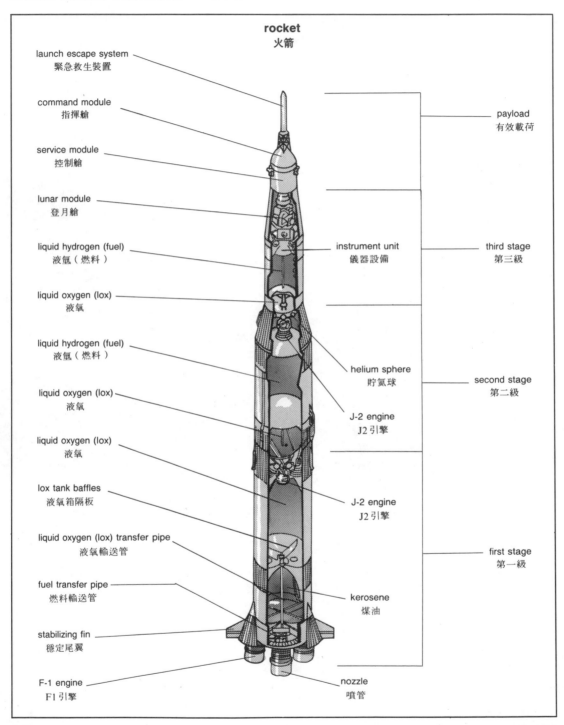

rocket
火箭

launch escape system
緊急救生裝置

command module
指揮艙

service module
控制艙

lunar module
登月艙

liquid hydrogen (fuel)
液氫（燃料）

liquid oxygen (lox)
液氧

liquid hydrogen (fuel)
液氫（燃料）

liquid oxygen (lox)
液氧

liquid oxygen (lox)
液氧

lox tank baffles
液氧箱隔板

liquid oxygen (lox) transfer pipe
液氧輸送管

fuel transfer pipe
燃料輸送管

stabilizing fin
穩定尾翼

F-1 engine
F1 引擎

instrument unit
儀器設備

helium sphere
貯氦球

J-2 engine
J2 引擎

J-2 engine
J2 引擎

kerosene
煤油

nozzle
噴管

payload
有效載荷

third stage
第三級

second stage
第二級

first stage
第一級

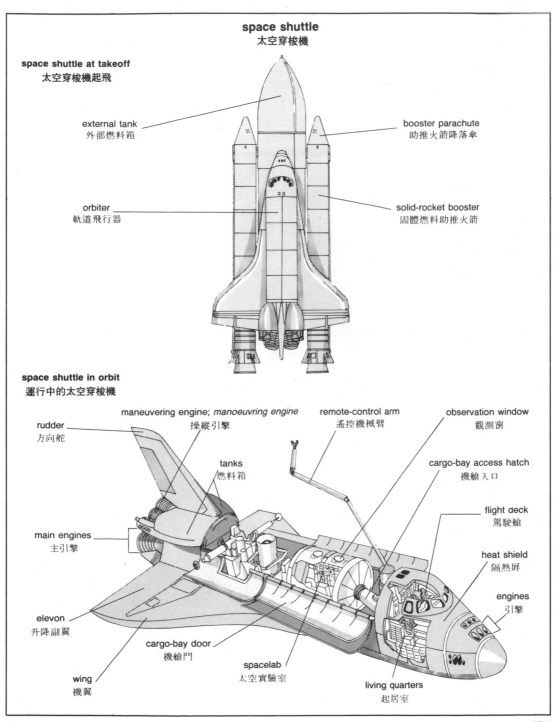

space shuttle
太空穿梭機

space shuttle at takeoff
太空穿梭機起飛

external tank
外部燃料箱

booster parachute
助推火箭降落傘

orbiter
軌道飛行器

solid-rocket booster
固體燃料助推火箭

space shuttle in orbit
運行中的太空穿梭機

maneuvering engine; *manoeuvring engine*
操縱引擎

remote-control arm
遙控機械臂

observation window
觀測窗

rudder
方向舵

tanks
燃料箱

cargo-bay access hatch
機艙入口

main engines
主引擎

flight deck
駕駛艙

heat shield
隔熱屏

elevon
升降副翼

engines
引擎

cargo-bay door
機艙門

spacelab
太空實驗室

living quarters
起居室

wing
機翼

space suit
太空衣

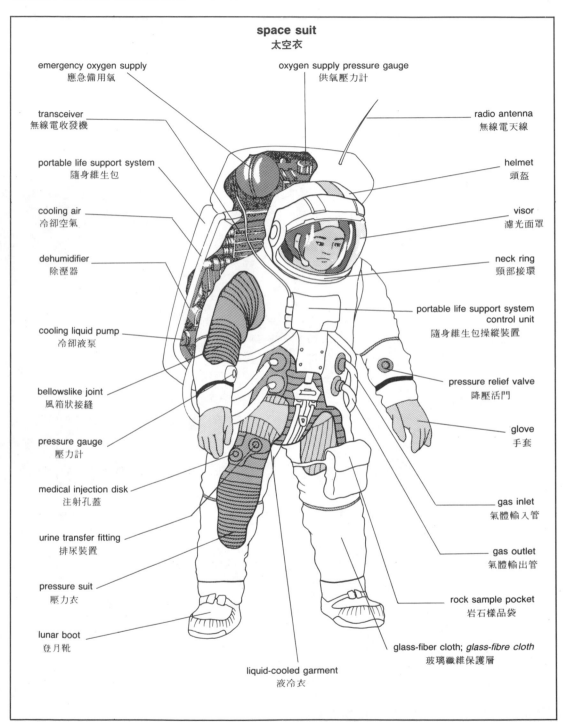

emergency oxygen supply
應急備用氧

oxygen supply pressure gauge
供氧壓力計

transceiver
無線電收發機

radio antenna
無線電天線

portable life support system
隨身維生包

helmet
頭盔

cooling air
冷卻空氣

visor
濾光面罩

dehumidifier
除溼器

neck ring
頸部接環

portable life support system
control unit
隨身維生包操縱裝置

cooling liquid pump
冷卻液泵

bellowslike joint
風箱狀接縫

pressure relief valve
降壓活門

pressure gauge
壓力計

glove
手套

medical injection disk
注射孔蓋

gas inlet
氣體輸入管

urine transfer fitting
排尿裝置

gas outlet
氣體輸出管

pressure suit
壓力衣

rock sample pocket
岩石樣品袋

lunar boot
登月靴

glass-fiber cloth; *glass-fibre cloth*
玻璃纖維保護層

liquid-cooled garment
液冷衣

OFFICE SUPPLIES AND EQUIPMENT

辦公室用品與設備

stationery
文具

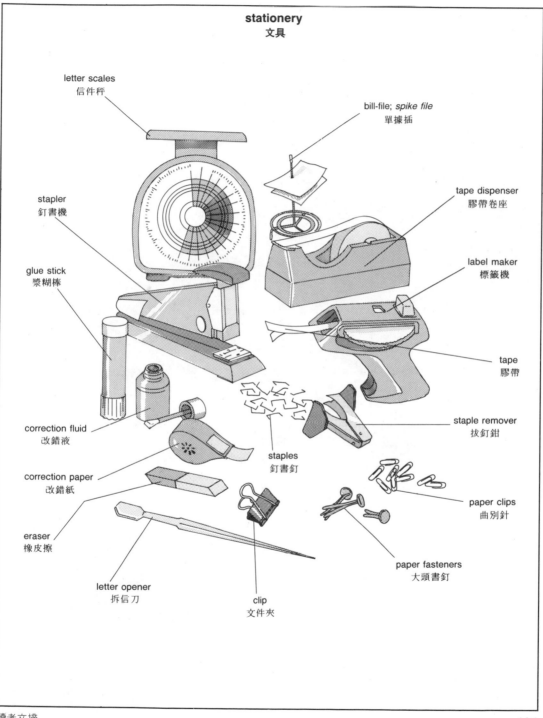

letter scales
信件秤

bill-file; *spike file*
單據插

tape dispenser
膠帶卷座

stapler
釘書機

glue stick
漿糊棒

label maker
標籤機

correction fluid
改錯液

tape
膠帶

correction paper
改錯紙

staples
釘書釘

staple remover
拔釘鉗

eraser
橡皮擦

paper clips
曲別針

letter opener
拆信刀

clip
文件夾

paper fasteners
大頭書釘

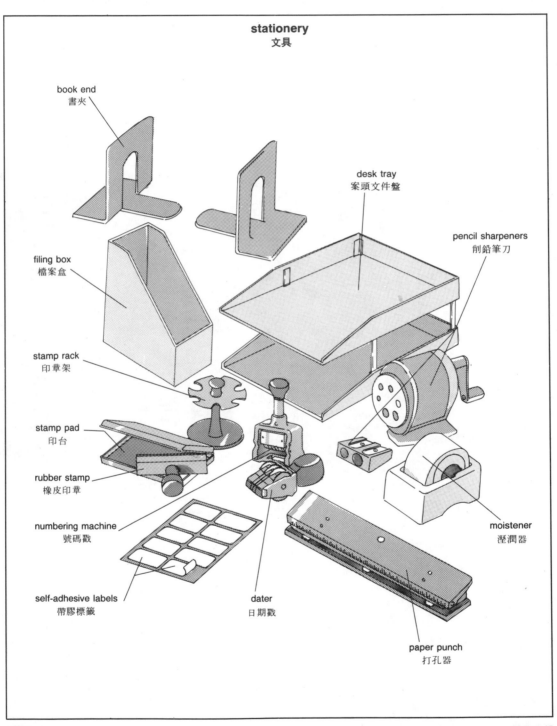

stationery
文具

book end
書夾

desk tray
案頭文件盤

pencil sharpeners
削鉛筆刀

filing box
檔案盒

stamp rack
印章架

stamp pad
印台

rubber stamp
橡皮印章

numbering machine
號碼戳

moistener
浥潤器

self-adhesive labels
帶膠標籤

dater
日期戳

paper punch
打孔器

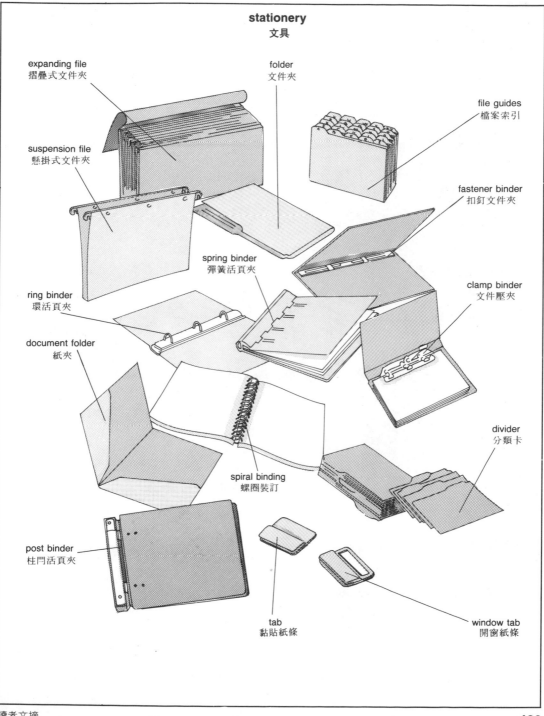

stationery
文具

expanding file
摺疊式文件夾

folder
文件夾

file guides
檔案索引

suspension file
懸掛式文件夾

fastener binder
扣釘文件夾

spring binder
彈簧活頁夾

clamp binder
文件壓夾

ring binder
環活頁夾

document folder
紙夾

divider
分類卡

spiral binding
螺圈裝訂

post binder
柱門活頁夾

tab
黏貼紙條

window tab
開窗紙條

stationery
文具

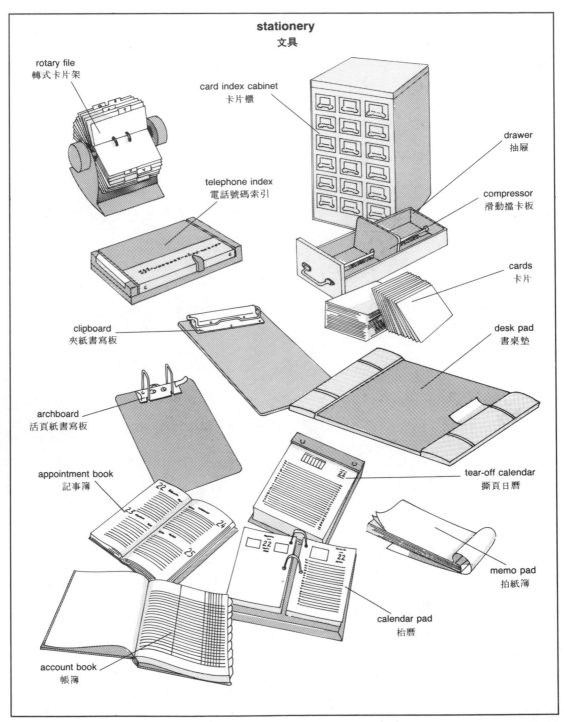

rotary file
轉式卡片架

card index cabinet
卡片櫃

drawer
抽屜

telephone index
電話號碼索引

compressor
滑動擋卡板

cards
卡片

clipboard
夾紙書寫板

desk pad
書桌墊

archboard
活頁紙書寫板

appointment book
記事簿

tear-off calendar
撕頁日曆

memo pad
拍紙簿

calendar pad
枱曆

account book
帳簿

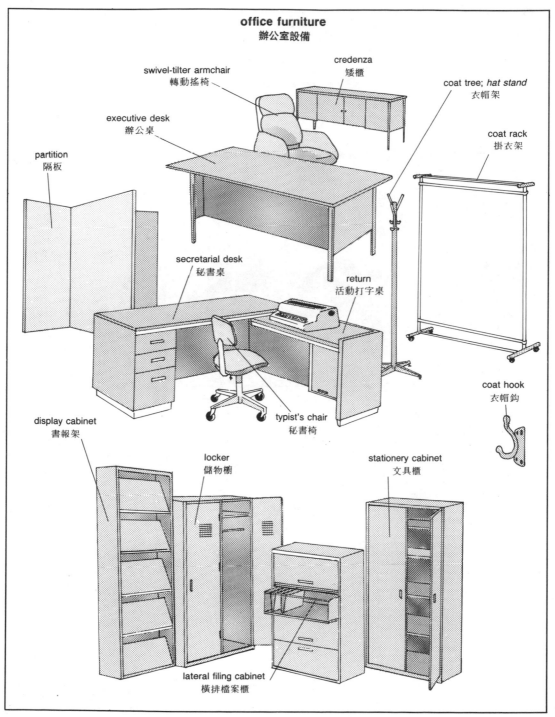

office furniture
辦公室設備

swivel-tilter armchair
轉動搖椅

credenza
矮櫃

coat tree; *hat stand*
衣帽架

executive desk
辦公桌

coat rack
掛衣架

partition
隔板

secretarial desk
秘書桌

return
活動打字桌

display cabinet
書報架

typist's chair
秘書椅

locker
儲物櫥

stationery cabinet
文具櫃

coat hook
衣帽鈎

lateral filing cabinet
橫排檔案櫃

typewriter
打字機

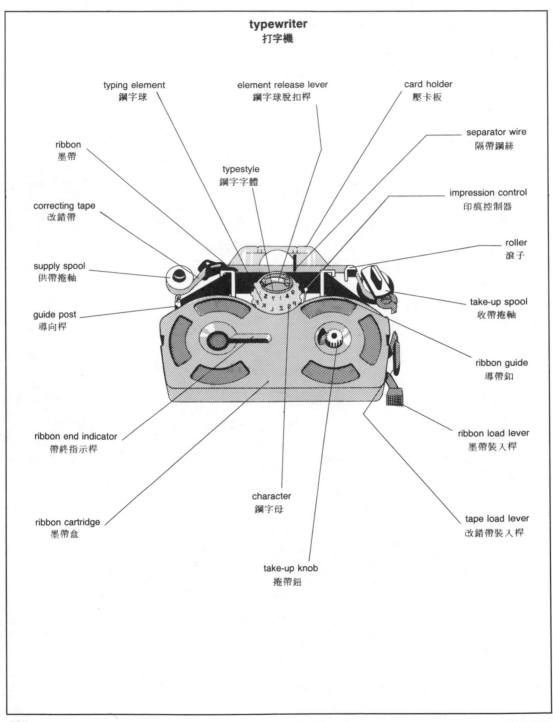

typing element
鋼字球

element release lever
鋼字球脫扣桿

card holder
壓卡板

separator wire
隔帶鋼絲

ribbon
墨帶

typestyle
鋼字字體

impression control
印痕控制器

correcting tape
改錯帶

roller
滾子

supply spool
供帶捲軸

take-up spool
收帶捲軸

guide post
導向桿

ribbon guide
導帶釦

ribbon end indicator
帶終指示桿

ribbon load lever
墨帶裝入桿

ribbon cartridge
墨帶盒

character
鋼字母

tape load lever
改錯帶裝入桿

take-up knob
捲帶鈕

typewriter
打字機

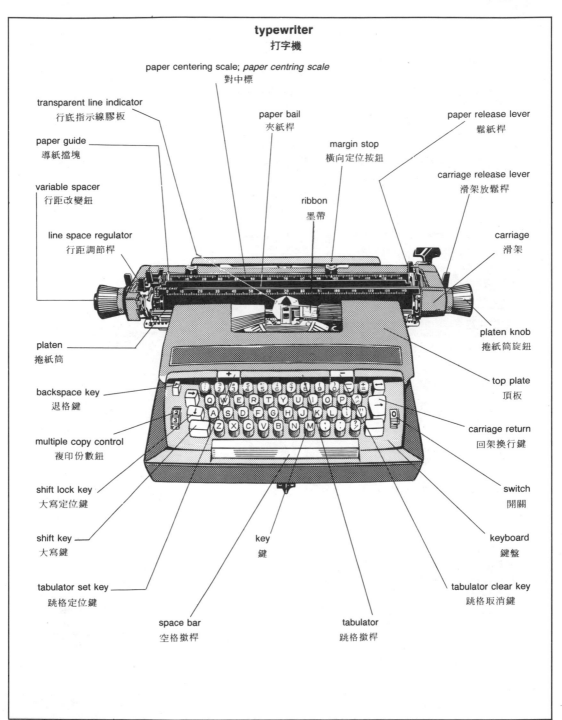

paper centering scale; *paper centring scale*
對中標

transparent line indicator
行底指示線膠板

paper bail
夾紙桿

paper release lever
鬆紙桿

paper guide
導紙擋塊

margin stop
橫向定位按鈕

carriage release lever
滑架放鬆桿

variable spacer
行距改變鈕

ribbon
墨帶

line space regulator
行距調節桿

carriage
滑架

platen knob
捲紙筒旋鈕

platen
捲紙筒

top plate
頂板

backspace key
退格鍵

carriage return
回架換行鍵

multiple copy control
複印份數鈕

switch
開關

shift lock key
大寫定位鍵

keyboard
鍵盤

shift key
大寫鍵

key
鍵

tabulator clear key
跳格取消鍵

tabulator set key
跳格定位鍵

space bar
空格撳桿

tabulator
跳格撳桿

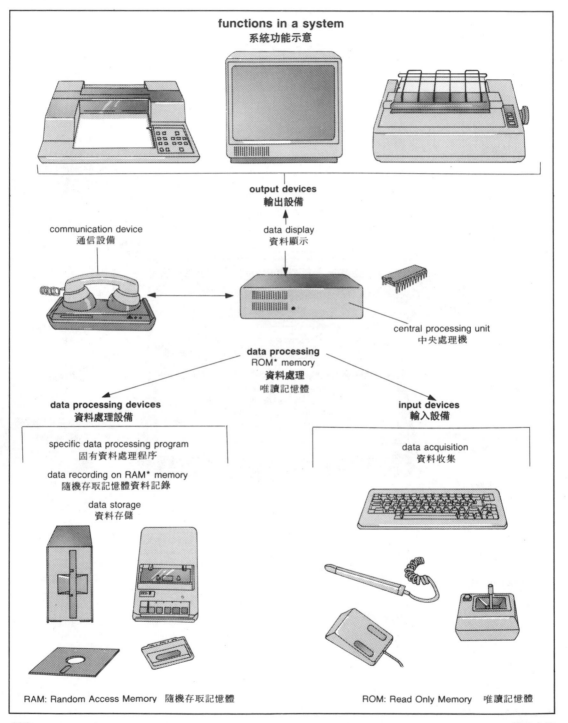

functions in a system
系統功能示意

output devices
輸出設備

communication device
通信設備

data display
資料顯示

central processing unit
中央處理機

data processing
ROM* memory
資料處理
唯讀記憶體

data processing devices
資料處理設備

input devices
輸入設備

specific data processing program
固有資料處理程序

data acquisition
資料收集

data recording on RAM* memory
隨機存取記憶體資料記錄

data storage
資料存儲

RAM: Random Access Memory　隨機存取記憶體

ROM: Read Only Memory　唯讀記憶體

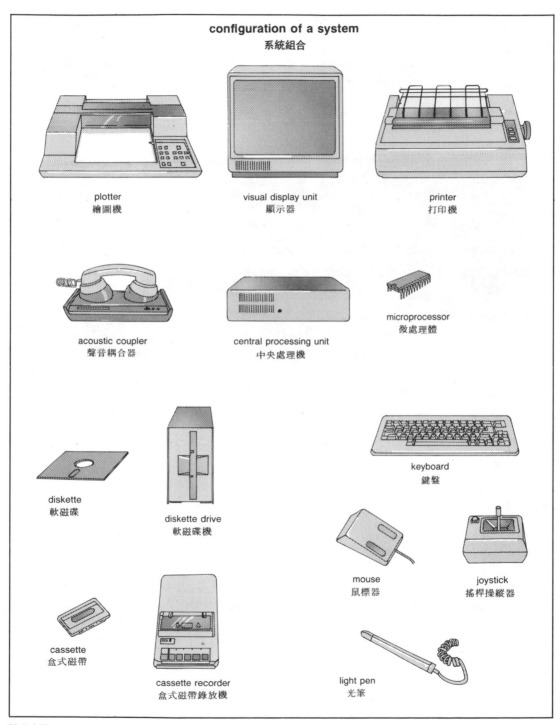

configuration of a system
系統組合

plotter
繪圖機

visual display unit
顯示器

printer
打印機

acoustic coupler
聲音耦合器

central processing unit
中央處理機

microprocessor
微處理體

diskette
軟磁碟

diskette drive
軟磁碟機

keyboard
鍵盤

mouse
鼠標器

joystick
搖桿操縱器

cassette
盒式磁帶

cassette recorder
盒式磁帶錄放機

light pen
光筆

keyboard
鍵盤

alphanumeric keyboard
字母數字鍵盤

numeric keypad
數字鍵台

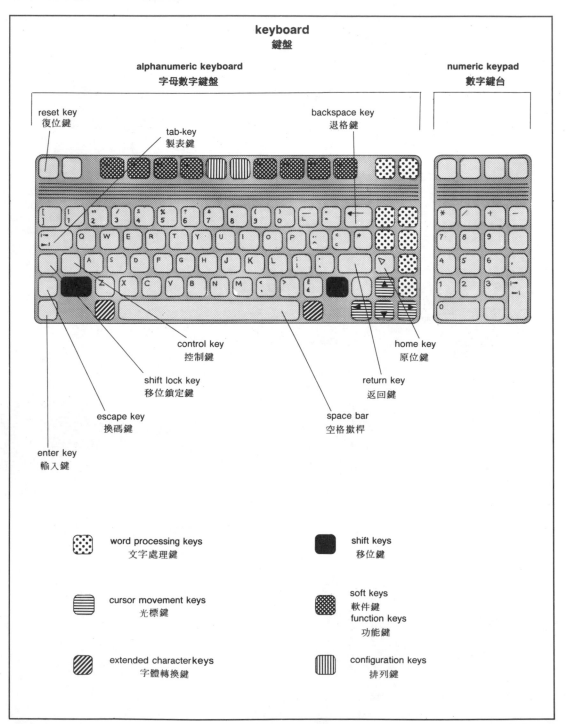

reset key
復位鍵

tab-key
製表鍵

backspace key
退格鍵

control key
控制鍵

home key
原位鍵

shift lock key
移位鎖定鍵

return key
返回鍵

escape key
換碼鍵

space bar
空格撥桿

enter key
輸入鍵

word processing keys
文字處理鍵

shift keys
移位鍵

cursor movement keys
光標鍵

soft keys
軟件鍵
function keys
功能鍵

extended character keys
字體轉換鍵

configuration keys
排列鍵

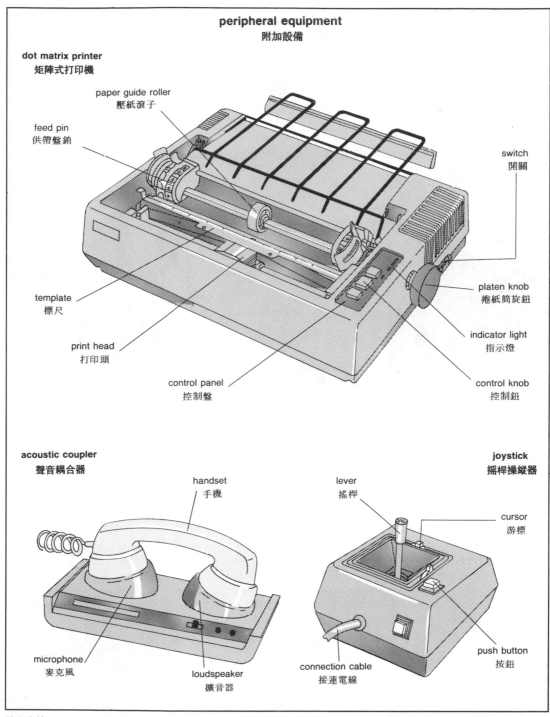

peripheral equipment
附加設備

dot matrix printer
矩陣式打印機

paper guide roller
壓紙滾子

feed pin
供帶盤銷

switch
開關

platen knob
捲紙筒旋鈕

template
標尺

indicator light
指示燈

print head
打印頭

control knob
控制鈕

control panel
控制盤

acoustic coupler
聲音耦合器

handset
手機

joystick
搖桿操縱器

lever
搖桿

cursor
游標

microphone
麥克風

loudspeaker
擴音器

connection cable
接連電線

push button
按鈕

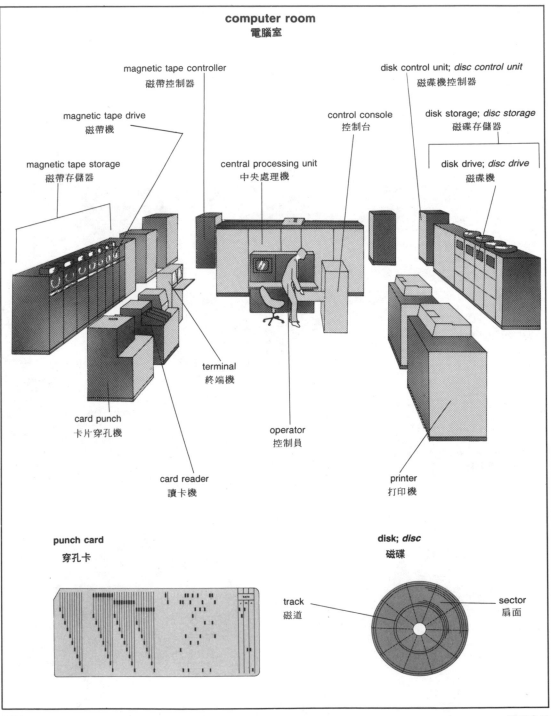

computer room
電腦室

magnetic tape controller
磁帶控制器

disk control unit; *disc control unit*
磁碟機控制器

magnetic tape drive
磁帶機

control console
控制台

disk storage; *disc storage*
磁碟存儲器

magnetic tape storage
磁帶存儲器

central processing unit
中央處理機

disk drive; *disc drive*
磁碟機

terminal
終端機

card punch
卡片穿孔機

operator
控制員

card reader
讀卡機

printer
打印機

punch card
穿孔卡

disk; *disc*
磁碟

track
磁道

sector
扇面

MUSIC

音樂

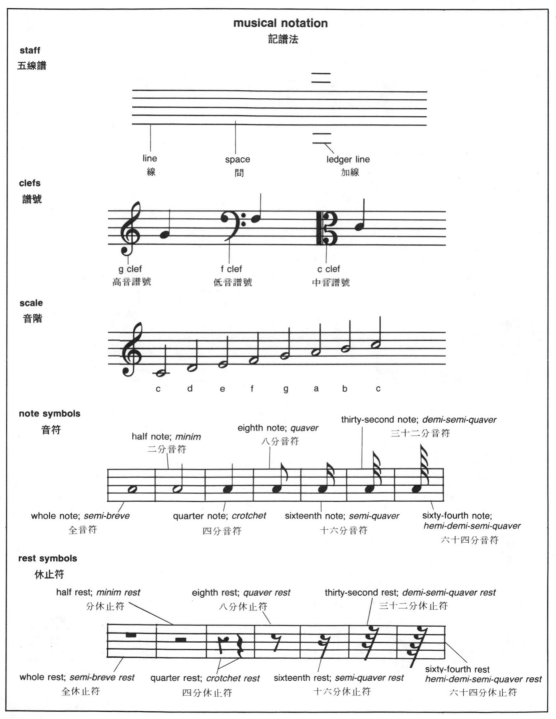

musical notation
記譜法

staff
五線譜

line 線

space 間

ledger line 加線

clefs
譜號

g clef 高音譜號

f clef 低音譜號

c clef 中音譜號

scale
音階

c d e f g a b c

note symbols
音符

half note; *minim*
二分音符

eighth note; *quaver*
八分音符

thirty-second note; *demi-semi-quaver*
三十二分音符

whole note; *semi-breve*
全音符

quarter note; *crotchet*
四分音符

sixteenth note; *semi-quaver*
十六分音符

sixty-fourth note;
hemi-demi-semi-quaver
六十四分音符

rest symbols
休止符

half rest; *minim rest*
分休止符

eighth rest; *quaver rest*
八分休止符

thirty-second rest; *demi-semi-quaver rest*
三十二分休止符

whole rest; *semi-breve rest*
全休止符

quarter rest; *crotchet rest*
四分休止符

sixteenth rest; *semi-quaver rest*
十六分休止符

sixty-fourth rest
hemi-demi-semi-quaver rest
六十四分休止符

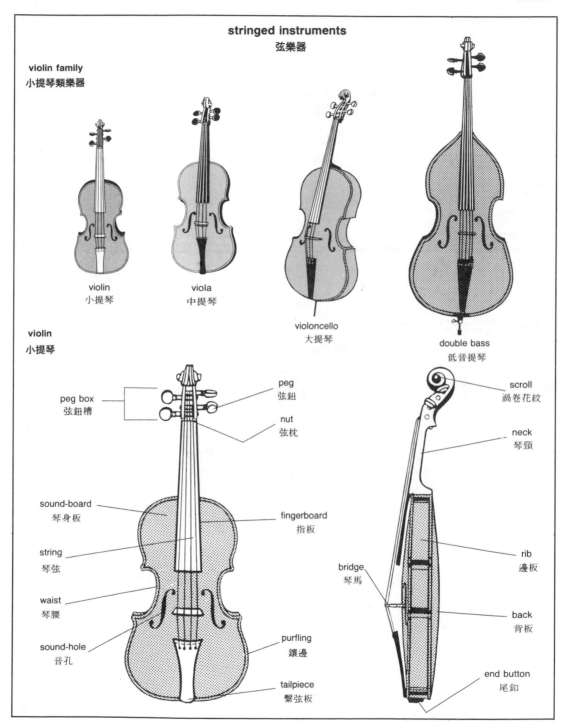

stringed instruments
弦樂器

violin family
小提琴類樂器

violin
小提琴

viola
中提琴

violoncello
大提琴

double bass
低音提琴

violin
小提琴

peg box
弦鈕槽

peg
弦鈕

nut
弦枕

sound-board
琴身板

fingerboard
指板

string
琴弦

waist
琴腰

sound-hole
音孔

purfling
鑲邊

tailpiece
繫弦板

scroll
渦卷花紋

neck
琴頸

rib
邊板

bridge
琴馬

back
背板

end button
尾鈕

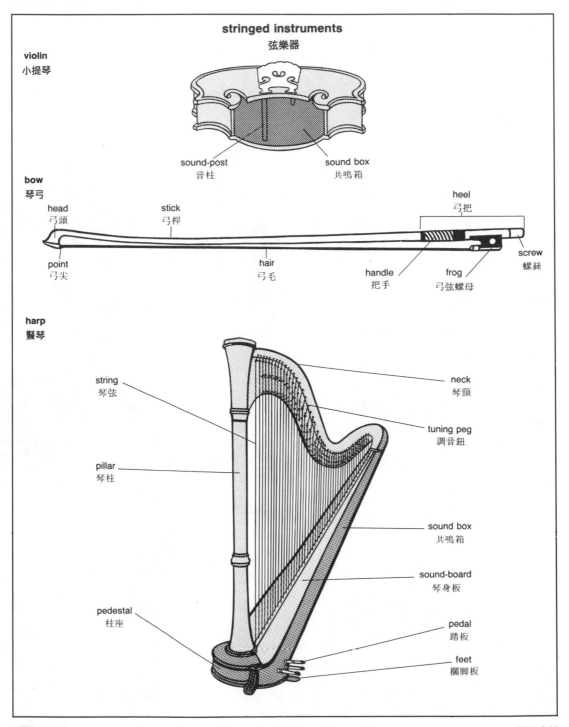

stringed instruments
弦樂器

violin
小提琴

sound-post
音柱

sound box
共鳴箱

bow
琴弓

head
弓頭

stick
弓桿

heel
弓把

point
弓尖

hair
弓毛

handle
把手

frog
弓弦螺母

screw
螺絲

harp
豎琴

string
琴弦

pillar
琴柱

pedestal
柱座

neck
琴頸

tuning peg
調音鈕

sound box
共鳴箱

sound-board
琴身板

pedal
踏板

feet
攔腳板

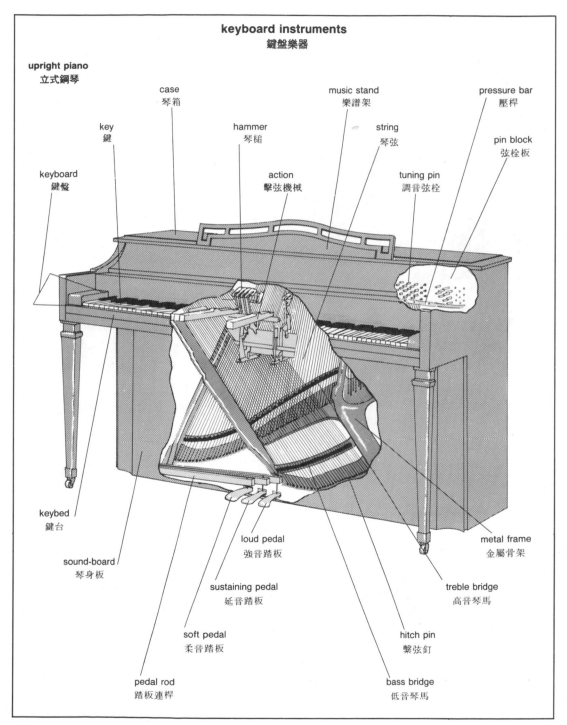

keyboard instruments
鍵盤樂器

upright piano
立式鋼琴

case
琴箱

music stand
樂譜架

pressure bar
壓桿

key
鍵

hammer
琴槌

string
琴弦

pin block
弦栓板

keyboard
鍵盤

action
擊弦機械

tuning pin
調音弦栓

keybed
鍵台

loud pedal
強音踏板

metal frame
金屬骨架

sound-board
琴身板

sustaining pedal
延音踏板

treble bridge
高音琴馬

soft pedal
柔音踏板

hitch pin
繫弦釘

pedal rod
踏板連桿

bass bridge
低音琴馬

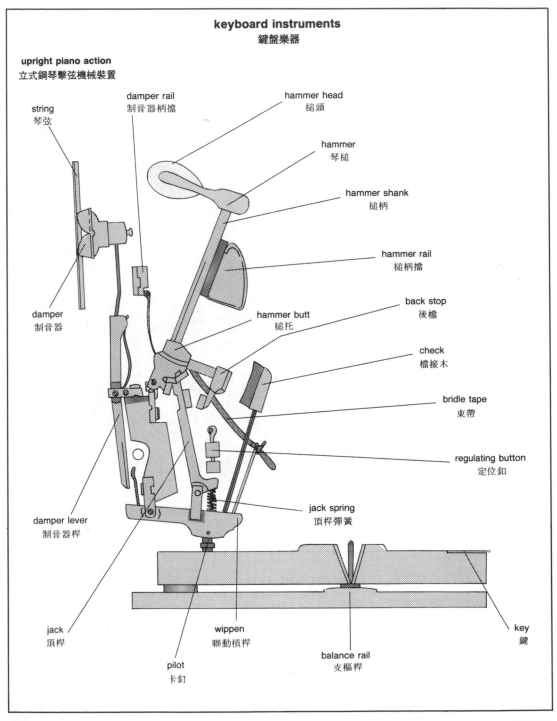

keyboard instruments
鍵盤樂器

upright piano action
立式鋼琴擊弦機械裝置

string
琴弦

damper rail
制音器柄擋

hammer head
槌頭

hammer
琴槌

hammer shank
槌柄

hammer rail
槌柄擋

damper
制音器

hammer butt
槌托

back stop
後擋

check
檔接木

bridle tape
束帶

regulating button
定位鈕

damper lever
制音器桿

jack spring
頂桿彈簧

jack
頂桿

wippen
聯動槓桿

pilot
卡釘

balance rail
支樞桿

key
鍵

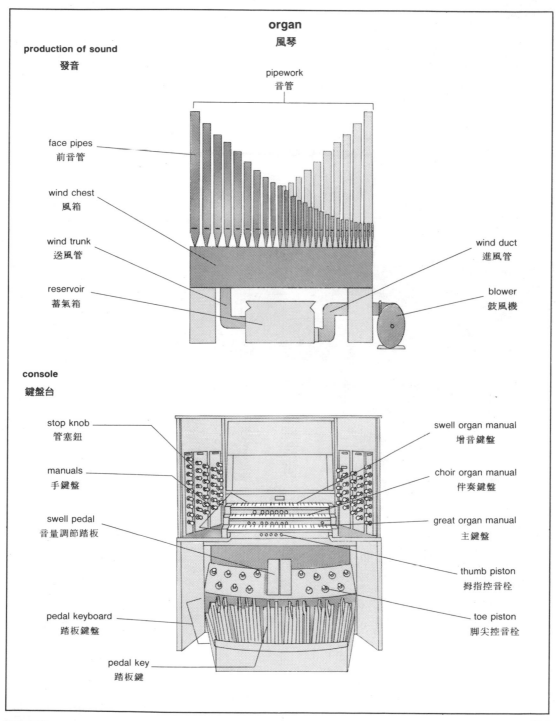

organ
風琴

production of sound
發音

pipework
音管

face pipes
前音管

wind chest
風箱

wind trunk
送風管

reservoir
蓄氣箱

wind duct
進風管

blower
鼓風機

console
鍵盤台

stop knob
管塞鈕

manuals
手鍵盤

swell pedal
音量調節踏板

pedal keyboard
踏板鍵盤

pedal key
踏板鍵

swell organ manual
增音鍵盤

choir organ manual
伴奏鍵盤

great organ manual
主鍵盤

thumb piston
拇指控音栓

toe piston
腳尖控音栓

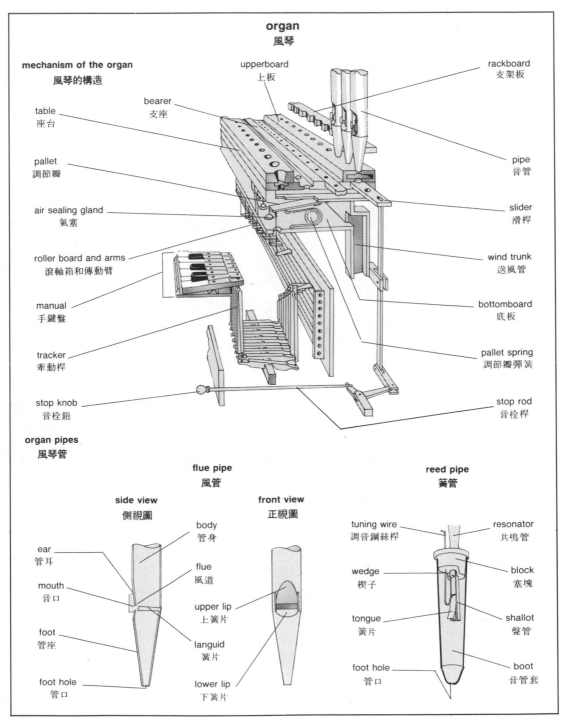

organ
風琴

mechanism of the organ
風琴的構造

upperboard
上板

rackboard
支架板

bearer
支座

table
座台

pipe
音管

pallet
調節瓣

slider
滑桿

air sealing gland
氣塞

wind trunk
送風管

roller board and arms
滾軸箱和傳動臂

manual
手鍵盤

bottomboard
底板

tracker
牽動桿

pallet spring
調節瓣彈簧

stop knob
音栓鈕

stop rod
音栓桿

organ pipes
風琴管

flue pipe
風管

reed pipe
簧管

side view
側視圖

front view
正視圖

tuning wire
調音鋼絲桿

resonator
共鳴管

body
管身

ear
管耳

flue
風道

wedge
楔子

block
塞塊

mouth
音口

upper lip
上簧片

tongue
簧片

shallot
聲管

foot
管座

languid
簧片

foot hole
管口

lower lip
下簧片

foot hole
管口

boot
音管套

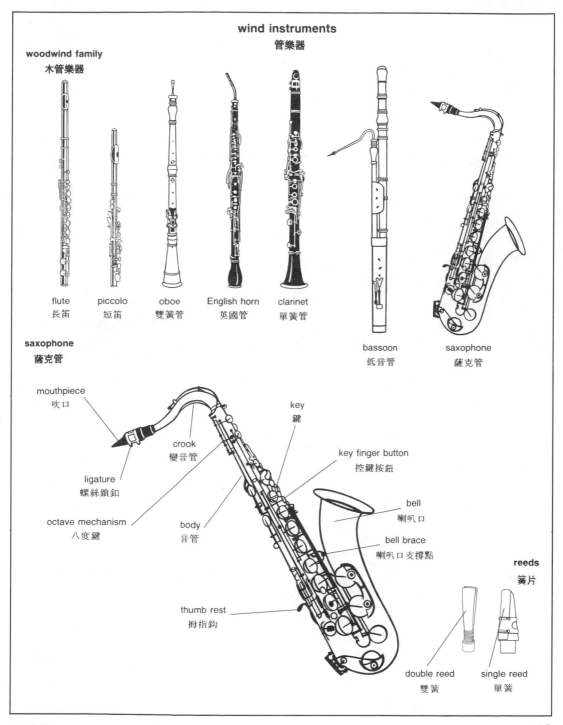

wind instruments
管樂器

woodwind family
木管樂器

flute
長笛

piccolo
短笛

oboe
雙簧管

English horn
英國管

clarinet
單簧管

bassoon
低音管

saxophone
薩克管

saxophone
薩克管

mouthpiece
吹口

key
鍵

crook
變音管

key finger button
控鍵按鈕

ligature
螺絲鎖釦

bell
喇叭口

octave mechanism
八度鍵

body
音管

bell brace
喇叭口支撐點

reeds
簧片

thumb rest
拇指鈎

double reed
雙簧

single reed
單簧

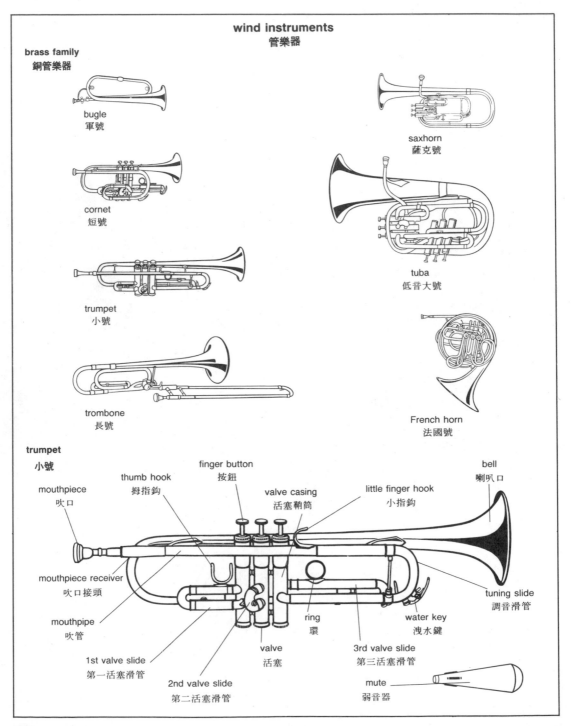

wind instruments
管樂器

brass family
銅管樂器

bugle
軍號

cornet
短號

trumpet
小號

trombone
長號

saxhorn
薩克號

tuba
低音大號

French horn
法國號

trumpet
小號

mouthpiece
吹口

thumb hook
拇指鉤

finger button
按鈕

valve casing
活塞鞘筒

little finger hook
小指鉤

bell
喇叭口

mouthpiece receiver
吹口接頭

mouthpipe
吹管

1st valve slide
第一活塞滑管

2nd valve slide
第二活塞滑管

valve
活塞

ring
環

3rd valve slide
第三活塞滑管

water key
洩水鍵

tuning slide
調音滑管

mute
弱音器

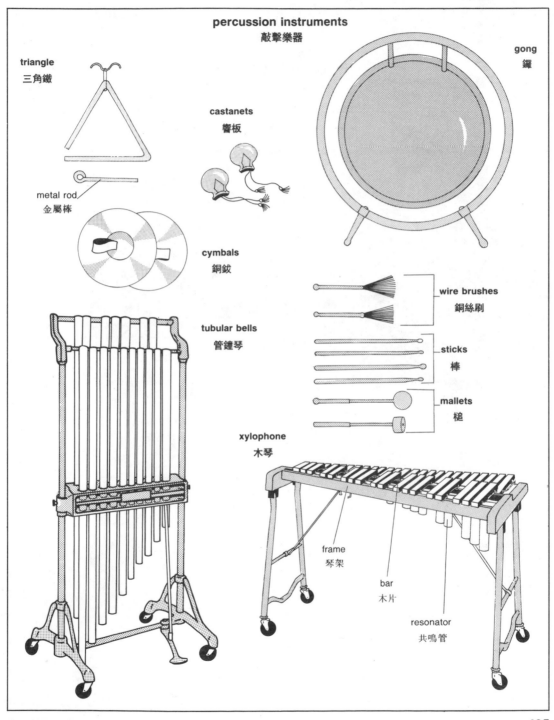

percussion instruments
敲擊樂器

triangle
三角鐵

metal rod
金屬棒

castanets
響板

gong
鑼

cymbals
銅鈸

tubular bells
管鐘琴

wire brushes
銅絲刷

sticks
棒

mallets
槌

xylophone
木琴

frame
琴架

bar
木片

resonator
共鳴管

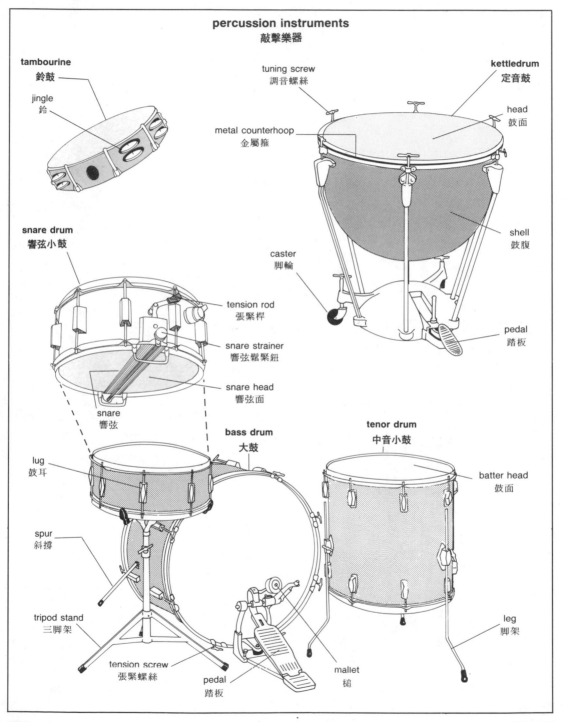

percussion instruments
敲擊樂器

tambourine
鈴鼓

jingle
鈴

tuning screw
調音螺絲

kettledrum
定音鼓

head
鼓面

metal counterhoop
金屬箍

shell
鼓腹

snare drum
響弦小鼓

tension rod
張緊桿

snare strainer
響弦鬆緊鈕

caster
腳輪

snare head
響弦面

snare
響弦

pedal
踏板

bass drum
大鼓

tenor drum
中音小鼓

lug
鼓耳

batter head
鼓面

spur
斜撐

tripod stand
三腳架

tension screw
張緊螺絲

pedal
踏板

mallet
槌

leg
腳架

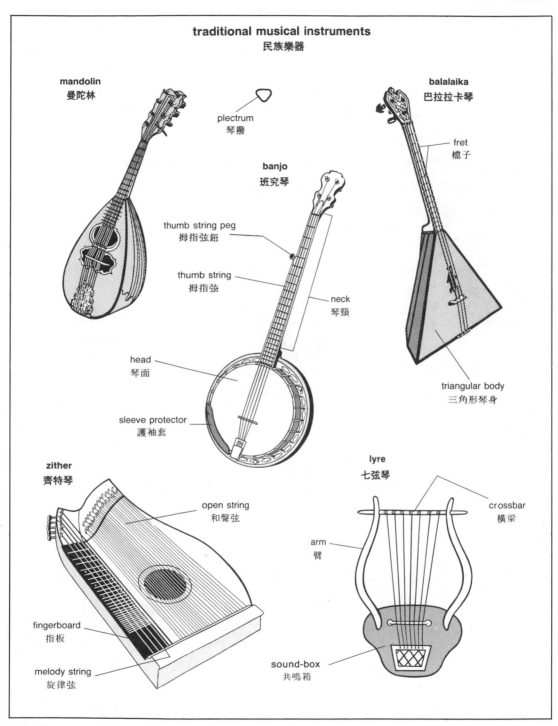

traditional musical instruments
民族樂器

mandolin
曼陀林

plectrum
琴撥

banjo
班究琴

thumb string peg
拇指弦鈕

thumb string
拇指弦

head
琴面

sleeve protector
護袖套

neck
琴頸

balalaika
巴拉拉卡琴

fret
檔子

triangular body
三角形琴身

zither
齊特琴

open string
和聲弦

fingerboard
指板

melody string
旋律弦

lyre
七弦琴

crossbar
橫梁

arm
臂

sound-box
共鳴箱

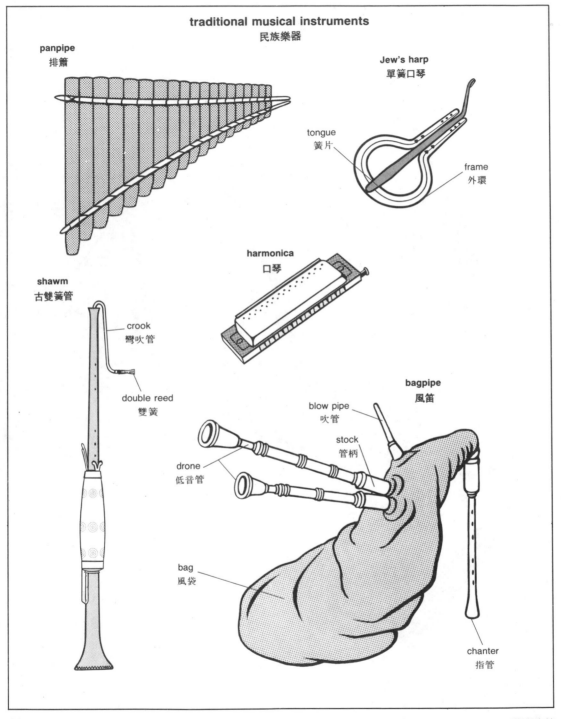

traditional musical instruments
民族樂器

panpipe
排簫

Jew's harp
單簧口琴

tongue
簧片

frame
外環

harmonica
口琴

shawm
古雙簧管

crook
彎吹管

double reed
雙簧

bagpipe
風笛

blow pipe
吹管

stock
管柄

drone
低音管

bag
風袋

chanter
指管

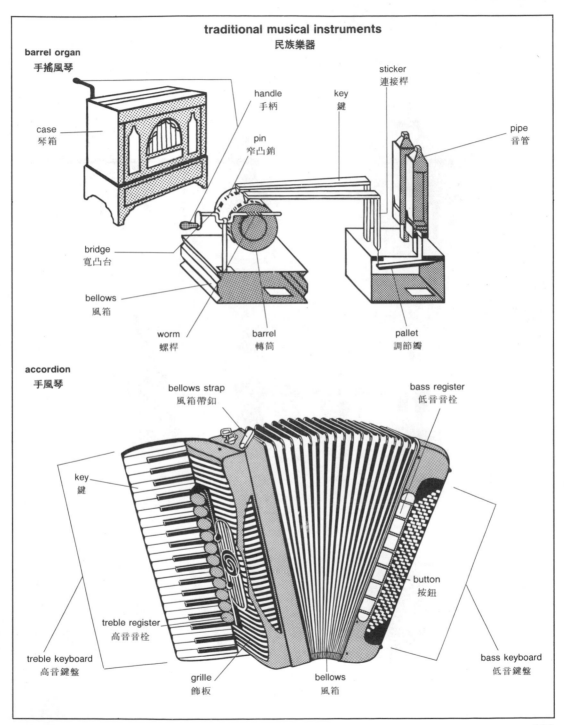

traditional musical instruments
民族樂器

barrel organ
手搖風琴

case
琴箱

handle
手柄

pin
窄凸銷

key
鍵

sticker
連接桿

pipe
音管

bridge
寬凸台

bellows
風箱

worm
螺桿

barrel
轉筒

pallet
調節瓣

accordion
手風琴

bellows strap
風箱帶釦

bass register
低音音栓

key
鍵

button
按鈕

treble register
高音音栓

treble keyboard
高音鍵盤

grille
飾板

bellows
風箱

bass keyboard
低音鍵盤

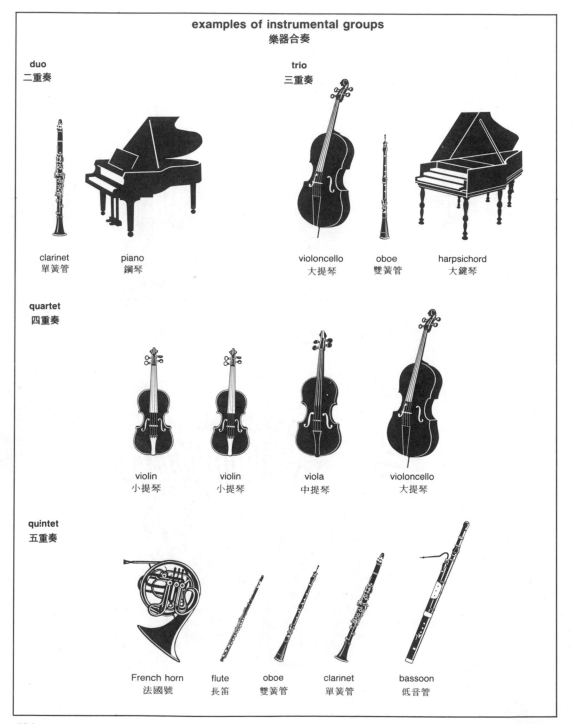

examples of instrumental groups
樂器合奏

duo
二重奏

trio
三重奏

clarinet
單簧管

piano
鋼琴

violoncello
大提琴

oboe
雙簧管

harpsichord
大鍵琴

quartet
四重奏

violin
小提琴

violin
小提琴

viola
中提琴

violoncello
大提琴

quintet
五重奏

French horn
法國號

flute
長笛

oboe
雙簧管

clarinet
單簧管

bassoon
低音管

examples of instrumental groups
樂器合奏

sextet
六重奏

jazz band
爵士樂隊

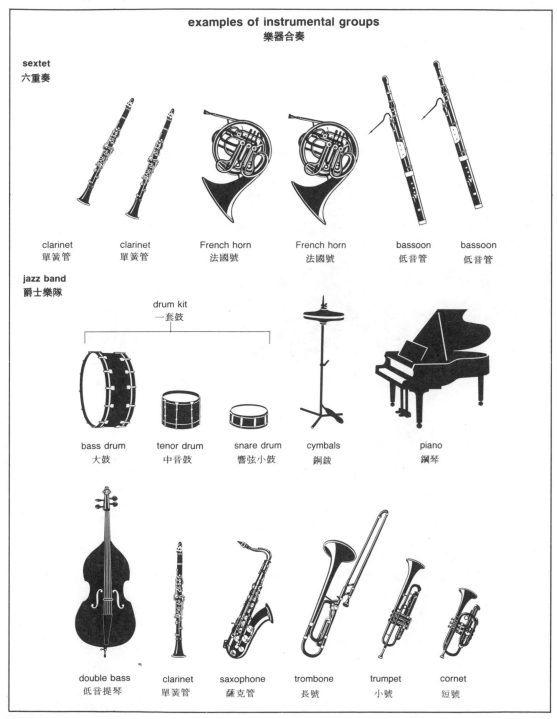

drum kit
一套鼓

clarinet	clarinet	French horn	French horn	bassoon	bassoon
單簧管	單簧管	法國號	法國號	低音管	低音管

bass drum	tenor drum	snare drum	cymbals	piano
大鼓	中音鼓	響弦小鼓	銅鈸	鋼琴

double bass	clarinet	saxophone	trombone	trumpet	cornet
低音提琴	單簧管	薩克管	長號	小號	短號

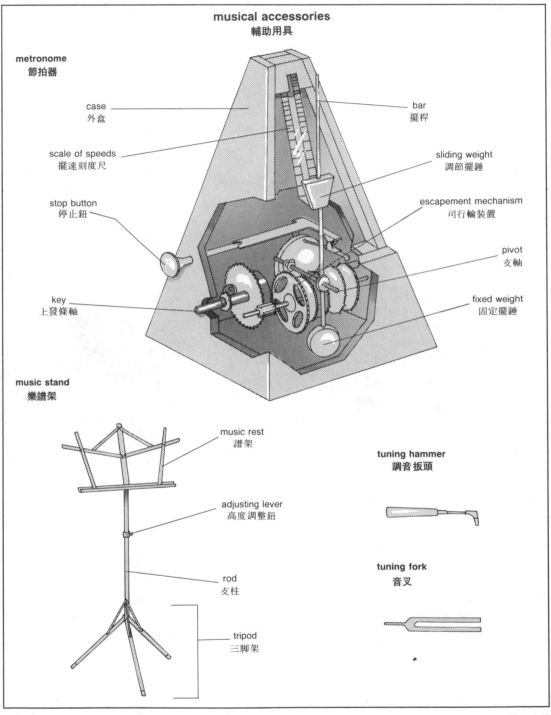

musical accessories
輔助用具

metronome
節拍器

case
外盒

bar
擺桿

scale of speeds
擺速刻度尺

sliding weight
調節擺錘

stop button
停止鈕

escapement mechanism
司行輪裝置

pivot
支軸

key
上發條軸

fixed weight
固定擺錘

music stand
樂譜架

music rest
譜架

tuning hammer
調音扳頭

adjusting lever
高度調整鈕

rod
支柱

tuning fork
音叉

tripod
三脚架

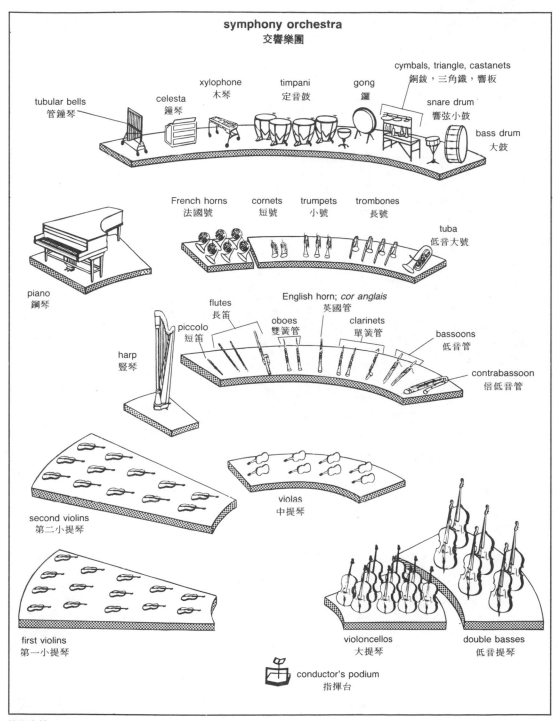

symphony orchestra
交響樂團

tubular bells
管鐘琴

celesta
鐘琴

xylophone
木琴

timpani
定音鼓

gong
鑼

cymbals, triangle, castanets
銅鈸，三角鐵，響板

snare drum
響弦小鼓

bass drum
大鼓

French horns
法國號

cornets
短號

trumpets
小號

trombones
長號

tuba
低音大號

piano
鋼琴

English horn; cor anglais
英國管

flutes
長笛

oboes
雙簧管

clarinets
單簧管

bassoons
低音管

piccolo
短笛

harp
豎琴

contrabassoon
倍低音管

second violins
第二小提琴

violas
中提琴

first violins
第一小提琴

violoncellos
大提琴

double basses
低音提琴

conductor's podium
指揮台

electric and electronic instruments
電樂器與電子樂器

electric guitar
電吉他

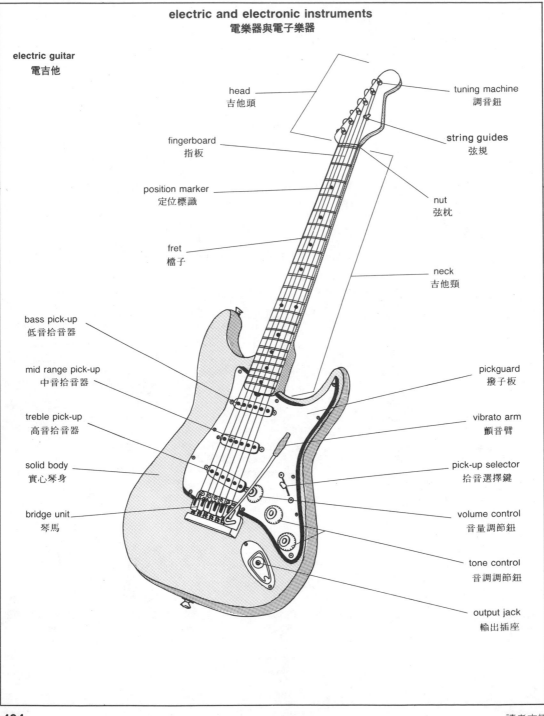

head
吉他頭

tuning machine
調音鈕

fingerboard
指板

string guides
弦規

position marker
定位標識

nut
弦枕

fret
檔子

neck
吉他頸

bass pick-up
低音拾音器

pickguard
撥子板

mid range pick-up
中音拾音器

vibrato arm
顫音臂

treble pick-up
高音拾音器

pick-up selector
拾音選擇鍵

solid body
實心琴身

volume control
音量調節鈕

bridge unit
琴馬

tone control
音調調節鈕

output jack
輸出插座

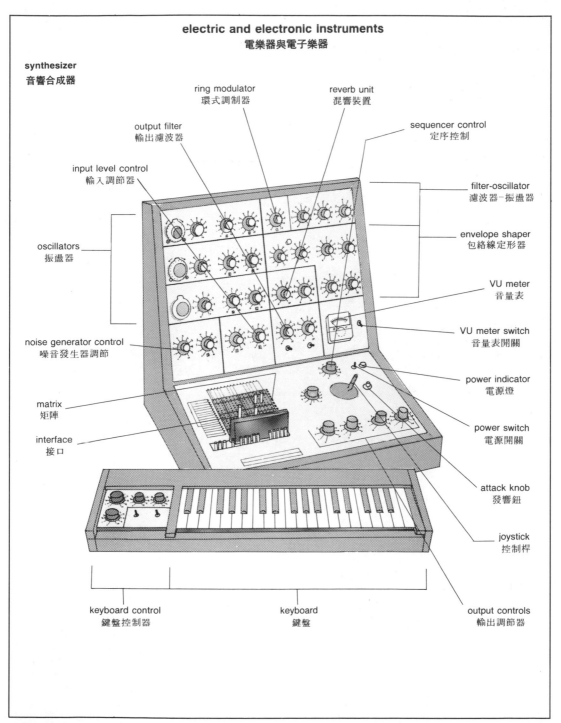

electric and electronic instruments
電樂器與電子樂器

synthesizer
音響合成器

ring modulator
環式調制器

reverb unit
混響裝置

sequencer control
定序控制

output filter
輸出濾波器

filter-oscillator
濾波器-振盪器

input level control
輸入調節器

envelope shaper
包絡線定形器

oscillators
振盪器

VU meter
音量表

VU meter switch
音量表開關

noise generator control
噪音發生器調節

power indicator
電源燈

matrix
矩陣

power switch
電源開關

interface
接口

attack knob
發響鈕

joystick
控制桿

keyboard control
鍵盤控制器

keyboard
鍵盤

output controls
輸出調節器

CREATIVE LEISURE ACTIVITIES

sewing
縫紉

sewing machine
縫紉機

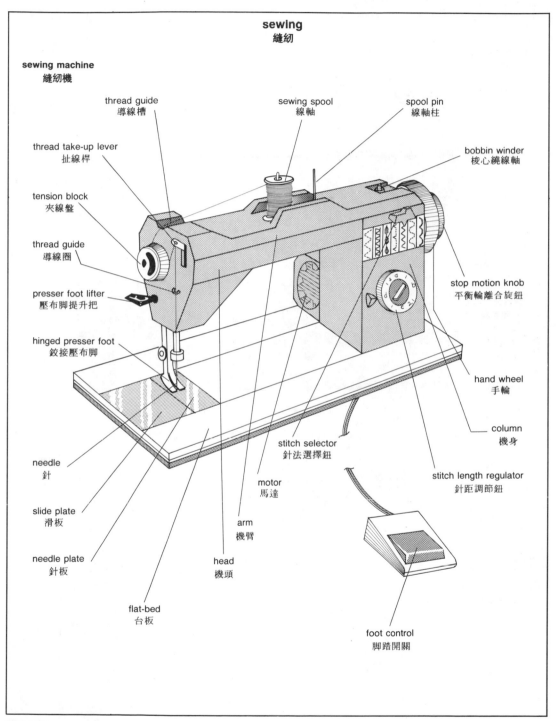

thread guide
導線槽

sewing spool
線軸

spool pin
線軸柱

thread take-up lever
扯線桿

bobbin winder
梭心繞線軸

tension block
夾線盤

thread guide
導線圈

stop motion knob
平衡輪離合旋鈕

presser foot lifter
壓布腳提升把

hinged presser foot
鉸接壓布腳

hand wheel
手輪

column
機身

stitch selector
針法選擇鈕

needle
針

motor
馬達

stitch length regulator
針距調節鈕

slide plate
滑板

arm
機臂

needle plate
針板

head
機頭

flat-bed
台板

foot control
腳踏開關

sewing
縫紉

sewing machine
縫紉機

tension block
夾線盤

thread guide
導線圈

tension disc
夾線片

tension dial
鬆緊旋鈕

tension spring
緩線彈簧

shuttle
梭子

bobbin
繞線筒

needle
針

presser foot
壓布脚

presser bar
壓桿

thread trimmer
割線刀口

needle clamp screw
夾針螺絲

hinged presser foot
鉸接壓布脚

feed dog
送布齒

needle bar
裝針桿

needle clamp
針夾

needle threader
穿線器

needle
針

shank
針桿

groove
槽

blade
針身

eye
針眼

point
針尖

latch lever
彈簧銷鈎柄

bobbin case
梭心匣

bobbin
梭心

hook
鈎

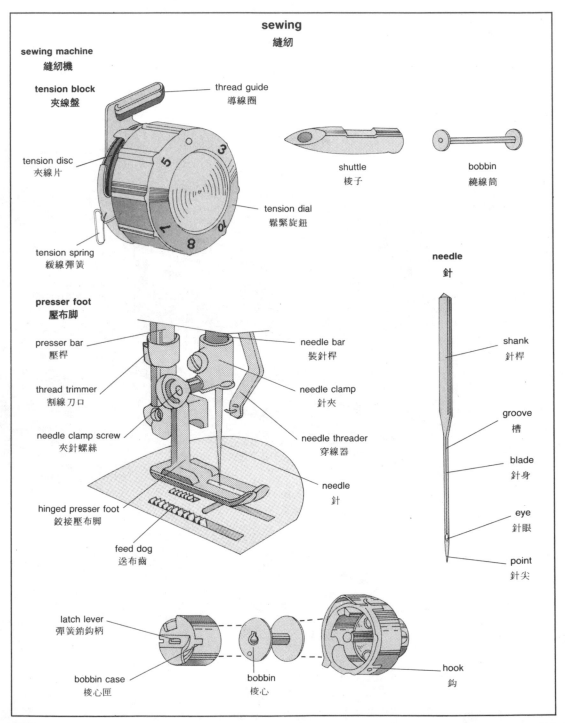

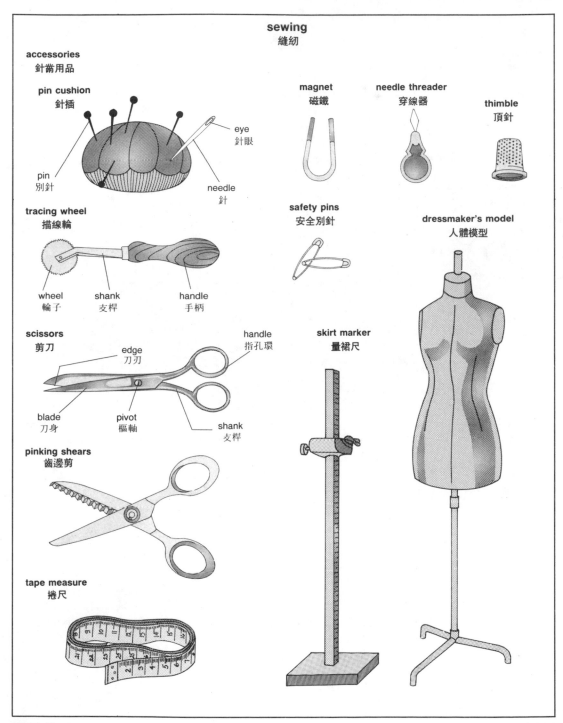

sewing
縫紉

accessories
針黹用品

pin cushion
針插

eye
針眼

pin
別針

needle
針

magnet
磁鐵

needle threader
穿線器

thimble
頂針

tracing wheel
描線輪

wheel
輪子

shank
支桿

handle
手柄

safety pins
安全別針

dressmaker's model
人體模型

scissors
剪刀

edge
刀刃

handle
指孔環

blade
刀身

pivot
樞軸

shank
支桿

skirt marker
量裙尺

pinking shears
齒邊剪

tape measure
捲尺

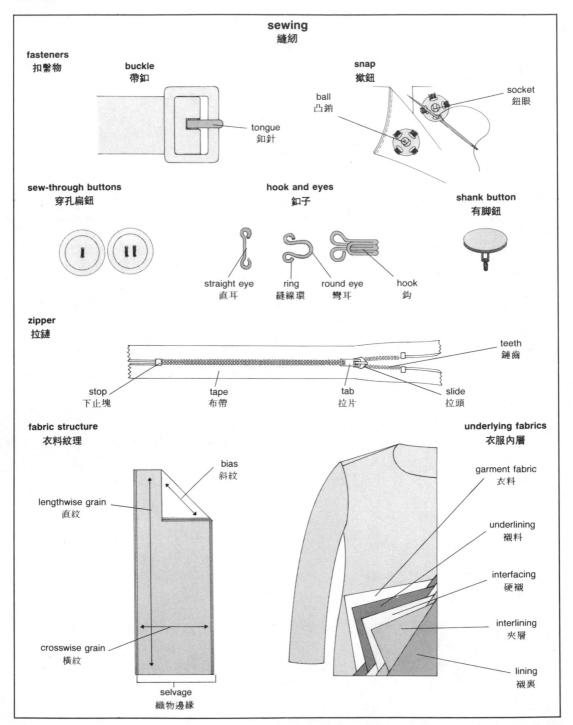

sewing
縫紉

fasteners
扣繫物

buckle
帶釦

tongue
釦針

snap
撳鈕

ball
凸銷

socket
鈕眼

sew-through buttons
穿孔扁鈕

hook and eyes
釦子

shank button
有腳鈕

straight eye
直耳

ring
縫線環

round eye
彎耳

hook
鈎

zipper
拉鏈

teeth
鏈齒

stop
下止塊

tape
布帶

tab
拉片

slide
拉頭

fabric structure
衣料紋理

underlying fabrics
衣服內層

bias
斜紋

garment fabric
衣料

lengthwise grain
直紋

underlining
襯料

interfacing
硬襯

interlining
夾層

crosswise grain
橫紋

lining
襯裏

selvage
織物邊緣

sewing
縫紉

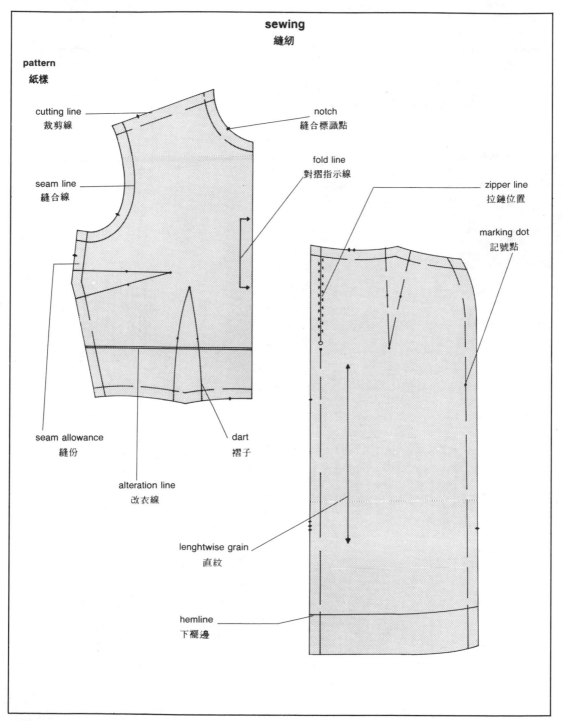

pattern
紙樣

cutting line
裁剪線

notch
縫合標識點

fold line
對摺指示線

seam line
縫合線

zipper line
拉鏈位置

marking dot
記號點

seam allowance
縫份

dart
褶子

alteration line
改衣線

lenghtwise grain
直紋

hemline
下襬邊

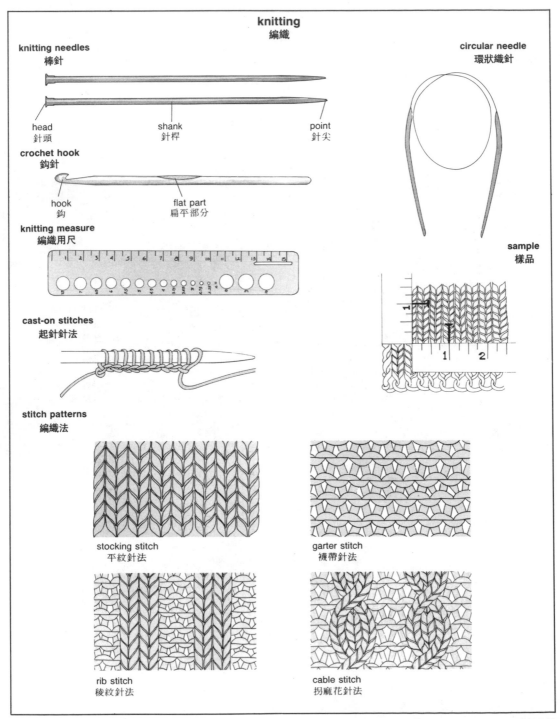

knitting
編織

knitting needles
棒針

head
針頭

shank
針桿

point
針尖

crochet hook
鈎針

hook
鈎

flat part
扁平部分

knitting measure
編織用尺

cast-on stitches
起針針法

stitch patterns
編織法

stocking stitch
平紋針法

garter stitch
襪帶針法

rib stitch
稜紋針法

cable stitch
拐廊花針法

circular needle
環狀織針

sample
樣品

knitting machine
編織機

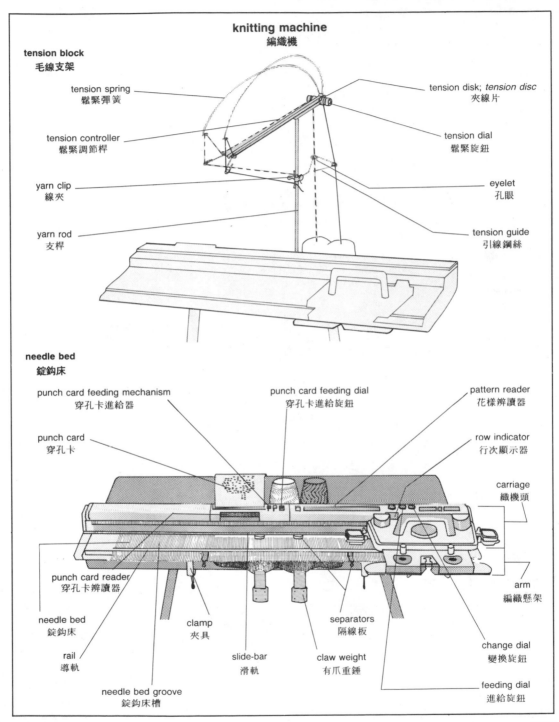

tension block
毛線支架

tension spring
鬆緊彈簧

tension disk; *tension disc*
夾線片

tension controller
鬆緊調節桿

tension dial
鬆緊旋鈕

yarn clip
線夾

eyelet
孔眼

yarn rod
支桿

tension guide
引線鋼絲

needle bed
錠鈎床

punch card feeding mechanism
穿孔卡進給器

punch card feeding dial
穿孔卡進給旋鈕

pattern reader
花樣辨讀器

punch card
穿孔卡

row indicator
行次顯示器

carriage
織機頭

punch card reader
穿孔卡辨讀器

arm
編織懸架

needle bed
錠鈎床

clamp
夾具

separators
隔線板

change dial
變換旋鈕

rail
導軌

slide-bar
滑軌

claw weight
有爪重錘

feeding dial
進給旋鈕

needle bed groove
錠鈎床槽

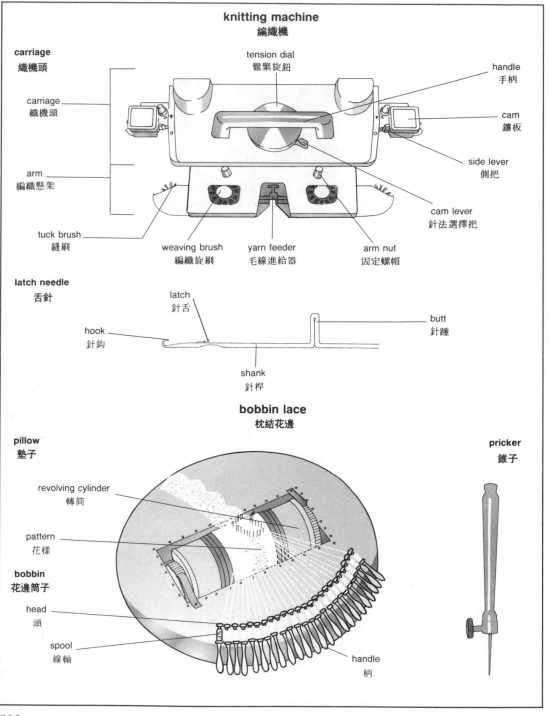

knitting machine
編織機

carriage
織機頭

tension dial
鬆緊旋鈕

handle
手柄

carriage
織機頭

cam
鑲板

side lever
側把

arm
編織懸架

cam lever
針法選擇把

tuck brush
縫刷

weaving brush
編織旋刷

yarn feeder
毛線進給器

arm nut
固定螺帽

latch needle
舌針

latch
針舌

hook
針鈎

butt
針踵

shank
針桿

bobbin lace
枕結花邊

pillow
墊子

pricker
錐子

revolving cylinder
轉筒

pattern
花樣

bobbin
花邊筒子

head
頭

spool
線軸

handle
柄

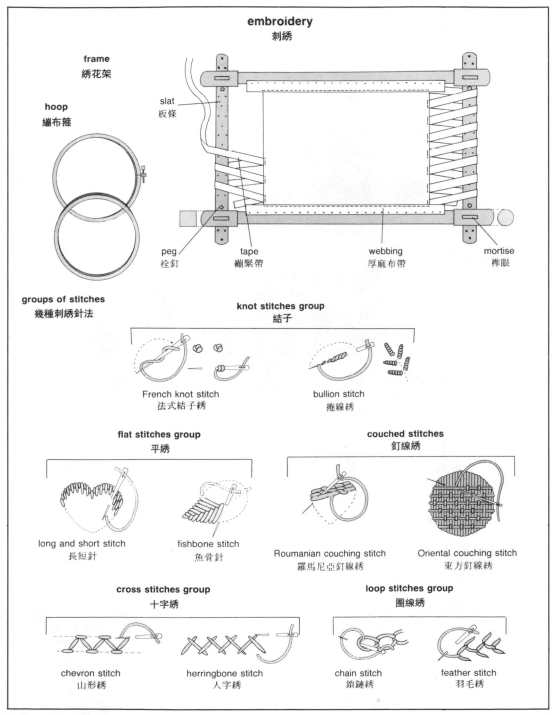

embroidery
刺綉

frame
綉花架

hoop
繃布箍

slat
板條

peg
栓釘

tape
繃緊帶

webbing
厚麻布帶

mortise
榫眼

groups of stitches
幾種刺綉針法

knot stitches group
結子

French knot stitch
法式結子綉

bullion stitch
捲線綉

flat stitches group
平綉

long and short stitch
長短針

fishbone stitch
魚骨針

couched stitches
釘線綉

Roumanian couching stitch
羅馬尼亞釘線綉

Oriental couching stitch
東方釘線綉

cross stitches group
十字綉

chevron stitch
山形綉

herringbone stitch
人字綉

loop stitches group
圈線綉

chain stitch
鎖鏈綉

feather stitch
羽毛綉

weaving
織造

low warp loom
臥經織機

heddle
綜絲

head roller
頂滾軸

harness
綜絖

warp
經紗

upright
支柱

harnesses
綜絖

leash rod
分經棒

beater handtree
筘座木

back beam
後經梁

reed
杼

warp roller
經紗捲軸

beater sley
筘座脚

beater
筘座支柱

weft
緯紗

handle
手柄

breast beam
撐梁

ratchet
棘爪

post
支柱

ratchet wheel
棘輪

crosspiece
橫檔

cloth roller
捲布軸

crossbeam
橫梁

lam
拉綜梁

treadle
踏板

frame　框架

treadle cord
踏板運動帶

screw eye
環首螺釘

take-up handle
提把

release treadle
放鬆踏板

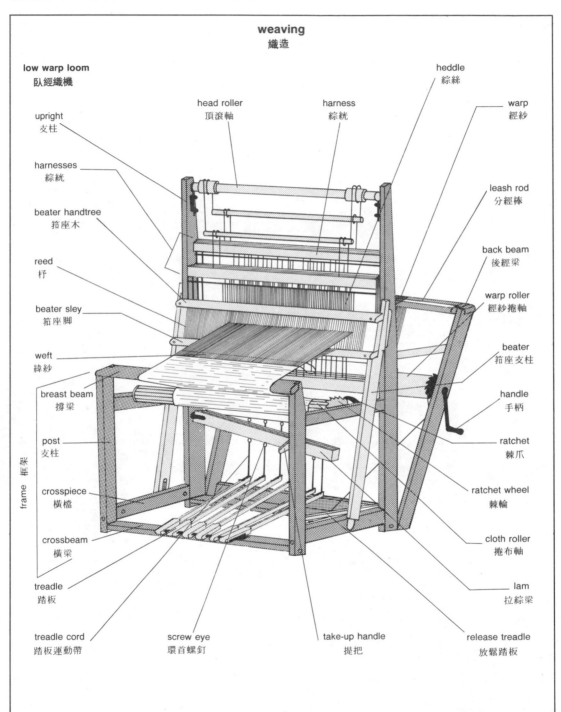

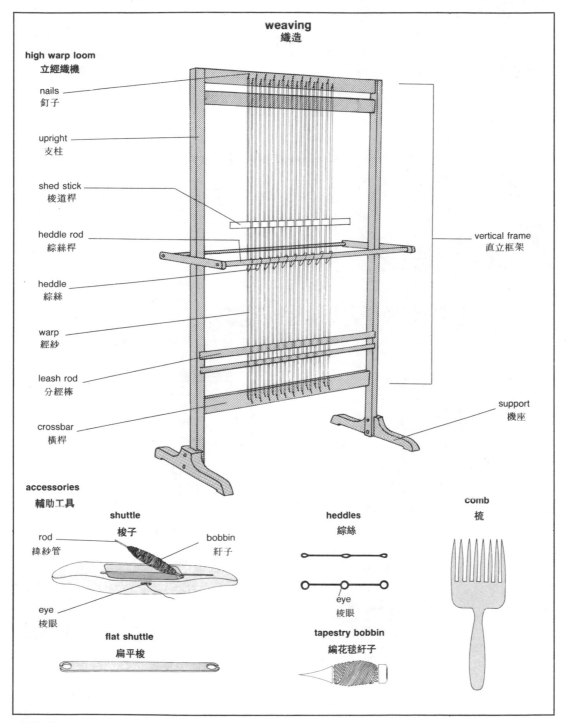

weaving
織造

high warp loom
立經織機

nails
釘子

upright
支柱

shed stick
梭道桿

heddle rod
綜絲桿

heddle
綜絲

warp
經紗

leash rod
分經棒

crossbar
橫桿

vertical frame
直立框架

support
機座

accessories
輔助工具

shuttle
梭子

rod
緯紗管

bobbin
紆子

eye
梭眼

flat shuttle
扁平梭

heddles
綜絲

eye
梭眼

tapestry bobbin
編花毯紆子

comb
梳

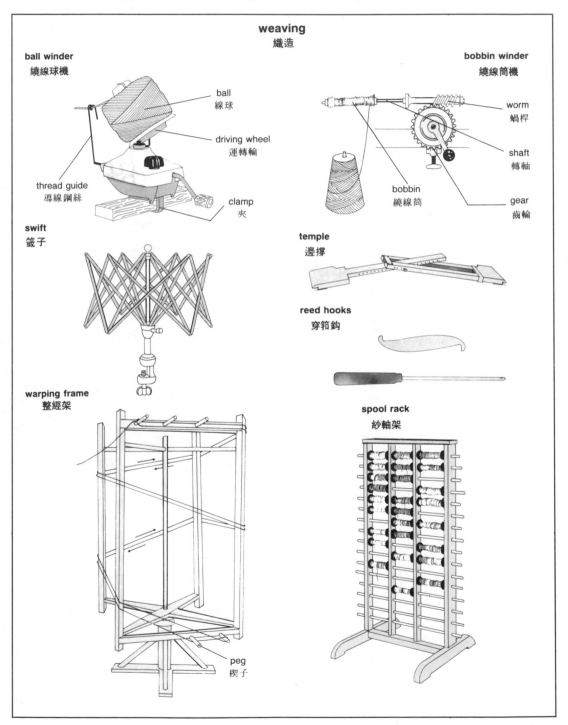

weaving
織造

ball winder
繞線球機

ball
線球

driving wheel
運轉輪

thread guide
導線鋼絲

clamp
夾

bobbin winder
繞線筒機

worm
蝸桿

shaft
轉軸

bobbin
繞線筒

gear
齒輪

swift
筬子

temple
邊撐

reed hooks
穿筘鉤

warping frame
整經架

peg
楔子

spool rack
紗軸架

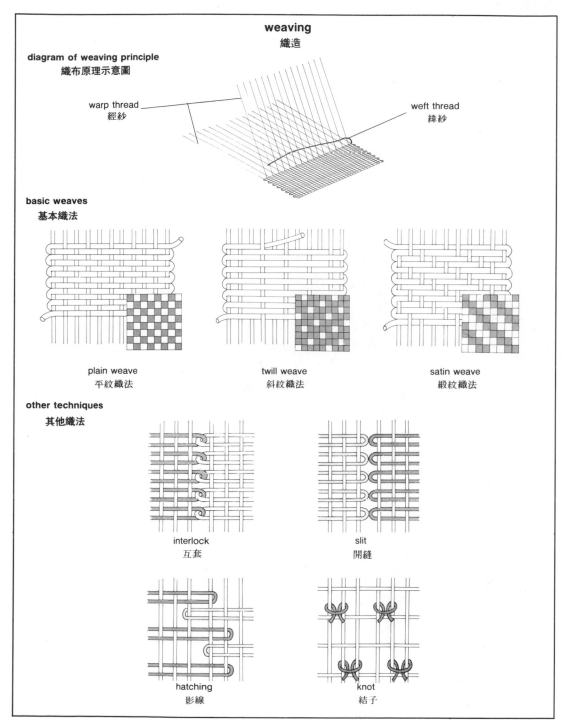

weaving
織造

diagram of weaving principle
織布原理示意圖

warp thread
經紗

weft thread
緯紗

basic weaves
基本織法

plain weave
平紋織法

twill weave
斜紋織法

satin weave
緞紋織法

other techniques
其他織法

interlock
互套

slit
開縫

hatching
影線

knot
結子

fine bookbinding
精裝書籍裝訂

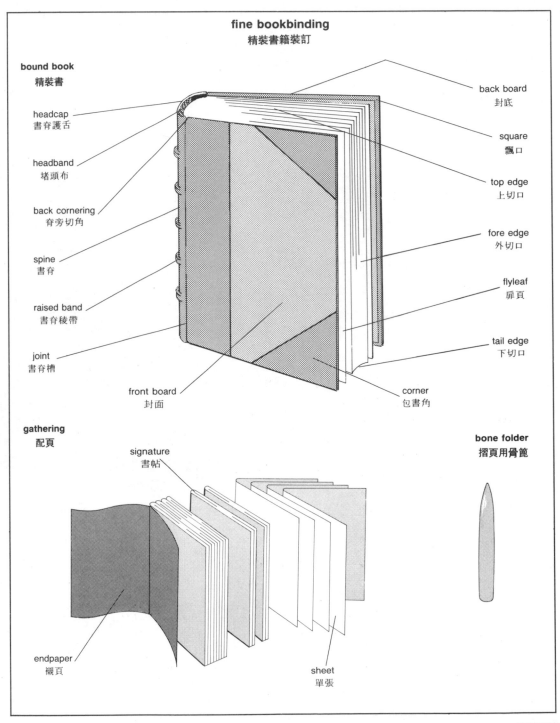

bound book
精裝書

headcap
書脊護舌

headband
堵頭布

back cornering
脊旁切角

spine
書脊

raised band
書脊稜帶

joint
書脊槽

front board
封面

back board
封底

square
飄口

top edge
上切口

fore edge
外切口

flyleaf
扉頁

tail edge
下切口

corner
包書角

gathering
配頁

signature
書帖

bone folder
摺頁用骨篦

endpaper
襯頁

sheet
單張

fine bookbinding
精裝書籍裝訂

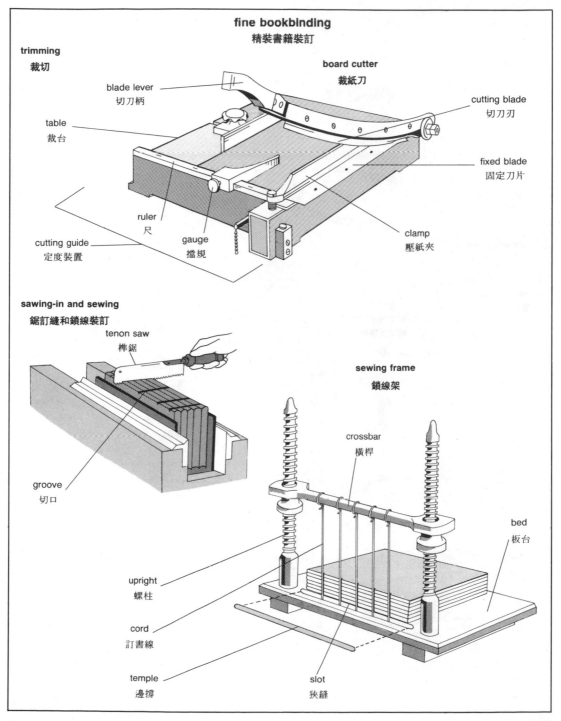

trimming
裁切

board cutter
裁紙刀

blade lever
切刀柄

cutting blade
切刀刃

table
裁台

fixed blade
固定刀片

ruler
尺

gauge
擋規

clamp
壓紙夾

cutting guide
定度裝置

sawing-in and sewing
鋸訂縫和鎖線裝訂

tenon saw
榫鋸

sewing frame
鎖線架

crossbar
橫桿

groove
切口

bed
板台

upright
螺柱

cord
訂書線

temple
邊撐

slot
狹縫

fine bookbinding
精裝書籍裝訂

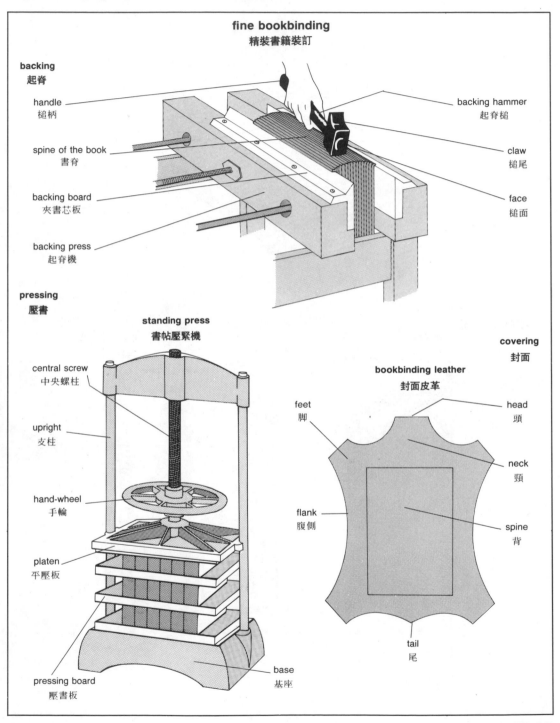

backing
起脊

handle
槌柄

spine of the book
書脊

backing board
夾書芯板

backing press
起脊機

backing hammer
起脊槌

claw
槌尾

face
槌面

pressing
壓書

standing press
書帖壓緊機

central screw
中央螺柱

upright
支柱

hand-wheel
手輪

platen
平壓板

pressing board
壓書板

base
基座

covering
封面

bookbinding leather
封面皮革

feet
腳

head
頭

neck
頸

flank
腹側

spine
背

tail
尾

intaglio printing process
凹版印刷

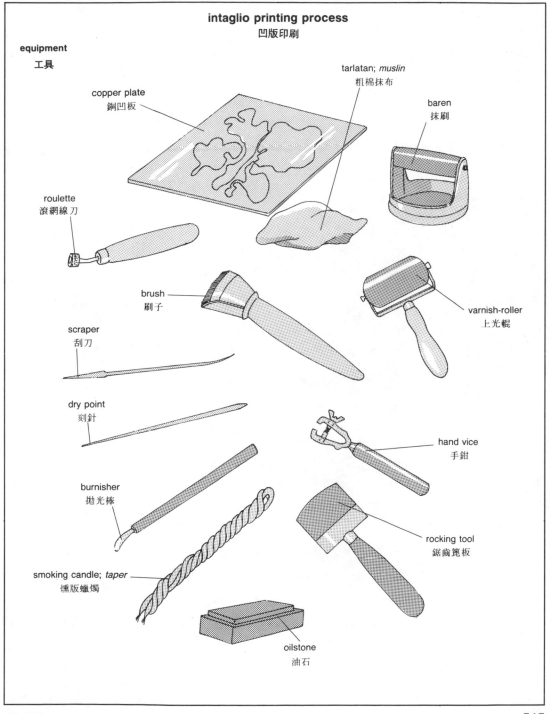

equipment
工具

copper plate
銅凹板

tarlatan; *muslin*
粗棉抹布

baren
抹刷

roulette
滾網線刀

brush
刷子

varnish-roller
上光棍

scraper
刮刀

dry point
刻針

hand vice
手鉗

burnisher
拋光棒

rocking tool
鋸齒篦板

smoking candle; *taper*
燻版蠟燭

oilstone
油石

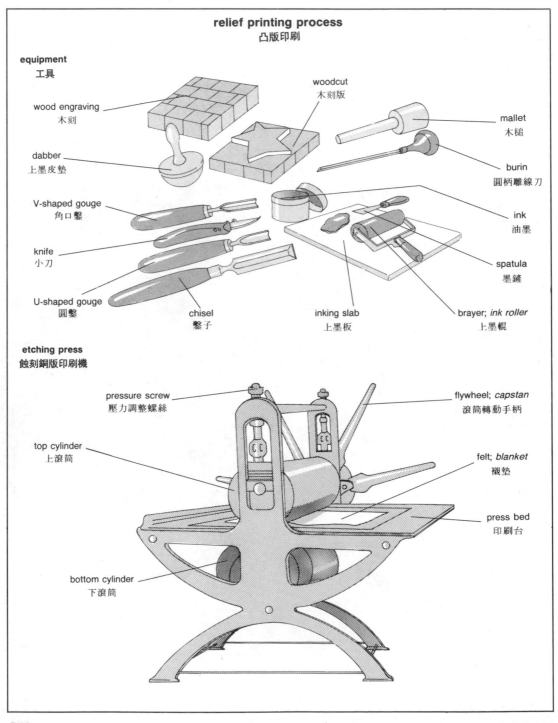

relief printing process
凸版印刷

equipment
工具

wood engraving
木刻

woodcut
木刻版

mallet
木槌

dabber
上墨皮墊

burin
圓柄雕線刀

V-shaped gouge
角口鑿

ink
油墨

knife
小刀

spatula
墨鏟

U-shaped gouge
圓鑿

chisel
鑿子

inking slab
上墨板

brayer; *ink roller*
上墨輥

etching press
蝕刻銅版印刷機

pressure screw
壓力調整螺絲

flywheel; *capstan*
滾筒轉動手柄

top cylinder
上滾筒

felt; *blanket*
襯墊

press bed
印刷台

bottom cylinder
下滾筒

lithography
平版印刷

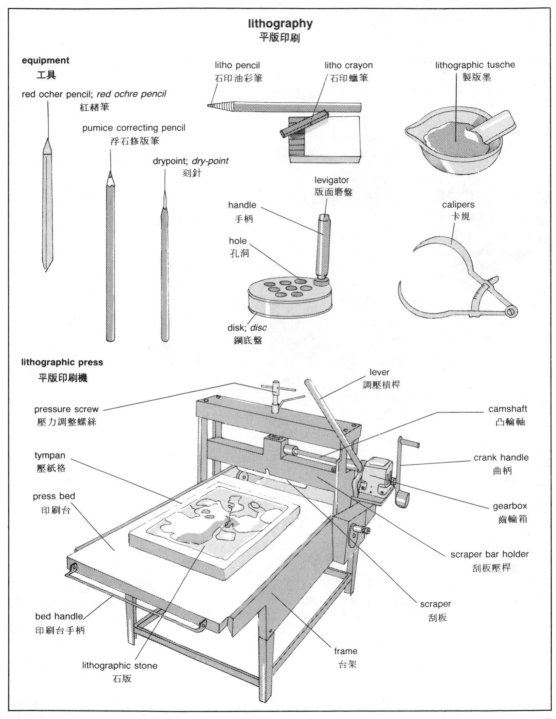

equipment
工具

red ocher pencil; *red ochre pencil*
紅赭筆

pumice correcting pencil
浮石修版筆

drypoint; *dry-point*
刻針

litho pencil
石印油彩筆

litho crayon
石印蠟筆

lithographic tusche
製版墨

levigator
版面磨盤

handle
手柄

hole
孔洞

calipers
卡規

disk; *disc*
鋼底盤

lithographic press
平版印刷機

lever
調壓槓桿

pressure screw
壓力調整螺絲

camshaft
凸輪軸

crank handle
曲柄

tympan
壓紙格

gearbox
齒輪箱

press bed
印刷台

scraper bar holder
刮板壓桿

scraper
刮板

bed handle
印刷台手柄

frame
台架

lithographic stone
石版

printing
印刷

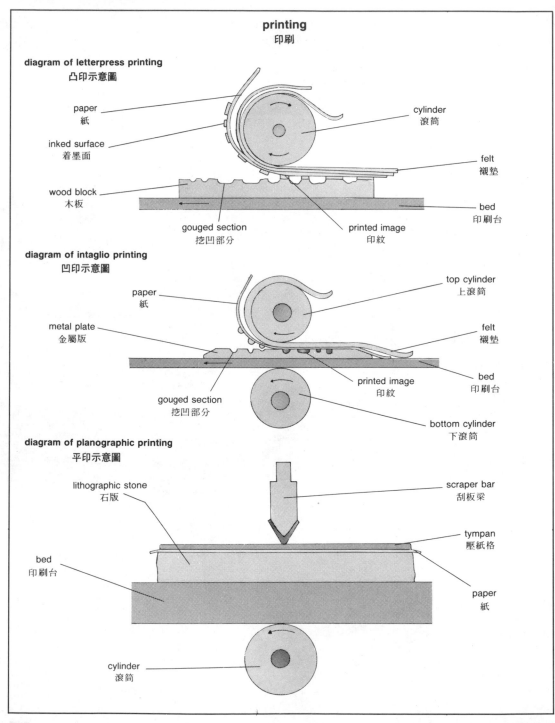

diagram of letterpress printing
凸印示意圖

paper
紙

inked surface
着墨面

cylinder
滾筒

wood block
木板

felt
襯墊

bed
印刷台

gouged section
挖凹部分

printed image
印紋

diagram of intaglio printing
凹印示意圖

paper
紙

metal plate
金屬版

top cylinder
上滾筒

felt
襯墊

bed
印刷台

gouged section
挖凹部分

printed image
印紋

bottom cylinder
下滾筒

diagram of planographic printing
平印示意圖

lithographic stone
石版

scraper bar
刮板梁

tympan
壓紙格

bed
印刷台

paper
紙

cylinder
滾筒

pottery
陶瓷工藝

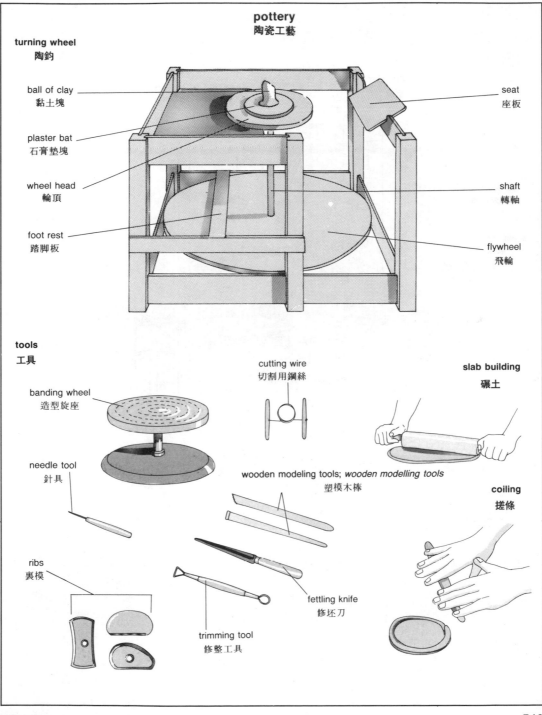

turning wheel
陶鈞

ball of clay
黏土塊

plaster bat
石膏墊塊

wheel head
輪頂

foot rest
踏腳板

seat
座板

shaft
轉軸

flywheel
飛輪

tools
工具

cutting wire
切割用鋼絲

slab building
碾土

banding wheel
造型旋座

needle tool
針具

wooden modeling tools; *wooden modelling tools*
塑模木棒

coiling
搓條

ribs
裏模

fettling knife
修坯刀

trimming tool
修整工具

pottery
陶瓷工藝

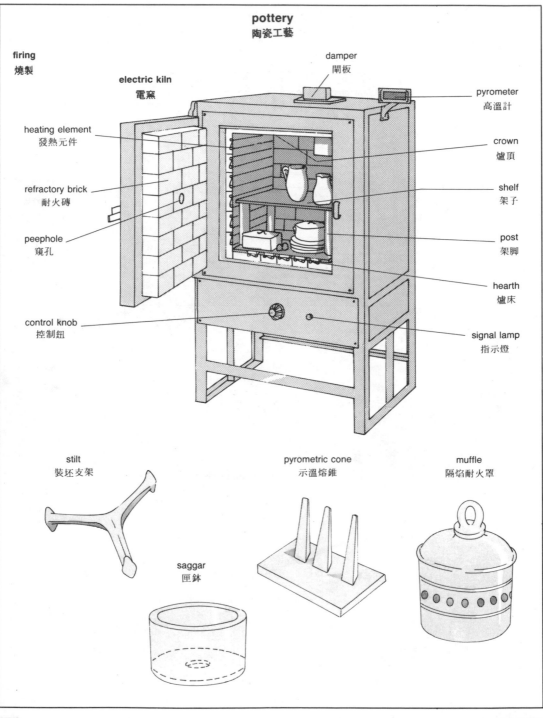

firing
燒製

electric kiln
電窯

damper
閘板

pyrometer
高溫計

heating element
發熱元件

crown
爐頂

refractory brick
耐火磚

shelf
架子

peephole
窺孔

post
架腳

hearth
爐床

control knob
控制鈕

signal lamp
指示燈

stilt
裝坯支架

pyrometric cone
示溫熔錐

muffle
隔焰耐火罩

saggar
匣鉢

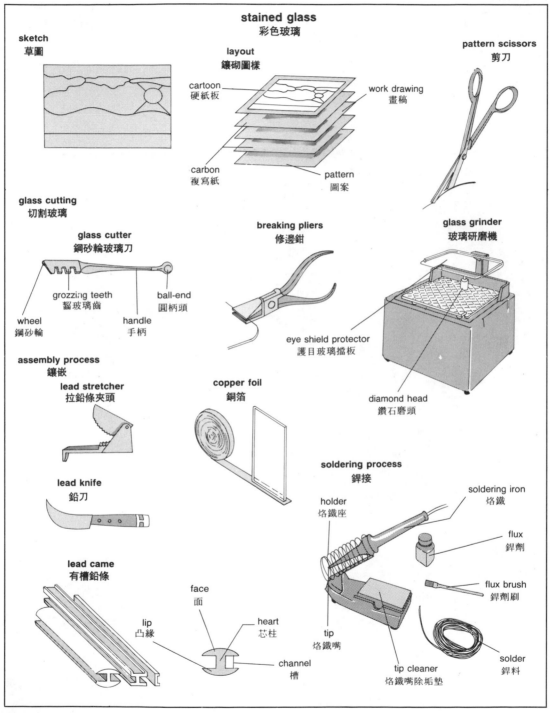

stained glass
彩色玻璃

sketch
草圖

layout
鑲砌圖樣

cartoon
硬紙板

carbon
複寫紙

work drawing
畫稿

pattern
圖案

pattern scissors
剪刀

glass cutting
切割玻璃

glass cutter
鋼砂輪玻璃刀

grozzing teeth
齧玻璃齒

ball-end
圓柄頭

wheel
鋼砂輪

handle
手柄

breaking pliers
修邊鉗

eye shield protector
護目玻璃擋板

glass grinder
玻璃研磨機

diamond head
鑽石磨頭

assembly process
鑲嵌

lead stretcher
拉鉛條夾頭

copper foil
銅箔

lead knife
鉛刀

soldering process
銲接

holder
烙鐵座

soldering iron
烙鐵

flux
銲劑

flux brush
銲劑刷

solder
銲料

tip
烙鐵嘴

tip cleaner
烙鐵嘴除垢墊

lead came
有槽鉛條

face
面

lip
凸緣

heart
芯柱

channel
槽

SPORTS
運動與遊戲

長度單位：yd＝碼，ft＝呎，in＝吋，m＝公尺，cm＝公分，mm＝公釐

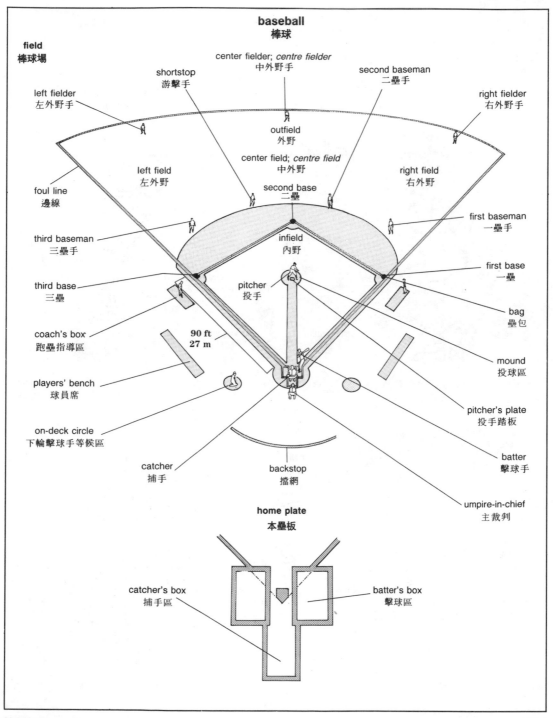

baseball
棒球

field
棒球場

center fielder; *centre fielder*
中外野手

shortstop
游擊手

second baseman
二壘手

left fielder
左外野手

right fielder
右外野手

outfield
外野

left field
左外野

center field; *centre field*
中外野

right field
右外野

foul line
邊線

second base
二壘

first baseman
一壘手

third baseman
三壘手

infield
內野

third base
三壘

first base
一壘

coach's box
跑壘指導區

pitcher
投手

bag
壘包

90 ft
27 m

mound
投球區

players' bench
球員席

pitcher's plate
投手踏板

on-deck circle
下輪擊球手等候區

batter
擊球手

catcher
捕手

backstop
擋網

umpire-in-chief
主裁判

home plate
本壘板

catcher's box
捕手區

batter's box
擊球區

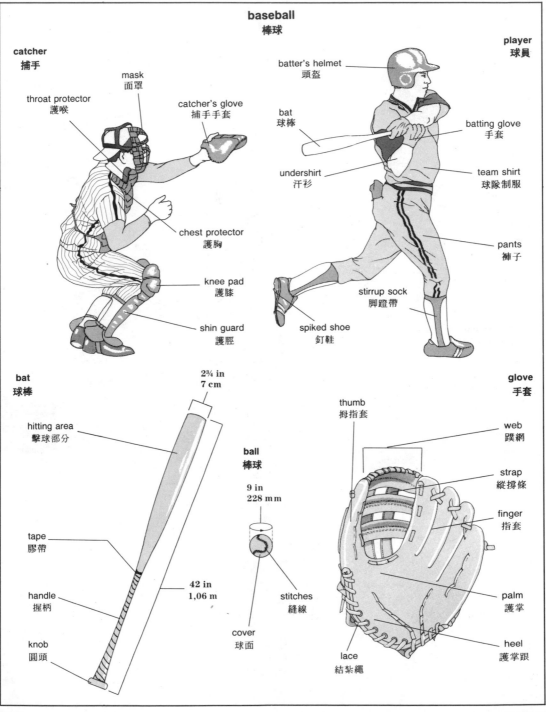

baseball
棒球

catcher
捕手

throat protector
護喉

mask
面罩

catcher's glove
捕手手套

chest protector
護胸

knee pad
護膝

shin guard
護脛

batter's helmet
頭盔

bat
球棒

undershirt
汗衫

stirrup sock
脚蹬帶

spiked shoe
釘鞋

player
球員

batting glove
手套

team shirt
球隊制服

pants
褲子

bat
球棒

2¾ in
7 cm

hitting area
擊球部分

tape
膠帶

handle
握柄

knob
圓頭

42 in
1,06 m

ball
棒球

9 in
228 mm

stitches
縫線

cover
球面

glove
手套

thumb
拇指套

web
蹼網

strap
縱撐條

finger
指套

palm
護掌

heel
護掌跟

lace
結紮繩

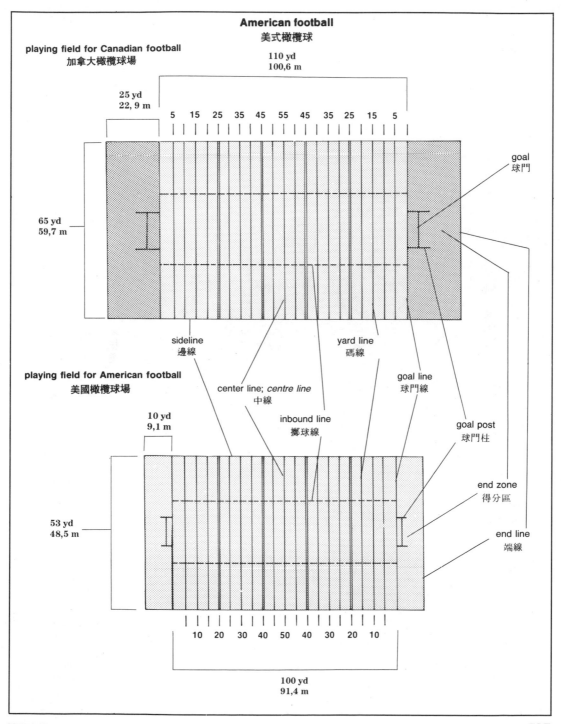

American football
美式橄欖球

playing field for Canadian football
加拿大橄欖球場

110 yd
100,6 m

25 yd
22, 9 m

5　15　25　35　45　55　45　35　25　15　5

goal
球門

65 yd
59,7 m

sideline
邊線

yard line
碼線

goal line
球門線

playing field for American football
美國橄欖球場

center line; *centre line*
中線

inbound line
擲球線

goal post
球門柱

10 yd
9,1 m

end zone
得分區

53 yd
48,5 m

end line
端線

10　20　30　40　50　40　30　20　10

100 yd
91,4 m

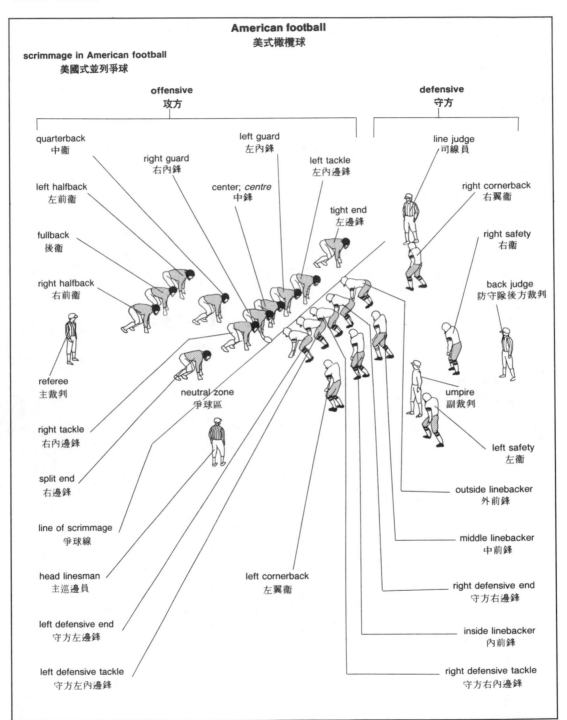

American football
美式橄欖球

scrimmage in American football
美國式並列爭球

offensive
攻方

defensive
守方

quarterback
中衛

left guard
左內鋒

line judge
司線員

right guard
右內鋒

left tackle
左內邊鋒

right cornerback
右翼衛

left halfback
左前衛

center; *centre*
中鋒

right safety
右衛

fullback
後衛

tight end
左邊鋒

back judge
防守隊後方裁判

right halfback
右前衛

referee
主裁判

neutral zone
爭球區

umpire
副裁判

right tackle
右內邊鋒

left safety
左衛

split end
右邊鋒

outside linebacker
外前鋒

line of scrimmage
爭球線

middle linebacker
中前鋒

head linesman
主巡邊員

left cornerback
左翼衛

right defensive end
守方右邊鋒

left defensive end
守方左邊鋒

inside linebacker
內前鋒

left defensive tackle
守方左內邊鋒

right defensive tackle
守方右內邊鋒

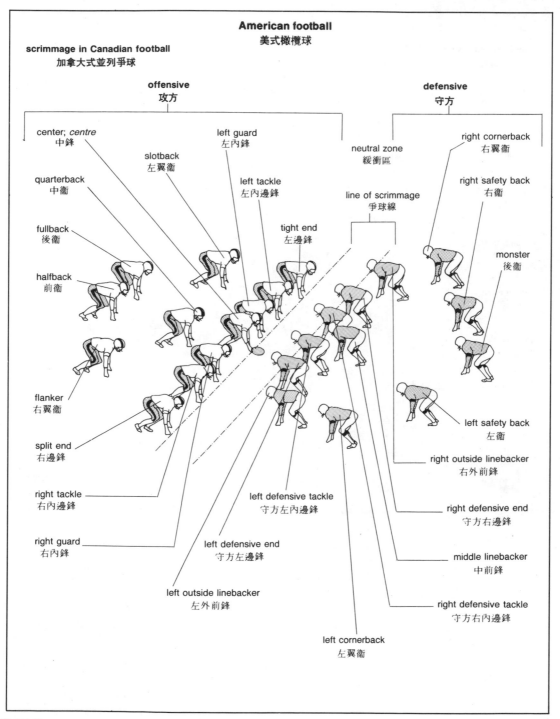

American football
美式橄欖球

scrimmage in Canadian football
加拿大式並列爭球

offensive
攻方

defensive
守方

center; *centre*
中鋒

left guard
左內鋒

right cornerback
右翼衞

slotback
左翼衞

neutral zone
緩衝區

right safety back
右衞

quarterback
中衞

left tackle
左內邊鋒

line of scrimmage
爭球線

fullback
後衞

tight end
左邊鋒

monster
後衞

halfback
前衞

flanker
右翼衞

left safety back
左衞

split end
右邊鋒

right outside linebacker
右外前鋒

right tackle
右內邊鋒

left defensive tackle
守方左內邊鋒

right defensive end
守方右邊鋒

right guard
右內鋒

left defensive end
守方左邊鋒

middle linebacker
中前鋒

left outside linebacker
左外前鋒

right defensive tackle
守方右內邊鋒

left cornerback
左翼衞

American football
美式橄欖球

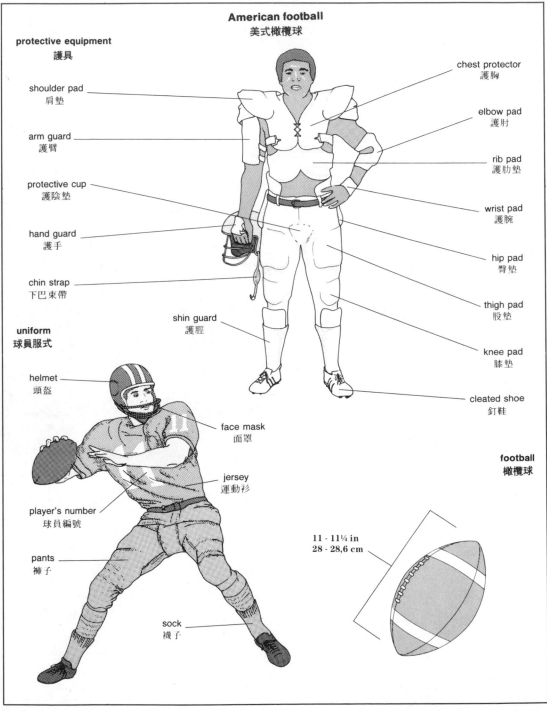

protective equipment
護具

shoulder pad
肩墊

arm guard
護臂

protective cup
護陰墊

hand guard
護手

chin strap
下巴束帶

chest protector
護胸

elbow pad
護肘

rib pad
護肋墊

wrist pad
護腕

hip pad
臀墊

thigh pad
股墊

knee pad
膝墊

shin guard
護脛

cleated shoe
釘鞋

uniform
球員服式

helmet
頭盔

face mask
面罩

jersey
運動衫

player's number
球員編號

pants
褲子

sock
襪子

football
橄欖球

11 - 11¼ in
28 - 28,6 cm

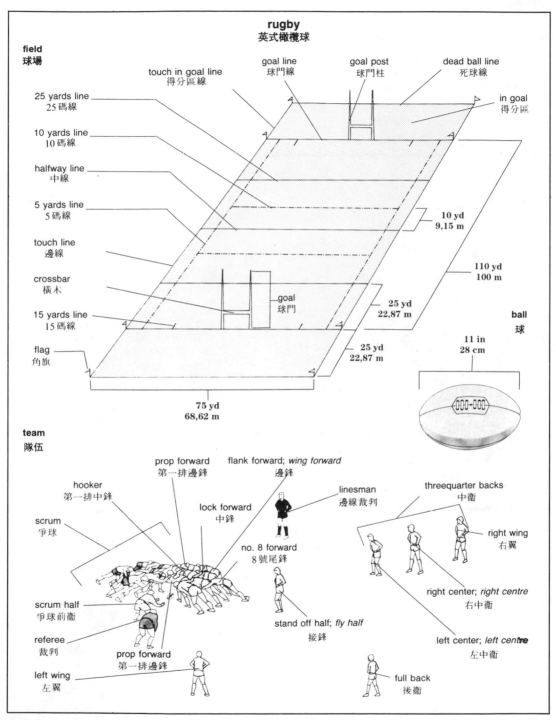

rugby
英式橄欖球

field
球場

touch in goal line
得分區線

goal line
球門線

goal post
球門柱

dead ball line
死球線

in goal
得分區

25 yards line
25 碼線

10 yards line
10 碼線

halfway line
中線

5 yards line
5 碼線

touch line
邊線

crossbar
橫木

15 yards line
15 碼線

flag
角旗

goal
球門

10 yd
9,15 m

110 yd
100 m

25 yd
22,87 m

25 yd
22,87 m

75 yd
68,62 m

ball
球

11 in
28 cm

team
隊伍

prop forward
第一排邊鋒

flank forward; *wing forward*
邊鋒

hooker
第一排中鋒

linesman
邊線裁判

threequarter backs
中衛

lock forward
中鋒

right wing
右翼

scrum
爭球

no. 8 forward
8 號尾鋒

scrum half
爭球前衛

right center; *right centre*
右中衛

referee
裁判

stand off half; *fly half*
接鋒

left center; *left centre*
左中衛

prop forward
第一排邊鋒

left wing
左翼

full back
後衛

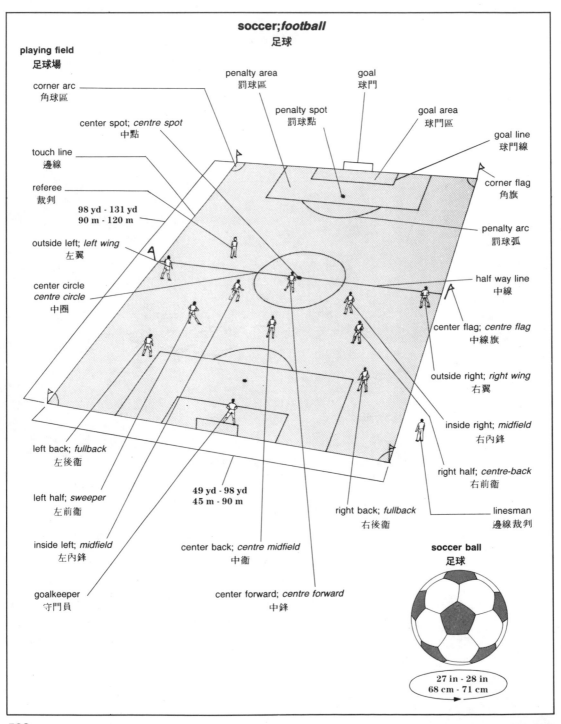

soccer;*football*
足球

playing field
足球場

corner arc
角球區

center spot; *centre spot*
中點

touch line
邊線

referee
裁判

98 yd - 131 yd
90 m - 120 m

outside left; *left wing*
左翼

center circle
centre circle
中圈

penalty area
罰球區

penalty spot
罰球點

goal
球門

goal area
球門區

goal line
球門線

corner flag
角旗

penalty arc
罰球弧

half way line
中線

center flag; *centre flag*
中線旗

outside right; *right wing*
右翼

inside right; *midfield*
右內鋒

right half; *centre-back*
右前衛

linesman
邊線裁判

left back; *fullback*
左後衛

left half; *sweeper*
左前衛

inside left; *midfield*
左內鋒

goalkeeper
守門員

49 yd - 98 yd
45 m - 90 m

center back; *centre midfield*
中衛

right back; *fullback*
右後衛

center forward; *centre forward*
中鋒

soccer ball
足球

27 in - 28 in
68 cm - 71 cm

ice hockey
冰球

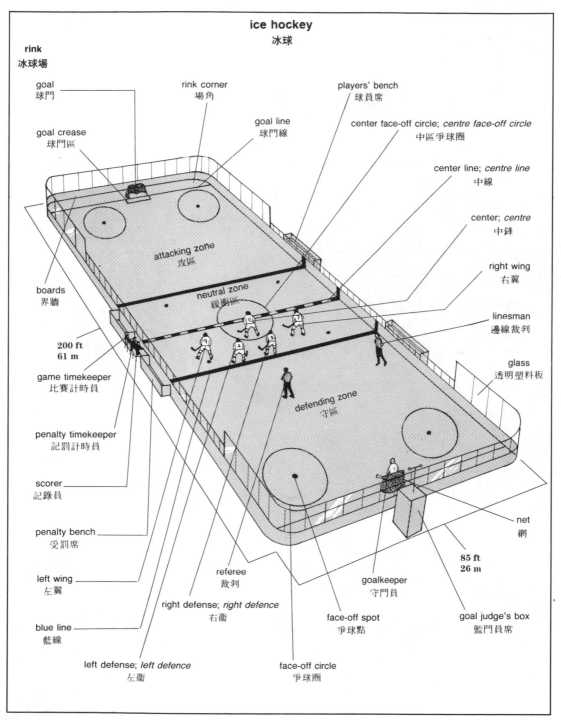

rink
冰球場

goal
球門

goal crease
球門區

rink corner
場角

goal line
球門線

players' bench
球員席

center face-off circle; *centre face-off circle*
中區爭球圈

center line; *centre line*
中線

center; *centre*
中鋒

right wing
右翼

linesman
邊線裁判

boards
界牆

attacking zone
攻區

neutral zone
緩衝區

200 ft
61 m

game timekeeper
比賽計時員

penalty timekeeper
記罰計時員

scorer
記錄員

penalty bench
受罰席

left wing
左翼

blue line
藍線

defending zone
守區

glass
透明塑料板

net
網

referee
裁判

right defense; *right defence*
右衛

left defense; *left defence*
左衛

goalkeeper
守門員

face-off spot
爭球點

face-off circle
爭球圈

85 ft
26 m

goal judge's box
監門員席

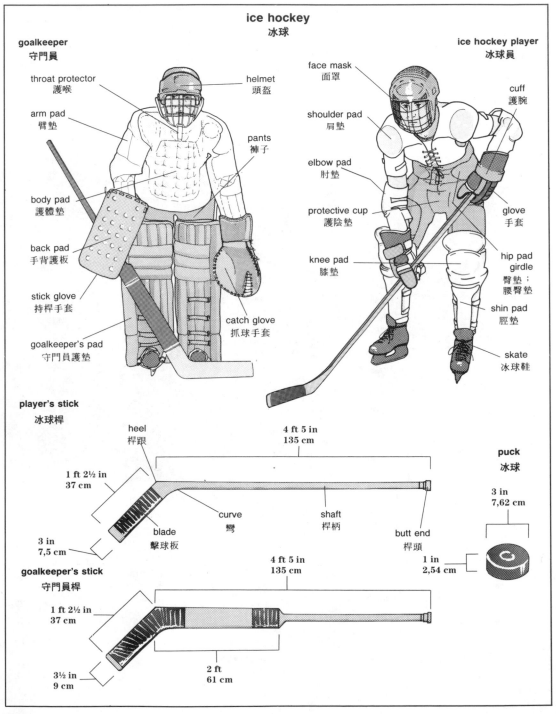

ice hockey
冰球

goalkeeper
守門員

throat protector
護喉

helmet
頭盔

arm pad
臂墊

pants
褲子

body pad
護體墊

back pad
手背護板

stick glove
持桿手套

catch glove
抓球手套

goalkeeper's pad
守門員護墊

ice hockey player
冰球員

face mask
面罩

cuff
護腕

shoulder pad
肩墊

elbow pad
肘墊

glove
手套

protective cup
護陰墊

knee pad
膝墊

hip pad
girdle
臀墊；
腰臀墊

shin pad
脛墊

skate
冰球鞋

player's stick
冰球桿

heel
桿跟

4 ft 5 in
135 cm

1 ft 2½ in
37 cm

curve
彎

shaft
桿柄

butt end
桿頭

3 in
7,5 cm

blade
擊球板

puck
冰球

3 in
7,62 cm

1 in
2,54 cm

goalkeeper's stick
守門員桿

1 ft 2½ in
37 cm

4 ft 5 in
135 cm

3½ in
9 cm

2 ft
61 cm

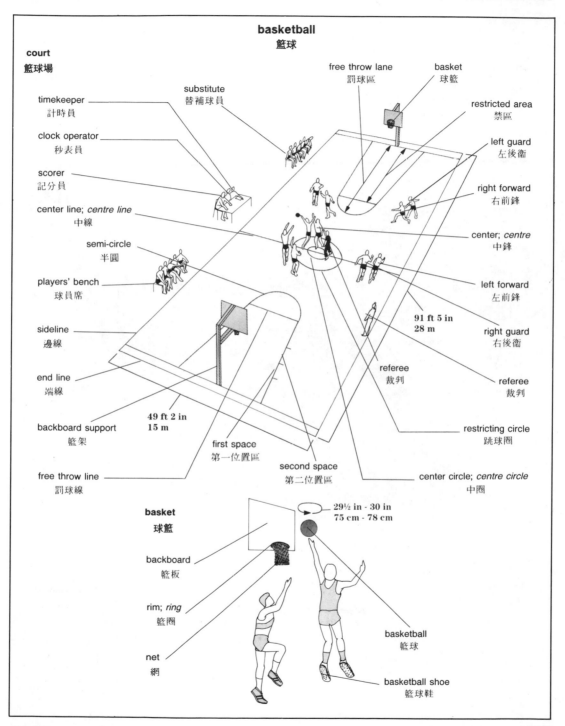

basketball
籃球

court
籃球場

timekeeper
計時員

clock operator
秒表員

scorer
記分員

center line; *centre line*
中線

semi-circle
半圓

players' bench
球員席

sideline
邊線

end line
端線

backboard support
籃架

free throw line
罰球線

substitute
替補球員

first space
第一位置區

second space
第二位置區

free throw lane
罰球區

basket
球籃

restricted area
禁區

left guard
左後衛

right forward
右前鋒

center; *centre*
中鋒

left forward
左前鋒

91 ft 5 in
28 m

right guard
右後衛

referee
裁判

referee
裁判

restricting circle
跳球圈

center circle; *centre circle*
中圈

49 ft 2 in
15 m

basket
球籃

backboard
籃板

rim; *ring*
籃圈

net
網

29½ in - 30 in
75 cm - 78 cm

basketball
籃球

basketball shoe
籃球鞋

volleyball
排球

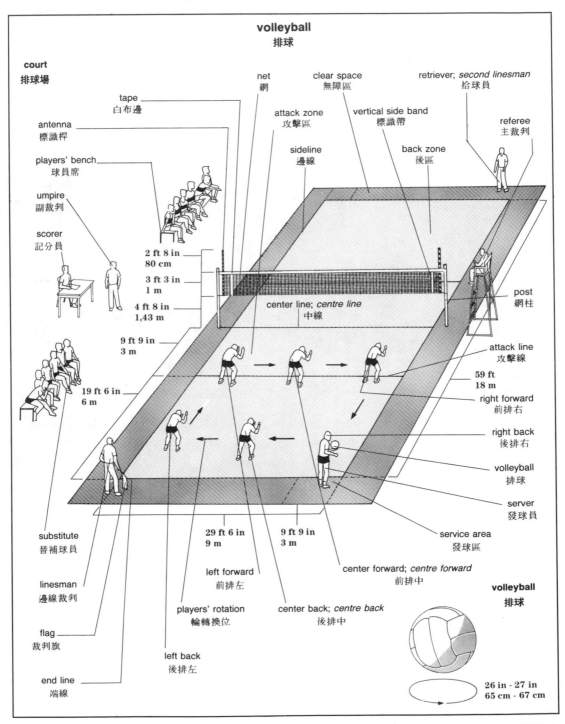

court
排球場

tape
白布邊

antenna
標識桿

players' bench
球員席

umpire
副裁判

scorer
記分員

net
網

clear space
無障區

attack zone
攻擊區

sideline
邊線

retriever; *second linesman*
拾球員

vertical side band
標識帶

back zone
後區

referee
主裁判

2 ft 8 in
80 cm

3 ft 3 in
1 m

4 ft 8 in
1,43 m

9 ft 9 in
3 m

19 ft 6 in
6 m

center line; *centre line*
中線

post
網柱

attack line
攻擊線

59 ft
18 m

right forward
前排右

right back
後排右

volleyball
排球

server
發球員

service area
發球區

substitute
替補球員

linesman
邊線裁判

flag
裁判旗

end line
端線

29 ft 6 in
9 m

9 ft 9 in
3 m

left forward
前排左

players' rotation
輪轉換位

center back; *centre back*
後排中

left back
後排左

center forward; *centre forward*
前排中

volleyball
排球

26 in - 27 in
65 cm - 67 cm

tennis
網球

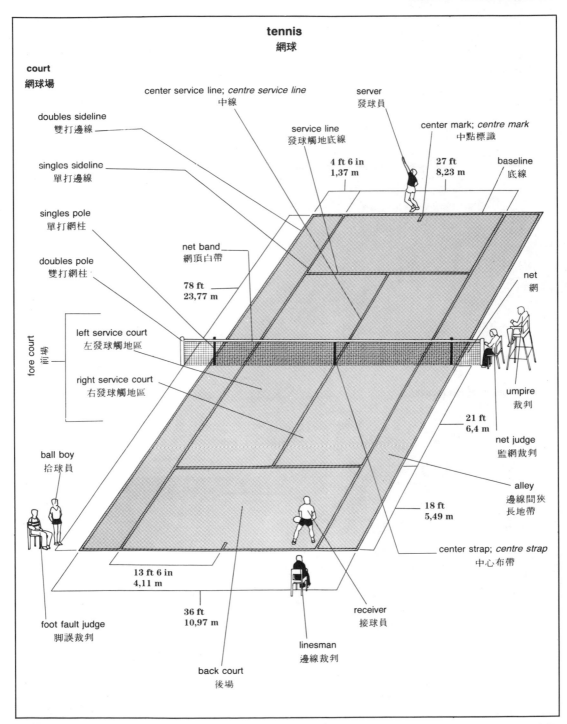

court
網球場

center service line; *centre service line*
中線

server
發球員

doubles sideline
雙打邊線

service line
發球觸地底線

center mark; *centre mark*
中點標識

singles sideline
單打邊線

4 ft 6 in
1,37 m

27 ft
8,23 m

baseline
底線

singles pole
單打網柱

net band
網頂白帶

doubles pole
雙打網柱

78 ft
23,77 m

net
網

fore court
前場

left service court
左發球觸地區

right service court
右發球觸地區

umpire
裁判

21 ft
6,4 m

net judge
監網裁判

ball boy
拾球員

alley
邊線間狹
長地帶

18 ft
5,49 m

center strap; *centre strap*
中心布帶

13 ft 6 in
4,11 m

receiver
接球員

foot fault judge
腳誤裁判

36 ft
10,97 m

linesman
邊線裁判

back court
後場

tennis
網球

tennis players
網球運動員

headband
束髮帶

shirt
男上衣

wristband
護腕

shorts
短褲

blouse
女上衣

skirt
網球裙

sock
襪子

tennis shoe
網球鞋

tennis racket; _tennis racquet_
網球拍

shoulder
拍肩

throat
拍頸

top
把頭

bevel
斜邊

flat side of the grip
平邊

frame
拍框

stringing
拍線

handle
握把

butt
柄尾

head
拍頭

shaft
拍柄

tennis ball
網球

press
球拍夾

7,85 in - 8,25 in
20 cm - 21 cm

handball
手球

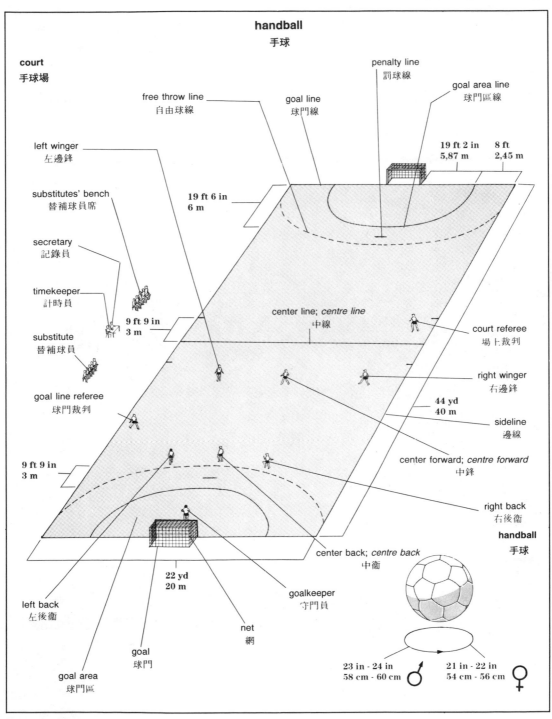

court
手球場

penalty line
罰球線

goal area line
球門區線

free throw line
自由球線

goal line
球門線

19 ft 2 in
5,87 m

8 ft
2,45 m

left winger
左邊鋒

19 ft 6 in
6 m

substitutes' bench
替補球員席

secretary
記錄員

timekeeper
計時員

center line; *centre line*
中線

court referee
場上裁判

9 ft 9 in
3 m

substitute
替補球員

right winger
右邊鋒

44 yd
40 m

sideline
邊線

goal line referee
球門裁判

center forward; *centre forward*
中鋒

9 ft 9 in
3 m

right back
右後衛

handball
手球

center back; *centre back*
中衛

left back
左後衛

22 yd
20 m

goalkeeper
守門員

net
網

goal
球門

23 in - 24 in
58 cm - 60 cm ♂

21 in - 22 in
54 cm - 56 cm ♀

goal area
球門區

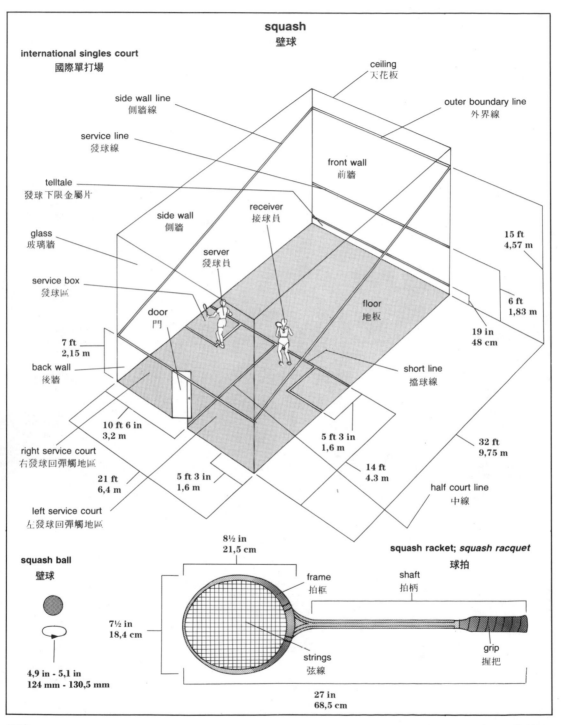

squash
壁球

international singles court
國際單打場

side wall line
側牆線

service line
發球線

telltale
發球下限金屬片

glass
玻璃牆

service box
發球區

door
門

7 ft
2,15 m

back wall
後牆

10 ft 6 in
3,2 m

right service court
右發球回彈觸地區

21 ft
6,4 m

left service court
左發球回彈觸地區

side wall
側牆

server
發球員

receiver
接球員

ceiling
天花板

front wall
前牆

outer boundary line
外界線

15 ft
4,57 m

6 ft
1,83 m

19 in
48 cm

floor
地板

short line
擋球線

5 ft 3 in
1,6 m

14 ft
4.3 m

32 ft
9,75 m

5 ft 3 in
1,6 m

half court line
中線

squash ball
壁球

4,9 in - 5,1 in
124 mm - 130,5 mm

8½ in
21,5 cm

squash racket; *squash racquet*
球拍

frame
拍框

shaft
拍柄

7½ in
18,4 cm

strings
弦線

grip
握把

27 in
68,5 cm

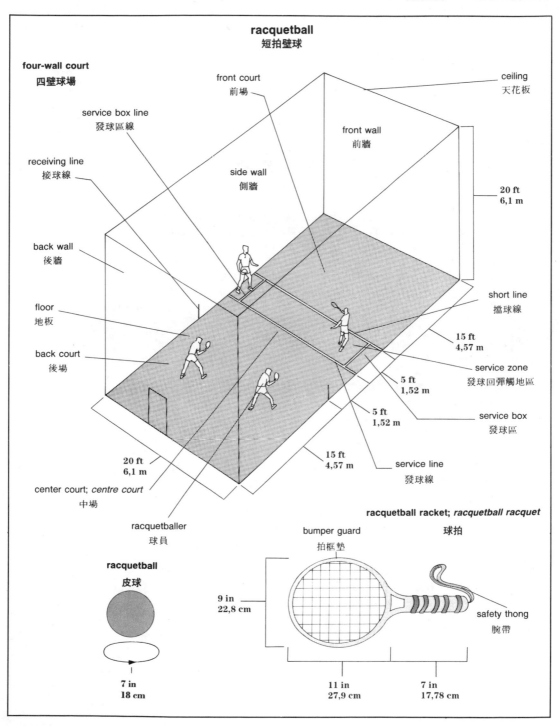

racquetball
短拍壁球

four-wall court
四壁球場

front court
前場

ceiling
天花板

service box line
發球區線

front wall
前牆

receiving line
接球線

side wall
側牆

20 ft
6,1 m

back wall
後牆

short line
擋球線

floor
地板

15 ft
4,57 m

back court
後場

service zone
發球回彈觸地區

5 ft
1,52 m

service box
發球區

5 ft
1,52 m

20 ft
6,1 m

15 ft
4,57 m

service line
發球線

center court; *centre court*
中場

racquetball racket; *racquetball racquet*

球拍

racquetballer
球員

bumper guard
拍框墊

racquetball

皮球

9 in
22,8 cm

safety thong
腕帶

7 in
18 cm

11 in
27,9 cm

7 in
17,78 cm

badminton
羽毛球

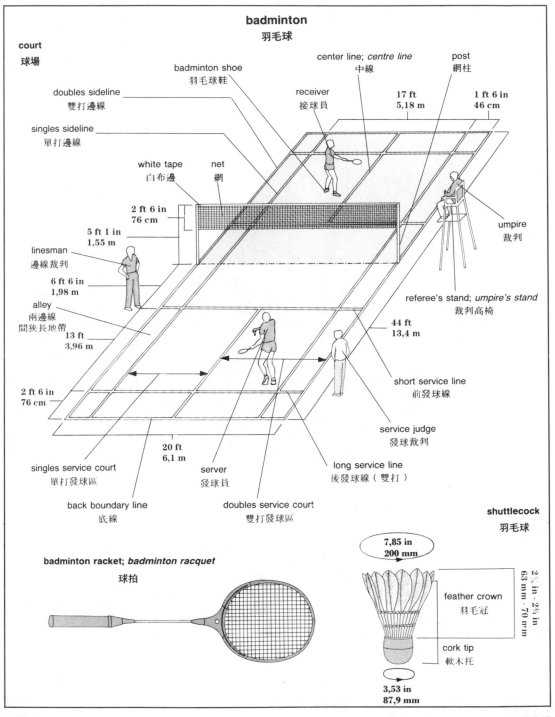

court
球場

doubles sideline
雙打邊線

singles sideline
單打邊線

badminton shoe
羽毛球鞋

white tape
白布邊

net
網

center line; *centre line*
中線

receiver
接球員

post
網柱

17 ft
5,18 m

1 ft 6 in
46 cm

2 ft 6 in
76 cm

5 ft 1 in
1,55 m

linesman
邊線裁判

6 ft 6 in
1,98 m

alley
兩邊線
間狹長地帶

13 ft
3,96 m

2 ft 6 in
76 cm

umpire
裁判

referee's stand; *umpire's stand*
裁判高椅

44 ft
13,4 m

short service line
前發球線

service judge
發球裁判

singles service court
單打發球區

20 ft
6,1 m

server
發球員

long service line
後發球線（雙打）

back boundary line
底線

doubles service court
雙打發球區

shuttlecock
羽毛球

badminton racket; *badminton racquet*
球拍

7,85 in
200 mm

2⅜ in - 2¾ in
63 mm - 70 mm

feather crown
羽毛冠

cork tip
軟木托

3,53 in
87,9 mm

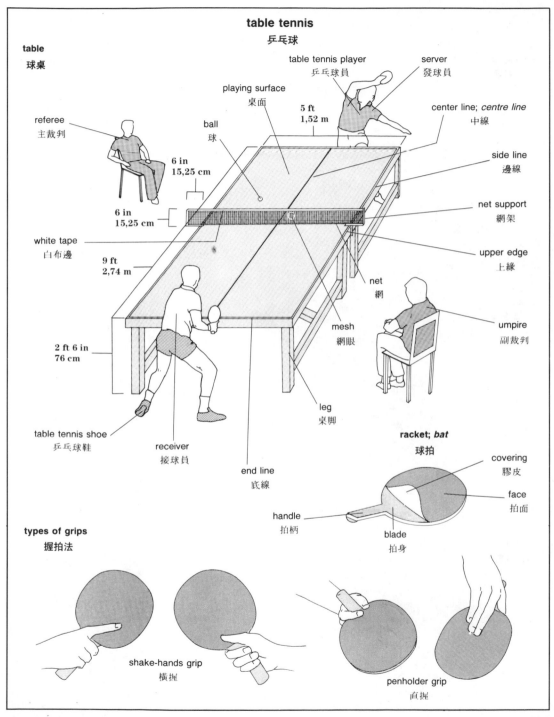

table tennis
乒乓球

table
球桌

table tennis player
乒乓球員

server
發球員

playing surface
桌面

center line; *centre line*
中線

5 ft
1,52 m

referee
主裁判

ball
球

side line
邊線

6 in
15,25 cm

net support
網架

6 in
15,25 cm

upper edge
上緣

white tape
白布邊

9 ft
2,74 m

net
網

2 ft 6 in
76 cm

mesh
網眼

umpire
副裁判

table tennis shoe
乒乓球鞋

receiver
接球員

end line
底線

leg
桌脚

racket; *bat*
球拍

covering
膠皮

face
拍面

handle
拍柄

blade
拍身

types of grips
握拍法

shake-hands grip
橫握

penholder grip
直握

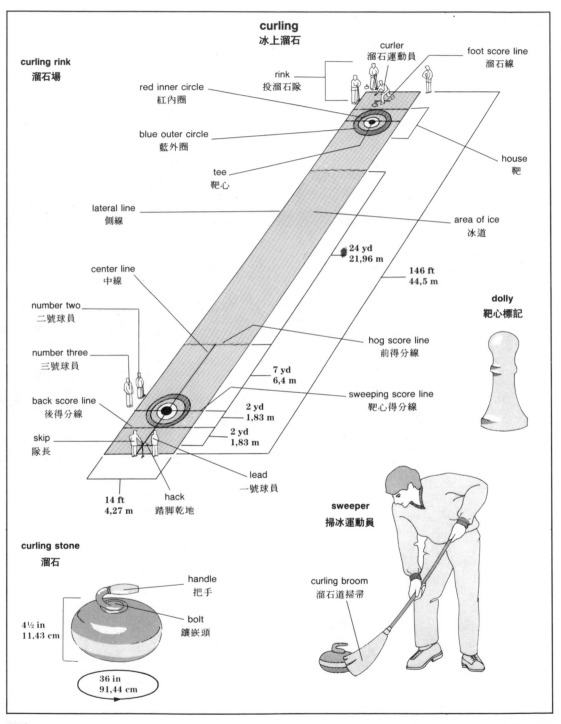

curling
冰上溜石

curler
溜石運動員

foot score line
溜石線

curling rink
溜石場

rink
投溜石隊

red inner circle
紅內圈

blue outer circle
藍外圈

house
靶

tee
靶心

lateral line
側線

area of ice
冰道

24 yd
21,96 m

146 ft
44,5 m

dolly
靶心標記

center line
中線

number two
二號球員

hog score line
前得分線

7 yd
6,4 m

sweeping score line
靶心得分線

number three
三號球員

back score line
後得分線

2 yd
1,83 m

skip
隊長

2 yd
1,83 m

lead
一號球員

sweeper
掃冰運動員

14 ft
4,27 m

hack
踏腳乾地

curling stone
溜石

handle
把手

curling broom
溜石道掃帚

4½ in
11,43 cm

bolt
鑲嵌頭

36 in
91,44 cm

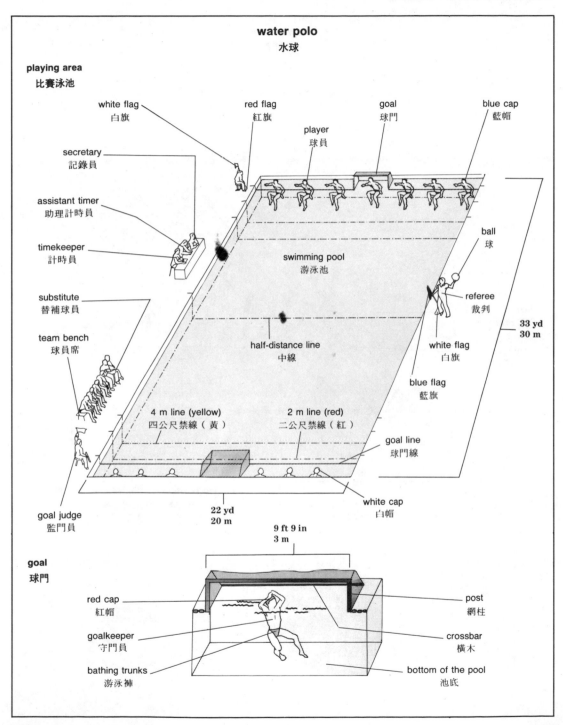

water polo
水球

playing area
比賽泳池

white flag
白旗

red flag
紅旗

goal
球門

blue cap
藍帽

player
球員

secretary
記錄員

assistant timer
助理計時員

timekeeper
計時員

ball
球

swimming pool
游泳池

referee
裁判

substitute
替補球員

team bench
球員席

half-distance line
中線

white flag
白旗

blue flag
藍旗

33 yd
30 m

4 m line (yellow)
四公尺禁線（黃）

2 m line (red)
二公尺禁線（紅）

goal line
球門線

white cap
白帽

goal judge
監門員

22 yd
20 m

9 ft 9 in
3 m

goal
球門

red cap
紅帽

post
網柱

goalkeeper
守門員

crossbar
橫木

bathing trunks
游泳褲

bottom of the pool
池底

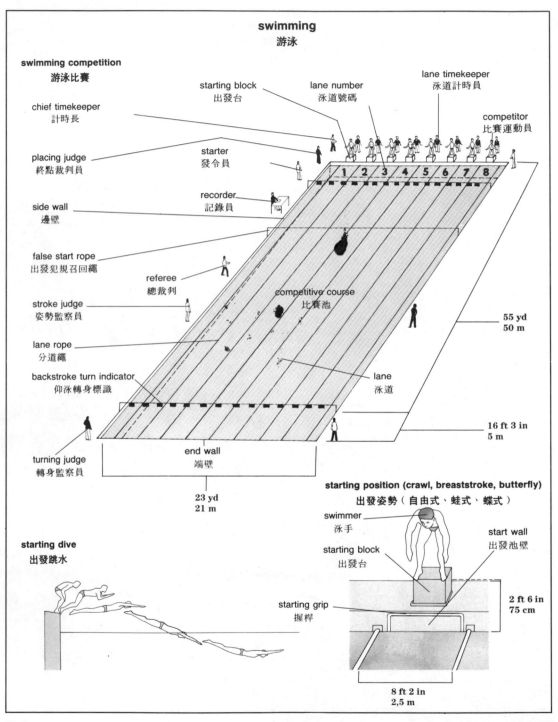

swimming
游泳

swimming competition
游泳比賽

chief timekeeper
計時長

starting block
出發台

lane number
泳道號碼

lane timekeeper
泳道計時員

competitor
比賽運動員

placing judge
終點裁判員

starter
發令員

side wall
邊壁

recorder
記錄員

false start rope
出發犯規召回繩

referee
總裁判

competitive course
比賽池

stroke judge
姿勢監察員

55 yd
50 m

lane rope
分道繩

lane
泳道

backstroke turn indicator
仰泳轉身標識

16 ft 3 in
5 m

turning judge
轉身監察員

end wall
端壁

23 yd
21 m

starting position (crawl, breaststroke, butterfly)
出發姿勢（自由式、蛙式、蝶式）

swimmer
泳手

start wall
出發池壁

starting block
出發台

starting dive
出發跳水

starting grip
握桿

2 ft 6 in
75 cm

8 ft 2 in
2,5 m

types of strokes
泳式

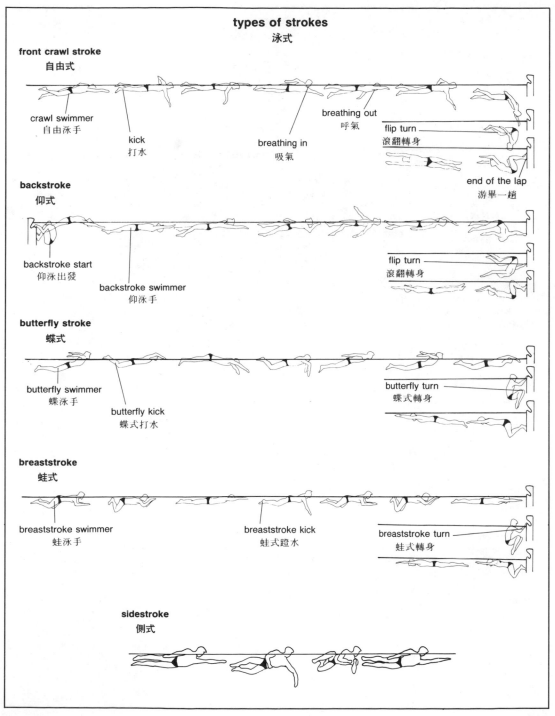

front crawl stroke
自由式

crawl swimmer
自由泳手

kick
打水

breathing in
吸氣

breathing out
呼氣

flip turn
滾翻轉身

end of the lap
游畢一趟

backstroke
仰式

backstroke start
仰泳出發

backstroke swimmer
仰泳手

flip turn
滾翻轉身

butterfly stroke
蝶式

butterfly swimmer
蝶泳手

butterfly kick
蝶式打水

butterfly turn
蝶式轉身

breaststroke
蛙式

breaststroke swimmer
蛙泳手

breaststroke kick
蛙式蹬水

breaststroke turn
蛙式轉身

sidestroke
側式

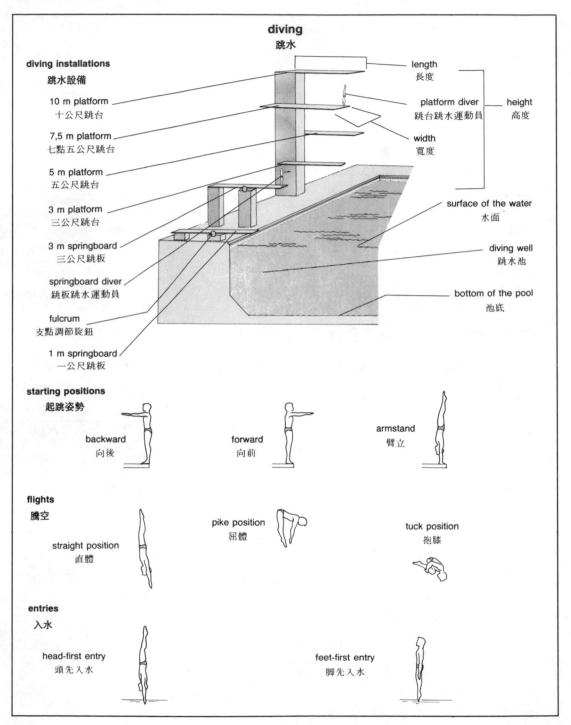

diving
跳水

diving installations
跳水設備

10 m platform
十公尺跳台

7,5 m platform
七點五公尺跳台

5 m platform
五公尺跳台

3 m platform
三公尺跳台

3 m springboard
三公尺跳板

springboard diver
跳板跳水運動員

fulcrum
支點調節旋鈕

1 m springboard
一公尺跳板

length
長度

platform diver
跳台跳水運動員

width
寬度

height
高度

surface of the water
水面

diving well
跳水池

bottom of the pool
池底

starting positions
起跳姿勢

backward
向後

forward
向前

armstand
臂立

flights
騰空

straight position
直體

pike position
屈體

tuck position
抱膝

entries
入水

head-first entry
頭先入水

feet-first entry
脚先入水

groups of dives
跳水動作

forward dive
向前跳水

backward dive
向後跳水

reverse dive
反身跳水

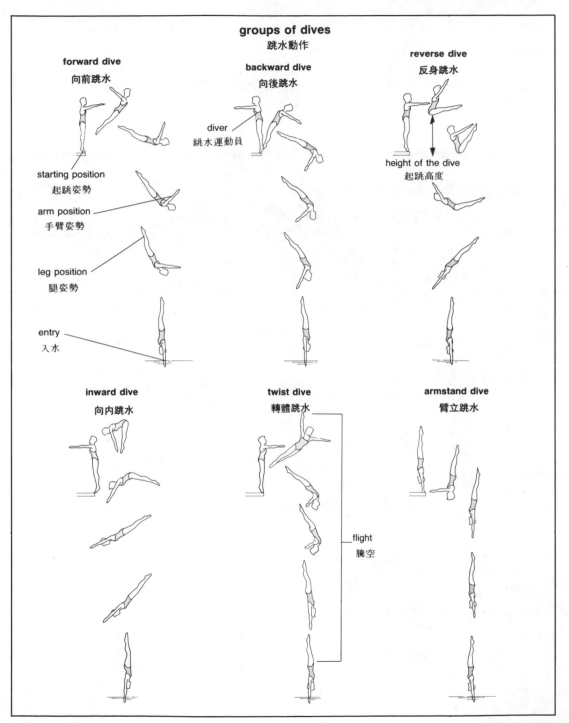

diver
跳水運動員

starting position
起跳姿勢

arm position
手臂姿勢

height of the dive
起跳高度

leg position
腿姿勢

entry
入水

inward dive
向內跳水

twist dive
轉體跳水

armstand dive
臂立跳水

flight
騰空

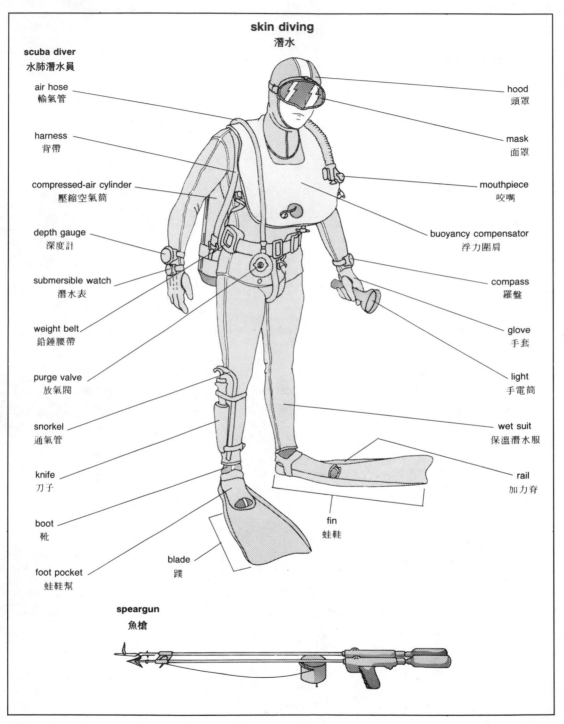

skin diving
潜水

scuba diver
水肺潜水員

air hose
輪氣管

harness
背帶

compressed-air cylinder
壓縮空氣筒

depth gauge
深度計

submersible watch
潜水表

weight belt
鉛錘腰帶

purge valve
放氣閥

snorkel
通氣管

knife
刀子

boot
靴

foot pocket
蛙鞋幫

blade
蹼

fin
蛙鞋

hood
頭罩

mask
面罩

mouthpiece
咬嘴

buoyancy compensator
浮力圍肩

compass
羅盤

glove
手套

light
手電筒

wet suit
保溫潜水服

rail
加力脊

speargun
魚槍

sailboard
帆板

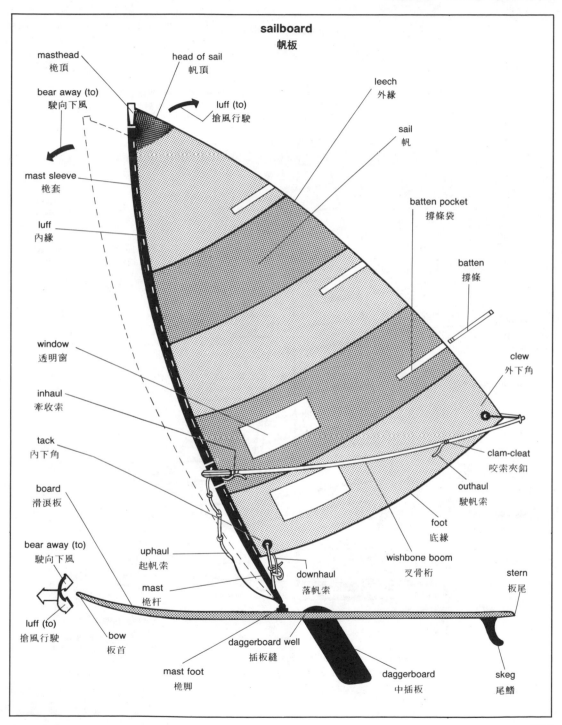

masthead
桅頂

head of sail
帆頂

bear away (to)
駛向下風

luff (to)
搶風行駛

leech
外緣

sail
帆

mast sleeve
桅套

luff
內緣

batten pocket
撐條袋

batten
撐條

window
透明窗

clew
外下角

inhaul
牽收索

clam-cleat
咬索夾鈕

tack
內下角

outhaul
駛帆索

board
滑浪板

foot
底緣

bear away (to)
駛向下風

uphaul
起帆索

wishbone boom
叉骨桁

downhaul
落帆索

stern
板尾

mast
桅杆

luff (to)
搶風行駛

bow
板首

daggerboard well
插板縫

mast foot
桅脚

daggerboard
中插板

skeg
尾鰭

one-design sailboat
帆船

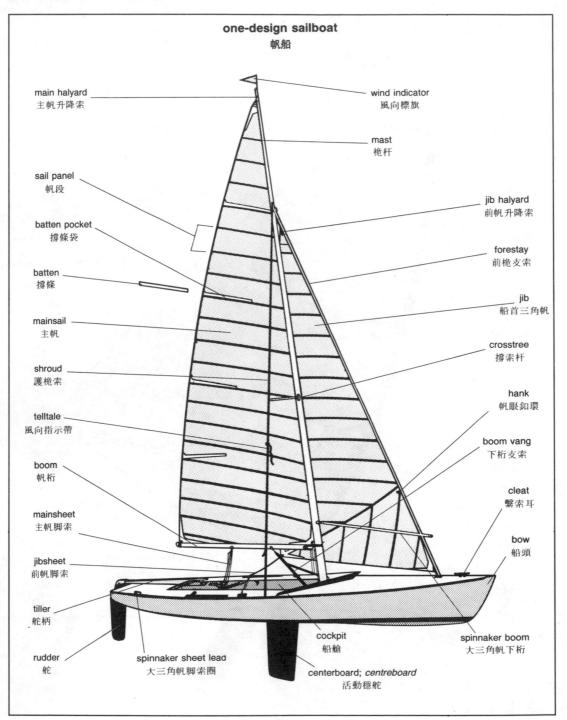

main halyard
主帆升降索

wind indicator
風向標旗

mast
桅杆

sail panel
帆段

jib halyard
前帆升降索

batten pocket
撐條袋

forestay
前桅支索

batten
撐條

jib
船首三角帆

mainsail
主帆

crosstree
撐索杆

shroud
護桅索

hank
帆眼鈕環

telltale
風向指示帶

boom vang
下桁支索

boom
帆桁

cleat
繫索耳

mainsheet
主帆腳索

bow
船頭

jibsheet
前帆腳索

tiller
舵柄

spinnaker boom
大三角帆下桁

rudder
舵

spinnaker sheet lead
大三角帆腳索圈

cockpit
船艙

centerboard; *centreboard*
活動穩舵

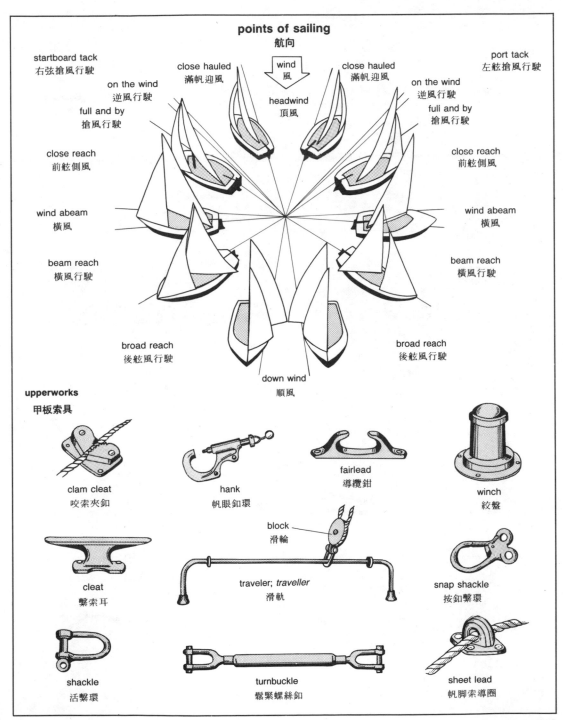

points of sailing
航向

startboard tack
右弦搶風行駛

close hauled
滿帆迎風

wind
風

close hauled
滿帆迎風

port tack
左舷搶風行駛

on the wind
逆風行駛

headwind
頂風

on the wind
逆風行駛

full and by
搶風行駛

full and by
搶風行駛

close reach
前舷側風

close reach
前舷側風

wind abeam
橫風

wind abeam
橫風

beam reach
橫風行駛

beam reach
橫風行駛

broad reach
後舷風行駛

broad reach
後舷風行駛

down wind
順風

upperworks
甲板索具

clam cleat
咬索夾釦

hank
帆眼釦環

fairlead
導纜鉗

winch
絞盤

block
滑輪

cleat
繫索耳

traveler; *traveller*
滑軌

snap shackle
按釦繫環

shackle
活繫環

turnbuckle
鬆緊螺絲釦

sheet lead
帆腳索導圈

water skiing
滑水

types of skis
滑水板

twin skis
雙板

toe piece
趾套

heel piece
踵套

mono-ski
單板

binding
脚套

fin
鰭板

front binding
前脚套

back binding
後脚套

figure ski
花式滑水板

jump ski
跳躍滑水板

tail
板尾

tip
板尖

bottom
板底

types of handles
拉把

handle
拉把

tow bar
拉桿

towrope
拖繩

figure skiing handle
花式滑水拉把

double handles
雙拉把

toe strap
趾帶

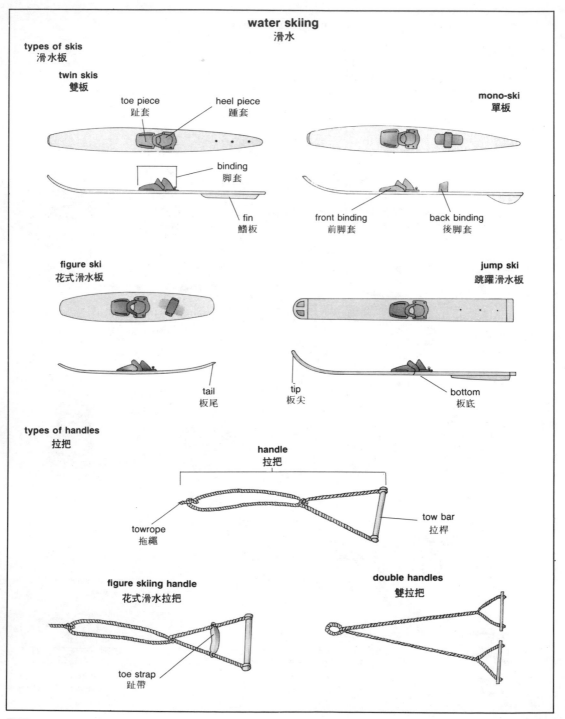

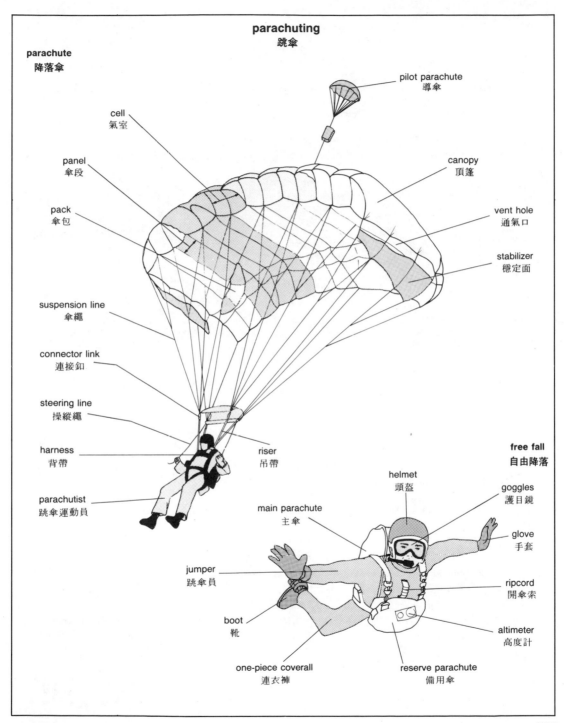

parachuting
跳傘

parachute
降落傘

pilot parachute
導傘

cell
氣室

panel
傘段

pack
傘包

canopy
頂篷

vent hole
通氣口

stabilizer
穩定面

suspension line
傘繩

connector link
連接釦

steering line
操縱繩

harness
背帶

riser
吊帶

free fall
自由降落

parachutist
跳傘運動員

helmet
頭盔

goggles
護目鏡

main parachute
主傘

glove
手套

jumper
跳傘員

ripcord
開傘索

boot
靴

altimeter
高度計

one-piece coverall
連衣褲

reserve parachute
備用傘

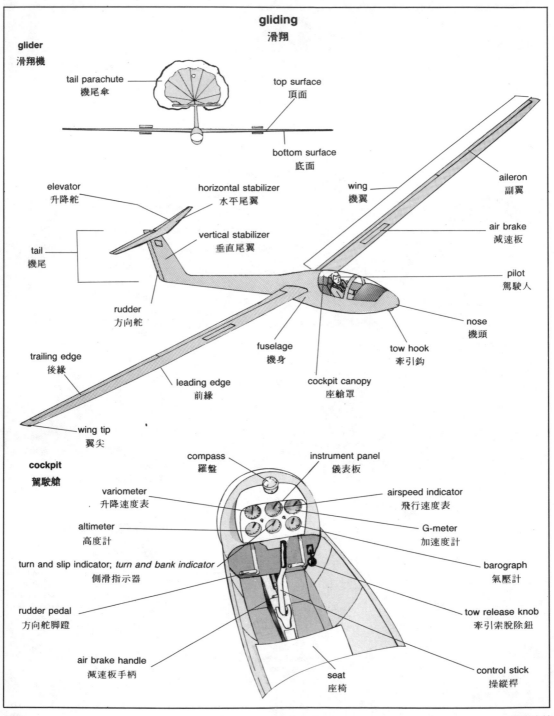

gliding
滑翔

glider
滑翔機

tail parachute
機尾傘

top surface
頂面

bottom surface
底面

elevator
升降舵

horizontal stabilizer
水平尾翼

wing
機翼

aileron
副翼

air brake
減速板

tail
機尾

vertical stabilizer
垂直尾翼

pilot
駕駛人

rudder
方向舵

nose
機頭

trailing edge
後緣

fuselage
機身

tow hook
牽引鈎

leading edge
前緣

cockpit canopy
座艙罩

wing tip
翼尖

cockpit
駕駛艙

compass
羅盤

instrument panel
儀表板

variometer
升降速度表

airspeed indicator
飛行速度表

altimeter
高度計

G-meter
加速度計

turn and slip indicator; *turn and bank indicator*
側滑指示器

barograph
氣壓計

rudder pedal
方向舵腳蹬

tow release knob
牽引索脫除鈕

air brake handle
減速板手柄

seat
座椅

control stick
操縱桿

hang gliding
翼滑翔

hang glider
滑翔翼

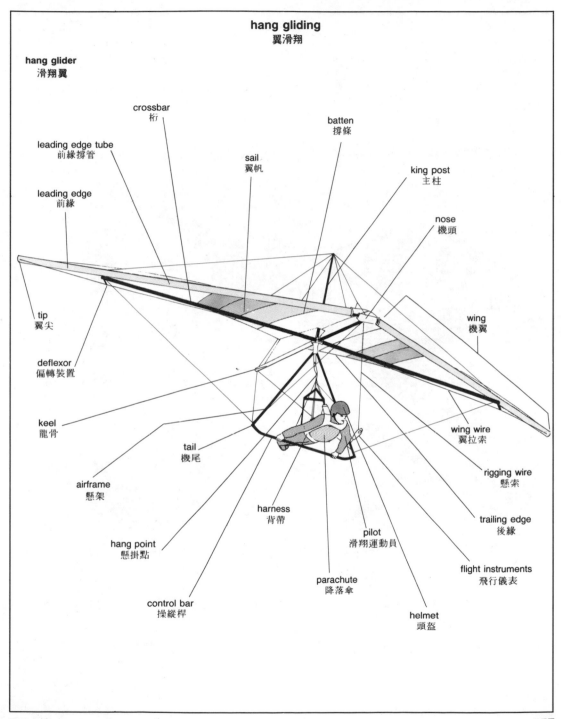

crossbar
桁

batten
撐條

leading edge tube
前緣撐管

sail
翼帆

king post
主柱

leading edge
前緣

nose
機頭

tip
翼尖

wing
機翼

deflexor
偏轉裝置

keel
龍骨

wing wire
翼拉索

tail
機尾

rigging wire
懸索

airframe
懸架

trailing edge
後緣

harness
背帶

hang point
懸掛點

pilot
滑翔運動員

flight instruments
飛行儀表

control bar
操縱桿

parachute
降落傘

helmet
頭盔

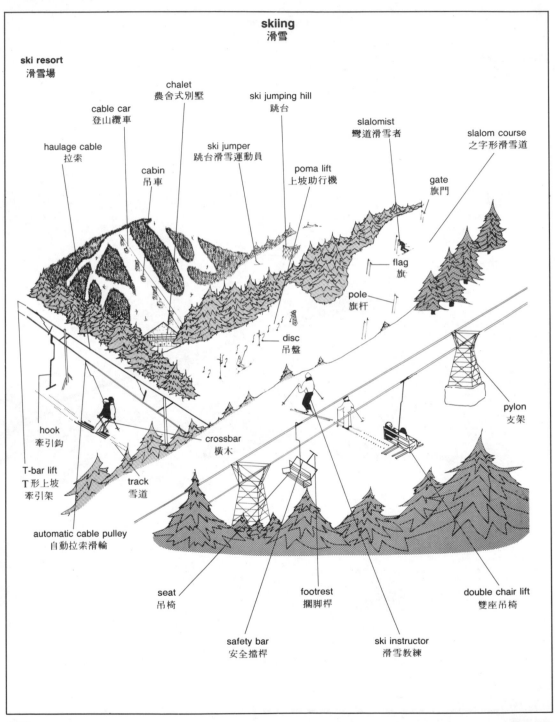

skiing
滑雪

ski resort
滑雪場

chalet
農舍式別墅

ski jumping hill
跳台

slalomist
彎道滑雪者

slalom course
之字形滑雪道

cable car
登山纜車

ski jumper
跳台滑雪運動員

poma lift
上坡助行機

gate
旗門

haulage cable
拉索

cabin
吊車

flag
旗

pole
旗杆

disc
吊盤

pylon
支架

hook
牽引鈎

crossbar
橫木

T-bar lift
T形上坡
牽引架

track
雪道

automatic cable pulley
自動拉索滑輪

seat
吊椅

footrest
攔脚桿

double chair lift
雙座吊椅

safety bar
安全擋桿

ski instructor
滑雪教練

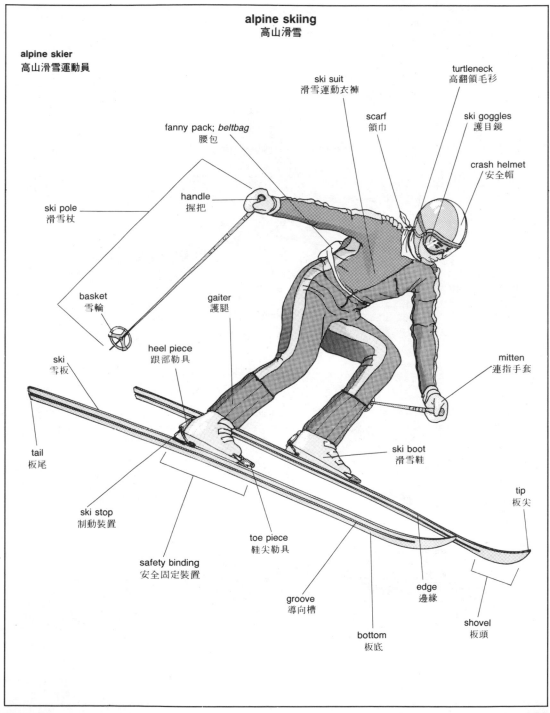

alpine skiing
高山滑雪

alpine skier
高山滑雪運動員

ski suit
滑雪運動衣褲

turtleneck
高翻領毛衫

scarf
領巾

ski goggles
護目鏡

crash helmet
安全帽

fanny pack; *beltbag*
腰包

handle
握把

ski pole
滑雪杖

basket
雪輪

gaiter
護腿

ski
雪板

heel piece
跟部勒具

mitten
連指手套

tail
板尾

ski boot
滑雪鞋

tip
板尖

ski stop
制動裝置

toe piece
鞋尖勒具

safety binding
安全固定裝置

groove
導向槽

edge
邊緣

bottom
板底

shovel
板頭

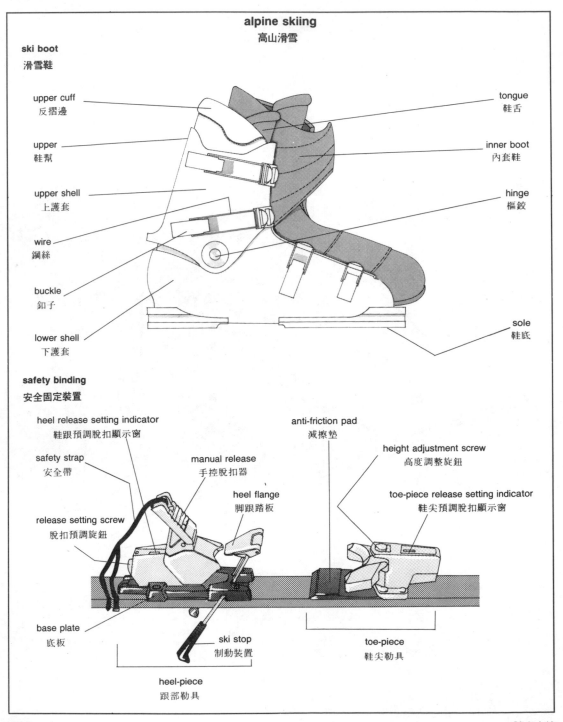

alpine skiing
高山滑雪

ski boot
滑雪鞋

upper cuff
反摺邊

upper
鞋幫

upper shell
上護套

wire
鋼絲

buckle
釦子

lower shell
下護套

tongue
鞋舌

inner boot
內套鞋

hinge
樞鈕

sole
鞋底

safety binding
安全固定裝置

heel release setting indicator
鞋跟預調脫扣顯示窗

safety strap
安全帶

release setting screw
脫扣預調旋鈕

base plate
底板

manual release
手控脫扣器

heel flange
脚跟踏板

ski stop
制動裝置

heel-piece
跟部勒具

anti-friction pad
減擦墊

height adjustment screw
高度調整旋鈕

toe-piece release setting indicator
鞋尖預調脫扣顯示窗

toe-piece
鞋尖勒具

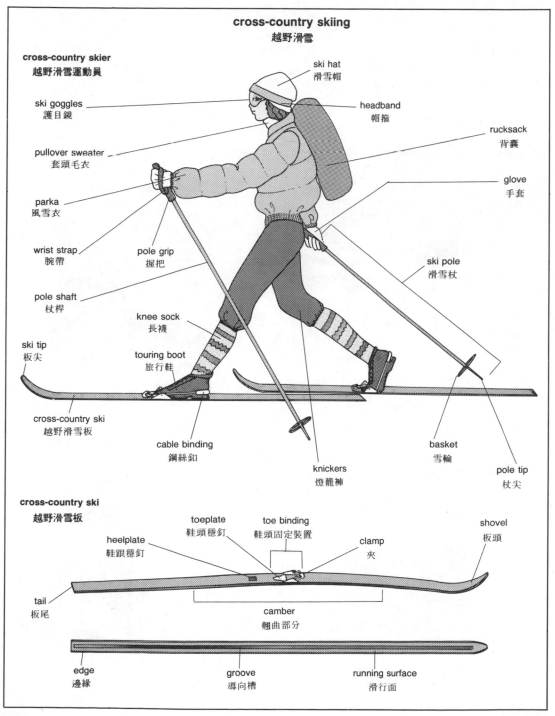

cross-country skiing
越野滑雪

cross-country skier
越野滑雪運動員

ski hat
滑雪帽

ski goggles
護目鏡

headband
帽箍

rucksack
背囊

pullover sweater
套頭毛衣

glove
手套

parka
風雪衣

wrist strap
腕帶

pole grip
握把

ski pole
滑雪杖

pole shaft
杖桿

knee sock
長襪

ski tip
板尖

touring boot
旅行鞋

cross-country ski
越野滑雪板

cable binding
鋼絲釦

knickers
燈籠褲

basket
雪輪

pole tip
杖尖

cross-country ski
越野滑雪板

toeplate
鞋頭穩釘

toe binding
鞋頭固定裝置

clamp
夾

shovel
板頭

heelplate
鞋跟穩釘

tail
板尾

camber
翹曲部分

edge
邊緣

groove
導向槽

running surface
滑行面

skating
溜冰

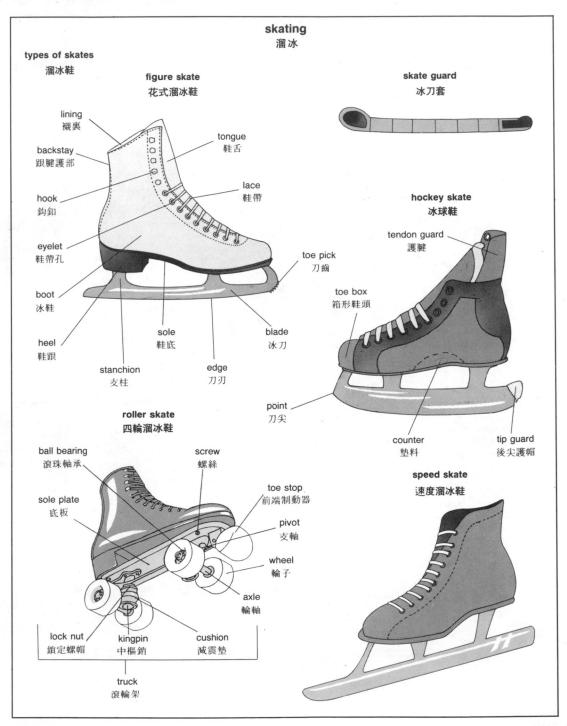

types of skates
溜冰鞋

figure skate
花式溜冰鞋

lining
襯裏

backstay
跟腱護部

hook
鈎釦

eyelet
鞋帶孔

boot
冰鞋

heel
鞋跟

stanchion
支柱

tongue
鞋舌

lace
鞋帶

toe pick
刀齒

sole
鞋底

edge
刀刃

blade
冰刀

skate guard
冰刀套

hockey skate
冰球鞋

tendon guard
護腱

toe box
箱形鞋頭

point
刀尖

counter
墊料

tip guard
後尖護帽

roller skate
四輪溜冰鞋

ball bearing
滾珠軸承

sole plate
底板

lock nut
鎖定螺帽

kingpin
中樞銷

truck
滾輪架

screw
螺絲

toe stop
前端制動器

pivot
支軸

wheel
輪子

axle
輪軸

cushion
減震墊

speed skate
速度溜冰鞋

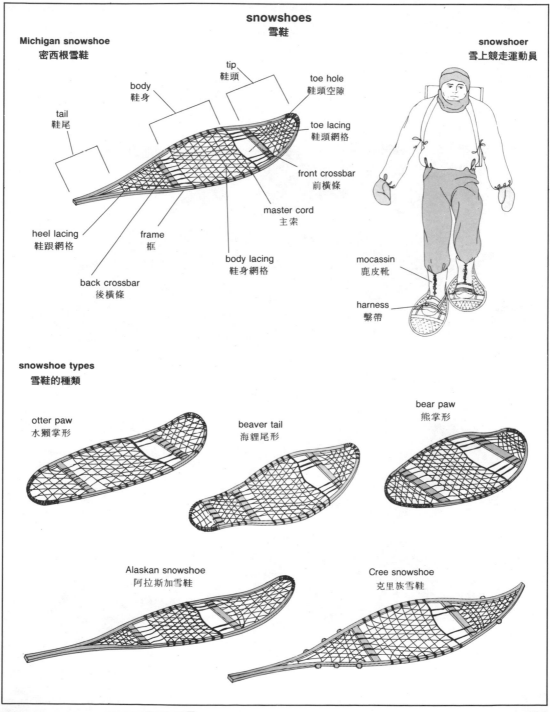

snowshoes
雪鞋

Michigan snowshoe
密西根雪鞋

snowshoer
雪上競走運動員

tip
鞋頭

toe hole
鞋頭空隙

body
鞋身

toe lacing
鞋頭網格

tail
鞋尾

front crossbar
前橫條

master cord
主索

heel lacing
鞋跟網格

frame
框

mocassin
鹿皮靴

back crossbar
後橫條

body lacing
鞋身網格

harness
繫帶

snowshoe types
雪鞋的種類

otter paw
水獺掌形

beaver tail
海狸尾形

bear paw
熊掌形

Alaskan snowshoe
阿拉斯加雪鞋

Cree snowshoe
克里族雪鞋

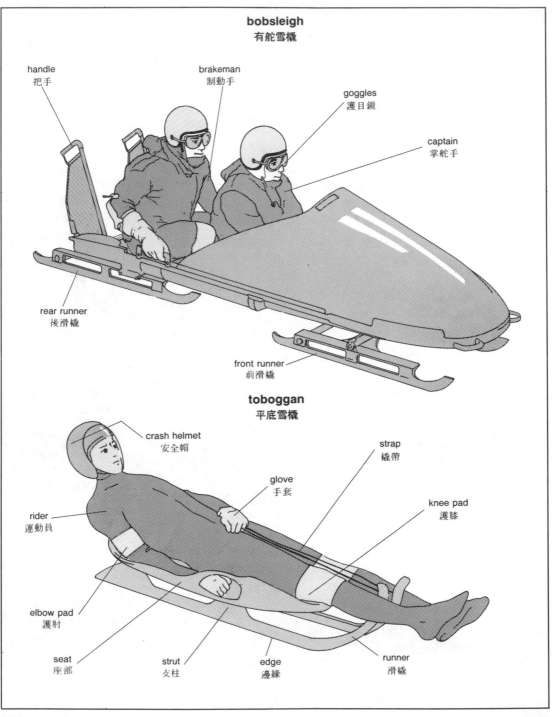

bobsleigh
有舵雪橇

handle
把手

brakeman
制動手

goggles
護目鏡

captain
掌舵手

rear runner
後滑橇

front runner
前滑橇

toboggan
平底雪橇

crash helmet
安全帽

strap
橇帶

glove
手套

knee pad
護膝

rider
運動員

elbow pad
護肘

seat
座部

strut
支柱

edge
邊緣

runner
滑橇

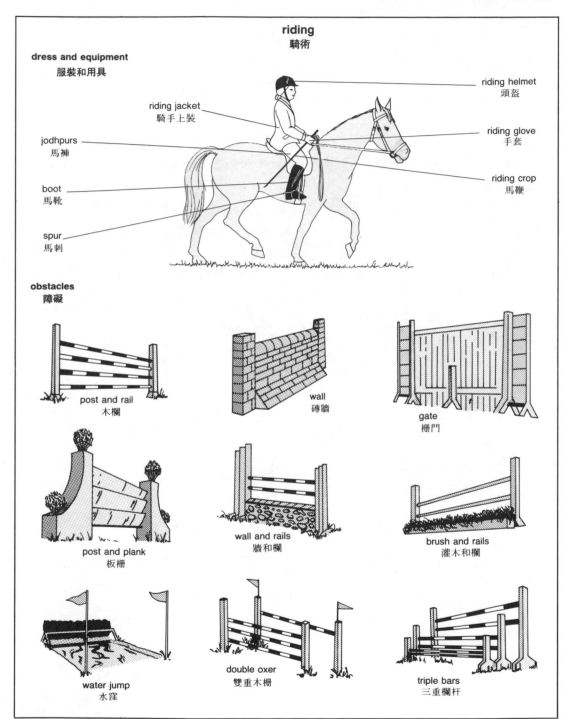

riding
騎術

dress and equipment
服裝和用具

riding helmet
頭盔

riding jacket
騎手上裝

riding glove
手套

jodhpurs
馬褲

riding crop
馬鞭

boot
馬靴

spur
馬刺

obstacles
障礙

post and rail
木欄

wall
磚牆

gate
柵門

post and plank
板柵

wall and rails
牆和欄

brush and rails
灌木和欄

water jump
水窪

double oxer
雙重木柵

triple bars
三重欄杆

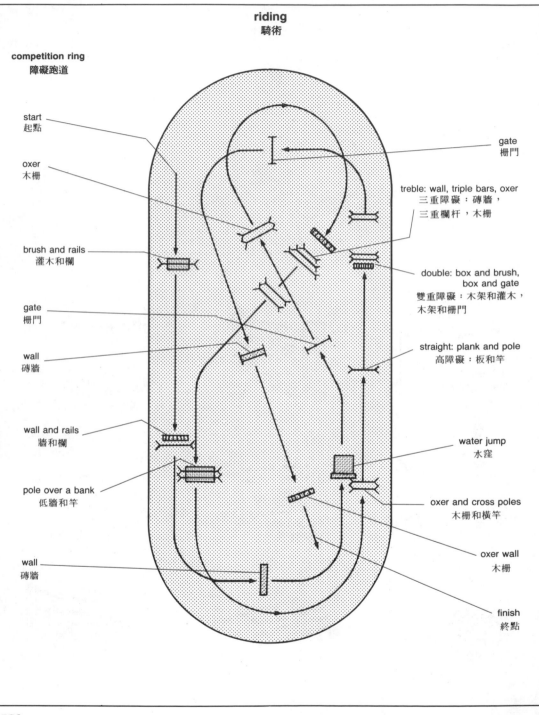

riding
騎術

competition ring
障礙跑道

start
起點

oxer
木柵

brush and rails
灌木和欄

gate
柵門

wall
磚牆

wall and rails
牆和欄

pole over a bank
低牆和竿

wall
磚牆

gate
柵門

treble: wall, triple bars, oxer
三重障礙：磚牆，
三重欄杆，木柵

double: box and brush,
box and gate
雙重障礙：木架和灌木，
木架和柵門

straight: plank and pole
高障礙：板和竿

water jump
水窪

oxer and cross poles
木柵和橫竿

oxer wall
木柵

finish
終點

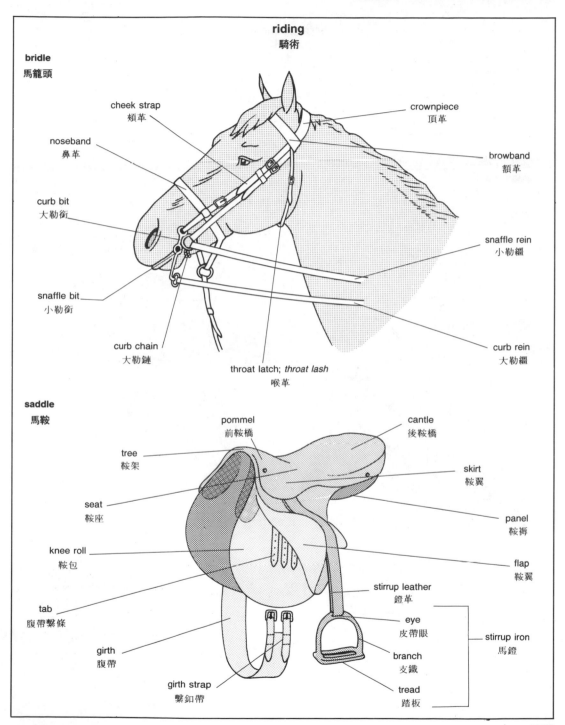

riding
騎術

bridle
馬籠頭

cheek strap
頰革

crownpiece
頂革

noseband
鼻革

browband
額革

curb bit
大勒銜

snaffle rein
小勒韁

snaffle bit
小勒銜

curb chain
大勒鏈

throat latch; *throat lash*
喉革

curb rein
大勒韁

saddle
馬鞍

pommel
前鞍橋

cantle
後鞍橋

tree
鞍架

skirt
鞍翼

seat
鞍座

panel
鞍褥

knee roll
鞍包

flap
鞍翼

tab
腹帶繫條

stirrup leather
鐙革

eye
皮帶眼

stirrup iron
馬鐙

girth
腹帶

branch
支鐵

girth strap
繫釦帶

tread
踏板

harness racing
賽馬車

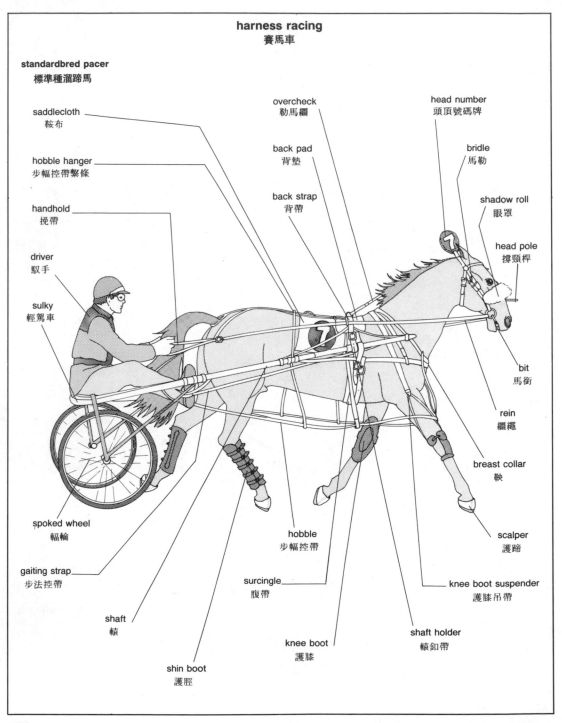

standardbred pacer
標準種溜蹄馬

saddlecloth
鞍布

hobble hanger
步幅控帶繫條

handhold
挽帶

driver
馭手

sulky
輕駕車

spoked wheel
輻輪

gaiting strap
步法控帶

shaft
轅

shin boot
護脛

overcheck
勒馬韁

back pad
背墊

back strap
背帶

hobble
步幅控帶

surcingle
腹帶

knee boot
護膝

head number
頭頂號碼牌

bridle
馬勒

shadow roll
眼罩

head pole
撐頸桿

bit
馬銜

rein
繮繩

breast collar
鞅

scalper
護蹄

knee boot suspender
護膝吊帶

shaft holder
轅釦帶

harness racing
賽馬車

racing programm
馬簿

morning line
預測賠率

horse's name
馬名

horse's pedigree
馬匹血統

trainer
練馬師

horse's number
馬匹號碼

driver's colors
馭手衣帽顏色

owner
馬主

temperature
氣溫

driver
馭手

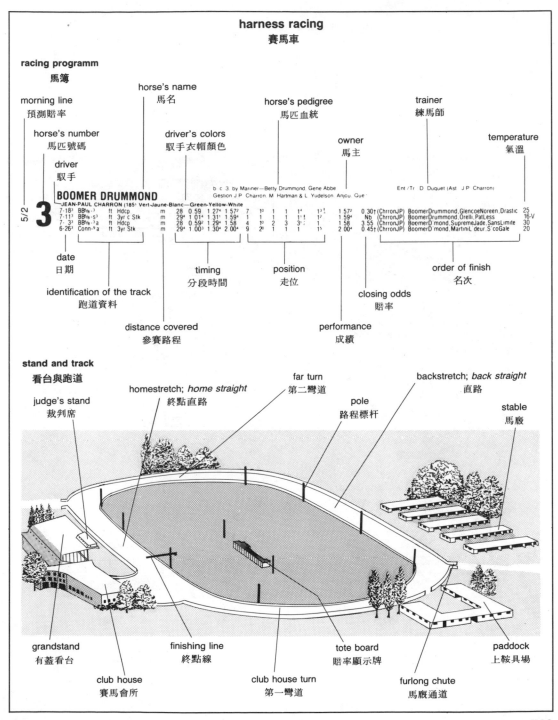

b c 3 by Mariner—Betty Drummond. Gene Abbe
Gestion J.P. Charron, M. Hartman & L. Yudelson, Anjou, Que

Ent./Tr. D. Duquet (Ast. J.P. Charron)

BOOMER DRUMMOND
JEAN-PAUL CHARRON (185) Vert-Jaune-Blanc—Green-Yellow-White

5/2 **3**

7-18³	BB⅝-³	ft	Hdcp	m	28	0.59	1.27⁴	1.57²	7	1⁰	1	1	1⁴	1³¼	1.57²	0.30†	(ChrronJP)	BoomerDrummond,GlencoeNoreen,Drastic	25
7-11³	BB⅝-s³	ft	3yr c Stk	m	29⁴	1.01⁴	1.31¹	1.59⁴	1	1	1	1	1²	1²	1.59⁴	Nb	(ChrronJP)	BoomerDrummond,Orelli,PatLess	16-V
7- 3³	BB⅝-³a	ft	Hdcp	m	28	0.59²	1.29⁴	1.58	4	1⁰	2	3	3¹¼	1.58	3.55	(ChrronJP)	BoomerD'mond,SupremeJade,SansLimite	30
6-26³	Conn-⁹a	ft	3yr Stk	m	29⁴	1.00³	1.30⁴	2.00⁴	9	2⁰	1	1	1⁵	2.00⁴	0.45†	(ChrronJP)	BoomerD'mond,MartiniL'deur,S'coGale	20

date
日期

timing
分段時間

position
走位

order of finish
名次

identification of the track
跑道資料

closing odds
賠率

distance covered
參賽路程

performance
成績

stand and track
看台與跑道

homestretch; *home straight*
終點直路

far turn
第二彎道

backstretch; *back straight*
直路

judge's stand
裁判席

pole
路程標杆

stable
馬廏

grandstand
有蓋看台

finishing line
終點線

tote board
賠率顯示牌

paddock
上鞍具場

club house
賽馬會所

club house turn
第一彎道

furlong chute
馬廏通道

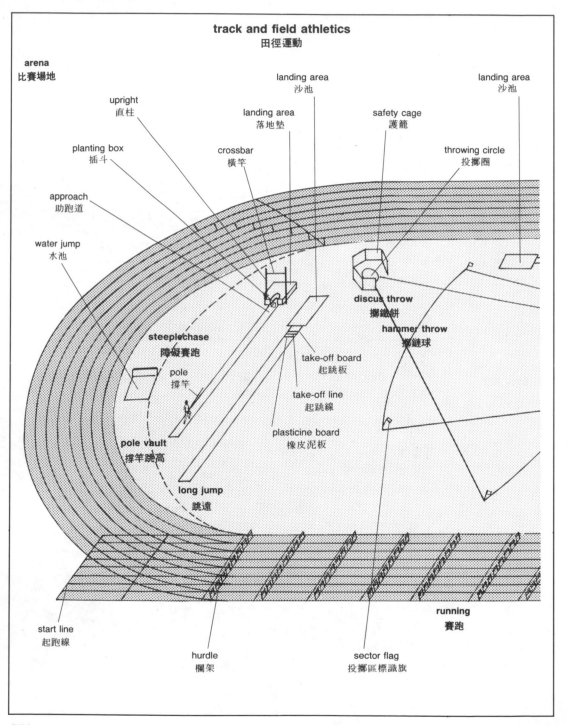

track and field athletics
田徑運動

arena
比賽場地

upright
直柱

landing area
沙池

landing area
沙池

planting box
插斗

crossbar
橫竿

landing area
落地墊

safety cage
護籠

throwing circle
投擲圈

approach
助跑道

water jump
水池

discus throw
擲鐵餅

steeplechase
障礙賽跑

hammer throw
擲鏈球

pole
撐竿

take-off board
起跳板

take-off line
起跳線

pole vault
撐竿跳高

plasticine board
橡皮泥板

long jump
跳遠

running
賽跑

start line
起跑線

hurdle
欄架

sector flag
投擲區標識旗

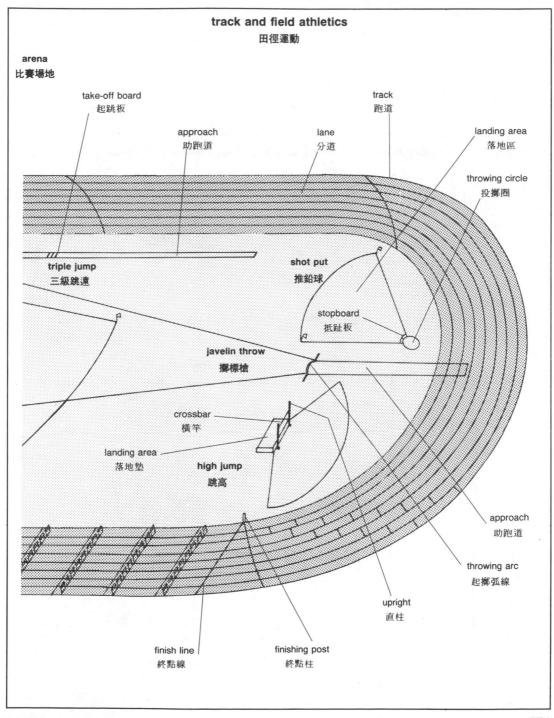

track and field athletics
田徑運動

arena
比賽場地

take-off board
起跳板

approach
助跑道

track
跑道

lane
分道

landing area
落地區

throwing circle
投擲圈

triple jump
三級跳遠

shot put
推鉛球

stopboard
抵趾板

javelin throw
擲標槍

crossbar
橫竿

landing area
落地墊

high jump
跳高

approach
助跑道

throwing arc
起擲弧線

upright
直柱

finish line
終點線

finishing post
終點柱

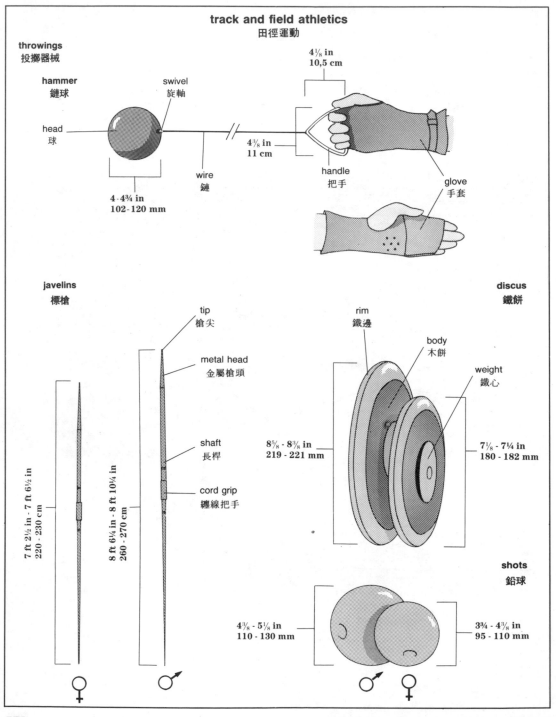

track and field athletics
田徑運動

throwings
投擲器械

hammer
鏈球

swivel
旋軸

head
球

wire
鏈

4 - 4¾ in
102 - 120 mm

4⅛ in
10,5 cm

4⅜ in
11 cm

handle
把手

glove
手套

javelins
標槍

tip
槍尖

metal head
金屬槍頭

shaft
長桿

cord grip
纏線把手

7 ft 2½ in - 7 ft 6½ in
220 - 230 cm

8 ft 6¼ in - 8 ft 10¼ in
260 - 270 cm

discus
鐵餅

rim
鐵邊

body
木餅

weight
鐵心

8⅝ - 8⅜ in
219 - 221 mm

7⅛ - 7¼ in
180 - 182 mm

shots
鉛球

4⅜ - 5⅛ in
110 - 130 mm

3¾ - 4⅜ in
95 - 110 mm

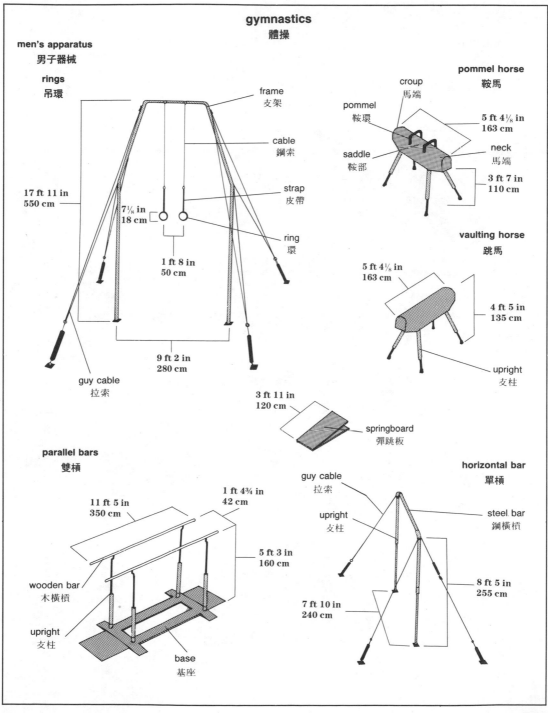

gymnastics
體操

men's apparatus
男子器械

rings
吊環

frame
支架

cable
鋼索

strap
皮帶

17 ft 11 in
550 cm

7 1/8 in
18 cm

ring
環

1 ft 8 in
50 cm

9 ft 2 in
280 cm

guy cable
拉索

pommel horse
鞍馬

croup
馬端

pommel
鞍環

saddle
鞍部

5 ft 4 1/8 in
163 cm

neck
馬端

3 ft 7 in
110 cm

vaulting horse
跳馬

5 ft 4 1/8 in
163 cm

4 ft 5 in
135 cm

upright
支柱

3 ft 11 in
120 cm

springboard
彈跳板

parallel bars
雙槓

11 ft 5 in
350 cm

1 ft 4¾ in
42 cm

5 ft 3 in
160 cm

wooden bar
木橫槓

upright
支柱

base
基座

horizontal bar
單槓

guy cable
拉索

upright
支柱

steel bar
鋼橫槓

8 ft 5 in
255 cm

7 ft 10 in
240 cm

gymnastics
體操

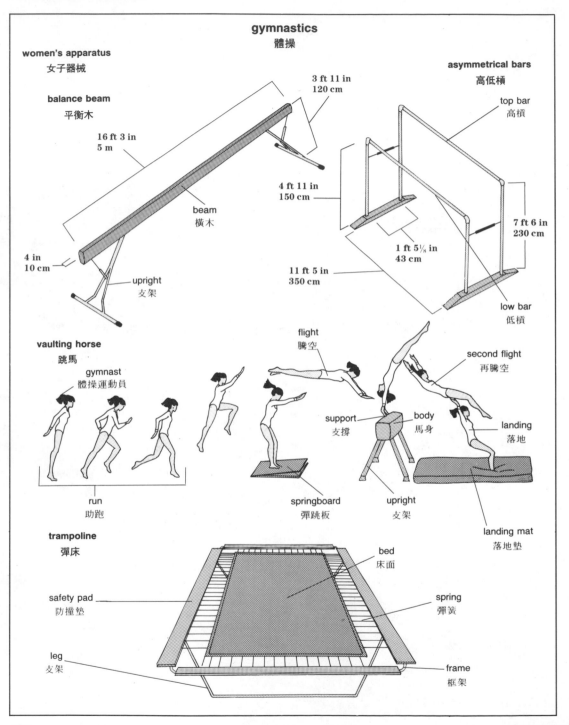

women's apparatus
女子器械

balance beam
平衡木

16 ft 3 in
5 m

4 in
10 cm

beam
橫木

upright
支架

3 ft 11 in
120 cm

asymmetrical bars
高低槓

top bar
高槓

4 ft 11 in
150 cm

7 ft 6 in
230 cm

1 ft 5⅛ in
43 cm

11 ft 5 in
350 cm

low bar
低槓

vaulting horse
跳馬

gymnast
體操運動員

run
助跑

flight
騰空

support
支撐

body
馬身

second flight
再騰空

landing
落地

springboard
彈跳板

upright
支架

landing mat
落地墊

trampoline
彈床

bed
床面

safety pad
防撞墊

spring
彈簧

leg
支架

frame
框架

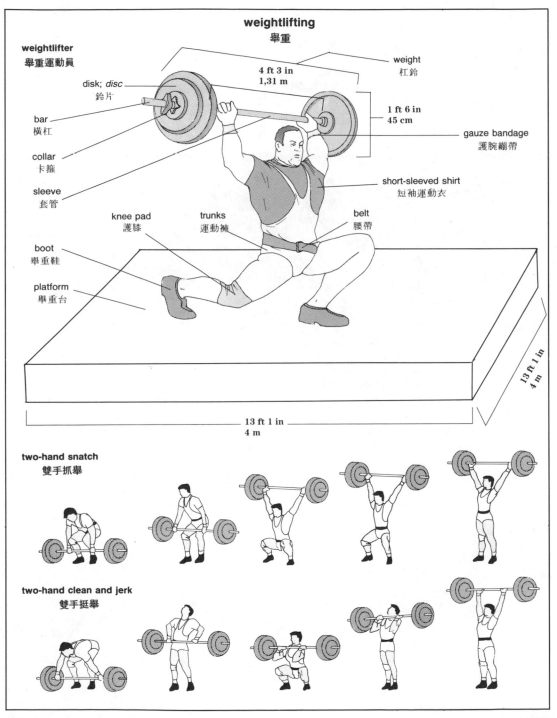

weightlifting
舉重

weightlifter
舉重運動員

weight
杠鈴

4 ft 3 in
1,31 m

disk; *disc*
鈴片

1 ft 6 in
45 cm

bar
橫杠

gauze bandage
護腕繃帶

collar
卡箍

short-sleeved shirt
短袖運動衣

sleeve
套管

knee pad
護膝

trunks
運動褲

belt
腰帶

boot
舉重鞋

platform
舉重台

13 ft 1 in
4 m

13 ft 1 in
4 m

two-hand snatch
雙手抓舉

two-hand clean and jerk
雙手挺舉

fencing
劍術

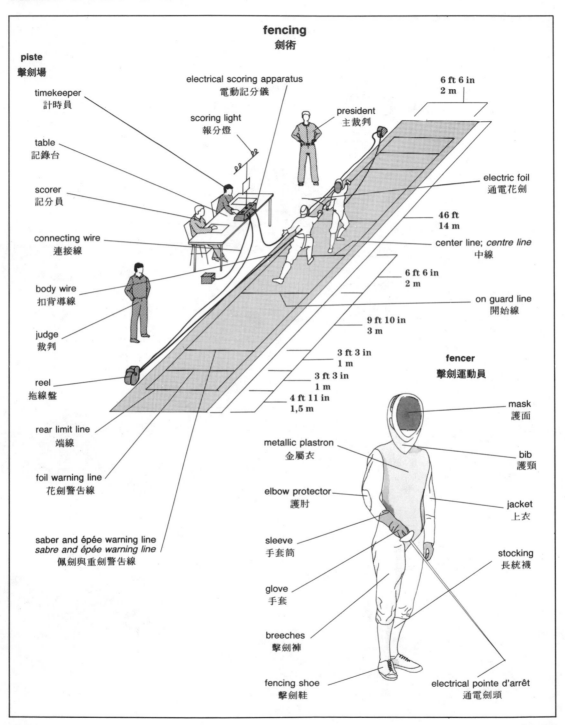

piste
擊劍場

electrical scoring apparatus
電動記分儀

timekeeper
計時員

scoring light
報分燈

president
主裁判

6 ft 6 in
2 m

table
記錄台

electric foil
通電花劍

scorer
記分員

46 ft
14 m

connecting wire
連接線

center line; *centre line*
中線

body wire
扣背導線

6 ft 6 in
2 m

on guard line
開始線

judge
裁判

9 ft 10 in
3 m

3 ft 3 in
1 m

fencer
擊劍運動員

reel
拖線盤

3 ft 3 in
1 m

4 ft 11 in
1,5 m

mask
護面

rear limit line
端線

metallic plastron
金屬衣

bib
護頸

foil warning line
花劍警告線

elbow protector
護肘

jacket
上衣

saber and épée warning line
sabre and épée warning line
佩劍與重劍警告線

sleeve
手套筒

stocking
長統襪

glove
手套

breeches
擊劍褲

fencing shoe
擊劍鞋

electrical pointe d'arrêt
通電劍頭

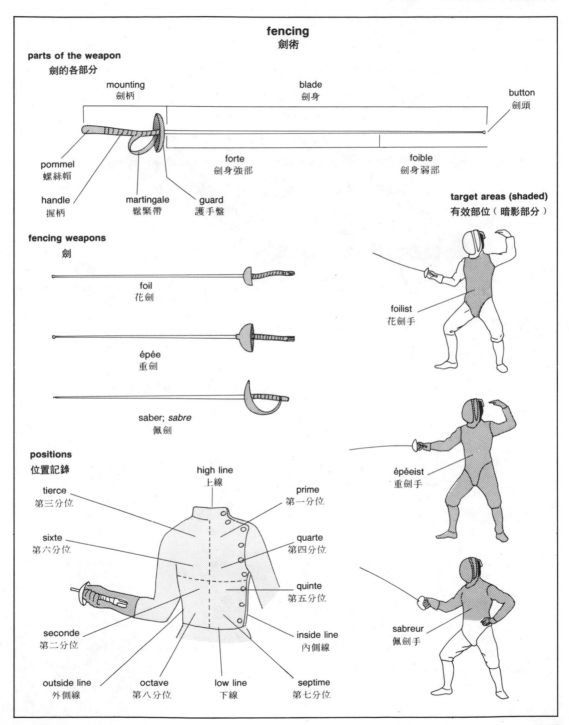

fencing
劍術

parts of the weapon
劍的各部分

mounting
劍柄

blade
劍身

button
劍頭

pommel
螺絲帽

forte
劍身強部

foible
劍身弱部

handle
握柄

martingale
鬆緊帶

guard
護手盤

target areas (shaded)
有效部位（暗影部分）

fencing weapons
劍

foil
花劍

épée
重劍

saber; *sabre*
佩劍

foilist
花劍手

épéeist
重劍手

positions
位置記錄

high line
上線

tierce
第三分位

prime
第一分位

sixte
第六分位

quarte
第四分位

quinte
第五分位

seconde
第二分位

inside line
內側線

outside line
外側線

octave
第八分位

low line
下線

septime
第七分位

sabreur
佩劍手

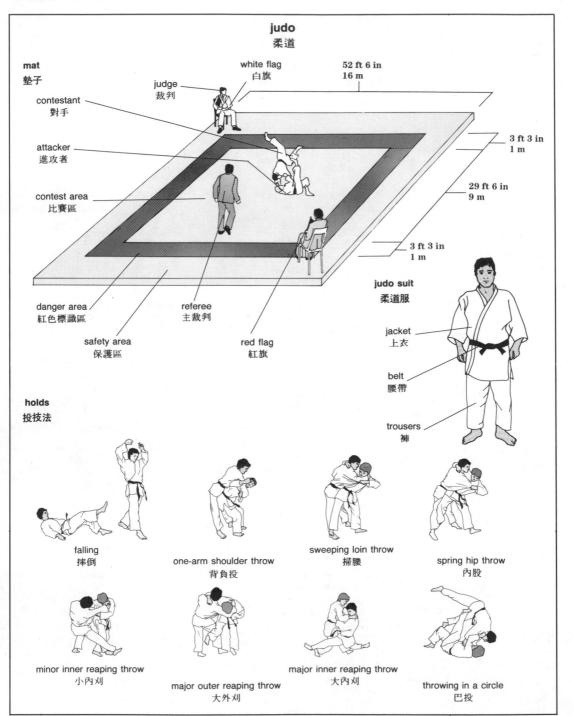

judo
柔道

mat
墊子

judge
裁判

white flag
白旗

52 ft 6 in
16 m

contestant
對手

attacker
進攻者

3 ft 3 in
1 m

29 ft 6 in
9 m

contest area
比賽區

3 ft 3 in
1 m

judo suit
柔道服

jacket
上衣

danger area
紅色標識區

referee
主裁判

belt
腰帶

safety area
保護區

red flag
紅旗

trousers
褲

holds
投技法

falling
摔倒

one-arm shoulder throw
背負投

sweeping loin throw
掃腰

spring hip throw
內股

minor inner reaping throw
小內刈

major outer reaping throw
大外刈

major inner reaping throw
大內刈

throwing in a circle
巴投

boxing
拳擊

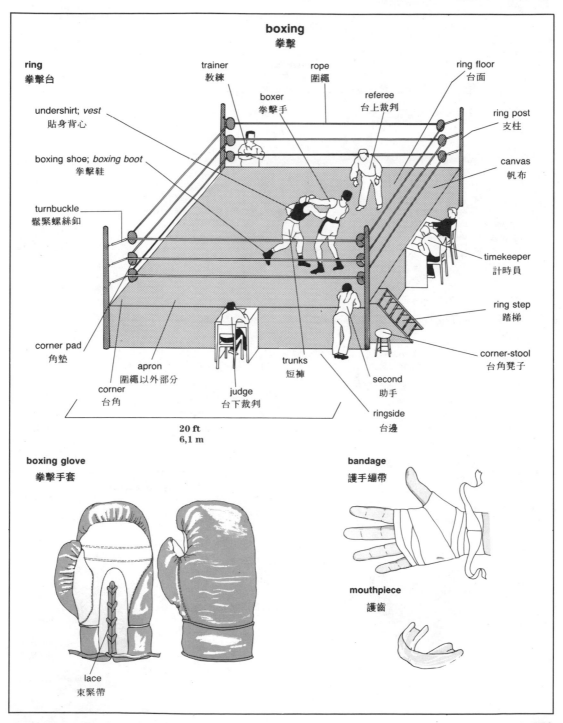

ring
拳擊台

trainer
教練

rope
圍繩

ring floor
台面

boxer
拳擊手

referee
台上裁判

ring post
支柱

undershirt; *vest*
貼身背心

canvas
帆布

boxing shoe; *boxing boot*
拳擊鞋

turnbuckle
鬆緊螺絲釦

timekeeper
計時員

ring step
踏梯

corner pad
角墊

apron
圍繩以外部分

trunks
短褲

corner-stool
台角凳子

corner
台角

judge
台下裁判

second
助手

ringside
台邊

20 ft
6,1 m

boxing glove
拳擊手套

bandage
護手繃帶

mouthpiece
護齒

lace
束緊帶

fishing
垂釣

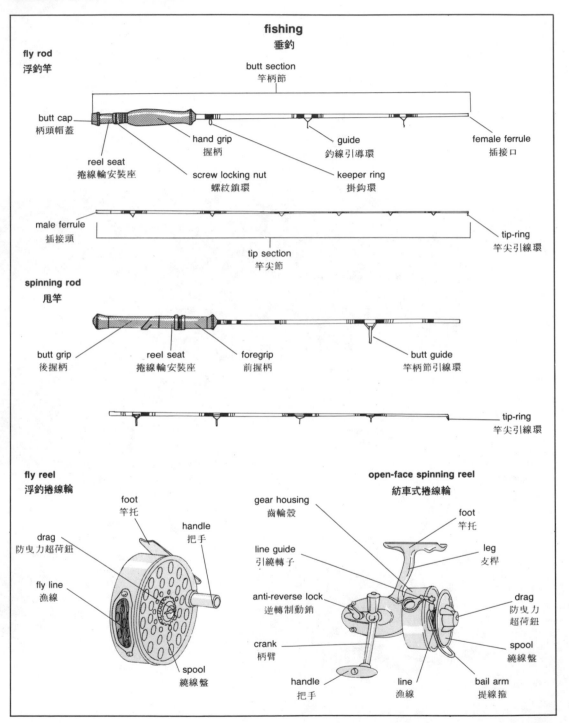

fly rod
浮釣竿

butt section
竿柄節

butt cap
柄頭帽蓋

hand grip
握柄

guide
釣線引導環

female ferrule
插接口

reel seat
捲線輪安裝座

screw locking nut
螺紋鎖環

keeper ring
掛鈎環

male ferrule
插接頭

tip-ring
竿尖引線環

tip section
竿尖節

spinning rod
甩竿

butt grip
後握柄

reel seat
捲線輪安裝座

foregrip
前握柄

butt guide
竿柄節引線環

tip-ring
竿尖引線環

fly reel
浮釣捲線輪

foot
竿托

handle
把手

drag
防曳力超荷鈕

fly line
漁線

spool
繞線盤

open-face spinning reel
紡車式捲線輪

gear housing
齒輪殼

foot
竿托

line guide
引繞轉子

leg
支桿

anti-reverse lock
逆轉制動銷

drag
防曳力
超荷鈕

crank
柄臂

spool
繞線盤

handle
把手

line
漁線

bail arm
提線箍

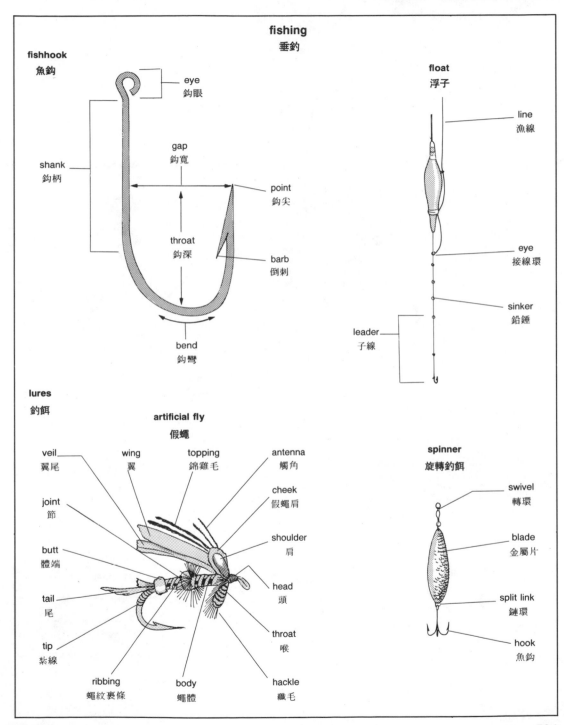

fishing
垂釣

fishhook
魚鈎

eye
鈎眼

shank
鈎柄

gap
鈎寬

point
鈎尖

throat
鈎深

barb
倒刺

bend
鈎彎

float
浮子

line
漁線

eye
接線環

sinker
鉛錘

leader
子線

lures
釣餌

artificial fly
假蠅

veil
翼尾

wing
翼

topping
錦雞毛

antenna
觸角

cheek
假蠅肩

joint
節

shoulder
肩

butt
體端

head
頭

tail
尾

throat
喉

tip
紮線

ribbing
蠅紋裹條

body
蠅體

hackle
纖毛

spinner
旋轉釣餌

swivel
轉環

blade
金屬片

split link
鏈環

hook
魚鈎

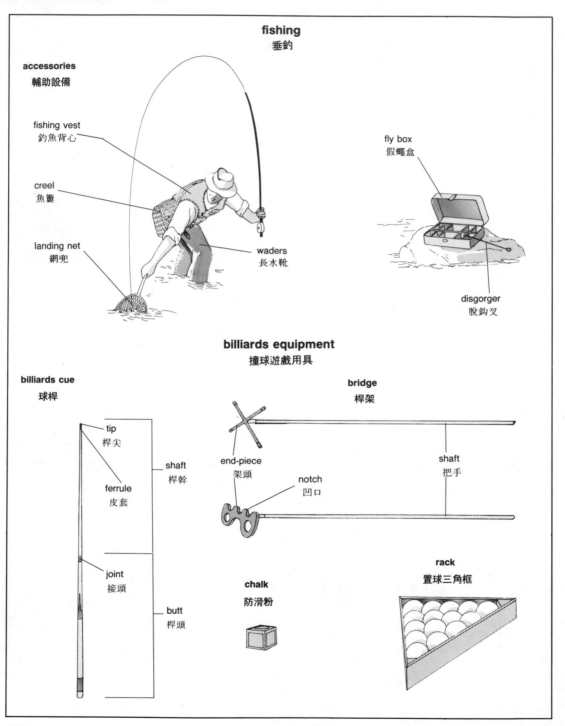

fishing
垂釣

accessories
輔助設備

fishing vest
釣魚背心

creel
魚簍

landing net
網兜

waders
長水靴

fly box
假蠅盒

disgorger
脫鈎叉

billiards equipment
撞球遊戲用具

billiards cue
球桿

tip
桿尖

shaft
桿幹

ferrule
皮套

joint
接頭

butt
桿頭

bridge
桿架

end-piece
架頭

notch
凹口

shaft
把手

chalk
防滑粉

rack
置球三角框

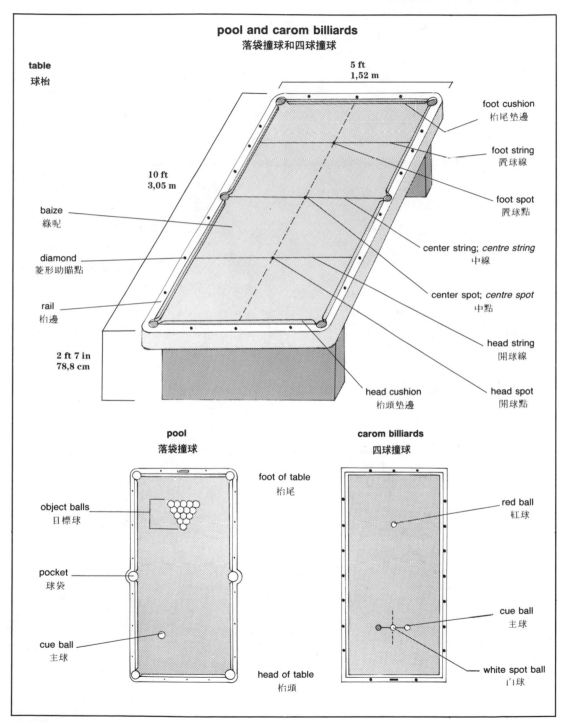

pool and carom billiards
落袋撞球和四球撞球

table
球枱

5 ft
1,52 m

foot cushion
枱尾墊邊

foot string
置球線

foot spot
置球點

10 ft
3,05 m

baize
綠呢

center string; *centre string*
中線

diamond
菱形助瞄點

center spot; *centre spot*
中點

rail
枱邊

head string
開球線

2 ft 7 in
78,8 cm

head cushion
枱頭墊邊

head spot
開球點

pool
落袋撞球

carom billiards
四球撞球

object balls
目標球

foot of table
枱尾

red ball
紅球

pocket
球袋

cue ball
主球

cue ball
主球

white spot ball
白球

head of table
枱頭

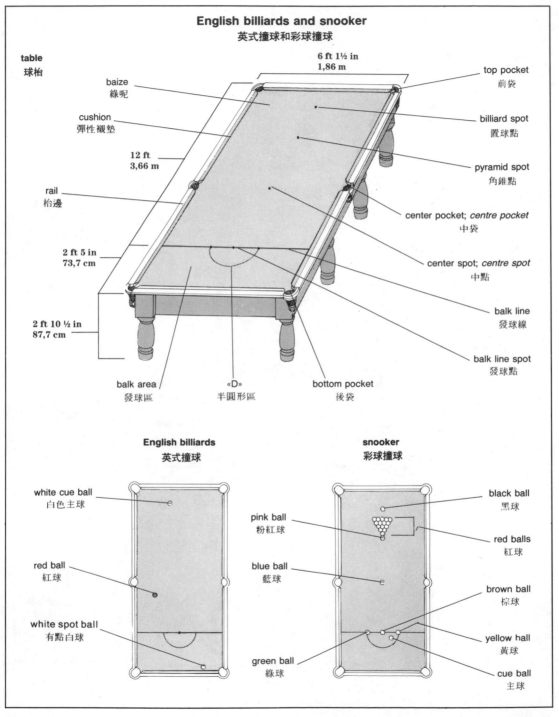

English billiards and snooker
英式撞球和彩球撞球

table
球枱

6 ft 1½ in
1,86 m

baize
綠呢

top pocket
前袋

billiard spot
置球點

cushion
彈性襯墊

pyramid spot
角錐點

12 ft
3,66 m

rail
枱邊

center pocket; *centre pocket*
中袋

center spot; *centre spot*
中點

2 ft 5 in
73,7 cm

balk line
發球線

2 ft 10 ½ in
87,7 cm

balk line spot
發球點

balk area
發球區

«D»
半圓形區

bottom pocket
後袋

English billiards
英式撞球

snooker
彩球撞球

white cue ball
白色主球

black ball
黑球

pink ball
粉紅球

red balls
紅球

red ball
紅球

blue ball
藍球

brown ball
棕球

white spot ball
有點白球

yellow ball
黃球

green ball
綠球

cue ball
主球

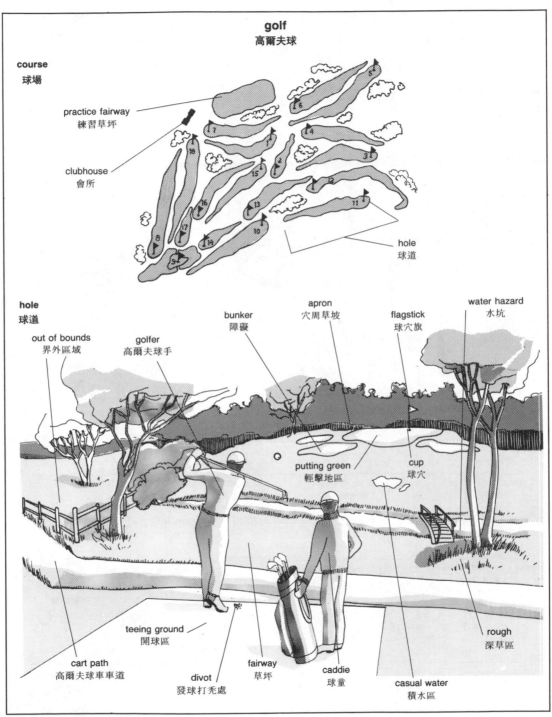

golf
高爾夫球

course
球場

practice fairway
練習草坪

clubhouse
會所

hole
球道

hole
球道

out of bounds
界外區域

golfer
高爾夫球手

bunker
障礙

apron
穴周草坡

flagstick
球穴旗

water hazard
水坑

putting green
輕擊地區

cup
球穴

rough
深草區

cart path
高爾夫球車車道

teeing ground
開球區

divot
發球打禿處

fairway
草坪

caddie
球童

casual water
積水區

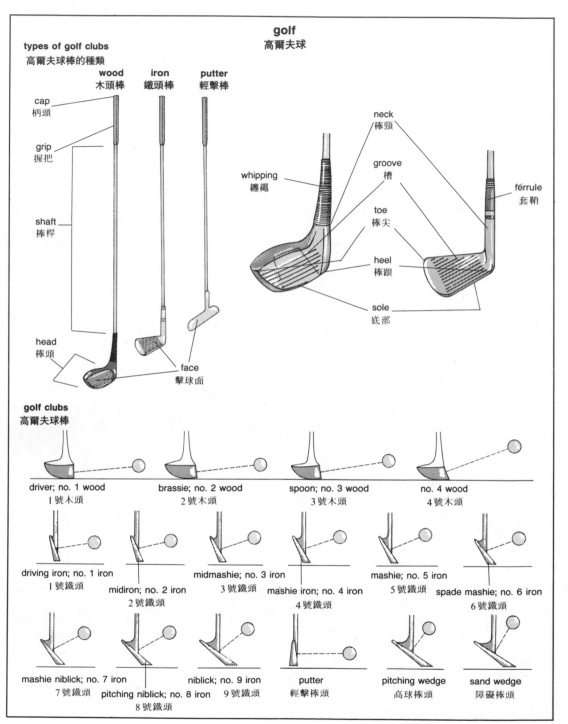

golf
高爾夫球

types of golf clubs
高爾夫球棒的種類

wood 木頭棒
iron 鐵頭棒
putter 輕擊棒

cap 柄頭

grip 握把

shaft 棒桿

head 棒頭

face 擊球面

neck 棒頸

whipping 纏繩

groove 槽

toe 棒尖

heel 棒跟

sole 底部

ferrule 套鞘

golf clubs
高爾夫球棒

driver; no. 1 wood
1號木頭

brassie; no. 2 wood
2號木頭

spoon; no. 3 wood
3號木頭

no. 4 wood
4號木頭

driving iron; no. 1 iron
1號鐵頭

midiron; no. 2 iron
2號鐵頭

midmashie; no. 3 iron
3號鐵頭

mashie iron; no. 4 iron
4號鐵頭

mashie; no. 5 iron
5號鐵頭

spade mashie; no. 6 iron
6號鐵頭

mashie niblick; no. 7 iron
7號鐵頭

pitching niblick; no. 8 iron
8號鐵頭

niblick; no. 9 iron
9號鐵頭

putter
輕擊棒頭

pitching wedge
高球棒頭

sand wedge
障礙棒頭

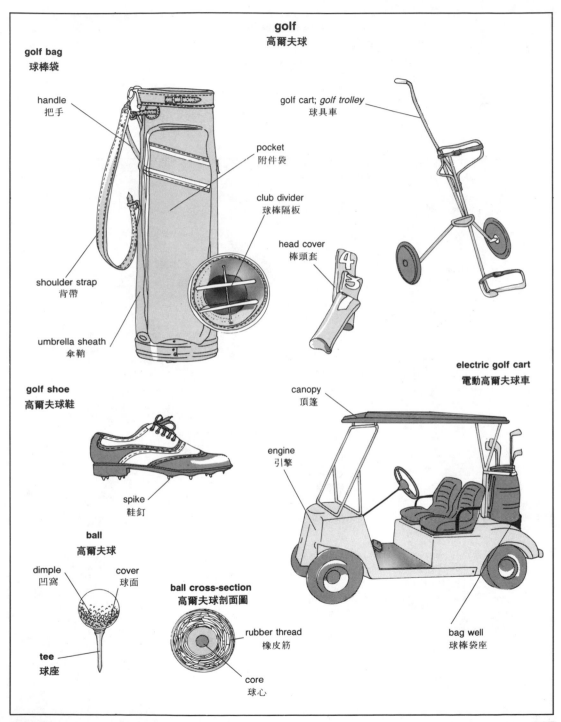

golf
高爾夫球

golf bag
球棒袋

handle
把手

pocket
附件袋

club divider
球棒隔板

golf cart; *golf trolley*
球具車

head cover
棒頭套

shoulder strap
背帶

umbrella sheath
傘鞘

electric golf cart
電動高爾夫球車

canopy
頂篷

engine
引擎

golf shoe
高爾夫球鞋

spike
鞋釘

ball
高爾夫球

dimple
凹窩

cover
球面

ball cross-section
高爾夫球剖面圖

rubber thread
橡皮筋

bag well
球棒袋座

tee
球座

core
球心

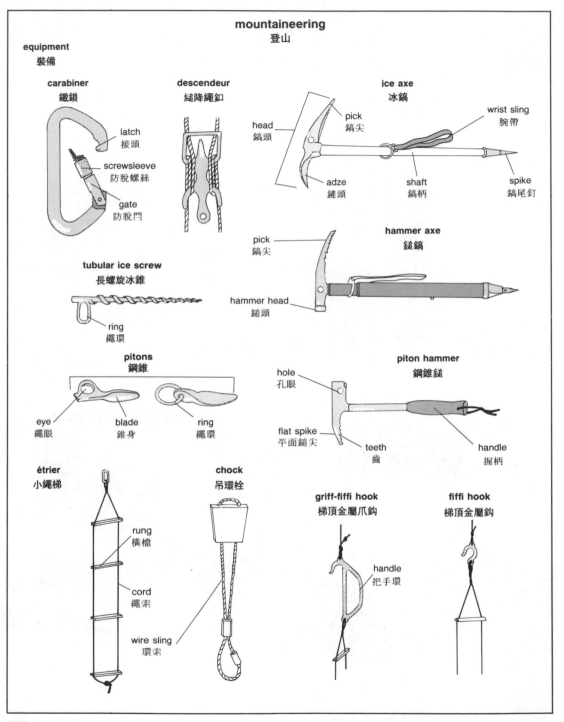

mountaineering
登山

equipment
裝備

carabiner
鐵鎖

latch
接頭

screwsleeve
防脫螺絲

gate
防脫門

descendeur
縋降繩釦

ice axe
冰鎬

head
鎬頭

pick
鎬尖

adze
鏟頭

shaft
鎬柄

wrist sling
腕帶

spike
鎬尾釘

tubular ice screw
長螺旋冰錐

ring
繩環

hammer axe
鎚鎬

pick
鎬尖

hammer head
鎚頭

pitons
鋼錐

eye
繩眼

blade
錐身

ring
繩環

piton hammer
鋼錐鎚

hole
孔眼

flat spike
平面鎚尖

teeth
齒

handle
握柄

étrier
小繩梯

rung
橫檔

cord
繩索

chock
吊環栓

wire sling
環索

griff-fiffi hook
梯頂金屬爪鈎

handle
把手環

fiffi hook
梯頂金屬鈎

mountaineering
登山

mountaineer
登山運動員

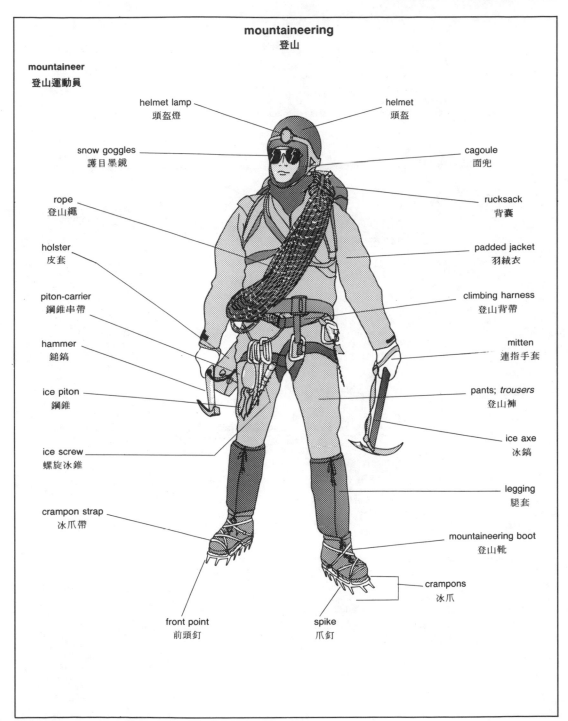

helmet lamp
頭盔燈

helmet
頭盔

snow goggles
護目墨鏡

cagoule
面兜

rope
登山繩

rucksack
背囊

holster
皮套

padded jacket
羽絨衣

piton-carrier
鋼錐串帶

climbing harness
登山背帶

hammer
鎚鎬

mitten
連指手套

ice piton
鋼錐

pants; *trousers*
登山褲

ice axe
冰鎬

ice screw
螺旋冰錐

legging
腿套

crampon strap
冰爪帶

mountaineering boot
登山靴

crampons
冰爪

front point
前頭釘

spike
爪釘

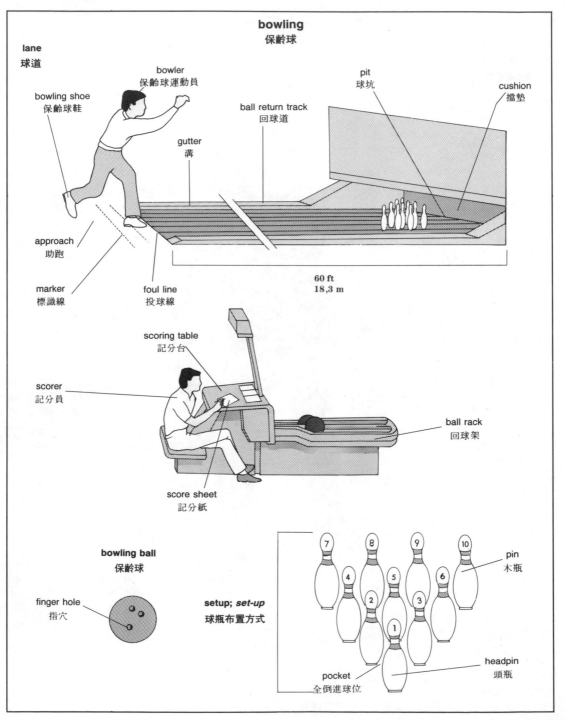

bowling
保齡球

lane
球道

bowler
保齡球運動員

bowling shoe
保齡球鞋

pit
球坑

cushion
擋墊

ball return track
回球道

gutter
溝

approach
助跑

marker
標識線

foul line
投球線

60 ft
18,3 m

scoring table
記分台

scorer
記分員

ball rack
回球架

score sheet
記分紙

bowling ball
保齡球

finger hole
指穴

setup; set-up
球瓶布置方式

7   8   9   10
4   5   6
2   3
1

pin
木瓶

pocket
全倒進球位

headpin
頭瓶

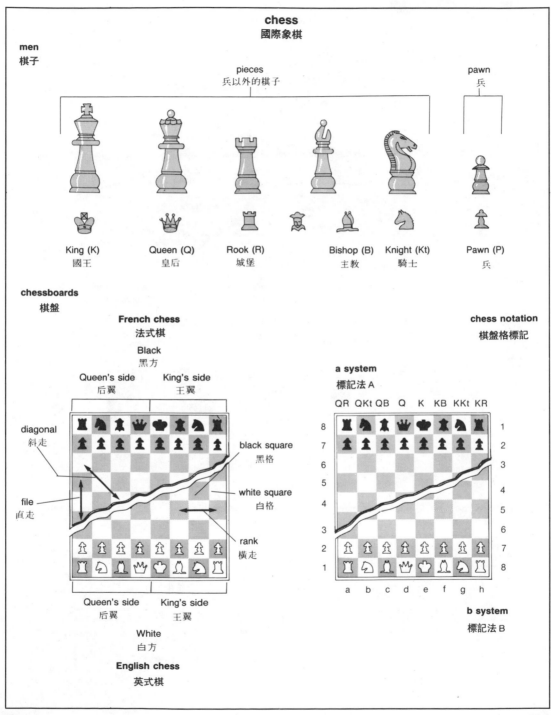

chess
國際象棋

men
棋子

pieces
兵以外的棋子

pawn
兵

King (K)	Queen (Q)	Rook (R)	Bishop (B)	Knight (Kt)	Pawn (P)
國王	皇后	城堡	主教	騎士	兵

chessboards
棋盤

French chess
法式棋

Black
黑方

chess notation
棋盤格標記

a system
標記法 A

Queen's side
后翼

King's side
王翼

diagonal
斜走

black square
黑格

white square
白格

file
直走

rank
橫走

Queen's side
后翼

King's side
王翼

White
白方

English chess
英式棋

b system
標記法 B

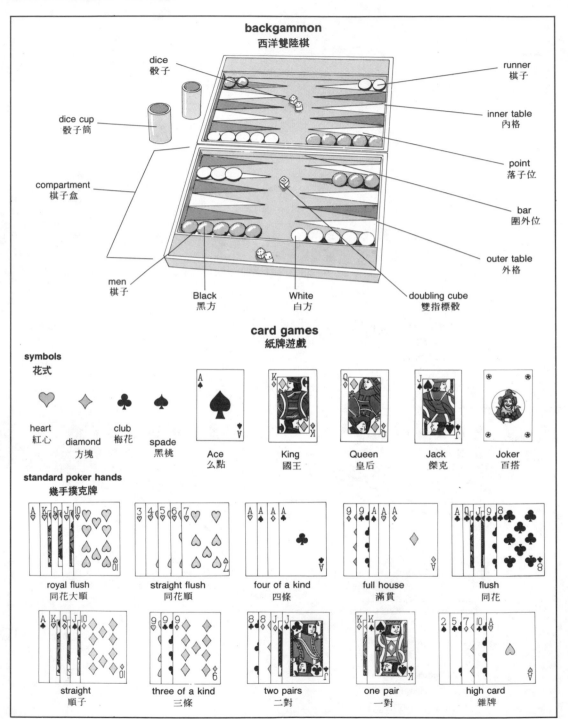

backgammon
西洋雙陸棋

dice
骰子

runner
棋子

dice cup
骰子筒

inner table
內格

compartment
棋子盒

point
落子位

bar
圍外位

outer table
外格

men
棋子

doubling cube
雙指標骰

Black
黑方

White
白方

card games
紙牌遊戲

symbols
花式

heart
紅心

diamond
方塊

club
梅花

spade
黑桃

Ace
么點

King
國王

Queen
皇后

Jack
傑克

Joker
百搭

standard poker hands
幾手撲克牌

royal flush
同花大順

straight flush
同花順

four of a kind
四條

full house
滿貫

flush
同花

straight
順子

three of a kind
三條

two pairs
二對

one pair
一對

high card
雜牌

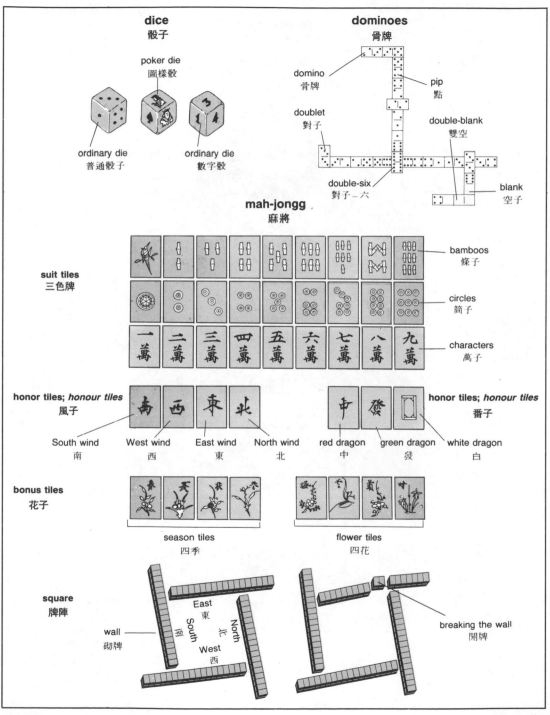

dice
骰子

poker die
圖樣骰

ordinary die
普通骰子

ordinary die
數字骰

dominoes
骨牌

domino
骨牌

pip
點

doublet
對子

double-blank
雙空

double-six
對子－六

blank
空子

mah-jongg
麻將

suit tiles
三色牌

bamboos
條子

circles
筒子

characters
萬子

honor tiles; *honour tiles*
風子

South wind
南

West wind
西

East wind
東

North wind
北

red dragon
中

green dragon
發

white dragon
白

honor tiles; *honour tiles*
番子

bonus tiles
花子

season tiles
四季

flower tiles
四花

square
牌陣

East
東

South
南

North
北

West
西

wall
砌牌

breaking the wall
開牌

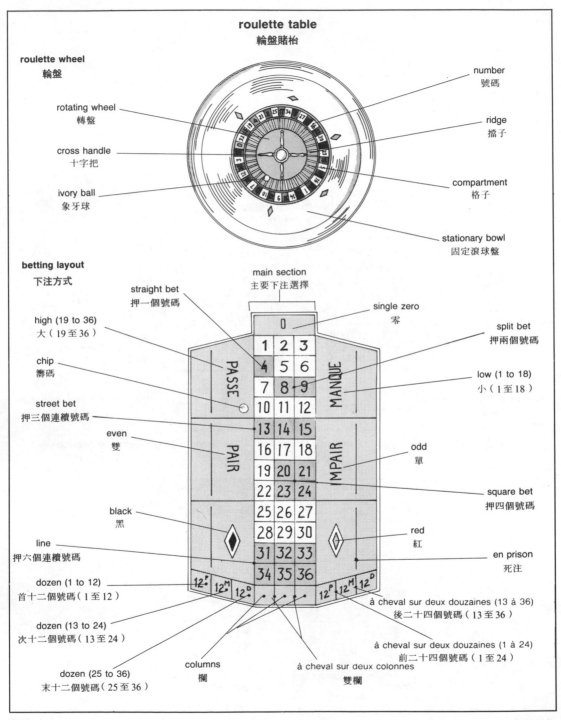

roulette table
輪盤賭枱

roulette wheel
輪盤

rotating wheel
轉盤

cross handle
十字把

ivory ball
象牙球

number
號碼

ridge
擋子

compartment
格子

stationary bowl
固定滾球盤

betting layout
下注方式

main section
主要下注選擇

straight bet
押一個號碼

single zero
零

high (19 to 36)
大（19至36）

split bet
押兩個號碼

chip
籌碼

low (1 to 18)
小（1至18）

street bet
押三個連續號碼

even
雙

odd
單

square bet
押四個號碼

black
黑

red
紅

line
押六個連續號碼

en prison
死注

dozen (1 to 12)
首十二個號碼（1至12）

à cheval sur deux douzaines (13 à 36)
後二十四個號碼（13至36）

dozen (13 to 24)
次十二個號碼（13至24）

à cheval sur deux douzaines (1 à 24)
前二十四個號碼（1至24）

à cheval sur deux colonnes
雙欄

columns
欄

dozen (25 to 36)
末十二個號碼（25至36）

PASSE
MANQUE
PAIR
IMPAIR

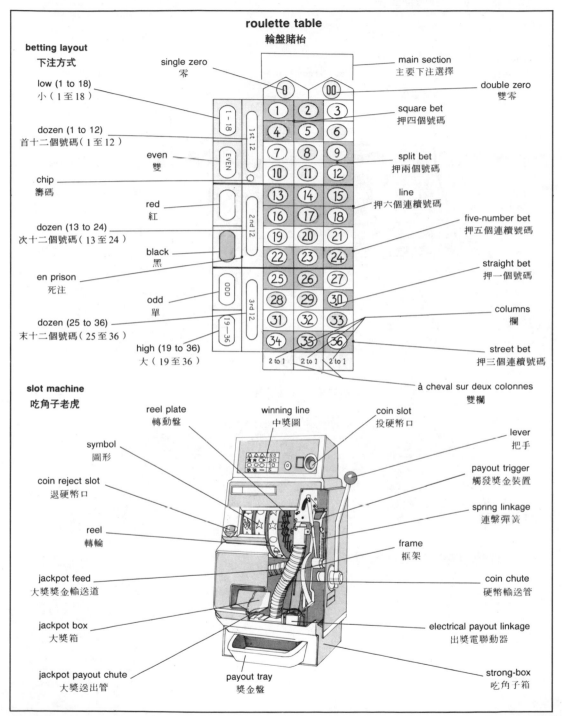

roulette table
輪盤賭枱

betting layout
下注方式

single zero
零

main section
主要下注選擇

double zero
雙零

low (1 to 18)
小（1至18）

square bet
押四個號碼

dozen (1 to 12)
首十二個號碼（1至12）

split bet
押兩個號碼

even
雙

line
押六個連續號碼

chip
籌碼

five-number bet
押五個連續號碼

red
紅

dozen (13 to 24)
次十二個號碼（13至24）

straight bet
押一個號碼

black
黑

en prison
死注

columns
欄

odd
單

dozen (25 to 36)
末十二個號碼（25至36）

street bet
押三個連續號碼

high (19 to 36)
大（19至36）

à cheval sur deux colonnes
雙欄

slot machine
吃角子老虎

reel plate
轉動盤

winning line
中獎圖

coin slot
投硬幣口

symbol
圖形

lever
把手

coin reject slot
退硬幣口

payout trigger
觸發獎金裝置

spring linkage
連繫彈簧

reel
轉輪

frame
框架

jackpot feed
大獎獎金輸送道

coin chute
硬幣輸送管

jackpot box
大獎箱

electrical payout linkage
出獎電聯動器

jackpot payout chute
大獎送出管

payout tray
獎金盤

strong-box
吃角子箱

tents
帳篷

family tents
家庭帳篷

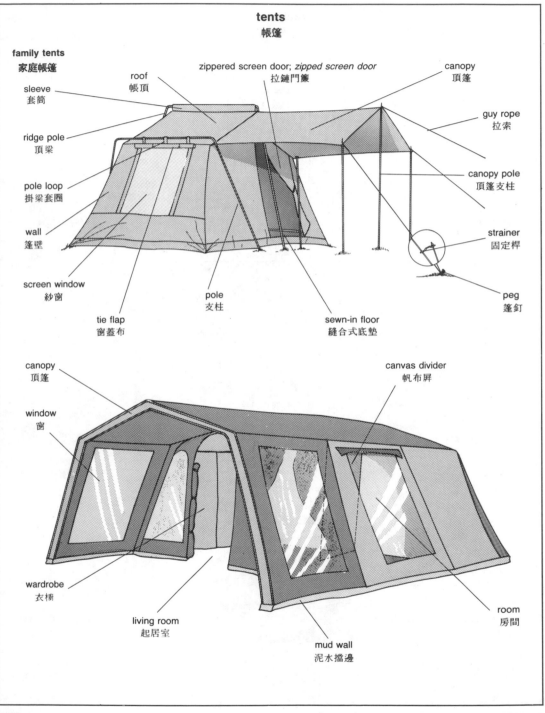

roof
帳頂

zippered screen door; *zipped screen door*
拉鏈門簾

canopy
頂篷

sleeve
套筒

guy rope
拉索

ridge pole
頂梁

pole loop
掛梁套圈

canopy pole
頂篷支柱

wall
篷壁

strainer
固定桿

screen window
紗窗

pole
支柱

peg
篷釘

tie flap
窗蓋布

sewn-in floor
縫合式底墊

canopy
頂篷

canvas divider
帆布屏

window
窗

wardrobe
衣櫥

room
房間

living room
起居室

mud wall
泥水擋邊

tents
帳篷

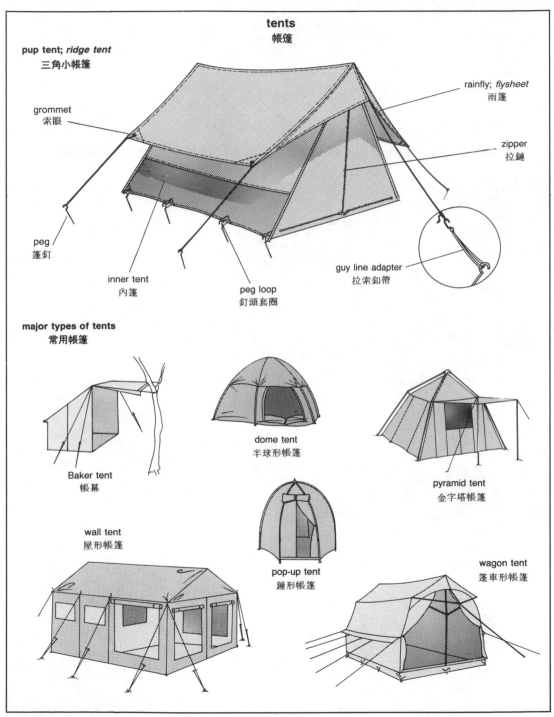

pup tent; *ridge tent*
三角小帳篷

grommet
索眼

rainfly; *flysheet*
雨篷

zipper
拉鏈

peg
篷釘

inner tent
內篷

peg loop
釘頭套圈

guy line adapter
拉索釦帶

major types of tents
常用帳篷

Baker tent
帳幕

dome tent
半球形帳篷

pyramid tent
金字塔帳篷

wall tent
屋形帳篷

pop-up tent
鐘形帳篷

wagon tent
篷車形帳篷

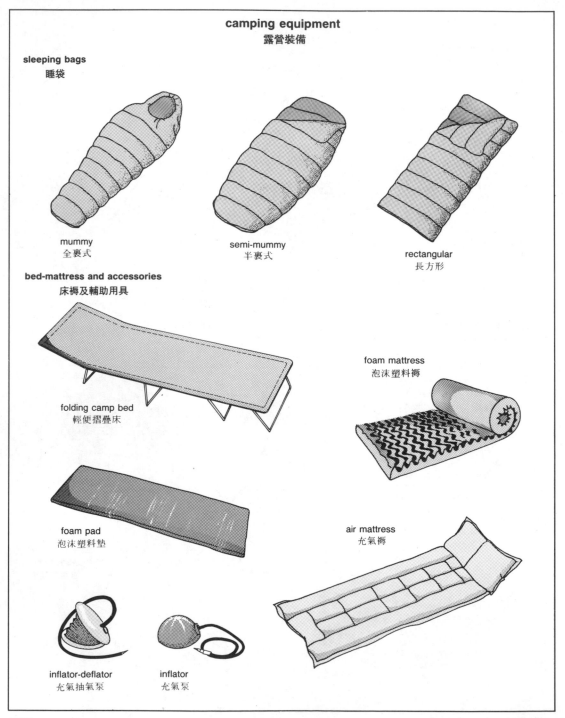

camping equipment
露營裝備

sleeping bags
睡袋

mummy
全裹式

semi-mummy
半裹式

rectangular
長方形

bed-mattress and accessories
床褥及輔助用具

folding camp bed
輕便摺疊床

foam mattress
泡沫塑料褥

foam pad
泡沫塑料墊

air mattress
充氣褥

inflator-deflator
充氣抽氣泵

inflator
充氣泵

camping equipment
露營裝備

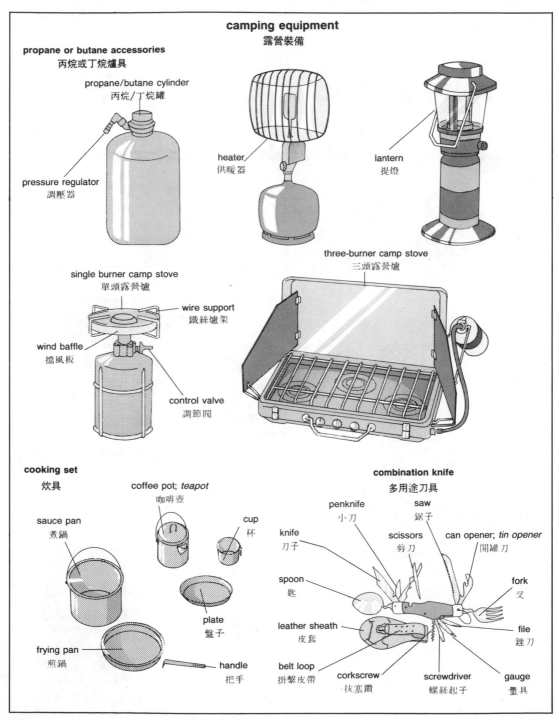

propane or butane accessories
丙烷或丁烷爐具

propane/butane cylinder
丙烷/丁烷罐

pressure regulator
調壓器

heater
供暖器

lantern
提燈

three-burner camp stove
三頭露營爐

single burner camp stove
單頭露營爐

wire support
鐵絲爐架

wind baffle
擋風板

control valve
調節閥

cooking set
炊具

coffee pot; *teapot*
咖啡壺

cup
杯

sauce pan
煮鍋

plate
盤子

frying pan
煎鍋

handle
把手

combination knife
多用途刀具

penknife
小刀

saw
鋸子

knife
刀子

scissors
剪刀

can opener; *tin opener*
開罐刀

spoon
匙

fork
叉

leather sheath
皮套

file
銼刀

belt loop
掛繫皮帶

corkscrew
拔塞鑽

screwdriver
螺絲起子

gauge
量具

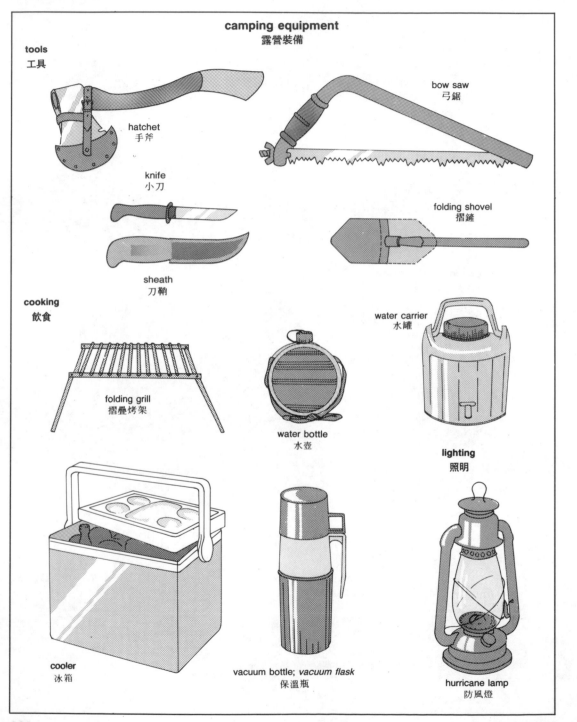

camping equipment
露營裝備

tools
工具

hatchet
手斧

bow saw
弓鋸

knife
小刀

folding shovel
摺鏟

sheath
刀鞘

cooking
飲食

water carrier
水罐

folding grill
摺疊烤架

water bottle
水壺

lighting
照明

cooler
冰箱

vacuum bottle; *vacuum flask*
保溫瓶

hurricane lamp
防風燈

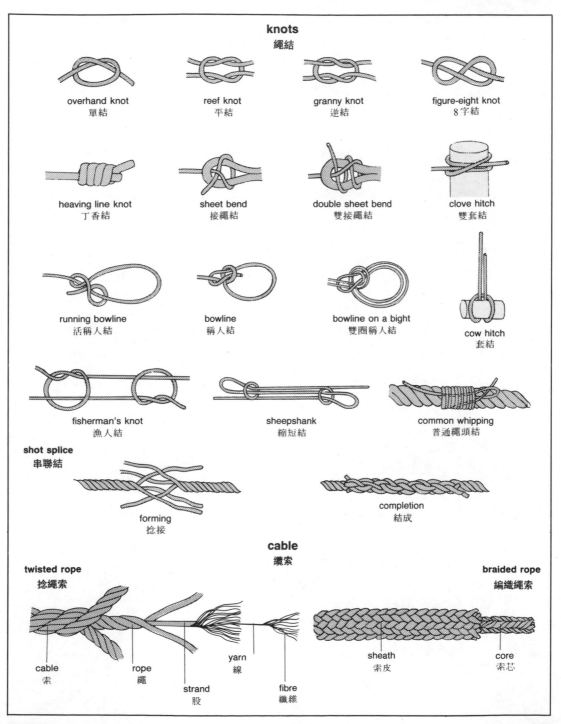

knots
繩結

overhand knot
單結

reef knot
平結

granny knot
逆結

figure-eight knot
8字結

heaving line knot
丁香結

sheet bend
接繩結

double sheet bend
雙接繩結

clove hitch
雙套結

running bowline
活稱人結

bowline
稱人結

bowline on a bight
雙圈稱人結

cow hitch
套結

fisherman's knot
漁人結

sheepshank
縮短結

common whipping
普通繩頭結

shot splice
串聯結

forming
捻接

completion
結成

cable
纜索

twisted rope
捻繩索

braided rope
編織繩索

cable
索

rope
繩

strand
股

yarn
線

fibre
纖維

sheath
索皮

core
索芯

MEASURING DEVICES

量度儀器

measure of time
計時

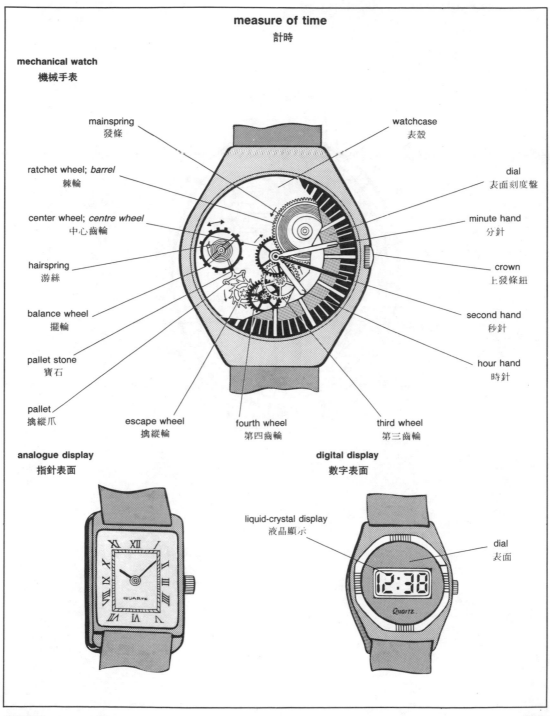

mechanical watch
機械手表

mainspring
發條

watchcase
表殼

ratchet wheel; *barrel*
棘輪

dial
表面刻度盤

center wheel; *centre wheel*
中心齒輪

minute hand
分針

hairspring
游絲

crown
上發條鈕

balance wheel
擺輪

second hand
秒針

pallet stone
寶石

hour hand
時針

pallet
擒縱爪

escape wheel
擒縱輪

fourth wheel
第四齒輪

third wheel
第三齒輪

analogue display
指針表面

digital display
數字表面

liquid-crystal display
液晶顯示

dial
表面

measure of time
計時

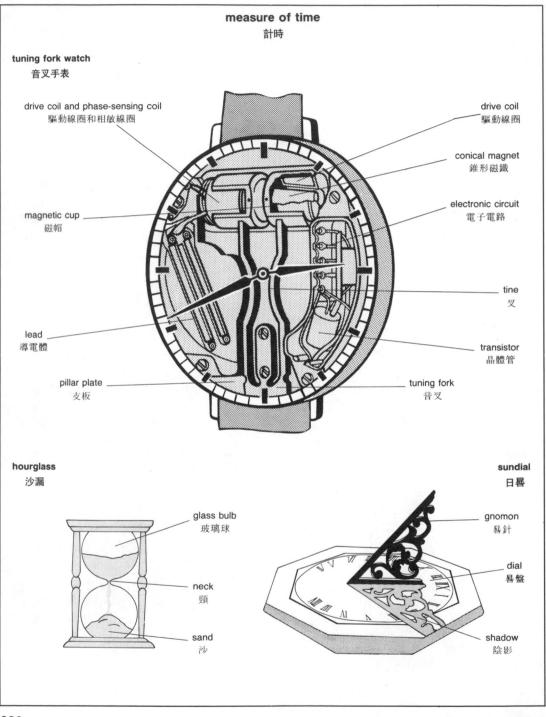

tuning fork watch
音叉手表

drive coil and phase-sensing coil
驅動線圈和相敏線圈

drive coil
驅動線圈

conical magnet
錐形磁鐵

electronic circuit
電子電路

magnetic cup
磁帽

tine
叉

lead
導電體

transistor
晶體管

pillar plate
支板

tuning fork
音叉

hourglass
沙漏

sundial
日晷

glass bulb
玻璃球

gnomon
晷針

dial
晷盤

neck
頸

sand
沙

shadow
陰影

measure of time
計時

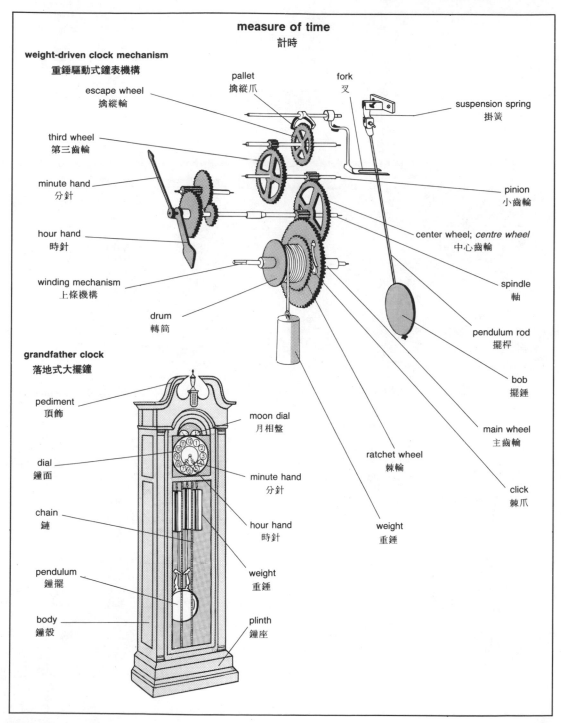

weight-driven clock mechanism
重錘驅動式鐘表機構

escape wheel
擒縱輪

third wheel
第三齒輪

minute hand
分針

hour hand
時針

winding mechanism
上條機構

drum
轉筒

pallet
擒縱爪

fork
叉

suspension spring
掛簧

pinion
小齒輪

center wheel; *centre wheel*
中心齒輪

spindle
軸

pendulum rod
擺桿

bob
擺錘

main wheel
主齒輪

click
棘爪

ratchet wheel
棘輪

weight
重錘

grandfather clock
落地式大擺鐘

pediment
頂飾

moon dial
月相盤

dial
鐘面

minute hand
分針

chain
鏈

hour hand
時針

pendulum
鐘擺

weight
重錘

body
鐘殼

plinth
鐘座

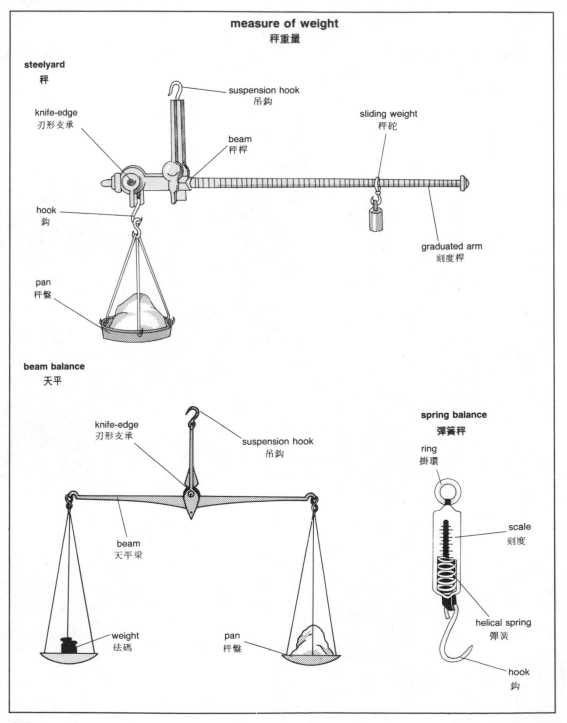

measure of weight
秤重量

steelyard
秤

suspension hook
吊鈎

knife-edge
刃形支承

sliding weight
秤砣

beam
秤桿

hook
鈎

graduated arm
刻度桿

pan
秤盤

beam balance
天平

knife-edge
刃形支承

suspension hook
吊鈎

spring balance
彈簧秤

ring
掛環

scale
刻度

beam
天平梁

helical spring
彈簧

weight
砝碼

pan
秤盤

hook
鈎

measure of weight
秤重量

Roberval's balance
托盤天平

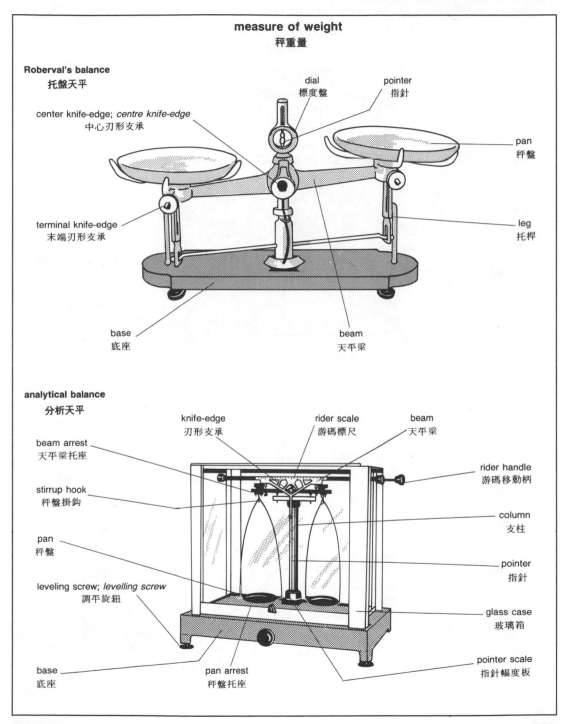

dial
標度盤

pointer
指針

center knife-edge; *centre knife-edge*
中心刃形支承

pan
秤盤

terminal knife-edge
末端刃形支承

leg
托桿

base
底座

beam
天平梁

analytical balance
分析天平

knife-edge
刃形支承

rider scale
游碼標尺

beam
天平梁

beam arrest
天平梁托座

rider handle
游碼移動柄

stirrup hook
秤盤掛鈎

column
支柱

pan
秤盤

pointer
指針

leveling screw; *levelling screw*
調平旋鈕

glass case
玻璃箱

base
底座

pan arrest
秤盤托座

pointer scale
指針幅度板

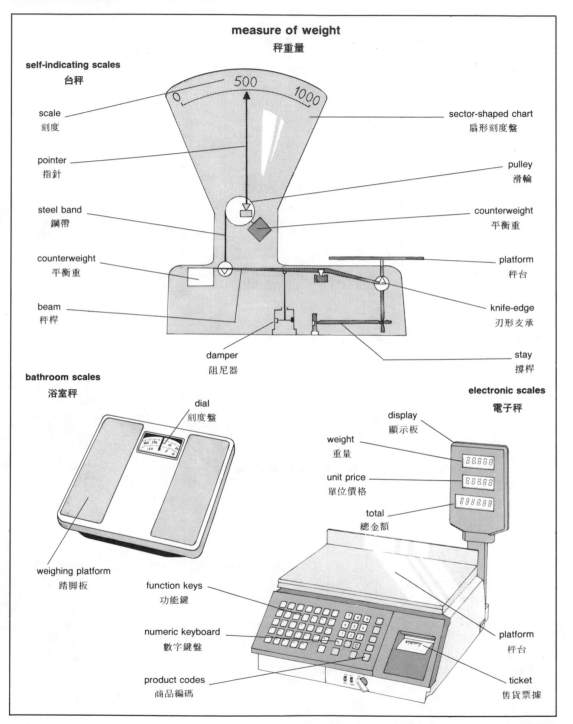

measure of weight
秤重量

self-indicating scales
台秤

scale
刻度

sector-shaped chart
扇形刻度盤

pointer
指針

pulley
滑輪

steel band
鋼帶

counterweight
平衡重

counterweight
平衡重

platform
秤台

beam
秤桿

knife-edge
刃形支承

damper
阻尼器

stay
撐桿

bathroom scales
浴室秤

dial
刻度盤

electronic scales
電子秤

display
顯示板

weight
重量

unit price
單位價格

total
總金額

weighing platform
踏腳板

function keys
功能鍵

numeric keyboard
數字鍵盤

platform
秤台

product codes
商品編碼

ticket
售貨票據

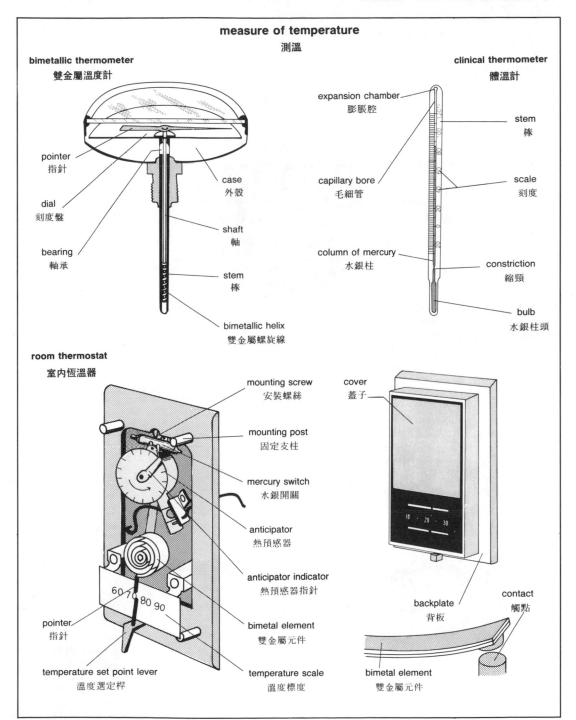

measure of temperature
測溫

bimetallic thermometer
雙金屬溫度計

pointer
指針

dial
刻度盤

bearing
軸承

case
外殼

shaft
軸

stem
棒

bimetallic helix
雙金屬螺旋線

clinical thermometer
體溫計

expansion chamber
膨脹腔

capillary bore
毛細管

column of mercury
水銀柱

stem
棒

scale
刻度

constriction
縮頸

bulb
水銀柱頭

room thermostat
室內恆溫器

mounting screw
安裝螺絲

mounting post
固定支柱

mercury switch
水銀開關

anticipator
熱預感器

anticipator indicator
熱預感器指針

bimetal element
雙金屬元件

temperature scale
溫度標度

pointer
指針

temperature set point lever
溫度選定桿

60 70 80 90

cover
蓋子

10 20 30

backplate
背板

contact
觸點

bimetal element
雙金屬元件

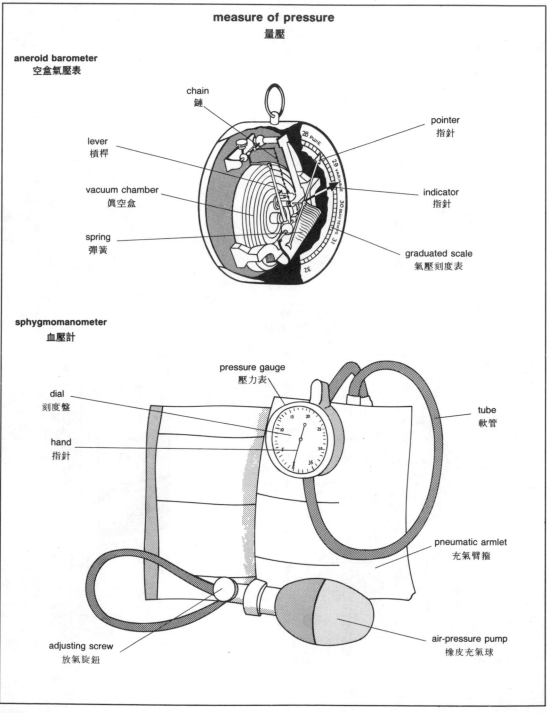

measure of pressure
量壓

aneroid barometer
空盒氣壓表

chain
鏈

pointer
指針

lever
槓桿

vacuum chamber
真空盒

indicator
指針

spring
彈簧

graduated scale
氣壓刻度表

sphygmomanometer
血壓計

pressure gauge
壓力表

dial
刻度盤

tube
軟管

hand
指針

pneumatic armlet
充氣臂箍

adjusting screw
放氣旋鈕

air-pressure pump
橡皮充氣球

measure of length and thickness
量度長度和厚度

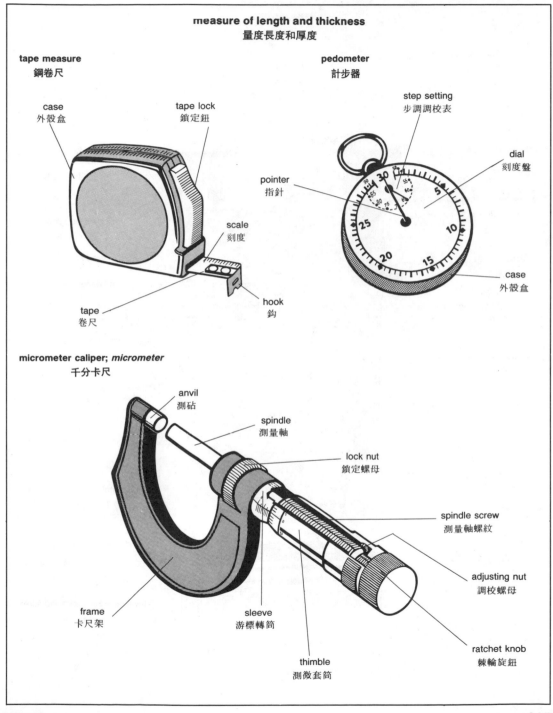

tape measure
鋼卷尺

case
外殼盒

tape lock
鎖定鈕

pointer
指針

step setting
步調調校表

dial
刻度盤

scale
刻度

hook
鉤

tape
卷尺

case
外殼盒

pedometer
計步器

micrometer caliper; *micrometer*
千分卡尺

anvil
測砧

spindle
測量軸

lock nut
鎖定螺母

spindle screw
測量軸螺紋

adjusting nut
調校螺母

frame
卡尺架

sleeve
游標轉筒

thimble
測微套筒

ratchet knob
棘輪旋鈕

theodolite
經緯儀

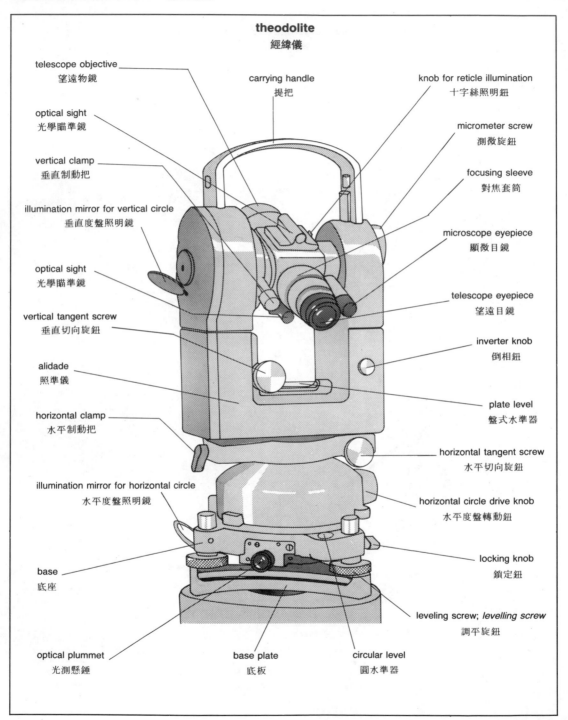

telescope objective
望遠物鏡

optical sight
光學瞄準鏡

vertical clamp
垂直制動把

illumination mirror for vertical circle
垂直度盤照明鏡

optical sight
光學瞄準鏡

vertical tangent screw
垂直切向旋鈕

alidade
照準儀

horizontal clamp
水平制動把

illumination mirror for horizontal circle
水平度盤照明鏡

base
底座

optical plummet
光測懸錘

carrying handle
提把

base plate
底板

circular level
圓水準器

knob for reticle illumination
十字絲照明鈕

micrometer screw
測微旋鈕

focusing sleeve
對焦套筒

microscope eyepiece
顯微目鏡

telescope eyepiece
望遠目鏡

inverter knob
倒相鈕

plate level
盤式水準器

horizontal tangent screw
水平切向旋鈕

horizontal circle drive knob
水平度盤轉動鈕

locking knob
鎖定鈕

leveling screw; *levelling screw*
調平旋鈕

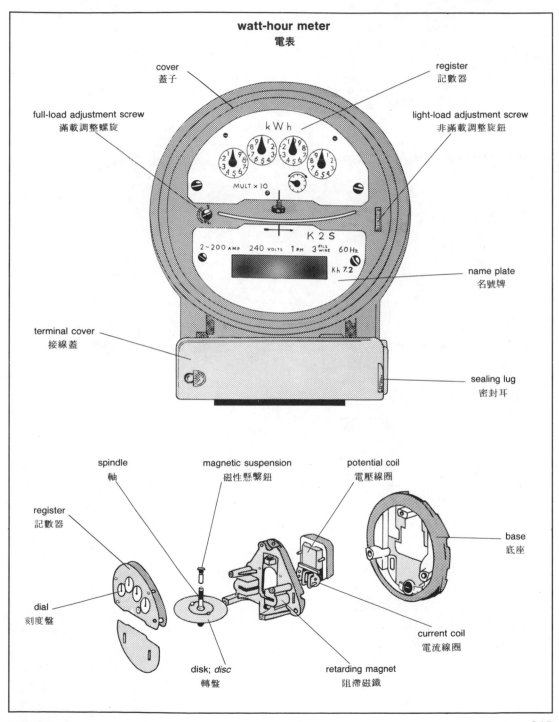

watt-hour meter
電表

cover
蓋子

register
記數器

full-load adjustment screw
滿載調整螺旋

kWh

light-load adjustment screw
非滿載調整旋鈕

MULT × 10

K 2 S

2-200 AMP 240 VOLTS 1 PH 3 WILS WIRE 60 Hz

Kh 7.2

name plate
名號牌

terminal cover
接線蓋

sealing lug
密封耳

spindle
軸

magnetic suspension
磁性懸繫鈕

potential coil
電壓線圈

register
記數器

base
底座

dial
刻度盤

disk; *disc*
轉盤

retarding magnet
阻滯磁鐵

current coil
電流線圈

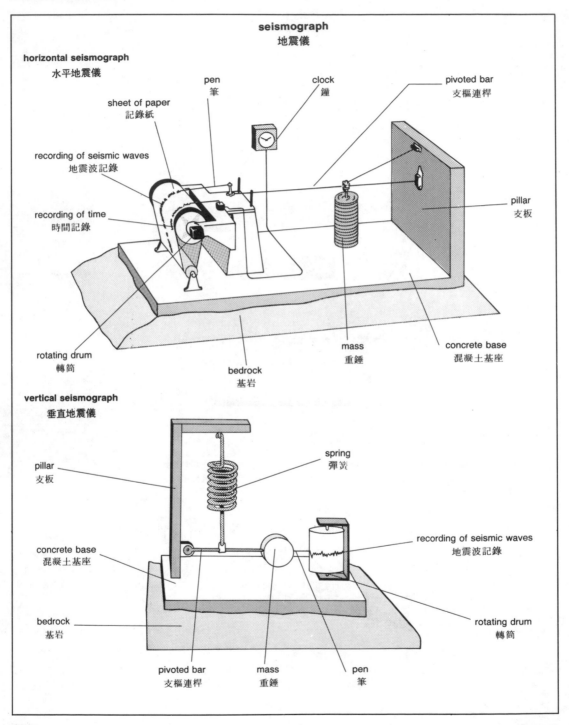

seismograph
地震儀

horizontal seismograph
水平地震儀

pen
筆

clock
鐘

pivoted bar
支樞連桿

sheet of paper
記錄紙

recording of seismic waves
地震波記錄

pillar
支板

recording of time
時間記錄

rotating drum
轉筒

bedrock
基岩

mass
重錘

concrete base
混凝土基座

vertical seismograph
垂直地震儀

spring
彈簧

pillar
支板

recording of seismic waves
地震波記錄

concrete base
混凝土基座

bedrock
基岩

rotating drum
轉筒

pivoted bar
支樞連桿

mass
重錘

pen
筆

OPTICAL INSTRUMENTS

光學儀器

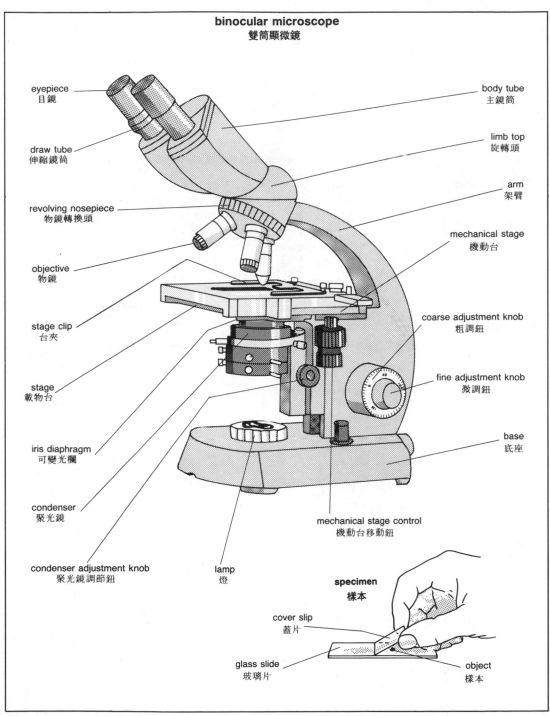

binocular microscope
雙筒顯微鏡

eyepiece
目鏡

draw tube
伸縮鏡筒

revolving nosepiece
物鏡轉換頭

objective
物鏡

stage clip
台夾

stage
載物台

iris diaphragm
可變光欄

condenser
聚光鏡

condenser adjustment knob
聚光鏡調節鈕

lamp
燈

body tube
主鏡筒

limb top
旋轉頭

arm
架臂

mechanical stage
機動台

coarse adjustment knob
粗調鈕

fine adjustment knob
微調鈕

base
底座

mechanical stage control
機動台移動鈕

specimen
樣本

cover slip
蓋片

glass slide
玻璃片

object
樣本

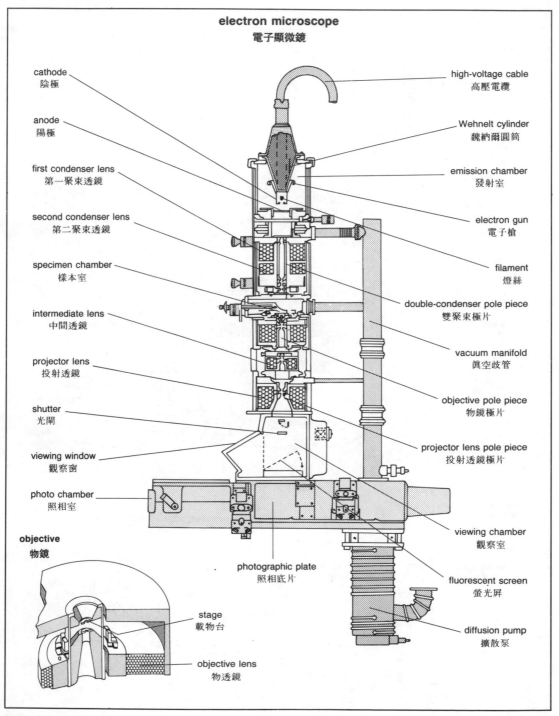

electron microscope
電子顯微鏡

cathode
陰極

anode
陽極

first condenser lens
第一聚束透鏡

second condenser lens
第二聚束透鏡

specimen chamber
樣本室

intermediate lens
中間透鏡

projector lens
投射透鏡

shutter
光閘

viewing window
觀察窗

photo chamber
照相室

objective
物鏡

stage
載物台

objective lens
物透鏡

photographic plate
照相底片

high-voltage cable
高壓電纜

Wehnelt cylinder
魏納爾圓筒

emission chamber
發射室

electron gun
電子槍

filament
燈絲

double-condenser pole piece
雙聚束極片

vacuum manifold
真空歧管

objective pole piece
物鏡極片

projector lens pole piece
投射透鏡極片

viewing chamber
觀察室

fluorescent screen
螢光屏

diffusion pump
擴散泵

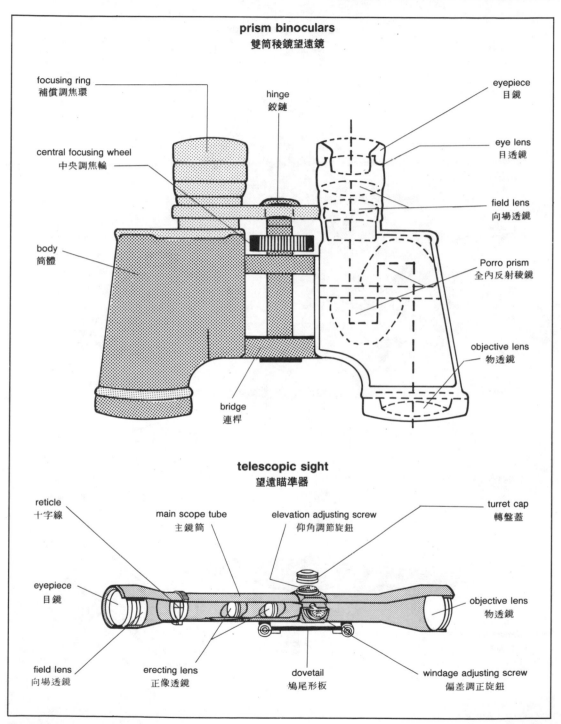

prism binoculars
雙筒稜鏡望遠鏡

focusing ring
補償調焦環

hinge
鉸鏈

eyepiece
目鏡

central focusing wheel
中央調焦輪

eye lens
目透鏡

field lens
向場透鏡

body
筒體

Porro prism
全內反射稜鏡

objective lens
物透鏡

bridge
連桿

telescopic sight
望遠瞄準器

reticle
十字線

main scope tube
主鏡筒

elevation adjusting screw
仰角調節旋鈕

turret cap
轉盤蓋

eyepiece
目鏡

objective lens
物透鏡

field lens
向場透鏡

erecting lens
正像透鏡

dovetail
鳩尾形板

windage adjusting screw
偏差調正旋鈕

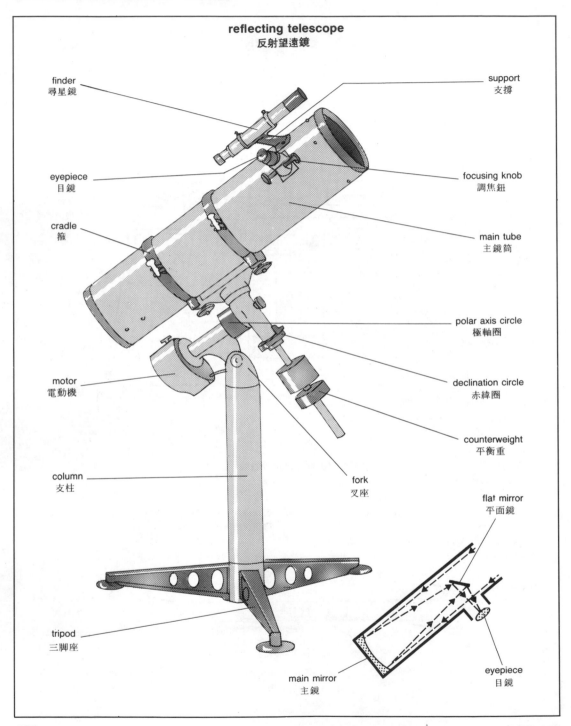

reflecting telescope
反射望遠鏡

finder
尋星鏡

support
支撐

eyepiece
目鏡

focusing knob
調焦鈕

cradle
箍

main tube
主鏡筒

motor
電動機

polar axis circle
極軸圈

declination circle
赤緯圈

counterweight
平衡重

column
支柱

fork
叉座

flat mirror
平面鏡

tripod
三腳座

main mirror
主鏡

eyepiece
目鏡

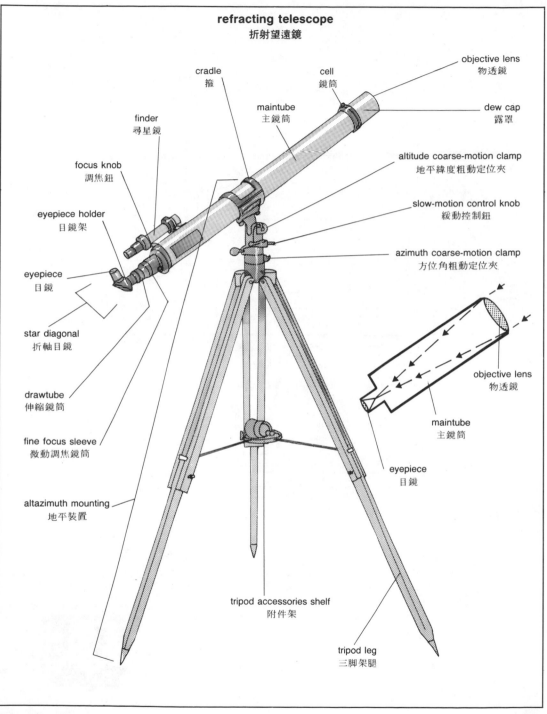

refracting telescope
折射望遠鏡

cradle
箍

cell
鏡筒

objective lens
物透鏡

maintube
主鏡筒

dew cap
露罩

finder
尋星鏡

altitude coarse-motion clamp
地平緯度粗動定位夾

focus knob
調焦鈕

slow-motion control knob
緩動控制鈕

eyepiece holder
目鏡架

azimuth coarse-motion clamp
方位角粗動定位夾

eyepiece
目鏡

star diagonal
折軸目鏡

objective lens
物透鏡

drawtube
伸縮鏡筒

maintube
主鏡筒

fine focus sleeve
微動調焦鏡筒

eyepiece
目鏡

altazimuth mounting
地平裝置

tripod accessories shelf
附件架

tripod leg
三腳架腿

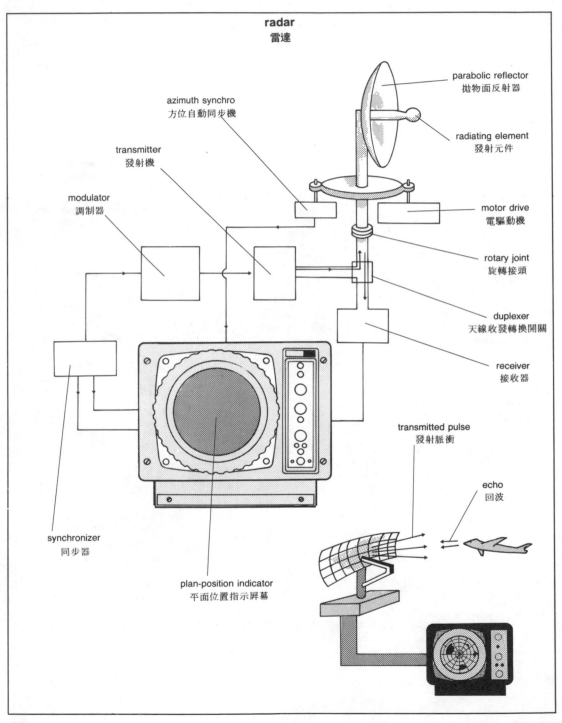

radar
雷達

parabolic reflector
拋物面反射器

azimuth synchro
方位自動同步機

radiating element
發射元件

transmitter
發射機

modulator
調制器

motor drive
電驅動機

rotary joint
旋轉接頭

duplexer
天線收發轉換開關

receiver
接收器

transmitted pulse
發射脈衝

echo
回波

synchronizer
同步器

plan-position indicator
平面位置指示屏幕

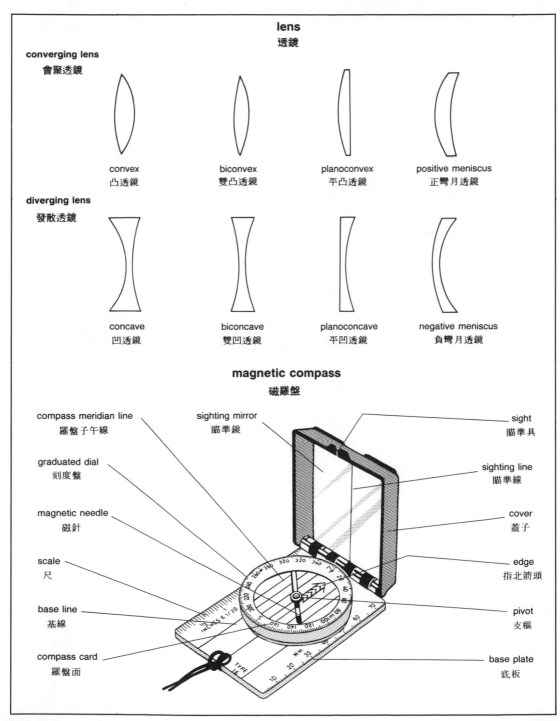

lens
透鏡

converging lens
會聚透鏡

convex
凸透鏡

biconvex
雙凸透鏡

planoconvex
平凸透鏡

positive meniscus
正彎月透鏡

diverging lens
發散透鏡

concave
凹透鏡

biconcave
雙凹透鏡

planoconcave
平凹透鏡

negative meniscus
負彎月透鏡

magnetic compass
磁羅盤

compass meridian line
羅盤子午線

graduated dial
刻度盤

magnetic needle
磁針

scale
尺

base line
基線

compass card
羅盤面

sighting mirror
瞄準鏡

sight
瞄準具

sighting line
瞄準線

cover
蓋子

edge
指北箭頭

pivot
支樞

base plate
底板

HEALTH
醫護復健

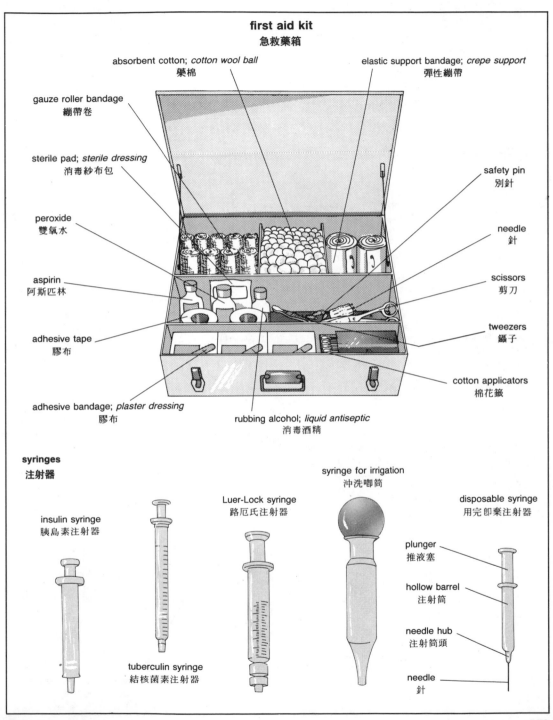

first aid kit
急救藥箱

absorbent cotton; *cotton wool ball*
藥棉

elastic support bandage; *crepe support*
彈性繃帶

gauze roller bandage
繃帶卷

sterile pad; *sterile dressing*
消毒紗布包

safety pin
別針

peroxide
雙氧水

needle
針

aspirin
阿斯匹林

scissors
剪刀

tweezers
鑷子

adhesive tape
膠布

cotton applicators
棉花籤

adhesive bandage; *plaster dressing*
膠布

rubbing alcohol; *liquid antiseptic*
消毒酒精

syringes
注射器

syringe for irrigation
沖洗唧筒

disposable syringe
用完即棄注射器

insulin syringe
胰島素注射器

Luer-Lock syringe
路厄氏注射器

plunger
推液塞

hollow barrel
注射筒

tuberculin syringe
結核菌素注射器

needle hub
注射筒頭

needle
針

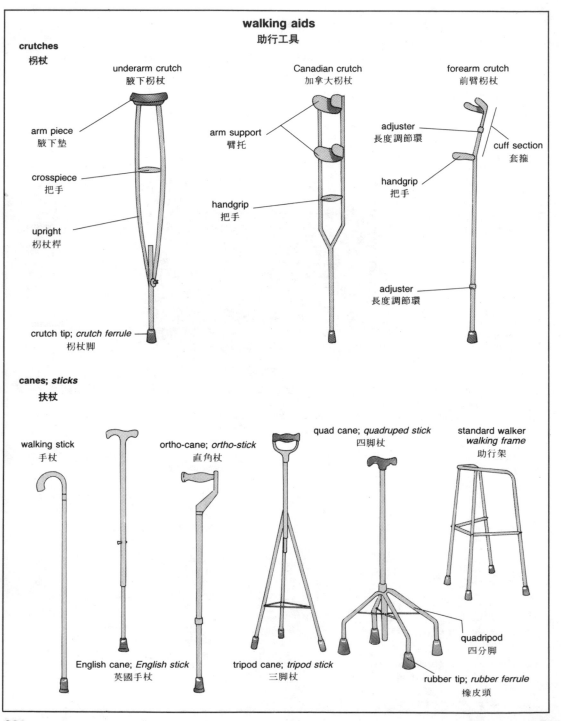

walking aids
助行工具

crutches
枴杖

underarm crutch
腋下枴杖

Canadian crutch
加拿大枴杖

forearm crutch
前臂枴杖

arm piece
腋下墊

arm support
臂托

adjuster
長度調節環

cuff section
套箍

crosspiece
把手

handgrip
把手

handgrip
把手

upright
枴杖桿

adjuster
長度調節環

crutch tip; *crutch ferrule*
枴杖腳

canes; *sticks*
扶杖

walking stick
手杖

ortho-cane; *ortho-stick*
直角杖

quad cane; *quadruped stick*
四腳杖

standard walker
walking frame
助行架

English cane; *English stick*
英國手杖

tripod cane; *tripod stick*
三腳杖

quadripod
四分腳

rubber tip; *rubber ferrule*
橡皮頭

wheelchair
輪椅

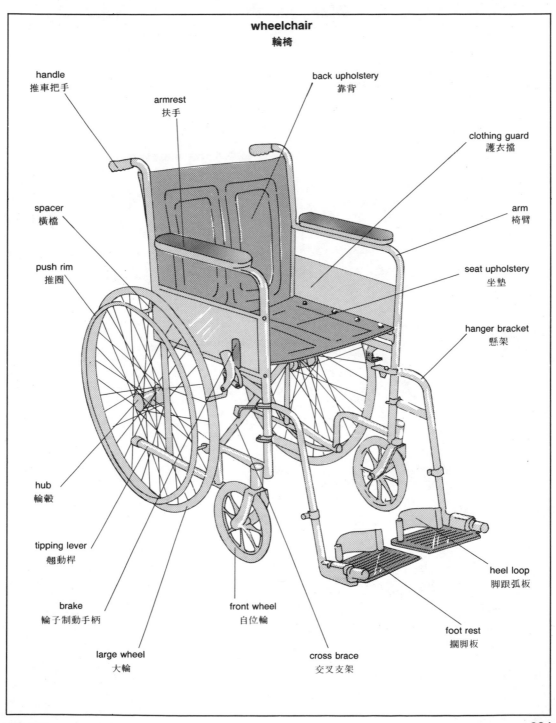

handle
推車把手

armrest
扶手

back upholstery
靠背

clothing guard
護衣擋

spacer
橫檔

arm
椅臂

push rim
推圈

seat upholstery
坐墊

hanger bracket
懸架

hub
輪轂

tipping lever
翹動桿

heel loop
脚跟弧板

brake
輪子制動手柄

front wheel
自位輪

foot rest
攔脚板

large wheel
大輪

cross brace
交叉支架

ENERGY
能源

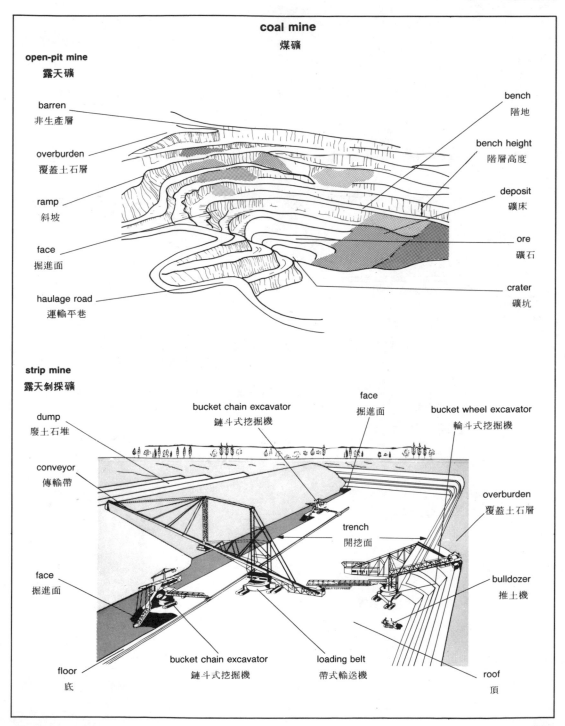

coal mine
煤礦

open-pit mine
露天礦

barren
非生產層

overburden
覆蓋土石層

ramp
斜坡

face
掘進面

haulage road
運輸平巷

bench
階地

bench height
階層高度

deposit
礦床

ore
礦石

crater
礦坑

strip mine
露天剝採礦

dump
廢土石堆

conveyor
傳輸帶

bucket chain excavator
鏈斗式挖掘機

face
掘進面

bucket wheel excavator
輪斗式挖掘機

overburden
覆蓋土石層

trench
開挖面

bulldozer
推土機

face
掘進面

bucket chain excavator
鏈斗式挖掘機

loading belt
帶式輸送機

floor
底

roof
頂

coal mine
煤礦

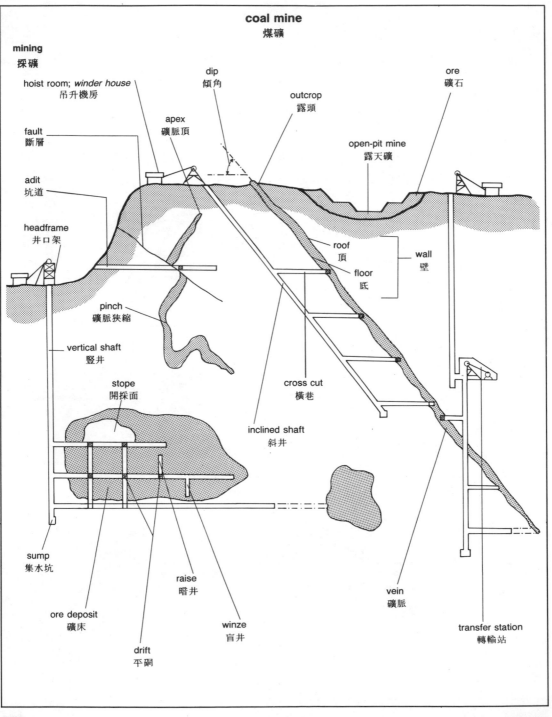

mining
採礦

hoist room; *winder house*
吊升機房

dip
傾角

outcrop
露頭

ore
礦石

apex
礦脈頂

open-pit mine
露天礦

fault
斷層

adit
坑道

headframe
井口架

roof
頂

wall
壁

floor
底

pinch
礦脈狹縮

vertical shaft
豎井

stope
開採面

cross cut
橫巷

inclined shaft
斜井

sump
集水坑

raise
暗井

vein
礦脈

ore deposit
礦床

winze
盲井

drift
平硐

transfer station
轉輪站

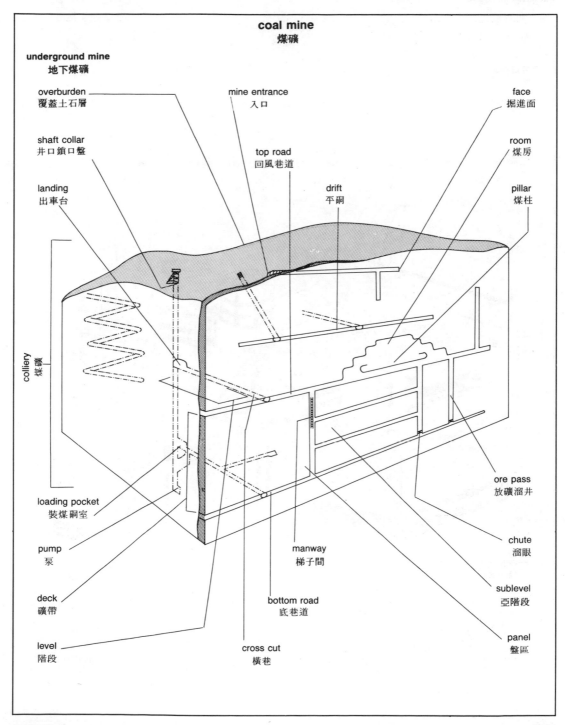

coal mine
煤礦

underground mine
地下煤礦

overburden
覆蓋土石層

shaft collar
井口鎖口盤

landing
出車台

colliery
煤礦

loading pocket
裝煤硐室

pump
泵

deck
礦帶

level
階段

mine entrance
入口

top road
回風巷道

drift
平硐

cross cut
橫巷

bottom road
底巷道

manway
梯子間

face
掘進面

room
煤房

pillar
煤柱

ore pass
放礦溜井

chute
溜眼

sublevel
亞階段

panel
盤區

coal mine
煤礦

pithead
礦井口加工設備

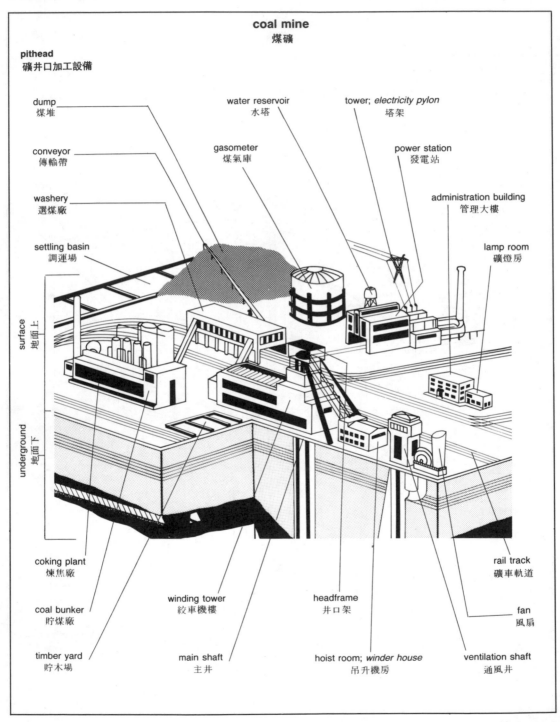

dump
煤堆

conveyor
傳輸帶

washery
選煤廠

settling basin
調運場

water reservoir
水塔

gasometer
煤氣庫

tower; *electricity pylon*
塔架

power station
發電站

administration building
管理大樓

lamp room
礦燈房

surface
地面上

underground
地面下

coking plant
煉焦廠

coal bunker
貯煤廠

timber yard
貯木場

winding tower
絞車機樓

main shaft
主井

headframe
井口架

hoist room; *winder house*
吊升機房

rail track
礦車軌道

fan
風扇

ventilation shaft
通風井

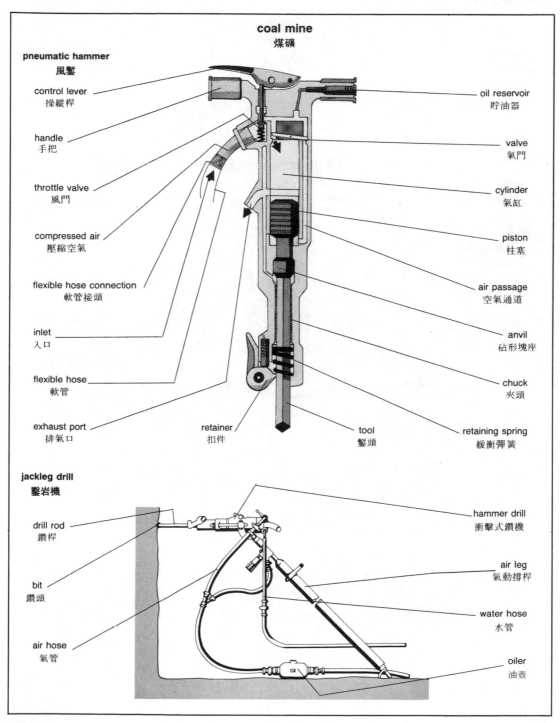

coal mine
煤礦

pneumatic hammer
風鑿

control lever
操縱桿

handle
手把

throttle valve
風門

compressed air
壓縮空氣

flexible hose connection
軟管接頭

inlet
入口

flexible hose
軟管

exhaust port
排氣口

retainer
扣件

tool
鑿頭

oil reservoir
貯油器

valve
氣門

cylinder
氣缸

piston
柱塞

air passage
空氣通道

anvil
砧形塊座

chuck
夾頭

retaining spring
緩衝彈簧

jackleg drill
鑿岩機

drill rod
鑽桿

bit
鑽頭

air hose
氣管

hammer drill
衝擊式鑽機

air leg
氣動撐桿

water hose
水管

oiler
油壺

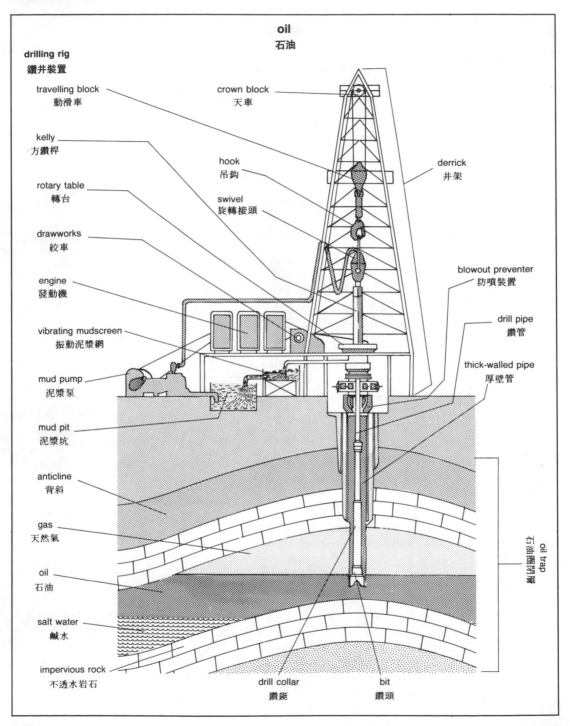

oil
石油

drilling rig
鑽井裝置

travelling block
動滑車

crown block
天車

derrick
井架

kelly
方鑽桿

hook
吊鈎

swivel
旋轉接頭

rotary table
轉台

drawworks
絞車

blowout preventer
防噴裝置

engine
發動機

drill pipe
鑽管

vibrating mudscreen
振動泥漿網

thick-walled pipe
厚壁管

mud pump
泥漿泵

mud pit
泥漿坑

anticline
背斜

gas
天然氣

oil trap
石油圈閉層

oil
石油

salt water
鹹水

impervious rock
不透水岩石

drill collar
鑽鋌

bit
鑽頭

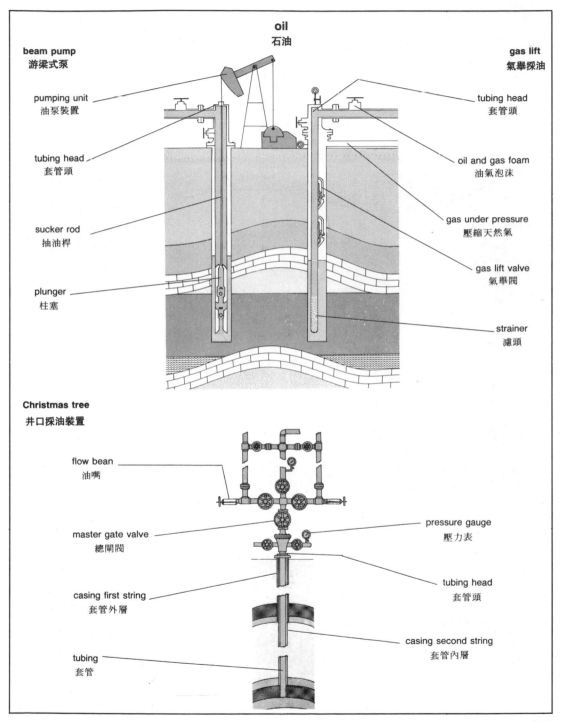

oil
石油

beam pump
游梁式泵

pumping unit
油泵裝置

tubing head
套管頭

sucker rod
抽油桿

plunger
柱塞

gas lift
氣舉探油

tubing head
套管頭

oil and gas foam
油氣泡沫

gas under pressure
壓縮天然氣

gas lift valve
氣舉閥

strainer
濾頭

Christmas tree
井口探油裝置

flow bean
油嘴

master gate valve
總閘閥

casing first string
套管外層

tubing
套管

pressure gauge
壓力表

tubing head
套管頭

casing second string
套管內層

oil
石油

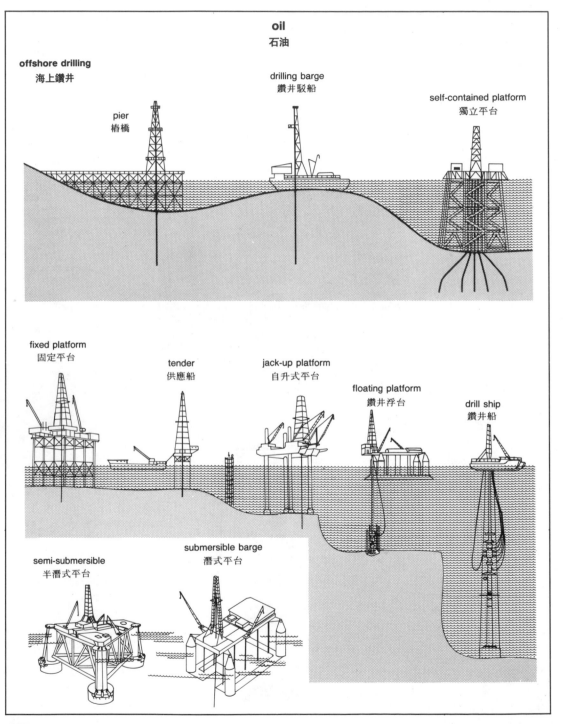

offshore drilling
海上鑽井

pier
樁橋

drilling barge
鑽井駁船

self-contained platform
獨立平台

fixed platform
固定平台

tender
供應船

jack-up platform
自升式平台

floating platform
鑽井浮台

drill ship
鑽井船

semi-submersible
半潛式平台

submersible barge
潛式平台

oil
石油

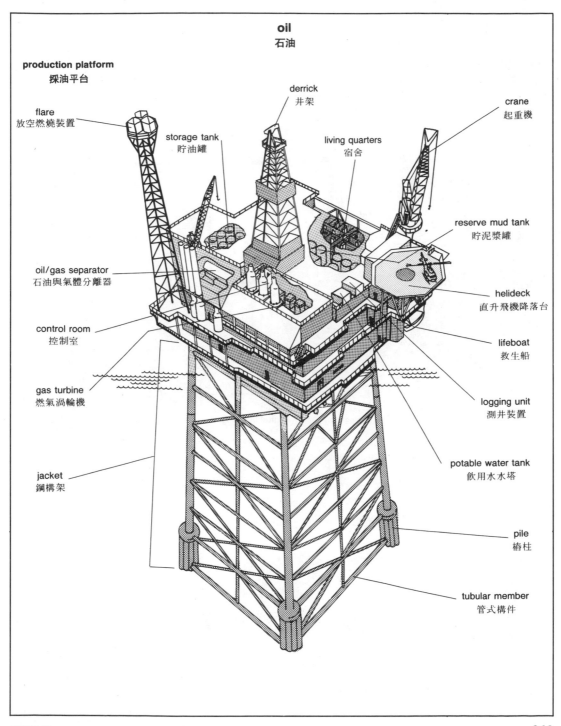

production platform
探油平台

flare
放空燃燒裝置

derrick
井架

crane
起重機

storage tank
貯油罐

living quarters
宿舍

reserve mud tank
貯泥漿罐

oil/gas separator
石油與氣體分離器

helideck
直升飛機降落台

control room
控制室

lifeboat
救生船

gas turbine
燃氣渦輪機

logging unit
測井裝置

potable water tank
飲用水水塔

jacket
鋼構架

pile
椿柱

tubular member
管式構件

oil
石油

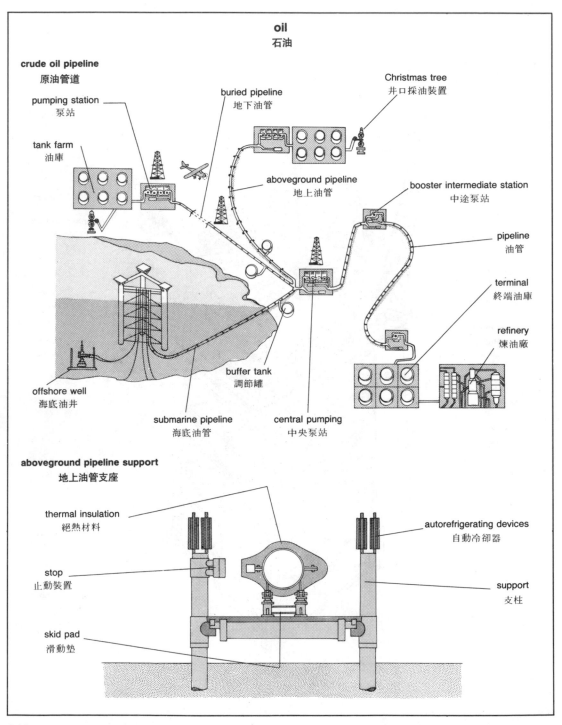

crude oil pipeline
原油管道

pumping station
泵站

tank farm
油庫

buried pipeline
地下油管

Christmas tree
井口採油裝置

aboveground pipeline
地上油管

booster intermediate station
中途泵站

pipeline
油管

terminal
終端油庫

refinery
煉油廠

offshore well
海底油井

buffer tank
調節罐

submarine pipeline
海底油管

central pumping
中央泵站

aboveground pipeline support
地上油管支座

thermal insulation
絕熱材料

autorefrigerating devices
自動冷卻器

stop
止動裝置

support
支柱

skid pad
滑動墊

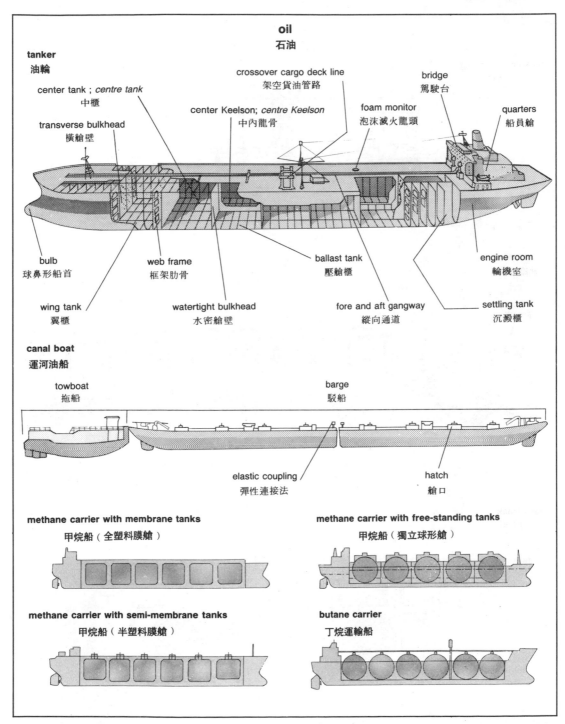

oil
石油

tanker
油輪

center tank ; *centre tank*
中櫃

transverse bulkhead
橫艙壁

crossover cargo deck line
架空貨油管路

center Keelson; *centre Keelson*
中內龍骨

foam monitor
泡沫滅火龍頭

bridge
駕駛台

quarters
船員艙

bulb
球鼻形船首

web frame
框架肋骨

ballast tank
壓艙櫃

engine room
輪機室

wing tank
翼櫃

watertight bulkhead
水密艙壁

fore and aft gangway
縱向通道

settling tank
沉澱櫃

canal boat
運河油船

towboat
拖船

barge
駁船

elastic coupling
彈性連接法

hatch
艙口

methane carrier with membrane tanks
甲烷船（全塑料膜艙）

methane carrier with free-standing tanks
甲烷船（獨立球形艙）

methane carrier with semi-membrane tanks
甲烷船（半塑料膜艙）

butane carrier
丁烷運輸船

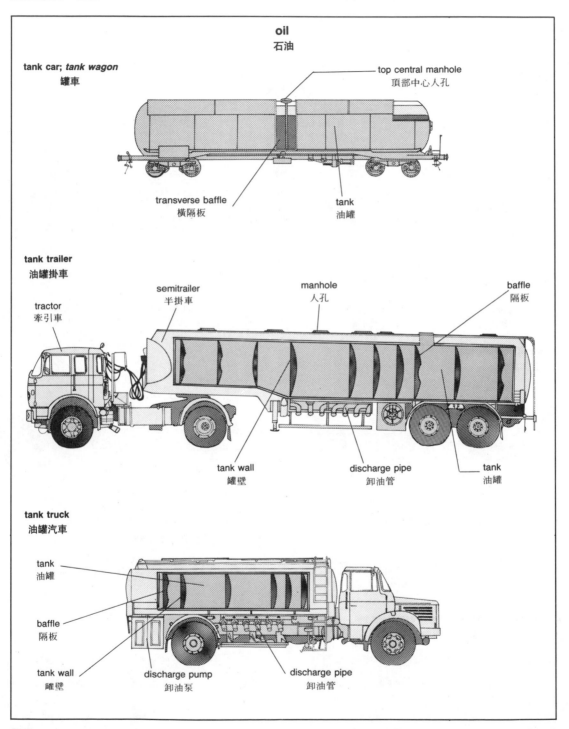

oil
石油

tank car; *tank wagon*
罐車

top central manhole
頂部中心人孔

transverse baffle
橫隔板

tank
油罐

tank trailer
油罐掛車

semitrailer
半掛車

manhole
人孔

baffle
隔板

tractor
牽引車

tank wall
罐壁

discharge pipe
卸油管

tank
油罐

tank truck
油罐汽車

tank
油罐

baffle
隔板

tank wall
罐壁

discharge pump
卸油泵

discharge pipe
卸油管

oil
石油

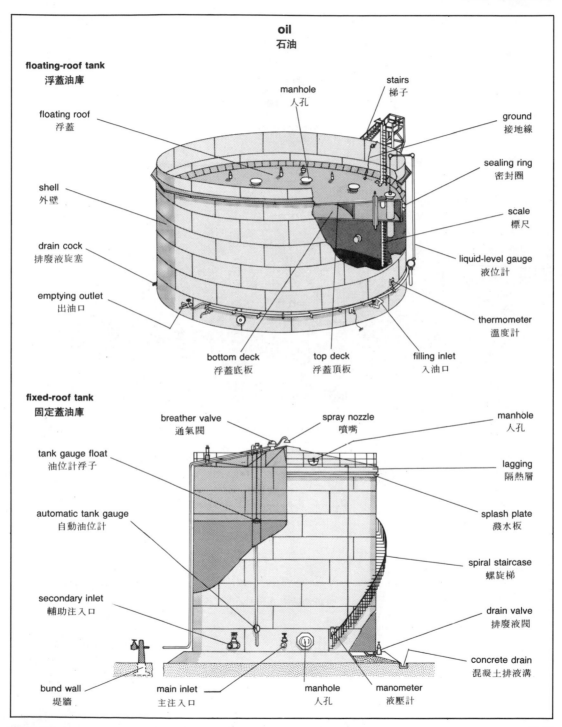

floating-roof tank
浮蓋油庫

floating roof
浮蓋

manhole
人孔

stairs
梯子

ground
接地線

sealing ring
密封圈

shell
外壁

scale
標尺

liquid-level gauge
液位計

drain cock
排廢液旋塞

emptying outlet
出油口

thermometer
溫度計

bottom deck
浮蓋底板

top deck
浮蓋頂板

filling inlet
入油口

fixed-roof tank
固定蓋油庫

breather valve
通氣閥

spray nozzle
噴嘴

manhole
人孔

tank gauge float
油位計浮子

lagging
隔熱層

automatic tank gauge
自動油位計

splash plate
潑水板

spiral staircase
螺旋梯

secondary inlet
輔助注入口

drain valve
排廢液閥

concrete drain
混凝土排液溝

bund wall
堤牆

main inlet
主注入口

manhole
人孔

manometer
液壓計

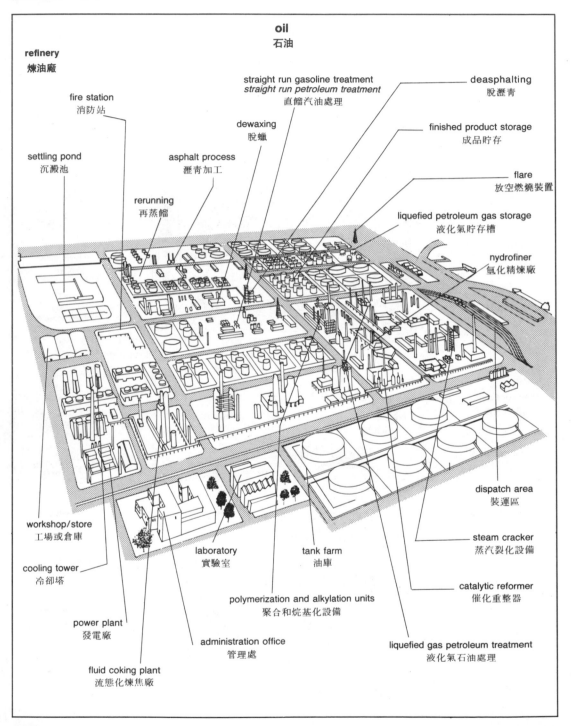

oil
石油

refinery
煉油廠

fire station
消防站

straight run gasoline treatment
straight run petroleum treatment
直餾汽油處理

deasphalting
脫瀝青

dewaxing
脫蠟

finished product storage
成品貯存

settling pond
沉澱池

asphalt process
瀝青加工

flare
放空燃燒裝置

rerunning
再蒸餾

liquefied petroleum gas storage
液化氣貯存槽

hydrofiner
氫化精煉廠

workshop/store
工場或倉庫

cooling tower
冷卻塔

laboratory
實驗室

tank farm
油庫

dispatch area
裝運區

steam cracker
蒸汽裂化設備

power plant
發電廠

polymerization and alkylation units
聚合和烷基化設備

catalytic reformer
催化重整器

fluid coking plant
流態化煉焦廠

administration office
管理處

liquefied gas petroleum treatment
液化氣石油處理

oil
石油

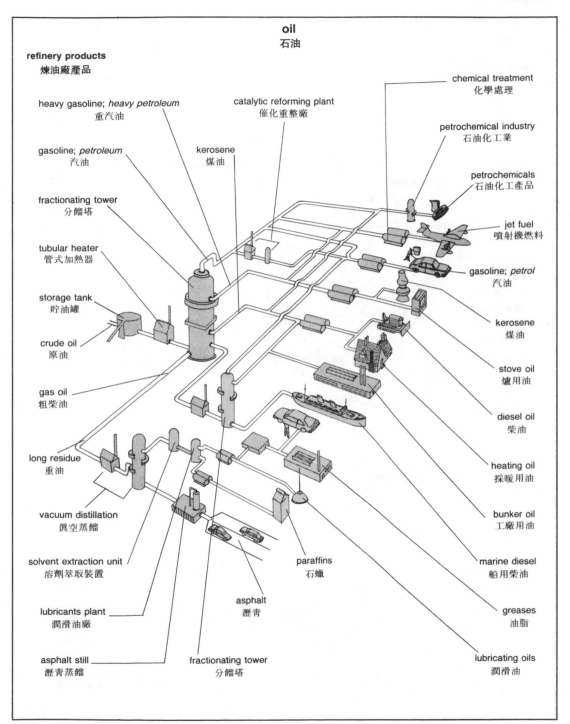

refinery products
煉油廠產品

heavy gasoline; *heavy petroleum*
重汽油

catalytic reforming plant
催化重整廠

chemical treatment
化學處理

petrochemical industry
石油化工業

gasoline; *petroleum*
汽油

kerosene
煤油

petrochemicals
石油化工產品

fractionating tower
分餾塔

jet fuel
噴射機燃料

tubular heater
管式加熱器

gasoline; *petrol*
汽油

storage tank
貯油罐

kerosene
煤油

crude oil
原油

stove oil
爐用油

gas oil
粗柴油

diesel oil
柴油

long residue
重油

heating oil
採暖用油

vacuum distillation
眞空蒸餾

bunker oil
工廠用油

solvent extraction unit
溶劑萃取裝置

paraffins
石蠟

marine diesel
船用柴油

lubricants plant
潤滑油廠

asphalt
瀝青

greases
油脂

asphalt still
瀝青蒸餾

fractionating tower
分餾塔

lubricating oils
潤滑油

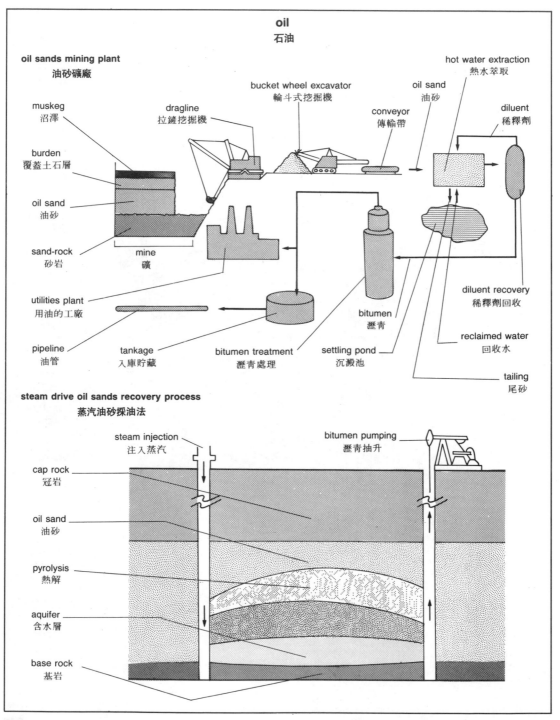

oil
石油

oil sands mining plant
油砂礦廠

hot water extraction
熱水萃取

bucket wheel excavator
輪斗式挖掘機

oil sand
油砂

dragline
拉鏟挖掘機

conveyor
傳輸帶

diluent
稀釋劑

muskeg
沼澤

burden
覆蓋土石層

oil sand
油砂

sand-rock
砂岩

mine
礦

diluent recovery
稀釋劑回收

utilities plant
用油的工廠

bitumen
瀝青

reclaimed water
回收水

pipeline
油管

tankage
入庫貯藏

bitumen treatment
瀝青處理

settling pond
沉澱池

tailing
尾砂

steam drive oil sands recovery process
蒸汽油砂採油法

steam injection
注入蒸汽

bitumen pumping
瀝青抽升

cap rock
冠岩

oil sand
油砂

pyrolysis
熱解

aquifer
含水層

base rock
基岩

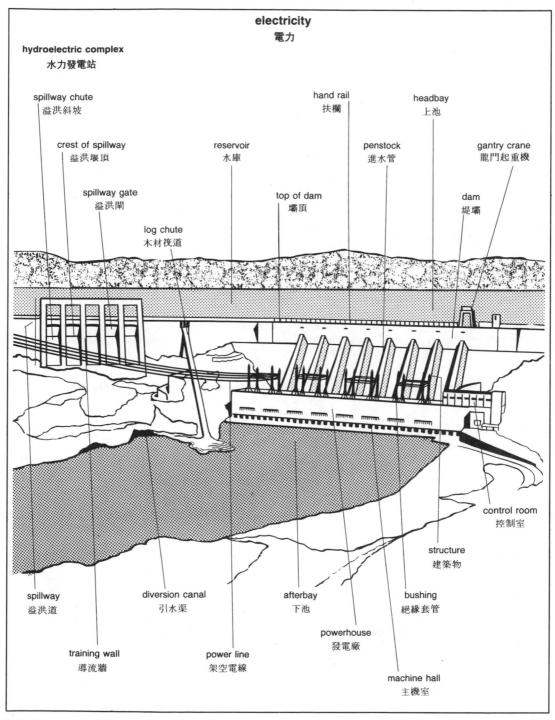

electricity
電力

hydroelectric complex
水力發電站

spillway chute
溢洪斜坡

crest of spillway
溢洪壩頂

spillway gate
溢洪閘

log chute
木材筏道

hand rail
扶欄

headbay
上池

reservoir
水庫

penstock
進水管

gantry crane
龍門起重機

top of dam
壩頂

dam
堤壩

spillway
溢洪道

diversion canal
引水渠

afterbay
下池

bushing
絕緣套管

control room
控制室

structure
建築物

training wall
導流牆

power line
架空電線

powerhouse
發電廠

machine hall
主機室

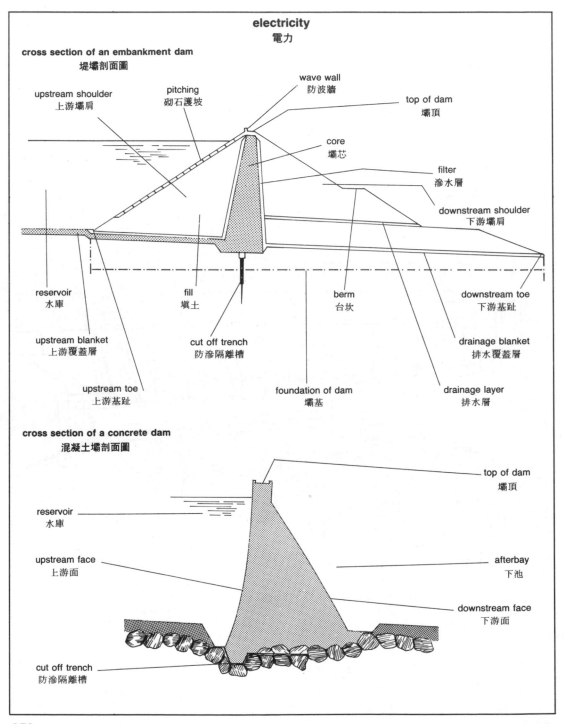

electricity
電力

cross section of an embankment dam
堤壩剖面圖

wave wall
防波牆

upstream shoulder
上游壩肩

pitching
砌石護坡

top of dam
壩頂

core
壩芯

filter
滲水層

downstream shoulder
下游壩肩

reservoir
水庫

fill
填土

berm
台坎

downstream toe
下游基趾

upstream blanket
上游覆蓋層

cut off trench
防滲隔離槽

drainage blanket
排水覆蓋層

upstream toe
上游基趾

foundation of dam
壩基

drainage layer
排水層

cross section of a concrete dam
混凝土壩剖面圖

top of dam
壩頂

reservoir
水庫

upstream face
上游面

afterbay
下池

downstream face
下游面

cut off trench
防滲隔離槽

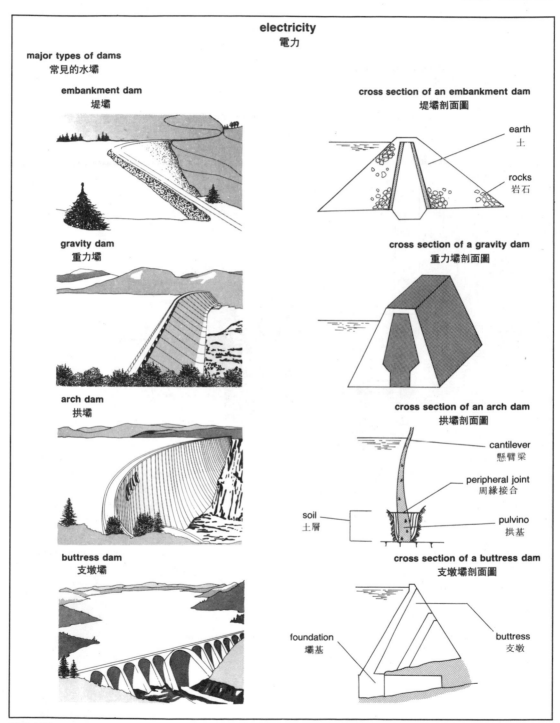

electricity
電力

major types of dams
常見的水壩

embankment dam
堤壩

cross section of an embankment dam
堤壩剖面圖

earth
土

rocks
岩石

gravity dam
重力壩

cross section of a gravity dam
重力壩剖面圖

arch dam
拱壩

cross section of an arch dam
拱壩剖面圖

cantilever
懸臂梁

peripheral joint
周緣接合

soil
土層

pulvino
拱基

buttress dam
支墩壩

cross section of a buttress dam
支墩壩剖面圖

foundation
壩基

buttress
支墩

electricity
電力

steps in production of electricity
水力發電示意圖

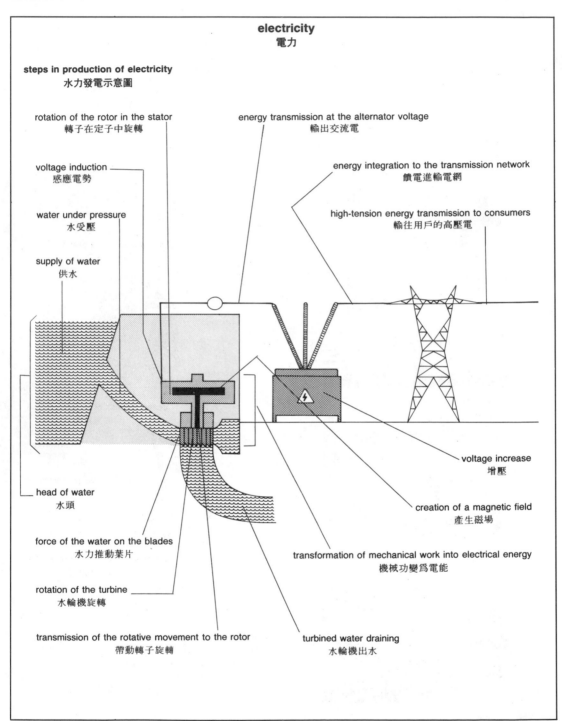

rotation of the rotor in the stator
轉子在定子中旋轉

energy transmission at the alternator voltage
輸出交流電

energy integration to the transmission network
饋電進輸電網

voltage induction
感應電勢

high-tension energy transmission to consumers
輸往用戶的高壓電

water under pressure
水受壓

supply of water
供水

voltage increase
增壓

head of water
水頭

creation of a magnetic field
產生磁場

force of the water on the blades
水力推動葉片

transformation of mechanical work into electrical energy
機械功變為電能

rotation of the turbine
水輪機旋轉

transmission of the rotative movement to the rotor
帶動轉子旋轉

turbined water draining
水輪機出水

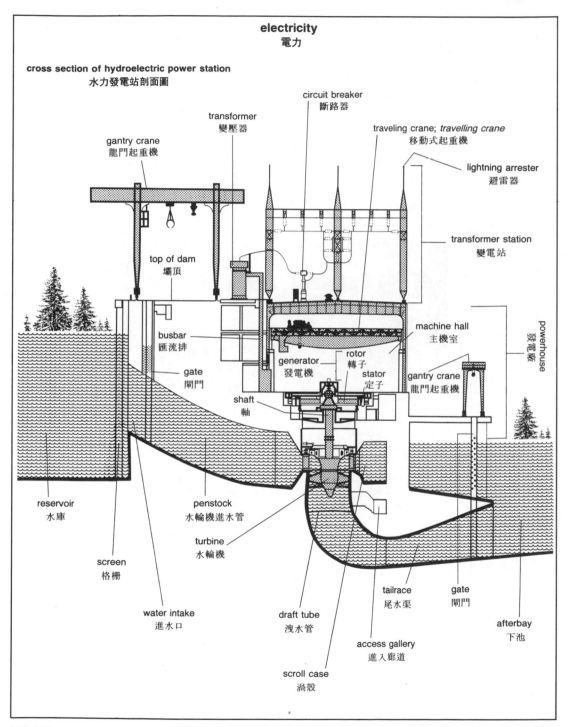

electricity
電力

cross section of hydroelectric power station
水力發電站剖面圖

circuit breaker
斷路器

transformer
變壓器

traveling crane; *travelling crane*
移動式起重機

gantry crane
龍門起重機

lightning arrester
避雷器

transformer station
變電站

top of dam
壩頂

machine hall
主機室

powerhouse
發電廠

busbar
匯流排

generator
發電機

rotor
轉子

gate
閘門

stator
定子

gantry crane
龍門起重機

shaft
軸

reservoir
水庫

penstock
水輪機進水管

turbine
水輪機

tailrace
尾水渠

gate
閘門

screen
格柵

afterbay
下池

water intake
進水口

draft tube
洩水管

access gallery
進入廊道

scroll case
渦殼

electricity
電力

generator
發電機

generator
發電機

salient pole
凸極

collector
集電器

rotor
轉子

stator
定子

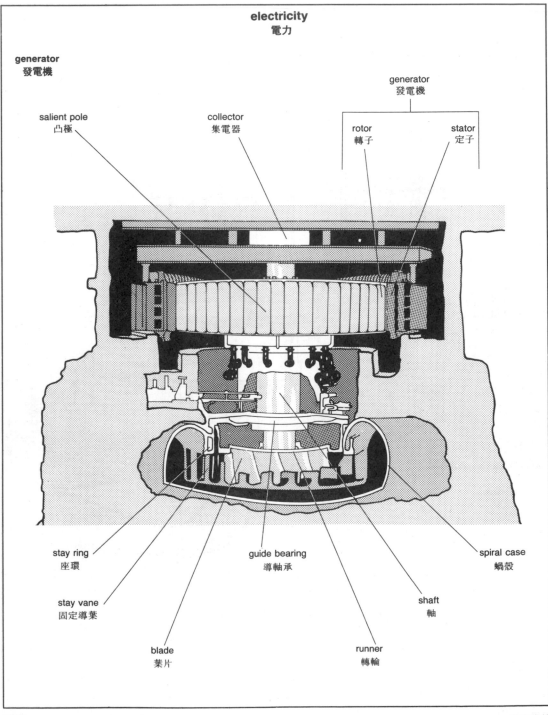

stay ring
座環

guide bearing
導軸承

spiral case
蝸殼

stay vane
固定導葉

shaft
軸

blade
葉片

runner
轉輪

electricity
電力

cross section of hydraulic turbine
水輪機剖面圖

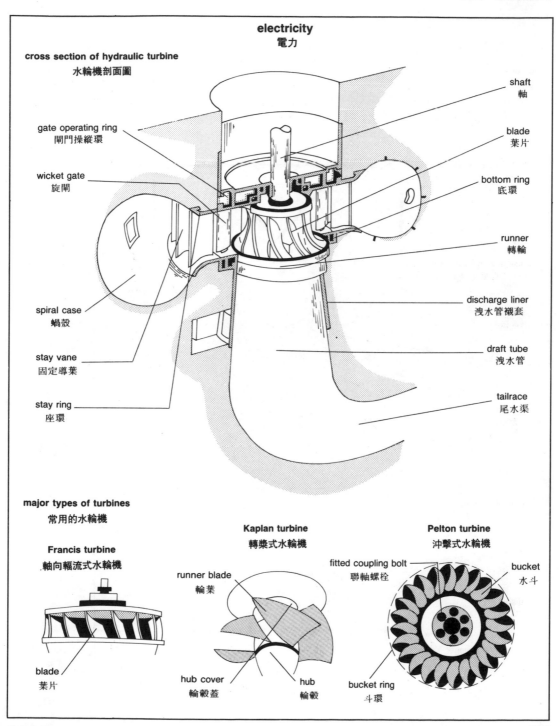

gate operating ring
閘門操縱環

wicket gate
旋閘

spiral case
蝸殼

stay vane
固定導葉

stay ring
座環

shaft
軸

blade
葉片

bottom ring
底環

runner
轉輪

discharge liner
洩水管襯套

draft tube
洩水管

tailrace
尾水渠

major types of turbines
常用的水輪機

Kaplan turbine
轉槳式水輪機

Pelton turbine
沖擊式水輪機

Francis turbine
軸向輻流式水輪機

runner blade
輪葉

fitted coupling bolt
聯軸螺栓

bucket
水斗

blade
葉片

hub cover
輪轂蓋

hub
輪轂

bucket ring
斗環

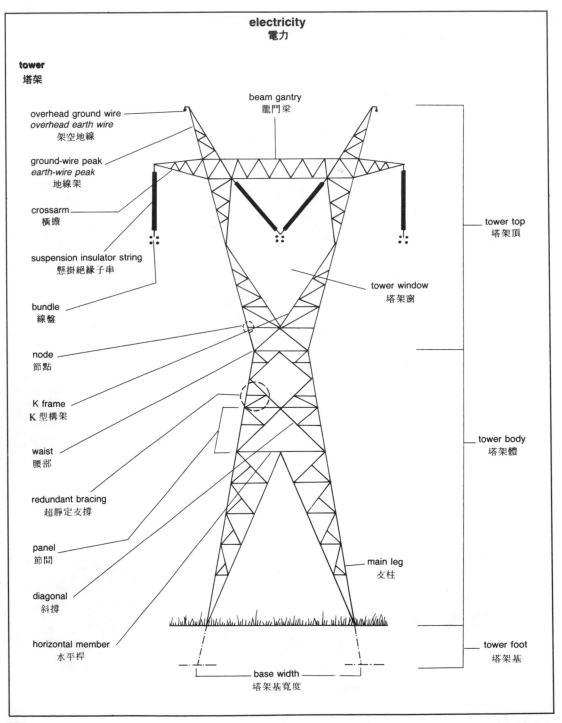

electricity
電力

tower
塔架

beam gantry
龍門梁

overhead ground wire
overhead earth wire
架空地線

ground-wire peak
earth-wire peak
地線架

crossarm
橫擔

suspension insulator string
懸掛絕緣子串

bundle
線盤

node
節點

K frame
K 型構架

waist
腰部

redundant bracing
超靜定支撐

panel
節間

diagonal
斜撐

horizontal member
水平桿

tower window
塔架窗

main leg
支柱

tower top
塔架頂

tower body
塔架體

tower foot
塔架基

base width
塔架基寬度

electricity
電力

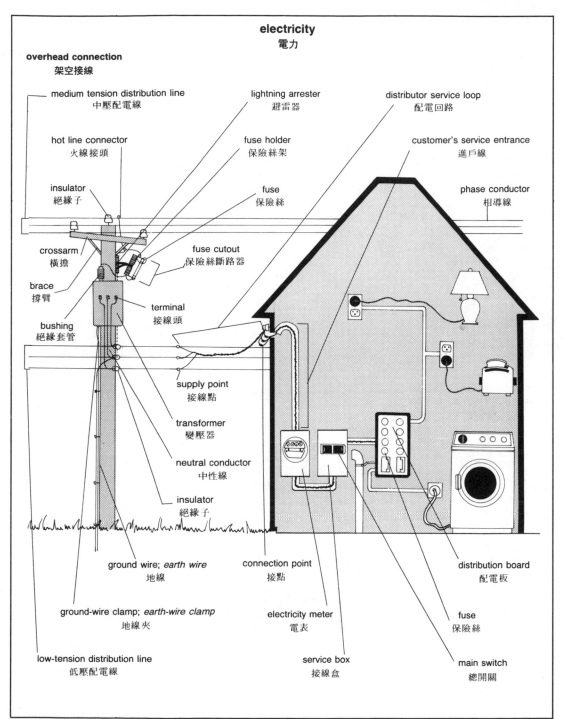

overhead connection
架空接線

medium tension distribution line
中壓配電線

lightning arrester
避雷器

distributor service loop
配電回路

hot line connector
火線接頭

fuse holder
保險絲架

customer's service entrance
進戶線

insulator
絕緣子

fuse
保險絲

phase conductor
相導線

crossarm
橫擔

fuse cutout
保險絲斷路器

brace
撐臂

bushing
絕緣套管

terminal
接線頭

supply point
接線點

transformer
變壓器

neutral conductor
中性線

insulator
絕緣子

ground wire; *earth wire*
地線

connection point
接點

distribution board
配電板

ground-wire clamp; *earth-wire clamp*
地線夾

electricity meter
電表

fuse
保險絲

low-tension distribution line
低壓配電線

service box
接線盒

main switch
總開關

electricity
電力

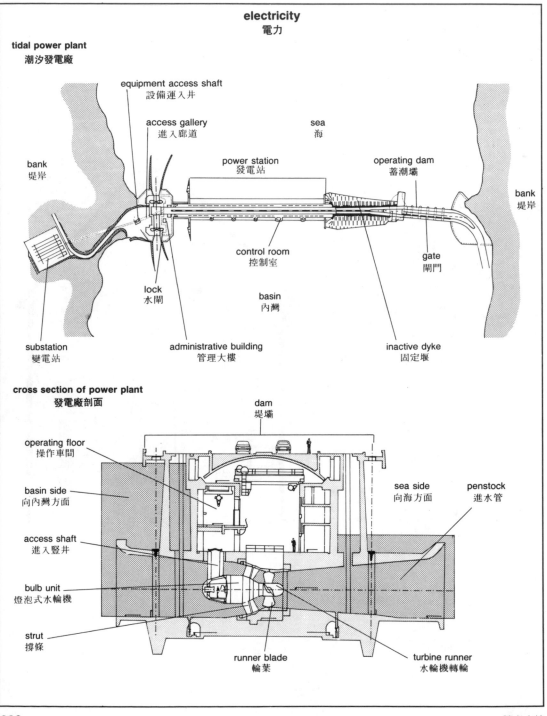

tidal power plant
潮汐發電廠

equipment access shaft
設備運入井

access gallery
進入廊道

sea
海

bank
堤岸

power station
發電站

operating dam
蓄潮壩

bank
堤岸

control room
控制室

gate
閘門

lock
水閘

basin
內灣

substation
變電站

administrative building
管理大樓

inactive dyke
固定堰

cross section of power plant
發電廠剖面

dam
堤壩

operating floor
操作車間

basin side
向內灣方面

sea side
向海方面

penstock
進水管

access shaft
進入豎井

bulb unit
燈泡式水輪機

strut
撐條

runner blade
輪葉

turbine runner
水輪機轉輪

nuclear energy
核能

CANDU nuclear generating station
加拿大重水－鈾核電廠

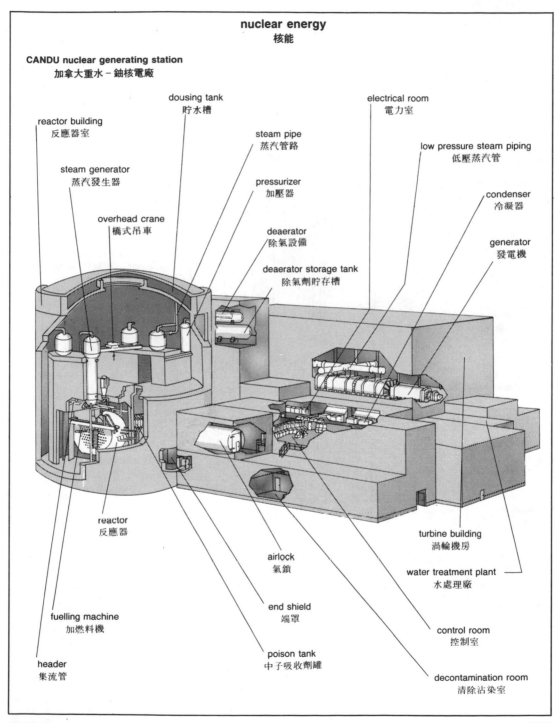

reactor building
反應器室

dousing tank
貯水槽

electrical room
電力室

steam pipe
蒸汽管路

low pressure steam piping
低壓蒸汽管

steam generator
蒸汽發生器

pressurizer
加壓器

condenser
冷凝器

overhead crane
橋式吊車

deaerator
除氣設備

generator
發電機

deaerator storage tank
除氣劑貯存槽

reactor
反應器

turbine building
渦輪機房

airlock
氣鎖

water treatment plant
水處理廠

fuelling machine
加燃料機

end shield
端罩

control room
控制室

header
集流管

poison tank
中子吸收劑罐

decontamination room
清除沾染室

nuclear energy
核能

CANDU reactor
加拿大重水－鈾反應器

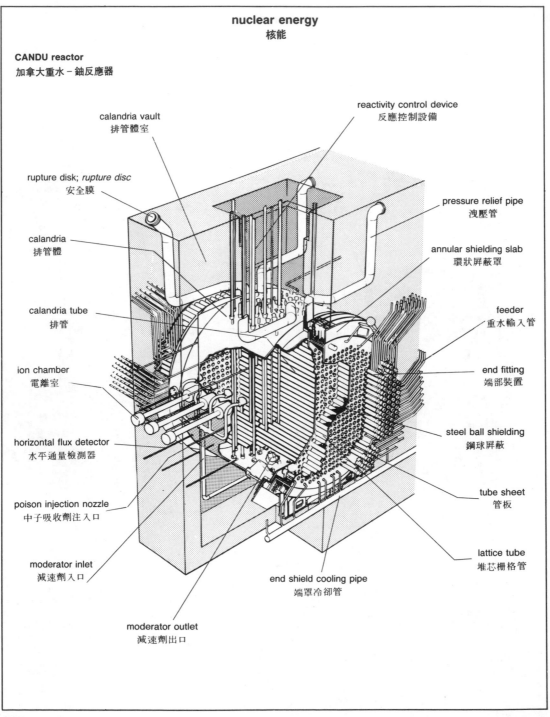

calandria vault
排管體室

reactivity control device
反應控制設備

rupture disk; *rupture disc*
安全膜

pressure relief pipe
洩壓管

calandria
排管體

annular shielding slab
環狀屏蔽罩

calandria tube
排管

feeder
重水輸入管

ion chamber
電離室

end fitting
端部裝置

horizontal flux detector
水平通量檢測器

steel ball shielding
鋼球屏蔽

poison injection nozzle
中子吸收劑注入口

tube sheet
管板

moderator inlet
減速劑入口

lattice tube
堆芯柵格管

end shield cooling pipe
端罩冷卻管

moderator outlet
減速劑出口

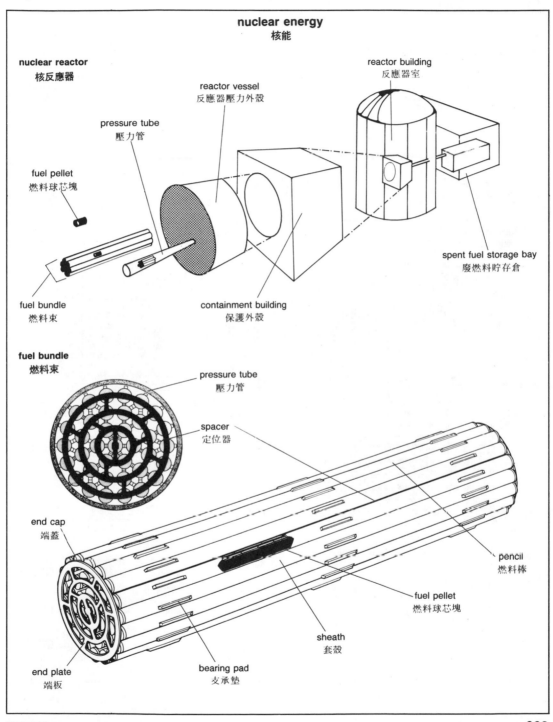

nuclear energy
核能

nuclear reactor
核反應器

fuel pellet
燃料球芯塊

pressure tube
壓力管

reactor vessel
反應器壓力外殼

reactor building
反應器室

fuel bundle
燃料束

containment building
保護外殼

spent fuel storage bay
廢燃料貯存倉

fuel bundle
燃料束

pressure tube
壓力管

spacer
定位器

end cap
端蓋

pencil
燃料棒

fuel pellet
燃料球芯塊

sheath
套殼

end plate
端板

bearing pad
支承墊

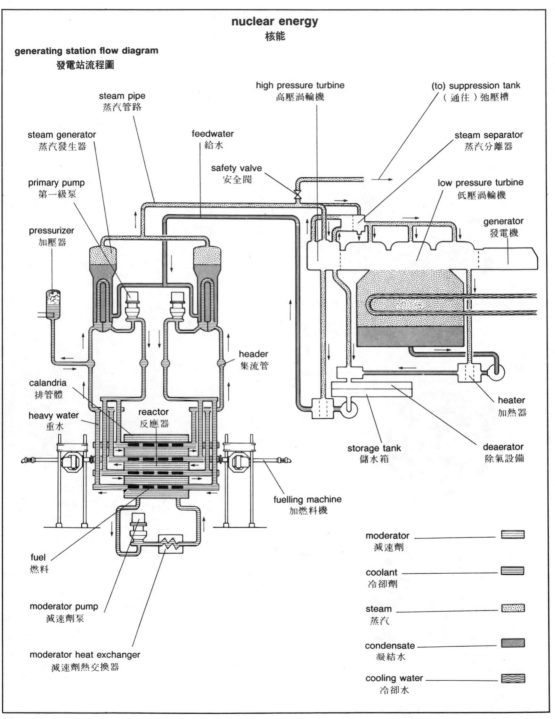

nuclear energy
核能

generating station flow diagram
發電站流程圖

high pressure turbine
高壓渦輪機

(to) suppression tank
（通往）弛壓槽

steam pipe
蒸汽管路

feedwater
給水

steam separator
蒸汽分離器

steam generator
蒸汽發生器

safety valve
安全閥

low pressure turbine
低壓渦輪機

primary pump
第一級泵

generator
發電機

pressurizer
加壓器

header
集流管

calandria
排管體

reactor
反應器

heavy water
重水

heater
加熱器

storage tank
儲水箱

deaerator
除氣設備

fuelling machine
加燃料機

fuel
燃料

moderator
減速劑

coolant
冷却劑

moderator pump
減速劑泵

steam
蒸汽

condensate
凝結水

moderator heat exchanger
減速劑熱交換器

cooling water
冷却水

nuclear energy
核能

fuel handling sequence
燃料裝卸程序

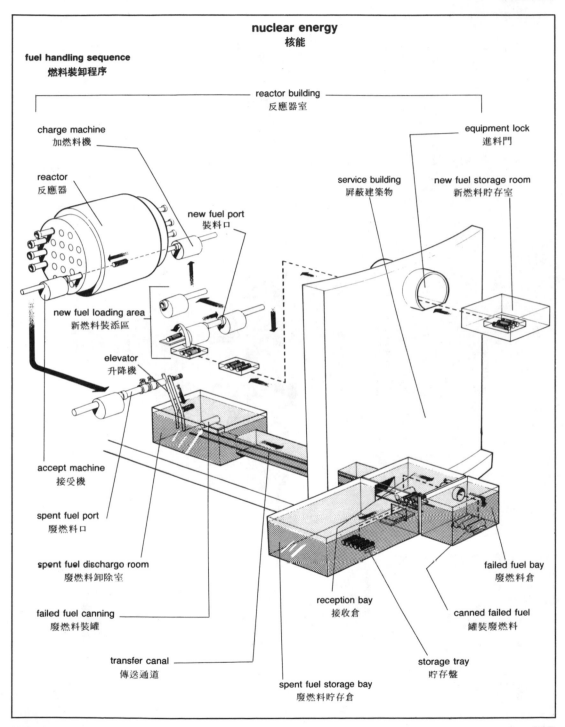

reactor building
反應器室

equipment lock
進料門

charge machine
加燃料機

service building
屏蔽建築物

new fuel storage room
新燃料貯存室

reactor
反應器

new fuel port
裝料口

new fuel loading area
新燃料裝添區

elevator
升降機

accept machine
接受機

spent fuel port
廢燃料口

spent fuel discharge room
廢燃料卸除室

failed fuel canning
廢燃料裝罐

transfer canal
傳送通道

reception bay
接收倉

spent fuel storage bay
廢燃料貯存倉

storage tray
貯存盤

failed fuel bay
廢燃料倉

canned failed fuel
罐裝廢燃料

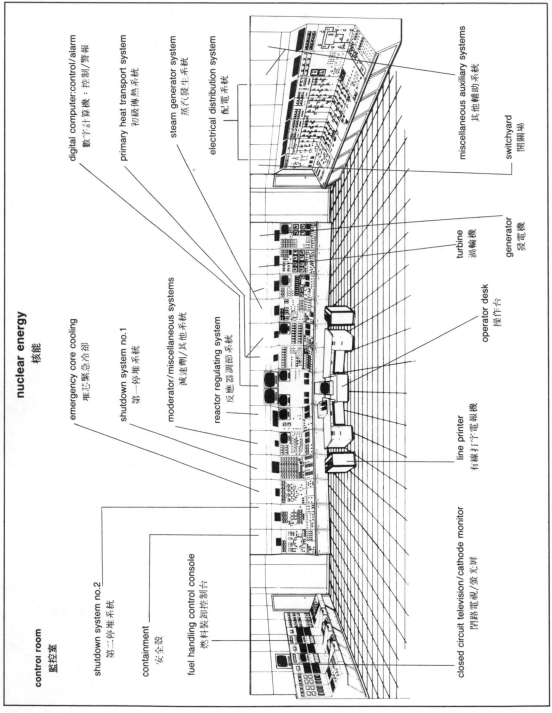

nuclear energy
核能

control room
監控室

digital computer:control/alarm
數字計算機：控制/警報

primary heat transport system
初級傳熱系統

steam generator system
蒸汽發生系統

electrical distribution system
配電系統

miscellaneous auxiliary systems
其他輔助系統

switchyard
開關場

generator
發電機

turbine
渦輪機

operator desk
操作台

line printer
有線打字電報機

closed circuit television/cathode monitor
閉路電視/螢光屏

emergency core cooling
堆芯緊急冷卻

shutdown system no.1
第一停堆系統

moderator/miscellaneous systems
減速劑/其他系統

reactor regulating system
反應器調節系統

shutdown system no.2
第二停堆系統

containment
安全殼

fuel handling control console
燃料裝卸控制台

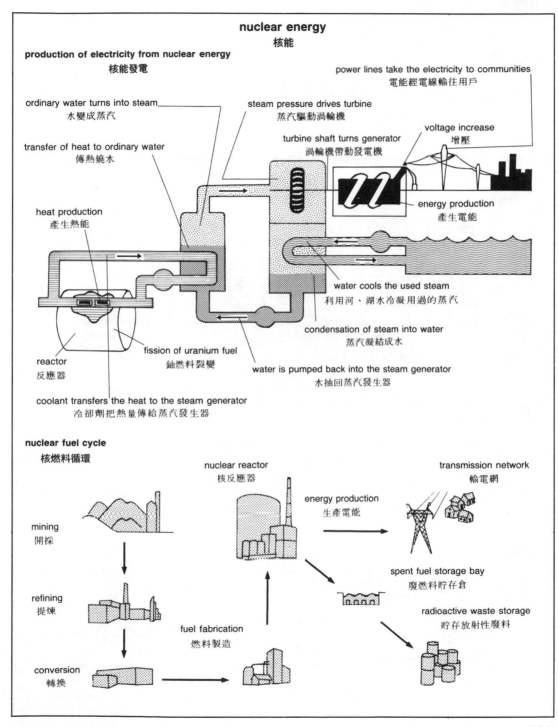

nuclear energy
核能

production of electricity from nuclear energy
核能發電

power lines take the electricity to communities
電能經電線輸往用戶

ordinary water turns into steam
水變成蒸汽

steam pressure drives turbine
蒸汽驅動渦輪機

voltage increase
增壓

transfer of heat to ordinary water
傳熱燒水

turbine shaft turns generator
渦輪機帶動發電機

energy production
產生電能

heat production
產生熱能

water cools the used steam
利用河、湖水冷凝用過的蒸汽

condensation of steam into water
蒸汽凝結成水

reactor
反應器

fission of uranium fuel
鈾燃料裂變

water is pumped back into the steam generator
水抽回蒸汽發生器

coolant transfers the heat to the steam generator
冷卻劑把熱量傳給蒸汽發生器

nuclear fuel cycle
核燃料循環

nuclear reactor
核反應器

transmission network
輸電網

energy production
生產電能

mining
開採

spent fuel storage bay
廢燃料貯存倉

refining
提煉

radioactive waste storage
貯存放射性廢料

fuel fabrication
燃料製造

conversion
轉換

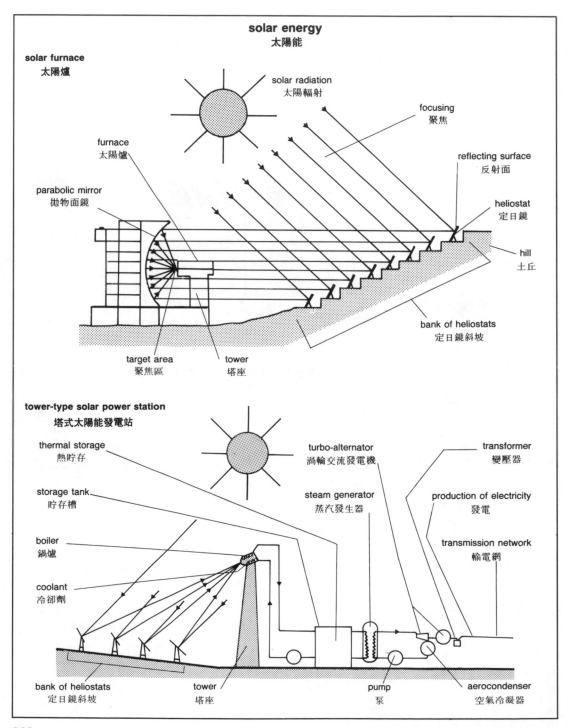

solar energy
太陽能

solar furnace
太陽爐

solar radiation
太陽輻射

focusing
聚焦

furnace
太陽爐

reflecting surface
反射面

parabolic mirror
拋物面鏡

heliostat
定日鏡

hill
土丘

bank of heliostats
定日鏡斜坡

target area
聚焦區

tower
塔座

tower-type solar power station
塔式太陽能發電站

thermal storage
熱貯存

turbo-alternator
渦輪交流發電機

transformer
變壓器

storage tank
貯存槽

steam generator
蒸汽發生器

production of electricity
發電

boiler
鍋爐

transmission network
輸電網

coolant
冷卻劑

bank of heliostats
定日鏡斜坡

tower
塔座

pump
泵

aerocondenser
空氣冷凝器

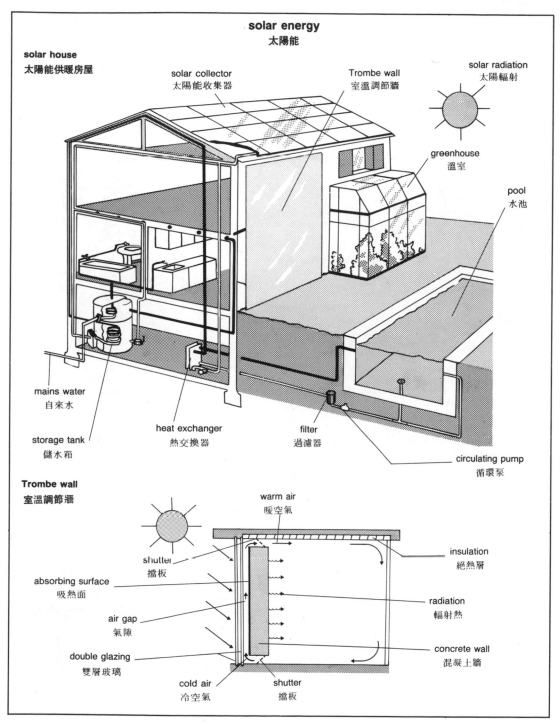

solar energy
太陽能

solar house
太陽能供暖房屋

solar collector
太陽能收集器

Trombe wall
室溫調節牆

solar radiation
太陽輻射

greenhouse
溫室

pool
水池

mains water
自來水

storage tank
儲水箱

heat exchanger
熱交換器

filter
過濾器

circulating pump
循環泵

Trombe wall
室溫調節牆

warm air
暖空氣

shutter
擋板

insulation
絕熱層

absorbing surface
吸熱面

radiation
輻射熱

air gap
氣隙

double glazing
雙層玻璃

concrete wall
混凝土牆

cold air
冷空氣

shutter
擋板

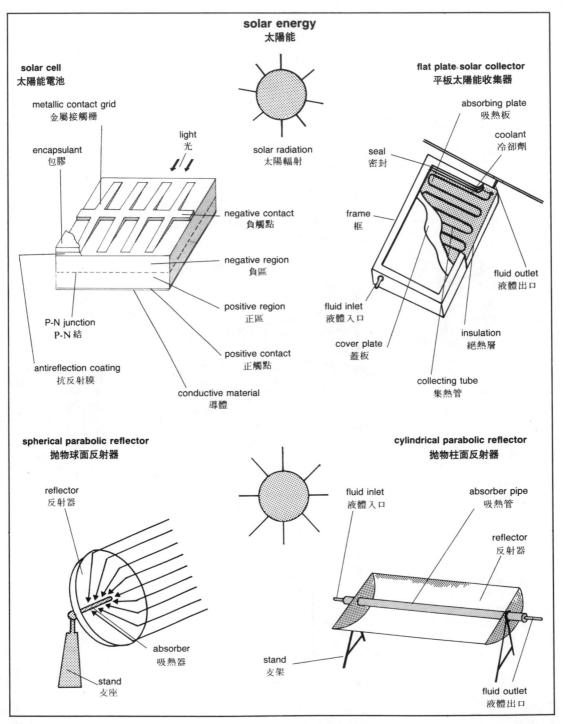

solar energy
太陽能

solar cell
太陽能電池

metallic contact grid
金屬接觸柵

encapsulant
包膠

light
光

negative contact
負觸點

negative region
負區

positive region
正區

P-N junction
P-N 結

positive contact
正觸點

antireflection coating
抗反射膜

conductive material
導體

solar radiation
太陽輻射

flat plate solar collector
平板太陽能收集器

absorbing plate
吸熱板

coolant
冷卻劑

seal
密封

frame
框

fluid outlet
液體出口

fluid inlet
液體入口

cover plate
蓋板

insulation
絕熱層

collecting tube
集熱管

spherical parabolic reflector
拋物球面反射器

reflector
反射器

absorber
吸熱器

stand
支座

cylindrical parabolic reflector
拋物柱面反射器

fluid inlet
液體入口

absorber pipe
吸熱管

reflector
反射器

stand
支架

fluid outlet
液體出口

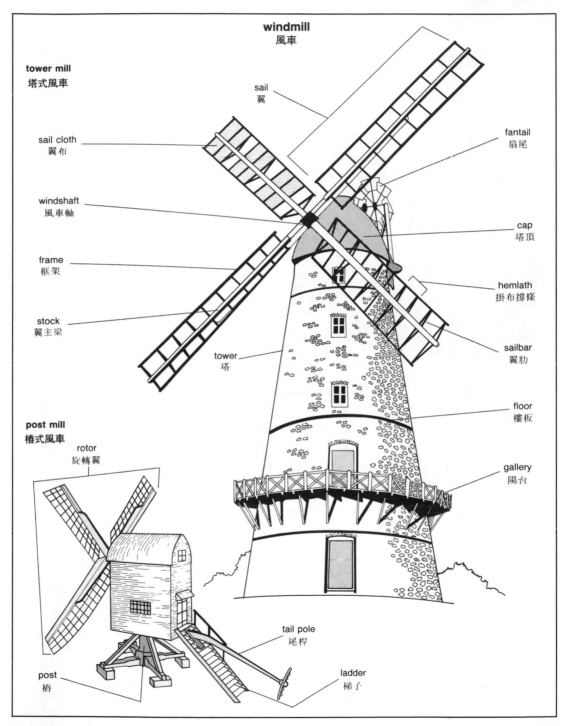

windmill
風車

tower mill
塔式風車

sail
翼

sail cloth
翼布

fantail
扇尾

windshaft
風車軸

cap
塔頂

frame
框架

hemlath
掛布撐條

stock
翼主梁

sailbar
翼肋

tower
塔

floor
樓板

post mill
椿式風車

rotor
旋轉翼

gallery
陽台

tail pole
尾桿

post
椿

ladder
梯子

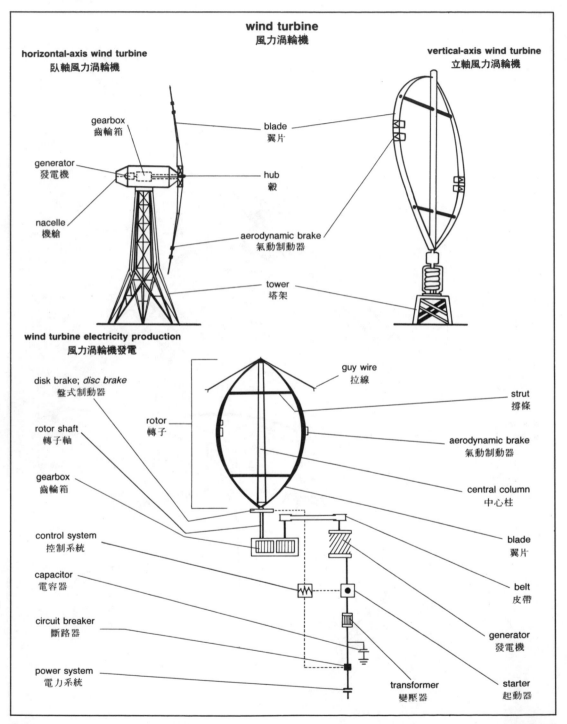

wind turbine
風力渦輪機

horizontal-axis wind turbine
臥軸風力渦輪機

vertical-axis wind turbine
立軸風力渦輪機

gearbox
齒輪箱

generator
發電機

nacelle
機艙

blade
翼片

hub
轂

aerodynamic brake
氣動制動器

tower
塔架

wind turbine electricity production
風力渦輪機發電

disk brake; *disc brake*
盤式制動器

rotor shaft
轉子軸

gearbox
齒輪箱

control system
控制系統

capacitor
電容器

circuit breaker
斷路器

power system
電力系統

guy wire
拉線

rotor
轉子

strut
撐條

aerodynamic brake
氣動制動器

central column
中心柱

blade
翼片

belt
皮帶

generator
發電機

starter
起動器

transformer
變壓器

HEAVY MACHINERY

重型機械

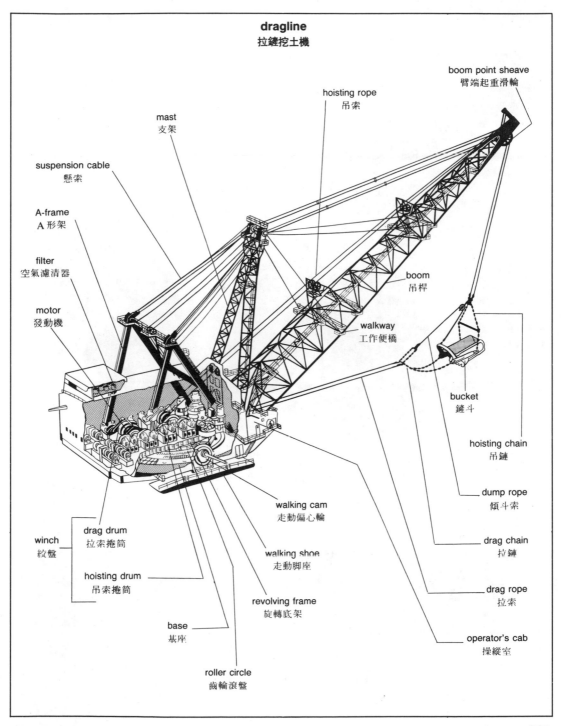

dragline
拉鏈挖土機

boom point sheave
臂端起重滑輪

hoisting rope
吊索

mast
支架

suspension cable
懸索

A-frame
A 形架

filter
空氣濾清器

motor
發動機

boom
吊桿

walkway
工作便橋

bucket
鏟斗

hoisting chain
吊鏈

dump rope
傾斗索

drag chain
拉鏈

drag rope
拉索

operator's cab
操縱室

walking cam
走動偏心輪

walking shoe
走動腳座

revolving frame
旋轉底架

drag drum
拉索捲筒

hoisting drum
吊索捲筒

winch
絞盤

base
基座

roller circle
齒輪滾盤

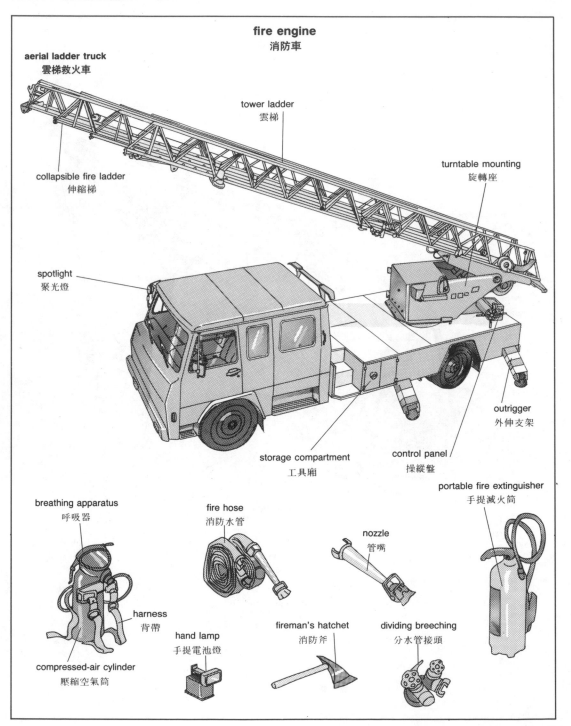

fire engine
消防車

aerial ladder truck
雲梯救火車

tower ladder
雲梯

turntable mounting
旋轉座

collapsible fire ladder
伸縮梯

spotlight
聚光燈

outrigger
外伸支架

storage compartment
工具廂

control panel
操縱盤

portable fire extinguisher
手提滅火筒

breathing apparatus
呼吸器

fire hose
消防水管

nozzle
管嘴

harness
背帶

hand lamp
手提電池燈

fireman's hatchet
消防斧

dividing breeching
分水管接頭

compressed-air cylinder
壓縮空氣筒

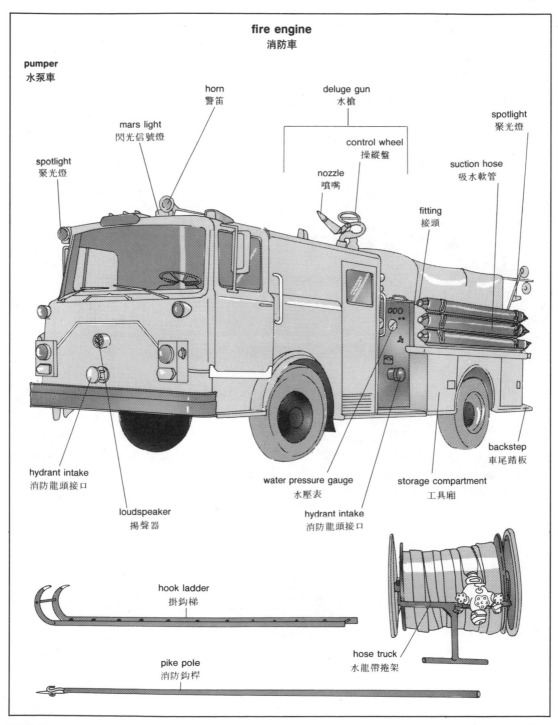

fire engine
消防車

pumper
水泵車

spotlight
聚光燈

mars light
閃光信號燈

horn
警笛

deluge gun
水槍

control wheel
操縱盤

nozzle
噴嘴

spotlight
聚光燈

suction hose
吸水軟管

fitting
接頭

spotlight
聚光燈

backstep
車尾踏板

hydrant intake
消防龍頭接口

loudspeaker
揚聲器

water pressure gauge
水壓表

hydrant intake
消防龍頭接口

storage compartment
工具廂

hook ladder
掛鈎梯

hose truck
水龍帶捲架

pike pole
消防鈎桿

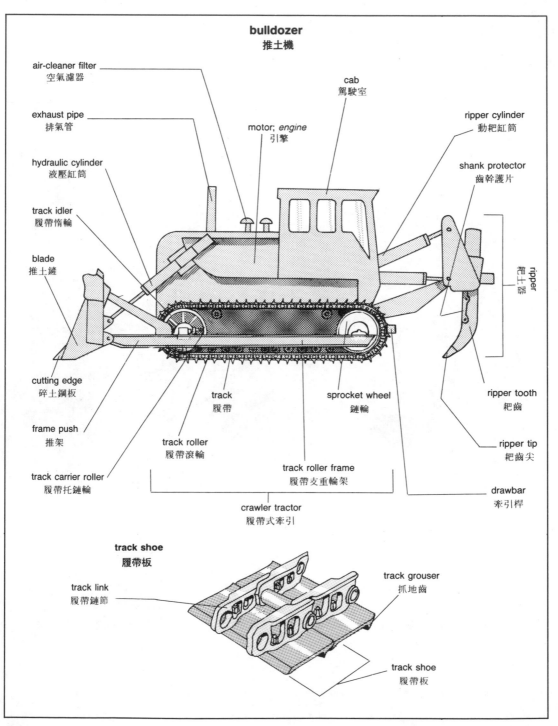

bulldozer
推土機

air-cleaner filter
空氣濾器

exhaust pipe
排氣管

hydraulic cylinder
液壓缸筒

track idler
履帶惰輪

blade
推土鏟

cutting edge
碎土鋼板

frame push
推架

track carrier roller
履帶托鏈輪

motor; *engine*
引擎

cab
駕駛室

ripper cylinder
動耙缸筒

shank protector
齒幹護片

ripper
耙土器

track
履帶

track roller
履帶滾輪

sprocket wheel
鏈輪

track roller frame
履帶支重輪架

ripper tooth
耙齒

ripper tip
耙齒尖

drawbar
牽引桿

crawler tractor
履帶式牽引

track shoe
履帶板

track link
履帶鏈節

track grouser
抓地齒

track shoe
履帶板

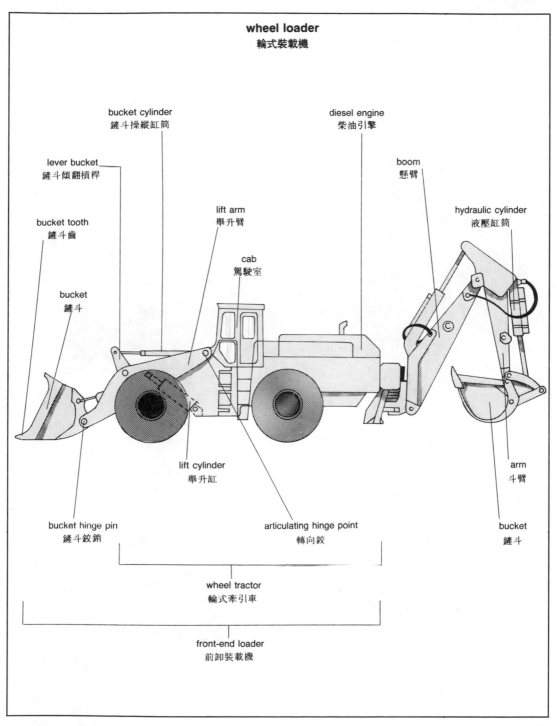

wheel loader
輪式裝載機

bucket cylinder
鏟斗操縱缸筒

diesel engine
柴油引擎

boom
懸臂

lever bucket
鏟斗傾翻槓桿

hydraulic cylinder
液壓缸筒

lift arm
舉升臂

bucket tooth
鏟斗齒

cab
駕駛室

bucket
鏟斗

lift cylinder
舉升缸

arm
斗臂

bucket hinge pin
鏟斗鉸銷

articulating hinge point
轉向鉸

bucket
鏟斗

wheel tractor
輪式牽引車

front-end loader
前卸裝載機

grader
平路機

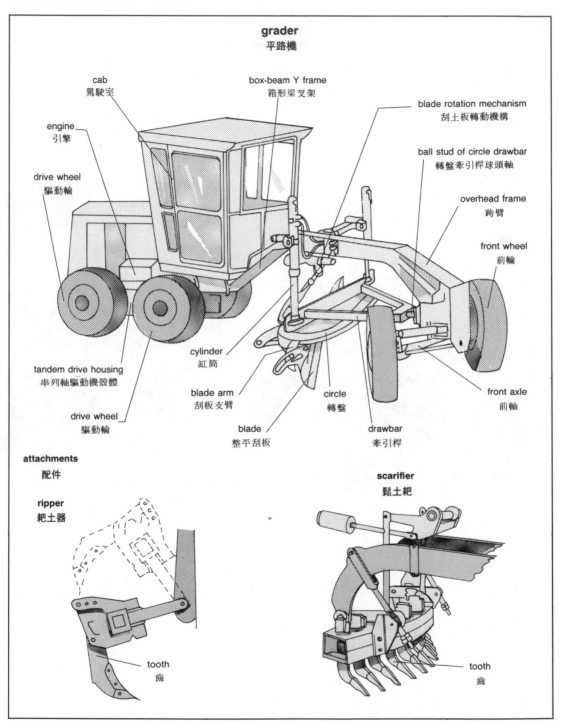

cab
駕駛室

box-beam Y frame
箱形梁叉架

blade rotation mechanism
刮土板轉動機構

engine
引擎

ball stud of circle drawbar
轉盤牽引桿球頭軸

drive wheel
驅動輪

overhead frame
跨臂

front wheel
前輪

tandem drive housing
串列軸驅動機殼體

cylinder
缸筒

drive wheel
驅動輪

blade arm
刮板支臂

circle
轉盤

front axle
前軸

blade
整平刮板

drawbar
牽引桿

attachments
配件

scarifier
鬆土耙

ripper
耙土器

tooth
齒

tooth
齒

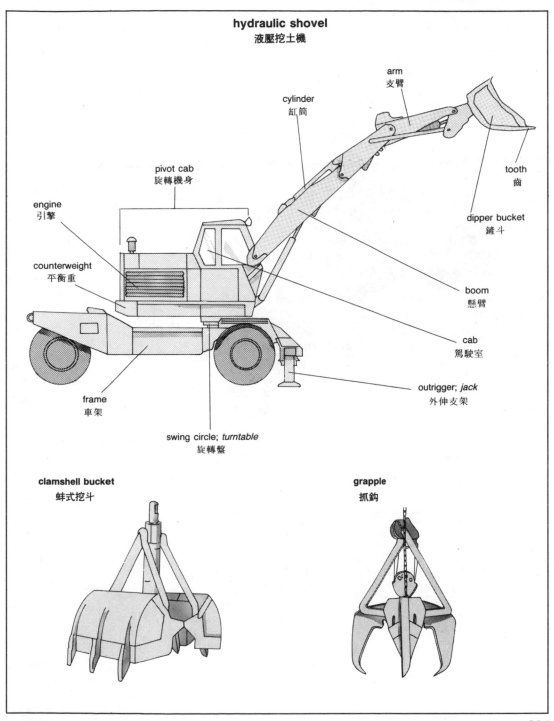

hydraulic shovel
液壓挖土機

arm
支臂

cylinder
缸筒

pivot cab
旋轉機身

tooth
齒

engine
引擎

dipper bucket
鏟斗

counterweight
平衡重

boom
懸臂

cab
駕駛室

outrigger; *jack*
外伸支架

frame
車架

swing circle; *turntable*
旋轉盤

clamshell bucket
蚌式挖斗

grapple
抓鈎

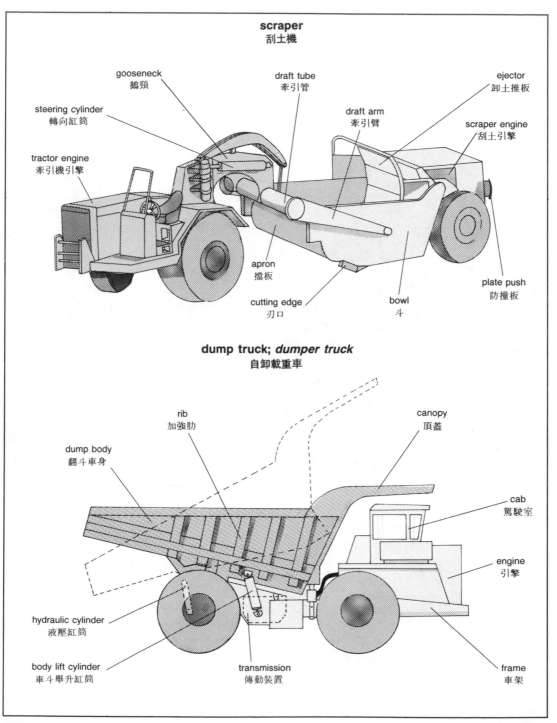

scraper
刮土機

steering cylinder
轉向缸筒

gooseneck
鵝頸

draft tube
牽引管

draft arm
牽引臂

ejector
卸土推板

scraper engine
刮土引擎

tractor engine
牽引機引擎

apron
擋板

cutting edge
刃口

bowl
斗

plate push
防撞板

dump truck; _dumper truck_
自卸載重車

rib
加強肋

canopy
頂蓋

dump body
翻斗車身

cab
駕駛室

engine
引擎

hydraulic cylinder
液壓缸筒

body lift cylinder
車斗舉升缸筒

transmission
傳動裝置

frame
車架

682

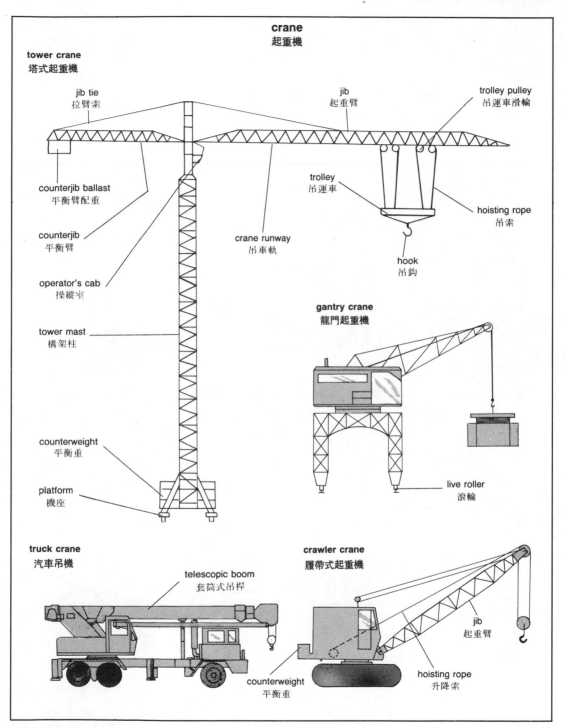

crane
起重機

tower crane
塔式起重機

jib tie
拉臂索

jib
起重臂

trolley pulley
吊運車滑輪

counterjib ballast
平衡臂配重

trolley
吊運車

hoisting rope
吊索

counterjib
平衡臂

crane runway
吊車軌

operator's cab
操縱室

hook
吊鈎

tower mast
構架柱

gantry crane
龍門起重機

counterweight
平衡重

platform
機座

live roller
滾輪

truck crane
汽車吊機

telescopic boom
套筒式吊桿

crawler crane
履帶式起重機

jib
起重臂

counterweight
平衡重

hoisting rope
升降索

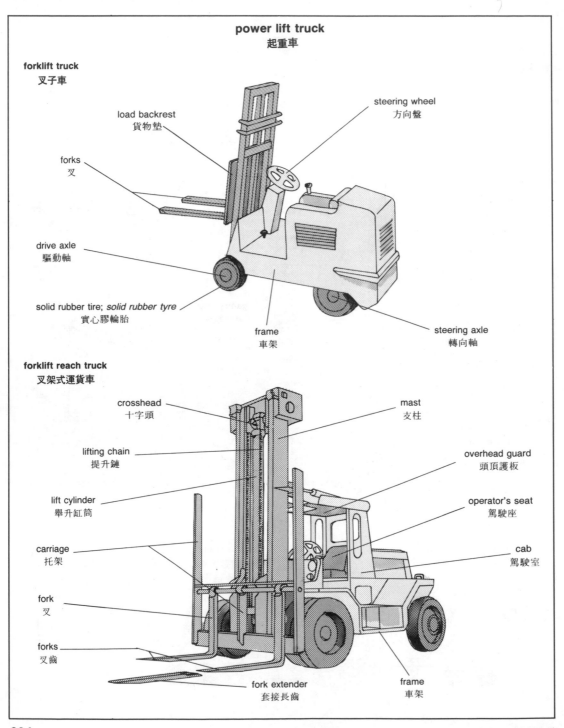

power lift truck
起重車

forklift truck
叉子車

load backrest
貨物墊

steering wheel
方向盤

forks
叉

drive axle
驅動軸

solid rubber tire; *solid rubber tyre*
實心膠輪胎

frame
車架

steering axle
轉向軸

forklift reach truck
叉架式運貨車

crosshead
十字頭

mast
支柱

lifting chain
提升鏈

overhead guard
頭頂護板

lift cylinder
舉升缸筒

operator's seat
駕駛座

carriage
托架

cab
駕駛室

fork
叉

forks
叉齒

fork extender
套接長齒

frame
車架

handling engines
手推車

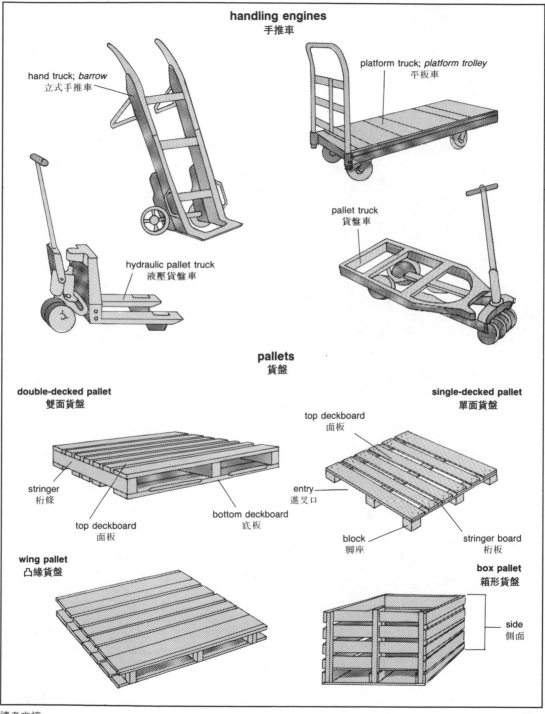

hand truck; *barrow*
立式手推車

platform truck; *platform trolley*
平板車

pallet truck
貨盤車

hydraulic pallet truck
液壓貨盤車

pallets
貨盤

double-decked pallet
雙面貨盤

single-decked pallet
單面貨盤

top deckboard
面板

stringer
桁條

entry
進叉口

top deckboard
面板

bottom deckboard
底板

block
腳座

stringer board
桁板

wing pallet
凸緣貨盤

box pallet
箱形貨盤

side
側面

WEAPONS

武器

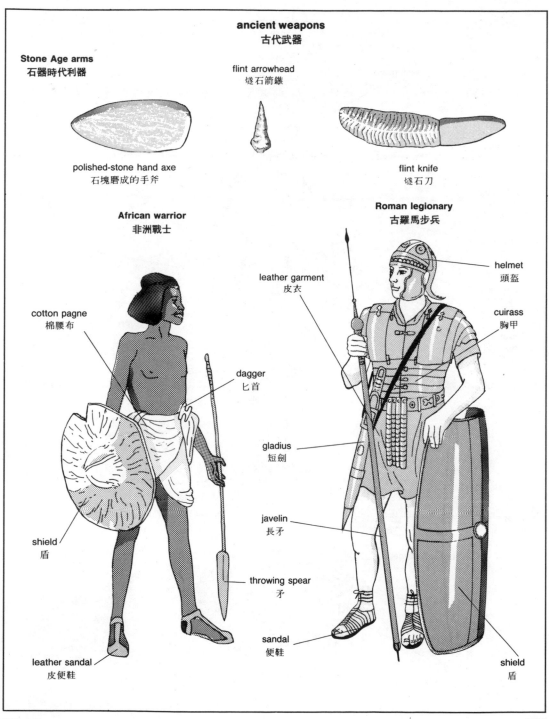

ancient weapons
古代武器

Stone Age arms
石器時代利器

flint arrowhead
燧石箭鏃

polished-stone hand axe
石塊磨成的手斧

flint knife
燧石刀

African warrior
非洲戰士

Roman legionary
古羅馬步兵

leather garment
皮衣

helmet
頭盔

cotton pagne
棉腰布

cuirass
胸甲

dagger
匕首

gladius
短劍

shield
盾

javelin
長矛

throwing spear
矛

sandal
便鞋

leather sandal
皮便鞋

shield
盾

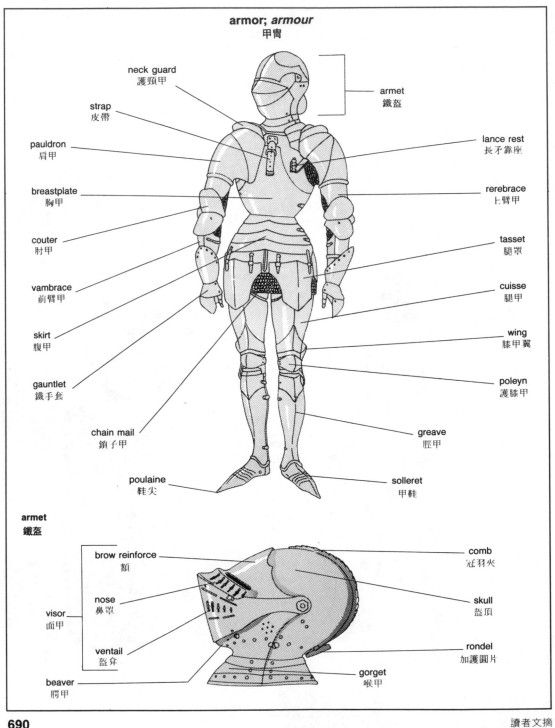

armor; *armour*
甲冑

neck guard
護頸甲

strap
皮帶

pauldron
肩甲

breastplate
胸甲

couter
肘甲

vambrace
前臂甲

skirt
腹甲

gauntlet
鐵手套

chain mail
鎖子甲

poulaine
鞋尖

armet
鐵盔

lance rest
長矛靠座

rerebrace
上臂甲

tasset
腿罩

cuisse
腿甲

wing
膝甲翼

poleyn
護膝甲

greave
脛甲

solleret
甲鞋

armet
鐵盔

brow reinforce
額

nose
鼻罩

visor
面甲

ventail
盔弇

beaver
腭甲

comb
冠羽火

skull
盔頂

rondel
加護圓片

gorget
喉甲

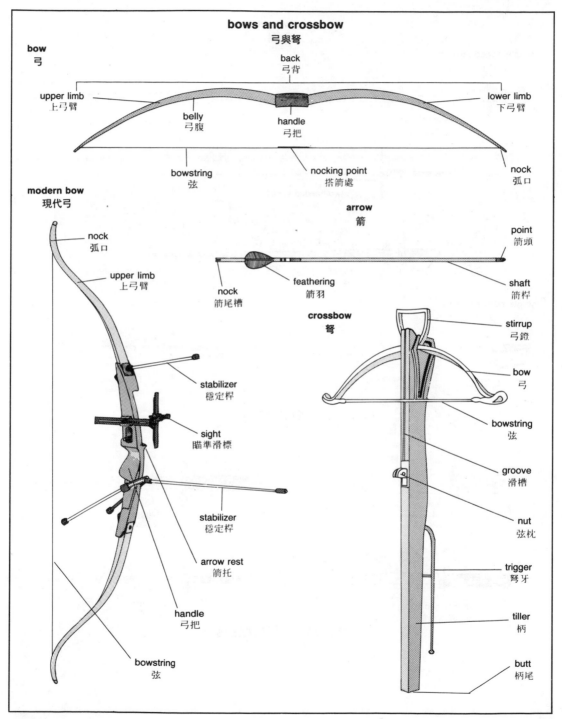

bows and crossbow
弓與弩

bow
弓

back
弓背

upper limb
上弓臂

lower limb
下弓臂

belly
弓腹

handle
弓把

bowstring
弦

nocking point
搭箭處

nock
弧口

modern bow
現代弓

nock
弧口

upper limb
上弓臂

stabilizer
穩定桿

sight
瞄準滑標

stabilizer
穩定桿

arrow rest
箭托

handle
弓把

bowstring
弦

arrow
箭

point
箭頭

nock
箭尾槽

feathering
箭羽

shaft
箭桿

crossbow
弩

stirrup
弓鐙

bow
弓

bowstring
弦

groove
滑槽

nut
弦枕

trigger
弩牙

tiller
柄

butt
柄尾

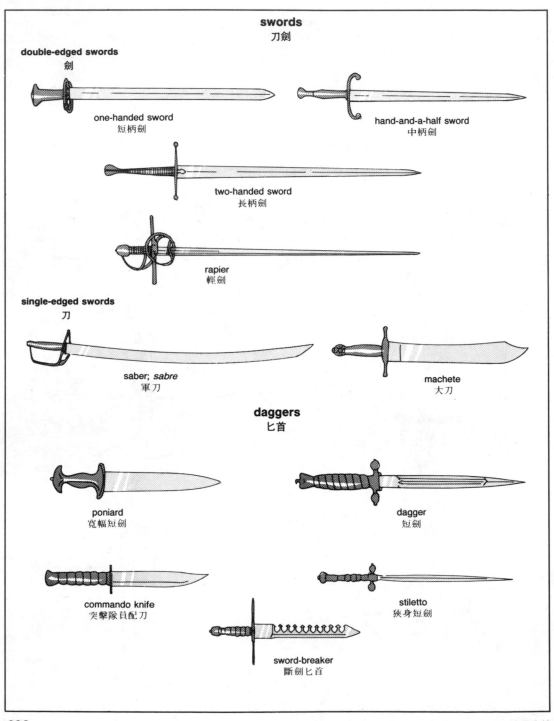

swords
刀劍

double-edged swords
劍

one-handed sword
短柄劍

hand-and-a-half sword
中柄劍

two-handed sword
長柄劍

rapier
輕劍

single-edged swords
刀

saber; *sabre*
軍刀

machete
大刀

daggers
匕首

poniard
寬幅短劍

dagger
短劍

commando knife
突擊隊員配刀

stiletto
狹身短劍

sword-breaker
斷劍匕首

bayonets
刺刀

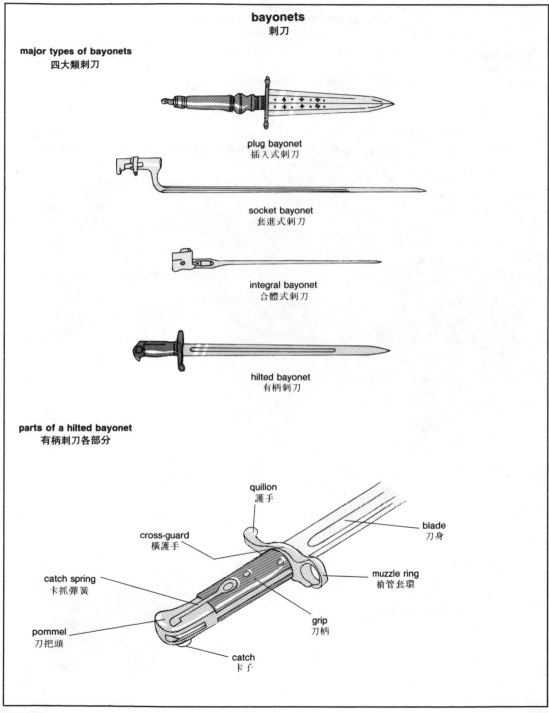

major types of bayonets
四大類刺刀

plug bayonet
插入式刺刀

socket bayonet
套進式刺刀

integral bayonet
合體式刺刀

hilted bayonet
有柄刺刀

parts of a hilted bayonet
有柄刺刀各部分

quillon
護手

cross-guard
橫護手

blade
刀身

catch spring
卡抓彈簧

muzzle ring
槍管套環

pommel
刀把頭

grip
刀柄

catch
卡子

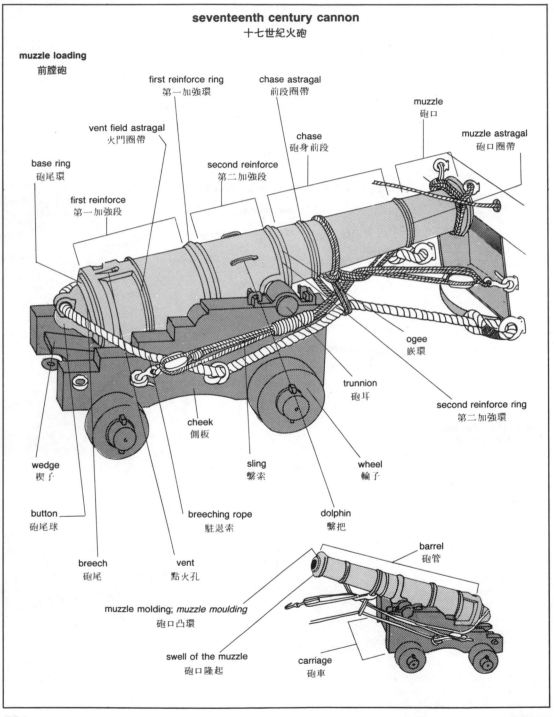

seventeenth century cannon
十七世紀火砲

muzzle loading
前膛砲

first reinforce ring
第一加強環

chase astragal
前段圈帶

muzzle
砲口

muzzle astragal
砲口圈帶

vent field astragal
火門圈帶

chase
砲身前段

second reinforce
第二加強段

base ring
砲尾環

first reinforce
第一加強段

ogee
嵌環

second reinforce ring
第二加強環

trunnion
砲耳

cheek
側板

sling
繫索

wheel
輪子

wedge
楔子

button
砲尾球

breeching rope
駐退索

dolphin
繫把

barrel
砲管

breech
砲尾

vent
點火孔

muzzle molding; *muzzle moulding*
砲口凸環

swell of the muzzle
砲口隆起

carriage
砲車

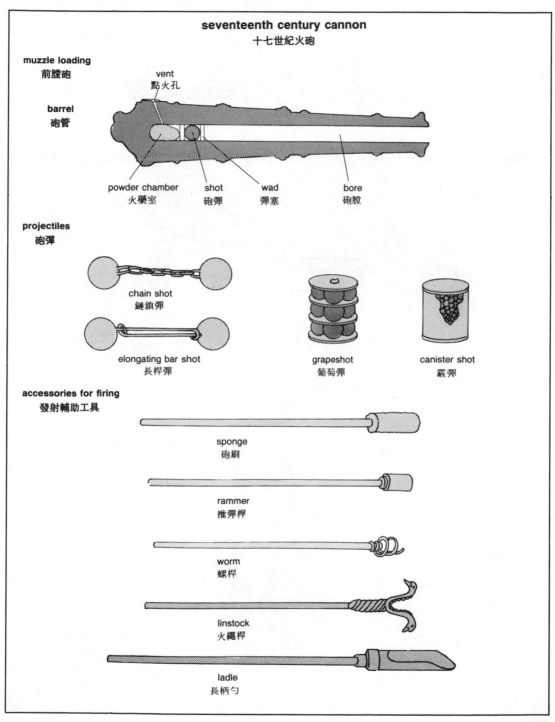

seventeenth century cannon
十七世紀火砲

muzzle loading
前膛砲

barrel
砲管

vent
點火孔

powder chamber
火藥室

shot
砲彈

wad
彈塞

bore
砲膛

projectiles
砲彈

chain shot
鏈鎖彈

elongating bar shot
長桿彈

grapeshot
葡萄彈

canister shot
霰彈

accessories for firing
發射輔助工具

sponge
砲刷

rammer
推彈桿

worm
螺桿

linstock
火繩桿

ladle
長柄勺

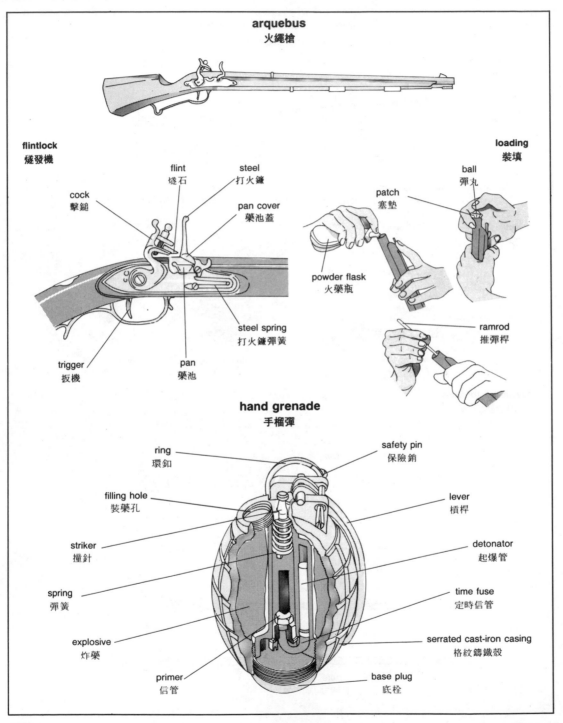

arquebus
火繩槍

flintlock
燧發機

cock
擊鎚

flint
燧石

steel
打火鐮

pan cover
藥池蓋

steel spring
打火鐮彈簧

trigger
扳機

pan
藥池

loading
裝填

ball
彈丸

patch
塞墊

powder flask
火藥瓶

ramrod
推彈桿

hand grenade
手榴彈

ring
環釦

safety pin
保險銷

filling hole
裝藥孔

lever
槓桿

striker
撞針

detonator
起爆管

spring
彈簧

time fuse
定時信管

explosive
炸藥

serrated cast-iron casing
格紋鑄鐵殼

primer
信管

base plug
底栓

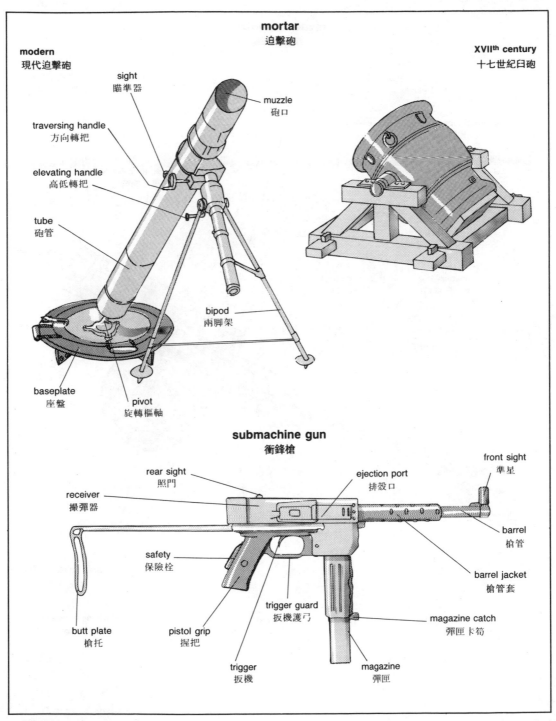

mortar
迫擊砲

modern
現代迫擊砲

sight
瞄準器

muzzle
砲口

XVIIth century
十七世紀臼砲

traversing handle
方向轉把

elevating handle
高低轉把

tube
砲管

bipod
兩腳架

baseplate
座盤

pivot
旋轉樞軸

submachine gun
衝鋒槍

front sight
準星

rear sight
照門

ejection port
排殼口

receiver
撮彈器

barrel
槍管

safety
保險栓

barrel jacket
槍管套

trigger guard
扳機護弓

magazine catch
彈匣卡筍

butt plate
槍托

pistol grip
握把

trigger
扳機

magazine
彈匣

modern howitzer
現代榴彈砲

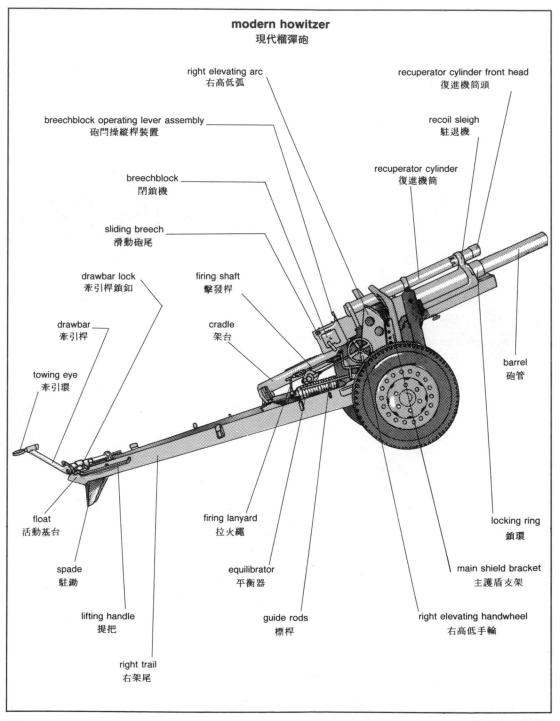

right elevating arc
右高低弧

recuperator cylinder front head
復進機筒頭

breechblock operating lever assembly
砲閂操縱桿裝置

recoil sleigh
駐退機

breechblock
閉鎖機

recuperator cylinder
復進機筒

sliding breech
滑動砲尾

drawbar lock
牽引桿鎖釦

firing shaft
擊發桿

drawbar
牽引桿

cradle
架台

barrel
砲管

towing eye
牽引環

float
活動基台

firing lanyard
拉火繩

locking ring
鎖環

spade
駐鋤

equilibrator
平衡器

main shield bracket
主護盾支架

lifting handle
提把

guide rods
標桿

right elevating handwheel
右高低手輪

right trail
右架尾

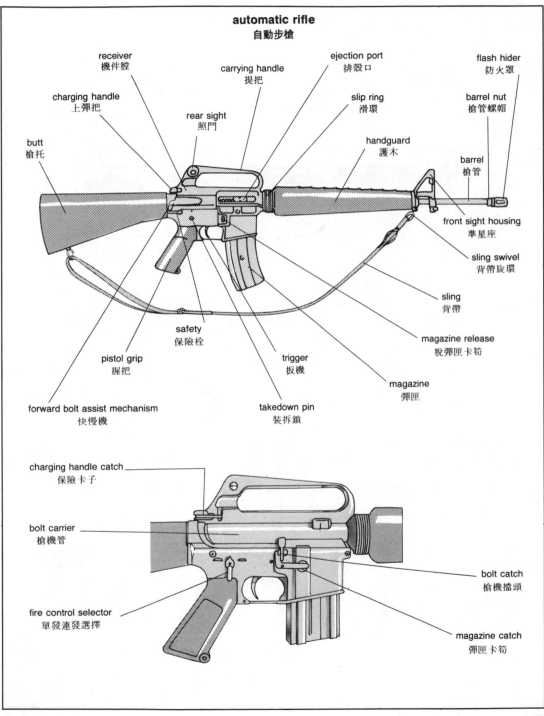

automatic rifle
自動步槍

receiver
機件膛

carrying handle
提把

ejection port
排殼口

flash hider
防火罩

charging handle
上彈把

slip ring
滑環

barrel nut
槍管螺帽

rear sight
照門

handguard
護木

barrel
槍管

butt
槍托

front sight housing
準星座

sling swivel
背帶旋環

sling
背帶

safety
保險栓

magazine release
脫彈匣卡筍

pistol grip
握把

trigger
扳機

magazine
彈匣

forward bolt assist mechanism
快慢機

takedown pin
裝拆鎖

charging handle catch
保險卡子

bolt carrier
槍機管

bolt catch
槍機擋頭

fire control selector
單發連發選擇

magazine catch
彈匣卡筍

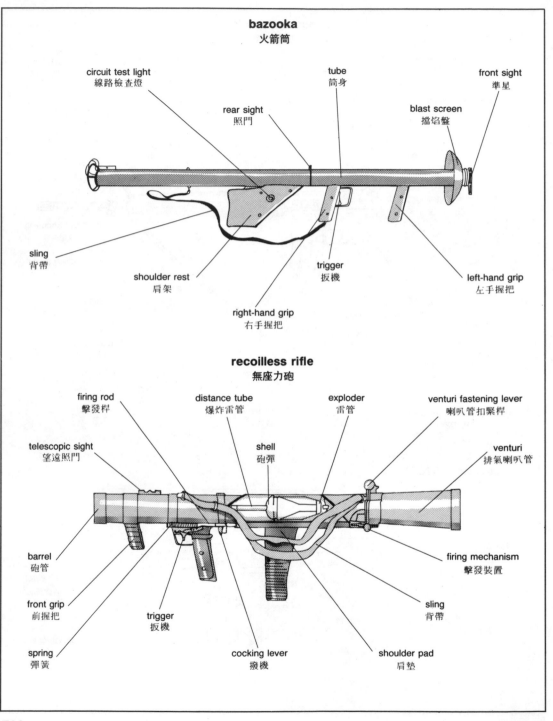

bazooka
火箭筒

circuit test light
線路檢查燈

tube
筒身

front sight
準星

rear sight
照門

blast screen
擋焰盤

sling
背帶

shoulder rest
肩架

trigger
扳機

left-hand grip
左手握把

right-hand grip
右手握把

recoilless rifle
無座力砲

firing rod
擊發桿

distance tube
爆炸雷管

exploder
雷管

venturi fastening lever
喇叭管扣緊桿

telescopic sight
望遠照門

shell
砲彈

venturi
排氣喇叭管

barrel
砲管

firing mechanism
擊發裝置

front grip
前握把

trigger
扳機

sling
背帶

spring
彈簧

cocking lever
撥機

shoulder pad
肩墊

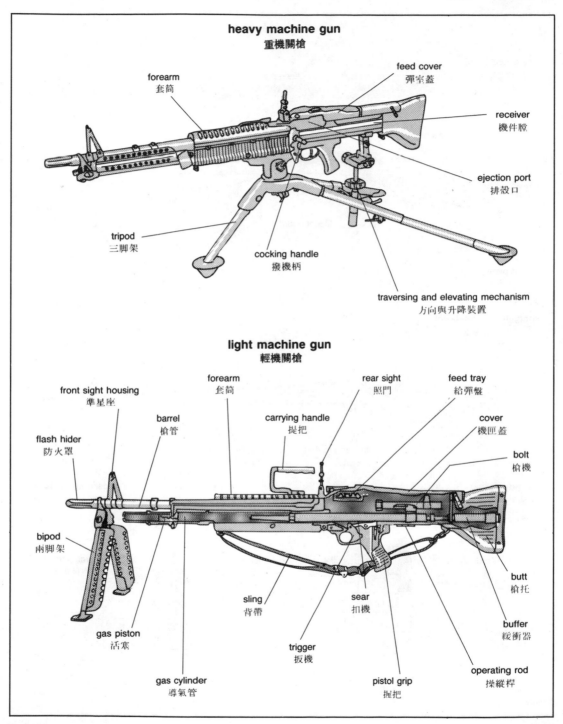

heavy machine gun
重機關槍

feed cover
彈室蓋

forearm
套筒

receiver
機件膛

ejection port
排殼口

tripod
三腳架

cocking handle
撥機柄

traversing and elevating mechanism
方向與升降裝置

light machine gun
輕機關槍

front sight housing
準星座

barrel
槍管

forearm
套筒

rear sight
照門

feed tray
給彈盤

carrying handle
提把

cover
機匣蓋

flash hider
防火罩

bolt
槍機

bipod
兩腳架

butt
槍托

buffer
緩衝器

gas piston
活塞

sling
背帶

sear
扣機

trigger
扳機

pistol grip
握把

operating rod
操縱桿

gas cylinder
導氣管

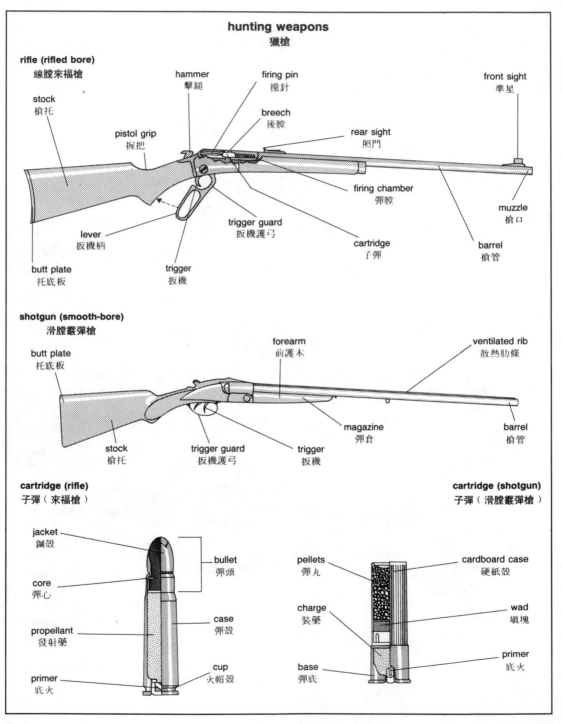

hunting weapons
獵槍

rifle (rifled bore)
線膛來福槍

hammer 擊鎚
firing pin 撞針
front sight 準星
stock 槍托
breech 後膛
pistol grip 握把
rear sight 照門
firing chamber 彈膛
lever 扳機柄
trigger guard 扳機護弓
cartridge 子彈
muzzle 槍口
butt plate 托底板
trigger 扳機
barrel 槍管

shotgun (smooth-bore)
滑膛霰彈槍

forearm 前護木
ventilated rib 散熱肋條
butt plate 托底板
magazine 彈倉
barrel 槍管
stock 槍托
trigger guard 扳機護弓
trigger 扳機

cartridge (rifle)
子彈（來福槍）

cartridge (shotgun)
子彈（滑膛霰彈槍）

jacket 鋼殼
bullet 彈頭
core 彈心
case 彈殼
propellant 發射藥
primer 底火
cup 火帽殼

pellets 彈丸
cardboard case 硬紙殼
charge 裝藥
wad 填塊
base 彈底
primer 底火

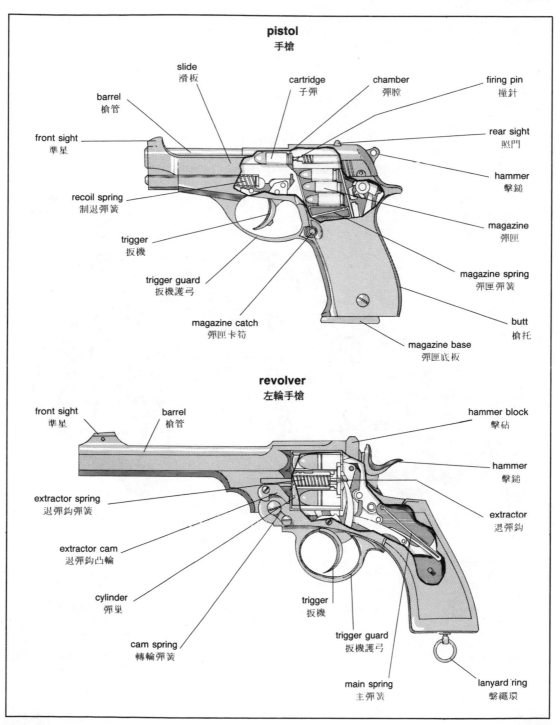

pistol
手槍

- slide 滑板
- barrel 槍管
- front sight 準星
- cartridge 子彈
- chamber 彈膛
- firing pin 撞針
- rear sight 照門
- hammer 擊鎚
- recoil spring 制退彈簧
- magazine 彈匣
- trigger 扳機
- trigger guard 扳機護弓
- magazine spring 彈匣彈簧
- magazine catch 彈匣卡筍
- butt 槍托
- magazine base 彈匣底板

revolver
左輪手槍

- front sight 準星
- barrel 槍管
- hammer block 擊砧
- hammer 擊鎚
- extractor spring 退彈鈎彈簧
- extractor 退彈鈎
- extractor cam 退彈鈎凸輪
- cylinder 彈巢
- trigger 扳機
- trigger guard 扳機護弓
- cam spring 轉輪彈簧
- main spring 主彈簧
- lanyard ring 繫繩環

tank
坦克

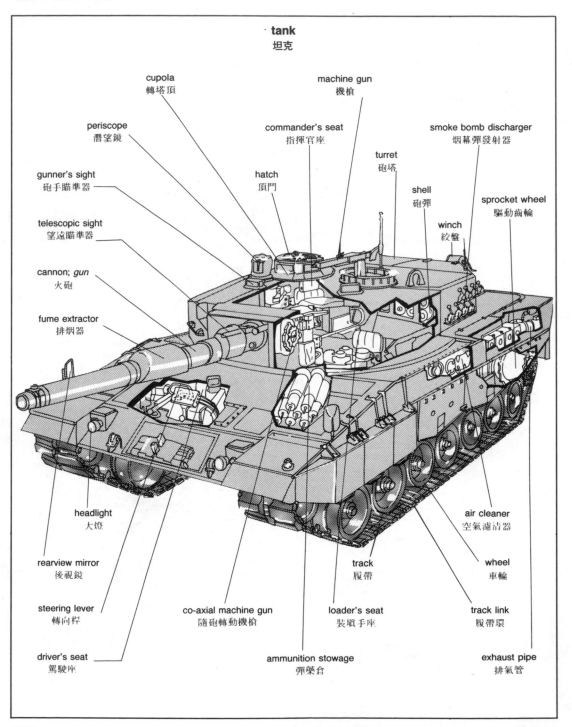

cupola
轉塔頂

machine gun
機槍

periscope
潛望鏡

commander's seat
指揮官座

smoke bomb discharger
烟幕彈發射器

gunner's sight
砲手瞄準器

hatch
頂門

turret
砲塔

shell
砲彈

sprocket wheel
驅動齒輪

telescopic sight
望遠瞄準器

winch
絞盤

cannon; *gun*
火砲

fume extractor
排烟器

headlight
大燈

air cleaner
空氣濾清器

rearview mirror
後視鏡

track
履帶

wheel
車輪

steering lever
轉向桿

co-axial machine gun
隨砲轉動機槍

loader's seat
裝填手座

track link
履帶環

driver's seat
駕駛座

ammunition stowage
彈藥倉

exhaust pipe
排氣管

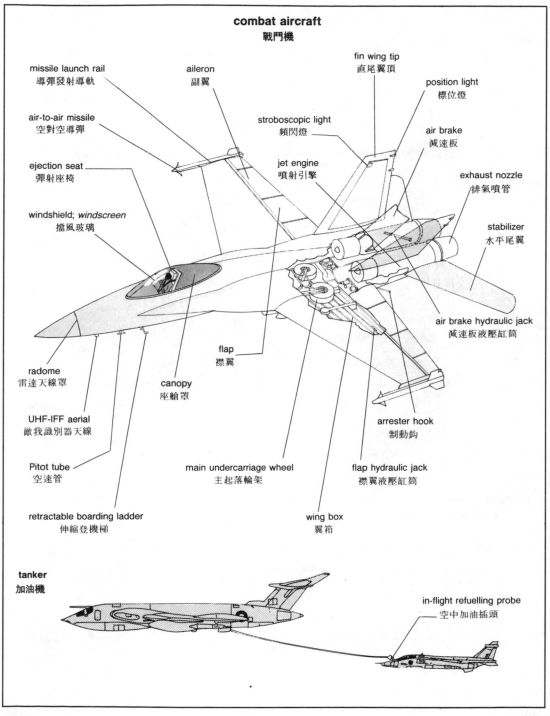

combat aircraft
戰鬥機

missile launch rail
導彈發射導軌

aileron
副翼

fin wing tip
直尾翼頂

position light
標位燈

air-to-air missile
空對空導彈

stroboscopic light
頻閃燈

air brake
減速板

ejection seat
彈射座椅

jet engine
噴射引擎

exhaust nozzle
排氣噴管

windshield; *windscreen*
擋風玻璃

stabilizer
水平尾翼

air brake hydraulic jack
減速板液壓缸筒

flap
襟翼

radome
雷達天線罩

canopy
座艙罩

arrester hook
制動鈎

UHF-IFF aerial
敵我識別器天線

Pitot tube
空速管

main undercarriage wheel
主起落輪架

flap hydraulic jack
襟翼液壓缸筒

retractable boarding ladder
伸縮登機梯

wing box
翼箱

tanker
加油機

in-flight refuelling probe
空中加油插頭

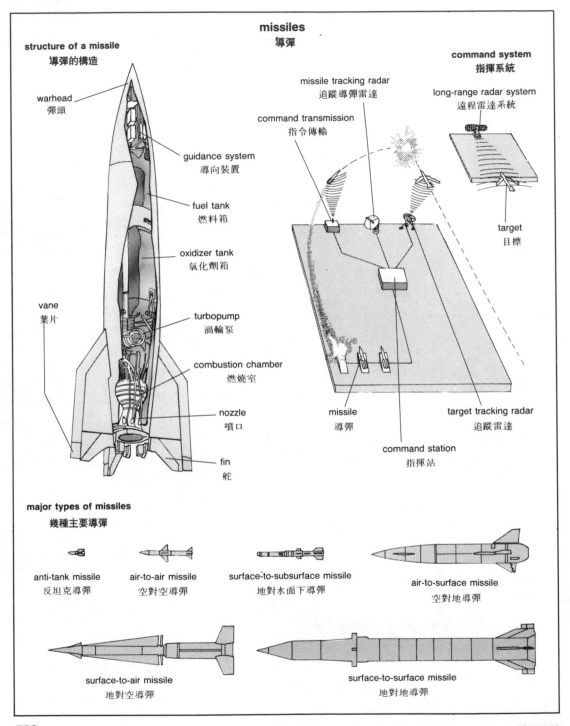

missiles
導彈

structure of a missile
導彈的構造

warhead
彈頭

guidance system
導向裝置

fuel tank
燃料箱

oxidizer tank
氧化劑箱

vane
葉片

turbopump
渦輪泵

combustion chamber
燃燒室

nozzle
噴口

fin
舵

command system
指揮系統

missile tracking radar
追蹤導彈雷達

command transmission
指令傳輸

long-range radar system
遠程雷達系統

target
目標

missile
導彈

command station
指揮站

target tracking radar
追蹤雷達

major types of missiles
幾種主要導彈

anti-tank missile
反坦克導彈

air-to-air missile
空對空導彈

surface-to-subsurface missile
地對水面下導彈

air-to-surface missile
空對地導彈

surface-to-air missile
地對空導彈

surface-to-surface missile
地對地導彈

SYMBOLS

標識

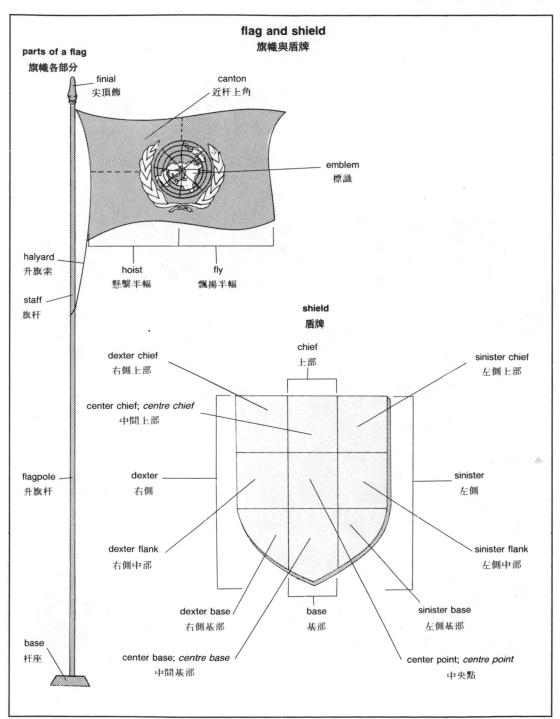

flag and shield
旗幟與盾牌

parts of a flag
旗幟各部分

finial
尖頂飾

canton
近杆上角

emblem
標識

halyard
升旗索

hoist
懸繫半幅

fly
飄揚半幅

staff
旗杆

shield
盾牌

dexter chief
右側上部

chief
上部

sinister chief
左側上部

center chief; *centre chief*
中間上部

flagpole
升旗杆

dexter
右側

sinister
左側

dexter flank
右側中部

sinister flank
左側中部

base
杆座

dexter base
右側基部

base
基部

sinister base
左側基部

center base; *centre base*
中間基部

center point; *centre point*
中央點

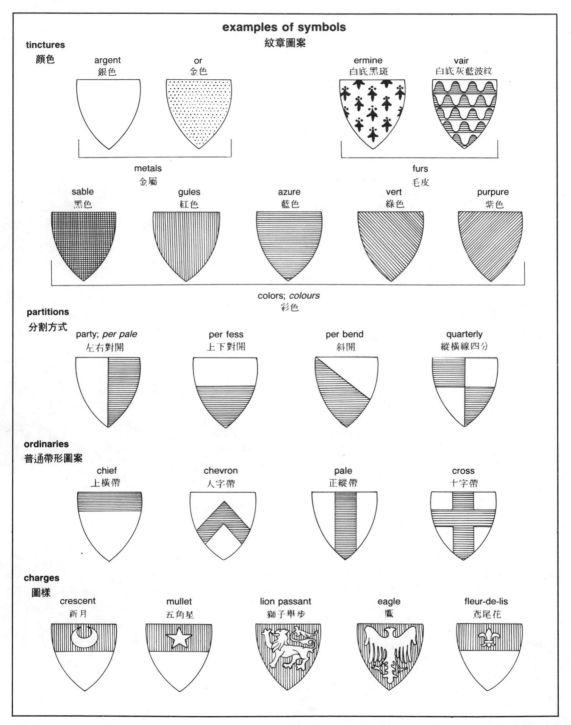

examples of symbols
紋章圖案

tinctures
顏色

argent
銀色

or
金色

ermine
白底黑斑

vair
白底灰藍波紋

metals
金屬

furs
毛皮

sable
黑色

gules
紅色

azure
藍色

vert
綠色

purpure
紫色

colors; *colours*
彩色

partitions
分割方式

party; *per pale*
左右對開

per fess
上下對開

per bend
斜開

quarterly
縱橫線四分

ordinaries
普通帶形圖案

chief
上橫帶

chevron
人字帶

pale
正縱帶

cross
十字帶

charges
圖樣

crescent
新月

mullet
五角星

lion passant
獅子舉步

eagle
鷹

fleur-de-lis
鳶尾花

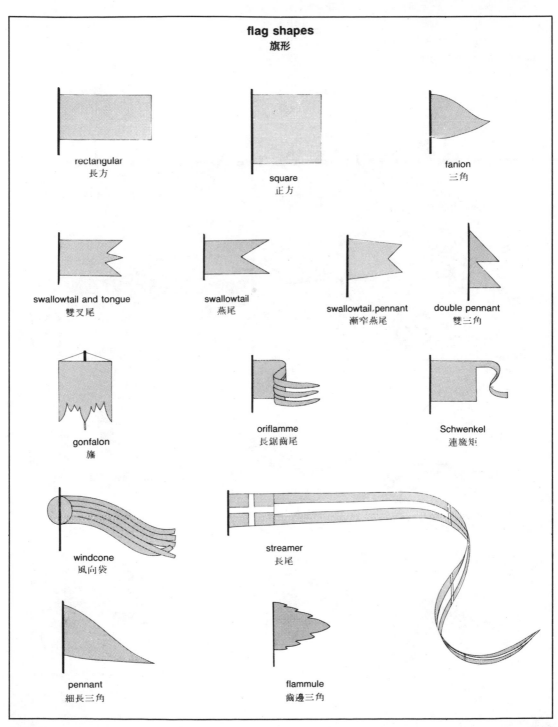

flag shapes
旗形

rectangular
長方

square
正方

fanion
三角

swallowtail and tongue
雙叉尾

swallowtail
燕尾

swallowtail, pennant
漸窄燕尾

double pennant
雙三角

gonfalon
旛

oriflamme
長鋸齒尾

Schwenkel
連旒矩

windcone
風向袋

streamer
長尾

pennant
細長三角

flammule
齒邊三角

constellations
星座

ancient and modern signs
古今標識

Aries, the Ram (March 21)
白羊座（3月21日）

Taurus, the Bull (April 20)
金牛座（4月20日）

Gemini, the Twins (May 21)
雙子座（5月21日）

Cancer, the Crab (June 22)
巨蟹座（6月22日）

Leo, the Lion (July 23)
獅子座（7月23日）

Virgo, the Virgin (August 23)
室女座（8月23日）

Libra, the Balance (September 23)
天秤座（9月23日）

Scorpio, the Scorpion (October 24)
天蠍座（10月24日）

Sagittarius, the Archer (November 22)
人馬座（11月22日）

Capricorn, the Goat (December 22)
摩羯座（12月22日）

Aquarius, the Water Bearer (January 20)
寶瓶座（1月20日）

Pisces, the Fishes (February 19)
雙魚座（2月19日）

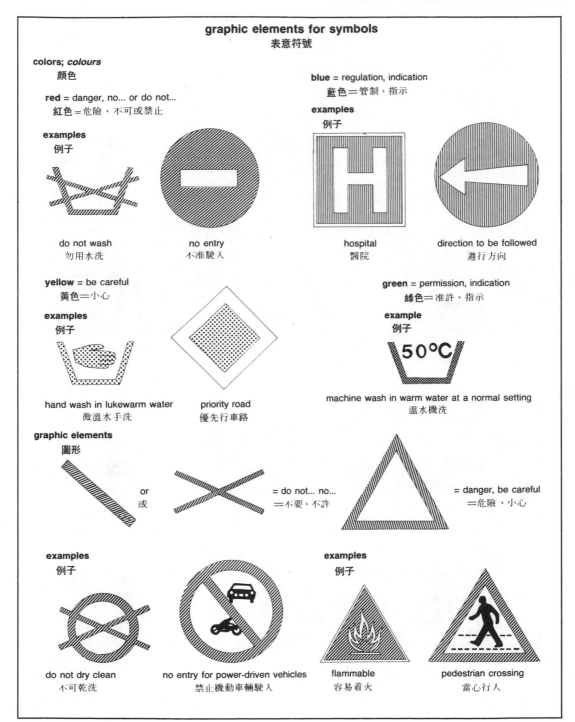

graphic elements for symbols
表意符號

colors; *colours*
顏色

red = danger, no... or do not...
紅色＝危險、不可或禁止

examples
例子

do not wash
勿用水洗

no entry
不准駛入

blue = regulation, indication
藍色＝管制、指示

examples
例子

hospital
醫院

direction to be followed
遵行方向

yellow = be careful
黃色＝小心

examples
例子

hand wash in lukewarm water
微溫水手洗

priority road
優先行車路

green = permission, indication
綠色＝准許、指示

example
例子

50°C

machine wash in warm water at a normal setting
溫水機洗

graphic elements
圖形

or
或

= do not... no...
＝不要、不許

= danger, be careful
＝危險、小心

examples
例子

do not dry clean
不可乾洗

no entry for power-driven vehicles
禁止機動車輛駛入

examples
例子

flammable
容易着火

pedestrian crossing
當心行人

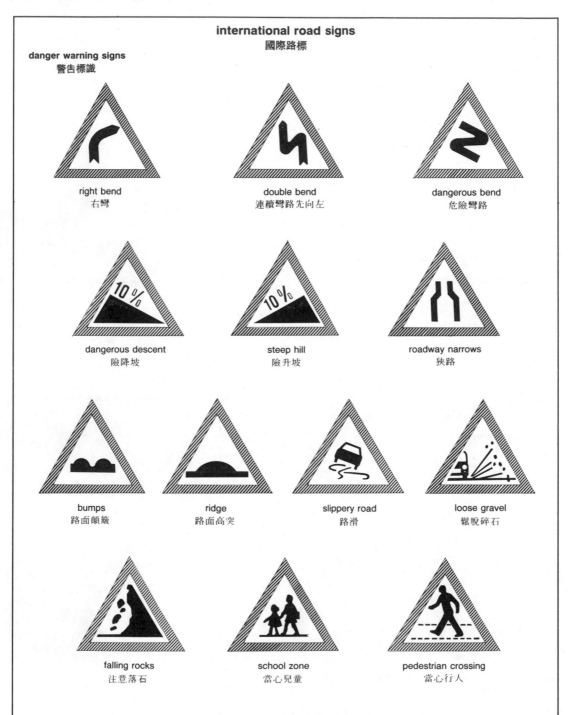

international road signs
國際路標

danger warning signs
警告標識

right bend
右彎

double bend
連續彎路先向左

dangerous bend
危險彎路

dangerous descent
險降坡

steep hill
險升坡

roadway narrows
狹路

bumps
路面顛簸

ridge
路面高突

slippery road
路滑

loose gravel
鬆脫碎石

falling rocks
注意落石

school zone
當心兒童

pedestrian crossing
當心行人

international road signs
國際路標

danger warning signs (cont.)
警告標識（續）

cyclists entering or crossing
當心腳踏車

cattle crossing
當心牛隻

wild animals crossing
當心野生動物

road works
修路

light signals
注意交通燈號

two-way traffic
雙向行車

other dangers
危險

traffic circle
前面迴旋處

priority intersection
前面十字路口

grade crossing
有柵門鐵路平交道

signs regulating priority at intersections
交叉路口行車先後標識

«give way» sign
讓路

stop at intersection
停車讓路

«priority road» sign
優先行車路

«end of priority» sign
優先行車路終止

international road signs
國際路標

prohibitory or regulatory signs
禁止或限制標識

no entry
不准駛入

no entry for mopeds
禁止機器脚踏兩用車進入

no entry for bicycles
禁止脚踏車進入

no entry for motorcycles
禁止摩托車進入

no entry for goods vehicles
禁止貨車駛入

no entry for pedestrians
行人止步

no entry for power-driven vehicles
禁止機動車輛駛入

width clearance
車輛寬度限制

overhead clearance
車輛高度限制

weight limitation
車輛總重限制

no left turn
禁止左轉

no U-turn
禁止迴車

passing prohibited
禁止超車

end of prohibition of passing
禁超車段完

maximum speed limit
最高速限

use of audible warning
devices prohibited
禁止響號

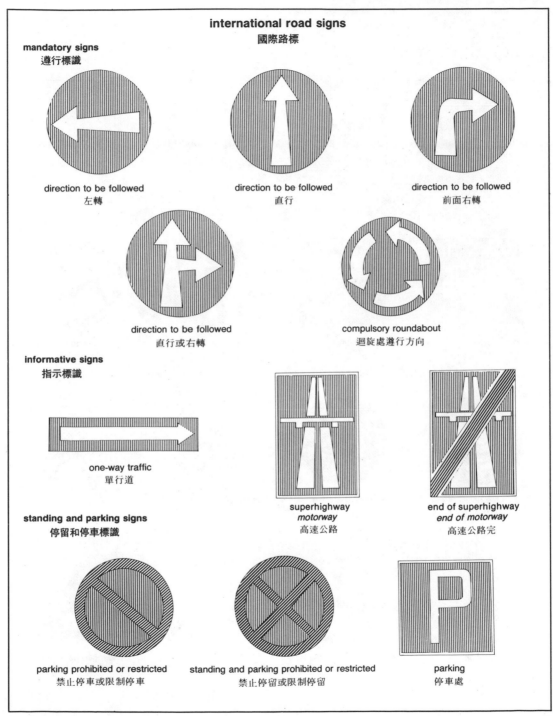

international road signs
國際路標

mandatory signs
遵行標識

direction to be followed
左轉

direction to be followed
直行

direction to be followed
前面右轉

direction to be followed
直行或右轉

compulsory roundabout
迴旋處遵行方向

informative signs
指示標識

one-way traffic
單行道

superhighway
motorway
高速公路

end of superhighway
end of motorway
高速公路完

standing and parking signs
停留和停車標識

parking prohibited or restricted
禁止停車或限制停車

standing and parking prohibited or restricted
禁止停留或限制停留

parking
停車處

common symbols
常用標識

information
服務台

first aid
救護站

hospital
醫院

police
警察

telephone
電話

do not enter
禁止進入

no dogs
禁止攜狗進入

fire hose
消防水帶

fire extinguisher
滅火筒

caution, pedestrian crossing
當心行人

caution, slippery floor
小心地滑

caution
小心

danger, electrical hazard
提防觸電

danger, poison
小心毒物

danger, flammable
小心易燃物

common symbols
常用標識

access for physically handicapped
殘疾人通道

do not use for wheelchairs
禁用輪椅

smoking permitted
准許吸烟

smoking prohibited
不准吸烟

toilet for men
男洗手間

toilet for women
女洗手間

toilet for men and women
男女洗手間

elevator for people; *passenger lift*
載客升降機

freight elevator; *goods lift*
載貨升降機

escalator, up
電動扶梯（上）

escalator, down
電動扶梯（下）

stairs
樓梯

restaurant
餐廳

coffee shop; *buffet*
咖啡店

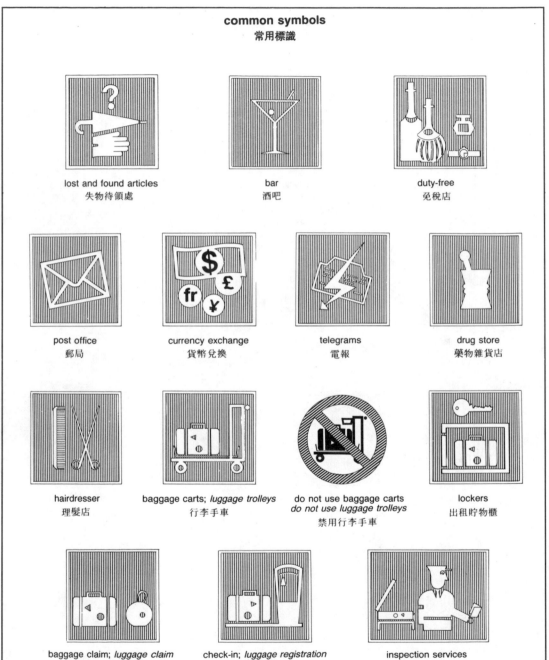

common symbols
常用標識

lost and found articles
失物待領處

bar
酒吧

duty-free
免稅店

post office
郵局

currency exchange
貨幣兌換

telegrams
電報

drug store
藥物雜貨店

hairdresser
理髮店

baggage carts; *luggage trolleys*
行李手車

do not use baggage carts
do not use luggage trolleys
禁用行李手車

lockers
出租貯物櫃

baggage claim; *luggage claim*
行李提取處

check-in; *luggage registration*
行李託運

inspection services
證件檢查

common symbols
常用標識

hotel information
旅館資料

car rental
汽車出租

taxi transportation
計程車服務

bus transportation
公共汽車

ground transportation
地面交通

air transportation
空運

helicopter transportation
直升機運輸

rail transportation
鐵路運輸

breakdown service
修理服務

service station
服務站

camping and caravan site
露營和旅行掛車營地

picnic area
野餐區

picnics prohibited
禁止野餐

camping area
露營區

camping prohibited
禁止露營

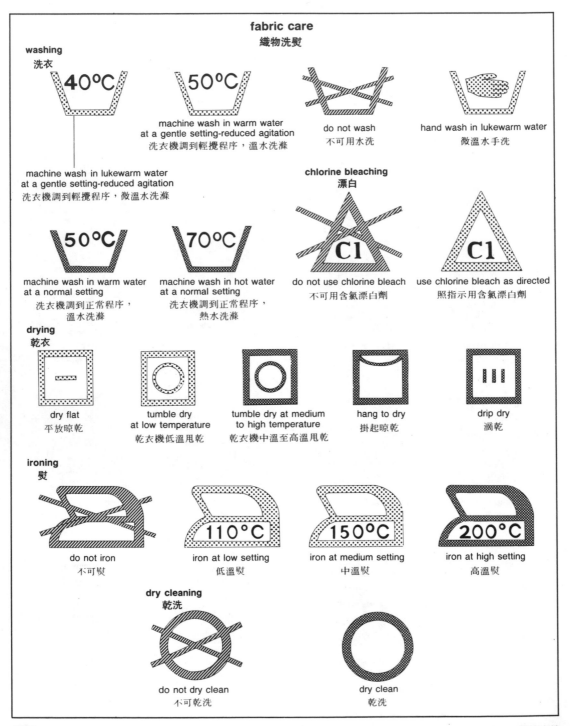

fabric care
織物洗熨

washing
洗衣

40°C

machine wash in lukewarm water
at a gentle setting-reduced agitation
洗衣機調到輕攪程序，微溫水洗滌

50°C

machine wash in warm water
at a gentle setting-reduced agitation
洗衣機調到輕攪程序，溫水洗滌

do not wash
不可用水洗

hand wash in lukewarm water
微溫水手洗

50°C

machine wash in warm water
at a normal setting
洗衣機調到正常程序，
溫水洗滌

70°C

machine wash in hot water
at a normal setting
洗衣機調到正常程序，
熱水洗滌

chlorine bleaching
漂白

C1

do not use chlorine bleach
不可用含氯漂白劑

C1

use chlorine bleach as directed
照指示用含氯漂白劑

drying
乾衣

dry flat
平放晾乾

tumble dry
at low temperature
乾衣機低溫甩乾

tumble dry at medium
to high temperature
乾衣機中溫至高溫甩乾

hang to dry
掛起晾乾

drip dry
滴乾

ironing
熨

do not iron
不可熨

110°C

iron at low setting
低溫熨

150°C

iron at medium setting
中溫熨

200°C

iron at high setting
高溫熨

dry cleaning
乾洗

do not dry clean
不可乾洗

dry clean
乾洗

**biology
生物學**

♂ male
雄性

♀ female
雌性

† death
死亡

✳ birth
出生

**mathematics
數學**

+ addition
加

− subtraction
減

× multiplication
乘

÷ division
除

± plus or minus
正負

= is equal to
等於

≠ is not equal to
不等於

≡ is identical with
恆等

≢ is not identical with
不恆等

≋ is approximately equal to
幾等於

≷ is equivalent to
等價

> is greater than
大於

≥ is equal to or greater than
相等或大於

< is less than
小於

≤ is equal to or less than
相等或小於

√² square root of
平方根

∞ infinity
無限大

% per cent
百分率

∪ union
并集

∩ intersection
交集

⊂ is contained in
子集

∈ is a member of
屬於

**miscellaneous
其他**

℞ prescription
配藥

& ampersand
與

© copyright
版權

® registered trademark
註冊商標

$ dollar
元

¢ cent
分

£ pound
鎊

→ reaction direction
產生反應

⇄ reversible reaction
可逆反應

+ positive charge
正電荷

− negative charge
負電荷

∅ empty set
空集

GENERAL INDEX

1

1-2 knots. 61.
10 knots. 61.
120-volt circuit. 288.
1st below-stage. 180.
1st valve slide. 484.

2

240-volt circuit. 288.
240-volt feeder cable. 288.
2nd below-stage. 180.
2nd metacarpal. 108.
2nd valve slide. 484.

3

3rd below-stage. 180.
3rd metacarpal. 108.
3rd valve slide. 484.

4

4th below-stage. 180.
4th metacarpal. 108.

5

5 knots. 61.
50 knots. 61.
5th metacarpal. 108.

6

6-point box end wrench. 258.

A

a. 475.
A-frame. 675.
a system. 591.
abacus. 170.
abdomen. 100, 103, 106, 114.
abdominal aorta. 125, 128.
abdominal rectus. 118.
abdominal segment. 100.
aboveground pipeline. 644.
aboveground pipeline support.
   644.
abruptly pinnate. 70.
absorbent cotton. 629.
absorber. 670.
absorber pipe. 670.
absorbing plate. 670.
absorbing surface. 669.
abutment. 175, 414, 415, 416.
abyssal hill. 50.
abyssal plain. 50.
acanthus leaf. 170, 210.
accelerator control. 253.
accelerator pedal. 400.
accent mark. 476.

accept machine. 665.
access for physically handicapped.
   719.
access gallery. 655, 660.
access panel. 205, 273.
access ramp. 187.
access shaft. 660.
accessories. 309, 320, 333, 412,
   501, 509, 582.
accessories for firing. 695.
accidentals. 476.
accommodation ladder. 434.
accordion. 489.
accordion bag. 348.
accordion pleat. 304.
accordion windows. 351.
account book. 464.
Ace. 592.
acetylene cylinder. 281.
acetylene valve. 282.
achene. 74, 78.
acorn nut. 264.
acoustic baffle. 435.
acoustic ceiling. 179.
acoustic coupler. 471.
acoustic coupler. 469.
acoustic echo. 442.
acoustic resistance. 387.
acromion. 121.
acroterion. 171.
action. 479.
action of wind. 58.
acute accent. 357.
Adam's apple. 114.
addition. 723.
adductor muscle. 102.
adhesive bandage. 629.
adhesive tape. 629.
adipose tissue. 117, 136.
adit. 636.
adjustable channel. 259.
adjustable foot. 383.
adjustable frame. 262.
adjustable lamp. 221.
adjustable pedestal. 205.
adjustable seat. 421.
adjustable spanner. 258.
adjustable spud wrench. 276.
adjustable waist tab. 293.
adjustable waistband. 317.
adjustable wrench. 258.
adjuster. 630.
adjusting knob. 257.
adjusting lever. 492.
adjusting nut. 613.
adjusting ring. 260.
adjusting screw. 259, 282, 612.
adjustment slide. 294.
adjustment wheel. 287.
administration building. 638.
administration office. 648.
administrative building. 660.
adrenal gland. 128.
adressee. 361.
advertising sign. 428.
adze. 588.

aerated filter. 277.
aerator. 271.
aerial. 397.
aerial ladder truck. 676.
aerocondenser. 668.
aerodynamic brake. 672.
affricate consonants. 358.
Africa. 49.
African warrior. 689.
Afro. 331.
Afro comb. 338.
aft stabilizer fin. 433.
afterbay. 651, 652, 655.
afterfeather. 96.
aftermast. 430.
agitation. 722.
agitator. 240.
agnolotti. 145.
agricultural machinery. 162, 163,
   164.
aiguillette de gîte à la noix. 149.
aiguillette de romsteck. 149.
aileron. 448, 556, 705.
air bladder. 99.
air brake. 556, 705.
air brake handle. 556.
air brake hydraulic jack. 705.
air bulb release. 374.
air cap. 280.
air chamber. 267, 272.
air-circulating fan. 206.
air cleaner. 704.
air-cleaner filter. 678.
air concentrator. 340.
air conditioning. 206.
air conditioning. 421.
air diffuser. 429.
air fan. 165.
air filter. 253, 405.
air gap. 669.
air hole. 107, 345, 367.
air hose. 550, 639.
air inlet. 450, 455.
air inlet control. 201.
air inlet grille. 340.
air intake. 42, 418, 436.
air leg. 639.
air lock. 437, 438.
air lock entrance hatch. 437.
air mattress. 598.
air outlet grille. 340.
air passage. 639.
air pressure adjusting screw. 280.
air-pressure pump. 612.
air scoop. 408.
air sealing gland. 482.
air space. 42, 97.
air tank. 437.
air temperature. 62, 63.
air-tight diaphragm. 405.
air-to-air missile. 705, 706.
air-to-surface missile. 706.
air transportation. 721.
air tube. 205.
air valve. 280.
air vent. 242.

air warning radar. 439.
aircraft gate. 452.
airframe. 557.
airlock. 42, 661.
airport. 452, 453.
airspeed indicator. 556.
aisle. 174.
ala. 133.
Alaskan snowshoe. 563.
albumen. 97.
alidade. 614.
alighting board. 107.
align horizontally. 362.
align vertically. 362.
all-in-one vest. 315.
alley. 537, 542.
almond. 75, 78.
alphabet. 386.
alphabet. 145.
alphanumeric keyboard. 470.
alpine skier. 559.
alpine skiing. 559, 560.
Alsace glass. 222.
Altar. 41.
altazimuth mounting. 623.
alteration line. 503.
alternator. 405, 418.
alternator indicator. 399.
altimeter. 555, 556.
altitude coarse-motion clamp. 623.
altitude control system. 65.
altitude scales. 47.
altocumulus. 52.
altostratus. 52.
alula. 96.
alveolar bone. 123.
amanita virosa. 73.
ambulatory. 174.
American bread. 146.
American Cheddar. 154.
American corn bread. 146.
American model. 359.
American proofreading model.
   365.
American white bread. 146.
ammeter. 410.
ammunition stowage. 704.
ampersand. 723.
amplifier. 389.
amplifier-tuner. 379.
ampulla. 136.
ampulla of fallopian tube. 117.
anal canal. 127.
anal fin. 98.
anal proleg. 100.
analogue display. 605.
analogue frequency meter. 379.
analytical balance. 609.
anatomy. 99.
anchor. 447.
anchor cable. 447.
anchor-windlass room. 433.
anchorage block. 416.
ancient. 367.
ancient and modern signs. 712.
anconeus. 119.

The terms in **bold type** indicate the title of an illustration; those in *italic* correspond to the British terminology.

725

andiron. 201.
Andromeda. 40.
anemometer. 63.
aneroid barometer. 612.
Anfrom. 154.
angle brace. 190.
angle scale. 263.
angle valve. 203.
Anik. 393.
animal cell. 113.
animal kingdom. 87.
ankle. 114.
ankle length. 297.
ankle sock. 311.
ankle-strap. 319.
anklet. 311.
annular combustion chamber. 450.
annular eclipse. 37.
annular shielding slab. 662.
annulet. 170.
anode. 273, 620.
Antarctic Circle. 35.
Antarctic Ocean. 49.
Antarctica. 49.
antefix. 171.
antenna. 100, 103, 106, 397, 448,
    581.
antennule. 103.
anterior chamber. 131.
anterior commissure. 130.
anterior end. 101.
anterior notch. 132.
anterior pulmonary plexus. 126.
anterior root. 130.
anterior tibial. 118.
anterior view. 114, 117, 118, 120,
    122.
anther. 72.
anti-aircraft gun. 439.
anti-collision light. 448.
anti-friction pad. 560.
anti-reverse lock. 580.
anti-skating device. 380.
anti-slip shoe. 278.
anti-submarine mortar. 439.
anti-tank missile. 706.
anti-torque tail rotor. 455.
anticipator. 611.
anticipator indicator. 611.
anticline. 640.
antihelix. 132.
antireflection coating. 670.
antitragus. 132.
antivibration handle. 253.
anus. 99, 102, 116, 117, 127.
anvil. 613, 639.
aorta. 126.
aperture. 101.
aperture scale. 372.
apex. 101, 104, 123, 134, 636.
apical foramen. 123.
apocrine sweat gland. 136.
apostrophe. 357, 363.
apple. 76.
apple. 76.
appoggiatura. 476.
appointment book. 464.
approach. 570, 571, 590.
approach ramp. 416.
apricot. 75.
apron. 209, 210, 213, 452, 579,
    585, 682.
apse. 174.
apsidiole. 174.
Aquarius, the Water Bearer. 712.
aquastat. 204.
aquatic bird. 97.
aquatic bird. 97.
aqueous humor. 131.
aqueous humour. 131.
aquifer. 650.
Arabic. 355.
arbor. 247.
arc tube. 284.
arc tube mount structure. 284.
arc welding. 281.

arc welding machine. 281.
arcade. 174.
arch. 42, 175, 415.
arch bridge. 415.
arch dam. 653.
arch of the aorta. 124.
archboard. 464.
Archer. 41.
arches. 172.
architectural styles. 170.
architecture. 167.
architrave. 170.
archivolt. 175.
Arctic. 49.
Arctic Circle. 35.
arctic continental. 62.
arctic maritime. 62.
Arctic Ocean. 49.
area of ice. 544.
arena. 570, 571.
Arenberg parquet. 196.
areola. 117.
argent. 710.
Aries, the Ram. 712.
arm. 91, 115, 210, 221, 447, 487,
    499, 505, 506, 619, 631, 679,
    681.
arm elevator. 380.
arm guard. 530.
arm nut. 506.
arm pad. 534.
arm piece. 630.
arm position. 549.
arm rest. 380, 400.
arm slit. 301.
arm stump. 210.
arm support. 630.
armchair. 210.
armchairs. 211.
Armenian. 355.
armet. 690.
armet. 690.
armhole. 297, 306.
armoire. 215.
armor. 690.
armored cord. 388.
armour. 690.
armpit. 114.
armrest. 631.
armstand. 548.
armstand dive. 549.
arpeggio. 476.
arquebus. 696.
array elevation and tensioning
    mechanism. 393.
arrester hook. 705.
arrivals concourse. 454.
arrivals schedule. 426.
arrivals timetable. 426.
arrow. 691.
Arrow. 40.
arrow rest. 691.
artichoke. 81.
articulated road train. 403.
articulated vehicule. 403.
articulating hinge point. 679.
articulation. 398.
artificial fly. 581.
artificial satellite. 47.
ASA/DIN exposure index. 372.
asbestos shingle. 195.
ascending aorta. 124.
ascending colon. 127.
ascot tiee. 295.
ash. 344.
ash layer. 53.
ash lid. 201.
ashtray. 344.
Asia. 49.
asparagus. 85.
asphalt. 649.
asphalt process. 648.
asphalt shingle. 195.
asphalt still. 649.
aspirin. 629.
assembly process. 521.

assistant timer. 545.
asterisk. 357.
asteroids. 36.
asthenosphere. 47.
astragal. 170, 445.
astronomical observatory. 42.
astronomy. 33.
asymmetrical bars. 574.
atenna. 536.
athletic shirt. 297.
Atlantic Ocean. 49.
atlas. 121.
atmosphere. 47.
atrium. 173.
attaché case. 350.
attached curtain. 217.
attachments. 680.
attack knob. 495.
attack line. 536.
attack zone. 536.
attacker. 578.
attacking zone. 533.
attic. 187.
attitude acquisition. 394.
aubergine. 81.
audio console. 389.
audio control room. 389.
audio input. 382.
audio operator. 389.
audio output. 382.
auditorium. 43.
auditory ossicles. 132.
auger bit. 260.
aunt by marriage. 138.
aunt-in-law. 138.
auricle. 106, 132.
auricular. 95.
Australia. 49.
auto answer indicator. 388.
auto/manual aperture (iris) control.
    384.
auto-manual focusing switch. 384.
automatic air vent. 204.
automatic cable pulley. 558.
automatic circulating pump. 204.
automatic control system
    computer. 436.
automatic cord reel. 244.
automatic drip coffee maker.
    234.
automatic fade control. 384.
automatic flex reel. 244.
automatic frequency control. 379.
automatic relief valve. 204.
automatic rifle. 699.
automatic shut-off. 206.
automatic tank gauge. 647.
automatic tweezers. 342.
automatically-controlled door. 454.
automobile. 397, 398, 399, 400.
automobile car. 420.
autopilot control. 451.
autorefrigerating devices. 644.
autumn. 35.
autumn squash. 81.
autumnal equinox. 35.
auxiliary handle. 261.
auxiliary projector. 43.
auxiliary tank. 402.
avocado. 80.
axial-flow compressor. 450.
axial rib. 101.
axillary artery. 125.
axillary bud. 69, 70.
axillary nerve. 129.
axillary vein. 125.
axis. 121.
axle. 418, 562.
axon. 135.
azimuth coarse-motion clamp. 623.
azimuth synchro. 624.
azure. 710.

B

b. 475.
b system. 591.
baby doll. 311.
baby shells. 145.
babygro. 315.
back. 91, 95, 115, 213, 224, 225,
    226, 227, 262, 265, 293, 304,
    477, 691.
back beam. 508.
back belt. 300.
back binding. 554.
back board. 512.
back boundary line. 542.
back cornering. 512.
back court. 537, 541.
back crossbar. 563.
back judge. 528.
back of a station wagon. 398.
back pack. 322.
back pad. 534, 568.
back pocket. 294.
back score line. 544.
back stop. 480.
back straight. 569.
back strap. 568.
back upholstery. 631.
back wall. 540, 541.
back zone. 536.
backboard. 535.
backboard support. 535.
backdrop. 180.
backgammon. 592.
background. 374.
backguard. 238, 240, 241.
backing. 514.
backing board. 514.
backing hammer. 514.
backing light. 162.
backing press. 514.
backplate. 611.
backrest. 400, 408.
backspace key. 467, 470.
backstay. 430, 562.
backstep. 677.
backstop. 525.
backstretch. 569.
backstroke. 547.
backstroke start. 547.
backstroke swimmer. 547.
backstroke turn indicator. 546.
backup light. 397.
backward. 548.
backward dive. 549.
badminton. 542.
badminton racket. 542.
badminton racquet. 542.
badminton shoe. 542.
baffle. 201, 646.
bag. 488, 525.
bag well. 587.
baggage cart. 454.
baggage carts. 720.
baggage check. 426.
baggage check-in counter. 454.
baggage claim. 720.
baggage claim area. 454.
baggage compartment. 455.
baggage conveyor. 453.
baggage lockers. 426.
baggage racks. 435.
baggage room. 426.
baggage trailer. 453.
baggage trolley. 454.
bagpipes. 488.
baguette cut. 327.
bail arm. 580.
bailey. 177.
Bailey bridge. 417.
baize. 583, 584.
bake element. 238.
Baker tent. 597.
baking utensils. 230.
balaclava. 314.
balalaika. 487.

The terms in **bold type** indicate the title of an illustration; those in *italic* correspond to the British terminology.

Balance. 41.
balance beam. 574.
balance control. 379.
balance rail. 480.
balance wheel. 605.
balcony. 188.
balk area. 584.
balk line. 584.
balk line spot. 584.
ball. 526, 531, 587.
ball. 502, 510, 543, 545, 696.
ball assembly. 271.
ball bearing. 367, 562.
ball boy. 537.
ball-cock supply valve. 268.
ball cross-section. 587.
ball-end. 521.
ball of clay. 519.
ball peen. 257.
ball peen hammer. 257.
ball rack. 590.
ball return track. 590.
ball stud of circle drawbar. 680.
ball winder. 510.
ballast. 422.
ballast tank. 645.
ballerina. 321.
ballerina. 319.
ballet slippers. 321.
balloon pants. 322.
ballpoint pen. 367.
baluster. 197.
balustrade. 182, 188.
bamboos. 593.
banana. 80.
band. 380.
band ring. 325.
band selectors. 379.
bandage. 579.
banding wheel. 519.
bands. 444.
bangs. 331.
banjo. 487.
bank. 660.
bank of heliostats. 668.
Banon. 155.
banquette. 212.
bar. 93, 485, 492, 575, 592, 720.
bar frame. 221.
bar line. 476.
bar nose. 253.
barb. 61, 96, 581.
barber comb. 338.
barbette. 176.
barbican. 177.
baren. 515.
barge. 645.
bark. 71.
barn. 161.
barn doors. 373.
barograph. 63, 556.
barometric pressure. 62.
barometric tendency. 62.
barred spiral galaxy. 39.
barrel. 605.
barrel. 340, 341, 367, 489, 694,
   697, 698, 699, 700, 701, 702,
   703.
barrel bag. 348.
barrel cuff. 306.
barrel jacket. 697.
barrel nut. 699.
barrel organ. 489.
barren. 635.
barrette. 343.
barrow. 427, 685.
bartizan. 177.
basaltic layer. 48.
base. 170, 200, 220, 242, 243,
   260, 261, 284, 340, 380, 392,
   422, 423, 514, 573, 609, 614,
   615, 619, 675, 702, 709.
base course. 413.
base elbow. 275.
base line. 625.
base of lamp. 372.

base of splat. 210.
base plate. 64, 263, 380, 560, 614,
   625.
base plug. 696.
base ring. 694.
base rock. 650.
base width. 658.
baseball. 525, 526.
baseboard. 376.
baseboard radiator. 203.
baseboard register. 202.
baseline. 537.
basement. 189.
basement membrane. 135.
basement window. 187.
baseplate. 697.
**basic plan of the Greek temple.
171.**
basic weaves. 511.
basil. 143.
basilic vein. 125.
basin. 660.
basin side. 660.
basin wrench. 276.
basket. 535.
basket. 233, 234, 240, 535, 559,
   561.
basket-handle. 172.
basket weave pattern. 196.
basketball. 535.
basketball. 535.
basketball shoe. 535.
bass bridge. 479.
bass drum. 486.
bass drum. 491, 493.
bass keyboard. 489.
bass pick-up. 494.
bass register. 489.
bass tone control. 379.
bassoon. 483, 490, 491.
bassoons. 493.
baster. 231.
bastion. 176.
bat. 108, 526.
bat. 543.
bat. 526.
bateau neck. 309.
bath. 269.
bathing trunks. 545.
bathing wrap. 315.
bathrobe. 311.
bathroom. 269.
bathroom. 189.
bathroom scales. 610.
bathtub. 269.
bathyscaphe. 437.
batrachian. 105.
batt insulation. 195.
batten. 180, 551, 552, 557.
batten pocket. 551, 552.
batter. 525.
batter head. 486.
batter's box. 525.
batter's helmet. 526.
battery. 372, 406.
battery. 65, 371, 437.
battery box. 402.
battery case. 406.
battery check meter. 383.
battery cover. 406.
batting glove. 526.
battlement. 177.
batwing sleeve. 306.
bavette. 149.
bay. 38.
bay antler. 89.
bayonet mount. 368, 370.
bayonets. 693.
bazooka. 700.
beach. 48, 51.
beach bag. 348.
Beacon antenna. 65.
bead wire. 407.
beam. 89, 163, 574, 608, 609, 610.
beam arrest. 609.
beam balance. 608.

beam bridge. 414.
beam gantry. 658.
beam pump. 641.
beam reach. 553.
bean bag (chair). 212.
bean sprouts. 85.
bear away (to). 551.
bear paw. 563.
bearer. 482.
bearing. 611.
bearing pad. 663.
beater. 165, 235, 508.
beater ejector. 235.
beater handtree. 508.
beater sley. 508.
beaters. 235.
Beatle cut. 331.
Beaumont. 155.
beaver. 90.
beaver. 690.
beaver tail. 563.
bed. 214.
bed. 513, 518, 574.
bed handle. 517.
bed lamp. 220.
**bed-mattress and accessories.
598.**
bedrock. 616.
bedroom. 189, 445.
bedside lamp. 220.
beef. 148, 149, 152.
beehive. 161.
beer mug. 222.
beet. 84.
beetroot. 84.
begin a new paragraph. 362.
belfry. 174.
bell. 483, 484.
bell bottoms. 310.
bell brace. 483.
bell buoy. 444.
bell roof. 191.
bell tower. 175.
bellows. 376, 489.
bellows strap. 489.
bellowslike joint. 458.
belly. 91, 95, 150, 153, 691.
belt. 294.
belt. 261, 291, 407, 575, 578, 672.
belt buckle. 291.
belt carrier. 291, 294, 316.
belt loop. 291, 294, 316, 599.
beltbag. 559.
belted radial tire. 407.
belted radial tyre. 407.
bench. 212, 428, 635.
bench height. 635.
bench saw. 262.
bend. 328, 581.
Berenice's Hair. 40.
beret. 314.
bergère. 210.
bergschrund. 56.
Bering Sea. 49.
berm. 652.
Bermuda shorts. 310.
bertha collar. 308.
best-end. 153.
betting layout. 594, 595.
between-the-lens shutter. 371.
bevel. 538.
bezel. 325.
bezel facet (8). 327.
bias. 502.
bias-ply tire. 407.
bias-ply tyre. 407.
bib. 315.
bib. 310, 316, 576.
bib necklace. 326.
bib tap. 271.
biceps of arm. 118.
biceps of thigh. 119.
biconcave. 625.
biconvex. 625.
bicycle. 411, 412.
bicycle horn. 412.

bifocal. 328.
big bowtie. 322.
Big Dog. 41.
bikini. 313.
bikini briefs. 297.
bill. 447.
bill compartment. 351.
bill-file. 461.
billboard. 178.
billfold. 351.
billhook. 252.
billiard spot. 584.
billiards cue. 582.
billiards equipment. 582.
bimetal element. 611.
bimetallic helix. 611.
bimetallic thermometer. 611.
binding. 298, 554.
binocular microscope. 619.
biology. 723.
bipod. 697, 701.
bird. 95, 96, 97.
Bird of Paradise. 41.
bird of prey. 97.
bird of prey. 97.
birth. 723.
biscuit. 157.
biscuit cutters. 230.
biscuit press. 230.
biscuit sheet. 230.
Bishop (B). 591.
bishop sleeve. 306.
bit. 260, 345, 568, 639, 640.
bitumen. 650.
bitumen pumping. 650.
bitumen treatment. 650.
bivalve shell. 101.
Black. 591, 592, 594, 595.
black ball. 584.
black currant. 74.
black rye bread. 146.
black salsify. 84.
Black Sea. 49.
black square. 591.
blackhead remover. 343.
blade. 70, 148, 206, 224, 227, 234,
   236, 252, 257, 258, 262, 263,
   285, 287, 337, 338, 500, 501,
   534, 543, 550, 562, 577, 581,
   588, 656, 657, 672, 678, 680,
   693.
blade arm. 680.
blade close stop. 338.
blade guard. 262, 280.
blade height adjustment. 262.
blade injector. 337.
blade lever. 513.
blade lift fan. 435.
blade-locking bolt. 263.
blade rotation mechanism. 680.
blade tilt lock. 263.
blade tilting mechanism. 262.
blank. 593.
blanket. 516.
blanket. 214.
blanket insulation. 195.
blanket sleepers. 315.
blast screen. 700.
blastodisc. 97.
blazer. 307.
bleeder valve. 203.
blender. 235.
blending attachment. 235.
bleu de Bresse. 154.
blind cloth. 219.
block. 482, 553, 685.
block bracket. 218.
blockboard. 195.
blood circulation. 124, 125.
blood vessel. 123, 136, 137.
blood vessels. 108.
bloomers. 317.
blouse. 538.
blouses. 305.
blow pipe. 488.
blower. 204, 205, 206, 481.

The terms in **bold type** indicate the title of an illustration; those in *italic* correspond to the British terminology.

blower motor. 205.
blowing snow. 60.
blowlamp. 281.
blowout preventer. 640.
blucher oxford. 320.
blue ball. 584.
blue beam. 392.
blue cap. 545.
blue flag. 545.
blue line. 533.
blue mussel. 102.
blue outer circle. 544.
blueberry. 74.
blusher brush. 332.
boa. 309.
board. 265.
board. 551.
board cutter. 513.
boarding joist. 196.
boarding step. 455.
boarding walkway. 452.
boards. 533.
boater. 314.
bob. 331, 607.
bobbin. 506.
bobbin. 500, 509, 510.
bobbin case. 500.
bobbin lace. 506.
bobbin winder. 510.
bobbin winder. 499.
bobby pin. 343.
bobeche. 220.
bobsleigh. 564.
bobstay. 430.
body. 134, 243, 260, 271, 359,
    361, 401, 421, 444, 482, 483,
    563, 572, 574, 581, 607, 621.
body lacing. 563.
body lift cylinder. 682.
body of nail. 137.
body pad. 534.
body shirt. 305.
body side molding. 397.
body stocking. 317.
body suit. 312.
body tube. 619.
body whorl. 101.
body wire. 576.
bogie. 418, 421.
bogie and track. 429.
bogie car-carrying wagon. 420.
bogie flat wagon. 420.
bogie frame. 418.
bogie open wagon. 420.
bogie tank wagon. 420.
bogie van. 420.
bogie wagon. 419.
bogie well wagon. 420.
boiler. 204.
boiler. 203, 438, 668.
boiler room. 439.
boilers. 433.
bold. 365.
bold capitals. 365.
boldface. 365.
boldface capitals. 365.
bole. 71.
bolero. 307.
bollard. 440.
bolster. 214, 224, 227.
bolt. 264.
bolt. 259, 544, 701.
bolt carrier. 699.
bolt catch. 699.
bolt follower. 266.
bonding jumper. 288.
bone folder. 512.
boning knife. 227.
bonnet. 397, 403.
bonnet. 271, 315.
bonus tiles. 593.
book end. 462.
bookbinding leather. 514.
booking hall. 426.
boom. 374, 552, 675, 679, 681.
boom operator. 390.

boom point sheave. 675.
boom truck. 453.
boom vang. 552.
booster intermediate station. 644.
booster parachute. 457.
boot. 397.
boot. 482, 550, 555, 562, 565,
    575.
boot jack. 320.
borage. 143.
bordeaux. 222.
bore. 695.
bottle cart. 281.
bottle opener. 229, 243.
bottom. 163, 554, 559.
bottom bracket axle. 412.
bottom cylinder. 516, 518.
bottom deck. 647.
bottom deckboard. 685.
bottom-end transverse member.
    425.
bottom face. 327.
bottom of collar. 305.
bottom of the pool. 545, 548.
bottom pocket. 584.
bottom rail. 198, 215.
bottom retainer. 419.
bottom ring. 657.
bottom road. 637.
bottom side rail. 425.
bottom surface. 556.
bottomboard. 482.
bouffant. 330.
bound book. 512.
Boursault. 154.
bow. 478, 691.
bow. 298, 551, 691.
bow collar. 308.
bow door ramp. 435.
bow rudder. 434.
bow saw. 600.
bow tie. 295.
bowl. 226, 236, 345, 443, 682.
bowl lid. 345.
bowl with serving spout. 236.
bowler. 590.
bowline. 601.
bowline on a bight. 601.
bowling. 590.
bowling ball. 590.
bowling shoe. 590.
bows. 145.
bows and crossbow. 691.
bowsprit. 430.
bowstring. 691.
box. 179.
box bag. 348.
box-beam Y frame. 680.
box car. 419.
box end wrench. 258.
box front lights. 179.
box pallet. 685.
box pleat. 217, 304.
box spring. 214.
boxer. 579.
boxer shorts. 297.
boxing. 579.
boxing boot. 579.
boxing glove. 579.
boxing shoe. 579.
bra. 313.
brace. 260.
brace. 192, 279, 431, 659.
brace clip. 294.
bracelet with curb chain. 325.
bracelets. 325.
braces. 294.
brachial. 118.
brachial artery. 125.
brachial plexus. 129.
brachioradial. 118, 119.
brachioradialis. 119.
bracket. 218, 219, 339, 442.
bracket base. 215.
bracket slot. 219.
brackets. 357.

bract. 78.
braided rope. 601.
braids. 330.
brail. 431.
Braille. 356.
brain. 99.
brake. 631.
brake cable. 411.
brake handle. 408.
brake lever. 411.
brake line. 407.
brake lining. 407.
brake pad. 407.
brake pedal. 400, 410.
brake shoe. 407.
brake van. 420.
brakeman. 564.
brakes. 407.
branch. 71, 85, 93, 267, 567.
branch duct. 202.
branch return pipe. 203.
branch supply pipe. 203.
branches. 71.
brandy. 222.
brass ball faucet. 271.
brass family. 484.
brass floor frange. 268.
brassie; no. 2 wood. 586.
brassiere cup. 313.
brattice. 177.
brayer. 516.
Brazil nut. 78.
bread. 146.
bread and butter plate. 223.
bread guide. 237.
bread knife. 227.
break line. 308.
breakdown service. 721.
breaker. 51.
breaking pliers. 521.
breaking the wall. 593.
breast. 117.
breast. 95, 114, 147, 151, 153.
breast beam. 508.
breast collar. 568.
breast dart. 292.
breast pocket. 292, 295, 305.
breast welt pocket. 293.
breastplate. 690.
breaststroke. 547.
breaststroke kick. 547.
breaststroke swimmer. 547.
breaststroke turn. 547.
breather valve. 647.
breathing apparatus. 676.
breathing in. 547.
breathing out. 547.
breech. 694, 702.
breechblock. 698.
breechblock operating lever
    assembly. 698.
breeches. 576.
breeching rope. 694.
Brick. 154, 193.
bridge. 582.
bridge. 218, 328, 438, 477, 489,
    621, 645.
bridge and chart room. 434.
bridge of nose. 133.
bridge unit. 494.
bridging. 192.
bridle. 567.
bridle. 568.
bridle tape. 480.
Brie. 155.
brig. 432.
brigantine. 432.
bright star projector. 43.
brightness control. 392.
brilliant cut facets. 327.
brilliant full cut. 327.
brim. 298, 314.
brioche. 156.

briolette cut. 327.
brisket. 148, 152.
bristle. 337, 338, 339, 341.
bristles. 280.
British cut. 152, 153.
British model. 361.
British proofreading model. 366.
broad beans. 85.
broad-leaved endive. 82.
broad ligament of uterus. 117.
broad reach. 553.
broad welt. 300.
broad welt side pocket. 291, 304.
broadest of back. 119.
broccoli. 81.
broil element. 238.
brooch. 325.
brood cell. 107.
brood chamber. 107.
broom. 201.
broom point downward. 446.
broom point upward. 446.
brother. 138.
brother/sister. 138.
brow brush and lash comb. 333.
brow reinforce. 690.
brow tine. 89.
browband. 567.
brown ball. 584.
Brunn's membrane. 133.
brush. 280.
brush. 79, 339, 515.
brush and rails. 565, 566.
Brussels sprouts. 82.
buck shots. 145.
bucket. 657, 675, 679.
bucket chain excavator. 635.
bucket cylinder. 679.
bucket hinge pin. 679.
bucket ring. 657.
bucket seat. 400.
bucket tooth. 679.
bucket wheel excavator. 635, 650.
buckle. 502.
buckle. 294, 349, 400, 560.
bud. 83.
buffer. 418.
buffer. 701.
buffer tank. 644.
bufferstop. 424.
buffet. 719.
buffet. 216.
bugle. 484.
building. 178.
building materials. 193, 194, 195.
building sewer. 267.
buildings. 161.
built-in microphone. 384.
bulb. 85, 93, 284, 322, 611, 645.
bulb dibber. 249.
bulb dibble. 249.
bulb unit. 660.
bulb vegetables. 83.
bulbil. 83.
bulk carrier. 441.
bulkhead. 402.
bulkhead deck. 434.
bulkhead flat car. 420.
bulkhead flat wagon. 420.
Bull. 40.
bull's eye. 187.
bulldozer. 678.
bulldozer. 635.
bullet. 702.
bullfighter. 321.
bullion stitch. 507.
bullseye. 446.
bulwark. 430.
bumper. 244, 397, 402, 403, 418,
    424.
bumper guard. 397, 541.
bumps. 714.
bun. 330, 331.
bun tin. 230.
bunch. 344.
bund wall. 647.

The terms in **bold type** indicate the title of an illustration; those in *italic* correspond to the British terminology.

bundle. 85, 658.
bungalow. 183.
bunk. 438.
bunker. 585.
bunker oil. 649.
bunker silo. 161.
bunting bag. 316.
buoyancy compensator. 550.
buoys. 444.
burden. 650.
bureau. 216.
burgundy. 222.
buried pipeline. 644.
burin. 516.
burner. 233.
burner ring. 233.
burnisher. 515.
burr. 89.
bus stop. 178.
bus transportation. 721.
busbar. 655.
bush. 247.
bushing. 651, 659.
butane carrier. 645.
butane tank. 344.
butt. 344, 506, 538, 581, 582, 691, 699, 703.
butt cap. 580.
butt end. 534.
butt grip. 580.
butt guide. 580.
butt hinge. 209.
butt plate. 697, 702.
butt portion. 150, 151.
butt section. 580.
butt-strap. 328.
butt welding. 282.
butte. 55.
butter compartment. 239.
butter curler. 227.
butter dish. 223.
butter knife. 224.
butterfly. 100.
butterfly kick. 547.
butterfly stroke. 547.
butterfly swimmer. 547.
butterfly turn. 547.
buttock. 115.
button. 284, 295, 489, 577, 694.
button loop. 294.
button notch. 243.
button strap. 316.
button-through smock. 305.
buttondown collar. 295.
buttoned placket. 295, 301, 305.
buttonhole. 291, 295, 296.
buttress. 174, 175, 653.
buttress dam. 653.
buttstock. 701.
by-pass taxiway. 452.
bypass contact. 385.

C

c. 475.
C-clamp. 259.
c clef. 475.
cab. 408, 678, 679, 680, 681, 682, 684.
cabbage lettuce. 82.
cabin. 434, 455, 558.
cabinet. 206, 240, 241, 242, 269, 378, 392.
cable. 601.
cable. 261, 322, 384, 442, 573, 601.
cable binding. 561.
cable car. 558.
cable release. 374.
cable ripper. 287.
cable sleeve. 261.
cable stay anchorage. 416.
cable-stayed bridge. 416.
cable stitch. 504.
cabochon cut. 327.

caboose. 420.
cabriole leg. 210.
cabriolet. 210.
cactus. 55.
caddie. 585.
caecum. 127.
café curtain. 217.
cage. 444.
cagoule. 589.
caisson. 441.
cake. 156.
cake mascara. 333.
cake pan. 230.
cake tin. 230.
calamus. 96.
calandria. 662, 664.
calandria tube. 662.
calandria vault. 662.
calcaneus. 92, 121.
calcar. 108.
calculator. 351, 372.
calculator/cheque book holder. 351.
calculator dial. 372.
calendar pad. 464.
calf. 115.
caliper. 407.
calipers. 517.
call director telephone. 388.
Callisto. 36.
calls indicator. 388.
callus. 101.
calm. 61.
calyx. 72, 74, 76, 79, 128.
cam. 506.
cam lever. 506.
cam ring. 260.
cam spring. 703.
camber. 561.
cambium. 71.
Camembert. 155.
camera 1. 391.
camera 2. 391.
camera 3. 391.
camera battery. 383.
camera body. 368.
camera crane. 390.
camera mount. 390.
camera platform. 374.
camera screw. 374.
cameraman. 390.
camisole. 312.
camping and caravan site. 721.
camping area. 721.
camping equipment. 598, 599, 600.
camping prohibited. 721.
camshaft. 405, 517.
can. 446.
can buoy. 444.
can opener. 243.
can opener. 229, 599.
Canadian Cheddar. 154.
Canadian crutch. 630.
Canadian elk. 89.
Canadian model. 360.
canal bed. 440.
canal boat. 645.
canal lock. 440.
canal lock. 441.
Cancer, the Crab. 712.
CANDU nuclear generating station. 661.
CANDU reactor. 662.
cane pen. 367.
canes. 630.
canine. 90, 123.
canister shot. 695.
canister vacuum cleaner. 244.
canned failed fuel. 665.
cannelloni. 145.
cannon. 91, 704.
canopy. 346, 448, 555, 587, 596, 682, 705.
canopy pole. 596.
Cantal. 155.

cantaloupe. 81.
cantilever. 653.
cantilever bridge. 414.
cantilever span. 414.
cantle. 649.
canton. 709.
canvas. 579.
canvas divider. 596.
cap. 73, 197, 275, 281, 285, 298, 314, 586, 671.
cap iron. 257.
cap rock. 650.
cap sleeve. 306.
capacitor. 672.
capillary bore. 611.
capital. 170.
capitals. 365.
capitals for initials, small capitals for the rest. 365.
capitulum. 72.
capless wig. 331.
caponiere. 176.
capped column. 57.
capped tee. 202.
cappelletti. 145.
Caprice des Dieux. 154.
Capricorn, the Goat. 712.
capstan. 516.
capstan. 439.
capsule. 79.
captain. 564.
captain's quarters. 433.
captain's seat. 451.
car. 397, 398, 399, 400.
car. 181, 425.
car anchor. 447.
car buffer. 181.
car coat. 300.
car deck. 435.
car guide rail. 181.
car parking. 188.
car rental. 721.
car safety device. 181.
car wash. 401.
carabiner. 588.
carafe. 234.
carapace. 103, 109.
caraway seeded rye bread. 146.
carbon. 521.
carbon copy. 359, 361.
carbon granules. 387.
carburetor. 404, 405, 409.
carburettor. 404, 405, 409.
card and photo case. 351.
card case. 351.
card games. 592.
card holder. 466.
card index cabinet. 464.
card punch. 472.
card reader. 472.
card support. 64.
cardan shaft. 162.
cardboard case. 702.
cardiac plexus. 126.
cardigan. 296, 307.
cardinal system of marking. 445.
cardoon. 85.
cards. 464.
cargo-bay access hatch. 457.
cargo-bay door. 457.
cargo boom. 434.
cargo hatch. 433.
cargo terminal. 452.
Caribbean Sea. 49.
caribou. 89.
carnassial. 90.
carnivore's jaw. 90.
carom billiards. 583.
carousel. 454.
carpal pad. 94.
carpentry. 265.
carpentry: fasteners. 264.
carpentry: tools. 257, 258, 259, 260, 261, 262, 263.

carpus. 92, 120.
carré. 150.
carré raccourci. 147.
carriage. 506.
carriage. 467, 505, 506, 684, 694.
carriage release lever. 467.
carriage return. 467.
carriageway. 413.
carrier. 291, 294, 295.
carrier. 218, 411.
carrier bag. 348.
carrot. 84.
carry handle. 341, 347.
carry-on bag. 347.
carrying handle. 614, 699, 701.
cart path. 585.
carton. 344.
cartoon. 521.
cartridge. 367, 371, 702, 703.
cartridge (rifle). 702.
cartridge (shotgun). 702.
cartridge fuse. 285.
cartridge stem. 271.
cartwheel hat. 314.
carving fork. 227.
carving knife. 227.
case. 337, 341, 342, 479, 489, 492, 611, 613, 702.
casement. 199.
casement window. 199.
cash readout. 401.
cashew. 78.
casing. 203, 206.
casing first string. 641.
casing second string. 641.
Caspian Sea. 49.
cassette. 371, 469.
cassette holder. 381.
cassette loading slot. 382.
cassette recorder. 469.
Cassiopeia. 40.
cast-on stitches. 504.
castanets. 485.
caster. 206, 244, 486.
castle. 177.
casual water. 585.
cat. 94.
catadioptric ring. 446.
catalytic reformer. 648.
catalytic reforming plant. 649.
catch. 693.
catch glove. 534.
catch spring. 693.
catcher. 526.
catcher. 525.
catcher's box. 525.
catcher's glove. 526.
catenary. 661.
catering vehicle. 453.
caterpillar. 100.
cathedral. 174.
cathode. 620.
cattle crossing. 715.
catwalk. 390.
caudal fin. 98.
caudal vertebrae. 92.
cauliflower. 81.
caution. 718.
caution, pedestrian crossing. 718.
caution, slippery floor. 718.
cave. 54.
cave. 51.
cavernous body. 116.
cecum. 127.
cedilla. 357.
ceiling. 540, 541.
ceiling collar. 202.
ceiling fan. 206.
ceiling fitting. 220.
ceiling grille. 202.
ceiling joist. 192.
ceiling register. 202.
celeriac. 84.
celery. 85.
celesta. 493.
celestial co-ordinate system. 35.

The terms in **bold type** indicate the title of an illustration; those in *italic* correspond to the British terminology.

celestial equator. 35.
celestial meridian. 35.
celestial sphere. 35.
celiac trunk. 124, 128.
cell. 100, 555, 623.
cell body. 135.
cell connector. 406.
cell membrane. 113.
cell wall. 113.
cellophane wrapped packet. 344.
cement. 194.
cement screed. 196.
cementum. 123.
cent. 723.
Centaur. 41.
center. 362, 528, 529, 533, 535.
center-aisle. 421.
center back. 532, 536, 539.
center back vent. 293.
center base. 709.
center bearing. 450.
center chief. 709.
center circle. 532, 535.
center console. 399.
center court. 541.
center cut. 150.
center electrode. 406.
center face-off circle. 533.
center field. 525.
center fielder. 525.
center flag. 532.
center forward. 532, 536, 539.
center hole. 380.
center Keelson. 645.
center knife-edge. 609.
center line. 527, 533, 535, 536,
    539, 542, 543, 544, 576.
center mark. 537.
center pocket. 584.
center point. 709.
center post. 215, 397.
center service line. 537.
center span. 416.
center spot. 532, 583, 584.
center strap. 537.
center string. 583.
center tank. 645.
center wheel. 605, 607.
centerboard. 552.
Central America. 49.
central column. 672.
central compartment. 349.
central console. 451.
central focusing wheel. 621.
central incisor. 123.
central instrument panel. 451.
central nervous system. 130.
central ply. 265.
central processing unit. 468, 469,
    472.
central pumping. 644.
central screw. 514.
centre. 362, 528, 533, 535.
centre-back. 532, 536, 539.
centre back vent. 293.
centre base. 709.
centre bearing. 450.
centre chief. 709.
centre circle. 532, 535.
centre console. 399.
centre court. 541.
centre electrode. 406.
centre face-off circle. 533.
centre field. 525.
centre fielder. 525.
centre flag. 532.
centre forward. 532, 536, 539.
centre hole. 380.
centre Keelson. 645.
centre knife-edge. 609.
centre line. 527, 533, 535, 536,
    539, 542, 543, 576.
centre mark. 537.
centre midfield. 532.
centre pocket. 584.
centre point. 709.

centre post. 215.
centre service line. 537.
centre span. 416.
centre spot. 532, 583, 584.
centre strap. 537.
centre string. 583.
centre tank. 645.
centre wheel. 605, 607.
centreboard. 552.
centriole. 113.
cep. 73.
cephalic vein. 125.
cephalothorax. 103.
Cepheus. 40.
cerebellum. 130.
**cerebrospinal axis (sagittal
    section). 130.**
cerebrum. 130.
cervical plexus. 129.
cervical vertebra (7). 121.
cervical vertebrae. 92.
chad container bin. 386.
chaffer sieve. 165.
chain. 220, 412, 607, 612.
chain brake. 253.
chain guide. 412.
chain mail. 690.
chain of dunes. 55.
chain pipe wrench. 276.
chain shot. 695.
chain stay. 411.
chain stitch. 507.
chain wheel. 412.
chainsaw. 253.
chainsaw chain. 253.
chaise longue. 213.
chalaza. 97.
chalet. 558.
chalk. 582.
chamber. 703.
Chameleon. 41.
champagne flute. 222.
champagne glass. 222.
chandelier. 220.
change dial. 505.
change machine. 426.
channel. 423, 521.
channel selector control. 382.
chanter. 488.
chanterelle. 73.
Chantilly parquet. 196.
chapel. 433.
character. 466.
characters. 593.
chard. 82.
charge. 702.
charge machine. 665.
charger. 337.
charges. 710.
charging handle. 699.
charging handle catch. 699.
charging light. 337.
Charioteer. 40.
charlotte. 156.
charm bracelet. 325.
charms. 325.
chase. 694.
chase astragal. 694.
chassis. 403.
check. 480.
check-in. 720.
check nut. 64.
check-rail. 422.
check valve. 277, 282.
checkbook holder. 351.
**checkbook/secretary clutch.
    351.**
checkers. 444.
checkmate. 351.
cheek. 91, 114, 257, 581, 694.
cheek strap. 567.
cheese knife. 224.
chela. 103.
chemical treatment. 649.
chemise. 177.
cheque book cover. 351.

cheque book holder. 351.
cherimoya. 80.
cherry. 75.
chervil. 143.
chess. 591.
chess notation. 591.
chessboards. 591.
chest. 91, 114.
chest of drawers. 216.
chest protector. 526, 530.
chesterfield. 211.
chestnut. 78, 91.
chevron. 710.
chevron stitch. 507.
chick peas. 85.
chicory. 82.
chief. 709, 710.
chief timekeeper. 546.
chiffonier. 216.
children. 138, 139.
**children's clothing. 315, 316,
    317.**
chilli. 81.
chimney. 202.
chimney. 187, 200.
chimney connection. 201.
chimney flue. 200.
chimney pot. 187.
chimney stack. 187.
chin. 95, 114.
chin strap. 530.
China Sea. 49.
Chinese. 355.
Chinese cabbage. 82.
chip. 594, 595.
chipboard. 265.
chisel. 516.
chive. 83.
chlorine bleaching. 722.
chloroplast. 113.
chock. 588.
choir. 174.
choir organ manual. 481.
choker. 326.
chopsticks. 233.
chord. 476.
choroid. 131.
christening set. 315.
Christmas tree. 641.
Christmas tree. 644.
chromatin. 113.
chromosphere. 37.
chrysalis. 100.
chuck. 148, 258, 260, 261, 639.
chuck key. 261.
chuck rib. 152.
chuck short rib. 148.
chukka. 320.
chump end. 153.
chute. 637.
cigar. 344.
cigar band. 344.
cigar box. 344.
cigarette. 344.
cigarette holder. 344.
ciliary process. 131.
ciliate. 70.
cine scale. 372.
cinema. 178.
cinematography. 383.
circle. 680.
circles. 593.
circuit breaker. 285.
circuit breaker. 655, 672.
circuit test light. 700.
circuit vent. 267.
circular level. 614.
circular needle. 504.
circular saw. 263.
circular saw blade. 263.
circulating pump. 203, 669.
circumflex accent. 357.
cirque. 38.
cirrocumulus. 52.
cirrostratus. 52.
cirrus. 52.

cistern lid. 269.
citrus juicer. 236.
citrus juicer. 228.
city houses. 183.
clafoutis. 157.
clam. 102.
clam-cleat. 551, 553.
clamp. 221, 277, 285, 341, 505,
    510, 513, 561.
clamp binder. 463.
clamp lever. 341.
clamping handle. 236.
clamping nut. 236.
clamshell bucket. 681.
clapper. 387.
clarinet. 483, 490, 491.
clarinets. 493.
clasp. 349, 350.
class ring. 325.
classic. 305.
classic bag. 349.
**classification of snow crystals.
    57.**
classification yard. 425.
clavicle. 120.
claw. 94, 95, 97, 100, 103, 106,
    108, 257, 325, 514.
claw hammer. 257.
claw weight. 505.
cleaning brush. 337.
cleaning tools. 244.
cleaning tools. 244.
cleanout. 270.
cleansing sponge. 333.
clear sky. 61.
clear space. 536.
clearance light. 402.
cleared ground. 63.
cleat. 552, 553.
cleated shoe. 530.
cleaver. 227.
clefs. 475.
clew. 551.
clew line. 431.
click. 607.
cliff. 38, 48, 51.
climates of the world. 59.
climbing harness. 589.
climbing iron. 320.
climbing plant. 247.
clinical thermometer. 611.
clip. 218, 294, 341, 367, 461.
clip earring. 325.
clipboard. 464.
clippers. 338.
clitoris. 117.
cloche. 314.
clock. 391, 399, 616.
clock operator. 535.
clock timer. 237, 238.
clog. 319.
close hauled. 553.
close reach. 553.
close up. 362.
close-up lens. 370.
closed circuit television/cathode
    monitor. 666.
closed expansion tank. 204.
closed stringer. 197.
closeness setting. 337.
closet. 188, 189, 216.
closet bend. 267.
closing odds. 569.
closing salutation. 361.
closure rail. 422.
cloth roller. 508.
clothing. 289.
clothing guard. 631.
cloud amount. 61, 62.
cloud of volcanic ash. 53.
**clouds and meteorological
    symbols. 52.**
**clouds of vertical development.
    52.**
cloudy sky. 61.
clove hitch. 601.

clown. 322.
clown shoe. 322.
club. 592.
club chair. 211.
club divider. 587.
club house. 569.
club house turn. 569.
clubhouse. 585.
clump of flowers. 247.
clutch bag. 348.
clutch lever. 410.
clutch pedal. 400.
co-axial machine gun. 704.
coach car. 421.
coach's box. 525.
coal bunker. 638.
coal mine. 635, 636, 637, 638, 639.
coarse adjustment knob. 619.
coast. 48.
coat dress. 302.
coat hook. 465.
coat rack. 465.
coat tree. 465.
coats. 300, 301.
cob. 85.
coccygeal nerve. 129.
coccyx. 120.
cochlea. 132.
cochlear nerve. 132.
cock. 696.
cocking handle. 701.
cocking lever. 700.
cockle. 102.
cockleshell. 210.
cockpit. 556.
cockpit. 552.
cockpit canopy. 556.
cocktail. 222.
cocktail cabinet. 216.
coconut. 78.
coeliac trunk. 124, 128.
coffee makers. 234.
coffee mill. 234.
coffee mug. 223.
coffee pot. 599.
coffee shop. 719.
coffee spoon. 226.
coil. 387.
coil spring. 219.
coiling. 519.
coin chute. 595.
coin purse. 351.
coin reject slot. 595.
coin return bucket. 388.
coin return knob. 388.
coin slot. 388, 595.
coinbox telephone. 388.
coking plant. 638.
colander. 228.
Colby. 154.
cold air. 669.
cold room. 189.
cold-water line. 268, 273.
cold-water riser. 267.
cold-water shutoff valve. 273.
cold-water supply line. 272.
collagenous fiber. 136.
collagenous fibre. 136.
collapsible fire ladder. 676.
collar. 308.
collar. 43, 69, 291, 293, 295, 337, 575.
collar bar. 326.
collar point. 295, 308.
collar stay. 295.
collaret. 308.
collateral. 135.
collecting funnel. 64.
collecting tube. 670.
collector. 656.
collet. 147, 151, 260, 374.
collet nut. 260.
colliery. 637.
colon. 357, 364, 386.
color analyzer. 375.

color filter. 370.
color filter set. 373.
color temperature switch. 384.
colors. 710.
colour analyser. 375.
colour filter. 370.
colour filter set. 373.
colour temperature switch. 384.
colours. 710.
columella. 101.
columella fold. 101.
column. 54, 57, 203, 220, 261, 374, 376, 415, 499, 609, 622.
column base. 170.
column crank. 374.
column lock. 374.
column of mercury. 611.
column radiator. 203.
columns. 594, 595.
coma. 39.
comb. 509.
comb. 690.
comb foundation. 107.
comb plate. 182.
combat aircraft. 705.
combination. 297.
combination box and open end wrench. 258.
combination knife. 599.
combination lock. 350.
combination pliers. 287.
combination spanner. 258.
combine harvester. 165.
combs. 338.
combustion chamber. 404, 450, 706.
comet. 39.
comfort contoured handle. 341.
comforter. 214.
comma. 357, 363, 386.
command antenna. 65, 393.
command module. 456.
command station. 706.
command system. 706.
command transmission. 706.
commander's seat. 704.
commando knife. 692.
commissure of lips of mouth. 134.
common carotid artery. 125.
common coastal features. 51.
common extensor of fingers. 119.
common hepatic artery. 125.
common iliac artery. 125, 128.
common iliac vein. 128.
common periwinkle. 104.
common peroneal nerve. 129.
common symbols. 718, 719, 720, 721.
common whipping. 601.
communicating rami. 130.
communication device. 468.
communications. 353.
company number. 361.
compartment. 350, 592, 594.
Compass. 41, 437, 550, 556.
compass card. 443, 625.
compass meridian line. 625.
compensating cables. 181.
competition ring. 566.
competitive course. 546.
competitor. 546.
completion. 601.
complex dune. 55.
complexus. 119.
complimentary close. 359.
compluvium. 173.
components of hair styles. 330, 331.
composite topmark. 446.
compound eye. 100, 106.
compound fleshy fruits. 74.
compound leaves. 70.
compressed air. 639.
compressed-air cylinder. 550, 676.
compression coupling. 270.
compression fitting. 274.

compressor. 204, 239, 404, 464.
compressor turbine. 404.
compulsory roundabout. 717.
computer room. 472.
Comté. 155.
concave. 165, 625.
concha. 132.
Concorde. 47.
concrete base. 616.
concrete block. 193.
concrete drain. 647.
concrete wall. 669.
condensate. 664.
condensation. 58.
condensation in water. 667.
condenser. 206, 376, 377, 619, 661.
condenser adjustment knob. 619.
condenser coil. 206, 239.
condensor. 204.
condominium. 183.
conductive material. 670.
conductor. 221.
conductor's podium. 493.
cone. 53, 378, 446.
configuration keys. 470.
configuration of a system. 469.
configuration of the continents. 49.
conical broach roof. 191.
conical buoy. 444.
conical magnet. 606.
conical snoot. 373.
conical washer. 268.
conjunctiva. 131.
connecting cable. 378.
connecting wire. 576.
connection and concentration equipment network. 394.
connection cable. 471.
connection point. 659.
connective tissue. 135, 136.
connector. 288.
connector link. 555.
console. 481.
constellations. 712.
constellations of the northern hemisphere. 40.
constellations of the southern hemisphere. 41.
constriction. 611.
contact. 611.
contact printer. 375.
container. 425.
container. 64, 235, 280, 434.
container car. 420.
container flat wagon. 420.
container hold. 434.
container-loading bridge. 441.
container ship. 434.
container ship. 441.
container terminal. 441.
containment. 666.
containment building. 663.
contest area. 578.
contestant. 578.
continental climates. 59.
continental margin. 50.
continental mass. 50.
continental rise. 50.
continental shelf. 48, 50.
continental slope. 48, 50.
continuity tester. 286.
continuous beam. 414.
continuous drizzle. 60.
continuous rain. 60.
continuous snow. 60.
contour feather. 96.
contrabassoon. 493.
contrast control. 392.
contre-filet. 149.
control bar. 557.
control cable. 412.
control column. 451.
control console. 43, 472.

control deck. 435, 438.
control key. 470.
control knob. 238, 471, 520.
control lever. 639.
control levers. 451.
control panel. 206, 237, 238, 240, 241, 242, 389, 390, 471, 676.
control room. 666.
control room. 43, 445, 643, 651, 660, 661.
control stand. 418.
control stick. 455, 556.
control system. 672.
control tower. 452.
control tower cab. 452.
control valve. 599.
control wheel. 677.
controller. 181, 182.
controls. 386.
convection zone. 37.
convector. 203.
converging lens. 625.
conversion. 667.
converter. 373.
convertible. 398.
convex. 625.
conveyor. 635, 638, 650.
cook's knife. 227.
cookie cutters. 230.
cookie press. 230.
cookie sheet. 230.
cooking. 600.
cooking set. 599.
cooking utensils. 232, 233.
cooking surface. 237.
cooktop. 238.
cool tip. 341.
coolant. 664, 668, 670.
coolant transfers the heat to the steam generator. 667.
cooler. 600.
cooling air. 458.
cooling fan. 377, 404, 405, 406.
cooling/heating coils. 204.
cooling liquid pump. 458.
cooling tower. 648.
cooling water. 664.
copper foil. 521.
copper pipe. 274.
copper plate. 515.
copper to plastic. 275.
copper to steel. 275.
copperplate. 515.
copy holder. 386.
copyright. 723.
cor anglais. 483.
corbel. 177.
corbel piece. 200.
cord. 243, 387, 513, 588.
cord grip. 572.
cord tieback. 217.
cordate. 70.
cordless shoe care kit. 320.
cordless telephone. 388.
core. 37, 76, 587, 601, 652, 702.
core plywood. 265.
corer. 231.
corinthian order. 170.
cork tip. 542.
corkscrew. 599.
corkscrew curls. 330.
corn. 85.
corn cutter. 342.
corn salad. 82.
cornea. 131.
corner. 512, 579.
corner arc. 532.
corner cap. 419.
corner cupboard. 216.
corner display cabinet. 216.
corner fitting. 425.
corner flag. 532.
corner lighting. 220.
corner pad. 579.
corner-stool. 579.
corner structure. 425.

The terms in **bold type** indicate the title of an illustration; those in *italic* correspond to the British terminology.

GENERAL INDEX

corner stud. 192.
corner tower. 177.
cornet. 484, 491.
cornets. 493.
cornice. 171, 187, 198, 215, 217.
corolla. 72.
corona. 37.
coronal suture. 122.
coronet. 91, 93.
corpus callosum. 130.
corpus cavernosum. 116.
correct a letter. 362.
correct a word. 362.
correcting tape. 466.
correction fluid. 461.
correction paper. 461.
corrections of diacritic symbols. 364.
corrections of errors. 362, 363.
corrections of punctuation marks. 363, 364.
corrections of type. 364.
corridor. 421.
corridor connection. 421.
corrugation. 378.
corsage. 317.
corselette. 312.
corset. 313.
corssbar. 487.
cortex. 128, 137.
corymb. 72.
cos lettuce. 82.
cosmetic sponge. 333.
cosmetic tray. 347.
costal shield. 109.
costumes. 321, 322.
côtelettes découvertes. 151.
côtelettes premières et secondes. 151.
côtes. 150.
côtes découvertes. 147.
cottage. 183.
cottage curtain. 217.
cotton applicators. 629.
cotton pagne. 689.
cotton wool ball. 629.
cotyledon. 69, 75, 79.
couched stitches. 507.
Coulommiers. 155.
coulter. 163.
counter. 318, 562.
counter memory button. 382.
counter reset button. 381.
counterguard. 176.
counterjib. 683.
counterjib ballast. 683.
counterscarp. 176.
countersink. 260.
countersunk. 264.
counterweight. 181, 380, 417, 422, 423, 610, 622, 681, 683.
counterweight guide rail. 181.
coupé. 398.
coupler head. 419.
coupler knuckle. 419.
coupler knuckle pin. 419.
courgette. 81.
course. 585.
court. 535, 536, 537, 539, 542.
court. 319.
court referee. 539.
couscous kettle. 232.
cousins. 138.
couter. 690.
cover. 346.
cover. 271.
cover. 236, 269, 345, 526, 587, 611, 615, 625, 701.
cover plate. 670.
cover slip. 619.
covered parapet walk. 177.
covered postern. 176.
covered way. 176.
covering. 514.
covering. 543.
covering disc. 164.

covering disk. 164.
cow hitch. 601.
cowl. 397.
cowl collar. 308.
Cowper's gland. 116.
cowshed. 161.
coxa. 100, 106.
Crab. 40, 103.
cradle. 219, 387, 622, 623, 698.
crak rye bread. 146.
crampon strap. 589.
crampons. 589.
cranberry. 74.
crane. 683.
Crane. 41, 42, 643.
crane runway. 683.
cranial nerves. 129.
crank. 260, 412, 440, 580.
crank handle. 517.
crash helmet. 559, 564.
crater. 38, 53, 635.
cravat. 295.
crawl swimmer. 547.
crawler crane. 683.
crawler tractor. 678.
crayfish. 103.
cream blush. 332.
cream jug. 223.
cream lipstick. 332.
creamer. 223.
crease. 294.
creation of a magnetic field. 654.
credenza. 465.
credit card wallet. 351.
Cree snowshoe. 563.
creel. 582.
cremaster. 100.
crème de Gruyère. 155.
crenate. 70.
crenel. 177.
crenulate margin. 101.
crepe support. 629.
crepidoma. 171.
crescent. 710.
crescentic dune. 55.
crest. 51, 54, 187.
crest of spillway. 651.
crevasse. 56.
crevice tool. 244.
crew cut. 331.
crew neck. 315.
crew neck sweater. 296.
crew quarters. 433.
crew sweater. 307.
cribriform plate of ethmoid. 133.
crimper. 287.
crinoline stretcher. 213.
crisper. 239.
crisscross curtains. 217.
crochet hook. 504.
croissant. 146.
crook. 483, 488.
crop elevator. 165.
cross. 710.
cross brace. 631.
cross-country ski. 561.
cross-country ski. 561.
cross-country skier. 561.
cross-country skiing. 561.
cross cut. 636, 637.
cross-guard. 693.
cross handle. 594.
cross head (Phillips). 264.
cross rail. 213.
cross rib. 148.
cross section of a buttress dam. 653.
cross section of a concrete dam. 652.
cross section of a gravity dam. 653.
cross section of a molar. 123.
cross section of a road. 413.
cross section of a stage. 180.
cross section of a street. 413.
cross section of a trunk. 71.

cross section of an arch dam. 653.
cross section of an embankment dam. 652, 653.
cross section of hydraulic turbine. 657.
cross section of hydroelectric power station. 655.
cross section of power plant. 660.
cross stitches group. 507.
cross stretcher. 213.
crossarm. 658, 659.
crossbar. 162, 411, 509, 513, 531, 545, 557, 558, 570, 571.
crossbeam. 508.
crossbow. 691.
crossbuck sign. 423.
crosse. 147, 149, 150.
crosshead. 684.
crossing. 174, 427.
crossing gate mechanism. 423.
crossover. 424.
crossover back straps dungarees. 316.
crossover cargo deck line. 645.
crosspiece. 209, 508, 630.
crosstree. 552.
crosswise grain. 502.
crotch. 297.
crotch piece. 305.
crotchet. 475.
crotchet rest. 475.
croup. 91, 573.
Crow. 41.
crown. 71, 95, 123, 298, 314, 327, 447, 520, 605.
crown block. 640.
crown tine. 89.
crownpiece. 567.
crude oil. 649.
crude oil pipeline. 644.
crus of helix. 132.
crustacean. 103.
crutch ferrule. 630.
crutch tip. 630.
crutches. 630.
crystal button. 220.
crystal drop. 220.
cubiculum. 173.
cubital vein. 125.
cucumber. 81.
cue ball. 583, 584.
cue screen. 391.
cuff. 294, 295, 310, 318, 534.
cuff section. 630.
cuirass. 690.
cuisse. 690.
cuisseau. 147.
culet. 327.
culotte. 149, 303.
cultivated mushroom. 73.
cultivator. 163.
cumulonimbus. 52.
cumulus. 52.
Cup. 41, 223, 387, 585, 599, 702.
cup conveyor. 164.
cupboard. 216.
cupola. 445, 704.
cupule. 78.
curb. 413.
curb bit. 567.
curb chain. 567.
curb rein. 567.
curled endive. 82.
curled kale. 82.
curler. 544.
curling. 544.
curling broom. 544.
curling brush. 341.
curling iron. 341.
curling rink. 544.
curling stone. 544.
curly hair. 330.
curly lasagna. 144.
currant. 74.

currency exchange. 720.
currency exchange counter. 454.
currency exchange office. 426.
current coil. 615.
cursor. 471.
cursor movement keys. 470.
curtain. 217.
curtain. 176, 347.
curtain pole. 218.
curtain track. 218.
curve. 534.
curved jaw. 259.
cushion. 562, 584, 590.
custard pie. 157.
custard tart. 157.
customer's service entrance. 659.
customs control. 454.
customs house. 441.
cut. 180.
cut off trench. 652.
cut-out button. 410.
cut ribbed macaroni. 145.
cut-throat razor. 337.
cutaway armhole. 306.
cuticle. 137.
cuticle knife. 342.
cuticle nippers. 342.
cuticle pusher. 342.
cuticle scissors. 342.
cutlery basket. 242.
cuts for gemstones. 327.
cutter. 287.
cutter bar. 165.
cutter link. 253.
cutting blade. 235, 513.
cutting cylinder. 252.
cutting edge. 224, 227, 338, 678, 682.
cutting guide. 513.
cutting line. 503.
cutting nozzle. 282.
cutting oxygen handle. 282.
cutting tip. 282.
cutting torch. 282.
cutting wheel. 243.
cutting wire. 519.
cyclists entering or crossing. 715.
cyclorama. 390.
cylinder. 266, 404, 409, 518, 639, 680, 681, 703.
cylinder-head. 409.
cylinder head cover. 405.
cylinder hole. 266.
cylinder lock. 266.
cylinder pressure gauge. 282.
cylindrical parabolic reflector. 670.
cymbals. 485.
cymbals. 491.
cymbals, triangle, castanets. 493.
cytoplasm. 113.

D

d. 475, 584.
dabber. 516.
dagger. 689, 692.
daggerboard. 551.
daggerboard well. 551.
daggers. 692.
dairy. 161.
dairy compartment. 239.
dam. 651, 660.
damper. 200, 202, 480, 520, 610.
damper lever. 480.
damper rail. 480.
dandelion. 82.
danger, electrical hazard. 718.
danger, flammable. 718.
danger, poison. 718.
danger area. 578.
danger warning signs. 714.
danger warning signs (cont.). 715.
dangerous bend. 714.

The terms in **bold type** indicate the title of an illustration; those in *italic* correspond to the British terminology.

dangerous descent. 714.
Danish. 355.
Danish rye bread. 146.
darkroom. 375.
dart. 503.
dash. 357, 386.
dashboard. 399.
dasher. 236.
data acquisition. 468.
data display. 468.
data processing. 468.
data processing devices. 468.
data recording on RAM* memory. 468.
data storage. 468.
date. 75, 569.
date line. 359.
dateline. 361.
dater. 462.
dating nail. 422.
daughter. 138.
daughter-in-law. 139.
davit. 430.
daylight filter control. 383.
dead ball line. 531.
dead bolt. 266.
deadly mushroom. 73.
deaerator. 661, 664.
deaerator storage tank. 661.
deaf-mute alphabet. 357.
death. 723.
decanter. 222.
deck. 402, 414, 415, 416, 637.
deck arch bridge. 415.
declination. 35.
declination axis. 42.
declination circle. 622.
décolleté bra. 313.
decontamination room. 661.
decorative sheet. 265.
deep fryer. 233.
deep peroneal nerve. 129.
deep-sea floor. 48.
deer antlers. 89.
deer family. 89.
defending zone. 533.
defensive. 528, 529.
deferent duct. 116.
deflexor. 557.
defrost heater. 239.
defrost timer. 239.
dehumidifier. 206.
dehumidifier. 458.
Deimos. 36.
delay indicator. 427.
delete. 363.
delicious lactarius. 73.
delta wing. 449.
deltoid. 118.
deluge gun. 677.
deluxe suite. 433.
demi-semi-quaver. 475.
demi-semi-quaver rest. 475.
demilune. 176.
demitasse. 223.
dendrite. 135.
denominations. 57.
dental alveolus. 123.
dental floss. 339.
dentate. 70.
dentil. 170.
dentin. 123.
department store. 178.
departure time indicator. 427.
departures concourse. 454.
departures room. 454.
departures schedule. 426.
departures timetable. 426.
deposit. 635.
depressed-center flat car. 420.
depth gauge. 550.
depth-of-field scale. 370.
depth of focus. 53.
depth stop. 261.
deputy sound supervisor. 389.
dermal papilla. 135, 136.

dermis. 135.
dermis. 136, 137.
derrick. 640, 643.
desasphalting. 648.
descendeur. 588.
descending aorta. 124.
descending colon. 127.
desert. 55.
desert. 59.
desk lamp. 221.
desk pad. 464.
desk tray. 462.
despin. 394.
dessert fork. 225.
dessert knife. 224.
dessert spoon. 226.
desserts. 156, 157.
dessus de côtes. 147, 149.
destination indicator. 427.
detachable control. 237.
detachable handle. 201.
detachable petrol tank. 437.
detergent dispenser. 242.
detonator. 696.
developer bath. 375.
developing film. 371.
developing tank. 375.
dew cap. 623.
dew claw. 94.
dew pad. 94.
dewaxing. 648.
dexter. 709.
dexter base. 709.
dexter chief. 709.
dexter flank. 709.
diacritic symbols. 357.
diagonal. 591, 658.
diagonal buttress. 175.
diagram of a circuit. 385.
diagram of intaglio printing. 518.
diagram of letterpress printing. 518.
diagram of planographic printing. 518.
diagram of weaving principle. 511.
dial. 386, 387, 605, 606, 607, 609, 610, 611, 612, 613, 615.
dial-type display. 442.
diamond. 446, 583, 592.
diamond head. 521.
diamond mesh metal lath. 194.
diamond point. 215.
diaper. 315.
diaphragm. 126, 127, 368, 378, 384, 387.
diaphram. 387.
diastema. 90.
dibber. 249.
dibble. 249.
dice. 593.
dice. 592.
dice cup. 592.
diesel-electric locomotive. 418.
diesel engine. 404.
diesel engine. 418, 436, 679.
diesel oil. 649.
diesel shop. 424.
diffuser. 373.
diffuser filter set. 373.
diffusion pump. 620.
digestive gland. 102.
digestive system. 127.
digging fork. 248.
digit. 94, 105.
digital clock. 382.
digital computer:control/alarm. 666.
digital display. 605.
digital frequency display. 379.
digital nerve. 129.
digital pad. 94.
digital pulp. 137.
dike. 53.
dill. 143.
diluent. 650.

diluent recovery. 650.
dimmer control. 389.
dimmer switch. 285.
dimmer switch. 400.
dimple. 587.
dining car. 421.
dining room. 189, 433, 434.
dining section. 421.
dinner fork. 225.
dinner knife. 224.
dinner plate. 223.
dinnerware. 223.
dioptric ring. 446.
dip. 636.
dip switch. 400.
dip switch. 410.
diphthongs. 358.
dipper bucket. 681.
dipstick. 405.
direct-reading rain gauge. 64.
direction in orbit. 65.
direction to be followed. 717.
directional sign. 428.
director's chair. 211.
disc. 407, 472, 517, 575, 615.
disc. 371, 558.
disc brake. 407, 409, 672.
disc camera. 369.
disc control unit. 472.
disc drive. 472.
disc seat. 271.
disc seat ring. 271.
disc storage. 472.
discharge line. 277.
discharge liner. 657.
discharge pipe. 646.
discharge pump. 646.
discharge spout. 162, 163.
discs. 236.
discus. 572.
discus throw. 570.
disgorger. 582.
dishwasher. 242, 272.
disk. 472.
disk. 407, 517, 575, 615.
disk brake. 407.
disk brake. 409, 672.
disk camera. 369.
disk control unit. 472.
disk drive. 472.
disk storage. 472.
diskette. 469.
diskette drive. 469.
disks. 236.
dispatch area. 648.
display. 610.
display cabinet. 465.
disposable fuel cylinder. 281.
disposable razor. 337.
disposable syringe. 629.
distal phalanx. 94, 120, 121, 137.
distal sesamoid. 92.
distance. 328.
distance covered. 569.
distance scale. 370.
distance tube. 700.
distribution board. 288.
distribution board. 659.
distribution field. 277.
distributor. 405.
distributor service loop. 659.
ditali. 145.
ditch. 413.
diver. 549.
diverging lens. 625.
diversion canal. 651.
diversity of jewellery. 325.
diversity of jewelry. 325.
diverter valve. 269.
divider. 165, 350, 463.
dividing breeching. 676.
diving. 548.
diving installations. 548.
diving suit. 322.
diving well. 548.
division. 723.

divot. 585.
do-it-yourself. 255.
do not dry clean. 722.
do not enter. 718.
do not use baggage carts. 720.
do not use chlorine bleach. 722.
do not use for wheelchairs. 719.
do not use luggage trolleys. 720.
do not wash. 722.
document folder. 463.
dog ear collar. 308.
dog tag. 325.
Dolby noise reduction switch. 381.
dollar. 723.
dolly. 544.
Dolphin. 40, 694.
dome roof. 191.
dome shutter. 42.
dome tent. 597.
domestic appliances. 235, 236, 237, 238, 239, 240, 241, 242, 243, 244.
domino. 593.
dominoes. 593.
door. 198, 400.
door. 187, 215, 237, 241, 397, 540.
door handle. 397.
door hasp. 419.
door hasp fastener. 419.
door lock. 397.
door mirror. 397, 403.
door operator. 181.
door panel. 215, 429.
door pillar. 397.
door shelf. 239.
door stop. 239, 419.
door switch. 241.
doorknob. 198.
doric order. 170.
dormant volcano. 53.
dormer. 187.
dorsal aorta. 99.
dorsal view. 101.
dorsum of nose. 133.
dorsum of tongue. 134.
dot. 386.
dot matrix printer. 471.
double: box and brush, box and gate. 566.
double bass. 477, 491.
double basses. 493.
double bend. 714.
double-blank. 593.
double boiler. 232.
double-breasted buttoning. 291, 301.
double-breasted jacket. 293.
double chair lift. 558.
double-condenser pole piece. 620.
double curtain rod. 218.
double-decked pallet. 685.
double-edge blade. 337.
double-edge razor. 337.
double-edged swords. 692.
double flat. 476.
double fluked anchor. 447.
double glazing. 669.
double handles. 554.
double kitchen sink. 267.
double-leaf bascule bridge. 417.
double oxer. 565, 566.
double pennant. 711.
double plate. 192.
double pole breaker. 288.
double reed. 483, 488.
double seat. 429.
double sharp. 476.
double sheet bend. 601.
double-six. 593.
double-twist auger bit. 260.
double zero. 595.
doubles pole. 537.
doubles service court. 542.

The terms in **bold type** indicate the title of an illustration; those in *italic* correspond to the British terminology.

733

doubles sideline. 537, 542.
doublet. 593.
doubling cube. 592.
doubly dentate. 70.
dough hook. 235.
doughnut. 156.
dousing tank. 661.
Doux de Montagne. 154.
Dove. 41.
dovetail. 621.
dowel hole. 328.
down. 188.
down tube. 411.
down wind. 553.
downhaul. 551.
downspout. 187.
downstream face. 652.
downstream shoulder. 652.
downstream toe. 652.
downtown. 178.
dozens. 594.
draft arm. 682.
draft tube. 655, 657, 682.
drag. 580.
drag chain. 675.
drag drum. 675.
drag rope. 675.
dragline. 675.
dragline. 650.
Dragon. 40.
drain. 267.
drain cock. 647.
drain hose. 240, 242, 272.
drain line. 204.
drain pan. 239.
drain tile. 192.
drain trap. 270.
drain valve. 204, 273, 647.
drainage blanket. 652.
drainage layer. 652.
draining spoon. 229.
draped neck. 309.
draped neckline. 309.
draw curtain. 217.
draw drapery. 217.
draw hoe. 248.
draw tube. 619.
drawbar. 678, 680, 698.
drawbar lock. 698.
drawbridge. 177.
drawer. 209, 216, 464.
drawers. 297.
drawstring. 292, 321, 349.
drawstring hood. 317.
drawtube. 623.
drawworks. 640.
dredger. 231.
dress. 315.
dress and equipment. 565.
dresser. 216.
dresses. 302.
dressmaker's model. 501.
drift. 636, 637.
drifting snow. 60.
drill. 260.
drill collar. 640.
drill pipe. 640.
drill press. 261.
drill rod. 639.
drill ship. 642.
drilling barge. 642.
drilling rig. 640.
drip bowl. 238.
drip dry. 722.
drip molding. 397.
drip moulding. 397.
drip stone. 187.
drive axle. 684.
drive belt. 240, 241, 380.
drive chain. 411.
drive coil. 606.
drive coil and phase-sensing coil. 606.
drive mechanism. 446.
drive shaft. 162.
drive shaft. 455.

drive sheave. 181.
drive wheel. 243, 260, 680.
driver. 568, 569.
driver; no. 1 wood. 586.
driver's cab. 418.
driver's colors. 569.
driver's seat. 704.
driveway. 188.
driving glove. 299.
driving iron; no. 1 iron. 586.
driving turbine. 404.
driving wheel. 510.
drone. 106.
drone. 488.
drop earring. 325.
drop-leaf. 209.
drop light. 221.
drop waist dress. 302.
drug store. 720.
drum. 170, 219, 236, 241, 407, 607.
drum brake. 407.
drum kit. 491.
drupelet. 74.
dry clean. 722.
dry cleaning. 722.
dry continental - arid. 59.
dry continental - semiarid. 59.
dry dock. 441.
dry flat. 722.
dry fruits: nuts. 78.
dry gallery. 54.
dry mounting press. 375.
dry-point. 517.
dry point. 515.
dry snow. 57.
dry subtropical. 59.
dryer. 241.
drying. 722.
drypoint. 517.
dual seat. 409.
dual swivel mirror. 340.
dual voltage selector switch. 337, 340.
duct. 136.
duct deferens. 116.
duffel bag. 349.
duffle coat. 292.
dump. 635, 638.
dump body. 682.
dump rope. 675.
dump truck. 682.
dumper truck. 682.
dune. 51.
dungarees. 310.
duo. 490.
duodenum. 127.
duplex. 183.
duplexer. 624.
dura mater of spinal cord. 130.
dural cul-de-sac. 130.
dust cover. 380.
dust tail. 39.
dusting brush. 244.
Dutch. 355.
Dutch oven. 232.
duty-free. 720.
duty-free shop. 454.
dynamic microphone. 384.
dynamics propeller. 435.
dynamo. 411.

E

e. 475.
Eagle. 40, 41, 710.
ear. 108, 114, 115, 213, 482.
ear cushion. 378.
ear drum. 132.
ear flap. 298.
ear loaf. 146.
earphone jack. 392.
earpiece. 328, 387.
earth. 385.
Earth. 36, 37, 38, 393, 653.

earth clamp. 281.
Earth co-ordinate system. 35.
earth lead. 380.
Earth's crust. 47, 53.
earth sensor. 393.
earth wire. 288, 659.
earth-wire clamp. 659.
earthquake. 53.
easel. 376.
easel. 375.
east. 445, 593.
east-west axis. 43.
East wind. 593.
eccrine sweat gland. 136.
échine. 150.
echinus. 170.
echo. 624.
echo sounder. 442.
edge. 265, 501, 559, 561, 562, 564, 625.
edger. 252.
edging. 247.
edible gyromitra. 73.
edible mushrooms. 73.
egg. 97.
egg. 107.
egg beater. 230.
egg poacher. 233.
egg slicer. 231.
egg timer. 229.
egg tray. 239.
eggplant. 81.
eggs. 99, 105.
eiderdown. 214.
eight cut. 327.
eighth note. 475.
eighth rest. 475.
ejaculatory duct. 116.
eject. 382.
eject button. 381.
ejection port. 697, 699, 701.
ejection seat. 705.
ejector. 682.
elastic. 214.
elastic ankle. 317.
elastic coupling. 645.
elastic leg opening. 315, 317.
elastic ligament. 94, 102.
elastic support bandage. 629.
elastic waistband. 315.
elastic webbing. 294.
elastic wristband. 317.
elasticized leg opening. 297.
elbow. 91, 108, 115, 201, 202, 203, 275.
elbow macaroni. 145.
elbow pad. 530, 534, 564.
elbow protector. 576.
electric and electronic instruments. 494, 495.
electric arc. 281.
electric cooker. 238.
electric current source. 385.
electric drill. 261.
electric foil. 576.
electric furnace. 205.
electric golf cart. 587.
electric grill. 237.
electric guitar. 494.
electric kiln. 520.
electric motor. 182, 205, 371, 437.
electric range. 238.
electric razor. 337.
electric supply. 204, 273.
electric switch. 285.
electric toothbrush. 339.
electric water-heater tank. 273.
electrical box. 285.
electrical connection. 402.
electrical distribution system. 666.
electrical payout linkage. 595.
electrical pointe d'arrêt. 576.
electrical power unit. 453.
electrical room. 661.
electrical scoring apparatus. 576.

electrically illuminated point signal. 423.
electrically illuminated switch signal. 423.
electrician's tools. 286, 287.
electricity. 284, 285, 286, 287, 288, 651, 652, 653, 654, 655, 656, 657, 658, 659, 660.
electricity cable. 413.
electricity meter. 659.
electricity pylon. 638.
electrified fence. 161.
electrode. 281, 284, 387.
electrode assembly. 205.
electrode holder. 281.
electrode lead. 281.
electromagnet. 385.
electron beam. 392.
electron gun. 392, 620.
electron microscope. 620.
electronic circuit. 606.
electronic flash. 372.
electronic scales. 610.
electronic viewfinder. 384.
electronic viewfinder display control. 384.
element. 406.
element release lever. 466.
elevating handle. 697.
elevation adjusting screw. 621.
elevator. 181.
elevator. 162, 448, 556, 665.
elevator for people. 719.
elevon. 457.
elk. 89.
ellipses. 357.
ellipsis. 357.
elliptical galaxy. 39.
elongating bar shot. 695.
embankment. 413.
embankment dam. 653.
emblem. 397, 709.
embrasure. 176.
embroidery. 507.
emerald cut. 327.
emergency brake lever. 429.
emergency core cooling. 666.
emergency niche. 428.
emergency oxygen supply. 458.
emery board. 343.
emission chamber. 620.
empty set. 723.
emptying outlet. 647.
en prison. 594, 595.
enamel. 123.
enameled hardboard. 194.
enamelled hardboard. 194.
encapsulant. 670.
enclosure line. 359.
end bracket. 218.
end button. 477.
end cap. 218, 663.
end door. 425.
end fitting. 662.
end grain. 265.
end joist. 192.
end ladder. 419.
end line. 527, 535, 536, 543.
end of motorway. 717.
[end of priority] sign. 715.
end of prohibition of passing. 716.
end of superhighway. 717.
end of the lap. 547.
end panel. 237.
end piece. 116, 582.
end plate. 663.
end shield. 661.
end shield cooling pipe. 662.
end stop. 218.
end wall. 546.
end zone. 527.
endocarp. 75, 76.
endoplasmic reticulum. 113.
endpaper. 512.
endpiece. 328.
energy. 633.

The terms in **bold type** indicate the title of an illustration; those in *italic* correspond to the British terminology.

energy integration to the transmission network. 654.
energy production. 667.
energy transmission at the alternator voltage. 654.
engagement ring. 325.
engine. 405.
engine. 165.
engine. 587, 640, 678, 680, 681, 682.
engine air intake. 435.
engine block. 405.
engine housing. 253.
engine instruments. 451.
engine mounting pylon. 449.
engine room. 438, 439, 645.
engines. 404.
engines. 457.
English. 355.
English billiards. 584.
English billiards and snooker. 584.
English cane. 630.
English chessboard. 591.
English horn. 483.
English horn; cor anglais. 493.
English loaf. 146.
English sitck. 630.
enlarger. 376.
enlarger. 375.
enlarger timer. 375.
enlarging lens. 376.
entablature. .170, 198.
entame de romsteck. 149.
enter key. 470.
entire. 70.
entrance. 107.
entrance slide. 107.
entrance turnstile. 428.
entrecôtes couvertes. 149.
entrecôtes découvertes. 149.
entries. 548.
entry. 549, 685.
envelope shaper. 495.
EP adaptor. 380.
épaule. 147, 151.
epaulet. 291, 321.
epaulet sleeve. 306.
épée. 577.
épéeist. 577.
epicalyx. 74.
epicenter. 53.
epicentre. 53.
epicondyle. 121.
epidermicula. 137.
epidermis. 135, 136, 137.
epiglottis. 126, 134.
ɔpitrochlea. 121.
eponychium. 137.
equalizer. 378.
equalizing buckle. 219.
equator. 35.
equilateral. 172.
equilibrator. 698.
equipment. 515, 516, 517, 588.
equipment access shaft. 660.
equipment lock. 665.
erase button. 388.
eraser. 461.
erecting lenses. 621.
ermine. 710.
escalator. 182.
escalator. 428.
escalator, down. 719.
escalator, up. 719.
escape key. 470.
escape wheel. 605, 607.
escapement mechanism. 492.
escutcheon. 101, 266, 270.
esophagus. 99, 102, 127.
espadrille. 319.
espresso coffee maker. 234.
estate car. 398.
etching press. 516.
Eton jacket. 317.
Eton suit. 317.

étrier. 588.
Eurasia. 49.
Europa. 36.
Europe. 49. `
European plug. 285.
Eustachian tube. 132, 133.
euthynteria. 171.
evaporation. 58.
evaporator. 206.
evaporator coil. 239.
evaporator coils. 206.
even. 594, 595.
evening glove. 299.
examples of branching. 272.
examples of instrumental groups. 490, 491.
examples of satellites. 393.
examples of symbols. 710.
exclamation mark. 357.
exclamation point. 357.
excretory pore. 104.
executive desk. 465.
executive length. 297.
exhaust cone. 450.
exhaust duct. 241, 450.
exhaust gas admission. 404.
exhaust gas outflow. 404.
exhaust hose. 241.
exhaust manifold. 404, 405, 406.
exhaust nozzle. 450, 705.
exhaust pipe. 404, 406, 409, 450, 455, 678, 705.
exhaust port. 639.
exhaust stack. 403.
exhaust system. 406.
exhaust tube. 284.
exhaust valve. 404.
exit turnstile. 428.
exocarp. 74, 75, 76.
exosphere. 47.
expandable file pouch. 350.
expanding file. 463.
expansion bolt. 264.
expansion chamber. 443, 611.
expansion space. 422.
expansion tank. 203.
exploder. 700.
explosive. 696.
exposure control. 371.
exposure meter. 372.
exposure-time scale. 372.
exposure value. 372.
exposure value scale. 372.
extendable solar array. 393.
extended character. 470.
extended claw. 94.
extension ladder. 278.
extension pipe. 244.
extension table. 209.
exterior dome shell. 42.
exterior door. 198.
exterior of a house. 187.
exterior pocket. 347, 350.
exterior sign. 428.
external acoustic meatus. 132.
external auditory meatus. 122.
external conductive coating. 392.
external ear. 132.
external ear. 132.
external gills. 105.
external iliac artery. 125.
external nose. 133.
external oblique. 118, 119.
external tank. 457.
external tooth lock washer. 264.
extractor. 703.
extractor cam. 703.
extractor fan. 375.
extractor spring. 703.
extrados. 172.
eye. 131.
eye. 104, 109, 114, 257, 500, 501, 509, 567, 581, 588.
eye lens. 621.
eye ring. 95.
eye shield protector. 521.

eye-socket. 91.
eyeball. 131.
eyeball. 105.
eyebrow. 131.
eyebrow pencil. 333.
eyebrow stripe. 95.
eyebrow tweezers. 342.
eyecup. 383, 384.
eyecups. 370.
eyeglasses. 328, 329.
eyelash. 131.
eyelash curler. 333.
eyelashes. 94.
eyelet. 318, 505, 562.
eyelet tab. 318.
eyelid. 109.
eyeliner. 332.
eyepiece. 371, 372, 619, 621, 622, 623.
eyepiece holder. 623.
eyepiece magnifier. 370.
eyeshadow. 332.
eyestalk. 104.

F

f. 475.
F-1 engine. 456.
f clef. 475.
fabric care. 722.
fabric guide. 243.
fabric structure. 502.
façade. 175.
face. 114, 176, 257, 351, 514, 521, 543, 586, 635, 637.
face mask. 530, 534.
face-off circle. 533.
face-off spot. 533.
face pipes. 481.
face ply. 265.
face shield. 283.
face side. 265.
faceplate. 266, 392.
facial nerve. 132.
facing. 293.
faculae. 37.
failed fuel bay. 665.
failed fuel canning. 665.
fairlead. 553.
fairway. 585.
fall. 308.
falling. 578.
falling rocks. 714.
fallopian tube. 117.
fallow. 161.
false rib (3). 121.
false start rope. 546.
false tuck. 315.
family relationships. 138, 139.
family tents. 596.
fan. 204, 205, 206, 239, 241, 429, 450, 638.
fan belt. 405, 406.
fan blade. 450.
fan brush. 333.
fan cable stays. 416.
fan control. 206.
fan housing. 340.
fan motor. 206.
fan trellis. 247.
fang. 109.
fanion. 711.
fanny pack. 559.
fantail. 671.
far side. 38.
far turn. 569.
farmhouse. 161.
farming. 159.
farmyard. 161.
fascia. 170.
fast forward. 382.
fast-forward button. 381, 388.
fastener binder. 463.
fasteners. 502.
fastening screw. 372.

father. 138, 139.
father-in-law. 139.
faucet body. 271.
fault. 48, 53, 636.
feather crown. 542.
feather stitch. 507.
feathering. 691.
fedelini. 144.
feed cover. 701.
feed dog. 500.
feed lever. 261.
feed pin. 471.
feed tray. 701.
feed tube. 236, 367.
feeder. 662.
feeding dial. 505.
feedwater. 664.
feet. 478, 514.
feet-first entry. 548.
felt. 516, 518.
felt hat. 298.
felt hat. 314.
female. 723.
female ferrule. 580.
female genital organs. 117.
femoral artery. 125.
femoral nerve. 129.
femoral vein. 125.
femur. 92, 100, 105, 106, 108, 120.
fencer. 576.
fencing. 576, 577.
fencing shoe. 576.
fencing weapons. 577.
fender. 397, 403, 411.
fennel. 85.
ferrule. 224, 280, 338, 346, 582, 586.
ferry. 434.
ferryboat. 441.
fertilizer distributor. 164.
fetlock. 91.
fetlock joint. 91.
fettling knife. 519.
fibre. 601.
fibula. 120.
field. 525, 531.
field heap spreader. 164.
field lens. 621.
field lenses. 621.
fiffi hook. 588.
fifth. 476.
fifth wheel. 403.
figure-eight knot. 601.
figure skate. 562.
figure ski. 554.
figure skiing handle. 554.
filament. 37, 72, 284, 620.
file. 591, 599.
file guides. 463.
filet. 150, 151.
filing box. 462.
fill. 652.
fill opening. 243.
filler. 344.
filler hole. 403, 405.
filler neck. 403.
filler plug. 443.
filler rod. 282.
filler tube. 268.
fillet. 152, 170, 187.
filleting knife. 227.
filling hole. 696.
filling inlet. 647.
film advance lever. 368.
film drying cabinet. 375.
film footage counter. 383.
film leader. 371.
film-pack. 371.
film path. 383.
film speed indicator. 368.
film transport sprocket. 368.
filming trigger. 384.
films. 371.
filter. 204, 205, 233, 345, 652, 669, 675.

The terms in **bold type** indicate the title of an illustration; those in *italic* correspond to the British terminology.

filter basket. 234.
filter drawer. 376.
filter-oscillator. 495.
filter tip. 344.
fin. 435, 448, 455, 550, 554, 706.
fin-mounted tail unit. 449.
fin wing tip. 705.
final limit cam. 181.
final limit switch. 181.
finder. 622, 623.
fine adjustment knob. 619.
fine bookbinding. 512, 513, 514.
*fine focus sleeve. 623.
fine tuning knob. 392.
finger. 162, 526.
finger button. 484.
finger hole. 590.
finger stop. 387.
fingerboard. 477, 487, 494.
fingerless mitt. 299.
fingerwaves. 330.
fingerwheel. 164.
finial. 423.
finial. 709.
finish. 566.
finish line. 571.
finished product storage. 648.
finishing line. 569.
finishing post. 571.
finned tube. 203.
Finnish. 355.
fire control selector. 699.
fire engine. 676, 677.
fire extinguisher. 718.
fire hose. 676, 718.
fire irons. 201.
fire station. 648.
firebox. 201.
firebrick. 205.
firebrick back. 200.
fireman's hatchet. 676.
fireplace. 200.
fireplace. 188.
firestopping. 192.
firing. 520.
firing chamber. 702.
firing lanyard. 698.
firing mechanism. 700.
firing pin. 702.
firing pine. 703.
firing rod. 700.
firing shaft. 698.
firn. 56.
first aid. 718.
first aid kit. 629.
first base. 525.
first baseman. 525.
first condenser lens. 620.
first dorsal fin. 98.
first floor. 188, 189.
first molar. 123.
first officer's seat. 451.
first premolar. 123.
first quarter. 38.
first reinforce. 694.
first reinforce ring. 694.
first space. 535.
first stage. 456.
first violins. 493.
fish. 98, 99.
fish-eye lens. 43, 370.
fish fork. 225.
fish kettle. 232.
fish knife. 224.
fish platter. 223.
fish poacher. 232.
fish wire. 287.
fishbone stitch. 507.
fisherman's knot. 601.
Fishes. 40.
fishhook. 581.
fishing. 580, 581, 582.
fishing vest. 582.
fishnet tights. 311.
fishplate. 422.
fishplate bolt. 422.

fission of uranium fuel. 667.
fitted coupling bolt. 657.
fitted sheet. 214.
fitting. 274, 349, 677.
fittings. 275.
fittings. 347.
five-number bet. 595.
fixed arch. 415.
fixed blade. 513.
fixed bridges. 414, 415, 416.
fixed distance marking. 452.
fixed jaw. 258, 259.
fixed platform. 642.
fixed-roof tank. 647.
fixed stairs. 428.
fixed weight. 492.
fixing bath. 375.
fixture drain. 267.
flag. 531, 536, 558.
flag and shield. 709.
flag shapes. 711.
flagpole. 709.
flagstick. 585.
flagstone. 247.
flame adjustment wheel. 344.
flame spreader tip. 281.
flammule. 711.
flan pan. 230.
flan tin. 230.
flanchet. 149.
flange bolt. 268.
flange nut. 274.
flank. 91, 95, 147, 148, 151, 176, 514.
flank forward. 531.
flanker. 529.
flanking tower. 177.
flap. 298, 349, 351, 567, 705.
flap guide rail. 449.
flap hydraulic jack. 705.
flap pocket. 292, 293, 304.
flap side pocket. 293.
flare. 37, 643, 648.
flare joint. 274.
flare nut. 274.
flare nut spanner. 258.
flare nut wrench. 258.
flash. 373.
flash bracket. 372.
flash hider. 699, 701.
flash lamp. 372.
flash meter. 373.
flash outlet. 372.
flash socket. 383.
flash synchronization terminal. 368.
flash umbrella. 373.
flash unit. 372.
flashbar socket. 371.
flashcube. 372.
flashing. 202.
flashing light. 423.
flashlight. 221.
flat. 476.
flat-back brush. 338.
flat-bed. 499.
flat cake. 156.
flat car. 420.
flat end pin. 219.
flat head. 264.
flat mirror. 42, 622.
flat part. 504.
flat pleat. 217.
flat roof. 190.
flat sheet. 214.
flat shuttle. 509.
flat side of the grip. 538.
flat spike. 588.
flat stitches group. 507.
flat tip. 258.
flat view. 116.
flat washer. 264.
flesh. 74, 75, 76.
fleshy fruits: berry fruits. 74.
fleshy fruits: citrus fruits. 77.
fleur-de-lis. 710.

flex. 220, 221, 243.
flex support. 243.
flexible hose. 244, 269, 639.
flexible hose connection. 639.
flexible rubber hose. 272.
flexible skirt. 435.
flies. 180.
flight. 175, 549, 574.
flight bag. 347.
flight deck. 451.
flight deck. 448, 455, 457.
flight engineer's panel. 451.
flight engineer's seat. 451.
flight information board. 454.
flight instruments. 557.
flight of stairs. 197.
flights. 548.
flint. 283, 696.
flint arrowhead. 689.
flint knife. 689.
flintlock. 696.
flip-flop. 319.
flip turn. 547.
float. 581.
float. 277, 443, 698.
float ball. 268.
float clamp. 277.
floating bridge. 417.
floating crane. 441.
floating dock. 441.
floating head. 337.
floating platform. 642.
floating rib. 120.
floating roof. 647.
floating-roof tank. 647.
floodlight. 390.
floor. 192, 540, 541, 635, 636, 671.
floor board. 196.
floor brush. 244.
floor crew. 390.
floor joist. 192.
floor lamp. 220.
floor manager. 390.
floor selector. 181.
floor tile. 195.
floorboard. 196.
flow bean. 641.
flower. 69.
flower bed. 247.
flower bud. 69.
flower tiles. 593.
flue. 482.
flue collar. 201.
flue damper. 201.
flue pipe. 482.
flue pipe. 201.
fluff trap. 241.
fluid adjustment screw. 280.
fluid coking plant. 648.
fluid inlet. 670.
fluid outlet. 670.
fluke. 447.
fluorescent lamp. 284.
fluorescent screen. 620.
flush. 592.
flush bushing. 275.
flush handle. 269.
flute. 260, 483, 490.
fluted land. 260.
fluted pole. 218.
fluted shaft. 398.
flutes. 493.
fluting. 170.
flux. 521.
flux brush. 521.
Fly. 41, 294, 297, 709.
fly agaric. 73.
fly box. 582.
fly front closing. 300, 317.
fly half. 531.
fly line. 580.
fly reel. 580.
fly rod. 580.
flying buttress. 174, 175.
Flying Fish. 41.

flying instruments. 451.
flying jib. 431.
flyleaf. 512.
flysheet. 597.
flywheel. 404, 405, 516, 519.
FM mode selector. 379.
FM stereo indicator. 379.
foam. 51.
foam insulation. 195.
foam mattress. 598.
foam monitor. 645.
foam pad. 598.
foam rubber insulation. 195.
foam windscreen. 384.
focus. 53.
focus knob. 623.
focus magnifier. 376.
focus setting ring. 384.
focusing. 668.
focusing control. 383.
focusing knob. 376, 377, 622.
focusing magnifier. 375.
focusing ring. 383, 621.
focusing sleeve. 614.
fodder corn. 161.
fog. 60.
fog light. 403.
foible. 577.
foil. 577.
foil warning line. 576.
foilist. 577.
fold line. 304, 503.
fold-out table. 421.
foldaway ladder. 278.
folder. 463.
folding. 198.
folding camera. 369.
folding camp bed. 598.
folding chair. 213.
folding door. 188.
folding grill. 600.
folding nail file. 343.
folding shovel. 600.
foliage. 71.
follicle. 79.
fondue fork. 225.
fondue pot. 233.
fondue set. 233.
food processor. 236.
food. 141.
foot. 95, 104, 108, 115, 150, 215, 315, 316, 482, 551, 580.
foot control. 499.
foot cushion. 583.
foot fault judge. 537.
foot hole. 482.
foot of table. 583.
foot pocket. 550.
foot rest. 519, 631.
foot rope. 430.
foot score line. 544.
foot spot. 583.
foot string. 583.
football. 527, 528, 529, 530.
footboard. 214, 408.
footbridge. 424, 428.
footing. 192.
footlights. 180.
footrest. 410, 558.
footstrap. 310.
footway. 413.
for grinding and grating. 228.
for measuring. 229.
for opening. 229.
for straining and draining. 228.
foramen caecum. 134.
foramen cecum. 134.
foramen ovale. 122.
force of the water on the blades. 654.
forced hot-water system. 203.
forced warm-air system. 202.
fore and aft gangway. 645.
fore court. 537.
fore edge. 512.
fore leg. 100, 106.

The terms in **bold type** indicate the title of an illustration; those in *italic* correspond to the British terminology.

fore rib. 152.
fore royal sail. 431.
fore wing. 100, 106.
forearm. 115, 701, 702.
forearm crutch. 630.
forecourt. 401.
foregrip. 580.
forehead. 95, 114.
foreleg. 94.
forelimb. 105.
forelock. 91.
foremast. 430.
foresail. 431.
forestay. 552.
fork. 225.
fork. 89, 411, 599, 607, 622, 684.
fork extender. 684.
fork pocket. 425.
forked tongue. 109.
forklift reach truck. 684.
forklift truck. 684.
forks. 684.
formeret. 175.
forming. 601.
forms. 57.
forte. 577.
forward. 548.
forward bolt assist mechanism. 699.
forward dive. 549.
forward/reverse switch. 383.
foul line. 525, 590.
foundation. 192, 653.
foundation of dam. 652.
foundation of tower. 416.
foundation slip. 312.
foundations. 192.
fountain pen. 367.
four blade beater. 235.
four-door saloon. 398.
four-door sedan. 398.
four-four time. 476.
four-masted bark. 430, 431.
four of a kind. 592.
four-wall court. 541.
fourchette. 299.
fourth. 476.
fourth wheel. 605.
fovea. 131.
fractionating tower. 649.
frame. 192, 507.
frame. 107, 163, 259, 279, 294, 346, 347, 350, 409, 443, 485, 488, 508, 517, 538, 540, 563, 573, 574, 595, 613, 670, 671, 681, 682, 684.
frame counter. 368.
frame push. 678.
frame rail. 403.
frame stile. 215.
framework. 446.
framing control. 383.
Francis turbine. 657.
franzipan. 156.
free fall. 555.
free margin. 137.
free throw lane. 535.
free throw line. 535, 539.
freezer bucket. 236.
freezer compartment. 239.
freezer door. 239.
freezing rain. 60.
freight elevator. 719.
freight hold. 433, 448.
freight station. 424.
French. 355.
French bread. 146.
French cheeses. 154, 155.
French chessboard. 591.
French cut. 327.
French horn. 484, 490, 491.
French horns. 493.
French knot stitch. 507.
French language signs. 356.
French loaf. 146.
French proofreading model. 366.

French twist. 331.
French window. 199.
fresh air inlet. 200.
fret. 487, 494.
fricative consonants. 358.
friction strip. 345.
frieze. 170, 215.
frigate. 439.
frilly pants. 315.
fringe trimming. 217.
frog. 105.
frog. 93, 163, 292, 308, 321, 422, 478.
front. 328.
front. 147, 151, 293, 295.
front apron. 295.
front axle. 680.
front bearing. 450.
front binding. 554.
front board. 512.
front brake. 411.
front brake lever. 410.
front court. 541.
front crawl stroke. 547.
front crossbar. 563.
front derailleur. 411, 412.
front-end loader. 679.
front fender. 409.
front flap. 345.
front foil. 436.
front foil control actuator. 436.
front footrest. 409.
front grip. 700.
front knob. 257.
front leg. 213.
front mudgard. 409.
front pipe. 406.
front point. 589.
front quarter. 148.
front runner. 564.
front sight. 697, 700, 702, 703.
front sight housing. 699, 701.
front spar. 449.
front tip. 243.
front top pocket. 310.
front view. 397, 482.
front wall. 540, 541.
front wheel. 631, 680.
frontal. 118, 120.
frontal bone. 122.
frontal sinus. 133.
fronts. 61.
frontwall. 402.
frost-free refrigerator. 239.
fruit cake. 157.
fruit-picking ladder. 279.
fruit vegetables. 81.
frying pan. 233.
frying pan. 599.
fuel. 664.
fuel bundle. 663.
fuel bundle. 663.
fuel fabrication. 667.
fuel handling control console. 666.
fuel handling sequence. 665.
fuel indicator. 399.
fuel injector pump. 404.
fuel pellet. 663.
fuel pump. 404.
fuel pump belt. 404.
fuel spray manifold. 450.
fuel tank. 253, 403, 409, 436, 445, 455, 706.
fuel transfer pipe. 456.
fuelling machine. 661, 664.
fulcrum. 548.
full and by. 553.
full back. 531.
full brisket. 148.
full house. 592.
full-load adjustment screw. 615.
full Moon. 38.
full stop. 357, 363, 386.
fullback. 532.
fullback. 528, 529.
fumarole. 53.

fume extractor. 704.
function keys. 470, 610.
function lever. 380.
function selector. 206.
functions in a system. 468.
funiculus. 74, 79.
funnel. 434.
funnel. 228, 392.
funnel aileron. 433.
fur hood. 314.
furlong chute. 569.
Furnace. 41, 202, 204, 668.
furs. 710.
fuse. 659.
fuse block. 205.
fuse cutout. 659.
fuse holder. 659.
fuse pullers. 286.
fuselage. 448, 556.
fuselage mounted tail unit. 449.
fuses. 285.

G

g. 475.
g clef. 475.
G-meter. 556.
gable. 175.
gable roof. 190.
gaff. 430.
gaff sail. 432.
gaff sail boom. 430.
gaff topsail. 431.
gaiter. 559.
gaiting strap. 568.
galaxy. 39.
gall-bladder. 127.
gall bladder. 99.
gallbladder. 127.
gallery. 175, 179, 445, 671.
galley. 448.
galosh. 320.
game timekeeper. 533.
gantry crane. 683.
gantry crane. 651, 655.
Ganymede. 36.
gap. 581.
garage. 187, 189, 433, 434.
garbage disposal sink. 270.
garbage disposal unit. 270.
garden. 173, 188.
garden hose. 250.
garden line. 249.
garden sorrel. 82.
gardening. 245.
garlic. 81.
garlic press. 228.
garment bag. 347.
garment fabric. 502.
garment strap. 347.
garrison cap. 298.
garter. 312, 313.
garter belt. 313.
garter stitch. 504.
gas. 284, 640.
gas cylinder. 701.
gas inlet. 458.
gas lift. 641.
gas lift valve. 641.
gas lighter. 344.
gas main. 413.
gas oil. 649.
gas-oil line. 404.
gas outlet. 458.
gas pedal. 400.
gas piston. 701.
gas tail. 39.
gas tank cap. 410.
gas tank door. 397.
gas turbine. 435, 643.
gas under pressure. 641.
gasket. 238, 240, 242, 271, 274.
gaskin. 91.
gasoline. 649.
gasoline engine. 405.

gasoline pump. 401.
gasoline pump. 401, 405.
gasoline pump hose. 401.
gasometer. 638.
gastrocnemius. 118, 119.
gastropod. 104.
gate. 558, 565, 566, 588, 655, 660.
gate arm. 423.
gate arm lamp. 423.
gate arm support. 423.
gate-leg. 209.
gate-leg table. 209.
gate operating ring. 657.
gateau. 156.
gather. 305.
gather skirt. 303.
gathering. 512.
gauchos. 310.
gauge. 513, 599.
gauntlet. 283, 299, 690.
gauze bandage. 575.
gauze roller bandage. 629.
gear. 510.
gear housing. 580.
gear selector. 411, 412.
gear shift. 410.
gear train. 371.
gearbox. 436, 517, 672.
gearchange lever. 399.
gearchange pedal. 409, 410.
gearshift lever. 399, 409.
gemelli. 145.
Gemini, the Twins. 712.
generating station flow diagram. 664.
generator. 656.
generator. 411, 655, 656, 661, 664, 666, 672.
genital pore. 104.
geography. 45.
geostationary orbit. 394.
geostationary orbit injection. 394.
germ. 79.
German. 355.
German rye bread. 146.
geyser. 53.
gigot. 151.
gill. 73.
gill cover. 98.
gill filament. 98.
gill raker. 98.
gills. 98.
gills. 99, 102.
gimbal ring. 443.
Giraffe. 40.
girder. 42, 192.
girdle. 313, 327.
girth. 567.
girth strap. 567.
gîte à la noix. 149.
gîte de derrière. 149.
gîte de devant. 149.
[give way] sign. 715.
glacial cirque. 56.
glacier. 56.
glacier tongue. 56.
glacis. 176.
gladius. 689.
glans penis. 116.
glass. 533, 540.
glass bulb. 372, 606.
glass case. 609.
glass cover. 239.
glass curtain. 217.
glass cutter. 521.
glass cutting. 521.
glass dome. 443.
glass-fiber cloth. 458.
glass-fibre cloth. 458.
glass filter. 443.
glass-fronted display cabinet. 216.
glass grinder. 521.
glass port. 322.
glass slide. 619.
glass sphere. 64.

glassware. 222.
glaze. 57.
glazed frost. 57.
glider. 556.
glides. 358.
gliding. 556.
globe. 220.
glove. 299, 526.
glove. 458, 534, 550, 555, 561, 564, 572, 576.
glove compartment. 399.
glove finger. 299.
glue. 196.
glue stick. 461.
gluteal nerve. 129.
gluteus maximus. 119.
gnomon. 606.
goal. 545.
goal. 527, 531, 532, 533, 539, 545.
goal area. 532, 539.
goal area line. 539.
goal crease. 533.
goal judge. 545.
goal judge's box. 533.
goal line. 527, 531, 532, 533, 539, 545.
goal line referee. 539.
goal post. 527, 531.
goalkeeper. 534.
goalkeeper. 532, 533, 539, 545.
goalkeeper's pad. 534.
goalkeeper's stick. 534.
gob hat. 314.
goggles. 283, 555, 564.
golf. 585, 586, 587.
golf bag. 587.
golf cart. 587.
golf clubs. 586.
golf hose. 311.
golf shoe. 587.
golf trolley. 587.
golfer. 585.
Golgi apparatus. 113.
gondola car. 420.
gonfalon. 711.
gong. 485.
gong. 387, 493.
goods lift. 719.
goose-neck. 197.
gooseberry. 74.
gooseneck. 682.
gored skirt. 303.
gorge. 54, 150, 176.
gorget. 690.
gothic cathedral. 174, 175.
gouge. 342.
gouged section. 518.
gour. 54.
Gournay. 155.
governor. 181.
grab handle. 403.
gracile. 119.
grade crossing. 715.
grade slope. 188.
grader. 680.
graduated arc. 443.
graduated arm. 608.
graduated dial. 625.
graduated scale. 612.
graduation. 613.
grafting knife. 252.
grain. 265.
grain auger. 165.
grain pan. 165.
grain sieve. 165.
grain tank. 165.
grain unloading auger. 165.
granddaughter. 139.
grandfather. 139.
grandfather clock. 607.
grandmother. 139.
grandson. 139.
grandstand. 569.
granitic layer. 48.
granivorous bird. 97.
granny knot. 601.

granulation. 37.
grape. 74.
grape. 74.
grapefruit. 77.
grapefruit knife. 227.
grapeshot. 695.
graphic elements for symbols. 713.
graphic symbols. 57.
grapnel. 447.
grapple. 681.
grass catcher. 252.
grass ley. 161.
grater. 228.
grater disc. 236.
grave accent. 357.
gravel. 192, 277.
gravity band. 447.
gravity dam. 653.
gravy boat and stand. 223.
grease trap. 277.
grease well. 237.
greases. 649.
great adductor. 119.
Great Bear. 40.
great foramen. 122.
great-granddaughter. 139.
great-grandfather. 139.
great-grandmother. 139.
great-grandson. 139.
great organ manual. 481.
great saphenous vein. 125.
great scallop. 102.
greater alar cartilage. 133.
greater covert. 96.
greater lip. 117.
greater pectoral. 118.
greater trochanter. 121.
greatest gluteal. 119.
greave. 690.
Greek. 355.
Greek temple. 171.
green ball. 584.
green beam. 392.
green bean. 81.
green cabbage. 82.
green dragon. 593.
green peas. 85.
green russula. 73.
green walnut. 78.
greenhouse. 161, 669.
Greenland Sea. 49.
grid. 180.
griddle. 237.
griff-fiffi hook. 588.
grill. 171.
grill and waffle baker. 237.
grill element. 238.
grille. 206, 378, 397, 489.
grip. 372, 540, 586, 693.
groin. 114.
grommet. 597.
groove. 237, 380, 500, 513, 559, 561, 586, 691.
grooved sleeve. 271.
gros bout de poitrine. 149.
ground. 385, 647.
ground airport equipment. 453.
ground bond. 288.
ground clamp. 281.
ground electrode. 406.
ground fault circuit interrupter. 288.
ground floor. 188, 189.
ground lead. 380.
ground moraine. 56.
ground/neutral bus bar. 288.
ground sill. 176.
ground transportation. 721.
ground wire. 288, 659.
ground-wire clamp. 659.
ground-wire peak. 658.
grounded receptacle. 277.
grounding prong. 285.
group retarders. 425.
groups of dives. 549.
groups of stitches. 507.

grow sleepers. 315.
growth line. 101, 104.
grozzing teeth. 521.
guard. 197, 221, 227, 577.
guard rail. 187, 239.
guardhouse. 177.
guava. 80.
guidance system. 706.
guide. 580.
guide bar. 253.
guide bearing. 656.
guide chain. 437.
guide post. 466.
guide rods. 698.
guiding and current bar. 429.
guiding tower. 417.
guillotine trimmer. 375.
gules. 710.
gully grate. 413.
gum. 123.
gun. 704.
gun body. 280.
gun director. 439.
gun flap. 291.
gunner's sight. 704.
gusset. 348.
gusset pocket. 304, 307.
gusseted pocket. 351.
Gutenberg discontinuity. 47.
guttae. 170.
gutter. 89, 187, 413, 590.
guy cable. 573.
guy line adapter. 597.
guy rope. 596.
guy wire. 672.
guyot. 50.
gym rompers. 317.
gymnast. 574.
gymnastics. 573, 574.
gypsum block. 193.

H

H stretcher. 213.
hack. 544.
hackle. 581.
hacksaw. 262.
hacksaw. 276.
hail. 57.
hail shower. 60.
hair. 137.
hair. 115, 136, 478.
hair bulb. 137.
hair clip. 343.
hair dryer. 340.
hair follicle. 137.
hair grip. 343.
hair roller. 343.
hair shaft. 137.
hair slide. 343.
hair styles. 330, 331.
hairbrushes. 338.
haircutting scissors. 338.
hairdresser. 720.
hairpieces. 331.
hairpin. 343.
hairsetter. 341.
hairspring. 605.
hairstyling implements. 343.
half barb. 61.
half court line. 540.
half-distance line. 545.
half-glasses. 329.
half handle. 227.
half hoe. 297.
half note. 475.
half rest. 475.
half-slip. 313.
half-through arch bridge. 415.
half way line. 532.
halfback. 529.
halfway line. 531.
hall. 179.
hall. 189, 433.
hallway. 189.

halyard. 431, 709.
ham knife. 227.
hammer. 572.
hammer. 287, 479, 480, 589, 702, 703.
hammer axe. 588.
hammer beam. 190.
hammer block. 703.
hammer butt. 480.
hammer drill. 639.
hammer head. 480, 588.
hammer rail. 480.
hammer shank. 480.
hammer throw. 570.
hampe. 149.
hand. 115, 612.
hand-and-a-half sword. 692.
hand blender. 235.
hand brake gear housing. 419.
hand brake wheel. 419.
hand brake winding chain. 419.
hand drill. 260.
hand fork. 249.
hand grenade. 696.
hand grip. 580.
hand guard. 530.
hand lamp. 676.
hand mixer. 235.
hand mower. 252.
hand rail. 651.
hand shield. 283.
hand truck. 427, 685.
hand vice. 515.
hand warmer pocket. 301.
hand warmer pouch. 304.
hand wash in lukewarm water. 722.
hand wheel. 499, 514.
handbags. 348, 349.
handball. 539.
handbrake lever. 399.
handgrip. 383, 384, 630.
handguard. 699.
handhold. 568.
handle. 554.
handle. 214, 221, 224, 225, 226, 235, 236, 237, 238, 239, 243, 244, 253, 257, 258, 259, 260, 262, 263, 271, 280, 282, 337, 339, 340, 341, 346, 347, 349, 350, 385, 478, 489, 501, 506, 508, 514, 517, 521, 526, 538, 543, 544, 559, 564, 572, 577, 580, 587, 588, 599, 631, 639, 691.
handle post. 350.
handlebars. 408, 411.
handling engines. 685.
handrail. 182, 197, 429.
handrail drive. 182.
handsaw. 262.
handset. 387, 388, 471.
handset cord. 387.
handsfree telephone. 388.
hang glider. 557.
hang gliding. 557.
hang point. 557.
hang to dry. 722.
hang-up ring. 340.
hanger. 377.
hanger bracket. 631.
hanger loop. 296.
hanging basket. 247.
hanging glacier. 56.
hanging hook. 347.
hanging pendant. 220.
hanging stile. 198, 199, 215.
hank. 552, 553.
harbor. 441.
harbor station. 441.
harbour. 441.
harbour station. 441.
hard palate. 122, 134.
hard shell clam. 102.
hardboard. 265.
hardboards. 194.

The terms in **bold type** indicate the title of an illustration; those in *italic* correspond to the British terminology.

hardtop. 398.
Hare. 41.
harmonica. 488.
harness. 508, 550, 555, 557, 563, 676.
harness racing. 568, 569.
harnesses. 508.
harp. 478.
Harp. 40, 493.
harp cable stays. 416.
harpsichord. 490.
harrow. 162.
hasp. 347.
hastate. 70.
hat. 321.
hat stand. 465.
hat veil. 314.
hatband. 298.
hatch. 645, 704.
hatchet. 600.
hatching. 511.
haulage cable. 558.
haulage road. 635.
haut de côtelettes. 151.
haut de côtes. 147.
hay turner. 164.
hazelnut. 78.
head. 94.
head. 39, 85, 100, 104, 106, 115, 116, 124, 153, 260, 264, 337, 339, 344, 345, 422, 478, 486, 487, 494, 499, 504, 506, 514, 538, 572, 581, 586, 588.
head band. 314.
head cover. 587.
head cushion. 583.
head-first entry. 548.
head linesman. 528.
head number. 568.
head of femur. 121.
head of frame. 199.
head of humerus. 121.
head of sail. 551.
head of table. 583.
head of water. 654.
head pole. 568.
head roller. 508.
head rotation lock. 376.
head spot. 583.
head string. 583.
head tube. 282, 411.
headband. 378, 512, 538, 561.
headbay. 651.
headboard. 214.
headcap. 512.
header. 198, 200, 661, 664.
headframe. 636, 638.
headgear. 298, 314.
headlamp bezel. 398.
headland. 51.
headlight. 398.
headlight. 397, 403, 408, 409, 427, 704.
headlight housing shell. 398.
headphone. 378.
headphone. 378.
headphone jack. 379, 381.
headpin. 590.
headrail. 219.
headrest. 400, 421.
heads. 257.
headwind. 553.
health. 627.
heart. 124.
heart. 99, 102, 521, 592.
hearth. 520.
heartwood. 71.
heat comfort control. 341.
heat deflecting disc. 284.
heat exchanger. 669.
heat pipe radiator. 393.
heat production. 667.
heat ready indicator dot. 341.
heat shield. 457.
heat/speed selector switch. 340.
heater. 599, 664.

heater control. 399.
heating. 200, 201, 202, 203, 204, 205.
heating duct. 241.
heating element. 204, 205, 241, 242, 520.
heating elements indicator. 204.
heating oil. 649.
heating room. 189.
heating unit. 203.
heaving line knot. 601.
heavy duty boot. 320.
heavy gasoline. 649.
heavy machine gun. 701.
heavy machinery. 673.
heavy petroleum. 649.
heavy thunderstorm. 60.
heavy water. 664.
Hebrew. 355.
heddle. 508, 509.
heddle rod. 509.
heddles. 509.
hedge. 247.
hedge shears. 249.
hedge trimmer. 252.
heel. 93, 115, 163, 227, 257, 262, 297, 318, 478, 526, 534, 562, 586.
heel calk. 93.
heel flange. 560.
heel grip. 318.
heel lacing. 563.
heel loop. 631.
heel of round. 148.
heel piece. 554, 559, 560.
heel release setting indicator. 560.
heel rest. 235, 243.
heelplate. 561.
height. 548.
height adjustment screw. 560.
height control. 376.
height of the dive. 549.
height scale. 376.
height sensor. 436.
helical spring. 608.
helicopter. 455.
helicopter hangar. 439.
helicopter transportation. 721.
helideck. 643.
heliostat. 668.
helium sphere. 456.
helix. 132.
helm roof. 191.
helmet. 322, 458, 530, 534, 555, 557, 589, 689.
helmet lamp. 589.
hem. 219.
hemi-demi-semi-quaver. 475.
hemi-demi-semi-quaver rest. 475.
hemibranch. 98.
hemispherical dome. 43.
hemlath. 671.
hemline. 503.
hepatic vein. 124, 125.
herbivore's jaw. 90.
herbs. 143.
Hercules. 40.
Herdsman. 40.
Hermes satellite. 393.
herringbone parquet. 196.
herringbone pattern. 196.
herringbone stitch. 507.
hex nut. 406.
hexagon bushing. 275.
hexagonal ring spanner. 258.
hidden pocket. 351.
high-back dungarees. 316.
high beam warning light. 410.
high card. 592.
high clouds. 52.
high focal plane buoy. 444.
high jump. 571.
high line. 577.
high-power light bulb. 43.
high pressure center. 62.
high pressure centre. 62.

high pressure turbine. 664.
high-rise apartment. 183.
high-rise block. 183.
high-rise office. 178.
high-speed exit taxiway. 452.
high street. 178.
high-temperature cutoff. 273.
high-tension energy transmission to consumers. 654.
high-voltage cable. 620.
high-voltage tester. 286.
high warp loom. 509.
highball. 222.
highland climates. 59.
highway crossing. 423.
highway crossing bell. 423.
hill. 54, 668.
hilted bayonet. 693.
hilus of kidney. 128.
hind leg. 100, 106, 108.
hind legs of the worker. 106.
hind limb. 105.
hind quarter. 148.
hind toe. 95, 97.
hind wing. 100, 106.
Hindi. 355.
hinge. 198, 199, 215, 237, 238, 242, 347, 349, 380, 560, 621.
hinge tooth. 101.
hinged door. 188.
hinged presser foot. 499, 500.
hip. 115, 148.
hip-and-valley roof. 191.
hip pad. 530.
hip pad; girdle. 534.
hip roof. 190.
hitch pin. 479.
hitting area. 526.
hive. 107.
hive body. 107.
hoarding. 178.
hoarding. 177.
hobble. 568.
hobble hanger. 568.
hock. 91, 150, 153.
hockey skate. 562.
hoe. 248.
hoe-fork. 248.
hog score line. 544.
hoist. 180, 390, 709.
hoist room. 636, 638.
hoist ropes. 181.
hoisting chain. 675.
hoisting drum. 675.
hoisting ring. 447.
hoisting rope. 278, 675, 683.
hold yard. 425.
holdall. 347.
holdback. 217.
holder. 521.
holding area marking. 452.
holds. 578.
hole. 585.
hole. 517, 585, 588.
hollow barrel. 629.
hollow-wood construction. 265.
holster. 589.
home key. 470.
home plate. 525.
home straight. 569.
homestretch. 569.
honey cell. 107.
honeybee. 106, 107.
honeycomb diffuser. 373.
honeycomb section. 107.
honor tiles. 593.
honour tiles. 593.
hood. 200, 244, 292, 397, 403, 550.
hood cover. 340.
hooded towelling robe. 315.
hoof. 93.
hoof. 91.
hook. 199, 218, 221, 248, 351, 500, 502, 504, 506, 558, 562, 581, 608, 613, 640, 683.

hook and eyes. 502.
hook ladder. 278, 677.
hooker. 531.
hoop. 507.
hoop earring. 325.
hopper. 164.
hopper car. 420.
hopper ore car. 420.
hopper ore wagon. 420.
hopper wagon. 420.
horizon mirror. 443.
horizon scanner. 65.
horizontal-axis wind turbine. 672.
horizontal bar. 573.
horizontal circle drive knob. 614.
horizontal clamp. 614.
horizontal end handhold. 419.
horizontal flux detector. 662.
horizontal member. 658.
horizontal pivoting. 199.
horizontal seismograph. 616.
horizontal stabilizer. 448, 455, 556.
horizontal tangent screw. 614.
horn. 325, 399, 418, 677.
horn button. 410.
horns. 104.
horny beak. 109.
hors d'oeuvre dish. 223.
horse. 90, 91, 92, 93.
horse's name. 569.
horse's number. 569.
horse's pedigree. 569.
horseradish. 84.
horseshoe. 93.
horseshoe. 172, 325.
horseshoe mount. 42.
hose. 311.
hose. 281, 311.
hose nozzle. 250.
hose reel. 250.
hose truck. 677.
hospital. 718.
host. 390.
hot-air register. 202.
hot bus bar. 288.
hot line connector. 659.
hot pepper. 81.
hot shoe. 372.
hot water extraction. 650.
hot-water heater. 267.
hot-water main. 204.
hot-water riser. 267.
hot-water supply. 272.
hot-water supply line. 272, 273.
hotel information. 721.
hotel reservation desk. 454.
hour angle gear. 42.
hour hand. 605, 607.
hourglass. 606.
house. 185, 188, 544.
house drain. 272.
house furniture. 207.
housing. 261, 337, 339, 340, 384, 387, 409, 442.
hovercraft. 435.
hub. 411, 631, 657, 672.
hub cover. 657.
Hubble's classification. 39.
hubcap. 397.
huckleberry. 74.
hull. 79.
human being. 111.
human body. 114, 115.
human denture. 123.
humerus. 92, 108, 120.
humid subtropical. 59.
humid temperate - long summer. 59.
humid temperate - short summer. 59.
humidifier. 204.
humidistat. 206.
humidity. 63.
hump. 425.
hump area. 425.

The terms in **bold type** indicate the title of an illustration; those in *italic* correspond to the British terminology.

Hungarian. 355.
Hunting Dogs. 40.
hunting weapons. 702.
hurdle. 570.
hurricane. 60.
hurricane deck. 434.
hurricane lamp. 600.
husband. 138.
husband and wife. 139.
husk. 78, 85.
hut. 169.
hydrant intake. 677.
hydraulic cylinder. 678, 679, 682.
hydraulic shovel. 681.
hydroelectric complex. 651.
hydrofiner. 648.
hydrofoil boat. 436.
hydrolic pallet truck. 685.
hydrologic cycle. 58.
hydrostatic pad. 42.
hygrograph. 63.
hypha. 73.
hyphen. 357, 364, 386.
hypogastric artery. 128.
hyssop. 143.

I

ice. 58.
ice axe. 588.
ice axe. 589.
ice-cream can. 236.
ice-cream freezer. 236.
ice cream spoon. 231.
ice cube tray. 239.
ice hockey. 533, 534.
ice hockey player. 534.
ice piton. 589.
ice pudding. 157.
ice screw. 589.
icing syringe. 230.
identification of the track. 569.
identification tag. 347.
idler pulley. 241.
idler wheel. 408.
igloo. 169.
igneous rocks. 48.
ignition switch. 410.
ignition transformer. 205.
ileum. 127.
iliohypogastric nerve. 129.
ilioinguinal nerve. 129.
ilium. 120.
illumination mirror for horizontal
  circle. 614.
illumination mirror for vertical
  circle. 614.
image dissector camera. 65.
immigration control. 454.
impeller. 242.
imperial roof. 191.
impervious rock. 640.
implement bar. 162.
impluvium. 173.
impost. 172.
impression control. 466.
in-flight refuelling probe. 705.
in goal. 531.
in km. 47.
in thousands of feet. 47.
inactive dyke. 660.
inbound line. 527.
incandescent lamp. 284.
incandescent lamp. 446.
incident-light measuring diffuser.
  372.
incisor. 90.
inclined shaft. 636.
incoming message cassette. 388.
index arm. 443.
index mirror. 443.
Indian. 41.
Indian chapati bread. 146.
Indian fig. 80.
Indian naan bread. 146.

Indian Ocean. 49.
Indication of types. 365.
indicator. 402.
indicator. 612.
indicator board. 427.
indicator lamp. 409.
indicator light. 397.
indicator light. 471.
indicator needle. 372.
indicator switch. 400.
indifferent cells. 137.
indoor/outdoor position. 384.
inert gas. 284.
inferior dental arch. 134.
inferior mesenteric artery. 128.
inferior nasal concha. 133.
inferior umbilicus. 96.
inferior vena cava. 124, 125, 128.
Inferior view. 122.
infield. 525.
Infiltration. 58.
infinity. 723.
inflated carrying tire. 429.
inflated carrying tyre. 429.
inflated guiding tire. 429.
inflated guiding tyre. 429.
inflator. 598.
inflator-deflator. 598.
Inflorescent vegetables. 81.
information. 718.
information counter. 454.
information office. 426.
Informative signs. 717.
infraorbital foramen. 122.
infrared spectrometer. 65.
infrared transmitter. 373.
infraspiatus. 119.
infraspinous. 119.
infundibulum of fallopian tube. 117.
inhaul. 551.
injector. 404.
injector pipe. 404.
ink. 367, 516.
ink roller. 516.
inked roller. 385.
inked surface. 518.
inking slab. 516.
inlaid parquet. 196.
inlet. 639.
inlet guide vanes. 450.
inlet hose. 240, 242.
inlet nozzle. 240.
inlet valve. 404, 405.
inner boot. 560.
inner core. 47.
inner edge. 93.
inner hearth. 200.
inner jib. 431.
inner lining. 407.
inner lip. 101.
inner ply. 265.
inner rail. 182.
inner root sheath. 137.
inner table. 592.
inner tent. 597.
inner toe. 95.
Input devices. 468.
input level control. 495.
input selectors. 379.
insectivorous bird. 97.
insert a letter. 362.
insert a word. 362.
insert here. 362.
insert space. 362.
inset pocket. 304.
inside. 226.
inside address. 359.
inside knob. 266.
inside left. 532.
inside-leg snap-fastening. 316.
inside line. 577.
inside linebacker. 528.
inside right. 532.
insole. 318, 320.
inspection chamber. 277.
inspection cover. 277.

inspection plug. 277.
inspection services. 720.
instep. 297.
Instrument board. 399.
instrument board. 399.
instrument panel. 399.
instrument panel. 556.
instrument shelter. 63.
instrument unit. 456.
insulated blade. 286.
insulated handle. 286, 287.
insulating material. 196.
insulating sleeve. 285.
insulation. 273, 669, 670.
insulator. 406, 659.
insulin syringe. 629.
Intaglio printing process. 515.
integral bayonet. 693.
Intelsat. 393.
interchangeable end assembly. 42.
interchangeable lens. 368.
Interchangeable lenses. 370.
interconnecting truss. 65.
intercostal nerve. 129.
interface. 495.
interfacing. 295, 502.
interfemoral membrane. 108.
interior dome shell. 42.
interior door handle. 400.
interior door lock button. 400.
interior pocket. 347, 351.
interlining. 502.
interlock. 511.
intermediate lens. 620.
intermittent drizzle. 60.
intermittent rain. 60.
intermittent snow. 60.
Internal and middle ear. 132.
internal ear. 132.
internal iliac artery. 124, 125.
internal iliac vein. 124.
internal jugular vein. 125.
internal tooth lock washer. 264.
**International phonetic alphabet.
  358.**
**International road signs. 714,
  715, 716, 717.**
International singles court. 540.
**International weather symbols.
  60, 61.**
internode. 69.
interplanetary space. 47.
interrogation recording and
  location system antenna. 65.
intersection. 723.
intertragic notch. 132.
Intervals. 476.
intervertebral foramen. 130.
intestine. 99, 102, 124.
intrados. 172.
intrusive rocks. 48.
Inuktitut. 355.
invert. 429.
inverted pleat. 217, 304.
inverter knob. 614.
Inward dive. 549.
Io. 36.
ion chamber. 662.
Ionic order. 170.
ionosphere. 47.
Iranian. 355.
iris. 131.
iris diaphragm. 619.
Irish bread. 146.
Iron. 586.
iron at high setting. 722.
iron at low setting. 722.
iron at medium setting. 722.
iron curtain. 180.
iron shot silo. 437.
Ironing. 722.
irregular crystal. 57.
irregular galaxy. 39.
is a member of. 723.
is approximately equal to. 723.

is contained in. 723.
is equal to. 723.
is equal to or greater than. 723.
is equal to or less than. 723.
is equivalent to. 723.
is greater than. 723.
is identical with. 723.
is less than. 723.
is not equal to. 723.
is not identical with. 723.
isba. 169.
ischium. 121.
isobar. 62.
isoseismal line. 53.
isthmus of fallopian tube. 117.
isthmus of fauces. 134.
Italian. 355.
italic. 365.
italic boldface capitals. 365.
italic capitals. 365.
ivory ball. 594.

J

J-2 engine. 456.
jabot. 308.
jack. 681.
jack. 378, 480, 592.
jack spring. 480.
jack staff. 439.
jack-up platform. 642.
jacket. 321, 576, 578, 643, 702.
jackleg drill. 639.
jackpot box. 595.
jackpot feed. 595.
jackpot payout chute. 595.
jalousie. 199.
jamb. 198, 199, 200.
jambon. 150.
jambonneau arrière. 150.
jambonneau avant. 150.
Japan plum. 76.
Japanese. 355.
Japanese persimmon. 80.
japonaise fancy. 156.
jar. 345.
jarret arrière. 147.
jarret avant. 147.
javelin. 689.
javelin throw. 571.
javelins. 572.
jaw. 258, 260, 261, 287, 343.
jazz band. 491.
jeans. 310.
jejunum. 127.
jersey. 530.
Jerusalem artichoke. 84.
jet deflector. 252.
jet engine. 705.
jet fuel. 649.
jet refueler. 453.
jet tip. 339.
Jew's harp. 488.
jewel cap. 443.
jewellery. 325, 326, 327.
jewelry. 325, 326, 327.
Jewish hallah. 146.
jib. 552, 683.
jib halyard. 552.
jib tie. 683.
jibsheet. 552.
jingle. 486.
job title. 361.
jockey roller. 412.
jodhpurs. 565.
joint. 367, 512, 581, 582.
joist. 196.
Joker. 592.
journal box. 418.
jowl. 150.
joystick. 471.
joystick. 469, 495.
judge. 576, 578, 579.
judge's stand. 569.
judo. 578.

The terms in **bold type** indicate the title of an illustration; those in *italic* correspond to the British terminology.

judo suit. 578.
juice extractor. 236.
juice sac. 77.
juicer. 236.
jumeaux. 149.
jump ski. 554.
jumper. 317.
jumper. 302, 555.
jumpsuit. 316.
jumpsuit. 310.
junction box. 423.
Jupiter. 36.

K

K frame. 658.
Kaplan turbine. 657.
keel. 557.
keep. 177.
keeper. 291, 294.
keeper ring. 580.
kelly. 640.
kerb. 413.
kerb weir. 413.
kerchief. 314.
kernel. 78, 85.
kerosene. 456, 649.
ketch. 432.
kettle. 243.
kettledrum. 486.
key. 266, 385, 467, 479, 480, 483, 489, 492.
key case. 351.
key finger button. 483.
key lock. 350.
key signature. 476.
keybed. 479.
keyboard. 470.
keyboard. 386, 467, 469, 479, 495.
keyboard control. 495.
keyboard instruments. 479, 480.
keystone. 172, 175.
keyway. 266.
kick. 547.
kick pleat. 304.
kickplate. 239.
kidney. 99, 124.
kill button. 410.
kilt. 303.
kimono. 311.
kimono sleeve. 306.
kinds of deer. 89.
kinds of hair. 330.
kinds of precipitation. 57.
King. 592.
King (K). 591.
king pin. 418.
king post. 557.
King's side. 591.
kingpin. 402, 562.
kiosk. 428.
kitchen. 173, 189, 421.
kitchen knife. 227.
kitchen scales. 229.
kitchen timer. 229.
kitchen utensils. 227, 228, 229, 230, 231.
kiwi. 80.
knee. 91, 108, 114.
knee boot. 568.
knee boot suspender. 568.
knee brace. 190.
knee pad. 526, 530, 534, 564, 575.
knee roll. 567.
knee sock. 561.
knickers. 310, 561.
knife. 224.
knife. 165, 516, 550, 599.
knife-blade cartridge fuse. 285.
knife-edge. 608, 609, 610.
knife pleat. 304.
knife sharpener. 231.
Knight (Kt). 591.
knit shirt. 296.
knitting. 504.

knitting machine. 505, 506.
knitting measure. 504.
knitting needles. 504.
knob. 209, 266, 526.
knob closure. 349, 351.
knob for reticle illumination. 614.
knob handle. 263.
knockout. 288.
knot. 511.
knot stitches group. 507.
knots. 601.
knuckle. 153.
knurled bolt. 280.
knurled button. 442.
kohl pencil. 332.
kohlrabi. 84.
kraft paper. 265.
kumquat. 77.

L

label. 344, 380.
label maker. 461.
labial palp. 100, 102.
labium majus. 117.
labium minus. 117.
laboratory. 648.
laccolith. 53.
lace. 526, 562, 579.
lace-up. 320.
lacrimal duct. 131.
lactiferous duct. 117.
ladder. 671.
laddor scaffold. 279.
ladders and stepladders. 278, 279.
ladle. 229, 695.
Lady chapel. 174.
lagging. 647.
lagoon. 51.
lake. 38.
lam. 508.
lamb. 151, 153.
lambdoid suture. 122.
lamina cribrosa. 133.
laminate board. 265.
laminboard. 265.
lamp. 376, 383, 619.
lamp changer. 446.
lamp-post. 178.
lamp room. 638.
lamp socket. 285.
lamphouse. 376.
lance rest. 690.
lanceolate. 70.
lancet. 172.
land. 260.
landing. 189, 197, 574, 637.
landing area. 570, 571.
landing light. 455.
landing mat. 574.
landing net. 582.
landside. 163.
lane. 590.
lane. 546, 571.
lane number. 546.
lane rope. 546.
lane timekeeper. 546.
languid. 482.
lantern. 247, 445, 599.
lantern of lighthouse. 446.
lantern pane. 445.
lanyard ring. 703.
lapel. 293, 308.
lapiaz. 54.
large intestine. 127.
large wheel. 631.
larger round. 119.
larva. 107.
larynx. 126.
lasagna. 144.
lasagna verde. 144.
LASH ship. 441.
last quarter. 38.
latch. 237, 238, 242, 506, 588.

latch bolt. 266.
latch follower. 266.
latch lever. 266, 500.
latch needle. 506.
lateen sail. 432.
lateral adjusting lever. 257.
lateral condyle of femur. 121.
lateral cutaneous nerve of thigh. 129.
lateral filing cabinet. 465.
lateral great. 118, 119.
lateral groove. 93.
lateral incisor. 123.
lateral line. 98, 544.
lateral moraine. 56.
lateral semicircular canal. 132.
lateral system of marking. 446.
lateral view. 122.
latissimus dorsi. 119.
latitude. 35.
latitude scale. 64.
lattice tube. 662.
launch escape system. 456.
launching orbit. 394.
laundry room. 189.
lava flow. 53.
lava layer. 53.
lava plateau. 53.
lavaliere. 326.
lavatory. 189.
lavatory truck. 453.
lawn. 188, 247.
lawn aerator. 251.
lawn edger. 248.
lawn mowers. 252.
lawn rake. 248.
layout. 521.
lead. 544, 606.
lead came. 521.
lead-in wire. 284, 372.
lead knife. 521.
lead pencil. 367.
lead screw. 260.
lead shot ballast. 437.
lead stretcher. 521.
leader. 581.
leading edge. 308, 448, 556, 557.
leading edge tube. 557.
leaf. 70.
leaf. 69, 85, 209, 440.
leaf axil. 69, 70.
leaf margin. 70.
leaf spring. 408.
leaf vegetables. 82.
lean-to roof. 190.
leash rod. 508, 509.
leather end. 294.
leather garment. 689.
leather goods. 350, 351.
leather sandal. 689.
leather sheath. 599.
LED peak level meter. 381.
ledger. 192.
ledger line. 475.
leech. 551.
leek. 83.
left atrium. 124.
left back. 532, 536, 539.
left bronchus. 126.
left center. 531.
left centre. 531.
left cornerback. 528, 529.
left defence. 533.
left defense. 533.
left defensive end. 528, 529.
left defensive tackle. 528, 529.
left field. 525.
left fielder. 525.
left forward. 535, 536.
left guard. 528, 529, 535.
left half. 532.
left halfback. 528.
left-hand grip. 700.
left kidney. 128.
left-luggage office. 426.
left lung. 124, 126.

left outside linebacker. 529.
left safety. 528.
left safety back. 529.
left service court. 537, 540.
left tackle. 528, 529.
left valve. 101.
left ventricle. 124.
left wing. 532.
left wing. 531, 533.
left winger. 539.
leg. 109, 115, 147, 150, 151, 153, 163, 209, 214, 297, 486, 543, 574, 580, 609.
leg, butt portion. 147.
leg, shank portion. 147.
leg-of-mutton sleeve. 306.
leg position. 549.
legging. 589.
lemon. 77.
lemon squeezer. 228, 236.
lenghtwise grain. 503.
length. 548.
lengthwise grain. 502.
lens. 625.
lens. 131, 371, 372, 377.
lens and accessories. 370.
lens aperture scale. 370.
lens cap. 370.
lens carriage. 446.
lens clock. 446.
lens hood. 370.
lens mount. 368.
lenticular galaxy. 39.
lentils. 637.
Leo, the Lion. 712.
leopard. 90.
lesser covert. 96.
lesser lip. 117.
let is stand. 363.
letter opener. 461.
letter scales. 461.
letterhead. 359, 361.
letters. 356, 357.
leucoplast. 113.
level. 637.
level controls. 378.
level crossing. 423.
level crossing sign. 423.
level crossing with automatic gates. 424.
leveling foot. 377.
leveling screw. 64, 609, 614.
levelling foot. 377.
levelling screw. 64, 609, 614.
lever. 237, 259, 270, 271, 343, 385, 401, 471, 517, 595, 612, 696, 702.
lever bucket. 679.
lever corkscrew. 229.
lever cover. 271.
lever tap. 271.
levigator. 517.
Libra, the Balance. 712.
lid. 232, 233, 234, 236, 237, 240, 341.
lid latch. 341.
Liederkranz. 154.
life buoy. 436.
life cycle of the frog. 105.
life raft. 435, 439.
lifeboat. 430, 643.
lift. 181.
lift. 430.
lift arm. 679.
lift bridge. 417.
lift buffer. 181.
lift cord. 219.
lift cord lock. 219.
lift cylinder. 679, 684.
lift-fan air intake. 435.
lift gate. 398.
lift guide rail. 181.
lift safety device. 181.
lift span. 417.
lifting chain. 684.
lifting handle. 698.

The terms in **bold type** indicate the title of an illustration; those in *italic* correspond to the British terminology.

lifting lever. 419.
ligature. 483.
light. 429, 444, 550, 670.
light bar. 340.
light from Sun. 38.
light-load adjustment screw. 615.
light machine gun. 701.
light pen. 469.
light-reading scale. 372.
light sensor. 372.
light signals. 715.
lightbox. 375.
lighted mirror. 340.
lighthouse. 445.
lighting. 600.
lighting and vision control room. 389.
lighting control panel. 389.
lighting director. 389.
lighting switch. 410.
lightning arrester. 655, 659.
lightning rod. 187.
lights. 220, 221.
lighttight box. 368.
limb. 71.
limb top. 619.
limousine. 398.
limpet. 104.
line. 385, 475, 580, 581, 594, 595.
line guide. 386, 580.
line judge. 528.
line map. 428.
line of scrimmage. 528, 529.
line printer. 666.
line space regulator. 467.
linear. 70.
lineman's pliers. 287.
linen. 214.
linen chest. 216.
lines. 385.
linesman. 531, 532, 533, 536, 537, 542.
lingual papillae. 134.
lingual tonsil. 134.
lining. 293, 318, 348, 350, 502, 562.
linstock. 695.
lint filter. 240.
lint trap. 241.
lintel. 175, 200.
Lion. 40.
lion passant. 710.
lip. 94, 266, 521.
lipbrush. 333.
lipid droplet. 113.
lipliner. 333.
lipstick. 333.
liquefied gas petroleum treatment. 648.
liquefied petroleum gas storage. 648.
liqueur. 222.
liquid compass. 443.
liquid consonants. 358.
liquid-cooled garment. 458.
liquid-crystal display. 605.
liquid foundation. 332.
liquid hydrogen (fuel). 456.
liquid-level gauge. 647.
liquid oxygen (lox). 456.
liquid oxygen (lox) transfer pipe. 456.
listen button. 388.
litchi. 80.
litho crayon. 517.
litho pencil. 517.
lithographic press. 517.
lithographic stone. 517, 518.
lithographic tusche. 517.
lithography. 517.
lithosphere. 47.
litter basket. 178.
litter bin. 178.
Little Bear. 40.
Little Dog. 40.
little finger hook. 484.

Little Horse. 40.
Little Lion. 40.
live roller. 683.
liver. 99, 124, 127.
livestock car. 420.
livestock van. 420.
living quarters. 445, 457, 643.
living room. 189, 596.
Lizard. 40.
load backrest. 684.
loader's seat. 704.
loading. 696.
loading belt. 635.
leading door. 201.
loading pocket. 637.
loafer. 320.
loam. 162.
lobate. 70.
lobate web. 97.
lobby. 454.
lobe. 97, 117.
lobster. 103.
lobule. 132.
lock. 266.
lock. 198, 215, 347, 412, 660.
lock-chamber. 440.
lock forward. 531.
lock keeper's building. 441.
lock nut. 64, 562, 613.
lock rail. 198.
lock ring. 377.
lock washer. 264.
locked groove. 380.
locker. 465.
lockers. 720.
locket. 326.
locking device. 278.
locking knob. 614.
locking nut. 268.
locking pliers. 259.
locking ring. 258, 698.
locknut. 270.
loculus. 76.
log carrier. 201.
log chute. 651.
log tongs. 201.
logging unit. 643.
loin. 91, 115, 147, 148, 150, 151, 153.
long adductor. 118.
long and short stitch. 507.
long cardigan. 307.
long extensor of toes. 118.
long johns. 297.
long jump. 570.
long-nose pliers. 287.
long palmar. 118.
long peroneal. 118.
long radial extensor of wrist. 119.
long-range jet. 448.
long-range radar system. 706.
long residue. 649.
long service line. 542.
longe. 147.
longitude. 35.
longitudinal dunes. 55.
lookout tower. 177.
loop. 295.
loop stitches group. 507.
loophole. 177.
loose curtain. 217.
loose fill insulation. 195.
loose gravel. 714.
loose powder. 332.
loose powder brush. 332.
loosely tied bow. 309.
lopping shears. 249.
lore. 95.
lorgnette. 329.
lost and found articles. 720.
loud pedal. 479.
loudness switch. 379.
loudspeaker. 378, 390, 471, 677.
lounge. 433.
louver. 206, 221.
louver-board. 175.

louvered window. 199.
louvre. 206, 221.
louvre-board. 175.
lovage. 143.
love seat. 211.
low bar. 574.
low clouds. 52.
low line. 577.
low pressure center. 62.
low pressure centre. 62.
low pressure steam piping. 661.
low pressure turbine. 664.
low-rise apartments. 183.
low-tension distribution line. 659.
low warp loom. 508.
lower berth. 421.
lower blade guard. 263.
lower bowl. 234.
lower chord. 415.
lower eyelid. 94, 105, 131.
lower fore topgallant sail. 431.
lower fore topsail. 431.
lower gill arch. 98.
lower girdle facet (16). 327.
lower guard retracting lever. 263.
lower heating element. 273.
lower landing plate. 182.
lower level. 440.
lower limb. 691.
lower lip. 134, 482.
lower lobe. 126.
lower mandible. 95.
lower mantle. 47.
lower mast. 430.
lower pan-head mounting screw. 374.
lower rudder. 438.
lower shell. 560.
lower side-rail. 402.
lower sphere clamp. 64.
lower support screw. 64.
lower thermostat. 273.
lox tank baffles. 456.
lubber's line. 443.
lubber's-line disk. 443.
lubricants plant. 649.
lubricating oils. 649.
Luer-Lock syringe. 629.
luff. 551.
luff (to). 551.
lug. 486.
luggage. 347.
luggage carrier. 347.
luggage claim. 720.
luggage label. 347.
luggage rack. 398.
luggage registration. 720.
luggage trolley. 347.
luggage trolleys. 720.
lumache. 145.
lumbar plexus. 129.
lumbar vertebra (5). 121.
lumbar vertebrae. 92.
lunar boot. 458.
lunar eclipse. 38.
lunar features. 38.
lunar module. 456.
lungs. 126.
lunula. 137.
lunule. 101.
lures. 581.
Lynx. 40.
lyre. 487.
lysosome. 113.

M

machete. 692.
machicolation. 177.
machine gun. 704.
machine hall. 651, 655.
machine wash in hot water at a normal setting. 722.
machine wash in lukewarm water at a gentle. 722.

machine wash in warm water at a gentle setting-reduced. 722.
machine wash in warm water at a normal setting. 722.
machinery. 165.
machinery store. 161.
macreuse. 149.
macro focusing knob. 383.
mafalde. 144.
mafaldine. 144.
magazine. 697, 699, 702, 703.
magazine base. 703.
magazine catch. 697, 699, 703.
magazine release. 699.
magazine spring. 703.
magma. 53.
magma chamber. 53.
magnesium alloy. 322.
magnesium wire. 372.
magnet. 501.
magnet. 443.
magnetic compass. 625.
magnetic cup. 606.
magnetic gasket. 239.
magnetic lid holder. 243.
magnetic needle. 625.
magnetic suspension. 615.
magnetic tape controller. 472.
magnetic tape drive. 472.
magnetic tape storage. 472.
magnifying mirror. 340.
mah-jongg. 593.
main beam warning light. 410.
main bevel drive gearbox. 435.
main breaker. 288.
main cable. 373.
main cleanout. 267.
main cord. 377.
main drive chain. 182.
main drive shaft. 182.
main duct. 202.
main electrode. 284.
main engines. 457.
main entrance. 188.
main gas tap. 410.
main generator. 418.
main halyard. 552.
main handle. 260.
main inlet. 647.
main landing gear. 448.
main leg. 658.
main line. 424.
main lower topgallant sail. 431.
main lower topsail. 431.
main mirror. 622.
main parachute. 555.
main petrol tap. 410.
main power cable. 288.
main return pipe. 203.
main royal sail. 431.
main running track. 425.
main sail. 431.
main scope tube. 621.
main section. 594, 595.
main sewer. 413.
main shaft. 638.
main shield bracket. 698.
main spar. 449.
main spring. 703.
main stand. 409.
main street. 178.
main supply pipe. 203.
main switch. 659.
main tube. 622.
main undercarriage mounting beam. 449.
main undercarriage wheel. 705.
main upper topgallant sail. 431.
main upper topsail. 431.
main wheel. 607.
mainmast. 430.
mains lead. 377.
mains water. 669.
mainsail. 552.
mainsheet. 552.
mainspring. 605.

The terms in **bold type** indicate the title of an illustration; those in *italic* correspond to the British terminology.

maintenance hangar. 452.
maintube. 623.
major inner reaping throw. 578.
major outer reaping throw. 578.
major types of bayonets. 693.
major types of berries. 74.
major types of citrus fruits. 77.
major types of dams. 653.
major types of forks. 225.
major types of knives. 224.
major types of missiles. 706.
major types of nuts. 78.
major types of spoons. 226.
major types of stone fruits. 75.
major types of tables. 209.
major types of tents. 597.
major types of tropical fruits. 80.
major types of turbines. 657.
make-up. 332, 333.
make-up kit. 332.
make-up products. 332.
make-up sponges. 333.
makeup. 332, 333.
makeup kit. 332.
makeup products. 332.
makeup sponges. 333.
malar bone. 120.
malar region. 95.
male. 723.
male ferrule. 580.
male genital organs. 116.
male urethra. 116.
mallet. 257.
mallet. 486, 516.
mallets. 485.
Malpighi's pyramid. 128.
mammary gland. 117.
mandarin. 77.
mandarin collar. 308.
mandatory signs. 717. ·
mandible. 92, 98, 100, 103, 106, 120, 122, 123.
mandolin. 487.
mane. 91.
maneuvering engine. 457.
mange-tout peas. 85.
mango. 75.
manhole. 413, 646, 647.
manicotti. 145.
manicure set. 342.
manicure stick. 342.
manicuring instruments. 343.
manoeuvring engine. 457.
manometer. 204, 647.
mansard roof. 191.
mantel. 200.
mantel shelf. 200.
mantle. 104.
mantle edge. 102.
manual. 482.
manual aperture control. 383.
manual release. 560.
manual zoom ring. 383, 384.
manually-operated points. 422.
manually-operated switch. 422.
manuals. 481.
manure spreader. 163.
manure spreader box. 163.
manway. 637.
Marconi cutter. 432.
margin. 70.
margin stop. 467.
marginal shield. 109.
marine diesel. 649.
maritime signals. 444, 445, 446.
marjoram. 143.
marker. 367, 590.
marker light. 403.
marking dot. 503.
marrow. 81.
Mars. 36.
mars light. 677.
martingale. 577.
mascara. 332.
mascara brush. 333.
mashie; no. 5 iron. 586.

mashie iron; no. 4 iron. 586.
mashie niblick; no. 7 iron. 586.
mask. 322, 526, 550, 576.
mass. 616.
masseter. 118.
mast. 423, 424, 455, 551, 552, 675, 684.
mast foot. 551.
mast sleeve. 551.
master bedroom. 189.
master carrier. 218.
master cord. 563.
master gate valve. 641.
master retarders. 425.
masthead. 430, 551.
masthead light. 434.
masting and rigging. 430.
mastoid process. 122.
mat. 578.
matchbook. 345.
matchbox. 345.
matchstick. 345.
maternal aunt. 138.
maternal uncle. 138.
maternity dress. 302.
mathematical symbols. 356.
mathematics. 723.
matinee length necklace (22 in.). 326.
matrix. 495.
mattress. 214.
mattress cover. 214.
maxilla. 98, 103, 120, 122, 123, 133.
maxilliped. 103.
maximum and minimum thermometers. 63.
maximum speed limit. 716.
measure of pressure. 612.
measure of temperature. 611.
measure of time. 605, 606, 607.
measure of weight. 608, 609, 610.
measuring cap. 235.
measuring cup. 341.
measuring cups. 229.
measuring devices. 603.
measuring spoons. 229.
measuring tube. 64.
meat grinder. 228.
meat keeper. 239.
meat thermometer. 229.
mechanical connectors. 274.
mechanical pencil. 367.
mechanical stage. 619.
mechanical stage control. 619.
mechanical watch. 605.
mechanism of the organ. 482.
medial condyle of femur. 121.
medial great. 118.
medial moraine. 56.
median groove. 93.
median lingual sulcus. 134.
median nerve. 129.
median vein of forearm. 125.
medical injection disc. 458.
medical injection disk. 458.
Mediterranean Sea. 49.
Mediterranean subtropical. 59.
medium format SLR (6 x 6). 369.
medium tension distribution line. 659.
medulla. 128, 137.
medulla oblongata. 130.
medullar axis of lumbar vertebra. 130.
Meissner's corpuscle. 136.
melanocyte. 136.
melody string. 487.
melting snow. 57.
meltwater. 56.
memo pad. 464.
memory button. 379.
men. 591.
men. 592.
men's apparatus. 573.

men's bag. 349.
men's clothing. 291, 292, 293, 294, 295, 296, 297, 298.
men's pompadour. 331.
mental foramen. 122.
Mercury. 36, 284.
mercury bath. 446.
Mercury capsule (USA). 47.
mercury switch. 611.
mercury-vapor lamp. 284.
mercury-vapour lamp. 284.
meridian. 35.
méridienne. 211.
meringue. 156.
meringue gateau. 156.
merlon. 177.
mesa. 55.
mesh. 543.
mesocarp. 74, 75, 76, 77.
mesosphere. 47.
mesothorax. 100.
metacarpus. 92, 94, 120.
metal A. 282.
metal B. 282.
metal counterhoop. 486.
metal frame. 479.
metal head. 572.
metal heat reflector. 200.
metal plate. 328, 518.
metal rod. 485.
metal washer. 270.
metal water pipe. 288.
metallic contact grid. 670.
metallic plastron. 576.
metals. 710.
metamorphic rocks. 48.
metatarsus. 92, 105, 120.
metathorax. 100.
meteorological ground. 63.
meteorological measuring instruments. 64.
meteorology. 62, 63.
meteors. 60.
methane carrier with free-standing tanks. 645.
methane carrier with membrane tanks. 645.
methane carrier with semi-membrane tanks. 645.
metope. 170.
metopic suture. 122.
metronome. 492.
mezzani. 144.
mezzanine. 179, 428.
Michigan snowshoe. 563.
micrometer caliper. 613.
micrometer screw. 613, 614.
microphone. 378, 388, 471.
microphone boom. 390.
microphone jack. 381.
microprocessor. 469.
microscope eyepiece. 614.
microwave oven. 237.
mid-calf length. 297.
mid range pick-up. 494.
middle clouds. 52.
middle covert. 96.
middle ear. 132.
middle jib. 431.
middle leg. 100, 106.
middle linebacker. 528, 529.
middle lobe. 126.
middle nasal concha. 133.
middle neck. 153.
middle panel. 198.
middle phalanx. 94, 120, 121.
middle piece. 116.
middle primary covert. 96.
middle rail. 215.
middle rib. 152.
middle sole. 318.
middle toe. 95.
middy. 305.
midfield. 532.
midiron; no. 2 iron. 586.
midmashie; no. 3 iron. 586.

midrange. 378.
midrib. 70, 79.
midriff band. 313.
milieu de poitrine. 149.
milieu de sous-noix. 147.
milk bread. 146.
Milky Way. 40.
Milky Way projector. 43.
Mimolette. 155.
minaudiere. 349.
mincer. 228.
mine. 650.
mine entrance. 637.
mini shirtdress. 305.
minim. 475.
minim rest. 475.
mining. 636.
mining. 667.
minor inner reaping throw. 578.
mint. 143.
minute hand. 605, 607.
mirror. 332, 347, 368, 409.
miscellaneous. 326, 723.
miscellaneous auxiliary systems. 666.
miscellaneous utensils. 231.
missile. 438, 706.
missile director. 439.
missile launch rail. 705.
missile launcher. 439.
missile tracking radar. 706.
missile tube. 438.
missiles. 706.
mist. 60.
miter gate. 440.
miter gauge. 262.
miter gauge slot. 262.
mitochondrion. 113.
mitral valve. 124.
mitre gauge. 262.
mitre gauge slot. 262.
mitt. 299.
mitten. 283, 299, 317, 559, 589.
mixing bowl. 235.
mixing bowls. 230.
mixing chamber. 282.
mizzen sail. 431.
mizzenmast. 430.
moat. 176, 177.
mob-cap. 314.
mobile passenger stairs. 453.
mobile septum of nose. 133.
mocassin. 563.
moccasin. 319.
mock pocket. 301.
moderator. 664.
moderator heat exchanger. 664.
moderator inlet. 662.
moderator/miscellaneous systems. 666.
moderator outlet. 662.
moderator pump. 664.
modern. 367, 697.
modern bow. 691.
modern howitzer. 698.
modesty. 308.
modillion. 170.
modulator. 624.
mogul base. 284.
Mohorovicic discontinuity. 47, 48.
moistener. 462.
molar. 90.
moldboard. 163.
mollusk. 102.
money clip. 351.
monitor. 391.
monitor bank. 391.
monitor indicator. 379.
monitor pusher. 390.
monitor roof. 191.
monitor speaker. 391.
monkey wrench. 276.
mono-ski. 554.
monocle. 329.
mons pubis. 117.
monster. 529.

The terms in **bold type** indicate the title of an illustration; those in *italic* correspond to the British terminology.

743

Monterey Jack. 154.
Moon. 38.
Moon. 36, 37, 38.
moon dial. 607.
Moon's orbit. 38.
moose. 89.
mordent. 476.
morel. 73.
morning line. 569.
morphology. 91, 95, 98.
Morse code. 386.
mortar. 697.
mortar. 193, 228.
mortise. 345, 507.
mortise lock. 266.
mother. 138, 139.
mother-in-law. 139.
motor. 165, 206, 240, 241, 244, 260, 261, 263, 377, 499, 622, 675.
motor car. 429.
motor cell. 135.
motor-compressor unit. 206.
motor drive. 624.
motor end plate. 135.
motor generator. 181.
motor generator set. 181.
motor mower. 252.
motor neuron. 135.
motor pulley. 380.
motor unit. 234, 235, 236.
motorcycle. 409, 410.
motorway. 717.
moulded insulation. 195.
moulded plywood. 265.
mound. 525.
mount frame blinder. 377.
mountain. 54.
mountain range. 38, 48.
mountain slope. 54.
mountain torrent. 54.
mountaineer. 589.
mountaineering. 588, 589.
mountaineering boot. 589.
mounting. 473.
mounting post. 611.
mounting screw. 611.
mouse. 469.
mousse. 157.
mouth. 134.
mouth. 102, 104, 105, 114, 482.
mouthparts. 106.
mouthpiece. 579.
mouthpiece. 387, 483, 484, 550.
mouthpiece receiver. 484.
mouthpipe. 484.
movable bridges. 417.
movable condenser. 376.
movable jaw. 258, 259.
movable maxillary. 109.
move to left. 363.
move to right. 363.
moving coil. 384.
Mt Everest. 47.
mud flap. 397, 402, 403.
mud pit. 640.
mud pump. 640.
mud wall. 596.
mudguard. 411.
muff. 349.
muffin pan. 230.
muffle. 520.
muffler. 253, 406.
mullet. 710.
multi-ply plywood. 265.
multimeter. 286.
multiple access station. 394.
multiple copy control. 467.
multiple-span beam bridge. 414.
multiplexing equipment. 394.
multiplication. 723.
multipurpose ladder. 278.
multipurpose tool. 287.
mummy. 598.
Munster. 155.
muntin. 198, 199.

murette. 445.
muscle arrector pili. 136, 137.
muscle fiber. 135.
muscle fibre. 135.
muscle scar. 101.
muscle segment. 99.
muscles. 118, 119.
musculocutaneous nerve. 129.
mushroom anchor. 447.
mushrooms. 73.
music. 473.
music rest. 492.
music stand. 492.
music stand. 479.
musical accessories. 492.
musical notation. 475, 476.
muskeg. 650.
muskmelon. 81.
muslin. 515.
mustard. 79.
mute. 484.
mutule. 170.
muzzle. 94, 694, 697, 702.
muzzle astragal. 694.
muzzle loading. 694, 695.
muzzle molding. 694.
muzzle moulding. 694.
muzzle ring. 693.
mycelium. 73.
myelin sheath. 135.

N

nacelle. 672.
nacreous cloud. 47.
nail. 137, 264.
nail. 109.
nail bed. 137.
nail brush. 342.
nail buffer. 342.
nail cleaner. 343.
nail clippers. 343.
nail file. 342.
nail hole. 93.
nail matrix. 137.
nail nippers. 342.
nail scissors. 342.
nail shaper. 342.
nail whitener pencil. 343.
nails. 509.
name of sender. 361.
name plate. 261, 615.
naos. 171.
nape. 95, 115.
nappy. 315.
naris. 133.
narrow cuff. 306.
narthex. 174.
nasal bone. 122, 133.
nasal cavity. 126.
nasal fossa. 122.
nasal fossae. 133.
nasal vowels. 358.
nasopharynx. 133.
natural. 476.
natural arch. 51.
natural sponge. 333.
nave. 174.
navel. 114.
navette cut. 327.
navigating bridge. 434.
navigation devices. 442, 443.
navigation light. 448.
navigational radar. 439.
Neapolitan coffee maker. 234.
near side. 38.
neck. 91, 109, 114, 116, 123, 147, 148, 151, 152, 153, 225, 226, 392, 477, 478, 487, 494, 514, 573, 586, 606.
neck end. 153, 295.
neck guard. 690.
neck of femur. 121.
neck of uterus. 117.
neck ring. 458.

neck-scrag end. 153.
neckhole. 297.
necklaces. 326.
necklines and necks. 309.
neckroll. 214.
necks. 309.
necktie. 295.
nectarine. 75.
needle. 500.
needle. 57, 499, 500, 501, 629.
needle bar. 500.
needle bed. 505.
needle bed. 505.
needle bed groove. 505.
needle clamp. 500.
needle clamp screw. 500.
needle hub. 629.
needle plate. 499.
needle threader. 501.
needle threader. 500.
needle tool. 519.
negative carrier. 376.
negative charge. 723.
negative contact. 670.
negative meniscus. 625.
negative plate. 406.
negative plate group. 406.
negative region. 670.
negative terminal. 406.
negligee. 311.
neon lamp. 286.
neon screwdriver. 286.
neon sign. 178.
neon tester. 286.
nephew. 138.
Neptune. 36.
nerve. 137.
nerve fiber. 135.
nerve fibre. 135.
nerve termination. 135.
nerveux de gîte à la noix. 149.
nerveux de sous-noix. 147.
nervous system. 129, 130.
nest of tables. 209.
Net. 41, 533, 535, 536, 537, 539, 542, 543.
net band. 537.
net judge. 537.
net stocking. 311.
net support. 543.
network. 387.
network management center. 394.
network management centre. 394.
neural spine. 121.
neural spine. 99.
neuron. 135.
neutral conductor. 659.
neutral service wire. 288.
neutral wire. 288.
neutral zone. 528, 529, 533.
new fuel loading area. 665.
new fuel port. 665.
new fuel storage room. 665.
new Moon. 38.
newel post. 197.
news dealer. 178.
newspaper vendor. 178.
nib. 367.
niblick; no. 9 iron. 586.
nictitating membrane. 94.
niece. 138.
nightdress. 311.
nightwear. 311.
nimbostratus. 52.
NIMBUS III meteorological satellite. 65.
nipple. 114, 117, 275.
Nissl bodies. 135.
nitrogen. 284.
no. 4 wood. 586.
no. 8 forward. 531.
no dogs. 718.
no entry. 716.
no entry for bicycles. 716.
no entry for goods vehicles. 716.

no entry for mopeds. 716.
no entry for motorcycles. 716.
no entry for pedestrians. 716.
no entry for power-driven vehicles. 716.
no left turn. 716.
no U-turn. 716.
nock. 691.
nocking point. 691.
noctilucent cloud. 47.
node. 69, 658.
node of Ranvier. 135.
noise generator control. 495.
noix. 147.
noix de hachage. 150.
noix pâtissière. 147.
non-skid spaghetti. 144.
noodles. 144.
normal mode acquisition. 394.
normal mode satellite. 394.
north. 445, 593.
North America. 49.
North American cheeses. 154.
North American cut. 147, 148, 150, 151.
North celestial pole. 35.
North pole. 35.
North Sea. 49.
North wind. 593.
Northern Crown. 40.
northern hemisphere. 35.
Norwegian. 355.
nose. 91, 114, 448, 556, 557, 690.
nose cone. 450.
nose landing gear. 448.
nose leaf. 108.
nose leather. 94.
nose of the quarter. 318.
nose pad. 328.
noseband. 567.
nosepad. 328.
nosing. 197.
nostril. 91, 95, 98, 105, 109.
notch. 293, 503, 582.
notched double-edged thinning scissors. 338.
notched lapel. 291, 301, 308.
notched single-edged thinning scissors. 338.
note symbols. 475.
notepad. 351.
nozzle. 282.
nozzle. 205, 280, 456, 676, 677, 706.
nuchal shield. 109.
nuclear energy. 661, 662, 663, 664, 665, 666, 667.
nuclear envelope. 113.
nuclear fuel cycle. 667.
nuclear reactor. 663.
nuclear reactor. 667.
nuclear whorl. 101.
nucleolus. 113.
nucleus. 39, 113, 135.
number. 594.
number of tracks sign. 423.
number three. 544.
number two. 544.
numbering machine. 462.
numbers. 357.
numerals. 356, 386.
numeric keyboard. 610.
numeric keypad. 470.
nut. 264, 422, 442, 477, 494, 691.
nut and bolt. 259.
nutcracker. 228.
nylon frilly tights. 315.
nylon rumba tights. 315.

O

o-ring. 271.
oasis. 55.
object. 619.
object balls. 583.

The terms in **bold type** indicate the title of an illustration; those in *italic* correspond to the British terminology.

objective. 620.
objective. 619.
objective lens. 372, 620, 621, 623.
objective pole piece. 620.
oboe. 483, 490.
oboes. 493.
obscured sky. 61.
observation deck. 454.
observation light. 437.
observation window. 457.
observer's seat. 451.
obstacles. 565.
obturator nerve. 129.
occipital. 119, 121.
occipital bone. 122.
occipital condyle. 122.
occluded front. 61.
ocean. 58.
ocean. 38.
ocean floor. 50.
Oceania. 49.
ocelli. 100.
Octant. 41.
octave. 476, 577.
octave mechanism. 483.
odd. 594, 595.
odd pinnate. 70.
odometer. 399.
oesophagus. 99, 102, 127.
off-on knob. 392.
offensive. 528, 529.
office furniture. 465.
office supplies and equipment. 459.
offset. 275.
offshore drilling. 642.
offshore well. 644.
ogee. 172, 694.
ogee roof. 191.
oil. 640, 641, 642, 643, 644, 645, 646, 647, 648, 649, 650.
oil. 640.
oil and gas foam. 641.
oil burner. 205.
oil drain plug. 405.
oil filter. 405.
oil/gas separator. 643.
oil indicator. 399.
oil pan. 253, 405.
oil pressure. 410.
oil pump. 205.
oil reservoir. 639.
oil sand. 650.
oil sands mining plant. 650.
oil supply line. 205.
oil tank cap. 410.
oil trap. 640.
oiler. 639.
oilstone. 515.
okra. 81.
old-fashioned. 222.
olecranon. 121.
olfactory bulb. 99, 133.
olfactory centre. 133.
olfactory membrane. 133.
olfactory nerve. 99, 133.
olive. 75.
on-deck circle. 525.
on guard line. 576.
on light. 341.
on-off switch. 277.
on-off switch. 221, 337, 339, 340, 341, 383, 384, 442.
on/play button. 388.
on the wind. 553.
one-arm shoulder throw. 578.
one-bar shoe. 319.
one-design sailboat. 552.
one-handed sword. 692.
one pair. 592.
one-piece coverall. 555.
one-piece sleepsuit. 317.
one way head. 264.
one-way traffic. 717.
onglet. 147, 149.
open-air terrace. 433.

open compartment. 349.
open end spanner. 258.
open end wrench. 258.
open-face spinning reel. 580.
open housing. 161.
open-pit mine. 635.
open-pit mine. 636.
open string. 487.
open stringer. 197.
opening. 299.
opening salutation. 361.
opera glasses. 329.
opera length necklace (30 in.). 326.
operating cord. 218.
operating dam. 660.
operating floor. 661.
operating rod. 701.
operator. 472.
operator desk. 666.
operator's cab. 675, 683.
operator's seat. 684.
operculum. 98, 105.
opisthodomos. 171.
opposite prompt side. 179.
optic chiasm. 130.
optic nerve. 131.
optical axis. 43.
optical instruments. 617.
optical plummet. 614.
optical sight. 614.
or. 710.
oral cavity. 126, 127.
oral hygiene center. 339.
orange. 77.
orange. 77.
orbicular of eye. 118.
orbicularis oculi. 118.
orbiculate. 70.
orbital cavity. 122.
orbiter. 457.
orchard. 161.
orchestra pit. 180.
orchestra seat. 179.
order. 175.
order of finish. 569.
ordinaries. 710.
ordinary die. 593.
ordinary water turns into steam. 667.
ore. 635, 636.
ore deposit. 636.
ore pass. 637.
oregano. 143.
organ. 481, 482.
organ pipes. 482.
Oriental couching stitch. 507.
oriflamme. 711.
Orion. 40, 41.
ornamental stitching. 349.
ornaments. 476.
ortho-cane. 630.
ortho-stick. 630.
oscillating sprinkler. 250.
oscillators. 495.
osteology of skull. 122.
ostium. 137.
other dangers. 715.
other signs. 476.
other techniques. 511.
other types. 367.
otolith. 99.
otter paw. 563.
ottoman. 212.
out of bounds. 585.
outbound. 425.
outcrop. 636.
outdoor condensing unit. 204.
outdoor sill cock. 267.
outer boundary line. 540.
outer core. 47.
outer edge. 93.
outer hearth. 200.
outer jib. 431.
outer lip. 101.
outer rail. 182.

outer root sheath. 137.
outer shell. 285.
outer table. 592.
outer toe. 95.
outfield. 525.
outgoing announcement cassette. 388.
outhaul. 551.
outlet. 285.
outlet grille. 203.
output controls. 495.
output devices. 468.
output filter. 495.
output jack. 494.
output lead. 380.
output monitor. 391.
outrigger. 676, 681.
outside counter. 318.
outside knob. 266.
outside left. 532.
outside line. 577.
outside linebacker. 528.
outside mirror. 397.
outside right. 532.
outside ticket pocket. 293.
outsole. 318.
outwash plain. 56.
oval cut. 327.
ovary. 72, 99, 117.
ovate. 70.
oven. 238.
oven lamp. 237, 238.
over-blouse. 305.
over curtain. 217.
overbridge. 414.
overburden. 635, 637.
overcast sky. 61.
overcheck. 568.
overcoat. 292.
overdrapery. 217.
overflow. 269.
overflow bend. 267.
overflow pipe. 273.
overflow protection switch. 242.
overflow tube. 268.
overhand knot. 601.
overhead clearance. 716.
overhead connection. 659.
overhead crane. 661.
overhead earth wire. 658.
overhead frame. 680.
overhead ground wire. 658.
overhead guard. 684.
overhead switch panel. 451.
overlap carrier. 218.
overlay flooring. 196.
overpass. 414.
overrider. 397.
overshirt. 305.
overshoe. 320.
ovule. 72.
owner. 569.
oxer and cross poles. 566.
oxer wall. 566.
oxidizer tank. 706.
oxyacetylene welding. 281.
oxygen cylinder. 281.
oxygen supply pressure gauge. 458.
oxygen valve. 282.
oyster. 102.
oyster fork. 225.
oyster knife. 227.
oyster mushroom. 73.
ozone. 47.

P

[P] trap. 267.
P-N junction. 670.
Pacific Ocean. 49.
Pacinian corpuscle. 136.
pack. 555.
packet of cigarette papers. 344.

packing. 271.
packing nut. 271.
packing retainer ring. 271.
pad. 328.
pad arm. 328.
padded jacket. 589.
paddle valve. 440.
paddock. 569.
padlock. 347.
page boy. 330.
pagoda sleeve. 306.
paint roller. 280.
painting upkeep. 278, 279, 280.
pajamas. 311.
palate. 133.
palatine tonsil. 134.
palatoglossal arch. 134.
palatopharyngeal arch. 134.
pale. 710.
paleron. 149.
palette. 150.
paling fence. 247.
pallet. 482, 489, 605, 607.
pallet and container transporter. 453.
pallet spring. 482.
pallet stone. 605.
pallet truck. 685.
pallets. 685.
pallial line. 101.
pallial sinus. 101.
palm. 89, 299, 447, 526.
palm grove. 55.
palmar pad. 94.
palmate. 70.
palmette. 210.
pan. 206, 608, 609, 696.
pan arrest. 609.
pan cover. 696.
pan handle. 374.
pancake. 157.
pancake pan. 233.
pancreas. 127.
pane. 199.
panel. 198, 217, 294, 313, 555, 567, 637, 658.
panoramic and tilting head. 374.
panoramic window. 421.
panpipe. 488.
pantee corselette. 312.
pantograph. 427.
pantry. 189.
pants. 294, 310.
pants. 321, 526, 530, 534, 589.
panty girdle. 313.
panty hose. 311.
papaya. 80.
paper. 344, 518.
paper bail. 467.
paper centering scale. 467.
paper centring scale. 467.
paper clips. 461.
paper fasteners. 461.
paper guide. 467.
paper guide roller. 471.
paper punch. 462.
paper release lever. 467.
paper safe. 375.
paper tape. 385, 386.
paper tape start button. 386.
papilla. 131, 137.
papillary muscle. 124.
parabolic antenna. 394.
parabolic dune. 55.
parabolic mirror. 668.
parabolic reflector. 373, 624.
parachute. 555.
parachute. 557.
parachuting. 555.
parachutist. 555.
parade ground. 176.
paraffins. 649.
parallel bars. 573.
parapet. 414.
parapet walk. 177.
parcels office. 426.

The terms in **bold type** indicate the title of an illustration; those in *italic* correspond to the British terminology.

745

parentheses. 357, 364.
parents. 139.
parents/children. 138.
parents-in-law. 139.
parfait. 156.
parietal. 121.
parietal bone. 122.
parietal foramen. 122.
parietal pleura. 126.
paring knife. 227.
Parisian cut. 147, 149, 150, 151.
parka. 292.
parka. 561.
parking. 717.
parking area. 452.
parking brake lever. 399.
parking meter. 178.
parking prohibited or restricted.
  717.
parsley. 143.
parsnip. 84.
parterre. 179.
partial eclipse. 37, 38.
particle board. 265.
particle board. 194.
partition. 78, 465.
partitions. 710.
partlow chart. 402.
parts. 210, 213, 214.
parts of a flag. 709.
parts of a hilted bayonet. 693.
parts of a shoe. 318.
parts of the weapon. 577.
party. 710.
pass. 54.
passenger cabin. 435, 448.
passenger car. 429.
passenger car interior. 429.
passenger lift. 719.
passenger liner. 433.
passenger platform. 427.
passenger seating. 436.
passenger station. 424.
passenger terminal. 454.
passenger terminal. 452.
passenger transfer vehicle. 453,
  454.
passengers-conductor
  communications. 429.
passing prohibited. 716.
passport case. 351.
passport control. 454.
pasta. 144, 145.
pasta maker. 228.
pastern. 91.
pastry bag and nozzles. 230.
pastry brush. 230.
pastry cutting wheel. 230.
patch. 696.
patch pocket. 300, 304, 316.
patch pocket with turn-down flap.
  300.
patella. 92, 120.
patera. 210.
paternal aunt. 138.
paternal uncle. 138.
path. 247.
patio. 188, 247.
patio door. 188.
pattern. 503.
pattern. 506, 521.
pattern reader. 505.
pattern scissors. 521.
pauldron. 690.
pause. 476.
pause button. 381.
pause/still. 382.
pavement. 413.
pavilion. 327.
pavilion facet (8). 327.
pavilion roof. 190.
pawl. 219, 260.
pawn. 591.
Pawn (P). 591.
payload. 456.
payout tray. 595.

payout trigger. 595.
pea. 79.
pea. 79.
pea jacket. 301.
peach. 75.
peach. 75.
Peacock. 41.
peak. 54, 298.
peaked lapel. 292, 293.
peanut. 78.
pear. 76.
pear-shaped cut. 327.
pearl. 89.
pearl screen. 377.
pecan nut. 78.
pecten. 106.
pectoral fin. 98.
pectoral limb. 124.
pedal. 411, 412, 478, 486.
pedal key. 481.
pedal keyboard. 481.
pedal pusher. 310.
pedal rod. 479.
pedestal. 401, 478.
pedestal type sump pump. 277.
pedestrian crossing. 178, 714.
pedicel. 72, 74, 76.
pedicle. 89.
pediment. 171, 607.
pedometer. 613.
peeled veneer. 265.
peeler. 227.
peep hole. 423.
peephole. 520.
peg. 215, 345, 477, 507, 510, 596,
  597.
peg box. 477.
peg loop. 597.
Pegasus. 40.
pelerine. 300.
pelerine. 300.
pellets. 702.
peltate. 70.
Pelton turbine. 657.
pelvic fin. 98.
pelvic girdle. 105.
pelvic limb. 124.
pelvis. 92, 128.
pen. 385, 616.
pen holder. 351.
penalty arc. 532.
penalty area. 532.
penalty bench. 533.
penalty line. 539.
penalty spot. 532.
penalty timekeeper. 533.
pencil. 663.
pencil point tip. 281.
pencil sharpeners. 462.
pendant. 326.
pendulum. 607.
pendulum rod. 607.
penholder grip. 543.
penis. 114, 116.
penknife. 599.
pennant. 61, 711.
pennine. 145.
pens. 145.
penstock. 651, 655, 660.
pentaprism. 368.
penumbra. 38.
penumbra shadow. 37.
pepper shaker. 223.
pepperpot. 223.
per bend. 710.
per cent. 723.
per fess. 710.
per pale. 710.
perching bird. 97.
percolator. 234.
**percussion instruments. 485,
  486.**
perforated gypsum lath. 194.
perforated hardboard. 194.
perforated pipe. 277.
perforated toe cap. 318.

perforation. 299, 371.
perforator. 386.
performance. 569.
pergola. 247.
pericardium. 126.
pericarp. 77, 78.
period. 357, 363, 386.
periodontal ligament. 123.
periople. 93.
peripheral equipment. 471.
peripheral joint. 653.
peripheral nervous system. 129.
periscope. 438, 704.
peristyle. 171, 173.
peritoneum. 116.
permanent magnet. 387.
permanent pasture. 161.
peroxide. 629.
perron. 187.
Perseus. 40.
personal adornment. 323.
personal articles. 335.
pestle. 228.
petals. 72.
Peter Pan collar. 308.
petiole. 70.
Petit-Suisse. 155.
petits fours. 156.
petrochemical industry. 649.
petrochemicals. 649.
petrol. 649.
petrol engine. 405.
petrol flap. 397.
petrol pump. 401, 405.
petrol pump hose. 401.
petrol tank cap. 410.
petroleum. 649.
phalange. 92.
phalanges. 105.
pharynx. 126, 127.
phase conductor. 659.
phases of the Moon. 38.
Phillips tip. 258.
philtrum. 133.
phloem. 71.
Phobos. 36.
Phoenix. 41.
phosphor coating. 284.
phosphor dot. 392.
photo chamber. 620.
photoelectric cell. 371.
photographic accessories. 374.
photographic picture. 377.
photographic plate. 620.
**photography. 368, 369, 370, 371,
  372, 373, 374, 375, 376, 377.**
photosphere. 37.
phrenic nerve. 126.
piano. 490, 491, 493.
piccolo. 483, 493.
pick. 248, 345, 588.
pick-up. 162.
pick-up automatic baler. 162.
pick-up loader. 162.
pick-up selector. 494.
pickguard. 494.
pickling onion. 83.
pickup automatic baler. 162.
pickup loader. 162.
pickup reel. 165.
picnic area. 721.
picnic shoulder. 150.
picnics prohibited. 721.
picture tube. 392.
pie. 156.
pie pan. 230.
pie tin. 230.
pieces. 591.
pied. 150.
piedmont glacier. 56.
pier. 172, 414, 415, 642.
pier foundation. 414.
pierce lever. 243.
pierced earring. 325.
piers. 175.
piggyback car. 420.

piggyback flat wagon. 420.
pigsty. 161.
pigtail. 321.
pigtails. 330.
pike pole. 677.
pike position. 548.
pile. 643.
pillar. 175, 478, 616, 637.
pillar plate. 606.
pillbox hat. 314.
pillion footrest. 409.
pillow. 506.
pillow. 214.
pillow protector. 214.
pillowcase. 214.
pilot. 480, 556, 557.
pilot light. 341.
pilot parachute. 555.
pilothouse. 436.
pin. 209, 266, 284, 489, 501, 590.
pin base. 284.
pin block. 479.
pin cushion. 501.
pinafore. 302, 317.
pinafore. 302.
pince-nez. 329.
pinch. 284, 636.
pinch pleat. 217.
pine seed. 78.
pineal body. 130.
pineapple. 80.
pinion. 260, 607.
pink ball. 584.
pink stocking. 321.
pinking shears. 501.
pinnacle. 174, 175, 423.
pinnatifid. 70.
pinocytotic vesicle. 113.
pip. 76, 77, 593.
pipe. 345.
pipe. 244, 274, 482, 489.
pipe cleaner. 345.
pipe coupling. 275.
pipe cross section. 345.
pipe rack. 345.
pipe section. 202.
pipe threader. 276.
pipe tools. 345.
pipe-wrapping insulation. 195.
pipe wrench. 276.
pipeline. 644, 650.
pipework. 481.
Pisces, the Fishes. 712.
pistachio nut. 78.
piste. 576.
pistil. 72.
pistol. 703.
pistol grip. 697, 699, 701, 702.
pistol grip handle. 261, 262.
pistol nozzle. 250.
piston. 404.
piston. 405, 407, 639.
pit. 590.
pita bread. 146.
pitch axis. 393.
pitch link. 455.
pitch nozzle. 65.
pitched roof. 190.
pitcher. 525.
pitcher's plate. 525.
pitchfork comb. 338.
pitching. 652.
pitching niblick; no. 8 iron. 586.
pitching wedge. 586.
pith. 71.
pithead. 638.
piton-carrier. 589.
piton hammer. 588.
pitons. 588.
Pitot tube. 705.
pituitary gland. 130.
pivot. 287, 337, 338, 443, 492,
  501, 562, 625, 697.
pivot cab. 681.
pivot spindle. 398.
pivoted bar. 616.

The terms in **bold type** indicate the title of an illustration; those in *italic* correspond to the British terminology.

placard board. 419.
placing judge. 546.
placket. 308.
plain gypsum lath. 194.
plain pole. 218.
plain weave. 511.
plan. 174.
plan-position indicator. 624.
plan reading. 188.
plan symbols. 198.
plane. 257.
planet projection system. 43.
planetarium. 43.
planetarium projector. 43.
planetarium projector. 43.
planets of the solar system. 36.
planoconcave. 625.
planoconvex. 625.
plant cell. 113.
plantar. 119.
plantar interosseous. 118.
plantar pad. 94.
plantar surface of the hoof. 93.
planting box. 570.
plantlet. 75.
plasmodesma. 113.
plaster. 194.
plaster bat. 519.
plaster dressing. 629.
plasterboard. 194.
plastic insulator. 288.
plastic-laminated hardboard. 194.
plastic pants. 315.
plasticine board. 570.
plastron. 109.
plat de côte couvert. 149.
plat de côte découvert. 149.
plate. 148, 152, 237, 599.
plate crystal. 57.
plate grid. 406.
plate level. 614.
plate push. 682.
plate strap. 406.
plateau. 54.
platen. 467, 514.
platen knob. 467, 471.
platform. 402.
platform. 279, 417, 548, 575, 610, 683.
platform diver. 548.
platform edge. 427, 428.
platform entrance. 426.
platform ladder. 279.
platform number. 427.
platform roofing. 427.
platform shelter. 424.
platform trolley. 427, 685.
platform truck. 427, 685.
platter. 223, 380.
play. 382.
play button. 381.
player. 526.
player. 545.
player's number. 530.
player's stick. 534.
players' bench. 525, 533, 535, 536.
players' rotation. 536.
playing area. 545.
playing field. 532.
playing field for American football. 527.
playing field for Canadian football. 527.
playing surface. 543.
playroom. 189, 433.
pleasure garden. 247.
pleat skirts. 304.
pleated heading. 217.
plectrum. 487.
plenum. 202.
pleural cavity. 126.
plinth. 607.
plotter. 469.
plow anchor. 447.
plug. 285.

plug. 261, 384.
plug adapter. 341.
plug bayonet. 693.
plug fuse. 285.
plum. 75.
plumbing. 267, 268, 269, 270, 271, 272, 273, 274, 275, 276, 277.
plumbing system. 267.
plumbing tools. 276.
plumbing wrench. 276.
plunger. 234.
plunger. 276, 387, 629, 641.
plunging neckline. 309.
plus or minus. 723.
Pluto. 36.
plywood. 194.
pneumatic armlet. 612.
pneumatic hammer. 639.
pneumostome. 104.
pocket. 351, 583, 587, 590.
pocket handkerchief. 293.
pocket instamatic camera. 369.
pocket sliding door. 188.
pockets. 304.
pogo stick. 403.
point. 225, 227, 367, 478, 500, 504, 562, 581, 592, 691.
point lever. 422.
point lock. 423.
point motor. 423.
point signal. 422.
point wire. 423.
pointed hat. 322.
pointed tab end. 295, 306.
pointer. 609, 610, 611, 612, 613.
pointer scale. 609.
points. 424.
points of sailing. 553.
poison injection nozzle. 662.
poison tank. 661.
poisonous mushroom. 73.
poitrine. 147, 150, 151.
poker. 201.
poker die. 593.
polar axis. 42.
polar axis circle. 622.
polar climates. 59.
polar ice cap. 59.
polar lights. 47.
polar tundra. 59.
polarizing filter. 370.
Polaroid Land camera. 371.
pole. 218, 430, 558, 569, 570, 596.
pole beacon. 444.
pole grip. 561.
pole loop. 596.
pole over a bank. 566.
pole piece. 387.
pole shaft. 561.
Pole Star. 40.
pole tip. 561.
pole vault. 570.
poleyn. 690.
police. 718.
Polish. 355.
polished-stone hand axe. 689.
pollen basket. 106.
pollen brush. 106.
pollen cell. 107.
pollen packer. 106.
pollen press. 106.
polo collar. 308.
polo shirt. 305.
polojama. 317.
polymerization and alkylation units. 648.
poma lift. 558.
pome fleshy fruits. 76.
pomegranate. 80.
pommel. 567, 573, 577, 693.
pommel horse. 573.
pompom. 314.
poncho. 301.
poniard. 692.
pons Varolii. 130.

Pont-l'évêque. 155.
pontoon. 417.
pony tail. 330.
poodle cut. 331.
pool. 583.
pool. 247, 669.
pool and carom billiards. 583.
poop. 430.
pop-up tent. 597.
poppy. 79.
porch. 174, 187.
pore. 79, 113, 136.
pork. 150, 153.
Porro prism. 621.
port. 222.
port sail plane. 438.
Port-Salut. 155.
port tack. 553.
portable fire extinguisher. 676.
portable life support system. 458.
portable life support system control unit. 458.
portable shower head. 269.
portal. 175.
portal bridge. 415.
portal frame. 415.
portal vein. 124, 125.
porter. 427.
porterhouse. 148.
portfolios. 350.
Portuguese. 355.
position. 569.
position light. 705.
position marker. 494.
position of the ligament. 101.
positions. 577.
positive charge. 723.
positive contact. 670.
positive meniscus. 625.
positive plate. 406.
positive plate group. 406.
positive region. 670.
positive terminal. 406.
post. 178, 508, 520, 536, 542, 545, 671.
post and plank. 565.
post and rail. 565.
post binder. 463.
post-hole digger. 248.
post lantern. 221.
post mill. 671.
post office. 718.
posterior chamber. 131.
posterior commissure. 130.
posterior cutaneous nerve of thigh. 129.
posterior end. 101.
posterior root. 130.
posterior rugae. 115.
posterior semicircular canal. 132.
posterior view. 115, 119, 121.
postern. 177.
postscript. 359, 361.
potable water tank. 643.
potable water truck. 453.
potato. 84.
potato masher. 229.
potato planter. 164.
potential coil. 615.
pothole lid. 201.
pottery. 519, 520.
pouch. 349.
pouch of Douglas. 117.
pouf. 212.
poulaine. 690.
poultry house. 161.
poultry shears. 231.
pound. 723.
powder chamber. 695.
powder flask. 696.
powder puff. 332.
power cord. 337, 378, 380.
power generators. 445.
power indicator. 495.
power lift truck. 684.
power line. 651.

power lines take the electricity to communities. 667.
power plant. 648.
power relay. 205.
power station. 638, 660.
power supply cord. 220, 221, 340.
power switch. 379, 381, 382, 495.
power system. 672.
power take off. 162.
power/timer off switch. 382.
power train. 412.
power zoom control. 384.
powerhouse. 651, 655.
practice fairway. 585.
pre-tuning control. 382.
preamplifier-amplifier. 378.
precipice. 54.
precipitation. 58.
precipitation area. 62.
premaxilla. 98.
premolar. 90.
prepuce. 116.
prescription. 723.
present state of weather. 62.
presenter. 390.
preset tuning button. 379.
president. 576.
press. 538.
press bed. 516, 517.
press camera. 369.
press-stud. 348, 351.
pressed powder compact. 332.
presser bar. 500.
presser foot. 500.
presser foot lifter. 499.
pressing. 514.
pressing board. 514.
pressure. 63.
pressure bar. 479.
pressure change. 62.
pressure cooker. 232.
pressure gauge. 458, 612, 641.
pressure regulator. 282.
pressure regulator. 232, 281, 599.
pressure relief pipe. 662.
pressure relief valve. 273, 458.
pressure screw. 516, 517.
pressure suit. 458.
pressure tube. 663.
pressurizer. 661, 664.
prestressed concrete. 193.
preview monitor. 391.
price per litre/gallon. 401.
pricker. 506.
primaries. 96.
primary covert. 96.
primary heat transport system. 666.
primary mirror. 42.
primary pump. 664.
primary root. 69.
prime. 577.
prime focus. 42.
prime focus observing capsule. 42.
primer. 696, 702.
princess dress. 302.
princess seaming. 312.
principal edible crustaceans. 103.
principal edible gastropods. 104.
principal edible mollusks. 102.
principal rafter. 190.
principal types of armchairs. 210, 211.
principal types of bills. 97.
principal types of eyeglasses. 329.
principal types of feet. 97.
principal types of pome fruits. 76.
principal types of shoes. 319, 320.
principal veins and arteries. 125.
print drying rack. 375.
print head. 471.
print washer. 375.

The terms in **bold type** indicate the title of an illustration; those in *italic* correspond to the British terminology.

printed circuit. 371.
printed image. 518.
printer. 469, 472.
printing. 518.
priority intersection. 715.
[priority road] sign. 715.
prism binoculars. 621.
prismatic section. 446.
probe receptacle. 237.
proboscis. 100.
processing rollers. 371.
producer. 391.
product codes. 610.
production control room. 391.
production control room. 389.
production of electricity. 668.
production of electricity from
nuclear energy. 667.
production of sound. 481.
production platform. 643.
products for make-up. 333.
products for makeup. 333.
profile of the Earth's
atmosphere. 47.
profiterole. 156.
programmable timer. 382.
programmer. 238, 240, 241, 242.
progressive wave. 51.
prohibitory or regulatory signs.
716.
projectiles. 695.
projection gallery. 43.
projection lamp. 377.
projection room. 43.
projection screen. 377.
projector lens. 620.
projector lens pole piece. 620.
projector zoom lens. 383.
proleg. 100.
prominence. 37.
prompt box. 180.
prompt side. 179.
pronaos. 171.
prong. 225.
proofreading. 362, 363, 364, 365,
366.
prop forward. 531.
prop stand. 409.
propane/butane cylinder. 599.
propane or butane accessories.
599.
propellant. 702.
propeller. 433, 436, 437, 438.
propeller gearbox. 435.
propeller shaft. 433, 434, 436.
property line. 188.
propman. 390.
proscenium. 180.
prostate. 116.
protective clothing. 283.
protective cup. 530, 534.
protective equipment. 530.
protective relay. 205.
protective sheet. 265.
protective window. 392.
prothorax. 100.
protoneuron. 135.
proximal phalanx. 94, 120, 121.
proximal sesamoid. 92.
pruning hook. 249.
pruning knife. 252.
pruning saw. 252.
pruning shears. 249.
psychrometer. 63.
pubis. 114.
public water main. 267.
puck. 534.
puff. 157.
puff pastry. 157.
puff sleeve. 306.
pull bail. 377.
pull rod. 422.
pull strap. 347.
pulley. 261, 278, 405, 610.
pulley safety guard. 261.
pullman case. 347.

pullover. 307.
pullover sweater. 561.
pullovers. 296.
pulmonary artery. 125, 126.
pulmonary trunk. 124.
pulmonary vein. 124, 125.
pulp. 77, 123.
pulp canal. 123.
pulp chamber. 123.
pulse button. 235.
pulse of sound. 442.
pulvino. 653.
pumice correcting pencil. 517.
pump. 319.
pump. 240, 242, 319, 637, 668.
pump attendant. 401.
pump island. 401.
pump motor. 277.
pump nozzle. 401.
pump suction head. 277.
pumper. 677.
pumpernickel bread. 146.
pumping station. 644.
pumping unit. 641.
pumpkin. 81.
punch card. 472.
punch card. 505.
punch card feeding dial. 505.
punch card feeding mechanism.
505.
punch card reader. 505.
punch hole. 294, 318.
punched paper tape reader. 386.
punctuation. 386.
punctuation marks. 356, 357.
pup tent. 597.
pupil. 94, 131.
purfling. 477.
purge valve. 550.
purlin. 190.
purlin cleat. 190.
purpure. 710.
purse. 351.
push-button. 266, 346, 367, 377,
471.
push-button control board. 242.
push-button release. 337.
push-button telephone. 388.
push buttons. 388.
push rim. 631.
push up bra. 313.
pusher. 236.
putter. 586.
putter. 586.
putting green. 585.
pygal shield. 109.
pylon. 435, 558.
pyjamas. 311.
pyloric caecum. 99.
pyloric cecum. 99.
pylorus. 127.
pyramid spot. 584.
pyramid tent. 597.
pyrolysis. 650.
pyrometer. 520.
pyrometric cone. 520.

Q

quad cane. 630.
quadriplex. 183.
quadripod. 630.
quadruped stick. 630.
quarte. 577.
quarter. 93, 318.
quarter note. 475.
quarter rest. 475.
quarter window. 397.
quarterback. 528, 529.
quarterly. 710.
quarters. 645.
quartet. 490.
quasi. 147.
quaver. 475.
quaver rest. 475.

quay ramp. 441.
quayside crane. 441.
quayside railway. 441.
queen. 106.
Queen. 592.
Queen (Q). 591.
queen cell. 107.
queen excluder. 107.
Queen's side. 591.
question mark. 357, 386.
quiche plate. 230.
quiche tin. 230.
quill. 260, 261, 367.
quill brush. 338.
quill lock. 261.
quillon. 693.
quince. 76.
quinte. 577.
quintet. 490.
quizzing glass. 329.
quotation marks. 357, 364.
quotation marks ((*csp*)). 386.

R

raceme. 72.
rachis. 96.
racing car. 398.
racing programm. 569.
rack. 582.
rack. 232, 238, 242, 446.
rackboard. 482.
racket. 543.
racks. 233.
racquetball. 541.
racquetball racket. 541.
racquetball racquet. 541.
racquetballer. 541.
radar. 624.
radar antenna. 438.
radar scanner. 435.
radial artery. 125.
radial nerve. 129.
radial passenger loading area. 452.
radial ply. 407.
radial tire. 407.
radial tyre. 407.
radial vein. 125.
radiating element. 624.
radiation. 669.
radiation zone. 37.
radiator. 406.
radiator. 406, 418.
radiator hose. 406.
radiator pressure cap. 406.
radicle. 69, 71.
radio antenna. 438, 458.
radioactive waste storage. 667.
radish. 84.
radius. 92, 108, 120.
radome. 705.
rafter. 190, 192.
raglan. 300.
raglan sleeve. 291, 300, 306, 316.
rail. 187, 422, 505, 550, 583, 584.
rail anchor. 422.
rail joint. 422.
rail track. 638.
rail transportation. 721.
railroad station. 424.
railroad track. 422, 423.
railway map. 426.
railway station. 424.
railway track. 422, 423.
rain. 57.
rain cap. 202.
rain gauge. 63.
rain shower. 60.
raincoat. 291.
rainfall. 63.
rainfly. 597.
raise. 636.
raised band. 512.
raised head. 264.
rake. 248.

rake comb. 338.
Ram. 40.
RAM: Random Access Memory.
468.
ramekin. 223.
rammer. 695.
ramp. 171, 424, 635.
rampart. 176, 177.
ramrod. 696.
rangefinder. 369.
rank. 591.
rapier. 692.
ratchet. 219, 258, 260, 508.
ratchet knob. 613.
ratchet wheel. 508, 605, 607.
ravioli. 145.
razor clam. 102.
razors. 337.
reaction control thruster. 393.
reaction direction. 723.
reactivity control device. 662.
reactor. 438, 661, 664, 665, 667.
reactor building. 661, 663, 665.
reactor deck. 438.
reactor regulating system. 666.
reactor vessel. 663.
reading. 328.
reamer. 236.
rear apron. 295.
rear brake. 411.
rear bumper. 408.
rear derailleur. 411.
rear foil. 436.
rear foil control actuator. 436.
rear leg. 213.
rear light. 397, 402, 409.
rear light. 411.
rear limit line. 576.
rear load area. 398.
rear of estate car. 398.
rear runner. 564.
rear seat. 400.
rear shock absorber. 409.
rear sight. 697, 699, 700, 701,
702, 703.
rear view. 397.
rear window. 397.
rear window frame. 397.
rearview mirror. 399, 704.
Reblochon. 154.
récamier. 211.
receiver. 385, 387.
receiver. 387, 537, 540, 542, 543,
624, 697, 699, 701.
receiver-indicator. 442.
receiving line. 541.
receiving station. 385.
receiving yard. 425.
receptacle. 72, 74.
receptacle analyzer. 286.
reception bay. 665.
receptor. 135.
recessed cooktop. 238.
reciprocating knife mower. 162.
reclaimed water. 650.
recoil sleigh. 698.
recoil spring. 703.
recoilless rifle. 700.
record. 380.
record. 382.
record announcement button. 388.
record button. 381.
record muting button. 381.
recorder. 546.
recording level button. 381.
recording of seismic waves. 616.
recording of time. 616.
recording reproducing head. 383.
recording switch. 383.
rectangular. 598, 711.
rectum. 116, 127, 128.
rectus femoris. 118.
recuperator cylinder. 698.
recuperator cylinder front head.
698.
red. 594, 595.

The terms in **bold type** indicate the title of an illustration; those in *italic* correspond to the British terminology.

red ball. 583, 584.
red balls. 584.
red beam. 392.
red cap. 545.
red dragon. 593.
red flag. 545, 578.
red inner circle. 544.
red marker light. 402.
red ocher pencil. 517.
red ochre pencil. 517.
red safelight filter. 376.
Red Sea. 49.
redan. 176.
redcap. 427.
redoubt. 176.
reduce space. 363.
reducing coupling. 275.
redundant bracing. 658.
reed. 508.
reed hooks. 510.
reed panicle. 367.
reed pipe. 482.
reeds. 483.
reef band. 431.
reef knot. 601.
reef point. 431.
reel. 164, 375, 576, 595.
reel plate. 595.
reel seat. 580.
referee. 528, 531, 532, 533, 535, 536, 543, 545, 546, 578, 579.
referee's stand. 542.
reference initials. 359.
reference station. 394.
refill. 367.
refill tube. 268.
refinery. 648.
refinery. 644.
refinery products. 649.
refining. 667.
reflecting screen. 373.
reflecting surface. 668.
reflecting telescope. 622.
reflector. 221, 284, 374, 402, 408, 670.
refracting telescope. 623.
refractory brick. 520.
refractory fire pot. 205.
refrigerant tubing. 204.
refrigeration unit. 402.
refrigerator car. 420.
refrigerator compartment. 239.
refrigerator van. 420.
register. 615.
registered office address. 361.
registered trademark. 723.
regulating button. 480.
rein. 568.
reindeer. 89.
reinforced concrete. 193.
relay. 206.
release bar. 403.
release button. 368.
release handle. 400.
release lever. 259.
release setting screw. 560.
release treadle. 508.
relief printing process. 516.
remote control. 377.
remote-control arm. 457.
remote control socket. 383.
remote-controlled points. 423.
remote-controlled switch. 423.
removable blade. 280.
removable lid. 277.
renal artery. 125, 128.
renal papilla. 128.
renal vein. 125, 128.
reniform. 70.
repair shop. 401.
repeat mark. 476.
reptile. 109.
rerebrace. 690.
rerunning. 648.
reserve gas tap. 410.
reserve mud tank. 643.

reserve parachute. 555.
reserve petrol tap. 410.
reservoir. 234, 481, 651, 652, 655.
reset button. 382.
reset key. 470.
resin-coated paper dryer. 375.
resonator. 406, 482, 485.
respiratory system. 126.
rest symbols. 475.
restaurant. 719.
restricted area. 535.
restricting circle. 535.
resurgence. 54.
retainer. 639.
retainer nut. 271.
retaining ring. 398.
retaining spring. 398.
retarding magnet. 615.
reticle. 621.
retina. 131.
retractable boarding ladder. 705.
retractable cord. 244.
retractable flex. 244.
retractable handle. 350.
retracted claw. 94.
retrenchment. 176.
retriever. 536.
return. 465.
return air. 205.
return duct. 204.
return elevator. 165.
return key. 470.
return main. 204.
return spring. 385, 407.
reverb unit. 495.
reverse dive. 549.
reversible reaction. 723.
reversing light. 162, 397.
revolution counter. 399.
revolver. 703.
revolving cylinder. 506.
revolving frame. 675.
revolving nosepiece. 619.
revolving sprinkler. 250.
rewind. 382.
rewind button. 381, 388.
rewind crank. 368.
rhinencephalon. 133.
rhomboid. 119.
rhomboideus. 119.
rhubarb. 85.
rib. 85, 147, 148, 151, 346, 477, 682.
rib eye. 148.
rib joint pliers. 259.
rib pad. 530.
rib portion. 150.
rib stitch. 504.
ribbing. 296, 301, 315, 316, 317, 581.
ribbing plough. 163.
ribbing plow. 163.
ribbon. 321, 466, 467.
ribbon cartridge. 466.
ribbon end indicator. 466.
ribbon guide. 466.
ribbon load lever. 466.
ribosome. 113.
ribs. 92, 120, 519.
rider. 564.
rider handle. 609.
rider scale. 609.
ridge. 50, 304, 594, 714.
ridge beam. 190.
ridge pole. 596.
ridge tent. 597.
riding. 565, 566, 567.
riding crop. 565.
riding glove. 565.
riding helmet. 565.
riding jacket. 565.
rifle (rifled bore). 702.
rift. 50.
rigging wire. 557.
right angle finder. 370.
right ascension. 35.

right atrium. 124.
right back. 532, 536, 539.
right bend. 714.
right bronchus. 126.
right center. 531.
right centre. 531.
right cornerback. 528, 529.
right defence. 533.
right defense. 533.
right defensive end. 528, 529.
right defensive tackle. 528, 529.
right elevating arc. 698.
right elevating handwheel. 698.
right field. 525.
right fielder. 525.
right forward. 535, 536.
right guard. 528, 529, 535.
right half. 532.
right halfback. 528.
right-hand grip. 700.
right kidney (sagittal section). 128.
right lung. 124, 126.
right outside linebacker. 529.
right safety. 528.
right safety back. 529.
right service court. 537, 540.
right side. 304.
right tackle. 528, 529.
right trail. 698.
right ventricle. 124.
right wing. 532.
right wing. 531, 533.
right winger. 539.
rigid board insulation. 195.
rigid frame. 43.
rim. 328, 407, 409, 411, 535, 572.
rim flange. 407.
rim soup bowl. 223.
rinceau. 210.
rind. 77.
ring. 579.
ring. 71, 73, 218, 346, 447, 484, 502, 573, 588, 608, 696.
ring binder. 463.
ring floor. 579.
ring modulator. 495.
ring nut. 274.
ring post. 579.
ring spanner. 258.
ring step. 579.
ringer coil. 387.
rings. 325, 573.
rings. 145.
ringside. 579.
rink. 533.
rink. 544.
rink corner. 533.
rinse-aid dispenser. 242.
rip fence. 262, 263.
rip fence adjustment. 262.
rip fence guide. 262.
rip fence lock. 262.
ripcord. 555.
ripper. 680.
ripper. 678.
ripper cylinder. 678.
ripper tip. 678.
ripper tooth. 678.
rise. 197.
riser. 43, 197, 555.
River Eridanus. 41.
rivet. 227, 259, 328.
road works. 715.
roadway narrows. 714.
roast sensor probe. 238.
roasting pans. 232.
Robertson tip. 258.
Roberval's balance. 609.
rock basin. 56.
rock garden. 247.
rock sample pocket. 458.
rock step. 56.
rocket. 456.
rocket. 47.
rocking chair. 211, 213.
rocking tool. 515.

rocks. 653.
rocky desert. 55.
rod. 206, 492, 509.
rodent's jaw. 90.
roe deer . 89.
roll. 308.
roll axis. 393.
roll bag. 347.
roll line. 308.
roll nozzle. 65.
roll of paper. 386.
roll-up blind. 219.
roller. 218, 219, 242, 251, 341, 446, 466.
roller blind. 219.
roller board and arms. 482.
roller circle. 675.
roller cover. 280.
roller frame. 280.
roller guides. 181.
roller pins. 343.
roller shade. 219.
roller skate. 562.
rolling ladder. 279.
rolling pin. 230.
ROM* memory. 468.
ROM: Read Only Memory. 468.
Roman house. 173.
Roman legionary. 689.
Roman metal pen. 367.
romsteck. 149.
rond de gîte à la noix. 149.
rondel. 690.
Rondelé. 154.
roof. 107, 397, 402, 425, 596, 635, 636.
roof flashing. 267.
roof structure. 190.
roof vent. 187, 275.
Rook (R). 591.
room. 596, 637.
room air conditioner. 206.
room thermostat. 611.
rooms of the house. 189.
root. 69.
root. 69, 83, 123, 134, 225.
root cap. 69.
root-hair zone. 71.
root hairs. 69.
root of hair. 137.
root of nail. 137.
root of nose. 133.
root rib. 449.
root vegetables. 84.
rope. 579, 589, 601.
rope (45 in.). 326.
rope belt. 316.
rope ladder. 278.
Roquefort. 154.
rose. 250, 266.
rose cut. 327.
rose window. 175.
rosemary. 143.
rosette. 170.
rostrum. 103.
rotary file. 464.
rotary hoe. 163.
rotary joint. 624.
rotary table. 640.
rotating auger. 165.
rotating dome. 42.
rotating dome truck. 42.
rotating drum. 616.
rotating wheel. 594.
rotation of the rotor in the stator. 654.
rotation of the turbine. 654.
rotisserie. 238.
rotor. 266, 655, 656, 671, 672.
rotor blade. 450, 455.
rotor head. 455.
rotor hub. 455.
rotor shaft. 672.
rotunda roof. 191.
rouelle. 147.
rough. 585.

The terms in **bold type** indicate the title of an illustration; those in *italic* correspond to the British terminology.

roulette. 515.
roulette table. 594, 595.
roulette wheel. 594.
Roumanian couching stitch. 507.
round. 148.
round brush. 338.
round end pin. 219.
round eye. 502.
round head. 264.
round ligament of uterus. 117.
round loaf. 146.
round neck. 309.
round pronator. 118.
router. 260.
routing cardboard. 419.
row. 339.
row indicator. 505.
royal antler. 89.
royal flush. 592.
royal mast. 430.
rub rail. 402.
rubber. 320.
rubber base. 338.
rubber ferrule. 630.
rubber gasket. 270.
rubber mat. 380.
rubber stamp. 462.
rubber thread. 587.
rubber tip. 630.
rubber wall. 407.
rubber washer. 270.
rubbing alcohol. 629.
rubbing strip. 407.
ruching. 315.
rucksack. 561, 589.
rudder. 433, 435, 448, 457, 552, 556.
rudder pedal. 451, 556.
ruffle. 217.
ruffled rumba pants. 315.
ruffled skirt. 303.
rug and floor nozzle. 244.
rugby. 531.
ruler. 513.
Rumanian. 355.
rump. 95, 148, 152, 153.
run. 197, 574.
run in. 362.
run on. 362.
rung. 278, 588.
runner. 209, 564, 592, 656, 657.
runner blade. 657, 660.
running. 570.
running bowline. 601.
running rail. 429.
running surface. 561.
running track. 425.
runway. 429, 452.
runway center line markings. 452.
runway centre line markings. 452.
runway designation marking. 452.
runway end lights. 452.
runway side stripe markings. 452.
runway threshold markings. 452.
runway touchdown zone marking. 452.
rupture disc. 662.
rupture disk. 662.
Russian. 355.
Russian pumpernickel. 146.
rutabaga. 84.

S

s-band antenna. 65.
S-scroll. 210.
saber. 577, 692.
saber and épée warning line. 576.
sable. 710.
sabre. 577, 692.
sabre and épée warning line. 576.
sabreur. 577.
sacral plexus. 129.
sacral vertebrae. 92.
sacrum. 120.

saddle. 567.
saddle. 153, 345, 377, 411, 573.
saddlecloth. 568.
safari jacket. 307.
safe and arm device. 393.
safelight. 375.
safety. 697, 699.
safety area. 578.
safety bar. 558.
safety binding. 560.
safety binding. 559.
safety cage. 570.
safety glasses. 329.
safety goggles. 329.
safety line. 428.
safety match. 345.
safety pad. 574.
safety pin. 629, 696.
safety pins. 501.
safety rail. 279.
safety scissors. 343.
safety strap. 560.
safety thermostat. 241.
safety thong. 541.
safety valve. 232, 664.
sage. 143.
saggar. 520.
sagittal section. 116, 117.
sagittal suture. 122.
Sagittarius, the Archer. 712.
sail. 551, 557, 671.
sail cloth. 671.
sail panel. 552.
sailbar. 671.
sailboard. 551.
sailor collar. 308.
sailor tunic. 305.
sails. 431.
Saint-Marcelin. 155.
Saint-Nectaire. 155.
Sainte-maure. 154.
salad bowl. 223.
salad fork. 225.
salad plate. 223.
salad shaker. 228.
salad spinner. 228.
salient angle. 176.
salient pole. 656.
saline lake. 55.
salivary glands. 127.
salon-style hair dryer. 340.
salsify. 84.
salt marsh. 51.
salt shaker. 223.
salt water. 640.
saltcellar. 223.
salutation. 359.
sample. 504.
sand. 606.
sand bar. 51.
sand island. 51.
sand-rock. 650.
sand shoe. 402.
sand wedge. 586.
sandal. 319, 689.
sandstorm or dust storm. 60.
sandy desert. 55.
saphenous nerve. 129.
sapwood. 71.
sarong. 303.
sartorius. 118.
sash. 321.
sash-frame. 199.
sash window. 199.
satellite launcher separation. 394.
satin weave. 511.
Saturn. 36.
sauce pan. 599.
saucepan. 232.
saucer. 223.
sauté pan. 233.
savarin. 156.
savory. 143.
saw. 599.
sawing-in and sewing. 513.
sawtooth roof. 191.

saxhorn. 484.
saxophone. 483.
saxophone. 483, 491.
scale. 475.
scale. 73, 97, 98, 109, 608, 610, 611, 625, 647.
scale leaf. 83.
scale of speeds. 492.
scallion. 83.
scallop. 102.
scalper. 568.
scampi. 103.
Scandinavian crak bread. 146.
scapula. 92, 120.
scapular. 96.
scarf. 559.
scarifier. 680.
scarp. 176, 177.
scatter cushion. 214.
scattered sky. 61.
schapska. 298.
schedules. 426.
schema of circulation. 124.
school zone. 714.
schooner. 432.
Schwenkel. 711.
sciatic nerve. 129.
scissors. 501.
scissors. 599, 629.
scissors crossing. 424.
scissors cut. 327.
scissors-glasses. 329.
sclera. 131.
sconce. 220.
scoop. 345.
score sheet. 590.
scorer. 533, 535, 536, 576, 590.
scoring light. 576.
scoring table. 590.
Scorpio, the Scorpion. 712.
Scorpion. 41.
scottia. 170.
scraper. 280, 682.
scraper. 515, 517.
scraper bar. 518.
scraper bar holder. 517.
scraper engine. 682.
screen. 271, 337, 384, 392, 655.
screen case. 377.
screen front. 315.
screen print. 316.
screen window. 596.
screw. 264.
screw. 266, 478, 562.
screw earring. 325.
screw eye. 508.
screw locking nut. 580.
screwdriver. 258.
screwdriver. 599.
screwsleeve. 588.
scrimmage in American football. 528.
scrimmage in Canadian football. 529.
script assistant. 391.
scroll. 477.
scroll case. 655.
scrotum. 114, 116.
scrum. 531.
scrum half. 531.
scuba diver. 550.
scuffle hoe. 248.
Sculptor. 41.
scum. 277.
scuttle panel. 397.
scythe. 252.
sea. 38, 660.
sea anchor. 447.
Sea Goat. 41.
sea level. 48, 50.
sea-level pressure. 62.
Sea Serpent. 41.
sea side. 660.
seal. 273, 670.
sealed-beam mounting ring. 398.
sealed cell. 107.

sealing lug. 615.
sealing ring. 647.
seam. 299, 344.
seam allowance. 503.
seam line. 503.
seam pocket. 300, 304.
seaming. 300.
seamount. 50.
sear. 701.
season tiles. 593.
seasons of the year. 35.
seat. 179, 210, 213, 269, 408, 519, 556, 558, 564, 567.
seat belt. 400.
seat post. 411.
seat stay. 411.
seat tube. 411.
seat upholstery. 631.
seats. 212, 400.
sebaceous gland. 136, 137.
secateurs. 249.
second. 476, 579.
second balcony. 179.
second base. 525.
second baseman. 525.
second condenser lens. 620.
second dorsal fin. 98.
second flight. 574.
second hand. 605.
second linesman. 536.
second molar. 123.
second premolar. 123.
second reinforce. 694.
second reinforce ring. 694.
second space. 535.
second stage. 456.
second violins. 493.
secondaries. 96.
secondary inlet. 647.
secondary root. 69.
secondary sheave. 181.
seconde. 577.
secretarial desk. 465.
secretary. 216, 539, 545.
section. 298.
section of a berry. 74.
section of a bulb. 83.
section of a capsule. 79.
section of a citrus fruit. 77.
section of a follicle. 79.
section of a grain of wheat. 79.
section of a hazelnut. 78.
section of a legume. 79.
section of a pome fruit. 76.
section of a silique. 79.
section of a stone fruit. 75.
section of a strawberry. 74.
section of a walnut. 78.
section of a wild blackberry or raspberry. 74.
section of the Earth's crust. 48.
sector. 472.
sector flag. 570.
sector-shaped chart. 610.
security check. 454.
sediment chamber. 406.
sedimentary rocks. 53.
seed. 74, 75, 76, 77, 78, 79.
seed coat. 75, 79.
seed drill. 164.
seed vegetables. 85.
seeder. 249, 251.
seeds. 145.
segment. 77.
seismic wave. 53.
self-adhesive labels. 462.
self-contained platform. 642.
self-indicating scale. 610.
self timer. 368.
selle. 151.
selvage. 502.
semaphore. 424.
semi-breve. 475.
semi-breve rest. 475.
semi-circle. 535.
semi-detached cottage. 183.

The terms in **bold type** indicate the title of an illustration; those in *italic* correspond to the British terminology.

semi-detached triplex. 183.
semi-fish-eye lens. 370.
semi-mummy. 598.
semi-quaver. 475.
semi-quaver rest. 475.
semi-submersible. 642.
semicircular arch. 172.
semicolon. 357, 364, 386.
semimembranosus. 119.
semimembranous. 119.
seminal vesicle. 116.
semitendinosus. 119.
semitendinous. 119.
semitrailer. 402.
semitrailer. 403, 646.
sender's reference. 361.
sending station. 385.
sense organs: hearing. 132.
sense organs: sight. 131.
sense organs: smell. 133.
sense organs: taste. 134.
sense organs: touch. 135.
sense receptor. 135.
senses of smell and taste. 133.
sensor probe. 237.
sensory impulse. 135.
sensory neuron. 135.
sepal. 74.
sepals. 72.
separator. 406.
separator wire. 466.
separators. 505.
septal cartilage of nose. 133.
septic tank. 277.
septic tank first compartment. 277.
septic tank second compartment. 277.
septime. 577.
septum. 79.
septum lucidum. 130.
septum of scrotum. 116.
septum pellucidum. 130.
sequencer control. 495.
serac. 56.
Serpent. 40, 41.
Serpent Bearer. 40, 41.
serrated cast-iron casing. 696.
server. 536, 537, 540, 542, 543.
service area. 536.
service box. 540, 541, 659.
service box line. 541.
service building. 665.
service judge. 542.
service line. 537, 540, 541.
service main. 413.
service module. 456.
service room. 445.
service station. 401.
service station. 721.
service zone. 541.
serving bowl. 223.
serving table. 209.
serving trolley. 209.
sesame seeded pita. 146.
set in boldface. 364.
set in capitals. 364.
set in italic. 364.
set in lightface. 364.
set in lower case. 364.
set in roman. 364.
set-in-sleeve. 291, 295, 296, 306.
set in small capitals. 364.
set of utensils. 229.
set-up. 590.
setting. 325.
setting-reduced agitation. 722.
setting ring. 370.
settling basin. 638.
settling pond. 648, 650.
settling tank. 645.
setup. 590.
seventeenth century cannon. 694, 695.
seventh. 476.
sew-through buttons. 502.
sewing. 499, 500, 501, 502, 503.

sewing frame. 513.
sewing machine. 499, 500.
sewing spool. 499.
sewn-in floor. 596.
sextant. 443.
sextet. 491.
shackle. 553.
shade. 220, 221.
shade cloth. 219.
shadow. 606.
shadow mask. 392.
shadow roll. 568.
shaft. 61, 170, 328, 510, 519, 534, 538, 540, 568, 572, 582, 586, 588, 611, 655, 656, 657, 691.
shaft collar. 637.
shaft holder. 568.
shag. 331.
shag-vac-rake. 244.
shake-hands grip. 543.
shallot. 83, 482.
shallow root. 71.
sham. 214.
shank. 147, 148, 150, 151, 152, 258, 260, 264, 318, 338, 345, 346, 447, 500, 501, 504, 506, 581.
shank button. 502.
shank portion. 150, 151.
shank protector. 678.
share. 163.
sharp. 476.
sharpening steel. 227.
shaving brush. 337.
shaving mug. 337.
shawl collar. 308.
shawm. 488.
sheath. 70, 91, 601, 663.
sheath dress. 302.
sheath knife. 600.
sheath of Schwann. 135.
sheath skirt. 303.
shed. 247.
shed stick. 509.
sheep shelter. 161.
sheepshank. 601.
sheepskin jacket. 292.
sheer curtain. 217.
sheet. 431, 512.
sheet bend. 601.
sheet lead. 553.
sheet of paper. 616.
shelf. 216, 239, 279, 520.
shelf channel. 239.
shell. 78, 97, 102, 104, 109, 243, 347, 486, 647, 700, 704.
shell membrane. 97.
shells. 145.
sherbet. 157.
SHF antenna. 393.
SHF beacon antenna. 393.
shield. 709.
Shield. 41, 328, 397, 689.
shift key. 467.
shift keys. 470.
shift lock key. 467, 470.
shifter. 411, 412.
shin. 152.
shin boot. 568.
shin guard. 526, 530.
shin pad. 534.
shingle. 195.
ship's anchor. 447.
Ship's Keel. 41.
ship's motor boat. 439.
Ship's Sails. 41.
Ship's Stern. 41.
shirred heading. 217.
shirt. 295.
shirt. 321, 538.
shirt collar. 305, 308.
shirt sleeve. 305.
shirttail. 295, 305.
shirtwaist dress. 302.
shirtwaist sleeve. 306.
shock absorber. 408.

shoe. 377.
shoe horn. 320.
shoe rack. 320.
shoe tree. 320.
shoelace. 318.
shoes. 318, 319, 320.
shoeshine kit. 320.
shoot. 69, 71.
shooting star. 47.
shop. 173.
shop sign. 178.
shop window. 178.
shopping bag. 348.
shore. 51.
short. 297.
short extensor of toes. 118.
short glove. 299.
short line. 540, 541.
short palmar. 118.
short peroneal. 119.
short radial extensor of wrist. 119.
short ribs. 148.
short service line. 542.
short-sleeved shirt. 575.
short sock. 311.
shortbread. 156.
shorts. 310, 538.
shortstop. 525.
shot. 695.
shot put. 571.
shot splice. 601.
shotgun (smooth-bore). 702.
shots. 572.
shoulder. 54, 91, 114, 147, 148, 150, 151, 153, 264, 413, 538, 581.
shoulder bag. 349.
shoulder blade. 115.
shoulder bolt. 264.
shoulder butt. 150.
shoulder pad. 530, 534, 700.
shoulder rest. 700.
shoulder-strap. 313, 346, 347, 349, 587.
shovel. 201, 248, 559, 561.
shower and tub fixture. 267.
shower head. 269.
shrimp. 103.
shroud. 430, 552.
shutdown system no. 1. 666.
shutdown system no. 2. 666.
shutoff switch. 277.
shutoff valve. 267, 268, 270, 272.
shutter. 199, 368, 620, 669.
shutter button. 371.
shutter release. 368.
shutter speed selector. 368.
shutters. 219.
shutting stile. 198.
shuttle. 509.
shuttle. 500.
shuttlecock. 542.
sickle. 252.
side. 150, 224, 430, 685.
side back vent. 293.
side chair. 213.
side chapel. 174.
side door. 425.
side entrance. 188.
side face. 327.
side handle. 260.
side handrail. 429.
side ladder. 419.
side ladder tread. 419.
side lever. 506.
side line. 543.
side-marker light. 397.
side mirror. 340.
side panel. 397.
side platform. 428.
side pocket. 291.
side post. 190.
side rail. 278.
side rib. 150.
side span. 416.
side-tilt lock. 374.

side view. 116, 482.
side wall. 93, 425, 440, 540, 541, 546.
side wall line. 540.
side window. 403.
sideboard. 216.
sidelight. 427.
sideline. 527, 535, 536, 539.
sidestroke. 547.
sidewalk. 413.
sidewall. 402.
sieve. 228.
sifter. 230.
sight. 625, 691, 697.
sight-glass tube. 243.
sighting line. 625.
sighting mirror. 625.
sigmoid colon. 127.
signal background plate. 423.
signal box. 424, 425.
signal gantry. 424.
signal lamp. 238, 242, 520.
signal light. 409.
signals. 423.
signature. 359, 512.
signature of sender. 361.
signet ring. 325.
signs regulating priority at intersections. 715.
silage harvester. 163.
silencer. 253, 406.
silk. 85.
sill. 53, 192.
sill of frame. 199.
sill plate. 192.
sill step. 419.
silverside. 152.
silverware. 224, 225, 226.
sima. 170.
simple leaves. 70.
simple-span beam bridge. 414.
simple topmarks. 446.
single-breasted coat. 293.
single burner camp stove. 599.
single curtain rod. 218.
single-decked pallet. 685.
single-edged swords. 692.
single-handle kitchen faucet. 271.
single-handle kitchen faucet. 270.
single-handle kitchen tap. 270, 271.
single-leaf bascule bridge. 417.
single-lens reflex camera. 368.
single pole breaker. 288.
single quotation marks. 357.
single reed. 483.
single seat. 429.
single twist. 260.
single zero. 594, 595.
singles pole. 537.
singles service court. 542.
singles sideline. 537, 542.
Sinhalese. 355.
sinister. 709.
sinister base. 709.
sinister chief. 709.
sinister flank. 709.
sink. 270.
sink. 269, 375.
sink hole. 54.
sink strainer. 270.
sinker. 581.
sinus of kidney. 128.
siphon. 54.
siphonal canal. 101.
siren. 436.
sirloin. 148, 152.
sirloin tip. 148.
sister. 138.
site plan. 188.
sixte. 577.
sixteenth note. 475.
sixteenth rest. 475.
sixth. 476.
sixty-fourth note. 475.

The terms in **bold type** indicate the title of an illustration; those in *italic* correspond to the British terminology.

sixty-fourth rest. 475.
skate. 534.
skate guard. 562.
skating. 562.
skeg. 551.
skeleton. 92, 120, 121.
skeleton of the hindlimb. 105.
sketch. 521.
ski. 408, 559.
ski boot. 560.
ski boot. 559.
ski cap. 298.
ski goggles. 329, 559, 561.
ski hat. 561.
ski instructor. 558.
ski jumper. 558.
ski jumping hill. 558.
ski pants. 310.
ski pole. 559, 561.
ski resort. 558.
ski stop. 559, 560.
ski suit. 559.
ski tip. 561.
skid. 455.
skid pad. 644.
skid ramp. 403.
skiing. 558.
skimmer. 163, 229.
skin. 135, 136.
skin. 74, 75, 76, 105, 135.
skin diving. 550.
skin surface. 135, 136.
skip. 544.
skirt. 538, 567, 690.
skirt finger. 435.
skirt marker. 501.
skirting board. 197.
skirting convector. 203.
skirting grille. 202.
skirts. 303.
skull. 92, 99, 114, 690.
skullcap. 298.
sky coverage. 61.
sky coverage. 62.
skylight. 187.
slab building. 519.
slalom course. 558.
slalomist. 558.
slash. 357, 386.
slash pocket. 294.
slat. 219, 507.
sleeper. 316.
sleeper. 422.
sleeping bags. 598.
sleeping car. 421.
sleeping-suit. 316.
sleepsuit. 315.
sleet. 57, 60.
sleeve. 293, 575, 576, 596, 613.
sleeve protector. 487.
sleeve strap. 291.
sleeve strap loop. 291.
sleeves. 306.
slender. 119.
slide. 377.
slide. 242, 502, 703.
slide-bar. 505.
slide chair. 422.
slide changer. 377.
slide mount. 377.
slide plate. 499.
slide projector. 377.
slide selector. 237, 243.
slide tray. 377.
slider. 482.
sliding. 198, 199.
sliding breech. 698.
sliding folding. 198, 199.
sliding roof. 397.
sliding weight. 492, 608.
sliding window. 421.
slightly covered sky. 61.
sling. 694, 699, 700, 701.
sling swivel. 699.
slip. 180, 312.
slip joint. 259.

slip joint pliers. 259.
slip-on. 320.
slip ring. 699.
slip-stitched seam. 295.
slipover. 296.
slipover. 307.
slippers. 321.
slippery road. 714.
slit. 511.
slit pocket. 294.
slope. 413.
sloped turret. 191.
sloping cornice. 171.
slot. 180, 225, 237, 264, 351, 513.
slot machine. 595.
slotback. 529.
slotted bracket. 219.
slotted wall bracket. 269.
slow-motion control knob. 623.
sludge. 277.
sluice hole. 440.
small bows. 145.
small capitals. 365.
small hand cultivator. 249.
small intestine. 127.
smaller round. 119.
smock. 302, 305.
smock. 305.
smoke. 60.
smoke bomb discharger. 704.
smoke dome. 200.
smoke filter. 433.
smoking accessories. 344, 345.
smoking candle. 515.
smoking permitted. 719.
smoking prohibited. 719.
snaffle bit. 567.
snaffle rein. 567.
snail. 104.
snail dish. 231.
snail tongs. 231.
snap. 502.
snap fastener. 299.
snap-fastening adjustable strap. 316.
snap-fastening front. 316.
snap-fastening shoulder strap. 316.
snap-fastening side. 315.
snap-fastening waist. 315.
snap shackle. 553.
snare. 486.
snare drum. 486.
snare drum. 491, 493.
snare head. 486.
snare strainer. 486.
sneaker. 319.
snooker. 584.
snorkel. 550.
snorkel exhaust. 438.
snorkel intake. 438.
snout. 105.
snow. 58.
snow goggles. 589.
snow guard. 408.
snow pellet. 57.
snow shower. 60.
snow tire. 407.
snow tyre. 407.
snowmobile. 408.
snowshoe types. 563.
snowshoer. 563.
snowshoes. 563.
snowsuit. 317.
soap dish. 269.
soccer. 532.
soccer ball. 532.
sock. 297.
sock. 311, 530, 538.
sock lining. 318.
socket. 285, 502.
socket bayonet. 693.
socket head (Robertson). 264.
sofa. 211.
soft-drink dispenser. 401.
soft keys. 470.
soft palate. 134.

soft pedal. 479.
soft ray. 98.
soft shell clam. 102.
softlight reflector. 373.
soil. 653.
soil-or-waste stack. 267.
solar cell. 670.
solar cell. 393.
solar collector. 669.
solar eclipse. 37.
solar energy. 668, 669, 670.
solar furnace. 668.
solar house. 669.
solar panel. 65.
solar panel deployment. 394.
solar radiation. 668, 669, 670.
solder. 283, 521.
soldering and welding. 281, 282, 283.
soldering gun. 281.
soldering iron. 281.
soldering iron. 521.
soldering process. 521.
soldering torch. 281.
sole. 93, 137, 297, 321, 560, 562, 586.
sole plate. 562.
soleplate. 422.
soleplate. 243.
soleus. 118.
solid body. 494.
solid-rocket booster. 457.
solid rubber tire. 684.
solid rubber tyre. 684.
solitaire ring. 325.
solleret. 690.
solvent extraction unit. 649.
something omitted. 363.
son. 138.
son-in-law. 139.
sorbet. 157.
soufflé. 157.
sound-board. 477, 478, 479, 487.
sound box. 478.
sound camera. 383.
sound control room. 389.
sound desk. 389.
sound engineer. 389.
sound-hole. 477.
sound-on-sound control. 383.
sound-post. 478.
sound projector. 383.
sound reproducing system. 378, 379, 380, 381.
sound supervisor. 389.
sounding balloon. 47, 63.
sounding gauge. 437.
soup bowl. 223.
soup spoon. 226.
soup tureen. 223.
south. 445, 593.
South America. 49.
South celestial pole. 35.
South pole. 35.
South wind. 593.
Southern Cross. 41.
Southern Crown. 41.
Southern Fish. 41.
southern hemisphere. 35.
Southern Triangle. 41.
southwester. 314.
soybeans. 85.
space. 475.
space achievements. 47.
space bar. 467, 470.
space probe. 47.
space shuttle. 457.
space shuttle at takeoff. 457.
space shuttle in orbit. 457.
space suit. 458.
spacelab. 457.
spacer. 631, 663.
spade. 248, 592, 698.
spade mashie; no. 6 iron. 586.
spading fork. 248.
spadix. 72.

spaghetti. 144.
spaghetti tongs. 231.
spandrel. 172.
Spanish. 355.
Spanish onion. 83.
spanker. 431.
spanners. 258.
spark plug. 406.
spark plug. 253.
spark plug body. 406.
spark plug cable. 405.
spark plug gap. 406.
spark plug gasket. 406.
spark plug terminal. 406.
spatial dendrite. 57.
spatula. 229, 516.
spatulate. 70.
speaker. 378.
speaker. 43, 383, 392.
speaker selector. 379.
speaking window membrane. 426.
spear. 85.
speargun. 550.
special effects. 391.
specific data processing program. 468.
specimen. 619.
specimen chamber. 620.
spectacles. 329.
speed control. 235.
speed selector. 236.
speed selector lever. 380.
speed skate. 562.
speedometer. 399, 410.
spencer. 307.
spent fuel discharge room. 665.
spent fuel port. 665.
spent fuel storage bay. 663, 665, 667.
spermatic cord. 116.
spermatozoon. 116.
sphenoid bone. 122.
sphenoidal sinus. 133.
sphere. 437, 446.
sphere support. 64.
spherical parabolic reflector. 670.
sphincter muscle of anus. 127.
sphygmomanometer. 612.
spicule. 37.
spider. 163.
spike. 72, 422, 587, 588, 589.
spike file. 461.
spike-tooth. 162.
spiked shoe. 526.
spillway. 651.
spillway chute. 651.
spillway gate. 651.
spinach. 82.
spinach lasagna. 144.
spinach noodles. 144.
spinal column. 120.
spinal cord. 99, 130, 135.
spinal ganglion. 135.
spinal nerve. 130, 135.
spindle. 213, 236, 266, 271, 380, 607, 613, 615.
spindle hole. 266.
spindle screw. 613.
spine. 101, 512, 514.
spine of scapula. 121.
spine of the book. 514.
spinnaker boom. 552.
spinnaker sheet lead. 552.
spinner. 581.
spinning rod. 580.
spinous process of vertebra. 121.
spiny lobster. 103.
spiny ray. 98.
spiracle. 100.
spiral. 258, 380.
spiral arms. 39.
spiral beater. 235.
spiral binding. 463.
spiral case. 656, 657.
spiral galaxy. 39.

The terms in **bold type** indicate the title of an illustration; those in *italic* correspond to the British terminology.

spiral-in groove. 380.
spiral ratchet screwdriver. 258.
spiral rib. 101.
spiral staircase. 647.
spire. 101, 104, 174.
spit. 51.
splash plate. 647.
splat. 210.
splay. 175.
splayed leg. 209.
splaying. 200.
spleen. 99, 124.
spleeping compartment. 421.
splenic artery. 125.
splenic vein. 125.
splenius muscle of head. 119.
spline. 406.
split bet. 594, 595.
split ond. 528, 529.
split link. 581.
split system heating pump. 204.
spoiler. 448.
spoke. 411.
spoke wheel. 403.
spoked wheel. 568.
sponge. 695.
sponge-tipped applicator. 332.
spongy body. 116.
spool. 506, 580.
spool pin. 499.
spool rack. 510.
spoon. 226.
spoon. 599.
spoon; no. 3 wood. 586.
spores. 73.
sports. 523.
spot. 221.
spot projector attachment. 373.
spot white ball. 584.
spotlight. 390, 436, 676, 677.
spotmeter. 372.
spouse. 138.
spout. 234, 243, 271.
spout assembly. 270.
spray. 243.
spray arm. 242.
spray button. 243.
spray head. 270.
spray hose. 270.
spray nozzle. 647.
spray paint gun. 280.
sprayer. 250.
spread collar. 295.
spreader. 251, 346.
spreader adjustment valve. 280.
spreading rotor. 163.
spring. 35, 221, 259, 266, 271,
   367, 418, 574, 612, 616, 696,
   700.
spring balance. 608.
spring binder. 463.
spring hip throw. 578.
spring linkage. 595.
spring onion. 83.
spring washer. 264.
spring washer. 422.
spring wing. 264.
springboard. 548, 573, 574.
springboard diver. 548.
springer. 172.
sprinkler hose. 250.
sprocket. 190, 408.
sprocket cluster. 412.
sprocket wheel. 678, 704.
spur. 54, 260, 486, 565.
squab. 400.
squall. 60.
squamous suture. 122.
square. 593.
square. 512, 711.
square bet. 594, 595.
square head plug. 275.
square neck. 309.
square root of. 723.
square sail. 432.
squash. 540.

squash ball. 540.
squash racket. 540.
squash racquet. 540.
St-George's cross. 446.
stabilizer. 434, 555, 691, 705.
stabilizer foot. 242.
stabilizing fin. 456.
stabilizing keel. 437.
stable. 569.
stack. 51, 434.
stack vent. 267.
stacking chairs. 213.
staff. 475.
staff. 709.
stage. 43, 180, 619, 620.
stage clip. 619.
stage curtain. 180.
stage-house. 180.
stained glass. 521.
stairs. 197.
stairs. 188, 647, 719.
stairwell. 189.
stake. 247.
stake pocket. 402.
stalactite. 54.
stalagmite. 54.
stalk. 74, 76, 85.
stalk vegetables. 85.
stalked eye. 103.
stamen. 72, 76.
stamp pad. 462.
stamp pocket. 351.
stamp rack. 462.
stanchion. 562.
stand. 220, 233, 235, 308, 341,
   347, 373, 374, 670.
stand and track. 569.
stand off half. 531.
stand-up collar. 308.
standard hardboard. 194.
standard lens. 370.
standard poker hands. 592.
standard walker. 630.
standardbred pacer. 568.
standing and parking prohibited or
   restricted. 717.
standing and parking signs. 717.
standing press. 514.
standpipe. 272.
staple remover. 461.
stapler. 461.
staples. 461.
star anise. 79.
star diagonal. 623.
star facet (8). 327.
star projection condenser. 43.
star projection lens. 43.
star sphere. 43.
starboard diving plane. 438.
starch. 79.
starch granule. 113.
stars. 145.
start. 566.
start line. 570.
start switch. 241.
start wall. 546.
startboard tack. 553.
starter. 405, 546, 672.
starter handle. 253.
starter pedal. 410.
starting block. 546.
starting dive. 546.
starting electrode. 284.
starting grip. 546.
starting position. 549.
**starting position (crawl,
   breaststroke, butterfly). 546.**
starting positions. 548.
starting resistor. 284.
starting signal. 427.
state of ground. 63.
station circle. 61, 62.
station concourse. 426.
station hall. 426.
station model. 62.
station name. 428.

station platform. 427.
station platform. 424.
station sign. 427.
station wagon. 398.
stationary bowl. 594.
stationary front. 61.
stationery. 461, 462, 463, 464.
stationery cabinet. 465.
stator. 266, 655, 656.
stator vane. 450.
statue. 171.
stay. 430, 610.
stay ring. 656, 657.
stay sail. 431.
stay vane. 656, 657.
staysail-stay. 430.
steak knife. 224.
steam. 664.
steam button. 243.
steam cracker. 648.
**steam drive oil sands recovery
   process. 650.**
steam generator. 661, 664, 668.
steam generator system. 666.
steam injection. 650.
steam iron. 243.
steam pipe. 661, 664.
steam pressure drives turbine. 667.
steam separator. 664.
steam turbine. 434.
steel. 193, 313, 696.
steel ball shielding. 662.
steel band. 610.
steel bar. 573.
steel hook. 322.
steel pen. 367.
steel safety wheel. 429.
steel spring. 696.
steel to plastic. 275.
steelyard. 608.
steep hill. 714.
steeplechase. 570.
steering. 400.
steering axle. 684.
steering column. 400.
steering cylinder. 682.
steering damper. 410.
steering lever. 704.
steering line. 555.
steering lock. 410.
steering track rod. 162.
steering wheel. 165, 399, 400,
   684.
stellar crystal. 57.
stem. 69.
stem. 69, 73, 83, 234, 284, 345,
   411, 430, 552, 611.
stem faucet. 271.
step. 182, 279, 403.
step chain. 182.
step chair. 212.
step cut. 327.
step groove. 197.
step setting. 613.
step stool. 279.
stepladder. 279.
steppe. 59.
**steps in production of
   electricity. 654.**
stereo camera. 369.
sterile dressing. 629.
sterile pad. 629.
stern. 551.
stern loading door. 434.
sternocleidomastoid. 118.
sternomastoid. 118.
sternum. 92, 120.
stick. 478.
stick glove. 534.
stick umbrella. 346.
sticker. 489.
stickpin. 325.
sticks. 485.
sticks. 630.
stiffening girder. 416.
stifle. 91.

stigma. 72, 78.
stile. 213.
stile groove of sash. 199.
stile tongue of sash. 199.
stiletto. 692.
still cameras. 369.
still water level. 51.
stilt. 520.
stilted. 172.
stimulator tip. 339.
sting. 106.
stipule. 70.
stirrup. 691.
stirrup hook. 609.
stirrup iron. 567.
stirrup leather. 567.
stirrup sock. 526.
stitch. 318.
stitch length regulator. 499.
stitch patterns. 504.
stitch selector. 499.
stitched pleat. 304.
stitches. 526.
stitching. 299.
stock. 447, 488, 671, 702.
stock pot. 232.
stockade. 177.
stocked anchor. 447.
stocking. 311.
stocking. 576.
stocking cap. 314.
stocking stitch. 504.
stockless anchor. 447.
stomach. 99, 102, 124, 127.
stone. 74, 75, 193.
Stone Age arms. 689.
stone fleshy fruits. 75.
stoner. 231.
stool. 212.
stop. 382, 502, 644.
stop at intersection. 715.
stop bath. 375.
stop button. 253, 381, 388, 492.
stop consonants. 358.
stop knob. 481, 482.
stop motion knob. 499.
stop rod. 482.
stopboard. 571.
stope. 636.
storage compartment. 676, 677.
storage door. 239.
storage furniture. 215, 216.
storage space. 189.
storage tank. 643, 649, 664, 668,
   669.
storage tray. 665.
storm collar. 202.
storm sewer. 413.
stove oil. 649.
straight. 592.
straight: plank and pole. 566.
straight bet. 594, 595.
straight eye. 502.
straight flush. 592.
straight hair. 330.
straight jaw. 259.
straight ladder. 278.
straight muscle of thigh. 118.
straight position. 548.
straight razor. 337.
straight run gasoline treatment.
   648.
*straight run petroleum treatment.
   648.*
straight skirt. 303.
straight-up ribbed top. 297.
straight wing. 449.
strainer. 236, 271, 596, 641.
strainer body. 270.
strainer coupling. 270.
strainer plug. 271.
strainer sleeve. 270.
strand. 601.
strap. 347, 351, 526, 564, 573,
   690.
strap handle. 346.

The terms in **bold type** indicate the title of an illustration; those in *italic* correspond to the British terminology.

strap wrench. 276.
strapless brassiere. 313.
stratocumulus. 52.
stratosphere. 47.
stratum basale. 136.
stratum corneum. 136.
stratum granular. 136.
stratum granulosum. 136.
stratum lucidum. 136.
stratum spinosum. 136.
stratus. 52.
straw walker. 165.
streamer. 711.
street bet. 594, 595.
street café. 178.
street light. 178.
street sign. 178.
stretcher. 209.
stretcher bar. 423.
stretchers. 213.
strike plate. 266.
striker. 283, 696.
striker wheel. 344.
string. 85, 314, 477, 478, 479, 480.
stringed instruments. 477, 478.
stringer. 449, 685.
stringer board. 685.
stringing. 538.
strings. 540.
strip flooring with alternate joints.
    196.
strip light. 221.
strip light. 390.
strip loin. 148, 152.
strip mine. 635.
striped trousers. 317.
stripes. 444.
stripper beater. 165.
strirrer cover. 237.
stroboscopic light. 705.
stroke judge. 546.
strong-box. 595.
structure. 190, 192, 199.
structure. 651.
structure of a flower. 72.
structure of a missile. 706.
structure of a mushroom. 73.
structure of a plant. 69, 70.
structure of a tree. 71.
structure of the Earth. 47.
structure of the Sun. 37.
strut. 190, 436, 564, 660, 672.
stub out. 268.
stud. 192, 407, 442.
studio. 389.
studio accessories. 374.
studio and control rooms. 389.
studio floor. 390.
studio lighting. 373.
study. 189.
stummel. 345.
stump. 71.
style. 72, 74, 75, 76, 79.
stylobate. 171.
stylus. 367.
stylus cartridge. 380.
sub-base. 64.
subarctic climates. 59.
subbase. 413.
subclavian artery. 125.
subclavian vein. 125.
subcutaneous tissue. 136.
subfloor. 192.
subgrade. 413.
subject. 361.
subject line. 359.
sublevel. 637.
sublimation. 58.
submachine gun. 697.
submarine. 438.
submarine canyon. 50.
submarine pipeline. 644.
submerged foils. 436.
submersible barge. 642.
submersible watch. 550.
subminiature camera. 369.

subpapillary network. 136.
subscript. 364.
subsidiary track. 424.
subsoil plough. 164.
subsoil plow. 164.
substation. 660.
substitute. 535, 536, 539, 545.
substitutes' bench. 539.
subterranean stream. 54.
subtraction. 723.
subtropical climates. 59.
suburban commuter railroad. 424.
suburban commuter railway. 424.
subway entrance. 178.
subway map. 428, 429.
subway station. 428.
subway to platforms. 426.
subway train. 429.
sucker rod. 641.
suction hose. 677.
suction regulator. 244.
sugar bowl. 223.
sugar spoon. 226.
suit tiles. 593.
suitcase. 347.
sulcus terminalis. 134.
sulky. 568.
summer. 35.
summer solstice. 35.
summer squash. 81.
summit. 54.
sump. 253, 405.
sump. 277, 636.
Sun. 37.
Sun. 35, 36, 37, 38, 65.
sun direction. 394.
sun roof. 397.
sun sensor. 65, 393.
sun visor. 399.
sundae spoon. 226.
sundeck. 433.
sundial. 606.
sundress. 302.
sunshine. 63.
sunshine recorder. 64.
sunshine recorder. 63.
sunspot. 37.
super. 107.
superciliary arch. 122.
superficial peroneal nerve. 129.
superhighway. 717.
superior dental arch. 134.
superior longitudinal sinus. 130.
superior mesenteric artery. 125,
    128.
superior nasal concha. 133.
superior semicircular canal. 132.
superior umbilicus. 96.
superior vena cava. 124, 125.
superior view. 122.
superscript. 364.
supertweeter. 378.
supplies. 285.
supply duct. 204.
supply line. 267.
supply of water. 654.
supply point. 659.
supply reel. 383.
supply spool. 466.
supply tube. 270.
support. 64, 213, 218, 284, 509,
    574, 622, 644.
support leg. 402.
support leg crank. 402.
support wheel. 241.
supraorbital foramen. 122.
suprarenal gland. 128.
suprascapular nerve. 129.
sural nerve. 129.
surcingle. 568.
surface. 638.
surface cold front. 61.
surface course. 413.
surface element. 238.
surface of the water. 548.
surface-piercing foils. 436.

surface runoff. 58.
surface-to-air missile. 706.
surface-to-subsurface missile. 706.
surface-to-surface missile. 706.
surface warm front. 61.
surface water drain. 413.
surlonge. 149.
surroyal antler. 89.
suspended span. 414.
suspender. 313.
suspender. 416.
suspender belt. 313.
suspender clip. 294.
suspenders. 294.
suspension bridge. 416.
suspension cable. 416, 675.
suspension file. 463.
suspension hook. 608.
suspension insulator string. 658.
suspension line. 555.
suspension spring. 607.
suspensory ligament. 131.
sustaining pedal. 479.
suture. 79, 101.
swagger bag. 349.
swagger bag. 349.
swagger stick. 346.
swallow-hole. 54.
swallowtail. 711.
swallowtail and tongue. 711.
swallowtail pennant. 711.
Swan. 40.
swede. 84.
Swedish. 355.
sweeper. 544.
sweeper. 532.
sweeping loin throw. 578.
sweeping score line. 544.
sweet bay. 143.
sweet corn. 85.
sweet pepper. 81.
sweet potato. 84.
sweetheart neckline. 309.
swell of the muzzle. 694.
swell organ manual. 481.
swell pedal. 481.
swept-back wing. 449.
swift. 510.
swimmer. 546.
swimmeret. 103.
swimming. 546.
swimming competition. 546.
swimming pool. 433, 545.
swing. 198.
swing bridge. 417.
swing circle. 681.
Swiss chard. 85.
Swiss roll. 157.
switch. 238, 239, 244, 260, 261,
    285, 372, 424, 467, 471.
switch engine. 425.
switch plate. 285.
switch point. 422.
switch point lock. 423.
switch signal. 422.
switch stand. 422.
switch tower. 424, 425.
switchboard. 394.
switcher. 391.
switchhook. 387.
switchyard. 666.
swivel. 572, 581, 640.
swivel base. 259.
swivel head. 259.
swivel lock. 259.
swivel-tilter armchair. 465.
swivel wall lamp. 220.
swiveling power supply cord. 341.
swivelling power supply cord. 341.
sword-breaker. 692.
Swordfish. 41.
swords. 692.
symbol. 595.
symbols. 592.
symbols. 707.
symbols of the planets. 36.
Symphony. 393.

symphony orchestra. 493.
symphysis pubis. 116, 117.
synapse. 135.
sync cable. 373.
synchro cord. 372.
synchronizer. 624.
synthesizer. 495.
synthetic sponge. 333.
syringe for irrigation. 629.
syringes. 629.
system elements. 378.

T

T. 446.
T-bar lift. 558.
T-bone. 148.
T-shirt. 305.
T-shirt dress. 302.
T-strap shoe. 319.
T-tail unit. 449.
tab. 346, 349, 350, 351, 463, 502,
    567.
tab-key. 470.
table. 209, 543, 583, 584.
table. 261, 262, 327, 482, 513,
    576.
table cut. 327.
table extension. 262.
table lamp. 220.
table-locking clamp. 261.
table mixer. 235.
table tennis. 543.
table tennis player. 543.
table tennis shoe. 543.
tablespoon. 226.
tablinum. 173.
tabulator. 467.
tabulator clear key. 467.
tabulator set key. 467.
tachometer. 410.
tack. 551.
tag. 318.
tail. 103, 108, 109, 116, 448, 514,
    554, 556, 557, 559, 561, 563,
    581.
tail assembly. 448.
tail boom. 455.
tail comb. 338.
tail edge. 512.
tail feather. 95.
tail of helix. 132.
tail-out groove. 380.
tail parachute. 556.
tail pipe. 406.
tail pipe extension. 406.
tail pole. 671.
tail shape. 449.
tailgate. 398.
tailing. 650.
taillight. 397, 402, 409.
tailored collar. 301, 308.
tailored sleeve. 306.
tailpiece. 270, 477.
tailrace. 655, 657.
take back to previous line. 363.
take-off board. 570, 571.
take-off line. 570.
take over to next line. 362.
take-up handle. 508.
take-up knob. 466.
take-up reel. 383.
take-up spool. 368, 466.
takedown pin. 699.
taking mirror. 371.
tall tumbler. 222.
talus. 121.
tam- o'-shanter. 314.
tambourine. 486.
tamper. 345.
tandem disc harrow. 164.
tandem disk harrow. 164.
tandem drive housing. 680.
tang. 224, 227.
tank. 704.

The terms in **bold type** indicate the title of an illustration; those in *italic* correspond to the British terminology.

tank. 646.
tank ball. 268.
tank car. 646.
tank car. 420.
tank farm. 644, 648.
tank gauge float. 647.
tank lid. 269.
tank sprayer. 250.
tank trailer. 646.
tank truck. 646.
tank wagon. 646.
tank wall. 646.
tankage. 650.
tanker. 645, 705.
tanks. 457.
tap body. 271.
tape. 219, 461, 502, 507, 526, 536, 613.
tape counter. 381, 382.
tape deck. 381.
tape deck. 378.
tape dispenser. 461.
tape load lever. 466.
tape lock. 613.
tape measure. 501, 613.
tape monitor switch. 379.
tape selector. 381.
tape speed selector. 382.
tape-type indicator. 381.
taper. 515.
tapered wing. 449.
tapestry bobbin. 509.
taproot. 71.
target. 706.
target area. 668.
target areas (dark). 577.
target tracking radar. 706.
tarlatan. 515.
tarpaulin covered gondola. 420.
tarpaulin covered open wagon. 420.
tarragon. 143.
tarsus. 92, 95, 100, 105, 106, 120.
tart. 156.
tassel. 217, 321.
tasset. 690.
Taurus, the Bull. 712.
taxi rank. 178.
taxi stand. 178.
taxi telephone. 178.
taxi transportation. 721.
taxiway. 452.
tea ball. 231.
tea infuser. 231.
team. 531.
team bench. 545.
team shirt. 526.
teapot. 599.
teapot. 223.
tear-off calendar. 464.
tear tape. 344.
teaser comb. 338.
teaspoon. 226.
technical director. 391.
technical terms. 74, 75, 76, 77, 78.
tee. 587.
tee. 272, 275, 544.
teeing ground. 585.
teeth. 123.
teeth. 262, 502, 588.
tele-converter. 370.
Telecom 1 satellite. 394.
telecommunication satellites. 393, 394.
telecommunications network. 394.
telecomputer. 394.
teleconference. 394.
telecopy. 394.
telegrams. 720.
telegraph. 385, 386.
Teleme. 154.
telemetry antenna. 393.
telephone. 718.
telephone answering machine. 388.

telephone booth. 178.
telephone box. 178.
telephone cable. 413.
telephone cord. 388.
telephone index. 464.
telephone line. 322.
telephone set. 387.
telephoto lens. 370.
teleprompter. 390.
Telescope. 41, 443.
telescope base. 42.
telescope control room. 42.
telescope eyepiece. 614.
telescope objective. 614.
telescopic antenna. 392.
telescopic boom. 683.
telescopic corridor. 452.
telescopic front fork. 409.
telescopic sight. 621.
telescopic sight. 700, 704.
telescopic umbrella. 346.
telescoping leg. 374.
telescoping uncoupling rod. 419.
teletex. 394.
television. 389, 390, 391, 392.
television set. 392.
telex: teleprinter. 386.
telltale. 540, 552.
telson. 103.
temperate climates. 59.
temperate marine. 59.
temperature. 569.
temperature control. 237, 341.
temperaturo dial. 243.
temperature indicator. 399.
temperature of dew point. 62.
temperature of the soil surface. 63.
temperature scale. 611.
temperature selector. 240, 241.
temperature sensing bulb. 238.
temperature set point lever. 611.
template. 471.
temple. 328, 510.
temple. 114, 513.
temporal. 120.
temporal bone. 122.
temporal fossa. 122.
tenaille. 176.
tender. 642.
tenderloin. 148, 152.
tenderloin portion. 150.
tendon. 94.
tendon guard. 562.
tendron. 147, 149.
tennis. 537, 538.
tennis ball. 538.
tennis players. 538.
tennis racket. 538.
tennis racquet. 538.
tennis shoe. 319, 538.
tenor drum. 486.
tenor drum. 491.
tension block. 500, 505.
tension block. 499.
tension controller. 505.
tension dial. 500, 505, 506.
tension disc. 505.
tension disc. 500.
tension disk. 505.
tension guide. 505.
tension pulley set. 218.
tension pulley wheel. 218.
tension rod. 486.
tension roller. 412.
tension screw. 486.
tension spring. 398, 500, 505.
tensor of fascia lata. 118.
tentacle. 104.
tents. 596, 597.
tepee. 169.
teres major. 119.
teres minor. 119.
terminal. 238, 285, 472, 644, 659.
terminal arborization. 135.
terminal bronchiole. 126.

terminal bud. 69.
terminal connections. 204.
terminal cover. 615.
terminal filament. 130.
terminal knife-edge. 609.
terminal moraine. 56.
terminal stopping switch. 181.
terminal stopping switch cam. 181.
terrace. 178, 187.
terreplein. 176.
terrestrial sphere. 35.
tertial. 96.
test-lamp. 286.
test pattern. 391.
tester probe. 286.
testicle. 116.
theater. 179, 180.
theater. 178, 433.
theatre. 179, 180, 433.
theodolite. 614.
theodolite. 63.
thermal control shutter. 65.
thermal insulation. 644.
thermal storage. 668.
thermometer. 647.
thermosphere. 47.
thermostat. 204, 205, 206.
thermostat control. 239.
thick flank. 152.
thick-walled pipe. 640.
thigh. 91, 95, 115.
thigh-high stocking. 311.
thigh pad. 530.
thimble. 501.
thimble. 613.
thin flank. 152.
thin macaroni. 144.
thin spaghetti. 144.
thin spring-metal insulation. 195.
thinning razor. 338.
third. 476.
third base. 525.
third baseman. 525.
third molar. 123.
third stage. 456.
third wheel. 605, 607.
thirty-second note. 475.
thirty-second rest. 475.
thong. 319.
thoracic leg. 100.
thoracic vertebra (12). 121.
thoracic vertebrae. 92.
thorax. 100, 106, 114.
thread. 264, 271.
thread guide. 499, 500, 510.
thread take-up lever. 499.
thread trimmer. 500.
threaded cap. 275.
threaded rod. 264.
three-branched air tube. 322.
three-burner camp stove. 599.
three-four time. 476.
three-hinged arch. 415.
three of a kind. 592.
three-quarter coat. 292.
three-quarter sleeve. 306.
threequarter backs. 531.
threshold. 187, 198.
throat. 95, 200, 259, 447, 538, 581.
throat lash. 567.
throat latch. 567.
throat protector. 526, 534.
throttle valve. 639.
through arch bridge. 415.
throwing arc. 571.
throwing circle. 570, 571.
throwing in a circle. 578.
throwing spear. 689.
throwings. 572.
thrust. 415.
thrust device. 367.
thrust tube. 367.
thumb. 108, 299, 526.
thumb hook. 484.
thumb piston. 481.

thumb rest. 243, 483.
thumb string. 487.
thumb string peg. 487.
thumbscrew. 258.
thunderstorm. 60.
thyme. 143.
tibia. 92, 100, 106, 108, 120.
tibial nerve. 129.
tibiofibula. 105.
ticket. 610.
ticket collector's booth. 428.
ticket counter. 426, 454.
ticket office. 426.
ticket pocket. 351.
tidal basin. 441.
tidal power plant. 660.
tie. 321, 346, 422, 476.
tie bar. 326.
tie beam. 190.
tie closure. 346.
tie flap. 596.
tie plate. 422.
tie tack. 326.
tieback. 217.
tieback hook. 217.
tierce. 577.
tight end. 528, 529.
tightening band. 64.
tights. 311.
tights. 321.
tile. 171, 195.
tiller. 251, 552, 691.
tilt-back head. 235.
tilt cord. 219.
tilt tube. 219.
timber. 171.
timber yard. 638.
time fuse. 696.
time signatures. 476.
timed outlet. 238.
timekeeper. 535, 539, 545, 576, 579.
timer. 375.
timer on switch. 382.
timetables. 426.
timing. 569.
timpani. 493.
tin opener. 229, 243, 599.
tinctures. 710.
tine. 606.
tip. 70, 85, 224, 226, 258, 263, 264, 281, 282, 294, 343, 346, 521, 554, 557, 559, 563, 572, 581, 582.
tip cleaner. 521.
tip cleaners. 283.
tip guard. 562.
tip of nose. 133.
tip-ring. 580.
tip section. 580.
tipping lever. 631.
tipping valve faucet. 271.
tipping valve tap. 271.
tire. 403, 411.
tire dolly. 401.
tire inflator. 401.
tire pump. 411.
tire valve. 412.
tires. 407.
tissue holder. 269.
Titan. 36.
title. 359.
(to) suppression tank. 664.
toaster. 237.
tobacco. 344.
tobacco hole. 345.
tobacco pouch. 345.
toboggan. 564.
toe. 93, 97, 114, 257, 262, 297, 321, 586.
toe binding. 561.
toe box. 562.
toe clip. 93, 411.
toe hole. 563.
toe lacing. 563.
toe pick. 562.

The terms in **bold type** indicate the title of an illustration; those in *italic* correspond to the British terminology.

toe piece. 554, 559, 560.
toe-piece release setting indicator. 560.
toe piston. 481.
toe rubber. 319.
toe stop. 562.
toe-strap. 319.
toe strap. 554.
toenail scissors. 343.
toeplate. 561.
toggle bolt. 264.
toggle fastening. 292.
toilet. 268.
toilet. 189.
toilet. 269, 421.
toilet bowl. 268, 269.
toilet cistern. 269.
toilet for men. 719.
toilet for men and women. 719.
toilet for women. 719.
toilet tank. 269.
toilet truck. 453.
tomato. 81.
tombolo. 51.
Tomme aux raisins. 154.
tone arm. 380.
tone control. 383, 494.
tongs. 231.
tongue. 99, 127, 133, 134, 294, 318, 349, 482, 488, 502, 560, 562.
tongue sheath. 109.
tool. 639.
tool tray. 279.
tools. 519, 600.
tools and equipment. 248, 249, 250, 251, 252.
tooth. 109, 164, 263, 338, 680, 681.
toothbrush. 339.
toothbrush shaft. 339.
toothbrush well. 339.
toothed jaw. 259.
toothed rotor. 164.
toothing stone. 187.
toothpaste. 339.
top. 71, 430, 538.
top bar. 574.
top central manhole. 646.
top coat. 300.
top collar. 293.
top cylinder. 516, 518.
top deck. 647.
top deckboard. 685.
top edge. 512.
top-end transverse member. 425.
top face. 327.
top hat. 298.
top lift. 318.
top of dam. 651, 652, 655.
top plate. 190, 467.
top pocket. 584.
top rail. 198, 213, 215.
top rail of sash. 199.
top road. 637.
top stitched pleat. 304.
top stitching. 294, 316.
top surface. 556.
topgallant mast. 430.
topmark. 444.
topmast. 430.
topping. 581.
topping lift. 430.
topside. 152.
toque. 314.
torch. 221.
torch. 276.
torpedo. 438.
torpedo room. 438.
tortellini. 145.
torus. 170.
total. 610.
total eclipse. 37, 38.
tote bag. 347, 348.
tote board. 569.
Toucan. 41.

touch in goal line. 531.
touch line. 531, 532.
toupee. 331.
touring boot. 561.
tourist-class cabin. 433.
tow bar. 554.
tow hook. 556.
tow release knob. 556.
tow tractor. 453.
towboat. 645.
towel bar. 269.
towel set. 269.
tower. 658.
tower. 174, 416, 638, 668, 671, 672.
tower body. 658.
tower crane. 683.
tower crane. 441.
tower foot. 658.
tower ladder. 676.
tower mast. 683.
tower mill. 671.
tower silo. 161.
tower top. 658.
tower-type solar power station. 668.
tower window. 658.
towing eye. 698.
towing fairlead. 437.
towing hook. 162.
towing truck. 401.
town house. 183.
towrope. 554.
tracery. 175.
trachea. 126.
tracing wheel. 501.
track. 218, 408, 427, 428, 472, 558, 571, 678, 704.
track and field athletics. 570, 571, 572.
track carrier roller. 678.
track grouser. 678.
track idler. 678.
track lighting. 221.
track link. 678, 704.
track roller. 678.
track roller frame. 678.
track shoe. 678.
track shoe. 678.
tracker. 482.
tracking control. 382.
traction motor. 418.
traction motor ventilator. 418.
tractor. 162.
tractor. 646.
tractor engine. 682.
tractor unit. 403.
trade sign. 178.
traditional houses. 169.
traditional musical instruments. 487, 488, 489.
traffic circle. 715.
traffic island. 178.
traffic light. 178.
tragus. 108, 132.
trailing edge. 448, 556, 557.
trailing edge flap. 448.
train delays notice board. 426.
train set. 424.
trainer. 569, 579.
training shoe. 319.
training wall. 651.
trajectory of a satellite. 394.
trampoline. 574.
tranche grasse. 149.
transceiver. 458.
transducer. 442.
transept. 174.
transfer. 394.
transfer canal. 665.
transfer dispensing machine. 428.
transfer of heat to ordinary water. 667.
transfer orbit satellite. 394.
transfer orbit solar cell. 393.
transfer scale. 372.

transfer station. 636.
transform fault. 50.
transformation of mechanical work into electrical energy. 654.
transformer. 373.
transformer. 205, 655, 659, 668, 672.
transformer station. 655.
transistor. 606.
transit shed. 441.
transition fittings. 275.
translation wave. 51.
transmission. 240, 682.
transmission-line contact. 385.
transmission network. 667, 668.
transmission of telegraph signals. 385.
transmission of the rotative movement to the rotor. 654.
transmitted pulse. 624.
transmitter. 385, 387.
transmitter. 387, 624.
transmitter-receiver. 394.
transmitter-receiver terminal. 394.
transparency slide. 377.
transparent line indicator. 467.
transpiration. 58.
transportation. 395.
transporter bridge. 417.
transpose lines. 363.
transpose two letters. 363.
transpose two words. 363.
transverse baffle. 646.
transverse bulkhead. 645.
transverse colon. 127.
transverse dunes. 55.
transverse process of vertebra. 121.
trap. 270, 275.
trap and drain auger. 276.
trap coupling. 270.
trapezius. 118.
traveler. 553.
traveling cables. 181.
traveling crane. 655.
traveller. 553.
travelling block. 640.
travelling cables. 181.
travelling crane. 655.
traverse arch. 175.
traverse rod. 218.
traversing and elevating mechanism. 701.
traversing handle. 697.
tray. 280.
tray. 233, 347.
tread. 197, 567.
tread design. 407.
treadle. 508.
treadle cord. 508.
treble: wall, triple bars, oxer. 566.
treble bridge. 479.
treble keyboard. 489.
treble pick-up. 494.
treble register. 489.
treble tone control. 379.
tree. 71.
tree. 567.
tree pruner. 249.
trefoil. 172, 175.
trench. 50, 635.
trench coat. 291.
triangle. 485.
Triangle. 40.
triangular body. 487.
triangular fossa. 132.
triceps of arm. 119.
triclinium. 173.
tricuspid valve. 124.
trifoliolate. 70.
triforium. 174, 175.
trigger. 253, 280, 383, 691, 696, 697, 699, 700, 701, 702, 703.
trigger guard. 697, 702, 703.
trigger switch. 263.
triglyph. 170.

trilby. 314.
trill. 476.
trim. 347.
trim collar. 201.
trim ring. 238.
trimmer. 337.
trimming. 513.
trimming. 351.
trimming tool. 519.
trio. 490.
trip lever. 268.
triple bars. 565.
triple jump. 571.
triple tail unit. 449.
triplex. 183.
tripod. 374.
tripod. 377, 492, 622, 701.
tripod accessories shelf. 623.
tripod cane. 630.
tripod leg. 623.
tripod stand. 486.
tripod stick. 630.
Triton. 36.
trochanter. 100, 106.
trolley. 417, 683.
trolley pulley. 683.
trolley wire. 427.
Trombe wall. 669.
Trombe wall. 669.
trombone. 484, 491.
trombones. 493.
tropic of Cancer. 35.
tropic of Capricorn. 35.
tropical climates. 59.
tropical fruits. 80.
tropical maritime. 62.
tropical rain forest. 59.
tropical savanna. 59.
tropical storm. 60.
troposphere. 47.
trotter. 153.
trough. 51, 62, 423.
trousers. 294, 310, 589.
trousers. 578.
trowel. 249.
truck. 418, 421, 562.
truck and track. 429.
truck crane. 683.
truck frame. 418.
truck level floor. 453.
truck tractor. 403.
truck trailer. 403.
truck trailer. 403.
true skin. 135.
truffle. 73.
trumpet. 484.
trumpet. 484, 491.
trumpets. 493.
trunk. 347.
trunk. 71, 115, 397.
trunk floor. 398.
trunks. 575, 579.
trunnion. 694.
truss. 182, 190.
truss rod adjustment. 494.
trussed arch. 415.
TT & C belt antenna. 393.
tub. 240, 242, 247.
tuba. 484, 493.
tube. 695.
tube. 377, 612, 697, 700.
tube bangle. 325.
tube cutter. 276.
tube end. 274.
tube flaring tool. 276.
tube sheet. 662.
tuber vegetables. 84.
tubercles. 101.
tuberculin syringe. 629.
tubing. 641.
tubing head. 641.
tubular bells. 485.
tubular bells. 493.
tubular element. 238.
tubular heater. 649.
tubular ice screw. 588.

The terms in **bold type** indicate the title of an illustration; those in *italic* correspond to the British terminology.

tubular lock. 266.
tubular member. 643.
tuck. 344.
tuck brush. 506.
tuck position. 548.
Tudor. 172.
tumble dry at low temperature. 722.
tumble dry at medium to high temperature. 722.
tumble dryer. 241.
tumbler. 222.
tumbler holder. 269.
tuner. 378.
tunic. 305.
tunic. 302, 305.
tuning buttons. 379.
tuning control. 442.
tuning fork. 492.
tuning fork. 606.
tuning fork watch. 606.
tuning hammer. 492.
tuning machine. 494.
tuning peg. 478.
tuning pin. 479.
tuning screw. 486.
tuning slide. 484.
tuning wire. 482.
turban. 314.
turbine. 438, 450, 655, 666.
turbine blade. 450.
turbine building. 661.
turbine-compressor shaft. 450.
turbine guide vane. 450.
turbine runner. 660.
turbine shaft turns generator. 667.
turbined water draining. 654.
turbo-alternator. 668.
turbo-charged engine. 404.
turbo-compressor engine. 404.
turbo-jet engine. 450.
turbo-jet engine. 448.
turbocharger. 418.
turbofan engine. 450.
turbopump. 706.
turn. 476.
turn and bank indicator. 556.
turn and slip indicator. 556.
turn signal. 402.
turn signal lever. 400.
turn-up. 294, 310.
turnbuckle. 423, 553, 579.
turner. 229.
turning handle. 260.
turning judge. 546.
turning wheel. 519.
turnip. 84.
turntable. 380.
turntable. 681.
turntable. 235, 378, 417.
turntable mounting. 676.
turret. 177, 704.
turret cap. 621.
turrets. 145.
turtle. 109.
turtleneck. 296, 307, 308, 559.
tutu. 321.
tweeter. 378.
tweezers. 343, 629.
twig. 69, 71.
twill weave. 511.
twin-lens reflex camera. 369.
twin-set. 307.
twin skis. 554.
twin turret. 439.
Twins. 40.
twist dive. 549.
twist drill. 260.
twist grip throttle. 410.
twisted macaroni. 144.
twisted rope. 601.
two-door saloon. 398.
two-door sedan. 398.
two-hand clean and jerk. 575.
two-hand snatch. 575.
two-handed sword. 692.

two-hinged arch. 415.
two pairs. 592.
two-seater settee. 211.
two-two time. 476.
two-way collar. 291.
two-way traffic. 715.
tympan. 517, 518.
tympanum. 105, 109, 171, 175.
type of fuel. 401.
type of high cloud. 62.
type of low cloud. 62.
type of middle cloud. 62.
type of the air mass. 62.
typed name. 359.
types of anchors. 447.
types of arch bridges. 415.
types of arches. 172, 415.
types of beam bridges. 414.
types of bodies. 398.
types of cars. 420.
types of chairs. 213.
types of collars. 308.
types of doors. 198.
types of freight wagons. 420.
types of gloves. 299.
types of golf clubs. 586.
types of grips. 543.
types of handles. 554.
types of headgears. 298.
types of inflorescences. 72.
types of jaws. 90.
types of kitchen knives. 227.
types of leaves. 70.
types of passenger cars. 421.
types of passenger coaches. 421.
types of rigs. 432.
types of roofs. 190, 191.
types of sails. 432.
types of skates. 562.
types of skis. 554.
types of strokes. 547.
types of telephones. 388.
types of windows. 199.
typestyle. 466.
typewriter. 466, 467.
typical letter. 359, 360, 361.
typing element. 466.
typist's chair. 465.
tyre. 411.
tyre inflator. 401.
tyre pump. 411.
tyre rack. 401.
tyre valve. 412.
tyres. 407.

U

U-bend. 275.
U-shaped gouge. 516.
UHF channel selector. 392.
UHF-IFF aerial. 705.
Ukrainian. 355.
ulna. 120.
ulnar artery. 125.
ulnar extensor of wrist. 119.
ulnar flexor of wrist. 118, 119.
ulnar nerve. 129.
umbel. 72.
umbilicus. 101.
umbo. 101.
umbra. 38.
umbra shadow. 37.
umbrella. 346.
umbrella diffuser. 373.
umbrella sheath. 587.
umbrella stand. 346.
umlaut. 357.
umpire. 528, 536, 537, 542, 543.
umpire-in-chief. 525.
umpire's stand. 542.
uncle by marriage. 138.
uncle-in-law. 138.
under tail covert. 95.
underarm crutch. 630.
underground. 638.

underground flow. 58.
underground map. 428, 429.
underground mine. 637.
underground railway. 429.
underground station. 428.
underground train. 429.
underlining. 502.
underlying fabrics. 502.
underpass. 414.
undershirt. 526, 579.
underwear. 297, 312, 313.
underwiring. 313.
Unicorn. 41.
uniform. 530.
union. 274.
union. 274, 723.
union nut. 274.
unison. 476.
unit price. 610.
univalve shell. 101.
universal step. 453.
unleavened bread. 146.
unmounted sleeve. 306.
uphaul. 551.
upholstery nozzle. 244.
upper. 560.
upper berth. 421.
upper blade guard. 263.
upper bowl. 234.
upper chord. 415.
upper cold front. 61.
upper cuff. 560.
upper deck. 434.
upper edge. 543.
upper eyelid. 94, 105, 131.
upper floor. 188, 189.
upper fore topgallant sail. 431.
upper fore topsail. 431.
upper gill arch. 98.
upper girdle facet (16). 327.
upper heating element. 273.
upper level. 440.
upper limb. 691.
upper lip. 134, 482.
upper lobe. 126.
upper mandible. 95.
upper mantle. 47.
upper rudder. 438.
upper shell. 560.
upper side-rail. 440.
upper sphere clamp. 64.
upper support screw. 64.
upper tail covert. 95.
upper thermostat. 273.
upper warm front. 61.
upperboard. 482.
upperworks. 553.
upright. 508, 509, 513, 514, 570, 571, 573, 574, 630.
upright piano. 479.
upright piano action. 480.
upstage. 179, 180.
upstream blanket. 652.
upstream face. 652.
upstream gate. 440.
upstream level. 440.
upstream shoulder. 652.
upstream toe. 652.
Uranus. 36.
ureter. 128.
urethra. 117, 128.
urinary bladder. 99, 116, 117, 128.
urinary meatus. 116.
urinary system. 128.
urine transfer fitting. 458.
urogenital aperture. 99.
uropod. 103.
urostyle. 105.
use chlorine bleach as directed. 722.
use of audible warning devices prohibited. 716.
user station. 394.
usual terms. 74, 75, 76, 77.
uterovesical pouch. 117.
uterus. 117.

utilities plant. 650.
utility case. 347.
utility speaker. 391.
uvula. 133, 134.

V

V-neck. 293, 296.
V-neck cardigan. 296.
V-shaped gouge. 516.
V-shaped neck. 309.
V-shaped row. 134.
vacherin. 156.
vacuole. 113.
vacuum bottle. 600.
vacuum chamber. 612.
vacuum coffee maker. 234.
vacuum distillation. 649.
vacuum flask. 600.
vacuum manifold. 620.
vagina. 117.
vagus nerve. 126.
vair. 710.
valance. 214, 217.
valance lighting. 220.
Valençay. 154.
valley. 54, 187.
valley gutter. 187.
valve. 79, 101, 344, 484, 639.
valve casing. 484.
valve seat. 271.
valve seat shaft. 268.
valve seat wrench. 276.
valve spring. 404, 405.
valve stem. 271.
vambrace. 690.
vamp. 318.
vane. 96, 187, 241, 706.
vanity case. 347.
vanity mirror. 399.
variable depth sonar. 439.
variable geometry wing. 449.
variable spacer. 467.
variometer. 556.
various dry fruits. 79.
varistor. 387.
varnish-roller. 515.
vas deferens. 116.
vastus lateralis. 118.
vastus medialis. 118.
Vauban fortification. 176.
vault. 175.
vaulting horse. 573, 574.
VCR pause switch. 384.
veal. 147, 153.
vegetable bowl. 223.
vegetable brush. 231.
vegetable garden. 161, 188.
vegetable kingdom. 67.
vegetable steamer. 232.
vegetables. 81, 82, 83, 84, 85.
veil. 581.
vein. 70, 636.
velum. 106.
velvet band chocker. 326.
Venetian blind. 219.
venom canal. 109.
venom-conducting tube. 109.
venom gland. 109.
venomous snake's head. 109.
vent. 53, 206, 399, 694, 695.
vent brush. 338.
vent cap. 406.
vent door. 402.
vent field astragal. 694.
vent hole. 280, 555.
vent line. 275.
ventail. 690.
ventilated rib. 702.
ventilating fan. 418.
ventilation shaft. 638.
ventral aorta. 99.
ventricular septum. 124.
venturi. 700.
venturi fastening lever. 700.

The terms in **bold type** indicate the title of an illustration; those in *italic* correspond to the British terminology.

757

Venus. 36.
vermicelli. 144.
vermiform appendix. 127.
vernal equinox. 35.
Versailles parquet. 196.
vert. 710.
vertebral column. 99, 105, 120.
vertebral shield. 109.
vertical-axis wind turbine. 672.
vertical clamp. 614.
vertical cord lift. 243.
vertical frame. 509.
vertical pivoting. 199.
vertical pupil. 109.
vertical seismograph. 616.
vertical shaft. 636.
vertical side band. 536.
vertical speed indicator. 437.
vertical stabilizer. 556.
vertical tangent screw. 614.
very cloudy sky. 61.
very large elbows. 145.
vest. 293, 315.
vest. 297, 579.
vest. 296, 307, 316, 317, 321.
vest pocket. 307.
vestibular nerve. 132.
vestibule. 132, 173, 421.
vestibule door. 421.
vests and pullovers. 307.
VHF aerial. 449.
VHF channel selector. 392.
viaduct. 414.
vibrating mudscreen. 640.
vibrato arm. 494.
vice. 259.
video camera. 384.
video input. 382.
video operator. 389.
video output. 382.
video tape recorder. 382.
video technician. 389.
video/TV selector. 382.
videotape recorder. 389.
Vienna bread. 146.
Vietnamese. 355.
view camera. 369.
viewfinder. 368, 383.
viewing chamber. 620.
viewing window. 620.
vine leaf. 82.
vinyl grip sole. 315, 316.
vinyl insulation. 195.
viola. 477, 490.
violas. 493.
violin. 477, 478.
violin. 477, 490.
violin family. 477.
violoncello. 477, 490.
violoncellos. 493.
Virgin. 40, 41.
Virgo, the Virgin. 712.
vise. 259.
visor. 423, 458, 690.
visual display unit. 469.
vitelline membrane. 97.
vitreous body. 131.
vocal cord. 126.
volcanic island. 50.
volcano. 53.
volcano. 48.
volcano during eruption. 53.
volleyball. 536.
volleyball. 536.
voltage increase. 654, 667.
voltage induction. 654.
voltage stabilizer. 376.
voltage tester. 286.
voltmeter. 286.
volume control. 378, 379, 383, 388, 394.
volume readout. 401.
volute. 170, 210.
volva. 73.
voussoir. 172.
vowels. 358.

voyager bag. 349.
VU meter. 495.
VU meter switch. 495.
vulva. 117.

W

wad. 695, 702.
waders. 582.
wading bird. 97.
waffle. 157.
wagon. 425.
wagon tent. 597.
waist. 115, 477, 658.
waistband. 294, 297, 301.
waistband extension. 294.
waistcoat. 293, 307.
waistcoat pocket. 307.
waistcoats and pullovers. 307.
waiting room. 426.
walking aids. 630.
walking cam. 675.
walking frame. 630.
walking leg. 103.
walking shoe. 675.
walking stick. 346.
walking stick. 630.
walkway. 675.
wall. 38, 77, 93, 565, 566, 593, 596, 636.
wall fitting. 220.
wall grille. 202.
wall lantern. 221.
wall register. 202.
wall stack section. 202.
wall stud. 192.
wall tent. 597.
wallet. 351.
wallet. 351.
wallet section. 351.
walnut. 78.
waning crescent. 38.
waning gibbous. 38.
wapiti. 89.
wardrobe. 216, 596.
warhead. 706.
warm air. 669.
warm-air comb. 338.
warming plate. 234.
warning light. 410.
warning plate. 261.
warp. 508, 509.
warp roller. 508.
warp thread. 511.
warping frame. 510.
wash tower. 242.
washer. 240, 272.
washer. 271.
washery. 638.
washing. 722.
washing machine. 240, 272.
WASP helicopter. 439.
Wassily chair. 210.
waste pipe. 268.
waste stack. 267.
waste tee. 272.
watch pocket. 293.
watchcase. 605.
Water Bearer. 41.
water bottle. 411, 600.
water bottle clip. 411.
water carrier. 600.
water cools the used steam. 667.
water cress. 82.
water ditch. 570.
water forms. 57.
water goblet. 222.
water hazard. 585.
water hose. 639.
water intake. 655.
water is pumped back into the
    steam generator. 667.
water jug. 223.
water jump. 565, 566.

water key. 484.
water level selector. 240.
water main. 413.
water meter. 267.
Water Monster. 40, 41.
water pitcher. 223.
water polo. 545.
water pressure gauge. 677.
water pump. 406.
water reservoir. 638.
water service pipe. 267.
water skiing. 554.
water table. 54.
water tank. 418, 421.
water treatment plant. 661.
water under pressure. 654.
waterfall. 54.
watering can. 250.
waterline. 439.
watermelon. 81.
waterproof pants. 315.
waterproofed electrical supply.
    277.
watertight bulkhead. 645.
watt-hour meter. 615.
wave. 51.
wave base. 51.
wave clip. 343.
wave height. 51.
wave length. 51.
wave wall. 652.
wavy hair. 330.
wax plate. 106.
wax seal. 268.
waxing crescent. 38.
waxing gibbous. 38.
weapons. 687.
wearing course. 413.
weather map. 62.
weather radar. 448.
weatherboard. 198, 199.
weaving. 508, 509, 510, 511.
weaving brush. 506.
web. 97, 422, 526.
web frame. 645.
web member. 190.
webbed foot. 105.
webbing. 507.
wedding ring. 325.
wedge. 482, 694.
wedge iron. 257.
wedge lever. 257.
weeder. 249.
weeding hoe. 248.
weekender. 347.
weft. 508.
weft thread. 511.
Wehnelt cylinder. 620.
weighing platform. 610.
weight. 572, 575, 607, 608, 610.
weight belt. 550.
weight-driven clock mechanism.
    607.
weight limitation. 716.
weightlifter. 575.
weightlifting. 575.
weld bead. 281, 282.
welding curtain. 283.
welding torch. 282.
welding torch. 281, 282.
well. 161.
Welsh. 355.
welt. 318.
welt pocket. 296, 304.
west. 445, 593.
West Coast mirror. 403.
West wind. 593.
wet dock. 441.
wet snow. 57.
wet suit. 550.
Whale. 40, 41.
whale boat. 432.
wheel. 407.
wheel. 347, 397, 501, 521, 562, 694, 704.
wheel chock. 453.

wheel cylinder. 407.
wheel head. 519.
wheel loader. 679.
wheel tractor. 679.
wheelbarrow. 251.
wheelchair. 631.
wheelhouse. 436.
wheels. 145.
whelk. 104.
whipping. 586.
whisk. 230.
whiskers. 94.
whistle buoy. 444.
White. 591, 592.
white balance control. 384.
white cabbage. 82.
white cap. 545.
white cue ball. 584.
white dragon. 593.
white flag. 545, 578.
white line. 93.
white spot ball. 583.
white square. 591.
white-tailed deer. 89.
white tape. 542, 543.
white wine. 222.
whiteface. 322.
whole loin. 147, 151.
whole note. 475.
whole rest. 475.
whole wheat bread. 146.
wholemeal bread. 146.
whorl. 101.
wicket gate. 657.
wide angle adapter. 372.
wide-angle lens. 370.
width. 548.
width clearance. 716.
wife. 138.
wigs and hairpieces. 331.
wigwam. 169.
wild animals crossing. 715.
winch. 434, 439, 553, 675, 704.
wind. 61.
wind. 55, 553.
wind abeam. 553.
wind arrow. 61.
wind baffle. 599.
wind chest. 481.
wind deflector. 403.
wind direction. 62.
wind direction and speed. 62.
wind duct. 481.
wind indicator. 552.
wind instruments. 483, 484.
wind scale. 61.
wind speed. 62, 63.
wind speed in knots. 61.
wind trunk. 481, 482.
wind turbine. 672.
wind turbine electricity
    production. 672.
wind vane. 63.
windage adjusting screw. 621.
windbreaker. 301.
windcheater. 301.
windcone. 711.
winder house. 636.
winding mechanism. 219.
winding mechanism. 607.
winding tower. 638.
windlass. 436.
windmill. 671.
window. 199.
window. 187, 188, 237, 238, 351, 397, 429, 448, 551, 596.
window accessories. 217, 218,
    219.
window regulator handle. 400.
window tab. 463.
window winder handle. 400.
windscreen. 397, 403, 408, 705.
windscreen. 42.
windscreen wiper. 398.
windscreen wiper blade. 398.
windshaft. 671.

The terms in **bold type** indicate the title of an illustration; those in *italic* correspond to the British terminology.

windshield. 397, 403, 408, 451, 705.
windshield wiper. 398.
windshield wiper blade. 398.
wine cellar. 433.
wine waiter corkscrew. 229.
wing. 96.
wing. 397, 403, 535.
wing. 95, 100, 108, 148, 448, 457, 556, 557, 581, 690.
wing box. 705.
wing covert. 95.
wing forward. 531.
wing membrane. 108.
wing nut. 264.
wing nut. 262.
wing pallet. 685.
wing rib. 152, 449.
wing shape. 449.
wing slat. 448.
wing structure. 449.
wing tank. 645.
wing tip. 449, 556.
wing vein. 100.
wing wire. 557.
wings. 179.
winning line. 595.
winter. 35.
winter solstice. 35.
winze. 636.
wiper. 398.
wiper arm. 398.
wiper blade rubber. 398.
wiper switch. 400.
wippen. 480.
wire. 560, 572.
wire beater. 235.
wire brushes. 485.
wire cutter. 259, 287.
wire sling. 588.
wire stripper. 287.
wire support. 599.
wishbone boom. 551.
withers. 91.
wok. 233.
wok set. 233.
Wolf. 41.
women's apparatus. 574.
women's clothing. 300, 301, 302, 303, 304, 305, 306, 307, 308, 309, 310, 311, 312, 313, 314.
women's pompadour. 331.
wood. 586.
wood. 194.
wood-based panel. 265.
wood block. 518.
wood chip car. 420.
wood engraving. 516.
wood flooring. 196.
wood flooring. 196.
wood flooring arrangements. 196.
wood flooring on cement screed. 196.
wood flooring on wooden structure. 196.
wood ray. 71.
wood stove. 201.
woodcut. 516.
wooden bar. 573.
wooden modeling tools. 519.
wooden modelling tools. 519.
woodwind family. 483.
woofer. 378.
word processing keys. 470.
work drawing. 521.
work lead. 281.
worker. 106.
working area. 43.
working pressure gauge. 282.
workshop. 189.
workshop/store. 648.
worktop surface. 242.
worm. 489, 510, 695.
worm gear. 219.
wrap-over dress. 302.

wrap-over skirt. 303.
wrap-over top. 305.
wrap over top. 305.
wraparound diaper shirt. 315.
wraparound dress. 302.
wraparound skirt. 303.
wrapper. 344.
wrenches. 258.
wrist. 108, 115.
wrist-length glove. 299.
wrist pad. 530.
wrist sling. 588.
wrist strap. 349, 350, 384, 561.
wristband. 538.
writing brush. 367.
writing case. 350.
writing instruments. 367.
writing systems of the world. 355.

X

X-15 (USA). 47.
XVIIth century. 697.
xylophone. 485.
xylophone. 493.

Y

Y-branch. 275.
yard. 425.
yard. 430.
yard line. 527.
yarn. 601.
yarn clip. 505.
yarn feeder. 506.
yarn rod. 505.
yaw axis. 393.
yaw nozzle. 65.
yellow ball. 584.
yoke. 218, 295, 305.
yoke skirt. 303.
yolk. 97.
yurt. 169.

Z

zenith. 43.
zest. 77.
zester. 227.
zipped screen door. 596.
zipper. 502.
zipper. 315, 316, 317, 342, 346, 347, 348, 597.
zipper line. 503.
zipper pocket. 350.
zippered screen door. 596.
zither. 487.
ziti. 144.
zoom lens. 370, 384.
zoom-speed selector. 384.
zucchini. 81.
zygomatic arch. 122.
zygomatic bone. 122.
zygomaticofacial foramen. 122.

The terms in **bold type** indicate the title of an illustration; those in *italic* correspond to the British terminology.

索 引

一 畫

一、二級肋肉 151
一公尺跳板 548
一束 85
一段樓梯 197
一套鼓 491
一號球員 544
一號攝影機 391
一對 592
一種金屬 282
一疊 525
一疊手 525
乙炔瓶 281
乙炔閥 282
乙狀結腸 127
乙烯絕緣材料 195

二 畫

丁香結 601
丁帶鞋 319
丁烷筒 344
丁烷運輸船 645
七分袖 306
七弦琴 487
七度 476
七點五公尺跳台 548
二公尺禁線（紅） 545
二分休止符 475
二分音符 475
二心外心桃尖拱 172
二心直線尖拱 172
二心邊心桃尖拱 172

二尖瓣 124
二拍二 476
二度 476
二重奏 490
二號球員 544
二號攝影機 391
二對 592
二樓樓座 179
二疊 525
二疊手 525
人 113
人工操縱轉轍器 422
人中 133
人孔 646, 647
人字形拼木地板 196
人字形排列 134
人字拖鞋 319
人字屋頂 190
人字紋地板 196
人字帶 710
人字閘門 440
人字繡 507
人字縫 122
人行道 413
人行橫道 178
人行橋 424, 428
人的齒列 123
人馬座 41
人馬座（3月21日） 712
人造海綿 333
人造衛星 47
人體 114, 115
人體模型 501
入口 107, 637, 639
入口滑板 107
入口轉柵 428
入水 548, 549
入油口 647

入射光測量感應罩 372
入庫貯藏 650
入境事務櫃枱 454
八分休止符 475
八分音符 475
八角茴香 79
八度 476
八度鍵 483
八斜面切磨 327
八邊階形切磨 327
刀 165, 224, 692
刀刃 224, 227, 338, 501,
　562
刀叉筐 242
刀子 550, 599
刀片 234, 236, 252, 337
刀片防護罩 280
刀尖 224, 227, 562
刀舌榫 224, 227
刀把 224
刀把頭 693
刀身 224, 227, 338, 501,
　693
刀柄 693
刀背 224, 227
刀面 224
刀跟 227
刀劍 692
刀輪 243
刀齒 162, 562
刀鞘 600
刀頭 337
刀頭組鬆脫鈕 337
匕首 689, 692
十七世紀火砲 694, 695
十七世紀臼砲 697
十二指腸 127
十六分休止符 475

十六分音符 475
十公尺跳台 548
十字形 213, 446
十字形尾翼組 449
十字把 594
十字帶 710
十字絲照明鈕 614
十字繡 507
十字槽頭 264
十字線 621
十字頭 684
十字頭螺絲起子 258

三 畫

三十二分休止符 475
三十二分音符 475
三叉空氣管 322
三公尺跳台 548
三公尺跳板 548
三心花瓣拱 172
三心拱 172
三列飛羽 96
三尖瓣 124
三色牌 593
三尾翼組 449
三角 711
三角小帳篷 597
三角帆 431
三角肌 118
三角形琴身 487
三角形簷飾 171
三角座 40
三角窩 132
三角褲 297, 313

三角牆 175
三角翼 449
三角鐵 485
三拍四 476
三度 476
三重奶油軟乾酪 154
三重奏 490
三重障礙：磚牆，三重欄
　杆，木柵 566
三重欄杆 565
三級台座 171
三級跳遠 571
三條 592
三通 275
三通管 272
三號球員 544
三號攝影機 391
三脚杖 630
三脚架 374, 377, 486, 492,
　701
三脚架腿 623
三脚座 622
三葉形飾 175
三鉸拱 415
三層樓住宅/三戶住宅 183
三頭露營爐 599
三疊 525
三疊手 525
三蹼葉 70
三隴板 170
下弓臂 691
下切口 512
下巴 114
下巴束帶 530
下止塊 502
下水位 440
下水道 267
下牙弓 134
下地幔 47
下池 651, 652, 655
下弦 415
下弦月 38
下恆溫器 273
下注方式 594, 595
下肢 124
下表面 265
下垂直舵 438
下桁支索 552
下唇 134
下唇鬚 100

下桅 430
下側梁 402
下基層 413
下眼瞼 94, 105, 131
下部支承螺絲 64
下部加熱元件 273
下部裝機螺絲 374
下雪裝 317
下喙 95
下游面 652
下游基趾 652
下游壩肩 652
下腔 234
下腔靜脈 124, 125, 128
下葉 126
下滾筒 516, 518
下端踏板 182
下頜片 293, 308
下鼻甲 133
下標 364
下樓 188
下線 577
下輪擊球手等候區 525
下鋪 421
下頜 98, 123
下頜骨 92, 120, 122
下橫檔 215
下機乘客入口大廳 454
下簧片 482
下臍 96
下鰓弧 98
下欄 198
下襬貼邊 301
下襬邊 503
下護套 560
下護蓋 263
下護蓋撥把 263
上下對開 710
上弓臂 691
上切口 512
上心拱 172
上水位 440
上牙弓 134
上主桅下帆 431
上主桅上帆 431
上半規管 132
上甲板 434
上矢狀竇 130
上光輥 515
上地幔 47

上池 651
上衣 305, 576, 578
上坡助行機 558
上弦 415
上弦月 38
上恆溫器 273
上承拱橋 415
上板 482
上胶 124
上肩肉 147, 150
上肩肋肉 151
上冒頭 198
上垂直舵 438
上唇 134
上梳直髮 331
上桅 430
上粉海綿 333
上側梁 402
上條機構 607
上眼瞼 94, 105, 131
上部 709
上部支承螺絲 64
上部加熱元件 273
上部肋肉 147, 149
上喙 95
上游水位 440
上游面 652
上游基趾 652
上游閘門 440
上游覆蓋層 652
上游壩肩 652
上發條軸 492
上發條鈕 605
上腔 234
上腔靜脈 124, 125
上菜缽 223
上楣 215
上腭 106
上腰肉 148, 152
上腰肋肉 149
上腹 114
上腹部肉 149
上葉 126
上跨通道 414
上滾筒 516, 518
上端股肉 152
上膊骨 92, 108
上頜 293
上鼻甲 133
上層 188, 189

上層活動架 107
上層游步甲板 434
上彈把 699
上標 364
上緣 543
上線 577
上鋪 421
上鞍具場 569
上領 123
上頜骨 98, 120, 122, 133
上墨皮墊 516
上墨板 516
上墨輥 516
上橫帶 710
上橫檔 215
上臂甲 690
上檻 199
上簧片 482
上臍 96
上鰓弧 98
上護套 560
上護蓋 263
凡爾賽式地板 196
么點 592
刃口 682
刃形支承 608, 609, 610
勺式傳送帶 164
千分卡尺 613
千呎 47
叉 225, 248, 599, 606, 607,
　684
叉子車 684
叉孔 425
叉尖 225
叉舌 109
叉把 225
叉架式運貨車 684
叉柄眼鏡 329
叉背 225
叉座 622
叉梳 338
叉骨桁 551
叉掌 89
叉標 423
叉齒 225, 684
叉齒根 225
叉頸 225
叉縫 225
口 102, 104, 105, 134
口角 134

口袋 304
口琴 488
口腔 126, 127
口腔保健器 339
口器 100, 106
土 653
土丘 668
土表溫度 63
土星 36
土層 653
土衛六 36
大（19至36） 594, 595
大刀 692
大三角帆下桁 552
大三角帆脚索圈 552
大小頭 275
大內刈 578
大內收肌 119
大切肉刀 227
大手提袋 348
大犬座 41
大功率燈泡 43
大外刈 578
大白菜 82
大皮箱 347
大衣 292
大衣式連衣裙 302
大西洋 49
大貝殼粉 145
大咖啡杯 223
大於 723
大門 188, 198
大洋洲 49
大扇貝 102
大氣現象 60
大氣層 47
大特寫調焦鈕 383
大勒銜 567
大勒韁 567
大勒鏈 567
大匙 226
大梁 192
大淺盤 223
大陸坡 48, 50
大陸性氣候 59
大陸架 48, 50
大陸隆 50
大陸塊體 50
大陸邊緣 50
大陰唇 117

大提琴 477, 490, 493
大街 178
大圓肌 119
大腸 127
大腭 100, 103
大腦 130
大葱 83
大雷雨 60
大鼓 486, 491, 493
大熊座 40
大腿 115
大腿中部肉 147
大腿肉 147, 148, 149, 150, 151, 152
大腿筋肉 147
大寫 365
大寫字母 356
大寫定位鍵 467, 470
大寫符號 356
大寫鍵 467, 470
大樓 178
大獎送出管 595
大獎獎金輸送道 595
大獎箱 595
大蝴蝶結 309, 322
大輪 631
大燈 704
大頭書釘 461
大翼軟骨 133
大鍵琴 490
大隱靜脈 125
大覆羽 96
大轉子 121
大觸角 103
大廳 433, 454
女 138
女上衣 538
女子器械 574
女性生殖器官 117
女洗手間 719
女裝 300, 301, 302, 303, 304, 305, 306, 307, 308, 309, 310, 311, 312, 313, 314
子 138
子女 138, 139
子午圈 35
子午線 35
子午線輪胎 407
子房 72
子室 76

子宮 113, 117
子宮腔 113
子宮圓韌帶 117
子宮膀胱陷凹 117
子宮寬韌帶 117
子宮頸 113, 117
子集 723
子葉 69, 75, 79
子彈 702, 703
子彈（來福槍） 702
子彈（滑腔霰彈槍） 702
子線 581
小（1至18） 594, 595
小刀 516, 599, 600
小丑裝 322
小丑鞋 322
小內刈 578
小孔 299
小心 718
小心地滑 718
小心易燃物 718
小心毒物 718
小手耙 249
小方山 55
小牛肉 147, 153
小犬座 40
小尖塔 174, 175
小行星 36
小貝殼粉 145
小咖啡杯 223
小於 723
小枝 71
小前犁 163
小室 173
小屋 247
小扁豆 85
小指鈎 484
小徑 247
小核果 74
小烤盆 223
小馬座 40
小勒銜 567
小勒韁 567
小圈粉 145
小甜餅成形擠管 230
小甜餅模 230
小陰唇 117
小提琴 477, 478, 490
小提琴類樂器 477
小結節 101

小號 484, 491, 493
小圓肌 119
小圓柱形鮮乾酪 155
小圓領 309
小圓翻領 308
小塔 177
小獅座 40
小節線 476
小腸 127
小腭 103
小腦 130
小熊座 40
小腿肉 147, 148, 150, 151, 152, 153
小腿筋肉 149
小蝶粉 145
小賣攤位 428
小齒輪 260, 607
小龍艾 143
小龍蝦 103
小翼羽 96
小臂 115
小覆羽 96
小鬈球 331
小繩梯 588
小觸角 103
小體大寫 365
山 54
山口 54
山丘 54
山地甜乾酪 154
山形繡 507
山谷 54
山坡 54
山肩 54
山洪 54
山峽 54
山峯 54
山脈 38, 48
山脊 54
山崖 54
山頂 54
山牆飾內的三角面 171
山牆飾物 171
山麓冰川 56
工字形 213
工作人員 390
工作台 261, 262
工作台車 453
工作台鎖夾 261

索 引

工作便橋 675
工作區 43
工作間 189, 445
工具 515, 516, 517, 519,
　600
工具廂 676, 677
工具袋 342
工具載台 279
工場或倉庫 648
工蜂 106
工蜂後足 106
工裝褲 310
工廠用油 649
弓 691
弓毛 478
弓尖 478
弓把 478, 691
弓弦螺母 478
弓架 42, 260
弓背 691
弓桿 478
弓腹 691
弓與弩 691
弓鋸 262, 276, 600
弓頭 478
弓鐙 691

四 畫

不可用水洗 722
不可用含氯漂白劑 722
不可乾洗 713, 722
不可熨 722
不同民族的房屋 169
不同管材的接頭 275
不恆等 723
不要、不許 713
不准吸烟 719
不准駛入 713, 716
不規則冰晶 57
不規則星系 39
不透水岩石 640
不透光沖洗罐 375
不等於 723
不漏光機腔 368
中 593
中三角帆 431

中子吸收劑注入口 662
中子吸收劑罐 661
中內龍骨 645
中心刃形支承 609
中心布帶 537
中心柱 672
中心粒 86
中心齒輪 605, 607
中文 355
中片單鏡反光照相機 369
中外野 525
中外野手 525
中央孔 380
中央凹 131
中央泵站 644
中央控制台 451
中央處理機 468, 469, 472
中央電極 406
中央調焦輪 621
中央操縱台 399
中央螺柱 514
中央點 709
中耳 132
中肋 70, 79
中足 100, 106
中性幹線 288
中性線 288, 659
中東空心麵包 146
中果皮 74, 75, 76, 77
中長大衣 292
中門齒 123
中前鋒 528, 529
中柄劍 692
中段 116
中段肉 150
中段低梁平板車 420
中段腰肉 150
中段嫩腰肉 148
中美洲 49
中音小鼓 486
中音拾音器 494
中音喇叭 378
中音鼓 491
中音譜號 475
中格 349
中桅 430
中耕機 163
中胸 100
中胸肋肉 148
中區爭球圈 533

中圈 532, 535
中梃 198, 199, 215
中統襪 297, 311
中袋 584
中趾 95
中趾骨 94
中途泵站 644
中部胸肉 149
中場 541
中插板 551
中提琴 477, 490, 493
中軸承 450
中間上部 709
中間基部 709
中間通道 421
中間透鏡 620
中間層 47, 265
中雲 52
中雲類型 62
中楣 215
中溝 93
中溫熨 722
中節指骨 121
中節趾骨 120
中葉 126
中跨 416
中隔 78
中獎圖 595
中鼻甲 133
中層 428
中樞神經系統（矢狀切
　面）130
中樞銷 562
中線 527, 531, 532, 533, 535,
　536, 537, 539, 540, 542,
　543, 544, 545, 576, 583
中線旗 532
中鋒 529, 531, 532, 533,
　535, 539
中橫檔 215
中磺 56
中衛 528, 529, 531, 532
中壓配電線 659
中點 532, 583, 584
中點標識 537
中櫃 645
中覆羽 96
丹麥文 355
丹麥裸麥麵包 146
之字形滑雪道 558

井口架 636, 638
井口探油裝置 641, 644
井口鎖口盤 637
井架 640, 643
互套 511
五公尺跳台 548
五斗櫃 216
五角星 710
五度 476
五重奏 490
五稜鏡 368
五線譜 475
仁 75, 78
元 723
內三角帆 431
內下角 551
內中堂 171
內外四心桃尖拱 172
內外線電話機 388
內耳 132
內耳和中耳 132
內衣 297, 312, 313, 315
內夾層 351
內把手 266
內底 318
內果皮 75, 76
內股 578
內前鋒 528
內胎氣門嘴 411
內軌 182
內唇 101
內套鞋 560
內容 359, 360, 361
內核 47
內格 592
內側腿肉 147
內側線 577
內側髁 121
內袋 347
內趾 95
內部通話揚聲器 391
內野 525
內層 265
內緣 93, 551
內線防禦工事 176
內質網 86
內齒鎖緊墊圈 264
內燃電力傳動機車 418
內篷 597
內爐床 200

內灣 660
六十四分休止符 475
六十四分音符 475
六分儀 443
六角孔閉口扳手 258
六角形襪套 275
六角螺母 406
六度 476
六重奏 491
公文皮包 350
公文箱 350
公主頭 331
公主縫 312
公司註册地址 361
公司註册編號 361
公用電話 388
公用電話亭 178
公共汽車 721
公里 47
公婆 139
公婆/岳父母 139
公寓大樓 183
分 723
分中 362
分切刀 227
分切叉 227
分水管接頭 676
分禾器 165
分析天平 609
分段 362, 380
分段時間 569
分段紋 380
分流閥 269
分音符號 357
分針 605, 607
分畦拉線 249
分割方式 710
分號 357, 364, 386
分經棒 508, 509
分道 571
分道繩 546
分隔板 350
分電器 405
分餾塔 649
分類卡 463
分體式冷暖氣機 204
切刀 287, 375
切刀刃 513
切刀柄 513
切口 513

切片刀 227
切圈刃 260
切蛋片器 231
切割用鋼絲 519
切割玻璃 521
切割滾刀 252
切割器 165
切管刀具 276
切餅輪 230
勿用水洗 713
化妝用具 333
化妝品 332, 333
化妝品盤 347
化妝海綿 333
化妝盒 332
化妝箱 347
化油器 404, 405, 409
化學處理 649
化糞池 277
化糞池次道隔間 277
化糞池頭道隔間 277
升力風機進氣口 435
升主動脈 124
升降台貨車 453
升降拉繩 219
升降座 180
升降索 431, 683
升降記號 476
升降副翼 457
升降舵 448, 556
升降速度表 556
升降速度指示器 437
升降裝置 43
升降機 181, 665
升降纜 181
升結腸 127
升號 476
升運器 162
升旗杆 709
升旗索 709
及膝襪 311
反光板 374
反光傘 373
反光器 221, 402
反光鏡 408
反自轉 394
反身跳水 549
反坦克導彈 706
反射片 284
反射屏 373

反射面 668
反射望遠鏡 622
反射器 670
反射鏡 368
反動推進器 393
反盒褶 217
反摺邊 560
反應控制設備 662
反應器 661, 664, 665,
  667
反應器室 661, 663, 665
反應器調節系統 666
反應器壓力外殼 663
反覆記號 476
天井 173
天文 35
天文台 42
天文館 43
天王星 36
天平 608
天平梁 608, 609
天平梁托座 609
天赤道 35
天車 640
天兔座 41
天花板 540, 541
天花板出氣口 202
天花板燈 220
天氣現狀 62
天氣雷達 448
天氣圖 62
天秤座 41
天秤座（9月23日） 712
天球 35
天球座標系 35
天然氣 640
天然海綿 333
天琴座 40
天窗 187
天象儀 43
天箭座 40
天線 397, 448
天線收發轉換開關 624
天壇座 41
天燕座 41
天貓座 40
天龍座 40
天鴿座 41
天鵝座 40
天蠍座 41

天蠍座（10月24日） 712
天爐座 41
天鶴座 41
天鷹座 40, 41
夫 138
夫妻 139
太平洋 49
太空火箭 47
太空成就 47
太空衣 458
太空穿梭機 457
太空穿梭機起飛 457
太空航行 456
太空實驗室 457
太陽 35, 36, 37, 38, 65
太陽方向 394
太陽系行星 36
太陽的構造 37
太陽能 668, 669, 670
太陽能收集器 669
太陽能吸收板 65
太陽能供暖房屋 669
太陽能電池 393, 670
太陽傳感器 65, 393
太陽電池板張開 394
太陽輻射 668, 669, 670
太陽爐 668
孔 79, 299
孔洞 517
孔屑箱 386
孔泰硬乾酪 155
孔眼 505, 588
孔雀座 41
尺 513, 625
尺神經 129
尺骨 120
尺側腕伸肌 119
尺側腕屈肌 118, 119
尺動脈 125
巴士站 178
巴西果 78
巴投 578
巴拉拉卡琴 487
幻燈片 377
幻燈片框 377
幻燈片盤 377
幻燈機 377
引入線 284
引水渠 651
引紋 380

引號 357, 364, 386
引線鋼絲 505
引橋坡道 416
引擎 404, 405, 457, 678, 680, 681, 682
引擎進氣口 435
引擎罩 397, 403
引擎儀表 451
引擎懸臂架 449
引繞轉子 580
心 99, 102
心土鏟 164
心包 126
心皮壁 77
心形 70
心材 71
心室中隔 124
心叢 126
心臟 124
戶內/外拍攝鈕 384
戶主共管的公寓 183
手 115
手叉 249
手把 639
手杖 346, 630
手制動輪 419
手制動齒輪罩 419
手制動鏈 419
手斧 600
手持式面罩 283
手持式蓮蓬頭 269
手柄 257, 258, 259, 260, 262, 263, 280, 282, 385, 489, 501, 506, 508, 517, 521
手背護板 534
手風琴 489
手套 299, 458, 526, 534, 550, 555, 561, 564, 565, 572, 576
手套指頭 299
手套筒 576
手套種類 299
手控脫扣器 560
手控光圈調節鈕 383
手控變焦環 383, 384
手推車 427, 685
手推割草機 252
手桿 244
手球 539
手球場 539

手掌部分 299
手提包 348, 349
手提滅火筒 676
手提電池燈 676
手提攪和機 235
手提攪拌機 235
手搖曲柄鑽 260
手搖風琴 489
手搖鑽 260
手煞車桿 399
手鉗 515
手電筒 221, 550
手榴彈 696
手槍 703
手槍式噴嘴 250
手輪 499, 514
手機 471
手鋸 262
手環 325
手臂姿勢 549
手鍵盤 481, 482
手鏈 325
手鐲 325
支承木 192
支承塊 341
支承墊 663
支承輪 241
支板 606, 616
支柱 64, 424, 436, 492, 508, 509, 514, 562, 564, 573, 579, 596, 609, 622, 644, 658, 684
支架 218, 219, 373, 374, 442, 446, 558, 573, 574, 670, 675
支架板 482
支座 482, 670
支座彎頭 275
支索 430
支索帆支索 430
支桿 501, 505, 580
支票夾 351
支票簿夾/秘書夾 351
支票簿夾層 351
支棒 247
支軸 492, 562
支幹 71
支管 202
支墩 653
支墩壩 653

支墩壩剖面圖 653
支撐 190, 574, 622
支樞 625
支樞桿 480
支樞連桿 616
支線軌道 424
支銷 407
支臂 221, 681
支點調節旋鈕 548
支鐵 567
文件皮夾 350
文件夾 461, 463
文件架 386
文件壓夾 463
文字處理鍵 470
文具 461, 462, 463, 464
文具櫃 465
斗 345, 682
斗形座椅 400
斗管 345
斗蓋 345
斗環 657
斗篷 301, 321
斗臂 679
方山 55
方向指示牌 428
方向舵 448, 457, 556
方向舵腳蹬 451, 556
方向與升降裝置 701
方向盤 399, 400, 684
方向轉把 697
方位自動同步機 624
方位角粗動定位夾 623
方形靠墊 214
方塊 592
方領 309
方銷頭 219
方頭螺絲起子 258
方鑽桿 640
日文 355
日光濾色片控制鈕 383
日芒 37
日珥 37
日冕 37
日常用語 74, 75, 76, 77
日晷 606
日期 359, 361, 569
日期戳 462
日間用長項鏈（22）吋 326

日照 63
日照計 63, 64
月台 424, 427, 428
月台行李車 427
月台頂 427
月台編號 427
月台蔭棚 424
月台邊緣 427, 428
月相 38
月相盤 607
月桂 143
月球 36, 37, 38
月球外貌 38
月球正面 38
月球背面 38
月球軌道 38
月蝕 38
木工 265
木工工具 257, 258, 259, 260, 261, 262, 263
木工緊固用具 264
木工鎚 257
木片 485
木瓜 80
木瓦 195
木地板 196
木地板拼法 196
木材 194
木材筏道 651
木刻 516
木刻版 516
木板 265, 518
木星 36
木架藤椅 210
木柵 247, 566
木柵和橫竿 566
木盆 247
木射線 71
木屐 319
木紋 265
木瓶 590
木廊 177
木琴 485, 493
木結構上鋪木地板 196
木塊芯膠合板 265
木構件 171
木槌 257, 516
木管樂器 483
木餅 572

木橫槓 573
木衛一 36
木衛二 36
木衛三 36
木衛四 36
木頭棒 586
木螺鑽頭 260
木欄 565
止動裝置 644
止推拱座 415
比目魚肌 118
比堅尼式三角褲 297
比賽池 546
比賽泳池 545
比賽計時員 533
比賽區 578
比賽場地 570, 571
比賽運動員 546
毛孔 137
毛皮 710
毛皮圍巾 309
毛皮質 137
毛地板 192
毛乳頭 137
毛根 137
毛根內鞘 137
毛根外鞘 137
毛球 137
毛細管 611
毛筆 367
毛幹 137
毛鉗 342
毛緣 70
毛線支架 505
毛線衫 307
毛線帽 314
毛線進給器 506
毛髮 136, 137
毛囊 137
毛髓質 137
水力推動葉片 654
水力發電示意圖 654
水力發電站 651
水力發電站剖面圖 655
水上起重機 441
水上運動 545
水井 161
水分循環 58
水手裝 305
水手領 308

水斗 657
水壺 223, 234, 411, 600
水壺夾架 411
水平切向旋鈕 614
水平地震儀 616
水平尾翼 448, 455, 556, 705
水平制動把 614
水平拉梁 190
水平度盤照明鏡 614
水平度盤轉動鈕 614
水平掃瞄器 65
水平桿 658
水平通量檢測器 662
水平腳架 377
水平搖窗 199
水池 570, 669
水位選擇鈕 240
水位觀察窗 243
水坑 585
水受壓 654
水抽回蒸汽發生器 667
水果奶油布丁 156
水果布丁 157
水果烘餅 156
水果蛋糕盤 230
水泥 194
水泥平面上鋪木地板 196
水泥抹平面 196
水狀液 131
水的形態 57
水肺潛水員 550
水芥子 82
水表 267
水星 36
水星號太空艙（美） 47
水泵 240, 242, 406
水泵車 677
水泵電動機 277
水面 548
水庫 651, 652, 655
水密艙壁 645
水桶 240
水球 545
水處理廠 661
水蛇座 41
水鳥 97
水晶玻璃垂飾 220
水晶玻璃珠 220
水晶體 131

水塔 638
水溫示警燈 399
水溫自動調節器 204
水落管 187
水路運輸 430
水道床 440
水道船閘 440, 441
水閘 660
水槍 677
水窪 565, 566
水管 101, 639
水管嘴 250
水銀柱 611
水銀柱頭 611
水銀開關 611
水銀槽 446
水銀燈泡 284
水槽 375
水箱 418
水箱注水管 268
水箱排水閥 268
水箱蓋 269
水輪機 655
水輪機出水 654
水輪機剖面圖 657
水輪機旋轉 654
水輪機進水管 655
水輪機轉輪 660
水頭 654
水龍帶捲架 677
水壓表 677
水翼船 436
水鍋 243
水獺 90
水獺掌形 563
水變成蒸汽 667
水罐 600
火山 48, 53
火山口 53
火山灰雲 53
火山島 50
火山道 53
火山噴發 53
火山錐 53
火石 283
火成岩 48
火車軌 422, 423
火車站 424
火花塞 253, 406
火花塞高壓導線 405

火花塞接頭 406
火花塞殼體 406
火花塞間隙 406
火花塞墊圈 406
火門圈帶 694
火星 36
火柴桿 345
火柴盒 345
火柴頭 345
火砲 704
火砲射擊瞄準器 439
火帽殼 702
火焰噴頭 281
火焰調節輪 344
火腿刀 227
火箭 47, 456
火箭筒 700
火線母線 288
火線接頭 659
火衛一 36
火衛二 36
火繩桿 695
火繩槍 696
火藥室 695
火藥瓶 696
爪 94, 95, 97, 100, 103, 106, 108, 109, 325
爪釘 589
父 138, 139
父母 139
父母/子女 138
片狀冰晶 57
牙 109
牙本質 123
牙刷 339
牙刷座 339
牙刷軸 339
牙周韌帶 123
牙冠 123
牙根 123
牙根尖 123
牙骨質 123
牙膏 339
牙槽 123
牙槽骨 123
牙線 339
牙齒 123
牙齒狀 70
牙頸 123
牙齦 123

索 引

牙齦按摩尖 339
牙髓 123
牛仔褲 310
牛奶房 161
牛奶麵包 146
牛皮紙 265
牛肉 148, 149, 152
牛至 143
牛肝菌 73
牛房 161
牛排刀 224
牛眼透鏡 446
牛腿 177
犬齒 90, 123
王翼 591

五畫

丙烷/丁烷罐 599
丙烷或丁烷爐具 599
世界各地文字 355
世界氣候 59
主人臥室 189
主井 638
主引擎 457
主支架 409
主交通壕 176
主帆 431, 552
主帆升降索 552
主帆腳索 552
主巡邊員 528
主注入口 647
主柱 557
主要下注選擇 594, 595
主要動靜脈 125
主要通堵塞口 267
主桅 430
主桅下帆 431
主桅上帆 431
主索 563
主起落架 448
主起落架安裝梁 449
主起落輪架 705
主動脈 126
主動脈弓 124
主動軸 182
主動鏈 182

主教 591
主球 583, 584
主頂帆 431
主傘 555
主幅前緣拉件 218
主焦點 42
主焦點觀察艙 42
主發電機 418
主裁判 525, 528, 536, 543,
　　576, 578
主幹 71
主幹橫斷面 71
主椽 190
主電極 284
主儀表板 451
主彈簧 703
主線軌道 425
主緩行器 425
主銷 402
主齒輪 607
主機室 651, 655
主燃油開關 410
主翼梁 449
主鍵盤 481
主斷路器 288
主鏡 42, 622
主鏡筒 619, 621, 622, 623
主護盾支架 698
主驅動傘齒輪箱 435
他種金屬 282
仙人球 80
仙人掌 55
仙女座 40
仙王座 40
仙后座 40
充氣支承輪胎 429
充氣抽氣泵 598
充氣泵 598
充氣救生筏 435
充氣導向輪胎 429
充氣褲 322
充氣褥 598
充氣臂箍 612
充電信號燈 337
充電器 337
兄弟 138
兄弟/姊妹 138
「兄弟」衛星 393
冬 35
冬至 35

冬季運動 558
冬葱 83
凹下的爐台 238
凹口 582
凹印示意圖 518
凹把 237
凹角堡 176
凹版印刷 515
凹面 226
凹透鏡 625
凹窩 587
凹頭 264
凹褶 348
出入口 176
出入坡道 187
出口格柵 203
出口高速滑行道 452
出口轉柵 428
出水口 271
出水管 277
出生 723
出灰台 201
出車台 637
出車軌道 425
出油口 647
出風口格柵 340
出租貯物櫃 720
出發台 546
出發犯規召回繩 546
出發池壁 546
出發姿勢（自由式、蛙
　　式、蝶式） 546
出發跳水 546
出獎電聯動器 595
凸印示意圖 518
凸角 176
凸角堡 176
凸版印刷 516
凸面切磨 327
凸透鏡 625
凸堞 177
凸極 656
凸緣 137, 266, 521
凸緣貨盤 685
凸緣螺母 274
凸輪軸 405, 517
凸銷 502
凸點文字 356
凸邊 197
加 723

加力脊 550
加托奶罩 313
加固大梁 416
加固懸跨 414
加油口 403
加油工人 401
加油車 453
加油機 705
加拿大式 360
加拿大式並列爭球 529
加拿大赤德乾酪 154
加拿大楓杖 630
加拿大重水－鈾反應器
　　662
加拿大重水－鈾核電廠
　　661
加拿大橄欖球場 527
加勒比海 49
加強肋 682
加強記號 476
加強檔 209, 210, 213
加速度計 556
加速控制器 253
加溼機 204
加熱元件 204, 205
加熱元件發熱指示燈 204
加熱管 241
加熱器 664
加線 475
加燃料門 201
加燃料機 661, 664, 665
加壓器 661, 664
加壓頭 260
加護圓片 690
功能鍵 470, 610
功率繼電器 205
包皮 116
包肩大衣 300
包肩袖 291, 300, 306, 316
包書角 512
包廂 179
包廂前照明燈 179
包絡線定形器 495
包跟皮 318
包裹部 426
包膠 670
包覆絕緣材料 195
北 445, 593
北天球星座圖 40
北天極 35

北半球 35
北回歸線 35
北美切割 147, 148, 150, 151
北美洲 49
北美乾酪 154
北海 49
北晃座 40
北極 35, 49
北極星 40
北極海 49
北極圈 35
北歐麵包 146
半人馬座 41
半月堡 176
半片刀柄 227
半片式眼鏡 329
半百葉窗 199
半沉頭 264
半穿式拱橋 415
半風羽 61
半掛車 646
半掛貨車 402, 403
半球形帳篷 597
半球形頂 43
半軟荷蘭乾酪 155
半魚眼鏡頭 370
半圓 535
半圓形室 174
半圓形區 584
半圓拱 172
半圓壁龕 174
半腱肌 119
半截窗簾 217
半裹式 598
半影 37, 38
半潛式平台 642
半膜肌 119
半鰓 98
卡子 693
卡尺架 613
卡爪 407
卡片 464
卡片夾 351
卡片穿孔機 472
卡片櫃 464
卡式膠卷 371
卡扣式插座 370
卡扣式鏡頭接環 368
卡抓彈簧 693
卡釘 480

卡規 517
卡箍 575
去果心刀 231
去果核器 231
去骨刀 227
可互換鏡頭 368, 370
可耳比多孔軟乾酪 154
可取下的控制器 237
可拆把手 201
可拆卸汽油箱 437
可放長的睡衣 315
可逆反應 723
可動上頜 109
可換的終端設備 42
可摺疊的太陽能電池組 393
可編程序的定時器 382
可調長短的按鈕帶 316
可調校座椅 421
可調節的腰帶 317
可調腳 383
可調鋸架 262
可縮下的提手 350
可變光欄 619
可變深度聲納 439
可變幾何形機翼 449
古今標識 712
古代 367
古洛米埃乾酪 155
古爾奈乾酪 155
古雙簧管 488
古羅馬步兵 689
古騰堡界面 47
右中衛 531
右內鋒 528, 529, 532
右內邊鋒 528, 529
右心房 124
右心室 124
右手握把 700
右支氣管 126
右水平舵 438
右外前鋒 529
右外野 525
右外野手 525
右弦搶風行駛 553
右肺 124, 126
右前衛 528, 532
右前鋒 535
右後衛 532, 535, 539
右架尾 698

右高低手輪 698
右高低弧 698
右側 709
右側上部 709
右側中部 709
右側基部 709
右移 362, 363
右發球回彈觸地區 540
右發球觸地區 537
右腎（矢狀切面） 128
右衛 528, 529, 533
右翼 531, 532, 533
右翼衛 528, 529
右邊鋒 528, 529, 539
右彎 714
司行輪裝置 492
司線員 528
叫計程車電話 178
台 43
台下裁判 579
台坎 652
台夾 619
台角 579
台角凳子 579
台板 499
台架 279, 517
台面 579
台面擴接件 262
台倉門 180
台秤 610
台基 171
台幕 180
台邊 579
句號 357, 363, 386
四大類刺刀 693
四公尺禁線（黃） 545
四分休止符 475
四分音符 475
四分腳 630
四片拌和桿 235
四角橫帆 432
四坡屋頂 190
四季 35, 593
四拍四 476
四花 593
四門轎車 398
四度 476
四重奏 490
四桅帆船 430, 431
四帶孔皮鞋 320

四條 592
四球撞球 583
四腳杖 630
四腳梯 279
四輪溜冰鞋 562
四壁球場 541
外三角帆 431
外下角 551
外分泌汗腺 136
外切口 512
外半規管 132
外皮 77, 85
外皮刀 342
外皮剪 342
外皮推棒 342
外皮鉗 342
外耳 132
外耳道 122, 132
外衣 300, 301
外衣袋 347
外伸支架 676, 681
外把手 266
外底 318
外果皮 74, 75, 76
外前鋒 528
外界線 540
外軌 182
外唇 101
外套 321
外套膜線 101
外套竇 101
外核 47
外格 592
外氣層 47
外側線 577
外側踝 121
外捲烟葉 344
外斜肌 118, 119
外盒 492
外票袋 293
外袋 347, 350
外趾 95
外部燃料箱 457
外野 525
外陰 117
外堡 177
外殼 78, 203, 206, 240,
　　241, 242, 243, 285, 337,
　　339, 384, 387, 406, 442, 611
外殼盒 613

外鼻 133
外緣 93, 551
外齒鎖緊墊圈 264
外壁 647
外牆 176, 177
外環 488
外螺紋接頭 274
外爐床 200
外鰓 105
失物待領處 720
奶油杯 223
奶油凍 157
奶油蛋白夾心蛋糕 156
奶油圓球蛋糕 156
奶油鬆餅 157
奶罩 313
孕婦裝 302
尼斯耳氏體 135
尼龍緊身褲襪 315
巨蛇座 40, 41
巨爵座 41
巨蟹座 40
巨蟹座（6月22日） 712
左中衛 531
左內鋒 528, 529, 532
左內邊鋒 528, 529
左心室 124
左手握把 700
左支氣管 126
左右對開 710
左外前鋒 529
左外野 525
左外野手 525
左肺 124, 126
左前衛 528, 532
左前鋒 535
左後衛 532, 535, 539
左側 709
左側上部 709
左側中部 709
左側基部 709
左移 362, 363
左舷搶風行駛 553
左殼瓣 101
左發球回彈觸地區 540
左發球觸地區 537
左腎 128
左衛 528, 529, 533
左輪手槍 703
左翼 531, 532, 533

左翼衛 528, 529
左轉 717
左邊鋒 528, 529, 539
市內住宅 183
布里軟乾酪 155
布帶 219, 502
布景格架 180
布景滑槽 180
布雷斯青黴乾酪 154
平凡細胞 137
平叉 411
平方根 723
平凹透鏡 625
平台 197, 247, 279
平交道閘口 423
平印示意圖 518
平底雪橇 564
平房 183
平放晾乾 722
平板 197
平板太陽能收集器 670
平板車 420, 685
平版印刷 517
平版印刷機 517
平肩領 309
平流層 47
平背刷 338
平面位置指示屏幕 624
平面圖 174, 188
平面圖上相應符號 198
平面鎚尖 588
平面鏡 622
平紋針法 504
平紋織法 511
平硐 636, 637
平移波 51
平頂 190
平頂海山 50
平頂硬草帽 314
平頂欄柵 192
平結 601
平視圖 116
平繡 507
平路機 680
平墊圈 264
平衡木 574
平衡重 181, 417, 422, 423,
　　610, 622, 681, 683
平衡重導軌 181
平衡控制鈕 379

平衡輪離合旋鈕 499
平衡器 378, 698
平衡臂 683
平衡臂配重 683
平衡纜 181
平頭 264, 331
平頭螺絲起子 258
平壓板 514
平褶 217
平穩腳 242
平邊 538
平鏡 42
幼蟲 107
打孔器 462
打孔機 386
打水 547
打火輪 344
打火機 344
打火鐮 696
打火鐮彈簧 696
打印機 469, 472
打印頭 471
打字機 466, 467
打蛋器 230
打緯支柱 508
打褶領 309
打褶領口 309
打褶褲 315
本位號 476
本堂 174
本影 37, 38
本線路線圖 428
本壘板 525
末十二個號碼（25至36）
　　594, 596
末梢分枝 135
末梢神經系統 129
末絲 130
末節指骨 121, 137
末節趾骨 120
末端 328
末端刃形支承 609
末端擋塊 218, 424
正中神經 129
正方 711
正方形閃光燈 372
正羽 96
正負 723
正面 175, 304, 328
正區 670

正常姿態 394
正常姿態衛星 394
正視圖 482
正極 273
正極板 406
正極板組 406
正極接頭 406
正電荷 723
正像透鏡 621
正線軌道 425
正縱帶 710
正轉/倒片鈕 383
正觸點 670
正彎月透鏡 625
正體字姓名 359, 360, 361
正廳前座 179
正廳後座 179
母 138, 139
母音 358
民族樂器 487, 488, 489
永久牧場 161
永久磁鐵 387
玄武岩層 48
玉夫座 41
玉蜀黍 85
玉蜀黍粒 85
瓦 171, 195
瓦朗賽乾酪 154
瓦檐飾 171
甘薯 84
生物學 723
生長線 101, 104
生產電能 667
生殖孔 104
用戶站 394
用完即扔的燃料筒 281
用完即棄刮鬍刀 337
用完即棄注射器 629
用油的工廠 650
甩竿 580
田徑運動 570, 571, 572
田間堆肥撒布機 164
甲上皮 137
甲床 137
甲周膜 137
甲弧影 136, 137
甲板索具 553
甲冑 690
甲根 137
甲基質 137

甲烷船（半塑料膜艙）
　645
甲烷船（全塑料膜艙）
　645
甲烷船（獨立球形艙）
　645
甲殼 109
甲殼類動物 103
甲鞋 690
甲體 137
白 593
白方 591, 592
白令海 49
白包體 86
白布邊 536, 542, 543
白羊座 40
白羊座（3月21日）712
白色主球 584
白色平衡調節 384
白色角質層 93
白卷心菜 82
白底灰藍波紋 710
白底黑斑 710
白格 591
白球 583
白帽 545
白葡萄酒杯 222
白旗 545, 578
白熾電燈 446
白熾燈 284
白臉 322
白蘭地酒杯 222
皮 74, 75, 76
皮下組織 136
皮手筒 349
皮扣襻 294
皮衣 689
皮夾 351
皮便鞋 689
皮革製品 350, 351
皮套 582, 589, 599
皮脂腺 136, 137
皮帶 261, 573, 672, 690
皮帶眼 567
皮帶鈕 349
皮帶輪 261, 405
皮帶輪安全罩 261
皮球 541
皮膚 105, 135, 136
皮膚表面 135, 136

皮質 128
皮襯條 318
目透鏡 621
目標 706
目標球 583
目鏡 372, 374, 619, 621,
　622, 623
目鏡放大器 370
目鏡架 623
矛 689
矢狀切面 116, 117
矢狀縫 122
石印油彩筆 517
石印蠟筆 517
石油 640, 641, 642, 643,
　644, 645, 646, 647, 648,
　649, 650
石油化工產品 649
石油化工業 649
石油圈閉層 640
石油與氣體分離器 643
石版 517, 518
石柱 54
石座 325
石料 193
石筍 54
石階 187
石塊磨成的手斧 689
石榴 80
石綿瓦 195
石膏板 194
石膏砌塊 193
石膏墊塊 519
石質荒漠 55
石器時代利器 689
石蠟 649
示溫熔錐 520
示廓燈 402
禾稈升運板 165
穴周草坡 585
立叉 411
立毛肌 136, 137
立式手推車 685
立式鋼琴 479
立式鋼琴擊弦機械裝置
　480
立軸風力渦輪機 672
立經織機 509
立領 308
立體照相機 369

六 畫

乒乓球 543
乒乓球員 543
乒乓球鞋 543
交叉支架 631
交叉四坡屋頂 191
交叉甬道 174
交叉背帶褲 316
交叉軌道 424
交叉路口行車先後標識
　715
交叉撩簾 217
交叉簾布層輪胎 407
交流發電機 405, 418
交流電線 378, 380
交通運輸 397
交通燈 178
交集 723
「交響樂」通訊衛星 393
交響樂團 493
伊朗文 355
休止符 475
休眠火山 53
休耕地 161
仰式 547
仰角調節旋鈕 621
仰泳手 547
仰泳出發 547
仰泳轉身標識 546
仰拱 429
光 670
光度表 372
光度調節 389
光度調節開關 285
光圈 368
光圈刻度 370, 372
光桿 218
光球 37
光斑 37
光測懸錘 614
光筆 469
光軸 43
光傳感器 372
光閘 620
光電池 371
光學瞄準鏡 614
光學儀器 619
光點曝光表 372

全內反射稜鏡 621
全休止符 475
全音符 475
全倒進球位 590
全麥粗麵包 146
全麥麵包 146
全景窗 421
全跨式拱橋 415
全蝕 37, 38
全裹式 598
全緣 70
共鳴管 482, 485
共鳴箱 478, 487
再蒸餾 648
再騰空 574
冰 58
冰刀 562
冰刀套 562
冰上溜石 544
冰川 56
冰川舌 56
冰斗 56
冰爪 589
冰爪帶 589
冰峽 56
冰淇淋勺 231
冰淇淋布丁 157
冰淇淋筒 236
冰球 533, 534
冰球員 534
冰球桿 534
冰球場 533
冰球鞋 534, 562
冰晶形態分類 57
冰塔 56
冰道 544
冰隙 56
冰箱 600
冰鞋 562
冰糕 157
冰鎬 588, 589
列車 424
列車時間表 426
列車誤點告示板 426
匈牙利文 355
印台 462
印地文 355
印刷 518
印刷台 516, 517, 518
印刷台手柄 517

索 引

印度洋 49
印度無酵硬麵包 146
印紋 518
印痕控制器 466
印第安座 41
印第安帳篷 169
印第安棚屋 169
印第安麵包 146
印章戒指 325
印章架 462
印製電路 371
危險 715
危險，小心 713
危險彎路 714
吉他頸 494
吉他頭 494
同步閃光燈接線端 368
同步接線 372
同步電線 372, 373
同步器 624
同花 592
同花大順 592
同花順 592
同度 476
同極連接片 406
吊升機房 636, 638
吊車 558
吊車軌 683
吊扇 206
吊索 430, 675, 683
吊索卷筒 675
吊帶 555
吊桿 206, 416, 675
吊腳褲 310
吊貨桿 434
吊廂 181
吊廂導軌 181
吊椅 558
吊鈎 608, 640, 683
吊艇架 430
吊運車 417, 683
吊運車滑輪 683
吊盤 558
吊橋 177
吊燈 220
吊燈桿 220
吊環 447, 572
吊環栓 588
吊環搹 447
吊襪帶 313

吊鏈 675
吊籃 247
各大洲輪廓 49
各部分名稱 210, 213, 214
各種常見的眼鏡 329
各種常見的鞋 319, 320
向下掃帚形 446
向上掃帚形 446
向內跳水 549
向內灣方面 660
向前 548
向前跳水 549
向後 548
向後跳水 549
向海方面 660
向場透鏡 621
名次 569
名號牌 261, 615
名稱 57
合體式刺刀 693
吃水線 439
吃角子老虎 595
吃角子箱 595
后髮座 40
后翼 591
回水支管 203
回水幹管 203, 204
回收水 650
回位彈簧 407
回波 624
回架換行鍵 467
回流管 204
回音 476
回風巷道 637
回氣 205
回動彈簧 385
回球架 590
回球道 589
回廊 174
回聲 442
回聲測深儀 442
回臂尾槽 380
地下水流 58
地下水面 54
地下河流 54
地下河復現 54
地下油管 644
地下室 189
地下室窗戶 187
地下廊道 54

地下煤礦 637
地下鐵路 429
地下鐵路入口 178
地下鐵路列車 429
地下鐵路車站 428
地下鐵路路線圖 428, 429
地下鐵路運輸 428
地上油管 644
地上油管支座 644
地中海 49
地中海副熱帶 59
地平裝置 623
地平緯度粗動定位夾 623
地平鏡 443
地板 192, 196, 443, 540, 541
地板地毯吸塵嘴 244
地板刷 244
地板攔柵 192
地表冷鋒 61
地表徑流 58
地表暖鋒 61
地段圖 188
地界線 188
地面下 638
地面上 638
地面交通 721
地面狀況 63
地面磚 195
地基 192
地球 35, 36, 37, 38, 393
地球大氣層縱剖面 47
地球同步軌道 394
地球座標系 35
地球傳感器 393
地球構造 47
地理 47
地殼 47, 53
地殼剖面 48
地對地導彈 706
地對空導彈 706
地線 385, 659
地線/中性線母線 288
地線夾 281, 659
地線架 658
地線連接線 288
地震 53
地震波記錄 616
地攔柵 196
地點和日期 360

地檻 176
在此插入 362
多孔石膏板 194
多孔纖維板 194
多爪錨 447
多用途人字梯 278
多用途刀具 599
多用途電線鉗 287
多串式項鏈 326
多角形尖塔屋頂 191
多雲 61
多跨橋 414
多路設備 394
多路衛星通訊站 394
多隙罩 337
多種飾物 325
多層板 265
多層塑料板 194
多邊形登機台 452
字母 356, 357, 386
字母粉 145
字母數字鍵盤 470
字體指示 365
字體轉換鍵 470
存水彎 275
存水彎及排水管通條 276
守方 528, 529
守方右內邊鋒 528, 529
守方右邊鋒 528, 529
守方左內邊鋒 528, 529
守方左邊鋒 528, 529
守車 420
守門員 532, 533, 534, 539, 545
守門員桿 534
守門員護墊 534
守區 533
安全火柴 345
安全守則銅板 261
安全別針 501
安全固定裝置 559, 560
安全恆溫器 241
安全島 178
安全剪刀 343
安全帶 400, 560
安全眼鏡 329
安全帽 559, 564
安全殼 666
安全閥 232, 664
安全線 428

安全膜 662
安全擋桿 558
安全燈 375
安全鋼輪 429
安全欄杆 279
安法倫乾酪 154
安裝管道工具 276
安裝螺絲 611
安樂椅 210
尖角下頜片 292, 293
尖軌連接桿 423
尖音符號 357
尖峯 54
尖頂 191, 423
尖頂帽 322
尖頂飾 709
尖筆 367
尖塔 174
尖端 243, 264
帆 431, 551
帆布 579
帆布便鞋 319
帆布屏 596
帆布摺椅 211
帆式 432
帆底邊索 430
帆板 551
帆的種類 432
帆段 552
帆桁 552
帆眼釦環 552, 553
帆船 552
帆頂 551
帆脚索 431
帆脚索導圈 553
年輪 71
成品貯存 648
成型膠合板 265
成績 569
扣件 639
扣背導線 576
扣釘文件夾 463
扣帶 349, 350
扣機 701
扣繫物 502
扣鏈齒輪組 412
扣襻 349, 351
托底板 702
托肩 200
托架 218, 219, 233, 684

托架槽 219
托座 215
托梁 196
托桿 377, 609
托葉 70
托飾 170
托盤 233
托盤天平 609
托樑楔塊 190
收片盤 383
收帆索 431
收舌音符號 357
收信人地址 359
收信人姓名、地址 360, 361
收帶捲軸 466
收報台 385
收報機 385
收發站 394
收發機 394
收費計算器 401
收聽按鈕 388
曲別針 461
曲柄 412, 440, 517
曲髮 330
有孔鞋頭 318
有爪重錘 505
有所遺漏 363
有拉鏈口袋 350
有肩螺栓 264
有柵門鐵路平交道 715
有柄刺刀 693
有柄刺刀各部分 693
有柄眼 103
有柄單片眼鏡 329
有柄磨刀石 231
有效部位（暗影部分）
　　577
有效載荷 456
有接地線插座 277
有桿錨 447
有舵雪橇 564
有頂垛後走道 177
有脚鈕 502
有蓋口袋 292, 293, 304
有蓋大湯碗 223
有蓋牛油碟 223
有蓋看台 569
有槽套管 271
有槽鉛條 521
有線打字電報機 666

有緩衝層子午線輪胎 407
有齒滾筒 164
有聲放映機 383
有褶貼袋 304, 307
有點白球 584
次十二個號碼（13至24）
　　594, 595
次叉 89
次生根 69
次列飛羽 96
死亡 723
死注 594, 595
死球線 531
氖燈泡測電燈 286
汗孔 136
汗衫 526
汗管 136
汗管壺腹 136
污水三通管 272
污水管 268
污水豎管 267
池底 545, 548
池塘 247
灰岩坑 54
灰岩溝 54
灰泥 194
灰塵刷 244
灰漿 193
灰膠紙柏板 194
百分率 723
百里香 143
百貨公司 178
百搭 592
百葉窗 175
百葉窗板 219
百慕達短褲 310
竹管筆 367
竹鱧 102
米粒組織 37
羊皮外套 292, 307
羊肉 151, 153
羊肚菌 73
羊棚 161
羊腿袖 306
羊膜 113
羊膜囊 113
羽毛冠 542
羽毛球 542
羽毛球鞋 542
羽毛綉 507

羽枝 96
羽狀半裂 70
羽絨衣 589
羽軸 96
羽管刷 338
羽管筆 367
老虎窗 187
耳 108, 114, 115
耳甲 132
耳石 99
耳羽 95
耳狀突 106
耳垂 132
耳屏 108, 132
耳屏間切跡 132
耳墊 378
耳廓 132
耳蝸 132
耳蝸神經 132
耳輪 132
耳輪尾 132
耳輪脚 132
耳機 378
耳機插座 379, 381, 392
肉汁碗連墊碟 223
肉質果：柑果 77
肉質果：漿果 74
肉穗 72
肉類保鮮室 239
肋甲 109
肋肉 147, 148, 150, 151
肋骨 92, 120
肋間神經 129
肌皮神經 129
肌肉 118, 119
肌肉塊 99
肌肉纖維 135
肌痕 101
自升式平台 642
自由式 547
自由泳手 547
自由降落 555
自由球線 539
自行修理用具 257
自位輪 206, 244, 631
自來水 669
自來水幹管 267, 413
自來水管 267
自卸載重車 682
自拍裝置 368

自動/手控光圈調節 384
自動安全閥 204
自動冷卻器 644
自動扶梯 182
自動步槍 699
自動或手控調焦鈕 384
自動拉索滑輪 558
自動油位計 647
自動門 454
自動洩氣口 204
自動停機裝置 206
自動捲線盤 244
自動淡變鈕 384
自動循環水泵 204
自動換燈器 446
自動答話指示燈 388
自動開關 277
自動駕駛儀 451
自動撿拾壓捆機 162
自動操縱系統電腦 436
自動斷路器 285
臼齒 90
臼齒剖面圖 123
舌 99, 127, 133, 134
舌正中溝 134
舌尖 134
舌乳頭 134
舌盲孔 134
舌扁桃體 134
舌界溝 134
舌背 134
舌根 134
舌神經 133
舌針 506
舌腭弓 134
舌鞘 109
舌體 134
色球 37
色溫鈕 384
血液循環 124, 125
血管 108, 123, 136, 137
血壓計 612
行 339
行人止步 716
行次顯示器 505
行李 347
行李小車 347
行李手車 720
行李手推車 454
行李架 435

行李託運 720
行李託運處 426
行李託運櫃台 454
行李寄存櫃 426
行李掛車 453
行李票 426
行李廂 397
行李廂板 398
行李提取處 720
行李艙 455
行李輸送帶 453
行車架 398
行車道 429
行車道橫斷面 413
行底指示線膠板 467
行星放映裝置 43
行星符號 36
行星際空間 47
行距改變鈕 467
行距調節桿 467
衣服 315
衣服內層 502
衣料 502
衣料紋理 502
衣被櫃 216
衣帽架 465
衣帽鈎 465
衣鈕槽口 243
衣領 291, 293, 295, 308
衣領款式 308
衣櫥 596
西 445, 593
西瓜 81
西洋雙陸棋 592
西班牙文 355
西裝上衣 307
西裝袖 306
西裝領 301, 308

七 畫

串列軸驅動機殼體 680
串聯結 601
位置記錄 577
伴奏鍵盤 481
伸手縫 301
伸爪 94

伸縮天線 392
伸縮走廊 452
伸縮桌 209
伸縮梯 278, 676
伸縮腳 374
伸縮傘 346
伸縮登機梯 705
伸縮電源線 244
伸縮箱 376
伸縮鏡筒 619, 623
低吹雪 60
低衩開襟領口 309
低音大號 484, 493
低音拾音器 494
低音音栓 489
低音控制鈕 379
低音喇叭 378
低音提琴 477, 491, 493
低音琴馬 479
低音管 483, 488, 490, 491, 493
低音鍵盤 489
低音譜號 475
低氣壓中心 62
低胸奶罩 313
低雲 52
低雲類型 62
低溫熨 722
低腰裝 302
低檻 574
低壓配電線 659
低壓渦輪機 664
低壓蒸汽管 661
低壓槽 62
低牆和竿 566
兌換亭 428
克里族雪鞋 563
免稅店 720
免稅商店 454
兵 591
兵以外的棋子 591
冷水截流閥 273
冷水管 272, 273
冷水豎管 267
冷空氣 669
冷卻水 664
冷卻或加熱盤管 204
冷卻空氣 458
冷卻風扇 377, 404, 405, 406

冷卻液泵 458
冷卻塔 648
冷卻劑 664, 668, 670
冷卻劑把熱量傳給蒸汽發生器 667
冷凍室 239
冷凍室門 239
冷凍劑管道 204
冷氣機 206
冷嘴 341
冷凝 58
冷凝桶 236
冷凝盤管 206, 239
冷凝器 204, 206, 661
冷藏車 420
冷藏室 189, 239
別針 501, 629
利用河、湖水冷凝用過的蒸汽 667
刪去 363
刨花膠合板 265
助手 579
助行工具 630
助行架 630
助行褶 304
助推火箭降落傘 457
助理計時員 545
助跑 574, 590
助跑道 570, 571
匣鉢 520
卵 97, 99, 105, 107
卵白 97
卵形 70
卵巢 99, 117
卵細胞 113
卵黃 97
卵黃膜 97, 113
卵黃繫帶 97
卵黃囊 113
卵圓孔 122
告示牌 427
告示標識 713
吹口 483, 484
吹口接頭 484
吹風機 340
吹草器 252
吹管 276, 484, 488
吹管頭 282
吻 105
吸力調節環 244

吸水軟管 677
吸氣 547
吸塵用具 244
吸塵器蓋 244
吸熱板 670
吸熱面 669
吸熱管 670
吸熱器 670
吸聲天花板 179
含水層 650
坑道 636
均布拉索 416
坐骨 121
坐骨神經 129
坐墊 631
夾 510, 561
夾子 221, 231, 294, 341
夾子耳環 325
夾心巧克力酥球 157
夾爪 260, 261
夾具 505
夾底 318
夾芯合板 265
夾相紙框 375, 376
夾套 260
夾套螺母 260
夾書芯板 514
夾紙書寫板 464
夾紙桿 467
夾針螺絲 500
夾鉗 258
夾管鉗 259
夾緊柄 236
夾鼻眼鏡 329
夾層 502
夾線片 500, 505
夾線盤 499, 500
夾髮針 343
夾頭 258, 260, 261, 639
夾頭鑰匙 261
尿布 315
尿殖孔 99
尿道 116, 117, 128
尿道口 116
尿道海綿體 116
尿道球腺 116
尾 103, 108, 109, 116, 514,
 581
尾上覆羽 95
尾水渠 655, 657

尾羽 95
尾形 449
尾足 100, 103
尾門 398
尾段 116
尾砂 650
尾桁 455
尾桅 430
尾骨 120
尾骨神經 129
尾桿 671
尾桿骨 105
尾鈕 477
尾椎 92
尾節 103
尾管 406
尾管延長部分 406
尾樓 430
尾燈 397, 402, 409, 411
尾翼組 448
尾鰭 98, 551
岔尖 422
岔尖鎖閉器 423
希伯來文 355
希臘文 355
希臘神廟 171
希臘神廟平面圖 171
床 214
床尾板 214
床面 574
床帷 214
床腳 214
床單 214
床墊 214
床墊面 214
床墊罩單 214
床鋪 438
床褥及輔助用具 598
床頭板 214
床頭燈 220
床邊燈 220
形成層 71
形狀 57
形態 91, 95, 98
快門 368
快門按鈕 368, 371
快門速度選擇鈕 368
快門線 374
快速正轉 382
快速正轉按鈕 388

快速正轉鈕 381
快慢機 699
戒指 325
抗反射膜 670
抗扭矩尾旋翼 455
技術指導 391
扶手 182, 188, 197, 210,
 400, 429, 631
扶手柱 210
扶手椅 210, 211
扶手驅動裝置 182
扶杖 630
扶梁 175
扶梁扶壁 174, 175
扶梁拱架 175
扶欄 182, 651
扭繩粉 145
把子 339, 340, 341, 346
把子插孔 339
把手 221, 235, 236, 237,
 238, 239, 244, 253, 383,
 384, 411, 478, 545, 564,
 572, 580, 582, 587, 595,
 599, 630
把手立管 411
把手門梃 198
把手樁 350
把手環 588
把頭 538
扳手 258
扳機 280, 383, 696, 697,
 699, 700, 701, 702, 703
扳機柄 702
扳機護弓 697, 702, 703
扯線桿 499
折反射環坑 446
折射望遠鏡 623
折焰板 201
折軸目鏡 623
折線形屋頂 191
投手 525
投手踏板 525
投技法 578
投射透鏡 620
投射透鏡極片 620
投球區 525
投球線 590
投硬幣口 595
投溜石隊 544
投幣孔 388

投擲區標識旗 570
投擲圈 570, 571
投擲器械 572
抓地齒 678
抓球手套 534
抓鉤 681
改正上下標符號 364
改正字體 364
改正標點 363, 364
改正錯誤 362, 363
改字母 362
改衣線 503
改為大寫 364
改為小寫 364
改為小體大寫 384
改為斜體 364
改為黑體 364
改為線體 364
改為羅馬體 364
改詞 362
改錯紙 461
改錯帶 466
改錯帶裝入桿 466
改錯液 461
攻方 528, 530
攻區 533
攻擊區 536
攻擊線 536
束口手提袋 349
束帶 347, 480
束緊帶 579
束髮帶 538
束頭帶 314
李子 75
杏 75
杏仁 78
杜比降噪鈕 381
杜鵑座 41
杖尖 561
杖桿 561
杆座 709
杠鈴 575
步足 103
步法控帶 568
步幅控帶 568
步幅控帶繫條 568
步調調校表 613
汞 284
沙 606
沙丘 51

沙池 570
沙拉叉 225
沙拉拌勺器 228
沙拉缽 223
沙拉盤 223
沙拉蔬菜晾乾籃 228
沙洲 51
沙島 51
沙海螂 102
沙漏 606
沙嘴 51
沙暴或塵暴 60
沙灘袋 348
沉音符號 357
沉澱池 648, 650
沉澱槽 406
沉澱櫃 645
沉積岩 48
沐浴裹巾 315
沖水扳手 269
沖水槓桿 268
沖洗唧筒 629
沖洗塔 242
沖擊式水輪機 657
汽車 397, 398, 399, 400
汽車出租 721
汽車甲板 435
汽車吊機 683
汽油 649
汽油引擎 405
汽油泵 401, 405
汽油計量表 401
汽油箱 409
汽油箱蓋 410
汽缸 404, 409
汽缸蓋 405, 409
汽缸殼體 409
汽缸體 405
汽笛 418, 436
牡蠣刀 227
牡蠣叉 225
男上衣 538
男女洗手間 719
男子器械 572
男用手提包 349
男性生殖器官 116
男洗手間 719
男裝 291, 292, 293, 294,
  295, 296, 297, 298
系統元件 378

系統功能示意 468
系統組合 469
肝 99, 124, 127
肝靜脈 124, 125
肝總動脈 125
肘 91, 108, 115
肘子 150, 153
肘甲 690
肘後肌 119
肘節螺栓 264
肘墊 534
肘靜脈 125
肛門 99, 102, 116, 117,
  125, 127
肛門括約肌 127
肛管 127
芒果 75
角口鑿 516
角形 325
角度標尺 263
角柱 192, 425
角面堡 176
角桿 89
角球區 532
角帽 419
角窗 398
角溝 89
角墊 579
角旗 531, 532
角閥 203
角撐 190
角樓塔 177
角膜 131
角質吻 109
角質層 136
角錐點 584
豆角 81
豆芽 85
豆莢 79
豆袋凳 212
貝殼粉 145
貝雷帽 314
赤經 35
赤道 35
赤緯 35
赤緯圈 622
赤緯軸 42
走位 569
走動偏心輪 675
走動腳座 675

走帶計數器 381, 382
走廊 174
足 95, 104, 108, 109
足球 532
足球場 532
車斗舉升缸筒 682
車外鏡 397
車行道 413
車尾踏板 677
車身 421
車身飾條 397
車門 397, 400
車門內側手柄 400
車門內鎖 400
車門後視鏡 403
車架 409, 681, 682, 684
車架下管 411
車架上管 411
車架大梁 403
車庫 433, 434
車站大廳 426
車站月台 427
車速表 399, 410
車頂 397
車頂支柱 397
車廂 425
車窗升降搖柄 400
車鈎 419
車道 188
車輛高度限制 716
車輛寬度限制 716
車輛總重限制 716
車輪 397, 407, 704
車輪粉 145
迂迴管 275
那不勒斯咖啡壺 234
里程計 399
防水褲 315
防火罩 699, 701
防守隊後方裁判 528
防曳力超荷鈕 580
防波牆 652
防空雷達 439
防雨套管 202
防雨罩 202
防風上衣 301
防風根 84
防風燈 600
防逆閥門 277, 282
防退頭 264

防脫門 588
防脫螺絲 588
防盜鎖 410
防溢開關 242
防滑粉 582
防滑裝置 380
防滑墊 278
防塵蓋 380
防滲隔離槽 652
防噴裝置 640
防墮安全裝置 181
防撞羊角 397
防撞板 682
防撞圈 244
防撞墊 574
防撞燈 448
防震把手 253
防擦胎邊 407
防擦擋條 402
防護手套 283
防護用具 283
防護屏 392
防護罩 262

八 畫

乳房 114
乳房矢狀切面 117
乳突 122
乳暈 117
乳腺 117
乳腺葉 117
乳酪刀 224
乳管 117
乳製品格 239
乳頭 114, 117
乳頭下毛細血管網 136
乳頭狀肌 124
事由 359, 360, 361
亞洲 49
亞美尼亞文 355
亞階段 637
依頓式套裝 317
依頓式短上衣 317
侍者用開瓶工具 229
供水 654
供水管 267, 268

供片軸 383
供油管 205
供氧壓力計 458
供帶捲軸 466
供帶盤銷 471
供暖 200, 201, 202, 203,
　204, 205
供暖設備 203
供暖調節鈕 399
供暖器 599
供電電纜 288
供墨水管 367
供應船 642
例子 713
來電指示燈 388
佩劍 577
佩劍手 577
佩劍與重劍警告線 576
兩用領 291
兩字母調換 363
兩行調換 363
兩門轎車 398
兩詞調換 363
兩腳架 697, 701
兩種電壓選擇開關 337,
　340
兩端有擋板的平板車 420
兩邊線間狹長地帶 537,
　542
其他 723
其他記號 476
其他種類 367
其他輔助系統 666
其他織法 511
刻度 608, 610, 611, 613
刻度弧 443
刻度紙托 64
刻度桿 608
刻度盤 610, 611, 612, 613,
　615, 625
刻針 515, 517
刷子 280, 515
刷毛 337, 338, 339, 341
刷毛箍 280
刷柄 339
刷鞋箱 320
刷頭 339
刺刀 693
刺菜薊 85
刺繡 507

到站時間表 426
到踝短襪 311
刮刀 515
刮土引擎 682
刮土板轉動機構 680
刮土機 682
刮斗勺 345
刮板 517
刮板支臂 680
刮板梁 518
刮板壓桿 517
刮鏟 229
刮鬍刀 337
制音器 480
制音器柄擋 480
制音器桿 480
制栓 266
制退彈簧 703
制動分泵缸 407
制動手 564
制動手柄 408, 411
制動鉤 705
制動裝置 559, 560
制動鼓 407
制動踏板 410
制動器 407
制動器管路 407
制動蹄片 407
制動鋼索 411
剁板 236
剁碎機 236
卷尺 613
卷心萵苣 82
卷軸 375
卷雲 52
卷層雲 52
卷盤 164
卷積雲 52
卸土推板 682
卸油泵 646
卸油管 646
卸載管 163
卸槽 162
卸穀螺旋 165
取景器 368, 383
叔伯 138
受話器 387
受精卵發育 113
受罰席 533
咖啡壺 599

咖啡店 719
咖啡匙 226
咖啡磨 234
咖啡籃 234
呼吸系統 126
呼吸器 676
呼氣 547
和弦 476
和服袖 306
和諧客機 47
和聲弦 487
和麵鉤 235
周緣接合 653
固有資料處理程序 468
固定刀片 513
固定支柱 611
固定平台 642
固定百葉窗 199
固定夾 218
固定拱 415
固定架 43
固定面蓋 266
固定旋鈕 372
固定桿 596
固定麥克風 384
固定堰 660
固定窗簾 217
固定鉗牙 258
固定鉗頭 259
固定滾球盤 594
固定箍 64
固定蓋油庫 647
固定導葉 656, 657
固定橋 414, 415, 416
固定螺帽 506
固定擺錘 492
固體燃料助推火箭 457
垃圾箱 178
坦克 704
夜光雲 47
奇異果 80
奇數羽狀 70
妻 138
姑丈 138
姑母 138
姓名牌 347
姊妹 138
定子 655, 656
定子葉片 450
定日鏡 668

定日鏡斜坡 668
定位卡 278
定位釦 480
定位標識 494
定位器 663
定序控制 495
定度裝置 513
定音鼓 486, 493
定時供電插座 238
定時信管 696
定時器 237, 238
定時器啟動鈕 382
定期客船 433
定距標識 452
定影液盆 375
尚蒂伊式地板 196
屈光環坑 446
屈體 548
岡下肌 119
岸 51
岩生植物圃 247
岩石 653
岩石圈 47
岩石樣品袋 458
岩床 53
岩流圈 47
岩盆 56
岩脈 53
岩階 56
岩蓋 53
岩漿 53
岩漿房 53
岬角 51
岳父 139
岳父母 139
並集 723
店鋪 173
底 635, 636
底支架軸 412
底木 192
底火 702
底片夾 376
底板 64, 243, 263, 376,
　380, 482, 560, 562, 614,
　625, 685
底巷道 637
底架 347
底面 327, 556
底座 200, 235, 260, 261,
　340, 380, 392, 609, 614,

615, 619
底座板 192
底栓 696
底紙板 345
底側梁 425
底帶 295
底部 586
底部托梁 192
底視圖 122
底層 188, 189
底盤座 64
底稿助理 391
底緣 551
底線 537, 543, 556
底礦 56
底環 657
延伸桿 244
延長記號 476
延音踏板 479
延髓 130
弦 691
弦枕 477, 494, 691
弦栓板 479
弦規 494
弦鈕 477
弦鈕槽 477
弦樂器 477, 478
弦線 540
弧口 691
弧形部分 175
弧面鉗牙 259
弧管支承架 284
弩 691
弩牙 691
往月台入口 426
往復式割刀機 162
或 713
房子 188
房屋 187
房屋外觀 187
房間 596
所有格或縮畧符號 356, 363
承枕 224, 227
拉手 209
拉火繩 698
拉片 502
拉把 214, 377, 554
拉把架 347
拉索 278, 558, 573, 596,

675
拉索卷筒 675
拉索釦帶 597
拉索錨墩 416
拉帶 347
拉桿 422, 554
拉鉛條夾頭 521
拉電線鈎 287
拉綜梁 508
拉維紀草 143
拉線 672
拉頭 502
拉臂索 683
拉簧 398
拉繩 218
拉繩鎖夾 219
拉鏟挖土機 675
拉鏟挖掘機 650
拉鏈 315, 316, 317, 342, 346, 347, 348, 502, 597, 675
拉鏈位置 503
拉鏈門簾 596
拌和桿 235
拌和桿彈出鈕 235
拌柵 236
抹刷 515
招牌 178
披水板 202
披肩 300
披肩大衣 300
披肩領 308
披風大衣 292
披針形 70
披裂形瞳孔 109
披頭 331
拔釘爪 257
拔釘鉗 461
拔瓶塞鑽 229
拔塞鑽 599
拋光棒 515
拋物柱面反射器 670
拋物面反射罩 373
拋物面反射器 624
拋物面天線 394
拋物面鏡 668
拋物球面反射器 670
拋物線狀砂丘 55
抽水馬桶 268, 269
抽吸器 277
抽油桿 641

抽風扇 375
抽氣扇 418
抽氣管 284
抽索 349
抽屜 209, 216, 464
抽帶兜帽 317
抽緊帶 321
拐廂花針法 504
拇指 299
拇指弦 487
拇指弦鈕 487
拇指套 526
拇指控音栓 481
拇指鈎 483, 484
拍子記號 476
拍片計數器 368
拍立得照相機 371
拍身 543
拍肩 538
拍柄 538, 540, 543
拍面 543
拍框 538, 540
拍框墊 541
拍紙簿 464
拍線 538
拍頸 538
拍頭 538
抵肩 295, 305
抵趾板 571
抱膝 548
拖曳車 401
拖拉機 162
拖架脫扣器 403
拖船 645
拖線盤 576
拖繩 554
拖纜拱架 437
拆信刀 461
拆電線器 287
放大定時器 375
放大透鏡 376
放大機 375, 376
放大鏡 340
放水閥 204, 273

放油孔塞 405
放空燃燒裝置 643, 648
放映室 43
放映廊 43
放映銀幕 377
放映機變焦鏡頭 383
放映燈 377
放射冠 113
放氣旋鈕 612
放氣窗 206, 550
放洩彎管 267, 270
放洩彎管接頭 270
放鬆桿 259
放鬆踏板 508
放礦溜井 637
易夾義大利麵 144
明梁 197
明斯特半軟乾酪 155
明溝 413
明線 294, 316
昇華 58
服務台 718
服務站 401, 721
服裝 291, 301
服裝和用具 565
枕巾 214
枕木 422
枕肌 119
枕骨 121, 122
枕骨大孔 122
枕骨髁 122
枕結花邊 506
枕墊 214
枕頭 214
枕頭套 214
東 445, 593
東方釘線綉 507
東西軸 43
果心 76
果汁機 236
果皮 77, 78
果皮絲刀 227
果托 74
果肉 74, 75, 76, 77
果核 74, 75, 76, 77
果柰 81
果園 161
枇杷 76
枝叉 89
枝角輪 89

枝狀冰晶 57
枝條 71, 85
枝葉狀飾 210
杯 236, 599
杯架 269
板台 513
板尖 554, 559, 561
板尾 551, 559, 561
板底 554, 559
板架排燈 221
板柵 565
板首 551
板條 180, 219, 507
板頭 559, 561
松子 78
松乳菇 73
松果體 130
析象攝影機 65
杵 228
杼 508
武仙座 40
武器 689
毒牙 109
毒液溝 109
毒液管 109
毒蛇頭部 109
毒腺 109
毒蕈 73
毒蠅傘 73
注入蒸汽 650
注水口 243
注油嘴 401
注射孔蓋 458
注射筒 629
注射筒頭 629
注射器 629
注液口塞子 443
注意交通燈號 715
注意落石 714
泳手 546
泳式 547
泳足 103
泳道 546
泳道計時員 546
泳道號碼 546
泌尿系統 128
泥水擋邊 596
泥漿坑 640
泥漿泵 640
泥鏟 249

沼澤 650
波江座 41
波谷 51
波底 51
波長 51
波段選擇按鈕 379
波音 476
波峯 51
波淚 51
波高 51
波爾多酒杯 222
波蘭文 355
法文 355
法文引號 357
法式 362, 363, 364
法式切割 147, 149, 150, 151, 327
法式午睡沙發 211
法式扭捲 331
法式校對舉例 366
法式棋 591
法式結子綉 507
法式躺椅 211
法國長麵包 146
法國乾酪 154, 155
法國號 484, 490, 491, 493
法國麵包 146
法語 358
法語音標 356
法蘭盤螺栓 268
油布篷貨車 420
油石 515
油位示警燈 399
油位計浮子 647
油門踏板 400
油門轉把 410
油炸鍋 233
油砂 650
油砂礦廠 650
油泵 205
油泵皮帶 404
油泵座階 401
油泵軟管 401
油泵裝置 641
油庫 644, 648
油桃 75
油氣泡沫 641
油脂 649
油脂孔 237
油壺 639

油漆噴槍 280
油漆盤 280
油漆罐 280
油管 644, 650
油價 401
油嘴 641
油箱門 397
油輪 645
油墨 367, 516
油壓示警燈 410
油爐 205
油罐 646
油罐汽車 646
油罐掛車 646
沿口加強鋼絲 407
泡沫 51
泡沫絕緣材料 195
泡沫塑料墊 598
泡沫塑料褲 598
泡沫滅火龍頭 645
泡沫橡膠絕緣材料 195
泡茶器 231
泛光燈 390
炊具 232, 233, 599
爬蟲類動物 109
爭球 531
爭球前衞 531
爭球區 528
爭球圈 533
爭球線 528, 529
爭球點 533
版面磨盤 517
版權 723
牧夫座 40
物透鏡 620, 621, 623
物鏡 372, 619, 620
物鏡極片 620
物鏡轉換頭 619
玫瑰切磨 327
盲井 636
盲腸 127
直升飛機 455
直升飛機降落台 643
直升飛機庫 439
直升機運輸 721
直立式排除積水泵 277
直立框架 509
直耳 502
直行 717
直行或右轉 717

直尾翼 448, 455
直尾翼頂 705
直角杖 630
直角取景器 370
直走 591
直柱 570, 571
直柱路燈 221
直展雲 52
直根 71
直紋 502, 503
直接讀數雨量計 64
直梯 278
直條紋浮標 444
直握 543
直筒裙 303
直稜紋襪口 297
直腸 116, 127, 128
直腸子宮陷凹 117
直路 569
直鉗牙 259
直髮 330
直褶裙 303
直餾汽油處理 648
直體 548
空子 593
空中加油插頭 705
空中運動 555
空心結構合板 265
空格撤桿 467, 470
空氣冷凝器 668
空氣通道 639
空氣過濾網 205
空氣過濾器 253
空氣管 205
空氣層 42
空氣調節設備 206
空氣調節機 421
空氣鎗 437
空氣濾清器 405, 675, 704
空氣濾器 678
空盒氣壓表 612
空速管 705
空集 723
空腸 127
空運 721
空對空導彈 705, 706
穹半肋 175
穹頂 175
肺 126
肺前叢 126

肺動脈 124, 125, 126
肺靜脈 124, 125
肥皂碟 269
肥厚胸肉 149
肥厚腹肉 152
肥腿肉 149
肢關節 91
肱三頭肌 119
肱肌 118
肱神經叢 129
肱骨 120
肱骨內上髁 121
肱骨外上髁 121
肱骨頭 121
肱動脈 125
肱橈肌 118, 119
股 91, 601
股二頭肌 119
股內側肌 118
股內側膜 108
股外側肌 118, 119
股肉 149
股直肌 118
股後皮神經 129
股神經 129
股骨 92, 105, 108, 120
股骨頸 121
股骨頭 121
股側皮神經 129
股動脈 125
股節 100, 106
股墊 530
股靜脈 125
股薄肌 119
肩 91, 114, 150, 264, 581
肩下肉 149
肩下肋肉 149
肩甲 690
肩羽 96
肩肉 147, 149, 150, 151,
　153
肩肋肉 152
肩披 291
肩後肋肉 148, 152
肩架 700
肩胛 115
肩胛上神經 129
肩胛肉 148
肩胛骨 92, 120
肩胛棘 121

肩峯 121
肩帶 313, 349
肩帶襯裙 312
肩部按鈕 316
肩部瘦肉 149
肩章袖 306
肩飾 321
肩飾帶 291
肩墊 530, 534, 700
肩膀肉 147, 148
肩頸 148
肯門貝鬆軟乾酪 155
臥車 421
臥具 214
臥室 189, 445
臥軸風力渦輪機 672
臥經織機 508
臥鋪間 421
芝士蛋糕盤 230
芝麻麵包 146
芭蕾舞裙 321
芭蕾舞裝 321
芭蕾舞鞋 321
芽 83
芹菜 85
花 69
花子 593
花式 592
花式滑水拉把 554
花式滑水板 554
花式溜冰鞋 562
花托 72
花序類型 72
花的構造 72
花柱 72, 74, 75, 76, 79
花格窗 175
花粉收集器 106
花粉刷 106
花粉室 107
花粉筐 106
花崗岩層 48
花絲 72
花莖 81
花鈕 308
花園 188, 247
花椰菜 81
花藥 72
花飾 210
花劍 577
花劍手 577

花劍警告線 576
花樣 506
花樣辨讀器 505
花壇 247
花壇邊緣 247
花蕾 69
花叢 247
花瓣 72
花邊內衣 312
花邊枕套 214
花邊筒子 506
芬蘭文 355
芥子 79
芯柱 284, 521
芯柱壓扁部分 284
芯軸 266
芯軸孔 266
芯閥桿 271
初生根 69
初列中覆羽 96
初列飛羽 96
初列覆羽 96
初級傳熱系統 666
返回鍵 470
近杆上角 709
近端籽骨 92
近端趾骨 94
金牛座 40
金牛座（4月20日） 712
金字塔帳篷 597
金色 710
金星 36
金橘 77
金屬 710
金屬水管 288
金屬片 328, 581
金屬包頭 346
金屬外殼 64
金屬衣 576
金屬防火幕 180
金屬版 518
金屬框 347
金屬框架 445
金屬骨架 479
金屬接觸柵 670
金屬嵌片 328
金屬棒 485
金屬絲 313
金屬墊圈 270
金屬槍頭 572

金屬箍 224, 486
長內收肌 118
長方 711
長方形 598
長水靴 582
長矛 689
長矛靠座 690
長尾 711
長沙發 211
長角果剖面 79
長度 549
長度調節環 630
長柄勺 695
長柄修枝剪 249
長柄眼鏡 329
長柄傘 346
長柄煮鍋 232
長柄劍 692
長音符號 357
長套筒 299
長桿 572
長桿彈 695
長條形燈 390
長條腰肉 148, 152
長笛 483, 490, 493
長統襪 311, 576
長蛇座 40, 41
長椅 212
長短板條錯縫地板 196
長短針 507
長短齒梳 338
長號 484, 491, 493
長罩衣 302
長罩衫 305
長葉萵苣 82
長凳 428
長劃 386
長嘴鉗 287
長燈籠袖 306
長鋸齒尾 711
長螺旋冰錐 588
長褲 297, 561
長襪 297
長襯褲 297
門 187, 198, 215, 241, 540
門下導夾 419
門口 175
門心板 198, 215
門式剛架 415
門把 397
門把手 198, 266

門板 198, 429
門柱 175
門架 239
門閂 238, 242
門框上鑲邊 198
門側處 175
門廊 171, 174
門鉤銷 237
門開閉設備 181
門開關 241
門間處 175
門搭釦 419
門搭釦鎖 419
門楣 175
門腳護板 239
門齒 90
門靜脈 124, 125
門檻 187, 198
門鎖 397
門襟 294, 297
門廳 173, 187, 189
門廳滑門 188
阿拉伯文 355
阿拉斯加雪鞋 563
阿倫貝格式地板 196
阿斯匹林 629
阿斯科特式領帶 295
阻尼器 610
阻滯磁鐵 615
附加設備 471
附加裝置 412
附件架 623
附件袋 587
附件註明 359, 360
附筆 359, 360, 361
附廢物清除器的洗滌盆 270
附屬小教堂 174
雨 57
雨水溝 413
雨水槽 397
雨衣 291
雨刮開關 400
雨刮臂 398
雨淞 57
雨帽 314
雨量 63
雨量計 63
「雨雲」三號氣象衛星 65
雨層雲 52

雨篷 597
青卷心菜 82
青花椰菜 81
青貯塔 161
青飼料收割機 163
青豌豆 85
非生產層 635
非洲 49
非洲戰士 689
非滿載調整旋鈕 615

九畫

亭部小面 327
亮度調節鈕 392
亮星放映機 43
信件秤 461
信號裝置 423
信號橋 424
信號燈襯板 423
信管 696
信標天線 65
侵入岩 48
便池注水管 268
便紙架 269
便帽 298, 314
便鞋 319, 320, 689
保安檢查 454
保留原樣 363
保溫板 234
保溫瓶 600
保溫潛水服 550
保險卡子 699
保險栓 697, 699
保險絲 285, 659
保險絲架 659
保險絲盒 205
保險絲鉗 286
保險絲斷路器 659
保險槓 397, 403
保險銷 696
保齡球 590
保齡球運動員 590
保齡球鞋 590
保護外殼 663
保護區 578

保護罩 221
保護層 265
保護繼電器 205
俄文 355
俄國裸麥粗麵包 146
俄羅斯木屋 169
冒號 357, 364, 386
冠叉 89
冠羽夾 690
冠岩 650
冠狀縫 122
冠柱狀 57
冠部小面 327
剃刀 337
剃鬚杯 337
削皮刀 227
削皮刨 227
削鉛筆刀 462
削線皮鉗 287
削壁 176, 177
前二十四個號碼（1至 24）594
前上桅下帆 431
前上桅上帆 431
前上頜骨 98
前叉 411
前中桅下帆 431
前中桅上帆 431
前切跡 132
前月面 101
前水翼 436
前水翼控制傳動裝置 436
前列腺 116
前帆升降索 552
前帆腳索 552
前臼齒 90
前把 257
前肋肉 152
前肘子 150
前足 100, 106
前制動桿 410
前制動器 411
前卸裝載機 679
前肢 105
前段圈帶 694
前背肉 149
前背鰭 98
前面十字路口 715
前面右轉 717
前面迴旋處 715

前面按鈕 316
前音管 481
前庭 132
前庭神經 132
前桅 430
前桅支索 552
前桅帆 431
前桅頂帆 431
前翅 100, 106
前胸 100
前得分線 544
前排中 536
前排右 536
前排左 536
前排氣管 406
前梁 449
前腳套 554
前舷側風 553
前袋 584
前連合 130
前部 147, 148, 151
前場 537, 541
前廊 174
前插袋 310
前握把 700
前握柄 580
前發球線 542
前視 114, 117
前視圖 118, 120, 122, 397
前軸 680
前軸承 450
前進波 51
前滑橇 564
前置擴音機連擴音機 378
前端 101
前端制動器 562
前管 411
前腿 91, 94, 213
前腿肉 149, 150
前腿脛肉 147
前緣 448, 556, 557
前緣地帶 176
前緣撐管 557
前膛砲 694, 695
前輪 680
前輪擋泥板 409
前衛 529
前鞍橋 567
前壁 402
前橫條 563

前燈 397, 398, 403, 408, 427
前燈近光開關 410
前燈殼體 398
前燈罩圈 398
前燈變光開關 400
前頭釘 589
前攔脚蹬 409
前牆 540, 541
前臂 115
前臂正中靜脈 125
前臂甲 690
前臂枴杖 630
前臂肉 149
前臂端肉 149
前覆片 345
前襟 293, 295, 317
前襟絹印圖案 315
前護木 702
前變速器 411, 412
勃艮第酒杯 222
南 445, 593
南十字座 41
南三角座 41
南天球星座圖 41
南天極 35
南半球 35
南瓜 81
南回歸線 35
南美洲 49
南美番荔枝 80
南海 49
南昆座 41
南魚座 41
南極 35
南極洲 49
南極座 41
南極海 49
南極圈 35
厚麻布帶 507
厚壁管 640
咬肌 118
咬索夾釦 551, 553
咬嘴 345, 550
咽 126, 127
咽峽 134
咽腭弓 134
咽鼓管 132, 133
哈勃分類法 39
垂耳領 308
垂直切向旋鈕 614

垂直地震儀 616
垂直尾翼 556
垂直制動把 614
垂直拉窗 199
垂直度盤照明鏡 614
垂直搖窗 199
垂釣 580, 581, 582
垂飾項鏈 326
垂簾 217
垂體 130
城市房屋 183
城堡 177, 591
埭後走道 177
姿勢監察員 546
姨 138
姨丈 138
娃娃裝睡衣 311
姪 138
威爾斯文 355
室女座 40, 41
室女座（8月23日）712
室內恆溫器 611
室內便帽 314
室內排水管 272
室內遊戲 591
室外冷凝裝置 204
室外灑水龍頭 267
室溫調節牆 669
客車 421
客車車廂 429
客車車廂內部 429
客套式結語 359, 361
客艙 435
封底 512
封面 512, 514
封面皮革 514
封閉式前燈固定圈 398
封墊壓緊環 271
屋內的房間 189
屋形帳篷 597
屋基 192
屋頂泛水 267
屋頂通氣孔 187
屋頂通氣管 275
屋頂結構 190
屋頂類型 190, 191
幽門 127
幽門盲囊 99
度盤式顯示器 442
建築材料 193, 194, 195

建築物 161, 169, 651
建築風格 170
後二十四個號碼（13至
　36）594
後水翼 436
後水翼控制傳動裝置 436
後半規管 132
後台 180
後尖護帽 562
後肘子 150
後足 100, 106, 108
後身 293
後身中衩 293
後身側衩 293
後制動器 411
後胺 105
後胺骨 105
後保險槓 408
後背鰭 98
後座 400
後座攔脚蹬 409
後桅 430
後桅帆 431
後翅 100, 106
後胸 100
後側腿肉 149
後區 536
後得分線 544
後掠翼 449
後排中 536
後排右 536
後排左 536
後脚套 554
後舷風行駛 553
後袋 294, 584
後趾 95, 97
後連合 130
後部 148
後場 537, 541
後握柄 580
後減震器 409
後發球線（雙打）542
後窗 397
後窗框 397
後視 115
後視圖 119, 121, 397
後視鏡 399, 409, 704
後傾頭 235
後滑橇 564
後經梁 508

後腰 115
後腰帶 300
後跟 318
後跟加固革 318
後跟襯 318
後端 101
後腿 91, 147, 150, 151, 213
後腿脛肉 147, 149
後腿膝關節 91
後撐 235, 243
後緣 448, 556, 557
後緣襟翼 448
後腔 702
後衛 528, 529, 531
後鞍橋 567
後橫條 563
後頸 95
後檔 480
後牆 540, 541
後穩定鰭板 433
後變速器 411
後廳堂 171
急救藥箱 629
恆星放映透鏡 43
恆星放映聚光鏡 43
恆星儀 43
恆等 723
恆淫器 206
恆溫控制器 239
恆溫器 204, 205, 206
扁平梭 509
扁平部 258
扁平部分 504
挖凹部分 518
按拇指處 243
按釦 299, 348, 351
按釦內縫 316
按釦繫環 553
按釦邊 315
按鈕 346, 367, 377, 388,
　471, 484, 489
按鈕板 242
按鈕開關 235
按鈕電話 388
持桿手套 534
指孔環 501
指令天線 393
指令傳輪 706
指北箭頭 625
指甲 137

指甲刷 342
指甲剔子 342
指甲剪 342
指甲塗白筆 343
指甲鉗 342, 343
指甲銼 342, 343
指示 713
指示標識 717
指示燈 238, 242, 341, 471, 520
指穴 590
指板 477, 487, 494
指狀突 108
指套 526
指神經 129
指針 372, 608, 609, 610, 611, 612, 613
指針表面 605
指針幅度板 609
指側皮條 299
指圈 338
指捲波紋 330
指旋調節螺絲 258
指揮天線 65
指揮台 437, 438, 452, 493
指揮台左水平舵 438
指揮系統 706
指揮官座 704
指揮站 706
指揮塔 452
指揮艙 456
指墊 137
指管 488
指標桿 443
指標鏡 443
指擋 387
指總伸肌 119
指嬰 137
拱 175, 415
拱扶垛 174, 175
拱券 172
拱券類型 172
拱的種類 415
拱肩 172
拱門緣飾 175
拱背 172
拱座 172
拱基 653
拱頂 175
拱頂石 172

拱頂式棚架 247
拱廊 174, 175
拱楔塊 172
拱脚石 172
拱腹 172
拱端托 172
拱橋 415
拱橋的種類 415
拱壩 653
拱壩剖面圖 653
括號 357
拾音選擇鍵 494
拾球員 536, 537
挑檐 171, 187, 198
施肥機 164
春 35
春分 35
星小面 327
星系 39
星系核 39
星狀冰晶 57
星星粉 145
星座 712
星號 357
柿 80
染色質 86
柱 175, 374, 376, 415, 423, 455
柱上楣構 170
柱子腰線 170
柱升降曲柄 374
柱列三級台階 171
柱式暖氣管 203
柱身 170
柱狀 57
柱門活頁夾 463
柱座 478
柱基 170
柱基凹線 170
柱梁 175
柱頂過梁 170
柱廊 171, 173
柱塞 639, 641
柱脚圓盤線脚 170
柱槽 170
柱頭 72, 78, 170, 213
柱頭飾 197
柱鎖 374
柔光反射罩 373
柔性圍裙 435

柔音踏板 479
柔道 578
柔道服 578
架子 232, 238, 242, 520
架台 698
架耳部分 328
架空地線 658, 659
架空貨油管路 645
架空電線 427, 651
架脚 520
架頭 582
架臂 619
柵門 565, 566
柄 74, 76, 85, 328, 337, 346, 506, 691
柄尾 538, 691
柄脚 328
柄頭 328, 586
柄頭帽蓋 580
柄臂 580
柑 77
柑橘剖面 77
枴杖 630
枴杖桿 630
枴杖脚 630
枱尾 583
枱尾墊邊 583
枱虎鉗 259
枱曆 464
枱燈 220
枱鋸 262
枱頭 583
枱頭墊邊 583
枱邊 583, 584
柳薄荷 143
洋 38
洋底 50
洋葱 83
流星 47
流音 358
流態化煉焦廠 648
流蘇 217
流體靜力墊 42
洗衣 722
洗衣房 189
洗衣筐 240
洗衣機 240, 272
洗衣機調到正常程序，溫
　水洗滌 722
洗衣機調到正常程序，熱

水洗滌 722
洗衣機調到輕攪程序，微
　溫水洗滌 722
洗衣機調到輕攪程序，溫
　水洗滌 722
洗車間 701
洗脚車 453
洗碗碟機 242, 272
洗滌盆 270
洗滌盆底用扳手 276
洗滌盆濾水器 270
洗滌液噴灑器 242
洗滌腔 242
洗臉盆 269
洗禮裝 315
洩水道口 440
洩水管 665, 657
洩水管襯套 657
洩水槽口雕飾 170
洩水鍵 484
洩水彎管 270
洩壓管 662
活芯鉛筆 367
活頁紙書寫板 464
活動刀片 280
活動支臂枱燈 221
活動打字桌 465
活動百葉窗 219
活動扳手 258, 276
活動便橋 417
活動基台 698
活動掛燈 221
活動登機梯 453
活動鉗牙 258
活動鉗頭 259
活動聚光鏡 376
活動腿 209
活動蓋 277
活動橋 417
活動穩舵 552
活桿壁燈 220
活塞 405, 407, 484, 701
活塞咖啡壺 234
活塞鞘筒 484
活稱人結 601
活繫環 553
炸藥 696
牲畜車 420
玻璃片 619
玻璃壺 234

玻璃泡 372
玻璃柱頭 284
玻璃研磨機 521
玻璃紙護封香烟包 344
玻璃球 64, 606
玻璃陳列窗 216
玻璃窗 322
玻璃圓頂 443
玻璃管 284
玻璃蓋板 239
玻璃箱 609
玻璃器皿 222
玻璃牆 540
玻璃濾光片 443
玻璃纖維保護層 458
玻璃體 131
甚高頻天線 449
甚高頻道選擇鈕 392
界外區域 585
界牆 533
皇后 591, 592
盆骨 92
省畧號 357
相片印製機 375
相片沖洗盆 375
相片乾燥架 375
相紙盒 375
相等或大於 723
相等或小於 723
相導線 659
眉 131
眉叉 89
眉弓 122
眉刷和睫毛梳 333
眉斑 95
眉筆 333
眉鉗 342
看台與跑道 569
看遠 328
盾 689
盾紋面 101
盾牌 709
盾牌座 41
砂岩 650
砂質荒漠 55
研磨和擦碎用具 228
砌石護坡 652
砌面 176
泵 637, 668
泵站 644

秒表員 535
秒格標度 372
秒針 605
秋 35
秋分 35
秋西葫蘆 81
秋葵莢 81
突擊隊員配刀 692
穿孔 318
穿孔卡 472, 505
穿孔卡進給旋鈕 505
穿孔卡進給器 505
穿孔卡辨讀器 505
穿孔耳環 325
穿孔扁鈕 502
穿孔紙帶讀出器 386
穿孔管 277
穿筘鈎 510
穿線器 500, 501
竿尖引線環 580
竿尖節 580
竿托 580
竿柄節 580
竿柄節引線環 580
紅 594, 595
紅內圈 544
紅心 592
紅外線分光儀 65
紅外線發射機 373
紅色 710
紅色＝危險、不可或禁止
　713
紅色安全濾鏡 376
紅色尾燈 402
紅色標識區 578
紅海 49
紅球 583, 584
紅帽 545
紅電子束 392
紅旗 545, 578
紅醋栗 74
紅赭筆 517
紆子 509
缸筒 680, 681
美式 362, 363, 364
美式校對舉例 365
美式橄欖球 527, 528, 529,
　530
美洲山核桃 78
美國玉米麵包 146

美國白麵包 146
美國式 359
美國式並列爭球 528
美國赤德乾酪 154
美國乾酪磚 154
美國橄欖球場 527
美國麵包 146
耐火磚 205, 520
耐火磚後壁 200
耐火爐膛 205
胚 67, 79
胚胎 113
胚珠 72
胚盤 97
胃 99, 102, 124, 127
背 91, 95, 115, 514
背大動脈 99
背心 293, 296, 297, 317,
　321
背心及其他 307
背心袋 307
背心裙 302, 317
背包 322
背甲 109
背肉 147, 150
背板 477, 611
背負投 578
背面 304
背側肉 148
背帶 294, 346, 347, 550,
　557, 568, 587, 676, 699,
　700, 701
背帶夾 294
背帶旋環 699
背帶裝 302
背斜 640
背景 374
背景畫幕 390
背景幕 180
背視圖 101
背墊 568
背闊肌 119
背護板 238, 240, 241
背囊 561, 589
胡椒瓶 223
胡蘿蔔 84
胎兒 113
胎面花紋 407
胎盤 113
茅屋 169

茄子 81
英文 355
英仙座 40
英式 362, 363, 364
英式切割 152, 153
英式校對舉例 366
英式棋 591
英式撞球 584
英式撞球和彩球撞球 584
英式橄欖球 531
英國手杖 630
英國式 361
英國管 483, 493
英國麵包 146
英語 358
苞片 78
虹膜 131
表小皮 137
表皮 135, 136, 137
表姊弟/表兄妹 138
表姊妹 138
表面 265, 605
表面刻度盤 605
表/堂兄弟 138
表/堂兄妹；表/堂姊弟
　138
表袋 293
表殼 605
表意符號 713
計步器 613
計時 605, 606, 607
計時長 546
計時員 535, 539, 545, 576,
　579
計時器 375
計程車服務 721
計程車停車處 178
計量用具 229
計量杯 229
計量匙 229
計量蓋 235
計算表度盤 372
計算器 372
計算機 351
計數記憶鈕 382
計數器回零鈕 381, 382
訂書線 513
訂婚戒指 325
負區 670
負極板 406

負極板組 406
負極接頭 406
負電荷 723
負觸點 670
負彎月透鏡 625
軍刀 692
軍號 484
軍裝雨衣 291
軌 218
軌卡 422
軌底 422
軌頂 422
軌腰 422
軌道 427, 428
軌道飛行器 457
軌道數目標識 423
迫擊砲 697
重力壩 653
重力壩剖面圖 653
重升號 476
重水 664
重水輸入管 662
重牙齒狀 70
重汽油 649
重油 649
重型牽引車 403
重型連掛車 403
重型機械 675
重降號 476
重量 610
重劍 577
重劍手 577
重機關槍 701
重錘 607, 616
重錘驅動式鐘表機構 607
門片 351
門桿 266
限位角鈕 425
限深規 261
降水 58
降水區 62
降水種類 57
降主動脈 124
降結腸 127
降號 476
降落板 107
降落傘 555, 557
降壓活門 458
面 351, 521
面甲 690

面板 209, 685
面神經 132
面兜 589
面帶 295
面罩 322, 526, 530, 534,
　550
面層 265
音叉 492, 606
音叉手表 606
音口 482
音孔 477
音柱 478
音栓桿 482
音栓鈕 482
音符 475
音程 476
音量表 495
音量表開關 495
音量調節 378, 379, 383,
　388
音量調節鈕 494
音量調節踏板 481
音階 475
音管 481, 482, 483, 489
音管套 482
音樂 475
音調調節 383
音調調節鈕 494
音響工程師 389
音響合成器 495
音響控制台 389
音響控制室 389
音響控制員 389
音響開關 383
音響器材 378, 379, 380,
　381
音響輸入 382
音響輸出 382
風 55, 61, 553
風力作用 58
風力渦輪機 672
風力渦輪機發電 672
風三角 61
風口 397
風子 593
風矢 61
風矢桿 61
風向 62
風向和風速 62
風向指示帶 552

風向袋 711
風向標 63, 187
風向標旗 552
風羽 61
風車 671
風車軸 671
風門 639
風雨板 198, 199
風扇 204, 205, 206, 239,
　241, 429, 450, 638
風扇皮帶 405, 406
風扇電動機 206
風扇調速鈕 206
風扇殼 340
風級 61
風笛 488
風袋 488
風速 62, 63
風速以浬計 61
風速計 63
風雪大衣 292
風雪衣 561
風雪帽 314
風琴 481, 482
風琴的構造 482
風琴管 482
風筒 340
風道 482
風管 482
風箱 481, 489
風箱狀接縫 458
風箱帶釦 489
風箱褶 304
風選機 165
風簾 42
風鑿 639
飛三角帆 431
飛行速度表 556
飛行儀表 451, 557
飛馬座 40
飛魚座 41
飛輪 404, 405, 519
飛檐托塊 170
食用大黃 85
食用鹿花菌 73
食用蕈 73
食肉動物的領 90
食肉鳥 97
食肉齒 90
食物 143

食草動物的領 90
食道 127
食管 99, 102
食穀鳥 97
食蟲鳥 97
首十二個號碼（1至12）
　594
首柱 430
香芹 143
香烟 344
香草 143
香蕉 80
香薄荷 143
香檳杯 222

十　畫

乘 723
乘客車長通話器 429
乘客座位 436
倍低音管 493
俯仰控制噴管 65
倚音 476
倒車燈 162, 397
倒刺 581
倒相鈕 614
倒帶 382
倒帶按鈕 381,
　388
個人用品 337
候車室 426
候機大廳 454
修甲刀 342
修甲桿 342
修車間 701
修坯刀 519
修枝刀 252
修枝剪 249
修枝鐮 249
修指甲工具 342, 343
修面刷 337
修理服務 721
修路 715
修髮梳 338
修整工具 519
修樹鋸 252
修邊鉗 521

修邊機 252
修鬢刀 337
修籬剪 249
修籬鋸 252
冥王星 36
凍雨 60
凍糕 156
准許 713
准許吸烟 719
剔子 345
剔甲尖 343
剝皮刀 287
剝線皮刀 287
原子筆 367
原生質連絡絲 86
原位鍵 470
原油 649
原油管道 644
哥林多柱型 170
哥德式教堂 174, 175
唇 94
唇膏 332, 333
唇膏刷 333
唇線筆 333
唇瓣 102
夏 35
夏至 35
夏西葫蘆 81
套几 209
套帶式扳手 276
套接長齒 684
套殼 663
套筒 596, 701
套筒式吊桿 683
套筒式減震前叉 409
套結 601
套進式刺刀 693
套裝毛衣 307
套管 260, 575, 641
套管內層 641
套管凸緣 201
套管外層 641
套管軸 261
套管軸鎖桿 261
套管頭 641
套播 630
套樓住宅/兩戶住宅 183
套膜 104
套膜邊緣 102
套鞘 586

套頭毛衣 307, 561
套頭披肩 301
套頭衫 296
娛樂室 189, 433
孫 139
孫女 139
家用電器 235, 236, 237,
　238, 239, 240, 241, 242,
　243, 244
家具 209
家具墊套吸塵頭 244
家庭帳篷 596
家常服 311
家譜室 173
容易着火 713
容器 235
射精管 116
峭壁 38
峨螺 104
席紋圖案地板 196
庭院 188
庭院門 188
庭園 173
座 387
座台 482
座位 179, 400, 408
座板 519
座柱 220
座枱攪拌機 235
座部 564
座椅 556
座殼 340
座管 411
座標系 35
座盤 697
座艙罩 556, 705
座環 656, 657
弱音器 484
恥骨 114
恥骨聯合 116, 117
捕手 525, 526
捕手手套 526
捕手區 525
捕鯨船式帆 432
扇尾 671
扇形刻度盤 610
扇形拉索 416
扇形格子架 247
扇貝 102
扇面 472

扇葉 450
拳擊 579
拳擊手 579
拳擊手套 579
拳擊台 579
拳擊鞋 579
振動泥漿網 640
振盪器 495
捏奶油花紋的袋和嘴 230
挽帶 568
挪威文 355
旁路觸點 385
旅行鞋 561
旅行轎車 398
旅行轎車後部 398
旅館資料 721
時角坐標轉換器 42
時針 605, 607
時間記錄 616
時鐘 391, 399
書夾 462
書帖 512
書帖壓緊機 514
書房 189
書信格式 359, 360, 361
書枱燈 221
書桌墊 464
書脊 512, 514
書脊稜帶 512
書脊槽 512
書脊護舌 512
書報架 465
書寫工具 367
書櫃寫字枱 216
校正姿態 394
校對符號 362, 363, 364,
　365, 366
核 113
核仁 86
核反應器 438, 663, 667
核反應器甲板 438
核孔 86
核心 37
核果 75
核果剖面 75
核桃 78
核桃肉 78
核桃剖面 78
核能 661, 662, 663, 664,
　665, 666, 667

核能發電 667
核膜 86
核燃料循環 667
核糖體 86
核螺層 101
案頭文件盤 462
框 563, 670
框架 107, 443, 446, 508,
　574, 671, 695
框架肋骨 645
框梃 215
根 69, 83
根毛 69
根毛區 71
根尖孔 123
根冠 69
根菜 84
根端 69, 71
根頸 69
梳 509
梳子 338
梳妝台櫃 216
梳妝鏡 399
梳狀板 182
栗 78
桌子 209
桌面 543
桌面形切磨 327
桌脚 543
桌腿 209
栽培菌 73
柴托架 201
柴油 649
柴油引擎 404, 418, 436,
　679
柴油機排氣管 438
柴架 201
柴鉗 201
柴爐 201
格 350
格子 594
格柵 171, 655
格紋鑄鐵殼 696
格鬥運動 576
格陵蘭海 49
格網 206
桁 557
桁板 685
桁架 182, 190
桁架拱 415

桁梁 42
桁條 449, 685
桃 75
桅杆 551, 552
桅杆後支索 430
桅杆與索具 430
桅套 551
桅頂 551
桅頂杆 430
桅脚 551
桅樓 430
桅燈 434
桅頭 430
栓釘 215, 507
氣孔 100, 104, 280, 345,
　367, 639
氣門彈簧 404, 405
氣室 97, 555
氣缸 639
氣動制動器 672
氣動撐桿 639
氣密膜片 405
氣球快門線 374
氣瓶車 281
氣腔 267, 272
氣象站 63
氣象測量儀器 64
氣象學 62, 63
氣塞 482
氣溫 62, 63, 569
氣罩 280
氣閘 42, 437, 438
氣閘艙口 437
氣隙 669
氣團類型 62
氣墊船 435
氣管 126, 639
氣閥 280
氣壓 62, 63
氣壓刻度表 612
氣壓計 63, 556
氣壓傾向 62
氣壓調節螺絲 280
氣壓變化 62
氣舉探油 641
氣舉閥 641
氣鎖 661
氣體 284
氣體彗尾 39
氣體輸入管 458

氣體輸出管 458
氧化劑箱 706
氧炔銲 281
氧瓶 281
氧閥 282
泰蘭米乾酪 154
消化系統 127
消化腺 102
消防水帶 718
消防水管 676
消防車 676, 677
消防斧 676
消防站 648
消防鈎桿 677
消防龍頭接口 677
消毒紗布包 629
消毒酒精 629
消音按鈕 388
消閒工藝 499
消閒運動 580
消噪音按鈕 381
消聲器 253, 406, 435
浸沉式水翼 436
海 660
海上鑽井 642
海王星 36
海王衛一 36
海平面 48, 50
海平面氣壓 62
海岸 48
海底山 50
海底油井 644
海底油管 644
海底峽谷 50
海洋 58
海脊 50
海豚座 40
海溝 50
海綿刷 332
海綿罩 384
海蝕拱 51
海蝕柱 51
海蝕洞 51
海狸尾形 563
海龜 109
海關櫃枱 454
海灘 48, 51
涉禽 97
浮力圍肩 550
浮子 277, 581

浮子卡 277
浮石修版筆 517
浮肋 120
浮動刀頭 337
浮動指標 443
浮球 268
浮球自動供水閥 268
浮釣竿 580
浮釣捲線輪 580
浮渣 277
浮塢 441
浮蓋 647
浮蓋底板 647
浮蓋油庫 647
浮蓋頂板 647
浮墩 417
浮標 444
浮標桿 444
浮箱式塢門 441
浮橋 417
浮錨 447
浮體 444
浴巾架 269
浴室 189, 269
浴室秤 610
浴缸 269
浴袍 311
烟 60
烟心 344
烟斗 345
烟斗架 345
烟斗柄 345
烟斗剖面 345
烟斗通條 345
烟斗頭 345
烟灰 344
烟灰缸 344
烟囱 187, 200, 202, 434
烟囱管 201
烟囱翼板 433
烟囱體 187
烟身 344
烟具 344, 345
烟絲 344
烟絲穴 345
烟絲袋 345
烟絲罐 345
烟腔 200
烟罩 200
烟蒂 344

烟葉 344
烟道 200
烟道頂 187
烟道調節板 201
烟幕彈發射器 704
烟嘴 344
烟頭 344
烘小甜餅板 230
烘板 237
烘焙電熱元件 238
烘爐 238
烤肉溫度計 229
烤肉澆油管 231
烤炙電熱元件 238
烤烘傳感探針 238
烤槽 237
烤鍋 232
烤麵包機 237
烙餅 156
烙鐵 281, 521
烙鐵座 521
烙鐵嘴 521
烙鐵嘴除垢墊 521
烏克蘭文 355
烏飯樹漿果 74
烏鴉座 41
特別效果 391
特拉比斯乾酪 155
特殊服裝 321,
　322
特細麵 144
特寫透鏡 370
狹身短劍 692
狹路 714
狹縫 513
班究琴 487
班級戒指 325
班機時間表 454
琉璃苣 143
留話播放按鈕 388
留話錄音帶盒 388
眞皮 135, 136,
　137
眞皮乳頭 135,
　136
眞空吸塵機 244
眞空咖啡壺 234
眞空歧管 620
眞空盒 612
眞空蒸餾 649

矩形翼 449
矩陣 495
矩陣式打印機 471
砵酒杯 222
砧形塊座 639
破折號 357
砲口 694, 697
砲口凸環 694
砲口圈帶 694
砲口隆起 694
砲手瞄準器 704
砲耳 694
砲尾 694
砲尾球 694
砲尾環 694
砲身前段 694
砲車 694
砲刷 695
砲垛 176
砲門操縱桿裝置 698
砲眼 176
砲塔 704
砲管 694, 695, 697, 698, 700
砲彈 695, 700, 704
砲腔 695
祖父 139
祖母 139
神幻乾酪 154
神經 137
神經元 135
神經末梢 135
神經交通支 130
神經系統 129, 130
神經乳頭 131
神經核 135
神經鞘 135
神經鍵 135
神經纖維 135
神像 171
秘書桌 465
秘書椅 465
秤 608
秤台 610
秤重量 608, 609, 610
秤砣 608
秤桿 608, 610
秤盤 595, 608, 609

秤盤托座 609
秤盤掛鈎 609
窄凸銷 489
站外標識 428
站名 428
站名牌 427
笊籬 233
粉底液 332
粉紅色襪 321
粉紅球 584
粉蒸鍋 232
粉餅盒 332
粉撲 332
紡車式捲線輪 580
紗窗 596
紗窗簾 217
紗軸架 510
紗籠 303
紋章圖案 710
索 601
索皮 601
索拉橋 416
索芯 601
索眼 597
紙 518
紙夾 463
紙卷 386
紙板火柴 345
紙帶 385, 386
紙帶起動鈕 386
紙牌遊戲 592
紙幣夾層 351
紙樣 503
缺角下頜片 291, 301, 308
缺刻緣 70
翅 100
翅室 100
翅脈 100
耙 162, 248
耙土器 678, 680
耙齒 162, 678
耙齒尖 678
脂肪組織 117, 136
脂類滴粒 86
胰 127
胰島素注射器 629
脅 95
胭脂 332
胭脂刷 332, 333
胸 91, 95, 100, 106, 114

胸大肌 118
胸甲 689, 690
胸肉 147, 148, 150, 151, 152, 153
胸肋肉 150, 152, 153
胸足 100
胸前口袋 292, 295, 305
胸針 325
胸骨 92, 120
胸側肉 152
胸側肋肉 147, 149, 151
胸排 148
胸部 148
胸部軟排骨 147, 149
胸椎 92
胸椎（12） 121
胸膜腔 126
胸膜壁 126
胸牆 177
胸鎖乳突肌 118
胸鰭 98
脈絡膜 131
能源 635
脊甲 109
脊肉 150, 151
脊柱 99, 105, 120
脊旁切角 511
脊神經 130, 135
脊神經前根 130
脊神經節 135
脊梁 190
脊飾 187
脊髓 99, 130, 135
臭氧 47
航向 553
航向標線 443
航向標線盤 443
航行燈 448
航空運輸 448
航海技術 601
航海儀器 442, 443
航海標識 444, 445, 446
航道浮標標記法 446
莨苕葉形飾 210
荒漠 55, 59
荔枝 80
草木棚 169
草地 188, 247
草地修邊切刀 248
草地鬆土耙 251

草坪 585
草莓剖面 74
草圖 521
茶杯 223
茶匙 226
茶壺 223
茶碟 223
茶藨子 74
蚌式挖斗 681
記分台 590
記分員 535, 536, 576, 590
記分紙 590
記事簿 351, 464
記號點 503
記溫圖 402
記罰計時員 533
記數器 615
記憶按鈕 379
記錄台 576
記錄員 533, 539, 545, 546
記錄紙 616
記錄頭 385
記譜法 475, 476
豺狼座 41
豹 90
起吊設備 390
起吊裝置 42
起帆索 551
起居室 189, 445, 457, 596
起柱 197
起重車 684
起重機 643, 683
起重臂 683
起首字母大寫，其餘的小
  體大寫 365
起脊 514
起脊槌 514
起脊機 514
起針針法 504
起動拉把 253
起動開關 241
起動踏板 410
起動器 672
起動機 405
起跑線 570
起落橋 455
起跳板 570, 571
起跳姿勢 548, 549
起跳高度 549
起跳線 570

起錨機 436
起點 566
起擲弧線 571
起爆管 696
迴旋處邊行方向 717
迴腸 127
送布齒 500
送風管 481, 482
送話器 387
逆風行駛 553
逆結 601
逆轉制動銷 580
迷迭香 143
迷走神經 126
退門連桿 266
退格鍵 467, 470
退硬幣口 595
退幣斗 388
退幣鈕 388
退彈鉤 703
退彈鉤凸輪 703
退彈鉤彈簧 703
追蹤雷達 706
追蹤導彈雷達 706
郎飛氏結 135
酒吧 720
酒吧間 433
酒窖 433
酒菜小車 209
酒精爐 233
酒櫃 216
配件 680
配重 380
配頁 512
配偶 138
配電回路 659
配電系統 666
配電板 659
配電盤 288
配藥 723
釘子 264, 509
釘孔 93
釘書釘 461
釘書機 461
釘線繡 507
釘鞋 525, 530
釘頭 264
釘頭套圈 597
針 499, 500, 501, 629
針尖 500, 504

針舌 506
針夾 500
針身 500
針具 519
針板 499
針法選擇把 506
針法選擇鈕 499
針狀 57
針桿 500, 504, 506
針眼 500, 501
針插 501
針距調節鈕 499
針鉤 506
針黹用品 501
針踵 506
針頭 504
針織衫 296
閃光表 373
閃光信號燈 423, 677
閃光器材 372
閃光燈 373
閃光燈托架 372
閃光燈泡 372
閃光燈插座 371
陣雨 60
陣雪 60
除 723
除氣組件 271
除氣設備 661, 664
除氣劑貯存槽 661
除粉刺針 343
除草叉 249
除草齒鋤 248
除溼器 458
除漆刮刀 280
除霜定時器 239
除霜發熱器 239
馬 90, 91, 92, 93
馬匹血統 569
馬匹號碼 569
馬主 569
馬可尼式縱帆 432
馬名 569
馬尾 330
馬身 574
馬車廂頂式屋頂 191
馬刺 565
馬勒 568
馬桶 268, 269
馬桶水箱 269

馬桶座圈 269
馬桶蓋 269
馬術運動 565
馬鹿 89
馬路 413
馬達 499
馬鈴薯 84
馬鈴薯種植機 164
馬靴 565
馬廄 569
馬廄通道 569
馬端 573
馬銜 568
馬鞍 567
馬褲 565
馬蹄上部 93
馬蹄中側 93
馬蹄形鏡架裝置 42
馬蹄拱 172
馬蹄蹠面 93
馬蹄鐵 93
馬鞭 565
馬簿 569
馬鐙 567
馬籠頭 567
骨架 279, 346
骨牌 593
骨骼 92, 120, 121
高山滑雪 559, 560
高山滑雪運動員 559
高氏體 86
高低槓 574
高低轉把 697
高吹雪 60
高枝剪 249
高空冷鋒 61
高空暖鋒 61
高度 197, 549
高度表 47
高度計 555, 556
高度控制器 65
高度傳感器 436
高度標尺 376
高度調節旋鈕 376, 560
高度調整器 492
高架橋 414
高背背帶褲 316
高音拾音器 494
高音音栓 489
高音控制鈕 379

高音喇叭 378
高音琴馬 479
高音鍵盤 489
高音譜號 475
高原 54
高原氣候 59
高射砲 439
高氣壓中心 62
高球棒頭 586
高脚水杯 222
高脚凳 212
高統鞋 320
高速公路 717
高速公路完 717
高速攪刀 235
高雲 52
高雲類型 62
高溫計 520
高溫截電器 273
高溫熨 722
高槓 574
高爾夫球 585, 586, 587
高爾夫球手 585
高爾夫球車車道 585
高爾夫球剖面圖 587
高爾夫球棒 586
高爾夫球棒的種類 586
高爾夫球鞋 587
高障礙：板和竿 566
高層雲 52
高導燈浮標 444
高積雲 52
高壓渦輪機 664
高壓試驗器 286
高壓電纜 620
高壓鍋 232
高翻領 308
高翻領毛衫 559
高翻領衫 296, 307
鬥牛裝 321

十一畫

乾大陸——半乾旱 59
乾大陸——乾旱 59
乾式壓褶機 375
乾衣 722

乾衣機 241
乾衣機中溫至高溫甩乾 722
乾衣機低溫甩乾 722
乾果：堅果 78
乾果蛋糕 157
乾果種類 79
乾洗 722
乾粉 332
乾粉刷 332
乾草原 59
乾雪 57
乾塢 441
乾溼計 63
乾酪叉 225
乾酪火鍋 233
乾酪鍋 233
乾燥副熱帶 59
偶數羽狀 70
停止 382
停止按鈕 381, 388
停止鈕 492
停車收費表 178
停車處 188, 717
停車間 187, 189
停車讓路 715
停放支架 402
停放支架曲柄 402
停放場 425
停留和停車標識 717
停機位 452
停機坪 452
停機區 452
停機鈕 253
停顯液盆 375
假肋（3） 121
假袋 301
假鼻 322
假髮 331
假褶 315
假蠅 581
假蠅肩 581
假蠅盒 582
側支架 409
側支索 430
側式 547
側扶手 429
側把 506
側板 694
側門 188, 425

側門齒 123
側柱 190
側柄 260
側面 327, 685
側面塔樓 177
側斜定位鎖 374
側梯 419
側梯橫檔 419
側桿 278
側條 93
側窗 403
側視圖 116, 122, 482
側溝 93
側滑指示器 556
側腹肉 147, 148, 151
側滾控制噴管 65
側線 98, 544
側壁 402, 425, 440
側燈 427
側磺 56
側牆 200, 540, 541
側牆線 540
側翼 176
側鏡 340
偏心撥禾輪 165
偏光濾鏡 370
偏流板 403
偏差調正旋鈕 621
偏航控制噴管 65
偏蝕 37, 38
偏轉軸 393
偏轉裝置 557
兜帽 292, 314
剪刀 501, 521, 599, 629
剪刀式切磨 327
剪刀桿 338
剪齒 338
副本 359, 360, 361
副羽 96
副寒帶氣候 59
副裁判 528, 529, 536, 543
副萼 74
副熱帶氣候 59
副機長座椅 451
副翼 448, 556, 705
勒馬韁 568
動力輸出軸 162
動力螺旋槳 435
動物 89
動物細胞 86

動耙缸筒 678
動圈 384
動圈式麥克風 384
動滑車 640
匙 226, 599
匙斗 226
匙尖 226
匙形 70
匙把 226
匙背 226
匙頸 226
參考站 394
參賽路程 569
曼陀林 487
商品編號 610
商業區 178
商標 344, 397
商標紙 344
商標圈 295
唱片 380
唱片盤 380
唱詩班席位 174
唱盤 378, 380
唱頭殼 380
唱臂 380
問訊處 426
問訊櫃台 454
問號 357, 386
唯讀記憶體 468
啤酒杯 222
售票大廳 426
售票處 426
售票櫃台 426, 454
售貨票據 610
圈狀耳環 325
圈線綉 507
國王 591, 592
國際天氣符號 60, 61
國際音標 358
國際單打場 540
國際象棋 591
國際路標 714, 715, 716, 717
國際電信衛星 393
堅果鉗 228
堆芯柵格管 662
堆芯緊急冷卻 666
基本方位浮標記法 445
基本織法 511
基岩 616, 650

基底層 136
基座 401, 423, 514, 573, 675
基部 709
基節 100, 106
基節趾骨 120, 121
基腳 192
基層 413
基線 625
基膜 135
婆 139
婆羅門參根 84
宿舍 643
密西根雪鞋 563
密封 670
密封耳 615
密封室 107
密封圈 238, 240, 242, 268, 647
密封墊 271, 273, 274
密封環 241
密紋唱片填心塊 380
密閉膨脹水箱 204
密雲 61
專業照相機 369
專線電報機 386
屏蔽建築物 665
巢箱 107
常平環 443
常用的叉 225
常用的水輪機 657
常用的扶手椅 210, 211
常用的廚刀 227
常用的餐刀 224
常用的羹匙 226
常用科學符號 723
常用帳篷 597
常用標識 718, 719, 720, 721
常見的水壩 653
常見的門 198
常見的柑果 77
常見的核果 75
常見的海岸地形 51
常見的堅果 78
常見的梨果 76
常見的窗 199
常見的漿果 74
常見的熱帶水果 80
常見食用甲殼類動物 103

常見食用軟體動物 102
常見食用腹足類動物 104
常見髮型 330, 331
帶 351
帶去屑槽刃口 260
帶式輪送機 635
帶尾 294
帶長調節鈕 294
帶限壓閥的加水口蓋 406
帶動轉子旋轉 654
帶圈 291, 294
帶條 294
帶終指示桿 466
帶釦 217, 219, 294, 400,
  502
帶傾注嘴杯 236
帶箍三通 202
帶墜耳環 325
帶槽軸 398
帶膠標籤 462
帶觸片管式保險絲 285
帳頂 596
帳幕 597
帳篷 596, 597
帳簿 464
康塔爾硬乾酪 155
張緊桿 486
張緊輥 412
張緊螺絲 486
強音踏板 479
彗星 39
彗核 39
彗髮 39
彗頭 39
彩色 710
彩色玻璃 521
彩球撞球 584
得分區 527, 531
得分區線 531
從動滑輪 181
御夫座 40
控制台 43, 389, 394, 418,
  438, 472
控制系統 672
控制板 237, 238, 240, 241,
  242, 390
控制室 43, 445, 643, 651,
  660, 661
控制員 472
控制桿 495

控制鈕 238, 471, 520
控制鈕板 206
控制盤 471
控制器 181, 182, 386
控制艙 456
控制鍵 470
控鍵按鈕 483
捲尺 501
捲片桿 368
捲片軸 368, 494, 508
捲帆索 431
捲式百葉窗 219
捲烟紙 344
捲紙筒 467
捲紙筒旋鈕 467, 471
捲動機械裝置 219
捲帶鈕 466
捲筒 219, 341
捲睫毛夾 333
捲葉甘藍 82
捲線綉 507
捲線輪安裝座 580
捲髮刷 341
捲髮鉗 341
捲縫鞋 319·
捲簾 219
探空氣球 63
探針插座 237
探測氣球 47, 64
探測儀器 624
探頭 286
接上文 362
接口 495
接水盤 206
接地插桿 285
接地電極 406
接地線 288, 380, 647
接地線故障斷路器 288
接收倉 665
接收器 624
接收機顯示器 442
接受機 665
接枝刀 252
接烟囱管 201
接送區 454
接球員 537, 540, 541, 542,
  543
接袖 291, 295, 296, 306
接連電線 471
接管方式數種 272

接線盒 423, 659
接線蓋 615
接線頭 204, 285, 659
接線環 581
接線點 659
接鋒 531
接頭 288, 582, 588, 677
接頭配件 275
接縫 344, 367
接褶裙 303
接點 659
接繩結 601
掘進面 635, 637
掩蔽通道 176
掃冰運動員 545
掃帚 201
掃腰 578
掛布撐條 671
掛衣架 465
掛衣棚 216
掛肩小袋 349
掛肩包 347
掛肩皮包 349
掛起晾乾 722
掛圈 296, 340
掛梁套圈 596
掛帽領 308
掛鈎 218, 221, 347
掛鈎梯 278, 677
掛鈎環 580
掛環 218, 608
掛斷鍵 387
掛簧 607
掛鎖 347
掛繫皮帶 599
推土機 635, 678
推土鏟 678
推式鋤 248
推車把手 631
推彈桿 695, 696
推架 678
推圈 631
推液塞 629
推鉛球 571
推管 367
推壓器 236
採光井 173
採光屋頂 191
採油平台 643
採暖用油 649

探礦 636
排水支管 267
排水瓦管 192
排水斜溝 187
排水軟管 272
排水溝 187, 413
排水管 204, 240, 242, 267
排水閥座 268
排水層 652
排水豎管 272
排水覆蓋層 652
排水彎頭 267
排列鍵 470
排成直行 362
排成橫行 362
排尿裝置 458
排放閥 203
排泄孔 104
排氣口 639
排氣系統 406
排氣歧管 404, 405, 406
排氣軟管 241
排氣喇叭管 700
排氣管 403, 404, 406, 409,
  450, 455, 678, 704
排氣管道 241
排氣閥 404
排氣噴管 450, 705
排烟器 704
排球 536
排球場 536
排殼口 669, 697, 701
排管 662
排管體 662, 664
排管體室 662
排廢液旋塞 647
排廢液閥 647
排簫 488
捻接 601
捻繩索 601
拼條錯縫地板 196
拼塊 298
拼縫 295
救生圈 436
救生船 643
救生筏 439
救生艇 430
救護站 718
教堂 174
教練 579

斜三通 275
斜井 636
斜切通心粉 145
斜方肌 118
斜帆駛帆杆 430
斜角規 262
斜角規槽 262
斜走 591
斜坡 413, 635
斜坡道 171
斜屋頂 190
斜桁 429
斜桁帆 431, 432
斜面 200
斜面牆 175
斜紋 502
斜紋織法 511
斜掛大三角帆 432
斜插袋 291, 294
斜裁袖窿 306
斜開 710
斜黑體大寫 365
斜滑面 403
斜撐 486, 658
斜撐橋 415
斜線號 357, 386
斜檐 171
斜邊 538
斜體 365
斜體大寫 365
旋切薄木 265
旋前圓肌 118
旋律弦 487
旋座鬆緊柄 259
旋脊 101
旋動卡頭 266
旋渦形飾 210
旋渦星系 39
旋渦臂 39
旋軸 572
旋開橋 417
旋閘 657
旋翼葉片 455
旋翼葉轂 455
旋翼葉轂體 455
旋轉式傳送帶 454
旋轉底架 675
旋轉芯子 266
旋轉座 259, 676
旋轉接頭 624, 640

旋轉釣餌 581
旋轉圓頂 42
旋轉鉋刀 260
旋轉樞軸 697
旋轉盤 681
旋轉鋤 163
旋轉機身 681
旋轉頭 259, 619
旋轉翼 671
旋轉灑水器 250
晚間用長項鏈（30吋）
  326
晨衣裝 302
望遠目鏡 614
望遠物鏡 614
望遠照門 700
望遠瞄準器 621, 704
望遠鏡 443
望遠鏡座 41, 42
望遠鏡控制室 42
望樓 177
脛 91
脛上腿肉 148
脛甲 690
脛神經 129
脛骨 92, 108, 120
脛骨前肌 118
脛腓骨 105
脛節 100, 106
脛墊 534
梁下橫檔 419
梁橋 414
梁橋的種類 414
梯子 647, 671
梯子和四腳梯 278, 279
梯子間 637
梯式腳手架 279
梯形翼 449
梯級 182, 197
梯級帶動鏈 182
梯頂金屬爪鈎 588
梯頂金屬鈎 588
梯凳 279
梯檔 278
桿 258, 260, 264
桿尖 582
桿架 581
桿柄 534
桿幹 582
桿跟 534

桿蓋 271
桿頭 218, 253, 534, 582
梗 72, 74, 76
梗節 89
棱子 500, 509
棱心 500
棱心匣 500
棱心繞線軸 499
棱眼 509
棱道桿 509
梅札尼通心粉 144
梅花 592
條子 593
條狀填料 282
條紋長褲 317
條裝香烟 344
條播機 164
梨 76
梨形切磨 327
梨果 76
梨果剖面 76
氫化精煉廠 648
涎巾 315
涼鞋 319
液化氣石油處理 648
液化氣貯存槽 648
液位計 647
液冷衣 458
液材 71
液泡 86
液流調節螺絲 280
液缸 443
液氧 456
液氧箱隔板 456
液氧輸送管 456
液氫（燃料）456
液晶顯示 605
液壓挖土機 681
液壓缸筒 678, 679, 682
液壓計 204, 647
液壓貨盤車 685
液體入口 670
液體羅盤 443
淤積物 277
淺口便鞋 321
淺根 71
清水噴灑器 242
清除沾染室 661
清理烟斗工具 345
清湯掛麵 330

清潔刷 337
淋浴及浴缸設備 267
混合管 282
混和盆 230, 235
混凝土砌塊 193
混凝土基座 616
混凝土排液溝 647
混凝土牆 669
混凝土壩剖面圖 652
混聲鈕 383
混響裝置 495
淚滴切磨 327
淚管 131
深水炸彈發射器 439
深度計 550
深海丘陵 50
深海平原 50
深海底 48
深海潛水器 437
深耕犁 164
深草區 585
淨膚海綿 333
烹煮用具 229
烹調定時器 229
牽引車 453, 646
牽引索脫除鈕 556
牽引桿 678, 680, 698
牽引桿鎖鈕 698
牽引鈎 162, 556, 558
牽引滑輪 218
牽引滑輪裝置 218
牽引電動機 418
牽引電動機通風器 418
牽引管 682
牽引機引擎 682
牽引環 698
牽引臂 682
牽收索 551
牽動桿 482
珠母雲 47
珠芽 83
珠柄 74, 79
珠粒 89
珠寶飾物 325, 326, 327
球 531, 543, 545, 572
球心 587
球穴 585
球穴旗 585
球坑 590
球形 446

球形燈罩 220
球形艙 437
球具車 587
球拍 540, 541, 542, 543
球拍夾 538
球芽甘藍 82
球門 527, 531, 532, 533,
　539, 545
球門柱 527, 531
球門區 532, 533, 539
球門區線 539
球門裁判 539
球門線 517, 527, 532, 533,
　539, 545
球架 64
球枱 583, 584
球面 526, 587
球員 526, 541, 545
球員服式 530
球員席 525, 533, 535, 536,
　545
球員編號 530
球座 587
球根穴播器 249
球桌 543
球桿 582
球瓶布置方式 590
球莖甘藍 84
球袋 583
球場 531, 542, 585
球棒 526
球棒袋 587
球棒袋座 587
球棒隔板 587
球童 585
球隊制服 526
球節 91
球道 585, 590
球鼻形船首 645
球類運動 525
球籃 535
理髮工具 338
理髮店 720
理髮剪刀 338
現代 367
現代弓 691
現代追擊砲 697
現代榴彈砲 698
瓶內氣壓表 282
甜瓜 81

甜品刀 224
甜品叉 225
甜品匙 226
甜炸麵圈 156
甜茴香 85
甜酒杯 222
甜菜根 84
甜點 156, 157
產生反應 723
產生電能 667
產生磁場 654
產生熱能 667
盔弇 690
盔頂 690
盒子 337, 341
盒式磁帶 469
盒式磁帶錄放機 469
盒狀褶 217
盒帶室 381
盒裝捲烟紙 344
盒裝感光片 371
盒裝膠片 371
盒墜項鏈 326
盛物門 239
盛物架 239
盛魚盤 223
眼 104, 109, 114, 131
眼先 95
眼前房 131
眼後房 131
眼柄 104
眼圈 95
眼球 105, 131
眼罩 383, 384, 370, 568
眼窩 91, 122
眼影 332
眼線液 332
眼線筆 332
眼輪匝肌 118
眼瞼 109
眼鏡 328, 329
眶下孔 122
眶上孔 122
票兜 351
移到下行 362
移到上行 363
移動式起重機 655
移密 362
移開 363
第一小提琴 493

第一分位 577
第一加強段 694
第一加強環 694
第一臼齒 123
第一位置區 535
第一前臼齒 123
第一活塞滑管 484
第一神經元 135
第一級 456
第一級泵 664
第一停堆系統 666
第一排中鋒 531
第一排邊鋒 531
第一聚束透鏡 620
第一彎道 569
第七分位 577
第二小提琴 493
第二分位 577
第二加強段 694
第二加強環 694
第二臼齒 123
第二位置區 535
第二前臼齒 123
第二活塞滑管 484
第二級 456
第二停堆系統 666
第二掌骨 108
第二聚束透鏡 620
第二彎道 569
第八分位 577
第三叉 89
第三分位 577
第三臼齒 123
第三活塞滑管 484
第三級 456
第三掌骨 108
第三齒輪 605, 607
第五分位 577
第五掌骨 108
第六分位 577
第四叉 89
第四分位 577
第四掌骨 108
第四齒輪 605
符邦堡壘 176
符號 57, 358
粒雪 56
粒線 86
粗毛耙 244
粗皮北風菌 73

粗扭花麵 144
粗呢上衣 301
粗柴油 649
粗細齒梳 338
粗棉抹布 515
粗調鈕 619
粗齒梳 338
粗糠篩 165
紮線 581
細扭花麵 144
細卷鴉葱 84
細長三角 711
細長形切磨 327
細胞 86
細胞核 86
細胞膜 86
細胞質 86, 113
細胞壁 86
細胞體 135
細香葱 83
細紋指甲銼 342
細斜切粉 145
細通心粉 144
細義大利麵 144
細麵 144
終末細支氣管 126
終站名牌 427
終端油庫 644
終端停止開關 181
終端機 472
終磧 56
終點 566
終點直路 569
終點柱 571
終點停機閘 181
終點裁判員 546
終點線 569, 571
朋 96
脫扣預調旋鈕 560
脫粒凹板 165
脫粒滾筒 165
脫鈎叉 582
脫鈎桿 419
脫靴板 320
脫彈匣卡筍 699
脫瀝青 648
脫蠟 648
腳 115, 514
腳先入水 548
腳尖控音栓 481

脚架 486
脚套 377, 554
脚座 685
脚趾 114
脚跟弧板 631
脚跟踏板 560
脚誤裁判 537
脚線嵌條 187
脚踏車 411, 412
脚踏車喇叭 412
脚踏開關 499
脚輪 486
脚燈 180
脚蹬帶 525
舵 433, 435, 552, 706
舵柄 552
舷 430
舷梯 434
舷牆 430
船用柴油 649
船帆座 41
船尾座 41
船尾裝載門 434
船形軍帽 298
船底座 41
船長艙 433
船首三角帆 552
船首汽車跳板門 435
船首斜桁 430
船首斜桁支索 430
船首舵 434
船首旗杆 439
船員艙 433, 645
船閘室 440
船閘管理處 441
船艙 434, 552
船頭 552
莙蓬菜 85
莢片 79
莢果剖面 79
莖 69, 83, 85
莖尖 85
莖菜 85
莖軸 69
莫氏界面 47, 48
荷葉裙 303
荷蘭文 355
荷蘭烤鍋 232
蛇夫座 40, 41
蛋奶格子餅 157

蛋奶餅烘爐 237
蛋奶糊酥餅 157
蛋白奶酥 157
蛋白餡餅 156
蛋箱 239
蛋糕 156
蛋糕烤盤 230
術語 74, 75, 76, 77, 78
袋口手絹 293
袖口貼邊 295
袖口搭扣帶 291
袖口搭扣帶圈 291
袖子 293, 306
袖衩尖頭貼邊 295, 306
袖珍自動裝片照相機 369
袖珍照相機 369
袖籠 297, 306
設自動柵欄的道口 424
設備運入井 660
貨車車廂 419
貨物墊 684
貨物臨時堆棧 441
貨運站 424, 452
貨運掛車 403
貨幣兌換 720
貨幣兌換處 426
貨幣兌換櫃台 454
貨盤 685
貨盤車 685
貨盤貨櫃搬運車 453
貨艙 433, 448
貨艙口 433
貨櫃 425, 434
貨櫃車 420
貨櫃站 441
貨櫃船 434, 441
貨櫃艙 434
趾 93, 94, 97, 105
趾甲剪 343
趾長伸肌 118
趾套 554
趾骨 92, 105
趾帶 554
趾鈕 93
趾短伸肌 118
趾墊 94
趾擋 411
趾攀涼鞋 319
軟木托 542

軟件鍵 470
軟音符號 357
軟帽 315
軟、硬窗簾 219
軟塑料鞋底 315, 316
軟矮凳 212
軟腭 134
軟墊長椅 212
軟磁碟 469
軟管 244, 269, 281, 612, 639
軟管捲盤 250
軟管接頭 639
軟銲吹管 281
軟銲和熔銲 281, 282, 283
軟邊帽 314
軟鰭條 98
軟體動物 102
通火工具 201
（通往）弛壓槽 664
通往郊區鐵路 424
通信設備 468
通風口 399
通風井 638
通氣口 42, 242, 555
通氣孔 107
通氣門 402
通氣窗 206
通氣管 275, 550
通氣蓋 406
通氣閥 647
通氣豎管 267
通訊 355
通訊網管理中心 394
通堵塞口 270
通話器 388
通道 189, 421
通電花劍 576
通電信號燈 341
通電劍頭 576
逗號 357, 363, 386
連字號 364, 386
連衣便褲 310, 316
連衣裙 302
連衣褲 555
連肩袖 306
連指手套 283, 299, 317, 559, 589
連島沙洲 51
連動測距照相機 369

連接桁架 65
連接桿 489
連接釦 555
連接管 270
連接線 576
連接線撐桿 403
連接導線 378
連接頭 275
連桿 621
連帽粗呢上衣 292
連旋矩 711
連短裙上衣 305
連結線 476
連廊 421
連廊門 421
連綿雨 60
連蓋座圈 269
連裹尿布衫 315
連燈鏡 340
連褲內衣 297
連褲襪子 315, 316
連繫彈簧 595
連續毛雨 60
連續降雪 60
連續梁 414
連續彎路先向左 714
連襯褲緊身胸衣 312
速度溜冰鞋 562
速度調節器 235
速度選擇盤 236
逐葉輪 165
逐葉器 165
造型旋座 519
造麵食機 228
透明幻燈片 377
透明夾 351
透明或半透明窗簾 217
透明窗 551
透明塑料板 533
透明隔 130
透明層 136
透聲網 378
透鏡 372, 625
透鏡型星系 039
透鏡座架 446
透鏡旋轉機構 446
野苣 82
野黑莓剖面 74
野餐區 721
釦子 349, 350, 502, 560

釦針 294, 349, 502
釦針孔 294
釦環 294
釣魚背心 582
釣餌 581
釣線引導環 580
釤刀 252
閉口扳手 258
閉孔神經 129
閉紋 380
閉剪止銷 338
閉殼肌 102
閉塞音 358
閉路電視/螢光屏 666
閉鎖機 698
陰天 61
陰阜 117
陰莖 114, 116
陰莖海綿體 116
陰莖兜 91
陰極 620
陰蒂 117
陰道 117
陰影 606
陰囊 114, 116
陰囊隔 116
陶立克柱型 170
陶瓷工藝 519, 520
陶鉤 519
雪 58
雪上競走運動員 563
雪地輪胎 407
雪地機車 408
雪板 559
雪加 344
雪加盒 344
雪道 558
雪維菜 143
雪輪 559, 561
雪鞋 563
雪鞋的種類 563
雪橇 408
頂 43, 635, 636
頂平台 242
頂板 190, 467
頂泌汗腺 136
頂芽 69
頂門 704
頂面 327, 556
頂革 567

頂風 553
頂桅 430
頂索 430
頂針 501
頂骨 121, 122
頂骨孔 122
頂梁 596
頂桿 480
頂桿彈簧 480
頂部 198
頂部中心人孔 646
頂視圖 122
頂罩殼 219
頂飾 607
頂滾軸 508
頂蓋 682
頂層樓座 179
頂標 444
頂篷 555, 587, 596
頂篷支柱 596
頂欄 199
魚 98, 99
魚刀 224
魚叉 225
魚尾板 422
魚尾板螺栓 422
魚骨針 507
魚眼鏡頭 370
魚鉤 581
魚雷 438
魚雷艙 438
魚槍 550
魚簍 582
鳥 95, 96, 97
鳥足主要類型 97
鳥喙主要類型 97
鳥蛤 102
鳥蛤殼狀飾 210
鹿皮靴 563
鹿角 89
鹿的種類 89
鹿科 89
鹿豹座 40
鹿彈粉 145
麥克風 378, 388, 471
麥克風活動桿 390
麥克風插座 381
麥芒 79
麥粒剖面 79
麻花通心粉 144

麻花鑽頭 260
麻將 593

十二畫

備用油箱 402
備用傘 555
備餐間 189
傑克 592
傘 346
傘包 555
傘段 555
傘套 346
傘骨 346
傘骨尖 346
傘桶 346
傘鞘 587
傘篷 346
傘繩 555
割水式水翼 436
割草機 252
割線刀口 500
博蒙乾酪 155
喇叭口 274, 483, 484
喇叭口支撐點 483
喇叭按鈕 410
喇叭按鍵 399
喇叭袖 306
喇叭管扣緊桿 700
喇叭管接頭 274
喇叭管螺母 274
喇叭褲 310
單 594, 595
單人沙發 211
單元 406
單元連接片 406
單引號 357
單爪犁錨 447
單片眼鏡 329
單打發球區 556
單打網柱 537
單打邊線 537, 542
單向褶 304
單行道 717
單位價格 610

單把式廚用龍頭 270, 271
單坡頂 190
單板 554
單面貨盤 685
單座位 429
單張 512
單排鈕西裝 293
單桿冷熱水龍頭 271
單眼 100
單殼貝 101
單發連發選擇 699
單結 601
單極斷路器 288
單葉 70
單跨橋 414
單樁 573
單層袖口 306
單幢住宅 183
單齒刃薄髮剪 338
單據插 461
單頭露營爐 599
單翼仰開橋 417
單螺旋 260
單簧 483
單簧口琴 488
單簧管 483, 490, 491, 493
單簾掛桿 218
單鏡頭反光照相機 368
單襻鞋 319
唾液腺 127
喉 95, 126, 581
喉甲 690
喉肉 150
喉革 567
喉結 114
喉塞音符號 357
圍外位 592
圍兜 310, 316
圍裙指 435
圍裙裝 302
圍椿 177
圍壁 445
圍繩 579
圍繩以外部分 579
堤岸 660
堤牆 647
堤壩 651, 653, 660
堤壩剖面圖 652, 653
報分燈 576
報販 178

堞口 177
堡內廣場 177
堡障 176
堵頭布 512
場上裁判 539
場地監督 390
場角 533
場院 161
壺嘴 234
壺碼 608
婿 139
尋星鏡 622, 623
嵌環 694
嵌鏡衣櫃 216
帽子 298, 321
帽子和頭巾 314
帽子面紗 314
帽子餡餅 145
帽貝 104, 298
帽冠 298, 314
帽帶 298
帽箍 561
帽蓋 285
帽檐 298, 314
幾手撲克牌 592
幾等於 723
幾種主要導彈 706
幾種刺繡針法 507
幾種常用桌子 209
幾種帽子 298
幾種無扶手椅 213
廁所 421
廂間通道 421
復位鍵 470
復進機筒 698
復進機筒頭 698
循軌道飛航方向 65
循環水泵 203
循環示意圖 124
循環泵 669
循環風扇 206
惰性氣體 284
惰輪 241
戟狀 70
扉頁 512
掌狀 70
掌長肌 118
掌骨 92, 94, 120
掌舵手 564
掌短肌 118

掌墊 94
描線輪 501
插入一個詞 362
插入字母 362
插入式刺刀 693
插入空位 362
插刀片器 337
插斗 570
插板縫 551
插架槽 239
插座 285, 372
插座測試器 286
插接口 580
插接頭 580
插桿 285
插袋 304
插筆套 351
插銷 284
插銷座 284
插頭 261, 285, 378, 384
插頭式保險絲 285
插縫 351
提升橋 417
提升橋面 417
提升鏈 684
提手 341, 347, 349, 350
提包 347
提示監控機 391
提把 236, 508, 614, 698,
   699, 701
提防觸電 718
提取行李處 454
提詞人隱席 180
提詞員 390
提煉 667
提線箍 580
提燈 599
握把 538, 540, 559, 561,
   586, 697, 699, 701, 702
握拍法 543
握柄 372, 526, 546, 577,
   580, 588
握桿 546
換片器 377
換形斷層 50
換值表 372
換能器 442
換碼鍵 470
揚聲器 43, 378, 383, 390,
   392, 677

揚聲器箱 378
揚聲器選擇按鈕 379
敞口格 349
敞開式農場 161
敞篷車 420
敞篷轎車 398
散氣口 429
散焰噴頭 281
散裝車 420
散裝貨船 441
散熱片管 203
散熱肋條 702
散熱管 203, 393
散熱器 406, 418
散熱器軟管 406
斑節蝦 103
斯庫納式縱帆 432
普洛凡斯酒味乾酪 155
普通尾翼組 449
普通帶形圖案 710
普通眼鏡 329
普通骰子 593
普通繩頭結 601
晴朗無雲 061
晶體管 606
景深刻度 370
暑針 606
暑盤 606
曾外孫 139
曾外孫女 139
曾外祖父 139
曾外祖母 139
最高速限 716
最高與最低溫度計 63
替換筆芯 367
替補球員 535, 536, 539,
   545
替補球員席 539
朝鮮薊 81
腓骨 120
腓骨長肌 118
腓骨短肌 119
腓淺神經 129
腓深神經 129
腓腸 115
腓腸肌 118, 119
腓腸神經 129
腓總神經 129
棕球 584
棕櫚叢 55

棘爪 219, 260, 508, 607
棘層 136
棘輪 219, 260, 508, 605,
   607
棘輪旋鈕 613
棘齒 258
棘鰭條 98
棗子 75
椅背 213
椅背底邊 210
椅背板 210
椅面 210, 213
椅腿 213
椅臂 631
棒 485, 611
棒尖 586
棒針 504
棒旋星系 39
棒桿 586
棒球 525, 526
棒球場 525
棒跟 586
棒頸 586
棒頭 586
棒頭套 587
棋子 591, 592
棋子盒 592
棋盤 591
棋盤格標記 591
棋盤圖案浮標 444
植物 69
植物細胞 86
植物構造 69, 70
椎骨棘突 121
椎骨橫突 121
椎間孔 130
棉毛衫褲 317
棉花籤 629
棉腰布 689
椏枝 69
殼 78, 97, 102, 104
殼口 101
殼斗 78
殼針 101
殼頂 101
殼膜 97
殼瓣 101
殼體 401
殘疾人通道 719
毯子 214

氫氣 284
港口 441
港口火車站 441
港口海關 441
游泳 546
游泳比賽 546
游泳池 433, 545
游泳褲 545
游梁式泵 641
游畢一趟 547
游絲 605
游標 471
游標鍵 470
游標轉筒 613
游碼移動柄 609
游碼標尺 609
游擊手 525
渡船 434
減 723
減少空位 363
減速板 556, 705
減速板手柄 556
減速板液壓缸筒 705
減速劑 664
減速劑入口 662
減速劑出口 662
減速劑/其他系統 666
減速劑泵 664
減速劑熱交換器 664
減逕機 206
減震墊 562
減震器 408
減壓閥 273
減擦墊 560
湖 38
渦卷花紋 477
渦輪 450
渦輪交流發電機 668
渦輪泵 706
渦輪風扇引擎 450
渦輪葉片 450
渦輪噴射引擎 448, 450
渦輪增壓引擎 404
渦輪增壓器 418
渦輪導向葉片 450
渦輪機 438, 666
渦輪機房 661
渦輪機帶動發電機 667
渦輪壓氣機軸 450
渦殼 655

湯勺 229
湯匙 226
湯鈢 223
湯鍋 232
測井裝置 643
測砧 613
測站圈 61, 62
測站圖式 62
測深儀 437
測量軸 613
測量軸螺紋 613
測微套筒 613
測微旋鈕 614
測微螺族 443
測溫 611
測溫頭 238
測試圖 391
測電氖燈泡 286
滋體麵 144
焦黃程度選擇器 237
無尾兩棲動物 105
無扶手椅子 213
無肩帶奶罩 313
無限大 723
無風 61
無座力砲 700
無草空地 63
無帶高跟鞋 319
無帶圓筒包 349
無桿錨 447
無袖襯裙 312
無鈕短背心 307
無罩假髮 331
無跟橡膠套鞋 319
無飾戒指 325
無酵餅 146
無障區 536
無領疊襟衫 305
無線電天線 438, 458
無線電收發機 458
無線電話 388
無簷軟帽 314
無霜電冰箱 239
無邊圓帽 298
煮咖啡壺 234
煮荷包蛋鍋 233
煮蛋定時器 229
煮魚鍋 232
煮鍋 599
牌行 593

牌形 325
牌陣 593
犁刀 163
犁托 163
犁柱 163
犁架 163
犁側板 163
犁壁 163
犁踵 163
犁轅 163
犁鏵 163
犁體 163
猶太白麵包 146
琺瑯質 123
琶音 476
琴弓 478
琴身板 477, 478, 479
琴弦 477, 478, 479, 480
琴柱 478
琴架 485
琴面 487
琴馬 477, 494
琴腰 477
琴槌 479, 480
琴撥 487
琴箱 479, 489
琴頸 477, 478, 487
甥女 138
畫面控制員 391
畫面控制鍵 391
畫格定位鈕 383
畫稿 521
番子 593
番石榴 80
番茄 81
登山 588, 589
登山背帶 589
登山運動員 589
登山靴 589
登山褲 589
登山繩 589
登山纜車 558
登月靴 458
登月艙 456
登車扶手 403
登機走廊 454
登機長廊 452
登機踏板 455
發 593
發令員 546

發光二極管電平表 381
發信人姓名首字母 359,
　360
發信人簽名 361
發信檔號 361
發音 481
發射元件 624
發射室 620
發射軌道 394
發射脈衝 624
發射輔助工具 695
發射機 624
發射藥 702
發動機 165, 640, 675
發動機殼 253
發條 605
發球下限金屬片 540
發球打禿處 585
發球回彈觸地區 541
發球員 536, 537, 540, 542,
　543
發球區 536, 540, 541, 584
發球區線 541
發球裁判 542
發球線 540, 541, 584
發球點 584
發球觸地底線 537
發報台 385
發報機 385
發散透鏡 625
發電 668
發電站 638, 660
發電站流程圖 664
發電廠 648, 651, 655
發電廠剖面 660
發電機 411, 445, 655, 656,
　661, 664, 666, 667, 672,
發熱元件 520
發響鈕 495
着陸區標識 452
着陸燈 455
着墨面 518
短大衣 300
短手套 299
短支管 268
短拍壁球 541
短柄活動扳手 276
短柄劍 692
短笛 483, 493
短袖 306

索 引

短袖運動衣 575
短通心粉 145
短項鏈 326
短號 484, 491, 493
短劍 689, 692
短髮 331
短褲 297, 310, 538, 579
短襪 297, 311
硬板絕緣材料 195
硬紙板 521
硬紙殼 702
硬脊膜 130
硬頂轎車 398
硬殼 347
硬腭 122, 134
硬幣輸送管 595
硬膜腔終部 130
硬質纖維板 265
硬襯 502
程序鈕 240, 241, 242
稀釋劑 650
稀釋劑回收 650
捆帶 346
窗 187, 188, 199, 237, 238,
　397, 429, 448, 596
窗台 199
窗玻璃 199
窗扇 199
窗框 199
窗帷 217
窗梃舌 199
窗梃槽 199
窗頂短帷 217
窗鈎 199
窗幔 217
窗蓋布 596
窗簾 217
窗簾安裝用具 218
窗簾軌 218
窗簾框架內燈 220
窗簾掛桿 218
窗簾罩 217
童裝 315, 316, 317
笱座木 508
笱座腳 508
等於 723
等候處標識 452
等價 723
等震線 053
等壓線 062

筆 616
筆尖 367
筆夾 367
筆芯 367
筆芯進退裝置 367
筆桿 367
筒子 593
筒身 700
筒狀手提包 348
筒體 621
筋 85
絞肉機 228
絞車 434, 439, 640
絞車機樓 638
絞盤 439, 553, 675, 704
結子 507, 511
結成 601
結尾敬辭 360
結核菌素注射器 629
結婚戒指 325
結紮繩 526
結構 190, 192, 199
結締組織 135, 136
結膜 131
結繭 101
結繩狀長項鏈（45吋）
　326
絨毛濾器 240
絨球 314
絨睡衣褲 315
絕熱材料 644
絕熱層 669, 670
絕緣子 659
絕緣材料 196, 273
絕緣柄 286, 287
絕緣套管 285, 651, 659
絕緣桿套 286
絕緣體 406
紫色 710
紫胎貝 102
絲瓜領 308
給水 664
給水支管 270
給彈盤 701
胼胝 91
胼胝體 130
腕 108, 115
腕骨 120
腕帶 349, 350, 384, 541,
　561, 588

腕墊 94
腋下枴杖 630
腋下墊 630
腋芽 69, 70
腋挾包 348
腋神經 129
腋動脈 125
腋窩 114
腋靜脈 125
腎 99, 124
腎上腺 128
腎形 70
腎乳頭 128
腎盂 128
腎門 128
腎動脈 125, 128
腎蓋 128
腎錐體 128
腎靜脈 125, 128
腎寶 128
脾 99, 124
脾動脈 125
脾靜脈 125
舒適把子 341
菠菜 82
菠菜寬麵 144
菠菜麵 144
華貴手提包 349
菱形 446
菱形肌 119
菱形助瞄點 583
菱形鋼絲網 194
菱格構件 162
萊茵白酒杯 222
萊菔 84
菌托 73
菌形錨 447
菌柄 73
菌傘 73
菌絲 73
菌絲體 73
菌輪 73
菌褶 73
菊芋 84
菊苣 82
菜圃 161
菜梗 85
菜園 188
菜盤 223
菜頭 85

蒸菜 82
蛙 105
蛙式 547
蛙式轉身 547
蛙式蹬水 547
蛙泳手 547
蛙的生活史 105
蛙鞋 550
蛙鞋幫 550
蛤 102
街道橫斷面 413
街邊咖啡店 178
裁切 513
裁台 513
裁判 531, 532, 533, 535,
　537, 542, 545, 576, 578
裁判席 569
裁判高椅 542
裁判旗 536
裁紙刀 513
裁剪線 503
視束交叉 130
視神經 131
視網膜 131
註冊商標 723
象牙球 594
貯木場 638
貯水槽 421, 660
貯存放射性廢料 667
貯存倉 161
貯存槽 668
貯存盤 665
貯泥漿罐 643
貯油器 639
貯油罐 643, 649
貯氫球 456
貯煤廠 638
貯蜜室 107
貼身衣 316
貼身背心 579
貼身窄腳裝 302
貼身連衣裙 302
貼面程度選擇鈕 337
貼袋 300, 304, 316
貼邊前袋 293
貼邊袋 296, 304
貴要靜脈 125
越南文 355
越野滑雪 561
越野滑雪板 561

越野滑雪運動員 561
越橘 74
超高音喇叭 378
超高頻天線 393
超高頻指向標天線 393
超高頻道選擇鈕 392
超廣角鏡頭 43
超靜定支撐 658
距 108
距骨 121
距離刻度 370
跑車 398, 452, 571
跑道中線 452
跑道末端燈 452
跑道指示標識 452
跑道起端標識 452
跑道側狹條標識 452
跑道資料 569
跑壘指導區 525
蹠骨 92, 95, 105, 112, 120
蹠節 100, 106
蹠關節 91
軸 380, 607, 611, 615, 655, 656, 657
軸向輻流式水輪機 657
軸承 611
軸流式壓氣機 450
軸索 135
軸索側突 135
軸脊 101
軸針 443
軸頸箱 418
軸褶 101
週末旅行箱 347
進入地球同步軌道 394
進入廊道 655, 660
進入豎井 660
進刃桿 261
進叉口 685
進戶線 659
進水口 240, 655
進水管 240, 242, 651, 660
進肉管 236
進攻者 578
進風口 340
進風管 481
進料門 665
進氣口 408, 418, 436, 450, 455
進氣閥 404, 405

進氣調節門 201
進氣導片 450
進給旋鈕 505
郵局 720
郵票兜 351
酥皮鬆餅 157
量具 599
量杯 341
量油尺 405
量度長度和厚度 613
量度儀器 605
量筒 64
量裙尺 501
量壓 612
鈔票夾 351
鈔票兜 351
鈕孔 291, 295, 296
鈕柄 263
鈕眼 502
鈕鈕 295
鈕鈕眼 294
鈕襻 292
鈍齒狀 70
鉤 500, 502, 504, 608, 613
鉤刀 252
鉤爪 419
鉤尖 581
鉤柄 581
鉤針 504
鉤深 581
鉤眼 581
鉤鈕 562
鉤寬 581
鉤銷 419
鉤彎 581
開口 308
開口扳手 258
開口桿 243
開口梅花扳手 258
開心果 78
開衩窄裙 303
開車信號 427
開車時間牌 427
開始線 576
開門限位銷 239
開挖面 635
開採 667
開採面 636
開球區 585
開球線 583

開球點 583
開瓶器 229, 243
開瓶罐用具 229
開閉口混合扳手 258
開傘索 555
開牌 593
開窗紙條 463
開縫 511
開縫刷 328
開襟毛線衫 296
開關 221, 238, 244, 260, 261, 263, 285, 337, 339, 340, 341, 372, 380, 383, 384, 392, 442, 467, 471
開關手柄 271
開關/放音按鈕 388
開關按鍵 237
開關桿 270, 271
開關盒 285
開關場 666
開關蓋板 285
開罐刀 599
間 475
間歇毛雨 60
間歇雨 60
間歇泉 53
間歇降雪 60
隊伍 531
隊長 544
階地 635
階形切磨 327
階段 637
階層高度 635
陽台 175, 187, 188, 445, 671
陽光 38
陽極 620
隅撐 190
隆起螺栓 280
雄性 723
雄蜂 106
雄蕊 72, 76
集水坑 636
集水漏斗 64
集合壕 176
集油槽 405
集流管 661, 664
集草囊 252
集絨毛器 241
集電器 656

集熱管 670
雲及其氣象符號 52
雲梯 676
雲梯救火車 676
雲量 61, 62
雲層密布 61
韌皮部 71
韌帶位置 101
項甲 109
項圈 326
項帶鈕環 368, 384
項鏈 326
順子 592
順風 553
飯廳 189
飲用水水塔 643
飲用水車 453
飲食 600
飲食供應車 453
飲料銷售機 401
飲液小泡 86
馭手 568, 569
馭手衣帽顏色 569
黃瓜 81
黃色＝小心 713
黃豆 85
黃油刀 224
黃油室 239
黃油球捲刀 227
黃油麵包碟 223
黃球 584
「黃蜂」直升飛機 439
黃道十二宮 712
黃銅法蘭盤 268
黃銅球閥龍頭 271
黑 594, 595
黑子 37
黑方 591, 592
黑色 710
黑格 591
黑桃 592
黑海 49
黑素細胞 136
黑球 584
黑醋栗 74
黑體 365
黑體大寫 365

十三畫

傳眞系統 394
傳送通道 665
傳送齒輪柱 368
傳動皮帶 240, 241
傳動帶 380
傳動軸 455
傳動裝置 240, 682
傳動輪系 412
傳動鏈 411
傳統式 305
傳感探針 237
傳熱燒水 667
傳導電報訊號 385
傳輸帶 635, 638, 650
傳輸線觸點 385
傾斗索 675
傾角 636
傾斜連桿 219
傾斜調節索 219
催化重整廠 649
催化重整器 648
匯流排 655
嗅神經 99
嗅球 99, 133
嗅腦 133
嗅膜 133
嗅覺和味覺 133
園圃用鋤 248
園藝 247
園藝工具和機械 248, 249,
  250, 251, 252
圓水準器 614
圓片腿肉 147
圓形 70
圓谷 38
圓刷 338
圓花窗 175
圓花飾 170
圓亭形屋頂 191
圓括號 357, 364
圓柱頂板 170
圓柄雕線刀 516
圓柄頭 521
圓珠 367
圓球下夾 64
圓球上夾 64
圓盒形小帽 314

圓頂 191, 445
圓頂內殼 42
圓頂天窗 42
圓頂外殼 42
圓頂旋轉驅動機 42
圓筒 236, 266
圓筒孔 266
圓筒形提包 347
圓筒鎖 266
圓領 315
圓領毛線衫 296, 307
圓餅乾酪 154
圓盤 407
圓銷頭 219
圓鋸 263
圓鋸片 263
圓錐形尖塔屋頂 191
圓錐飾 170
圓雕花飾 210
圓頭 257, 264, 526
圓頭鎚 257
圓鑽式切磨小面 327
圓繫 516
塞塊 482
塞墊 696
塞擦音 358
塑料絕緣體 288
塑料褲 315
塑模木棒 519
塗刷 230
塔 671
塔式太陽能發電站 668
塔式風車 671
塔式起重機 441, 683
塔柱 435
塔架 416, 638, 658, 672
塔架基 658
塔架基寬度 658
塔架頂 658
塔架窗 658
塔架體 658
塔座 668
塔基 416
塔頂 671
塔樓 174
填土 652
填密螺母 271
填塊 702
塊根芹 84
塊莖菜 84

塊菌 73
媳 139
幹管 202
幹線 424
微波散射器蓋 237
微波爐 237
微型電腦 468
微動調焦鏡筒 623
微處理體 469
微溫水手洗 713, 722
微調鈕 392, 619
感光指數 372
感受器 135
感嘆號 357
感應電勢 654
感覺神經元 135
感覺脈衝 135
感覺器官：味覺 134
感覺器官：視覺 131
感覺器官：嗅覺 133
感覺器官：觸覺 135
感覺器官：聽覺 132
愛斯基摩文 355
愛斯基摩雪屋 169
愛奧尼亞柱型 170
愛爾蘭麵包 146
搋子 276
搓條 519
搪瓷纖維板 194
搭接片 288
搭釦 347
搭箭處 691
搬運工人 427
搶風行駛 551, 553
搖柄 260
搖桿 471
搖桿器 470, 471
搖桿操縱器 469, 471
搖椅 211, 213
搖擺式灑水器 250
攜環 346
新月 38, 710
新月形砂丘 55
新月形麵包 146
新聞照相機 369
新枝 71
新燃料貯存室 665
新燃料裝添區 665
新鮮空氣入口 200
暗井 636

暗夾層 351
暗房 375
暗門襟 300, 307
暗梁 197
暗條 37
暗道 176, 177
暖手插兜 304
暖手插袋 301
暖空氣 669
會所 585
會厭 126, 134
會聚透鏡 625
楔子 482, 510, 694
楔桿 257
楔鐵 257
極地冰蓋 59
極地凍原 59
極地氣候 59
極板 406
極限止位鍵 181
極限控制軸 181
極軸 42
極軸圈 622
極光 47
椰子 78
楞條 170
楯狀 70
橡 190, 192
溢洪斜坡 651
溢洪堰頂 651
溢洪道 651
溢洪閘 651
溢流口 269
溢流管 268, 273
溢流彎頭 267
溶洞 54
溶酶體 86
溶劑萃取裝置 649
溝 590
溝渠進口柵 413
滅火筒 718
溼度 63
溼度計 63
溼雪 57
溼塢 441
溼潤副熱帶 59
溼潤溫和──夏季長 59
溼潤溫和──夏季短 59
溼潤器 462
溫水機洗 713

溫室 161, 669
溫度刻度盤 243
溫度計 647
溫度標度 611
溫度調節鈕 341
溫度選定桿 611
溫度選擇鈕 240, 241
溫度選擇器 237, 243
溫帶氣候 59
溫帶海洋性 59
滑水 554
滑水板 554
滑行面 561
滑行旁道 452
滑行道 452
滑板 499, 703
滑門 198
滑架 467
滑架放鬆桿 467
滑軌 505, 553
滑軌框架 221
滑軌燈 221
滑音 358
滑淚板 551
滑動砲尾 698
滑動接點 259
滑動頂板 397
滑動窗 199, 421
滑動墊 644
滑動擋卡板 464
滑動環 346
滑動轍枕 422
滑桿 482
滑雪 558
滑雪杖 559, 561
滑雪教練 558
滑雪場 558
滑雪帽 298, 561
滑雪運動衣褲 559
滑雪鞋 559, 560
滑雪褲 310
滑雪護目鏡 329
滑翔 556
滑翔運動員 557
滑翔機 556
滑翔翼 557
滑道 209
滑槽 242, 691
滑膛霰彈槍 702
滑輪 218, 242, 278, 553,

610
滑輪夾 218
滑輪旅行箱 347
滑橇 564
滑環 218, 699
準星 697, 700, 702, 703
準星座 699, 701
溜石 544
溜石場 544
溜石運動員 544
溜石道掃帚 545
溜石線 544
溜冰 562
溜冰鞋 562
溜眼 637
煎烤板 237
煎盤 237
煎薄餅鍋 233
煎鍋 233, 599
煤房 637
煤油 456, 649
煤柱 637
煤氣庫 638
煤氣總管 413
煤堆 638
煤礦 635, 636, 637, 638,
639
煉油廠 644, 648
煉油廠產品 649
煉焦廠 638
照明 600
照明設備 220, 221
照明開關 410
照明燈插座 383
照門 697, 699, 700, 701,
702, 703
照指示用含氯漂白劑 722
照相底片 620
照相室 620
照相室照明設備 373
照相室輔助器材 374
照相機 369
照相機台架 374
照準儀 614
煞車踏板 400
獅子座 40
獅子座（7月23日） 712
獅子頭 331
獅子舉步 710
獅足形彎腿 210

瑞士卷 157
瑞典文 355
當心牛隻 715
當心行人 713, 714, 718
當心兒童 714
當心野生動物 715
當心脚踏車 715
睫毛 94, 131
睫毛刷 333
睫毛液 332
睫毛膏 333
睫狀突 131
睪丸 116
矮脚凳 212
矮櫃 465
碎土鋼板 678
碎泥器 163
碎料板 194
碎浪 51
碎褶裙 303
碰插門板 266
碉樓 177
禁止左轉 716
禁止或限制標識 716
禁止迴車 716
禁止停車或限制停車 717
禁止停留或限制停留 717
禁止貨車駛入 716
禁止野餐 721
禁止超車 716
禁止進入 718
禁止携狗進入 718
禁止脚踏車進入 716
禁止摩托車進入 716
禁止機動車輛駛入 713,
716
禁止機器脚踏兩用車進入
716
禁止露營 721
禁止響號 716
禁用行李手車 720
禁用輪椅 719
禁區 535
禁超車段完 716
萬子 593
萬用梯 453
萬用螺絲起子 258
萬向傳動軸 162
萬向頭 374
萬向頭控制把 374

禽舍 161
禽剪 231
稜紋 296, 301, 315, 316,
317
稜紋針法 504
稜紋通心粉 145
稜堡 176, 241
稜鏡切面 446
筷子 233
節 69, 581
節目主持人 390
節拍器 492
節間 69, 658
節點 658
綉花架 507
經度 35
經紗 508, 509, 511
經紗捲軸 508
經緯儀 63, 64, 614
經濟客艙 433
絹印圖案 316
置球三角框 582
置球線 583
置球點 583, 584
罩下鬆緊帶 313
罩杯 313
罩柵 221
罩衫 305
罩帽 271
罩蓋 281, 408
罩頭式吹風機 340
義大利文 355
義大利春卷 145
義大利圓水餃 145
義大利餛飩 145
義大利麵 144
聖內克泰爾半硬乾酪 155
聖代匙 226
聖母峯 47
聖母堂 174
聖馬塞蘭羊乳酪 155
聖摩爾乾酪 154
腭 133
腭甲 690
腭足 103
腭扁桃體 134
腰 91, 95, 115, 148, 150
腰下小面 327
腰上小面 327
腰包 559

索 引

腰末肋肉 148
腰尖肉 148
腰肉 147, 149, 150, 151, 153
腰肋肉 152
腰果 78
腰後 148
腰神經叢 129
腰脊 147, 151
腰脊肉 152
腰帶 105, 291, 294, 321, 575, 578
腰帶絆 291, 294, 316
腰帶釦 291
腰部 658
腰部按鈕 315
腰椎 92
腰椎（5）121
腰椎脊髓 130
腰稜 327
腰腹細肉 149
腰窩 91
腰箍 313
腰褶 292
腱 94
腸 99, 102, 124
腸系膜下動脈 128
腸系膜上動脈 125, 128
腹 91, 95, 114
腹大動脈 99
腹主動脈 125, 128
腹甲 109, 690
腹肉 149, 152
腹足 100
腹足類動物 104
腹直肌 118
腹側 514
腹帶 567, 568
腹帶繫條 567
腹桿 190
腹部 100, 103, 106
腹腔動脈 124, 128
腹節 100
腹膜 116
腹鰭 98
腦 99
腦神經 129
腦橋 130
腩肉 148, 150, 153
舅 138

舅母 138
落子位 592
落水洞 54
落地 574
落地式大擺鐘 607
落地區 571
落地窗 199
落地墊 570, 571, 574
落地燈 220
落帆索 551
落花生 78
落袋撞球 583
落袋撞球和四球撞球 583
葉 69, 70, 85
葉片 70, 206, 219, 656, 657, 706
葉片型升力風機 435
葉尖 70
葉的類型 70
葉柄 70
葉脈 70
葉腋 69, 70
葉菜 82
葉距操縱桿 455
葉綠體 86
葉緣 70
葉輪 242
葉鞘 70
葛魯耶乾酪 155
萼 72, 74, 76, 79
萼片 72, 74
葡萄 74
葡萄牙文 355
葡萄柚 77
葡萄柚刀 227
葡萄皮硬乾酪 154
葡萄酒瓶 222
葡萄葉 82
葡萄彈 695
葱形屋頂 191
堇 83
黃蒿子黑麵包 146
號碼 594
號碼戳 462
號碼鎖 350
號燈 445
號燈玻璃窗 445
蛹 100
蜂后 106
蜂后室 107

蜂后隔板 107
蜂巢剖面 107
蜂巢漫射片 373
蜂窩板 107
蜂箱 107, 161
蜂箱體 107
裙子 303
裙襯架形 213
補償調焦環 621
裝坯支架 520
裝拆鎖 699
裝物盤 347
裝柄螺環 337
裝料口 665
裝烟囱口 201
裝針桿 500
裝備 588
裝嵌孔壁 377
裝嵌盤 266
裝填 696
裝填手座 704
裝煤碉室 637
裝照相機螺絲 374
裝運區 648
裝飾音 476
裝飾層 265
裝飾縫 300
裝飾縫線 349
裝鉸鏈門梃 215
裝燈板 340
裝牆路燈 221
裝鎖橫檔 198
裝藥 702
裝藥孔 696
裏海 49
裏模 519
解剖 99
試電筆 286
話筒 387
詢問記錄與定位系統天線 65
資料存儲 468
資料收集 468
資料處理 468
資料處理設備 468
資料顯示 468
跟骨 92, 121
跟部 257, 262
跟部勒具 559, 560
跟腱護部 562

跟蹤、遙測和指令天線 393
跨臂 680
路厄氏注射器 629
路肩 413
路面高突 714
路面層 413
路面顛簸 714
路基 413
路堤 413
路牌 178
路程標杆 569
路滑 714
路緣石 413
路線牌 419
路燈 178, 247
路燈柱 178
跳水 548
跳水池 548
跳水動作 549
跳水設備 548
跳水運動員 549
跳台 558
跳台滑雪運動員 558
跳台跳水運動員 549
跳板跳水運動員 548
跳格取消鍵 467
跳格定位鍵 467
跳格撤桿 467
跳馬 573, 574
跳高 571
跳球圈 535
跳傘 555
跳傘員 555
跳傘運動員 555
跳遠 570
跳躍滑水板 554
載半掛車的平板車 420
載台 417
載台面板 402
載台掛車 402
載物台 619, 620
載物架 411
載客升降機 719
載客車廂種類 421
載貨升降機 719
載貨車廂種類 420
載貨報表牌 419
載運汽車的多層車 420
載駁母船 441

載盤 236
農舍 161
農舍式別墅 558
農場 161
農業機械 162, 163, 164
運行中的太空穿梭機 457
運河油船 645
運送橋 417
運動上衣連裙 302
運動甲板 433
運動衣領 308
運動衫 305, 530
運動員 564
運動神經元 135
運動神經細胞 135
運動終板 135
運動連衣褲 317
運動與遊戲 525
運動鞋 319
運動褲 575
運穀螺旋 165
運輸平巷 635
運轉輪 510
道口 427
道岔 424
道岔底座 423
道具管理員 390
道釘 422
道路交通 397
道碴 422
過肘長手套 299
過腕手套 299
過膝長襪 311
過膝燈籠褲 310
過膝褲 310
過濾器 204, 669
鉗 341
鉗口 343
鉗牙 287
鉗曲夾 343
鉗架 259
鉗架高 259
鉗柄 341
鈾燃料裂變 667
鉚釘 227, 259, 328
鉛刀 521
鉛丸壓載 437
鉛球 572
鉛筆 367
鉛錘 581

鉛錘腰帶 550
鉋 257
鉋刀 257
鉋口深淺調平桿 257
鉋底面 257
鈴 486
鈴片 575
鈴鼓 486
鈴錘 387
閘口柵欄操縱器 423
閘口警鐘 423
閘板 520
閘門 655, 660
閘門閥 440
閘門操縱環 657
閘臂 423
閘臂支撐肘 423
閘臂信號燈 423
隔布 347
隔板 406, 465, 646
隔脂池 277
隔帶鋼絲 466
隔焰耐火罩 520
隔熱屏 457
隔熱層 647
隔線板 505
隔膜 79
隔壁相連的三層樓住宅
　183
隔壁相連的房屋 183
雉蝶 177
雷雨 60
雷達 624
雷達天線 438
雷達天線罩 705
雷達旋轉天線 435
雷管 700
電力 651, 652, 653, 654,
　655, 656, 657, 658, 659
電力系統 672
電力室 661
電力裝置 453
電力檢查表 383
電子束 392
電子取景器 384
電子取景器顯象控制 384
電子秤 610
電子閃光燈 372
電子槍 392, 620

電子顯微鏡 620
電工工具 286, 287
電工鉗 287
電文廣播 394
電平調節鈕 378
電吉他 494
電池 65, 371, 372, 437
電池伸撐機械 393
電池組操作裝置 393
電池蓋 406
電池箱 402
電池鞋刷 320
電吹風機 340
電弧 281
電弧管 284
電弧銲 281
電弧銲機 281
電表 615, 659
電信一號衛星 394
電信衛星 393, 394
電流示警燈 399
電流表 410
電流線圈 615
電容器 672
電氣 284, 285, 286, 287,
　288
電能經電線輸往用戶 667
電動扶梯 428
電動扶梯（下） 719
電動扶梯（上） 719
電動刮鬍刀 337
電動烤叉 238
電動記分儀 576
電動高爾夫球車 587
電動開罐刀 243
電動機 182, 205, 206, 234,
　240, 241, 244, 260, 261,
　263, 371, 377, 437, 622
電動機發電機 181
電動機發電機組 181
電動機裝置 235, 236
電動機滾輪 380
電動壓縮裝置 206
電動變焦開關 384
電接頭 238
電報 385, 386, 720
電報線 385
電視 389, 390, 391, 392
電視機 392
電視攝影機 384

電開關 285
電極 284, 387
電極組件 205
電源 204, 385
電源/定時器斷路鈕 382
電源插座 285
電源開關 379, 381, 382,
　495
電源線 220, 221, 243, 273,
　340
電源燈 495
電腦 472
電腦室 472
電話 718
電話號碼索引 464
電話鈴線圈 387
電話線 322, 388
電話機 387
電話機數種 388
電話錄音機 388
電話纜 413
電路接頭 402
電路圖 385
電鈴 387
電磁鐵 385
電影攝影 383
電樂器與電子樂器 494,
　495
電熱水器水箱 273
電熱絲 241, 242
電窰 520
電線 261, 337, 373, 377,
　387
電線夾 285
電線套 261
電線剪 287
電壓表 286
電壓線圈 615
電離室 662
電離層 47
電爐 205
電爐竈 238
電驅動機 624
電籬 161
電纜 413
電纜溝 423
電鑽 261
雹 57
雹陣 60
零 594, 595

零散雲 61
零錢口袋 351
零錢包 351
零錢兌換機 426
零雜用具 231
靶 544, 550, 555
靶心 544
靶心得分線 544
靶心標記 544
預定旅館房間櫃台 454
預測睹率 569
預播監控機 391
預熱指示點 341
預選調諧按鈕 379
預應力混凝土 193
飼用穀物 161
飾板 489
飾釘 349
馴鹿 89
鳩尾形板 621
鼓式制動器 407
鼓耳 486
鼓形柱 170
鼓面 486
鼓風機 204, 205, 206, 481
鼓風機電動機 205
鼓腹 486
鼓膜 105, 109, 132
鼠標器 469
鼠蹊 114

嫩煎鍋 233
嫩腰肉 150, 152
嫩腰軟肉 148
孵化室 107
實心琴身 494
實心膠輪胎 684
實驗室 648
對子 593
對子－六 593
對中標 467
對分劉海 331
對手 578
對比度調整鈕 392
對耳屏 132
對耳輪 132
對行紙夾 386
對角拱 175
對流式供暖器 203
對流層 37, 47
對接銲 282
對焦套筒 614
對話窗口 426
對摺指示線 503
對褶 304
幕前部分 180
幕牆 176
截流墊 271
截流墊座 271
截流閥 267, 268, 270, 272
截割吹管 282
截割管嘴 282
摘果梯 279
摔倒 578
摟草耙 248
摺門 188, 198
摺面板 209
摺面桌 209
摺頁用骨篦 512
摺桌 421
摺椅 213
摺鏈 600
摺疊口袋 351
摺疊包 348
摺疊式文件夾 463
摺疊式文件袋 350
摺疊式指甲銼 343
摺疊式照相機 369
摺疊烤架 600
摺疊梯 278
摺疊窗 199

蔽脫式孔蓋片 288
蔽擊樂器 485, 486
旗 558
旗形 711
旗杆 558, 709
旗門 558
旗袍領 308
旗幟各部分 709
旗幟紋章 709
旗幟與盾牌 709
槓桿 259, 385, 612, 696
構架 192
構架柱 683
榛子 78
榛子剖面 78
樺釘孔 328
樺眼 345, 507
樺眼鎖 266
樺鋸 513
樺頭 345
榠桴 76
槍口 702
槍尖 572
槍托 697, 699, 701, 702, 703
槍把形手柄 261, 262
槍眼 177
槍管 697, 699, 701, 702, 703
槍管套 697
槍管套環 693
槍管螺帽 699
槍機 701
槍機管 699
槍機撞頭 699
槌 485, 486
槌托 480
槌尾 514
槌柄 480, 514
槌柄擋 480
槌面 514
槌頭 257, 480
榨汁錐 236
榨蒜鉗 228
榨橙汁器 228, 236
歌王牌乾酪 154
演播室 389, 390
演播室和控制室 389
滾子 446, 466
滾花旋鈕 442

滾珠軸承 562
滾動軸 393
滾筒 241, 518
滾筒架 280
滾筒絨層 280
滾筒轉動手柄 516
滾軸箱和傳動臂 482
滾網線刀 515
滾輪 408, 683
滾輪架 562
滾壓筒 241, 251
滾翻轉身 547
滴水石 187
滴注咖啡壺 234
滴乾 722
漏勺 229
漏斗 228
漏斗形罩 392
漏斗車 420
漏斗礦車 420
漏匙 229
漂白 722
滿月 38
滿帆迎風 553
滿貫 592
滿圓鑽式切磨 327
滿載調整螺旋 615
滯留鋒 61
漸盈的凸月 38
漸盈的蛾眉月 38
漸窄燕尾 711
漸虧的凸月 38
漸虧的蛾眉月 38
漫射片 373
漫射濾光片 373
漁人結 601
漁線 580, 581
滲水區 277
滲水層 652
滲潤作用 58
滲濾咖啡壺 234
滲濾管 234
滲濾籃 234
熔岩流 53
熔岩高原 53
熔銲吹管 281, 282
熊掌形 563
監門員 545
監門員席 533
監控室 666

十 四 畫

僧伽羅文 355
凳、椅 212
圖形 595, 713
圖案 521
圖樣 710
圖樣骰 593
塵埃彗尾 39
墊 328
墊子 506, 578
墊板 422
墊料 562
墊圈 271
墊臂 328
獎金盤 595

監控機 391
監控機組 391
監控機操作員 390
監網裁判 537
監製 391
監製室 389, 391
監聽指示燈 379
監聽揚聲器 391
瞄準具 625
瞄準滑標 691
瞄準線 625
瞄準器 697
瞄準鏡 625
睡衣 311, 316
睡衣褲 311
睡袍 311
睡袋 598
磁性吸蓋盤 243
磁性密封圈 239
磁性懸繫鈕 615
磁針 625
磁帶存儲器 472
磁帶控制器 471
磁帶機 472
磁帶錄影機 389
磁帽 606
磁極片 387
磁道 472
磁道調鈕 382
磁碟 472
磁碟存儲器 472
磁碟機 469, 472
磁碟機控制器 472
磁羅盤 625
磁鐵 443, 501
碟式底片照相機 369
碟式膠片 371
碳粒 387
種子 74, 75, 76, 77, 78, 79
種子葉 85
種子箱 164
種皮 75, 79
稱人結 601
稱呼 359, 360, 361
端底橫梁 425
端板 237, 663
端門 425
端架 218
端面水平扶手 419
端紋 265

端梯 419
端部 257, 262
端部裝置 662
端頂橫梁 425
端罩 661
端罩冷卻管 662
端蓋 663
端線 527, 535, 536, 546,
　576
管 377
管口 482
管子 274
管式加熱器 649
管式保險絲 285
管式構件 643
管式鎖 266
管耳 482
管扳手 276
管身 482
管制 713
管底 284
管板 662
管柄 488
管段 202
管座 482
管接頭 274
管理大樓 638, 660
管理處 648
管帽 275
管塞 275
管塞鈕 481
管道 274
管道工程 267, 268, 269,
　270, 271, 272, 273, 274,
　275, 276, 277
管道系統 267
管道纏繞絕緣材料 195
管嘴 282, 676
管嘴清通器 283
管樂器 483, 484
管螺紋切削器 276
管鐘琴 485, 493
箋頭 359, 360, 361
箋 510
箍 622, 623
精子 116
精索 116
精裝書 511
精裝書籍裝訂 512, 513,
　514

精囊 116
綜絖 508
綜絲 508, 509
綜絲桿 509
綠皮西葫蘆 81
綠色 710
綠色＝准許、指示 713
綠呢 583, 584
綠洲 55
綠球 584
綠電子束 392
綠蓋紅菇 73
緊束背心 307
緊身裙 313
緊身衣褲 305
緊身背心 307
緊身胸衣 312
緊身胸衣連三角褲 312
緊身連衣襪褲 317
緊身短上衣 307
緊身短襪褲 313
緊身褲 313
緊急制動手柄 429
緊急救生裝置 456
緊袖口 306
緊髮夾 343
綴飾 313, 321
網 533, 535, 536, 537, 539,
　542, 543
網柱 536, 542, 545
網架 543
網罟座 41
網兜 582
網球 537, 538
網球拍 538
網球場 537
網球裙 538
網球運動員 538
網球鞋 319, 538
網眼 543
網頂白帶 537
網罩 271, 384
網路 387
網襪 311
維也納麵包 146
維修庫 452
罰球弧 532
罰球區 532, 535
罰球線 535, 539
罰球點 532

聚合和烷基化設備 648
聚光罩 373
聚光燈 221, 373, 376, 390,
　436, 619, 676, 677
聚光鏡調節鈕 619
聚風罩 340
聚焦 668
聚焦放大鏡 375, 376
聚焦區 668
膀胱 99, 116, 117, 128
膈柱肌肉 147, 149
膈神經 126
腿 95, 115
腿甲 690
腿肉 147, 153
腿姿勢 549
腿套 589
腿罩 690
腿端肉 147, 149, 150
與 723
舞台 180
舞台下第一層 180
舞台下第二層 180
舞台下第三層 180
舞台下第四層 180
舞台右側 179
舞台左側 179
舞台兩側及後方 179
舞台後方 179, 180
舞台剖面圖 180
蒔蘿 143
蓄水池 173
蓄氣箱 481
蓄電池 406
蓄潮壩 660
蒙古包 169
蒙特雷乾酪 154
蒲公英葉 82
蒜頭 83
蓋 341
蓋子 232, 233, 234, 236,
　237, 611, 615, 625
蓋片 345, 349, 351, 619
蓋板 240, 670
蓋門鍵 341
蓋鐵 257
蒸汽 664
蒸汽分離器 664
蒸汽油砂採油法 650
蒸汽渦輪機 434

蒸汽發生系統 666
蒸汽發生器 661, 664, 668
蒸汽裂化設備 648
蒸汽管路 661, 664
蒸汽熨斗 243
蒸汽凝結成水 667
蒸汽驅動渦輪機 667
蒸架 233
蒸發 58
蒸發盤管 239
蒸發器 206
蒸發器盤管 206
蒸餾咖啡壺 234
蒸騰 58
蒼蠅座 41
蘋果 79
蘋果剖面 79
脣葵 79
脣葵果剖面 79
蜜蜂 106, 107
蝕刻銅版印刷機 516
裸麥粗麵包 146
裸麥黑麵包 146
裸麥麵包 146
製冰淇淋機 236
製冰盤 239
製冷裝置 402
製版墨 517
製表鍵 470
製麵包糕餅用具 230
誤點告示牌 427
豪華大轎車 398
豪華套房 433
赫米斯衛星 393
輔助工具 509
輔助手柄 261
輔助用具 492
輔助放映機 43
輔助注入口 647
輔助消聲器 406
輔助設備 582
輔助攝影器材 374
輕便公文包 350
輕便手杖 346
輕便台梯 279
輕便摺疊床 598
輕劍 692
輕駕車 567
輕機關槍 701
輕擊地區 585

輕擊棒 586
輕擊棒頭 586
辣根 84
辣椒 81
遠光警告燈 410
遠程雷達系統 706
遠程噴射機 448
遠距離通訊會議 394
遠距離通訊電腦 394
遠距離通訊網 394
遠端籽骨 92
遠端趾骨 94
遠攝鏡頭 370
遙控插座 383
遙控器 377
遙控機械臂 457
遙控轉轍器 423
遙測天線 393
酸模 82
鉸合齒 101
鉸接 398
鉸接壓布脚 499, 500
鉸銷 337, 338
鉸臂 242
鉸鏈 198, 199, 209, 215, 237,
　　238, 347, 349, 380, 621
鉸鏈門 188
鉸鏈梃 198, 199
銀色 710
銀河 40
銀河放映機 43
銀幕 377
銀幕護匣 377
銀餐具 224, 225, 226
銅凹板 515
銅球閥 271
銅絲刷 485
銅鈸 485, 491
銅鈸，三角鐵，響板 493
銅管 274
銅管接塑料管 275
銅管接鋼管 275
銅管樂器 484
銅箔 521
閣樓 187
閣樓小圓窗 187
閥座 271
閥座扳手 276
閥桿 271
閥桿式龍頭 271

閥鍵 344
障礙 565, 585
障礙棒頭 586
障礙跑道 566
障礙賽跑 570
雌性 723
雌蕊 72
鞅 568
領口 297
領口與領子 309
領巾 559
領片鑲面 293
領尖 295, 308
領尖硬襯 295
領夾 326
領底 305
領座 308
領座翻摺 308
領座翻摺線 308
領缺嘴 293
領帶 295, 321
領帶別針 325
領帶夾 326
領帶針 326
領圈 295
領飾 326
領緣 308
颮 60
餅乾 157
駁船 645
骰子 592, 593
骰子筒 592
鳴笛浮標 444
鳶尾花 710
鳳凰座 41
鳳梨 80
鼻 91, 114
鼻口部 94
鼻中隔皮部 133
鼻中隔軟骨 133
鼻孔 91, 95, 98, 105, 109, 133
鼻母音 358
鼻尖 133
鼻咽 133
鼻革 567
鼻根 133
鼻骨 122
鼻梁 133
鼻梁架 328
鼻腔 126

鼻嗅區上皮 133
鼻罩 690
鼻葉 108
鼻墊 328
鼻窩 122, 133
鼻端韌皮 94
鼻翼 133
齊平襯套 275
齊特琴 487

十五畫

儀表板 399, 556
儀容修飾 325
儀器百葉箱 063
儀器板 399
儀器設備 456
劇毒蕈 73
劇院 179, 180, 433
劍 577, 692
劍身 577
劍身弱部 577
劍身強部 577
劍的各部分 577
劍柄 577
劍術 576, 577
劍魚座 41
劍頭 577
嘴 114
噴口 706
噴口調節錐 450
噴水口 243
噴水按鈕 243
噴汽按鈕 243
噴油器 404
噴射引擎 705
噴射機燃料 649
噴氣孔 53
噴槍 280
噴漆調節閥 280
噴管 456
噴嘴 205, 280, 339, 647, 677
噴霧器 250
噴灑水管 270
噴灑器 242
噴灑頭 270
增加空位 362

增音鍵盤 481
增距鏡頭 370
增壓 654, 667
寬口長手套 299
寬大晨衣 311
寬凸台 489
寬底腳座 402
寬度 549
寬腳綴片裙 303
寬幅短劍 692
寬貼邊 300
寬搭裙 303
寬緣湯匙 223
寬髮夾 343
寬鬆長上衣 305
寬鬆掛簾 217
寬邊斜插袋 291, 304
寬麵 144
層雲 52
層積雲 52
層壓板 265
履帶 408, 678, 704
履帶支重輪架 678
履帶式起重機 683
履帶式牽引 678
履帶托鏈輪 678
履帶板 678
履帶惰輪 678
履帶滾輪 678
履帶環 704
履帶鏈節 678
廢土石堆 635
廢物清除器 270
廢氣出口 404
廢氣進口 404
廢燃料口 665
廢燃料卸除室 665
廢燃料倉 665
廢燃料貯存倉 663, 665, 667
廢燃料裝罐 665·
廚刀 227
廚房 173, 189, 421, 448
廚房用具 227, 228, 229, 230, 231
廚房秤 229
廣告牌 178, 428
廣角擴散片 372
廣角鏡頭 370
彈丸 696, 702

彈心 702
彈匣 697, 699, 703
彈匣卡筍 697, 699, 703
彈匣底板 703
彈匣彈簧 703
彈床 574
彈底 702
彈性連接法 645
彈性韌帶 94, 102
彈性繃帶 629
彈性襯墊 584
彈室蓋 701
彈倉 702
彈射座椅 705
彈巢 703
彈殼 702
彈塞 695
彈跳板 573, 574
彈膛 702, 703
彈頭 702, 706
彈簧 221, 259, 266, 271, 367, 418, 574, 608, 612, 616, 696, 700
彈簧卡 346
彈簧床座 214
彈簧活頁夾 463
彈簧門 266
彈簧秤 608
彈簧墊圈 422
彈簧銷鉤柄 500
彈簧翼 264
彈藥倉 704
影象技術員 389
影象投射鏡 371
影象輸入 382
影象輸出 382
影線 511
德文 355
德國裸麥麵包 146
摩托車 409, 410
摩爾斯電碼 386
摩羯座 41
摩羯座（12月22日） 712
摩擦子音 358
摩擦面 345
摩擦塊 407
摩擦襯片 407
撞針 696, 702, 703
撞球遊戲用具 582
撐架 213

撐竿 570
撐竿跳高 570
撐索桿 552
撐骨 346
撐梁 508
撐桿 192, 610
撐條 284, 551, 552, 557, 660, 672
撐條袋 551, 552
撐頸桿 568
撐臂 659
撥子板 494
撥火棍 201
撥號盤 386, 387
撥機 700
撥機柄 701
撕封帶 344
撕頁日曆 464
撒布器 251
撒肥箱 163
撒肥機 163
撒肥轉盤 163
撒粉器 231
撒爾維亞 143
撮彈器 697
撳鈕 502
播出監控機 391
播放 382
播放按鈕 381
播種器 249, 251
敵我識別器天線 705
敷設日期標識釘 422
數字 356, 357, 386
數字表面 605
數字計算機：控制/警報 666
數字符號 356
數字骰 593
數字鍵台 470
數字鍵盤 610
數字鐘 382
數種車身 398
數碼頻率顯示 379
數學 723
數學符號 356
暫停/定鏡 382
暫停按鈕 381
樣本 619
樣本室 620
樣品 504

椿 671
椿孔挖掘器 248
椿式風車 671
椿柱 643
椿橋 642
樞 287
樞椎 121
樞軸 501
樞鉸 560
標尺 471, 647
標位燈 705
標度盤 443, 609
標記法 A 591
標記法 B 591
標桿 698
標準種溜蹄馬 568
標準鏡頭 370
標準纖維板 194
標槍 572
標點 386
標點符號 356, 357
標識 709
標識帶 536
標識桿 536
標識線 590
標識燈 403
標籤 380
標籤機 461
槽 500, 521, 586
槽口 264
槽車 420
槽紋 380
槽紋桿 218
槽鉋 260
模擬頻率表 379
樓板 671
樓板管周圈 202
樓座 179
樓梯 188, 197, 428, 719
樓梯井 189
樓梯平台 189
樓層選擇器 181
槳式活門 440
樂隊席 180
樂器合奏 490, 491
樂譜架 479, 492
歐亞大陸 49
歐洲 49
歐洲式插頭 285
漿果剖面 74

漿糊棒 461
潟湖 51
澆水壺 250
澆水軟管 250
潛水 550
潛水表 550
潛水裝 322
潛式平台 642
潛望鏡 438, 704
潛艇 438
潮水塢 441
潮汐發電廠 660
潤滑油 649
潤滑油廠 649
潤滑油槽 253
熱馬鈴薯搗爛器 229
熱反射金屬罩 200
熱水支管 203
熱水萃取 650
熱水幹管 203, 204
熱水管 272, 273
熱水豎管 267
熱水器 267
熱交換器 669
熱成層 47
熱折射片 284
熱度與風速選擇鈕 340
熱度調節鈕 341
熱風梳 338
熱氣出口 202
熱氣增壓室 202
熱帶水果 80
熱帶雨林 59
熱帶風暴 60
熱帶氣候 59
熱帶稀樹草原 59
熱貯存 668
熱解 650
熱預感器 611
熱預感器指針 611
熨 722
瘦果 74, 78
皺葉菊萵苣 82
皺褶飾 217
皺邊領 308
皺邊雙層掛簾 217
皺麵 144
盤子 599
盤式水準器 614
盤式制動器 407, 409, 672

盤花鈕釦 292
盤區 637
盤管電熱線 238
磌土 519
碼線 527
碼頭坡道 441
碼頭區鐵路 441
碼頭邊起重機 441
穀物升運器 165
穀倉 161
穀粒貯槽 165
穀粒盤 165
穀粒篩 165
箭 691
箭托 691
箭羽 691
箭尾槽 691
箭桿 691
箭塔 177
箭頭 691
箱形梁叉架 680
箱形貨盤 685
箱形鞋頭 562
箱狀手提包 348
箱框 347, 350
箱頂 107, 402, 425
練馬師 569
練習草坪 585
緯度 35
緯度尺 64
緯紗 508, 511
緯紗管 509
編花毯籽子 509
編組場 425
編組緩行器 425
編織 504
編織用尺 504
編織法 504
編織旋刷 506
編織機 505, 506
編織繩索 601
編織懸架 505, 506
緣甲 109
線 475, 601
線夾 505
線形 70
線圈 387
線球 510
線軸 499, 506
線軸柱 499

線路 385
線路檢查燈 700
線盤 658
線膛來福槍 702
線縫 79, 318
緞紋織法 511
緩坡 188
緩動控制鈕 623
緩線彈簧 500, 639
緩衝柱 181
緩衝區 529, 533
緩衝層 407
緩衝器 418, 701
膜片 378, 384, 387
膜突 106
膝 91, 108, 114
膝甲翼 690
膝骨 92
膝墊 530, 534
膠片反捲曲柄 368
膠片感光速度指示器 368
膠布 629
膠皮 543
膠合板 194, 265
膠卷 372
膠卷計尺器 383
膠卷乾燥櫃 375
膠卷筒 371
膠卷頭 371
膠原纖維 136
膠帶 461, 526
膠帶卷座 461
膠黏劑 196
蕨藥藍 143
蓮蓬頭 250, 269
蓮蓬頭架 269
蔬果保鮮室 239
蔬菜 81, 82, 83, 84, 85
蔬菜刷 231
蔬菜缽 223
蔬菜蒸籠 232
蔭罩 392
蔓越橘 74
蓬萊韋克半軟乾酪 155
蓬蓬頭 330
蝴蝶 100
蝴蝶粉 145
蝴蝶結 298
蝴蝶領 308
蝴蝶領結 295

蝶式 547
蝶式打水 547
蝶式轉身 547
蝶形螺母 264
蝶泳手 547
蝶骨 122
蝶竇 133
蜻蜓座 41
蝦 103
蝸牛 104
蝸牛鉗 231
蝸牛碟 231
蝸桿 510
蝸殼 656, 657
蝸輪轉動裝置 219
蝙蝠 108
蝙蝠袖 306
衝鋒槍 697
衝擊式鑽機 639
複印份數鈕 467
複合砂丘 55
複合頂標 446
複眼 100, 106
複葉 70
複寫紙 521
複漿果 74
複褶 304
調平旋鈕 609, 614
調平螺絲 64
調正螺母 64
調車場 425
調車機車 425
調制器 624
調音扳頭 492
調音弦栓 479
調音鈕 478, 494
調音滑管 484
調音鋼絲桿 482
調音螺絲 486
調校柄 400
調校螺母 613
調速器 181
調焦鈕 376, 377, 383, 622, 623
調焦環 383, 384
調號 476
調溫百葉窗 65
調溫鈕 238
調節定位槽 259
調節板 200, 202

調節高度支座 205
調節鈕 257
調節閥 599
調節輪 287
調節環 260, 370
調節螺絲 282
調節擺錘 492
調節瓣 482, 489
調節瓣彈簧 482
調節罐 644
調運場 638
調整螺絲 423
調諧按鈕 379
調諧旋鈕 442
調諧器 378
調頻立體聲指示燈 379
調頻單聲立體聲選擇 379
調壓槓桿 517
調壓器 281, 282, 599
豌豆 79
豌豆角 85
豎井 636
豎板 197
豎柱凹槽 402
豎琴 478, 493
豎鉸鏈窗 199
豎線膠筒 243
賠率 569
賭金顯示牌 569
踝 114
踝襻涼鞋 319
踢脚板 197
踢脚板出氣口 202
踢脚板暖氣管 203
踏步板槽紋 197
踏板 411, 412, 478, 486,
  508, 567
踏板高椅 212
踏板連桿 479
踏板運動帶 508
踏板鍵 481
踏板鍵盤 481
踏梯 579
踏脚板 403, 519, 610
踏脚乾地 544
輪子 347, 501, 562, 694
輪子制動手柄 631
輪斗式挖掘機 635, 650
輪式牽引車 679
輪式裝載機 679

輪作草地 161
輪胎 403, 407, 411
輪胎充氣泵 401
輪胎架 401
輪胎氣泵 411
輪梯台 279
輪頂 519
輪椅 631
輪軸 418, 562
輪楔 453
輪葉 657, 660
輪盤 407, 594
輪盤賭枱 594, 595
輪輞 407, 409, 411
輪輞邊圈 407
輪機室 645
輪轂 411, 631, 657
輪轂罩 397
輪轂蓋 657
輪轉換位 536
輥子導引器 181
遮布 297
遮禿假髮 331
遮窗板 199
遮陽板 399
遮陽罩 423
遮護板 270
遮護圈 270
銷釘 209
鋪砌層 413
鋪路扁石 247
鋤 248
鋤鎬 248
銲料 283, 521
銲接 521
銲接地線 281
銲接防護幕 283
銲條 281
銲條夾 281
銲條電源線 281
銲槍 281
銲槍尖 281
銲劑 521
銲劑刷 521
銲縫 281, 282
銼刀 599
鋒 60
閱讀 328
震央 53
震波 53

震源 53
震源深度 53
靠背 400, 408, 631
靠背框柱 213
靠背連扶手長沙發 211
靠背頂梁 213
靠背橫梁 213
鞍包 567
鞍布 568
鞍式牽引架 403
鞍架 567
鞍座 411, 567
鞍座支柱 411
鞍馬 573
鞍部 573
鞍褥 567
鞍環 573
鞍翼 567
鞍囊形手提包 349
鞋 318, 319, 320
鞋尖 690
鞋尖勒具 559, 560
鞋尖預調脫扣顯示窗 560
鞋舌 318, 560, 562
鞋尾 563
鞋身 563
鞋身網格 563
鞋具 320
鞋底 321, 560, 562
鞋底中腰 318
鞋底釘 320
鞋拔 320
鞋的各部分 318
鞋架 320
鞋面 318
鞋套 320
鞋釘 587
鞋帶 318, 562
鞋帶孔 318, 562
鞋帶孔片 318
鞋帶包頭 318
鞋楦 320
鞋跟 562
鞋跟底革 318
鞋跟預調脫扣顯示窗 560
鞋跟網格 563
鞋跟穩釘 561
鞋墊 320
鞋頭 321, 563
鞋頭固定裝置 561

鞋頭空隙 563
鞋頭網格 563
鞋頭穩釘 561
鞋幫 560
鞋幫側面 318
翬膜 131
頰 95
頰孔 122
頜的類型 90
駝峯調車場 425
駝峯調車場地 425
駐退索 694
駐退機 698
駐鋤 698
駛向下風 551
駛帆索 551
駕駛人 556
駕駛台 434, 435, 438, 645
駕駛台與海圖室 434
駕駛室 418, 436, 678, 679,
  680, 681, 682, 684
駕駛座 684, 704
駕駛桿 451
駕駛盤 165
駕駛艙 448, 451, 455, 457,
  556
骶神經叢 129
骶骨 120
骶椎 92
髮夾 343
髮刷 338
髮卷 341, 343
髮卷插針 343
髮型 330, 331
髮剪 338
髮髻 331
墨水 367
墨帶 466, 467
墨帶盒 466
墨帶裝入桿 466
墨輥 385
墨鏈 516
齒 588, 680, 681
齒孔 371
齒尖 263
齒形飾 170
齒軌 424
齒幹護片 678
齒隙 90
齒輪 510

索 引

齒輪組 371
齒輪殼 580
齒輪滾盤 675
齒輪箱 436, 517, 672
齒邊三角 711
齒邊剪 501

十六畫

凝結水 664
噪音發生器調節 495
器材搬運 683
壁 636
壁球 540
壁燈 220
壁櫥 188, 189
壁爐 188, 200
壁爐架 200
寰椎 121
導升塔架 417
導向供電條 429
導向桿 162, 466
導向裝置 705
導向槽 559, 561
導向螺絲 260
導流牆 651
導軌 422, 429, 505
導軌接頭 218
導風弧板 403
導氣管 701
導紙擋塊 467
導航雷達 439
導帶釦 466
導桿 253
導傘 555
導軸承 656
導電弓 427
導電外層 392
導電線 221
導電體 606
導彈 438, 706
導彈的構造 706
導彈發射指揮儀 439
導彈發射管 438
導彈發射器 439
導彈發射導軌 705
導線 372, 384, 442

導線圈 499, 500
導線槽 499
導線鋼絲 510
導棍 412
導鏈 437
導體 670
導纜鉗 553
戰鬥機 705
擋子 594
擋火建材 192
擋光板 373
擋板 239, 669, 682
擋泥板 397, 402, 403, 411
擋門塊 419
擋風板 599
擋風玻璃 397, 403, 408, 451, 705
擋風玻璃雨刮 398
擋球線 540, 541
擋規 513
擋雪板 408
擋焰盤 700
擋墊 590
擋網 525
操帆索 431
操作台 666
操作車間 660
操作開關 206
操桿員 390
操縱引擎 457
操縱室 676, 683
操縱柄 408
操縱桿 401, 451, 455, 556, 557, 639, 701
操縱盤 676, 677
操縱鋼索 412
操縱繩 555
擒縱爪 605, 607
擒縱輪 605, 607
撿拾裝載機 162
撿拾器 162
整平刮板 680
整流器 373
整經架 510
整髮工具 343
橙 77
橫木 192, 531, 545, 558, 574
橫向定位按鈕 467
橫向拱 175

橫向砂丘 55
橫杠 575
橫走 591
橫巷 636, 637
橫竿 570, 571
橫風 553
橫風行駛 553
橫桁 430
橫紋 502
橫帶 170
橫排檔案櫃 465
橫梁 487, 508
橫桿 162, 218, 374, 509, 513
橫條紋浮標 444
橫握 543
橫結腸 127
橫隔板 402, 646
橫膈膜 126, 127
橫撐 209, 279
橫擔 658, 659
橫艙壁 645
橫檔 209, 213, 508, 588, 631
橫檔板 279
橫護手 693
樹 71
樹皮 71
樹枝 71
樹狀突 135
樹的構造 71
樹冠 71
樹脂面相紙乾燥機 375
樹頂 71
樹鳥 97
樹幹 71
樹葉 71
樹椿 71
樹籬 247
橄欖 75
橄欖球 530
橢圓大麵包 146
橢圓形切磨 327
橢圓星系 39
橡皮充氣球 612
橡皮印章 462
橡皮泥板 570
橡皮基 338
橡皮軟管 272
橡皮筋 587

橡皮墊 270
橡皮墊圈 270
橡皮頭 630
橡皮擦 461
橡膠刮片 398
橡膠底帆布鞋 319
橡膠套鞋 320
橡膠墊 380
橡膠壁 407
橋下通道 414
橋台 414, 415, 416
橋式吊車 661
橋式貨櫃吊車 441
橋面 414, 415, 416
橋墩 414, 415
橋墩基座 414
橈帶 564
橈神經 129
橈骨 92, 108, 120
橈側腕短伸肌 119
橈動脈 125
橈靜脈 125
機件膛 699, 701
機匣蓋 701
機尾 448, 556, 557
機尾傘 556
機身 368, 448, 499, 556
機車車廂 429
機車庫 424
機具桿 162
機油注入口 405
機油箱蓋 410
機油壓示警燈 399
機油濾清器 405
機長座椅 451
機柱 261
機座 242, 509, 683
機動台 619
機動台移動鈕 619
機動割草機 252
機械手表 605
機械功變爲電能 654
機械員座椅 451
機械員儀表板 451
機械庫 161
機械構造 165
機殼 206, 261
機場 452, 453
機場大樓 452, 454
機場地勤設備 453

機槍 704
機箱 392
機艙 438, 439, 448, 455, 672
機艙入口 457
機艙門 457
機頭 448, 499, 556, 557
機頭起落架 448
機頭旋轉定位鎖 376
機翼 448, 457, 556, 557
機翼結構 449
機臂 499
澱粉 79
澱粉粒 86
澳洲 49
燒製 520
燈 429, 444, 619
燈光指導 389
燈光與影象控制室 389
燈自動開關 239
燈泡 284, 376, 383
燈泡式水輪機 660
燈泡頭 284
燈座 220, 372
燈插座 285
燈絲 284, 620
燈塔 445
燈塔號燈 446
燈罩 220, 221
燈箱 375, 376
燈橋 390
燈籠袖 306
燈籠椒 81
燈籠褲 317, 561
燕尾 711
燙髮工具 341
燙髮器 341
燃油泵 404
燃油貯藏室 445
燃油種類 401
燃油管路 404
燃油槽 436
燃油箱 403, 455
燃料 664
燃料束 663
燃料球芯塊 663
燃料棒 663
燃料裝卸控制台 666
燃料裝卸程序 665
燃料製造 667

燃料噴射歧管 450
燃料箱 253, 457, 706
燃料輸送管 456
燃氣渦輪機 435, 643
燃燒室 404, 450, 706
獨石戒指 325
獨立平台 642
獨輪手推車 251
盥洗用品包 347
盥洗室 189
磨刀鋼條 227
磨臼 228
磚 193
磚牆 565, 566
積水坑 277
積水區 585
積雨雲 52
積雲 52
窺孔 520
篩 230
篩子 228
篩板 133
糖衣擠管 230
糖缸 223
糖匙 226
糖霜小蛋糕 156
縋降繩釦 588
翮 96
膨脹水箱 203
膨脹室 443
膨脹腔 611
膨脹間隙 422
艙口 645
艙頂配電板 451
艙罩 448
艙壁甲板 434
蕈的構造 73
蕈類 73
蕪菁 84
蕪菁甘藍 84
蕎頭 83
螢光屏 392, 620
螢光塗層 284
螢光幕 392
螢光燈管 284
螢光點 392
融水 56
融水蒸發盤 239
融雪 57
衛兵樓 177

衛星軌道 394
衛星與運載火箭分離 394
衛星數種 393
褲 294, 310, 321, 578
褲子 526, 530, 534
褲腰 294, 297
褲腰蓋片 294
褲腳反褶 294
褲裙 303
褲襠 297
褲襠片 305
褲襪 311, 321
親屬關係 138, 139
豬肉 150, 153
豬腳 150, 153
豬棚 161
貓 94
蹄 91, 93
蹄冠 91, 93
蹄側 93
蹄楔 93
蹄跟 93
蹄跟防滑尖鐵 93
蹄壁 93
蹄鐵形 325
蹄鐵側 93
踵 115
踵革 318
踵套 554
輻射區 37
輻射熱 669
輻條 411
輻條車輪 403
輻輪 568
輸入設備 468
輸入管 204
輸入調節器 495
輸入選擇器 379
輸入鍵 470
輸片槽 383
輸出引線 380
輸出交流電 654
輸出氣壓表 282
輸出設備 468
輸出插座 494
輸出調節器 495
輸出濾波器 495
輸卵管 117
輸卵管峽 117
輸卵管壺腹 117

輸卵管漏斗 117
輸尿管 128
輸往用戶的高壓電 654
輸氣管 550
輸氧開關柄 282
輸電組件 285
輸電網 667, 668
輸精管 116
輸導密集儀器網 394
辦公室用品 461
辦公室用品與設備 459
辦公室設備 465
辦公桌 465
遵行方向 713
遵行標識 717
選台鈕 382
選速鍵 380
選煤廠 638
錠鈎床 505
錠鈎床槽 505
鋸子 599
鋸片 262, 263
鋸片固定螺絲 293
鋸片高度調節柄 262
鋸片斜度固定鈕 263
鋸片傾斜裝置 262
鋸背 262
鋸訂縫和鎖線裝訂 513
鋸齒 262, 263
鋸齒形屋頂 191
鋸齒形鉗牙 259
鋸齒狀邊緣 101
鋸齒篦板 515
鋸鏈 253
鋸鏈鉸接頭 253
錢夾 351
鋼字母 466
鋼字字體 466
鋼字球 466
鋼字球脫扣桿 466
鋼材 193
鋼卷尺 613
鋼底盤 517
鋼板彈簧 408
鋼砂輪 521
鋼砂輪玻璃刀 521
鋼軌 422
鋼軌接頭 422
鋼索 573
鋼帶 610

鋼球屏蔽 662
鋼殼 702
鋼琴 490, 491, 493
鋼筆 367
鋼筋混凝土 193
鋼絲 313, 560
鋼絲剪 259
鋼絲圈拌和桿 235
鋼絲釦 561
鋼鉤 322
鋼摺床 213
鋼構架 643
鋼管帆布椅 210
鋼管接塑料管 275
鋼橫楨 573
鋼錐 588, 589
鋼錐串帶 589
鋼錐鎚 588
錄音放音磁頭 383
錄音按鈕 381
錄音座 378, 381
錄音帶彈出鈕 381
錄音帶監聽鈕 379
錄音帶種類指示燈 381
錄音帶選擇鈕 381
錄音輸入電平鈕 381
錄音攝影機 383
錄影 382
錄影帶盒放入口 382
錄影帶盒彈出鈕 382
錄影帶/電視選擇鈕 382
錄影機 382
錄影機暫停鈕 384
錐口鑽 260
錐子 506
錐形 446
錐形浮標 444
錐形墊圈 268
錐形磁鐵 606
錐形聚光罩 373
錐身 588
錐體 378
錮囚鋒 61
錦雞毛 581
隨身維生包 458
隨身維生包操縱裝置 458
隨砲轉動機槍 704
隨機存取記憶體 468
隨機存取記憶體資料記錄
　468

隨艦艇 439
險升坡 714
險降坡 714
雕帶 170
雕帶裝飾 170
雕飾衣櫃 215
霓虹燈招牌 178
靜水位 51
頰 91, 95, 114
頰肉 150
頰革 567
頸 91, 109, 114, 116, 150,
　392, 514, 567, 606
頸內靜脈 125
頸肉 147, 148, 149, 151,
　152, 153
頸背 115
頸根肉 153
頸神經叢 129
頸部接環 458
頸椎 92
頸椎（7） 121
頸飾 309
頸墊 214
頸環 43, 170
頸總動脈 125
頻閃燈 705
頻率自動控制 379
頻道預調器 382
頭 94, 100, 104, 106, 115,
　116, 124, 258, 506, 514, 581
頭巾 314
頭巾帽 314
頭半棘肌 119
頭先入水 548
頭夾肌 119
頭枕 400, 421
頭狀 72
頭面護罩 283
頭胸甲 103
頭胸部 103
頭骨 92, 99
頭帶 378
頭瓶 590
頭盔 322, 458, 526, 530, 534,
　555, 557, 565, 589, 689
頭盔燈 589
頭部 113
頭頂 95
頭頂號碼牌 568

頭頂護板 684
頭筆 367
頭罩 340, 550
頭銜 359, 360
頭髮 115
頭髮類型 330
頭錐 450
頭靜脈 125
頭頸肉 153
頭顱 114
餐刀 224
餐叉 225
餐車 421
餐具 223
餐具櫃 216
餐前小吃盤 223
餐廳 173, 421, 433, 434,
　719
餡卷 145
餡餅 156
餡餅烤盤 230
餡餃 145
餃 91
髻 330
髹漆和粉刷 278, 279, 280
髹漆滾筒 280
鴨絨被 214
龍門起重機 651, 655, 683
龍門梁 658
龍骨 557
龍蝦 103
龍頭 271
龍頭組合件 270
龜頭 116

十 七 畫

優先行車路 713, 715
優先行車路終止 715
壕溝外崖 176
壓力衣 458
壓力表 612, 641
壓力計 458
壓力暖風系統 202
壓力管 663
壓力熱水系統 203
壓力調節旋鈕 232

壓力調整螺絲 516, 517
壓卡板 466
壓布脚 500
壓布脚提升把 499
壓衣帶 347
壓扁鉗頭 287
壓書 514
壓書板 514
壓烟絲棒 345
壓紙夾 513
壓紙格 517, 518
壓紙滾子 471
壓桿 343, 479, 500
壓緊式連接 274
壓緊式管接頭 270
壓線飾邊褶 304
壓線褶 304
壓艙櫃 645
壓縮天然氣 641
壓縮空氣 639
壓縮空氣筒 550, 676
壓縮器 204, 404
壓縮器渦輪 404
壓縮機 239
嬰兒暖套 316
應急設備壁龕 428
應急備用氧 458
應答錄音帶盒 388
戲院 178
擊弦機械 479
擊砧 703
擊球手 525
擊球板 534
擊球面 586
擊球區 525
擊球部分 526
擊發桿 698, 700
擊發裝置 700
擊劍場 576
擊劍運動員 576
擊劍鞋 576
擊劍褲 576
擊鎚 696, 702, 703
擠褶 217
擦碎板 228
擦碎盤 236
攔板 216
攔柵栅 192
攔脚板 408, 478, 631
攔脚桿 558

攔脚蹬 410
攔臂座 380
檁 190
檔子 487, 494
檔板 402
檔案索引 463
檔案盒 462
檔接木 480
檔號 360
檢查井 277
檢查井口塞 277
檢修孔口 413
檢修蓋板 205
檢視門 273
檐溝 187
檐緣支撐木 190
濱螺 104
氈帽 298, 314
燧石 696
燧石刀 689
燧石箭鏃 689
燧發機 696
燭台式吊燈 220
燭碟 220
爵士樂隊 491
牆內豎管 202
牆內壕溝 176
牆角食櫥 216
牆角陳列櫃 216
牆角燈 220
牆和欄 565, 566
牆筋 192
牆壁出氣口 202
環 484, 573
環式調制器 495
環形山 38
環形燃燒室 450
環形螺母 274
環狀屏蔽罩 662
環狀織針 504
環活頁夾 463
環首螺釘 508
環索 588
環鈕 696
環路通氣管 267
環蝕 37
環層小體 136
瞳孔 94, 131
瞬膜 94
瞭望塔 177

穗形麵包 146
穗狀 72
穗絲 85
穗軸 85
篷車形帳篷 597
篷釘 596, 597
篷壁 596
縮爪 94
縮帆複帶 431
縮帆點 431
楄短結 601
縮頭 611
縮縫簾頂 217
總下水道 413
總狀 72
總金額 610
總裁判 546
總開關 659
總閘閥 641
縱向砂丘 55
縱向通道 645
縱割導桿 262
縱割擋板 262, 263
縱割擋板固定裝置 262
縱割擋板調節器 262
縱撐條 526
縱橫線四分 710
繃布箍 507
繃帶卷 629
繃緊帶 507
縫隙吸塵嘴 244
縫份 503
縫匠肌 118
縫合式底墊 596
縫合標識點 503
縫合線 299, 503
縫刷 506
縫紉 499, 500, 501, 502,
 503
縫紉機 499, 500
縫飾 299
縫線 79, 346, 526
縫線暗袋 300, 304
縫線環 502
縫翼條 448
縫邊 219
翼 95, 96, 108, 581, 671
翼子板 397, 403
翼片 672
翼主梁 671

翼布 671
翼尖 556, 557
翼帆 557
翼肋 449, 671
翼尾 581
翼形 449
翼形螺母 262
翼拉索 557
翼根肋 449
翼梢 449
翼部 174
翼滑翔 557
翼箱 705
翼膜 108
翼櫃 645
聲波 442
聲阻器 387
聲音耦合器 469, 471
聲帶 126
聲管 482
聯合收割機 165
聯動槓桿 480
聯軸螺栓 657
聯管節 274
聯管螺母 274
聯管螺栓 274
臂 115, 487
臂立 548
臂立跳水 549
臂托把手 630
臂板信號 424
臂墊 534
臂端起重滑輪 675
臀 91, 115
臀大肌 119
臀甲 109
臀肉 147, 148, 149, 150,
 151, 152, 153
臀神經 129
臀棘 100
臀溝 115
臀墊 530
臀墊：腰臀墊 534
臀鰭 98
膽囊 99, 127
腋 114
舉升缸 679
舉升缸筒 684
舉升臂 679
舉重 575

舉重台 575
舉重運動員 575
舉重鞋 575
舉臂桿 380
薄大衣 300
薄片木芯夾板 265
薄荷 143
薄絕緣金屬卷材 195
薄雲 61
薄煎餅 157
薄髮剃刀 338
螯 103
螯針 106
螺母 264
螺母帽 264
螺形彈簧 219
螺柱 513
螺栓 259, 264, 442
螺栓頭 264
螺紋 264, 271
螺紋接套 275
螺紋桿 264
螺紋帽 275
螺紋槽 260
螺紋鎖環 580
螺圈裝訂 463
螺旋冰錐 589
螺旋拌和桿 235
螺旋粉 145
螺旋梯 647
螺旋電源線 341
螺旋飾 170
螺旋槳 433, 436, 437, 438
螺旋槳軸 433, 436
螺旋槳齒輪箱 435
螺旋鬢 330
螺桿 258, 259, 489, 695
螺頂 101, 104
螺帽 422, 442
螺帽和螺栓 259
螺絲 264, 266, 478, 562
螺絲耳環 325
螺絲起子 258, 599
螺絲帽 577
螺絲頭 264
螺絲鎖釦 483
螺軸 101
螺塔 101, 104
螺層 101
螺縫 101

褶子 503
褶紋 378
褶痕 294
褶稜 304
褶裙 304
褶裥 305
褶裥飾邊 315
褶裥簾頂 217
賽車手套 299
賽馬車 568, 569
賽馬會所 569
賽跑 570
購物長袋 348
購物袋 348
轂 672
轅 568
轅釦帶 568
避雷針 187
避雷器 655, 659
鎂合金 322
鎂絲 372
錨 447
錨爪 447
錨爪尖 447
錨定銷 236
錨的種類 447
錨冠 447
錨桿 447
錨喉 447
錨掌 447
錨幹 447
錨墩 416
錨機間 433
錨環 447
錨臂 447
錨鏈 447
鍵 385, 467, 479, 480, 483, 489
鍵台 479
鍵鈎 387
鍵槽 406
鍵盤 386, 467, 469, 470, 479, 495
鍵盤台 481
鍵盤控制器 495
鍵盤樂器 479, 480
鍋底 243
鍋嘴 243
鍋鏟 229
鍋爐 203, 204, 433, 438,

668
鍋爐房 189
鍋爐艙 439
鍋體 243
闊筋膜張肌 118
闊葉菊萵苣 82
闊邊帽 314
闌尾 127
隱神經 129
隱縫縫線 295
顆粒層 136
颶風 60
糜 89
黏土塊 519
黏貼紙條 463
點 386, 593
點火孔 694, 695
點火開關 410
點火端 344
點火器 283
點火變壓器 205
點弧電阻 284
點弧電極 284
點播器 249

十八畫

儲水箱 664, 669
儲物家具 215, 216
儲物櫥 465
儲備燃油開關 410
儲藏室 189
疊包 525
疊道 176
嬸 138
擴音電話 388
擴音調諧器 379
擴音器 471
擴音機 389
擴散泵 620
擴開螺栓 264
擴管口器 276
擲球線 527
擲標槍 571
擲鏈球 570
擲鐵餅 570
擾流片 448

擺桿 492, 607
擺速刻度尺 492
擺輪 605
擺錘 607
斷裂 50
斷路器 655, 672
斷劍匕首 692
斷層 48, 53, 636
斷線檢查器 286
旙 711
櫃腳 215
檸檬 77
濾水和晾乾用具 228
濾水套筒 270
濾水器 270
濾水器接頭 270
濾片夾 376
濾汁器 236
濾光面罩 458
濾色片 373
濾色鏡 370
濾波器－振盪器 495
濾烟器 433
濾罩 271
濾罩塞 271
濾管 345
濾網 233, 271
濾嘴 344
濾頭 641
濾鍋 228
濺水板 647
瀑布 54
燭版蠟燭 515
獵戶座 40, 41
獵犬座 40
獵裝 307
獵槍 702
禮拜堂 433
禮帽 298
簧片 482, 483, 488
簧管 482
簡單頂標 446
繐 321
織布原理示意圖 511
織物洗熨 722
織物熨溫指示 243
織物邊緣 502
織造 508, 509, 510, 511
織機頭 505, 506
轍形 72

轍房 72
繞線球機 510
繞線筒 500, 510
繞線筒機 510
繞線盤 580
翹曲部分 561
翹動桿 631
翻下部分 308
翻土叉 248
翻土機 251
翻斗車身 682
翻草機 164
翻摺線 308
翻摺邊 298
翻領 295
翻轉軸 393
翻邊 310
翻邊貼袋 300
職銜 361
臍 101, 114
臍帶 113
薩夫瓦軟乾酪 154
薩瓦蘭蛋糕 156
薩克號 484
薩克管 483, 491
藍外圈 544
藍色 710
藍色＝管制、指示 713
藍紋半硬羊乾酪 154
藍球 584
藍帽 545
藍電子束 392
藍旗 545
藍線 533
覆土盤 164
覆羽 95
覆蓋土石層 635, 637, 650
覆疊式透明卡片袋 351
蹠 93
蹠肌 119
蹠骨 92, 105, 120
蹠骨間肌 118
蹠墊 94
軀幹 115
轉子 655, 656, 672
轉子在定子中旋轉 654
轉子軸 672
轉子葉片 450
轉台 417, 640
轉向主銷 418

轉向阻尼器 410
轉向指示燈 397, 402, 409
轉向指示燈桿 400
轉向柱 400
轉向架 418, 421
轉向架框 418
轉向架與軌道 429
轉向缸筒 682
轉向桿 704
轉向筒 260
轉向軸 684
轉向� 679
轉向機構 400
轉式卡片架 464
轉身監察員 546
轉車車票機 428
轉送客車 453, 454
轉動搖椅 465
轉動腿 209
轉動盤 595
轉動螺旋 165
轉接插頭 341
轉移 394
轉移軌道太陽能電池 393
轉移軌道衛星 394
轉速表 410
轉換 667
轉筒 219, 236, 489, 506,
　　607, 616
轉軸 236, 510, 519
轉塔頂 704
轉節 98, 100, 106
轉數計 399
轉槳式水輪機 657
轉盤 235, 594, 615, 680
轉盤牽引桿球頭軸 680
轉盤蓋 621
轉輪 595, 656, 657
轉輪彈簧 703
轉輪站 636
轉環 581
轉轍信號 422
轉轍信號燈 423
轉轍控制樓 424, 425
轉轍電動機 423
轉轍器座 422
轉轍器導線 423
轉體跳水 549
轍岔 422
醫院 713, 718

醫護復健 629
鎚子 287
鎚面 257
鎚眼 257
鎚頭 588
鎚幫 257
鎚鎬 588, 589
鎊 723
鎖 198, 215, 266, 347, 412
鎖子甲 690
鎖快門旋鈕 368
鎖定套崗 374
鎖定鈕 613, 614
鎖定螺母 64, 613
鎖定螺帽 562
鎖門手柄 419
鎖門按鈕 266
鎖門 266
鎖門板 266
鎖骨 120
鎖骨下動脈 125
鎖骨下靜脈 125
鎖緊鉗 259
鎖緊墊圈 264
鎖緊螺母 268, 270
鎖蓋板 266
鎖線架 513
鎖環 258, 398, 698
鎖鏈綉 507
鎧裝電線 388
鎬尖 588
鎬尾釘 588
鎬柄 588
鎬頭 588
離合器桿 410
離合器踏板 400
離站時間表 426
雜物箱 399
雜牌 592
雙 594, 595
雙人沙發 211
雙人鞍座 409
雙三角 711
雙刃刀片 337
雙刃刮鬍刀 337
雙叉尾 711
雙子座 40
雙子座（ 5 月 21 日 ） 712
雙手抓舉 575
雙手挺舉 575

雙爪錨 447
雙凹透鏡 625
雙凸透鏡 625
雙打發球區 542
雙打網柱 537
雙打邊線 537, 542
雙母音 358
雙列圓盤耙 164
雙向行車 715
雙向滑桿 218
雙拉把 554
雙板 554
雙空 593
雙金屬元件 611
雙金屬溫度計 611
雙金屬螺旋線 611
雙指標骰 592
雙重木柵 565
雙重障礙：木架和灌木，
　　木架和柵門 566
雙重簾掛桿 218
雙面貨盤 685
雙面鏡 340
雙套結 601
雙套樓住宅/四戶住宅 183
雙座吊椅 558
雙座位 429
雙桅橫帆 432
雙桅縱帆 432
雙桅縱橫帆 432
雙氧水 629
雙圈稱人結 601
雙接繩結 601
雙排鈕 291, 301
雙排鈕西裝 293
雙魚座 40
雙魚座（ 2 月 19 日 ） 712
雙廊花木鑽頭 260
雙殼貝 101
雙焦點鏡片 328
雙筒稜鏡望遠鏡 621
雙筒顯微鏡 619
雙開門 198
雙極斷路器 288
雙零 595
雙摺門 198
雙槓 573
雙聚束極片 620
雙鉸拱 415
雙層玻璃 669

雙層鍋 232
雙齒刃薄髮剪 338
雙頭肌 118
雙翼仰開橋 417
雙聯式廚房洗滌盆 267
雙聯砲塔 439
雙臂犂 163
雙褶捲邊 304
雙簧 483, 488
雙簧管 483, 490, 493
雙鏡頭反光照相機 369
雙辮子 330
雙欄 594, 595
雙疊袖口 306
雞心領口 309
雞尾酒杯 222
雞油菌 73
雞眼刀 342
額 95, 114, 690
額肌 118
額狀縫 122
額革 567
額骨 120, 122
額劍 103
額髮 91
額寶 133
顏色 710, 713
顏色測定器 375
騎士 591
騎手上裝 565
騎兵帽 298
騎術 565, 566, 567
鬃 91
鬃毛 280
鬆土耙 680
鬆紙桿 467
鬆脫碎石 714
鬆散填充絕緣材料 195
鬆緊彈簧 505
鬆緊帶 214, 294, 577
鬆緊旋鈕 500, 505, 506
鬆緊袖口 317
鬆緊腰帶 315
鬆緊腰襻 293
鬆緊腿孔 315, 317
鬆緊調節桿 505
鬆緊褲腳 297, 317
鬆緊螺絲釦 553, 579
鬆餅烤盤 230
鬆髮 330

鬖髮梳 338
魏納爾圓筒 620
鯉魚鉗 259
鵝頭 682
鵝頸彎 197

十九畫

攀緣植物 247
曝光表 372
曝光值 372
曝光值刻度 372
曝光時間刻度 372
曝光調節 371
曝氣濾池 277
櫛 106
櫥窗 178
瀝青 649, 650
瀝青加工 648
瀝青瓦 195
瀝青抽升 650
瀝青頁岩絕緣材料 195
瀝青處理 650
瀝青蒸餾 649
爆炸雷管 700
爆炸頭 331
瓣 77
瓣蹼 97
穩定尾翼 456
穩定面 555
穩定桿 691
穩定裝置 434
穩定龍骨 437
穩壓器 376
簾布 219
簾布夾 218
簾布層 407
簾蛤 102
簽名 359, 360
繫把 694
繫弦板 477
繫弦釘 479
繫索 694
繫索耳 552, 553
繫帶 217, 321, 563
繫帶便鞋 320
繫帶鉤 217

繫釦帶 316, 567
繫帽帶 292, 314
繫鈕門襟 301
繫鈕貼邊 295
繫鈕領 295
繫鈕襻 305
繫繩環 703
繫纜樁 440
韁繩 568
繩 601
繩索 588
繩帶 316
繩梯 278
繩眼 588
繩結 601
繩環 588
繪圖機 469
羅馬尼亞文 355
羅馬尼亞釘線繡 507
羅馬房屋 173
羅馬金屬筆 367
羅馬甜瓜 81
羅勒 143
羅盤 437, 550, 556
羅盤子午線 625
羅盤面 625
羅盤座 41
藤架 247
藥池 696
藥池蓋 696
藥物雜貨店 720
藥棉 629
蠋 100
蠅紋裹條 581
蠅體 581
蠍虎座 40
蟹 103
襟飾領 308
襟翼 705
襟翼液壓缸筒 705
襟翼導軌 449
譜架 492
譜號 475
證件和相片套 351
證件檢查 720
蹼 97, 550
蹼趾 105
蹼網 526
蹼瓣 97
蹬帶 310

邊石塘 54
邊板 477
邊框 198, 199
邊跨 416
邊飾 351
邊撐 510, 513
邊緣 265, 559, 561, 564
邊線 525, 527, 531, 532,
  535, 536, 539, 543
邊線裁判 531, 532, 533,
  536, 537, 542
邊鋒 531
邊齒石 187
邊壁 546
鏡子 332, 347
鏡框 328
鏡筒 623
鏡箱 269
鏡頭 371, 377
鏡頭及附件 370
鏡頭插座 368
鏡頭間快門 371
鏡頭蓋 370
鏡頭遮光罩 370
鏈 248
鏈子 201
鏈斗 675, 679, 681
鏈斗傾翻槓桿 679
鏈斗鉸銷 679
鏈斗齒 679
鏈斗操縱缸筒 679
鏈頭 588
鏈 571, 607, 612
鏈斗式挖掘機 635
鏈式管扳手 276
鏈制動器 253
鏈狀砂丘 55
鏈條 220, 412
鏈條起動扳機 253
鏈條導夾 412
鏈球 572
鏈墜 325
鏈輪 408, 412, 678
鏈齒 502
鏈鋸 253
鏈環 581
鏈鎖彈 695
钁頭 639
關引擎鈕 410
霧 60

霧燈 403
髂下腹神經 129
髂內動脈 124, 125, 128
髂內靜脈 124
髂骨 120
髂腹股溝神經 129
髂總動脈 125, 128
鯨魚座 40, 41
麒麟座 41

二十畫

寶石 605
寶石切磨法 327
寶石管座 443
寶瓶座 41
寶瓶座（1月20日） 712
懸冰川 56
懸吊設備 180
懸架 557, 631
懸索 416, 557, 675
懸索橋 416
懸崖 38, 48, 51
懸掛式文件夾 463
懸掛絕緣子串 658
懸掛鉤 377
懸掛點 557
懸韌帶 131
懸雍垂 133, 134
懸墊 94
懸縋索 181
懸蹄 94
懸臂 679, 681
懸臂托梁 190
懸臂梁 653
懸臂跨度 414
懸臂橋 414
懸繫半幅 709
攙酒高杯 222
攙酒矮杯 222
爐子 202, 204
爐台 238
爐用油 649
爐床 520
爐門 237
爐門頂磚 200
爐面電熱元件 238

爐圈 233, 238
爐頂 520
爐頂梁 200
爐喉 200
爐膛 201
爐膛蓋 201
爐燈 237, 238
爐額 200
爐襯盤 238
礦 650
礦井口加工設備 638
礦石 635, 636
礦坑 635
礦床 635, 636
礦車軌道 638
礦脈 636
礦脈狹縮 636
礦脈頂 636
礦帶 637
礦燈房 638
礫石 192, 277
籌碼 594, 595
籃板 535
籃架 535
籃圈 535
籃球 535
籃球場 535
籃球鞋 535
辮子 321
辮子頭 330
繼電器 206
耀斑 37
蘆筍 85
蘆管筆 367
蘋果 76
蘇格蘭便帽 314
蠔 102
觸手 104
觸角 100, 104, 106, 581
觸發獎金裝置 595
觸點 611
觸覺小體 136
警告標識 714
警告標識（續） 715
警笛 677
警察 718
罌粟 79
鐘 616
鐘形屋頂 191
鐘形帳篷 597

鐘形帽 314
鐘形圓飾 170
鐘乳石 54
鐘面 607
鐘座 607
鐘殼 607
鐘琴 493
鐘樓 174, 175
鐘擺 607
鐘響浮標 444
鐙革 567
霰 57
霰彈 695
飄口 512
飄揚半幅 709
饋電進輪電網 654
騰空 548, 549, 574
鰲甲 91
鰓 98, 99, 102
鰓耙 98
鰓絲 98
鰓蓋 98, 105
鰓蓋骨 98
鹹水 640
麵包 146
麵包刀 227
麵包插入口 237
麵包導架 237
麵食 144, 145
麵條 144
麵條夾 231

二十一畫

屬於 723
攝影 368, 369, 370, 371, 372,
　　373, 374, 375, 376, 377
攝影師 390
攝影開關 384
攝影機升降車 390
攝影機座 390
攝影機電池 383
櫻桃 75
欄 594, 595
欄杆 187, 197
欄杆小柱 197
欄架 570

灌木 247
灌木和欄 565, 566
纏線把手 572
纏繩 586
蠟狀外膜 93
蠟腺板 106
襪子 311, 530, 538
襪底 297
襪背 297
襪帶 312, 313
襪帶針法 504
襪跟 297
襪管 297
襪頭 297
護手 227, 530, 693
護手盤 577
護手繃帶 579
護木 699
護目玻璃擋板 521
護目墨鏡 589
護目鏡 283, 329, 555, 559,
　　561, 564
護肋墊 530
護衣擋 631
護肘 530, 564, 576
護角 347
護具 530
護城壕 177
護柵 397
護軌 422
護面 576
護桅索 552
護胸 526, 530
護圈螺母 271
護脛 526, 530, 568
護條 397
護袖套 487
護陰墊 530, 534
護喉 526, 534
護掌 526
護掌跟 526
護腕 530, 534, 538
護腕繃帶 575
護照夾 351
護照檢查處 454
護腱 562
護腿 559
護膝 526, 564, 568, 575
護膝甲 690
護膝吊帶 568

護齒 579
護齒用品 339
護蹄 568
護頸 576
護頸甲 690
護牆 177
護臂 530
護欄 187, 414
護籠 570
護體墊 534
鐮刀 252
鐵丸筒艙 437
鐵心 572
鐵手套 690
鐵盔 690
鐵絲爐架 599
鐵路交通圖 426
鐵路運輸 418, 721
鐵餅 572
鐵頭棒 586
鐵鍬 248
鐵鎖 588
鐵邊 572
鐲片小圈鏈 325
露天剝採礦 635
露天座 178
露天礦 635, 636
露台 433
露指長手套 299
露罩 623
露頭 636
露營 596
露營和旅行掛車營地 721
露營區 721
露營裝備 598, 599, 600
露點溫度 62
響弦 486
響弦小鼓 486, 491, 493
響弦面 486
響弦鬆緊鈕 486
響板 485
響度鈕 379
驅動渦輪 404
驅動軸 434, 684
驅動滑輪 181
驅動線圈 606
驅動線圈和相敏線圈
　　606
驅動輪 680
驅動齒輪 243, 260, 704

索 引

驅逐艦 439
鰭板 435, 554
鶴嘴鋤 248
齧玻璃齒 521
齧齒動物的頜 90

二十二畫

彎 534
彎耳 502
彎吹管 488
彎形通心粉 145
彎道滑雪者 558
彎管粉 145
彎管溝 54
彎頭 201, 202, 203, 275, 328
攢尖式屋頂 190
灑水軟管 250
瓤囊 77
疊幅前緣拉件 218
疊椅 213
籠架 444
聾啞人手語 357
聽小骨 132
聽筒 387
聽筒托架 387
聽筒電線 387
襯衫 295, 321
襯衫下襬 295, 305
襯衫袖 305, 306
襯衫連裙 302
襯衫領 305, 308
襯頁 512
襯料 502
襯裙 313
襯裏 293, 308, 313, 318, 338, 350, 407, 502, 512, 516, 518, 562
襯墊 318, 516, 518
襯襟 308
讀卡機 472
鑄塑絕緣材料 195
鑊 233
鑊及輔助用具 233
顫音 476
顫音臂 494

鬃 94
鰾 99

二十三畫

攪刀罩 235
攪和機 235
攪拌器 230
攪動器 240
纓 217
纖毛 581
纖維 601
纖維板 194
變阻器 387
變音符號 357
變音管 483
變速桿 399, 409, 410, 411, 412
變換旋鈕 505
變焦速度選擇鈕 384
變焦鏡頭 370, 384
變電站 655, 660
變質岩 48
變壓器 205, 655, 659, 668, 672
顯示板 610
顯示器 469
顯象管 392
顯微目鏡 614
顯影中的感光片 371
顯影液盆 375
顯影滾軸 371
驗收場 425
髓 71
髓室 123
髓棘 99
髓管 123
髓質 128
髓鞘 135
體育運動 570
體溫計 611
體端 581
體操 573, 574
體操運動員 574
體螺層 101
鱗 97, 98, 109
鱗片 73

鱗狀縫 122
鱗柄白毒傘 73
鱗莖 85
鱗莖剖面 83
鱗莖蔬菜 83
鱗葉 83

二十四畫

壩芯 652
壩基 652, 653
壩頂 651, 652, 655
罐式噴霧器 250
罐形 446
罐形浮標 444
罐車 646
罐裝廢燃料 665
罐壁 646
罐頭刀 229
蠶豆 85
讓路 715
靄 60
髖骨 92, 120
鷹 710
鷹嘴 121
鷹嘴豆 85
鹽沼 51
鹽瓶 223
鹽湖 55

二十五畫

欖形切磨 327
灣 38
觀測窗 457
觀察孔 423
觀察室 620
觀察員座椅 451
觀察窗 620
觀察照明燈 437
觀劇望遠鏡 329
觀眾席 43, 179
鑲板 506
鑲砌圖樣 521

鑲嵌 521
鑲嵌地板 196
鑲嵌座 325
鑲嵌頭 545
鑲邊 298, 318, 477
鑰匙 266
鑰匙孔 266
鑰匙包 351
鑰匙圈 351
鑰匙鎖 350
顱骨構造 122
髖 115

二十六至二十九畫

鑷子 343, 629
鑷尖 343
纜索 322, 601
顴骨 120, 122
顴窩 122
顴顳 114
鑽井浮台 642
鑽井船 642
鑽井裝置 640
鑽井駁船 642
鑽石磨頭 521
鑽床 261
鑽底 327
鑽亭 327
鑽冠 327
鑽面 327
鑽面狀飾 215
鑽桿 639
鑽管 640
鑽鋌 640
鑽頭 260, 639, 640
鑽頭刃帶 260
鑼 485, 493
顴弓 122
顴面孔 122
顴骨 120, 122
鱷梨 80
鑿子 516
鑿岩機 639
鬱金香形香檳杯 222

英文字母序

A 形架 675
C 形夾鉗 259
F1 引擎 456
J2 引擎 456
K 型構架 658
P-N 結 670
S 形椅腿 210
S 波段天線 65
T 字形 446
T 形上坡牽引架 558
T 形尾翼組 449
T 骨嫩肉 148
U 形彎頭 275
V 形領口 293, 296
V 領開襟毛衣 296
X-15 型飛機（美） 47

阿拉伯數字序

1 號木頭 586
1 號鐵頭 586
2 號木頭 586
2 號鐵頭 586
3 號木頭 586
3 號鐵頭 586
4 號木頭 586
4 號鐵頭 586
5 號鐵頭 586
5 碼線 531
6 號鐵頭 586
7 號鐵頭 586
8 字結 601
8 號尾鋒 531
8 號鐵頭 586
9 號鐵頭 586
10 碼線 531
15 碼線 531
25 碼線 531
120 伏電線 288
240 伏供電電纜 288
240 伏電線 288

The editors are grateful for the assistance provided by the following manufacturers and organizations:

Air Canada — **Archambault Musique** — Aréo-feu Ltée — **ASEA Inc.** — Atelier Lise Dubois — **Atomic Energy of Canada Ltd** — Automobiles Renault Canada Ltée — **Banque de terminologie du Québec** — Bell Canada — **Bombardier Inc.** — Botanical Garden of Montreal — **Camco Inc.** — Canada Mortgage and Housing Corporation — **Canadian Broadcasting Corporation** — Canadian Coleman Supply Inc. — **Canadian General Electric Company Ltd** — Canadian Government Terminology Bank — **Canadian National** — Canadian Pacific — **François Caron Inc.** — CKAC Radio — **CNCP Telecommunications** — Control Data Canada Ltd — **Department of National Defence** — Dow Planetarium — **Eaton** — Fédération québécoise de badminton — **Fédération québécoise de canot-camping** — Fédération québécoise de handball olympique — **Fédération québécoise de la montagne** — Fédération québécoise de ski nautique — **Fédération québécoise de soccer football** — Fédération québécoise des sports aériens Inc. — **Fédération québécoise de tennis** — Fédération de tennis de table du Québec — **Ford du Canada Ltée** — General Motors of Canada Ltd — **G.T.E. Sylvania Canada Ltée** — Gulf Canada Ltd — **Hewitt Equipment Ltd** — Hippodrome Blue Bonnets Inc. — **Honeywell Ltd** — Hudson's Bay Company — **Hydro-Québec** — IBM Canada Ltd — **Imperial Oil Ltd** — Institut de recherche d'Hydro-Québec (IREQ) — **Institut Teccart Inc.** — Institut de tourisme et d'hôtellerie du Québec — **International Civil Aviation Organization** — Johnson & Johnson Inc. — **La Maison Casavant** — Nissan — **Office de la langue française du Québec** — J. Pascal Inc. — **Petro-Canada Inc.** — Quebec Cartier Mining Company — **RCA Inc.** — Shell Canada Products Company Ltd — **Smith-Corona Division of SMC (Canada) Ltd** — Société d'énergie de la Baie James — **Société de transport de la Communauté urbaine de Montréal** — Teleglobe Canada — **Translation Bureau: Department of the Secretary of State of Canada** — Via Rail Canada Inc. — **Volvo Canada Ltd** — Wild Leitz Canada Ltd — **Xerox Canada Inc.** — Yamaha Canada Music Ltd.

A special thanks to **Alan Goodworth**, Managing Director of **Facts on File Publications** (Oxford), for providing the British terminology.

SELECTIVE BIBLIOGRAPHY

Dictionaries:

Gage Canadian Dictionary, Toronto, Gage Publishing Limited, 1983, 1313 p.

Larousse Illustrated International, Paris, Larousse, McGraw-Hill, 1972.

The New Britannica/Webster Dictionary and Reference guide, Encyclopedia Britannica, 1981.

The Oxford Illustrated Dictionary, Oxford, Clarendon Press, 1967.

The Random House Dictionary of the English Language, the unabridged Edition, 1983, 2059 p.

Webster's New Collegiate Dictionary, Springfield, G. @ C. Merriam Company, 1980, 1532 p.

Webster's New Twentieth Century Dictionary of the Language, unabridged, Cleveland, Collins World, 1975.

Webster's new world dictionary of the American language, New York, The World Pub., 1953.

French and English Dictionaries:

Belles-Isle, J.-Gerald. *Dictionnaire thématique général anglais-français*, Paris, Dunod, Montréal, Beauchemin, 2e édition, 1977, 553 p.

Collins-Robert. *French-English, English-French Dictionary*, London, Glasgow, Cleveland, Toronto, 1978, 781 p.

Dubois, Marguerite-Marie. *Dictionnaire moderne français-anglais*, Paris, Larousse, 1960.

Harrap's *New Standard French and English Dictionary*, part one, French-English, London, 1977, 2 vol., part two, English-French, London, 1983, 2 vol.

Harrap's *Shorter French and English Dictionary*, London, Toronto, Willington, Sydney, George G. Harrap and Company, 1953, 940 p.

Encyclopedias:

Academic American Encyclopedia, Princeton, Arete Publishing Company, Inc., 1980, 21 vol.

Chamber's Encyclopedia, New rev. edition, London, International Learning Systems, 1969.

Collier's Encyclopedia, New York, Macmillan Educational Company, 1984, 24 vol.

Compton's Encyclopedia, F.E. Compton Company, Division of Encyclopedia Britannica Inc., The University of Chicago, 1982, 26 vol.

Encyclopedia Americana, Danbury, International ed., Conn.: Grolier, 1981, 30 vol.

Encyclopedia Britannica, E. Britannica, Inc., USA, 1970.

How it works — The illustrated science and invention encyclopedia, New York, H.S. Stuttman, Co., Inc. publishers, 1974.

McGraw-Hill Encyclopedia of Science @ Technology, New York, McGraw-Hill Book Company, 1982, 5th edition.

Merit Students Encyclopedia, New York, Macmillan Educational Company, 1984, 20 vol.

New Encyclopedia Britannica, Chicago, Toronto, Encyclopedia Britannica, 1985.

The Joy of Knowledge Encyclopedia, London, Mitchell Beazleg Encyclopedias, 1976, 7 vol.

The Random House Encyclopedia, New York, Random House, 1977, 2 vol.

The World Book Encyclopedia, Chicago, Field enterprises educational Corporation, 1973.

Illustrations:

In addition to the above sources, we also consulted many specialized works recognized both nationally and internationally such as **Diagram Group, Maloine, Reader's Digest, Time-Life, Bornemann, Rand McNally, Elsevier, Eyrolles, McMillan**, etc.